CATALOGUE

OF THE

LIBRARY

OF THE

STATE HISTORICAL SOCIETY

OF WISCONSIN.

PREPARED BY

DANIEL S. DURRIE, Librarian, and ISABEL DURRIE, Assistant.

MADISON.

PUBLISHED BY ORDER OF THE STATE.

M.DCCC.LXXIII.

MADISON:
ATWOOD & CULVER, STATE PRINTERS AND STEREOTYPERS.
1873.

PREFATORY.

The present volume has been prepared with a view to meet the immediate wants of the large number of persons who have occasion to consult the Library. The necessity of this catalogue has long been apparent, as without it a great portion of the volumes were no better than sealed books to every inquirer who had not time or patience to seek among the undigested mass of materials for such facts as he desired; and in its preparation, it has been a prime object to make the arrangement as simple as possible, the more readily to facilitate all classes of inquirers.

The system adopted is the alphabetical form, in connection with a full list of subjects, under their appropriate heads. A work is first catalogued under the author's name, if known, with the title-page, place and date of publication, omitting superfluous words. It is then placed, in abbreviated title, under its proper heading or subject, referring to the author's name for full title; and if a pamphlet, reference is made to the volume containing it, of works of that particular character. When the author's name is wanting, the work can be found under the prominent name of the subject or topic. Books are often cross-referenced under various heads, so that the student can, with little experience, ascertain whether the work he may desire is in the Library, and also to learn the full strength of the Library in any given department.

In order to make the catalogue as useful as possible to the general reader, some of the more important papers of an historical character are catalogued from the publications of the various historical societies, the historical and other magazines of the country, and also important papers from the publications of the various American scientific and learned societies. Many valuable articles upon important subjects are thus brought to the notice of the general reader, who would otherwise probably have remained ignorant of them.

A synopsis of the more important portion of the Tank Collection, of some 5,000 volumes, mostly in the Holland language, presented to the society by Mrs. C. L. A. Tank, of Fort Howard, Wisconsin, has been kindly prepared by Prof. William F. Allen, of the State University, and for convenience, has been appended to the work. In the appendix will also be found, grouped together, works of a religious and theological character — many of them pamphlets from 1600 to the present time, rich in the early polemic literature of that period, when so much attention was paid to such matters, and which left such a marked impress upon the English mind, and the early Puritans and other primitive settlers of the American colonies.

The present volume has been prepared by the librarian, Mr. D. S. Durrie, with the aid of his daughter, Miss Isabel Durrie, assistant librarian, and every pains taken to make the work one of value and convenience to all persons consulting the Library.

The number of volumes and pamphlets in the library on Jan. 1, 1873, was 54,224; of which number 25,671 were bound volumes, and 28,553 pamphlets and unbound documents. Since which, over two thousand additions have been made, which are included in this catalogue up to the time of going to press.

L. C. DRAPER,
D. S. DURRIE,
O. M. CONOVER,
Library Committee.

MADISON, WIS., July 1, 1873.

CATALOGUE.

A.

ABBOT, Rev. Abiel. Address before the Mass. Soc'y for the Suppression of Intemperance, June 2, 1815. Cambridge, 1815. 12mo. Temp. Pamph. Vol. 3.

—— History of Andover, Mass., from its first settlement to 1829. Andover, 1829. 12mo.

ABBOT, Rev. A. and Rev. E. General Register of Abbott Family. Boston, 1847. 8vo.

ABBOTSFORD. — See IRVING, W. Abbotsford and Newstead Abbey.

ABBOTT, A. O. Prison Life in the South: at Richmond, Savanah, Andersonville, etc. New York, 1865. 12mo.

ABBOTT, Jacob. Lecture before the American Institute of Instruction. Boston, 1834. 12mo. Educa. Pamph. Vol. 6.

ABBOTT, John S. C. Confidential Correspondence of the Emperor Napoleon and the Empress Josephine. New York, 1858. 12mo.

—— History of Frederick the 2d of Prussia. New York, 1871. 8vo.

—— History of Napoleon Bonaparte. New York, 1855. 2 vols. 8vo.

—— History of the Civil War in America. Vol. 1. New York, 1864. 8vo.

—— The Empire of Austria: its rise and present power. 3d ed. New York, 1859. 12mo.

—— The Empire of Russia: from the remotest period to the present time. New York, 1860. 12mo.

ABEEL, Rev. John N. Discourse before the N. York Missionary Soc'y. With Appendix. New York, 1801. 8vo. Indian Pamph. Vol. 3.

ABENAKI INDIANS. — See KIDDER, F.

—— —— See RASLES, Father S. Dictionary.

ABERCROMBIE, Dr. John. Contributions to the Pathology of the Heart. Edinburgh, 1823. 8vo, Med. Pamph. Vol. 13.

—— Inquiries concerning the Intellectual Powers. Harpers' Fam. Lib. New York, 1860. 18mo.

—— Philosophy of the Moral Feelings. Harpers' Fam. Lib. New York, 1854. 18mo.

ABERDEEN, Scotland. Collections for a Hist. of the Shires of Aberdeen and Banff. Printed by the Spalding Club. Aberdeen, 1843. 4to.

—— Colleges of. Collection of Papers relating to the proposal for uniting the King's and the Marischal Colleges. London, 1787. 4to. Eng. Miscell. Pamph. Vol. 24A.

—— See COURAGE, A. Guide to Important Places in. 1855.

—— Illustrations of the Topogr. and Antiquities of the Shires of Aberdeen and Banff. Aberdeen, 1869. 4 vols. 4to.

ABERNETHY, Dr. John. The Hunterian Oration of 1819. Delivered before the Royal College of Surgeons, London. London, 1819. 8vo. Pamphleteer. Vol. 14. Med. Pamph. Vol. 23.

ABERT, J. J. Report on the Surveys of the Mouths of the Milwaukee, Root, and other Rivers. With Maps. Washington, 1838. 8vo. Wis. Miscell. Pamph. Vol. 5. See also SENATE Doc. No. 175, 2d Sess., 25th Cong.

ABERT, Lieut. J. W. Report of an Exped. on the Upper Arkansas, and through the Country of the Camanche Indians, in 1845. Senate Doc. No. 438, 1st Sess. 29th Cong., 1846.

—— Report and Map of the Examination of New Mexico. Maps, etc. Senate Doc. No. 23, 1st Sess. of 30th Congress, 1848.

ABERT, S. T. Is a Ship Canal Practicable? Notes on the Projected Routes for an Inter-Oceanic Canal between the Atlantic and Pacific Oceans. Cincinnati, 1870. 8vo.

ABINGDON, Earl of. Thoughts on the Letter of Edmund Burke to the Sheriffs of Bristol, on the Affairs of America. Oxford, Eng., 1776 (?). 8vo. Eng. Polit. Pamph. Vol. 18.

ABINGTON, Mass. — See HOBART, B. History of.

—— Hist. and Descrip. of. Mass. Hist. Soc. Trans. 2d ser. Vol. 7.

ABITOL, M. Observations on the Gaming Act of 1854. London, 1854. 8vo. Strangford Pamph. Vol. 66.

ABOLITION (The). Conspiracy to Destroy the Union; or, Ten Years' Record of Repub. Party. 1863. Rebell'n Pamph. Vol. 74.

ABOLITION AND SECESSION; or, Cause and Effect, with the Remedy for Sectional Troubles. 1862. Rebell'n Pamph. Vol. 74.

ABOTT, A. A. The Assassination and Death of Abraham Lincoln. New York, 1865. 12mo. Rebell'n Pamph. Vol. 110.

ABOUT THE WAR: Plain Words to Plain People. Phila., 1863. 8vo. Rebell'n Pamph. Vol. 3.

ABRAHAM AFRICANUS I. His Secret Life, etc. New York, 1864. 12mo. Rebell'n Pamph. Vol. 97.

ABRAHAM, Rob't John. Popular Explanation of the System of Land Registration under Lord Westbury's Act. London, 1864. 8vo. Law Pamph. Vol. 21.

ABRAHAM, R. T. Proofs in relation to Contingent Remainders. London, 1829. 8vo. Law Pamph. Vol. 16.

ABSALOM'S CONSPIRACY; or, the Tragedy of Treason. London, 1680. Fol. Eng. Pol. Pamph. Vol. 2.

ABSTRACT (An) Laws of New England as they are now established, 1641. – FORCE'S HISTORICAL TRACTS. Vol. 3.

ABYSSINIA. — See HEAD, F. B. Life and Advent. of J. Bruce.
—— RUSSELL, M. History of Nubia and.
ACADIA. — See WHITE, W. Hist. of Belfast and Acadia.
ACADIAN EXILES; or, French Neutrals in Penn. — See REED, Wm. B.
ACCOUNT of a Journey to Niagara, Montreal and Quebec in 1765. N. York, 1846. 8vo. Pamphlets—Amer. Travel. Vol. 1.
—— of an Egyptian Mummy, presented to the Museum of the Leeds Philos. and Literary Soc'y. Leeds, 1828. 8vo. Scientific Pamph. Vol. 42.
—— of Early Voyages, made by the Portuguese, Spaniards, &c., to Africa, East and West Indies. London, 1790. 4to.
—— of that part of Africa inhabited by Negroes, with remarks on the Slave Trade. 3d Ed. London, 1768. 8vo.
—— of the Management of the Poor in Hamburgh, since 1788. Dublin, 1796. 8vo. Eng. Miscell. Phamph. Vol. 13.
—— of the manner in which persons confined in the prisons of Paris, were tried and executed, Sept. 2d and 3d, 1792. London, 1792. 8 vo. Eng. Polit. Pamph. Vol. 24.
—— of the Charity Schools in G. Britain and Ireland. London, 1712. 4to. 11th Ed. Educa. Pamph. Vol. 40.
—— of the meetings held in Hyde Park, in favor of Parliamentary Reform. London, 1866. 8vo. Eng. Miscell. Pamph. Vol. 11.
—— (An) of the Opera. of the Corps under the Duke of Brunswick, from the time of its formation. London, 1810. 8vo. Eng. Polit. Pamph. Vol. 30.
—— of the Private League of Chas. 2d., of Eng., with the French King, 1672. London, 1669. Fol. Eng. Polit. Pamph. Vol. 1.
—— (Authentic) of the Proceedings of the Congress held at New York in 1775, on the American Stamp Act. London, 1767. American Tracts. Vol. 2.
—— of the subversion of the Legal Gov't at Madras, by Imprisoning the Governor. Lord Pigot in 1777. 4to. Eng. Polit. Pamph. Vol. 4.
ACCOUNTS and Extracts of MSS. in the Library of the King of France. Vol. 2. London, 1779. 8vo.
ACLAND, Dr. H. W. Fever in Agricultural Districts. Being a Report on Cases in Great Horwood, Eng. Oxford, 1858. 8vo. Med. Pamph. Vol. 17.
—— Letter to W. E. Gladstone, concerning an Initiative Board for the University of Oxford. Ox., 1854. 8vo. Strangford Pamph. Vol. 66.
ACRELIUS, Rev. Israel. New Sweden, or the Swedish Settlements on the Delaware. N. York Hist. Soc. Coll. New Ser. Vol. 1.
ACROSS THE CONTINENT. — See BOWLES, Samuel.
ACTON, Mass. — See ADAMS, Josiah. Centen. Address, 1835.
—— SHATTUCK, L.
ADAIR, Jas. History of Amer. Indians; more particularly those on the Mississippi, and in Southern States. London, 1775. 4to.
ADAIR, Gen. John, and JACKSON, Gen. A. Letters relative to the Charges of Cowardice brought against the Ky. Troops at New Orleans, 1815, 17. 8vo. Congr. and Polit. Pamph. Vol. 111.

ADAIR, Robt. Two Letters to the Bishop of Winchester, in answer to the charge of a high Treasonable Misdemeanor. London, 1821. 8vo. Eng. Polit. Pamph. Vol. 35.

ADAM GENEALOGY. — See ADAMS, William.

ADAM, L. De L'Abolition de l'Esclavage aux Etats—Unis, 1861. Rebell'n Pamph. Vol. 75.

ADAM, William. Genealogy of the Adam Family. Albany, 1848. 8vo. Genealog. Pamph. Vol. 11. Same with emendations. Genealog. Pamph. Vol. 14.

—— Speech at Edinburgh, Jan. 22, 1816, on Trial by Jury. London, 1816. 8vo. Law Pamph. Vol. 20.

ADAM'S ROMAN ANTIQUITIES. Index of Phrases and Sentences which are explained or illustrated. Cambridge, 1832. 8vo. Scientific Pamph. Vol. 42.

ADAMS, Mrs. Abigail. Letters: with a memoir by her Grand-son, Charles Francis Adams. 4th Ed. Boston, 1848. 12mo.

ADAMS, Rev. C. Address to Abolitionists of the M. E. Church. Boston, 1843. 8vo. Addresses, &c. Vol. 23.

ADAMS, Prof. C. B. Catalogue of Genera, and Species of Recent shells in his Collection. Middlebury, 1847. 8vo. Scientific Pamph. Vol. 6.

ADAMS, Charles Francis. Address at Quincy, July 4, 1856. Boston, 1856. 8vo. Addresses, &c. Vol. 27.

—— Lecture at New York, Jan. 30, 1855, on the subject of Slavery. Boston, 1852. 8vo. Addresses and Orations. Vol. 1.

—— Speech at Phila., Aug. 28, 1860, on Conservatism and Reform. Congr. and Polit. Pamph. Vol. 87.

—— The Struggle for Neutrality in America: an Address delivered before the N. York Hist. Soc'y, Dec. 13, 1870. N. York, 1871. 8vo.

ADAMS Co. WIS. PRESS. Newspaper. Friendship, Wis., 1865—1873. 2 Vols., folio.

ADAMS, Daniel, M.D. Medical and Agricultural Register for the years 1806 and 1807. Boston. 8vo.

ADAMS, Rev. Eliphalet. — See CAULKINS, F. M

ADAMS, George. Genealogy of the Adams Family, of Kingston, Mass. Boston, 1861. 8vo.

—— Maine Register, for the year 1855; Embracing State and County Officers, with a Bus. Direc. Portland, 1855. 12mo.

ADAMS, G. J. Letter to Pres. Tyler on the Signs of the Times, &c. N. York, 1844. 12mo. Mormon Pamph. Vol. 1.

ADAMS, Hannah. Abridgment of History of New England. Boston, 1805. 12mo.

ADAMS, John. — See ADAMS' MEMORIAL.

—— Correspondence with Wm. Cunningham, 1803–1812. Boston, 1823. 8vo. Congr. and Polit. Pamph. Vol. 109.

—— Correspondence Concerning Impressmemt and matters of interest during his Administration. Baltimore, 1809. 8vo. Congr. and Polit. Pamph. Vol. 199.

—— CRANCH, W. Memoir of Life and Character.

—— Discourses on Davila: a series of papers on Political History, written in 1809. Boston; 1805. 8vo.

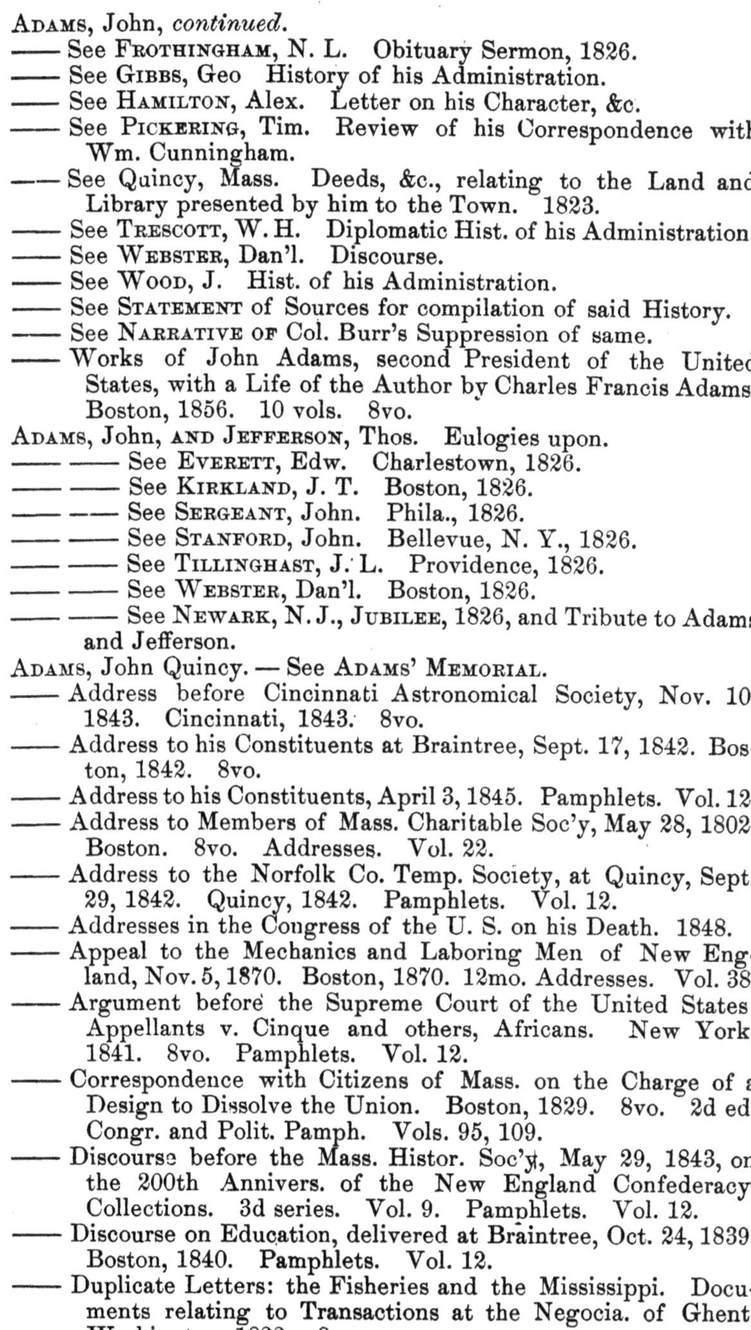

ADAMS, John, *continued.*
—— See FROTHINGHAM, N. L. Obituary Sermon, 1826.
—— See GIBBS, Geo History of his Administration.
—— See HAMILTON, Alex. Letter on his Character, &c.
—— See PICKERING, Tim. Review of his Correspondence with Wm. Cunningham.
—— See Quincy, Mass. Deeds, &c., relating to the Land and Library presented by him to the Town. 1823.
—— See TRESCOTT, W. H. Diplomatic Hist. of his Administration.
—— See WEBSTER, Dan'l. Discourse.
—— See WOOD, J. Hist. of his Administration.
—— See STATEMENT of Sources for compilation of said History.
—— See NARRATIVE OF Col. Burr's Suppression of same.
—— Works of John Adams, second President of the United States, with a Life of the Author by Charles Francis Adams. Boston, 1856. 10 vols. 8vo.
ADAMS, John, AND JEFFERSON, Thos. Eulogies upon.
—— —— See EVERETT, Edw. Charlestown, 1826.
—— —— See KIRKLAND, J. T. Boston, 1826.
—— —— See SERGEANT, John. Phila., 1826.
—— —— See STANFORD, John. Bellevue, N. Y., 1826.
—— —— See TILLINGHAST, J. L. Providence, 1826.
—— —— See WEBSTER, Dan'l. Boston, 1826.
—— —— See NEWARK, N. J., JUBILEE, 1826, and Tribute to Adams and Jefferson.
ADAMS, John Quincy. — See ADAMS' MEMORIAL.
—— Address before Cincinnati Astronomical Society, Nov. 10, 1843. Cincinnati, 1843. 8vo.
—— Address to his Constituents at Braintree, Sept. 17, 1842. Boston, 1842. 8vo.
—— Address to his Constituents, April 3, 1845. Pamphlets. Vol. 12.
—— Address to Members of Mass. Charitable Soc'y, May 28, 1802. Boston. 8vo. Addresses. Vol. 22.
—— Address to the Norfolk Co. Temp. Society, at Quincy, Sept. 29, 1842. Quincy, 1842. Pamphlets. Vol. 12.
—— Addresses in the Congress of the U. S. on his Death. 1848.
—— Appeal to the Mechanics and Laboring Men of New England, Nov. 5, 1870. Boston, 1870. 12mo. Addresses. Vol. 38.
—— Argument before the Supreme Court of the United States; Appellants v. Cinque and others, Africans. New York, 1841. 8vo. Pamphlets. Vol. 12.
—— Correspondence with Citizens of Mass. on the Charge of a Design to Dissolve the Union. Boston, 1829. 8vo. 2d ed. Congr. and Polit. Pamph. Vols. 95, 109.
—— Discourse before the Mass. Histor. Soc'y, May 29, 1843, on the 200th Annivers. of the New England Confederacy. Collections. 3d series. Vol. 9. Pamphlets. Vol. 12.
—— Discourse on Education, delivered at Braintree, Oct. 24, 1839. Boston, 1840. Pamphlets. Vol. 12.
—— Duplicate Letters: the Fisheries and the Mississippi. Documents relating to Transactions at the Negocia. of Ghent. Washington, 1822. 8vo.

ADAMS, John Quincy, *continued.*

—— Eulogy on the Life and Character of Jas. Madison, at Boston, Sept. 27, 1836. Boston, 1836. 8vo. Addresses. Vol. 24. Pamphlets. Vol. 11.

—— Eulogy on the Life and Character of James Monroe, Aug. 25, 1831. Boston, 1831. 8vo. Pamphlets. Vol. 11. Addresses. Vol. 24.

—— Jubilee of the Constitution. A Discourse before the N. York Hist. Soc'y, April 30, 1839. New York, 1839. 8vo. N. York Hist. Soc. Addresses. Vol. 2. Another copy. Pamphlets. Vol. 11.

—— Lectures on Rhetoric and Oratory, delivered in Harvard University. Cambridge, 1810. 2 vols. 8vo.

—— Letter to Hon. Harrison G. Otis on the State of our National Affairs. Newburyport, 1808. 12mo. Congress. and Polit. Pamph. Vol. 96.

—— Letter read at the Celebra. of West India Emancipation in Bangor, Me. 8vo. Pamphlets. Vol. 12.

—— Letters on the Masonic Institution. Boston, 1847. 8vo.

—— Letters to his Constituents, including his Speech in Congress, Feb. 9, 1837. Boston, 1838. 12mo.

—— Lives of James Madison and James Monroe. Buffalo, 1851. 12mo.

—— See LUNT, W. P. Obituary Discourse, 1848.

—— Oration addressed to the Citizens of the Town of Quincy, July 4, 1831. Boston, 1831. 8vo. Pamphlets. Vol. 12. Addresses. Vols. 2, 17.

—— Oration before the Cincinnati Astronom. Soc'y, Nov. 10, 1843. Cincinnati, 1843. 8vo. Addresses, etc. Vol. 35.

—— Oration on the Life, etc., of Gilbert Motier de Lafayette, before Congress, Dec. 31, 1834. Washington, 1835. 8vo. Pamphlets. Vol. 11. Other copies. Addresses, etc. Vols. 12, 28.

—— See QUINCY, Josiah. Memoir of Life of.

—— Report of Select Comm. in House of Repr. on the Smithsonian Bequest, March 5, 1840. Pamphlets. Vol. 12.

—— Report of Minority Comm. on Manufactures in the House of Representatives, Feb. 28, 1833. Boston, 1833. Pamphlets. Vol. 11.

—— See SEWARD, W. H. Life and Public Services.

—— See —— ORATION on.

—— Speech in Congress, 1834, on Removal of Deposits. Washington, 1834. 8vo. Speeches. Vol. 4. Another copy. Pamph. Vol. 11.

—— Speech on the Fortification Bill, delivered in the House of Repr., Jan. 22, 1836. Washington, 1836. Pamphlets. Vol. 11.

—— Speech in Congress, June 16, 1838, on the Freedom of Speech and Annexa. of Texas. Washington, 1838. 8vo. Pamphlets. Vol. 11.

—— Speech in Congress, Dec. 28, 1840, in relation to the Navy Pension Fund. Pamphlets. Vol. 12.

ADAMS, John Quincy, *continued.*
—— Substance of a Speech in Congress on the Bill to insure the more faithful Execution of the Laws relating to the Collection of Duties. Boston, 1849. 8vo. Pamphlets. Vol. 12.
—— The New England Confederacy of 1643. A Bi-Centennial Discourse before the Mass. Hist. Soc'y, May 29, 1843. Mass. Hist. Soc. Coll. 3d series. Vol. 9.
—— The Social Compact Exemplified in the Constitution of the Commonwealth of Mass. A Lecture. Pamphlets. Vol. 12. Providence, 1842. 8vo.
—— See WALKER, T. Oration on.
ADAMS, John Q. and Chas. F. Life of John Adams. Phila., 1871. 2 vols. 12mo.
ADAMS, Joseph. Account of Huntington County, Pa. Hist. Soc. of Pa. Collec. Vol. 1.
ADAMS, Josiah. Centen. Address at Acton, Mass., July 21, 1835. Boston, 1835. 8vo. Mass. Hist. Discourses. Vol. 4.
—— Genealogy of the Descendants of Rich'd Haven, of Lynn, Mass. Boston, 1843. 8vo. Genealog. Pamph. Vol. 8.
ADAMS' MEMORIAL: containing Sketches of John Adams and John Quincy Adams. Boston, 1848. 8vo. Congr. and Polit. Pamph. Vol. 75.
ADAMS, Nathan'l. Annals of Portsmouth for Two Hundred Years. Portsmouth, 1825. 8vo.
—— Memoir of Hon. Sam'l Penhallow. Maine Hist. Soc. Collections. Vol. 1.
ADAMS, Nehemiah, D. D. Discourse and Address on the Death of Hon. Rufus Choate. Boston, 1859. 12mo. Sermons. Vol. 51.
—— Sermon at Boston, Oct. 31, 1852, on the Death of Dan'l Webster. Boston, 1852. 8vo. Sermons. Vol. 32.
—— Sermon at Boston, Dec. 9, 1846, on the Death of Wm. J. Armstrong, D. D. Boston, 1846. 8vo. Sermons. Vol. 35.
ADAMS, Sam'l. — See CORRESPONDENCE with John Adams, 1790.
—— Petition to Cong. in relation to his Exploration of the Colorado River of the West. 1870. Congr. and Political Pamph. Vols. 108, 116.
—— See WELLS, W. V. Life and Pub. Services of.
ADAMS, Stephen. Speech in Congress, Dec. 11, 1854, on the Nat uraliza. Laws. Speeches. Vol. 5.
ADAMS, Rev. Wm. — See CAULKINS, F. M.
ADDERLEY, C. B. Reflections on the Speech of Lord Russell on Colonial Policy. London, 1850. 8vo. Strangford Pamph. Vol. 54.
—— The Australian Colonies Gov't Bill discussed. London, 1849. 8vo. Strangford Pamph. Vol. 54.
ADDEY, M. Life of Gen. Thomas J. Jackson. New York, 1863. 12mo.
ADDISON Co., VT., BAPTIST ASSOC. Minutes of the 18th and 19th Anniversaries, held in 1851–52. Middlebury. 8vo.
ADDISON Co., VT. — See LAMB, Rev. D. List of Cong. Ministers.
—— See SWIFT, S. Statis. and Hist. Acc.

ADDISON, Joseph. — See AIKEN, L. Life of.

—— Letter from Italy to Charles, Lord Halifax. London, 1709. 12mo. Poetry. Vol. 20.

—— Memoir of. n. d. 8vo. Biograph. Pamph. Vol. 18.

—— The Spectator: edited with Notes by George W. Greene. New York, 1858. 2 vols. 12mo.

ADDRESS AND RECOMMENDATIONS to the States by Congress. Philadelphia, 1783. American Tracts. Vol. 4.

ADDRESS from one of the Secretaries to the Stockholders of the Fire Insurance Companies of N. York. N. York, 1858. 8vo. N. York City Miscell. Pamph. Vol. 5.

—— of Members of the U. S. House of Repr. to their Constituents, on the subject of War with G. Britain. Boston, 1812. 8vo. Congr. and Polit. Pamph. Vol. 123.

—— of Members of the House of Representatives on the War with Great Britain. Alexandria, 1812. 8vo. Congress. Pamph. Vol. 97.

—— of Members of House of Representatives of U. S. on the War with Great Britain. New York, 1812. 8vo. Addresses, etc. Vol. 8.

—— of Ohio Soldiers in the Army of the Cumberland, to the People of Ohio. Toledo, 1863. 8vo. Rebell'n Pamph. Vol. 48.

—— of the Comm. appointed at a public meeting held in Boston, Dec. 19, 1823, for the Relief of the Greeks. Boston. 8vo. Addresses, etc. Vol. 32.

—— of the People of Sheffield, Eng., to the British Nation, on Parliamentary Reform. Sheffield, 1794. 12mo. Eng. Polit. Pamph. Vol. 74.

—— of the Republicans of the City and County of N. York, to Republicans of the U. S. N. York, 1808. 8vo. Congr. and Polit. Pamph. Vols. 75, 134.

—— of Democratic Members of Congress to Democracy of the U. States. Rebell'n Pamph. Vol. 61.

—— of the Democratic State Central Committee of Penn. Phila., 1863. 8vo. Rebell'n Pamph. Vol. 10.

—— of Penn. Democratic State Central Committee. 1864. Rebell'n Pamph. Vol. 46.

—— of the Union State Central Committee of Maryland. Baltimore. n. d. 8vo. Rebell'n Pamph. Vol. 108.

—— of the Young Men of Philadelphia to the Young Men of the United States. Philadelphia, 1834. 8vo. Speeches. Vol. 4.

—— of the People's Club of Philadelphia, in favor of Gen. Simon Cameron for President. Philadelphia, 1859. 8vo. Addresses, etc. Vol. 13.

—— of Committee appointed at a public meeting at Boston, Sept. 24, 1846, on the recent case of Kidnapping. Boston, 1846. 8vo. Addresses, etc. Vol. 1.

—— of the Young Men's Temperance Society to the Young Men of Boston. 1832. 8vo. Addresses, etc. Vol. 1.

—— on Laying the Foundation Stone of Highbury College, with Addresses. London, 1826. 8vo. Addresses, etc. Vol. 12.

ADDRESS, *continued.*

—— to the Anti-Slavery Christians of the U. S. N. York, 1852. 8vo. Congr. and Polit. Pamph. Vol. 139.

—— to the Electors and other Free Subjects of G. Britain; occasioned by the late Secession. London, 1733. 8vo. Eng. Polit. Pamph. Vol. 68.

—— to the English Nation; with a Sketch of the Existing Grievances, &c. London, 1796. 8vo. Eng. Polit. Pamph. Vol. 75.

—— to the Inhabitants of St. James' Westminister, on Sanatory Affairs. London, 1847. 8vo. Eng. Miscell. Pamph. Vol. 30.

—— to the Knights, Citizens, and Burgesses, elected to represent the Commons in the ensuing Parliament. London, 1734. 8vo. Eng. Polit. Pamph. Vol. 67.

—— to the People, by the Democracy of Wisconsin, Sept. 3, 1862. Madison, 1862. 8 vo. Wis. Miscell. Pamph. Vol. 6.

—— to the People of England; in which the Conduct of Lord Sackville is considered. London, 1759. 8vo, Eng. Polit. Pamph. Vol. 71.

—— to the People of Mass., by Members of the Legislature of the State. n. d. 8vo. Congr. and Polit. Pamph. Vol. 139.

—— to the People of Massachusetts, by the Friends of Temperance. Boston, 1838. 8vo. Mass. Miscell. Pamph. Vol. 4.

—— to the People of the County of Hampshire, Mass., by a Committee appointed for that purpose. Northampton, 1809. 8vo. Miscell. Tracts. Vol. 1.

—— to the Republican Citizens of the State of New York, 1828. Congr. and Polit. Pamphlets. Vol. 97.

—— to Christians throughout the World, by the Clergy of the Confederate States. London. (n. d.) Rebell'n Pamph. Vol. 29.

—— to the Parliament of G. Britain, on the Claims of Authors to their own Copyright. London, 1813. 8vo. Pamphleteer. Vol. 2.

—— to the Citizens of Boston and Vicinity, on the subject of a Rural Cemetery. Boston, 1850. 8vo. Boston Miscell. Pamph. Vol. 2.

—— to the Democracy of the United States on the duty of the Democratic Party. 1863. Rebell'n Pamph. Vol. 15.

—— to the Parishioners of St. Peter's Church, Pittsburgh, Penn. 1864. Rebell'n Pamph. Vol. 29.

—— to the People of R. Island, &c., to promote the establishment of a State Constitution. Providence, 1834. 8vo. R. I. Miscell. Pamph. Vol. 1.

—— to the People of the State of N. York, on the subject of the Constitution agreed upon at Phila., Sept. 17, 1787. N. York. (n. d.) 4to. N. York Miscell. Pamph. Vol. 2.

—— to the People of the U. States, by Democratic Members of Congress. Washington, 1864. 8vo. Rebell'n Pamph. Vol. 38.

—— to the Bishops, upon a late Letter from Lord ——, to certain Clergy, &c. London, 1790. 8vo. Eng. Polit. Pamph. Vol. 23.

ADDRESS, *continued.*
—— to the Voters of the Fourth Congress'l District. Boston, 1860. 8vo. Mass. Miscell. Pamph. Vol. 2.
—— to the Young Men of the City of New York, friendly to the Election of Gen. Andrew Jackson to the Presidency. 1828. Addresses, &c. Vol. 12.
—— to the People; occasioned by "A Letter to the Queen, from a Friend of the People." London, 1839. 8vo. Eng. Polit. Pamph. Vol. 42.
—— to the Members of the House of Commons, upon the Necessity of Reforming our Financial System, &c. London, 1822 8vo. Eng. Polit. Pamph. Vol. 36.
—— to the Princess Charlotte on her Marriage: showing the Cause of the present distress, and its remedy. London, 1816. 8vo. Pamphleteer. Vol. 8.
—— to the Community on the Necessity of Legalizing the Study of Anatomy. Boston, 1829. 8vo. Med. Pamph. Vol. 9.
—— to De Cadogan, occasioned by his Dissertation on the Gout, &c. London, 1771. 8vo. Med. Pamph. Vol. 23.

ADDRESSES AND MESSAGES of the Presidents of the U. States, from Washington to Harrison. N. York, 1841. 8vo.

ADDRESSES at the Inauguration of Rev. James Walker. D.D., as President of Harvard College, May 23, 1853. Cambridge, 1853. 8vo. Addresses, &c. Vol. 10.
—— at the Inauguration of Geo. F. Magoon, as President of Iowa College, July 9th, 1865. Chicago, 1865. 8vo. Addresses, &c. Vol. 19.
—— at the Inauguration of Hon. Thos. Frelinghuysen as President of Rutgers College, July 24, 1850. Addresses. Vol. 12.
—— by Gov. J. A. Andrew, Hon. E. Everett, Hon. B. F. Thomas and Hon. R. C. Winthrop. Aug. 27, 1862, in aid of recruiting. Boston, 1862. 8vo. Rebell'n Pamph. Vol. 66.
—— delivered at the Organization Meeting of the Department of Public Instruction, N. York, Apr. 29, 1871. N. York, 1871. 8vo. N. York City Pamph. Vol. 6.
—— in Cong., and Funeral Solemnities on the Death of J. Q. Adams. Washington, 1848. 8vo. Addresses. Vol. 24.
—— in Cong., Apr. 1, 1850, on the Death of J. C. Calhoun. Washington, 1850. 8vo. Addresses. Vol. 17.
—— in Cong., May 30 and 31, 1850, on the Death of F. H. Elmore. Cong. and Polit. Pamph. Vol. 90.
—— in Cong., Dec. 8, 1853, on the Death of Wm. R. King. Washington, 1854. 8vo.
—— in Cong., Dec. 3, 1856, on the Death of Hon. J. M. Clayton. Cong. and Polit. Pamph. Vol. 88. Also, Addresses. Vol. 17.
—— in Cong., July 10, 1859, on the Death of Zachary Taylor. Washington. 8vo. Addresses. Vol. 5.
—— in Cong., July 9, 1861, on the Death of Hon. Stephen A. Douglas. Washington, 1861. 8 vo. Rebell'n Pamph. Vol. 31. Addresses, &c. Vol. 19.
—— in Cong., Dec. 11, 1862, on the Death of Hon. Edw. D. Baker. Washington, 1862. 8vo. Reb. Pam. Vols. 60 and 80.

ADDRESSES, *continued*.

—— in Cong., Mar. 28, 1864, on the Death of Hon. Owen Lovejoy. Washington, 1864. 8vo. Addresees. Vol. 17.

—— in Cong., Dec. 14, 1865, on the Death of Hon. J. Collamer. Washington, 1866. 8vo. Cong. and Polit. Pamph. Vol. 121.

—— in Cong., Apr. 12, 1866, on the Death of Hon. Solomon Foote. Washington, 1866. 8vo. Addresses. Vol. 17.

—— in Cong., Feb. 9, 1871, on the Death of Hon. John Covode. Washington, 1871. 8vo.

—— of Hon. W. D. Kelley, Miss Anna E. Dickinson and Frederick Douglass, July 4, 1863, at Philadelphia. Rebell'n Pamph. Vol. 91.

—— on the Presentation of the Sword of Gen. Andrew Jackson to Congress, Feb. 26, 1855. Addresses. Vol. 5. Congr. and Polit. Pamph. Vols. 56 and 88.

—— Memorial Day. — See ANDERSON, Col. E. F. 1870.

—— See SHEPARD, Gen. I. F. Jefferson Barracks. 1870.

—— to the Legislature of Indiana on Education. Terre Haute, 1849. 8vo. Indianapolis, 1852. 8vo. Indiana Miscell. Pamph. Vol. 1.

ADIRONDAC MOUNTAINS — See STEVENS, Geo. T. The Flora of.

ADMIRAL ALPIN, Indiaman. — See LETTERS Intercepted on Board the Vessel, &c.

—— See PLAYFAIR, Wm. Proof relative to the Falsification of the Intercepted Correspondence, &c.

ADMISSION OF CALIFORNIA, New Mexico, &c. — See CONGRESSIONAL SPEECHES.

ADSHEAD, Joseph. On Juvenile Criminals, Reformatories, &c. Manchester, Eng. 1856. 8vo. Eng. Miscell. Pamph. Vol. 14.

—— Our present Gaol System. London. 1847. 8vo. Strangford Pamph. Vol. 43.

ADVANTAGES for a Division of the County of Ulster, N. Y., and for the Formation of the County of Highland. 1860.

ADVENTURER (The). By Dr. Hawkesworth and other contributors. London, 1752–4, folio.

ADVENTURES on the Prairie and Life among the Indians. Glasgow. n. d. 8vo.

AELFRIC'S GRAMMAR AND GLOSSARY. — See PHILLIPS, Sir T. Fragment of.

AERON, (The). — See ANDREWS, S. Letter to Cong. 1864.

AERONAUTICS — See MASON, M. Account of a late Expedition from London to Weilburg.

—— See SHELDON, W. Aerial Navigation.

—— See WISE, John. System of. 1850.

AESTHETICS. — See FIELD, Geo.

—— See MOFFAT, J. C. Introduc. to Study of.

—— See SIMMS, W. G. The Sense of the Beautiful. An Address.

AFFGHAN PAPERS. — See NEWCASTLE FOREIGN AFFAIRS Assoc.

AFFGHAN WAR. Causes and Consequences of the. London. 1842. 8vo. Strangford Pamph. Vol. 38.

—— See URQUHART, D. Edinburgh Review and the Affghan War. 1843.

AFRICA. — See Account of. 1768.
—— See AFRICAN REPOSITORY.
—— See ALGOA BAY AND ALBANY.
—— See APPEAL to the Churches in behalf of Africa. 1834.
—— See BOWEN, T. J. On the Country and People of Yoruba.
—— See COATES, B. Cotton Cultivation in.
—— See COLONIZATION.
—— See COOMBS, J. H. Livingstone's Explorations.
—— See DUNCAN, J. Travels in Western A.
—— See ENTICK, J. Hist. of Late War.
—— See HARRIS, W. C. Expedition into Southern Africa. 1836.
—— See HEAD, F. B. Bruce. Life and Advent.
—— See HODGSON, W. B. Sketch of the Berbers and their Language.
—— See JAMESON, Robt. Commerce with Liberia.
—— See LANDER, R. and J. Expedit. to Source of Niger.
—— See BRYANT, Rev. J. C. Zulu Language.
—— See GROUT, Rev. Lewis. Zulu and other Dialects.
—— See WILSON, Rev. J. L. Negro Dialects of Africa.
—— See MAUROY, M. Du Commerce des peuples de l'Afrique.
—— See MOFFAT, R. Missionary Labors in South A.
—— See PARK, M. Travels after the Source of the Niger.
—— See Proposals for Letting and Preserving the British Trade to Africa. London. Folio. *Circa.* 1750. Eng. Miscell. Pamph. Vol. 37.
—— See SHALER, W. On the Language, Customs, &c , of the Berbers of Africa.
AFRICA. — The Deserts of. Chambers' Papers for the People. n. d. 8vo. Hist. Pamph. Vol. 20.
—— See TRACY. J, State of Society in West Africa
—— See U. S. House of Repr. Report of Naval Comm. in regard to Mail Steamships. 1850.
AFRICAN COLONIZATION. — See CONGRESSIONAL Speeches.
—— —— See MITCHELL, Jas. Letter to the President.
—— Institution. Extracts from the 18th and 19th Reports of the Directors, read at London, 1824–5. Phila., 1826. 8vo. Pamph. on Colonization. Vol. 1.
—— Repository. Vols. 31–48. Washington, 1855–72. 18 vols. 8vo.
—— Slave Trade in Jamaica, and comparative treatment of Slaves. Read before the Md. Hist. Soc., Oct. 1854. Baltimore, 1854. Md. Hist. Soc. Addresses. Vol. 3.
—— Slave Trade: the Secret Purpose of the Insurgents to Revive it. 1863. Rebell'n Pamph. Vol. 75.
—— See TEXUGO, F. T. Letter on. 1839.
AGASSIZ, Louis. Address delivered on the Centen. Annivers. of the Birth of Alexander von Humboldt, under the auspices of the Boston Soc'y of Nat. History. Boston, 1869. 8vo. Scientific Pamph. Vol. 40.
—— A Journey in Brazil. Illustrated. Boston, 1871. 8vo.
—— BACHMAN, J.
—— Contributions to the Natural History of the United States of America. Boston, 1858–62. 4 vols. 4to.

AGASSIZ, Louis, *continued.*
—— HARTT, C. F., and AGASSIZ, L.
—— Introduction to the Study of Natural History, with a Short Biography of the Author. N. York, 1847. 8vo. Scientific Pamph. Vol. 19.
—— Lake Superior: its Physical Character, Vegetation, and Animals; with a Narrative of the Tour, by J. Elliot Cabot. Boston, 1850. 8vo.
—— On the Classification of Insects from Embryological Data. Smithson. Contr. Vol. 2.
AGGAWAM. — See WARD, N. Simple Cobbler of.
AGNEW, Dan'l. Our National Constitution: its Adaptation to a State of War or Insurrection. Phila., 1863. 8vo. Rebell'n Pamph. Vols. 26, 28, 66, 91.
AGRICULTURAL BUREAU: Establishment of. — See CONGRESSIONAL Speeches.
—— Education. — See KLIPPART, J. H. Addresses. 1866.
—— Essays. — See ESSEX, Mass., AGR. SOC'Y.
—— Occupation: dignity of. — See MARSHALL, J. T. Address, 1838.
—— Science. — See HENKLE, M. M. Dignity and Claims of.
AGRICULTURE. — See ADAMS, D. Med. and Agric. Register. 1806–7.
—— ALLEN, R. L. Domestic Animals.
—— American Agriculturist. 1842–49. 1865–68.
—— BLAKE, J. L. Farmers' Every-Day Book.
—— Bristol Co. Agr. Soc.
—— Essex Co. Agr. Soc.
—— Franklin Co. Agr. Soc.
—— Norfolk Co. Agr. Soc.
—— Various States.
—— CAMPENS, E. Opbrenging en Bestiering, etc.
—— Canadian Agriculturist.
—— Chicago Jour. and Prairie Farmer. 1858–61.
—— Chinese Sugar Cane, etc.
—— Cincinnatus. 1857–60.
—— COLMAN, H. European Agr.
—— Cultivator (The). 1838–1841.
—— Culture of Grapes.
—— DARLINGTON, W. Agricul. Botany.
—— DAVIS, N. S. Text-Book on.
—— DAVIS, T. View of Agr. of Wiltshire, Eng.
—— FRAAS, Dr. Geschichte Landwirthschaft.
—— France. Exposit. 1855.
—— Gen. View of Lincolnshire, Eng.
—— Genessee Farmer and Gardeners' Journal. 1831.
—— GUERNSEY and WILLARD. Hist. of Rock Co. Agr. Soc., Wis.
—— HARRIS, T. M. Insects Injurious to Vegetation.
—— Louisville, Ky., Dollar Farmer. 1842–3.
—— Michigan Farmer.
—— MIDDLETON, J. View of Agr. of Middlesex, Eng.

AGRICULTURE, *continued.*
—— MOLL, M. L. Handboch voor den Landbouwer.
—— Monthly Journal of. 1846–8.
—— MORRELL, L. A. Amer. Shepherd.
—— MORSE, A. Agr. and the Corn Law.
—— Papers on Agrcul. Boston, 1801. 8vo. Agr. Pam. Vol. 11.
—— PITKIN, T. Statistical view of Commerce and.
—— PITT, W. View of Worcester Co., Eng.
—— SALISBURY, J. H. History, etc., of Maize. 1849.
—— SERRA, J. C. de. Observa. on the Soil of Kentucky.
—— Soil of the South.
—— SOMERVILLE, R. Gen. View of East Lothian.
—— Transactions of N. Y. Soc.
—— U. S. Agricult. Soc. 1859.
—— U. STATES Comm'r of Agr.
—— U. S. Patent Office Reports.
—— VIELE, E. L. On Refuse of Cities.
—— WASHINGTON, G. Letters on.
—— WATSON, E. On Modern Agricul. Societies.
—— WATSON, W. C. Treatise on Practical Husbandry.
—— Wisconsin and Western Farmer. 1849–72.
—— WHITTLESEY, C. On the Agr. of Ohio.
—— Wisconsin Agr. Soc. Trans. 1851–9.
—— VARIOUS STATES. Reports Board of Agr., etc.

AIKEN, Chas. A., D. D. — See UNION COLLEGE.

AIKEN, Rev. S. C. The Laws of Ohio in respect to Colored People, shown to be unjust, etc. Address at Cleveland. 1845. Ohio Miscell. Pamph. Vol. 2.

AIKIN, Arthur. Address at the Ann. Distribution of Rewards by the Soc'y for the Encouragement of Arts, etc. 1817. London. 8vo. Scientific Pamph. Vol. 29.

AIKIN, Lucy. Life of Joseph Addison. Phila., 1846. 12mo.

AIKIN, Wm. E. A. Geology of the Country between Baltimore and the Ohio River. 1834. Silliman's Journ. Vol. 26.

AIKMAN, Wm. The Father of the Colored Race in America. 1862. Rebell'n Pamph. Vol. 74.

AITKIN, Wm. B. Remarks in the New York Assembly on the Canal Fund. n. d. 8vo. Addresses, etc. Vol. 19.

AIX LA CHAPELLE, France. — See DEFINITE TREATY. 1748.

AKERMAN, A. T. Opinion on the Reimbursement of Interest upon Union Pacific R. R. Bonds. Washington, 1871. 8vo. Congr. and Polit. Pamph. Vol. 138.

AKERMAN, John Y. Archæological Index to Remains of Antiquity of the Celtic, Romano-British, and Anglo-Saxon Periods. London, 1847. 8vo.
—— Glossary of Provincial Words and Phrases in use in Wiltshire. London, 1842. 12mo.
—— Intro. to the Study of Ancient and Modern Coins. London, 1848. 12mo.
—— Remains of Pagan Saxondom. London, 1855. 4to.
—— Remarks on the coins of Ephesus, struck during the Roman Dominion. London, 1841. 8vo. Scientific Pamph. Vol. 39.

ALABAMA — Acts of the 7th Biennial Session of General Assembly. Montgomery, 1860. 8vo.

—— Ann. Report of Supt. of Education for 1856. Montgomery, 1857. 8vo.

—— and Chattanooga Railroad Prospectus. Boston, 1870. 8vo. Alabama Pamph. Vol. 1.

—— and Tennessee River Railroad. Letter of the Chief Engineer in relation to. Selma, Ala., 1850. 8vo. Alabama Pamph. Vol. 1.

—— Auditors' Report for 1870. Montgomery, 1870. 8vo.

—— See BALDWIN. J. G. Flush Times in.

—— See BREWER, G. Ala., her Hist., Resources. etc. 1540—1872.

—— See BUREAU OF REFUGEES AND FREEDMEN.

ALABAMA CLAIMS — Award of the Geneva Tribunal for the Settlement of Private Alabama Claims. Englewod, N. J., 1873. 8vo. Congr. and Polit. Pamph. Vol. 8.

—— See BEAMAN, C. C. National and Private Alabama Claims.

—— CONGRESS'L SPEECHES.

—— JOHNSON, Reverdy. Reply to Sir Roundell Palmer.

—— LORING, C. G. England's Liability for Indemnity.

—— Memorandum showing the manner in which the Alabama Claims have been treated by the Gov't, until the Geneva Award. n. d. 8vo. Congr. and Polit. Pamph. Vol. 68.

—— Official Correspondence on the Claims of the U. S. in respect to the Alabama. London, 1867. 8vo.

—— See PARKER, J. A. Argument, etc.

—— The Question. An Imaginary Letter to the "Times." London. 1872. 8vo. Congr. and Polit. Pamph. Vol. 140.

—— REBEL STEAMER — See Story of the Kearsage and Alabama.

—— Comptroller's Report for 1866. Montgomery, 1866. 8vo.

—— CONSTITUTION OF. Reprint of the Official Constitution, as revised and amended Nov. 5, 1867. Washington. n. d. 8vo.

—— Same Ala. Newspaper Extra. Ala. Pamph. Vol. 1.

—— Ordinances and Constitution of, with the Constitution of the Confed. Statos. Montgomery, 1861. 8vo. Ala. Miscell. Pamph. Vol. 2.

—— See DARBY, W. Geograph. Descrip. of.

—— Geology. — See HALE, S. C. Geol· of South Alabama.

—— Laws passed at Session of 1865 and 1866--7. Mobile. 2 Vols. 8vo.

—— See LEA, Isaac. Contributions to Geology of. 1833.

—— LOCAL HISTORY — See Mobile.

—— Memorial of Gen. Assem. of Ala., to Cong. Nov. 2, 1872, against Domestic Violence. Ala. Miscell. Pamph. Vol. 2.

—— Messages and Documents. 1869--70. Montgomery, 1870. 8vo.

—— or Here we Rest. An Indian Legend of Olden Times. Cleveland, O., 1863. Indian Pamph. Vol. 3.

—— See PATTON, R. M. Address to People of. 1868.

—— Penal Code adopted by Gen. Assembly in 1865--66. Montgomery. 1866. 8vo.

ALABAMA, *continued.*
—— See PICKETT, A. J. History of.
—— Construction Bill.—See Congress'l Speeches.
—— University of. Historical Catalogue of the Officers and Alumni, from 1821 to 1870. Tuscaloosa. 1870. 8vo.
ALASKA — Cession of to U. S. — See Congress'l Speeches.
—— See DALL. W. H. Alaska and its Resources.
—— Report of Special Agent of Alaska on the Fur Seal Fisheries. Washington. 1870. Sec. of Treas. Miscell. Rep'ts.
—— See SUMNER, C. Speech in U. S. Senate. 1867.
—— See WHYMPER, Geo. Travels and Adventures.
ALBACH, James R. Annals of the West; or Accounts of Events in the Western States and Territories from the Discovery of the Mississippi Valley to the year 1856. Pittsburgh, 1857. 8vo. — See PERKINS, J. H.
ALBANY ACADEMY. — Catalogue for 1851–52, 1852–53. Celebration of the Semi Centennial Anni. 1863. Statutes and Register for 1871–2. Albany. 8vo.
—— and Schenectady R. R. Co. *vs.* Mayor of the City of Albany before N. Y. Court of Appeals. Law Pamphlets. Vol. 2.
—— and Susquehanna R. R. Co. Considerations on the proposed construction of. 1852.
—— —— By-Laws. 1853.
—— —— Remarks on the Prospects of. 1854.
—— —— Address by the Directors. 1856. Albany. v. d. 8vo.
—— and West Stockbridge R. R. Co. Act of Incorporation, etc. Albany. 1840. 8vo.
—— Annual Register for 1849 and 1850. Albany. 12mo. 1849 and 1850. 2 Vols.
—— Argus. Newspaper. Feb. 1844. Dec. 1845. Folio. 2 Vols.
—— Army Relief Bazaar. Catalogue of Rare and Valuable Curiosities for Sale. Feb. 22, 1864. Albany. 1864. 8vo. Rebell'n Pamph. Vol. 107.
—— Balance, and New York State Journal of. Newspaper. Jan. to Dec. 1809. Folio.
—— —— Same. Jan. to Dec. 1810. Folio.
—— See BARNES, W. Address on Early History of. 1850.
—— Basin. Report of Commissioners. Publications of Albany. 1842. 8vo.
—— Bridge Case. HILL, Nicholas. Argument before U. S. Circuit Court. 1858.
—— SEWARD, W. H. Argument before U. S. Circuit Court. 1858.
—— Chamberlain Reports for the years 1821, 1835–6, 1838–53. Publications of Albany.
—— Children's Friend Soc'y. 1st. Ann. Report of the Industrial School. 1857. 8vo. Albany Miscell. Pamph. Vol. 1.
—— Church Brotherhood. Constitution and By-Laws. Albany, 1853. 8vo. Albany Miscell. Pamph. Vol. 1.
—— City and County Census. 1720. See Doc. Hist. of N. York. Vol. 1.
—— City Directories. 1840, 45, 47, 50, 51, 52, 53, 54, 55, 58, 60. Albany, 1840–1860. 12mo.

ALBANY ACADEMY, *continued.*

—— Directory. Collected etc., by J. Fry. Albany, 1813. 8vo. Reprinted, 1853.

—— City Missionary Soc'y, Abstract from the 8th Ann. Report, 1851. 17th Ann. Report, 1860. Albany, 1860. 8vo.

—— City Park, MURRAY, D. Olmsted, Vaux & Co.

—— City Salt Manufacturing Co. of Michigan. Articles of Assoc., and By-Laws. Albany, N. Y., 1864. 8vo. Mich. Miscell. Pamph. Vol. 1.

—— Tract Society. Seventeenth and Eighteenth Annual Reports for 1852, & 3 Publications of Albany.

—— Tract Soc'y. 19th Ann. Report for 1854. Albany, 1855. 8vo.

—— Tract & Missionary Soc'y. Ann. Reports for 1857, '58, '63, '66, '68, '69, '70. Albany, 1858–1871. 8vo.

—— Classis. Report of the Committee on Ministerial Support. Albany, 1854. 8vo. Albany Miscell. Pamph. Vol. 2.

—— Common Council. Report of the Water Committee, 1846, 1851. 8vo.

—— Congregational Convention. Report of the Sec'y and Treasurer of the Central Committee etc. N. York, 1856. 8vo. Albany Miscell. Pamph. Vol. 2.

—— Co. Bible Soc'y. See BROWN, S. D. Sermon, 1864.

—— ——. 4th, 49th, 53d, 57th, 58th, 59th, 60th, Ann. Reports, Albany. 8vo. 1815, 1861–71.

—— Co.Board of Supervisors. Journal for 1858. Albany, 1859. 8vo.

—— Co. Medical Soc'y. See ARMSBY, J. H. Address, 1851. WILLARD, S. D.

—— Medical Society. By-Laws. Albany, 1851. 8vo. Med. Pamph. Vol. 33.

—— Statistical Report of the County of Albany for the year 1820. 2d Ed. Albany, 1824. Publications of Albany.

—— Evangelical Luth. Ebenezer Church. Rules and Regulations for the Govt. of. Albany, 1851. 8vo. Albany Miscell. Pamph. Vol. 1.

—— Evening Journal Almanac. Albany, 1867. 8vo.

—— Exchange Bank. Articles of Association, and the General Banking Law of the State of N. York. Albany, 1838. 8vo. Albany Miscell. Pamph. Vol. 1.

—— Female Academy. Exercises of the Alumnae for the years 1846, '47, '48. 8vo. Albany. Pamphlets. Vol. 2.

—— Exercises of the Alumnae, 1846, '53, '56, '57. Catalogue for 1856, '58, '59, '64, 72. Report of Ann. Examinations, 1857, '63, '64. Albany. 8vo.

—— Circular and Catalogue of, for the year 1850. Albany, 1850. 8vo. Pamphlets. Vol. 2.

—— 1st Cong. Church. Articles of Faith and Covenant, etc. Albany, 1853. 8vo. N. York Hist. Discourses, etc. Vol. 4.

—— 1st Presbyt'n Ch. Catalogue of Communicants to 1843. Albany, 1843. Pamph. Vol. 2.

—— Report on the subject of building a new Church edifice. 1847. 8vo. Albany Miscell. Pamph. Vol. 1.

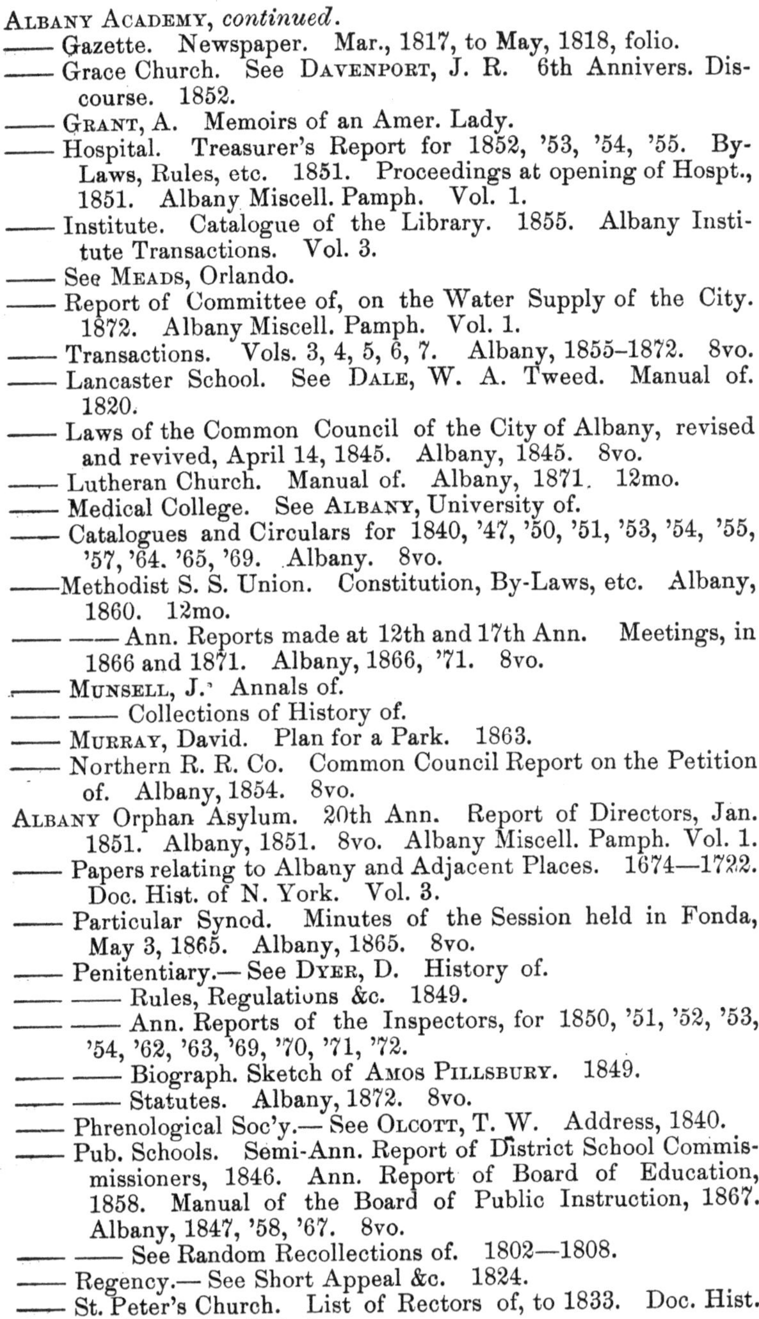

ALBANY ACADEMY, *continued.*

—— Gazette. Newspaper. Mar., 1817, to May, 1818, folio.

—— Grace Church. See DAVENPORT, J. R. 6th Annivers. Discourse. 1852.

—— GRANT, A. Memoirs of an Amer. Lady.

—— Hospital. Treasurer's Report for 1852, '53, '54, '55. By-Laws, Rules, etc. 1851. Proceedings at opening of Hospt., 1851. Albany Miscell. Pamph. Vol. 1.

—— Institute. Catalogue of the Library. 1855. Albany Institute Transactions. Vol. 3.

—— See MEADS, Orlando.

—— Report of Committee of, on the Water Supply of the City. 1872. Albany Miscell. Pamph. Vol. 1.

—— Transactions. Vols. 3, 4, 5, 6, 7. Albany, 1855–1872. 8vo.

—— Lancaster School. See DALE, W. A. Tweed. Manual of. 1820.

—— Laws of the Common Council of the City of Albany, revised and revived, April 14, 1845. Albany, 1845. 8vo.

—— Lutheran Church. Manual of. Albany, 1871. 12mo.

—— Medical College. See ALBANY, University of.

—— Catalogues and Circulars for 1840, '47, '50, '51, '53, '54, '55, '57, '64. '65, '69. Albany. 8vo.

——Methodist S. S. Union. Constitution, By-Laws, etc. Albany, 1860. 12mo.

—— —— Ann. Reports made at 12th and 17th Ann. Meetings, in 1866 and 1871. Albany, 1866, '71. 8vo.

—— MUNSELL, J. Annals of.

—— —— Collections of History of.

—— MURRAY, David. Plan for a Park. 1863.

—— Northern R. R. Co. Common Council Report on the Petition of. Albany, 1854. 8vo.

ALBANY Orphan Asylum. 20th Ann. Report of Directors, Jan. 1851. Albany, 1851. 8vo. Albany Miscell. Pamph. Vol. 1.

—— Papers relating to Albany and Adjacent Places. 1674—1722. Doc. Hist. of N. York. Vol. 3.

—— Particular Synod. Minutes of the Session held in Fonda, May 3, 1865. Albany, 1865. 8vo.

—— Penitentiary.— See DYER, D. History of.

—— —— Rules, Regulations &c. 1849.

—— —— Ann. Reports of the Inspectors, for 1850, '51, '52, '53, '54, '62, '63, '69, '70, '71, '72.

—— —— Biograph. Sketch of AMOS PILLSBURY. 1849.

—— —— Statutes. Albany, 1872. 8vo.

—— Phrenological Soc'y.— See OLCOTT, T. W. Address, 1840.

—— Pub. Schools. Semi-Ann. Report of District School Commismissioners, 1846. Ann. Report of Board of Education, 1858. Manual of the Board of Public Instruction, 1867. Albany, 1847, '58, '67. 8vo.

—— —— See Random Recollections of. 1802—1808.

—— Regency.— See Short Appeal &c. 1824.

—— St. Peter's Church. List of Rectors of, to 1833. Doc. Hist. of N. York. Vol. 3.

ALBANY Orphan Asylum, *continued.*
—— St. Peter's Church. Report of Lay Delegates to the Diocesan Convention at N. York, in Sept., 1845. Albany, 1845. 8vo. Albany Pamph. Vol. 2.
—— 2d Presb. Ch.— See SPRAGUE, Rev. W. B. Hist. of.
—— Proceedings of Citizens of Albany, Nov. 27, 1847. On M. Vattemare's plan of Interna. Exchange. Albany, 1849. 8vo. Albany Miscell. Pamph. Vol. 1.
—— Scotch Light Infantry.— Constitution & By-Laws. Albany, 1851. 12mo. Albany Miscell. Pamph. Vol. 1.
—— State Street High School.— Circular, 1866. Albany. 4to.
—— Presb. Church.— Covenant & Membership. Albany, 1863. 8vo. N. York Hist. Discourses, &. Vol. 4.
ALBANY. University of. Catalogue & Circulars of the Law School for 1852–3, 1853–4, 1854–5, 1858–9, 1860–1, 1861–2, 1862–3. 1864–5. 1865–6, 1866–7, 1867–8, 1871–2, 1872–3. Albany, v. d. 8vo.
—— —— Hist. Sketches of the Medical College, the Law School, & the Dudley Observatory. Albany, 1868. 8vo.
—— —— Law Department. Annual Circular for 1855. Publications of Albany.
—— —— Speeches in behalf of.
—— —— What it is? What it has done? &c. And what it wants? Albany, 1870. 8vo.
—— Water Supply.— Report by De Witt Clinton. 1832. Albany, 1832. 8vo.
—— Water Commissioners. Reports, 1850, '52, '53, '54, '55, '60.
—— Young Ladies' Institute. Catalogue & Circular, 1857. Albany. 8vo.
—— —— See SPRAGUE, W. B. Address, 1861.
—— Young Mens' Association. Catalogue of Library, 1848. 8vo. Pamphlets. Vol. 2.
—— —— Charter of. Albany, 1847. 8vo. Pamphlets. Vol. 2.
—— Ann. Reports, 1839, '40, '41, '42, '43, '45, '46, '47, '48, '49, '50, '53, '54, '55, '56, '57, '58, '59, '60, '61, '62, '63, '65, '66, '69.
—— —— Charter, 1835, '47, '53.
—— —— Catalogue of Library, 1848—1853.
—— Oration by A. OAKEY HALL, July 4, 1859; with the Prize Essays, &c. Albany, 1859. 8vo.
—— Young Men's Christian Assoc. Constitution & By-Laws, 1857,
—— —— 1st & 6th Ann. Reports, 1858—1863. Albany, 1857—'63.
—— —— Temperance Society. Proceedings at Annual Meeting, 1836. Publications of Albany.
ALBEMARLE. GEO. THOMAS, Earl of. Memoirs of the Marquis of Rockingham and his contemporaries. London, 1852. 2 Vols. 8vo.
ALBERT, PRINCE. [Defence of Prince Albert from the Public Press.] London, 1854. 8vo. Strangford Pamph. Vol. 66.
ALBIN, JOHN. Companion to the Isle of Wight. London, 1823. 12mo. 9th ed. Guide Books. Vol. 21.
ALBION, Mich., Commercial College. Circular. Detroit, 1866. 8vo.

ALBRO, Rev. J. A. Commemoration of the 25th Anniv. of his Pastorate in Cambridge, Mass., Apr., 1860. Cambridge, 1860. 8vo. Mass. Hist. Discourses &c. Vol. 11.

—— Sermon on the Death of WASHINGTON ALLSTON, delivered at Cambridge, Mass., July 16, 1843. Boston, 1843. 8vo. Sermons. Vols. 31, 36.

ALCORN, JAS. L. Letter & Resolution Memorializing Congress, relative to overflowed lands on the Miss. River. Jackson, Miss., 1870. 8vo. Congr. & Polit. Pamph. Vol. 120.

—— Mississippi Levees. Speech in U. S. Senate, Jan. 21, 1873. Washington, 1873. 8vo, Congr. & Polit. Pamph. Vol. 68.

ALDEN, EBENEZER, M. D. Biograph. Notices of Deceased Physicians in Mass. 1847. N. Eng. Hist. & Gen. Register. Vol. 1.

—— Memorials of the Descendants of Hon. JOHN ALDEN. Randolph, 1867. 8vo.

—— ALDEN Genealogy.—See ALDEN, E., and Vinton Memorial.

ALDEN, J. DEANE. Proceedings at the Dedication of Charter Oak Hall, at Hartford, Conn. Hartford, 1856. 8vo. Conn. Hist. Discourses &c. Vol. 4.

ALDEN, Rev. TIMOTHY. Account of the Captivity of HUGH GIBSON, among the Delaware Indians, 1756–7. Boston, n. d. 8vo. Mass. Hist. Soc. Coll. 3d Ser. Vol. 6.

—— Account of Sundry Missions performed among the Senecas and Munsees. New York, 1827, 18mo.

—— A collection of American Epitaphs and Inscriptions with notes. New York, 1814. 5 Vols. 12mo.

—— Account of the Religious Societies in Portsmouth, N. H., to 1805. Mass. Hist. Soc. Collec. 1st Ser. Vol. 10.

ALDERNEY, Isle of. — See BERRY, Wm. Hist. of Guernsey.

—— New Parish Church of St. Ann: its Origin and Symbolism. Guernsey, 1850, 12mo. Hist. Pamph. Vol. 19.

ALEXANDER, Dr. Archibald. Biographical Sketches of the Founder and Principal Alumni of the Log College.

—— Brief Compend of Bible Truth. Phila., 1846. 12mo.

ALEXANDER, Archibald. — See ALEXANDER, J. W. Life of.

—— Reminiscence of. Va. Hist. Register. Vol. 5.

—— Reminiscenses of Patrick Henry. Virginia Hist. Register. Vol. 3.

ALEXANDER, C. A. Outline of the Origin and History of the Royal Society of London. Smithsonian Report, 1863.

ALEXANDER, Jas. E. Sketches of Portugal, during the War of 1834. Waldo's Circulating Library. Vol. 5.

ALEXANDRIA, Va. — See OLMSTEAD, L. G. Reminiscenses of Early Hist. of.

ALEXANDER, John Henry. Index to the Calendar of Maryland State Papers. Baltimore, 1861. 8vo. Md. Miscell. Pamph. Vol. 1.

—— International Coinage of Great Britain and the United States. Baltimore, 1855. 8vo. Congress. & Polit. Pamph. Vol. 96.

—— See PINCKNEY, Rev. Wm. Memoir of.

ALEXANDER, Rev. J. W. Life of Archibald Alexander, D. D.. Professor in Princeton Theolog. Seminary. New York, 1854. 8vo.
ALEXANDER, Dr. W. Picture of Royalty: or a Key to open the Progeny of the Royal Line, &c. Edinburgh, 1704. Small. 4to. Eng. Miscell. Pamph. Vol. 1.
ALEXANDER, Rev. Walter S. See POMFRET, Conn. 1st Church.
ALEXANDER, Wm., Earl of Sterling. Selections from his Correspondence. N. Jersey Hist. Soc. Proceed. Vols. 5, 6, 7.
ALFORD, LODOVIC P. — See PASCHAL, Geo. W. Letter in behalf of.
ALFRED, King of Angland. — See Memorials of.
ALFRED, N. Y. University and Academy. Catalogue for 1857–8. Elmira, 1858. 8vo.
ALFRIEND, Frank H. Life of Jefferson Davis. Cincinnati & Chicago, 1868. 8vo.
ALGER, Andrew. — See MAYBERRY, D. F.
ALGER, Francis. See JACKSON, C. T.
—— Notes on the Mineralogy of Nova Scotia. 1827. Silliman's Journ. Vol. 12.
ALGER, Wm. R. Sermon at Boston, Apr. 1861, on the civil war. Rebell'n Pamph. Vol. 67.
—— An American Voice on the late War in the East. Boston, 1856. 8vo. Histor. Pamphlets. Vol. 7.
—— Oration at Boston, July 4, 1857. 8vo. Addresses, &c. Vol. 1.
ALGIERS. — See Almanac, 1856.
—— See France.
ALGOA BAY & ALBANY, South Africa. — See PHILIPPS, Thos.
ALGONKIN Language. See TRUMBULL, J. H. Ind. Geog. Names.
—— Grammar. — See TRUMBULL, J. H. Mistaken Notion of.
—— Indians. — See SQUIER, E. G. Traditions of.
ALISON, Sir Arch'd. History of Europe from the French Revolution in 1779, to the Restoration of the Bourbons in 1815. 9th Ed. With Index. Edinburgh, 1864. 13 vols. 12mo.
—— Same, from the Fall of Napoleon in 1815, to the Accession of Louis Napoleon in 1852, with Index. Edinburgh, 1866. 8 vols. 12mo.
—— History of Europe from 1789 to 1815. Abridged from the last London Ed. New York, 1844. 8vo.
—— Miscellaneous Essays. Philadelphia, 1848. 8vo.
ALITERATIVE Poem on the Deposition of Richard II. — See Camden Society Publications.
ALLAN, Geo. Life of Sir Walter Scott, with Critical Notices of his Writings. Waldies Circulating Library. Vol. 6.
ALLAN, John. Catalogue of his Library. N. York, 1864. 8vo. Bibliograph. Pamph. Vol. 6.
ALLEGHANIA. — See TAYLOR, Jas. W.
ALLEGHANY COLLEGE, Meadville, Pa. Catalogue, 1869–70. Meadville. 8vo.
ALLEGHANY MOUNTAINS. — See LANMAN, C.
ALLEGHANY RAILROAD & COAL Co.Third Report of Directors. Phila., 1855. 8vo. Penn. Miscell. Pamph. Vol. 3.

ALLEN, Miss A. J. Ten Years in Oregon; or Adventures of Dr. Elijah White among the Rocky Mountains, &c. New York, 1859. 12mo.

ALLEN, Asa W. Genealogy of the Allen and Witter Families. Salem, O., 1872. 12mo.

ALLEN, Col. Eben. — See BARNES, Dr. M. Biography of.

ALLEN, Ethan. — See MOORE, Memoir of.

—— Narrative of his Captivity. 4th Ed. Burlington, 1846. 12mo.

—— See SPARKS, J. Life of.

ALLEN, Ethan, D. D. Maryland Toleration; or Sketches of the Early History of Maryland to 1650. Baltimore, 1855. 8vo. Md. Miscell. Pamph. Vol. 2.

—— Who were the Early Settlers of Maryland: a paper before the Md. Histor. Soc'y, Oct. 5, 1865. Baltimore, 1866. 8vo. Md. Hist. Soc. Addresses. Vol. 2.

ALLEN, Rev. E. D. Address before Young Men's Association at Albany, Nov. 30, 1841. 8vo. Addresses, &c. Vol. 1.

ALLEN, E. H. Speeches in Cong. July 11 & 25, 1842, on the Army Bill. Washington, 1842. 8vo. Congr. & Polit. Pamph. Vol. 24.

ALLEN, Frederick. The Early Lawyers of Lincoln and Kennebeck Counties, Maine. Maine Hist. Soc. Collec. Vol. 6.

ALLEN. Genealogy. — See VINTON Memorials. — See ALLEN, A. W.

ALLEN, Rev. Geo. H. Centen. Address delivered before the 1st Baptist Church, South Chelmsford, Mass., Oct. 22, 1871. Lowell, 1871. 8vo. Mass. Hist. Discourses, &c. Vol. 20.

ALLEN, Geo. W. Letter to Senator Howe on Specie Payments. Milwaukee, 1868. 8vo. Congr. & Polit. Pamph. Vol. 101.

—— SEYMOUR. His past and present position. Speech at Milwaukee, Oct. 10, 1868. Congr. & Polit. Pamph. Vol. 137.

ALLEN, Gen. Henry. — See DORSEY, Sarah A. Recollections of.

ALLEN, Ira. Miscellaneous Remarks on the Proceedings of the State of N. York against the State of Vermont, &c. 1777. Vermont Hist. Soc. Collections. Vol. 1.

—— National & Political History of the State of Vermont, 1798. Vermont Hist. Soc. Collections Vol. 1.

—— Same. London 1798. 8vo.

ALLEN, Lieut. J. & SCHOOLCRAFT, H. R. Map and Report of Visit to N. West Indians in 1832. Ex. Doc. 1833–4, No. 323.

ALLEN, Dr. J. Adams. Introductory Address to the Third Session of the College of Medicine & Surgery of the University of Mich., Oct. 1852. Detroit, 1852. 8vo. Mich. University Catalogues, &c.

ALLEN, Jos. D. D. Half Century Sermon. Order of Exercises & Commem. Discourse at the Fiftieth Annivers. of his Settlement, Cambridge, 1867. 8vo. Mass. Hist. Discourses. Vol. 5. Another copy Addresses, &c., Vol. 19.

—— Genealog. Sketches of Allen Family. Boston, 1869. 8vo.

ALLEN, Rev. Joseph. Histor. Account of Northborough, Mass. Worcester Magazine. Vol. 2.

ALLEN, Julian. Autocrasy in Poland and Russia, including the Experience of an Exile. New York, 1854. 12mo.

ALLEN, L. Essay on Motion and Force, read before the Albany Institute, Apr. 24, 1865. Scientific Pamph. Vol. 15.

ALLEN, Myron O. History of Wenham, Mass., 1639–1860. Boston, 1860. 12mo.

ALLEN, Nathan, M. D. The Opium Trade, including a Sketch of its History, &c., in India & China. Lowell, 1853. 8vo. Hist. Pamph. Vol. 3.

ALLEN, Paul. History of the American Revolution. Baltimore, 1819. 2 Vols. 8vo.

ALLEN, Dr. R. L. Analysis of the Principal Mineral Fountains at Saratoga Springs. N. York, 1858. 12mo. Med. Pamph. Vol. 6.

—— Domestic Amimals; History and Description of the Horse, Mule, Cattle, Sheep, &c. New York, 1849. 12mo.

ALLEN, Lieut. Sam'l.—See — BARNES, Dr. M. Biography of 1852.

ALLEN, Samuel C. Oration, delivered July 6, 1812, in Commem. of Amer. Independence. Greenfield, Mass., 1812. 8vo. Miscellaneous Tracts. Vol. 1.

ALLEN, Stephen M. Myles Standish, with an Account of the Exercises of Consecration of the Monument Ground in Duxbury, Aug. 17, 1871. Boston, 1871, 8vo. Mass. Hist. Discourses, &c. Vol. 19.

ALLEN, Rev. Stephen T. Centenn. Address, delivered at Merrimack, N. H., Apr. 3, 1846. Boston, 1846. 8vo. N. H. Hist. Discourses. Vol. 3.

ALLEN, Thos. Address before the Mo. Hist. Soc'y on, Japan & the Expedition. St. Louis, 1853. 8vo.

ALLEN, Rev. Thos. Hist. Sketch of the County of Berkshire, and Town of Pittsfield. Boston, 1808. 8vo. Mass. Hist. Discourses, &c. Vol. 20.

ALLEN, Thos. History of the County of Surrey, Eng., illustrated. London, 1830. 2 vols. 8vo.

—— New and complete History of the County of York. London, 1828. 6 vols. in 3. 8vo.

ALLEN, W. Killing no Murder, &c. London, 1659. 4to. Eng. Polit. Pamph. Vol. 65.

ALLEN, W. B. History of Kentucky; embracing Gleanings, Reminiscences, Antiquities, &c. Louisville, 1872. 8vo.

ALLEN, Rev. Wm. Bi-Centen. Address at Northampton, Mass., Oct. 29, 1854. Northampton, 1855. 8vo. Mass. Hist Discourses. Vols. 6 & 15.

—— Hist. Discourse, delivered in Dorchester, Jan. 2, 1848, on the 40th Annivers. of the 2d Church, Boston, 1848. 8vo. Mass. Hist. Discourses. Vol. 20.

—— The American Biographical Dictionary. Boston, 1857. 8vo. 3d Edition.

—— See DUNN, Henry. Life of, 1848.

—— Memoir of Hon. Nahum Mitchell. N. Eng. Hist. & Gen. Register. Vol. 18.

—— Letter to the Young Men's Democrat. Convent., held at Columbus, O., July 28, 1842. Washington, 1842, 8vo. Congr. & Polit. Pamph. Vol. 25.

ALLEN, Rev. Wm., *continued.*

—— Speech in U. S. Senate, Feb. 11, 1840, on the Public Debt. Congr. & Polit. Pamp. Vol. 92.

—— Speech in U. S. Senate, Mar. 15, 1842, on the Tariff. Congr. & Polit. Pamph. Vol. 25.

—— Speech in U. S. Senate, Feb. 10 & 11, 1846, on our Relations with England. Congr. & Polit. Pamph. Vol. 90.

—— Journal of the Expedition to Quebec in 1775. Maine Hist. Soc. Coll. Vol. 1.

ALLEN, Prof. Wm. F. The Rural Population of England, as Classified in Doomsday Book. Trans. Wis. Acad. of Sciences, 1870–2.

ALLEN, William H. Address before American Peace Society, May 29, 1854. 8vo. Addresses, &c. Vol. 1.

—— Eulogy on the Character and Services of Daniel Webster, Jan. 18, 1853. Phila., 1853. 8vo. Addresses, &c. Vol. 13.

ALLEN, Zach. Memorial of Roger Williams. Read before R. Island Hist. Soc., May 18, 1860. Providence. n. d. 8vo. R. I. Hist. Soc, Addresses. Vol. 1.

ALLERTON, Isaac. Memoir of. Mass. Hist. Soc. Coll. 3d Series. Vol. 7.

ALL HALLOWS' COLLEGE, near Dublin. Annals for 1860. Dublin. 8vo. Eng. Religious Pamph. Vol. 59.

ALLIES, Jabez. The British, Roman and Saxon Antiquities and Folks' Lore of Worcestershire, Eng. 2d Ed. London, 1856. 8vo.

ALLOUEZ, *Father* Claudius.— See Shea, J. G. Discov. of Mississippi Valley.

ALLPORT, W. W. Address to Graduates of Ohio College of Dental Surgery, 1858–9. Cincinnati, 1859. 8vo.

ALLSTON, Washington.— See ALBRO, Rev. J. A. Sermon on his death, 1843.

ALLYN, Rob't. — See R. Island Public Schools.

ALMANACH, de l'Algerie, 1852. Paris, 1852. 18mo.

—— Same. 1856. Paris, 1856. 18mo.

ALMANACS. See Amer. Calendar, 1794.

—— American A., 1843–60.

—— Annuarie Historique, 1837.

—— Boston, 1840–1865, (except 1862).

—— British Almanac, 1828–1869.

—— Childs' National Almanac, 1863–64.

—— Collection of, 1842–49. 12mo.

—— DISTURNELL, J. U. S. Register, 1851–2.

—— DOWNES, J. U. S. Almanac, 1843.

—— FORCE, P. Nat. Calendar, 1813.

—— HOMANS, J. S. Merch. & Bankers Alm., 1862–64.

—— Kalendar, (Chinese) for 1853.

—— National Almanac, 1863–64.

—— N. Y. Observer Almanac, 1871.

—— Pokrok: Kalendar, 1867.

—— Royal Kalendar for 1775, 79, 80, 90, 99 & 1806.

—— STICKNEY (M. A.). — Almanacs and their authors.

ALMANACH, de l'Algerie, *continued.*
—— STOKES (C) Continental 1862, 3, 4.
—— Texas almanac, 1867.
—— Tribune Almanac, 1859, 61, 62.
—— United States Phil'a, 1844, 1845.
—— Whig Almanac, 1843–53.
—— Wisconsin Almanac, 1856; 1857.
ALMON J. See Collection of authentic Papers, etc.
—— The Remembrancer; a Repository of Passing Events. London, 1775—1784. 17 Vol's. 8vo. Same for 1780. Part 2.
—— See Two Letters to him on Libels, &c. 1765, '70.
ALOFSEN (Solomon). Origin of the name "Pavonia." N. Jersey Hist. Soc. Proceed. Vol. 9.
ALSOP. (Geo.) Character of the Province of Maryland with notes by J. G. Shea.—New York, 1869. 8vo. pr. printed.
ALSTEAD, N. H. Hist. Sketches of the town, from 1826 to 1836.—Keene, N. H., 1836. 8vo. N. Hampshire Hist. Discourses, &c. Vol. 1.
ALTA CALIFORNIA: With Notices of Northern Mexico, & Military & Naval Opera of 1846–47. Phil'a., 1847 8vo. Mex. War Pamph. Vol. 2.
ALTHORPIANA; or a few facts relative to the late Northamptonshire Election. London, 1831. 8vo. Eng. Polit. Pamph. Vol. 37.
ALTO, Wis. See West (G. M.) Hist. of.
ALTON, (Ill.) See Beecher, (Rev. E.) Narrative of Riots at Alton.
ALVORD GENEALOGY. See BOUTELLE (J. A.)
ALVORD (Rev. J. W).—Hist. Address at Stamford, Ct., at Celebra. of 2d, Centen. Anniver., Dec. 22, 1841. N. Y., 1842, 8vo. Conn. Hist. Discourses. Vol. 2.
—— Letters from the South, relating to the Condition of the Freedmen. Washington, 1870. 8vo. Congr. & Polit. Pamph. Vols., 114, 118.
AMAZON RIVER. See EDWARDS, (W. H.) Voyage up.
—— —— See HERNDON, (Lieut.) Exploration of Valley of. 1853.
AMENDMENTS to the Internal Revenue Act of the U. S., proposed by the Comm. of the Associated Conveyancers of Phil'a.—1862. Rebell'n Pamph. Vol. 93.
AMERICA and EUROPE. 1857. See GUROWSKI (Adam.)
—— her Commmentators. See TUCKERMAN (H. T.)
—— its Peculiarities.—Amsterdam 1781. 4 Vols. 8vo.
AMERICA and THE AMERICANS. See MURAT.
AMERICA, Discovery in. See CABOT (S) Memoir and Hist. of Martine Discov.
—— —— CAMPE, (J. H. Discovery of America.
—— —— BEAMISH, (N. L.) Discovery by Northmen.
—— —— COLUMBUS, C. Letter on Discovery of New World.
—— —— DAVIS, A. Northmen in America.
—— —— DE COSTA, B. F. Pre-Columbian Discovery of.
—— —— DE SOTO, H. Information from Florida 1575.

AMERICA, *continued.*
—— —— DE VRIES, D. P. Voyage from Holland to America, 1632–1644.
—— —— Discovery of New Britaine, 1651.
—— —— EVERETT, Edw. Discovery & Colonization of America. 1853.
—— —— GORDON, T. F. Hist. of Spanish Discoveries.
—— —— HENNEPIN, L. Discovery of a Vast Country, &c.
—— —— IRVING, W. Life and Voyages of Columbus.
—— —— JONES, G. Hist. of Ancient America.
—— —— JOUTEL. — Journal du Voyage pour de Mississippi.
—— —— LA SALLE, M. de. Last Expedition, 1698.
—— —— LEDERER, F. Discoveries, 1667–70.
—— —— LESTER, C. E. Life and Voyages of Vespucius.
—— —— MORSE, Abner. — Traces of Northmen.
—— —— Narrative of De Vaca.
—— —— NEWMAN, J. B. Ancient Hist. & Discov. of America.
—— —— OTTO, Mr. Memoir on Discov. of America.
—— —— PARKER, H. F. Discoveries of America.
—— —— Phenicans in America.
—— —— PRITTS, J. Mirror of Old Time.
—— —— RAFN, C. C. Discovery in 10th century.
—— —— ROBERTSON, W. Hist. of Discovery and Conquest.
—— —— SIMMS, W. G. Huguenots in Florida.
—— —— SMITH, J. T. Discovery by Northmen.
—— —— SQUIER, E. G. Rare and Original Documents.
—— —— STEVENS, H. Histor. and Geograph. Notes. 1453–1530.
—— —— SYLLACIUS, N. 2d Voyage of Columbus.
—— —— THORNTON, J. W. Anglo-Amer. Colonization.
—— —— TYTLER, P. F. Progress of Discovery on Northern Coasts of Amer.
—— —— VERAZZANO, J. de. Voyage on Coast of Verazzano, N. America. 1524.
—— —— WILLIAMS, J. Enquiry into Claims of Prince Madog.
—— —— ZESTERMANN, Dr. C. A. Colonization in Ante-Historic Times.
—— —— See VOYAGES.
AMERICA. History of, Travels in, etc. — See AMERICAN Notes and Queries. 1857.
—— —— BACQUEVILLE, M. de. Historie de l'Amerique. 1753.
—— —— BARBER, J. W. Hist. Amer. Scenes, etc.
—— —— —— Incidents in Amer. History.
—— —— BRACKENRIDGE, H. M. Recollec. of Persons and Places. 1835.
—— —— British Empire in America. 1741.
—— —— BURKE E. European Settlements in America. 1765.
—— —— CALLENDER, J. T. Sketches of History of Amer. 1798.
—— —— CHALMERS, Geo. Political Annals to 1763.

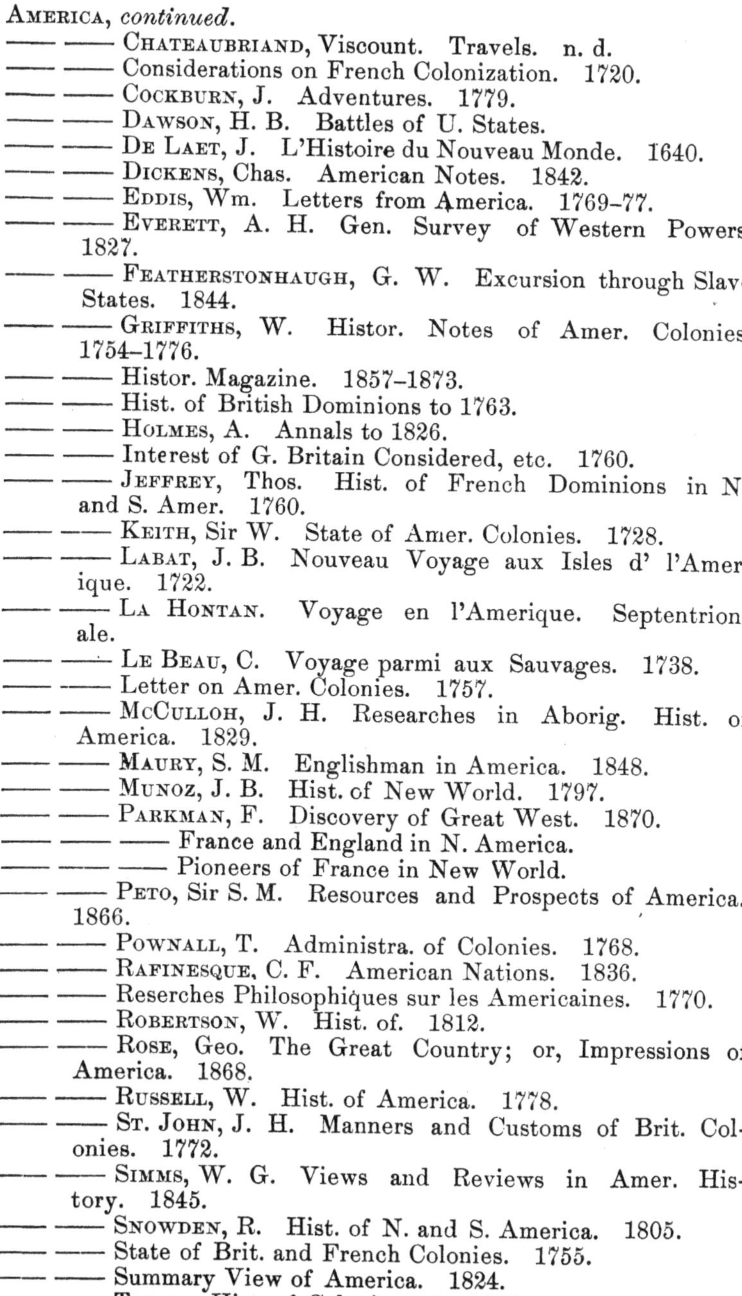

AMERICA, *continued.*

—— —— CHATEAUBRIAND, Viscount. Travels. n. d.

—— —— Considerations on French Colonization. 1720.

—— —— COCKBURN, J. Adventures. 1779.

—— —— DAWSON, H. B. Battles of U. States.

—— —— DE LAET, J. L'Histoire du Nouveau Monde. 1640.

—— —— DICKENS, Chas. American Notes. 1842.

—— —— EDDIS, Wm. Letters from America. 1769–77.

—— —— EVERETT, A. H. Gen. Survey of Western Powers. 1827.

—— —— FEATHERSTONHAUGH, G. W. Excursion through Slave States. 1844.

—— —— GRIFFITHS, W. Histor. Notes of Amer. Colonies. 1754–1776.

—— —— Histor. Magazine. 1857–1873.

—— —— Hist. of British Dominions to 1763.

—— —— HOLMES, A. Annals to 1826.

—— —— Interest of G. Britain Considered, etc. 1760.

—— —— JEFFREY, Thos. Hist. of French Dominions in N. and S. Amer. 1760.

—— —— KEITH, Sir W. State of Amer. Colonies. 1728.

—— —— LABAT, J. B. Nouveau Voyage aux Isles d' l'Amerique. 1722.

—— —— LA HONTAN. Voyage en l'Amerique. Septentrionale.

—— —— LE BEAU, C. Voyage parmi aux Sauvages. 1738.

—— —— Letter on Amer. Colonies. 1757.

—— —— McCULLOH, J. H. Researches in Aborig. Hist. of America. 1829.

—— —— MAURY, S. M. Englishman in America. 1848.

—— —— MUNOZ, J. B. Hist. of New World. 1797.

—— —— PARKMAN, F. Discovery of Great West. 1870.

—— —— —— France and England in N. America.

—— —— —— Pioneers of France in New World.

—— —— PETO, Sir S. M. Resources and Prospects of America. 1866.

—— —— POWNALL, T. Administra. of Colonies. 1768.

—— —— RAFINESQUE, C. F. American Nations. 1836.

—— —— Reserches Philosophiques sur les Americaines. 1770.

—— —— ROBERTSON, W. Hist. of. 1812.

—— —— ROSE, Geo. The Great Country; or, Impressions of America. 1868.

—— —— RUSSELL, W. Hist. of America. 1778.

—— —— ST. JOHN, J. H. Manners and Customs of Brit. Colonies. 1772.

—— —— SIMMS, W. G. Views and Reviews in Amer. History. 1845.

—— —— SNOWDEN, R. Hist. of N. and S. America. 1805.

—— —— State of Brit. and French Colonies. 1755.

—— —— Summary View of America. 1824.

—— —— TALVI. Hist. of Coloniza. of. 1851.

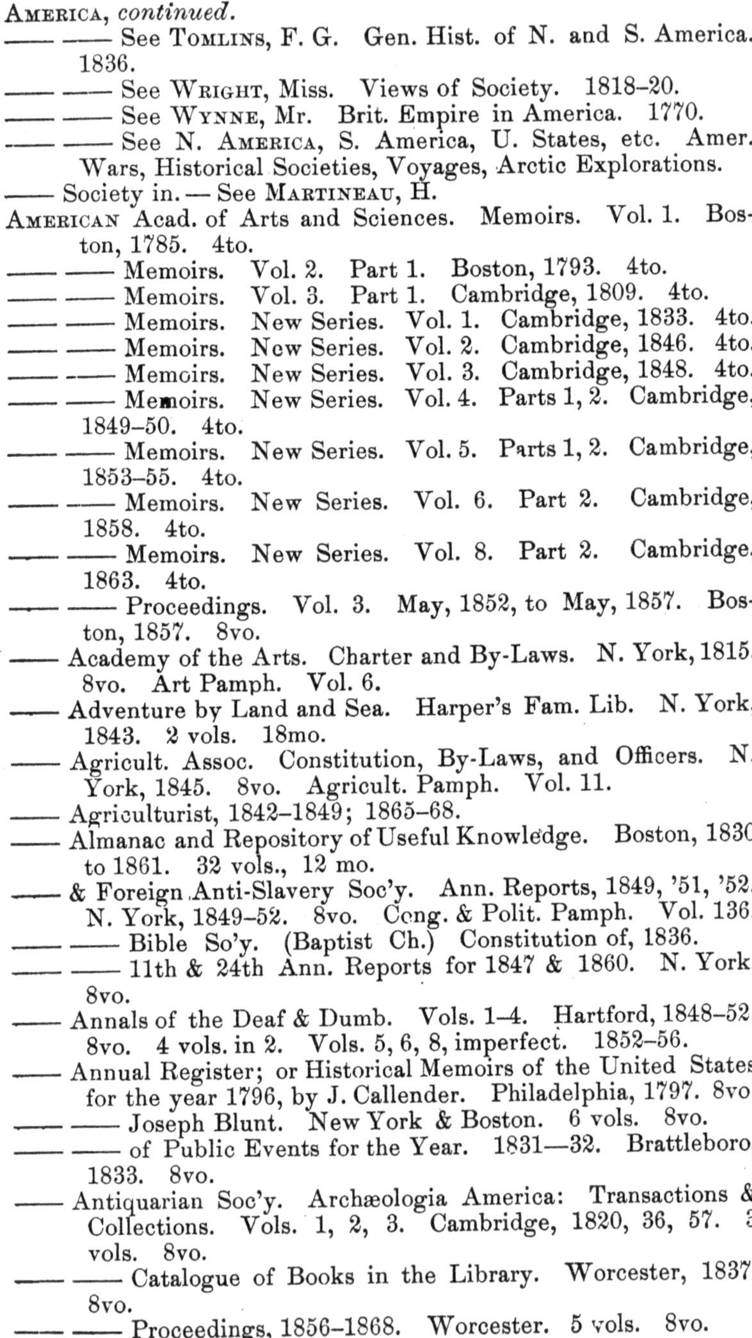

AMERICA, *continued.*

—— —— See TOMLINS, F. G. Gen. Hist. of N. and S. America. 1836.

—— —— See WRIGHT, Miss. Views of Society. 1818–20.

—— —— See WYNNE, Mr. Brit. Empire in America. 1770.

—— —— See N. AMERICA, S. America, U. States, etc. Amer. Wars, Historical Societies, Voyages, Arctic Explorations.

—— Society in. — See MARTINEAU, H.

AMERICAN Acad. of Arts and Sciences. Memoirs. Vol. 1. Boston, 1785. 4to.

—— —— Memoirs. Vol. 2. Part 1. Boston, 1793. 4to.

—— —— Memoirs. Vol. 3. Part 1. Cambridge, 1809. 4to.

—— —— Memoirs. New Series. Vol. 1. Cambridge, 1833. 4to.

—— —— Memoirs. New Series. Vol. 2. Cambridge, 1846. 4to.

—— —— Memoirs. New Series. Vol. 3. Cambridge, 1848. 4to.

—— —— Memoirs. New Series. Vol. 4. Parts 1, 2. Cambridge, 1849–50. 4to.

—— —— Memoirs. New Series. Vol. 5. Parts 1, 2. Cambridge, 1853–55. 4to.

—— —— Memoirs. New Series. Vol. 6. Part 2. Cambridge, 1858. 4to.

—— —— Memoirs. New Series. Vol. 8. Part 2. Cambridge, 1863. 4to.

—— —— Proceedings. Vol. 3. May, 1852, to May, 1857. Boston, 1857. 8vo.

—— Academy of the Arts. Charter and By-Laws. N. York, 1815. 8vo. Art Pamph. Vol. 6.

—— Adventure by Land and Sea. Harper's Fam. Lib. N. York, 1843. 2 vols. 18mo.

—— Agricult. Assoc. Constitution, By-Laws, and Officers. N. York, 1845. 8vo. Agricult. Pamph. Vol. 11.

—— Agriculturist, 1842–1849; 1865–68.

—— Almanac and Repository of Useful Knowledge. Boston, 1830 to 1861. 32 vols., 12 mo.

—— & Foreign Anti-Slavery Soc'y. Ann. Reports, 1849, '51, '52. N. York, 1849–52. 8vo. Cong. & Polit. Pamph. Vol. 136.

—— —— Bible So'y. (Baptist Ch.) Constitution of, 1836.

—— —— 11th & 24th Ann. Reports for 1847 & 1860. N. York. 8vo.

—— Annals of the Deaf & Dumb. Vols. 1–4. Hartford, 1848–52. 8vo. 4 vols. in 2. Vols. 5, 6, 8, imperfect. 1852–56.

—— Annual Register; or Historical Memoirs of the United States for the year 1796, by J. Callender. Philadelphia, 1797. 8vo.

—— —— Joseph Blunt. New York & Boston. 6 vols. 8vo.

—— —— of Public Events for the Year. 1831—32. Brattleboro, 1833. 8vo.

—— Antiquarian Soc'y. Archæologia America: Transactions & Collections. Vols. 1, 2, 3. Cambridge, 1820, 36, 57. 3 vols. 8vo.

—— —— Catalogue of Books in the Library. Worcester, 1837. 8vo.

—— —— Proceedings, 1856–1868. Worcester. 5 vols. 8vo.

AMERICAN Antiquarian Society, *continued.*
—— —— Proceedings on Death of Hon. Edw. Everett, Jan. 17, 1865.
Proceedings, 1862–5.
—— —— Remarks and Resolutions on the Death of Hon. Josiah Quincy.
Worcester, 1864. 8vo.
—— Apollo, Periodical. 1792. Boston, 1792. 8vo.
—— Archives: a Documentary History of the English North American Colonies. 4th series, 1774–76. Vol. 1–6. Washington, 1846. 6 vols. folio.
—— See Amer. State Papers.
—— Art Union. Bulletins for Nov. & Dec., 1848, and Oct. & Dec., 1849. N. York. 8 vo. Art Pamph. Vol. 1.
—— —— Transactions for 1847, 48, 49. New York. 8vo. Pamphlets. Vol. 1.
—— Assoc. for Advancement of Science. Daily Programmes of 17th & 18th Annual Meetings, 1868 & 1869. Scientific Pamph. Vol. 17.
—— —— See PIERCE, Prof. Benj. Valedictory Address. n. d.
—— —— Proceedings of 1st to 16th meetings, inclusive, except the 14th & 15th meetings. Phila., Cambridge, &c., 1849–1868. 14 vols. 8vo.
—— See Assoc. of Amer. Geologists & Naturalists.
—— Assoc. for the Cure of Inebriates. Proceedings of 2d Meeting held in N. Y., 1871. Philadelphia, 1872. 8vo. Temp. Pamph. Vol. 5.
—— Asylum (Hartford), for Deaf and Dumb. Reports presented in 1819, '43, '55, '56, '57, '59, '61, '62, '63. Hartford, Conn., 1819-1863. 8vo.
—— Baptist Hist. Soc'y. See BAILEY, Rev. Silas. BLISS, Rev. Geo. R. EDDY, Rev. D. C. HOWELL, Rev. B. C.
—— —— Free Mission Soc'y. 7th Ann. Meeting held in Bristol. N. Y., 1850. Utica, 1850. 8vo.
—— —— Home Missionary Soc'y. Proceedings of First Anniver., Apr. 27, 1832.
—— —— Ann. Reports for 1836, 37, 39, 40, 41, 42–55. N. York v. d. 8vo.
—— —— Missionary Convention. Report of the 15th Annivers. held in Phila., 1855. Providence, 1855. 8vo.
—— —— Missionary Union. Ann. Report for 1847–1857. Boston, 1848–1858. 8vo.
—— —— See Gen. Convention.
—— —— Publication Soc'y. 5th, 29th, 30th, 39th, 40th, 41st Ann. Reports. Phila., 1844–1865. 8vo.
—— —— Year-Books, 1869–1870. Phila. 8vo.
—— Bastile. — See MARSHALL, J. A.
—— Bible Soc'y. Addresses at the Celebration of the Fifty-Fourth Anniversary. N. York, 1870. 8vo.
—— —— Ann. Reports. 1816–71 inclusive. 4 Vols. 8vo. N. York, 1838–71.
—— Do. 1872. Pamph.

AMERICAN Bible Society, *continued.*
—— —— Bible Agent's Manual. n. d. 8vo.
—— —— Bible Society, Manual. 1860–71. 8vo.
—— —— Bible Visitors, or Local Agent's Book. n. d. 12o.
—— —— Brief View of the Plan &. Operations of. n. d. 8vo.
—— —— Expose of the Rise & Proceedings of. N. York, 1830. 8vo. 2d. Ed.
—— —— Report on the History & Recent Collation of the Eng. Version of the Bible, etc. N. York, 1852. 8vo.
—— —— Statements & Documents concerning the Standard edition of the Eng. Scriptures, etc. New York, 1858. 8vo.
—— Bibliopolist.—See SABIN, J.
—— Board of Commiss'rs for Foreign Missions. Ann Reports for 1810–1820, 1827, 1830, 1832, 1833–1861 & 1865, 1870. Boston & Cambridge, 1821–1870. 8vo.
—— Abstract of Report for 1831. 12mo.
—— —— Historical Sketch of the Missons to the Mahrattas of Western India. N. York, 1862. 8vo.
—— —— Letters on Receiving Donations from Slave-holders. n. d. 12mo.
—— —— Maps of the Missions. Sept., 1852. 8vo.
—— —— Missionary Papers. Nos. IX & XXII. Boston, 1831–1837. 12mo.
—— —— Missionary Schools. 1861. 8vo.
—— —— Report of the Special Committee on the Deputation to India. 1st and 2d Editions. Boston & N. York, 1856. 8vo.
—— Calendar & U. S. Register for the year 1794. London, 1794. 12mo.
—— Christian Commission Document No. 8. 1869 8vo. Religious Pamph. Vol. 16.
—— Civilization. — See THORNTON, J. W. First Records of.
—— See Civilization
—— Coinage. — See HICKCOX, J. H. Historical Acc. of.
—— Colonial Church. — See PERRY, W. S. Historical Collections.
—— Colonization Society. Address of the Manager. 1832. Addresses, Vol. 11.
—— —— A Few Facts respecting the Amer. Col. Soc., & the Colony at Liberia. Boston, 1830. 8vo. Pamph. on Colonization, Vol 1.
—— —— See CAREY, M. Letters on. EVERETT, E. Address, 1853.
—— —— Memorial of the Semi-Centennial Anniversary. Jan. 15, 1867. Washington, 1867. 8vo.
—— —— 14th Annual Report, 1831.
—— —— 16th Annual Report, 1833.
—— —— 24th Annual Report, 1841.
—— —— 28th to 52d Annual Report, 1845–1869, inclusive. Washington, 1831–69. 8vo.
—— —— FULLER, Rich'd. Address. 1851.
—— —— Proceedings of a Public Meeting in New York City. 1829. Congress & Polit. Pamphlets. Vol 103.
—— ——Sketch of the Origin & Progress of, etc. Hartford, 1833. 12mo. Pamph. on Colonization, Vol. 1.

AMERICAN Conflict.—See Amer. War of Rebellion. GREELEY, H. Hist. of.
—— Congregational Assoc. 12th, 14th, 15th, 16th, 17th, 18th Ann. Reports of the Directors. Boston, 1865–1871. 8vo.
—— Congregational Union. 7th–16th Ann. Reports of the Trustees. N. York, 1860–1869. 8vo. And Manual, 1870.
—— Congregational Year-Book. 1854–59. 8vo.
—— Convention of Cattle Commissioners. Proceedings & Debates at Springfield, Ill., 1868. Springfield, 1869. 8vo.
—— Crisis (The). London, 1777. 8vo. Cong. & Polit. Pamph. Vol. 74.
—— (New) Cyclopedia. Vols. 1—16. N. York. D. Appleton & Co. 1858–63. 8vo.
—— (The) Annual Cyclopedia & Register for 1861 to 1870, inc. N. York, 1865–71. 10 vols. 8vo.
—— Dialogues of the Dead; and Dialogues of the American Dead. Phila., 1814. 8vo. Cong. & Polit. Pamph. Vol. 71.
—— Documents relative to Mr. Henry's Mission collected and reprinted. London, 1812. 8vo.
—— Education Soc'y. Address to the Friends of Religion in behalf of. Andover, 1825. 8vo. Religious Pamph. Vol. 16.
—— —— 39th Ann. Report of the Directors, May, 1855. Boston, 1855. 8vo.
—— —— and Society for Promotion of Collegiate & Theolog. Educa. at the West. Plan of Union agreed upon by the Joint Committee, at their meeting in New Haven, Jan. 4, 1854: with the Committee's Report.
—— —— 16th Ann. Report, 1832. Boston, 1832. 8vo. Educa. Pamph. Vol. 9.
—— Educational Year-Book. Feb., 1858. Boston, 1858. 12mo.
—— Electro-Magnetic Telegraph.—See KENDALL, Amos.—See TELEGRAPH.
—— Epitaphs.—See ALDEN, Timothy, Collection of.—See EPITAPHS.
—— Equal Rights Asso. Proceedings at the Ch. of the Puritans, N. Y., May 9 & 10, 1867. N. York, 1867. 8vo. Cong. & Polit. Pamph. Vol. 128.
—— Ethnological Soc'y. Transactions, Vols. 1 & 2. Vol. 3, Part 1. N. York, 1845, 1848, 1853. 8vo.
—— Extracts. A Scrap Book of Newspaper Cuttings relative to America. 1752–1833.
—— Female Guardian Society.—See N. York City.
—— Fire-Alarm Telegraph.—See CHANNING, W. F.
—— Flag. HAMILTON, S., History of.
—— —— See NASON, E., Monogram on.
—— Forest Scenes.—See HEAD, Geo.
—— Free Trade League. Polit. and Cong. Pamph. Vol. 73.
—— Gazetteer. London, 1762. 3 vols. 12mo.
—— Genealogist.—See WHITMORE, W. H.
—— Geograph. Society. Bulletin, 1852–1856. N. York. 4to.
—— —— and Statistical Society. By-Laws of. N. Y., 1855. 8vo.
—— —— Catalogue of the Library. N. York, 1857.

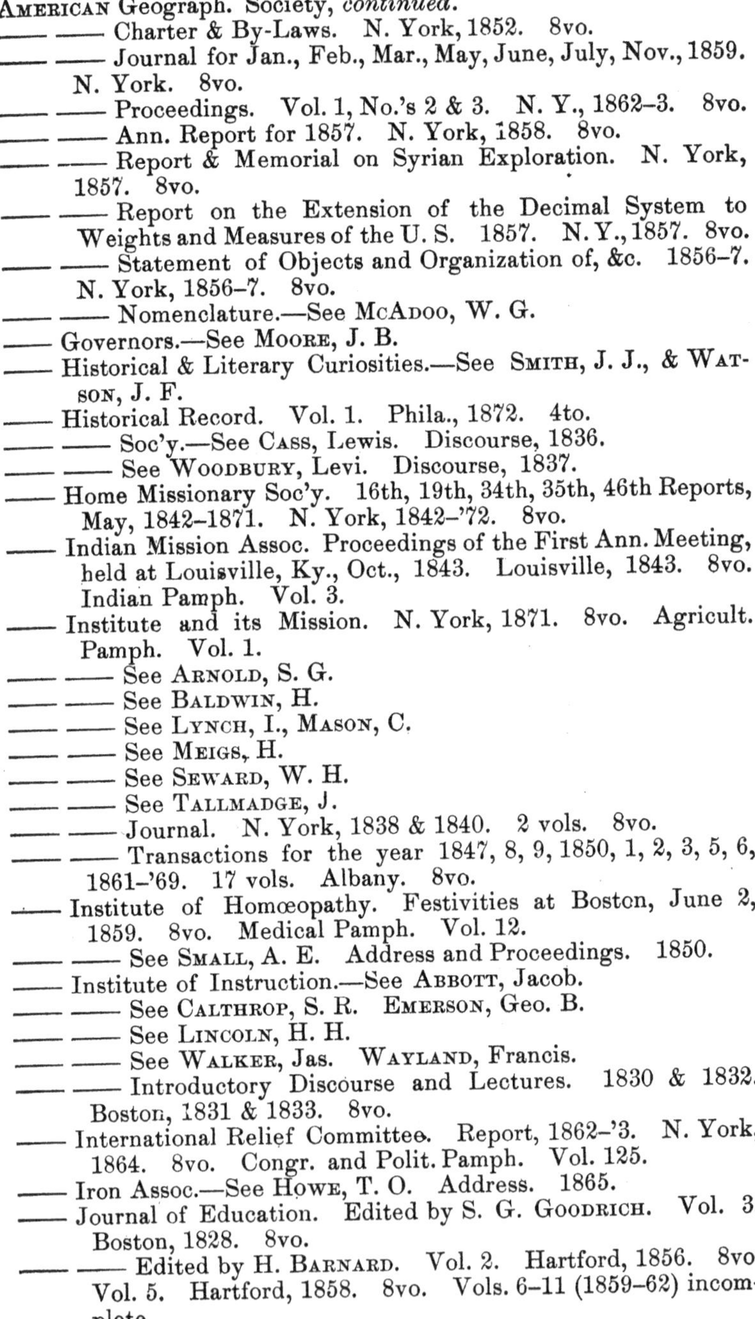

AMERICAN Geograph. Society, *continued.*

—— —— Charter & By-Laws. N. York, 1852. 8vo.

—— —— Journal for Jan., Feb., Mar., May, June, July, Nov., 1859. N. York. 8vo.

—— —— Proceedings. Vol. 1, No.'s 2 & 3. N. Y., 1862–3. 8vo.

—— —— Ann. Report for 1857. N. York, 1858. 8vo.

—— —— Report & Memorial on Syrian Exploration. N. York, 1857. 8vo.

—— —— Report on the Extension of the Decimal System to Weights and Measures of the U. S. 1857. N. Y., 1857. 8vo.

—— —— Statement of Objects and Organization of, &c. 1856–7. N. York, 1856–7. 8vo.

—— —— Nomenclature.—See MCADOO, W. G.

—— Governors.—See MOORE, J. B.

—— Historical & Literary Curiosities.—See SMITH, J. J., & WATSON, J. F.

—— Historical Record. Vol. 1. Phila., 1872. 4to.

—— —— Soc'y.—See CASS, Lewis. Discourse, 1836.

—— —— See WOODBURY, Levi. Discourse, 1837.

—— Home Missionary Soc'y. 16th, 19th, 34th, 35th, 46th Reports, May, 1842–1871. N. York, 1842–'72. 8vo.

—— Indian Mission Assoc. Proceedings of the First Ann. Meeting, held at Louisville, Ky., Oct., 1843. Louisville, 1843. 8vo. Indian Pamph. Vol. 3.

—— Institute and its Mission. N. York, 1871. 8vo. Agricult. Pamph. Vol. 1.

—— —— See ARNOLD, S. G.

—— —— See BALDWIN, H.

—— —— See LYNCH, I., MASON, C.

—— —— See MEIGS, H.

—— —— See SEWARD, W. H.

—— —— See TALLMADGE, J.

—— —— Journal. N. York, 1838 & 1840. 2 vols. 8vo.

—— —— Transactions for the year 1847, 8, 9, 1850, 1, 2, 3, 5, 6, 1861–'69. 17 vols. Albany. 8vo.

—— Institute of Homœopathy. Festivities at Boston, June 2, 1859. 8vo. Medical Pamph. Vol. 12.

—— —— See SMALL, A. E. Address and Proceedings. 1850.

—— Institute of Instruction.—See ABBOTT, Jacob.

—— —— See CALTHROP, S. R. EMERSON, Geo. B.

—— —— See LINCOLN, H. H.

—— —— See WALKER, Jas. WAYLAND, Francis.

—— —— Introductory Discourse and Lectures. 1830 & 1832. Boston, 1831 & 1833. 8vo.

—— International Relief Committee. Report, 1862–'3. N. York, 1864. 8vo. Congr. and Polit. Pamph. Vol. 125.

—— Iron Assoc.—See HOWE, T. O. Address. 1865.

—— Journal of Education. Edited by S. G. GOODRICH. Vol. 3. Boston, 1828. 8vo.

—— —— Edited by H. BARNARD. Vol. 2. Hartford, 1856. 8vo. Vol. 5. Hartford, 1858. 8vo. Vols. 6–11 (1859–62) incomplete.

AMERICAN Journal of Education, *continued.*

—— —— & College Review. Edited by A. PETERS. Vol. 1. N. York, 1856. 8vo. Vol. 2, parts, incomplete.

—— Journal of Insanity. Vols. 1–14. 1844–1858. 8vo.

—— Journal of Science and Arts. Conducted by Benj. Silliman & Son. Vols. 1 to 44, 1st series. New York and New Haven, 1819–1843.

—— Same. Vols. 3, 4, 5, 6, 7. Second series. 5 Vols. 1847–49.

—— —— Second series. Vol. 25, No. 73, Jan., 1858.

—— —— " " " 26, " 78, Nov., 1858.

—— —— " " Vols. 43, 44, complete. 1867.

—— —— " " Vol. 45, No. 135, May, 1868.

—— —— " " " 47, " 140, March, 1869.

—— —— " " " 50, " 150, Nov., 1870.

—— —— Third Series. Vol. 1. Nos. 4 and 11. Apr. and Nov., 1871.

—— Lakes. See COLTON, C.

—— —— See DISTURNELL, J. Great Lakes.

—— —— WHITTLESEY, C. On Fluctuations of Level of.

—— —— See Lake Mich., etc.

—— Law Register. Vol. 1. Nos. 2, 3, 4. Phila. 1852–3. 8vo. Law Pamph. Vol. 6.

—— Life Underwriters' Convention. Proceedings at N. York. 1859. N. York, 1859. 8vo. Insurance Pamph. Vol. 1.

—— Linguistics. See SHEA, J. G. Library of.

—— Literary Gazette and Publishers' Circular. May, 1866.—Oct. 1871. 5 Vols. 8vo. Phila.

—— Loyalists. See SABIN, L. Loyalists of the Revolution.

—— Magazine. Phila., 1758. 8vo.

—— Med. Assoc. Code of Ethics adopted May, 1847. Phila., 1848. 12mo. Med. Pamph. Vol. 8.

—— —— Manual for the Meeting in New Haven. N. Haven, 1860. 12mo. Med. Pamph. Vol. 8.

—— —— Memorial to Congress on the Cultivation of the Cinchona Tree in the U. States. Phila., 1870. 8vo. Congr. and Polit. Pamph. Vol. 131.

—— —— PARSONS, U. Address. 1854.

—— —— Proceedings relative to the Memorial of Ninian Pinkney, on Assimilated Rank. 1852. (n. p.) 8vo. Med. Pam. Vol. 8.

—— —— Reception at Independence Hall, Phila. May 2, 1855. Phila., 1855. 8vo. Med. Pamph. Vol. 8.

—— —— Report of the Committee on Ophthalmology, by Dr. Jos. Hildreth, at the Session at Washington, 1868. Chicago, 1869. 8vo. Med. Pamph. Vol. 8.

—— —— See WARREN, J. C. Address, 1850.

—— —— See WOOD, G. B. " 1856.

—— Medical Biography — See THACHER, JAS.

—— See WILLIAMS, S. W.

—— Migration — See HELLWALD, FRED.

—— Military Biography. Including a Life of Gen. La Fayette. Pub. for Subscribers. 1825. 12vo.

—— Mining Gazette. June, 1864. Apr., 1866. Vols. 1, 2, 3. (Incomplete.) N. York, 1864–66. 3 Vols. 8vo.

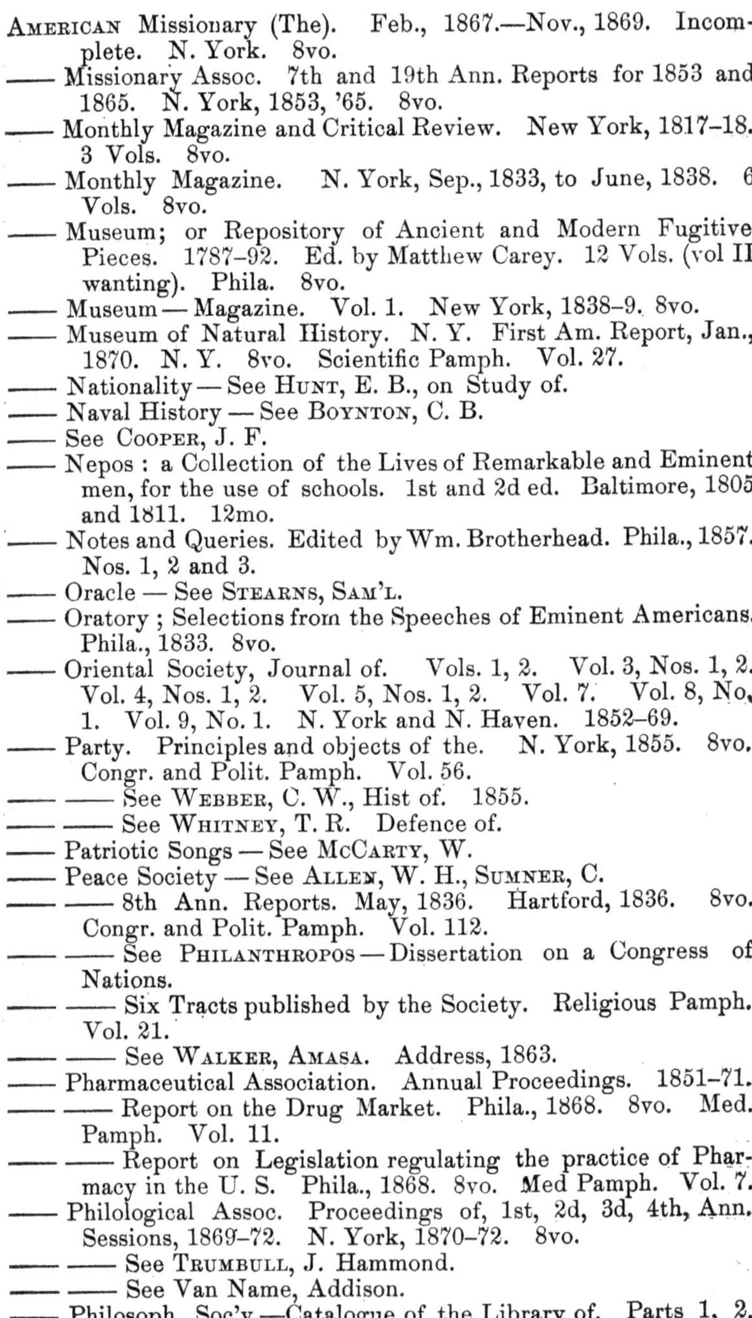

AMERICAN Missionary (The). Feb., 1867.—Nov., 1869. Incomplete. N. York. 8vo.

—— Missionary Assoc. 7th and 19th Ann. Reports for 1853 and 1865. N. York, 1853, '65. 8vo.

—— Monthly Magazine and Critical Review. New York, 1817–18. 3 Vols. 8vo.

—— Monthly Magazine. N. York, Sep., 1833, to June, 1838. 6 Vols. 8vo.

—— Museum; or Repository of Ancient and Modern Fugitive Pieces. 1787–92. Ed. by Matthew Carey. 12 Vols. (vol II wanting). Phila. 8vo.

—— Museum — Magazine. Vol. 1. New York, 1838–9. 8vo.

—— Museum of Natural History. N. Y. First Am. Report, Jan., 1870. N. Y. 8vo. Scientific Pamph. Vol. 27.

—— Nationality — See HUNT, E. B., on Study of.

—— Naval History — See BOYNTON, C. B.

—— See COOPER, J. F.

—— Nepos: a Collection of the Lives of Remarkable and Eminent men, for the use of schools. 1st and 2d ed. Baltimore, 1805 and 1811. 12mo.

—— Notes and Queries. Edited by Wm. Brotherhead. Phila., 1857. Nos. 1, 2 and 3.

—— Oracle — See STEARNS, SAM'L.

—— Oratory; Selections from the Speeches of Eminent Americans. Phila., 1833. 8vo.

—— Oriental Society, Journal of. Vols. 1, 2. Vol. 3, Nos. 1, 2. Vol. 4, Nos. 1, 2. Vol. 5, Nos. 1, 2. Vol. 7. Vol. 8, No. 1. Vol. 9, No. 1. N. York and N. Haven. 1852–69.

—— Party. Principles and objects of the. N. York, 1855. 8vo. Congr. and Polit. Pamph. Vol. 56.

—— —— See WEBBER, C. W., Hist of. 1855.

—— —— See WHITNEY, T. R. Defence of.

—— Patriotic Songs — See McCARTY, W.

—— Peace Society — See ALLEN, W. H., SUMNER, C.

—— —— 8th Ann. Reports. May, 1836. Hartford, 1836. 8vo. Congr. and Polit. Pamph. Vol. 112.

—— —— See PHILANTHROPOS — Dissertation on a Congress of Nations.

—— —— Six Tracts published by the Society. Religious Pamph. Vol. 21.

—— —— See WALKER, AMASA. Address, 1863.

—— Pharmaceutical Association. Annual Proceedings. 1851–71.

—— —— Report on the Drug Market. Phila., 1868. 8vo. Med. Pamph. Vol. 11.

—— —— Report on Legislation regulating the practice of Pharmacy in the U. S. Phila., 1868. 8vo. Med Pamph. Vol. 7.

—— Philological Assoc. Proceedings of, 1st, 2d, 3d, 4th, Ann. Sessions, 1869–72. N. York, 1870–72. 8vo.

—— —— See TRUMBULL, J. Hammond.

—— —— See Van Name, Addison.

—— Philosoph. Soc'y.—Catalogue of the Library of. Parts 1, 2. Phila., 1865–6. 8vo.

AMERICAN Philosoph. Society, *continued.*
—— —— Laws and Regulations. Phila., 1860. 8vo.
—— —— List of Members from 1769 to Jan., 1860. Phila., 1860. 8vo.
—— —— Proceedings 1854–1870., beings Vols. 6, 7, 8, 9, 10, 11. Phila., 1854–70. 6 vols. 8vo. Also in parts, Vol. 12, Nos. 86, 87, 88, 89, for 1871–2.
—— —— Transactions, Vol. 1, 2 and 5, 1769 to 1802. Phila., 1771, 1786, 1802. 3 vols. 4to.
—— —— Same, N. Series, Vols. 1–12, complete. Phila., 1818–1863. 12 vols. 4to.
—— Physiological Soc'y.—See BARTLETT. E. Lecture, 1838.
—— Pioneer, a Monthly Periodical, devoted to the objects of the Logan Historical Society. 1842–43. Cincin. 2 vols. 8vo.
—— Politics.—See Congressional Speeches.
—— —— See Politics & Gov't.
—— Prime Meridian.—See DAVIS, C. H. Establishment of. 1849.
—— Primitive Methodist Magazine, Oct., Nov., Dec., 1863, Jan.–Dec., 1864. Vols. 2, 3. Mineral Point, Wis. 8vo.
—— Printing House for the Blind. Louisville, Ky. Circular and 3d Report of Trustees. Louisville & Frankfort. 1870. 8vo.
—— Privateers.—See COGGESHALL, G. History of.
—— Protestant Reformation Soc'y., N. York, Report for 1842. N. York. 8vo.
—— Publishers' Circular. Phila., 1855–1871. 17 vols. 8vo.
—— Pulpit.– See SPRAGUE, W. B. Annals of.
—— Quarterly Church Review & Ecclesiastical Register. Oct. 1865, Jan. 1866. 2 numbers. Vol. 17, Jan., Oct. 1866, complete. N. York. 8vo.
—— Quarterly Observer. July, 1833 to Oct., 1834. Boston. 3 vols. 8vo.
—— Quarterly Register and Journal. Andover & Boston, 1829–1839. 12 vols. 8vo.
—— Quarterly Review. March, 1827 to Dec., 1831. Phila. 10 vols. 8vo.
—— —— Sept., 1832 to Dec., 1833. Phila. 3 vols. 8vo.
—— —— Philadelphia, 1834–1837. Incomplete, viz.: Mar. & June, 1834, Mar. & Dec., 1835, Mar. & June, Sep. & Dec., 1836, Mar., June, Sept, 1837.
—— Register: or General Repository of History, Politics & Science. Phila., 1806–9. 6 vols. 8vo.
—— —— Or Summary Review of History, Politics & Literature. Phila., 1817. 2 Vols. 8vo.
—— Repertory of Arts, Science and Manufactures. New York. 1840–42. 4 vols. 8vo.
—— Review: a Whig Journal of Politics, Literature, &c., vols. 1–16, except vol. 14. New York, 1845–1852. 15 vols. 8vo.
—— Review of History and Politics, and Gen. Repository of Literature and State Papers. Vols. 1, 2, 3, 4. Phila. 1811, 1812. 8vo.
—— Scenery.—See BARTLETT, W. H.

AMERICAN Seamen's Friend Soc'y.—36th, 38th & 39th Ann. Reports, including Reports from the Boston Seamen's Friend and kindred Societies. N. York, 1864, '66, '67. 8vo.

—— Senator.—See CARPENTER, F.

—— Slave Trade.—See BUXTON, T. F. Ancient Slave Trade.

—— —— See Slavery.

—— Social Science Assoc.—See SPOFFORD, A. R. Public Libraries of the U. S.

—— —— WASHBURNE, E. Paper, 1868.

—— —— WHARTON, J. Address, 1870.

—— Soc'y for Civilization, &c., of the Indians, Constitution, &c., of the Soc'y. Washington, D. C., 1822. Indian Pamph., Vol, 1.

—— Society for Educating Pious Youth. Constitution and Address, 1816. 8vo. Religious Pamph., Vol. 16.

—— Society for Encouragement of Domestic Manufactures. Address to the People of the U. States. N. York., 1817. 8vo. Addresses, &c., Vol. 5.

—— Society for Meliorating the Condition of the Jews, Constitution, &c., 1820.

—— —— Ann. Reports for 1859 & 1860. N. York, n. d. 8vo.

—— State Papers. Documents, Legislative and Executive of the U. States, in Relation to Public Lands, 1789 to 1834. Washington. 5 vols. Folio.

—— —— Same, 1827 to 1837. Washington. 5 vols. Folio.

—— —— Finance, 1789–1822 and 1822–1828. 5 vols. Folio.

—— —— Naval Affairs, 1789–1825 and 1827–1836. 4 vols. Folio.

—— —— Foreign Relations, 1789–1822 and 1789–1859. 6 vols. Folio.

—— —— Military Affairs, 1819–1832 and 1823–1838. 6 vols. Folio.

—— —— Indian Affairs, 1789–1827. 2 vols. Folio.

—— —— Commerce & Navigation, 1789–1824. 2 vols. Folio.

—— —— Claims, 1789–1822. 1 vol. Folio.

—— —— Post Office, 1789–1833. 1 vol. Folio.

—— —— Miscellaneous, 1789–1823. 2 vols. Folio.

—— —— See U. S. State Papers.

—— —— In relation to the Berlin and Milan Decrees, 1810. London reprint, 1812. 8vo.

—— Statistical Association.—See WALLEY, S. H.

—— S. S. Union. 24th, 30th, 31st, 32d, Ann. Reports, May, 1848, 1856. Phila., 1848–1856. 8vo.

—— —— Sketch of Missionary Operations, 1855–6. Phila., 1856. 12mo. Religious Pamph., Vol. 17.

—— Tableaux, No. 1, Sketches of Aboriginal Life. New York, 1846. 12mo.

—— Temperance Jour. Phila., 1837–1842, 1846–1848. 3 vols. 4to.

—— —— Society. Annual Report, 1829, 1831, 1832, 1833. Temp. Pamph's., Vols. 1, 5.

—— —— Union. Report of Ex. Committee, 1843. New York, 1843. 8vo. Temp. Pamph., Vol. 1.

—— Tract Society, Boston. Ann. Reports for 1858, '63, 67, 68. Boston, 1859–1869. 8vo.

AMERICAN Tract Society. See New England Tract Soc'y.
—— —— Brief Survey of History and Operations of, for Ffty years. 1859. 12mo.
—— Tract Society, New York. Ann. Reports for 1847. 48, 49, 58, 59, 60, 65. New York, 1848-1866, 8vo.
—— —— Ninth Ann. Report of the Chicago Agency. 1863. 8vo.
—— —— and Slavery.
—— —— See BLISS, Seth. Letters on Tract Controversy.
—— —— See HARTFORD, Conn. 1st Cong. Ch. Remonstrance on Policy of the Soc'y.
—— —— See HARTFORD Branch of Amer. Tract Soc'y.
—— Tracts, 1776-1788, containing:

1. De Tumultibus Americanis. Oxford, 1776. 8vo.
2. Review of Claim of American Loyalists. London, 1788. 8vo.
3. The Case and Claim of American Loyalists considered. n. d.
4. Proposals for Establishing Colonies in Canada.
5. Observations, etc., on the Losses of American Loyalists. 1783. 8vo.
6. PAINE'S Letter to ABBE RAYNAL on Amer. Rev. London, 1782. 8vo.
7. Reply to Gen. HOWE'S, "Observa. on Letters to a Noblemen." London, 1780. 8vo.
8. Letters to a Nobleman on the Conduct of the War. London, 1779. 8vo.
9. Letter to Lord HOWE on his Naval Conduct in the War. London, 1779. 8vo.
10. Examination of Jos. GALLOWAY before House of Commons. London. 1779. 8vo.

—— Tramp in the Fall of 1864. Edinburgh, 1868. 8vo.
—— Union Academy of Literature, Science and Art.
—— See PASCHAL, G. W. Lecture. 1870.
—— Union Commission.
—— Speeches of W. DENNISON, J. R. DOOLITTLE, and others, in Hall of Repr., Washington, Feb. 12, 1865. New York. 8vo. Congr. ond Polit. Pamph. Vol. 104.
—— Unitarian Assoc.
—— Quarterly Journal. Vols. 1-6. Incomplete. Boston, 1853-1858. 8vo.
—— —— 9th, 16th, 24th, 25th, 28th, 46th, Ann. Reports. Boston, 1834-71. 12mo.
—— —— Circular of Assoc. respecting the Book and Tract Fund. Boston, 1854. 12mo.
—— —— The Mission to India. Boston, 1851. 12mo.
—— Universal Magazine. Vol. 3. July, 1797—Nov. 1797.
—— —— Vol. 4. Dec. 1797—Mar. 1798. New York. 2 Vols. 8vo.
—— WAR OF 1744, etc. (French and Indian.)
—— —— See BAYARD & LODOWICK. Journal of Actions in Canada.
—— —— Beginning, Progress and Conclusion of.
—— —— Brief View of Penn. in BRADDOCK'S Exped. 1755.
—— —— CRAFT, Benj. Journal of Siege of Louisburg, 1745.

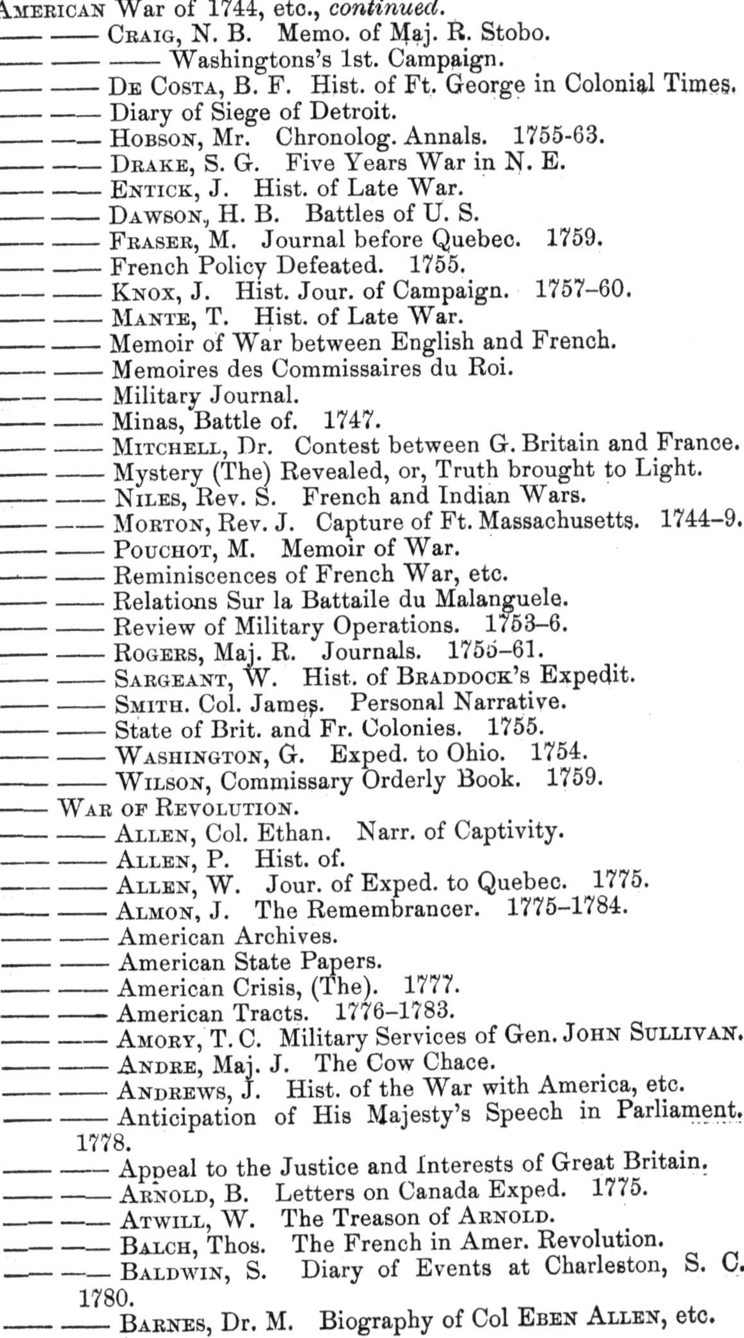

AMERICAN War of 1744, etc., *continued.*
—— —— CRAIG, N. B. Memo. of Maj. R. Stobo.
—— —— —— Washingtons's 1st. Campaign.
—— —— DE COSTA, B. F. Hist. of Ft. George in Colonial Times.
—— —— Diary of Siege of Detroit.
—— —— HOBSON, Mr. Chronolog. Annals. 1755-63.
—— —— DRAKE, S. G. Five Years War in N. E.
—— —— ENTICK, J. Hist. of Late War.
—— —— DAWSON, H. B. Battles of U. S.
—— —— FRASER, M. Journal before Quebec. 1759.
—— —— French Policy Defeated. 1755.
—— —— KNOX, J. Hist. Jour. of Campaign. 1757–60.
—— —— MANTE, T. Hist. of Late War.
—— —— Memoir of War between English and French.
—— —— Memoires des Commissaires du Roi.
—— —— Military Journal.
—— —— Minas, Battle of. 1747.
—— —— MITCHELL, Dr. Contest between G. Britain and France.
—— —— Mystery (The) Revealed, or, Truth brought to Light.
—— —— NILES, Rev. S. French and Indian Wars.
—— —— MORTON, Rev. J. Capture of Ft. Massachusetts. 1744–9.
—— —— POUCHOT, M. Memoir of War.
—— —— Reminiscences of French War, etc.
—— —— Relations Sur la Battaile du Malanguele.
—— —— Review of Military Operations. 1753–6.
—— —— ROGERS, Maj. R. Journals. 1755–61.
—— —— SARGEANT, W. Hist. of BRADDOCK's Expedit.
—— —— SMITH. Col. James. Personal Narrative.
—— —— State of Brit. and Fr. Colonies. 1755.
—— —— WASHINGTON, G. Exped. to Ohio. 1754.
—— —— WILSON, Commissary Orderly Book. 1759.
—— WAR OF REVOLUTION.
—— —— ALLEN, Col. Ethan. Narr. of Captivity.
—— —— ALLEN, P. Hist. of.
—— —— ALLEN, W. Jour. of Exped. to Quebec. 1775.
—— —— ALMON, J. The Remembrancer. 1775–1784.
—— —— American Archives.
—— —— American State Papers.
—— —— American Crisis, (The). 1777.
—— —— American Tracts. 1776–1783.
—— —— AMORY, T. C. Military Services of Gen. JOHN SULLIVAN.
—— —— ANDRE, Maj. J. The Cow Chace.
—— —— ANDREWS, J. Hist. of the War with America, etc.
—— —— Anticipation of His Majesty's Speech in Parliament. 1778.
—— —— Appeal to the Justice and Interests of Great Britain.
—— —— ARNOLD, B. Letters on Canada Exped. 1775.
—— —— ATWILL, W. The Treason of ARNOLD.
—— —— BALCH, Thos. The French in Amer. Revolution.
—— —— BALDWIN, S. Diary of Events at Charleston, S. C. 1780.
—— —— BARNES, Dr. M. Biography of Col EBEN ALLEN, etc.

AMERICAN War of Revolution, *continued.*
—— —— BARTON, Lieut. W. Journal. 1779.
—— —— BELDING, S. Ms. Orderly Book. 1779.
—— —— BENSON, E. Vindic. of Maj. ANDRE's Captors.
—— —— BENTALOU, P. PULASKI Vindicated.
—— —— BIDDLE, C. J. The Case of Maj. ANDRE Considered.
—— —— BLEECKER, Capt. L. Order Book. Campaign of. 1779.
—— —— BOTTA, Chas. History of War of Independence.
—— —— BRAYMAN, J. O. Deeds of Amer. Heroes.
—— —— BURGOYNE, Gen. Orderly Book, 1777.
—— —— BURKE, A. Address to Freemen of South Carolina, 1783.
—— —— BURKE, Edmund. Speech in Parl't, 1775.
—— —— BUSHNELL, C. I. Series of Biographies of Soldiers.
—— —— Calendar of Histor. Manuscripts.
—— —— CAMPBELL, Mrs. M. Revolu. Life of Gen. W. Hull.
—— —— CARROLL, Chas. Journal of Visit to Canada, 1776.
—— —— CARRUTHERS, E. W. Life of Rev. D. Caldwell and Revolu. Incidents.
—— —— —— Rev. Incidents in N. C.
—— —— CASE, Rev. W. Revolu. Memorials.
—— —— Celebration of Bat. King's Mountain.
—— —— CHALMERS, Geo. Intro. to History of Revolt of Colonies.
—— —— CLARK, Col. Geo. R. Expedit. to Illinois, 1778–9.
—— —— CLARK, Jos. Diary, 1778–9.
—— —— CLEMENT, J. Noble Deeds of Amer. Women.
—— —— CLINTON, Sir H. Narr. of Campaign, 1781.
—— —— Conduct of the late Administration Examined.
—— —— CONWAY, Gen. Speech in Parliam't, 1780.
—— —— COOPER, Rev. Mr. Hist. of N. America, 1795.
—— —— CORNWALLIS, Lord. Campaign in Virginia, 1781.
—— —— —— Correspondence.
—— —— CRAIG, N. B. Life and Service of Maj. I. Craig.
—— —— Crisis, The. Addressed to People of England, 1775.
—— —— DALZELL, J. M. Acc't of J. Gray, Rev. Soldier.
—— —— DAVIS, W. H. Sketch of Life of J. Lacy.
—— —— DAWSON, H. B, Assault on Stony Point.
—— —— —— Battles of U. S.
—— —— —— British Prison Ships, etc.
—— —— —— Gleanings, etc., of Amer. Hist.
—— —— —— Putnam. Correspondence.
—— —— —— Sons of Liberty in N. Y.
—— —— DAY, T. Reflections on State of England and Indepen. of America, 1783.
—— —— DECOSTA, B. F. Hist. of Ft. George in Revolution.
—— —— DENNY, W. H. Military Journal of Maj. E. Denny.
—— —— DICKINSON, J. Letters from Penn. Farmer.
—— —— DONNE, W. B. Corr. of Geo. III. and Lord North. 1768–1783.
—— —— DRAYTON, J. Memoirs of Amer. Revolution.
—— —— DUER, W. A. Life of Earl of Stirling.
—— —— DULANEY, D. Taxation of British Colonies.

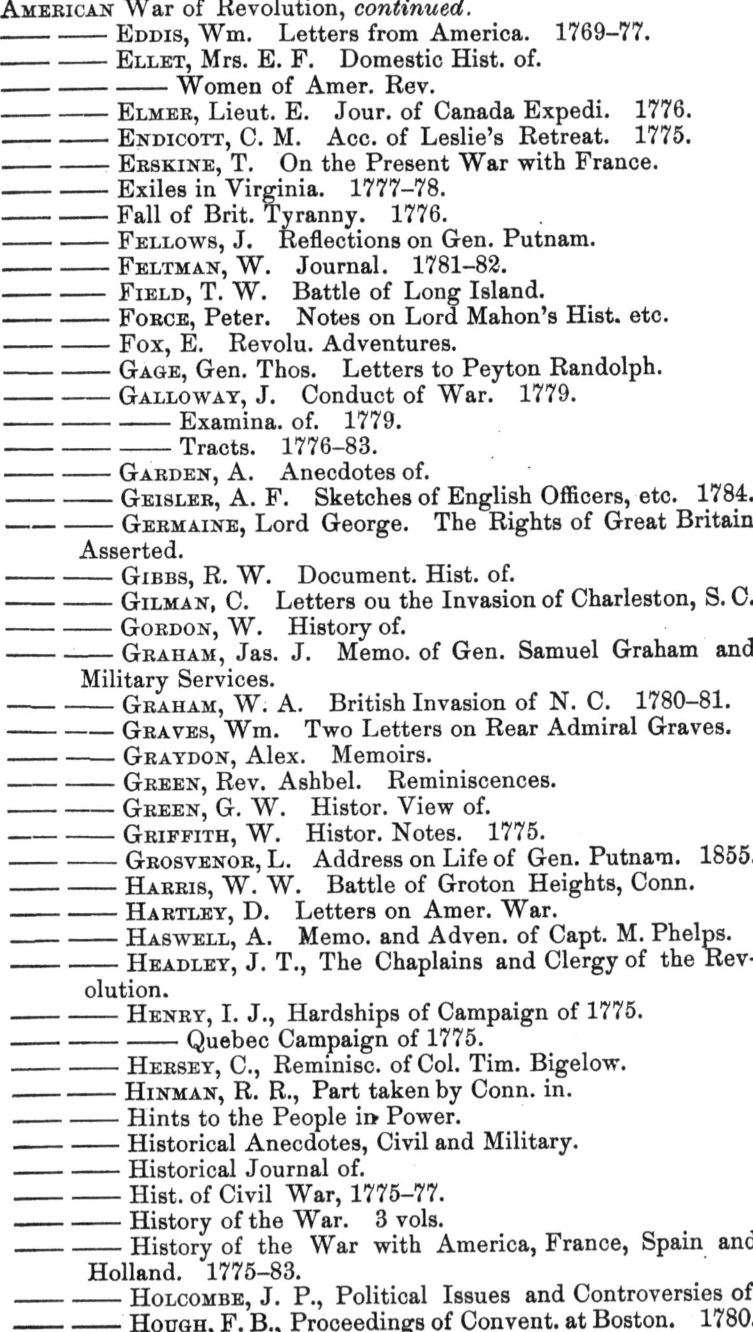

American War of Revolution, *continued.*
—— —— Eddis, Wm. Letters from America. 1769–77.
—— —— Ellet, Mrs. E. F. Domestic Hist. of.
—— —— —— Women of Amer. Rev.
—— —— Elmer, Lieut. E. Jour. of Canada Expedi. 1776.
—— —— Endicott, C. M. Acc. of Leslie's Retreat. 1775.
—— —— Erskine, T. On the Present War with France.
—— —— Exiles in Virginia. 1777–78.
—— —— Fall of Brit. Tyranny. 1776.
—— —— Fellows, J. Reflections on Gen. Putnam.
—— —— Feltman, W. Journal. 1781–82.
—— —— Field, T. W. Battle of Long Island.
—— —— Force, Peter. Notes on Lord Mahon's Hist. etc.
—— —— Fox, E. Revolu. Adventures.
—— —— Gage, Gen. Thos. Letters to Peyton Randolph.
—— —— Galloway, J. Conduct of War. 1779.
—— —— —— Examina. of. 1779.
—— —— —— Tracts. 1776–83.
—— —— Garden, A. Anecdotes of.
—— —— Geisler, A. F. Sketches of English Officers, etc. 1784.
—— —— Germaine, Lord George. The Rights of Great Britain Asserted.
—— —— Gibbs, R. W. Document. Hist. of.
—— —— Gilman, C. Letters ou the Invasion of Charleston, S. C.
—— —— Gordon, W. History of.
—— —— Graham, Jas. J. Memo. of Gen. Samuel Graham and Military Services.
—— —— Graham, W. A. British Invasion of N. C. 1780–81.
—— —— Graves, Wm. Two Letters on Rear Admiral Graves.
—— —— Graydon, Alex. Memoirs.
—— —— Green, Rev. Ashbel. Reminiscences.
—— —— Green, G. W. Histor. View of.
—— —— Griffith, W. Histor. Notes. 1775.
—— —— Grosvenor, L. Address on Life of Gen. Putnam. 1855.
—— —— Harris, W. W. Battle of Groton Heights, Conn.
—— —— Hartley, D. Letters on Amer. War.
—— —— Haswell, A. Memo. and Adven. of Capt. M. Phelps.
—— —— Headley, J. T., The Chaplains and Clergy of the Revolution.
—— —— Henry, I. J., Hardships of Campaign of 1775.
—— —— —— Quebec Campaign of 1775.
—— —— Hersey, C., Reminisc. of Col. Tim. Bigelow.
—— —— Hinman, R. R., Part taken by Conn. in.
—— —— Hints to the People in Power.
—— —— Historical Anecdotes, Civil and Military.
—— —— Historical Journal of.
—— —— Hist. of Civil War, 1775–77.
—— —— History of the War. 3 vols.
—— —— History of the War with America, France, Spain and Holland. 1775–83.
—— —— Holcombe, J. P., Political Issues and Controversies of.
—— —— Hough, F. B., Proceedings of Convent. at Boston. 1780.

AMERICAN War of Revolution, *continued.*
—— —— Howe, Sir W., Exam. before House of Commons. 1779.
—— —— HUBLEY, F., Hist. of Amer. War.
—— —— HUTCHINSON, K. M., Memoir of Abijah Hutchinson.
—— —— JOHNSON, WM., Life and Corr. of Gen. Nath. Greene.
—— —— JOHNSON, J., Traditions and Reminiscences.
—— —— JOHNSTONE, Gov., Colony of Mass. Bay in Rebellion.
—— —— JONES, J. S., Defence of N. Carolina against Jefferson's Aspersions.
—— —— JUNIUS. Letters, &c.
—— —— HALL, Henry., Evacuation of Ticonderoga in 1777.
—— —— HEATH, Gen. Wm., Memoirs of.
—— —— JONES, Alex., The Cymry of 76.
—— —— JONES, John Paul, Life of. 1869.
—— —— KEACH, Rev. I., Annivers. Address on Battle of Bennington.
—— —— KIDDER, F., Hist. of 1st N. H. Regt.
—— —— Military Opera. in Me.
—— —— KING, C., Battle of Monmouth, N. J.
—— —— King's Mountain, Celebration of Battle of.
—— —— KNIGHT, Dr. & SLOVER, John, Perils among the Indians during the War.
—— —— LAMB, R., Jour. of Occurrences to 1783.
—— —— Late Occurrences in North America Considered.
—— —— LAURENS, H., Acc. of his Capture and Confinement.
—— —— LEAKE, J. Q., Memories of John Lamb.
—— —— LEE, Maj. Gen. Chas., Court Martial of. 1778.
—— —— LEE, Henry, Campaign of, 1781, in the Carolinas.
—— —— LEE, Gen. H., Champe's Adventures.
—— —— LEE, Henry, Memoirs of War.
—— —— LEGGETT, Maj. A., Personal Narrative, &c.
—— —— LEMOINE, J. M., The Sword of Gen. Montgomery.
—— —— LENDRUM, J., Concise and Impartial History.
—— —— Letters by an Amer. Spy, 1764–1785.
—— —— Long Island, Battle of.
—— —— L. I. Histor. Soc., Battle of L. I.
—— —— LOSSING, B. J., Pictorial Field Book of.
—— —— —— 1776; or, the War of the Rev.
—— —— LOXLEY, Capt., Campaign to Amboy. 1776.
—— —— LUNT, Paul., Diary. 1775.
—— —— MACAULEY, C., Address to People of Great Britain. 1775.
—— —— MACKENZIE, A. S., Life of Paul Jones.
—— —— MACKENZIE, R. TARLETON'S Campaigns.
—— —— MAGOON, E. L., Orators of.
—— —— MARBOIS, B., Complot D'ARNOLD.
—— —— Maryland Provincial Convention. 1774–6.
—— —— Mass. Provincial Congress Journals. 1771–5.
—— —— MEIGS, R. J., Journal of Canada Exped. 1775.
—— —— MELVIN, J., Journal of Quebec Exped. 1775.
—— —— Minutes of Court Martial of André.
—— —— MOORE, F., Corresp. of H. Laurens.

AMERICAN War of Revolution, etc., *continued.*

—— —— —— Songs, &c., of Amer. Rev.

—— —— —— Diary of.

—— —— —— Patriot Preachers.

—— —— MOORE, G. H., On the Employment of Negroes.

—— —— —— Treason of Gen. Chas. Lee.

—— —— MORRIS, M., Private Journal.

—— —— MOORE, M. A., Life of Gen. E. Lacy & S. C. Revolutionary War Hist.

—— —— MORSE, JED., Annals of Amer. Revolution.

—— —— MORGAN, W., Facts for people of Gr. Britain respecting Expenses of War.

—— —— MOTT, Capt. Edw., Journal.

—— —— MOULTRIE, W., Amer. Revolution in N. & S. Carolina.

—— —— MUHLENBERG, H. M., Journal 1776–7.

—— —— Narrative of the Excursion and Ravages of the King's Troops.

—— —— NEILSON, C., Burgoyne's Campaigns.

—— —— NELL, W. C., Colored Patriots of the Revolution.

—— —— N. Jersey Official Registers of Officers, &c.

—— —— New York Provincial Congress.

—— —— NILES, H., Principles and Acts of the.

—— —— Notices of Sullivan's Campaigns.

—— —— Observations on the Justice and Policy of the.

—— —— On a Reconcilia. of G. Brit. and the Colonies.

—— —— ONDERDONK, H., Revolu. Hist. of Kings Co., N. Y.

—— —— Orderly Book at Williamsburg, Va.

—— —— Orderly Book of Northern Army.

—— —— OTIS, J,, The Rights of the Colonies.

—— —— —— Vindication of Brit. Colonies.

—— —— PAGE, Capt. Sam'l, Journal, 1779.

—— —— PAINE, T., Common Sense.

—— —— —— The Amer. Crisis.

—— —— —— Letter to the Abbé Raynal.

—— —— PETERSON, C. J., Military Heroes of the Revolution.

—— —— PINCKNEY, Chas., Recent Captures by British Cruisers.

—— —— Plain Truth to the Inhabitants of America. 1776.

—— —— PRICE, Rev. Rich'd, Observa. on Civil Liberty, the Justice of the War, &c.

—— —— —— Additional Observation on the.

—— —— Private Recollections of.

—— —— Protests against Bill to Repeal Amer. Stamp Act.

—— —— PULTENEY, W., Thoughts on Present State of Affairs.

—— —— PURVIANCE, R., Narr. of Events at Baltimore.

—— —— RAMSAY, D., History of.

—— —— RAYNAL, Abbé, Revolution in America.

—— —— REED & CADWALLADER Pamphs.

—— —— REED, J., Life and Correspondence.

—— —— REED, Wm. B., Reprint of Washington's Letters.

—— —— Regula. concerning the British Colonies, considered 1765.

—— —— Relations, &c., Battle Monongahela.

—— —— Revolutionary Relics, or Clinton Correspondence.

AMERICAN War of Revolution, *continued.*
—— —— RICHMOND, J. W., Revolu. Debt of R. Island.
—— —— RIEDESEL, Gen. and Mad., Letters and Journals relat. to.
—— —— ROBBINS, Rev. Ammi R., Journal. 1776.
—— —— ROBIN, Abbé, Campaign de l'Armée. 1781.
—— —— SABINE, L., Amer. Loyalists.
—— —— SAFFELL, W. T. R., Records of Rev. War.
—— —— ST. CLAIR, Gen. A., Indian Campaign. 1791.
—— —— SCHROEDER, J. F., Life & Times of Washington.
—— —— SCHUYLER, G. L., On Bancroft's Hist. of Northern Campaign of 1777.
—— —— SENTER, Dr. Isaac, Journal, 1775.
—— —— Sexagenary; or Reminiscences of Amer. Rev.
—— —— SHELBY, I., Battle of King's Mountain. 1780.
—— —— SHEPHERD, Rev. Dr., History of.
—— —— SHEPPARD, J. H., Life of Comm. S. Tucker.
—— —— SHORT, A. History of the Opposition during last Session of Parl't. 1779.
—— —— SIMMS, W. G. S. Carolina in Rev. War.
—— —— SMITH, H. W. Nuts to Crack.
—— —— SMITH, Joshua H. Record of his Trial, &c.
—— —— SMITH, T. Marshall Legends of.
—— —— SOULE'S, F. Hist. des troubles de l'Amerique.
—— —— SPARK'S, J. Correspondence of.
—— —— STAPLES, W. R. Destruction of the Gaspee.
—— —— STARK, C. Mem. and Official Corr. of Gen. J. Stark.
—— —— STEADMAN, C. Hist. of the Rise, Progress, etc.
—— —— STONE, E. M. Invasion of Canada.
—— —— STONE, W. L. Border Wars of.
—— —— Stories of Indians during the.
—— —— STREET, A. B. Battle of Saratoga.
—— —— SUMNER, W. H. Reminis. of Warren and Bunker Hill.
—— —— SWETT, S. Hist. of Battle of Bunker Hill.
—— —— —— Who Commanded at Bunker Hill?
—— —— TARLETON, B. Campaigns. 1780–81.
—— —— TAYLOR, G. Martyrs to Revolution.
—— —— Ten Chapters of Life of John Hancock.
—— —— THACHER, Dr. J. Military Journal.
—— —— THOMAS, E. S. Reminiscences of 60 years.
—— —— THORNTON, J. W. The Pulpit of Amer. Rev.
—— —— Thoughts of a Traveller on Amer. Disputes.
—— —— THOMPSON, J. L. Hist. of Wars of U. S.
—— —— Traditions of.
—— —— Trenton, Battle of.
—— —— TRESCOTT, W. H. Diplomacy of the Revolution.
—— —— TRUMBULL, J. Autobiog. and Reminiscences.
—— —— TRUMBULL, J. H. Origin of Expedition against Ticonderoga.
—— —— TUCKER, J. Tracts on.
—— —— TYSON, J. R. Moral and Social Influences of.
—— —— U. S. Census of Pensioners.
—— —— U. S. Report on Revolu. Claims.

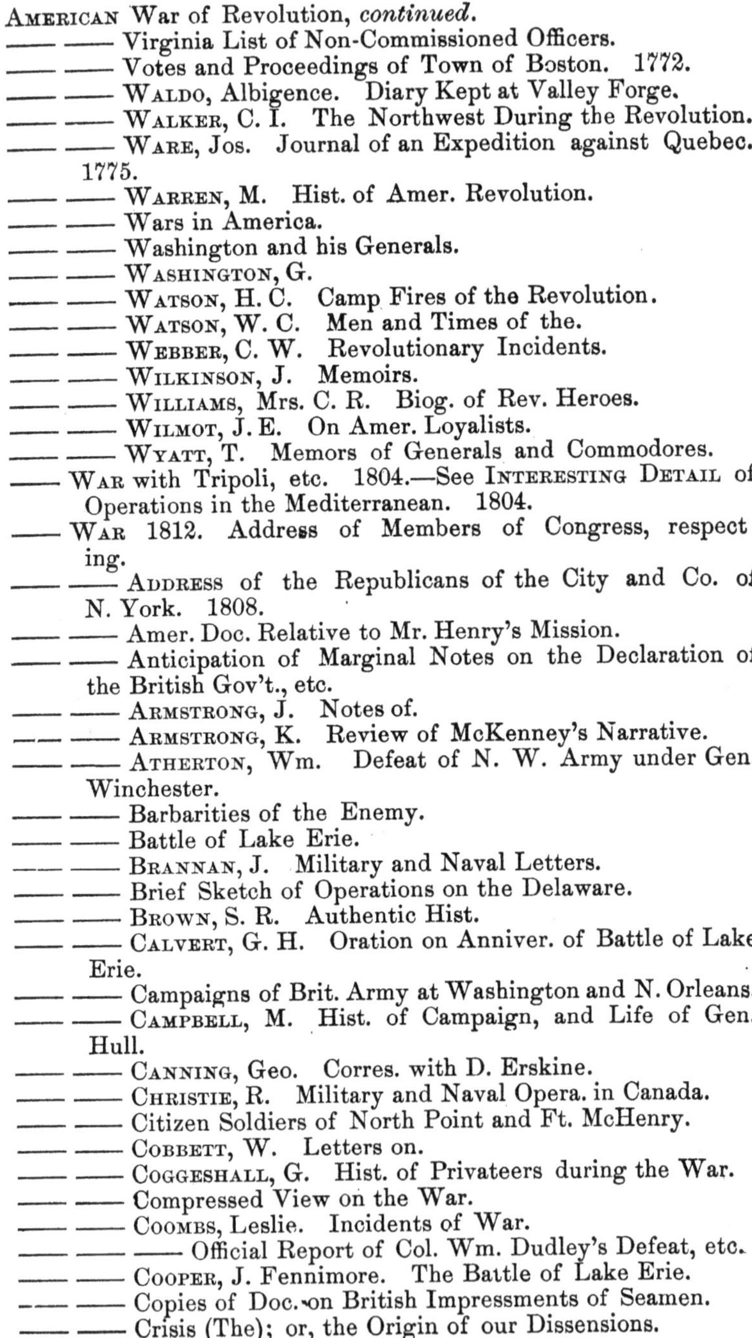

AMERICAN War of Revolution, *continued.*
—— —— Virginia List of Non-Commissioned Officers.
—— —— Votes and Proceedings of Town of Boston. 1772.
—— —— WALDO, Albigence. Diary Kept at Valley Forge.
—— —— WALKER, C. I. The Northwest During the Revolution.
—— —— WARE, Jos. Journal of an Expedition against Quebec. 1775.
—— —— WARREN, M. Hist. of Amer. Revolution.
—— —— Wars in America.
—— —— Washington and his Generals.
—— —— WASHINGTON, G.
—— —— WATSON, H. C. Camp Fires of the Revolution.
—— —— WATSON, W. C. Men and Times of the.
—— —— WEBBER, C. W. Revolutionary Incidents.
—— —— WILKINSON, J. Memoirs.
—— —— WILLIAMS, Mrs. C. R. Biog. of Rev. Heroes.
—— —— WILMOT, J. E. On Amer. Loyalists.
—— —— WYATT, T. Memors of Generals and Commodores.
—— WAR with Tripoli, etc. 1804.—See INTERESTING DETAIL of Operations in the Mediterranean. 1804.
—— WAR 1812. Address of Members of Congress, respecting.
—— —— ADDRESS of the Republicans of the City and Co. of N. York. 1808.
—— —— Amer. Doc. Relative to Mr. Henry's Mission.
—— —— Anticipation of Marginal Notes on the Declaration of the British Gov't., etc.
—— —— ARMSTRONG, J. Notes of.
—— —— ARMSTRONG, K. Review of McKenney's Narrative.
—— —— ATHERTON, Wm. Defeat of N. W. Army under Gen. Winchester.
—— —— Barbarities of the Enemy.
—— —— Battle of Lake Erie.
—— —— BRANNAN, J. Military and Naval Letters.
—— —— Brief Sketch of Operations on the Delaware.
—— —— BROWN, S. R. Authentic Hist.
—— —— CALVERT, G. H. Oration on Anniver. of Battle of Lake Erie.
—— —— Campaigns of Brit. Army at Washington and N. Orleans.
—— —— CAMPBELL, M. Hist. of Campaign, and Life of Gen. Hull.
—— —— CANNING, Geo. Corres. with D. Erskine.
—— —— CHRISTIE, R. Military and Naval Opera. in Canada.
—— —— Citizen Soldiers of North Point and Ft. McHenry.
—— —— COBBETT, W. Letters on.
—— —— COGGESHALL, G. Hist. of Privateers during the War.
—— —— Compressed View on the War.
—— —— COOMBS, Leslie. Incidents of War.
—— —— —— Official Report of Col. Wm. Dudley's Defeat, etc.
—— —— COOPER, J. Fennimore. The Battle of Lake Erie.
—— —— Copies of Doc. on British Impressments of Seamen.
—— —— Crisis (The); or, the Origin of our Dissensions.

AMERICAN War of 1812, *continued*.
—— —— CROKER, J. W. Letters on the Naval War.
—— —— Correspondence with the Editor of the *Times*, etc.
—— —— DALLIBA, Jas. Battle of Brownstown.
—— —— DARNELL, E. Sufferings, etc., of Kentucky Volunteers.
—— —— DAVIS, P. M. Authentic Hist. of War.
—— —— Dispassionate Inquiry as to Causes of War.
—— —— DUDLEY, T. P. Battle at Frenchtown, Mich.
—— —— ELLIOTT, Com. J. D. Speech in Hagerstown, Md. 1843.
—— —— Embargo Act. 1808.
—— —— Exposition of Causes of the Late War.
—— —— ESSEX Co., Mass. Declara., etc., July 12, 1812.
—— —— FAY, H. A. Official Accounts of Battles.
—— —— FOSTER, J. Hist. of Hull's Exped.
—— —— HATCH, W. A Chapter of Hist. of the War.
—— —— HEADLEY, J. T. Second War with G. B.
—— —— Hist. of the Late War.
—— —— HULL, W. Hist. of N. W. Army.
—— —— HUNT, G. J. Historical Reader.
—— —— INGERSOLL, C. J. Histor. Sketch of War.
—— —— INGRAHAM, E. D. The Capture of Washington, D. C.
—— —— JAMES, W. Full Acc. of Late War.
—— —— JAMES, Wm. Military Occurrences, etc.
—— —— —— Naval Transactions between G. Britain and the U. S.
—— —— JAY, Wm. Table of the Killed and Wounded.
—— —— LATOUR, A. L. Memoir of War in W. Florida and Louisiana.
—— —— Letters of Vetus. 1812–14.
—— —— LOSSING, B. J. Pictorial Field-Book.
—— —— LOWELL, J. Enquiry into the Question of the Chesapeake, etc.
—— —— —— Perpetual War; the Policy of Mr. Madison, etc.
—— —— McLEOD, Alex. Scriptural View of.
—— —— MANN, J. Medical Sketches of Campaigns. 1812–14.
—— —— Military Opera. on the Delaware.
—— —— N. York Convention of Soldiers of the War. 1856.
—— —— Papers relating to. Western Reserve Hist. Soc. Tracts.
—— —— Papers relating to Naval Engagements.
—— —— PARSONS, U. On Battle of Lake Erie.
—— —— PERKINS, T. Hist. of the Late War.
—— —— Philadelphia, Hist. of; with Account of the War.
—— —— PREBLE, Capt. G. H. The First Cruise of the Frigate Essex.
—— —— Proceedings of Convention of Soldiers. 1857.
—— —— QUINCY, Josiah. Speech in Cong., Jan. 5, 1813.
—— —— RICHARDSON, M. War of 1812. Canadian Army.
—— —— RIGHT and Practice of Impressment.
—— —— SCOTT, Gen. W., and Gen. Z. Taylor.
—— —— Sketches of the War.
—— —— STEPHENS, Jas. Observations on John Randolph's Speech.

AMERICAN War of 1812, *continued.*
—— —— The War. Newspaper.
—— —— THOMPSON, J. L. Hist. of the Wars of the U. S.
—— —— TODD and DRAKE's Military Hist. of Gen. Harrison.
—— —— U. S. House of Repr. Address of Members to their Constituents. 1812.
—— —— U. S. Sec'y of Interior. Report of Commiss'r of Indian Affairs on Bounty Lands. 1840.
—— —— VAN RENSSELAER, S. Affair at Queenstown, N. Y.
—— —— WALKER. Adam. Journals of Campaigns in Mich. and Ind. Territories.
—— —— WALKER, Alex. Jackson and New Orleans.
—— —— WHITTLESEY, E. Defence or Fort Stephenson.
—— —— "Why are We Still at War?" etc.
—— —— WILLIAMS, J. S. History of Invasion of City of Washington.
—— —— WILLIAMS, Sam'l. Two Western Campaigns.
—— —— WYATT, T. Memoirs of Generals and Commodores of Army and Navy.
AMERICAN WAR OF REBELLION.—See ABBOTT, A. O. Prison Life in the South.
—— —— ABBOTT, J. S. C. History of.
—— —— ALFRIEND, F. H. Life of Jeff. Davis.
—— —— Amer. Tramp in 1864.
—— —— ANDREWS, C. C. Campaign of Mobile.
—— —— ANDREWS, S. South Since the War.
—— —— Antietam National Cemetery. History, etc.
—— —— Army and Navy Offic. Cazette. 1863–4.
—— —— Army of the Cumberland. Tennessee, etc.
—— —— AUGLEY, J. H. Slavery and Secession.
—— —— BADEAU, A. Military Hist. of. Gen. Grant.
—— —— BAKER, S. C. Hist. of U. S. Secret Service.
—— —— BARBEIRE, Jos. Scraps from the Prison Table at Camp Chase, etc. 1868.
—— —— Battle Fields of the South.
—— —— BICKHAM, W. D. Rosekrans' Campaign with 14th Army Corps.
—— —— BILL, S. Pen Pictures of the War.
—— —— BISHOP, J. S. Concise Hist. of the War.
—— —— BLAKE, H. N. Army of Potomac.
—— —— BLEDSOE, A. T. Is Davis a Traitor?
—— —— BOTTS, J. M. The Great Rebellion.
—— —— BOUDRYE, L. N. Hist. Records of 5th N. Y. Cavalry.
—— —— BOWMAN AND IRWIN. Sherman and his Campaigns.
—— —— BOYD, Belle. In Camp and Prison.
—— —— BOYNTON, C. R. Hist. of Navy in War of Rebell'n.
—— —— BREARLEY, W. H. Recollections of the East Tennessee Campaign.
—— —— BREWER, G. Hist., War Record, etc., of Alabama. 1872.
—— —— BRIGHT, J. Speech at Rockdale.
—— —— BROCKETT, L. P. Camp, Battlefield, and Hospital.
—— —— BROWNE, Dunn. Experiences in the Army.

AMERICAN War of Rebellion, *continued.*
—— —— BROWNE, J. H. Four Years in Secessia. 1865.
—— —— BROWNLOW, W. G. Rise, Progress and Decline of Secessia. 1862.
—— —— BUCHANAN, Isaac. Canada Relations with U. S. 1864.
—— —— BUTLER, Gen. B. F. Campaign before Richmond. 1864.
—— —— BUTLER, L. C. Memorial Record of Essex, Vermont.
—— —— CAREY, Jas. P. Record of the Great Rebellion. 1866.
—— —— CARPENTER, S. D. Logic of Hist. ' Causes of the War.
—— —— CASTLEMAN, A. L. Army of the Potomac.
—— —— CAVADA, F. F. Libby Prison Life.
—— —— CHIPMAN, N. P. Claims of Loyal Citizens.
—— —— Chronicles of.
—— —— CLARK, J. H. Hist. of 115th N. York Reg't.
—— —— CLARK, P. H. Black Brigade of Cincin.
—— —— CLEVELAND, H. A. H. Stephens, Public and Private.
—— —— COFFIN, C. C. Four Years of Fighting.
—— —— Conn. Volunteer Organizations.
—— —— CONYNGHAN, D. P. Sherman's March through the South.
—— —— COOK, Joel. Siege of Richmond. 1862.
—— —— COOK, John E. Personal Portraits.
—— —— COPPEE, H. Gen. Grant and his Campaigns.
—— —— COWELL, B. The Spirit of '76 of R. I.
—— —— CRAWFORD, J. M. Adventures of Mosby and his Men.
—— —— CROFFUT and MORRIS. Conn. in the War.
—— —— CUDWORTH, W. H. Hist. of 1st Mass. Infantry. 1861–64.
—— —— CUMMING, Kate. Hospital Life in Confed. Army.
—— —— DABNEY, Rev. A. L. Campaigns of Lt. Gen. Thos. J. Jackson.
—— —— DANIELS, —. Life of Stonewall Jackson.
—— —— DAVIS, Jeff., and Stonewall Jackson.
—— —— DAVIS, W. W. H. Hist. of 104th Penn. Reg't.
—— —— DAY, S. P. Down South: an Englishman's Experience.
—— —— DENISON, C. W. Winfield, the Lawyer's Son.
—— —— DENSON, A. C. Westmoreland; or, Secession Ferocity.
—— —— DE PEYSTER, J. W La Royale. Parts i, vi, viii.
—— —— —— Military Hist. of Gen. Phil. Kearney.
—— —— DORSEY, S. A. Recollections of Gen. Allen, C. S. A.
—— —— DOWLEY, M. F. Hist. of 12th Reg't N. G. N. Y.
—— —— DRAPER, J. W. Hist. of Amer. Civil War.
—— —— DUKE, B. W. Hist. of Morgan's Cavalry.
—— —— DUYCKINCK, E. L. Hist. of the War.
—— —— EARLY, Gen. J. A. Campaigns of Gen. R. E. Lee.
—— —— —— Mem. of Last Year of War.
—— —— Echoes from the South.
—— —— EDDY, R. Hist. of N. York 60th Vol. Reg't.
—— —— EDWARDS, Rev. J. E. The Confederate Soldier.
—— —— EDWARDS, J. N. Shelby and his Men.
—— —— ELLIS, T. T. Leaves from the Diary of an Army Surgeon. 1863.
—— —— ELY, Alfred. Journal while a Prisoner at Richmond.

AMERICAN War of Rebellion, *continued.*
—— —— ESTVAN, B. War Pictures from the South.
—— —— Farragut and our Naval Commanders.
—— —— FARRAR, C. C. S. The War: its Causes, etc.
—— —— FAULKNER, T. C. Hist. of. 1861.
—— —— FERREE, P. V. The Heroes of the War for Uuion.
—— —— FISCH, Geo. Nine Months in U. S. 1863.
—— —— FITCH, John. Annals of the Army of the Cumberland.
—— —— FOOTE, H. S. Causes of Civil War.
—— —— FOSTER, J. Y. N. Jersey in Rebellion.
—— —— Four Miscellaneous Scrap-Books of Newspaper Cuttings. Folio. 1861–64.
—— —— Ten volumes do. of the Part taken by Wisconsin in the War. 4to.
—— —— FOWLER, W. Sectional Controversy; the Causes of the War, etc.
—— —— FREEMANTLE, Col. Three Months in So. States. 1863.
—— —— FREMONT, Jesse B. Story of the Guard. 1862.
—— —— FROST, Mrs. J. B. Rebellion in U. States.
—— —— GASPARIN, A. America before Europe. 1862.
—— —— —— Uprising of a Great People.
—— —— GEER, J. J. Beyond the Lines: a Yankee Prisoner loose in Dixie.
—— —— GIDDINGS, J. R. Hist. of Rebellion.
—— —— GILMOR, H. Four Years in the Saddle.
—— —— GILMORE, Q. A. Siege, etc., of Ft. Pulaski.
—— —— GLAZIER, W. W. Capture, Prison Pen, and Escape.
—— —— GOLDSBOROUGH, W. W. The Maryland Line in Confed. Army.
—— —— GOODRICH, F. B. Tribute Book: Record of Munificence, etc., of Amer. People.
—— —— GOODWIN, T. S. Nat. Hist. of Secession.
—— —— GOSS, E. H. Melrose, Mass., Memorial.
—— —— Grand Army of Republic.
—— —— GRANT, U. S. GREELEY, H. Amer. Conflict.
—— —— GREENE, C. S. Thrilling Stories of the Great Rebellion. 1864.
—— —— GUROWSKI, A. Diary 1861–62, 1862–63.
—— —— HAMERSLY, L. R. Navy Biography, and Opera. in Rebellion.
—— —— HAMLIN, A. C. Martyria; or, Andersonville Prison.
—— —— HANAFORD, E. Hist. 6th Ohio Vol. Infantry.
—— —— HANSON, J. W. Hist. of 6th Mass. Volunteers.
—— —— Harper's Ferry Invasion.
—— —— HARPERS' Pictorial History of.
—— —— Harvard Memorial Biographies.
—— —— HEADLEY, J. T. Grant and Sherman: their Campaigns.
—— —— —— Farragut and Naval Commanders.
—— —— HELPER, H. R. Compendium of Impending Crisis. 1860.
—— —— HEPWORTH, Geo. H. Whip, Hoe, and Sword.
—— —— HILLIARD, G. S. McClellan's Life and Campaigns.
—— —— HOGE, Mrs. A. H. The Boys in Blue.

AMERICAN War of Rebellion, *continued.*

—— —— HOLMES, M. Soldier of the Cumberland.

—— —— HOSMER, J. K. The Color Guard: a Corporal's Notes.

—— —— Hospital Transports: a Memoir, etc.

—— —— HOTCHKISS and ALLAN. Battlefields of Va.

—— —— HOUGH, Dr. F. B. Hist. of Duryee's Brigage in Va. and Md.

—— —— HOWE, H. The Western States in the War.

—— —— HUNT, C. E. The Shenandoah; or, last Confed. Cruiser.

—— —— Illinois in the Rebellion.

—— —— JACKSON, Gen. T. J. Life of.

—— —— JACOBS, M. Rebel Invasion of Md. and Pa.

—— —— JOHNS, H. T. Life with 49th Mass. Vol.

—— —— JONES, C. C. Hist. of Chatham Artillery.

—— —— JONES, E. R. Personal Recollections.

—— —— JORDAN and PRYOR. Campaigns of Gen. N. B. Forrest and his Cavalry.

—— —— JULIAN, G. W. Select Speeches.

—— —— KEILEY, A. M. In Vinculis; or, the Prisoner of War.

—— —— KEIM, B. R. Sheridan's Troopers on the Borders.

—— —— KELLOGG, R. H. Life and Death in Rebel Prisons.

—— —— KELSO, Isaac. Stars and Bars: the Reign of Terror in Mo.

—— —— KIRKE, E. Down in Tennessee.

—— —— —— My Southern Friends. 1863.

—— —— KNOX, T. W. Camp Fires.

—— —— LANMAN, C. Red Book of Michigan.

—— —— LAUGEL, A. U. States during the War.

—— —— LAWRENCE, Geo. Border and Bastile.

—— —— LEE, R. E.

—— —— Libby Prison: Prisoners, etc.

—— —— Life in the South, from Commencement of the War.

—— —— Light and Dark of the Rebellion. 1863.

—— —— LINCOLN, A.

—— —— LOCKE, W. H. Story of the Penn. 11th.

—— —— LOSSING, B. J. Pictorial Hist. of War.

—— —— LOVE, W. D. L. Wisconsin in the War.

—— —— LUNT, Geo. Origin of the Late War.

—— —— LYON, Gen. Nathan.

—— —— MCCLELLAN, G. B.

—— —— MCPHERSON, E. Polit. Hist. of U. S. during the Rebellion.

—— —— Maine Military Records.

—— —— Maps of Operations of Armies of Potomac and James. 1864–5.

—— —— Marginalia: Gleanings from an Army Note Book. 1864.

—— —— Mkars, J. J. Peninsular Campaigns in Va.

—— —— MARSHALL, J. A. Amer. Bastile.

—— —— MASSIE, J. W. Origin of Present Conflict.

—— —— Military Science.

—— —— Medical and Surgical Hist. of the War.

—— —— MITCHELL, D. W. An Englishman's Views, etc. 1862.

AMERICAN War of Rebellion, *continued.*
—— —— MOORE, F. Women of the War.
—— —— MOTLEY, J. L. Causes of Amer. Civil War.
—— —— Narr. of Suffering, etc., of Union Prisoners.
—— —— New Jersey in the Rebellion.
—— —— N. York. Presentation of Flags to Legislature. 1864.
—— —— —— State Bureau of Military Statistics.
—— —— —— State Bureau of Military Record.
—— —— —— State Soldiers' Depot. Report. 1864.
—— —— NICHOLS, G. W. Story of Sherman's Great March.
—— —— NOTT, C. C. Sketches of the War.
—— —— NOYES, Geo. F. Bivouac and Battlefield.
—— —— 112 Volumes of Pamphlets on the Rebellion.
—— —— Opening of the Mississippi.
—— —— O'REILLY, H. Great Questions of the Times.
—— —— PARTON, Jas. Gen. Butler in New Orleans.
—— —— PECKHAM, Jas. Gen. N. Lyon and Missouri in 1861.
—— —— Penn. War Claims. Correspondence on. 1872.
—— —— PERRINE, C. O. Topograph. War Map and Chronology.
—— —— PEYTON, J. L. The American Crisis.
—— —— PIERCE, S. W. Battle Fields and Camp Fires.
—— —— PIKE. Scout and Ranger.
—— —— PITTENGER, W. Daring and Suffering.
—— —— POLLARD, E. A. First and Last Years of the War.
—— —— —— Life of Jeff. Davis.
—— —— —— Observations in the North, etc.
—— —— —— Southern Hist. of.
—— —— —— Lost Cause, and Lost Cause Regained.
—— —— QUINER, E. B. Wisconsin Military Hist.
—— —— QUINT, Rev. A. H. The Potomac and Rapidan.
—— —— RAWLINS, C. E., Jr. Amer. Disunion. 1862.
—— —— Rebellion Pamphlets.
—— —— Rebellion Record.
—— —— Rebuke (The) of Secession Doctrines, etc.
—— —— Red Tape and Pigeon-Hole Generals.
—— —— REED, Wm. H. Hospital Life in Army of Potomac.
—— —— REID, W. Ohio in the War.
—— —— Rejected Stone (The) Insurrection *vs.* Resurrection.
—— —— RICHARDSON, A. D. Secret Service, etc.
—— —— REYNOLDS, E. W. True Hist. of the Barons of the South. 1862.
—— —— Richmond During the War.
—— —— Roll of Honor: Names of Soldiers who Died in Defence of the Union. 1866–69. 6 vols.
—— —— Ross, Fitzgerald. Visit to Confed. States. 1865.
—— —— SABRE, G. E. Nineteen Months a Prisoner of War.
—— —— SCHALK, E. Campaigns of 1862 and 1863.
—— —— SCHMUCKER, S. S. Hist. of Civil War in U. S.
—— —— SENOUR F. Morgan and his Captors.
—— —— SHANKS, W. F. G. Recollections of Generals.
—— —— SHEA, John G. The Fallen Brave.
—— —— SHOULER, Wm. Mass. in the War.

AMERICAN War of Rebellion, *continued.*
—— —— Slavery.
—— —— SNOW, Wm. P. Southern Generals.
—— —— SOMERS, R. So. States Since the War.
—— —— S. Carolina. Report of Destruction of Churches in.
—— —— Southern Hist. of the War. 1863.
—— —— Southern Soldiers' Song Book.
—— —— SPENCE, Jas. Amer. Union. 1862.
—— —— SPRAGUE, Maj. J. T. Texas Treason.
—— —— STACKE, Henry. Story of Amer. War. 1866.
—— —— STANTON, B. Letter on Gen. W. T. Sherman.
—— —— STEPHENS, A. H. Constitu. View of Late War.
—— —— STEVENSON, Geo. A. Thirteen Months in Rebel Army.
—— —— STEWART, G. T. Lessons of the War.
—— —— STONE, E. W. R. I. in the War.
—— —— Story of the Kearsage and the Alabama.
—— —— SUMNER, C. Oration at N. York. 1861.
—— —— SWINTON, Jas. Twelve Decisive Battles.
—— —— SYPHER, J. R. Hist. of Pa. Reserve Corps.
—— —— TAYLOR, Wm. Causes and Probable Results of the Civil War, etc. 1862.
—— —— TELFER, W. D. First Battle of Manassas.
—— —— Three Years Among the Working Classes during the War. 1865.
—— —— TOWNSEND, Geo. A. Campaigns of a Non-Combatant.
—— —— TRUMBULL, H. C. Life of Maj. H. W. Camp.
—— —— U. States Conduct of the War.
—— —— U. S. Sanitary Commission.
—— —— U. S. Senate Report on Conduct of the War.
—— —— U. States Service Magazine.
—— —— VALLANDIGHAM, C. L. Trial.
—— —— VICTOR, O. J. History of.
—— —— WAITE, O. F. R. Claremont, N. H., War History.
—— —— —— New Hampshire in the Rebell'n.
—— —— —— Vermont in the Rebell'n.
—— —— WARDER, T. B., and CATLETT, J. M. Battle of Young's Branch, or Manassas Plain. 1861.
—— —— —— Battle of Young's Branch.
—— —— War Songs for Freemen.
—— —— WATSON, W. C. Military Hist. of Essex Co. N. Y.
—— —— "W. D. B." Rosekrans' Campaign with 40th Army Corps.
—— —— Western Sanitary Commission.
—— —— WHITING, Wm. War Power of the President, etc.
—— —— WHITNEY, J. H. E. Hawkins Zouaves.
—— —— WILSON, J. G. Biogr. of Illinois Officers.
—— —— WILLARD, Joseph.
—— —— Wisconsin Volunteers.
—— —— Wisconsin War Correspondence.
—— —— "With Gen. Sheridan in Lee's Last Campaign."
—— —— WOOD, G. L. Record of 7th Ohio Reg't.
—— —— WOODBURY, A. Campaign of 1st R. I. Reg't in 1861.

AMERICAN WHIG REVIEW. New York 1850–51. 4 vols. 8vo. — See AMERICAN REVIEW.

AMERICANS as They Are: described in a Tour through the Valley of the Mississippi. London, 1828. 12mo.

AMERICUS VESPUCIUS. — See SANTAREM, Viscount.

AMES, Rev. Chas. G. Address before National Union Association of Cincinnati, Mar. 6. 1863. Rebell'n Pamph. Vols. 66, 91.

AMES, Ellis. Descendants of William Ames. Tabular Pedigree. Easton, Mass., 1851. Sheet. Genealog. Pamph., etc. Vol. 14.

AMES, Fisher. Speech in the House of Repr. of the U. S., April 28, 1796, on the Treaty between the U. States and G. Britain. Phila., 1796. 8vo. Pamphlets. Vol. 5.

—— Works of; to which are prefixed Notices of his Life and Character. Boston, 1809. 8vo.

—— Works of; with a Selection from his Speeches and Correspondence. New York, 1869. 2 vols. 8vo.

AMES GENEALOGY.— See AMES, Ellis. Decendants of Wm. Ames. 1851.

AMES, Oakes, and others. — See BOSTON. Meeting of the Ames Creditors. 1871.

AMHERST, Mass., Charitable Institution. Brief Account of the Origin of. n. d. 8vo. Mass. Miscell. Pamph. Vol. 3.

—— College, Amherst, Mass. Annals of the College. 1860. 12mo.

—— —— Catalogue of the Officers and Students for 1833–4, 1856–7, 1857–8, 1858–9.

—— —— Triennial Catalogues for 1842, 1845.

—— —— Phi Beta Kappa Soc'y.— See MARCH, F. A. Address. 1868.

—— —— STEARNS, Wm. A.

—— —— HUMPHREY, Rev. H. Sermon at Dedication of College Chapel. 1827.

AMHERST, N. H.— See FARMER, J. Historical Sketch of.

AMHURST, N. Terrae-Filius; or, the Secret History of the University of Oxford. 3d ed. London, 1754. 12mo.

ARMISTAD CASE.— See ADAMS, J. Q., BALDWIN, R. S.

—— —— Congress'l Document containing Correspondence, etc., in relation to the Captured Africans. N. York, 1840. 8vo. Congr. and Polit. Pamph. Vol. 107.

—— —— U. S. Supreme Court. BALDWIN, R. S. Argument. 1841.

AMORY FAMILY.— See D'AMERIE, EMERY, AMORY.

AMORY, Thos. C. Life of James Sullivan, with Selections from his Writings. Boston, 1859. 2 vols. 8vo.

—— Gen. John Sullivan: a Vindication of his Characters as a Soldier and a Patriot. Hist. Magazine. Vol. 10. See, also, Mass. Hist. Soc. Proceed. 1866–7.

—— Military Services and Public Life of Gen. John Sullivan. Boston, 1868. 8vo.

AMOS, A. Introduc. Lecture delivered in the Univer. of London, Nov. 8, 1830, on the Study of the English Law. London, 1830. 8vo. Law Pamph. Vol. 21.

AMOS, A. Observa. on the Case of the King and Geddington, relative to the Law of Parochial Settlement. London, 1823. 8vo. Law Pamph. Vol. 11.
—— Report of Trials in the Courts of Canada, relative to the Destruction of the Earl of Selkirk's Settlement on Red River. London, 1820. 8vo.
AMOSKEAG VETERANS. Constitution of. Manchester, 1855. 8vo.
—— —— Charter and By-Laws. Manchester, 1860. 12mo. N. H. Miscell. Pamph. Vol. 1.
—— —— POTTER, C. E.
AMSDEN'S Hydrostatic Scale.— See N. Y. CANAL Comm'rs. Report on.
AMSTERDAM. History of the City of, in Dutch. Amsterdam, 1760. 13 vols. 8vo.
—— European Mercury. Newspaper, in Dutch language. Amsterdam, 1691–1756. 67 vols. 4to.
—— Mercury. Newspaper, in Dutch. Amsterdam, 1807–1815.
ANACHARSIS' TRAVELS.— See BARTHELEMI, Abbe.
ANÆSTHETICS.— See DISCOVERY of Dr. H. Wells.
—— Examina. of Memorial of C. T. Wells.
—— FORBES, J. Etherization in Surgery, etc. 1847.
—— GAY, Dr. M. Statement of Claims of C. T. Jackson, etc.
—— LORD, J. T. and H. C. Defence of Dr. C. T. Jackson's Claim for Discovery.
—— Morton Testimonial Assoc.
—— MORTON, Dr. Wm. T. G. Memorial to Congress.
—— Points and Proofs urging Compensation for the Use of Anæsthetics in the Army and Navy. Washington, 1864. 8vo. Med. Pamph. Vol. 9.
—— SIMPSON, Dr. J. T. Superinduction of Anæsthesia, etc.
—— SMITH, Truman.
—— SNOW, Dr. J. Narcotism by Inhalation of Vapors.
—— U. S. House of Rep. Report of Comm.
—— WARREN, E. Discoverer of.
—— —— Account of the Letheon.
ANALECTIC MAGAZINE for 1813 to 1820, inclusive. (Complete.) Phila., 1816–1820. 16 vols. 8vo.
ANALYSIS of the late Correspondence between our Administration and Great Britain and France. Boston, n. d. Miscell. Tracts. Vol. 1.
ANATOMY.— See AUZOUX, Dr. Reports on his Artificial Anatomy.
—— GRISCOM, J. H. Animal Mechanism.
—— Importance of the Study of.
—— LOOMIS, J. R. Elements of.
—— PINNOCK'S Catechism of.
ANCIENT and Honorable Artillery Co. of Mass.— See PIERPONT, Rev. J., SANDERS, Rev. D. C., STEARNS, Rev. W. A., THACHER, Peter, VINTON, Rev. A. H., WHITMAN, Bernard, THAYER, Rev. T. B., TYLER, Rev. T. P.
ANCIENT and Modern History of the Balearic Islands; or, the Kingdom of Majorica. London, 1716. 8vo.

ANDERSON, Alex. C. Notes on the Indian Tribes of Brit. North America and the Northwest Coast. Read before the N. York Hist. Soc'y, Nov. 1862. Hist. Magazine. Vol. 7.

ANDERSON, —. Ancient Constitutions of Free and Accepted Masons. Alton, Ill., 1854. 12mo.

ANDERSON, Mr. History of Life and Adventures in Europe and America. Berwick, 1772. 12mo.

ANDERSON, Chas. Letter to the Opera House Meeting at Cincinnati. N. Y., 1863. 8vo. Rebell'n Pamph. Vols. 23, 90.

—— The Cause of the War. Speech at Dayton, O., May 2, 1863. N. Y., 1863. 8vo. Rebell'n Pamph. Vol. 90.

ANDERSON, Col. E. F. Memorial Address delivered at Antietam National Cemetery, May 30, 1870. Baltimore, 1870. 8vo. Rebell'n Pamph. Vols. 107, 110.

ANDERSON, Geo. General View of the Variations made in the Affairs of East India Co. since 1784. 1792. 8vo. Eng. Polit. Pamph. Vol. 24.

ANDERSON, Henry J. Address before Columbia College Alumni Association. 1855. Addresses, etc. Vol. 12.

ANDERSON, John, D. D. The Course of Creation; with a Glossary of Scientific Terms. Cincinnati, 1851. 12mo.

ANDERSON, J. B. Bible Tetotalism, and the Voice of Facts. London, 1868. 8vo. Temp. Pamph. Vol. 4.

ANDERSON, Rob't. Exposition of the Present State of the Coal Trade between the North of England and London. Newcastle-upon-Tyne, 1839. 8vo. Strangford Pamph. Vol. 18.

ANDERSON, Rufus. Memoir of Catherine Brown, a Christian Indian of the Cherokee Nation. York, Eng., 1827. 18mo.

—— The Missionary Age: a Half-Century Discourse. Boston, 1851. 8vo. Sermons. Vol. 23.

ANDERSON, Wm. Genealogy and Surnames; with Heraldic and Biograph. Notices. Edinburgh, 1865. 8vo.

—— The Scottish Nation; or, the Surnames, Families, Literature, Honours, and Biograph. History of the People of Scotland. Edinburgh, 1862. 3 vols. 4to.

ANDERSON, Dr. W. J. On Canadian History and Biography. Read before the Quebec Lit. and Hist. Soc'y, Dec. 19, 1866. Transactions. New Series. Part 5.

—— On the Coal-like Substance found at Point Lewis, Canada. Quebec Lit. and Hist. Society Trans. N. Series. Part. 4.

ANDERSONVILLE PRISON.—See HAMLIN, A. C. Martyria.

ANDOVER, Mass.—See ABBOT, A. History of.

—— Theological Seminary. Catalogues for 1866–67, 1867–8, 1868–9, 1869–70, 1870–1, 1871–2, 1872–3. Andover, 1867–1872. 8vo.

—— —— Triennial Catalogue. 1870. Andover, 1870. 8vo.

—— —— Constitution and Associate Statutes. Boston, 1808. Andover, 1817. 8vo.

—— —— Laws of the Institution. Andover, 1817–1870. 8vo.

—— —— DANA, R. H., GRIFFIN, E. D., STUART, Moses, TAYLOR, J. L.

—— —— Memorial of Semi-Centennial Celebration of the Founding. Andover, 1859. 8vo.

ANDOVER, N. H.—See MOORE, J. B. Topogr. and Hist. Sketch of.
ANDRE, Maj. John.—See BENSON, E. Vindica. of Captors.
—— BIDDLE, Chas. J. The Case of.
—— Minutes of a Court of Inquiry upon the Case of, with accompanying Documents; with plates. Albany, 1865. Sm. 4to.
—— PAULDING, John. Paper on the Capture of.
—— Revolutionary Relics, etc.
—— SARGENT, Winthrop. Life and Career.
—— SEWARD, A. Monody on.
—— THACHER, Jas. Observations on his Execution.
—— The Cow Chace. Cincinnati, 1869. 8vo. Rev. War Pamph. Vol. 3.
ANDREW COUNTY, Mo.—See SWAN, A. M. Advantages of, for Immigration. 1869.
ANDREW, John A. Address before Legislature of Mass., Nov. 11, 1863. Rebell'n Pamph. Vol. 36.
—— Address before the New Eng. Hist. Gen. Soc'y, at Boston, Jan. 2, 1867. Boston, 1867. 8vo. Addresses. Vol. 17.
—— Address to the Graduating Class of the Medical School in the University at Cambridge, Mar. 9, 1864. Boston, 1864. 8vo. Harvard Coll. Pamph.
—— and others. Addresses at the Mass Meeting in Aid of Recruiting, held on Boston Common, Aug. 27, 1862. Boston, 1862. 8vo. Rebell'n Pamph. Vol. 106. Addresses, etc. Vol. 9.
—— BURNHAM, Sam. Address at Boston. 1869.
—— —— Memoir of.
—— Letter to S. F. Wetmore, on Massachusetts Enlistments, Feb. 3, 1863. Rebell'n Pamph. Vol. 67.
—— NASON, E. Discourse on Life and Character.
—— N. York Union League Club.
—— The Errors of Prohibition. Argument before Joint Special Comm. of Mass. Gen. Court, 1867. Boston. 1867. 8vo. Temp. Pamph. Vol. 5.
ANDREW, WM. Theories intended to Unfold Nature and her Operations. Milwaukee. 1864. 8vo. Scientific Pamph. Vol. 42.
ANDREWS, Alfred. Genealogy and Ecclesiastical History of New Britain, Conn. Chicago. 1867. 8vo.
ANDREWS, ——. Slavery and Domestic Slave Trade in the U. S.
ANDREWS, C. C. History of the Campaign of Mobile, and operations of Gen. Wilson's Cavalry in Alabama. N. Y. 1867. 8vo.
—— Speeches Delivered in Texas and Arkansas 1863–5, on Reconstruction. Washington. 8vo. Congr. and Polit. Pamph. Vol. 137.
ANDREWS, Rev. David. Centennial Discourse at Pepperell, Mass., Jan. 29, 1847. Boston, 1847. 8vo. Mass. Hist. Discourses Vol. 5.
ANDREWS, Prof. E. A.—See WINSLOW, Hubbard. Eulogy on. 1858.
ANDREWS, E. B. Report on the Econom. Geology of Southern Ohio, traversed by the Marietta & Cincinnati R. R. Cincinnati, 1865. 8vo. Ohio Miscell. Pamph. Vol. 2.

ANDREWS, Rev. Erastus. Hist. Discourse delivered at N. Leverett, Aug. 18, 1847, on the 80th Annivers. of the Baptist Ch. Amherst. 1847. 8vo. Mass. Hist. Discourses. Vol. 20.

ANDREWS, I. D. Report on the Trade and Commerce of the British North Amer. Colonies since 1829.

—— Same for 1850 and '51. Washington. 1851, '54. 8vo.

ANDREWS, Israel W. Why is Allegiance due? And where is it due? Cincinn. 1863. 8vo. Rebellion Pamph. Vol. 3. Rebellion Pamph. Vol. 80.

ANDREWS, John. History of the War with America, France, Spain and Holland, 1775–83. London. 1785. 4 vols. 8vo.

—— Letters of, 1772–76. Mass. Hist. Soc. Proceedings. 1863–64

ANDREWS, John W. Oration before the Conn. Alpha of the Phi Beta Kappa Soc'y at Yale College, Aug. 14, 1850. New Haven. 1850. 8vo. Yale College Pamphlets.

ANDREWS, S. Letter to Cong., Jan. 1864, on the Aereon. Congr. and Polit. Pamph. Vol. 90.

ANDREWS, Sidney. The South Since the War; or 14 weeks residence in Georgia, etc. Boston. 1866. 12mo.

ANDREWS, Stephen P. Discoveries in Chinese; or the Symbolism of the Primitive Characters of the Chinese System of Writing. New York. 1854. 12mo.

ANDROS, Sir Edmund. — See BRODHEAD, J. R. Paper on his Gov't in N. Eng., in 1688–9.

—— Commission of King James the 2d as Governor of Massachusetts Bay. — See FORCE'S Histor. Tracts. Vol. 4.

ANDROS TRACTS. A Collection of Pamphlets and Official Papers. Boston. 1868. 2 vols. 4to. — See PRINCE SOCIETY Publications.

ANECDOTES AMERICAINES: Ou Histoire Anglais Abrigee des Principaux Evenements depuis sa decouverte jusqu'a a' l'Epoque presente. Paris. 1776. 12mo.

ANECDOTES AND TRADITIONS. — See CAMDEN SOCIETY Publications.

ANGELL, Avery F. Genealogy of Descendants of Thos. Angell of Providence. R. I. Providence. 1872. 8vo.

ANGLICAN (The) Bishopric of Jerusalem. Letter to the Archbishop of Canterbury. London. 1843. 8vo. Strangford Pamph. Vol. 32.

ANGLING. --- See WESTWOOD, Thos. Bibliotheca Piscatoria.

ANGLO-AMERICAN: A Journal of Literature, News and Politics. April 29, 1843, to Oct. 19, 1844. New York. 3 vols. Folio.

—— Magazine. Toronto. 1852--55. 7 vols. 8vo.

—— New Church Repository. Feb.--Dec., 1850. Feb.--Dec., 1851. Jan.--Dec., 1852. Jan.--Dec., 1853. Jan.--Apr., July. Oct., 1854. N. York. 8vo.

—— New Church Repository. --- See New Church Herald.

—— See NEW CHURCH REPOSITORY.

ANGLO-CHRISTIANA SOCIETY PUCLICATIONS: 1 Giraldus Cambrensis de Instructione Principum.

—— —— 2 Chronicon Monasterri de Bello.

—— —— 3 Liber Eliensis ad Fidem Codicum Variolum. Vol. 1.

—— NORMAN CHRONICLE. --- See CAXTON SOCIETY Publications.

ANGLO-SAXON DICTIONARY --- See BOSWORTH, Jos.
—— —— LANGUAGE, BARNES, W. Anglo-Saxon Delectus. VERNON, E. J.
—— —— LITERATURE. --- See NORTH, Simeon.
—— —— SAGAS. --- See HAIGH, D. H. Their Value in History.
ANIMAL MAGNETISM. --- See YORKE, A.
ANNALS OF AMERICA. --- HOLMES, Abiel.
—— OF AMER. PULPIT. — See SPRAGUE, Rev. W. B.
—— OF EUROPE for the years 1739, '40, '41, '42, '43. London, 1740–44. 6 vols. 8vo.
—— OF IOWA. — See Iowa.
—— OF NEW ENGEAND. — See PRINCE, Thos.
—— OF THE CONGRESS of the United States from March 3, 1789, to March 3, 1823, being the 1st to the 17th Congress inclusive. Washington. 1834–56. 40 vols. 8vo.
—— OF THE WEST. 2d Ed. Revised and Enlarged by Rev. John M. Peck. St. Louis. 1850. 8vo.
—— —— See ALBACH, Jas. R.
—— —— See PERKINS, Jas. H.
ANNAPOLIS, MARYLAND, GAZETTE. Newspaper. April 1760 to Dec. 1762. Folio.
—— —— Same. Jan. 1763 to Dec. 1767. Folio.
—— —— Jan. 1783 to Dec. 1784.
—— NAVAL SCHOOL. — See U. S. Naval Academy.
—— See RIDGELY, D. Annals of.
—— See U. S. Naval Academy.
ANNE (QUEEN). Instructions to Gov. Dudley in 1702. Mass. Hist. Soc. Coll. 3d Series. Vol. 9.
ANNEXATION OF SAN DOMINGO. N. York. 1870. 8 vo. Congr. and Polit. Pamph. Vol. 120.
ANNIVERSARY (THE) WEEK AT BLOOMINGTON. The Agr. Convention, etc. Chicago. 1860. 8vo. Ill. Miscell. Pamph. Vol. 2.
ANNUAL BIOGRAPHY AND OBITUARY. London. 1817–37. 21 vols. 8vo.
—— OBITUARIES. Dutch Language. Amsterdam. 1721–54. 67 vols. 18mo.
—— REGISTER, (DODSLEY and others); or a View of History Politics and Literature. London. 1758–1826. 68. vols. 8vo.
—— —— Same. 1831–54. 24 vols. 8vo.
—— —— " . Index. 1758–1819. 8vo.
—— —— " . " . 1758–92. 8vo.
—— —— " . " . 1758–80. 8vo.
—— —— " . " . 1781–92. 8vo.
—— View of History and Politics. London, 1855–62. 8 vols. 8mo.
ANNUARE HISTORIQUE POUR L'ANNEE. 1837. Paris. 1837. 24mo.
ANONYMOUS JOURNALISM. London. 1855. 8vo. Eng. Polit. Pamph. Vol. 53.
"ANOTHER INVESTIGATION." London. 1815. 8vo. Eng. Polit. Pamph. Vol. 32.
ANOTHER LETTER TO MR. ALMON, in Matter of Libel. London. 1770. Political Tracts. Vol. 2.
ANSON, Geo. Journal of a Voyage to South Seas, in Dutch. Amsterdam, 1766. 4to.

ANSON, Geo. Travels Around the World — in Dutch. Delft, 1754. 4to.

—— —— Another ed. Amsterdam, 1748. 4to.

ANSWER to a Letter from a Freeholder of Buckinghamshire, on the Election of Knights, etc. n. d. Folio. Eng. Polit. Pamph. Vol. 1.

—— to a Letter by a Scottish Freeholder, addressed to the Marquis of Huntly. Edinburgh, 1821. 8vo. Eng. Polit. Pamph. Vol. 35.

—— to a Pamphlet, entitled, "Considerations on the Public Expediency of a Bridge from one Part of Boston to the other." Boston, 1806. 8vo. Boston Miscell. Pamph. Vol. 2.

—— to Dr. Sherlock's Vindica. of the Case of Allegiance due to Sovereign Powers. London, 1692. Sm. 4to. Eng. Polit. Pamph. Vol. 64.

—— to Mr. Falconer, on the Assumption of Surnames without Royal License. London, 1863. 8vo.

—— to the Letter from a "By-Stander," in Refutation of his Misrepresentation of Facts in the Time of K. Charles II, etc. London, 1742. 8vo. Eng. Polit. Pamph. Vol. 68.

ANTHON, Chas. E. Narrative of the Settlement of George C. Anthon in America. N. York, 1872. 8vo. Genealog. Pamph. Vol. 12.

ANTHON Family Genealogy.— See ANTHON, C. E. Narrative of Settlement of G. C. Anthon in America.

ANTHON, Geo. C. Narrative and Documents connected with his Displacement from the Greek Professorship in the University of the City of N. York. N. York, 1851. 8vo. (N. Y. College Catalogues, etc.)

ANTHON, Henry. Sermon on the Death of Rev. Hugh Smith, D. D., at N. York, April 1, 1849. N. York, 1849. 8vo. Sermons. Vol. 54.

ANTHON, John. Report of Court Martial in Cases of Surgeon Jacques and Lt. Col. De La Montagnie. N. York, 1812. 8vo. N. York City Pamph. Vol. 6.

ANTHROPOLOGY.— See LONDON Anthropolog. Soc'y.

—— N. York Anthropolog. Institute.

ANTICIPATION. Containing the substance of his M——y's speech to both Houses of P—l—t. 6th Ed. London, 1778. American Tracts. Vol. 5. Eng. Polit. Pamph. Vol. 18. (Same Ed.)

—— of Marginal Notes on the Declaration of Gov't. of the 9th of Jan. 1813, in the Amer. National Intelligencer. London, 1813. 8vo. Pamphleteer. Vol. 1.

ANTICOSTI, Island of—See ROCHE, A. R.—Resources and Capabilities of.

ANTIDOTE (An.) to Poison, or a full Reply to Nathan'l Jeffery's Attack on the Conduct of the Prince of Wales. London, 1806. 8vo. 2nd Ed., Eng. Polit. Pamph. Vol. 28.

ANTIETAM, Battle of—See OUR SOLDIERS AND SAILORS. What they said and did. 1872.

—— National Cemetery. See ANDERSON, E. F. Memorial Address. 1870.

ANITETAM National Cemetery, *continued.*
—— —— History of, with Descriptive Lists of Loyal Soldiers buried therein. Baltimore. 1869. 8vo.
ANTIOCH COLLEGE, Yellow Springs, Ohio. Catalogue for 1856–7, 1857–8, 1858–9, 1859–60, 1860–1, 1861–2, 1862–3, 1863–4, 1865–6.
—— —— See HILL, T. Baccalaureate Address, 1860
ANTIQUARIAN REPERTORY: A Miscellany designed to preserve and illustrate the Valuable Remains of Olden Times, with Engravings. London, 1780. 2 vols. quarto.
ANTIQUITIES AND ARCHÆOLOGY.—See AKERMAN, J. Y. Archæolog. Index to Celtic and other Antiquities.
—— —— Remains of Pagan Saxondom.
—— —— ALLIES, JABEZ. Antiq. of Worcestershire. Eng.
—— —— Amer. Antiquarian Soc'y.
—— —— Antiquarian Repertory. 1780.
—— —— Archæologia Cambrensis. 1846–67.
—— ARTHUR, Rev. W., The Antiquarian.
—— Asiatic Researches. Transactions of Bengal Soc'y.
—— Asiatic Journal. 1816–41.
—— ATWATER, C. Descrip. of, in Ohio.
—— See BAGG, S. C. Canadian Archæol.
—— BALDWIN, J. D. Ancient America. 1872.
—— BARRANDT, A. Ancient Earthworks on the Upper Missouri.
—— BARTON, B. S. Ancient N. American Remains.
—— BATEMAN, Thos. Antiq. of Derbyshire, Eng.
—— BLARAMBERG, M. De. Objects d'Antiquite decouverts en Tauride. 1822.
—— BRADFORD, A. W. American.
—— BRACKENRIDGE, H. H., on the Popula. and Tumuli of Aborigines of N. A.
—— BRINTON, D. J. The Mound-Builders of the Mississippi Valley.
—— Bulletin des Sciences Historique.
—— Carleon Antiq. Soc.
—— Callington Church, Cornwall.
—— Cambro—Briton and Celtic Repository.
—— CEAN, J. A. Roman Antiq. in Spain.
—— CIST, C. Cincinnati Miscell. and Antiquities.
—— CLERK, Johanne. Dissertatio de Monumentis quibusdam Romanis in Parte Brittaniæ. 1731.
—— CLERK, D. J. Dissertatio de Stylis Veterum, etc.
—— DAVIS, A. Lectures on Amer. Antiq.
—— Remarkable Discoveries in the East. 1852
—— DE COSTA. B. F. Moabitish Stone.
—— DELAFIELD, J. J. Origin of Antiquities of America.
—— DESOR, E. Lacustrian Constructions of the Lake of Neuchatel, Switz.
—— DILLE J. Sketch of Ancient Earthworks.
—— DRYDEN, H. E. L. Antiq. of Steeple Aston. Oxfordshire.
—— Egyptian Monuments. 5 Nos.

ANTIQUITIES AND ARCHÆOLOGY, *continued.*
—— Essex Archæolog. Soc.
—— ESTES, L. C. Antiquities near Lake Pepin.
—— EWBANK, Thos. North American Rock Writing.
—— FERGUSSON J. Rock Cut Temples of India.
—— FINCH, John. Celtic Antiq. of America.
—— FINCK, Hugo. Antiquities in Vera Cruz, Mexico.
—— FOSBROKE, T. D. Encyclopedia of.
—— GIBSON, Wm. S. Notices of Northumbrian Castles, &c.
—— GILBERT, W. B. Antiquities of Maid Stone Eng.
—— GLIDDON G. R. Ancient Egypt.
—— GODWYN, T. Antiq. of Ancient Hebrew.
—— GUEST, W. E. Ancient Indian Remains, near Prescott, C. W.
—— HAKEWELL, H. Roman Remains in Oxfordshire, Eng.
—— HALLIWELL, J. O. Ancient Stone Circles of Isle of Man.
—— —— —— Rambles in Western Cornwall, Eng.
—— —— —— The Archæologist, Vol. 1. 1841-2.
—— HERBERT, A. Cyclops Christianus.
—— HAVEN, S. F. Archæology of the U. S.
—— HILL, Ira. Antiq. of America Explained.
—— HOYT, E. Antiquarian Researches.
—— JONES, C. C. Ancient Tumuli on Savannah River.
—— —— Monumental Remains of Georgia.
—— JOSEPHUS, F. Jewish Antiq.
—— KELLER, Dr. On Lacustrian Settlements. Switzerland.
—— KENRICK, John. Roman Sepulchral Inscriptions.
—— Papers on Yorkshire Archæol.
—— KILKENNY and S. East of Ireland Arch. Soc.
—— LAPHAM, I. A. Man-Shaped Mounds of Wis.
—— —— On Antiquities of Wisconsin.
—— LAYARD, A. H. Discov. in Nineveh and Babylon.
—— LETHIEULLIER, S. Antiquities found in Essex Co., Eng., 1796.
—— —— Letters on Indian Antiquities.
—— LOFTUS, W. K. Researches in Chaldea.
—— LONDON Society of Antiquaries. 1843-69.
—— LUBBOCK, J. Civilization and Primitive Cond. of Man.
—— —— Pre-Historic Times.
—— —— —— North American Archæology.
—— LYMNE, Kent Co., Eng. Excavations, 1850.
—— LYON, S. S. Mounds in Union Co., Ky.
—— M'BRIDE, Jas. Ancient Fortifications in Butler Co., Ohio.
—— MCCULLOH, J. H. Researches in Aborig. Hist.
—— MARSH, (O. C.) Description of Ancient Mound near Newark, O.
—— MATILE, G. A. On the Study of Amer'n Antiq.
—— MAYER, B. Observa. on Mexican Archæology.
—— Mexican Antiquities.
—— MORLOT, A. General Views on.
—— MORRISON, W. Recovery of Jerusalem.
—— Mural Painting at Burlington, Norfolk. 1856.
—— OLMUTZ. Antiquities of.

ANTIQUITIES AND ARCHÆOLOGY, *continued.*
—— PARK, Saml. American Antiquities.
—— PEGGE, Saml. Dissertations on Anglo-Saxon Remains. 1756.
—— PETRIE, Geo. Notices of the Brochs and Picts' Houses of Orkney.
—— PIDGEON, W. Antiquarian Researches.
—— POWNALL, Gov. Antiquities of the Provincia Romana of Gaul.
—— PRIEST, J., Amer. Antiquities.
—— RAFINESQUE, C. S., Alleghanian Monuments in Ky.
—— RAFN, C. C., Antiquities Americaines.
—— Recent Aboriginal Discoveries in Missouri. 1870.
—— RIVERO & TSCHUDI, Peruvian Antiquities.
—— Royal Society of Northern Antiquaries.
—— SALMON, N., Roman Antiquities in Midland Co's of Eng.
—— SARGENT, W., Drawings of Articles found in a Mound at Cincinnati, O., 1794.
—— —— Fortifications at Marietta, O.
—— SCHOOLCRAFT, H. R., Observ. on Grave Creek Mound.
—— —— On the Antiquities of the Western Country.
—— Scientific and Learned Societies.
—— SMITH, H. E., Remains of Roman Isurium at Oldborough.
—— SMITH, J. J., Amer. Hist. & Lit. Curiosities.
—— SMITH, W., School Ed. of Greek & Roman Antiq.
—— —— Smithsonian Reports, 1867, 1870.
—— —— Somerset Arch. and Nat. Hist. Soc'y.
—— SQUIER, E. G., Aborig. Monum. of Mississippi Valley.
—— —— Antiq. of New York.
—— —— On Aboriginal Monuments of N. York.
—— —— Nicaragua: Its Monuments, &c.
—— —— Serpent Symbol. Uses of the Mounds of the West.
—— SQUIER, and DAVIS, Ancient Monuments of Mississippi Valley.
—— STEVENS, Geo., The Old Northern Runic Monuments.
—— STEVENS, Edward T., Flint Chips, Pre-Historic Archæology.
—— SURREY, Eng., Archæology Collections.
—— SURRIDGE, Rev. T., Roman Inscriptions in Northumberland.
—— TAYLOR, R. C., Indian Mounds, etc., in Wis. Terr.
—— TAYLOR, S., Wisconsin Mounds.
—— TOMLINSON, A. B., Antiquities of Grave Creek Mound.
—— TROOST, G., Acc. of Remains found in Tenn.
—— TROYON, M. F. Lacustrian Cities of Switzerland.
—— Ulster Journal of Archæology. 1853–1861.
—— VALASQUEZ, P. Expedition to Central America. 1848.
—— Virginia. Indian Relics.
—— WALBRIDGE, T. C. Mounds of Southern Ill. & Ohio.
—— WARNE, C. Celtic Tumuli of Dorset.
—— WESTALL, W. Hist. of Carisbrook Castle, Isle of Wight. 1839.
—— Western Reserve Hist. Society.
—— WHITTLESEY, Chas. Ancient Inscriptions in Ohio.
—— WHITTLESEY, Chas. Ancient Mining on the Shores of Lake Superior.

ANTIQUITIES AND ARCHÆOLOGY, *continued.*
—— WHITTLESEY, C. Descrip. of Ancient Works in Ohio.
—— WHITTLESEY, Chas. Earth Forts of the Cuyahoga Valley, Ohio.
—— WHITTLESEY, C. On Delafield's Antiquities.
—— WILLIAMS, J. Essays on Archæol.
—— WILLIS, G. Current Notes.
—— WINSTON, C. Lincoln Cathedral.
—— WRENCH. F. Antiquities of Stowting, Kent Co., Eng., 1845.
—— WRIGHT, Thos. Essays on Archæology.
—— YOUNG, Dr. Thos. Observa., &c., on Ancient Greek Manuscript, &c.
—— ZESTERMAN, A. Coloniza. of America, etc.
ANTIQUITY OF MAN.—See LYELL, Chas. Geolog. Evidences of.
—— —— Ethnology and kindred subjects.
—— —— WHITTLESEY, Chas. Evidences of in U. S.
ANTISELL, T. Cyclopædia of the Useful Arts. New York, 1855. 12mo.
—— ANTONINI ITER BRITANNIARUM.—Commentaries Illustratum. THOMAS GALE. London, 1809. 4vo.
—— ANTRIM, N. H. See WHITON, Rev. J. M. Brief notices of.
ANTROBUS, N. H. London, its Danger and its Safety; suggestions for its present and future protection, &c. London, 1848. 8vo., 3d Ed. Eng. Miscel. Pamph. Vol. 6.
APACHE COUNTRY.—See BROWNE, J. Ross. Adventures in.
APACHE INDIANS.—See COLYER, Vincent. Peace with Apaches of N. Mexico, &c.
—— —— CREMONY, J. C. Life among the Apaches.
—— —— Outrages perpetrated by the Apache Indians in Arizona, in 1869 and 1870. San Francisco, 1871. 8vo. Indian Pamph. Vol. 5.
APESS Wm. Experience of Five Christian Indians of the Pequod Tribe. Boston, 1837. 8vo. Indian Pamph. Vol. 3.
—— Indian Nullification of the Unconstitutional Laws of M ass. relative to the Marshpee Tribe. Boston, 1835. 12mo.
APOLLO Assoc. for Promotion of Fine Arts. Catalogue of Exhibition at N. York, 1840. 8vo. Art Pamph. Vol. 1.
APOLOGIE des Dominicains Missionaries de la Chine: ou reponse au Livre du Pere Le Tellier Jesuite intitule " Defense des Nouveaux Chretiens. Cologne, 1699. 12mo.
APPEAL for a Charitable Trusts Act of Parliament, in behalf of Dulwich College. 1852. 8vo. Eng. Polit. Pamph. Vol. 49.
—— for Rectitude in Primary Politics. Boston, 1863. 8vo. Rebell'n Pamph. Vol. 39.
—— for the Rights of Conscience. [In regard to Quakers bearing Arms.] Richmond, Ind., 1863. 12mo. Sermons, &c. Vol. 23.
—— from a Countryman to the Union Men of the South. 1861. Rebell'n Pamph. Vol. 53.
—— from the Country to the City, for the Preservation of the King's Person, &c., and the Protestant Religion. (n. d.) Folio. Eng. Polit, Pamph. Vol. 2.

APPEAL in behalf of the Greeks: with a Letter from Lord Erskine to Prince Mavrocordato. 1823. London, 1824. 8vo. Pamphleteer. Vol. 23.

—— on behalf of British Subjects residing in and connected with the River Plate. London, 1846. 8vo. Strangford Pamph. Vol. 41.

—— to Repub. Senators by Repub. Leaders of Georgia. Washington, 1870. 8vo. Congr. and Polit. Pamph. Vol. 120.

—— to the Citizens of Pennsylvania to provide additional Accommoda. for the Insane. Phila., 1854. 12mo. Penn. Miscell. Vol. 3.

—— to England against the New Indian Stamp Act. London, 1828. 8vo. Strangford Pamph. Vol. 3.

—— to the Legislature for the Repeal of the Act regulating the Marriage of the Royal Family. London, 1814. 8vo. Pamphleteer. Vol. 3.

—— to Democrats and Union Men. From the Democracy of Boston and Suffolk. Boston, 1855. 8vo. Congr. and Polit. Pamph. Vol. 135.

—— to the Medical Soc'y of R. Island, in behalf of Female Physicians. (n. p.) 1850–1. 12mo. Med. Pamph. Vol. 8.

—— to the People: containing the Letter of Admiral Byng to the Sec'y of the Admiralty. London, 1856. 8vo. Part 1. Eng. Polit. Pamph. Vol. 71.

—— to the People of the State of N. York, for the Financial Reform of the City and Co. of N. York. N. York, 1871. 8vo. N York City Pamph. Vol. 6.

—— to the Public on the Conduct of the Banks in the City of N. York. N. York, 1815. 8vo. N. York City Miscell. Pamph. Vol. 5.

—— to the Moral and Intellectual Classes of the Kingdom, in favor of a Repeal of the Reform Bill. London, 1838. 8vo. Eng. Polit. Pamph. Vol. 42.

—— to the Patriotism of the Citizens of Missouri. (n. d.) Rebell'n Pamph. Vol. 46.

—— to the People of Penn'a for Sick and Wounded Soldiers. Phila. (n. d.) Pebell'n Pamph. Vol. 60.

—— to the People of the North. Louisville, Ky., 1861. Rebell'n Pamph. Vol. 19.

—— to the Patrons of Science and the Friends of Humanity in raising a fund for Dr. W. T. G. Morton. Scientific Pamph. Vol. 14.

—— to the Reason and Religion of American Christians against the American Anti-Slavery Society. N. York, 1838. 8vo. Congress. and Polit. Pamph. Vol. 103.

—— to the Justice and Interests of the People of Great Britain, in the present Disputes with America. London, 1774. Political Tracts. Vol. 4.

—— —— Also, same. 4th Ed. London, 1776.

—— —— Same. Second appeal. On same subject. London, 1775.

APPELLATE (the) Jurisdiction. Scotch Appeals. Edinburgh, 1851. 8vo. Strangford Pamph. Vol. 62.

APPENDIX to the Present State of the Republic of Letters for Dec., 1736. London, 1737. 8vo. Eng. Polit. Pamph. Vol. 11.

APPLETON'S, D., Companion Hand Book of Travel to the United States and British Provinces. New York, 1861. 8vo.

—— Cyclopedia. See American Cyclopedia.

—— —— American Ann. Register

APPLETON, D. & Co. Library Manual; a Catalogue Raisonné of 12,000 works, &c. New York, 1847. 8vo.

—— Modern Atlas of the Earth, with 34 beautifully engraved maps, etc. New York (n. d.), 1847. 8vo.

—— Railway and Steam Navigation Guides, Oct., 1856; July, 1858, Dec., 1859. New York. 12vo. Guide Books, Vol. 17.

APPLETON, Nathan. Corres. with John G. Palfrey. Boston, 1846. 8vo. Congr. and Polit. Pamph. Vols. 102 and 124.

—— GANNETT, Rev. E. S. Obit. Sermon.

—— Memoir of Hon. Abbot Lawrence. Boston, 1856. 8vo. Biograph. Pamph. Vol. 8.

—— —— Mass. Hist. Soc. Proceedings, 1855–58.

—— —— Mass. Hist. Soc. Collections. 4th Series. Vol. 4.

—— Remarks on Currency and Banking. Boston, 1841. 8vo. 2d Ed. Banking and Currency Pamph. Vol. 2.

—— —— Same. 3d Edition. 1857. 8vo. Banking and Currency Pamph. Vol. 2.

—— SHEPPARD, I. N. Sketch of.

—— Speech in Cong. July 5, 1842, on the Tariff and Compromise Act. Washington, 1842. 8vo. Congr. and Polit. Pamph. Vol. 24.

—— WINTHROP, R. C. Memoir of.

APPLETON, Saml.—See LOTHROP, S. K. Memoir of.

—— Notice of. N. Eng. Gen. and Hist. Register. Vol. 8.

APPLETON, Wm.—See ROBBINS, Rev. C. Memoir.

—— SHEPPARD, J. H. Sketch of.

—— WELLS, E M. P. Discourse on his Death. 1862.

APPLETON, W. S. Ancestry of Mary Oliver. 1640–1698. Cambridge, 1867. Small 4to.

—— Ancestry of Priscilla Baker, who lived 1674–1731, and was Wife of Isaac Lawrence, of Ipswich, Mass. Cambridge, 1870. 8vo.

—— Memorials of the Cranes ot Chilton. Cambridge, 1868. 4to.

APPLETON, Wis. Crescent, Newspaper, Jan. 1854 to Dec. 1856. Folio.

—— Same Jan. 1857 to Dec. 1873. Folio.

—— Lawrence University.

—— Motor, Newspaper, Aug. to Dec. 1859. Folio. 1860–1866.

—— Post, Newspaper. Appleton, 1866–1873. Folio.

—— Public Schools. Rules and Regulations, 1869–70. Appleton, 1869. 8vo.

APPOMATTOX RIVER.—See STEIN, Albert. Remarks on Improvement of. 1854.

APTHORP, Rev. East. Considerations on the Institution and Conduct of the Soc'y for Propagation of the Gospel in Foreign Parts. Boston, 1763. 8vo. Religious Pamph. Vol. 3.

APTHORP, George H. Topographical Description of the Dutch Colony of Surrinam. Mass. Hist. Soc. Collec. 1st Series. Vol. 1.
AQUARIA.—See BUTLER, H. D.
—— LLOYD, W. A.
—— MELIA P.
ARABIA.—See BONAR, H. Desert of Sinai.
—— BURTON, R. F. Pilgrimage to Mecca.
—— CRICHTON, A. History of.
ARABIC LANGUAGE.—See ST. DAVIDS, T. Arabic Alphabet, etc.
ARACAN, INDIA.—See COMSTOCK, G. S. Notes on.
ARAGO Francis. Autobiography of. Smithsonian Report, 1870.
—— Eulogy on Thos. Young, read before the French Academy of Sciences, Nov. 26, 1832. Smithsonian Report, 1869.
—— Popular Lectures on Astronomy, with Additions and Corrections, by DIONYSIUS LARDNER. Scientific Pamph. Vol 15.
ARAM, Eugene. His Trial and Defence; Executed Feb. 8, 1745, for the Murder of Dan'l. Clark. London, 1824. 8vo. Pamphleteer, Vol. 23.
ARCHÆOLOGY.—See Antiquities and Archæology.
ARCHÆOLOGIA Æliana; or Miscellaneous Tracts, relating to Antiquity, published by the Society of Antiquaries of New Castle-upon-Tyne. New Castle, 1822–55. 4 Vols. 4to. 1857–65. 6 Vols., 8vo.
—— AMERICANA.—See Amer. Antiquarian Society.
ARCHÆOLOGIA CAMBRENSIS.—A Record of the Antiquities of Wales and its Marches; and Journal of the Cambian Archælogical Association. 1st, 2d and 3d Series. London, 1846–67. 22 Vols. 8vo.
ARCHER, Major Edw. Letter to Lord Russell on Emigration from India to the Mauritius. London, 1840. 8vo. Strangford Pamph. Vol. 23.
ARCHER FAMILY.—Memorials of the Families of the Surname of Archer. London, 1861. 4to.
ARCHDALE, John. New Description of that Fertile and Pleasant Province of Carolina, with a Brief Account of the Discovery and Settling of that Government. London, 1707. CARROLL, B. R., Hist. Coll. of S. C.
ARCHER, Wm. Relation of Capt. Barth. Gosnold's Voyage to Virginia in 1602. Mass. Hist. Soc. Coll. 3d Series, Vol. 8.
ARCHER, Wm. S. Speech in U. S. Senate, Feb. 9, 1842, on the Veto Power of the President. Washington, 1842. 8vo. Cong. and Polit. Pamph. Vol. 24.
ARCHITECTURE.—See BARNARD, H. School Architecture.
—— BROWN, Rich'd. On Drawing Ornaments. 1822.
—— CHAMBERLAIN, N. H. Paper on N. Eng. Architecture. 1858.
—— DOWNING, A. J. Cottage Residences.
—— Few Words to Church Builders.
—— HATFIELD, R. G. Amer. House Carpenter.
—— HODGINS, J. G. School Architecture. 1858.
—— Institute of British Architects.
—— JOHONNOT, J. School Houses and Architecture.

ARCHITECTURE. N. York Crystal Palace. Descrip. of.
—— Penn. School Architecture.
—— PORTER, C. H. On Building Stones.
—— RANDALL, G. P. Prospective Plans of Cottages, School Houses, etc.
—— REID, D. B. College of Architecture.
—— RUSKIN, J. Beauties of.
—— RUSKIN, J. Stones of Venice.
—— SILLOWAY, T. W. Text Book of Carpentry.
—— STUART, R. Cyclopœdia of.
—— U. S. Sec. of Treasury. Reports of Supervising Architect.
—— WEST, Benj. Memorandum on Lord Elgin's Pursuits in Greece.
—— WHEELER, G. Homes for the People.
—— —— Rural Homes.
ARCHIVO Americano y espiritu de la preusa del mundo. Buenos Ayres, 1849. 8vo.
ARCTIC EXPLORATION.—See ELLIS, H. Voyage de la Baye de Hudson. 1846–7.
—— FORSTER, J. R. Hist. of Voyages to the North. 1786.
—— GODFREY, W. C. 2d Grinnell Exped. 1853–5.
—— HUISH, R. Last Voyage of Sir John Ross. 1829–33.
—— KANE, E. K. Astronom. Observations, 1853–5: Magnetical, Meteorolog., Tidal.
—— —— Grinnell Expedition.
—— —— Paper before Amer. Geograph. Soc. 1852.
—— LESLIE, Prof. Polar Seas and Regions.
—— MCCLINTOCK, Capt. Fate of Sir John Franklin.
—— MCCLINTOCK, Leopold. Meteorolog. Observations, 1857–9.
—— MACKENZIE A. Voyages to Frozen Ocean. 1789–90.
—— MARKHAM, C. R. Franklin's Footsteps.
—— Northern Regions: or, etc.
—— OSBORN, S. Polar Regions.
—— PARRY, W. E. Second Voyage. 1821–3.
—— —— Three Voyages. 1821–3.
—— Ross, Sir John. Second Voyage. 1829.
ARCTIC OCEAN.— See HAYES, I. I. Physical Observations. 1860–61.
—— WRANGELL, F. Narr. of Exped. in 1820.
ARGALL SAMUEL. Expedition to the French Settlements in Acadia. and to Manhattan Island, A. D. 1613. N. York Hist. Soc. Coll. 2d Series, Vol. 1.
ARGENTINE CONFEDERATION.—See Archivo Americano, 1849.
—— Exposicion dirigida a las Provincias Unidas del Rio de la Plata. London, 1829. 8vo. Strangford Pamph. Vol. 6.
ARGUMENT against Mr. Dudley Moor, in the Queen's Bench, 1713. Small 4to. Eng. Polit. Pamph. Vol. 8.
—— against the Abolition of the Constitution of the U. S. 1864. Rebellion Pamph., Vol. 20.
—— concerning the Militia. (n. d.) 4to. Eng. Polit. Pamph. Vol. 53A.
—— for Self-Defence, etc. London, 1710. 12 mo. Eng. Religious Pamph. Vol. 10A.

ARGUMENT in Defence of Edw. P. Grayson before a Navy General Court Martial at Philadelphia. 1863. Rebellion Pamph. Vol. 88.

—— in the Supreme Court of the U. States in the Case of the Bank of the U. States v. ——. Mobile, 1838. 8vo. Law Pamph. Vol. 5.

—— on the Case of Marshal Ney, with Reference to the 12th Article of the Convention of Paris, and the Treaty of Nov. 20, 1815. London, 1816. 8vo. Eng. Polit. Pamph. Vol. 33.

—— showing that a Standing Army is inconsistent with a Free Government. 1697. London, Reprinted. 1817. 8vo. Pamphleteer, Vol. 10.

ARGUMENTS and Statements addressed to the Members of the Legislature, in regard to bringing into Boston the Water of Long Pond. Boston, 1845. 8vo. Boston Miscell. Pamph. Vol. 1.

ARISTOCRACY (The) of Boston; who they are, and what they were. Boston, 1848. 8vo. Mass. Hist. Discourses, etc. Vol. 15.

ARISTOCRACY (Rights of the.) See NOAKES, J.

ARISTÓTLE.—See WORSELDINE, Wm. Lecture on Life and Genius of. 1845.

ARIZONA AND SONORA.—See BROWNE, J. Ross. Tour through.

—— MOWRY, S. Geog. Hist. etc., of. 1864.

ARIZONA.—Apache Outrages in Arizona. 1869–70.

—— HUMPHREYS, A. A. Report on Explorations and Surveys. 1871.

—— MOWRY, Sylvester. Geography and Resources of. 1859.

—— Preliminary Report on Explorations in Nevada and Arizona. Washington, 1871. 4to.

ARKANSAS.—Acts passed at 11th Session of General Assembly. Little Rock, 1857. 8vo.

—— Auditor's Biennial Report for 1864, '65, '66. Little Rock, 1866. 8vo.

—— Auditor's Report on Public Debt of the State. Little Rock, 1868. 8vo.

—— Constitution of the State, adopted Feb. 11, 1868. Little Rock, 1868. 8vo. Ark. Pub. Docs.

—— Debates and Proceedings of Legislature of Arkansas on the Public Debt of the State. Little Rock, 1869. 8vo. Ark. Pub. Docs.

—— —— of Constitutional Convention. Little Rock, 1868. 8vo.

—— Geolog. Survey. 1st Report on the Geol. of the Northern Counties, made by DAVID D. OWEN and others, in 1857 and 1858. Little Rock, 1858. 8vo.

—— —— 2d Report on the Geol. of the Southern and Middle Counties, made by DAVID D. OWEN and others, in 1859 and 1860. Phila., 1860. 8vo.

—— See HENRY, J. P. Resources of, etc. 1872.

—— Homes in Arkansas. Lands for sale by Little Rock & Fort Smith R. R. Co. Little Rock, 1871. 8vo. Ark. Miscell. Pamph. Vol. 1.

—— Hot Springs of. See U. S. Sec. of Interior. Report. 1850.

ARKANSAS.—Laws of the State. 1843–46, '53. Little Rock, 2 Vols. 8vo.

—— Message of the Governor, 1866. Biennial Message, 1871. Little Rock, 1866–71. 8vo. Ark. Pub. Docs.

—— Natural Resources of Arkansas. Little Rock, 1869. 8vo. Arkansas Misscell. Pamph. Vol. 1.

—— NUTTALL, T. Journal of Travels. 1819.

—— SCHOOLCRAFT, H. R. On the Geology and Mineralogy of.

—— River—ALBERT, J. W. Report of an Expedition, etc. 1845.

ARMENDARIS, Pedro. See WATTS, John S. Memorial to Cong.

ARMENIA.—See LAYARD, A. H. Nineveh and Babylon, and Travels in.

ARMISTEAD, Rev. John. Popular Education: Its Present Condition and Future Prospects considered. Oxford, 1856. 8vo. Educa. Pamph. Vol. 33.

ARMITAGE, Bishop W. E. The German Sunday. Trans. Wis. Acad. of Sciences. 1870–2.

ARMS of the Goodwin and Bradbury Families. Fac simile ——. Broadside. Washington, ——.

ARMSBY, Dr. J. H. Hospitals: Their Rise and Progress. Address before the Albany Med. Soc'y., Nov. 1851. Albany, 1852. 8vo. Med. Pamph. Vols. 10 and 31.

ARMSTRONG, Edw. Address before the Hist. Soc'y. of Penn., Nov. 8, 1851, on the 169th Anniversary of the Landing of Wm. Penn. Phila., 1852. 8vo. Penn. Hist. Soc. Addresses. Vol. 1.

—— Record of Upland Court; 1676–1681. Penn. Hist. Soc. Memoirs. Vol. 6.

ARMSTRONG, Gen. John. See ARMSTRONG, Kosciusko.

—— Life of Gen. Anthony Wayne. SPARKS' Amer. Biog. 1st Series. Vol. 4.

—— Life of Gen. Richard Montgomery. SPARKS Amer. Biog. 1st Ser. Vol. 1.

—— Notices of the War of 1812. New York, 1840. 2 Vols. 12 mo.

ARMSTRONG, J. W. Oration at Lowville, N. Y., July 4, 1861. Lowville, 1861. 8vo. Addresses, etc. Vol. 18.

ARMSTRONG, Kosciusko. Review of T. L. McKenney's Narrative of the Cause of Gen. Armstrong's Resignation of the War Office in 1814. New York, 1846. 8vo. Congr. and Polit. Pamph. Vol. 135.

ARMSTRONG, M. K. History and Resources of Dakota, Montana and Idaho. Yankton, 1866. 12mo.

—— Information Circular on Dakota Territory. Sioux City, 1870, 8vo.

ARMSTRONG, W. C. Life and Adventures of Capt. John Smith. Hartford, 1855. 12mo.

ARMSTRONG, W. J., D. D. See ADAMS, Rev. Nehemiah. Sermon on his death.

ARMY and Navy Pensions. See Pensions.

ARMY Appropriations. See Congressional Speeches.

ARMY Life and Stray Shots: by a Staff Officer of the 8th Wisconsin Volunteers, 15th Army Corps. Nos. 1 and 2. Memphis, 1863. 8vo. Rebell'n Pamph. Vol. 6.

—— —— in the West. See MARCY, R. B.

—— Lists of the Roundheads and Cavaliers of 1642. London, 1863. Small, 4to.

—— Meteorological Register. See LAWSON, Dr. Thos. 1826–30.

—— LOVELL, Dr. Jos. 1822–25.

—— —— —— U. S. Secretary of War.

—— of Georgia. See Army Reunion. 1868.

—— of the Cumberland. See Army Reunion. 1868.

—— —— Reports of 1st, 3d, 4th and 5th Reunions, held in 1868, 69, 70, 71, 72. Cincinnati, 1868–72. 8vo.

—— —— FITCH, John.

—— —— "W. D. B." Rosekrans' Campaign.

ARMY of the Ohio. See Army Reunion. 1868.

ARMY of the Potomac. See JOINVILLE, Prince de.

—— —— McCLELLAN, G. B. Report. 1864.

—— —— Report of the Congress. Comm. on its operations, &c. N. York, 1863. 8vo. Rebell'n Pamph. Vol. 106.

—— the Tennessee. See Army Reunion. 1868.

—— Report of Proceedings of 3d and 5th Ann. Meeting, held at Chicago, Dec. 15 and 16, 1868; Apr. 6 and 7, 1871. Cincinnati, 1869 and 1872. 8vo.

—— Officers' Pocket Companion. New York, 1862. 12mo.

—— Registers, U. S. See U. States. Sec. of War.

—— Regulations. See U. S. Army.

—— Reunion: with Reports of the Meetings of the Army of the Cumberland, Army of the Tennessee, Amy of the Ohio and Army of Georgia, at Chicago, 1868. Chicago, 1869. 8vo.

ARNETT, Rev. W. W. Sermon on the death of Rev. S. G. Gassaway. Milwaukee, 1854. 8vo.

—— at the opening of the 8th Ann. Convention of P. E. Church in Wisconsin. Milwaukee, 1854. 8vo. Wis. Miscell. Pamph. Vol. 4.

ARNOLD, Benedict. A Love Affair of. From the N. Eng. Register, Jan., 1857. Biograph. Pamph. Vol. 11.

—— ATWILL, W. Treason of.

—— HILL, G. C. Biograph of.

—— Letters on the Expedition across the State of Maine to Attack Quebec in 1775; with Col. Montresor's Journal of a Tour from the St. Lawrence to the Kennebec. 1760. Maine. Hist. Soc. Coll. Vol. 1.

—— MARBOIS, B. Complot d'Arnold.

—— SPARKS, J. Life and Treason of.

ARNOLD, I. N. See Chicago Hist. Soc'y.

—— History of Abraham Lincoln; and the Overthrow of Slavery. Chicago, 1866. 8vo.

—— Speech in Congress, Jan. 6, 1864, on Slavery in the Rebel States. Rebell'n Pamph. Vols. 9 and 34.

ARNOLD, Sam'l G. Anniversary Address at Amer. Institute, N. York, Oct. 11, 1850. Addresses, &c. Vol. 5.

ARNOLD, Sam'l G., *continued.*
—— Greene—Staples—Parsons. An Address before the R. I. Hist. Soc'y, June 1, 1869. Providence, 1869. 8vo. R. I. Hist. Soc'y Addresses. Vol. 1.
—— The Spirit of Rhode Island History. A Discourse before the R. I. Hist. Soc'y, Jan. 17, 1853. Providence, 1853. 8vo. R. I. Hist. Soc'y Addresses. Vol. 1.
—— History of the State of Rhode Island and Providence Plantations. New York, 1859–60. 2 vols. 8vo.
ARNOLD, Rev. Thos. Inaugural Lecture at Oxford, Dec. 2, 1841, on the Study of Modern History. Oxford. 8vo. Hist. Pamph. Vol. 15.
—— Lectures on Modern History. N. York, 1843. 4to.
—— ROLLO, Rev. E. M. Address on Arnold a Model Teacher. 1859.
ARNOT, Hugo. Letter to the Lord Advocate of Scotland. 1777. 4to. Eng. Polit. Pamph. Vol. 18.
ARNOTT, Arch'd, M. D. Account of the last Illness and Death of Napoleon Bonaparte. London, 1822. 8vo. Strangford Pamph. Vol. 3.
ARNY, W. F. M. Interesting Items regarding New Mexico. Sante Fe, 1873. 8vo.
AROOSTOOK Territory, Maine. See HOLMES, E. Explora. and Survey of. 1838.
ARRINGTON, A. W. Argument in case O. S. Hough *vs.* Western Transportation Co., before U. S. District Court. Chicago, 1858. 8vo. Law Pamph. Vol. 5.
ARROWSMITH, Jas. Paper Hanger's Companion. Phila., 1852. 12mo.
"ART AND ARTISTS." See HASKINS, R. W.
ART. See Amer. Art Union. Trans. and Bulletin.
—— BIDDLE, H. P. Discourse on Art. 1854.
—— British Institution for Promoting Fine Arts.
—— Chicago Exhibition. 1859.
—— Cosmopolitan Art Union.
—— DELGADO, A. Memoria Sobre el Gran disco, de Theodosio.
—— ELLET, Mrs. Women Artists of the World.
—— GREELEY, H. Art and Industry at N. Y. Crystal Palace.
—— HUNTINGTON, D. Manual of.
—— Illustrated Exhibitor.
—— KERATRY, M. Les Arts d'Imitation.
—— LESTER, C. E. Artists of America.
—— LOSSING, R. J. Outline Hist. of.
—— MILMAN, H. H. Comparative Estimate of Sculpture and Painting.
—— MORSE, S. F. B.
—— N. York Gallery and Exhib. Cat. 1844.
—— Observations on the Probable Decline or Extinction of British Historical Painting. 1825.
—— PERKINS, C. C. Amer. Art Museums.
—— Penn. Acad. of Fine Arts.
—— R. I. Art Association.
—— RIPLEY & TAYLOR. Cyclopæ. of.

ART.—RUSKIN, J. Beauties of.
—— Society of British Artists. 3d Exhibition. 1826.
—— SPOONER, S. Anecdotes of Painters, &c.
—— TUCKERMAN, H. T. Book of Artists.
—— YAPP, G. W. Art Education, &c.
—— Manual of.
ART of War in Europe. See DELAFIELD, Maj. R.
ARTIFICIAL Clock Maker. A Treatise on Watch and Clock Works. London, 1714. 12mo.
ARTESIAN Wells. See WETHERELL, C. M.
ARTHUR, T. S., & CARPENTER, W. H. History of Georgia from its Earliest Settlement. Phila., 1858. 18mo.
—— History of Kentucky from its Earliest Settlement. Phila., 1858. 18mo.
—— Virginia from its Earliest Settlement. Phila., 1858. 18mo.
ARTHUR, Wm. An Etymolog. Dictionary of Family and Christian Names, with an Essay on their Deriva. and Import. N. York, 1857. 12mo.
—— The Antiquarian and General Review. Vol. 1. Schenectady, 1846. 8vo.
—— The Antiquarian. Vol. 3. Lansingburg, 1847. 8vo.
ARTICLES from the London Times on the Feelings Entertained by by the U. S. toward England, &c. Boston, 1847. 12mo. Congr. and Polit. Pamph. Vol. 75.
ARTICLES relating to Social Science and Political Economy as bearing on the Subjects of Labor, &c. Chicago, 1867. 8vo. Scientific Pamph. Vol. 15.
ARUNDEL, Eng. See TIERNEY, Rev. M. A. Hist. and Antiquities of.
ARUNDEL Manuscripts. See British Museum.
ASGILL, John. De Jure Divino: on the Title of the House of Hanover to the Succession of the Crown. London, 1710. 8vo. Eng. Miscell. Pamph. Vol. 1.
ASHBRIDGE, Elizabeth. Life of, written by herself. Concord, 1810. 12mo. Biograph. Pamph. Vol. 16.
ASHE, E. D. Notes of a Journey across the Andes, in Peru. Read before the Quebec Lit. and Hist. Soc'y, Apr. 3, 1861. Transactions, Vol. 5, Part 1.
—— Paper on Solar Spots. Read before the Quebec Lit. and Hist. Soc'y, Nov. 7, 1866. Transactions, N. Series, Part 5.
—— Water Power of Quebec. Read before the Quebec Lit. and Hist Soc'y, Nov., 1854. Transactions, Vol. 4, Part 3.
ASHE, Thos. Travels in America. 1806. London, 1808. 8vo.
ASHER & ADAMS. New Commer. and Statistic. Atlas and Gazetteer of the U. States. N. York, 1872. 2 vols. 5to.
ASHER, Dr. G. M. Sketch of Henry Hudson, the Navigator. Brooklyn. 1867. 8vo. Biograph. Pamph. Vol. 12.
ASHLAND Co., O. See KNAPP, H. S.
—— Mutual Fire Insurance Co. Instructions to their Agents. 1853, 1857. Ashland and Columbus, 1853, 1857. 8vo. Ohio Miscell. Pamph. Vol. 2.
—— Press. Newspaper. 1870–72. 1 vol. Ashland and Bayfield, bound together.

ASHLEY, C. Speech in Congress, Apr. 3, 1864, on Oregon. Speeches. Vol. 1.

ASHLEY, J. M. Speech in Congress March 30, 1864, on Reconstruction. Rebell'n Pamph. Vol. 31.

—— Speech at Toledo, Nov. 26, 1861, on the Rebell'n. Rebell'n Pamph. Vol. 36.

ASHMEAD, John W. Opening Speech in the case of the U. States *vs.* Castner Hanway, indicted for Treason. Phila., 1851. 8vo. Law Pamph. Vol. 5.

ASHMUN, R. R. Gurley, R. R., Life of.

ASHTABULA (O.) Sentinel. Newspaper. 1868. 1 vol.

ASHTON, R. Memo. of Rev. John Robinson. Mass. Hist. Colls. 4th Ser. Vol. 1.

ASIA. See Asiatic Ann. Register. 1800.

—— BURNES, Alex. Travels in Bokhara, &c. 1831–3.

—— ENTICH, J. Hist. of War. 1763.

—— HUMBOLTD, A. Travels and Researches.

—— MURRAY, H. Ancient Geography of Cent. and Eastern Asia.

—— PERKINS, Justin. Journal of Tour in 1849.

—— PALO, Marco. Travels in.

—— SEDDON, F. Language and Literature of.

ASIA MINOR. See TAYLOR, B. Lands of the Saracen.

ASIATIC Annual Register; or View of the History of Hindustan, for the year 1800. London, 1801. 8vo.

—— Journal. 1816–41. 55 vols. 8vo. London, 1816, etc.

—— Researches; or, Transactions of the Society Instituted in Bengal for Inquiring into the Hist., Antiquities, &c., of Asia. London, 1806. 8vo. 12 vols.

ASK and You Shall Have; or, the Source of Public Grievances Displayed. London. (n. d.) 8vo. Eng. Polit. Pamph. Vol. 75.

ASPER, Joel F. Speech in Congress, Jan. 21, 1871, on Revenue Reform. 8vo. Congr. Polit. Pamph. Vol. 119.

—— Speech in Cong., Feb. 13, 1871, on a Bill in regard to Duty on Wool, &c. Congr. and Polit. Pamph. Vol. 119.

ASPINWALL Papers. Mass. Hist. Soc'y Coll. 4th Series. Vols. 9, 10.

ASPINWALL, Col. Thos. Papers on the Narraganset Patent of 1643. Mass. Hist. Soc'y Proceedings. 1862–63.

ASPLUND, John. Ann. Register of the Baptist Denomina. in America to 1790. (n. d.)

ASSEY, Chas. On the Trade to China, and the Indian Archipelago. London, 1819. 8vo. Pamphleteer. Vol. 14.

ASSOCIATION for the Restoration of Amer. Shipping Interests. Memorial to Cong. on the Ship Building Interests of the U. S. San Francisco, 1870. 8vo. Congr. Pamph. Vol. 120.

—— of Amer. Geologists and Naturalists. See Amer. Asso. for Advancement of Science.

—— Proceeding, 1840, 41 and 42. Boston, 1843. 8vo.

—— See ROGERS, H. D.

—— of Banks for the Suppression of Counterfeiting. 6th Ann. Report of the Board of Managers. Boston. 1859. 8vo. Banking and Currency Pamph. Vol. 3.

ASSOCIATION of Medical Superintendents of Amer. Institutes for the Insane. Procee. at Baltimore, May 10, 1853. 8vo. Med. Pamph. Vol. 12.
—— Report of the Committee on the Distribution of Lunatic Hosp. Reports; by Dr. E. Jarvis. Dorchester, Mass., 1857. 8vo. Med. Pamph. Vol. 8.
—— of Men of Progress. Proposed Positive and Practical Reforms. N. York, 1856. 8vo. Congr. and Polit. Pamph. Vol. 75.
—— of 1774, in favor of Non-importation, &c. Charleston, S. C., 1859. 8vo. Congr. and Polit. Pamph. Vol 109.
—— to promote a Communica. between the Districts lying North and South of Hyde Park. London, 1860. 8vo. Eng. Miscell. Pamph. Vol. 9.
ASSOLLANT, A. Canonniers a vos Pieces! Paris, 1861. Rebell'n Pamph. Vol. 72.
ASSYRIA. See FRASER. History of.
ASTOR Library, New York. Ann. Report of the Trustees, 1850–58. Albany and N. York, 1850–58. 8vo.
—— Catalogue, A—Z. With Supplementary vol. and Index. N. York, 1857–66. 8vo.
ASTORIA, Oregon. See IRVING, W. Astoria.
ASTRONOMY. See ADAMS, J. Q. Address at Cincinn. 1843.
—— Amer. Philos. Soc'y.
—— ARAGO, M. Popular Lectures.
—— BARTLETT, W. H. C. Spherical Astronomy.
—— BRAYLEY, E. W. Luminous Prominences on the Sun.
—— BRENT, Chas. Compendious Astronomer.
—— CHALMERS, T. Astronom. Discourses.
—— DICK, J. Celestial Scenery.
—— Practical Astronomer.
—— Sidereal Heavens.
—— The Solar System.
—— GOULD, B. A. Report on Discov. of Neptune.
—— HACKLEY, Prof. Notes on.
—— HIND, J. R. The Solar System.
—— HOUGH, G. W. Descrip. of Cataloguing Machine.
—— KANE, E. K. Astronom. Observa. in Arctic Seas.
—— KIDDLE, H. Manual of Astronomy.
—— LEE, T. J. Tables and Formulae for.
—— MERCERON, O. S. Copernicus Refuted.
—— MITCHELL, O. M. Planetary Words.
—— MITCHELL, O. M. Sidereal Messenger.
—— NORTON, W. A. Treatise on.
—— OLMSTED, D. Rudiments of Philos. and Astron.
—— PAINE, R. T. Massachusetts Astronom. Obser.
—— RITTENHOUSE, D. Astronom. Obser.
—— RUNKLE, J. D. New Tables for Determining the Value of Co-efficients, &c.
—— U. S. Navy. Astron. Exped. to Southern Hemisphere.
—— WILLIAMSON, H. Essay on Comets.
—— WATSON, A. Lecture delivered at Albany.

ASTRONOMY. WHEWELL, W. Astronomy and General Physics.
—— —— Astronomy and Nat. Theology.

ASYLUMS for Foundlings: Their Supporters. 1860. 8vo. Eng. Miscell. Pamph. Vol. 9.

ATCHISON, Nathan'l. American Encroachments on British Rights. London, 1808. 8vo. Pamphleteer, Vol. 6.

ATCHISON, Thos. Statement in defence of his Military Integrity, etc. London, 1834. 8vo. Eng. Polit. Pamph. Vol. 40.

ATCHISON & St. Joseph and Weston & Atchison R. R. Co.'s. Let-Letter from the Presidents to the Governor of Missouri. St. Louis, 1865. 8vo. Mo. Miscell. Pamph. Vol. 1.

ATCHISON, Topeka & Santa Fe R. R. Co. Petition by C. K. Halliday, to the U. S. Senate, in relation to the Osage Indian Reservation. Washington, 1869. 8vo. Congr. and Polit. Pamph. Vol. 112.

ATHENÆUM: A Journal of Literature, Science and the Fine Arts. London, 1838, '41, '42, '44, '45, '49, '58. 7 vols. 4to.

ATHENEUM: Magazine. New York, 1831–2. 8vo.

ATHENS—See COLTON, Rev. W. Views of.

ATHENS Co., Ohio.—See WALKER, C. M. History of.

ATHENS, Tenn.—Post, Newspaper. June 1854, to Oct. 1858. Folio.

ATHERTON, C. G. Obituary Addresses in Congress, Dec. 19, 1853, on his Death. Washington. 8vo. Cong. and Polit. Pamph. Vol. 89.

—— Speech in Cong., Dec. 23, 1841, on the Tariff. Washington, 1841. 8vo. Cong. and Polit. Pamph. Vol. 25.

—— Speech in Cong., May 3, 1842, on the Apportionment Bill. Washington, 1842. 8vo. Cong. and Polit. Pamph. Vol. 25.

—— Address delivered before New Hamp. Hist. Society, June 8, 1831. Collections. Vol. 3.

—— Memoir of Hon. Joshua Atherton. Boston, 1852. 8vo. Biograph. Pamph. Vol. 7.

—— Memoir of the Hon. Saml. Dana. N. Hampshire Hist. Soc. Collections. Vol. 3.

—— Memoir of Wiseman Clagett. N. Hampshire Hist. Soc. Collections. Vol. 3.

—— Oration at Amherst, N. H., July 4, 1798. Amherst, 1798. Addresses, etc. Vol 29.

ATHERTON. Joshua. See ATHERTON, C. H.

ATHERTON, Wm. Narrative of Defeat of N. W. Army, under Gen. Winchester. Frankfort, Ky., 1842. 12mo. Pamphlets War of 1812. Vol. 2.

ATHOL, Mass. See Norton, J. F. Address at the Reconsecration of the Ancient Cemetery. 1859.

ATKINSON, Edw. Memorandum in regard to the Case between the Govt. and the Union Pacific R. R. (n. p.) 1871. 8vo. Cong. and Polit. Pamph. Vol. 127.

—— On the Collection of Revenue. Boston, 1867. 8vo. Banking and Currency Pamphlets. Vol. 4.

—— Report on the Cotton Manufacture of 1862. Rebelln. Pamph. Vol. 92.

—— Speech at Worcester, Mass., Sept. 9, 1868, on the National Debt. Washington. 8vo. Cong. and Polit. Pamph. Vol. 122.

ATKINSON, N. H. See COGSWELL, Rev. W. History of.

ATKINSON, Wm. Principles of Political Economy, or the Laws of the Formation of National Wealth. 1843. 8vo. Scientific Pamph. Vol. 11.

"ATLANTA."—Rebel Steam Ram. See History of.

ATLANTIC Co., N. J. See MICKLE, I. Reminiscences of.

—— Magazine. May, 1824 to April, 1825. New York, 1824–5. 2 vols. 8vo.

—— Monthly. Nov., 1857, to Dec., 1868. Boston. 22 vols. 8vo.

—— Steam Ships. See TOWN, Ithiel. 1838.

ATLASES.—Appleton's Modern Atlas. (n. d.)

—— See ASHER & ADAMS. Atlas and Gazetteer. 1872.

ATLAS, MAJOR. Amsterdam, 1709, etc. 4 vols., folio.

—— FADEN, W. No. American Atlas. 1777.

—— See FINDLAY, A. G. Modern Atlas. 1850.

—— General Atlas of the World. No title. 1733–5. Folio.

—— General Atlas. London, 1773. Folio.

—— Another. Amsterdam, 1696. Folio.

—— Another. Amsterdam, 1739, etc. 2 vols. Folio.

—— —— JEFFERY, T. Atlas. 1776. 8vo. HARRISON & WARNER, State Map of Wis., 1873. Dane County, Wis., 1873.

—— KITCHEN, T. General Atlas. 1783.

—— LOTTERI, T. C. Atlas Minor. (n. d.)

—— Atlas Maritime. La petit Atlas Maritime recueil de cartes et plans des quatre parties du monde. Paris, 1764. 5 vols. 4to.

—— Atlas of German Provinces, in Portfolios. 2 vols., folio. (n. d.)

—— Atlas of Spanish Provinces and Possessions. No title. 1770, etc. Folio.

—— Atlas Universel. Paris, 1849. Folio.

—— Benton Co., Iowa.

—— BOWEN, E. Atlas of World. 1752.

—— COLTON, G. W. Atlas of World. 1854–56.

—— DEWITT, F. Atlas. (n. d.)

—— MOLL, H. World Described. 1714.

—— —— Atlas. 1719.

—— PALAIRET, J. Atlas Methodique. 1755.

—— ROBERT M. Atlas Universel. 1755.

—— SANSON, S. 1674, etc.

—— SAYER, R. Atlas. 1787.

—— Theatrum, Orbis, Terrarum. 1570.

ATMOSPHERE.—Influence on Diseases. See FORSTER, Thos.

ATTACK ON PETERSBURG.—See U. States House of Reps. Report on.

ATTEMPT (An) at Vocal English, or English Spelled as Spoken. London, 1844. 8vo. Strangford Pamph. Vol. 35.

ATTERBURY, Bishop F. Antonius Musa's Character, Represented by Virgil, etc. London, 1740. 8vo. Eng. Miscell. Pamph. Vol. 23.

ATTILA.—Theology, Logic, Anatomy, etc., Combined, to Establish the Truism that the Woman is no Human Being. N. York, 1871. 8 vo. Cong. and Polit. Pamph. Vol. 128.

ATTLEBOROUGH, Mass. See DAGGETT, I. Sketch of the History of.

ATWATER, Caleb. Descrip. of Antiquities Discovered in Ohio and other Western States. Amer. Antiquarian Soc. Coll. Vol. 1.

—— Facts and Remarks on the Climate, Geology, etc., of Parts of Ohio. 1826. Sillimann's Jour. Vol. 11.

—— HILDRETH, S. P. Letters to, on Ohio. 1819.

—— History of the State of Ohio, Natural and Civil. 2d Ed. Cincinnati, 1839.

—— Remarks made on a Tour to Prairie du Chien, and thence to Washington City, in 1829. Columbus, 1831.

ATWATER, Dorence. List of Union Soldiers Buried at Andersonville, from the Official Record in the Surgeon's Office at Andersonville, 1866. Rebell'n Pamph. Vol. 55.

ATWATER, Rev. Lyman H. Discourse at the Funeral of Hon. Roger Minott Sherman, Jan. 2, 1845. N. Haven, 1845. 8vo. Sermons. Vol. 51.

ATWILL, Winthrop. The Treason of Benedict Arnold. A Lecture. Northampton, 1837. 8vo. Rev. War Pamph. Vol. 5. Another Copy, Addresses. Vol. 23.

ATWOOD, Thos. History of the Island of Dominica. London, 1791. 8vo.

AUB. Theodore. Plan for the Insurance of Titles and Mortgages. N. York, 1871. 8vo. Insurance Pamph. Vol. 1.

AUBURN.—See PRINCE, Fred. Story. of Fort Hill.

AUCHINCLOSS, Wm. S. See Paris Universal Exposition, 1867. Report on Steam Engineering.

AUCKLAND ISLANDS.—See ENDERBY, C. Climate, Soil and Pro ductions of. 1849.

AUDUBON, J. J. Ornithological Biography; or, Birds of the U. S. London, 1831–9. 5 vols. 8vo.

——Ornithological Biography of the U. S. Edinburgh. Vol. 3, 1835. Edinburgh. Vol. 5, 1839. 2 vols. 8vo.

—— Synopsis of the Birds of N. America. Edinburgh, 1839. 8vo.

AUGHEY, J. H. Iron Furnace; or Slavery and Secession. Phila., 1863. 12mo.

AUGUSTA Co., Virginia. Scraps from the Records. Virginia Hist. Register. Vol. 3.

AUGUSTA, Ga. Chronicle, Newspaper. Augusta, 1861–2. Folio.

AUGUSTA, Me. See WORTH, J. W. History of.

AUGUSTAN AGE.—See MEIGS, C. D. Lecture on.

AULNEY AND LA TOUR.—Governors of Nova Scotia. Papers Relative to. Mass. Hist. Soc. Coll. 3d Series. Vol. 7.

AUPAUMUT, Hendrick. Narrative of an Embassy to the Western Indians. 1791. Penn. Hist. Soc. Memoirs. Vol. 2. Part 1.

AUSTIN, F. W. G. On some of the Fishes of the St. Lawrence. Read before the Quebec Lit. and Hist. Soc'y, Apr. 4, 1866. Transactions. N. Series. Part 4.

AUSTIN, James T. The Life of Elbridge Gerry, with Contemporary Letters to the Close of the American Revolution. Boston, 1828. 8vo.

AUSTIN, Saml. Oration Pronounced at Worcester, July. 4, 1798. Worcester, Mass., 1798. 8vo. Addresses, etc. Vol. 29.

AUSTRALIA.—See ADDERLEY, C. B. Australian Colonies Gov't Bill Discussed. 1849.

—— MATHESON, M. Facts from the Gold Diggings. 1852.

—— and its Gold Regions. Edinburgh. (n. d.) 12mo. Hist. Pamph. Vol. 20.

—— Emigration to. GREY, Earl. Speech in House of Lords, 1848.

—— MOSSMAN. Saml. Emigrants Letters, etc.

—— SMITH, Sidney. Whether to go, and Whither?

—— Patriotic Assoc. Letter to C. Buller, Jr., M. P., on Transportation of Convicts. Sydney, 1843. 8vo. Strangford Pamph. Vol. 31.

AUSTRIA.—See ABBOTT, J. S. C. The Empire of.

—— and Central Italy. London, 1849. 8vo. Strangford Pamph. Vol. 48.

—— Coup d Oeil Geologique sur les Mines de la Monanarchie Autrichienne. Vienna, 1855. 4to.

AUTHENTIC (An) Exposition of the "K. G. C."—Knights of the Golden Circle; or, a History of Secession from 1834 to 1861, Illustrated. Indianapolis, 1861. 12mo. Reb. Pam. Vol. 11.

—— Narrative of the Captivity of Mrs. Horn and her Two Children by the Camanche Indians. Cincinnati, 1853. 8vo.

AUTHORS.—See BULL, E. Hints to.

AUTOGRAPHS FOR FREEDOM.—See GRIFFITHS, Julia.

AVON, N. Y., Mineral Springs. See SALISBURY, S.

AWARD (The) of Mr. Sergeant Frere, on a Cause pending between Wm. Adair and Lieut.-Gen. Money, with Observations thereon, etc. Norwich, Eng., 1813. 8vo. Law Pamph. Vol. 12.

AYDELOTT, B. P., D.D. Address on Collegiate Departments of the English Languages and Literature. Cincinnati, 1838. 8vo. Educa. Pamph. Vol. 3.

—— Duties of American Citizens—An Address. Cincinnati, 1840. Addresses, etc. Vol. 12.

—— Incidental Benefits of Denomina Division. Cincinnati, 1846. 8vo.

—— Our Country's Evils, and their Remedy. Cincinnati, 1843. 12mo. Cong. and Polit. Pamph. Vol. 135.

—— The Secret of a Sound Judgment; an Address delivered at Woodward College, June 28, 1844. Cincinnati, 1844. 12mo. Addresses, Vol. 30.

AYNGE, G. A. The Death of Tecumseh, and Poetical Fragments on Various Subjects. Dartmouth, 1821. 12mo. Indian Pamph. Vol. 4.

AYSCOUGH, Samuel. Catalogue of the MSS. Preserved in the British Museum, hitherto undescribed, including the Collection of Sir Hans Sloan and Rev. Thos. Birch. London. 1782. 2 vols. 4to.

B.

BABBAGE, Chas. Ninth Bridgewater Treatise—a Fragment. Lond., 1837. 8vo.

BABBIDGE, Rev. Chas. Centen. Address in Vindica. of the 1st Ch. in Pepperell, Feb. 9, 1847. Boston, 1847. 8vo. Mass. Hist. Discourses. Vol. 5.

BABCOCK. Remarks on the R. Cath. Ch. Prop. Bill, in N. Y. Senate, June 24, 1853. Albany, 1853. 8vo. Addresses. Vol. 15.

BABCOCK, Jas. F. Address on Jas. Brewster, at N. Haven, Dec. 19, 1866. N. Haven, 1867. 8vo. Addresses. Vol. 35.

BABSON, J. J. History of the Town of Gloucester, Cape Ann,

BABYLON and the Banks of the Euphrates. Lond. (n. d.) 12mo. Hist. Pamph. Vol. 8.

—— LAYARD, A. H. Discoveries, &c.

—— Relation of the Late Siege and taking of the City by the Turk. Lond., 1639. sm. 4to. Eng. Polit. Pamph. Vol. 6. Mass. Gloucester, 1860. 8vo.

BACHE, Alex. Dallas. See HENRY, Jos. Eulogy on.

—— Lecture on Switzerland. Smithsonian Report. 1870.

—— Paper on the Gulf Stream, read before the Amer. Geograph. and Statist. Soc'y, Jan. 27, 1856. Bulletin. Vol. 2.

—— Report on Educa. in Europe, to the Educa. Trustees of Girard College. Phila., 1839. 8vo.

—— Records and Results of a Magnetic Survey of Penn. Smithsonian Contrib. Vol. 13.

BACHMAN, John. Examina. of Characteristics of Genera and Species, &c., of the Human Race. Charleston, 1855. 8vo. Scientific Pamph. Vol. 11.

——Examination of Prof Agassiz's Sketch of the Natural Provinces of the Animal World. Charleston, 1855. 8vo. Scientific Pamph. Vol. 11.

BACKUS, Isaac. Church History of N. E. (Baptist,) from 1620 to 1800, with a Memoir of Author. Phila., 1839. 12mo.

BACKUS, Rev. J. S. Disc. on Secret Societies; with a Reply to the same by Rev. H. B. KENYON. Albany, 1850. 8vo. Sermons. Vol. 11.

BACON'S Rebellion. The Beginning, Progress and Conclusion of Bacon's Reb. in Va., in 1675–6. Force's Hist. Tract's. Vol. 1.

—— See BERKLEY, Sir Wm.

BACON, Benj. C. Statistics of the Colored People of Phila. Phila., 1856. 8vo. Phila. Misc. Pamph. Vol. 2.

BACON, D. Francis. Disc. on the History, Philosophy and Tendency of Amer. Politics. N. York, 1844. 8vo. Addresses, &c. Vol. 12.

BACON, Francis, Lord. Essays, Moral, Economical and Political, with an Introductory Essay by A. POTTER, D. D. Harper's Fam. Lib. N. York, 1860. 18mo.

—— History, Natural and Experimental, of Life and Death. Med. Pamph. Vol. 4. N. York. (n. d.)

BACON, Lord—See NAPIER, M. Writings of. 1818.
—— or, the Case of Private and National Corruption and Bribery, impartially considered. Lond., 1721. 8vo. Eng. Polit. Pamph. Vol. 67.
BACON, Maj. Gen. Francis. See FULLER, Rev. Sam'l. Obit. Disc. 1849.
BACON, Leonard. Christianity in History. A Disc. to the Alumni of Yale Coll., Aug. 16, 1848. N. Haven, 1848. 8vo. Yale Coll. Pamph.
—— Disc. on the Death of Wm. Henry Harrison, at N. Haven, Apr. 17, 1841. N. Haven, 1841. 8vo. Addresses. Vol. 31.
—— Hist. Disc. on the 200th Ann. of the Founding of the Hopkins Gramm. School, N. Haven, with Appendix. N. Haven, 1860. 8vo. Yale Coll. Pamph.
—— Thirteen Hist. Disc. on 200 years of the 1st Ch. in N. Haven. N. Haven, 1839. 8vo.
BACON, Nathaniel. See WARE, W. Memoir of.
BACON, Oliver N. History of Natick, from 1651 to the Present Time. Boston, 1856. 8vo.
BACON'S Guide to Amer. Politics; or, a complete View of the Fundamental Principles of National and State Governments. Lond., 1864. 12mo. Congr. and Polit. Pamph. Vol. 73.
BACON'S Mercantile Coll., Cincinnati. Circular and Catalogue. Cin., 1853. 8vo.
BACQUEVILLE, M. de. De la Potherie. Historie de l'Amerique Septentrionale. Maps and Engravings. Paris, 1853. 4 vols. 18mo.
BADCOCK Genealogy. From N. E. Histor. and Genealog. Reg. 1865. Genealog. Pamph. Vol. 1.
BADEAU, Adam. Military History of Gen. U. S. Grant, from Apr. 1, 1861, to Apr., 1865. N. York, 1868. Vol. 1.
BADGER, G. E. Speech in U. S. Senate, Feb. 16, 1854, on Nebr. Bill. Congr. and. Polit. Pamph. Vol. 93.
BADGER, Stephen C. Juridical Statistics of Merrimack Co., N. H. 1847. N. E. Hist. and Gen. Reg. Vol. 1.
BADGERS. Home of the. See Sketches of the West.
BADHAM, Dr. Chas. Observations on the Inflammatory Affections of the Mucous Membrane of the Bronchiæ. Lond., 1808.
BADDELEY, Lieut. Observations on the Geognosy of a part of the Saguenay Country, Canada. Quebec Lit. and Hist. Soc'y Trans. Vol. 1.
—— Geology of a portion of the Labrador Coast. Quebec Lit. and Hist. Soc'y Trans. Vol. 1.
BAEGERT, Jacob. Account of the Aboriginal Inhabitants of the Californian Peninsula. Smithsonian Reports, 1863–64.
BAGG, Stanley C. Canadian Archæology. Montreal, 1864. 8vo. Archæolog. Pamph. Vol. 2.
—— Notes on Coins: before the Montreal Numismatic Soc'y. Montreal, 1863. 12mo. Scientific Pamph. Vol. 42.
—— The Antiq. and Legends of Durham, Eng., before the Antiq. Soc'y of Montreal. Montreal, 1866. 8vo. Addresses. Vol. 17.

BAIGENT, Francis J. History and Antiq. of Parish Ch. of Wyke, near Winchester. Winchester, 1865. 8vo.

BAILEY, Rev. A. J. Sermon on Politics and Politicians. Monroe. Wis. (n. d.) 8vo. Wis. Misc. Pamph. Vol. 8.

BAILEY, Alex. H. Speech in N. Y. Senate, Jan. 29, 1863, on Gov. Seymour's Message. Rebell'n Pamph. Vol. 11.

BAILEY Genealogy. See POOR (A).

BAILEY, J. W. Knox Coll., by whom Founded and Endowed; also, a Review of a pamphlet on the Right on Congregationalists, &c. Chicago, 1860. 8vo.

BAILEY, Nathan. Universal Etymological Dictionary. Lond., 1773. 8vo.

BAILEY, Silas D. D. Address before the Amer. Bap. Hist. Soc'y, May 12, 1857, on the Amer. Bapt. Preaching of the 17th and 18th Centuries. Phila., 1858. 8vo.

BAILEY, Wm. Records of Patriotism and Love of Country. Washington, 1826. 8vo.

BAILLIE, Rt. Hon. Geo., and Lady BAILLIE. See MURRAY, Lady. Memoirs of.

BAILY, Francis. Journal of a Tour in the Unsettled parts of America. 1796–97. Lond., 1856. 8vo.

—— Tables for Purchasing and Renewing of Leases, &c. Lond., 1807. 8vo. 2d Ed. Law Pamph. Vol. 14.

BAINES, Edward. The History of the County Palatine and Dutchy of Lancaster, new revised and improved Ed. Lond., 1868. 2 vols. 4to.

BAINES, Edward, Jr. History of the Cotton Manufacture in G. Britain. London. (n. d.) 8vo.

—— Letters to Lord Russell, on State Education. Lond., 1846. 8vo. Educa. Pamph. Vol. 36.

—— The Social, Educational and Religious State of the Manufacturing Dists. Lond., 1843. 8vo. Strangford Pam. Vol. 32.

BAINES, Thos. Present State of Affairs of the River Plate. Livpool, 1845. 8vo. Strangford Pamph. Vol. 38.

BAIRD. Genealog. Colls. Concerning the Sir-name of Baird. Lond., 1870. 4to.

BAIRD, Chas. W. History of Rye, Westchester, Co., N. Y., 1660 and 1870, including Harrison and the White Plains till 1788. N. York, 1871. 8vo.

BAIRD, Henry S. On the Early History of Wis. See Wis. Hist. Soc'y Colls. Vol. 2.

—— Recollections of the Early History of Northern Wis. Wis. Hist. Soc'y. Colls. Vol. 4.

BAIRD, Rob't D. D. Memoir of. From Holden's Mag., Mar., 1859. Biograph. Pamph. Vol. 11.

BAIRD, S. F., and GIRARD, C. Catalogue ot North Amer. Reptiles in the Smithsonian Institution. Part 1. Washington, 1853. 8vo. Congr. and Polit. Pamph. Vol. 36.

BAIRD, Rev. S. J. Southern Rights and Northern Duties in the Present Crisis. 1861. Rebell'n Pamph. Vol. 82.

BAIRD, Thos. H. Memo. to Congress for Enactment of Measures to Preserve the Union. 1864. Rebell'n Pamph. Vol. 16.

BAKER, Anne E. Glossary or Northamptonshire Words and Phrases. London, 1855. 2 vols. 8vo.
—— Index Locorum. BAKER's Hist. of Northampton. Northampton, 1867. 8vo.
BAKER, Edward D. See Addresses on the Death of.
—— Speech in U. S. Senate, Jan. 2, 1861, on Secession. Rebell'n Pamph. Vol. 34.
BAKER Genealogy. See APPLETON, W. S. Ancestry of Priscilla Baker.
—— BAKER, N. M.
BAKER, Geo. E. See SEWARD, W. H. Works.
BAKER, Jas. Military Educa. with the Universities. Cambridge, Eng., 1861. 8vo. Educa. Pamph. Vol. 36.
BAKER, J. L. Exports and Imports, as showing the Relative Advancement of Nations. Phila., 1859. 8vo. Congr. and Polit. Pamph. Vols. 100, 104.
BAKER, Gen. L. C. History of the U. S. Secret Service. Phila., 1867. 8vo.
BAKER, Nelson M. Genealogy of Descendants of Edward Baker, of Lynn, Mass. 1860. Syracuse, 1867. 8vo.
BAKER, R. L. Description of Economy, Beaver Co., Pa. Penn. Hist. Soc'y. Mem. Vol. 4, Part 2.
BAKERSTOWN, Me. See Ladd, W. Annals of.
BAKEWELL, R. H. Visit to the Purton Spa. Purton, Wilts, 1865. 8vo. Guide Books. Vol. 31.
BALANCE (The) and Columbian Repository. Newspaper for the year 1802. Hudson, 1802. 4to.
BALANCE (The) and State Journal. 1811. Albany, 1811. 4to.
BALANCE of Power. Plan for Establishment of, in Europe. Lond., 1814. 8vo. Pamphleteer. Vol. 4.
BALBOA, Miguel Cavello. Histoire de Perou. See Ternaux. Voyages. Vol. 14.
BALCH, Thos. Les France en Amerique pendant la guerre de l'Independence des Etats Unis. 1777–83. Paris, 1872. 8vo.
BALDAEUS, P. Description of Malabar and Ceylon, in Dutch. Amsterdam, 1672. Folio.
BALDWIN, Rev. A. C. Review of a Pamphlet purporting to be "A Statement of Facts in Relation to the [New Haven] Howe Street Society." N. Haven, 1846. 8vo. Conn. Hist. Discourse. Vol. 7.
—— The Review Reviewed, &c. Reply to the above. N. Haven, 1846. 8vo. Conn. Hist. Discourses. Vol. 7.
BALDWIN, B. A. Nathaniel Baldwin and One Line of his Descendants. Boston, 1871. 8vo. Genealog. Pamph. Vol. 2.
BALDWIN, Ebenezer. Annals of Yale Coll. to 1831. N. Haven, 1831. 8vo.
BALDWIN GENEALOGY.—See BALDWIN, B. A.
BALDWIN, Rev. Geo. C. Representative Women. New York, 1857 12mo.
BALDWIN, Henry. Address before Amer. Institute, N. Y., Oct. 9. 1834. Addresses. Vol. 11.
BALDWIN Institute, Berea, Ohio. See Baldwin University.

BALDWIN, J. D. Ancient America, in Notes on Amer. Antiquities. N. York, 1872. 12mo.

—— Speech in Cong., Mar. 5, 1865, on State Sovereignty. Rebell'n Pamph. Vol. 34.

—— Speech in Cong., Jan. 11, 1868, on Human Rights, etc. Congr. and Polit. Pamph. Vol. 122.

BALDWIN, J. G. Party Leaders: Sketches of Jefferson, Hamilton, Jackson, Clay, Randolph and others. N. Y., 1868. 12mo.

—— Flush Times of Alabama and Mississippi; a Series of Sketches. N. Y., 1854. 12mo.

BALDWIN, R. S. Argument in Case of U. S. *vs.* Cinque, *et al.*, of the Armistad. N. Y., 1841. 8vo. Congr. and Polit. Pamph. Vol. 107. Law Pamph. Vol. 3.

—— Speech in the U. S. Senate, Mar. 27, and Apr. 3, 1850, on Admission of Cal. Congr. and Polit. Pamph. Vol. 86.

—— Speech in U. S. Senate, July 25, 1850, on Texas' Claim to New Mexico. Congr. and Polit. Pamph. Vol. 83.

BALDWIN, Samuel. Diary of Events in Charleston, S. C., from Mar. 20 to Apr. 20, 1780, during the Siege of the British. N. J. Hist. Soc. Proceed. Vol. 2.

BALDWIN, School. See St. Paul, Minn.

BALDWIN, Simeon. See DUTTON, S. W. S. Funeral Disc. 1851.

BALDWIN, Rev. Thos. Disc. in 2d Bapt. Meeting-House, Boston, Jan., 1824; with Hist. Sketches of the Ch. Boston. 8vo. (n. d.) Boston Hist. Discourses. Vol. 1.

BALDWIN UNIVERSITY.—Catalogues for 1853–4 (Baldwin Institute), 1866–7. Cleveland. 8vo.

BALDWIN, W. H. Protest on the Extension of the Hillsborough & Cincinnati R. R. Co. 1853. 8vo. Ohio Misc. Pamph. Vol. 2. Baldwin's Free R. R. Guide. Jan., 1869. Guide Books. Vol. 16.

BALEARICK ISLANDS—See Anc. and Mod. Hist. of.

BALESTIER, J. N. Annals of Chicago. Lecture before Chicago Lyceum, Jan. 21, 1840. Chicago, 1840. 8vo. Ill. Local Histories. Vol. 1.

BALL, Alonzo S. Address before Homœpathic Med. Soc. of N. Y., Feb. 14, 1854. Albany, 1854. 8vo. Med. Pamph. Vol. 2.

BALL, John. Address to the Public, on behalf of the Poor. Dublin, 1815. 8vo. Eng. Polit. Pamph. Vol. 32.

—— Remarks on the Geol. and Physical Features of the Country West of the Rocky Mountains. 1834. Silliman's Jour. Vol. 28.

—— Salem Provident Assoc.

BALLANCE, C. History of Peoria, Ill. Peoria, 1870. 12mo.

BALLARD, Bland. Obit. Address at Frankfort, Ky. 1854.

BALLARD, Rev. Edward. Early History of the Epis. Ch. in Maine. Maine Hist. Soc. Coll. Vol. 6.

BALLINGALL, Jas. Shipwrecks; their Causes, and the Means of Prevention. Melbourne, 1857. 8vo. Eng. Misc. Pamph. Vol. 9.

BALLOT-Box (The)—the Palladium of our Liberties. N. Orleans, 1863. 8vo. Rebell'n Pamph. Vol. 38.

BALLOT (The) Weighed in the Balance: Estimate of the Value of a Secret Suffrage. Lond., 1853. 8vo. Strangford Pamph. Vol. 65.
BALMERINO, Scotland. See CAMPBELL, J. Balmerino and its Abbey.
BALTIC (Battle of the). 1658. See DE PEYSTER, J. W.
BALTIMORE, Lord. See KENNEDY, J. P., Dis. on. 1845.
—— MAYER, Brantz. Disc. on. 1852.
—— NEILL, E. D, Memoir of. 1869.
—— Relation of Md. 1634.
—— Remarks of U. S. Catholic Mag. of J. P. Kennedy.
—— Review of J. P. Kennedy's Disc.
—— Virginia and Md., etc.
BALTIMORE American and Commercial Daily Advertiser, Jan. and Feb., 1811. Folio.
—— and Ohio R. R. Co. See GARRETT, J. W.
—— Proceed. of Railway Meetings at Pittsburg, Uniontown, &c. 1870. 8vo.
—— 46th Ann. Report of President and Directors, 1872. Baltimore. 1872. 8vo.
—— Assoc. for Improving Condition of Poor. 8th and 9th Ann. Reports. Baltimore, 1857–58. 8vo. Baltimore Pamph. Vol. 1.
—— Board of Trade. Statistics of the Trade and Commerce of Baltimore, for 1857. Baltimore, 1858. 8vo. Baltimore Pamph. Vol. 1.
—— City Directory for the year 1858. Baltimore, 1858. 8vo.
—— Coll. of Dental Surgery. 15th Ann. Announcement and Catalogue. 1854–5. Baltimore, 1854. 8vo.
—— Commercial Convention, held Dec. 18, 1852. Baltimore, 1852. 8vo. Baltimore Pamph. Vol. 1.
—— Commissioners of Pub. Schools. Ann. Reports for 1856, '57, '62.
—— Rules and Regulations, 1857.
—— Evening Post. Newspaper. Sept., 1808 to March, 1809. Folio.
—— —— Mar., 1810, to May, 1810. Folio.
—— Federal Gazette and Daily Advertiser. Newspaper. Aug., 1799, to Dec., 1799. Folio.
—— —— Nov., 1808, to Dec., 1808. Folio.
—— Female Coll. 11th Ann. Catalogue. 1859. Baltimore, 1859, 8vo.
—— Gazette. Newspaper. 1794. Folio.
—— High School. See MAYER, Brantz.
—— LATROBE, J. H. B. Laying Corner Stone of City Hall. 1867.
—— London Park Cemetery.
—— Magazine. The Portico, a Repository of Science and Literature. 4 vols. 8vo. Baltimore, 1816–18.
—— Memoranda concerning Baltimore and its Surroundings. Baltimore, 1860. 12mo. Baltimore Pamph. Vol. 1.
—— Monument. Magazine. 1839. Vols. 1 and 2. 8vo.
—— Same. Vols. 1 and 2. 1839. 4to. 1837–8.

BALTIMORE—or, Long, Long Time Ago. Baltimore, 1853. 8vo. Md. Hist. Soc. Addresses, &c. Vol. 2.

—— PEABODY, Geo. Letter. 1857.

—— Peabody Institute.

—— Plan for Formation of a "Citizens' Assoc. for Diffusion of Knowledge." Baltimore. (n. d.) 8vo. Baltimore Pamph. Vol. 1.

—— Reports on the Improvement of Jones' Falls. Baltimore, 1870. 4to.

—— Republican, or Anti-Democrat. Newspaper.

—— —— Jan., 1802, to Mar. 1802. July to Dec., 1802. Folio.

—— Sun. Newspaper. Jan., 1845, to May, 1847. Folio.

—— Same. Jan., 1848, to June, 1848. Folio.

—— Same. June, 1847, to Dec., 1847. Folio.

—— WINANS, R. How to prevent Floods in.

BALY, Dr. Wm. Lecture at St. Bartholomews Hospt., London, Oct. 2, 1848. Lond., 1848. 8vo. Med. Pamph. Vol. 29.

BAMFORD, Saml. Dialect of So. Lancashire; or Tim Robbins' Tummus and Meary. 2d Ed. Lond., 1854. 12mo.

BAMPTON, Eng. See GILES, Rev. J. A. Hist. of.

BANBURY, Eng. See BEESLEY, Alfred. History of.

BANBURY, Wm. Letter to the Duke of Wellington, on the Silk Trade, in 1829. Lond., 1831. 8vo. Strangford Pamph. Vol. 7.

BANCROFT, Aaron, D.D. Sermon at Worcester, Jan. 31, 1836, on Fifty Years of his Ministry. Worcester, 1836. 8vo. Mass. Hist. Discourses. Vol. 1.

—— Disc. before the 2d Cong. Soc. in Worcester, Apr. 8, 1827, after the Ordination of Rev. Alonzo Hill. Worcester, Mass.. 1827. 8vo. Mass. Hist. Discourses. Vol. 16.

—— HILL, Rev. Alonzo. Disc. on Life and Character of. 1839.

—— Life of George Washington, Commander-in-Chief of the American Army, etc. Lond., 1808. 8vo.

—— Sermon before the 2d Christian Ch. and Soc., in Worcester, Jan. 6, 1811. Worcester, Mass.. 1811. 8vo. Mass. Hist. Discourses. Vol. 16.

BANCROFT, George. Hist. of the U. S., from the Discovery of the Amer. Continent. Boston, 1857. 13th Ed. 9 vols. 8vo.

—— See HUNT, C. H. Life of Edw. Livingston.

—— JOSEPH REED. An Hist. Essay. N. York, 1867. 8vo.

—— League for the Union.

—— Memorial Address on Abraham Lincoln, before Congress. Washington, 1866. 8vo.

—— Oration at N. Y., Feb. 22, 1862. Rebell'n Pamph. Vol. 99.

—— REED, Wm. B. Rejoinder to his Hist. Essay on Pres. Reed.

—— Remarks on the Genius and Character of Wm. H. Prescott, before the N. Y. Hist. Soc. Hist. Mag. Vol. 3.

—— SCHUYLER, Geo. L., on the Northern Campaign of 1777, etc.

—— SWETT, S. Defence of Pickering.

BANDORY, Pere. Oeuvres Diverses. Nouvelle Edition. Paris, 1762. 18mo.

BANERJEA, Rev. K. M. Remarks on the Speech of the Earl of Ellenborough, on the Bengal Petition. Calcutta, 1853. 8vo. Eng. Polit. Pamph. Vol. 50.

BANFF, Scotland. Collections for a History of Aberdeen and Banff, printed for the Spalding Club. Aberdeen, 1843–4.

—— Illustrations of the Topogr. and Antiq. of Aberdeen and Banff. Aberdeen, 1869. 4 vols. 4to.

BANGOR, Me. Centen. Celebra., Sept. 30, 1869. Bangor, 1870. 8vo.

BANGS, Isaac. Extract from the Journ. of. 1776. N. J. Hist. Soc. Proceed. Vol. 8.

BANGS Nathan, D.D. History of the Meth. Epis. Ch., 1796 to 1840. 12th Ed. N. Y., 1860. 4 vols. 12mo.

—— Original Church of Christ. N. Y. 12mo.

BANK (The) of England Case, under Marsh & Co.'s Commission. Lond., 1825. 8vo. Eng. Miscell. Pamph. Vol. 28.

BANK of the U. States. Report on. 1830. Washington, 1830. 8vo. Congress. Pamph. Vol. 50.

—— Same. 1832. Congress. Pamph. Vol. 40.

—— See Congress. Speeches.

—— Considerations in favor of a Nat. Bank. N. Y., 1834. 8vo. Congr. and Polit. Pamph. Pol. 71.

—— Constitu. Power to Repeal Charter of the Bank vindicated. Philadelphia, 1837. 8vo. Congr. and Polit. Pamph. Vol. 100.

—— INGERSOLL, C. J. Opinion on, etc.

—— N. Y. Union Committee. 1834.

—— Ohio Legis. Report on. 1821. Richmond, 1821. 8vo. Congr. and Polit. Pamph. Vol. 71.

—— Outline of a Plan for a Nat. Bank, with Remarks on the Bank of the U. S. N. York, 1833. 8vo. Congr. and Polit. Pamph. Vol. 71.

—— Proceed. of Friends of a Nat. Bank, at Boston, July, 1841. Boston, 1841. 8vo. Banking and Curr. Pamph. Vol. 1.

—— Proceed. at N. Y. to establish a Nat. Bank. 1863. Rebell'n Pamph. Vol. 83.

—— Proceed. at N. Y. to establish a Nat. Bank. 1864. Rebell'n Pamph. Vol. 7.

—— Report of a Committee of Directors of the Bank of the U. S. (n. d). Speeches, etc. Vol. 4.

—— "Second (The) War of Revolution."

BANK (The) Question—from the Amer. Quar. Rev., March, 1832. Banking and Currency Pamph. Vol. 3.

BANKERS' Mag. and Statist. Reg. Jan., 1854, to June, 1866, except from July, 1854, to July, 1856. 22 vols. 8vo. N. York, 1854–1866.

BANKING AND CURRENCY.—See APPLETON, N. Remarks on, and Currency.

—— —— BRONSON, I. Letter on Banking.

—— —— BROSS, Wm. History and Influence of Banking. 1852.

—— —— Chronolog. History of the Currency.

—— —— CLEWS, H. Our Monetary Evils, etc. 1872.

BANKING AND CURRENCY, *continued.*

—— —— Considera. on Abolishing Damages on Protested Bills of Exchange. 1829.

—— —— Crisis (The), and the Remedy. 1842.

—— —— DAVIS, R. M. Credit and Banking, their Abuses. 1869.

—— —— Decimal Assoc. Proceed. 1854.

—— —— Examina. of the Currency Question. 1830.

—— —— FELT, J. B. Hist. Acc. of Mass. Currency.

—— —— FIELD, Justice. Legal Tender Act Considered.

—— —— GALLATIN, A. Suggestions on.

—— —— GALLATIN, Jas. Letter to J. R. Doolittle. 1866.

—— —— GOUGE, Wm., on Bank Agency with the U. S.

—— —— GRANT, John P. Essays, etc.

—— —— HAMILTON, A. Letter on Currency and Banking.

—— —— HOMANS, J. S. Bankers Almanac. 1862–64.

—— —— HURD, J. R., on Nat. Bank.

—— —— INGHAM, S. D. Observa. on.

—— —— Letter on—to A. Gallatin.

—— —— LEVERSON, M. R. Uses, etc., of Money.

—— —— MASON, J. Economy, Exchange and Distribution of Wealth. 1847.

—— —— Merchants and Banker's Register. 1857.

—— POTTER, C. N. Treasury Notes a Legal Tender. N. Y. Safety Fund Law.

—— QUINCY, S. M. People's Banks of Germany.

—— SCROPE, G. D. Examina of the Bank Charter System (England), 1833.

—— SMITH, J. Y. Depreciation of the Currency.

—— STANSFIELD, H. Money and the Money Market Explained.

—— SULLIVAN, Geo. Explanation of the System of Circulating Medium, 1839.

—— SINCLAIR, Sir John. The Approaching Crisis.

—— —— Cash Payments.

—— SMITH, Thos. Address to the Hon. Robert Peel. 1819.

—— —— Letter on the New Coinage. 1817.

—— SULLIVAN, J. E. Consid. for Nat. Bank.

—— TATHAM, W. P. Restoration of Standard of Value.

—— TIMOTHY, E. Banks; their Construction, Purposes, etc.

—— Treasury Notes a Legal Tender.

—— WALKER, Amasa. Claims of the Bondholders, 1868.

—— —— Corn, Cotton and Currency, 1871.

—— —— Expansion or Contraction? 1870.

—— —— Money and Mixed Currency.

—— What Banks are Constitutional.

—— WHITNEY, R. M. Memorial, etc., U. S. Bank.

—— WILLSON, Hugh B. Plea for Uncle Sam's Money.

—— Wisconsin Bank Comptroller's Reports. Banking Assoc. and Uniform Currency Bill, 1861–2. Rebellion Pamph. Vol. 93.

BANKRUPTCY—Act to Establish a Uniform System of, through the U. S., 1867. Congr. and Polit. Pamph. Vol. 67.

—— Congress. Report on Establishment of a Uniform System of. 1866. Congr. and Polit. Pamph., vol. 61.

BANKRUPTCY. Considerations upon Commissions of Bankrupts, 1727.
—— FANE, C. Letters to Sir Robt. Peel, 1838.
—— JAMES, E. Suggestion for Law.
—— Proposed Gen. Bankrupt Act, 1861.
—— BANKS, Andrew. Letter to Hist. Soc. of Pa. on the Early History of Juniata County. Pa. Hist. Soc. Coll., Vol. 1.
—— BANKS, Sir Joseph. HUMPHREY, D. Letters on the Sea Serpent.
—— —— Cause of the Blight in Corn. Lond., 1815. 8vo. Pamphleteer., vol. 6.
—— BANKS, N. P. Reconstruction of States; Letter to Hon. J. H. Lane, N. Y., 1865. 8vo. Rebell'n Pamph.,Vol. 23.
—— —— Speech in Cong., May 23, 1854, on the Kansas and Nebr. Bill. Washington, 1854. 8vo. Speeches, Vol. 3.
—— —— Speech in Cong., July 17, 1854, on Army Appropriations. Congr. and Polit. Pamph., Vol. 87.
—— —— Speech in Cong., Dec. 18, 1854, on Amer. Politics. Speeches, Vol. 5.
—— —— Speech in Cong., 1866, on the Representation of the U. S. the Paris Exposition, 1867. 8vo. Cong. and Pol. Pamph., at Vol. 80.
BANKS—The National. The System Unmasked. Greenbacks forever. 1869. 8vo. Banking and Currency Pamph.,Vol. 2.
BANKS, Sir T. C. Baronia Anglica Concentrata; an Acc't of of all Baronies called Baronies in Fee. Ripon Eng. 1844. 2 vols., 4to.
BANNANTINE, Jas. Opinions of His Majesty's Ministers respecting the French Revolution, the War, etc. Lond., 1801. 8vo. Eng. Polit. Pamph.,Vol. 76.
BANNEKER, Benjamin. LATROBE, J. H. B. NORRIS, J. S.
BANNING, Dr. E. P. Common Sense on Chronic Diseases. N. Y., 1846. 12mo. 9th Ed. Med. Pamph,Vol. 6.
—— Banquet to Anson Burlingame by the Citizens of N. Y., June 23, 1868. N. Y. 1868. 8vo. Addresses, etc.,Vol. 18.
BAPTIST CHURCH—Addison Co., Vt., Bapt. Assoc.
—— Amer. and Foreign Bible Soc.
—— Amer. Bapt. Free Miss. Soc.
—— Amer. Bapt. Hist. Soc.
—— Amer. Bapt. Home Miss. Soc.
—— Amer. Bapt. Miss. Conven.
—— Amer. Bapt. Miss. Union.
—— Amer. Bapt. Year Book, 1869–70.
—— ASPLUND, J., Ann. Reg. of 1790.
—— BACKUS, I. Ch. Hist. of N. Eng.
—— Bear Creek Assoc.
—— BENEDICT, D. Fifty Years among Baptists.
—— Berkshire, Mass., Bapt. Assoc.
—— Dane Bapt. Assoc., Wis.
—— Dover Bapt. Assoc.
—— DENNISON, Rev. F. Notes on the Baptists.
—— EDWARDS, Rev. M. Materials for Hist. of the Ch. in R. I.

BAPTIST CHURCH. HAYNES, D. C. Bapt. Denom.
—— Ill. Bapt. Gen. Assoc.
—— Ind. Bapt. Gen. Assoc.
—— JACKSON, Rev. H. Address at 215th Annivers. of Ch. in America.
—— —— Churches in R. I.
—— —— Hist. Disc. 1854.
—— La Crosse Valley, Wis., Bapt. Assoc.
—— La Fayette Bapt. Assoc., Wis.
—— Lake Shore Bapt. Assoc., Wis.
—— LEHMANN, Rev. G. W. History of, in Germany.
—— McCOY, I. History of Bapt. Indian Missions. Marquette, Wis., Bapt. Assoc.
—— Md. Bapt. Union Assoc.
—— Maumee Bapt. Assoc.
—— Minn. Bapt. Assoc.
—— Milwaukee Bapt. Assoc.
—— N. Y. Bapt. Educa. Soc.
—— Racine, Wis., Bapt. Assoc.
—— Rensselaerville, N. Y., Bapt. Assoc.
—— Rock River Bapt. Assoc.
—— Stephentown, N. Y., Bapt. Assoc.
—— TAYLOR, J. B. Va. Bapt. Ministers, 1838.
—— Tippecanoe Bapt. Assoc.
—— Va. Gen. Assoc, 1859.
—— Va. (Southern) Bapt. Conven, 1846.
—— Walworth, Wis., Bapt. Assoc.
—— Warren, R. I., Assoc.
—— WAYLAND, F. Miss. Organizations of.
—— Wayne Bapt. Assoc.
—— Wis. Bapt. Educa. Soc.
—— Wis. Bapt. Ministerial Union.
—— Wis. Bapt. State Conventions.
—— Wis. River Bapt. Assoc.
—— WRIGHT, S. History of Shaftsbury Assoc.
—— Gen Conven. for Foreign Miss. Reports for 1825, '30, '31, '32, '34, '38, '39, '42, '43, '45. Boston, 1826–46. 8vo.
—— Amer. Bapt. Miss. Union.
BARABOO, Wis.,—See CANFIELD, Wm. H.
—— Independent and Republican Newspapers, 1867–69.
—— Republic, Newspaper, May 1855 to Dec. 1859. Folio.
—— Same, May 1860 to Dec. 1866. Folio.
—— Same, May 1870 to Dec. 1872. Folio.
BARBARITIES, of the Enemy. Documents accompanying the Report of Comm. of House of Repr. Lexington, Mass., 1814. 12mo.
——BARBAROUX, C. O. Le Histoire des Etats—Unis de Amerique. Boston, 1832. 12mo.
BARBARY.—See RUSSELL, M. History of.
—— SUMNER, C. White Slavery in.
BARBEIRE, Jas. Scraps from the Prison Table at Camp Chase and Johnson's Island. Doyleston, Pa., 1868. 8vo.

BARBER, E. H. Claims of Sir Philip Francis to the Authorship of Junius disproved; with Enquiry into the Claim of Chas. Lloyd, Esq. Lond., 1828. 12mo.

BARBER, G. D. Suggestions on Ancient Britons. Lond., 1854. 8vo.

BARBER, John W. European Hist. Collections; comprising England, Scotland, Holland, etc. N. Haven, 1855. 8vo.

—— Hist. Collection of Mass. Worcester, 1841. 8vo.

—— Do. of N. Jersey. N. Y., 1854. 8vo.

—— Historical, Poetical and Pictorial American Scenes. N. Haven, 1851. 12mo.

——History and Antiquities of N. E., N. Y., N. J. and Penn. 3rd Ed. Hartford, 1846. 8vo.

—— Conn. Hist.Collections; relating to the History and Antiquities of every Town in Conn. N. Haven. (n. d.) 8vo.

—— History and Antiquities of N. Haven, Conn., to the Present Time. N. Haven, 1831. 12mo.

—— Same by BARBER, J. W., and PUNDERSON, L. S. N. Haven, 1856. 12mo.

—— Incidents in American History. 3d Ed. N. Y., 1847. 12mo.

—— Pictorial History of the State of N.Y. Cooperstown, 1846. 8vo.

——Hist. Collections of the State of N. Y., 1844. 8vo.

BARBOUR, P. P. Speech in Cong., March, 1830, on the Nat. Road Bill. Congr. and Polit. Pamph., vol. 87.

BARCLAY, Anthony. Wilde's Summer Rose; or, the Lament of the Captive. Savannah, 1871. 8vo. Georgia Hist. Soc. Pamph.

BARCLAY, Jas. J. Address at Organization of the Normal School, Phila., Jan. 13, 1848. 8vo. Penn. Misc. Pamph, vol. 3.

—— Address at laying the Corner stone of the House of Refuge, Phila., July 1st, 1848. Phila., 1848. 8vo.

BARCLAY, Robt. Short Account of his Life and Writings. Dublin, 1834. 12mo. Eng. Religious Pamph., vol. 46.

BARD, Saml. Letter to President Grant on the Situation in Georgia and the South, 1870. Congr. and Polit. Pamph., vol. 129.

—— Discourse before the Coll. of Physicians and Surgeons of the State of N. Y., Apr. 6, 1819. N.Y., 1819. 8vo. Med. Pamph. Vol. 31.

BARD, Saml. Letter to Prest. Grant on the Situation in Ga. and the South, 1870. Congress. Pamph. Vol. 129.

BARD, Wm. Letter on Life Insurance. N. Y., 1832. 12mo. Insurance Pamph., Vol. 1.

BARDEN, Rev. Stillman. See HANAFORD, Mrs. P. A. Sketch of.

BARDS and Druids of Britain. See NASH, D. W. Taliesin; Early Welsh Bards.

BARKER, Edmund H. Letter to Rev. T. S. Hughes on his Address in the Cause of the Greeks. Lond., 1822. 2d Ed. Pamph., Vol. 21.

BARKER, Genealogy. See EDES, H. H. Memorial of Josiah Barker.

BARKER, George P. See BRYANT, G. J. Life of.

BARKER, H. Matlock and its Environs. Lond., 1828. 12mo. 5th Ed. Guide Books, Vol. 6.

BARKER, Jacob. Incidents in the Life of J. Barker of N. Orleans, from 1800 to 1855.

BARKER, Col. Joseph. See HILDRETH, S. P. Early Ohio Settlers.

BARKER, Josiah. See EDES, H. H. Memorial of.

BARLOW, J. Connection between Physiology and Intellectual Science. Phila., 1846. 12mo. Scientific Pamph., Vol. 4.

—— Vision of Columbus. A Poem. Lond., 1787. 12mo.

BARLOW, T. Worthington. Sketch of the History of the Church at Holmes Chapel, Cheshire. Manchester, 1853, 8vo.

BARNARD, A. P. J. Letter to the President of the U. S., by a Refugee. N. Y., 1863. 8vo. Rebellion Pamph.,Vol. 65.

BARNARD, Daniel D. Address before Literary Societies of Rutgers Coll., July 18, 1837. 8vo. Addresses, Vols. 7 and 16.

—— Lecture on the Character and Services of Jas. Madison, at Albany, Feb. 28, 1837. Albany, 1837. 8vo. Addresses,Vols. 7 and 14.

—— Address before Young Men's Association. Albany, Jan. 7, 1834. 8vo. Addresses,Vols. 7 and 8.

—— Disc. on the Life of Gen. Stephen VanRensselaer, 1839. 8vo. Sermons, etc.,Vol. 10.

—— Disc. on the Life of Ambrose Spencer at Albany, Jan. 5, 1849. Addresses, Vol. 7.

—— Oration at Albany, July 4, 1835. 8vo. Addresses, Vol. 3.

—— Speech in Cong., Apr. 28, 1842, on the Election of Representatives. Washington, 1842. 8vo. Congr. and Polit. Pamph., Vol. 24.

—— Speeches in Cong.,July 1 and 6, 1842,on the Tariff Bill. Washington, 1842. 8vo. Congr. and Polit. Pamph., Vol. 24.

BARNARD, F. A. P. Letter to the Board of Trustees of the University of Mississipi. Oxford, 1858. 8vo. Miss. Pamph.,Vol. 1.

—— Letters on College Government. N. Y., 1855. 8vo. Educa. Pamph., Vol. 7.

—— Report on Collegiate Educa., to the University of Alabama. N. Y., 1854. 8vo. Educa. Pamph., Vol. 7.

—— On the Pendulum; with a Description of an Electric Clock. N. Y., 1859. 8vo. Scientific Pamph. Vol. 27.

—— Oration at Tuscaloosa, Ala., July 4, 1851. Tuscaloosa, 1851. 8vo. Addresses, Vol. 27.

BARNARD, Henry. Disc. on the Life and Character of Rev. Thos. H. Gallaudet, LL. D. Hartford, 1852. 8vo.

—— Legal Provision respecting Children in Factories, etc. Hart ford, 1842. 8vo. Conn. Misc. Pamph. Vol. 1.

—— Memoir of. From the Mass. Teacher, 1858. Biograph. Pamph. Vol. 11.

—— National Educa. in Europe; Account of the Organization, etc., of Public Schools in the Principal States. 2d Ed. N. Y., 1854. 8vo.

—— Normal Schools in U. S. and British Provinces. Hartford, 1851. 8vo. Educa. Pamph. Vol. 4.

—— School Architecture; or, Contributions to the Improvement of School Houses in the U. S. 6th Ed. Cincin., 1854. 8vo. Also, 2d Ed. Lond., 1854. 8vo.

BARNARD, J. G. Eulogy on the late Jos. G. Totten, Maj. Gen., &c. Smithsonian Report, 1865.

BARNARD, J. G., *continued.*
—— Dangers and Defences of N. Y. N. Y., 1859. 8vo. N. Y. City, Misc. Pamph. Vol. 3.
—— The Peninsular Campaign and its Antecedents, as Developed by Gen. McClellan's Report. N. Y., 1864. 12mo. Rebell'n Pamph. Vols. 13, 21, 52.
—— The Isthmus of Tehauntepec. Maps. N. Y., 1852. 2 vols. 8vo.
BARNES, Albert. Oration on the Progress and Tendency of Science, at N. Haven, Aug. 18, 1840. Phila., 1840. 8vo. Yale Coll. Pamph.
BARNES, Alfred. Inquiry into the Scriptural Views of Slavery. Phila., 1857. 12mo.
BARNES, D. M. The Metropolitan Police; their Services during the Draft Riots in N. Y., 1863. Rebell'n Pamph. Vol. 69.
BARNES, Isaac O. Address at Bedford, N. H., on 100th Anniversary of the Town, May 19, 1850. Boston, 1850. 8vo. N. H. Hist. Discourses. Vol. 1.
BARNES, Dr. Melvin. Short Biography of Col. Eben. Allen, of the N. A. Grants and its Rangers in 1777, etc. (n.p.) 1851. 8vo.
—— Reprint of same, with Biographies of Lt. Saml. Allen and Dr. Jacob Roebeck. Plattsburg, 1852. 8vo. Rev. War Pamph. Vol. 5.
BARNES, S. W. Remarks in the Wis. Senate, Feb. 19, 1857, on the Bill to Amend the Charter of the Watertown and Madison R. R. Wis. Misc. Pamph. Vol. 1.
BARNES, Wm. Settlement and Early History of Albany; Essay before the Y. M. Assoc., Dec. 26, 1850. Albany, 1851. 8vo. N. York Hist. Discourses. Vol. 2. See also Addresses. Vol. 8.
—— Grammar and Glossary of Dorset Dialect, with the History, etc., of Southwestern English. Berlin, 1863.
—— Notes on Ancient Britain and the Britons. Lond., 1853. 8vo.
—— Philolog. Grammar, grounded on the English, and formed from a comparison of more than Sixty Languages. London, 1854. 8vo.
—— Poems of Rural Life in the Dorset Dialect. 2d and 3d Collections. Lond., 1863, 1869. 2 vols. 12mo.
—— Same. Lond., 1866. 12mo.
—— Se Gefylsta (the Helper), an Anglo-Saxon Delectus. 2d Ed. Lond., 1866. 8vo.
—— Tiw: a View of Roots and Stems of the English as a Teutonic Language. Lond., 1862. 12mo.
BARNES, William H. History of the 39th Congress, U. S. N. Y., 1868. 8vo.
—— The Body Politic. Cincin., 1866. 12mo.
BARNEY, Joshua. Survey of a Route from St. Louis to the Big Bend of the Red River. 1852. War Department Misc. Reports.
BARNEY, Com. J. See BARNEY, Mary.

BARNEY, Mary. Biograph. Memoir of Com. Joshua Barney. Boston, 1832. 8vo.

—— Letter to Pres't Jackson in Vindica. of her Husband. 1829. 8vo. Congr. and Polit. Pamph. Vol. 58.

BARNSTABLE Co., Mass. Description of the Eastern Coast of Mass. Hist. Soc. Coll. Vol. 8. 1st Series.

—— See FREEMAN, Fred. Annals of.

—— PRATT, E. Hist. of Towns.

BARNSTABLE, Mass. Cape Cod Centen. Celebration at Barnstable, Sept. 3, 1839. Barnstable, 1840. 8vo. Mass. Hist. Discourses, etc. Vol. 4.

—— See MELLEN, Rev. Mr. Topog. Descr. of.

—— PALFREY, J. G. Hist. Address. 1839.

BARNWELL, Robt. G. Sketch of the Life and Times of John De-Witt, Grand Pensioner. N. Y., 1856. 12mo.

BARNUM, E. M. Memoirs of Clarksfield, Ohio. Fire Lands Pioneer. Vol. 1.

BARONIA Anglica Concentrata. See BANKS, T. C.

BARRANDT, A. Sketch of Ancient Earthworks on the Upper Missouri. Smithsonian Report. 1870.

BARRE, Lt. Col. Isaac. See BRITTON, J.

BARRE, Mass. See THOMPSON, Jas. '50th Annivers. Disc. 1854.

BARRE, W. L. Life and Pub. Services of Millard Fillmore. Buffalo, 1856. 12mo.

BARRETT, Jas. Memorial Address on the Hon. Chas. Marsh, before Vt. Hist. Soc., Oct. 11, 1870. Proceedings Soc., 1870.

—— Memorial Address on Hon. Jacob Collamer, before the Vt. Hist. Soc., Oct. 20, 1868. Rutland, 1868. 8vo. Vt. Hist. Soc. Addresses. Vol. 1. Another Copy Addresses and Orations. Vol. 21.

BARRETT, Joseph H. Life of Abraham Lincoln, with his Messages, Proclamations, etc. Cincin., 1865. 8vo.

—— The Soldier Bird: a History of "Old Abe," the Live War Eagle of the 8th Wis. Reg't. Chicago, 1865, p. 61.

BARRET, Walter, pseud. The Old Merchants of N. Y. City. N. Y., 1863. 12mo. Another Ed. N. Y, 1870. 3 vols. 12mo.

BARRIER Treaty. Remarks on the Treaty between Her Majesty and the States-General, with the Treaty, 1712. Dublin, 1741. Sm. 4to. Eng. Polit. Pamph. Vol. 8.

BARRINGER, Daniel M. Speech in Cong., July 1, 1846, on the Tariff. Washington, 1846. 8vo. Speeches. Vol. 1.

BARRINGTON, Daines. Probability of reaching the North Pole discussed: Two Papers. Lond., 1775. 4to. Hist. Pamph. Vol. 21.

BARRINGTON, Sir Jonah. Personal Sketches of his own Times. N. Y., 1858. 12mo.

BARRON, Henry D. Biograph. Sketch of. Wis. Mis. Pam. Vol. 4.

BARRON, Com. Jas. Brief Account of. Va. Hist. Reg. Vol. 4.

—— See DECATUR, Com. Stephen. Corres. with.

—— Proceed. of Gen. Court Martial on the Trial of Com. Barron, Capt. Chas. Gordon, Wm. Hook, and Capt. John Hall. Washington, 1822.

BARROW, John. Memoir of the Life of Peter the Great. Harper's Fam. Lib. N. Y., 1858. 18mo.

—— Summer Tours in Central Europe, 1855–6. Part 3. Lond., 1857. 8vo. Guide Books. Vol. 26.

—— Case of Queen's College, Oxford; in a Letter to Hon. W. E. Gladstone. Oxford, 1854. 8vo. Strangford Pamph. Vol. 66.

BARROW, John, Jr. Visit to Iceland in 1834. Waldie's Circulating Library. Vol. 7.

BARROWS, Wm. Disc. at Reading, Mass., Dec. 28, 1862, on the War and Slavery. Rebell'n Pamph. Vol. 40.

BARRY, Ex-Governor. Letter on the Principles of the Repub. Party. 1864. Broadside. Rebell'n Pamph. Vol. 52.

BARRY, A. Constantine. Address before State Agricult. Soc. of Wis., Oct. 1856. Transactions, 1856.

BARRY, John Stetson. Genealog. and Biograph. Sketch of the Name and Family of Stetson, 1634–1847. Boston, 1847. 8vo. Another Copy, Genealog. Pamph. Vol. 10.

—— Hist. Sketch of Hanover, Mass., with Genealogies. Boston, 1853. 8vo.

—— History of Mass. Colonial Period. Boston, 1855. 8vo.

—— Same. Commonwealth Period. Boston, 1857. 8vo.

BARRY, William. History of Framingham, Mass., from 1640 to the Present, with Appendix and Genealog. Register. Boston, 1847. 8vo.

BARRY, W. T. See Obit. Address at Frankfort, Ky., 1854.

BARSTOW, George. History of N. H. from 1614, to the Passage of the Toleration Act, in 1819. 2d Ed. Boston, 1853. 8vo.

BARSTOW, John. See CASWELL, Alexis. Memoir of.

BARTHELEMI, Abbe. Travels of Anacharsis the Younger, in Greece, in the 4th Century before the Christian Era. Lond., 1796. 4 vols. 8vo.

BARTHOLOW, Dr. Robt. Case of Davis B. Lawler. Amnesia of Written Language, etc. From Lancet and Observer, Nov., 1869. 8vo. Med. Pamph. Vol. 8.

BARTLETT, David W. Life of Gen. Frank Pierce. Auburn, 1852. 12mo. Biograph. Pamph. Vol. 13.

—— Life of Lady Jane Grey. N. Y., 1858. 12mo.

—— Modern Agitators; or Pen Portraits of Living Amer. Reformers. N. Y., 1856. 12mo.

—— Life of Joan of Arc, the Maid of Orleans. N. Y., 1853. 12mo.

—— Paris, with Pen and Pencil; its People, Literature, Life and Business. N. Y., 1858. 12mo.

—— What I saw in London; or Men and Things in the Great Metropolis. Auburn, 1852. 12mo.

BARTLETT Elisha, M. D. Lecture before Amer. Physiolog. Soc'y, Jan. 30, 1838. Boston. (n. d.) 12mo. Med. Pamph. Vol. 31.

BARTLETT, John R. Bibliography of R. Island. Providence, 1864. 8vo.

BARTLETT, John R. Dictionary of Americanisms, a Glossary of Words and Phrases peculiar to the U. S. 3d Ed. Boston, 1860. 8vo.

—— Personal Narrative of Explorations in Texas, N. Mexico, etc. N. Y., 1854. 2 vols. 8vo.

—— Progress of Ethnology; Account of Archæolog. Philolog. and Geograph. Researches in Various Parts of the Globe. N. Y., 1847. 8vo. 2d Ed.

—— Same. Archæolog. Pamph. Vol. 1.

—— Report on the Boundary Line between the U. S. and Mexico. 1853. 8vo. Washington. Sec. of Interior Rep'ts.

BARTLETT, Josiah. Hist. Sketch of Charlestown, Co. of Middlesex, Mass. Mass. Hist. Soc. Coll. Vol. 2. 2d Series.

—— Historical Sketch of Med. Science in Mass., to 1813. Mass. Hist. Soc. Coll. Vol. 1. 2d Series.

BARTLETT, J. M. On Propelling Vessels by Windmill Sails. London, 1819. 8vo. Pamphleteer. Vol. 14.

BARTLETT, Richard. Remarks and Documents relating to the Preservation and Keeping of the Public Archives. N. H., Hist. Soc. Coll. Vol. 5.

BARTLETT, W. H. Amer. Scenery from Drawings. Lond., 1852. 2 vols. 4to.

BARTLETT, William H. C. Account of the Observatory of the U. S. Military Academy, with Observa. of the Comet of 1843. Amer. Philos. Soc. Trans. U. S. Vol. 9.

BARTLETT, Rev. Wm. S. Contribution to the History of Bath, Me. Maine Hist. Soc. Coll. Vol. 3.

—— Frontier Missionary; a Life of Rev. Jacob Bailey. Boston, 1853.

BARTOL, C. A. Disc. in Memory of Rev. Thos. Starr King, at Boston, Mar. 6, 1864. Boston, 1864. 8vo. Sermons. Vol. 32.

—— Tribute to Brig. Gen. Chas. R. Lowell, Jr., at Boston, Oct. 30, 1864. Boston, 1864. 8vo. Rebell'n Pamph. Vol. 8.

—— Tribute to Maj. Sidney Willard, at Boston, Dec. 21, 1862. Boston, 1862. 8vo. Addresses. Vol. 26.
Rebell'n Pamph. Vol. 64.

BARTON, Dr. Benj. S. Observations on Articles taken from an Old Indian Grave at Cincinnati. Amer. Philos. Soc. Trans. Vol. 4.

—— Observations on some parts of Nat. History, with an Acct. of Ancient Remains found in N. America. Part 1. Lond., 1787. 8vo. Scientific Pamph. Vol. 27.

BARTON, David. Speech in U. S. Senate, Feb. 9, 1830, on Mr. Foote's Resolution on the Sale of the Public Lands. Congr. and Polit. Pamph. Vol. 139.

BARTON, Jas. L. Address before Y. M. Assoc. of Buffalo, Feb. 16, 1848, on Early Reminiscences of Western N. York, etc. Buffalo, 1848. 8vo. N. York Hist. Discourses. Vol. 2.

—— Commerce of the Lakes and Erie Canal. Buffalo, 1847 and 1851. 8vo. N. York Misc. Pamph. Vol. 6.

—— Letter to the Hon. Robert McClelland. Buffalo, 1846. 8vo. Addresses, etc. Vol. 15.

BARTON, Wm. Dissertation on the Freedom of Navigation and Maritime Commerce. Phila., 1802. 8vo.
—— Memoirs of the Life of David Rittenhouse, LL. D., F. R. S., with Appendix containing sundry Philosoph. Papers. Phila., 1813. 8vo.
BARTON, Gen. William. See WILLIAMS, Mrs. C. R. Biography of.
BARTON, Lieut. Wm. Journal kept during Gen. Sullivan's Expedition against the Indians in 1779. N. J. Hist. Soc. Proceed. Vol. 2.
BARTON, W. S. Epitaphs from Worcester, Mass., Cemetery. Worcester, 1848. 8vo.
BARTRAM, John. DARLINGTON, W. Memorials of.
—— Observations made in his Travels from Penn. to Onondaga, etc., with P. KALM's Account of the Cataract of Niagara. London, 1751. 12mo.
BARTRAM, Wm. Travels through N. and S. Carolina, Georgia, and E. and W. Florida. Lond., 1792. 8vo.
BASCOM FAMILY GENEALOGY.—See HARRIS, E. D.
BASCOME, Dr. Edw. Cholera; its Nature, Treatment, etc. Lond., 1853. 8vo. Med. Pamph. Vol. 27.
BASNAGE, J. Continuation of Josephus' History, in Dutch. Amsterdam, 1726. 2 vols. Folio.
BASSETT, Francis. Reminiscences of an Octogenarian. N. Eng. Hist. and Gen. Reg. Vol. 25.
BASSETT, Geo. W. Disc. on the Wickedness and Folly of the Present War, at Ottawa, Ill., Aug. 11, 1861. Rebell'n Pamph. Vol. 41.
—— A Northern Plea for the Right of Secession, 1861. Rebell'n Pamph. Vol. 89.
BAST, A. P. London: a Poem. London, 1818. 8 vo. Eng. Misc. Pamph. Vol. 3.
BASTICK, Wm. Exposure of the Adulteration of the Preparations of the Pharmacopœia. Lond., 1845. 8vo. Med. Pamph. Vol. 29. .
BASTILE (The). See DE LATUDE, H. M.
—— MARSHALL, J. A. Amer. Bastile.
—— in America; or Democratic Absolutism. Lond., 1861. 8vo. Rebell'n Pamph. Vol. 73.
BASTILES (The) of the North, by a Member of Md. Legislature. 1863. Rebell'n Pamph. Vol. 73.
BATCHELLER, W. Descriptive Picture of Dover; or the Visitor's New Guide. Dover, Eng., 1837. 12mo. Guide Books. Vol. 20.
—— Same. 1838. Guide Books. Vol. 8.
BATEMAN, Thos. Vestiges of the Antiquities of Derbyshire; and the Sepulchral Usages of the Inhabitants. Lond., 1848. 8vo.
BATES, Edward. What Constitutes Citizenship? Hartford, 1863. 12mo. Rebell'n Pamph. Vol. 24.
BATES, Isaac C. Oration at Northampton, July 4, 1805. Northampton, 1805. 8vo. Addresses. Vol. 29.
—— Oration at Northampton, 1812, in Commem. of the Nativity of Washington. Northampton, 1812. 8vo. Misc. Tracts, vol. 1.

BATES, Rev. Joshua. Annivers. Disc. at Dudley, Mass., Mar. 20, 1853, with Topograph. and Hist. Notices. Boston, 1853. 8vo. Mass. Hist. Discourses. Vol. 8.

—— See Boston, Mass. Memorial of.

—— Tribute of Boston Merchants to.

BATES, Thos. Letter to the Bishop of Durham, on the Sale of Ridley Hall Estate, Northumberland. Newcastle-upon-Tyne, 1830. 8vo. Eng. Misc. Pamph. Vol. 36.

BATH, Eng. See WARNER, Rev. R. Guide Book, 1811.

BATH and West of England Soc. for Promotion of Agriculture. Journ. for 1867. Lond. 8vo. Agr. Pamph. Vol 7.

BATH, Me. See BARTLET, Rev. W. S. Hist. of.

—— SEWALL, J. Hist. of.

—— SUTHERLAND, D. Geograph. Sketch of.

BATH, N. H. See SUTHERLAND, Rev. D. Hist. Address, 1854.

BATHURST, H. Remonstrance addressed to the Duke of Norfolk, on behalf of Himself and his Father. Lond., 1841. 8vo. Strangford Pamph. Vol. 32.

BATHURST, Rev. Ralph. See WARTON, Thos. Life and Remains.

BATT, John Thos., M. D. Oratio Anniversaria Harveiana; in Theatro Collegii Regalis Medicorum Londinensium, habita. 1754. Lond. 1755. 4to. Latin Pamph. Vol. 5.

BATTIE, Wm. Oratio Anniversaria in Theatro Collegii Regalis Medicorum Londinensium ex Harvaei Instituto habita Oct. 18, 1746. Lond., 1746. 4to. Latin Pamph. Vol. 5.

BATTEL ABBEY. See LOWER, M. A. Chronicle of.

—— See THORPE, Thos. Charters, Royal Grants, etc.

BATTLE. The Field of Shiloh—Account of 1862. Rebell'n Pamph. Vol. 53.

—— Fields of the South from Bull's Run to Petersburg. N. Y., 1864. 8vo.

—— of Lake Erie Monument Assoc. Account of Organization and Proceedings on 45th Annivers., Sept. 10, 1858. Sandusky, 1858. 8vo. Ohio Hist. Discourses, etc. Vol. 1.

—— Roll. See PERCE, E.

BATTLES of U. States. See DAWSON, H. B.

BATTY, Lt. Col. Family Tour through South Holland, up the Rhine, and across the Netherlands. 1832? Waldie's Circulating Library. Vol. 1.

BAUGHER, H. L. Disc. to Graduating Class of Penn. Coll., 1861. Gettysburg, 1861. 8vo, Rebell'n Pamph. Vol. 64.

BAURY, Rev. Alfred L. 25th Annivers. Disc. in St. Mary's Ch., Newton Lower Falls, Mass., 1847. Boston, 1847. 8vo. Mass. Hist. Discourses. Vol. 19.

BAXTER, D. W. C. School of the Soldier—in German. Phila., 1861. 12mo. Rebell'n Pamph. Vol. 103.

—— Volunteers' Manual. N. Y., 1863. 12mo.

BAXTER, Rev. Jos. Journal of Visits to the Indians on the Kennebec River, 1717. With Notes by Rev. E. Nason. Boston, 1867. 8vo. Indian Pamph. Vol. 5.

BAXTER, R. D. Results of Railway Extension—read before Statist. Soc. of Lond., 1866. Scientific Pamph. Vol. 16.

BAY STATE MILLS. Report of Investigating Committee to the Stockholders, Feb. 5, 1858. Boston, 1858. 8vo. Mass. Misc. Pamph. Vol. 4.

BAYARD, Jas. A. Speech in U. S. Senate, Mar. 20, 1861, on the Condition of the Country. Rebell'n Pamph. Vol. 35.

—— Speech in U. S. Senate, July 19, 1861, on Executive Usurpation. Rebell'n Pamph. Vol. 34.

—— Speech in Cong., Apr. 3, 1863, on Slavery in Dist. of Columbia. Rebell'n Pamph. Vol. 61.

—— Two Speeches in U. S. Senate, Feb, 28 and March 3, 1863, on the Conscription Bill and Habeas Corpus. Baltimore, 1863. 8vo. Rebell'n Pamph. Vol. 30.

—— Speech in U. S. Senate, Jan. 19, 1864, on the Validity of the Test Oath. Phila., 1864. Rebell'n Pamph. Vol. 30.

BAYARD, N. & LODOWICK, C. Journ. of the Late Actions of the French at Canada.—Reprint. N. Y., 1868. 4to.

BAYEN, Pierre. Opuscules Chimiques. Paris. 2 vols. 8vo.

BAYFIELD, Capt. H. W. Outlines of Geology of Lake Superior. Quebec. Lit. and Hist. Soc. Trans. Vol. 1.

BAYFIELD Press. 1870–2. 1 Vol. Ashland and Bayfield Bound Together.

BAYLE, Bishop. Kyng Johan. See Camden Soc. Publications.

BAYLEY, Bishop J. R. Address before the N. J. Catholic Total Abstinence Union, Nov. 28, 1871. N. Y. 8vo. Tem. Pam. Vol. 5.

—— Memoirs of Rt. Rev. Simon William Gabriel Brute, D. D., First Bishop of Vincennes. N. Y., 1861. 12mo.

—— Sketch of the History of the Catholic Ch. on the Island of N. Y. N. Y., 1853. 12mo.

BAYLEY, Thos. Butterworth. Biograph. Memoirs of. Manchester, Eng., 1802. Sm. 4to. Biograph. Pamph. Vol. 2.

BAYLIES, Francis. Hist. Memoir of Colony of New Plymouth, with Notes by S. G. Drake. N. Y., 1866. 2 vols. 8vo.

—— Remarks on the Life and Character of Gen. David Cobb, at the Taunton Lyceum, July 2, 1830. N. Eng. Hist. and Gen. Reg. Vol. 18. See also Biograph. Pamph. Vol. 7.

BAYLY, Thomas H. Speech in Cong., June 30, 1846, on the Tariff Bill. Washington. 1846. 8vo. Speeches. Vol. 1.

—— Speech in Congress, Mar. 11, 1846, on the Harbor Bill. Washington, 1846. 8vo. Speeches. Vol. 1.

—— Speech in Cong., May 25, 1852, on the Fugitive Slave Bill. Congr. and Polit. Pamph. Vol 84.

—— Speech in Congress, June 20, 1854. on the Mexican Treaty. Washington, 1854. 8vo. Speeches. Vol. 2.

—— Speech in Congress, Mar. 8, 1854, on the Public Lands. Washington, 1854. 8vo. Speeches. Vol. 2.

BAYNE, Peter. Essays in Biography and Criticism. 2d Series. Boston, 1858. 12mo.

BAYNES, Alderman. The Cotton Trade. Two Lectures Blackburn, 1857. 8vo. Eng. Polit. Pamph. Vol. 54.

BAYNES, Rev. J. W. Sermon at St. Catherines, C. W., at the Funeral of Mrs. Hester Ann Phelps. St. Catherines, 1849. 8vo. Sermons. Vol. 22.

BAZIN, C. Notice sur un Insecte qui a Cause les plus Grands Ravages dans nos Dernieres Recolte de ble sur pied. Paris, 1856. 8vo.

BEACH, Lewis. A Word or Two about the War. 1862. Rebell'n Pamph. Vol. 20.

BEAL, Jas. Free Trade in Land: Influence of the Laws of Succession, and the System of Entail. Lond., 1855. 8vo. Eng. Polit. Pamph. Vol. 53.

BEALE. C. L. Speech in Cong., May 6, 1852, on the Homestead Bill. Congress. Pamph. Vol. 83.

BEAMAN, Rev. C. C. Sketch of the Branch, or Howard St. Church, Salem. Essex Institute Coll. Vol. 3.

BEAMAN, Chas. C., Jr. The National and Private "Alabama Claims." and their "Final and Amicable Settlement." Washington, 1871. 8vo.

BEAMAN, E. A. The Law of Nature, the Law of Development, (with reference to Female Education). Boston, 1854. 8vo. Educa. Pamph. Vol. 3.

BEAMISH, N. L. Discovery of America by the Northmen in the 10th Century, with Notices of Early Settlements of the Irish in the West. Lond., 1841. 8vo.

BEAR Creek Assoc. of United Baptists. Minutes of 2d and 4th Ann. Meetings, 1855–57. Mo. Pamph. Vol. 2.

BEARDMORE, Nathan'l. Suggestions for a New Street through London, with an Aqueduct, Sewer, etc. London, 1850. 8vo. Eng. Misc. Pamph. Vol. 7.

BEARDSLEE, Geo. W. On the Rejection of the Application for a Re-issue of Letters Patent to Barnabas Langdon. Law Pamphlets. Vol. 2.

BEARDSLEY, Rev. E. E. Hist. Address on the 25th Ann. Commencement of Trinity Coll., Hartford, July 30, 1851. Hartford, 1851. 8vo. Conn. Hist. Discourses. Vol. 1.

—— History of P. Episcopal Church of Conn., to the Death of Bishop Seabury. N. Y., 1869. 2 vols. 8vo.

BEARDSLEY, L. Reminiscences of Early Settlement of Otsego Co., N. York. N. Y., 1852. 8vo.

BEARSE GENEALOGY.—See NEWCOMB, J. B.

BEATSON, R. Naval and Military Memoirs of G. Britain, 1727 to 1783. Lond., 1783. 6 vols. 8vo.

BEAUCHAMP, Lord. Letter to the Belfast First Company of Volunteers. Belfast, 1782. 8vo. Eng. Polit. Pamph. Vol. 73.

BEATTIE, James. Dissertations, Moral and Critical. Phila., 1809. 3 vols. 18mo.

—— Elements of Moral Science. Phila., 1809. 3 vols. 18mo.

—— Essays on Truth, Poety, Music, and Classical Learning. Phila., 1809. 3 vols. 18mo.

BEATTY, Adam. Essays on Practical Agriculture. Marysville, Ky., 1844. 12mo.

BEAUHARNAIS, Hortense. Ex-Queen of Holland. Memoirs of. Translated from the French. Waldie's Cir'ng Lib. Vol. 1.

BEAUJOUR, Felix De. Sketch of the U. S. at the Commencement of the 19th Century, 1800–1810. Lond., 1814. 8vo.

BEAUMARCHAIS and his Times. See DE LOMENIE, L.

BEAUMONT, ELI de. Memoir of Legendre. Smithsonian Report. 1867.

BEAUMONT, J. T. B. Essay on Criminal Jurisprudence, with the Draft of a new Penal Code. Lond., 1821. 8vo. Pamphleteer. Vol. 18.

—— Essay on Provident or Parish Banks for Savings. Lond., 1816. 8vo. Pamphleteer. Vol. 7.

BEAUMONT, G. de., and TOCQUEVILLE, A. de. Penitentiary System in the U. S., and its Application in France, with Notes by F. LIEBER. Phila., 1833. 8vo.

BEAUMONT, Jas. Letter to the Lord High Chancellor, occasioned by his Allusions to the "Independence" and "Disinterestedness" of Attornies and Solicitors. Lond., 1833. 8vo. Eng. Polit. Pamph. Vol. 40.

BEAUMONT, John. Treatise on Spirits, Apparitions and Witchcraft. Lond., 1705. 8vo.

BEAUMONT, L. Elie de. Observations Geologiques; sur les differentes Formations daus de Systeme des Vosges. Paris, 1828. 8vo.

BEAVER Dam, Wis.—Argus, Newspaper. 1860–63. 1867–70. Folio.

—— See Fox Lake, Wis.

—— Republican and Citizen, Newspaper. 1860–63. Folio.

—— Dodge County Citizen, Newspaper. May, 1856, to Dec., 1859. Folio.

—— Republican and Sentinel, Newspaper. Mar., 1854, to Mar., 1857. Folio.

—— Democrat, Newspaper. April to Dec., 1859. Folio.

—— See Wayland University.

BEICHARD, M. Ferdinand. De la Reform Administrative et Electorale. Paris, 1848. 8vo. Strangford Pamph. Vol. 68.

BECK, Justice. Opinion in Joseph Hollman *et al., vs.* Harry Fulton, on Habeas Corpus. Keokuk, Iowa, 1869. 8vo. Iowa Misc. Pamph. Vol. 1.

BECK'S Guide to Kenilworth Castle. Leamington, Eng. (n. d.) 12mo. Guide Books. Vol. 2.

BECK, Jas. B. Speech in Cong., Jan. 6, 1871, on the Imprisonment of Bliss and Masterman in Paraguay, etc. Congr. and Polit. Pamph. Vol. 129.

—— Speech in Cong., Feb. 18, 1871, on the Claim of Wm. McGarrahan. 8vo. Congr. and Polit. Pamph. Vol. 132.

—— Expenditures of the Gov't. Speech in Cong., June 8, 1872. Chicago, 1872. 8vo. Congr. and Polit. Pamph. Vol. 130.

BECK, Lewis C. Contributions towards the Botany of Illinois and Missouri. 1825. Silliman's Journ. Vols. 10, 11, 14.

—— Gazetteer ot the Illinois and Missouri, with Map Engravings. Albany, 1823. 8vo.

—— THEODORIC R. BECK. See VAN CORTLANDT, Mrs. C. E. Lives of.

BECK, Dr. T. Romeyn. Statistics of the Deaf and Dumb in N. Y. State, the U. States, and in Europe. 1837 (?) 8vo.

BECKER, Abraham. Address at Worcester, N. Y., July 26, 1852, on the Death of Capt. Leslie Chase. Albany. 8vo. Sermons. Vol. 10.

—— Address before the N. Y. Conference Seminary, Charlotteville, N. Y., July 5, 1852. Albany, 1852. 8vo. Addresses. Vol. 27.

BECKET, Andrew. Public Prosperity; Arguments for Raising Six Millions Sterling, etc. Lond., 1813. 8vo. Pamphleteer. Vol. 2.

BECKET, Thomas á. See MILMAN, H. H. Life of.

BECKFORD, Wm. See BRITTAN, J. Fonthill Abbey.

—— Italy; with Sketches of Spain and Portugal. Waldie's Circulating Library. Vol. 4.

—— See RUTTER, J. Descrip. of Fonthill Abbey.

BECKLEY, Hosea. History of Vermont, with Descriptions Physical and Topographical. Brattleboro, 1846. 12mo.

BECKMAN, Johann W. Den. Una Swenska Psalmboker. Stockholm, 1845. 4to. 4 no's.

BECKWITH, George C. Eulogy on Wm. Ladd, late President of the Amer. Peace Society. Boston, 1841. 8vo. Sermons. Vol. 1.

—— Peace Manual; or, War and its Remedies. Boston, 1847. 12mo. Congr. and Polit. Pamph. Vol. 2.

BECKWITH, Leonard and Arthur. See Paris Universal Exposition, 1867.

BECKWOURTH, Jas. P. Life and Adventures of J. P. Beckwourth, Scout, Pioneer, and Chief of Crow Nation of Indians. N.Y., 1858. 12mo.

BECQUEREL, M. Traite de Physique Considerie dans les Rapports avec la Chimie et les Sciences Naturelles. Paris, 1842, 1844. 2 Vols. 8vo.

BEDELL, Gregory T. Sermon at Phila., Jan. 18, 1824, on the Cause of the Greeks. Phila., 1824. 8vo. Sermons. Vol. 24.

BEDFORD, Gunning S., M. D. Lecture before the Med. Depart. of the N. Y. University, Oct. 29, 1847. N. Y., 1847. 8vo. Medical Pamph. Vol. 2.

—— Lecture before Albany Med. Coll., Oct. 1, 1839. 8vo. Addresses. Vol. 7.

—— Valedict. Address before the Med. Class of the N. Y. University, Feb. 28, 1845. N. Y., 1845. 8vo. Med. Pamph. Vol. 2.

BEDFORD, John, Duke of. Correspondence. With an Introduction by Lord John Russell. Lond., 1842. 3 Vols. 8vo.

BEDFORD, Mass. See SHATTUCK, L.

BEDFORD, N. H. See BARNES, I. O. Centen. Address, 1850.

—— FOSTER and WOODBURY. Topogr. and Hist. Sketch of.

—— History of, and Centenn. Annivers. Boston, 1851. 8vo.

BEDLOW, Capt. Wm. His Examina. Relating to the Popish Plot, taken by Sir Francis North. Lond., 1680. Folio. Eng. Polit. Pamph. Vol. 63.

BEECHER, Catharine E. Essay on the Educa. of Female Teachers. N. Y., 1835. 8vo. Educa. Pamph. Vol. 3.

BEECHER, Catharine E. Evils Suffered by Amer. Women and Amer. Children. Addresses. Vol. 12.

BEECHER, Edw. Address at the 8th Annivers. of the Auxiliary Educa. Soc. of Boston, Feb. 10, 1827. Boston, 1827. 8vo. Addresses. Vol. 33.

—— Narrative of Riots at Alton; in connexion with the death of Rev. Elijah P. Lovejoy. Alton, 1838. 12mo.

BEECHER, Rev. Henry Ward. Defence of Kansas. Washington, 1856. 8vo. Congr. and Polit. Pamph. Vol. 93.

—— England and America. Speech at Manchester, Eng., Oct. 9, 1863. Boston, 1863. 12mo. Rebell'n Pamph. Vol. 4.

—— Lectures to Young Men on Various Important Subjects. N. Y., 1857. 12mo.

—— Memoir from Holden's Mag., Sept., 1848. Biog. Pam. Vol. 11.

—— Oration at the Raising of the Old Flag over Fort Sumpter, Apr. 14, 1865. Rebell'n Pamph. Vol. 47.

—— Report of Speeches at Manchester, Glasgow, Edinburgh, Liverpool and London. Manchester, 1864. 8vo. Rebell'n Pamph. Vol. 30.

BEEDE, Rev. Thomas. Topograph. and Hist. Description of Wilton, N. H. Farmer and Moore's N. H. Hist. Collec. Vol. 1.

BEEKE, Rev. H. Observa. on the Produce of the Income Tax. Lond., 1799. 8vo. Eng. Polit Pamph. Vol. 75.

BEEKMAN, Jas. W. Address before N. Y. St. Nicholas Soc., Dec. 4, 1867, on the Founders of N. Y. N. Y., 1870. 8vo.

BEESLEY, Alfred. History of Banbury; including copious Hist. and Antiq. notices of the neighborhood. Lond., 1841. 8vo.

BEESON, Henry W. Speech in Cong., July 9, 1842, on the Tariff. Washington, 1842. 8vo. Congr. and Polit. Pamph. Vol. 25.

BEGGS, Rev. S. R. Pages from the Early History of the West and N. West, with Reference to the History of Methodism. Cincin., 1868. 12mo.

BEGINNING, Progress, and Conclusion of the Late War. Lond., 1770. 4to.

BEHAIM, Martin. See MORRIS, John G.

BEHARRELL, Thomas G. Die Bruderschaldt. Cincin., 1861. 12mo.

BEHNES, Wm. The "Nelson Testimonial." Lond., 1839. 8vo. Eng. Miscell. Pamph. Vol. 30.

BELCHER, Rev. Joseph. Religious Denominations in the U. S.; their History, Doctrine, and Statistics. Phila., 1854. 8vo.

BELCHERTOWN, Mass. See DOOLITTLE, M. Hist. of Cong. Ch.

BELCOURT, Rev. G. A. Department of Hudson Bay. Minn. Hist. Soc. Coll. Vol. 1.

BELDEN, E. P. New York; its Past, Present, and Future. N. Y., 1849. 12mo.

BELDING, Maj. Simeon. Orderly Book, 1779. Ms.

BELFAST, Me. See WHITE, Wm. History of.

BELGIUM. Apercu des Principales Publications Statistique, faites sur la Belgique depuis l'Incorporation de ce Pays. A la France en 1794. Bruxelle. 4to.

—— Catalogue Systematique de la Bibliotheque de la Chambre des Representants. Brussels, 1844. 8vo. Avec Supplemente.

BELGIUM. Commune de Berchem: Rapport par la Commission de Salubrite Publique. Bruxelles, 1850. 8vo.

—— Comptes Rendu, des Recette et Dispenses du Royaume, Pendant l'Annees, 1835, '36, '37, '38, '39, '41, 45, '46, '47, '48, '49. Bruxelles, 1837–52. 11 vols. Folio.

—— Congres des Economistes Reuni a Bruxelles par les Soins de la Association Belge pour la Liberte Commerciale. Session de 1847. Bruxelles, 1847. 8vo.

—— Congres De Hygiene Publique. Session de 1851. Brussels, 1851. 4to.

—— Des Naissances dans la Ville de Bruxelles, Considerees dans leur Rapport avec la Population. Bruxelles, 1843. 4to.

—— See DUMORTIER, B. C. Belgium and the 24 Articles. 1838.

—— Essai sur la Statistique Generale de la Belgique. Brussels, 1844. 4to.

—— Extrait du Rapport Decennal sur la Situation Administrative du Royaume, 1841–50. Caltes. Bruxelles, 1850. 4to.

—— See FROMENT, Chas. Etudes sur la Revolution Belge. 1834.

—— MEURSIUS, J. Historica Danica and Belgica.

—— Inspection des Chemins Vincinaux. Flandre Occidentale—Flandre Orientale. Bruxelles, 1848. 8vo.

—— Institutions de Bien faisance de la Belgique: Resume Statistique. Bruxelles, 1852. 4to.

—— Memoir a Propos du projet de Loi sur le enseignement Secondaire par une Reunion de Delegues de Societies Flamandes Bruxelles, 1849. 4to.

—— Notice Statisque sur la Maison Penitentiare des Jeunes Delinquants. Bruxelles, 1852. 4to.

—— Memoire a l'appui du projet de loi sur les Prisons. Bruxelles, 1845. 8vo.

—— Statisque du Royaume, de Baviere. Bruxelles. 4to.

—— Statistique Commerciale. Instruction Generales pour les Entreposeurs et les Receveurs. Bruxelles, 1841. 4to.

—— Statistique des Prisons de la Belgique. Bruxelles, 1852. 4to.

—— Sur le Mouvement de l'etat civil en Belgique pendant les quatre Annees, 1841 and 1844. Bruxelles. 4to.

—— Programme de la Distribution Solennelle des Recompenses aux Exposants et aux Travailleurs Agricoles, 1848. 4to.

—— Observations des Phenomenes Periodiques. Bruxelles, 1850. 4to.

—— De l'Impot sur le Revenu. Nouvelles Considerations par X. Heuschling. Brussels, 1848. 4to.

—— Statistique Territoriale du Royaume de Belgique, Basée sur les Resultats des Operations Cadastrales. Bruxelles, 1853. Folio.

—— Question des Flandres. Communication aux Conseils Provinciaux, 1848. Brussels, 1848. 8vo.

—— Extrait du Rapport sur le Police et Surete Publique, 1841–50. Brussels, 1850. 4to.

—— Des Mesues, Propres A Restreindre la Maladie Syphilitique. Brussels, 1843. 8vo.

—— Projet de Loi sur les Brevets de Priorite. Brussels, 1849. 8vo.

BELGIUM. Chemins de Fer. l'Etat Transport des Marcnandises. Bruxelles, 1850. Folio.

—— Compte—Rendu des Operations de le Exercise, 1844, '46, '47, '49, '50. Rapport Presente aux Chambres Legislatives par le Ministre des Tavaux Publies. Brussels. 7 vols. Folio.

—— Chemin de Fer de Louvain a la Sambre. Memoire a l'Appui du projet. Bruxelles, 1845. Folio.

—— Chemin de Fer de Bruxelles Vers Gaud par Alost. Memoire a la Appui du projet. Bruxelles, 1846. Folio.

—— Coup d'œil sur la Situation des Chemins de Fer, Belges. Brussels, 1844. 8vo.

—— Itineraire General. Topographique et Descriptif des Chemins de Fer, Belges. Brussels, 1843. Small 4to.

—— Comptes Rendus par les Ministres Sur la Comptabilite de l'etat. Bruxelles, 1855. Folio.

—— Tableau General du Commerce avec les pays Etrangers Pendant l'Annee, 1851. Bruxelles, 1852. Folio.

BELKNAP, Jeremy, D. D. Amer. Biography: with Additions and Notes by F. M. Hubbard. Harpers Fam. Lib. N. Y., 1855. 3 vols. 18mo.

—— Descrip. of the White Mountains in N. H. Amer. Philos. Soc. Trans. Vol. 2.

—— History of N. H., Comprehending the Events of one Complete Century. Boston, 1792. 3 vols. 8vo.

—— See KIRKLAND, J. T. Obit. Discourse. 1798.

BELL, Dr., and LANCASTER, Mr. See FOX, Jos. Comparative View of their Plans of Educa'n.

BELL, Sir Charles. The Hand: Its Mechanism, etc., as Evincing Design. Lond., 1834. 8vo.

BELL, Chas. H. Biograph. Notice of Hon. Saml. D. Bell. N. Eng. Hist. and Gen. Reg. Vol. 23.

—— Disc. Before the N. Eng. Hist. Gen. Soc., Mar. 18, 1871, at the Dedica. of the Society's House, etc. N. E. H. and G. Register. Vol. 25.

BELL, Henry G. Life of Mary, Queen of Scots. Harper's Fam. Lib. N. Y., 1859. 2 vols. 18mo.

BELL, Hiram. Speech in Cong., Mar. 11, 1852, on the Homestead Law. Congr. and Polit. Pamph. Vol. 83.

—— Speech in Cong., July 20, 1852, on the Presidency. Cong. and Polit. Pamph. Vol. 89.

—— Speech in Cong., Jan. 11, 1853, on the Acquisition of Cuba. Congr. and Polit. Pamph. Vol. 88.

BELL, Jacob. Chemical and Pharmaceutical Processes and Products. 1851 8vo. Med. Pamph. Vol. 19.

BELL, John His "Past History connected with the Public Service." (n. d.) 8vo. Congr. and Polit. Pamph. Vol. 76.

—— Memorial to the Trustees of the University of Penn. Phila., 1850. 8vo. Penn. University Pamph.

—— Speech in House of Repr., Feb. 4, 1846, on the Oregon Question. Washington, 1846. 8vo. Speeches. Vol. 1.

—— Speech in U. S. Senate, July 3 and 5, 1850, on the Compromise. Cong. and Polit. Pamph. Vol. 94.

BELL, John. Speech in the U. S. Senate, Mar. 18, 1858, on the Lecompton Constitution. Congr. and Polit. Pamph. Vol. 93.

—— Thoughts on the Proposed Alteration in the Court of Chancery. Lond., 1830. 8vo. Law Pamph. Vol. 14.

BELL, Lincoln and Douglas: An Address to the Patriotism of the Country. 1860. Rebell'n Pamph. Vol. 77.

BELL, Luther V., M. D. See ELLIS, Rev. G. E. RAY, J.

BELL, Marcus A. South-Side View of Cotton is King; and the Philosophy of African Slavery. Atlanta, 1860. 8vo. Congr. and Polit. Pamph. Vol. 58.

BELL, Saml. D. Address before the N. H. Hist. Soc., June 13, 1849. Hist. Mag. 2d Ser. Vol. 4.

—— See BELL, Chas. H. Biograph. Notice of.

BELL, W. A. New Tracks in No. America; a Journey for a Survey for the Southern Pacific R. R. in 1867. Maps and Plates. Lond., 1869. 2 vols. 8vo.

BELLE Isle. Impartial Narrative of the Reduction of Belle Isle. Lond., 1761. 8vo. Eng. Polit. Pamph. Vol. 15.

BELLENGER, J. M. See Shea's Library of Liguistics.

BELLERS, F. A Delineation of Universal Law. Lond., 1754. 4to. Law Pamph. Vol. 25.

—— of the Ends of Society. To a Member of Parliament. Lond., 1759. 4to. Eng. Polit. Pamph. Vol. 66.

BELLEVUE Hospital Med. Coll. N. Y. Ann. Report of the Med. Board. 1856.

—— Annual Announcement, 1864–5.

BELLONI, Jerome. Dissertation on Commerce, Demonstrating the True Sources of National Wealth and Power. Lond., 1752. 8vo. Eng. Misc. Pamph. Vol. 35.

BELLOWS, Rev. H. W. Address at N. Y., 1835, in behalf of the Inebriate Asylum. N. Y., 1857. 8vo. Temp. Pamph. Vol. 1.

—— Address at the Academy of Music, Phila., Feb. 24, 1863. Phila., 1863. 8vo. Rebell'n Pamph. Vol. 66.

—— Discourse on the Death of Rev. William E. Channing, at N. Y., Oct. 1842. N. Y., 1842. 8vo. Sermons. Vol. 19.

—— Hist. Sketch of Col. Benj. Bellows, and Account of Family Meeting. N. Y., 1855. 8vo.

—— Unconditional Loyalty. N. Y., 1863. 8vo. Rebell'n Pamph. Vols. 38 and 65.

Belmont, Mass. Speeches in Mass. Legisla. on Incorporating the Town. 1857. Boston, 1857. 8vo. Mass. Mis. Pamp. Vol. 5.

BELMONT. Penn., Hospt. Proceedings at Laying the Corner Stone of. With Addresses by Bp. Potter and Rev. B. Dorr. Phila., 1856. 8vo. Addresses. Vol. 13.

BELOIT & Madison R. R. Co. 1st and 2d Ann. Reports. Chicago, 1854–5. 8vo.

BELOIT College. See CARPENTER, Matt. H. Speech at Dedica., Memorial Hall, 1869.

—— —— Catalogues of Officers and Students for 1849–50, 1850–51, 1852–3, 1853–4, 1856–7, 1859–60, 1860–61, 1861–2, 1862–3, 1863–4, 1864–5, 1865–6, 1866–7, 1868–9, 1869–70, 1870–1, 1871–2. Beloit, 1850–1871. 8vo.

BELOIT College. First Annual Report of Trustees. Beloit, 1849.
—— —— See CHAPIN, A. L. Address, EMERSON, J.
—— —— Exercises at the Quarter-Centennial Annivers. of the Coll., July 9, 1872. Beloit, 1872. 8vo. Beloit Coll. Pamph.
—— —— Monthly. Vols. 1 to 18 inclusive, incomplete. Beloit, 1853–72. 18 vols. Vols. 1-3, 4to; others 8vo.
—— —— See PAGE, H. M. Address.
—— —— Palladium. Dec. 1863. Vol. 2. No. 1. Beloit. 8vo.
—— —— Proceedings at 10th Anniversary of the College, including an Address by Prof. J. Emerson. Beloit, 1857. 8vo. Beloit Coll. Pamph.
—— —— Register for 1862–3, 1866–7, 1869–70. Beloit. 8vo.
—— —— SCHURZ, Carl. Address. 1858.
—— —— SQUIER, Miles P. Address.
—— —— Journal, Newspaper. Mar., 1854, to Dec., 1859. 2 vols. Folio.
—— —— and Courant, Newspaper. Beloit, 1860–3. Folio.
BELTRAMI, Constantine. See HILL, A. J. Sketch of.
—— Life and Writings of. In Italian. Bergamo, 1864. 12mo.
BELTRAMI, J. C. Pilgrimage in Europe and America, Leading to the Discovery of the Mississippi and Bloody Rivers. Lond., 1828. 2 vols 8vo.
BENBOW, Wm. The Whigs Exposed; or Truth by Daylight. Lond., 1820. 8vo. Eng. Polit. Pamph. Vol. 35.
BENCH AND BAR.—Vol. 1. 1869–70. 3 Nos.
—— —— Vol. 2. 1870–71. Complete.
—— —— N. Series. Vol. 1. 1871–72. 2 Nos.
—— —— N. Series. Vol. 2. 1872–73. 4 Nos. Chicago, 1869–73. 8vo.
BENEDICT, Rev. David, D.D. Fifty Years Among the Baptists. N. Y., 1860. 12mo.
BENEDICT, Erastus C. Address at the Closing of the N. York Normal School, July 8, 1858. Albany. 1858. 8vo. Addresses. Vol. 16.
—— See New York City. Board of Education.
—— Remarks on the Act Revising the School Laws of State of N. Y., 1851. Congr. and Polit. Pamph. Vol. 96.
BENEDICT GENEALOGY.—See BENEDICT, H. M.
BENEDICT, Henry M. Genealogy of the Benedicts in America. Albany, 1870. 8vo.
BENEDICT, Rev. Judson D. See HALL, Judge N. K.
BENEDICT, Julius. Sketch of the Life and Works of the late Felix Mendelssohn Bartholdy. Lond., 1853. 8vo. 2d Ed. Biograph. Pamph. Vol. 4.
BENEDICT, Lewis. See PORTER, John K. Argument before N. Y. Canal Appraisers. 1862.
—— Proceedings of Albany Bar, on the Death of. Albany, 1864. 8vo. Rebell'n Pamph. Vol. 8.
BENEDICT Platt. Memoir of the Township of Norwalk, Ohio. Fire Lands Pioneer. Vol. 1.
BENETT, John. Essay on the Commutation of Tithes. Lond., 1814. 8vo. Pamphleteer. Vol. 16.

BENGAL, India.—Proceedings of the Governor and Council, respecting the Administration of Justice in Bengal. 1774. 4to. Eng. Misc. Pamph. Vol. 24A.

—— —— See SCRAFTON, Luke.

BENJAMIN, John F. Speech in Cong., Mar. 15, 1870, on the Payment of Pensions. Congr. and Polit. Pamph. Vol. 119.

BENJAMIN, J. P. Speech in U. S. Senate, Dec. 31, 1860, on the Right of Secession. Rebell'n Pamph. Vol. 113.

BENNETT, Mr. Boston in 1840: Extracts from the History of N. Eng. Mass. Hist. Soc. Proceed. 1860–2.

BENNETT, David S. Speech in Cong., Apr. 1, 1870, on the Improvement of the Erie and Oswego Canals. Cong. and Polit. Pamph. Vol. 119.

BENNETT, Henry. Speech in Cong., May 27, 1850, on Admission of California. Cong. and Polit. Pamph. Vol. 86.

—— Speech in Cong., June 8, 1852, on Public Lands. Congr. and Polit. Pamph. Vol. 84.

BENNETT, H. G. Letter on Abuses in Newgate. Lond., 1818. 8vo. 2d Ed. Pamphleteer. Vol. 11.

BENNETT, Jas. Gordon. Memoirs of, and of his Times. N. Y., 1855. 12mo.

BENNETT, John C. The History of the Saints; or an Expose of Joe Smith and Mormonism. 3d Ed. Boston, 1842. 12mo.

BENNETT, Dr. J. H. Researches on Inflammation of the Nervous Centres. Edinburgh. (n. d.) 8vo. Med. Pamph. Vol. 13.

—— Present State of the Theory and Practice of Medicine. Edinburgh, 1855. 8vo. 2d Ed. Med. Pamph. Vol. 13.

BENNINGTON, (Battle of). See BUTLER, J. D.

—— Celebra. in 1778, of the Bennington Victory of 1777. Vt. Hist. Soc. Vol. 1.

—— See KEACH, Rev. Israel. 52d Annivers. Address. 1829.

BENNINGTON, Vt. See JENNINGS, I. Early Hist. of.

BENONI, Lorenzo. Passages in the Life of an Italian. 3d Ed. N. Y., 1857. 12mo.

BENSON, Benj. Hist. Sketch of Townsend, Ohio. Fire Lands Pioneer. Vol. 2.

—— Sketch of Clarksfield, Ohio. 1858. Fire Lands Pioneer. Vol. 1.

BENSON, EGBERT. Memoir on Names, before the N. Y. Hist. Soc., Dec. 31, 1816. N. Y. Hist. Soc. Coll. 2d Ser. Vol. 2.

—— Vindica. of the Captors of Maj. André. N. Y., 1817. 8vo. N. Y., Reprint 1865. 8vo.

BENSON GENEALOGY.—See GARRISON, W. P.

BENSON, Henry C. Life smong the Choctaws, and Sketches of the Southwest. Cincin., 1860. 12mo.

BENT, Lieut. Paper on the Japanese Gulf Stream. Amer. Geograph. and Statis. Soc. Bulletin. Vol. 2.

BENTALOU, Paul. Pulaski Vindicated. Two Pamphlets in Reply to Judge Johnson. Baltimore, 1825 to 1826. 8vo. Rev. War Pamph. Vol. 2.

BENTHAM, Edw. Introduction to Moral Philosophy. Oxford, 1746. 8vo.

BENTHAM, Edw. Letter to a Young Gentleman of Oxford. Lond., 1749. 12mo. Eng. Polit. Pamph. Vol. 69.

BENTHAM, Geo. Observa. on the Registration Bill before Parliament. Lond., 1831. 8vo. Law Pamph. Vol. 18.

BENTHAM, Jeremy. Defence of Economy against the late Mr. Burke. Lond., 1817. 8vo. Pamphleteer. Vol. 9.

—— Defence of Economy against the Rt. Hon. Geo. Rose. Lond., 1817. 8vo. Pamphleteer. Vol. 10.

—— Indications respecting Lord Eldon. Lond., 1825. 8vo. Eng. Polit. Pamph. Vol. 77.

—— Leading Principles of a Constitutional Code, for any State. Lond., 1823. 8vo. Pamphleteer. Vol. 22.

—— Observa. on Mr. Sec. Peel's House of Commons Speech, Mar. 25, 1825. Lond., 1825. 8vo. Eng. Misc. Pamph. Vol. 28.

—— Observa. on Sir Robt. Peel's Speech in Parliament, Mar. 21, 1825, on the Magistrates' Salary Bill, etc. Lond., 1825. 8vo. Pamphleteer. Vol. 25.

BENTLEY, Rich'd. Account of late Proceedings in the University of Cambridge. London, 1719. 8vo. Eng. Misc. Pamph. Vol. 23.

BENTLEY, Robt. Two Lectures before the Pharmaceutical Soc. of G. B., Feb. 24, and Mar. 23, 1864. Lond., 8vo. Med. Pamph. Vol. 22.

BENTLEY, William. Descrip. and Hist. of Salem, Mass. Mass. Hist. Soc. Coll. Vol. 6. 1st Ser.

BENTON, Charles S. Speech in Congress, June 30, 1846, on the Tariff. Washington, 1846. 8vo. Speeches. Vol. 1.

BENTON Co., (Iowa) Atlas and R. R. Map, of Iowa. Marshalltown, Ia., 1872. 4to.

BENTON, Nathaniel S. History of Herkimer County, including the Upper Mohawk Valley, to present time. Albany, 1856. 8vo.

BENTON, Thos. H. Abridgement of the Debates of Congress, 1789–56. N. Y., 1857–1861. 16 vols. 8vo.

—— Hist. and Legal Examination of the "Dred Scott Case," and Uuconstitutionality of Missouri Compromise. N. Y., 1837. 8vo.

—— Letter to People of Missouri, on Pacific R. R. (n. d.) 8vo. Congr. and Polit. Pamph. Vol. 90.

—— Speeches in U. S. Senate, Jan. 2, 3, 6, 7, 1834, on the Removal of the Deposits. Speeches. Vol. 5.

—— Speech in U. S. Senate, Mar. 14, 1838, on the U. S. Bank. Speeches. Vol. 5.

—— Speech in U. S. Senate, Jan. 13, 1842, on Plan for a Federal Exchequer. Washington, 1842. 8vo. Congr. and Polit. Pamph. Vol. 25.

—— Speech in U. S. Senate, May 22, 25 and 28, 1846, on the Oregon Question. Washington, 1846. 8vo. Speeches. Vol. 1.

—— Speech at Jefferson, Mo., May 26, 1849, on the Compromise. Congr. and Polit. Pamph. Vol. 94.

—— Speech in Congress, Apr. 25, 1854, on Kansas and Nebraska Bill. Congr. and Polit. Pamph. Vol. 84.

BENTON, Thos. H. Speech in U. S. Senate, June 10, 1850, on the Compromise. Congr. and Polit. Pamph. Vol. 94.
—— Speech in U. S. Senate, July 15, 1850, on the Texas Boundary, Congr. and Polit. Pamph. Vol. 83.
—— Speech in Congress, April 25, 1854, on the Kansas and Nebr. Bill. Washington, 1854. 8vo. Speeches. Vol. 3.
—— Speech in Congress, Jan. 16, 1855, on the Pacific R. R. Bill. Speeches. Vol. 5.
—— Thirty Years View; or History of the Working of the Amer. Gov't, from 1820 to 1850. N. Y., 1854–57. 2 vols. 8vo.
BERBERS.—Language of. See SHALER, Wm. HODGSON, W. B.
BERENDT, C. H. Report of Explorations in Central Amer. Smithsonian Report. 1867.
BERGEN, N. Y. See TAYLOR, B. C. Annals and Civil History.
BERGEN, T. G. Bergen Family Genealogy. N. Y., 1867. 8vo.
—— Genealogy of the Van Brunt Family, 1653–1867. Albany, 1867. 8vo.
BERKLEY, Mass. See SANFORD, Rev. E. History of.
BERKLEY, Sir William. List of those Executed for the late Rebellion in Va., 1676. Force's Hist. Tracts. Vol. 1.
BERKS Co., Pa. See RUPP, I. D. History of.
BERKSHIRE, Eng. See BERRY, W. Co. Genealogies.
BERKSHIRE, County, Mass. See ALLEN, Thos. Hist. Sketch of. 1808.
—— History of—Containing a Gen. View of the County, and an Account of the Several Towns. Pittsfield, 1829. 12mo.
—— HOLLAND, J. G.
—— The Jubilee, at Pittsfield, Mass., Aug. 22 and 23, 1844. Albany, 1845. 8vo.
—— Agr. Soc. See WATSON, E. History of. 1819.
—— Assoc. of Cong. Ministers. Proceedings at Centen. Commemora., held at Stockbridge, Oct. 28, 1863. Boston, 1864. 8vo. Mass. Hist. Discourses, etc. Vol. 11.
—— Bapt. Assoc. 30th and 31st Anniversaries, held in 1857–8. North Adams, 1857–8. 8vo. Mass. Misc. Pamph. Vol 4.
—— Medical Journal. Vol. 1. Pittsfield, 1861. 8vo.
BERLIN, Germany. Guide du Voyageur a Berlin Potsdam et aux Environs. Berlin, 1844. 12mo. Guide Books. Vol. 15.
—— and Milan Decrees. See Amer. State Papers. 1810.
—— Interna. Statist. Congress. See RUGGLES, S. B. Report on Resources of U. S. 1863.
BERLIN, O. See PHILLIPS, X. Memoir of.
BERLIN, Wis. Courant, Newspaper. Berlin, 1859–73.
BERMUDA Island. See COTTER, Rich'd. Sketches of.
—— Plain Description of, etc. 1613.
BERNALDEZ, Andres. Extract from the History of Ferdinand and Isabella. Mass. Hist. Soc. Coll. 3d Ser. Vol. 8.
BERNARD, Gov. Select Letters on the Trade and Govt. of Amer., and the Law and Polity Applied to the Amer. Colonies, Written in 1763–8. Lond., 1784. 8vo.
BERNARD, Sir Thos. Acc. of a Supply of Fish for the Manfacturing Poor. Lond., 1813. 8vo. Pamphleteer. Vol. 1.

BERRIEN, John M. Speech in U. S. Senate, Jan. 26, 1842, on the Bankrupt Law. Washington, 1842. 8vo. Cong. and Polit. Pamph. Vol. 24.

—— Speech in U. S. Senate, Mar. 4, 1842, on the Veto Power of the President. Washington, 1842. 8vo. Cong. ond Polit. Pamph. Vol. 24.

BERRY, Maj. Gen. Hiram G. Sketch of. From the Northern Monthly, Mar., 1864. Biograph. Pamph. Vol. 11.

BERRY, Wm. County Genealogies; Pedigrees of the Co. of Hants, Lond., 1833. Folio.

—— County Genealogies; Pedigrees of the Families of the Co. of Kent, Eng. Lond., 1830. Folio.

—— of the Families of Berkshire, Buckingham and Surrey. Lond., 1837. Folio.

—— County Genealogies; Pedigrees of the Families of Sussex. Lond., 1830. Folio.

—— Hist. of the Island of Guernsey, to 1814, with an Account of Islands of Alderney, Serk and Jersey. Lond., 1815. 4to.

—— Pedigrees of Hertfordshire Families. London. (n. d.) Folio.

BERTIE, Lord Robt. See Letter on his Defence of Admiral Byng.

BERTRAND, M. Kepler: His Life and Works. Smithsonian Report. 1869.

BESCHKE, Wm. Memorial to Cong. Concerning European Navies, and the Amer. Navy, etc. Phila., 1852. 8vo. Congr. and Polit. Pamph. Vol. 139.

BESTE, J. R. The Wabash; or Adventures of an English Gentleman's Family in America. Lond., 1855. 2 vols. 12mo.

BETHUNE, A. N., D.D. The Clergy Reserve Question in Canada. Lond., 1853. 8vo. Strangford Pamph. Vol. 64.

BETHUNE, Rev. G. W. Address before Hamilton Lit. and Theolog. Institution, June 5, 1833. Addresses. Vol. 12.

BETTINGER, J B. Responsibility of Society for the Causes of Crime. N. Y., 1871. 8vo.

BETTLE, Edw. Negro Slavery, as connected with Penn. Paper before the Penn. Hist. Soc., Aug. 7, 1826. Penn. Hist. Soc. Mem. Vol. 1. Part 2.

BETTRIDGE, Rev. Wm. Brief Hist. of the Ch. in Upper Canada. Lond., 1838. 8vo. Canada Pamph. Vol. 1.

BETTS, Rev. Xenophon. Early Settlement of Wakeman, O. Address before the Fire Lands Hist. Soc., Dec., 1867. Fire Lands Pioneer. Vol. 9.

BEVER, Thos. Introduct. Disc. on Jurisprudence, and the Civil Law. Oxford, 1766. 4to. Law Pamph. Vol. 25.

BEVERLEY, Carter. See JACKSON, A.

BEVERLY, Mass. See RANTOUL, Robt.

—— STONE, E. M. Hist. Lecture.

—— —— Hist. of.

—— THAYER, C. T. 200th Annivers. Address. 1867.

—— —— Valedict. Disc. in 1st Ch., 1858.

BEVERLY, Robt. Hist. of Virginia and its Gov't to 1706, and the Present State of the Country, etc., to June, 1722. Lond., 8vo.

BEVERLEY, R. M. Letter to the Duke of Gloucester, on the Corrupt State of the University of Cambridge. Lond., 1833. 8vo. 3d Ed. Eng. Polit. Pamph. Vol. 39.

BIARD, *Pere* Pierre. Missio Canadensis. Epistola ex Portu Regali in Acadia transmissa ad Præpositum Generalem Societatis Jesu. Dillingen, 1612. 8vo. Albany, 1870. 8vo. Reprinted.

—— See Canadicæ Missionis Relatio, etc.

—— Relation de la Nouvelle France, de ses Terres, Nature du Pays, de ses Habitans, Item, Du Voyage des Peres Jesuites Ausdictes Contrees, et de ce quils y ont faict jusques a leur Prinse par les Anglois. Lyons, 1616. 8vo. Albany. Fac simile Reprint. 1870 or 1871. 8vo.

BIBLE (The) against Slavery; or an Inquiry into the Genius of the Mosaic Systems. Pittsburgh, 1864. 12mo. Rebell'n Pamph. Vol. 47.

BIBLE, and Parts thereof. Bibelen eller deu Hellige Skrist. Christiana, 1844. 8vo.

—— Biblia Sacra. 1720.

—— BRADY and TATE. Version of Psalms.

—— in Danish Language. N. Y., 1870. 8vo.

—— in Hungarian. Koszegen, 1850. 8vo.

—— in Polish Language. Leipsic, 1846. 8vo.

—— in French. N. Y., 1849. 8vo.

—— in Irish. Dublin, 1830. 12mo.

—— in Latin. London, 1857. 12mo.

—— in Bohemian. Prague, 1867. 8vo.

—— in Italian. Lond., 1859. 8vo.

—— in Swedish. Lond., 1847. 8vo.

—— Testament, in Spanish. N. Y., 1851–2. 8vo.

—— in Norwegian. Christiana, 1844. 8vo.

—— in Dutch. Harlem, 1637. Folio.

—— in Dutch. Amsterdam, 1696. Folio.

—— in Dutch. Amsterdam, 1714. Folio.

—— in Dutch. Gorinchem, 1748. 2 vols. Folio.

—— Gospel According to St. Luke, in Tamil. Madras, 1845. 12mo.

—— Gospel of Luke and Acts in Grebo. N. Y. (n. d.)

—— New Testament in Chinese. N. Y. 12mo.

—— New Testament, Danish and English. N. Y., 1849. 12mo.

—— Testament in French and English. N. Y., 1852. 12mo.

—— Genesis Liber Hebraica. Romae, 1836. 8vo. Eng. Religious Pamph. Vol. 48A.

—— Iu Otoshki.—Kik in diuin au Kitogimaminan gae bemafiin ung Jesus Krist ima ojibue inueuining ghzhitong. The New Testament Trans. into the Language of the Ojibwas. N. Y., 1844. 12mo.

—— Das Neue Testament unfres herrn und Heilandes Jesu Christi Bielefeld, 1846. 8vo.

—— Genesis, Exodus, Proverbs and Acts Translated into the Mpongwe Language, at the Mission of the Gaboon, West Africa. N. Y., 1859. 12mo.

BIBLE. LOOKUP, John. New Transla. of Genesis.
—— PEILE, T. W. New Transla. of Romans.
—— Early Editions of King James' Bible in folio. Hist. Mag. Vol. 5.
—— GLEIG, G. R. History of Bible.
—— HUGHES, E. Scripture Geog. and Hist.
BIBLE in Schools. See Arguments in favor of Abolishing Religious Instruction, etc.
—— —— Arguments in Case of J. D. Minor *vs.* Cincinnati Board of Educa. Cincin., 1870. 8vo.
—— —— See DUNN, Henry.
—— —— HURLBUT, E. P.
—— —— JACOBUS, M. J. Popery against Common Schools. MAYO, A. D.
—— —— Proceedings and Addresses at Mass Meeting, at Cincinnati, 1869. 8vo. Sermons, etc. Vol. 25.
—— —— See Religion in Public Instruction.
BIBLE. O'CALLAGHAN, E. B. List of Amer. Editions printed previous to 1860.
—— on the Present Crisis. Rebell'n Pamph. Vol. 76.
—— TOWNSEND, Howard. The Sinai Bible.
—— PRIME, S. I. Bible in the Levant.
BIBLIA Sacra e Vulgata Editione, Latinisque Translationabus. Venice, 1720. Folio.
BIBLIOGRAPHY.—Accounts, etc., of Libr'y of King of France.
—— ALLAN, John. Priv. Libr. Cat.
—— Amer. Philo. Soc. Cat.
—— Appleton's Library Manual.
—— BARTLETT, J. R. Bibliog. of R. I.
—— Belgium. Bibliotheque de la Chambres. Representants.
—— Bibliotheca Americana.
—— Bibliotheca Americana Vetustissima.
—— Bibliotheca Americo, Septentrionalis.
—— Book Buyers Manual.
—— BOYNE, Wm. Yorkshire Library.
—— BRADFORD, A. W. Priv. Libr. Cat.
—— BROCKHAUS, F. A. Cat. of Americana prior to 1700.
—— BRUNET, J. C. Manuel du Libraire.
—— BUCHANAN, Robt. Cat. Priv. Libr'y. 1872.
—— Catalogues of Public Libraries.
—— CHOATE, Rufus. Priv. Libr. Cat.
—— CHOULES, Rev. J. O. Priv. Libr. Cat.
—— COLBURN, Jeremiah. Bibliography of Mass. Local Hist.
—— COLLIER, J. P. Bibliogr. Acct. of Rare Books.
—— CORNER, Wm. H. Priv. Libr. Cat.
—— COXE, J. R. Priv. Libr. Cat.
—— DEAN, Amos. Priv. Libr. Cat.
—— DE BRY'S Voyages.
—— DEBURY, R. Philobiblon.
—— DEETH, S. G. Priv. Libr. Cat.
—— DRAKE, S. G. Priv. Libr. Cat.
—— DURRIE, Danl. S. Bibliog. of Wis.

BIBLIOGRAPHY. EDWARDS, E. Memoir of Libraries.
—— Essay towards an Indian Bibliog.
—— FAIRBAULT, G. B. Cat. d'Ouvrages, sur l'Histoire de l'Amerique.
—— FARNHAM, Luther. Glance at Private Libraries. 1855.
—— FISHER, J. B. Priv. Libr. Cat.
—— FLEMING, Aug. Priv. Libr. Cat.
—— FOWLE, Wm. F. Priv. Libr. Cat.
—— FRANCIS, J. W. Priv. Libr. Cat.
—— GIRARD, Chas. Bibliog. of Amer. Nat. Hist. for 1851.
—— GOWANS, Wm.
—— GREENE, Albert G. Priv. Libr. Cat.
—— GRISWOLD, Rev. R. W. Priv. Libr. Cat.
—— GUILD, R. A. Librarian's Manual.
—— HALLECK, Fitz-Greene. Priv. Libr. Cat.
—— HERVEY, J. B. Priv. Libr. Cat.
—— HODGSON, T. Index to London Cat.
—— HOWELL, E. English Book Cat.
—— HUNNEWELL, J. F. Bibliog. of Hawaian Islands.
—— Iowa Grand Lodge Libr. Cat. 1873.
—— JEWETT, C. C. Report on Catalogues.
—— —— Notices of Public Libraries in U. S. 1851.
—— KELLY, Jas. American Catalogue. 1866–1871.
—— LECLERC, C. Bibliotheca Americana.
—— LOWNDES, W. T. Manual of Eng. Literature.
—— LUDEWIG, H. E. Bibliog. of Amer. Local Hist. 1846.
—— —— Bibliotheca Glottica.
—— —— Priv. Libr. Cat.
—— Lumley's Bibliog. Advertiser.
—— LYLE, Rev. J. K. Priv. Libr. Cat.
—— MAYER, Brantz. Priv. Libr. Cat.
—— MEDING, H. Bibliotheque du Paris. Medical.
—— MITCHELL, A. Private Libr. Cat.
—— MORRELL, T. H. Priv. Libr. Cat.
—— MULLER, Fred. Cat. of Books on America and Early Voyages, etc.
—— MUNSELL, Joel. Priv. Libr. Cat.
—— NORTON, C. B. Cat. of Books on America. 1862.
—— —— Literary Registers. 1852–4.
—— Notes for Bibliog. of New France.
—— O'CALLAGHAN, E. B. Amer. Editions of Bibles Printed prior to 1860.
—— Philo-Biblion. 1862–1863.
—— POOLE, H. W. Priv. Libr. Cat.
—— POOLE, W. F. Index to Period. Literature.
—— POTTER, A. Hand Book for Students.
—— PRATT, G. W. Priv. Libr. Cat.
—— PYCROFT, Rev. J. Course of English Reading.
—— QUARITCH, B. Book Catalogues.
—— QUERARD, J. M. Dictionnaire Bibliographique.
—— RICE, John A. Priv. Lib. Cat.
—— RICH, O. Biblioth. American. Nova and Vetus.

BIBLIOGRAPHY. ROCHE, R. W. Priv. Libr. Cat.
—— ROORBACH, O. A. Bibliotheca Americana.
—— SABIN, J. Amer. Bibliopolist.
—— —— Dict. of Amer. Books.
—— SCHMIDT, L. W. Bibliog. Guide to Litera. of Science.
—— SMITH, J. R. Bibliotheca Americana.
—— —— Bibliotheca Cantiana.
—— —— Bibliog. of Eng. Provincial Dialects, etc.
—— —— Cat. of Amer. Books. 1870.
—— SOBOLEWSKI, M. S. Cat. 1873.
—— SOTHERAN, H. Book Cat.
—— STEVENS, Henry. Amer. Bibliographer. Vol. 1, Nos. 1 and 2. 1854.
—— —— Bibliotheca Geographica.
—— —— Hist. Nuggets.
—— —— My English Library.
—— TRUBNER, N. Bibliog. Guide to Amer. Liter.
—— TUCKERMAN, H. T. Priv. Libr. Cat.
—— WATTS, R. Bibliotheca Brittanica.
—— WESTCOTT, Thompson. Ante-Revolutionary.
—— WHITE, R. G. Priv. Libr. Cat.
—— WHITMORE, W. H. Hand Book of Amer. Genealogy.
—— WRIGHT, Andrew. Priv. Libr. Cat.
—— WILLIAMS, J. F. Bibliog. of Minn. 1870.
—— WILLIS, Wm. Bibliograph. Essay on Collections of Voyages to America.
—— WOODWARD, W. E. Priv. Libr. Cat.
—— WYNNE, J. Private Libraries of N. York. 1860.
—— 68 Pamphlet Volumes of Catalogues of Private Libraries, Trade Lists, Autographs, etc., Assorted, and the most Important Cat'd.

BIBLIOTHECA Americana; or a Chronolog. Catalogue of Books, Pamphlets, State Papers, etc., on N. and S. America. Lond., 1789. 4to.
—— —— Vetustissima; a Description of Works Relating to America, published between 1492 and 1551. N. Y., 1866. 8vo.
—— Americo—Septentrionalis; being a Choice Collection of Books in Various Languages. Paris, 1820. 8vo.
—— Cantiana. See SMITH, J. Russell.
—— Monensis. See HARRISON, W. Books Relating to Isle of Man.
—— Sacra & American Biblical Repository. Jan.—Oct., 1854. Jan.—July, 1855. Oct., 1855. Jan., 1860. Andover, 1854–60. 8vo.

BICKHAM, Geo. Deliciae Britannicae; or, the Curiosities of Kensington, Hampton Court and Windsor Castle. 2d Ed. Lond., (n. d.) 12mo.

BICKHAM, W. D. Rosecran's Campaign with the 14th Army Corps; Narrative of Personal Observations. Cincin., 1863. 12mo.

BICKLEY, Geo. W. L. History of the Settlement, and Indian Wars of Tazewell County, Va. Cincin., 1852. 8vo.

BIDDEFORD, Me. See FOLSOM, G. History of.

BIDDLE, Chas. Eulogy on Hon. Geo. Mifflin Dallas, delivered before the Phila. Bar, Feb. 11, 1865. 8vo. Addresses. Vol. 20.

BIDDLE, Chas. Speech in Cong., Mar. 6, 1862, on State of the Union. Rebell'n Pamph. Vols. 32, 52, 61.

—— Speech in Cong., June 5, 1862, on Appointing Consul Generals to Liberia and Hayti. Rebell'n Pamph. Vol. 61.

—— The Case of Major Andre. With a Review of the Statements of Lord Mahon. Penn. Hist. Soc. Memoirs. Vol. 6. See also Hist. Mag. Vol. 1.

BIDDLE, Geo. W. Lecture at the Law Acad. of Phila., May 6, 1863. Rebell'n Pamph. Vol 31.

BIDDLE, Horace P. Discourse on Art, delivered at the Melodeon Hall, La Fayette, Dec. 30, 1854. La Fayette, 1855. 8vo. Art Pamph. Vol. 2.

BIDDLE, John. Discourse Delivered before the Hist. Soc. of Michigan. (n. d.) See Sketches of Michigan.

BIDLACK, B. A. Speech in Cong., July 5, 1842, on the Revenue Bill. Washington, 1842. 8vo. Congr. and Polit. Pamph. Vol. 25.

BIEDMA, Luis H. Narrative of the Expedition of Hernando de Soto into Florida. French's Hist. Coll. of La. Vol. 2.

BIERCE, Lucius V. Hist. Reminiscences of Summit County, Ohio. Akron, 1854. 18mo.

BIFFE, Dr. Thos. See LEWIS, J. Defence of the Eng. Liturgy, &c.

BIGELOW, E. R. The Tariff Question in regard to the Policy of England and the Interests of the U. S. Boston, 1862. 4to.

BIGELOW, Henry J., M. D. Lecture on Surgery, at the Mass. Med. Col., Nov. 6, 1849. Boston, 1850. 8vo. Med. Pam. Vol. 2.

BIGELOW, Jacob. Brief Expositions of Rational Medicine. Boston, 1858. 8vo.

—— Florula Bostoniensis ; or Plants of Boston. Boston, 1824. 8vo.

—— History of the Cemetery at Mount Auburn. Boston, 1860. 12mo.

—— Lecture on the Treatment of Disease. Boston, 1852. 8vo. Med. Pamph. Vol. 12.

BIGELOW, Col. Timothy. See HERSEY, C. Reminiscences of.

—— Oration at Boston, July 4, 1853. Boston, 1853. 8vo. Addresses. Vols. 3 & 27.

BIGLER, Wm. Address at New Hope, Penn., Sept. 17, 1863. Rebell'n Pamph. Vol. 37.

BIGLOW, Wm. History of Sherburne from 1674 to 1830. Milford, 1830. 8vo. Mass. Hist. Discourses, etc. Vol. 12.

—— Hist. of Natick, from 1650 to 1830. Boston, 1830. 8vo. Mass. Hist. Discourses, etc. Vol. 10.

BIGNOLD, Thos. Exposure of the Unjustifiable Proceedings of Mr. Thorpe and Others. Lond., 1818. 8vo. Eng. Polit. Pamph. Vol. 34.

BIGNON, M. Les Cabinets et les Peuples. 1815—1822. Lond., 1823. 8vo. Pamphleteer. Vol. 22.

BIGOT, R. P. Jacque. Relation de ce qui S'est Passé de plus Remarquable dans la Mission Abnaquise de Sainct Joseph de Sillery et de Sainct Francois de Sales, 1685. N. Y., 1858. 4to. Printed by J. G. Shea.

BIGOT, Père Vincent. Relation de ce qui Passé de plus Remarquable dans la Mission des Abnaquis à L'Acadie, l'année, 1701. N. Y., 1858. 4to. Shea's Ed.

BIGSBY, John. Geology and Mineralogy of the N. West Portion of Lake Huron, 1820. Silliman's Journ. Vol. 3.

—— Minerals and Organic Remains in the Canadas, 1824. Silliman's Journ. Vol. 8.

BILL, Ledyard. Genealogy of the Bill Family. N. Y., 1867. 8vo.

—— Minnesota; its Character and Climate; with Hints to Tourists and Emigrants. N. Y., 1871. 12mo.

—— Pen Pictures of the War. N. Y., 1866. 8vo.

—— Winter in Florida. 4th Ed. N. Y., 1870. 12mo.

BILLED MAGAZINE. (Scandinavian.) Madison, 1869. 4to.

BILLERICA, Mass. Celebration of the 200th Annivers. of the Town, May 29, 1855. Lowell, 1855. 8vo. Mass. Hist. Discourses, Vol. 7.

—— See FARMER, J. Sketches of History of.

BILLIARDS. Laws & Regulations of the Game. London. 12mo. (n. d.) Eng. Misc. Pamph. Vol. 17.

BILLOT, Fred. Frankish Letters to Napoleon III. Translated from the French. Lond., 1853. 12mo. Eng. Pol. Pam. Vol. 51.

BINEAU, M. Rapport sur l'Emploi de la tourbe pour le Puddlage de la Fonte et le Travail du Fer, etc. Paris, 1835.

BINGHAM, Hiram. Residence of Twenty-one Years in the Sandwich Islands. 3d Ed. Roy. Hartford, 1849. 8vo.

BINGHAM, J. A. & STEVENS, T. Remarks in Cong., July 9, 1867, on Reconstruction. Congr. and Polit. Pamph. Vol. 122.

—— Argument in Trial of Conspirators for the Assassination of Pres't Lincoln. 1865.

—— Remarks in Cong., Feb. 22, 1868, on the Impeachment of the President. Congr. and Polit. Pamph. Vol. 122.

—— Speeches in Cong., Jan. 13 & 14, 1868, on the Judiciary and Reconstruction Bills. Congr. and Polit. Pamph. Vol. 122.

—— Speech in Cong., Jan. 15, 1862, on the Rebellion. Rebell'n Pamph. Vols. 61, 66.

—— Speech in Cong., Jan. 20, 1868, on Reconstruction. Congr. and Polit. Pamph. Vol. 122.

—— Speech in Cong., Jan. 13, 1863, on Reconstruction. Rebell'n Pamph. Vol. 57.

BINGLEY, W. Travels in N. America. Selected from Modern Writers. Lond., 1821. 12mo.

BINKERD, A. D. The Mammoth Cave and its Denizens. Cincin., 1869. 8vo. Ky. Misc. Pamph. Vol. 1.

BINNEY. C. J. F. History and Genealogy of Prentice or Prentiss Family, 1631—1852. Boston, 1862. 8vo.

BINNEY, Horace. Eulogy on the Life and Character of John Marshall, Chief Justice. Waldie's Circulating Library. Vol. 6.

—— Another Copy. Addresses. Vol. 13.

—— Letter to Union League of Phila., 1863. Rebell'n Pamph. Vol. 91.

—— Privilege of the Writ of Habeas Corpus. Parts 1 and 2. Phila., 1862. 8vo. Rebell'n Pamph. Vols. 27 & 60.

BINNEY, Horace. Speech in Cong., Jan., 1834, on the Removal of the Deposites. Congress. and Polit. Pamph. Vol. 88.

BIOGRAPHIA Brittanica. See KIPPIS, Andrew.

BIOGRAPHIA Brittanica Literaria; a Biography of Literary Characters of G. Britain and Ireland. Anglo-Saxon and Anglo-Norman Periods. Lond., 1842–46. 2 vols. 8vo.

BIOGRAPHICAL Dictionary. Containing an Account of the Life and Writings of most Eminent Persons of all Nations. Lond., 1795. 8 vols. 8vo.

—— Same. Enlarged, 1798. 15 vols. 8vo.

BIOGRAPHICAL Dictionaries. See ALLEN, W. H. BLAKE, John L. CHAMBERS, R. DRAKE, F. S. ELIOTT, John. GORDON, John. LANMAN, Chas.

—— See Univers. Biogr. Dict.

BIOGRAPHICAL Sketches of Leading Men in Chicago. Photographically Illustrated. Chicago, Roy. 8vo.

—— Sketches of Eccentric Characters. Cooperstown. (n. d.) 18mo.

BIOGRAPHY, Collective. See ABBOTT, J. S. C. Kings and Queens.

—— Amer. Milit. Biogr., 1825.

—— American Nepos.

—— ANDERSON, W. Scottish Nation.

—— Annual Biogr. and Obituary,1817–37.

—— BARTLETT, D. W. Modern Agitators.

—— BELKNAP, J. Amer. Biography.

—— Biograph. Dictionaries.

—— Biograph. Pamphlets. 18 vols.

—— Biog. Sketches of Eccent. Charac.

—— Biog. of Distin. Men.

—— BUNGAY, G. W. Off Hand Takings.

—— BREWSTER, D. Martyrs of Science.

—— BROUGHAM, Lord. Men of Letters, Philosophers and Statesmen, Time of George 3d.

—— BRUCE, J. Classic and Historic Portraits.

—— CHILD, L. M. Biog. of Good Wives.

—— Choice English Biog.

—— Collection of Interesting Biog. 1791.

—— COOPER, J. F. Lives of Amer. Naval Officers.

—— COOPER, T. Men of the Time, 1872.

—— Court and Camp of Bonaparte.

—— CROSBY, N. Annual Obit. Notices.

—— CUNNINGHAM, A. Eminent British Painters.

—— CUNNINGHAM, G. G. Eminent Englishmen.

—— DAVISON, Jas. W. Living Writers of the South.

—— DELAPLAINE, J. Repository of Distin. Americans.

—— Disting. Men of Modern Times.

—— DIX, J. R. Pulpit Portraits.

—— DWIGHT, N. Lives of the Signers.

—— ELLET, Mrs. E. F. Pioneer Women of the West.

—— —— Women of the Revolution.

—— —— Queens of Amer. Society.

—— Evangelical Biog.

—— FENELON. Lives of Ancient Philosophers.

BIOGRAPHY, Collective. FLANDLERS, H. Lives of Ch. Justices U. S.
—— FROST, J. Heroic Women of the West.
—— FULLER, Thos. Worthies of England.
—— Georgian Era.
—— GODWIN, P. Cyclopedia of.
—— GOODMAN, Rev. J. R. Penn. Biog.
—— GOODRICH, C. A. Lives of Signers.
—— GOODRICH, Frank. Republican Court.
—— GOODRICH, S. G. Popular Biog.
—— GORRIE, P. D. Biog. Methodist Ministers.
—— GRISWOLD, R. W. The Republican Court.
—— HARSHA, D. A. Orators and Statesmen.
—— Harvard Memorial Biography.
—— HEADLEY, J. T. Washington and his Generals.
—— —— Chaplains and Clergy of Revolution.
—— HERBERT, H. W. Captains of Old World.
—— —— Capt's of Roman Republic.
—— HERRING, J. Portrait Gallery of Americans.
—— HEWITT, M. E. Heroines of History.
—— HILDRETH, R. Lives of Atrocious Judges.
—— HUNT, W. Amer. Biogr. Panorama.
—— JAMIESON, Mrs. Lives of Female Sovereigns.
—— JOHNSON, S. Lives of the Poets.
—— JONES, A. D. Illust. Amer. Biog.
—— KIPPIS, A. Biographia Britannica.
—— KNAPP, S. L. Female Biogr.
—— KNIGHT, C. Gallery of Portraits and Memoirs.
—— LANCELOT, F. Queens of England.
—— LANMAN, C. Dict. of U. S. Congress.
—— LAWRENCE, E. Lives of British Historians.
—— LESTER, C. E. Artists of America.
—— LINCOLN, R. W. Lives of Presidents and Signers.
—— LODGE, E. Illustrious Personages of G. B.
—— LOSSING, B. J. Eminent Americans.
—— —— Lives of the Signers.
—— —— Our Countrymen.
—— LOWER, M. A. Sussex Worthies.
—— MAGOON, E. L. Orators of Amer. Rev.
—— MARSHALL, J. Royal Naval Biog.
—— N. Y. Genealog. and Biograph. Record.
—— Old English Worthies.
—— Orators of France.
—— PARKER, H. F. Discoverers of America.
—— PARKER, Theo. Historic Americans. 1870.
—— PARTON, Jas. Famous Americans of Recent Times. 1871.
—— —— Men of Progress.
—— PEIRCE, B. K. The Eminent Dead.
—— PLUTARCH'S Lives.
—— PRIDHAM, T. L. Devonshire Celebrities.
—— Public Characters.
—— ROBERTSON, I. L. Sketches of Pub. Characters.
—— ROGER, J. Monument of Patriotism.

BIOGRAPHY, Collective. ROGERS, T. J. Amer. Biog. Dict.
—— SABINE, L. Amer. Loyalists.
—— ST. JOHN, J. A. Lives of Celebrated Travellers.
—— SANDERSON, J. Lives of the Signers.
—— SHEIL, R. L. Sketches of the Irish Bar.
—— SIGOURNEY, L. H. Examples of 18th and 19th Centuries.
—— SPARKS, J. Amer. Biog.
—— SPRAGUE, W. B. Annals of Amer. Pulpit.
—— STANTON, H. B. Sketches of Reformers.
—— STRICKLAND, A. Queens of England.
—— SUMMERS, T. O. Biogr. of Methodist Ministers.
—— THACHER, Jas. Amer. Med. Biogr.
—— TOWNSEND, W. Descendants of the Stuarts.
—— TUCKERMAN, H. T. Book of the Artists.
—— VICKARS, J. England's Worthies, 1642–47.
—— WALTON, I. Choice English Biog.
—— Washington and Amer. Generals.
—— WHEELER, H. G. History of Cong.
—— WILLIAMS, S. W. Amer. Medical Biogr.
—— WILLS, J. Illustrious Irishmen.
—— WILSON, H. Wonderful Characters.
—— WILSON, J. G. Ill. Officers in War of Rebellion.
—— WILSON, Thos. Amer. Milit. and Naval Biog. 1817.
—— WRIGHT, Thos. Biograph. Britann. Literaria.
—— WYATT, Thos. Generals, Coms., etc., of Am. Army and Navy.

BIOGRAPHY, Exemplary and Instructive, of Distinguished Men. Phila., 1854. 12mo.

BIRBECK, Morris. Extracts from a Supplementary Letter from the Illinois, etc. London, 1819. 8vo. 2d Ed. Pamph.
—— See FLOWER, Rich'd.
—— Letters from Illinois. Phila., 1818. 12mo.
—— Notes on a Journey in America from Va. to Illinois. Lond., 1818. 8vo.

BIRCH, Jas. H. Speech in Cong., June 1, 1864, in his Contested Election Case. Congr. and Polit. Pamph. Vol. 121.

BIRKENHEAD Dock Co. To Merchants, Ship Owners, and Others, Trading to the Mersey. Birkenhead, 1846. 8vo. Eng. Polit. Pamph. Vol. 45.

BIRD, F. W. The Road to Ruin; or, the Decline and Fall of the Hoosac Tunnel. Boston, 1862. 8vo. 2d Ed. Mass. R. R. Reports, etc. Vol 2.

BIRDSALL, A. Speech in Cong., July 24, 1848, on the Wilmot Proviso. Congress. and Polit. Pamph. Vol. 89.

BIRKS, Rev. T. R. Modern Astronomy. London, 1850. 12mo. Scientific Pamph. Vol. 26.

BIRMINGHAM, Eng. Chamber of Commerce. Memorials addressed to Sir Robt. Peel, on the Currency Question, 1842. Birmingham, 1843. 8vo.
—— See SMITH, Toulmin. Memorials of, 1864.

BIRMINGHAM, Ohio. See HAWLEY, Uriah. Memoirs of.

BIRNIE, John. Account of the Families of Birnie and Hamilton, of Broomhill. Edinburgh, 1838. 4to.

BISCHOFF, Jas. Foreign Tariffs; their Injurious Effects on British Manufactures, etc. Lond., 1843. 8vo. Strangford Pamph. Vol. 31.

BIRT, John. Letter to Sir Geo. Grey, on Slavery in the British Colonies. Lond., 1837. 8vo. Strangford Pamph. Vol. 15.

BISHOP, George. New England Judged by the Spirit of the Lord; Containing a Relation of the Sufferings of Quakers from 1656 to 1660. Lond., 1702. 12mo.

BISHOP, Jas. Abstract of the New County Courts Act, for the Recovery of Small Debts, etc. Lond., 1847. 12mo. Law Pamph. Vol. 10.

BISHOP, J. S. Concise History of the War, with new War Map of the U. States. Indianapolis, 1864. 12mo.

BISHOP, J. W. History of Fillmore Co., Minn. Chatfield, Minn., 1858. 8vo.

BISHOP, Rev. Pierpont E. See SAYE, Rev. J. H. Memorial Sermon. 1859.

BISHOP, R. H. Introductory to a Course of Lectures on History at Transylva. University. Lexington, 1823. 12mo. Pamphlets. Vol. 4.

BISHOP, Saml. G. Eulogium on the Death of Geo. Washington at Pittsfield, N. H., Feb. 22, 1800. Roxbury, 1856. 8vo. Reprint.

BISSELL, Champion. Poem before the Phi Beta Kappa Soc'y of Yale Coll., July 24, 1861. N. Haven, 1861. 8vo. Yale Coll. Pamph.

BISSELL Genealogy. See STILES, H. R.

BISSELL, W. H. Speech in Cong., Feb. 21, 1850, on Slavery. Cong. and Polit. Pamph. Vol. 85.

BISSET, Rev. Thos. Suggestions on University Reform. Lond., 1850. 8vo. Strangford Pamph. Vol. 54.

BISSET, Rev. Wm. The Modern Fanatic, with an Account of Dr. Sacheverell. Lond,, 1710. 12mo. Eng. Religious Pamph. Vol. 81.

BIZARRE, for Fireside and Wayside. Conducted by J. M. Church. Philadelphia, 1852–1855. 6 vols. 8vo.

"BLACKBEARD." See TEACH, Edw.

"BLACK BOB" Band of Shawnee Indians. Memorial to Congress. 1870. 8vo. Congr. and Polit. Pamph. Vol. 117.

BLACK Code of Dist. of Columbia. See SNETHAN, W. G. 1848.

BLACK Earth Wis., Advertiser, Newspaper. 1870–72. 1 vol.

BLACK HAWK.—Account of Black Hawk, and the Sac and Fox Indians, with the Narrative of a Lady taken Prisoner. Phila., 1834.

—— See DRAKE, B. Life of.

—— SMITH, Elbert H. Black Hawk, and Scenes in the West: A Poem.

—— PATTERSON, J. B. Life of.

—— Purchase. See LEA, A. M. Notes on Wisconsin Terr'y, etc. 1836.

—— War. See DAWSON, H. B. Battles of U. S.

—— —— FORD, Gov. T. Hist. of, etc.

Black Hawk War. Smith, W. R. Hist. of Wisconsin.
—— —— Wakefield, J. A. Hist. of.
—— —— Wis. State Hist. Soc. Coll. Vols. 2 and 5.
Black's Guide to the English Lakes. Edinburgh, 1854. 12mo. Guide Books. Vol. 25.
Black, Jere. S. Speech at Phila., Oct. 24, 1864, on Doctrines of Political Parties. Rebell'n Pamph. Vol. 37.
—— Speech at Dem. Mass Convention at Lancaster, Pa., Sept. 17, 1863. Congr. and Polit. Pamph. Vol. 90.
Black, Samuel W. Address at Washington, Pa., Sept. 25, 1850, Pittsburgh, 1850. 8vo. Addresses, etc. Vol. 13.
Black, Wm. Reflections on the Relics of Ancient Grandeur in South Wales. Lond., 1823. 12mo. Eng. Misc. Pamph. Vol. 12.
Blacker, Wm. Best Mode of Improving the Condition of the Laboring Classes in Ireland. Lond., 1846. 8vo. Eng. Polit. Pamph. Vol. 45.
Blackmore, Sir Rich'd. Disc. upon the Plague, with an Account of Malignant Fevers. Lond., 1722. 12mo. 2d Ed. Med. Pamph. Vol. 27.
Blackshear, Gen. David. Memoir, with Letters of U. S. Officers. 1812–14.
Blackstone Monument Assoc. See Newman, S. C.
Blackstone, Wm. Disc. on the Study of the Law. Oxford, 1758. 4to. Eng. Polit. Pamph. Vol. 10.
Blackwell, J. K. Explosions in Coal Mines: Their Causes and Prevention. Lond., 1853. 8vo. Strangford Pamph. Vol. 64.
Blackwell, Thos. E. Hydrology of the Basin of the River St. Lawrence. Trans. Amer. Philosoph. Soc. N. S., Vol. 13.
Blackwood *vs.* Carlyle. A Vindication. Lond., 1850. 8vo. Eng. Misc. Pamph. Vol. 36.
Blackwood's Edinburgh Monthly Magazine, from Apr., 1817, to Dec., 1870. Edinburgh. 108 vols. 8vo.
—— Same Index to first 50 vols. Edinburgh, 1855. 8vo.
Blagden, Geo. W., D.D. Memoir of Rev. Wm. Jenks. Mass. Hist. Soc. Proceed. 1867–69.
Blain, Wm. J. Sermon at the Funeral of Dr. A. W. Hull, Apr. 15, 1867. Albany, 1867. 8vo. Sermon. Vol. 20.
Blaine, J. G. Letter of Acceptance of his Nomination for Congress, 1870. 8vo. Congr. and Polit. Pamph. Vol. 116.
—— Speech in Congress, Apr. 21, 1864, on War Debts of Loyal States. Rebell'n Pamph. Vol. 9.
—— Republican Economy *vs.* Democratic Extravagance: Speech in Cong., July 2, 1868. Congr. and Polit. Pamph. Vol. 84.
Blair, Austin. Speech in Congr., Mar. 16, 1870, on the Tariff. Congr. and Polit. Pamph. Vol. 87.
Blair, F. P. Remarks in Cong., 1862, on the Case of Gen. Fremont. Rebell'n Pamph. Vol. 15.
Blair, Hugh, D.D. Abridgment of his Lectures on Rhetoric. Salem, 1818. 12mo.
Blair, Montgomery. Speech at Union Meeting at Rockville, Md., 1863. Rebell'n Pamph. Vol. 54.

BLAKE, A. P. To the Rescue of Amer. Commerce. [In Regard to the Steamship Ontario.] Boston, 1869. 8vo. Pamphlets. Vol. 13.

BLAKE Family Genealogy. See BLAKE, Saml.

BLAKE, Francis. Oration at Worcester, Mass., July 4, 1812. Worcester. 8vo. Addresses. Vol. 29.

BLAKE, H. G. Speech in Congress, Apr. 11, 1862, on Slavery in the District of Columbia. Rebell'n Pamph. Vol. 68.

BLAKE, H. N. Three Years in Army of Potomac. Boston, 1865. 12mo.

BLAKE, James. Annals of Dorchester, 1870. Dorchester Antiq. Soc. Coll. Vol. 2.

BLAKE, Rev. John L. Farmer's Every-Day Book; or Sketches of Social Life in the Country. 1857. 8vo.

BLAKE, Jonathan. Paper on the Early History of Warwick, Mass. N. Eng. Hist. and Gen. Reg. Vol. 21.

BLAKE, Rev. Mortimer. Centurial History of Mendon Assoc. of Congrega. Ministers. Boston, 1853. 8vo.

—— Sermon before the Taunton and Raynham Volunteers, June 2, 1861. Taunton. 8vo. Mass. Hist. Disc. Vol. 1.

BLAKE, Samuel. Genealog. History of William Blake, of Dorchester, Mass. Boston, 1847. 8vo.

BLAKE, William J. History of Putnam Co., N. Y. N. Y., 1849. 12mo.

BLAKE, Wm. P. See Paris Universal Exposition. 1867.

BLAKESLEE, Jos. W. Catholicity and Protestanism. Sermon at Trinity Coll., Dec. 16, 1841. Cambridge, 1842. 8vo. Strangford, Pamph. Vol. 32.

BLACKSTONE, W. J. Speech in Md. State Conven., Mar. 22, 1851, on the Basis of Representation. Cong. and Pol. Pam. Vol. 88.

BLANCHARD, John. Speech in Congress, June 29, 1846, on the Tariff. Washington, 1846. 8vo. Speeches. Vol. 1.

BLANCHARD, J. P. The War of Secession. Portland. (n. d.) Rebell'n Pamph. Vol. 102.

BLANCHARD, Rufus. Map of the U. S., Sheet Form. 1854.

—— R. R. Map of Wisconsin. 1858.

—— Map of Western Part of the U. S. 1795.

BLANCHARD'S Guide Map. 1868. Chicago Mis. Pamp., etc. Vol. 1.

BLAND, John. Letter to the Friends: in which the Conduct of Lord Geo. Sackville is Defended. Lond., 1759. 8vo. Eng. Polit. Pamph. Vol. 71.

BLAND Papers; or Selections from the MSS. of Col. Theodoric Bland. Petersburgh, Va., 1840.

BLANE, Sir Gilbert. Causes and Remedies of the Scarcity and High Price of Provisions. Lond., 1817. 8vo. 2d Ed. Pamphleteer. Vol. 9.

BLAQUIERE, Ed. Report on the State of the Greek Confederation, and its Claims on the Christian World. Lond., 1823. 8vo. Pamphleteer. Vol. 22.

BLAREMBERG, M. De. Notice sur Quelques Objets D'Antiquite, Decouverts en Tauride. Paris, 1822. 8vo. Strangford Pamph. Vol. 42.

BLATCHFORD, John. See BUSHNELL, C. I. Life and Imprisonment.

BLEDSOE, Albert Taylor. Essay on Liberty and Slavery. Phila., 1857. 12mo.

—— Is Davis a Traitor? or was Secession a Constitutional Right, etc. Baltimore, 1866. 12mo.

BLEDSOE, Jesse Lecture on Common and Statute Law, at Transylva. University. Nov., 1823. Lexington, Ky. 12mo. Pamphlets. Vol. 4.

BLEEKER, Anthony J. Documents in favor of his Appointment as Assessor for the District including N. Y. City, 1865, 1868. 8vo. Congr. and Polit. Pamph. Vol. 79.

BLEEKER, Capt. Leonard. Orderly Book in the Early Part of the Expedition under Gen. Jas. Clinton, in the Campaign of 1779. N. Y., 1865. Small 4to.

BLENHEIM, Eng. New Description of, with an Acc't of the Paintings, Tapestry, etc. Lond., 1800. 12mo. Guide-Books. Vol. 6.

BLENHEIM & NUNEHAM, Eng. See Oxford University and City Guide, etc.

BLENNERHASSETT, Harman. See HILDRETH, S. P. Early Ohio Settlers.

—— SAFFORD, W. H. Blennerhasset Papers.

—— —— Life of.

BLIND. See N. England Institution Reports.

—— Perkins Instit. and Mass. Asylum Reports.

—— Reports of Various States.

BLISS, George. Address at the Opening of the Town Hall in Springfield, Mar. 24, 1828, with Hist. Sketches. Springfield, 1828. 8vo. Mass. Hist. Discourses. Vol. 12.

—— Hist. Address before the Hampshire, Franklin and Hampden Bar, Sept., 1826. Springfield, 1827. 8vo. Mass. Hist. Discourses. Vol. 6.

—— Speech in Cong., Apr. 18, 1854, on the Kansas and Nebr. Bill. Congr. and Polit. Pamph. Vol. 84.

BLISS, Geo. R., D. D. The Place of Baptists in Protestant Christendom. Address before the Amer. Bapt. Hist. Soc., 1862. Phila., 1862. 8vo.

BLISS, Leonard. History of Rehoboth, Bristol County, Mass., including Seekonk and Pawtucket. Boston, 1836. 8vo.

BLISS, P. Speech in Cong., Jan. 7, 1858, on Slavery, etc. Congr. and Polit. Pamph. Vol. 88.

BLISS, Philemon. Inauguration of Dan'l Read, as President of the University of Missouri, June 26, 1867. Columbia, 1867. 8vo. Addresses, etc. Vol. 16.

BLISS, Porter C, & MASTERMAN, Geo. F. Congress. Report relative to their Imprisonment in Paraguay, etc. Washington, 1870. 8vo. Congr. and Polit. Pamph. Vol. 131.

BLISS, Seth. Letters to the Members of the American Tract Society, on the Tract Controversy. Boston, 1858. 8vo.

BLIZARD, Sir Wm. Oration before the Hunterian Society, Feb. 9, 1826. Lond., 1826 (?) 4to. Med. Pamph. Vol. 34.

BLOFIELD, J. H. & FORBES, E. Notes on St. Helena. From the Quar. Journ. of the Geolog. Soc. of Lond., 1852. Scientific Pamph. Vol. 3.

BLODGET, Lorin. Commercial and Financial Strength of the U. S. Phila., 1864. 8vo. Rebell'n Pamph. Vols. 7 and 20.

—— Paper on Compulsory Educa., read before the Social Science Assoc. of Phila., Jan. 19, 1871. 8vo. Educa. Pamph. Vol. 5.

BLOIS, John T. Gazetteer of Michigan. Detroit, 1839. 12mo. Another Copy. Detroit, 1840. 12mo.

BLOMFIELD, Bishop Chas. Jas. Sermon at the Coronation of Queen Victoria, in the Abbey Ch. of Westminster, June 27, 1838. Lond. 8vo. 4th Ed. Eng. Sermons. Vol. 41.

BLOOD, Henry A. History of Temple, N. H., 1758—1858. Boston, 1860. 8vo.

BLOODGOOD, S. D. W. The Sexagenary; or Reminiscences of the Amer. Revolution. Albany, 1866. 8vo.

BLOODY (The) Week; Account of the Outrages on Life and Property at the Riots in N. Y. City, 1863. Rebel'n Pam. Vol. 69.

BLOOMFIELD, Conn. See STILES, H. R. Ancient Windsor.

BLOOMINGDALE Asylum for the Insane. See N. York Hospital and Bloomingdale Asylum.

BLOOMINGTON, Ill. See (The) Anniversary Week at Bloomington, 1860.

BLOSS, C. A. Heroines of the Crusades. Auburn, 1853. 8vo.

BLOUNT, Chas. Legality of Marriage with a Deceased Wife's Sister. Lond., 1871. 12mo. Eng. Religious Pamph. Vol. 92.

BLOUNT, Wm. Proceedings on the Impeachment of Wm. Blount, for High Crimes and Misdemeanors. Phila., 1799. 8vo.

BLOW, Henry T. Speech in Cong., Feb. 23, 1864, in Reply to F. P. Blair. Congr. and Polit. Pamph. Vol. 121. Rebell'n Pamph. Vol. 34.

"BLUE BOOKS"—U. States. See U. S. Official Registers.

—— DISTURNELL, John.

—— Wisconsin Legislative Manuals.

BLUE LAWS of New Haven Colony, usually called Blue Laws of Connecticut; Quaker Laws of Plymouth and Massachusetts, etc. Hartford, 1838. 12mo.

—— Or the Code of 1650. Hartford, 1822. 12mo.

—— —— Another Copy. Hartford, 1832. 12mo.

BLUNDELL, B. Review of the Contribution of John Lewis Peyton to the History of Va., and the Civil War in America, 1861—1865. Lond., 1868. 8vo. Rebell'n Pamph. Vol. 57.

BLUNT, Joseph. Historical Sketch of the Formation of the Confederacy. N. Y., 1825. 8vo.

—— History of the Cessions by the States of the North Western Territory. "Olden Time." Vol. 1.

BLUNT, Walter. The Education Question Practically Considered. London, 1850. 8vo. Educa. Pamph. Vol. 34.

BLYTH, Eng. See RAINE, John. Hist. and Antiq. of, 1860.

BOADEN, Jas. Letter to Geo. Stevens, with an Examina. of the Papers of Shakspeare, published by Sam'l Ireland. Lond., 1796. 8vo. 2d Ed. Eng. Misc. Pamph. Vol. 20.

BOADEN, Jas. Memoirs of the Life of John Philip Kemble, Esq.; including a History of the Stage. Lond., 1825. 2 vols. 8vo.
BOARDMAN, Rev. Geo. D. Address on Re-establishing of the National Flag at Fort Sumpter, 1865. Phila., 1865. 8vo. Rebell'n Pamph. Vol. 15.
BOARDMAN, H. A. Intervention tried by the Teachings of Washington. Address at Phila., Feb. 23, 1852. Phila., 1852. 8vo. Addresses. Vol. 10.
—— Sermon at Phila., Sept. 14, 1862. Rebell'n Pamph. Vol. 29.
—— Thanksgiving Sermon at Phila., Nov. 29, 1860. Rebell'n Pamph. Vol. 71.
—— Thanksgiving in War; Sermon at Phila., Nov. 28, 1861. Rebell'n Pamph. Vols. 71 & 80.
—— The Federal Judiciary; a Thanksgiving Disc. Phila., 1862. 8vo. Rebell'n Pamph. Vol. 64.
—— The Peace-Makers; a Thanksgiving Sermon at Phila., Apr. 9, 1865. Rebell'n Pamph. Vol. 40.
BOARDMAN, S. L. Agriculture and Industry of Kennebec County, Maine, with Notes upon its History and Nat. Hist. Augusta, 1867. 8vo. Agr. Pamph. Vol. 6.
BOARD of Nat. Popular Educa. 2d, 4th, 5th, 6th Ann. Reports. Cleveland, O., 1849—1853. 8vo. Educa. Pamph. Vol. 1.
BOCKH, August. Enquiry into the Cosmic System of Plato. Berlin, 1852. 8vo. Scientific Pamph. Vol. 39.
BODIAM, Eng., and its Lords. See LOWER, M. A.
BODLEY, Rachel L. Cat. of Plants in the Herbarium of Jos. Clark, of Cincin., O., 1865. Scientific Pamph. Vol. 15.
—— Introduct. Lecture in Women's Med. Coll. of Pa., October 15, 1868. Phila., 1868. 8vo. Addresses. Vol. 14.
BODY, John E. The Inter-Oceanic Canal, via Nicaragua. Address delivered June 24, 1870. N. Y., 1870. 8vo.
BOGNOR, Eng., Eight Views of Bognor and Neighborhood. 12mo. (n. d.) Guide Books. Vol. 4.
BOGOTA in 1836–7. See STEWART, J.
BOHN, Henry G. The Paper Duty Considered in Reference to the Literature and Trade of G. Britain. Lond., 1860. 8vo. Eng. Polit. Pamph. Vol. 58.
—— Sale Catalogue of Books. Lond., 1841. 8vo. pp. 1948.
—— Catalogue of Books, Vol. 1. Nat. Hist., etc. London, 1847. 8vo.
—— —— Part 2, Sec. 1, Greek and Latin Classics. London, 1850. 8vo.
BOILEAU, M. Letter to M. de Maucroix, with his Reply to the Same, 1695. 12mo. Eng. Miscell. Pamph. Vol. 14.
BOILEAU, D. Remarks on Mr. Hayward's English Prose Translation of Goethe's Faust. London, 1834. 8vo. Eng. Misc. Pamph. Vol. 20.
BOKER, Geo. H. Corres. with Phila. Union League, 1863. Rebell'n Pamph. Vol. 54.
BOKUM, H. Testimony of a Refugee from E. Tennessee.
—— Same in German, 1863. Rebell'n Pamph. Vol. 91.
—— Wanderings North and South. Phila., 1864. 8vo. Rebell'n Pamph. Vol. 12.

BOLLER, H. A. Among the Indians. Eight Years in the Far West, 1858—1866. Phila., 1868. 12mo.
BOLLES, J. A. Bolles' Genealogy. Boston, 1865. 4to.
BOLLING, Robt. Memoirs and Genealogy of Bolling Family of Va. Photographically Illustrated. Richmond, 1868. 4to. Genealog. Pamph. Vol. 5.
BOLTON, Robt. Jr. Hist. of the Co. of Westchester, N. Y., with Genealogies. N. Y., 1848. 2 vols. 8vo.
—— Hist. of the Epis. Ch., Westchester Co., N. Y., 1693—1853. N. Y., 1855. 8vo.
BOLWELL. John. The Worthing Guide. Worthing, Eng. (n. d.) 12mo. Guide Books. Vol. 21.
BOMBAY Catholic Education and Orphan Soc'y. Proceedings, etc. Bombay, India, 1847. 8vo. Educa. Pamph. Vol. 37.
BONAPARTE, Chas. Louis Napoleon. Hist. of Julius Cæsar. N. Y., 1866. 2 vols. 8vo.
—— —— See Napoleon III and the State of Europe, 1860.
—— —— In Italy.
—— —— PASCAL, A. Histoire de.
BONAPARTE in Egypt. See Copies of Intercepted Letters.
BONAPARTE, Louis. Reply to Sir Walter Scott's Hist. of Napoleon. Phila., 1829. 8vo. Biograph. Pamph. Vol 14.
BONAPARTE, Napoleon. See ABBOTT, J. S. C. Corres. with Josephine.
—— ARNOTT, Dr. A. Last Illness and Decease of.
—— Court and Camp of. Harper's Family Library. N. York, 1859. 18mo.
—— See DE SEGUR, Count. Hist. of Russian Expedition.
—— FORSYTH, W. Hist. of Captivity of.
—— HAZLITT, W. Life of.
—— HEADLEY, J. T. Imperial Guard of.
—— —— Napoleon and Marshals.
—— HEADLEY, P. C. Life of.
—— Island Empire; or Scenes at Elba.
—— LAS CASES, Count. Memoirs of.
—— LOCKHART, J. G. Life of.
—— Napoleon and Marshals of the Empire.
—— Napoleon Dynasty.
—— POORE, B. P. Early Life and Campaigns.
—— THIERS, M. A. Hist. of Consulate.
—— WHATELY, Rev. R. Historic Doubts, etc.
BONAPARTE, Prince Napoleon Louis. Authentic Memoirs of. Providence, 1848. 12mo. Biograph. Pamph. Vol. 14.
BONAR, Horatius. Desert of Sinai; Notes of a Spring Journey from Cairo to Beersheba. N. Y., 1857. 12mo.
—— Land of Promise; Notes of a Spring Journey from Beersheba to Sidon. N. Y., 1858. 12mo.
BONCHAMPS, Marchioness de.— See GENLIS, Countess de. Memoirs of.
BOND, Rev. ALVAN.— Hist. Disc. on the 100th Anniver. of the Organiza. of 2d Congrega. Ch., Norwich, Conn. July, 1860. 8vo. Conn. Hist, Discourses. Vol. 5.

BOND, GEO.— See LOTHROP, S. K. Obit. Sermon. 1842.

BOND, Dr, HENRY.— Genealogies of Early Settlers of Watertown, Mass., including Waltham and Weston. Boston, 1855. 8vo.

—— See PALMER, JOS. Sketch of Life of.

BOND, JOHN W.— Meteorology of Minnesota. Minn. Hist. Soc. Coll. Vol. 1.

—— Minn. and its Resources. N. Y., 1853. 12mo.

BOND, L. M.— Catalogue of his Library, to be sold at N. Y., May 3, 1870. Bibliograph. Pamph. Vol. 34.

BONHEUR, ROSA.— See De Bois Gallais, F. L. Biog.

BONNEFOUX, L.— Extracts from a Treatise on the Constitution of U. States. New York, 1863. Rebelln. Pamph. Vol, 28.

BONNEVILLE, Capt.— See Irving, W.

BONNEY, EDW. Banditti of the Prairies, &c. [Murder of Col. Davenport at Rock Island.] Chicago, 1850. 8vo.

BONNYCASTLE, CHAS.— Lecture Introduc. to the Course of Mathematics, of the Univer. of Va. 1837. Charlottesville, Va. 8vo. Scientific Pamph. Vol. 21.

BONNYCASTLE, Capt.— Observa. on Certain Rocks and Minerals of Upper Canada. Quebec Lit. & Hist. Soc'y Trans. Vol. 1.

BONNYCASTLE, Sir R. H.— The Canada's in 1847. Lond., 1847. 2 Vols. 8vo.

BOOK Buyers Manual. N. Y., 1853. 8vo.

—— The, for the Nation and the Times. Phila., 1864. 12mo. Rebell'n Pamph. Vol. 4.

—— of Amer. Indians, with Comprehensive Details of Indian Battles &c. Dayton, O., 1854. 12mo.

—— of Common Prayer. Lond. 1776. 12mo.

—— of Family Crests, comprising nearly every Bearing, with its Blazonry, with upwards of 4000 engravings. 7th ed. enlarged Lond. 1854. 2 vols. 12mo.

—— of Mormon. Account written by the Hand of Mormon upon Plates, taken from the Plates of Nephi. 4th ed. Liverpool 1854. 12mo.

—— of Sports. The King's Majesties Declaration concerning Lawful Sports. Phila. 1866. Sm. 4to. Eng. Mis. Pamph. Vol. 36.

—— of the Prophet Stephen, Son of Douglass. Books, 1, 2. Rebelln. Pamph. Vol. 97.

—— —— River Axe, Eng. See Pulman, G. P. R.

—— —— Signers. Brotherhead, W.

BOOKER, GEO. W.— See Tucker, G.

BOONE, DAN'L.— See ELLIS, E. S. Life and Times of. FLINT, Tim. Life and Adventures. HARTLEY, C. B. Life and Times of. HAYCRAFT, S. Speech on Boone Monument, 1860. HILL, G. C. Biog. of. IMLAY, G. Adventures of. Life and Times of. 1860. PECK, J. M. Life of. MCCLUNG, I. A. & PRATT'S J.

BOONESBOROUGH, Ky. Attack upon Boonsborough by the Indians, in 1778. Western Review. Vol. 3.

—— See Morehead, J. T. Address. 1840.

BOOT, The, On the other Leg; or Loyalty above Party. 1863. Rebelln. Pamph. Vol. 91.

BOOTH, DAVID. Observations on the English Jury Laws in Criminal Cases. Lond. 1833. 8vo. 2d ed. Law Pamph. Vol. 18.

BOOTH. Genealogy. See Smith, Columbus. Report of the Booth Assoc.

BOOTH, Dr. JAS. Female Educa. of the Industrial Classes. Lond. 1855. 8vo. Educa. Pamph. Vol. 33.

BOOTH, James C. & Morfit C. On Recent Improvements in the Chemical Arts. Washington, 1852. 8vo. Congress Pamph. Vol. 36.

—— Letter to the President of the U. S. in reply to charges of Prof. R. S. McColloh, 1853. Congress, Pamph. Vol. 49.

BOOTH, Rev. John. Metrical Epitaphs. Lond. 1868. 12mo.

BOOTH, John Wilkes. See Townsend, G. A. Life, Crime and Capture of.

BOOTH, Mary L. History of the City of N. Y. to the Present Time. 100 engravings. N. Y. 1860. 8vo.

BOOTH, S. M. Speech in the Assembly Chamber, Madison, Apr. 3, 1867. on his Claim &c. Wis. Misc. Pamph. Vol. 1. Cong. & Polit. Pamph. Vol. 87.

BOOTHE. Genealogy. See Swan, Rev. B. L.

BOQUET, Col. Expedition, 1764. See Whittlesey, Chas.

BORDEAUX, France. Deliberation sur l'en quete, relative a l'etablissement de la Gare du Chemin de Fer de Paris a Bordeaux. Bordeaux 1846. 4to.

BORDEN, M. B. Addr. before B'd of Aldermen, Fall River, Mass. 1858. 8vo. Addr. Vol. 1.

BORDER & BASTILE, See Lawrence, Geo.

—— Life. See Mirror of Olden Time.

—— Warfare of New York. See CAMPBELL, W. W.

BORDLEY Family. See GIBSON, Mrs. E. B. Biograph. Sketches of.

BORLAND, S. Speech in U. S. Senate, May 12 & 17, 1852, on the Collins Line of Steamers. Congr. & Polit. Pamph. Vol. 89.

—— Speech in U. S. Senate, May 27, 1852, on the Deficiency Bill. Congr. & Polit. Pamph. Vol. 90.

BORRING. Laurett Etienne. Notices on the Life and Writings of Carl Christian Rafn. Copenhagen, 1864. 8vo. Addresses &c. Vol. 19.

BORROW, George. The Bible in Spain; or Journeys, Adventures &c., in circulating the Scriptures. N. Y. 1859. 8vo.

BORS, P. Wars of the Netherlands, 1500—1600, in Dutch. Amsterdam 1679. 4 vols. 8vo.

BOSCAWEN, N. H. Academy. 1st Catalogue, 1857. Concord, 1857. 8vo.

BOSCAWEN, N. H. See PRICE, E. Chronolog, Register. 1823.

BOSCOBEL, Wis., Broadaxe. Newspaper. 1863–6. Folio.

BOSQUETT, Abraham. Treatise on Duelling; with the Annals of Chivalry. Lond. 1818. 8vo. Pamphleteer. Vol. 12.

BOSS, Henry R. Early Newspapers in Ill.; read before the Franklin Soc. of Chicago. 1870. Chicago 1870. 4to.

Bossu, Mr. Travels thro' that part of N. America formerly called Louisiana. Lond. 1771. 2 vols. 8vo.

Bostock, Dr. John. Heat: its Nature, Properties, &c. n. d. n. p. 4to. Scientific Pamph. Vol. 38.

Boston. Daily Advertiser. Newspaper. Boston, 1858—1867. 15 vols. Folio.

—— Weekly Advertiser. Newspaper. 1872. 1 vol. Bound with Boston Spectator. 1871.

—— American Traveller, Newspaper. Aug., 1850, to Mar., 1854.

—— Almanac. 1840—1865. Except 1862. 25 vols. 12mo.

—— & Lowell R. R. Corporation. Remonstrance in regard to the Construction of R. R's. between Lowell & Andover. 1845.

—— —— Ann. Report for 1865. Mass. R. R. Reports &c. Vol. 3. Boston. 8vo.

—— & Maine, R. R. Report of Directors, Sept. 10, 1856. Boston, 1859. 8vo. Mass. R. R. Reports. Vol. 3.

—— & Providence R. R. Corporation. 3d Ann. Report. Boston, 1834. 8vo. Mass. R. R. Reports. Vol. 3.

—— & Worcester R. R. Co. Report of a Committee of Directors. 1840.

—— —— 20th, 21st, 25th, 28th, 33d, 36th, Ann. Reports. Boston, 1840.—1866. 8vo. Mass. R. R. Reports. Vol. 2.

—— —— Communication by Directors to Stockholders. Boston, 1860. 8vo. Mass R. R. Reports &c. Vol. 2.

—— See Aristocracy The, of Boston.

—— Arlington St. Ch. See Gannett, E. S. 40th Annivers. Discourse. 1864.

—— Artillery Company. See Vinton, A. H. 207th Annivers. Discourse. 1845.

—— Assoc. for Relief of Aged Indigent Females. Act of Incorporation, By-Laws, etc. 1850.

Ann. Reports. 1850–1869.

—— Memorial in Behalf of. 1849.

—— See Rogers, H. B.

—— Asylum and Farm School for Indigent Boys. Reports, Act of Incorporation, etc. Boston, 1849. 8vo.

—— Atheneum. Catalogue of Books in Library. Boston, 1827.

—— —— Catalogue of Exhibition of Paintings and Statuary. 1866. Boston, 1866. 8vo. Bibliograph. Pamph. Vol. 21.

—— Auditor's Reports of Receipts and Expenditures, for 1833, 1835, 1847–8, 1849–50, 1850–1, 1851–, 1852–3, 1853–4, 1854–5, 1855–6, 1856–7, 1858–9, 1859–60, 1862–3, 1868–9, 1870–71. Boston, 1833–1871. 8vo.

—— Benev. Fraternity of Churches. 4th, 11th, 17th, 18th, 22d, 23d, 24th, 25th, 26th, 28th, 29th, 31st, 33d, 37th Ann Reports, 1845–1871. Boston. 8vo. and 12mo.

—— See Bigelow, Jacob. Hist. of Mt. Auburn Cemetery.

—— Board of Aldermen. See Mayor's Addresses. Municipal Registers.

—— Board of Trade. Act of Incorporation, By-Laws, etc. 1854.

—— —— Ann. Reports for 1854, '56, '58, '66, '67, '70.

BOSTON. Board of Trade. Appeal to Capitalists and others, on Steam Communication between Boston and New Orleans. Boston, 1860. 8vo. Boston Misc. Pamph. Vol. 2.

—— —— Proceedings Relative to a Canal from the Lakes to the Mississippi, etc. Boston, 1870. 8vo. Boston Misc. Pamph. Vol. 2.

—— —— Report of Com. on Am. Shipping Interests. Boston, 1871. 8vo. Boston Misc. Pamph. Vol. 5.

—— Bowdoin St. Ch. Articles of Faith, Covenant, etc., with a Hist. of the Ch. Boston, 1843 and 1856. 8vo.

—— Brattle, St Ch. See LOTHROP, S. K. Hist. of, and THACHER, Peter. Centen. Sermon. 1799.

—— BRIDGMAN, T. Memorials of Dead, in.

—— Pilgrims of.

—— Brown's Guide Book. 1869.

—— Bullfinch, St. Church. See GRAY, F. T.

—— —— Letter to Friends of F. S. Gray.

—— Cape Cod Assoc. Constitution of, with an Account of the Celebration of its First Annivers., Nov. 11, 1851, Including an Oration by H. A. Scudder. Boston, 1852. 8vo. Boston Hist. Discourses, etc. Vol. 2.

—— Catalogue of Lots, Wharves, etc., to be sold by the Mill Pond Wharf Corporation, May 28, 1840. Boston, 1840. 8vo. Boston Misc. Pamph. Vol. 3.

—— Celebra. of the Centen, Anivers. of the Birth of Robt. Burns, Jan. 25, 1859. Boston, 1859. 8vo. Addresses, etc. Vol. 26.

—— Census of Boston for 1845, 1850, 1855.

—— Central Cong. Church. Confession of Faith and Covenant. Boston, 1842. 8vo. Sermons, etc. Vol. 8.

—— Chambers Street Chapel. Report of the Supt. of. Apr., 1866. Boston, 1866. 12mo. Boston Misc. Pamph. Vol. 4.

—— Channing Home. 1st, 2d and 3d Reports, 1869, '70, 71. Boston, 1869–1871. 12mo.

—— Charter and Ordinances of the City. Boston, 1856. 8vo.

—— Children's Aid Soc'y. 5th and 6th Ann. Reports. Boston, 1869–1870. 8vo.

—— Children's Hospital. 1st, 2d and 3d Ann. Reports for 1869, '70, '71. Boston, 1870–72. 8vo.

—— Children Mission to the Children of the Destitute. Ann. Reports of the Executive Committee, 1827, '59, '60, '61, '65, '68, '69, '71. Boston. 12mo.

—— Christ Church. See EATON, Rev. Asa. Historical Account of.

—— Christian Contributor and Free Missionary. Newspaper. 1846–7. Folio.

—— —— Watchman, Newspaper. April, to Dec., 1864.

—— Chronicle, Newspaper. Dec., 1767, to Dec., 1768. 4to.

—— Church Home for Orphan and Destitute Children. 9th Ann. Report. Boston, 1866. 8vo.

—— —— of the Advent. See BOLLES, J. A.

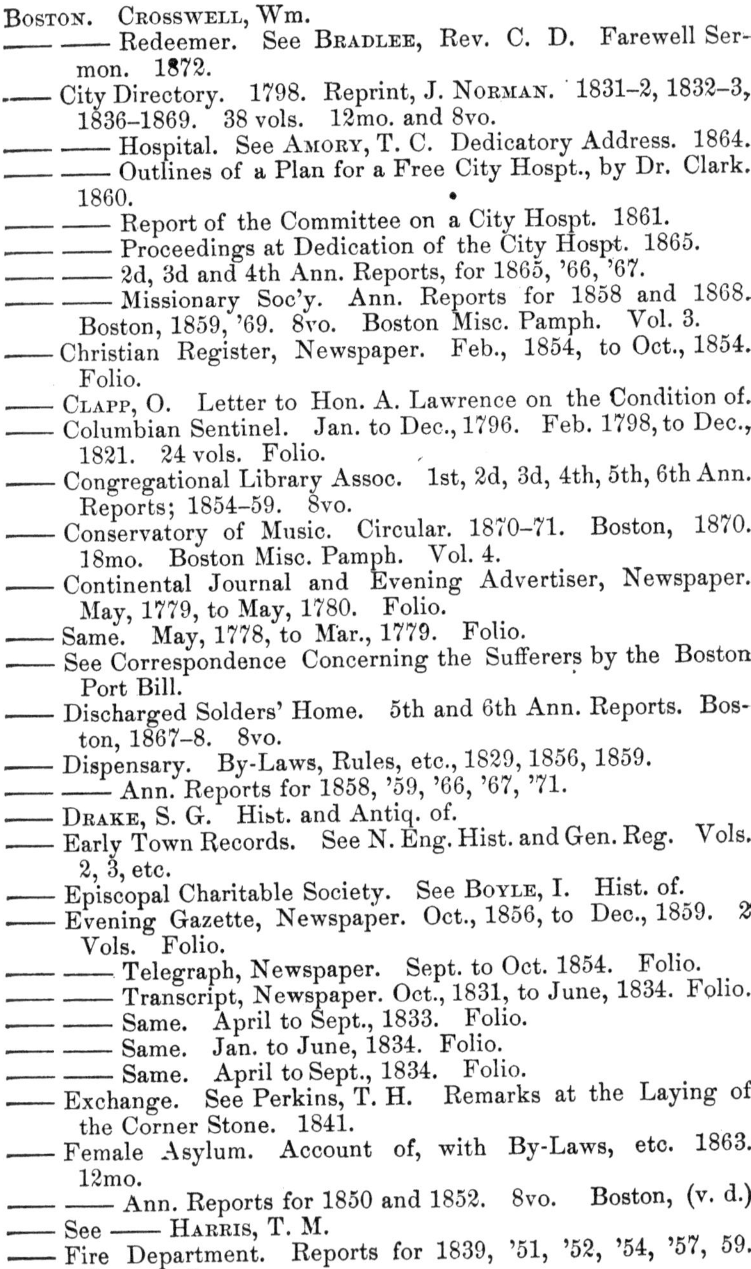

BOSTON. CROSSWELL, Wm.
—— —— Redeemer. See BRADLEE, Rev. C. D. Farewell Sermon. 1872.
—— City Directory. 1798. Reprint, J. NORMAN. 1831–2, 1832–3, 1836–1869. 38 vols. 12mo. and 8vo.
—— —— Hospital. See AMORY, T. C. Dedicatory Address. 1864.
—— —— Outlines of a Plan for a Free City Hospt., by Dr. Clark. 1860.
—— —— Report of the Committee on a City Hospt. 1861.
—— —— Proceedings at Dedication of the City Hospt. 1865.
—— —— 2d, 3d and 4th Ann. Reports, for 1865, '66, '67.
—— —— Missionary Soc'y. Ann. Reports for 1858 and 1868. Boston, 1859, '69. 8vo. Boston Misc. Pamph. Vol. 3.
—— Christian Register, Newspaper. Feb., 1854, to Oct., 1854. Folio.
—— CLAPP, O. Letter to Hon. A. Lawrence on the Condition of.
—— Columbian Sentinel. Jan. to Dec., 1796. Feb. 1798, to Dec., 1821. 24 vols. Folio.
—— Congregational Library Assoc. 1st, 2d, 3d, 4th, 5th, 6th Ann. Reports; 1854–59. 8vo.
—— Conservatory of Music. Circular. 1870–71. Boston, 1870. 18mo. Boston Misc. Pamph. Vol. 4.
—— Continental Journal and Evening Advertiser, Newspaper. May, 1779, to May, 1780. Folio.
—— Same. May, 1778, to Mar., 1779. Folio.
—— See Correspondence Concerning the Sufferers by the Boston Port Bill.
—— Discharged Solders' Home. 5th and 6th Ann. Reports. Boston, 1867–8. 8vo.
—— Dispensary. By-Laws, Rules, etc., 1829, 1856, 1859.
—— —— Ann. Reports for 1858, '59, '66, '67, '71.
—— DRAKE, S. G. Hist. and Antiq. of.
—— Early Town Records. See N. Eng. Hist. and Gen. Reg. Vols. 2, 3, etc.
—— Episcopal Charitable Society. See BOYLE, I. Hist. of.
—— Evening Gazette, Newspaper. Oct., 1856, to Dec., 1859. 2 Vols. Folio.
—— —— Telegraph, Newspaper. Sept. to Oct. 1854. Folio.
—— —— Transcript, Newspaper. Oct., 1831, to June, 1834. Folio.
—— —— Same. April to Sept., 1833. Folio.
—— —— Same. Jan. to June, 1834. Folio.
—— —— Same. April to Sept., 1834. Folio.
—— Exchange. See Perkins, T. H. Remarks at the Laying of the Corner Stone. 1841.
—— Female Asylum. Account of, with By-Laws, etc. 1863. 12mo.
—— —— Ann. Reports for 1850 and 1852. 8vo. Boston, (v. d.)
—— See —— HARRIS, T. M.
—— Fire Department. Reports for 1839, '51, '52, '54, '57, 59. Boston. 8vo.

BOSTON. First Church. See FROTHINGHAM, N. L. Bi-Centen. Sermon, 1830, and

—— —— 20th Anniv. Disc. 1835.

—— First Baptist Church. WINCHELL, Rev. J. M. Hist. Sketch of. 1818.

—— First Church, Chauncy St. ELLIS, Rev. Rufus. Last Sermon in the Ch. 1868.

—— Forts During the Revolution. See FINCH, J. Account of.

—— Gas Light Co. *vs.* Wm. Gault. Boston, 1848. 8vo. Law Pamphlets. Vol. 1.

—— Gazette, Newspaper. 29 Nos. 1724. March 8, 1725, and June 21, 1736. Small Folio.

—— —— Jan., 1764, to Oct., 1769.

—— —— Jan. to Dec., 1801; Feb., 1802, to Dec., 1803, with parts of the Years 1805, 1807, 1809, 1812, 1860–65.

—— Gen. Theolog. Library. 2d, 6th, 7th, 8th, Ann. Reports: 1864, '68, '69, 70. Boston. 8vo.

—— Guardian for Friendless Girls. 1st Ann. Report. Boston, 1855. 8vo.

—— Hanover, St. Church. See Recent Attempt to Defeat the Constitutional Provisions in Favor of Religious Freedom, etc.

—— Home for Aged Colored Women. 4th Ann. Report. Boston, 1864. 12mo.

—— —— Men. By-Laws, etc.,.1861, and Reports for 1862, '63, '64, '66, '67, 68. 8vo.

—— Horticult. School for Women. 1st Ann. Report. Boston, 1871. 8vo. Agr. Pamph. Vol. 1.

—— House of the Angel Guardian. 2d Ann. Report. Boston, 1853. 8vo.

—— —— Good Samaritan. 6th Ann. Report for 1866. Boston, 1867. 8vo.

—— —— Good Shepherd. Account of. 1869. 8vo.

—— Houses of Industry and Reformation. Ann. Reports for 1846–7, 1847–8, 1851–2, 1853–4. Boston, 1847-1854. 8vo.

—— Howard Benevolent Soc'y. Ann. Reports for 1866, '69, '70. Boston. 12mo.

—— In 1740. See BENNETT. Mr.

—— Independent Chronicle and Universal Advertiser. Newspaper. Aug. 1782 to May 1784. Folio.

—— —— Jan. 1794.—Dec. 1769. 3 vols. Folio. Jan.,–Dec., 1803. Jan. 1809.—Dec. 1810. 2 vols. Folio.

—— Independent Co. of Cadets. LATHROP. Rev. SAML. K.—Centen. Address. 1841.

—— Industrial Aid Soc. Reports for 1852. 55, 56, 57, 58, 59, 60, 61, 62, 63, 64, 65, 66, 68, 69, 70.

—— Industrial Journal of the Soc'y. for Feb. 1851. HALE, Rev. E. E.—Sermon. 1852.

—— LEACH, J.—Journal kept in Boston Gaol. 1775.

—— Liberator. Newspaper. Boston, 1833. Folio.

—— Lists of Persons. Copartnerships & Corporatious, in the City, in 1848, '54, '55, '56, '57, '58. 8vo.

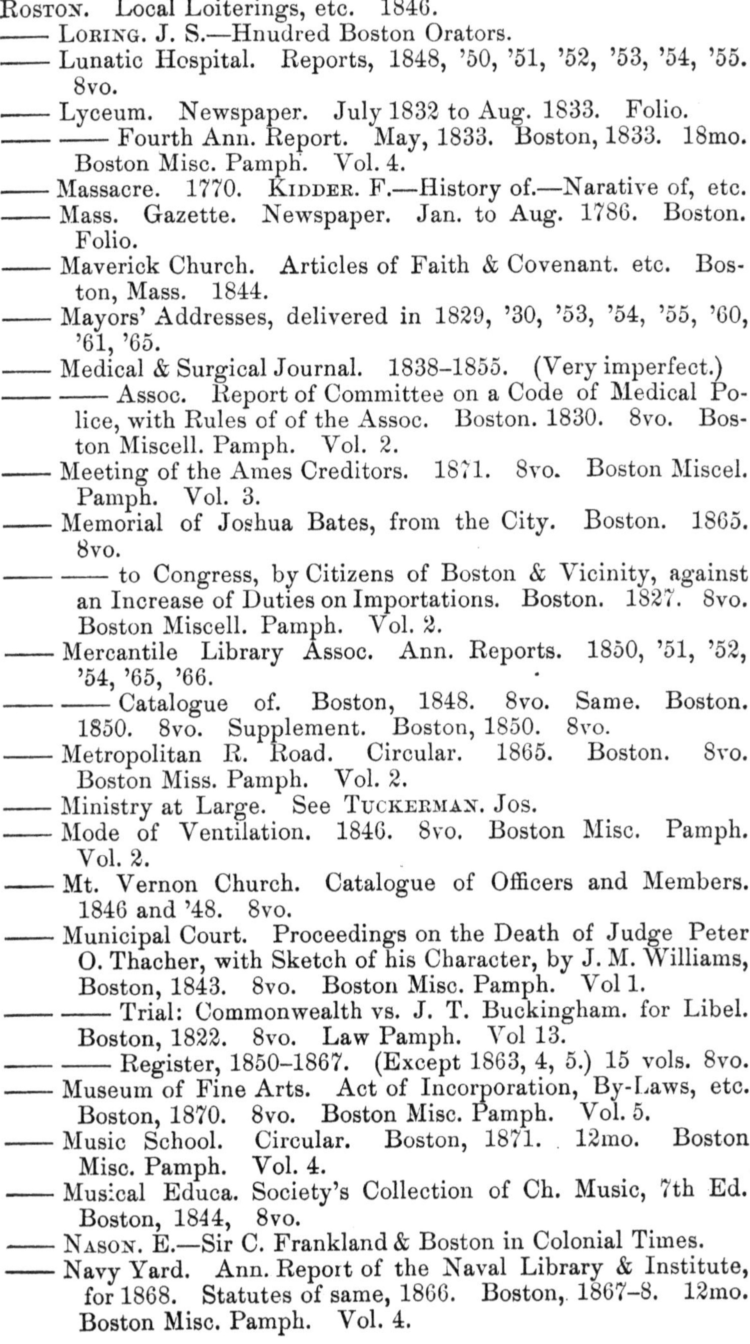

ROSTON. Local Loiterings, etc. 1846.
—— LORING. J. S.—Hnudred Boston Orators.
—— Lunatic Hospital. Reports, 1848, '50, '51, '52, '53, '54, '55. 8vo.
—— Lyceum. Newspaper. July 1832 to Aug. 1833. Folio.
—— —— Fourth Ann. Report. May, 1833. Boston, 1833. 18mo. Boston Misc. Pamph. Vol. 4.
—— Massacre. 1770. KIDDER. F.—History of.—Narative of, etc.
—— Mass. Gazette. Newspaper. Jan. to Aug. 1786. Boston. Folio.
—— Maverick Church. Articles of Faith & Covenant. etc. Boston, Mass. 1844.
—— Mayors' Addresses, delivered in 1829, '30, '53, '54, '55, '60, '61, '65.
—— Medical & Surgical Journal. 1838–1855. (Very imperfect.)
—— —— Assoc. Report of Committee on a Code of Medical Police, with Rules of of the Assoc. Boston. 1830. 8vo. Boston Miscell. Pamph. Vol. 2.
—— Meeting of the Ames Creditors. 1871. 8vo. Boston Miscel. Pamph. Vol. 3.
—— Memorial of Joshua Bates, from the City. Boston. 1865. 8vo.
—— —— to Congress, by Citizens of Boston & Vicinity, against an Increase of Duties on Importations. Boston. 1827. 8vo. Boston Miscell. Pamph. Vol. 2.
—— Mercantile Library Assoc. Ann. Reports. 1850, '51, '52, '54, '65, '66.
—— —— Catalogue of. Boston, 1848. 8vo. Same. Boston. 1850. 8vo. Supplement. Boston, 1850. 8vo.
—— Metropolitan R. Road. Circular. 1865. Boston. 8vo. Boston Miss. Pamph. Vol. 2.
—— Ministry at Large. See TUCKERMAN. Jos.
—— Mode of Ventilation. 1846. 8vo. Boston Misc. Pamph. Vol. 2.
—— Mt. Vernon Church. Catalogue of Officers and Members. 1846 and '48. 8vo.
—— Municipal Court. Proceedings on the Death of Judge Peter O. Thacher, with Sketch of his Character, by J. M. Williams, Boston, 1843. 8vo. Boston Misc. Pamph. Vol 1.
—— —— Trial: Commonwealth vs. J. T. Buckingham. for Libel. Boston, 1822. 8vo. Law Pamph. Vol 13.
—— —— Register, 1850–1867. (Except 1863, 4, 5.) 15 vols. 8vo.
—— Museum of Fine Arts. Act of Incorporation, By-Laws, etc. Boston, 1870. 8vo. Boston Misc. Pamph. Vol. 5.
—— Music School. Circular. Boston, 1871. 12mo. Boston Misc. Pamph. Vol. 4.
—— Musical Educa. Society's Collection of Ch. Music, 7th Ed. Boston, 1844, 8vo.
—— NASON. E.—Sir C. Frankland & Boston in Colonial Times.
—— Navy Yard. Ann. Report of the Naval Library & Institute, for 1868. Statutes of same, 1866. Boston, 1867–8. 12mo. Boston Misc. Pamph. Vol. 4.

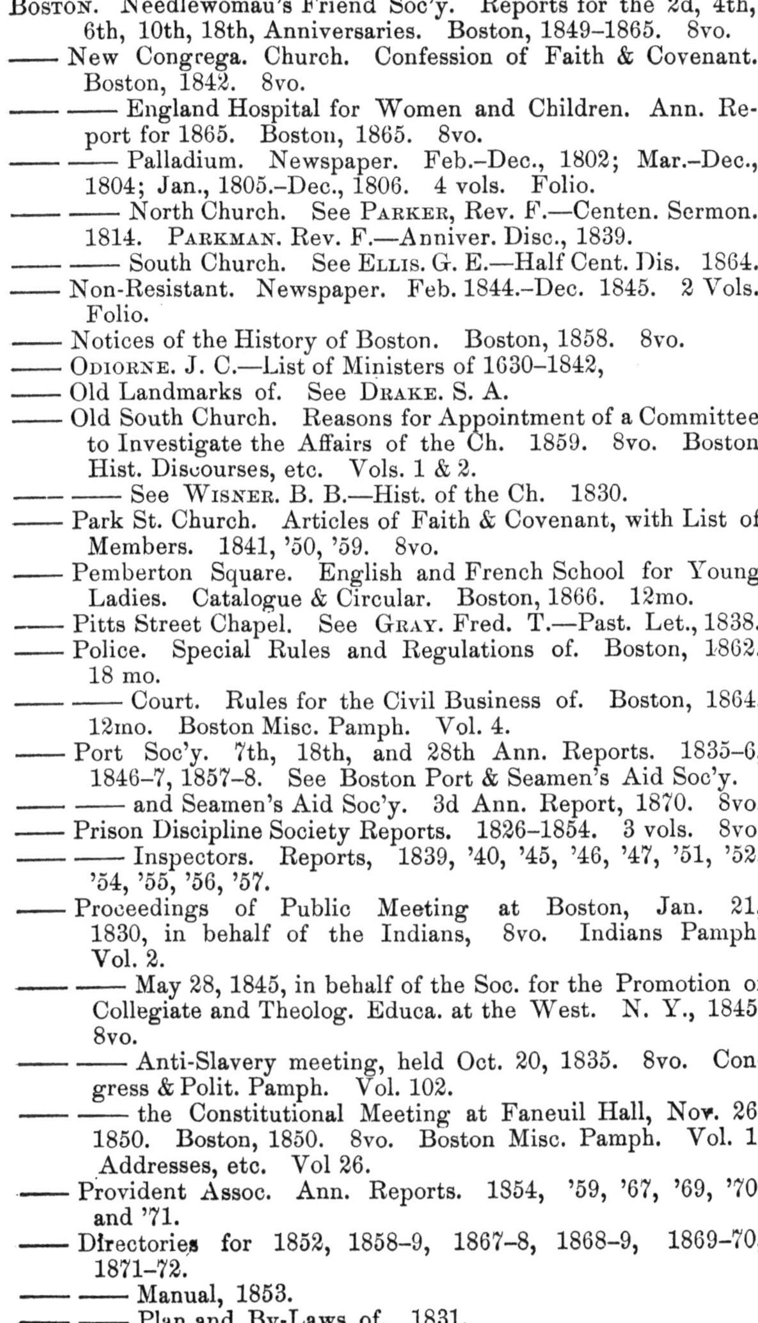

BOSTON. Needlewomau's Friend Soc'y. Reports for the 2d, 4th, 6th, 10th, 18th, Anniversaries. Boston, 1849–1865. 8vo.

—— New Congrega. Church. Confession of Faith & Covenant. Boston, 1842. 8vo.

—— —— England Hospital for Women and Children. Ann. Report for 1865. Boston, 1865. 8vo.

—— —— Palladium. Newspaper. Feb.–Dec., 1802; Mar.–Dec., 1804; Jan., 1805.–Dec., 1806. 4 vols. Folio.

—— —— North Church. See PARKER, Rev. F.—Centen. Sermon. 1814. PARKMAN. Rev. F.—Anniver. Disc., 1839.

—— —— South Church. See ELLIS. G. E.—Half Cent. Dis. 1864.

—— Non-Resistant. Newspaper. Feb. 1844.–Dec. 1845. 2 Vols. Folio.

—— Notices of the History of Boston. Boston, 1858. 8vo.

—— ODIORNE. J. C.—List of Ministers of 1630–1842,

—— Old Landmarks of. See DRAKE. S. A.

—— Old South Church. Reasons for Appointment of a Committee to Investigate the Affairs of the Ch. 1859. 8vo. Boston Hist. Discourses, etc. Vols. 1 & 2.

—— —— See WISNER. B. B.—Hist. of the Ch. 1830.

—— Park St. Church. Articles of Faith & Covenant, with List of Members. 1841, '50, '59. 8vo.

—— Pemberton Square. English and French School for Young Ladies. Catalogue & Circular. Boston, 1866. 12mo.

—— Pitts Street Chapel. See GRAY. Fred. T.—Past. Let., 1838.

—— Police. Special Rules and Regulations of. Boston, 1862. 18 mo.

—— —— Court. Rules for the Civil Business of. Boston, 1864. 12mo. Boston Misc. Pamph. Vol. 4.

—— Port Soc'y. 7th, 18th, and 28th Ann. Reports. 1835–6, 1846–7, 1857–8. See Boston Port & Seamen's Aid Soc'y.

—— —— and Seamen's Aid Soc'y. 3d Ann. Report, 1870. 8vo.

—— Prison Discipline Society Reports. 1826–1854. 3 vols. 8vo.

—— —— Inspectors. Reports, 1839, '40, '45, '46, '47, '51, '52, '54, '55, '56, '57.

—— Proceedings of Public Meeting at Boston, Jan. 21, 1830, in behalf of the Indians, 8vo. Indians Pamph. Vol. 2.

—— —— May 28, 1845, in behalf of the Soc. for the Promotion of Collegiate and Theolog. Educa. at the West. N. Y., 1845. 8vo.

—— —— Anti-Slavery meeting, held Oct. 20, 1835. 8vo. Congress & Polit. Pamph. Vol. 102.

—— —— the Constitutional Meeting at Faneuil Hall, Nov. 26, 1850. Boston, 1850. 8vo. Boston Misc. Pamph. Vol. 1. Addresses, etc. Vol 26.

—— Provident Assoc. Ann. Reports. 1854, '59, '67, '69, '70, and '71.

—— Directories for 1852, 1858–9, 1867–8, 1868–9, 1869–70, 1871–72.

—— —— Manual, 1853.

—— —— Plan and By-Laws of. 1831.

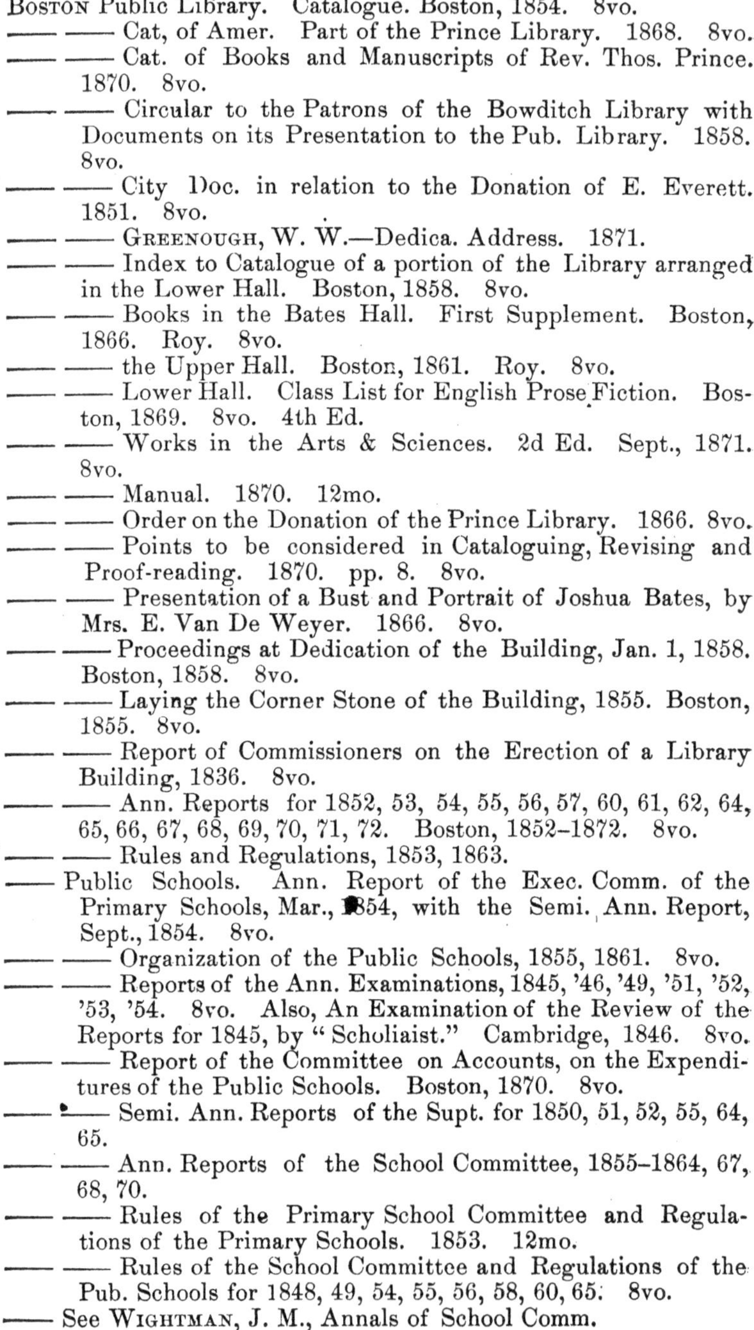

BOSTON Public Library. Catalogue. Boston, 1854. 8vo.

—— —— Cat, of Amer. Part of the Prince Library. 1868. 8vo.

—— —— Cat. of Books and Manuscripts of Rev. Thos. Prince. 1870. 8vo.

—— —— Circular to the Patrons of the Bowditch Library with Documents on its Presentation to the Pub. Library. 1858. 8vo.

—— —— City Doc. in relation to the Donation of E. Everett. 1851. 8vo.

—— —— GREENOUGH, W. W.—Dedica. Address. 1871.

—— —— Index to Catalogue of a portion of the Library arranged in the Lower Hall. Boston, 1858. 8vo.

—— —— Books in the Bates Hall. First Supplement. Boston, 1866. Roy. 8vo.

—— —— the Upper Hall. Boston, 1861. Roy. 8vo.

—— —— Lower Hall. Class List for English Prose Fiction. Boston, 1869. 8vo. 4th Ed.

—— —— Works in the Arts & Sciences. 2d Ed. Sept., 1871. 8vo.

—— —— Manual. 1870. 12mo.

—— —— Order on the Donation of the Prince Library. 1866. 8vo.

—— —— Points to be considered in Cataloguing, Revising and Proof-reading. 1870. pp. 8. 8vo.

—— —— Presentation of a Bust and Portrait of Joshua Bates, by Mrs. E. Van De Weyer. 1866. 8vo.

—— —— Proceedings at Dedication of the Building, Jan. 1, 1858. Boston, 1858. 8vo.

—— —— Laying the Corner Stone of the Building, 1855. Boston, 1855. 8vo.

—— —— Report of Commissioners on the Erection of a Library Building, 1836. 8vo.

—— —— Ann. Reports for 1852, 53, 54, 55, 56, 57, 60, 61, 62, 64, 65, 66, 67, 68, 69, 70, 71, 72. Boston, 1852–1872. 8vo.

—— —— Rules and Regulations, 1853, 1863.

—— Public Schools. Ann. Report of the Exec. Comm. of the Primary Schools, Mar., 1854, with the Semi. Ann. Report, Sept., 1854. 8vo.

—— —— Organization of the Public Schools, 1855, 1861. 8vo.

—— —— Reports of the Ann. Examinations, 1845, '46, '49, '51, '52, '53, '54. 8vo. Also, An Examination of the Review of the Reports for 1845, by "Scholiaist." Cambridge, 1846. 8vo.

—— —— Report of the Committee on Accounts, on the Expenditures of the Public Schools. Boston, 1870. 8vo.

—— —— Semi. Ann. Reports of the Supt. for 1850, 51, 52, 55, 64, 65.

—— —— Ann. Reports of the School Committee, 1855–1864, 67, 68, 70.

—— —— Rules of the Primary School Committee and Regulations of the Primary Schools. 1853. 12mo.

—— —— Rules of the School Committee and Regulations of the Pub. Schools for 1848, 49, 54, 55, 56, 58, 60, 65. 8vo.

—— See WIGHTMAN, J. M., Annals of School Comm.

BOSTON. See QUINCY, Josiah, Bi-Centen. Address, 1830.
—— QUINCY, J., Municipal Hist. of.
—— QUINCY, J., 2d Centen. Address.
—— Railways. See GRANT, E. B.
—— Registration Reports of Births, Marriages and Deaths for 1853, '54, '55, '56, '57, '59, '68.
—— Repertory. Newspaper. July, 1808 to Dec. 27, 1808. Folio.
—— Report of Committee of Delegates from the Benev. Societies of Boston. Boston, 1834. 8vo. Boston Mis. Pamph. Vol. 4.
—— —— The Celebra., July 4, 1858, with the Oration of Rufus Choate and John S. Holmes. Boston, 1858. 8vo. Addresses. Vol. 27.
—— St. Stephen's Chapel. Reports of the Mission to the Poor in 1848, 49, 50, 51. 52, 69, 70. Boston, n. d. 8vo. Religious Pamph. Vol. 24.
—— Salem Church. Article of Faith and Covenant, etc. 1852. Boston, 1853. 12mo.
—— School for the Ministry (Unitarian) Catalogue for 1868–9. 12mo.
—— Seamen's Aid Soc'y, 7th, 12th, 14th, 15th, 16th, 19th, 20th, 21st and 22d Ann. Reports. 1840–1855. 8vo.
—— —— See Boston Port and Seamen's Aid Soc'y.
—— Seamen's Friend Sor'y. Fourteenth Ann. Reports, 1841–2. Boston, 1842. 8vo.
—— —— See Amer. Seamen's Friend Soc'y.
—— Second Ch.
—— —— See Our Pastor's Offering.
—— —— ROBBINS, Rev. C., History.
—— —— ROBBINS, C., 25th Anniver. Disc., 1858.
—— —— WARE, H., Hist. Discourses. 1921.
—— Second Bapt. Ch.
—— —— BALDWIN, Thos. Discourse with Histor. Sketehes. 1824.
—— Siege of 1775–6.
—— —— See CRAFT, Benj., Journal of.
—— —— NEWELL, Tim., Journal of.
—— Soc'y of Nat. His. Act of Incorporation, Constitution and By-Laws. Boston, 1836. 8vo.
—— —— Condition and Doings of, as shown in Reports of the Custodian, etc. Boston, 1867. 8vo.
—— —— GOULD, A. A.
—— —— Journal Vol. 6. Nos. 1, 2, 3. Boston, 1850–1853. 8vo.
—— —— Objects and Claims of. Boston, 1861. 8vo.
—— —— Proceedings 1854–56. Vol. 4. Wants Index. Boston, 1856. 8vo.
—— —— Proceedings 1856–62. Vols. 6, 7, 8. Incomplete. Boston, 1859–62. 8vo.
—— —— WARREN, J. C.
—— Society for Prevention of Pauperism.
—— —— See Boston Industrial Aid Soc.
—— Soldiers' Fund Assoc. Appeal of, with Constitution and By-Laws. Boston, 1862. 12mo. Boston Mis. Pamph. Vol. 4.

BOSTON "Statesman Party."
—— —— See DERBY, J. B.
—— Stock Market. See Martin J. G.
—— Stranger's Guide in the City of Boston. Boston, 1849. 12mo. Vol. 1. No. 2.
—— Sumner, Gen. W. H. See Hist. of East Boston.
—— Supreme Judicial Court. Report of Trial of Theodore Lyman. jr., for Libel on Dan'l Webster. Boston, 1828. 12mo. Congr. & Polit. Pamph. Vol. 134.
—— Temporary Home for the Destitute. Ann. Reports of the Board of Managers for 1851, '53, '56, '57, '58, '59, '60, '61, '67, '68, '69, '70.
—— Thursday Evening Club. Proceed. on Death of Edw. Everett, Jan. 26, 1865. Boston, 1865. 8vo. Addresses, &c. Vol. 25.
—— Lecture. See Frothingham, N. L. Bi–Centen. Sermon. 1833.
—— Topograph. and Hist. Descrip. of. 1794. Mass. Hist. Soc. Coll. 1st Ser. Vol. 3.
—— Tremont St. Medical School. Catalogue. March, 1851, '53, '54, '55. Boston 1851–55. 8vo.
—— Trinity Church. Protest of the Laity against the Election of any Ass't Bishop. Boston, 1838. 8vo. Boston Misc. Pamph. Vol. 5.
—— Union Church. Confession of Faith, Covenant, and Brief Hist. of. Boston, 1830. 12mo.
—— —— Club. Constitution and By-Laws. 1866. Rebell'n Pamph. Vol. 58.
—— —— Maternal Assoc. 7th Ann. Report. Boston, 1868. 12mo.
—— U. S. Literary Gazette. Newspaper. April 1824 to March 1825. 4to.
—— Votes and Proceedings of Freeholders and other Inhabitants. Lond. re-printed 1773. Amer. Tracts. Vol. 5.
—— Warren St. Chapel Assoc. 18th, 19th, 21st Ann. Reports. Boston, 1855—1858. 12mo.
—— Washingtonian Home. Ann. Report for 1870. Boston, 1870. 8vo.
—— Water Commissioners. Reports, 1837, '44, '48; with Reports of the Cochituate Water Board, for 1850, '52, '53, '54, '55, '57, '59.
—— Water Power Company. Report of the Directors to the Stockholders, 1855. Boston, 1855. 8vo. Boston Miscell. Pamph. Vol. 1.
—— —— Supply. Arguments &c., in regard to the Long Pond. Channing, W. How shall we vote on the Water Supply?
—— See Hubbard, W. J. Argument on. Shattuck, L. Letters on.
—— Weekly Magazine. Vols. 1–3. Boston 1838–41. 4to. 2 Vols.
—— —— Oct. 29, 1803 to April, 1805. 4to.
—— —— Messenger. Newspaper. Oct. 1811 to Oct. 1814. Folio. Oct. 1817 to Oct. 1818. 8vo.
—— Weekly Spectator. Newspaper. 1871. 1 Vol. Bound with Boston Advertiser. 1872.

BOSTON, West Ch. and its Ministers. Fiftieth Annivers. of the Ordination of Chas. Lowell. Boston, 1856. 12mo. See Lowell, Rev. Chas.

—— Yankee Farmer. Newspaper. Jan. to Dec., 1841.

—— Y. Men's Benev. Soc. 29th, 35th, 38th, 39tn, 42d Ann. Rep. Boston 1857–70. 12mo.

—— —— Christian Assoc. 1st & 13th Ann. Reports. Boston, 1853, 1864. 8vo. Boston Misc. Pamph. Vol. 3.

—— —— Constitution and By-Laws. Boston. 1852 12mo. Boston Misc. Pamph. Vol. 3.

—— —— Union. Reports for 1853, 1870, 1872. Boston, 1853, '70, '72. 8vo. Boston Misc. Pamph. Vol. 3.

BOSWELL, Capt. Narrative of the Captain of the Diamond Rock, by Sir Sam'l HOOD, in the Centaur. Waldie's Circulating Libr. Vol. 4.

BOSWELL, James. Life of Samuel JOHNSON, L. L. D., including a Journal of his Tour to the Hebrides. New Ed., with additions and Notes by John WILSON Croker. 1858. 4 Vols. 12mo.

BOSWORTH, Jas. Compendious Anglo Saxon and English Dictionary. Lond. 1868. 8vo.

BOSWORTH, Newton. Hochelaga Depicta; Early History of the Early and Present State of Montreal. Montreal, 1839. 12mo.

BOTANY. See AGASSIZ. (L.) Lake Superior.

—— BECK, L. C. Botany of Illinois and Missouri. 1825.

—— BIGELOW, J. Flora Bostoniensis.

—— BODLEY, R. L. Cat. of Clark's Herbarium of Cincin.

—— CLARK. J. Plants near Cincinnati.

—— CLINTON, G. W. Plants of Buffalo, N. Y.

—— DARLINGTON, W. Agricult. Botany.

—— —— Flora Cestrica.

—— —— Memorials of Bartram and Marshall.

—— —— Reliquæ Baldwinianæ.

—— FLINT, C. L. Grasses & Forage Plants.

—— GRAY, A. Botanical Text Book.

—— —— Botan. Excursion to N. C. Mountains.

—— —— How Plants Grow.

—— HARVEY, W. H. Nereis Boreali — Americana.

—— HOOKER, Wm. J. Botany of America.

—— LAPHAM, I. A. On the Classification of Plants.

—— —— Plants found near Milwaukee.

—— NUTTAL, Thos. N. Amer. Plants.

—— PECK, Chas. H. Paper on. 1872.

—— PURSH, Fred. Flora Americæ. Septentrionalis.

—— STEVENS, GEO. T. Flora of the Adirondacks.

—— WALTER, T, Flora Carolina.

BOTELLER, A. R. Speech in Congress, Jan. 25, 1860, on the organization of the House. Rebellion Pamph. Vol. 31.

BOTH SIDES of the Controversy between the Roman and Reformed Churches; being 1, "A Doctrinal Catechism" approved by Bishop Hughes and 2, "The other Side," by Rev. T. S. Bacon. N. Y. 1859. 12mo.

BOTT, Arthur. Prussia & the German System of Education, Albany Institute Trans. Vol. 6. See also Ed. Pamph. Vol. 3.

BOTTA, Chas. History of the War of Independence in the U. S. Boston, 1826. 2 Vols. 8vo.

BOTTA, Vicenzo. Accôunt of the System of Education in Sardinia. Hartford, 1858. 8vo. Educa. Pamph. Vol. 3.

BOTTS, J. M. Speech at Powhattan Court House, Va., June 15th, 1850. Congr. and Polit. Pamph. Vol. 87.

—— Speech in Cong., July 12, 1842, on the Tariff Bill. Washington, 1842. 8vo. Congr. and Polit. Pamph. Vol. 24.

—— The Great Rebellion; its Secret History, Rise, Progress, and and Disastrous Failure. N. Y. 1866. 8vo.

BOUCHETTE, Joseph. British Dominions in N. America; or, A Topograph. and Statis. Descrip. of Canada and the other British Provinces. Lond.: 1832. 2 Vols. 4to.

—— Topograph. Dictionary of the Province of Lower Canada. Lond.: 1832. 4to.

BOUDRYE, L. N. Hist. Records of 5th N. Y. Cavalry. Albany. 1865. 12mo.

BOUNDARIES of Empires. See FINCH, John. Natural Boundaries, etc.

BOUNTY. Mutiny of the. See Description of Pitcairn's Island.

BOUQUET, Col. Henry. Hist. Account of Expedition Against the Ohio Indians in 1764. Cincin.: 1868. 8vo. Another copy. Dublin. 1769. 12mo.

—— Expedition. 1764. See WHITTLESEY, C.

BOURBONS. See LEOPARD, P. S. Coup D'Oeil Historical sur-les Bourbons de Naples. 1847.

BOURDIN, Mark A. A Guide to the Redemption of the Land Tax. Lond. 1853. 8vo. Eng. Pol. Pamph. Vol. 52.

—— Exposition of the Land Tax. Lond. 1854. 12mo. Eng. Misc. Pamph. Vol. 32.

BOURNE, A. On the Prairies and Barrens of the West. Silliman's Journ. Vol. 2.

BOUTELLE, Chas. English Heraldry. 450 Engravings. Lond. 1867. 8vo.

—— John A. Genealog. Account of the Descendants of Richard Burke, of Sudbury, Mass., and Alexander Alvord, of Windsor, Conn. Boston, 1864. 8vo.

BOUTON, Nathan'l, D. D. Disc. before the N. H. Hist. Soc., June 12, 1833, on Educa. in N. H. Concord. 1833. 8vo.

—— Hist. Disc. Preached Before the Gen. Assoc. of N. H., Aug. 22, 1848. Concord. 1848. 8vo. N. H. Hist. Discourses. Vol. 3.

—— —— In Commemora. of the Two Hundredth Anniver. of the Settlement of Norwalk, Conn., in 1651. N. Y. 1851. 8vo. Conn. Hist. Discourses. Vol. 2.

—— History of Concord, N. H., from 1725 to 1853. Concord. 1856. 8vo.

—— Memoir of Hon. C. E. Potter. Boston. 1869. 8vo. Biograph. Pamph. Vol. 2.

BOUTON, N. See N. Hampshire Provincial Papers.
—— Two Sermons Preached Nov. 21, 1830, in Commemora., etc., of the First Church in Concord, N. H. Concord. 1831. 8vo. N. H. Hist. Discourses. Vol. 2.
BOUTWELL, Geo. S. Address at Berlin, Oct. 3, 1853, on the New Constitution.. Boston. 8vo. Congr. and Polit. Pamphlet. Vol. 87. Addresses. Vol. 1.
—— Address before the Emancipation League at Boston, Dec. 16, 1861. Rebell'n Pamph. Vol. 75.
—— Address at Concord, Mass., Sept. 18, 1850, on Agriculture. Addresses. Vol. 1.
—— Address before Hillsborough Agr. and Mechan. Soc., Sept. 30, 1852. Boston. 1853. 8vo. Addresses. Vol. 1.
—— Address at Worcester, Sept. 22, 1853. Addresses. Vol. 1.
—— —— On Education at Salem, Mass., 1854.
—— —— On Dedication of a Monument to Capt. Wadsworth, Nov. 23, 1852.
—— —— On Dedication of Davis' Monument, at Acton, Oct., 1851.
—— —— At Dedication of Power's Institute, Bernardston, 1858. Addresses. Vol. 1.
—— Argument on the Division of Middlesex and Worcester Counties, Mass., 1858. Addresses. Vol. 1.
—— and others. Debate in Congress, July 11, 1868, on Counting the Electoral Votes. Congr. and Polit. Pamph. Vol. 122.
—— Speeches in Cong. on the Admission of Tennessee. Washington. 1866. 8vo. Congr. and Polit. Pamph. Vol. 121.
—— Speech in Congr. Dec. 5 and 6, on the Impeachment of the President. Congr. and Polit. Pamph. Vol. 121.
—— Thoughts on Educa. Topics and Institutions. Boston. 1859. 12mo.
—— Rev. W. T. Extracts from his Journal of an Exploring Tour to Itasca Lake, in 1832. Minn. Hist. Soc. Coll. Vol. 1.
BOWDITCH, Dr. Henry I. Address at Greenfield, Mass., Aug. 4, 1858, on the Life and Character of Jas. Deane, M.D. Greenfield. 1858, 8vo. Addresses. Vol. 31.
—— Brief Plea for an Ambulance System for U. S. Army. 1863. Rebell'n Pamph. Vols. 18, 72.
BOWDITCH, Nathan'l. See Bowditch, N. I. Memoir of.
—— Memoir of. Boston. 1841. 12mo.
—— See Young, Alex. Memoir of.
BOWDITCH, Nathan'l I. See Lothrop, Rev. S. K.
—— Memoir of Nathan'l Bowditch. 2d Ed. Boston. 1840. 4to.
—— Suffolk Surnames. 2d Ed. Enlarged. Boston. 1858. 8vo.
BOWDITCH, William I. Slavery and the Constitution. Boston. 1849. 8vo. Congr. and Polit. Pamph. Vol. 102.
—— The Rendition of Anthony Burns. Boston. 1854. 8vo. Congr. and Polit. Pamph. Vol. 102.
BOWDOIN COLLEGE. Brunswick. Catalogue of the Fraternity of Phi Beta Kappa, Alpha of Maine. 1849. Brunswick. 1849. 8vo. Bowdoin Coll. Pamph.
—— Catalogus Collegii Bowdoinensis. 1849. 1864. 8vo.
—— See HARRIS, Sam'l.

BOWDOIN COLLEGE. NEWMAN, S. P.
—— PACKARD, A. S.
—— SPRAGUE, W. B.
—— WINTHROP, R. C.
—— The Bugle. Nov. 1867. Portland. 1867. 8vo. Bowdoin Coll. Pamph.
BOWDOIN, Genealogy. See Whitmore, W. H.
BOWDOIN, James. See HARRIS, T. M. Tribute to.
—— Philosoph. Disc. before Amer Academy of Arts and Sciences. Boston. Nov. 8, 1780. Memoirs of Soc. Vol. 1. 1785.
—— See THATCHER, Rev. Peter. Obit. Sermon. 1790.
BOWEN, Eli. Pictorical Sketch Book of Pennsylvania, or its Scenery, Internal Improvements, etc. Phila. 1853. 8vo.
—— —— Same. 8th Ed. Phila. 1854. 8vo.
—— See U. S. Post Office Directories.
BOWEN, Emmanuel. Geography of Amer. Map. London. 1714. Folio.
—— Complete Atlas of the World. Lond. 1752. Folio. Two Copies.
BOWEN, Francis. See De Tocqueville, A. Democracy in America.
—— Life of Baron Steuben. Sparks Amer. Biog. 1st Ser. Vol. 9.
—— Life of Gen. Benjamin Lincoln. Sparks Amer. Biog. 2nd Series. Vol. 13.
—— Life of Sir William Phipps. Sparks Amer. Biog. 1st Ser. Vol. 7.
—— Life of James Otis. Sparks Amer. Biog. 2d Ser. Vol. 2.
BOWEN, Geo. F. Ithaca in 1850. Lond. 1851. 8vo. 2d ed. Strangford Pamph. Vol. 63.
BOWEN, Rev. T. J. Grammar and Dictionary of the Yoruba Language, with a Descrip. of the Country and People of Yoruba. Smithson. Contr. Vol. 10.
BOWER, Archibald. Brief Refutation of Charges brought against him by his Enemies. 1761. 4to. Eng. Polit. Pamph. Vol. 4.
BOWER, J. Descrip. of the Abbeys of Melrose and Old Melrose. Edinburgh, 1827. 8vo.
BOWERS, Lieut. W. Naval Adventures during Thirty-five Years Service. Waldie's Circulation Library. Vol. 5.
BOWLES, Chas. See Lewis, J. W. Life, Labors & Travels.
BOWLES. Genealogy. See Thornton, J. W, Tabular Pedigree.
BOWLES, John. Observa. on the Corres. between Wm. Adam, & Mr. Bowles. Lond., 1804. 8vo. Eng. Polit. Pam. Vol. 27.
BOWLES, Samuel. Across the Continent; Journey to the Rocky Mountains, the Mormons and the Pacific States. Springfield, 1868. 12mo.
—— Our New West; Records of Travel between the Mississippi River and the Pacific Ocean. Hartford, 1870. 8vo.
—— Summer Vacation in the Parks and Mountains of Colorado. Springfield, Mass., 1869. 12mo.
BOWLES, Rev. W. L. Hermes Brittanicus; a Dissertation on Celtic Deity Tentates, the Mercurious of Cæsar. Lond., 1828. 8vo.

BOWLES, Rev. W. L. Two Letters to Lord Byron, on his Life and Writings of Pope. Lond., 1821. 8vo. Pamphleteer. Vol. 18.
—— Letter to T. Campbell & Others, on Poetical Criticism &c.; in Reference to Pope. Lond., 1822. 8vo. Pamphleteer. Vol. 20.
—— Letters to Lord Byron in Answer to his Letter on Pope. Lond., 1821. 8vo. Strangford Pamph. Vol. 2.
—— Observations on the Poetical Character of Pope. Lond. 1821(?). 8vo. Pamphleteer. Vol. 17.
—— Reply to the Charges .... in the Quarterly Review, Oct., 1820, against the last Editor of Pope's Works; &c. Lond., 1820. 8vo. Pamphleteer. Vol. 17.
—— Vindication of Winchester Coll., in Reply to H. Brougham on Charitable Abuses. Bath, 1818. 8vo. Eng. Misc. Pamph. Vol. 27.
—— —— In a Letter to Hen. Brougham. Lond., 1819. 8vo. 2d ed. Pamphleteer. Vol. 13.
—— Thoughts on the Increase of Crimes, the Education of the Poor, &c. Lond., 1819. 8vo. 2d ed. Pamphleteer. Vol. 15.
BOWLING GREEN, O. See Licking Co. Pioneers.
BOWLING, W. K. Hist. Address to the Graduating Class of 1868, in the Med. Depart. of the University of Nashville. Nashville, 1868. 8vo. Addresses. Vol. 19.
BOWMAN, Jas. L. History of Redstone Old Fort, Ky. Ameri. Pioneer. Vol. 2.
BOWMAN, S. M., & IRWIN, R. B. Shermam and his Campaigns; a Military Biography. N. Y. 1865. 8vo.
BOWRING, John. Account of the State of the Prisons in Spain & Portugal. Lond., 1824. 8vo. Pamphleteer. Vol. 23.
BOYCE, William W. Speech in Cong. Feb. 16, 1854, on the Tariff. Washington, 1854. 8vo. Speeches. Vol. 3.
BOYD, Belle. In Camp and Prison. N. Y., 1867. 12mo.
BOYD, B. M. Speech in Cong., June 30, 1868, on Public Expenditures. Congr. & Polit. Pamph. Vol. 84.
BOYD, Rev. James R. See Barron, W.
BOYD, Mark. Reminiscences of 50 Years in G. Britain & Colonies. N. Y., 1871. 12mo.
BOYE, Martin H. Treatise on Pneumatics. Phila., 1856. 8vo. Scientif. Pamph. Vol. 13.
BOYD, W. H. Directory of Richmond City, and Business Directory of 50 Counties of Va. Richmond, 1869. 8vo.
BOYLE, Isaac, D. D. Hist. Memoir of the Boston Epis. Charitable Soc. Boston, 1840. 8vo. Boston Hist. Discourses &c. Vol. 2.
BOYLSTON Genealogy. See Vinton Memorials.
—— Med. School. Catalogues of Officers and Students, 1851—1853. Boston, 1851-53. 8vo.
BOYNE, Wm. The Yorkshire Library; a Bibliograph. Account of Books on Topography &c., of County of York. Pr. printed. Lond., 1869. 4to.
BOYNTON, Rev. Oration before the N. E. Soc. of Cincinnati, Dec. 22, 1847. Cincin., 1848. 8vo. Addresses &c. Vol. 34.

BOYNTON, Rev. C. B. History of the Navy during the Rebellion. N. Y., 1867-8. 2 vols. 8vo.

—— Our Country, the Herald of a New Era. Lecture at Cincinnati, Jan. 19, 1847. Cin., 1847. 8vo. Addresses, &c. Vol. 38.

—— The Navies of England, France, America and Russia. N. Y. 1865. 8vo. Rebell'n Pamph. Vol. 8.

—— & Mason, T. B. Journey through Kansas, with Sketches of Nebraska. Cincin., 1855, 12mo.

BOYS, Capt. Edw. Narrative of Captivity & Adventures in France & Flanders, between 1803 & 1809. Waldie's Circulating Library. Vol. 7.

BOZMAN, John L. History of Md. from 1633 to 1660. Baltimore, 1837. 2 vols. 8vo.

—— Sketch of the History of Md. for the three first years after its settlement. Baltimore, 1811. 8vo.

BRACE, Charles L. Home Life in Germany. N. Y., 1856. 12mo.

—— Hungary in 1851; with an Experience of the Austrian Police. N. Y., 1853. 12mo.

BRACE, Rev. J. Half Century Dis.; History of the Ch. in Newington, Conn. Hartford, 1855. 8vo. Conn. Hist. Discourses. Vol. 5.

BRACKENRIDGE, Hugh H. Incidents of the Insurrection in the Western Part of Penn. Phila., 1795. 8vo.

—— Recollections of Persons and Places in the West. Phila. 1835. 12mo.

—— Views of Louisiana; with a Journal of a Voyage up the Missouri River in 1811. Pittsburgh, 1814. 8vo.

BRADBURN, Geo. Statement of his Connection with the "True Democrat," & J. C. Vaughan. Cleveland, 1853. 8vo. Ohio Misc. Pamph. Vol. 1.

BRADBURY. See Arms of Goodwin & Bradbury.

BRADBURY & Guild's R. R. Charts. No. 1. Boston to Albany. Boston, 1847. 8vo. Guide Books. Vol. 30.

BRADBURY, John. Travels in the Interior of America in 1809, 1810, 1811, with Description of Upper Louisiana. Liverpool, 1817. 8vo.

BRADBURY, J. W. Speech in U. S. Senate, Apr. 23, 1850, on Removals and Appointments to Office. Congr. & Polit. Pamph. Vol. 84.

—— Speech in U. S. Senate, Apr. 15, 1852, on French Spoliations. Congr. & Polit. Pamph. Vol. 84.

Braddock's Defeat. See CRAIG, N. B. Sargeant, Winthrop.

BRADFORD, Alden. Biograph. Notices of Distinguished Men in N. E. Boston, 1842. 12mo.

—— Biography of Hon. Caleb Strong. Boston, 1820. 8vo. Biograph. Pamph. Vol. 7.

—— Descrip. of Wiscasset, and of the River Sheepscot, Me. Mass. Hist. Soc. Coll. Vol. 7. 1st series.

—— History of Mass. Vol. 1. 1764—1775. Vol. 2. 1775—1789. Boston, 1822—1825. 2 vols. 8vo.

—— Notes on Duxbury, Plymouth Co. Mass. Mass. Hist. Soc. Soc. Coll. 2d Ser. Vol. 10.

BRADFORD, Alexander W. Amer. Antiquities and Researches into the Origin and History of the Red Race. N. Y. 1841. 8vo.

—— Cat. of his Private Library. N. Y. n. d. 8vo. Bibliograph. Pamph. Vol. 61.

BRADFORD, Allen. History of the Federal Gov't from March 1789, to March 1839. Boston, 1840. 8vo.

BRADFORD, Andrew. See Jones, H. G.

BRADFORD, Gov. A. W. Inaug. Address as Gov. of Md. at Baltimore, Jan. 8, 1862. Rebell'n Pamphs. Vols. 36, 66.

BRADFORD, Gamaliel, M. D. See FRANCIS, Convers.

BRADFORD, Mass. See PERRY, Rev. G. B. Hist. Disc. 1820.

BRADFORD, Penn. Reporter, Newspaper. June, 1855, to Dec., 1859. Folio.

BRADFORD, S. D. Letters to Hon. Abbott Lawrence, with Letters on Free Trade. Boston, 1846. 8vo. Speeches. Vol. 1.

—— Works of. Boston, 1858. 8vo.

BRADFORD, Sarah H. History of Peter the Great, Czar of Russia. N. Y., 1858. 12mo.

BRADFORD, Gov. Wm. Dialogue Concerning "The Church, and the Gov't thereof." Mass. Hist. Soc. Proceed. 1869–70.

—— History of Plymouth Plantation. Mass. Hist. Soc. Coll. 4th Series. Vol. 3.

—— Letter Book, (in Reference to Plymouth Colony). Mass. Hist. Soc. Coll. 1st Ser. Vol. 3.

—— See Penn. Hist. Soc. 1863.

—— Sketch of His Life, with a Catalogue of Works Printed by him. Hist. Mag. Vol. 3.

—— Some Account of "The Book of Common Prayer," printed by him in 1710. Phila., 1870. 8vo. Religious Pamph. Vol. 3.

—— See WALLACE, J. W. Bi.-Centen. Address. 1863.

BRADFORD, Wm. J. A. Notes on the Northwest, or the Valley of the Upper Mississippi. N. Y., 1846. 12mo.

BRADISH, L. Speech in N. Y. Legisla., May 25, 1836, on Public Lands. Congr. and Polit. Pamph. Vol. 87.

BRADLEE, Rev. C. D. Farewell Sermon at Boston, Apr. 21, 1872. with Sketch of the "Ch. of the Redeemer." Boston, 1872. 8vo. Boston Hist. Soc. Vol. 2.

—— Order of Exercises at his Installation, at Boston, Apr. 2, 1873. Boston Hist. Discourses, etc. Vol. 2.

—— Sermon at Boston, Sept. 3, 1871, on the Late R. R. Disaster. Boston, 1871. 12mo. Sermons. Vol. 53.

—— Life, Writings and Character of Rev. Thos. Starr King. Boston, 1870. 8vo. Addresses. Vol. 31.

BRADLEY, Joseph. Address before Literary Societies of Rutger's College. N. Brunswick, 1849. 8vo. Addresses, etc. Vol. 14.

BRADLEY, Rev. Joseph P. Hist. Disc. at Centen. Celebra. at Rutger's Coll., June 21, 1870. Albany, 1870. 8vo.

BRADSHAW'S Hand Book of G. Britain and Ireland. Section II. Lond., (n. d.) 12mo. Guide Books. Vol. 2.

BRADSHAW'S Railway Guide for England, Wales and Scotland. Lond., 1865. 12mo. Guide Books. Vol. 11.

—— for Gt. Britain and Ireland, Aug., 1869. London. 12mo. Guide Books. Vol. 26.

BRADSTREET, Gen. Statement on Indian Affairs, Dec. 17, 1764, and Papers Relating to the Indian Wars of 1763 and 1764, and the Conspiracy of Pontiac. Albany, (n. d.) Sm. 4to.

BRADSTREET'S, Expedition. 1764. See WHITTLESEY, Chas.

BRADY, Jas. See JEFFRIES, C. Wabash Captives.

BRADY N. and TATE, N. New Version of the Psalms of David. Boston, 1813. 8vo.

BRADY, Capt. Samuel. Sketches of his Life; Military and Hunting Adventures. See PRITTS, J. Border Life.

BRAE, Andrew E. Electrical Communication in Railway Trains. London, 1865. 4to. Scientific Pamph. Vol. 7.

BRAGDON, O. D. Facts and Figures for the People of Louisiana. N. Orleans, 1872. 8vo. La. Pamph. Vol. 1.

BRAHE, Tycho. See BREWSTER, D.

BRAINARD, Rev. David. See EDWARDS, Rev. J. Account of Life of.

—— PEABODY, W. B. O. Life of.

BRAINARD, John. See BRAINARD, Rev. Thos. Life of. 1865.

BRAINARD, Rev. Thos. Life of John Brainard, Brother of David Brainard, and Successor as Missionary to the Indians of N. Jersey. Phila., 1865. 12mo.

—— Fast Day Sermon at Phila., 1863. Rebellion Pamph. Vols. 3 and 80.

BRAINARD, Rev. Dr. Remarks at the Funeral of Lieut. John T. Greble, U. S. A. 1861. Rebell'n Pamph. Vol. 88.

BRAINARD, Cephas. The Customs Revenue Laws; Suggestions for their Amendment. N. Y., 1872. 8vo. Congr. and Polit. Pamph. Vol. 129.

BRAINARD Genealogy. See FIELDS. Rev. D.D.

BRAINARD, Prof. Jehu. Origin of Quartz Pebbles of the Sandstone Conglomerate, and Stratified Sand Rocks. Cleveland, 1854. 8vo. Scientific Pamph. Vol. 21.

BRAMAN, Rev. Isaac. Semi-Centen. Disc. at Georgetown, Mass., June 7, 1847. Georgetown, 1847. 8vo. Mass. Hist. Discourses. Vol. 2.

BRANDENBURG. Memoirs of the House of. Lond., 1748. 8vo. Biograph. Pamph. Vol. 15.

BRANDON, Vt. Telegraph, Newspaper. Oct., 1835, to Sept., 1837. Folio.

BRANDON, Wis. Times, Newspaper. Brandon, 1866–73. Folio.

BRANDYWINE, Battle of. See Penn. Hist. Soc.

BRANNAN, John. Official Letters of Military and American Naval Officers of the U. S. during the War with Gt. B., in 1812–15. Washington, 1823. 8vo.

BRANNON, G. Pleasure Visitor's Companion for the Isle of Wight. Wootton, 1848. 12mo. Guide Books. Vol. 1.

BRANSBY, Rev. James Hews Acc. of the Fanaticism at Water-Stratford in 1694. Carnarvon, 1835. 12mo. Eng. Religious Pamph. Vol. 46A.

BRANT, Jos. Principal Events in the Life of. N. Eng. Hist. and Gen. Reg. Vols. 2 and 3.
—— STONE, W. L. Life of.
BRANTLEY, Rev. W. T. Our National Troubles; Thanksgiving Sermon at Phila., 1860. Rebell'n Pamph. Vol. 80.
BRATIANO, D. Documents Concerning the Danubian Principalities. London, 1849. 8vo. Strangford Pamph. Vol. 55.
BRATTLE Genealogy. See HARRIS, E. D.
BRATTLE, Thos. Account of the Delusion Called Witchcraft; and of the Trials and Executions at Salem. Mass. Hist. Soc. Coll. Vol. 5. 1st Series.
—— HARRIS, E. D. Descendants of.
BRAXFIELD, Lord. See Letter to, etc. 1780.
BRAY, Chas. Education of the Body; Address to the Working Classes. Coventry, 1847. 8vo. Educa. Pamph. Vol. 28.
BRAYLEY, E. W. Relation of the Luminous Prominences to the Faclae of the Sun. London, 1869. 8vo. Scientific. Pamph. Vol. 6.
BRAYMAN, James O. Daring Deeds of Amer. Heroes, with Biograph. Sketches. N. Y., 1858. 12mo.
—— Thrilling Adventures by Land and Sea. N. Y., 1858. 12mo.
BRAZER, John. Disc. at Salem, April 4, 1829, on the Death of Edward A. Holyoke, M. D. LLD. Salem, 1829. Sermon. Vols. 5 and 30.
—— Disc. on the Life and Character of Hon. Leverett Saltonstall, May 18, 1845. Salem, 1845. 8vo. Sermons. Vol. 5.
—— Sermon on the Annivers. of his Ordination in the North Ch. Salem, 1837. 8vo. Mass. Hist. Discourses. Vol. 17. Another Copy. Sermons. Vol. 7.
BRAZIL. See Agassiz, L. Journey in. 1871.
—— DE PRAT, M. Les Six Dernier Mois du Brésil.
—— HARTT, C. F., and AGASSIZ. L. Journey in. 1870.
—— KIDDER and FLETCHER. Brazil and Brazilians.
—— MAGALHANES, P. Histoire de la Province.
—— RENDU, A. Etudes Topograph. sur le Bresil.
BRAZILIAN Improvements, particularly as regards Espirito Santo. London, 1825. 8vo. Strangford Pamph. Vol. 1.
BREAD'S New Guide and Hand Book to Worthing and Vicinity. London, (n. d.) 8vo. Guide Books. Vol. 4.
BREARLEY, Wm. H. Recollections of East Tenn. Campaign. Detroit, 1871. 8vo. Rebell'n Pamph. Vol. 110.
BRECK, R. L. Habeas Corpus and Martial Law. Cincin., 1862. 8vo. Rebell'n Pamph. Vol. 27.
BRECK, Samuel. Hist. Anecdote of John Harris, Sr.; first European Letter of Harrisburg, Penn. Penn. Hist. Soc. Memoirs. Vol. 2. Part 1.
—— See INGERSOLL, J. R. Memoir of.
BRECKINRIDGE, J. C. Address on Removal of the Senate from the Old to the New Chamber, Jan. 4, 1859. Rebell'n Pamph. Vol. 37.
—— Address to the People of Kentucky. 1861. Rebell'n Pamph. Vol. 31.

BRECKENRIDGE and LANE, Gen. Joseph. Biograph. Sketches of. Rebell'n Pamph. Vol. 77.

—— See MAURY, M. F.

—— Oration at Transylvania University, Feb. 22, 1820, on George Washington. Western Rev. Vol. 2.

—— Speech in Cong., Mar. 4, 1852, on the Presidency, etc. Congr. and Polit. Pamph. Vol. 88.

—— Speech in Cong., March 23, 1854, on the Kansas and Nebr. Bill. Congr. and Polit. Pamph. Vol. 93.

BRECKINRIDGE, Robt., D.D. Oration at Laying the Corner Stone of the Nat. Monument to Henry Clay, near Lexington, Ky., 1857. Cincin., 1857. 8vo. Ky. Pamph. Vol. 1.

—— Our Country: Its Peril and its Deliverance. Cincin., 1861. 8vo. Rebell'n Pamph. Vol. 29.

BREED, Wm. P. Sermon for the Times. Phila., 1863. 8vo. Rebellion Pamph. Vol. 65.

BREESE, Sydney. Speech in Congress, March 2, 1846, on the Oregon Question. Washington, 1846, 8vo. Speeches. Vol. 1.

BREMEN, Germany. See Neuester Wegweiser Durch Bremen.

BREMER, Frederika, Homes in the New World; or Impressions of America. N. York, 1853. 2 vols. 8vo.

BENTON, Edward P. Naval History of Gt. Britain, 1783 to 1836. London, 1837. 2 vols. 8vo.

BRENTS, Maj. J. A. Patriots and Guerillas of East Tennessee and Ky, and Experience in the Union Army. 1863. Rebell'n Pamph. Vol. 76.

BRERETON, M. John. Relation of the Discovery of Va. by Capt. Barth. Gosnold, in 1602. Mass. Hist. Soc. Coll. 3d Series. Vol. 8.

BRERETON, John A.—Florae Columbianae Prodromus. Washington, 1830. 12mo.

BRESSANY, F. J.—Relation Abregee de Quolques Missions des Peres de la. Compagnie de Jesus, dans la Nouvelle France. Montreal, 1852. 8vo.

BRETT, Rev. W. H.—Indian Tribes of British Guiana. N. Y., 1856. 18mo.

BREWER, Rev. Dr.—Guide to Roman History from the Earliest Period to the close of the Western Empire. N. Y., 1857. 12mo.

—— Guide to the Scientific Knowledge of Things Familiar. N. Y., 1859. 12mo.

BREWER, F. P.—Memoir of David L. Swain, L. L. D. N. Eng. Hist. & Gen. Reg. Vol. 24. Also Biograph. Pamph. Vol. 7.

BREWER, G.—Alabama. Her History, Resources, War Record and Public Men. 1540–1872. Montgomery, 1872. 8vo.

BREWER, J. N.—London and Middlesex. A Hist. Commer. and Descrip. Survey of the Metropolis of G. Britain. Lond., 1816. 4 vols. 8vo. Vol. 4.

—— Topograph and Hist. Descrip. of the Co. of Oxford. 30 Engravings. Lond., 1813. 8vo.

—— Topograph and Hist. Descrip. of to Co. of Warwick. Lond., 1820. 8vo.

BREWSTER, G. Douglass.—The War in Kansas. A Rough Trip to the Border among New Homes and a Strange people. N. Y., 1856. 12mo.

BREWSTER, B. H.—Address before Alumni of High School. Phila., Feb. 12, 1863. Rebelln, Pamph. Vol. 30.

—— Speech at Inauguration of Nat. Union Club. Phila., 1863. Rebelln. Pamph. Vol. 68.

BREWSTER. C. W.—Rambler about Portsmouth, N. H., with Brograph. Sketch of Author, by W. H. T. Sackett. 2d Ser. Portsmouth, 1869. 8vo.

BREWSTER, Sir David.—Letters on Natural Magic. Harper. Fam. Lib. N. Y., 1858. 18mo.

—— Life of Sir Isaac Newton. Harper Fam. Lib. N. Y. 18mo.

—— Martyrs of Science or Lives of Galileo, Tycho Brahe and Kepler. Harper Fam. Lib. N. Y., 1860. 18mo.

BREWSTER, David P.—Speech in Cong., July, 1842, on the Tariff. Washington, 1842. 8vo. Congr. and Polit. Pamph. Vol 25.

BREWSTER, F. C.—Oration before the Literary Societies of La Fayette Coll. Easton, Pa., 1861. Rebelln. Pamph. Vol. 68.

BREWSTER, Jas.—See BABCOCK, J. F.—Address on. 1866.

BREWSTER, Mass.—See SIMPKINS, Rev. J.—Topog. Descrip. of.

BREWSTER, Wm.—See STEELE, A.—Life and Times of.

BRICE, W. A.—History of Fort Wayne, Indiana. Ft. Wayne, 1868. 8vo.

BRICKELL, John.—Narrative of his Captivity among the Delaware Indians. Amer. Pioneer. Vol. 1.

BRICKNELL, Dr. John.—Nat. Hist of N. Carolina, with an Acc. of the Trade, Manners, etc. of the Christian and Indian Inhabitants. Dublin, 1737. 8vo.

BRIDESBURG Armory for the Manufacture of N. S. Springfield Rifle Muskets. 1863. Rebelln. Pamph. Vol. 16.

BRIDGE, Saml.—Suggestions for Forming an Army of 250,000 men for the Govt. Service. Lond., 1808. 8vo. Eng. Polit. Pamph. Vol. 29.

BRIDGES. See HERVEY, H. L.—Descrip. of.

BRIDGEMAN, Laura.—See LIEBER, F., Vocal Sounds of.

BRIDGEWATER, Mass. Celebra. of the 200th Annivers. of the Town, June 3, 1856. Boston, 1856. 8vo. Mass. Hist. Discourses, etc. Vol. 4.

—— Description of. See Mass. Hist. Soc. Coll. Vol 7. 2d Ser.

—— See HODGES, R. M.—Semi-Centen. Disc. 1871.

—— MITCHELL, N.—Early Settlement of.

BRIDGEWATER TREATISES, on the Power, Wisdom, and Goodness of God, as manifested in the Creation. London, 1835, etc. 13 vols. 8vo. Contents—Dr. Chalmers on the Wisdom of God. 2 vols. Kidd on the Adoption of Nature to Man—Whewell's Astronomy—Bell on the Hand—Roget's Physiology. 2 vols. Goodness of God. 2 vols. Prout's Chemistry—Babbage's Ninth Bridgewater Treaties.

BRIDGEMAN, C. D. W.—Words at the Obsequies of the late Col. Lewis Benedict. Albany, May 2, 1864. Rebelln. Pamph. Vol. 40.

BRIDMAN, John.—Hist. and Topograph. Sketch of Knole in Kent, with a Brief Geneal. of the Sackville Pamily. Lond., 1817. 8vo.

BRIDGMAN, Thomas.—Inscriptions on Grave Stones in Northampton, and other Towns in Conn. Valley. Northampton, 1850. 12mo.

—— Pilgrims of Boston. The Name, etc., of many who fell on Bunker Hill. Also Inscriptions from Monuments of Copp's Hill. Boston, 1856. 12mo.

—— Pilgrims of Boston and their Descendants. N. Y., 1856. 8vo.

—— Memorials of the Dead in Boston. Containing Inscriptions from the Scpul. Monuments in the Kings's Chapel Burial Ground. Boston, 1853. 12mo.

BRIEF Acct. of an Opthalmic Institution at Macao, China, from 1827 to 1833. Canton, China, 1834. Med. Pamph. Vol 7. 8vo.

—— and True Narrative of the Indians Conduct of the Barbarous Natives Americans towards the Dutch Nation. Albany, 1863, 8vo.

—— Enquiry into the Nature and Character of our Federal Govt. Petersburg, 1840. 8vo.

—— Narrative of Incident in the War in Missouri, and Experience of one who has Suffered. Boston, 1863. 8vo. Rebelln. Pamph. Vol 40.

—— —— of the Late Campaigns in Germany and Flanders. In a Letter to a Member of Parliament. Lond., 1751. 12mo. Eng. Polit. Pamph. Vol. 70.

—— Observations on the Copy-Right Bill. Lond., 1821. 8vo. Pamphleteer. Vol. 18.

—— Remarks on the Slave Registry Bill; and upon a Special Report of the African Institution. Lond., 1816, 8vo. Pamphleteer. Vol. 7.

—— Review of the Action of Labour, Production, Commerce, and Consumption. Phila., 1849. 8vo. Congr. & Polit. Pamph. Vol. 104.

—— Sketch of the Military Operations on the Deleware during the late War, with Muster-Rolls, etc. Phila. 1820. 12mo. Pamphlets, War of 1812. Vol. 3.

—— State of the Province of Penn.. Lond., 1755. Also an answer to an Invidious Pamphlet, Entitled, "Brief State," etc. Lond., 1755. 2 vols. 12mo.

—— View of Constitutional Powers. Phila., 1864. 8vo. Rebelln. Pamph. Vol. 26.

—— —— of the Conduct of Penn. in Gen. Braddock's Expedition, 1755. Lond., 1756. 12mo.

BRIGGS, G. N.—Speech in Cong., June 30, 1842, on the President's Veto of the Tariff Bill. Washington, 1842. 8vo. Congr. & Polit. Pamph. Vol 24.

BRIGGS, Geo. W.—Memoir of Danl. A. White. Essex. Institute Coll. Vol. 6.

BRIGGS, Robt. M.—Resolutions and Addresses Relative to his Death, Feb. 23, 1869. Cincin., 1869. 8vo. Aderesses etc. Vol. 21.

BRIGHAM, Amariah, M. D.—See GOODRICH, Rev. C. E.—Obit. Sermon. 1849.

BRIGHAM GENEALOGY. See MORSE, A.

BRIGHAM, Wm.—Centen. Addresses at Grafton, Apr. 29, 1835. Boston, 1835. 8vo. Mass. Hist. Discourses. Vol. 13.

BRIGHT, John.—The Letter of John Bright on the War, Verified and Illustrated. Lond., 1854. 8vo. Strangford Pamph. Vol. 67.

—— —— Speech at Rockdale, Dec. 4, 1861, on the Amer. Crisis. N. Y., 1862. 8vo. Rebelln. Pamph. Vol. 61. Congs. & Polit. Pamph. Vol. 99.

BRIGHT, Jonathan B.—The Brights of Suffolk, England, Represented in America by Descendants of Henry Bright, Jun. who came to N. E. in 1630. Boston, 1848. 8vo.

BRIGHTON, Eng. Strangers' Guide in Brighton, for 1844. Brighton, Eng. 12mo. Guide Books. Vol 2.

—— Same. n. d. Guide Books, Vols. 7, 8.

—— Mass. Holton Library. Rules and Regulations, 1864. 1st, 2d, 3d, 4th, 5th, 6th Ann. Reports, 1865–1870. Brighton, 1864–'70.

—— Pub. Schools. 21st and 23d Reports of the School Comm. for 1858–9 and 1860–1. Cambridge, 1859, 61. 8vo.

—— See WHITNEY, F. A.

BRIMFIELD Mass. Annals of the Ch. in Brimfield. Sprinfield, 1856. 8vo. Mass. Hist. Discourses, etc. Vol. 11.

—— See BROWN, Rev. C. Topog. Descrip. of.

BRIND, Geo. True Philosophy of Vegetation. Albany, 1857. 8vo. Agri. Pamph. Vol. 7.

BRINGIER, L. Notices of the Geol., Topog., Inhabitants, etc., of the Region of the Mississippi. 1818. Silliman's Journ. Vol. 3.

BRINTON, D. G. Grammar of the Choctaw Language of Rev. C. Byington. Edited from original MSS. Phila., 1870. 8vo.

—— Notes on the Floridan Peninsular. Phila., 1859. 12mo.

—— The Mound-Builders of the Mississippi Valley. Hist. Mag. Vol. 10.

—— Myths of the New World. Treatise on Symbolism or of the Red Race of America. N. Y., 1868. 12mo.

—— The Shawnees and their Migrations. Hist, Mag. Vol. 10.

BRISBIN, Jas. S. Belden, the White Chief, or Twelve Years among the Indians of the Plains. Cincin., 1872. 12mo.

BRISSOT, J. P. Letter to his Constituents on the National Convention. Influence of the Anarchist, etc. Dublin, 1793. 8vo. Hist. Pamph. Vol. 8.

BRISTOL, C. C. Traveller's Guide through the U. S. & Canadas. Buffalo, 1848. 18mo. Guide-Books. Vol. 29.

BRISTOL, Conn. Cong. Ch. See IVES, Dea. C. G. Semi-Centen. Celebra. 1859.

BRISTOL, Co., Mass., Agr. Soc y. Transactions for 1852, with the Address by R. C. Winthrop. Boston, 1853. 8vo, Agr. Pamph. Vol. 13.

—— Eng. See CORRY, J., History of, 1816.

BRISTOL. Facts Relating to the present Local Gov't of Bristol. Bristol, 1831. 8vo, Strangford Pamph. Vol. 7.
—— See MANCHEE, T. J. Origin of the Bristol Riots.
—— MUELLER, Geo. Facts concerning his Orphan Houses.
—— SOMERTON, W. H. Narr. of Bristol Riots. 1831.
BRISTOL, R. I. Acc. of the Settlement of the Town, and of the Cong. Ch. therein. Providence, 1785. 8vo. R. I. Hist. Discourses &c. Vol. 1.
BRISTOL, Jas. Narrative of the Sufferings and Captivity of, in India. Phila., 1801. 12mo. Hist. Pamph. Vol. 10.
BRITISH ALMANAC of the Society for the Diffusion of Useful Knowledge, with Companions to the Almanac. Lond., 1828–1869. 39 Vols. Except 1834.
—— America. TAYLOR, J. W. B. America and Minnesota. See Canada, etc.
—— American Guide Book. A Guide to Canada, Western States and N. Y. 1869. 8vo.
—— And Foreign Bible Soc'y. Abridged Statement of Leading Transactions, etc. Lond., 1815. 8vo. Pamphleteer. Vol. 6.
—— —— Institute. 4th Ann. Report, 1847. 8vo. Eng. Misc. Pamph. Vol. 30.
—— —— —— Transactions. Lond., 1845. 4to.
—— —— Mission. Records of Proceedings, Correspondence, etc. from March 16, to June 16, 1837. Lond., 12mo. Eng. Religious Pamph. Vol. 48.
—— and Foreign School Society. Defence of against the Edinburgh Review. Lond., 1821. 8vo. Strangford Pamph. Vol. 50.
—— —— Manual of System of. Phila., 1817. 8vo.
—— —— Report, 1853. Lond., 8vo. Educa. Pamph. Vol. 35.
—— Apollo. Newspaper. 1709–10. And Spectator. Aug., Sept., 1711.
—— Archæolog. Assoc. Chester Congress. Visit to Liverpool, 1849. 8vo. Scientific Pamph. Vol. 25.
—— Army List. List of all Officers of the Army and Marines on Full and Half Pay. Jan. 1, 1802. Glasgow, 1864. 3 Vols. 8vo.
—— Assoc. for Advancement of Science. Address of Gen. Secretaries, at the 8th Meeting. Newcastle, n. d. 8vo. Strangford Pamph. Vol. 29.
—— —— Ann. Reports. Lond., 1833–1869. 39 Vols. 8vo.
—— —— Lithographed Signatures of Members of the Assoc., who met at Cambridge, June 1833, with Report. Cambride, 1833. 4to.
—— —— Proceedings of 5th Meeting, at Dublin, 1835. Dublin, 1835. 4to.
—— —— See WHEWELL, Rev. W. Address, 1833.
—— Church Establishment. Lond., 1834. 8vo. Strangford Pamph. Vol. 9.
—— Colonial Slavery compared with that of Pagan Antiquity. Lond., 1830. 8vo. Strangrord Pamph. Vol. 21.

BRITISH Colonies in America. See ANDERSON, I. D., Trade and Commerce of.
—— —— BOUCHETTE, J., Brit. Domin. in America. British Empire in America, 1741.
—— —— Conduct of the Late Administration.
—— —— See Canada.
—— —— DULANEY, D., Propriety of Taxing the.
—— —— Interest (The) of G. B. considered. 1770.
—— —— Late Occurrences considered.
—— —— Letter from Penn. Farmer.
—— —— MARTIN, R. M., History of.
—— —— Memorials of the Eng. and French Commissaries, 1755.
—— —— MURRAY, H., Hist. and Descrip. Acc. of.
—— —— OTIS, J., Rights of asserted and proved, 1766.
—— —— OTIS, J., Vindica. of 1769.
—— —— PALAIRET, J., Descrip. of, 1755.
—— —— POWNALL, T., Topog. Descrip. of.
—— —— Regulations concerning considered. 1765.
—— —— State of. 1755.
—— —— TUCKER, J., Tracts respecting.
—— —— Two Papers on Taxing the.
—— Diplomacy and Turkish Independence. Lond., 1838. 8vo. Strangford Pamph. Vol. 14.
—— —— Illustrated in the Affair of the "Vixen." Lond.,1838. 8vo. Strangford Pamph. Vol. 16.
—— —— In the River Plate. Lond., 1847. 8vo. Strangford Pamph. Vol. 45.
—— Empire in America; History of the Discovery, Settlement, etc., of British Colonies in America. Lond., 1741. 2 Vols. 8vo.
—— Essayists; with Prefaces, Historical and Biographical, by A. CHALMERS. Vols. 13, 14, 15. The Tatler. Vols. 22, 23, 24. The World. Boston, 1856. 6 vols. 12mo.
—— Expedition to Egypt. See WILSON, R. T.
—— India: her Claims upon the Promoters of Commerce & Friends of Justice. Manchester, 1841. 8vo. Eng. Polit. Pamph. Vol. 43.
—— Institute. See BUCKINGHAM, J. S. Prospectus for.
—— Magazine: or Monthly Repository. Jan. & Dec., 1761. Lond., 8vo.
—— Metre (The) and its Derivatives; a Sketch of a proposed Reforma. in Weights, Measures, etc. Lond., 1820. 8vo. Pamphleteer. Vol. 16.
—— Museum (The). 1859 (?) 4to. Guide Books. Vol. 10.
—— —— New Reading Room and Libraries. Lond., 1857. 12mo. Eng. Miscell. Pamph. Vol. 32.
—— —— AYSCOUGH, S. Cat. of Mss., 1782.
—— —— Cat. of Mss., formerly in Possession of Francis Hargrave. Lond., 1818. 4to.
—— —— Cat. of Mss. New Series, Vol. 1, comprising the Arundel and Burney Mss. with Index, in Three Parts. Lond., 1834. 4to. 3 vols. Folio.

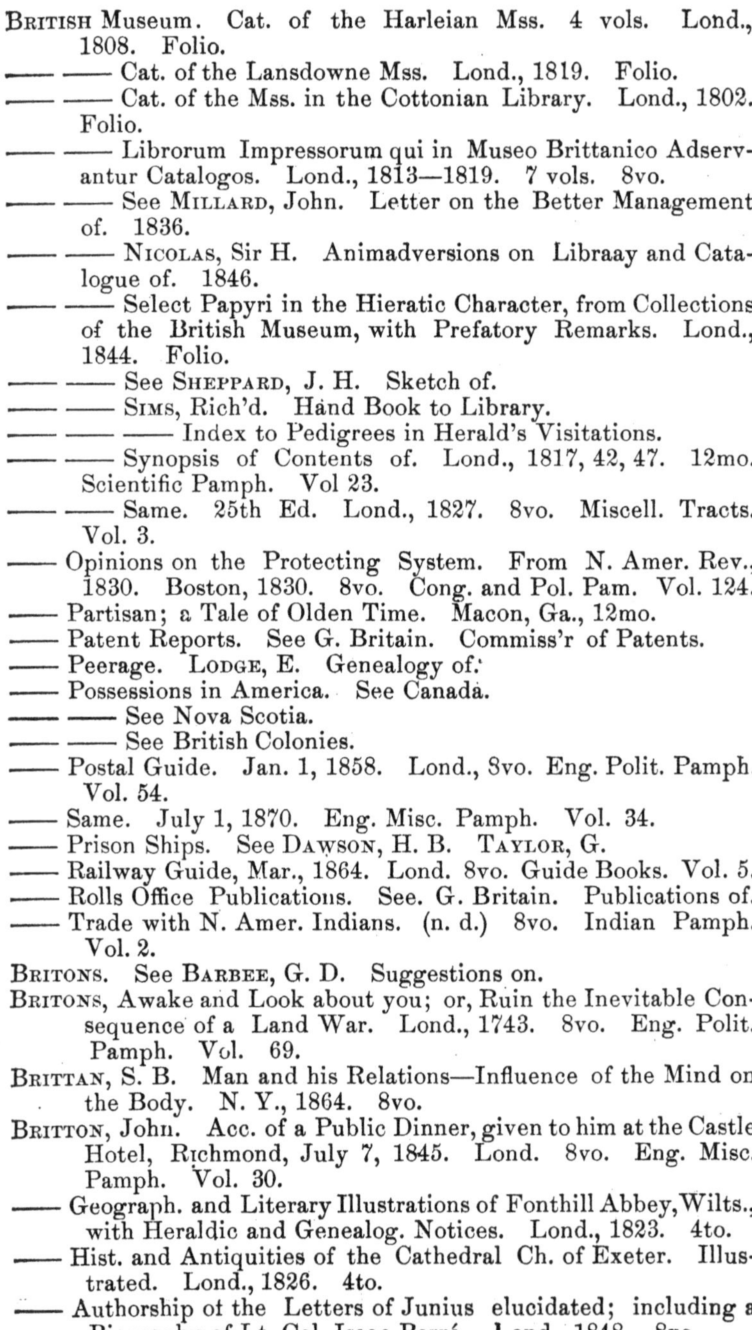

BRITISH Museum. Cat. of the Harleian Mss. 4 vols. Lond., 1808. Folio.

—— —— Cat. of the Lansdowne Mss. Lond., 1819. Folio.

—— —— Cat. of the Mss. in the Cottonian Library. Lond., 1802. Folio.

—— —— Librorum Impressorum qui in Museo Brittanico Adservantur Catalogos. Lond., 1813—1819. 7 vols. 8vo.

—— —— See MILLARD, John. Letter on the Better Management of. 1836.

—— —— NICOLAS, Sir H. Animadversions on Libraay and Catalogue of. 1846.

—— —— Select Papyri in the Hieratic Character, from Collections of the British Museum, with Prefatory Remarks. Lond., 1844. Folio.

—— —— See SHEPPARD, J. H. Sketch of.

—— —— SIMS, Rich'd. Hand Book to Library.

—— —— —— Index to Pedigrees in Herald's Visitations.

—— —— Synopsis of Contents of. Lond., 1817, 42, 47. 12mo. Scientific Pamph. Vol 23.

—— —— Same. 25th Ed. Lond., 1827. 8vo. Miscell. Tracts. Vol. 3.

—— Opinions on the Protecting System. From N. Amer. Rev., 1830. Boston, 1830. 8vo. Cong. and Pol. Pam. Vol. 124.

—— Partisan; a Tale of Olden Time. Macon, Ga., 12mo.

—— Patent Reports. See G. Britain. Commiss'r of Patents.

—— Peerage. LODGE, E. Genealogy of.

—— Possessions in America. See Canada.

—— —— See Nova Scotia.

—— —— See British Colonies.

—— Postal Guide. Jan. 1, 1858. Lond., 8vo. Eng. Polit. Pamph. Vol. 54.

—— Same. July 1, 1870. Eng. Misc. Pamph. Vol. 34.

—— Prison Ships. See DAWSON, H. B. TAYLOR, G.

—— Railway Guide, Mar., 1864. Lond. 8vo. Guide Books. Vol. 5.

—— Rolls Office Publications. See. G. Britain. Publications of.

—— Trade with N. Amer. Indians. (n. d.) 8vo. Indian Pamph. Vol. 2.

BRITONS. See BARBEE, G. D. Suggestions on.

BRITONS, Awake and Look about you; or, Ruin the Inevitable Consequence of a Land War. Lond., 1743. 8vo. Eng. Polit. Pamph. Vol. 69.

BRITTAN, S. B. Man and his Relations—Influence of the Mind on the Body. N. Y., 1864. 8vo.

BRITTON, John. Acc. of a Public Dinner, given to him at the Castle Hotel, Richmond, July 7, 1845. Lond. 8vo. Eng. Misc. Pamph. Vol. 30.

—— Geograph. and Literary Illustrations of Fonthill Abbey, Wilts., with Heraldic and Genealog. Notices. Lond., 1823. 4to.

—— Hist. and Antiquities of the Cathedral Ch. of Exeter. Illustrated. Lond., 1826. 4to.

—— Authorship ot the Letters of Junius elucidated; including a Biography of Lt. Col. Isaac Barré. Lond., 1848. 8vo.

BROADHURST, Rev. Thos. Britons Exhorted to the Defence of their Country, Aug. 28, 1803. Bath. 8vo. Eng. Polit. Pamph. Vol. 27.

BROADSIDE, A. For the Times, 1861. Rebell'n Pamph. Vol. 96.

BROADWAY Tabernacle. See THOMPSON, J. P. Last Sabbath in.

BROCK, Rev. Wm. Biograph. Sketch of Sir Henry Havelock, K. C. B. N. Y., 1858. 12mo.

BROCK, Gen. Sir Isaac. TUPPER, F. B. Life and Corres. of.

BROCKETT, L. P. Life and Times of Abraham Lincoln. Phila., 1865. 12mo.

—— The Camp, the Battle Field, and the Hospital; or Lights and Shadows of the Great Rebellion. Phila., 1866. 8vo.

BROCKHAUS, F. A. Bibliotheque Americaine. Cat. of Books on America prior to 1700. Leipsic, 1861. 8vo. Bibliograph. Pamph. Vol. 22.

BROCKMEYER, H. C. Speech in Senate of Missouri, Feb. 8, 1872, on the Usury Law. Jefferson City (?) 1872. 8vo. Missouri Pamph. Vol. 2.

BROCKWAY College, Ripon, Wis. Catalogue, 1854. Ripon. 8vo.

BROCKWAY, J. Lecture before the 3d. Dist. Dental Assoc. of N. Y.. Jan. 12, 1869. Albany, 1869. 8vo. Addresses. etc. Vol. 21.

BROCKWAY, John H. Speech in Cong., June 20, 1842, on the Tariff. Washington, 1842. 8vo. Congr. and Polit. Pamph. Vol. 24.

BRODHEAD, Col. Dan'l. Extracts from his Correspondence, 1780–81. "Olden Time." Vol. 2.

—— Papers relating to his Expedition against the Indians in 1779. "Olden Time." Vol. 2.

BRODHEAD, J. R. Address before N. Y. Hist. Soc., at 40th Annivers., Nov. 20, 1844. N. Y., 1844. 8vo. N. Y. Hist. Soc. Addresses. Vol. 2.

—— Address before the Clinton Hall Assoc. and Merc. Lib. Assoc. June 8, 1854. N. Y. 8vo.

—— Documents relative to the Colonial History of the State of N. Y., procured in Holland, England and France, Edited by E. B. O. Callaghan, M. D., LL. D. Albany, 1853–58. 10 vols. 4to. With Gen. Index. Albany, 1861. 4to.

—— History of the State of N. Y, First Period, 1609—1664. N. Y., 1853. 8vo.

—— The Government of Sir Edmund Andros over N. Eng. in 1688 and '89, Read before the N. Y, Hist. Soc., Dec. 4, 1866. Hist. Mag. 2d Ser. Vol. 1.

BRODHEAD, R. Speech in Cong., June 25, 1846, on the Tariff. Washington, 1846. 8vo. Speeches. Vol. 1.

—— Speech in Cong., June 3, 1848, on Compromise Bill. Congr. and Polit. Pamph. Vol. 94.

—— Speech in U. S. Senate, March 15, 1852, on Land Grants, &c. Congr. and Polit. Pamph. Vol. 83.

—— Speech in U. S. Senate, Feb. 28, 1854, on Kansas and Nebr. Bill. Congr. and Polit. Pamph. Vol. 93.

BRODHEAD, Wis. Weekly Reporter, Newspaper, from June, 1859, to Dec., 1860. Folio.

BROMFIELD, John. Reminiscences of.
BROMWELL, William J. History of Immigration to the U. S. from 1819 to 1855. N. Y., 1856. 8vo.
BRONSON, Alvin. Commerce and Transportation of Valleys of the Great Lakes and Rivers of the Northwest. Oswego, N. Y., 1868. 8vo. Pamphlets. Vol. 13.
BRONSON, Dr. Henry. History of Waterbury, Conn., with Appendix of Biography, Genealogy and Statistics. Waterbury, 1858. 8vo.
BRONSON, Isaac. Letter to Sec. of the Treasury on Currency and Banking. N. Y., 1837. 8vo. Congr. Pamph. Vol. 99.
BRONSON, Ohio. See KELLOGG, M. Memoir of.
BRONSON, S. A., D, D, Address before the Fire Lands Hist. Soc., May 8, 1859. Fire Lands Pioneer. Vol. 2.
BROOKE, Sir Jas. Vindica. of his Character and Proceedings, in reply to Jos. Hume. Lond., 1853. 8vo. Strangford Pamph. Vol, 64.
BROOKE, Richard. Liverpool as it was during the last Quarter of the 18th Century, 1775—1800. Liverpool, 1853. 8vo.
BROOKES, R. General Gazetteer. Boston, 1816. 18mo.
—— Same. Baltimore, 1815. 18mo.
BROOKFIELD, Mass. See FISKE, Rev. N. Hist. of the Settlement of.
—— FOOT, J. I. Hist. Disc., 1843.
—— Hist. Sketch of the Baptist Church in Brookfield. (n. d.) 8vo. Mass. Hist. Discourses, etc. Vol. 10.
—— See STONE, M. 50th Annivers. Disc., 1851.
—— Same. 80th Birthday Disc., 1850.
—— WHITING, LYMAN. Bi Centen. Oration, 1848.
—— See West Brookfield.
BROOKLINE, Mass. List of Taxes assessed for 1854 & '55.
—— Treasurer's Report of Receipts and Expenditures, List of Taxes etc., for 1867–8.
—— Report of School Committee for 1857–8, and By-Laws of the same, 1858.
—— Report on the Repair of Roads. 1865.
—— See PIERCE, Rev. J. Half Century Ch. Dis., 1847.
—— —— Hist Sketch of.
BROOKLYN, Conn. Trinity Ch. See FOGG, T. B. Memorial Sermon, 1871.
—— N. Y. Benev. Assoc. of the Ch. of the Holy Trinity. Proceedings at 1st, 2d, 3d, 4th, 5th, Annivers. Meetings. 1851–55. N. Y., 1851–55. 8vo. Brooklyn City Pamph. Vol. 1.
—— Business Women's Union. 1st Annual Report. 1871. 12mo.
—— City Directories for 1846–7, 1849–50, 1853–4, 1858–9, 1864–5.
—— DE VOE, THOS. F. Reminiscences of Old Brooklyn.
—— FIELD, T. W. Hist. and Antiq. Scenes.
—— FURMAN, G. Geograph. and Hist. Notes.
—— Juvenile House of Industry. Ann. Report of the Supt. for 1864. Brooklyn, 1865. 8vo. Brooklyn City Pamph. Vol. 1.
—— See STILES, H. R. History of

BROOKLYN N. Y. Water Works. Report of Drainage of Supply Basin. Brooklyn, 1865, 8vo. Brooklyn Pamph. Vol. 1.
—— Y. M. C. A. 1st Ann. Report, 1854. Brooklyn, 1854. 8vo. Brooklyn City Pamph. Vol. 1.
BROOKS, Rev, Charles. History of Medford, Middlesex Co., Mass., from 1630, to 1855, with Family Registers. Boston, 1855. 8vo.
—— Laws of Reproducton, and Intermarriage of near Blood Relations. Cambridge 1856. 8vo. Med. Pamph. Vol. 8.
—— Memoir of John Brooks, Gov. of Mass. n. d. 8vo. Rev. War Pamph. Vol. 4.
—— Moral Education. Paper before the Amer. Assoc., for the Advancement of Education. 1856. 8vo. Educa. Pamph. Vol. 3.
—— Reasons for Establishment of a Nat. System of Education. Boston, 1869. 8vo. 2d Ed. Educa. Pamph. Vol. 1.
—— Statement of Facts respecting Ministers' Salaries in N. E. Boston, 1854. 8vo. Religious Pamph. Vol. 16.
—— The Tornado of 1851, in Medford, West Cambridge and Waltham, Mass. Boston, 1852. 18mo.
—— Two Lectures on State Normal Schools, & on Nat. Educa. Boston, 1864. 8vo. Educa. Pamph. Vol. 1.
BROOKS, David. Facts & Influences relating to Lightning and Lightning Rods. Phila., 1872. 8vo. Scientific Pamph. Vol. 6.
BROOKS, Edward. See LOWELL, John A.
BROOKS, Jas. Speech before Democratic Union Assoc. Sep. 29, 1862, at N. Y. Rebell'n Pamph. Vol. 74.
—— Speech in Cong. May 14, 1850. on Reciprocity. Congr. & Polit. Pamph. Vol. 92.
—— Speech in Cong., Jan. 4, 1853, on Acquisition of Cuba. Congr. and Polit. Pamph. Vol. 90.
—— Speech in Cong., Mar. 24, 1864, on the Currency. Rebell'n Pamph. Vol. 32
—— Speech in Congress Apr. 18, 1864 on the Tax Bill. Rebell'n Pamph. Vol. 32.
BROOKS, Gov. John. See BROOKS, Chas. — Memoir of.
—— Discourse before the Humane Soc'y of Mass., June 9, 1795. Boston. 1795. 8vo. Sermons. Vol. 40
BROOKS, Peter C. See FROTHINGHAM, N. S. — Obit. Sermon.
—— Memoir of. N. Eng. Hist. & Gen. Reg. Vols. 8, 9.
BROOM, W. W. An Englishman's Thoughts on the Crimes of the South, &c. N. Y. 1865. 8vo. Loyal Publica. Soc. Rebellion Pamph. Vol. 90 A.
—— N. Y. History of, from 1806 to 1867. Syracuse. 1867. 8vo. N. York Hist. Discourses &c. Vol. 2.
BROSS, Lt. Col. John A. Memorial of — with a Sermon by Rev. Arthur SWAZEY. Chicago, 1865. 8vo. Rebell'n Pamph. Vols. 10 and 13.
BROSS, Wm. Address before the Alumni of Williams Col., July 31, 1866. Chicago, 1866. 8vo. Addresse. Vol. 17.

BROSS, Wm. Banking, its History, Importance, &c. Lecture at Chicago, 1852. Chicago, 1852. 8vo. Banking & Currency Pamph. Vol. 3.

—— Resources of the Far West & the Pacific Railway; delivered at N. Y., Jan. 25, 1866. N. Y., 1866. 8vo. Addresses. Vol. 16.

BROTHERHEAD, Wm. See Amer. Notes and Queries.

—— Book of the Signers. Fac Simile Letters of the Signers of the Declar. of Independence. Phil'a 1861. 4to.

—— General Fremont and the Injustice done him. Phil'a, 1862. Rebell'n Pamph. Vols. 82 & 88.

BROTHERS, Rich'd. See BRYAN, Wm. HALHEAD, N. B. HORNE, Geo. MOSER, Jos.

—— Revealed Knowledge of the Prophecies & Times. Lond., 1794. 8vo. Eng. Religious Pamph. Vol. 27.

BROUGH, J. Speech at Union Mass Meeting at Marietta, O., June 10, 1863. Rebell'n Pamph. Vol. 48.

—— Speech at Circleville, O., Sept. 3. 1864, on the Chicago Platform, &c. Cincin. 1864. 8vo. Congr. & Polit. Pamph. Vol. 137. Rebell'n Pamph. Vol. 9.

BROUGHAM, Lord. Answer to Lord Londonderry's Letter [on his Historical Sketches.] London. 1839. 8vo. Strangford Pamph. Vol. 17.

—— Appendix to his Minutes of Evidence taken before the Educa. Committee. Lond. 1818. 8vo. Eng. Misc. Pamph. Vol. 27.

—— Complete Works. Lond. 1855–7. 10 Vols.

—— George IV. & Queen Caroline. Abuses of the Press. Waldie's Circulating Libr. Vol. 12.

—— See GLOVE, Wm. Lord Brougham's Law Reforms, &c.

—— Hist. & Polit. Dissertations. Lond. 1855. 12mo.

—— Inaugural Disc. on being installed Lord Rector of the University of Glasgow, Apr. 6, 1825. Glasgow. 1825. 8vo. Addresses. Vol. 34.

—— Introductory Disc. on the Objects, Pleasures, & Advantages of Sciences. n. d. folio. Scientific Pamph. Vol. 7.

—— Letter to the Marquess of Landsdowne, on the late Revolution in France. Lond. 1848. 8vo. Strangford Pamph. Vol. 48.

—— Letter to Sir Sam'l ROMILLY on the Abuse of Charities. Lond. 1818. 8vo. 9th Ed. Pamphleteer. Vol. 13.

—— Letters on Law Reform, to Sir J. R. G. GRAHAM. Lond. 1843. 8vo. Law Pamph. Vol. 21.

—— Men of Letters of Time of George 3d. Lond. 1855. 8vo.

—— Philosophers of Time of George 3d. London, 1855. 12mo.

—— See POTTER, A.

—— Rhetorical and Literary Dissertations. Lond. 1855. 12mo.

—— Social and Political Speeches. Lond. 1857. 12mo.

—— Speech at the Dover Festival, Eulogizing the Duke of Wellington. Lond. 1839. 8vo. Strangford Pamph. Vol. 19.

—— Speech in Parl't, June 29, 1820, on the Educa. of the Poor. Lond. 1820. 8vo. Pamphleteer. Vol. 16.

BROUGHAM, Lord. Speech in Parl't, Dec. 2, 1830, on Legal Abuses. Lond. n. d. 8vo. 2d Ed. Eng. Polit. Pamph. Vol. 77.

—— —— July 21, 1834, on the Poor Laws. Lond., 1834. 1st and 2d Eds. Eng. Polit. Pamph. Vol. 40.

—— —— Jan. 18, 1838, upon Canada. Lond., 1838.8vo. 2d Ed. Canada Pamph. Vol. 2.

—— —— Apr. 11, 1848, on Italian and French Affairs. Lond., 1848. 8vo. Strangford Pamph. Vol. 46.

—— Statesmen of Time of George 3d. Lond., 3 vols., 12o.

—— See also Waldie's Circulating Libr. Vol. 14.

BROUGHTON's Monthly Planeter, Reader and Astrolog. Journal for July and Aug., 1863, with Nativity of Hon. W. H. Seward. Rebell'n Pamph. Vol. 88.

BROUGHTON, R. E. Letter to G. W. Hall, on Agricult. Assoc. of G. B. Lond., 1821. 8vo. Pamphleteer. Vol. 18.

BROWN, Aaron V. Speech in Cong., June 18, 1842, on the Tariff. Washington, 1842, 8vo. Congr. and Polit. Pamph. Vol. 25.

BROWN, ABIEL. Genealog. History of Early Settlers of West Simsbury now Canton, Ct. Hartford, 1856. 8vo. Genealog. Pamph. Vol. 3.

BROWN, A. G. Letter to his Constituents. 1850. Congr. and Polit. Pamph. Vol. 87.

—— Speech at Elwood Springs, Miss., Nov. 2, 1850. Washington, 8vo. Congr. and Polit. Pamph. Vol. 90.

—— Speech in Cong., Mar. 14, 1852, on Capitol Enlargement. Congr. and Polit. Pamph. Nol. 87.

—— Speech in Cong., Apr. 28, 1852, on the Homestead Bill. Cong. and Polit. Pamph. Vol. 83.

—— Speech in Miss. Legislature, Nov. 8, 1859, on State of Parties in Miss. Congr. and Polit. Pamph. Yol. 89.

BROWN, B. Gratz. Addres at St. Louis, Sept. 22, 1865, on Universal Suffrage. St. Louis, 1865. 8vo. Rebellion Pamph. Vol. 25.

BROWN, Chas. Speech in Cong., Mar 17, 1842, on the Loan Bill. Washington, 1842. 8vo. Congr. and Polit. Pamph. Vol. 25.

—— Speeches in Cong., May 20, and June 24, 1842, on Navy Appropriation Bill. Washington, 1842. 8vo. Congr. and Polit. Pamph. Vol. 25.

BROWN, Charles Brockden. See PRESCOTT, W. H. Life of.

BROWN, Chas. P. Essay on the Language and Literature of the Telugus. Madras, India, 1839. 8vo. Scientific Pamph. Vol. 25.

BROWN, Rev. Clark. Topograph. Description of Brimfield, Hampshire Co. Mass. 1803. Mass. Hist Soc. Coll., 1st. Ser. Vol. 9.

—— Topograph. Descrip. of Catskill N. Y, 1803. Mass. Hist. Soc. Coll. 1st. Ser. Vol. 9.

—— Topograph. Descrip. of Newtown, N. Y. 1803. Mass. Hist. Soc. Col. 1st. Ser. Vol. 9.

BROWN Co., Wis. See Resources of Brown, Door, etc. 1870.

BROWN, David P. Eulogium on Jos. R. Ingersoll, Sept. 2, 1869, at the University of Penn. Phila., 1869. 8vo. Penn Hist. Soc. Misc. Papers.

—— Eulogium on William Rawle, Dec. 31, 1836. Phil'a 1837. 8vo. Addresses. Vol. 13.

—— Reply to H. Binney on Habeas Corpus. Phil'a 1862. 8vo. Rebell'n Pamph. Vol. 27.

BROWN, Mrs. D. C. Memoirs of the late Rev. Lemuel Covell and Rev. Alanson L. Covell. Brandon, 1839. 12mo.

BROWN Family Genealogy. See SMITH, Columbus. Report to Brown Assoc.

BROWN, Francis H. See Harvard Coll.

BROWN, George Wm. Address before the Literary Societies of St. Johns College, July 27, 1869. Baltimore, 1869. 8vo. Addresses. Vol. 34.

—— Origin and Growth of Civil Liberty in Maryland. Baltimore, 1850. 8vo. Md. Hist. Soc. Addresses. Vol. 3.

BROWN, H. A. Guide-Book for the City and Vicinity of Boston. Boston, 1869. 12mo.

BROWN, Henry. History of Illinois, from its First Discovery and Settlement. N, Y., 1844. 8vo.

BROWN, Isaac V. Biography of Rev. Rob't Finley, D. D., Author of the Amer. Colonization Soc. Phil'a, 1857. 12mo.

—— Hist. Vind. of the Abrogation of the Plan of Union, by the Presb. Ch., in the U. S. Phil'a, 1855. 8vo.

BROWN, Gen. Jacob. See Life of, etc.

BROWN, J. N. Memoirs of Ripley, Ohio. Fire Lands. Pioneer. Vol. 4.

BROWN, Capt. John. See REDPATH, Jas. Public Life of. 1860.

—— WEBB, R. D. Life and Letters.

BROWN, Dr. John. The Enterkin. Edinburgh, 1865. 12mo. Hist. Pamph. Vol. 19.

BROWN, John P. ET TABARY'S Conquest of Persia by the Arabs. Amer. Oriental Soc. Jour. Vols. 1, 2.

BROWN, Milton. Speech in Cong., July 7, 1842, on the Tariff. Washington, 1842. 8vo. Cong. and Polit. Pamph. Vol. 24.

BROWN, Capt. Moses, U. S. N. See SWETT. S.

BROWN, Nicholas. See Wayland, Rev. F.

BROWN, Orlando. Memorandum of Preston Family. Albany. Genealog. Pamph. Vol. 5.

BROWN, Rich'd. Principles of Drawing Ornaments exemplified. Lond. 1822. 4to. Eng. Miscell. Pamph. Vol. 39.

BROWN, Sam'l Gilman, D. D. See Hamilton College.

BROWN, SAM'L R. Authentic History of Second War for Independence. Auburn. 1815. 2 Vols. 12mo.

—— Chinese Culture or Remarks on the Causes of the Peculiarities of the Chinese. Amer. Oriental Soc. Journ. Vol. 2.

—— Western Gazetteer; or Emigrants' Directory of Western States. Auburn. 1817. 8vo.

BROWN, Tarleton. See BUSHNELL, C. I. Rev. War Memoirs.

BROWN, Thos. Lectures on the Philosophy of the Human Mind. Hallowell. 2 Vols. 1830. 8vo.

BROWN UNIVERSITY. Ann. Reports to the Corporation, made Sept. 3, 1829, Mar. 28, 1850. Report of Comm. of the Corporations appointed to raise $125,000. 1850.

—— —— Catalogues for 1830–1, 1834–5, 1844–5, 1845–6, 1846–7, 1847–8, 1848–9, 1850–1, 1852–3, 1853–4, 1855–6, 1857–8, 1864–5, 1869–70. Providence.

—— —— Catalogus Senatus Academici. Providence, 1860.

—— —— Catalogue of Library. Providence, 1843. 8vo.

—— —— Charter granted in 1764. Providence, 1834. 8vo.

—— —— See GUILD, R. A. History of. 1858.

—— —— History & Laws of the Library. Providence, 1843. 8vo.

—— —— PARSONS, U. — Med. Lecture, 1826.

—— —— Pitman, John.

—— —— Proceedings on the Resignation of Pres't Wayland, the Induction of Pres't Sears. Providence, 1856. 8vo.

—— —— Society of the United Brothers. Trien. Catalogue, 1848. Providence. 8vo.

—— —— Trien. Catalogues, 1846. 1852, 1856, 1860, 1866. Boston & Providence. 8vo.

—— —— Under the Presidency of Asa Messer. Boston, 1867. 8vo. R. I. Hist. Discourses, &c. Vol. 1.

BROWN, Wm. Address in the Ill. Legisla., on Importance of Education. Vandalia, Ill., 1839. 8vo. Addresses. Vol. 24.

BROWN, Wm. Memorial to Congr. in behalf of Manufacturers of Distilled Spirits in Ky. and Penn. Washington, 1870. 8vo. Congr. and Polit. Pamph. Vol. 118.

BROWN, Wm. H. Historical Sketch of Slavery in Ill., before Chicago Hist. Soc., Dec. 5, 1864. 8vo. Chicago Hist. Soc. Pamph. See also Congr. and Polit. Pamph. Vol. 107.

—— Memoir of Hon. D. P. Cook, before Chicago Hist. Soc., June 9, 1857. Chicago, 1857. 8vo.

BROWN, W. K. Four Papers on "Protection to Agriculture." Maidstone, 1845. 8vo. Strangford Pamph. Vol. 40.

BROWN, Rev. W. S. Address on Freemasonry, before Bloomfield Lodge, No. 57, Feb. 22, 1854. Louisville, 1854. 8vo. Masonic Pamph. Vol. 1.

BROWN, W. W. Sketches of Places and People Abroad, with Memoir of the Author. N. Y., 1855. 12mo.

BROWNE, Benj. F. Acc. of Salem Common, and the Leveling of the same in 1802. Essex Institute Coll. Vol. 4.

—— Memorials of Nathan'l Ward. Essex Institute Coll. Vol. 2.

BROWNE, Dunn. Experiences in the Army. Boston, 1866. 12mo.

BROWNE, J. Ross. Adventures in the Apache Country. Tour Through Arizona and Sonora. N. Y., 1869. 12mo.

—— Resources of the Pacific Slope: Mines, Minerals, etc., West of the Rocky Mountains. N. Y., 1869. 8vo.

—— Crusoe's Island: A Ramble in the Footsteps of Alex. Selkirk, with Adventures in Cal. and Washoe. N. Y., 1867. 12mo.

—— Report of Debate in Cal. Convention. Washington, 1850. 8vo.

—— and TAYLOR, J. W. Reports on Mineral Resources of U. S. Washington, 1867. 8vo.

BROWNE, Junius H. Four Years in Secessia: Adventures within and beyond the Union Lines. Hartford, 1865. 8vo.

BROWNE, N. B. Address before Union League. Phila., 1863. Rebell'n Pamph. Vol. 91.

BROWNE, Peter A. Essays on the Physical History of the Globe. Its Great Antiquity. Scientific Pamph. Vol. 3.

—— Lecture on the Naturalization Laws of the U. S. Phila., 1845. 8vo. Congr. Pamph. Vol. 100.

BROWNE, Thos. The Garden of Cyrus; or, Net Work Plantations of the Ancients, considered. Lond., 1736. 8vo. English Miscell. Pamph. Vol. 36.

BROWNE, Wm., of Tavistock. Whole Works; with a Memoir and Notes, by W. Carew Hazlitt. Printed for Roxburghe Library. Lond., 1868. 2 Vols. 4to.

BROWNELL, Chas. DeWolf. The Indian Races of N. and S. Amer. Boston, 1853. 8vo.

BROWNELL, Thos. Church, D. D. See WILLIAMS, (Bishop.) Obit. Sermon. 1865.

BROWNING, O. H. Speech in U. S. Senate, June 25, 1862, on Confiscation. Rebell'n Pamph. Vol. 10.

BROWNING, Reuben. The Finances of Gt. Britain considered. London, 1859 8vo. Eng. Polit. Pamph. Vol. 56.

BROWNING, W. S. History of the Huguenots during the 16th Century. London, 1839. 2 vols. 8vo.

BROWNLOW, W. G. The Irreligious Character of the Rebell. Address at N. Y., 1862. Rebell'n Pamph. Vol. 102.

—— Speech at N. Y., May 15, 1862, on the Sufferings of Union Men. Rebell'n Pamph. Vol. 102.

—— The Great Iron Wheel examined. Nashville, 1856. 12mo.

—— Rise, Progress and Decline of Secessia, with a Narrative of Personal Adventures. Phila., 1862. 12mo.

—— See TILTON, Theo.

—— and the Unionists of E. Tennessee. N. Y., 1862. Rebellion Pamph. Vol. 103.

BROWNRIGG, Wm., M. D. Considerations on Pestilential Contagion. London, 1771. 8vo. Med. Pamph. Vol. 33.

BROWNSTOWN, Battle of. 1812. See DALLIBA, James. Narrative of.

BRUCE, James. Classic and Historic Portraits. N. Y., 1854. 12mo.

—— See HEAD, F. B. Life and Adven. in Africa.

—— See WHARTON, R. Authenticity of his Travels in Abyssinia, etc.

BRUCE, John. Letter to the Fellows and Lord Mahon, Pres. of Soc. of Antiquaries, on Payments to the Soc. London, 1852. 8vo. Strangford Pamph. Vol. 62.

—— Speech in Comm. of House of Commons, on India Affairs, May 31, 1813. London, 1813. 8vo. Pamphleteer. Vol. 2.

BRUCE, Peter H. Memoirs: Account of his Travels in Germany, Russia, Tartary, Turkey, West Indies, etc. Dublin, 1783. 8vo.

BRUNET, Jacques Charles. Manuel du Libraire, et de l'Amateur de Livres. Paris, 1838. 4 vols. in 2. 8vo.

BRUNSON, Rev. Alfred. Communica. relating to his Travels in the N. Western Wilderness of Wisconsin, Dec. 6, 1843. Wis. House Jour., Sess. 1849. Appendix p. 30.

—— Early History of Wisconsin. Wis. Hist. Soc. Coll. Vol. 4.

—— Prairie du Chien: Its Present Position and Future Prospects. Milwaukee, 1857. 12mo. Wis. Local Hist. Vol. 1.

—— Western Pioneer: Incidents of Life and Times of Rev. Alfred Brunson, D. D., Embracing a Period of Seventy Years. Vol. 1. Cincin., 1872. 8vo.

BRUSH, Capt. Henry. See WILLIAMS, Saml. Two Western Campaigns.

BRUTE, Bishop. See BAYLEY, J. R. Memoir of.

BRUYAS, Jas. Radical Words of the Mohawk Language. N. Y., 1862. 4to. Shea's Libr. of Linguistics.

BRUYERE, Jean-Baptiste. Noticc sur M. Jean-Baptiste Bruyere, de Montreal. Montreal, 1859. 18mo. Canada Pamph. Vol. 3.

BRYAN, George J. Life of George P. Barker, with Sketches of some of his Speeches. Buffalo, 1849. 12mo.

BRYANT, C. S. Indian Massacres in Minn. Cincin., 1864. 12mo.

BRYANT, Edwin. What I saw in California; or Journal of a Tour Across the Continent in 1846–7. 4th Ed. N. Y., 1849. 12mo.

BRYANT, Rev. Jas. C. The Zulu Language. Amer. Oriental Soc. Journ. Vol. 1.

BRYANT, Wm. Cullen. Disc. on the Life, Character and Writings of Gulian C. Verplanck, before N. Y. Hist. Soc., May 17, 1870. N. Y., 1870. 8vo.

—— Selections from the Amer. Poets. Harper's Fam. Lib. N. Y., 1860. 18mo.

BRYDGES, Sir Edgerton. Arguments in favor of Relieving the Able-Bodied Poor, by Finding them Employment London, 1817. 8vo. Pamphleteer. Vol. 11.

—— Reasons for a Farther Amendment of the Copyright Act. London, 1817. 8vo. Pamphleteer. Vol. 10.

—— What are Riches? Examination of the Definitions of Modern Economists. London, 1822. 8vo. Pamphleteer. Vol. 20.

BUBBLES from the Brunnens of Nassau. See HEAD, Sir F. B.

BUCCANEERS.—See OEXMELIN, A. O. Histoire des Bucaniers.

BUCHAN, Geo. Hist. Sketch of Ecclesiastical Establishment in Scotland. Edinburgh, 1840. 8vo. Strangford Pamph. Vol. 19.

BUCHANAN, Rev. Claudius. See PEARSON, Rev. H. Memoir of.

BUCHANAN, Dr. Geo. Oration on Slavery at Baltimore, July 4, 1791. See POOLE, W. F.

BUCHANAN, Isaac. Relations of Industry of Canada with the Mother Country and the U. S. Montreal, 1864. 8vo.

BUCHANAN, James. His Administration on the Eve of Rebellion. N. Y., 1866. 8vo.

—— His Doctrines and Policy as exhibited by himself and Friends. (n. d.) 8vo. Congr. and Polit. Pamph. Vol. 76.

BUCHANAN, James. Life and Public Services of, Including the most Important of his State Papers. Portrait. 12mo. New York, 1856.

—— See JACKSON, A. Letter to Carter Beverley, etc.

—— Speech in U. S. Senate, Feb. 2, 1842, on the Veto Power. Washington, 1842. 8vo. Congr. and Polit. Pamph. Vol. 25.

—— Speech in U. S. Senate, May 9, 1842, on Remedial Justice in U. S. Courts. Washington, 1842. 8vo. Congr. and Polit. Pamph. Vol. 25.

—— and BRECKINRIDGE, John C. Lives of. Cincin., 1856. 12mo. Biograph. Pamph. Vol. 13.

BUCHANAN, J. R. Journal of Man. Vols. 1, 2, 3, 4. Cincin., 1849–1853. 8vo.

BUCHANAN, Robt. Catalogue of his Library. Cincin., 1872. 8vo. Bibliograph. Pamph. Vol. 49.

—— The Culture of the Grape and Wine-Making. 5th Ed. Cincin., 1856. 12mo.

BUCK, Alfred E. Speech in Congr., Feb. 14, 1871, on the Condition of the South Ku-Klux Klan, etc. 8vo. Congr. and Polit. Pamph. Vol. 119.

BUCKE, Wm. J. History of Montgomery Co., Penn. Norristown, 1859. 8vo.

—— History of Mooreland, Penn., from its First Settlement. Hist. Soc. of Pa. Coll. Vol. 1.

BUCKE, Charles. Beauties, Harmonies and Sublimities of Nature. Harper's Fam. Lib. N. Y., 1858. 18mo.

—— Ruins of Ancient Cities; their Rise, Fall and Present Condition. Harper's Fam. Lib. N. Y., 1854. 2 vols. 18mo.

BUCKINGHAM Co., Eng. See BERRY, W. Co. Genealogies.

—— BYRNE, Wm. Brittania Depicta. Buckinghamshire. 1806.

—— LIPSCOMBE, G. Hist. and Antiq. of. 1847.

—— SHEAHAN, J. J. Hist. and Topog. 1862.

BUCKINGHAM, Duke of. Extracts from his Household Book, with a Description of Thornbury, 1507. London, 1833. 4to. Hist. Pamph. Vol. 22.

—— See Hope, A. J. B. Richelieu Compared with.

BUCKINGHAM Genealogy.—See CHAPMAN, F. W.

BUCKINGHAM, J. S. Account of his Farewell Meeting with his Constituents, etc., 1837. Broadside. Eng. Polit. Pamph. Vol. 42.

—— Address in Defence of his Lectures on Palestine. N. Y., 1840. 8vo. Addresses. Vol. 22.

—— America, Historical, Statistical and Descriptive. London, 1842. 3 vols. 8vo.

—— Bills for Promoting the Sobriety, Recreation and Instruction of the Laboring Classes. London, 1835. 8vo. Eng. Misc. Pamph. Vol. 29.

—— The British Institute: Prospectus, Etc. London, (n. d.) 8vo. Eng. Misc. Pamph. Vol. 9.

—— Canada, Nova Scotia, New Brunswick, and the other British Provinces of America. London, 1843. 8vo.

BUCKINGHAM, J. S. Correspondence with Lord Durham. London, 1837. 8vo. Eng. Misc. Pamph. Vol. 29.

—— Debate in the House of Commons in 1833, on the National Debt, etc. London, 1853. 8vo. Eng. Polit. Pamph. Vol. 50.

—— His Defence against the Charge of having received a Retainer from the East India Co. London, 1830. 8vo. Eng. Misc. Pamph. Vol. 29.

—— History and Progress of the Temperance Reformation, with a Plea for a Maine Law. London, 1854. 8vo. Temperance Pamph. Vol. 2.

—— Irish Improvidence encouraged by English Bounty, with a Plan of Relief for Ireland. London, (n. d.) 8vo. Eng. Polit. Pamph. Vol. 45.

—— Outline Sketch of his Voyages, Travels, Writings, etc. London. (n. d.) 8vo.

—— Outlines of a new Budget, for raising Eighty Millions. London, 1831. 8vo. Eng. Misc. Pamph. Vol. 29.

—— Petition to the House of Commons for Redress from Certain Injuries, June 31, 1847. London. 8vo. Eng. Polit. Pamph. Vol. 46.

—— Plan for the Future Gov't of India. London, 1853. 8vo. 2d Ed. Eng. Polit. Pamph. Vol. 50.

—— Plan of an Improved Income Tax and Real Free Trade, etc. London, 1845. 8vo. 2d Ed. Eng. Polit. Pamph. Vol. 44.

—— Prospectus of an Institution to be called the British Institute. London, (n. d.) 8vo. Eng. Misc. Pamph. Vol. 29.

—— Reasons for Legislative Interference to prevent the Practice of Duelling. London, (n. d.) 8vo. Eng. Misc. Pamph. Vol. 29.

—— See RUSSELL, Lord John.

—— Sketch of a Plan for effecting a Voyage Round the Globe. London, 1830. 8vo. Eng. Misc. Pamph. Vol. 29.

—— Sketch of his Life, Travels and Lectures on the Oriental World. London, 1831. 8vo. Eng. Misc. Pamph. Vol. 29.

—— Slanders of "Punch." Address to the British Public in Regard to the British and Foreign Institute. London, 1846. 8vo. 4th Ed. Eng. Polit. Pamph. Vol. 45.

—— Speech at the Peace Convention at Brussels, Sept. 20, 1848. (n. p.) 8vo. Eng. Polit. Pamph. Vol. 46.

—— Speech in Parl't, June 3, 1834, on the Extent, Causes and Effects of Drunkenness. Temp. Pamph. Vol. 5.

—— Speech in House of Commons, March 9, 1837, on Establishment of a Marine Board. London, 1837. 8vo. Eng. Misc. Pamph. Vol. 29.

—— The Justice, Policy and Safety of a Marine Law for England. Manchester. 8vo. (n. d.) Eng. Polit. Pamph. Vol. 50.

—— The Slave States of America. London, 1842. 2 vols. 8vo.

—— The Eastern and Western States of America. London, 1842. 3 vols. 8vo.

BUCKINGHAM and Solebury, Penn. See WATSON, J. First Settlement of.

BUCKINGHAM, Wm. A. Letter to the Legislature of Conn., May, 1863. Hartford, 1863. 8vo. Rebell'n Pamph. Vol. 66.

BUCKLAND, Rev. Wm. Geology and Mineralogy considered in relation to Nat. Theology. Lond., 1836. 2 vols. 8vo.

BUCKMINSTER, Rev. J. S. Extract from a Disc. at Boston, Oct., 1811, on the Death of Hon. James Bowdoin, 1848. 8vo. Sermons. Vol. 10.

—— Memoir of. Mass. Hist. Soc. Coll. 2d Ser. Vol. 2.

BUCKMINSTER, Lydia N. Genealog. Account of the Descendants of Thos. Hastings. Boston, 1866. 8vo.

BUDD, Thos. Good Order Established in Penn. and N. Jersey; being a True Account of the Country, etc., 1683. Hist. Mag. Vol. 6.

BUDDHISM. See SALISBURY, E. E.

BUDGETT, Dr. J. B. The Tobacco Question, Morally, Socially and Physically Considered. Lond., 1827. 8vo. Eng. Polit. Pamph. Vol. 54.

BUDINGTON, Rev. William I. History of the 1st Ch., Charlestown. Boston, 1858. 8vo.

BUEL, Alex. W. Speech at Detroit, Nov. 19, 1850, in Defence of the Constitution and Union. Washington. 8vo. Congr. & Polit. Pamph. Vol. 90.

—— Speech in Cong., Feb. 20, 1850, on Hungarian Independence. Congr. and Polit. Pamph. Vol. 92.

BUEL, Jesse. See DEAN, A. Eulogy on, 1840.

BUELL, Gen. D. C. Review of Evidence before Military Commission, Nov., 1862, on Campaigning in Ky.,Tenn.,etc. Rebell'n Pamph. Vol. 12.

BUENA VISTA, Battle of. See GIBSON, Capt. J.W. Letter Descriptive of, 1847.

BUENOS AYRES. See Appeal on Behalf of British Subjects, etc., 1846.

—— Asesinato del Gobernador de la Buenos Ayres. Lond., 1829. 8vo. Strangford Pamph. Vol. 6.

—— See BAINES, T. Affairs of the River Plate, 1845.

—— MALLALIEU, A. Rosas and his Calumniators, etc., 1845.

—— Monarchical Projects; or a Plan to Place a Bourbon on the Throne of Buenos Ayres, etc. Lond., 1820. 8vo. Strangford Pamph. Vol. 1.

—— Official Note from the French Consul in Buenos Ayres. With Documents, etc. 4 Pamphlets. Lond., 1838, 1839. 8vo. Strangford Pamph. Vol. 18.

—— See PFEIL, A. R. Résumé des Affairs de la Plata, 1849.

BUFFALO Co., Wis., Papers. 1856, '64, '69, '70. 1 vol.

—— Republican, Newspaper. 1870–72. 1 vol.

BUFFALO, N. Y. Board of Trade. History of, by S. S. Guthrie. Address by C. G. Curtiss, etc. Buffalo, 1870. 8vo. Buffalo City Pamph. Vol. 1.

—— —— Report of Comm. on the Niagara Ship Canal, 1871. 8vo. Buffalo City Pamph. Vol. 1.

—— —— Statement of Trade and Commerce of Buffalo, for 1869 & '71. Buffalo, 1870–72. 8vo. Buffalo City Pamph. Vol. 1.

BUFFALO N. Y. Business Directories. Buffalo, 1855. 8vo.
—— City Directory, 1838-9, '42, '44, '48-9, '49-50, '50-51, '52, '53, 54. 9 vols. 12mo.
—— Same, 1855—69. 15 vols. 8vo.
—— Same, 1871.
—— See CLINTON, G. W. Plants of Buffalo and Vicinity.
—— Commercial Advertiser and Directory. Buffalo, 1850. 12mo.
—— Comptroller's Report of Fiscal Affairs for 1870. Buffalo, 1871. 8vo. Buffalo City Pamph. Vol. 1.
—— 1st Presb. Ch. See CLARKE, Rev. W.
—— 1st Unitarian Church. Account of the Quarter Centen. Celebration, Oct. 16, 1861, with Rev. Dr. Hosmer's two Discourses. Buffalo, 1861. 8vo. N. Y. Hist. Discourses. Vol. 3.
—— Forest Lawn Cemetery. By-Laws, Rules, etc. Buffalo, 1866. 8vo. Buffalo City Pamph. Vol. 1.
—— See HAYES, G. E. Geology of.
BUFFALO Hist. Society. Brief Resumè of its History, etc. From the Buffalo Courier, Mar. 6, 1873.
—— See CLINTON, Judge.
—— Constitution and By-Laws. Buffalo. 1863. 8vo.
—— Proceedings at Ann. Meeting, Jan. 11, 1871. Buffalo, 1871. 8vo.
—— See HAYES, G. E.
—— MARSHALL, O. H.
—— NORTON, C. D.
—— PROSSER, E. S.
—— STEELE, O. G.
—— SELLSTEDT, L. G.
—— WILKESON, J.
—— HOSMER, G. W.
BUFFALO Horticult. Soc'y. See CLINTON, Geo. W. Address, 1846.
—— Constitution and By-Laws. Buffalo, 1846. 8vo. Agr. Pamph. Vol. 1.
BUFFALO, N. York. See KETCHUM, W. Hist. of.
—— NORTON, C. D. The Old Ferry at the Black Rock.
—— Old Settlers' Festival, held Jan. 23-6, 1867. Buffalo. 8vo. (n. d.) N. Y. Hist. Discourses, etc. Vol. 3.
—— Park Commissioners. 1st Ann. Report. Buffalo, 1871. 8vo. Buffalo City Pamph. Vol. 1.
—— Public Schools. See STEELE, O. G. Hist. of, 1863.
—— SALISBURY, Guy H. Buffalo in 1836 and 1862.
—— Soc. of Nat. Sciences. Bulletin. Vol. 1, No. 1. Buffalo, 1873. 8vo.
—— STEELE, O. G. Buffalo City Sewerage, etc.
—— Manufacturing Interests of the City of Buffalo. Sketches of Buffalo, 1866. 8vo. 2d Ed. N. Y. Hist. Discourses, etc. Vol. 4.
—— See WILKESON, John. Manufacture of Iron in.
—— WILKESON, S. Early Incidents of.
—— Y. M. Assoc. See BARTON, J. L. Address, 1848.
—— —— Bulletin of Books added to the Library, Mar. 1 to June 1, 1870. Buffalo, 1870. 8vo. Bibliograph. Pamph. Vol. 69.

BUFFALO Y. M. Assoc. 7th, 11th and 34th Ann. Reports, 1843, '47, '70. Buffalo. 8vo. Buffalo City Pamph. Vol. 1.

BUFFON, George Louis, Count de. Histoire Naturelle Générale et partiulière Sixieme Edition. Paris, 1759–68. 32 vols.

—— Supplement, 1744–82. 12 vols. Paris. 44 vols. 18mo.

—— Histoire Naturelle des Minéraux. Paris, 1783–87. 8vols. 12mo.

BUFORD, H. M. Rights of Property of Married Women, under the Laws of Ky. Cincin., 1871. 8vo. Law Pamph. Vol. 22.

BUGLE (The): its Utility in Battery Evolutions. N. Y.,1862. 12mo. Rebell'n Pamph. Vol. 105.

BULFINCH, Thomas. The Age of Chivalry. Boston, 1859. 12mo.

BULKELEY, Gershom. The People's Right to Election or Alteration of Gov't in Conn., argued, etc. Conn. Hist. Soc. Coll. Vol. 1.

BULKLEY, Rev. John. Inquiry into the Right of the Aborig. Natives to the Lands in America. Mass. Hist. Soc. Coll. 1st Ser. Vol. 4.

BULKLEY, Rev. Justice. Hist. Sketch of Shurtleff College, delivered June 15, 1865, Upper Alton, Ill. 8vo. Addresses, etc. Vol. 23.

BULL, Edw. Hints and Directions for Authors in Writing, Printing and Publish'g. Lond., 1842. 8vo. Strang. Pam. Vol. 48.

BULLARD, E. F. The Nation's Trial: The Proclamation: Dormant Powers of the Government, etc. N. Y., 1863. 8vo. Rebell'n Pamph. Vols. 2 and 74.

BULLARD, H. A. Disc. before Hist. Soc., La., Jan 13, 1836. French's Hist. Coll. of La., Vol. 1.

—— Disc. on the Life, Character and Writings of F. X. Martin. French's Hist. Coll., La., Vol. 2.

—— Louisiana Hist. Researches. From De Bow's Review, Jan., 1847. La. Misc. Pamph. Vol. 1.

BULLARD, O. A. Views in N. Y. City. (n. d.) 8vo. N. Y. City Misc. Pamph. Vol. 3.

BULLETIN des Sciences Historique, Antiquités, Philology. Paris, 1824–29. 11 vols. 8vo.

BULLFINCH, Thos. Oregon and Eldorado. Boston, 1866. 12mo.

BULLITT, J. C. Review of Mr. Binney on Habeas Corpus. Phila., 1862. 8vo. Rebell'n Pamph. Vols. 27 and 60.

BULLOCK, Rufus B. Address to the People of Georgia (n. p.) 1872. 8vo. Congr. and Polit. Pamph. Vol. 130.

—— Have the Reconstruction Acts been fully executed in Georgia? 1868. Rebell'n Pamph. Vol. 41.

—— Letter in Reply to John Scott, U. S. S. Atlanta, Ga., 1871. 8vo. Congr. and Polit. Pamph. Vol. 138.

—— Letter to Repub. Members of Congress who Sustain the Reconstruction Acts. Washington, 1870. 8vo. Congr. and Polit. Pamph. Vol. 120.

—— See TIFT, N.

BUNDLING, See STILES, Henry R.

BUNDY, H. S. Speech in Cong., Jan. 5, 1867, on the Financial Interests of the Country. Congr. and Polit. Pamph. Vol. 121.

BUNDY, J. M. Are we a Nation? The Question as it stood before the War. With a Hist. Letter from Sen. Howe. N. Y.,1870. 8vo. Congr. and Polit. Pamph. Vol. 120.

BUNGAY, Geo. W. Off-hand Takings; or Noticeable Men of Our Age, with Portraits. N. Y., 1854. 12mo.
BUNKER HILL, Battle of. See DAWSON, H. B.
—— DEARBORN, H
—— PUTNAM, Dan.
—— SUMNER, W. H.
—— SWETT, S.
BUNKER Hill Declaration, Sept. 10, 1840. 8vo. Congr. and Polit. Pamph. Vol. 135.
BUNKER HILL Monument. See PACKARD, A. S. Hist. of.
—— SWETT, S. Original Plan and Construction.
BUNKER HILL Monument Association. Ceremonies on Displaying the Nat. Flag, June 17, 1861. Rebell'n Pamph. Vol. 17.
—— Proceedings at Ann. Meeting, June 17, 1862. Rebell'n Pamph. Vol. 17.
—— Act of Incorporation, By-Laws, etc. Boston, 1830. 8vo. Boston Misc. Pamph. Vol. 3.
—— Proceed. on 40th Annivers., June 17, 1863. Boston, 1863. 8vo. Boston Misc. Pamph. Vol. 3.
—— See WARREN, G. W. Address, 1865.
BUNNER, E. History of Louisiana, from its First Discovery and Settlement. Harper's Fam. Libr. N. Y. 1846. 18mo.
BUNNER, R. Disc. before Alumni of Columbia Coll., Oct. 8, 1834. Addresses. Vol. 12.
BUNSEN, Chevalier. Life of Martin Luther, with an Estimate of his Character and Genius, by Thos. CARLYLE. N. Y., 1859. 18 mo.
——Constitutional Rights of the Duchies of Schleswig and Holstein. London, 1848. 8vo. Strangford Pamph. Vols. 46 and 55.
BUNSEN, C. C. Outlines of the Philosophy of Universal History Applied to Language and Religion. London, 1854. 2 vols. 8vo.
—— Signs of the Times on the Dangers to Religious Liberty. London, 1856. 8vo.
BUNSEN, C. C. J. The Law of Slavery in the U. S. Boston, 1863. 8vo. Rebellion Pamph. Vol. 18.
BURBANK, Lt. Col. Gardner. Defence before General Court-Martial, Worcester, Mass., Sept. 8, 1818. Congr. and Polit. Pamph. Vol. 77.
BURBANK, Judge. Speech in the Senate of Cal. on the Crittenden Compromise, 1861. Rebell'n Pamph. Vols. 36 and 68.
BURCHELL, Wm. J. Hints on Emigration to the Cape of Good Hope. London, 1820. 8vo. Pamphleteer. Vol. 17.
BURDER, Geo. The Welch Indians; Papers Respecting a People whose Ancestors Emigrated from Wales to America in 1170. London, 1797. 8vo. Indian Pamph. Vol. 2.
BURDETT, Chas. Life of Kit (Christopher) Carson, the Great Western Hunter and Guide. Phila., 1869. 12mo.
BURDETT, Sir Francis. Speech at London, Feb. 22, 1819. 8vo. Eng. Polit. Pamph. Vol. 35.
BUREAU of Refugees and Freedmen. See U. S. Sec. of War.

Bureau of Refugees and Freedmen. Report of the Asst. Comm'r for Alabama, 1866. Rebell'n Pamph. Vol. 16.

—— —— Eighth Semi-Ann. Report on Schools for Freedmen, July 1, 1869. Congr. and Polit. Pamph. Vol. 79.

Bureau of Statistics. See U. S. Sec. of Treasury.

Burford, J. & R. Description of a View of the City of Mexico. London, 1825. 8vo.

Burge, W. Speech in the House of Commons, April 22, 1839, on the Gov't of Jamaica. London, 1839. 8vo. Strangford Pamph. Vol. 17.

Burges, Tristam. Memoir of. From Amer. Quar. Rev., June, 1835. Biograph. Pamph. Vol. 17.

—— Speeches in Congr., Jan., 1831, on General Appropriation Bill. Congr. and Polit. Pamph. Vol. 88.

Burgess, E. Memorial of Family of Thomas and Dorothy Burgess, of Sandwich, 1637. Boston, 1865. 8vo.

Burgess, Rev. George, D. D. Disc. before Maine Hist. Soc., Aug. 2, 1854. Collections. Vol. 4.

—— Pages from the Ecclesiastical Hist. of N. England. Boston, 1847. 8vo. Religious Pamph. Vol. 17.

Burgess, Rich'd. Metropolis Schools for the Poor. Letter to the Bishop of London. London, 1846. 8vo. Strangford Pamph. Vol. 46.

Burgon, John W. Life and Times of Sir Thomas Gresham. London, 1839. 2 vols. 8vo.

—— Remarks on Art with reference to the Studies of the University. Oxford, 1846. 8vo. Art Pamph. Vol. 2.

Burgoyne, Gen. John. Invasion of Vermont, 1777. Documents in Relation to. Vt. Hist. Soc. Coll. Vol. 1.

Burgoyne's Campaigns. See Neilson, C. Account of.

Burgoyne, Lieut. Gen. John. Orderly Book, from the Entry of his Army into the State of N. Y., until the Surrender at Saratoga, Oct. 16, 1777. Albany, 1860. 4to.

Burgoyne, Sir John. A Sacrifice to "The Slanders of a Ribald Press," etc London, 1855. 8vo. Eng. Polit. Pamph. Vol. 53.

Burk, John. History of Virginia from its First Settlement to the Present time. Petersburg, 1804–5, '16, 22. 4 vols. 8vo.

Burke, Aedanus. Address to the Freemen of S. Carolina. Phila., 1783. Amer. Tracts. Vol. 4.

Burke, Sir Bernard. Book of Orders of Knighthood and Decorations of Honor of all Nations, with fac simile colored illustrations, etc. London, 1858. 8vo.

—— Genealog. and Heraldic Dic. of the Peerage and Baronetage of the British Empire. 16th Revised Ed. London, 1854. 8vo.

—— Genealog. and Heraldic Dict. of the Landed Gentry of G. Britain and Ireland. London, 1858. 8vo.

—— Same. 5th Ed. London, 1871. 8vo.

—— See Burke, John.

Burke, Edmund. Account of European Settlements in America. London, 1765. 2 vols. 8vo.

BURKE, Edmund. Short Account of a Late Short Administration. London, 1765. Scarce Tracts. Vol. 2.

—— Correspondence of, between 1744 and 1797. Edited by Chas. Earl Fitzwilliam and Gen. Sir Rich'd Bourke. Lond., 1844. 4 vols. 8vo.

—— Letter ——— respecting the Effect of the Quebec Bill upon the Boundary of N. Y. N. Y. Hist. Soc. Coll. New Ser. Vol. 2.

—— Letter to Sir H. Langrishe, on the Admission of Roman Catholics of Ireland to the Elective Franchise. Dublin, 1792. 8vo. Eng. Polit. Pamph. Vol. 24.

—— Speech in Parl't, March 22, 1775, on Conciliation with the Colonies. London, 1775. 4to. Eng. Polit. Pamph. Vol. 66.

—— See Speeches of Burke and others.

—— Speech in Parliament, Feb. 11, 1780, on Public Economy, etc. London, (n. d.) 8vo. Eng. Polit. Pamph. Vol. 73.

—— Three Memorials on French Affairs, written in 1791, '92 and '93. London, 1797. 8vo. Eng. Polit. Pamph. Vol. 26.

—— Works of. 1st Amer. Ed. Boston, 1806. 4 vols. 8vo.

—— Essays on the Protective System and the Present Tariff. 1846. 8vo. Congr. and Polit. Pamph. Vol. 92.

—— Speech in Cong., July 8, 1842, on the Tariff. Washington, 1842. 8vo. Congr. and Polit. Pamph. Vol. 25.

BURKE, Edward. Report on Tobacco Manufacture, adopted at N. Y., Dec. 7, 1864. N. Y., 1864. 8vo. Rebel'n Pamp. Vol. 7.

BURKE Genealogy. See BOUTELLE, John A.

BURKE, John, and John BERNARD. Encyclopœdia of Heraldry, or General Armory of England, Scotland and Ireland. 3d Ed. London, 1844. 8vo.

— Genealog. and Heraldic Hist. of the Extinct and Dormant Baronetcies of England, Ireland and Scotland. 2d Ed. London, 1844. 8vo.

—— Heraldic Illustrations, Comprising the Armorial bearings of the Principal Families of the Empire with Pedigrees. London, 1844–6. 3 vols. 8vo.

—— The Patrician. London, 1846–8. 6 vols. 8vo.

—— See BURKE, Sir Bernard.

BURKE, John Daly. See CAMPBELL, Chas. Memoir of.

BURKE, Rev. T. N. Froude's Crusade. Lecture in Brooklyn, Dec. 17, 1872. N. Y., 1872. 8vo. Addresses. Vol. 39.

—— Lectures on Temperance, with Sketch of his Life, by J. W. O'BRIEN. N. Y., 1872. 8vo. Temp. Pamph. Vol. 5.

BURKE, W. S. Directory of Council Bluffs, and Emigrant's Guide to the Gold Regions of the West. Council Bluffs, 1866. 8vo.

BURLEIGH, Joseph B., LLD. The Legislative Guide; Rules for Conducting Business in Congress, etc. 4th Ed. Phila., 1858. 8vo.

BURLINGAME, Anson. Memorial of. Boston, 1870. 8vo. Biograph. Pamph. Vol. 11.

—— Speech in Congress, June 21, 1856, on the State of the Union. Congr. and Polit. Pamph. Vol. 85.

BURLINGTON, Iowa. Proceedings of the Rapids Convention, at Burlington, Iowa, Oct. 23 and 24, 1851. Burlington, 1852. 8vo. Iowa Misc. Pamph. Vol. 1.

BURLINGTON, N. J., St. Mary's Hall. Catalogues for 1848 and 1868. Burlington and Phila., 1848–1868. 8vo.

—— See SMITH, J. J.

BURLINGTON, Wis. Gazette, Newspaper, Aug. to Dec., 1859. Folio. Bound with Racine Papers.

—— —— Burlington, 1859–1860. Folio.

—— Standard. 1869–72. 1 vol.

BURN, John S. History of Parish Registers in England; also of the Registers of Scotland, Ireland, and E. and W. Indies. 2d Ed. London, 1862. 8vo.

BURN, Dr. Rich'd. Observa. on the Proposed Bill for the Relief of the Poor. London, 1776. 8vo. Eng. Polit. Pamph. Vol. 18.

BURNABY, Rev. Andrew. Travels through the Middle Settlements of N. America in 1759–60. 3d Ed. London, 1798. 4to.

BURNAP, Geo. W. Lectures on the Hist. of Christianity. Phila., 1850. 12mo.

—— Lectures to Young Men on the Cultivation of the Mind, etc. 5th Ed. Baltimore, 1854. 12mo.

—— Life of Leonard Calvert, 1st Gov. of Md. Sparks' Amer, Biog. 2d Ser. Vol. 9.

—— Memoir of Henry A. Ingalls, with Selections from his Writings. Boston, 1846. 12mo.

—— Miscell. Writings. Baltimore, 1844. 12mo.

—— Origin and Causes of Democracy in America; Read before Maryland Hist. Soc., Dec. 20, 1853. Baltimore, 1854. 8vo. Md. Hist. Soc. Addresses. Vol. 3.

BURNES, Lieut. Alex. Travels into Bokhara; Account of a Journey to Cabool, Tartary and Persia, etc., 1831–3. Waldie's Circulating Libr. Vol. 5.

BURNET, Bishop Gilbert. Defence from a Speech Imputed to him on Occasional Conformity. London, 1704. Folio. Eng. Polit. Pamph. Vol. 2.

—— See ELLIOT, Robt. Specimen of his Posthumous History.

—— Reasons for Abrogating the Test imposed on all Members of Parl't. (n. d.) Small 4to. Eng. Misc. Pamph. Vol. 1.

—— Obedience to the Present King, Notwithstanding our Oaths to the Former. London, 1689. Sm. 4to. Eng. Polit. Pamph. Vol. 65.

—— Pastoral Letter Concerning the Oaths of Allegiance and Supremacy to King William and Queen Mary. London, 1689. Sm. 4to. Eng. Religious Pamph. Vol. 79.

—— Reasons against Repealing the Acts of Parliament Concerning the Test, etc. 6 Papers. 1687. Small 4to. Eng. Polit. Pamph. Vol. 7.

—— See Remarks on his History, etc. 1723.

—— Speech in the House of Lords, on the 1st Article of Impeachment of Dr. Henry Sacheverell. London, 1710. Small 4to. Eng. Misc. Pamph. Vol. 1.

BURNET, Jacob. Letters Relating to the Early Settlement of tne Northwest Territory. Ohio Hist. and Philos. Soc. Trans. Part 2. Vol. 1.

—— Notes on the Settlement of the N. Western Territory. N. Y. 1847. 8vo.

BURNET, Rev. John. Lecture Apr. 27, 1847, on Geology and Christianity. Lond.? 8vo, Scientific Pamph. Vol. 34.

BURNETT, Peter H. Amer. Theory of Gov't, with Reference to the Present Crisis. 2d Ed. N. Y., 1863. 8vo. Rebell'n Pamph. Vol. 1.

BURNETT, Thomas P. See BRUNSON, Rev. A. Memoir of.

BURNETT, Dr. Waldo J. Origin and Development of the Spermatic Particles among the Vertebrated Animals. 1850. 4to. Scientific Pamph. Vol. 38.

BURNEY Manuscripts. See British Museum.

BURNHAM, Rev. A. W. Address at Centen. Celebra. at Dunbarton, N. H., Sept. 13, 1865. 8vo. N. H. Hist. Discourses. Vol. 1.

BURNHAM, Carrie S. Suffrage the Citizens' Birthright. Address before the Constitutional Convention of Penn., Jan. 16, 1873. Phila., 1873. 8vo. Congr. and Polit. Pamph. Vol. 68.

—— Woman Suffrage. Argument in Penn. Supreme Court, Apr., 1873. Phila. 1873. 8vo.

BURNHAM, R. H. Burnham Family Genealogy. Hartford, 1869. 8vo.

BURNHAM, Sam'l. Memoir of John A. Andrew. From the N. Eng. Hist. and Gen. Reg., Jan., 1869. Addresses. Vol. 21.

BURNS, Anthony. See WILLSON, Rev. E. B.

BURNS, Barnet. Brief Narrative of a New Zealand Chief; a Personal History. Birmingham, 1842. 8vo. Biograph. Pamph. Vol. 15.

BURNS, Robert. See Boston Celebra., 1859.

—— CARLYLE, T. Life of.

—— Milwaukee Celebra. in honor of, 1859.

—— N. Y. Celebra. in honor of, 1869.

BURNSIDE, Gen. A. E. See Men of the Time.

BURNSIDE, Saml. M. Memoir of Isaiah Thomas, LL. D. Amer. Antiq. Soc. Coll. Vol. 2.

BURR, Aaron. See DAVIS, M. L. Private Journ. of.

—— —— —— Memoirs of.

—— Examination of Charges against, 1804. Congr. and Polit. Pamph. Vol. 75.

—— See GREENWOOD, John. Personal Recollections of.

—— Report of Trial of, for Treason, etc. Phila., 1808. 2 vols.

—— Narrative of Suppression of "Wood's Administration of J. Adams."

—— PARTON, J. Life and Times of.

—— SAFFORD, W. H. Expedition of.

—— WIRT, Wm. Two Arguments on Trial of Burr.

BURR, C. C. History of the Union and the Constitution. N. Y., 1863. Rebell'n Pamph. Vol. 98.

—— Notes on the Constitution of the U. S., 1864. Rebell'n Pamph. Vol. 97.

BURR, C. C. Speech at a Festival in Bergen Co., N. J., 1863. Rebell'n Pamph. Vol. 54.

BURR, Thos. Wm. Lecture, Nov. 8, 1856, on the History of the Law of Gravitation. Lond. 8vo. Scientific Pamph. Vol.28.

BURRITT, Elihu. Ocean Penny Postage; its Necessity Shown and its Feasibility Demonstrated. Lond., 1848. 12mo. Congr. and Polit. Pamph. Vol. 81.

BURROUGHS, Rev. Charles, D. D. Address before the N. H. Hist. Soc., June 14, 1843. Coll. Vol. 6.

BURROWS, Jas. Essay on Punctuation. Lond., 1768, 1772. Educa. Pamph. Vol. 40.

BURROWS, Thos. H. Against Compulsory School Attendance. From Penn. School Journ., 1858. Educa. Pamph. Vol. 7.

BURROWS, E. J. The Great Rebellion of 1861. Twelve Months History of the U. S. Phila., 1862. Rebell'n Pamph. Vol. 99.

BURROWS, John. On National Prejudices; their Good and Bad Effects. Lond., 1817. 8vo. Pamphleteer. Vol. 9.

BURT, Rev. Federal. Sketches of the Civil and Eccles. History of Durham. N. H. Hist. Soc. Coll. Vol. 5.

BURT, John T. Results of the System of Separate Confinement, as Administered at the Pentonville Prison, Eng. Lond., 1852. 8vo.

BURTON, Richard F. Personal Narrative of a Pilgrimage to El-Medinah and Mecca; with an Introduction by Bayard Taylor. N. Y., 1856. 12mo.

—— City of the Saints: and across the Rocky Mountains to California. N. Y., 1862. 8vo.

BURY, Viscount. Exodus of the Western Nations. Lond., 1865. 2 vols. 8vo.

BUSBY, C. A. Essay on the Propulsion of Navigable Bodies. N. Y., 1818. 8vo. Scientific Pamph. Vol. 13.

BUSBY, Thos. Arguments demonstrating that the Letters of Junius were written by John Lewis De Lolme. Lond., 1816. 8vo.

BUSH, Rev. George. Life of Mohammed, Founder of the Religion of Islam. Harpers Fam. Libr. N. Y,, 1858. 18mo.

BUSH, Rev. Robt. W. England's Two Great Military Captains—Marlborough and Wellington. Lond., 1853. 8vo. Biograph. Pamph. Vol. 10.

BUSHE, G. P. Considerations on the Income Tax. Lond., 1845. 8vo. Strangford Pamph. Vol, 42.

BUSHNELL, Chas. I. Adventures of Christopher Hawkins; Details of his Captivity by the British, his Sufferings, and his Escape from Jersey Prison Ship. N. Y., 1864. 8vo.

—— Arrangement of Tradesmen's Cards, Political Tokens; also Election Medals current in the U. S. N. Y., 1858. 8vo.

—— Hist. Account of the First Three Business Tokens issued in the City of N. York. N. Y., 1859. 12mo. N. Y. Hist. Discourses, etc. Vol. 3.

—— Journal of Exped. against Quebec, under Gen. Arnold, 1775, by Maj. Return J. Meigs, with an Introduction and Notes. Pr. Printed N. Y., 1864. 8vo.

BUSHNELL, Chas. I. Journ. of Sol. Nash, a Soldier of the Revolution, 1776–77, with Notes and Introduction. Pr. Printed N. Y., 1861. 8vo.

—— See LEGGETT, Maj. A.

—— Narrative of Eben. Fletcher, a Soldier of the Revolution, written by Himself, with Notes, etc. Pr. Printed N. Y., 1866. 8vo.

—— Narrative of John Blatchford; his Sufferings in the Revolutionary War while a Prisoner with the British: related by Himself, etc. With Notes. Pr. Printed N. Y., 1865. 8vo.

—— Narrative of Life and Adventures of Levi Hanford, a Soldier of the Revolution. With Notes, etc. Pr. Printed N. Y., 1863. 8vo.

—— Narrative of Sufferings of Lieut. Jas. Moody, in the Cause of Government, since 1776. Written by Himself, with Notes, etc. Pr. Printed N. Y. 1865. 8vo.

—— Tarleton Brown, a Capt. in the Rev. Army. Written by Himself, with Notes, etc. Pr. Printed N. Y., 1862. 8vo.

BUSHNELL, Horace, D. D. Commem. Disc. in the North Church of Hartford, May 22, 1853. Hartford, 1853. 8vo. Conn. Hist. Discourses. Vol. 1.

—— Hist. Estimate of Conn.; Speech before the Legislature, etc., June 4, 1851. Hartford, 1851. 8vo. Conn. Misc. Pamph. Vol. 1.

—— Disc. before the Alumni of Yale Coll., Aug. 16, 1843. N. Y., 1843. Addresses. Vol. 11.

—— The Fathers of N. England. Oration before the N. E. Soc. of N. Y., Dec. 21, 1849. N. Y., 1850. 12mo. Addresses, etc. Vol. 38.

—— See Yale Coll. Celebra., 1865.

BUSHWICK, N. Y. See STILES, H. R. Hist. of Brooklyn.

BUSTED, Richard. See SMITH, Robt. H. Review of Evidence against.

BUTLER, Gen. Journ. kept during an Expedition to the Miami in 1785. "Olden Time." Vol. 2.

BUTLER, Andrew P. Speech in U. S. Senate, Feb. 24 and 25, 1854, on the Kansas and Nebr. Bill. Congr. and Polit. Pamph. Vol. 93. Speeches. Vol. 3.

—— Speech in U. S. Senate, Mar., 18, 1856, on Naval Affairs. Congr. and Polit. Pamph. Vol. 87.

—— Speech in U. S. Senate, June 12 and 13, 1856, on the Difficulty of Messrs. Brooks and Sumner. Congr. and Polit. Pamph. Vol. 87.

BUTLER, Benj. F. Address on the Present Relations of Parties, at Boston, Nov. 23, 1870. Lowell, (n. d.) 8vo. Congr. and Polit. Pamph. Vol. 114.

—— Outline of the Constitutional Hist of N. Y. N. Y., 1848. 8vo. N. Y. Hist. Soc. Addresses. Vol. 2. Collections, 2d Series. Vol. 2.

—— Life and Public Services of. (n. d.) Rebell'n Pamph. Vol. 95.

—— See MACKENZIE, W. L. Life and Opinions of.

BUTLER, Benj. F. Men of the Time.
—— Representative Democracy in the U. S. Address at Union College, July 26, 1841. Albany, 1841. 8vo. Pamphlets. Vol. 3.
—— Speech at Academy of Music, N. York, Apr. 2, 1862. Rebell'n Pamph. Vols. 30 and 66.
—— Letter to the Hon. Dan'l S. Richardson, 1862, on Recruiting. Rebell'n Pamph. Vol. 68.
—— Speech at Cleveland, Ohio, Sept. 29, 1866, on the President's Policy. Washington, 1866. 8vo. Congr. and Polit. Pamph. Vol. 121.
—— Speech at Lowell, Mass., Aug. 10, 1860. Rebell'n Pamph. Vol. 77.
—— Speech at N. Y. on the War, Jan., 1863. Rebell'n Pamph. Vols. 9 and 90.
—— Speech at Lowell, Mass., Mar. 26, 1863. Rebell'n Pamph. Vol. 91.
—— Speech in Cong., Nov. 26 and 27, 1867, on the Currency. Congr. and Polit. Pamph. Vol. 121.
—— Speech in Cong., Dec. 20 and 21, 1869, on Reconstruction of Georgia. Congr. and Polit. Pamph. Vol. 122.
—— Speeches in Cong., March 4 and 8, 1870, on the Admission of Georgia. Congr. and Polit. Pamph. Vol. 119.
—— Speech upon the Campaign before Richmond, 1864, at Lowell, Mass., Jan. 29, 1865. Boston, 1865. 8vo. Rebell'n Pamph. Vol. 111.
—— See Tyrant, (The) of N. Orleans.
—— and HOYT, Jesse. See MACKENZIE, W. L. Lives and Opinions of, etc.
BUTLER, Caleb. History of the Town of Groton, including Pepperell and Shirley, with Family Registers, etc. Boston, 1848. 8vo.
BUTLER, Chas. Inaugural Oration, Nov. 4, 1815, at the Laying of the first Stone of the London Institution for Diffusion of Science, etc. London, 1816. 8vo. Pamphleteer. Vol. 7.
—— On the Legality of Impressing Seamen. London, 1824. 8vo. Pamphleteer. Vol. 23.
BUTLER Co., Ohio. See MCBRIDE, Jas. Ancient Fortifications in.
—— MCBRIDE, Jas. Pioneer Biography.
BUTLER, Frederick. Complete History of the U. S. to 1820. Hartford, 1821. 3 vols. 8vo.
BUTLER, Geo. B. Sewerage of New York. From Hunt's Merchants' Mag., 1845. 8vo. N. Y. City Misc. Pamph. Vol. 1.
—— The Conscription Act. N. Y., 1862. Rebell'n Pamph. Vol. 14 and 90.
BUTLER, Henry D. Family Aquarium; or Aqua Vivarium. New York, 1858. 12mo.
BUTLER Hospital, for the Insane, Providence, R. I. Charter, Reports of Trustees, etc, 1847–1869, except the Report of Jan., 1849. Providence. 8vo.
BUTLER, Rev. Jas. Sermon at Norwich, Vt., on the Death of Col. Truman B. Ransom.

BUTLER, James Davie, and HOUGHTON, Geo. F. Addresses on the Battle of Bennington, and the Life, etc., of Col. Seth Warner Burlington, 1849, 8vo. Vt. Hist. Soc'y Addresses. Vol. 1.

—— Address before the Vt. Hist. and Antiq. Soc., Oct. 16, 1846. Montpelier, 1846. 8vo. Vt. Hist. Soc. Addresses. Vol. 1.

—— Incentives to Mental Culture among Teachers. Boston, 1853. 8vo. Educa. Pamph. Vol. 3.

—— Nebraska: Its Characteristics and Prospects. (n. p.) 1872. 8vo.

—— Remarks at the Dinner of the Semi-Centen. Celebra. of Middlebury Coll.

—— Scenes in the Life of Christ, etc. Description of an Engraving. Chicago, 1866. 8vo. Art Catalogues, etc. Vol. 6.

BUTLER, Rev. John. Fast-Day Sermon before the House of Commons, Dec. 13, 1776. London, 1777. 4to. Eng. Sermons. Vol. 27.

—— Fast-Day Sermon before the House of Lords, Feb. 27, 1778, on the War with America.. London, 1778. 4to. Eng. Sermons. Vol. 27.

BUTLER, Dr. Acct. of the Character of Rt. Hon. Henry Bilson Legge. London, 1762. Scarce Tracts. Vol. 1.

BUTLER, L. C. Memorial Record of the Town of Essex, Vt. Burlington, 1866. 8vo. Rebell'n Pamph. Vol. 55.

BUTLER, Mann. History of the Commonwealth of Kentucky. Louisville, 1834. 8vo.

—— Same. 2d Ed., Revised and Enlarged. Cincin., 1836. 8vo.

BUTLER, Dr. R. Advantages of Blood-Letting. London, 1834. 8vo· Med. Pamph. Vol. 21.

BUTLER, Samuel, D. D. Geographia Classica; or the Application of Ancient Geography to the Classics. Phila., 1843. 8vo.

BUTLER, T. B. Speech in Cong., March 12, 1850, on Slavery. Congr. and Polit. Pamph. Vol. 85.

BUTTERFIELD, C. W. History of Seneca Co., Ohio. Sandusky, 1848. 12mo.

BUTTERWORTH, Jos. See SIBTHORP, Rev. R. W.

BUTT, Isaac. Irish Corporation Bill. Speech in House of Lords, May 15, 1840. London, 1840. 8vo. Strangford Pamph. Vol. 25.

—— Irish Municipal Reform. Speech at Dublin, Feb. 13, 1840. Dublin, 1840. 8vo. Strangford Pamph. Vol. 23.

BUTTS, Isaac. Brief Reasons for Repudiation, applicable to the War Debts of all Countries. Rochester, 1869. 8vo. Rebellion Pamph. Vol. 41. Cong. and Polit. Pamph. Vol. 104.

BUXTON, Maine. Records of the Ch. in Buxton, Me., during the Pastorate of Paul Coffin, D. D. Cambridge, 1868. 8vo. Maine Hist. Discourses, etc. Vol. 1.

BUXTON, Thos. F. The Amer. Slave Trade. Phila., 1839. 12mo.

BYAM, Geo. Wanderings in some of the Western Republics of America, and Remarks on the Ship Canal through Central America. London, 1850. 12mo.

BYBERRY, Penn. See COMLY, Isaac. Sketches of Hist. of.

Byfield, Nathaniel. Account of the late Revolution in New England, 1689. Force's Historical Tracts. Vol. 4. N. Y., Reprint, 1865.
—— See also Hist. Magazine. Vol. 6.
Byington, Rev. Cyrus. Grammar of the Choctaw Language. Edited by Dr. D. G. Brinton. Phila., 1870. 8vo. Indian Pamph. Vol. 1.
Byng, Admiral John. See Appeal to the People, etc.
—— Candid Examination of the Court-Martial of.
—— Letter to a Gentleman in the Country, —— on his Death.
—— Letter to a Member of Parliament, etc.
—— Letter to Lord Bertie, on his Defence of.
—— Modest Apology for the Conduct of a certaid Admiral, etc.
—— Parallel between his Case and that of Lord Geo. Sackville.
—— Real Defence of.
Byrd, Wm. History of the Dividing Line between Va. and N. Carolina. 1728–9. Richmond Reprint, 1867. 2 vols. 4to.
—— The Westover Manuscripts, Containing the History of the Dividing Line between Va. and N. Carolina. 1728. Petersburg, 1841. 8vo.
Byrne, John A. American Lands: The Emigrant's Home in the West. Clonmel, 1862. 12mo. Wis. Misc. Pamph. Vol. 1.
Byrne, Oliver. Treatise on Spherical Trigonometry. London, 1835. 8vo. Educa. Pamph. Vol. 36.
Byrne, Wm. Brittannia Depicta, a Series of Views of Picturesque Objects in G. Britain. Part 1. Buckinghamshire. London, 1806. 4to.
Byron, Lord. See Galt, J. Life of.
—— Gordon, Sir C. Life and Genius of.
—— Letter on the Rev. W. L. Bowles' Strictures on Pope. Lond., 1821. 8vo. Strangford Pamph. Vol. 2.
—— Letter of Expostulation to Lord Byron, on his Pursuits, Writings, etc. London, 1822. 8vo. Pamphleteer. Vol. 19.
—— Painted by his Compeers; or, All about Lord Byron, from his Marriage to his Death. London, 1869. 8vo. Biograph. Pamph. Vol. 10.
—— See Scott, Sir Walter. Character of.

C.

Cabeca de Vacca. See Smith, Buckingham. Relation of.
Cabell, E. C. Speech in Cong., Dec. 21, 1852, on Fortifying Key West and Tortugas. Congr. and Polit. Pamph. Vol. 90.
—— Speech in Cong., Mar. 5, 1850, on Slavery. Congr. and Polit. Pamph. Vol. 86.
—— Speech in Cong., Feb. 3, 1852, on Political Parties. Congr. & Polit. Pamph. Vol. 89.

CABLE, Jos. Speech in Cong., Mar. 11, 1852, on the Homestead Bill. Congr. and Polit. Pamph. Vol. 83.
CABOT, Geo. See KIRKLAND, John T., D. D. Disc. on his Death.
CABOT, J. S. Address before Essex Co., Mass., Agr. Soc. (n. d.)
CABOT, Sebastian. See HAYWARD, C. Life of.
—— Memoir of; with a Review of the History of Maritime Discovery. 2d Ed. Lond., 1832. 8vo.
CADOGAN, Rev. Wm. Dissertation on the Gout and all Chronic Diseases. Lond., 1771. 8vo. 5th Ed. Med. Pam. Vol. 17.
CADOGAN, Rev. W. B. Funeral Sermon on the Death of Rev. W. Romaine, preached Aug. 9, 1795. Lond., 1795. 8vo. Eng. Sermons. Vol. 57.
CADWALLADER, J. Speech in Cong., Mar. 5, 1856, on the Compromise. Congr. and Polit. Pamph. Vol. 94.
CADY, Daniel. Opinions in the Supreme Court—The People of the State of N. Y. vs. George Clarke, 1851. Law Pamph. Vol. 2.
CAERLAVEROCK, Siege of, 1300. See WRIGHT, Thos. Roll of Arms, etc.
CAERLEON Antiq. Soc. See MORGAN, O. Excavations within the Walls of Caerwent, 1855.
CAESAR, Julius. See BONAPARTE, Louis Napoleon. History of.
—— Commentaries. Latin. No Title. Vellum. 12mo.
—— LIDDELL, H. G. Life of.
—— See POST, Rev. B. Cæsar's Place of Landing in Britain.
—— SURTEES, Rev. S. F. Did he Cross the Channel?
CAIRNES, Prof. J. E. Speech at Dublin on the Amer. Question. n. d. Rebell'n Pamph. Vol. 39.
—— The Amer. Revolution; a Lecture. N. Y., 1862. 8vo. Rebell'n Pamph. Vol. 66.
—— The Slave Power; its Character, Career, and Probable Designs. 1862. Rebell'n Pamph. Vol. 75.
CAIRO, Ill. Engineers' Reports, relating to the Cairo City Property, etc. n. p. 1848. 8vo. Ill. Misc. Pamph. Vol. 2.
CALAMY, Rev. Benj. See SHERLOCK, Rev. Wm. Sermon at his Funeral, 1685–6.
CALDWELL, Chas. See COATES, B. H.
—— Disc. on the Genius and Character of Rev. Horace Holley, LL. D. Boston, 1828. 8vo.
—— Thoughts on Quarantine and Other Sanitary Systems. Boston, 1834. 8vo. Harvard Coll. Pamph.
—— Thoughts on the Original Unity of the Human Race. N. Y., 1830. 8vo.
—— Memoirs of the Life and Campaigns of Hon. Nathan'l Greene, Maj. Gen. in the U. S. Army. Phila., 1819. 12mo.
—— WARNER, H. W. Autobiog. of.
CALDWELL, Rev. David, D. D. See CARUTHERS, Rev. E. W.
CALDWELL, G. A. Speech in Cong., June 7, 1850, on the Admission of Cal. Congr. and Polit. Pamph. Vol. 86.
CALDWELL, Rev. James. See MURRAY, Rev. N. Memoir of.
CALDWELL, Rev. S. L. Discourse at Warren, R. I., on the 1st Century of the Warren Assoc., Sept. 11, 1867. Providence, 1867. 8vo. R. I. Hist. Discourses. Vol. 1.

CALDWELL, Rev. S. L. Hist. Disc. on the 1st Baptist Meeting House, Providence, R. I., May 28, 1865. Boston, 1865. 8vo. R. I. Hist. Discourses, Vol. 1.

CALENDAR of Hist. Mss. in the Office of the Sec. of State of N. Y. Part 1. Dutch Mss., 1630—1664.

—— Part 2. English Mss., 1664—1776. Albany, 1865–6. 2 vols. 4to.

CALENDAR of N. Y. Colonial Mss. Indorsed, Land Papers and Papers in the Office of the Sec. of State of N. Y., 1643—1803. Albany, 1864. 8vo.

CALENDARIUM Genealogicum, for the Reigns of Henry III and Edward I. Lond., 1865. 2 vols. 4to.

CALHOUN, Geo. A., D. D. Celebra. at North Coventry, Conn., Mar. 10, 1859, of the Settlement of Geo. A. Calhoun, D. D. Hartford, 1859. 8vo. Conn. Hist. Discourses, etc. Vol. 3.

—— Hist. Address before the Ch. in North Coventry, Conn., at their Centen. Celebra., Oct. 9, 1845. Hartford, 1846. 8vo. Conn. Hist. Discourses. Vol. 3.

CALHOUN, John C. Address in U. S. Senate, Mar. 4, 1850, on Slavery. Congr. Pamph. Vol. 96.

—— Addresses in Cong. on his Death.

—— See JACKSON, Gen. A. Corres. with, on Seminole War, 1831.

—— HAMILTON, Jas. Corres. on State Interposition.

—— JENKINS, J. S. Life of.

—— Life of, with Hist. of Polit. Events, from 1811 to 1843. N.Y., 1843. 8vo. Biograph Pamph. Vol. 12.

—— Opinions of Vice President of U. S. on the Relation of the States to the Gen. Gov. Charleston, 1831. 12mo. Nullification Tracts.

—— Speech in U, S. Senate, Mar. 21, 1834, on the Bank of the U. S. Congr. and Polit. Pamph. Vol. 90.

—— Same, Jan. 13, 1834. Speeches. Vol. 5.

—— Speech in U. S. Senate, Jan. 25, 1842, on the Treasury Note Bill. Washington, 1842. 8vo. Congr. and Polit. Pamph. Vol. 25.

—— Speech in U. S. Senate, Feb. 28, 1842, on the Veto Power. Washington, 1842. 8vo. Congr. and Polit. Pamph. Vol. 25.

—— Speech in U. S. Senate, Aug., 1842, on the Treaty of Washington. Congr. and Polit. Pamph. Vol. 112.

—— Speeches in U. S. Senate, Mar. 16 and Aug. 5, 1842, on the Tariff. Washington, 1842. 8vo. Congr. and Polit. Pamph. Vol. 25.

—— Speech in U. S. Senate, Jan. 4, 1848, on the Mexican War. Congr. and Polit. Pamph. Vol. 83. And Mar. 4, 1850, on Slavery. Same. Vol. 85.

—— The Works of. N. Y., 1854–59. 6 vols. 8vo.

CALIFORNIA. Academy of Sciences. Proceedings, Vol. II, Vol. III. Parts 3 & 5. Vol. IV. Parts 1 & 2. San Francisco, 1863–70. 8vo.

—— See Alta California.

—— Bill. See Congress'l Speeches.

—— BROWNE, J. Ross. Adventures, etc.

CALIFORNIA. BROWN, J. Ross. Debates in Cal. Convention, 1850.
—— BRYANT, E. What I Saw in.
—— Central Pacific Railroad. Description of the Route, and Account of the Organization, Resources, and Prospects of the Co. N. Y., 1868. 8vo. Cal. Misc. Pamph. Vol. 1.
—— COLTON, Rev. W. Three Years in.
—— Controller. Ann. Reports, 1854–55. Bien. Report, 1869–71.
—— CRONISE, T. F. Nat. Wealth of, 1868.
—— DANA, J. D. Notes on Upper Cal.
—— Descript, of Petroleum Region of Cal.
—— EMORY, W. A. Military Reconnoissance of Cal. and New Mexico.
—— FARNHAM, J. T. Life and Adventures in.
—— FORBES, Alex. History of, 1839.
—— FREMONT, J. C. & EMORY, W. H. Notes of Travel.
—— —— Exploring Exped.
—— —— Geograph. Memoir on Upper Cal., 1848.
—— Geological Survey. Letter of the State Geologist on the Progress of the Survey. San Francisco, 1862. 8vo.
—— —— Report by John B. Trask on the Geol. of N. and So. Cal. 1856. Scientific Pamph. Vol. 14.
—— —— Report by Philip B. Tyson. Baltimore, 1851. 8vo.
—— —— Report by John B. Trask on the Geol. of the Coast Mts. and Part of the Sierra Nevada. Cal. Senate Journ., 1854–55.
—— —— WHITNEY, J. D. Address on, 1861.
—— Gold Regions; with a Full Account of its Mineral Resources, etc. Phiia., 1849? 8vo. Cal. Misc. Pamph. Vol. 1.
—— GREENHOW, R. Hist. of Oregon and Cal.
—— HARRIS, J. M. Paper on, 1849.
—— See Hesperian, The.
—— HITTELL, G. S. Resources of, etc.
—— HOMES, H. A. Cal. and the N-West Coast 100 Years Since.
—— INDIANS. See BAEGERN, Jacob. Account of.
—— Insane Asylum. Report of Trustees, 1853 and 1854.
—— —— Bien. Reports of Directors, etc., 1867, 1869. Sacramento, 1867, '70. 8vo.
—— Insurance Comm'r. 2d and 3d Annual Reports, 1869, 1870. Sacramento, 1870, '71. 2 vols. 8vo.
—— See JOHNSON, T. F. Cal. and Oregon, 1865.
—— JONES, W. C. Report on Land Titles in, 1850.
—— Journals of Senate and Assembly, 1854–61, '66, '67, '69, '70. Sacramento, v. d. 8vo.
—— Appendix to Senate Journ., 1856–61. Sacramento. 6 vols. 8vo.
—— Appendix to Senate and Assembly, 1856, 1868. Sacramento. 6 vols. 8vo.
—— Appendix to Assembly Journ., 1855, '57–61. Sacramento, 1855–61. 6 vols.
—— See KING, J. B. Cal.; the Wonder of the Age, etc., 1850.
—— KIP, L. Cal. Sketches.
—— Laws of the Legislature, passed in 1851, 1854–59, 1863, 1867–8, 1869–70. Sacramento, v. d. 8vo. 13 vols.

CALIFORNIA. See LESQUEREUX, Leo. Masses of.
—— Local Hist. See San Francisco.
—— Lunatic Asylum. See WILKINS, E. T.
—— See Insane Hospital.
—— MAYER, B. History of Mexico, and Notices of.
—— NORDHOFF, Chas. Cal. for Health, Pleasure and Recreation. 1873.
—— Notes on Cal. and the Placers. N. Y., 1850. 8vo. Cal. Misc. Pamph. Vol. 1.
—— PARKMAN, F. Cal. and Oregon Trail.
—— Public Schools. 1st, 9th, 13th Ann. Reports of the Supt. of Pub. Instr., 1852, '59, '63. Sacramento, 1852–63. 8vo.
—— —— Revised School Law, 1866. Sacramento, 1866. 8vo.
—— See RINGGOLD, C. Charts of Rivers and Bays.
—— ROBINSON, Fayette. Cal. and its Gold Regions, 1849.
—— Ross and GARY. From Wis. to Cal.
—— RUFFIN, E. Sketches of Lower No. Cal.
—— SAGE, R. B. Scenes in Oregon and Cal.
—— Society of Cal. Pioneers. See FARWELL, W. B. 9th Annivers. Address, 1859.
—— —— FREELON, T. W. 7th Annivers. Address, 1857.
—— —— HITTELL, J. S. 19th Annivers. Address, 1869.
—— —— MIZNER, L. B. 20th Annivers. Address, 1870.
—— See SQUIER, E. G. Antiq. or N. Mexico and Cal.
—— State Teachers' Institute. Proceedings at San Francisco, May 4–9, 1863. Sacramento, 1863. 8vo. Educa. Pamph. Vol. 9.
—— State Treasurer. Ann. Reports, 1854–5.
—— Surveyor General. Statistical Reports ot Surveyor Gen. for 1869, '70, '71. Sacramento, 1870, '71. 8vo.
—— TAYLOR, B. Eldorado; or Travels in.
—— TODD, Rev. J. Sunset Land, etc.
—— TORREY, Dr. John. Plants collected by J. C. Fremont.
—— TRASK, J. B. Report cf Geol. of, 1856.
—— TUTHILL, F. Hist. of, 1866.
—— TYSON, P. T. Geol. and Resources.
—— See U. S. Sec. of War. Report on Geol. and Topog. of, 1850.
—— VENEGAS, M. Nat. and Civil Hist., 1759.
—— Voices from Cal. The Public Lands for Homesteads. 1865–6. 8vo. Cal. Misc. Pamph. Vol. 1.
—— WISE, H. A., Jr. Los Gringos: an Inside View, etc. 1849.
CALKIN, Hervey C. Speech in Cong., Jan. 28, 1871, on the Alabama Claims. 8vo. Congr. and Polit. Pamph. Vol. 119.
CALL (A) to my Countrywomen. From Atlantic Monthly, Mar., 1863. N. Y., 1863. 12mo. Rebell'n Pamph. Vol. 100.
CALL, R. K. Letter to John S. Littell, on Union, Slavery, and Secession, 1861. Rebell'n Pamph. Vol. 89.
CALLCOTT, Wm. H. Facts in the Life of Handel. Lond., 1859. 12mo. Biograph. Pamph. Vol. 16.
CALLENDER, Geo. W. On the Present System of Med. Educa. in England. Lond., 1864. 8vo. Med. Pamph. Vol. 14.
CALLENDER, James T. Political Register; or Proceedings in Cong. from Nov. 3, 1794, to Mar. 3, 1795. Phila., 1795. 2 vols. 8vo.

CALLENDER, James T. Sketches of the Hist. of America. Phila., 1798. 8vo.

CALLENDER, John. Hist. Disc. on the Civil and Religious Affairs of the Colony of R. Island. R. I. Hist. Soc. Coll. Vol. 4.

CALLERY, M. History of the Insurrection in China. N. Y., 1853. 12mo.

CALLICOT, T. Carey. Cyclopedia of Universal Geog. 2d Ed. N. Y., 1854. 12mo.

CALLINGTON, Ch., Cornwall. See HUTCHISON, Rev. Aeneas B. Monograph, etc., 1861.

CALM Enquiry into the Chesapeake Question, and the Necessity of War. Boston, 1807. 8vo. Congr. and Polit. Pamph. Vol. 110.

CALTHROP, S. R. Lecture before the Amer. Institute of Instruction, Aug. 20, 1858. Boston, 1859. 12mo. Educa. Pamph. Vol. 6.

CALUMET, Wis. Republican, Newspaper. Calumet, 1860–61. Folio.

CALVERT, Sir George. See Baltimore, Lord.

—— Oration on the 40th Annivers. of the Battle of Lake Erie, at Newport, R. I., Sept. 10, 1853. 1st and 2d Editions. Cambridge, 1853. 8vo. Providence, 1854. 8vo. Pamphlets War of 1812. Vol. 4.

CALVERT, Leonard. See BURNAP, G. W. Life of.

CALVIN, M. V. Recent Progress of Public Educa. in the South. Augusta, 1870. 8vo. Educa. Pamph. Vol. 7.

CAMBRENSIS Eversus seu Potius Historica. See KELLY, Rev. M.

CAMBRIAN Archæolog. Assoc. See Archæologia Cambrensis.

CAMBRIDGE Camden Soc'y. Acct. of the Sixth Annivers. Meeting, May 8, 1845. Cambridge. 8vo. Eng. Misc. Pamph. Vol. 5.

—— —— Hints on the Study of Ecclesiastical Antiquities. Cambridge, 1842. 8vo. Scientific Pamph. Vol. 28.

—— —— See Letter to a non-Resident Member of the Soc'y, 1845.

—— —— Paper before the Soc., Nov. 22, 1841, on the History of Pews. Cambridge, 1841. 8vo. Eng. Religious Pamph. Vol. 49.

—— —— Reports for 1841, 1842, 1843 and 1844. Cambridge. 8vo. Eng. Misc. Pamph. Vol. 5.

—— —— Words for the Parish Clerks and Sextons of Country Parishes. Cambridge, 1843. 8vo. Eng. Religious Pamph. Vol. 49.

—— —— Words to Church Wardens on Churches and Church Ornaments. Nos. 1 & 2. Cambridge, 1841. 8vo. Eng. Religious Pamph. Vol. 49.

—— Coronation Festival. Account of Proceedings at Cambridge in Honor of the Coronation of Queen Victoria. Cambridge, 1838. 8vo. Eng. Misc. Pamph. Vol. 50.

CAMBRIDGE Co., Eng. See LYSONS, D. & S. Topograph. Account, of, 1808.

CAMBRIDGE, Eng., University. See BEVERLY, R. M. Letter on Corrupt State of, 1833.

—— —— See CHRISTIAN, E. Law of Elections in, 1822.

—— —— HALLIWELL, J. O. Mss. Rarities.

CAMBRIDGE Camden Soc'y. Letter on Examination of Students at. Lond., 1822. 8vo. Pamphleteer. Vol. 20.

—— —— Thoughts on the Present System of Educa. Lond., 1821. 8vo. Pamphleteer. Vol. 20.

CAMBRIDGE, Mass. See ALBRO, Rev. J. A. 25th Anniv. Disc., 1860.

—— Ann. Reports of the Receipts and Expenditures, 1843, 1846. 8vo.

—— Charter and Ordinances, Municipal Register, etc., for 1857. 8vo.

—— Act to Establish the City of Cambridge, 1846.

—— Christ Ch. See HOPPIN, N. Annivers. Sermon, 1860.

—— Controversy between the 1st Parish and Dr. Holmes.

—— Directory and Almanac for 1856. 12mo.

—— Federal Street Soc. Report of Committee of Assoc., on the Theolog. School in Cambridge. Cambridge, 1825. 8vo.

—— HARRIS, W. T. Epitaphs from Old Burying Ground.

—— High School. Classed Catalogue of the Library of; with an Alphabetical Index. Cambridge, 1853. 8vo.

—— See HOLMES, A. Hist. of.

—— Mayors' Addresses on the Organization of the City Gov't in 1846, '47, '49, 52, '54, '55, '57, '58, '60, '61. Cambridge. 8vo.

—— See NEWELL, Wm. Annivers. Discourses, 1833, '46, '55.

—— Old Cambridge and New. New Eng. Hist. and Gen. Reg. Vol. 25.

—— School, Comm. Reports for 1847, '58, '67. Regulations of Pub. Schools, adopted Apr., 1855, Jan., 1866.

—— —— Address from the School Committee on Corp. Punishment. 1866.

—— Theolog. School. See Cambridge. Federal St. Soc.

—— Water Works. See GREEN, J. D.

CAMBRO British Biog. See RICHARDS, Rev. Wm.

CAMBRO Briton; and General Celtic Repository. Lond., 1820–21. 3 vols. 8vo.

CAMDEN, Lord. Discussion of his Opinion in case of Allen and the Duke of Newcastle. Lond., 1774. 4to. Law Pamph. Vol. 25.

CAMDEN, Me. See CHASE, B. C., LOCKE, J. L.

CAMDEN Co., N. J. See MICKLE, I. Reminiscences of.

CAMDEN & AMBOY Monopoly, See Raritan and Delaware R. R. Co. Reasons, etc.

—— & Atlantic R. R. Engineer's Report, 1852. Phila., 1852. 8vo. N. J. Misc. Pamph. Vol. 1.

—— See FISLER, L. F. Hist. of. 1858.

—— Journal. Newspaper. Camden, 1860–62. Folio.

CAMDEN Society. Publications of the Camden Society, being reprints of exceedingly rare and curious books, and publications of inedited MSS. etc., with copious Introductions and Notes. 46 vols. small 4to. London, 1838–60.

CONTENTS:

Edward IV.'s Restoration.
Bishop Bale's Kynge Johan.
Maydiston's Richard II.
Plumpton Correspondence.
Leycester's Correspondence.
Correspondence of James I. and Cecil.
Pilgrimage of Sir R. Guylford.

CAMDEN Society, *continued.*
Anecdotes and Traditions.
Hayward's Annals of Elizabeth.
Ecclesiastical Documents.
Norden's Essex.
Warkworth's Chronicle.
Kemp's Nine Days' Wonder.
Egerton Papers.
Chronica Jocelini de Brakelonda.
Irish Narratives, 1641–90.
Rishanger's Chronicle.
Poems of W. Mapes.
Travels of N. Nucius.
Three Metrical Romances.
Diary of Dr. Dee.
Apology for the Lollards.
Rutland Papers.
Diary of Bp. Cartwright.
Letters of Eminent Men.
Household Roll of Bishop Swinfield.
Secret Services of Charles II. and James II.
Suppression of Monasteries.
French Chronicle of London.
Polydore Vergil, Vol. I.
Thornton's Romances.
Verney's Long Parliament.
James Earl of Perth's Correspondence.
Liber de Antiquis Legibus.
Chronicle of Calais.
Polydore Vergil, an Early English Translation, Vol. 2.
Letters of George Lord Carew.
Blonde on Oxford.
Camden Miscellany, Vol. I.
Life of Lord Grey.
Diary of Walter Yonge.
Liber Famelicus of Sir J. Whitelocke.
Twysden on English Government.
Diary of John Rous, 1625–42
Trevelyan Papers.
Dean Davies' Jonrnal.

CAMEL, The.—His Organization, etc. See MARSH, G. P.

CAMELS for Military Transportation. See U. States War Department.

CAMERON, A.—Cultivation of Flax and Preparation of Flax Cotton. N. Y., 1852. Agr. Pamph. Vol. 2.

CAMERON, Simon.—See Address of Phil'a. Club, 1859.

CAMILLUS. A Dialogue on the Navy. Lond., 1748. 8vo. Eng. Misc. Pamph. Vol. 24.

CAMMAN, H. J., and CAMP, H. N.—The Charities of New York, Brooklyn, and Staten Island. N. Y., 1868. 8vo.

CAMP, George S.—Democracy. Harper's Fam. Libr. N. Y., 1859. 18mo.

CAMP, Maj. Henry Ward—See TRUMBULL, Rev. H. C. Biog. of. 1871.

CAMPAIGNS of the British Army at Washington and N. Orleans in 1814–15. 3d Ed. revised. Lond., 1827. 12mo.

CAMPBELL, A.—True Amer. System of Finance, etc. Chicago, 1864. 8vo. Cong. and Polit. Pamph. Vol 76.

CAMPBELL, C.—Geneal. of Spotswood Family of Scotland and Virginia. N. Y., 1868. 8vo. Geneal. Pamph. Vol 14.

—— Hist. of the Colony and Ancient Dominion of Va. Phila., 1860. 8vo.

—— Materials for a Brief Memoir of John Daly Burke. Albany, 1868. 8vo.

CAMPBELL, Hugh Y.—Ossiana, or Fingal ascertained and traced in Ulster. Lond., 1819. 8vo. Pamphleteer. Vol. 15.

CAMPBELL, Jas.—Balmerino and its Abbey; A Parochial History. Edinburgh, 1867. 12mo.

CAMPBELL, Sir Jas. Memoirs of. An Autobiography. Waldie's Circulating Lib. Vol. 3.

CAMPBELL, Jas. Speech at Scranton, Pa., Sept., 17, 1863. Rebell'n Pamph. Vol. 68.

CAMPBELL, John. Speech in Congr. Apr. 15, 1842, on the General Appropria. Bill. Washington, 1842. 8vo. Congr. and Polit. Pamph. Vol. 24.

—— Speech in Congr. July 6, 1842, on the Apportionment Bill. Washington, 1842. 8vo. Congr. and Polit. Pamph. Vol. 25.

—— The Political Parties of Phila. Phila., 1861. 8vo. Rebell'n Pamph. Vols. 38 and 72.

CAMPBELL, J. L., and HADLEY, A. M. Teachers' Miscellany; Selection of Articles from Proceedings of the College of Teachers. Cinn., 1856. 12mo.

CAMPBELL, John N., D. D. See SPRAGUE. Wm. B. Obit. Disc. 1864.

CAMPBELL, J. W. Hist. of Va. from its Discovery to 1781, with Biog. Sketches. Phila., 1813. 12mo.

CAMPBELL, L. D. Speech in Congr., Feb. 19, 1850, on Slavery, etc. Congr. and Polit. Pamph. Vol. 84.

—— Speech in Congr. Mar. 5, 1852, on Internal Improvements. Congr. and Polit. Pamph. Vol. 89.

—— Speech in Congr. Mar. 7, 1854, on Grants of Pub. Lands to R. Roads. Congr. and Polit. Pamph. Vol. 83.

CAMPBELL, L. J. Historical Sketch of Minn. Boston, 1868. 12mo. Minn. Pamph. Vol. 1.

CAMPBELL, Mrs. Maria. Revolu. Services and Civil Life of Gen. William Hull, with the Hist. of the Campaign of 1812, and Surrender of Detroit. N. Y., 1848. 8vo.

CAMPBELL, Thos. Biograph. Sketch of. From Chambers' Papers for the People. Biograph. Pamph. Vol. 10.

—— Letters from the South. (Algiers, etc.) Waldie's Circula. Library. Vols. 6, 7, 8.

CAMPBELL, Thompson. Speech in Congr. July 22, 1852, on River and Harbor Improvements. Congr. and Polit. Pamph. Vol. 83.

—— Speech in Congr. May 28, 1852, on the Keokuk and Dubuque R. R. Congr. and Polit. Pamph. Vol. 90.

CAMPBELL, W. F. Letter to a Protectionist Peer, on the Naviga. Laws. Lond., 1849. 8vo. Strangford Pamph. Vol. 49.

—— Speech Vindicating the House of Lords on the Jewish Quest. Lond., 1849. 8vo. Strangford Pamph. Vol. 51.

CAMPBELL, W. W. Lecture on Life and Military Services of Gen. Jas. Clinton, before N. Y. Hist. Soc., Feb., 1839. N. Y., 1839. 8vo. N. Y. Hist. Soc. Discourses. Vol. 2.

—— Life and Writings of DeWitt Clinton. N. Y., 1849. 8vo.

—— Border Warfare of N. Y., or the Annals of Tryon County. N. Y., 1849. 12mo.

CAMP, J. H. The Discovery of America; for the use of Children and Young Persons. Lond., 1799. 12mo.

CAMPEUS, Ed. Opbrenging en bestiering der nuttige huisdieren. Ghent, 1850.

CANADA. A Brief Outline of her Geograph. Position, Productions, Climate, etc. Toronto, 1857. 8vo. Canada Pamph. Vol. 1.
—— Act to Amend and Consolidate the Judicature Acts of Lower Canada. Toronto, 1858. Folio.
—— Act to Provide for the Better Establishment of Agricultural Societies in Lower Canada. Quebec, 1852. 8vo. Canada Pamph. Vol. 2.
—— Affairs of the Canadas. In a Series of Letters. Lond., 1837. 8vo. Strangford Pamph. Vol. 13.
—— AMOS, A. Destruction of the Earl of Selkirks Settlement. 1820.
—— and the Continental Congress. See DUANE, Wm. Address. 1850.
—— ANDERSON, W. J. Coal in.
—— —— Canadian Hist. and Biog.
—— BAGG, S. C. Canadian Archaeol.
—— BETHUNE, A. N. Clergy Reserves in Canada. 1853.
—— BETTRIDGE, Rev. Wm. History of the Ch. in Upper Canada. 1838.
—— BIARD, P. Missio Canadensis. 1612.
—— —— Relation de la Nouvelle France. 1616.
—— BONNYCASTLE, Sir R. H. The Canadas in 1847.
—— —— Rocks and Minerals of.
—— BOUCHETTE, J. Topog. Descrip. of Lower Canada.
—— BROUGHAM, Lord. Speech in House of Lords. 1838.
—— BUCKINGHAM, J. S. Travels in.
—— Canadian Free Holder.
—— Canadicæ Missionis Relatio. 1611–13.
—— Canal Commissioners. Letter to the Sec. of State, on Inland Navigation. Ottawa, 1871. 8vo.
—— See CAVENDISH, Sir H. Parliament Debates, 1774.
—— Champlain. Voy. de la Nouvelle. France.
—— CHAPPELL, Ed. Voyage to Hudson's Bay, 1817.
—— CHARLEVOIX, Father. Account of, 1763. Hist. of New France.
—— Voyage to America.
—— CHESTER, G. J. Sketches in U. S. & Canada, 1869.
—— CHRISTIE, R. History of Lower Canada.
—— —— Military Operations, 1807–15.
—— COKE, E. T. Travels in, 1832.
—— COLDEN, C. Hist. of Five Nations of.
—— Collection de Memoires et de Relations sur l'Histoire du Canada. Pub. by Quebec Histor. Soc., 1840. 8vo.
—— COOK, J. W. Paper on the Hist. of.
—— CRESPEL, E. Voyage au Nouveau Monde.
—— Creusius, F. Historiæ Canadensis.
—— De Regione ac Moribus Canadensium, seu Barbarorum Novæ Franciæ. From Jouvency Historia Societatis Jesu. Rome, 1810. 8vo. Albany, Reprint, 1870. 8vo.
—— Detailed Estimates of the Dominion of Canada for 1868–9.
—— DOUGLASS, Jas. Gold Fields of.
—— DOYLE, M. Hints on Emigration to, 1831.
—— DUNCAN, J. M. Travels in, and U. S.

CANADA. Educational Directory. See HODGINS, Thos., 1857–8.
—— Emigration. Practical Advice to Emigrants. Lond., 1834. 8vo. Strangford Pamph. Vol. 11.
—— Excursion through U. S. & Canada in 1822–23.
—— Facts, etc., relative to Canadian Indians.
—— FERGUSON, A. Tour in Canada, 1831.
—— Five Papers on Fur Trade of Canada. 1823. Canadian Magazine. Vol. 1
—— GARNEAUX, F. H. History of.
—— Geolog. Survey. Report of Progress for 1857. Toronto, 1858. 8vo.
—— —— Report of Progress from its Commencement to 1863. Montreal, 1863. 8vo.
—— —— Report of Progress 1863 to 1866. Ottawa, 1866.
—— Geology. See BIGSBY, J. I. Geol., etc., of N. Western Portion of L. Huron. 1820.
—— —— Minerals and Organic Remains in the Canadas. 1824.
—— Grand Trunk Railway Co. Proceedings of Shareholders, at Toronto, Dec. 15, 1858. Montreal, 1858. 8vo. Canada Pamph. Vol. 2.
—— GRAY, H. Letters from 1806–8.
—— Great Western Railway. Report of Directors, July 31, 1859. Hamilton, 1859. 8vo. Canada Pamph. Vol. 2.
—— HALL, Francis. Travels in. 1818.
—— HEAD, F. B. Narrative.
—— —— The Emigrant.
—— HENRY, A. Travels in, and the Indian Territories.
—— HERIOT, G. Hist. of.
—— —— Travels in 1807.
—— HIND, HENRY T. Red River Explor. Exped.
—— Hints on the Case of Canada for the Consideration of Parliament. Lond., 1838. 8vo. Strangford Pamph. Vol. 14.
—— Historical Notes on Colony of Detroit.
—— Howison, J. Sketches of Upper Canada. 1821.
—— Insurrection, 1837. Patriot War. See Gould, N. Letter on. 1838.
—— —— Snow, Sam'l. Narrative of his Banishment.
—— —— Wright, S. S. Narr. of Captivity, &c.
—— Invasion of. Stone, E. M. Army under Arnold.
—— Jackson, J. W. Polit. Situation of. 1809.
—— JACOBS, Rev. Peter. Journal of.
—— JAMESON, Mrs. Sketches in. 1852.
—— See Jesuit Relations.
—— KIRKE, H. Eng. Conquest of Canada.
—— LALLEMANT, Pere Chas. Trois Lettres, 1625–6, &c.
—— LAMBERT, J. Travels in, and U. S.
—— LANGTON, John. Timber of.
—— The Law of 1855 relating to R. Catholic Separate Schools in U. Canada. Toronto, 1858. 8vo. Canada Pamph. Vol. 2.
—— LE BEAU, C. Adventures et Description du Canada.
—— LE CLERQ. Relation de la Gaspesie.

CANADA Legislative Assembly. Rules, Orders, & Forms of Assembly. Ottawa, 1866. 12mo.
—— LE MOINE, J. M. Birds of.
—— LESCARBOT M. Histoire de la Nouvelle, France.
—— LIANCOURT,, Duke. Travels in, andU. S.
—— Library of Parliament. Cat. of the Library. Toronto. 2Vols. 8vo.
—— LOCAL HIST. See Montreal.
—— —— Shipton.
—— —— Quebec.
—— —— Red River Settlement.
—— London Interna. Exhibition, 1862.
—— MACKEY, C. Tour in, 1857.
—— McMULLEN, J. Hist. of, 1855, 1869.
—— MARCOU, J. Taconic & Silurian Rocks of Canada.
—— MARTIN, R. M. Hist., Statistics, &c., of, 1838.
—— Messages, Fortifications and Defenses, San Juan Island, Canada Claims, &c, 1869. Ottawa, 8vo.
—— Minister of Finance. Report on Reciprocity Treaty with the U. S., 1862. 8vo. Congr. & Polit. Pamph. Vol. 59.
—— Nova Scotia. See Present State of, &c., 1787.
—— O'CALLAGHAN, E. B. Relations des Jesuites. 1611–72.
—— PALMER, J. Travels in, and U. S., 1817.
—— (Two) Papers on the Chronology of Canada, 1823. Canadian Magazine. Vol. 1.
—— Patent Office. Rules and Regulations, Sept. 1, 1872. Pamph. 8vo.
—— Polit. Annals of Lower Canada. Montreal, 1828. 8vo. Canada Pamph. Vol. 1.
—— Prisons in. 1st Ann. Report of the Directors of Penitentiaries for 1868. Ottawa, 1870. 8vo.
—— —— MINES & DWIGHT. Prisons in U. S. & Canada, 1867.
—— Public Accounts of the Province for 1866–7. Ottawa, 1867. 8vo.
—— Pub. Schools. TREMENHEERE, H. S. Notes on, 1852.
—— —— Special Reports on Separate School Provisions of the School Law of Upper Canads. Toronto, 1858. 8vo.
—— —— Ann. Reports of the Normal, Model, Grammar & Common Schools in Upper Canada, for 1853, '54, '55, '56, '57, '58 '67. Toronto, &c., 1854–1867. 8vo.
—— —— Reports of the Sup't. of Educa. for Lower Canada, for 1850–1, 1853 '54, '55, '56, '64, '65. Quebec, &c., 1852–1866. 8vo.
—— —— Report of Supt. of Public Schools for U. Canada, on Elementary Instruction. Montreal, 1847. 8vo.
—— —— Gen. Cat. of Books for Pub. Sch. Libraries in U. Canada. Toronto, 1858. 8vo.
—— —— Gen Provisions of the Law and Rules respecting Pub. School Libraries in U. Canada. Toronto, 1854. 12mo.
—— Reciprocity Mining Company. Circular. 1864. n. p. 8vo. Canada Pamph. Vol. 2.
—— Relatio Rerum Gestarum in Novo Francica Missione. 1613–14.

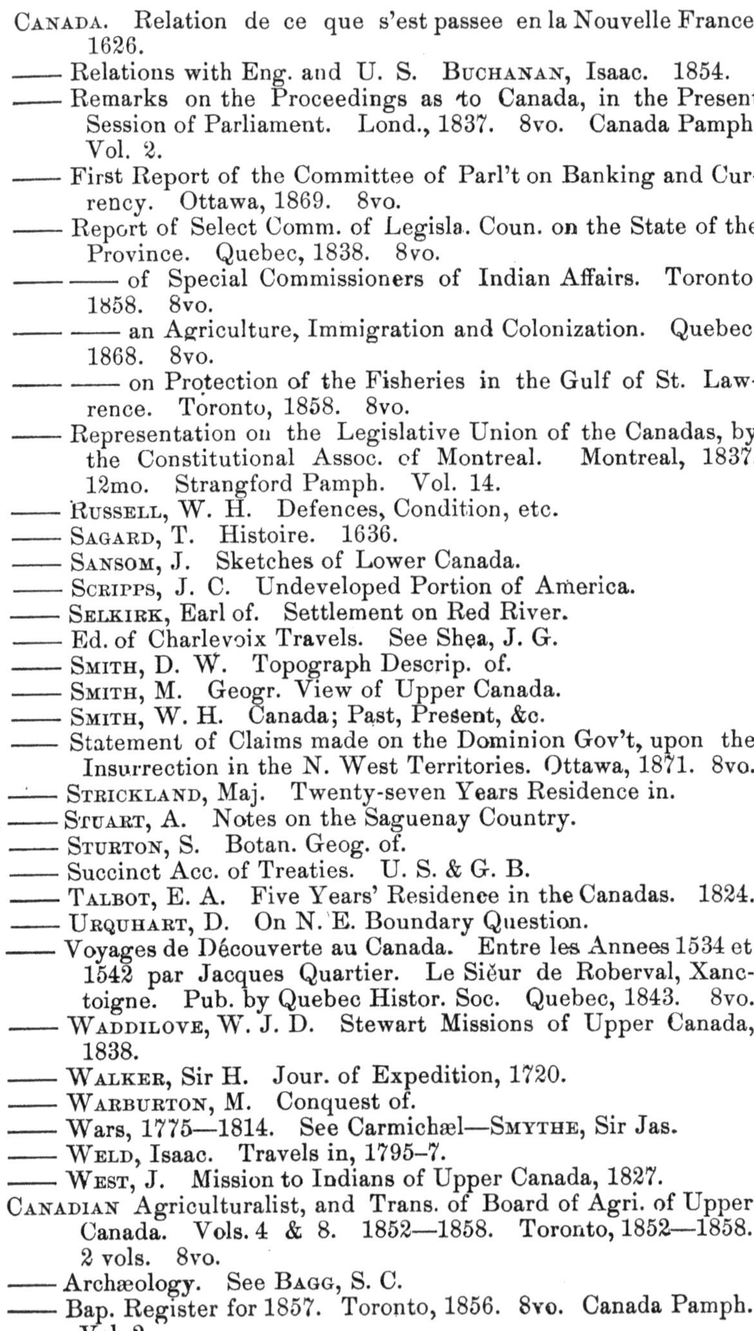

Canada. Relation de ce que s'est passee en la Nouvelle France. 1626.

—— Relations with Eng. and U. S. Buchanan, Isaac. 1854.

—— Remarks on the Proceedings as to Canada, in the Present Session of Parliament. Lond., 1837. 8vo. Canada Pamph. Vol. 2.

—— First Report of the Committee of Parl't on Banking and Currency. Ottawa, 1869. 8vo.

—— Report of Select Comm. of Legisla. Coun. on the State of the Province. Quebec, 1838. 8vo.

—— —— of Special Commissioners of Indian Affairs. Toronto. 1858. 8vo.

—— —— an Agriculture, Immigration and Colonization. Quebec. 1868. 8vo.

—— —— on Protection of the Fisheries in the Gulf of St. Lawrence. Toronto, 1858. 8vo.

—— Representation on the Legislative Union of the Canadas, by the Constitutional Assoc. of Montreal. Montreal, 1837. 12mo. Strangford Pamph. Vol. 14.

—— Russell, W. H. Defences, Condition, etc.

—— Sagard, T. Histoire. 1636.

—— Sansom, J. Sketches of Lower Canada.

—— Scripps, J. C. Undeveloped Portion of America.

—— Selkirk, Earl of. Settlement on Red River.

—— Ed. of Charlevoix Travels. See Shea, J. G.

—— Smith, D. W. Topograph Descrip. of.

—— Smith, M. Geogr. View of Upper Canada.

—— Smith, W. H. Canada; Past, Present, &c.

—— Statement of Claims made on the Dominion Gov't, upon the Insurrection in the N. West Territories. Ottawa, 1871. 8vo.

—— Strickland, Maj. Twenty-seven Years Residence in.

—— Stuart, A. Notes on the Saguenay Country.

—— Sturton, S. Botan. Geog. of.

—— Succinct Acc. of Treaties. U. S. & G. B.

—— Talbot, E. A. Five Years' Residence in the Canadas. 1824.

—— Urquhart, D. On N. E. Boundary Question.

—— Voyages de Découverte au Canada. Entre les Annees 1534 et 1542 par Jacques Quartier. Le Siĕur de Roberval, Xanctoigne. Pub. by Quebec Histor. Soc. Quebec, 1843. 8vo.

—— Waddilove, W. J. D. Stewart Missions of Upper Canada, 1838.

—— Walker, Sir H. Jour. of Expedition, 1720.

—— Warburton, M. Conquest of.

—— Wars, 1775—1814. See Carmichæl—Smythe, Sir Jas.

—— Weld, Isaac. Travels in, 1795–7.

—— West, J. Mission to Indians of Upper Canada, 1827.

Canadian Agriculturalist, and Trans. of Board of Agri. of Upper Canada. Vols. 4 & 8. 1852—1858. Toronto, 1852—1858. 2 vols. 8vo.

—— Archæology. See Bagg, S. C.

—— Bap. Register for 1857. Toronto, 1856. 8vo. Canada Pamph. Vol. 2.

CANADIAN Biography. See MORGAN, H. J. Celebrated Canadians.
—— Fisheries. See Review of President GRANT's Recent Message. 1870.
—— Free Holder; Dialogues between an Englishman and a Frenchman. Lond., 1777. 3 vols. 8vo.
—— Literature. See FABRE, Hector. (Written in French.)
—— Magazine and Literary Repository. Vol. 1· July–Dec., 1823. Montreal. 8vo.
—— Plants. Catalogue of, 1827. Quebec Lit. and Hist. Soc. Trans. Vol. 1.
CANADICAE Missionis Relatio, 1611–13 in Acadiâ, cum Vitâ Petri Biardi. From Jouvency Historia Societatis Jesu. Rome, 1710. 8vo. Albany reprint, 1871. 8vo.
CANALS. See STEVENS, Col. John. Advantages of Railways over Canals. 1812.
—— TANNER, H. S. Descrip. of in U. S.
—— WATSON, Elkanah.
CANDIA. See FLETCHER, Edw. T. Twenty years Siege of.
CANDIA, N. H. See EATON, F. B. Hist. of.
CANDID EXAMINATION of the Court Martial of Admiral Byng. Lond., 1757. 8vo. Eng. Polit. Pamph. Vol. 71.
—— Review of Mr. Pitt's Twenty Resolutions. Dublin, 1785. 12mo. Eng. Polit. Pamph. Vol. 22.
CANDLISH, Rob't S., D. D. Narrative relating to certain recent Negotiations for the settlement of the Scottish Ch. Question. Edinburgh, 1841. 8vo. Strangford Pamph. Vol. 27.
CANFIELD, Wm. H. Baraboo and its Water Powers. Baraboo, Wis., 1871. 8vo. Wis. Local Hist. Vol. 2.
—— Catalogue of Birds of Sauk Co., Wis. Wis. Misc. Pamph. Vol. 3.
—— Outline Sketches of Sauk County, Wis. Nos. 1, 2, 3. Baraboo, 1861. 8vo.
CANNING, Geo. Corres. with Hon. D. Erskine on Amer. Affairs. Lond., 1811. 8vo.
—— GOLDSMITH, Lewis. On the Appointment of 1822.
—— Speech in Parl't, Jan. 29, 1817, on an Address to the Prince Regent. Lond., 1817. 8vo. Pamphleteer. Vol. 10.
—— Speech in Parliament, Apr. 25, 1822, on Parliamentary Reform. Lond., 1822. 8vo. Pamphleteer. Vol. 21.
—— Speech at Liverpool, Mar. 18, 1820, on his Re-election. Lond., 1820. 8vo. 4th Ed. Pamphleteer. Vol. 16.
—— Speeeh in Parl't, Apr. 1823, on Negotiations at Verona, Paris, & Madrid. With Accompanying Papers. Lond., 1823. 8vo. Strangford Pamph. Vol. 4.
—— Speeches in Parl't, Dec. 12, 1826, on an Address to the King. Lond., 1827. 8vo. Eng. Polit. Pamph. Vol. 37.
CANNING, Elizabeth. Account of the Case of. Lond., 1754. 8vo. Eng. Misc. Pamph. Vol. 25.
CANNING, Elizabeth. See Gascoigne, Sir Crisp. See Hall, Dr.
CANSICK, F. P. Collection of Curious Epitaphs, from Chur. of St. Pancras. Lond., 1872. 2 Vols. 12mo.

CANTERBURY, Eng. Goulden's Hand Book and Guide.
—— Guide; or, Travelers' Pocket Companion. Canterbury, Eng., n. d. 12mo. Guide Books, Vols. 9 and 20.
—— Representation of the Present State of Religion, by the Upper House of Convocation. Lond., 1711. Folio. Eng. Polit. Pamph. Vol. 3.
CANTERBURY, N. H. See Patrick, Rev. W. Sketches of Hist. of.
CANTERBURY Settlement. New Zealand. Brief Information Relating to. Lond., 1850. 8vo. Eng. Misc. Pamph. Vol. 7.
CANTON, Conn. See BROWN, Abiel. Genealog. Hist. of West Simsbury.
—— PHELPS, N. A. Hist. of.
CAPE ANNE, Mass. See THORNTON, J. W. Hist. of 1st Colony at.
CAPE COD Centen. Celebra. BARNSTABLE.
—— —— FREEMAN, F. Hist. of Cape Cod.
—— —— GRAHAM, J. D. Military and Hydrograph. Chart. 1838.
CAPE GIRARDEAU CO. AND CITY, Mo. Hist. and Descrip. Resources of. St. Louis, 1867. 12mo.
—— —— Western Eagle, Newspaper. Cape Girardeau, 1849–52. Folio.
CAPE TOWN, South Africa. Advertiser, Newspaper. Cape Town, 1857–58.
CAPEN, Nahum. Indissoluble Nature of the Amer. Union. Boston, 1862. 8vo. Rebell'n Pamph. Vol. 1.
—— Letter to Rev. Nath. Hall, on Politics and the Pulpit. Boston, 1855. 8vo. Congr. and Polit. Pamph. Vol. 74.
—— Plain Facts and Considera. in Favor of the Election of James Buchanan. Boston, 1856. 8vo. Congr. and Polit. Pamph. Vol. 74.
CAPITAL PUNISHMENT. See DOLE, B. Examination of Rantoul. 1837.
—— —— DYMOND, J. Essays on Morality, etc.
—— —— Use and Abuse of. From Amer. Monthly Magaz., July, 1833.
—— —— MONTAGU, Basil. Inquiries into the Punishm. of Death.
—— —— The Penalty of Death Retained, etc. 1841.
—— —— POLIDORI, J. W. On the Punishment of Death.
—— —— Report Against Cap. Punishment, made to Maine Legislature, in 1836. Washington, 1852. 8vo.
—— —— Reports Made to Massachusetts Legislature in 1835–6, on the Expediency of Abolishing Cnpit. Punishment. (Majority and Minority Reports. Mass. Pub. Docs. 1835–6.
—— —— Report of Select Comm. of House of Commons, on Cap. Punishment in Felonies. Lond., 1820. 8vo. Pamphleteer. Vol. 15.
—— —— ROMILLY, Sir Sam'l. Crim. Law of England in Relation to, etc.
—— —— Speech in Penn. Legisla., Dec., 1796, against Cap. Punishment. n. d. sm. 4to, Penn. Miscell. Pamph. Vol. 3.
—— —— STEVENS, J. L. Remarks in Maine Legisla., 1869.
—— —— WRIGHTSON, Thos. Pamphlet against the Punishment of Death, 1833.

CAPITAL PUNISHMENT. Strictures on the Indiscriminate Denunciation of Cap. Punishment. Lond., 1814. 8vo. Pamphleteer. Vol. 3.

CAPPE, Catherine. Thoughts on Ladies Visiting the Female Wards of Hospitals and Lunatic Asylums. Lond., 1816. 8vo. Pamphleteer. Vol. 8.

CAPRON FAMILY GENEALOGY. See HOLDEN, F. A.

CAPTAINS OF THE OLD WORLD. See HERBERT, H. W.

CAPTIVITY and Redemption of Mrs. Elizabeth Hanson of Dover Township, by N. E. Indians in 1724. Stanford, N. Y., 1803. 18mo.

CARAUSIUS. See DePeyster, J. W.

CARBOLIC Acid as an Agent in the Destruction of Insects affecting Vegetation. N. Y., 1869. 8vo. Agr. Pamph. Vol. 11.

CARBON Co., Pa. See RUPP, I. D. History of.

CARDIGAN Co. Wales. See MEYRICK, S. R. Hist. of & Antiq. 1810.

CARDOZO, J. N. Reminiscences of Charleston, S. C. Charleston, 1866. 12mo.

CARDWELL, Edward. Coinage of the Greeks and Romans. Oxford, 1832. 8vo.

CAREY, Henry C. French and Amer. Tariffs Compared. 1861. Rebell'n Pamph. Vol. 87.

—— Letters to Schuyler Colfax on the Currency Question. Phila. 1865. 8vo. Congr. & Polit. Pamph. Vol. 89.

—— Letters on the Iron Question, 1865. Congr. & Polit. Pamph. Vol. 101.

—— Letters on the Paper Question, 1865. Congr. & Polit. Pamph. Vol. 6.

—— Letters to same on the R. R. Question. Congr. & Pamph. Vol. 74.

—— Letters to the President on the Foreign and Domestic Policy of the Union. Phil'a., 1858. 8vo. Rebell'n Pamph. Vol. 25.

—— Letters to the President Elect of the U. S.—Peace, Financial and Political. Phila., 1869. 8vo. Rebell'n Pamph. Vol. 41.

—— Letters on International Copyright. Phila., 1853. 8vo. Congress. Pamph. Vol. 100.

—— Review of Report of Hon. D. A. Wells, on the Revenue. Phila., 1869. 8vo. Congr. & Polit. Pamph. Vol. 80.

—— Letters of Michel Chevalier, on French & Amer. Tariffs. Detroit, 1861. 8vo. Congr. & Polit. Pamph. Vol. 74.

—— The Finance Minister, the Currency, & the Public Debt. Phila., 1868. 8vo. 2d ed. Banking & Currency Pamph. Vol. 3.

—— The Resources of the Union. Phila., 1866. 8vo. Rebell'n Pamph. Vol. 1.

—— The Past, the Present and the Future. Phila., 1848. 8vo.

—— The Slave Trade, Domestic and Foreign; Phila., 1853. 12mo.

—— —— Another Copy. Phila., 1856.

—— and LEA, I. Geography, History and Statistics of America and the West Indies. Lond., 1824. 8vo.

CAREY, Jas. P. Record of the Great Rebellion; a Chronolog. Hist. of the War. N. Y., 1866. 8vo. Rebell'n Pamph. 112.

CAREY, Matt. Essays on the Public Charities of Phila. Phila., 1830. 8vo. 5th edition. Phila. Mis. Pamph. Vol. 2.

—— Letters on the Colonization Society; and of its probable Results. Phila., 1832. 8vo. Pamph. on Colonization. Vol. 1.

—— Review of the Evidence of a Conspiracy of the Roman Catholics of Ireland to Massacre the Protestants. Oct. 23 1641. Phila., 1833. 8vo. Hist. Pamph. Vol. 4.

—— The New Olive Branch; or an Identity of Interest between Agriculture, Manufactures and Commerce. Phila., 1820. 8vo.

—— The Olive Branch; or Fault on Both Sides, Federal and Democratic. 6th ed. Phila., 1815. 8vo.

—— —— Same. Boston, 1815. 12mo.

—— —— The Porcupiniad; a Hudibrastic Poem Addressed to W. Cobbett. Phil. 1799. Congr. Pamph. Vol. 95. 8vo.

CARLETON College. Northfield, Minn. See Whiting, Rev. L. Oration, 1871.

CARLISLE, Anthony. On the Connection between the Leaves and Fruit of Vegetables, &c. Lond., 1816. 4to. Scientific Pamph. Vol. 37.

CARLISLE, J. S. Speech at Indiana Dem. State Convention, July 30, 1862. Rebell'n Pamph. Vol. 54.

CARLISLE, Mass. See Shattuck, L.

CARLOS, Prince of Spain & his Father Philip II. Hist. Sketch of. Canadian Magazine. Vol. 1.

CARLTON, Robert. New Purchase; or Early Years in the Far West. N. Albany, Ind., 1855. 12mo.

CARLYLE, Thos. See BLACKWOOD *versus* CARLYLE.

—— Life of Robert Burns. N. Y., 1860. 18mo.

—— On Heroes. Hero-Worship, and the Heroic in History. N. Y., 1859. 12mo.

—— On the Character and Genius of Milton. See BUNSEN, Chev.

CARMICHAEL — SMYTHE, Sir Jas. Precis of the Wars in Canada from 1775 to the Treaty of Ghent in 1814. Lond. 1862. 8vo.

CARNAHAN, Rev. Jas. Pennsylvania Insurrection of 1794, commonly called the "Whisky Insurrection." N. J. Hist. Soc. Proceed. Vol. 6.

CARNARVON, Lord. On Prison Discipline; a Report adopted at the Hampshire Quarter Sessions, 1864. With Notes, &c. Lond. 1864. 8vo. Eng. Polit. Pamph, &c. Vol 60.

CARNE, John. Letters from Switzerland and Italy, during a Late Tour. Waldie's Circulating Libr. Vol. 4.

—— Letters from the East, Turkey, Egypt, &c., 1826. Wildie's Circulating Libr. Vol. 10.

CARNOCHAN, J. M. Elephantiasis Arabum of the Right Inferior Extremity. N. Y., 1852. 8vo. Med. Pamph. Vol. 4.

CARNOT, M. Memorial addressed to the King of France in July, 1814. Lond., 1815. 8vo. Pamphleteer. Vol. 5.

CAROLANA. See COXE, D.

CAROLINA. Brief Descrip. of the Province of Carolina, on the Coasts of Florida, &c., 1666. Carroll's Hist. Coll. of S. C.

—— A Description of the Present State of that Country, &c., 1682. Carroll's Hist. Coll. of S. C.

—— See WILSON, S. Acc. of, 1682.

CAROLINE, Queen. See BROUGHAM, Lord.—George IV. & Queen Caroline.

—— Hist. Fragment relative to Queen Caroline. Lond., 1824. Biograph. Pamph. Vol. 2.

—— See Journ. of an Eng. Traveller, &c.

CARPENTER, Capt. E. J. Letter and Documents Relating to the Screw Propeller, used in the Royal Navy. Lond., 1855. 8vo. Eng. Misc. Pamph. Vol. 32.

CARPENTER, F. B. Six Months at the White House with Abraham Lincoln. N. Y., 1866. 12mo.

CARPENTER, Hugh S. Eulogy on Pres't. Harrison, before the University of N. Y., May 28, 1841. N. Y., 1841. 8vo. Addresses. Vol. 24.

CARPENTER, Rev. H. S. Relations of Religion to War. Fast Day Sermon at Brooklyn, Sept. 26, 1861. Rebell'n Pamph. Vol. 29.

CARPENTER, Matt H. Address to the Graduating Class of Columbian Law Coll., June 8, 1870. 8vo. Law Pamph. Vol. 13.

—— Argument in U. S. Supreme Court, in Case of Wm. H. McCardle, 1868. 8vo. Congr. & Polit. Pamph. Vol. 101.

—— Speech at Janesville, June 28, 1783, on the Back Pay Bill. Milwaukee, 1873. 8vo. Congr. & Polit. Pamph. Vol. 140.

—— Speech at Milwaukee Oct. 4, 1866. Rebelln. Pamph. Vol. 37.

—— Speech at Milwaukee, Oct. 4, 1866, on Reconstruction. Congr. and Polit. Pamph. Vol. 79.

—— Speech at N. Orleans, 1873, on Louisiana Polit. Affairs. La. Misc. Pamph. Vol. 2.

—— Speech at the Dedication of Memorial Hall, Beloit College, July, 1869, on the Mission and Future Policy of the U. S. Milwaukee, Wis., 1869. Congr. and Polit. Pamph. Vol. 79.

—— Speech in U. S. Senate, Dec. 15, 1869, on Neutrality between Spain and Cuba. Congr. and Polit. Pamph. Vol. 122.

—— Speech in U. S. Senate, Feb. 3, 1870, on Laws of Neutrality. Congr. and Polit. Pamph. Vol. 129.

—— Speech in the U. S. Senate, Feb. 14 and 16, 1870, on Admission of Mississippi. Congr. and Polit. Pamph. Vol. 119.

—— Speech in U. S. Senate, April 5, 1870, on Admission of Georgia. Congr. and Polit. Pamph. Vols. 88 and 119.

—— Speech in U. S. Senate, Jan. 18, 1872, on Civil Service Reform. Congr. and Polit. Pamph. Vols. 129, 138.

CARPENTER, S. C.—Select Amer. Speeches, Forensic and Parliamentary. Phila., 1815, 2 Vols. 8vo.

CARPENTER, S. D.—Logic of History, or 500 Political Texts, etc. 2d Ed. Madison, Wis., 1864. 8vo.

CARPENTER, Prof. Stephen H.—English of the XIVth Century, illustrated by Notes, Grammatical and Philological on Chaucer's Prologue and Knight's Tale. Boston, 1872. 12mo.

CARPENTER, Thos.—The American Senator. Report of Debates in the Cong. of the U. S. of the 2d Sess. of the 4th Cong. Phil. 1796–7. 4 Vols. 8vo.

CARPENTER, W. B.—Use and Abuse of Alcoholic Liquors, with a Preface by D. F. Condie, M. D. Phila., 1838. 12mo.

CARPENTER, W. H. and ARTHUR, T. S.—History of Conn. from its Earliest Settlement. Phila., 1858. 18mo.

—— —— History of Mass. from the Earliest Settlement. Phila., 1858. 18mo.

—— —— History of N. J. from its Earliest Settlement. Phila., 1858. 18mo.

—— —— History of Penn. from its Earliest Settlement. Phila., 1857. 18mo.

—— —— History of Tenn. from its Earliest Settlement. Phila., 1857. 18mo.

—— —— History of Vt. from its Earliest Settlement. Phila., 1858. 18mo.

—— —— History of N. Y. from its Earliest Settlement. Phila., 1858. 18mo.

—— —— History of Ohio from its Earliest Settlement. Phila., 1858. 18mo.

—— —— History of Ill. from its Earliest Settlement. Phila., 1857. 18mo.

CARPENTRY. See Architecture.

CARR, E. S.—Inaug. Address before the Regents of Wis. Madison, 1856. 8vo. Wis. Misc. Pamph. Vol 3.

CARR, John. Early Times in Middle Tenn. Nashville, 1857. 18mo.

CARR, Rev. Spencer. Brief Sketch of LaCrosse, Wis. LaCrosse, 1854. 8vo. Wis. Local Hist. Vol. 1.

CARRINGTON, Margaret I. Ab-sa-ra-ka (Wyoming) Home of the Crows; Experience of an Officer's Wife on the Plains. Phila., 1869. 12mo.

CARROLL, Anna E. Amer. Nominations: Fillmore & Donelson. N. Y., 1856. 12mo. Congr. and Polit. Pamph. Vol. 104.

—— Review of Pierce's Administration. Boston, 1856. 8vo. Congr. and Polit. Pamph. Vol. 73.

—— The Star of the West; or National Men and National Measures. Boston, 1856. 12mo.

—— The Union of States. Boston, 1856. 12mo. Congress. and Polit. Pamph. Vol. 95.

CARROLL, B. R. Hist. Collections of S. Carolina, embracing many rare Pamphlets, etc. N. Y., 1836. 2 vols. 8vo.

CARROLL, Chas. Journ. of his Visit to Canada in 1776, with a Memoir and Notes by Brantz Mayer. Baltimore, 1845. 8vo. Md. Hist. Soc. Papers. Vol. 1.

CARROLL, Chas. H. Speech in Cong., July 1, 1846, on the Tariff. Washington, 1846. 8vo. Speeches. Vol. 1.

CARROLL College, Waukesha, Wis. Ann. Catalogues for 1855–6, 1856–7, 1857–8. 8vo.

—— —— See SAVAGE, Rev. J. A.

CARRUTHERS, Rev. J. J. The War: Its Evils and their Compensations. Portland, 1862. 8vo. Rebell'n Pamph. Vol. 70.

CARSON City Branch Mint. Petition Addressed to Cong., against Unlawful Practices at the Mint. San Francisco, 1873. 8vo. Congr. and Polit. Pamph. Vol. 66.

CARSON, Kit. See BURDETT, Chas. Life of.

CARTIE, Cornelius S. Elements of Map-Drawing, designed for Schools and Academies. Boston, 1849. Oblong 4to.

CARTER, Rev. T. T. Rome Catholic, and Rome Papal. Oxford, 1850. 8vo. Eng. Religious Pamph. Vol. 91.

CARTER, W. C., and GLOSSBRENNER, A. J. History of York Co., Penn., from its Erection to the Present Time. York, Penn., 1834. 12mo.

CARTHAGENA, New Granada. See Remarks on Canal Navigation.

CARTIER, Jacques. Documents of. Quebec Lit. and Hist. Soc. Trans. Vol. 5. Part 1.

CARTTER, D. K. Speech in Cong., May 25, 1852, on the Compromise Bill. Congr. and Polit. Pamph. Vol. 88.

CARTWRIGHT, Bishop. Diary. See Camden Soc. Publica.

CARTWRIGHT, Major John. Address to the Electors of Westminster. London, 1819. 8vo. Eng. Misc. Pamph. Vol. 4.

—— Letter to Sir Francis Burdett, for the Relief of Sufferers under the Suspension Act. 1818. London. 8vo. Eng. Misc. Pamph. Vol. 3.

—— Letter to Lord John Russell, on Reform. London, (n. d.) 8vo. Eng. Misc. Pamph. Vol. 6.

—— Letters to the Lord Mayor, with Analysis and New Classifica. of the House of Commons. No. 1. London, 1817. 8vo. Eng. Misc. Pamph. Vol. 3.

—— Summary of his Treatise, entitled "The People's Barrier against Undue Influence, etc. 1780. 8vo. Eng. Misc. Pamph. Vol. 2.

CARTWRIGHT, Peter. Autobiog. of. Edited by W. P. STRICKLAND. N. Y., 1857. 12mo.

CARTWRIGHT, S. A. Essay on the Prognathous Race.

—— See TANEY, R. B.

CARUTHERS, Rev. E. W. Interesting Revolutionary Incidents, chiefly in the Old North State. 1st and 2d Series. Phila., 1854 and 1856. 2 vols. 12mo.

—— Life and Character of David Caldwell, D. D., with Account of Revolutionary Transac., in which he was Concerned. Greensborough, N. C., 1842. 8vo.

CARUTHERS, Robt. L. Speech in Cong., July 1, 1842, on the Tariff. Washington, 1842. 8vo. Congr. and Polit. Pamph. Vol. 24.

CARVALHO, E. N. The Patriot's Referee, containing the Declaration of Independence, Constitution, etc. N. Y., 1861. 12mo. Congr. and Polit. Pamph. Vol. 81.

CARVER, Grant. Minn. Hist. Soc. Coll. Vol. 1.

CARVER, John. See SHURTLEFF, N. B. Notice of.

CARVER, Capt. Jonathan, and the "Carver Grant." See DURRIE, D. S.

—— Minn. Hist. Soc. Celebra. of Carver Centenary. 1867.

—— Travels in N. America. 1764. Walpole, N. H., 1813. 8vo.

CARVER, Jonathan. Travels through the Interior Parts of N. America in 1766, 1767 and 1768. Lond., 1778. 8vo.

—— Same. Lond, 1781. 8vo.

CARVER, Mass. Topog. and Hist. of. Mass. Hist. Soc. Coll. 2d Ser. Vol. 4.

CARY, Saml. Address to the Merrimack Humane Soc., at Newburyport, Sept. 2, 1806. Newburyport, 1806. 8vo. Addresses. Vol. 28.

CARY, Thos. G. Gold from California, and its Effects on Prices. N. Y., 1856. 8vo. Banking and Currency Pamph. Vol. 4.

—— Oration at Boston, July 5, 1847. Boston, 1847. 8vo. Addresses. Vol. 24.

—— Speech in Mass. Senate on the Hoosac Tunnel, May 18, 1853. Boston, 8vo. Addresses. Vol. 9.

CARYSPORT, Lord. Letter to the Huntingdonshire Committee, etc. 1780. 8vo. Eng. Polit. Pamph. Vol. 19.

CASANOVA Inocencio. Memorandum of Wrongs received by him from the Spanish Gov't. N. Y., 1871. 8vo. Congr. and Polit. Pamph. Vol. 138.

CASCO BAY, Me. See Chronicles of.

CASE and Claim of Amer. Loyalists, and Review of the same. See Amer. Tracts, 1776–1778.

—— of Individual Sacrifice, and of Natural Ingratitude. Sir Jos. Douglas. Lond., 1847. 8vo. Eng. Misc. Pamph. Vol. 30.

—— stated between the Public Libraries and the Booksellers. London, 1813. 8vo. Pamphleteer. Vol. 2.

CASE, Rev. Wheeler. Revolu. Memorials, embracing Poems published in 1778, with other Papers. Edited by Rev. S. DODD. N. Y., 1852. 12mo.

CASES of Personal Identity. Albany, 1854. 8vo.

CASEY, Jos. Speech in Cong., March 18, 1850, on Admission of Cal. Congr. and Polit. Pamph. Vol. 86.

CASEY, Gen. S. Infantry Tactics. N. Y., 1863. 3 vols. 18mo.

CASH, Wm. and Fred. G. The Search for a Publisher; or Counsels for a Young Author. Lond., 1855. 8vo. 2d Ed. Eng. Misc. Pamph. Vol. 20.

CASKET, (The). Magazine. Phila., 1827–1836 and 1840. 11 vols. 8vo.

CASPARI, C. P. Symbols and Rules of Christian Belief in German. Christiana, 1869. 2 vols. 8vo.

CASS, LEWIS. Address on Slavery in U. S. Senate, March, 1850. Congr. and Polit. Pamph. Vol. 97.

—— Address before Kalamazoo Co., Mich. Agr. Soc., Oct. 11, 1850. Congr. and Polit. Pamph. Vol. 90.

—— Biog. of. N. Y., 1843. 8vo. Congr. and Polit. Pamph. Vol. 109.

—— Disc. Delivered before Hist. Soc. of Mich., at its 1st Annivers. Sketches of Michigan.

—— Disc. at Washington, Jan. 30, 1836, before the Amer. Hist. Soc. Washington, 1836. 8vo. Addresses. Vol. 33.

—— France—its King, Court and Gov't. 3d Ed. N. Y., 1848. 8vo.

CASS, Lewis. Outlines of the Life and Character of. Albany, 1848. 8vo. Biograph. Pamph. Vol. 7.
—— Sketch of his Life and Public Services. 1848. 8vo. Congr. and Polit. Pamph. Vol. 69.
—— SMITH, W. L. G. Life and Times of.
—— Speech in U. S. Senate, Jan. 4, 1850, on Relations with Austria. Congr. and Polit. Pamph. Vol. 90.
—— Speeches in U. S. Senate, Dec. 11 and 12, 1851, on the Resolution in honor of Kossuth. Congr. and Polit. Pamph. Vol. 92.
—— Speech in U. S. Senate, Jan. 11, 1854, on the Central Amer. Treaty. Congr. and Polit. Pamph. Vol. 87. Speeches. Vol. 3.
—— Speech in U. S. Senate, Feb. 20, 1854, on Slavery in the Territories. Washington, 1854. 8vo. Speeches. Vol. 3. Congr. and Polit. Pamph. Vol. 93.
—— Speech in U. S. Senate, May 15, 1854, on the Relig. Rights of Amer. Citizens in Foreign Countries. Washington, 1854. 8vo. Speeches. Vol. 3.
—— Speech in U. S. Senate, Feb. 20, 1855, on European Affairs. Speeches. Vol. 5.
—— Speech in U. S. Senate, May 12 and 13, 1856, on the Kansas and Nebr. Bills. Cong. and Polit. Pamph. Vol. 93.
—— See YOUNG, W. T. Life and Pub. Services of.
CASSEDAY, B. Hist. of Louisville, Ky., from Early Settlement to 1852. Louisville, 1852. 8vo.
CASSERLY, Eugene. Letter to T. T. Davenport on "The Issue in Cal. San Francisco, 1861. 8vo. Rebell'n Pamph. Vol. 6.
CASTANEDA DE NAGERA, Pedro. Relation du Voyage de Cibola. See TERNAUX. Voyages. Vol. 9.
CASTE. See MORTON, Rev. W.
CASTELL, William. Petition to Parl't for the Propaga. of the Gospel in America. 1641. See Force's Hist. Tracts. Vol. 1.
CASTILLO, Conquistador B. D. del. Memoirs of, containing a full Account of Mexico and New Spain. Lond., 1844. 2 Vols. 8vo.
CASTINE, Me. See WILLIAMSON, J. Acc. of, etc.
CASTLETON, Derbyshire, Eng. See HEDINGER, J. M. Short Descript. of.
CASTLETON, N. Y., Med. Coll. Announcements and Catalogues for 1844, '45, '46, '47. Albany and Troy, 1844–47. 8vo.
CASWALL, Henry. The Prophet of the 19th Century; or the Rise, Progress, etc., of the Mormons. London, 1843. 12mo.
CASWELL, Alexis. Memoir of John Barstow. N. Eng. Hist. and Gen. Reg. Vol. 18.
—— Meteorolog. Observa. at Providence, R. I., 1831-1860. Smithsonian Contrib. Vol. 12.
CATALOGUE of Amer. Minerals, (title page gone.) (n. d.) 8vo. Scientific Pamph. Vol. 5.
—— of Books on the Masonic Institution, in Pub. Libraries; Anti-Masonic in Arguments and Conclusions. Boston, 1852. 8vo.

CATALOGUE of Designs for the New Houses of Parliament. Lond., 1836. 4to. 4th Ed. Eng. Polit. Pamph. Vol. 53A.

—— of Papers relating to Penn. and Del., deposited in the State Paper Office. London. Hist. Soc. of Penn. Memoirs. Vol. 4. Part 2.

CATALOGUES, Construction of. See JEWETT, C. C. Report on. 1853.

—— of Private Libraries, Trade Lists, Autographs, etc. 68 Pamplet Volumes. Assorted.

—— of Public Libraries. See Albany Institute Lib.

—— —— Albany Y. M. Assoc.

—— —— Amer. Antiq. Soc.

—— —— Amer. Philosoph. Soc.

—— —— Astor Library.

—— —— Belgium. Libr. of Chamber of Dept.

—— —— See Bibliography.

—— —— of Boston Atheneum.

—— —— Boston Pub. Libr.

—— —— British Museum.

—— —— Brown University.

—— —— Cambridge High School.

—— —— Canada Library of Parliament.

—— —— Groton, (Mass.) Libr.

—— —— Harvard College.

—— —— Libr. of Cong.

—— —— Loganian Libr.

—— —— London Institution.

—— —— Lowell (Mass.) School Libr.

—— —— Madison (Wis.) Institute.

—— —— Marietta (O.) Coll. Libr.

—— —— Mass. Hist. Soc.

—— —— Mass. State Libr.

—— —— Mich. State Libr.

—— —— Milwaukee Y. M. Asso.

—— —— N. Y. Hist. Soc.

—— —— N. Y. Merc. Libr. Assoc.

—— —— N. Y. Soc. Libr.

—— —— N. Y. State Lib.

—— —— Ohio State Lib.

—— —— Penn. Hist. Soc.

—— —— Penn. State Libr.

—— —— Phila. Libr. Co.

—— —— Petersburg (Va.) Libr.

—— —— Prince Libr.

—— —— Providence (R. I.) Atheneum.

—— —— St. Louis Merc. Libr. Assoc.

—— —— Salem Atheneum.

—— —— Smithsonian Institution.

—— —— S. Kensington Museum.

—— —— Tenn. State Libr.

—— —— Wayland (Mass.) Libr

—— —— Wis. State Libr.

CATCOTT, A. S. Tractacus, in quo tentatur Conamen Recuperandi Notitiam Principiorum Veteris et Veræ Philosophiæ, etc. Lond., 1738. 4to. Latin Pamph. Vol. 6.
CATHEDRAL Institutions. See SELWYN, Rev. G. A. Use of. 1838.
—— Reform. Observations on Plans proposed for. Cambridge, 1840. 8vo. Strangford Pamph. Vol. 23.
CATHOLIC Directory and Ann. Register for 1843. Lond. 8vo. Eng. Rel. Pamph. Vol. 69.
CATLIN, Geo. Fourteen Ioway Indians. Lond., 1844. 12mo. Indian Pamph. Vol. 3.
—— See GURLEY, R. R. Memorial on Purchase of his Indian Portraits. 1848.
—— Illustra. of Manners, Customs and Condition of the N. Amer. Indians. 19th Ed. Lond, 1866. 2 Vols. 8vo.
—— Last Rambles among the Indians of the Rocky Mountains and the Andes. N. Y., 1867. 12mo.
—— Letters and Notes on Manners, Customs and Condition of the N. Amer. Indians. Phila., 1857. 2 Vols. 8vo.
—— Life among the Indians, Illustrated. N. Y., 1867. 12mo.
—— Notes of Eight Years' Travels and Residence in Europe, with his N. Amer. Collection. 2d Ed. Lond., 1848. 2 Vols. 8vo.
—— O-kee-pa; a Religious Ceremony, and other Customs of the Mandans. 13 Plates. Lond., 1867. 4to.
CATON, John D. The Last of the Illinois, and a Sketch of the Pottawatomies. Read before Chicago Hist. Soc., Dec. 13, 1870. Chicago, 1870. 8vo.
—— and SPRINGER, Wm. M. Speeches at Chicago, Aug. 27, 1872, on the Presidential Campaign. Chicago, 1872. 8vo. Congr. and Polit. Pamph. Vol. 130.
CATON, Dr. T. M. Prevention and Cure of Asthma. Lond., 1813. 8vo. 4th Ed. Med. Pamph. Vol. 25.
CATS, Jacob. Complete Works—in Dutch. Amsterdam, 1661. 4to.
CATSKILL Mountain. See DWIGHT, H. E. Account of.
—— —— PIERCE. Jas. Memoir on.
—— N. Y. Amer. Eagle, Newspaper. Jan., 1808, to Oct., 1810. Folio.
—— See BROWN, Rev. C. Topog. Descrip. of.
—— DWIGHT, B. W. Great Storm of 1819.
—— Western Constellation, Newspaper. May, 1802, to May, 1803. Folio.
—— Recorder, Newspaper. Mar., 1839, to Dec., 1840. Folio.
CATTARAUGUS Co., N. Y. See MAULEY, J. History of.
CATTELL, A. G. Speech in U. S. Senate, Jan. 22, 1867, on the Tariff. Congr. and Polit. Pamph. Vols. 84 and 92.
CATTLE Disease. See N. Y. State Cattle Comm'rs. 1869.
—— —— U. S. Commr. of Agriculture. Report on. 1870.
CAUCASIAN (The) Mountains and their Inhabitants. See DITSON, G. L.
CAULKINS, Francis M. See HAVEN, H. P. Biograph. Sketch of.
—— History of New London, Conn., from 1612 to 1852. N. London, 1852. 8vo.

CAULKINS, Francis M. Same, 2d Ed. Continued to 1860. N. London, 1860. 8vo.
—— History of Norwich, Conn., from 1660 to 1845. Norwich, 1845. 12mo.
—— Same, New Ed. Hartford, 1866. 8vo.
—— Memoirs of Rev. Wm. and Rev. Eliphalet Adams. Cambridge, 1849. 8vo. Genealog. Pamph. Vol. 2.
—— See also Mass. Hist. Soc. Coll., 4th Ser. Vol. 1.
CAUSES of the Reduction of the Amer. Tonnage. Washington, 1871. 8vo.
CAUSTEN, Jas. H. Claims of Amer. Citizens on U. S. Gov't for Indemnity for French Spoliations. Washington, 1871. 8vo. Congr. and Polit. Pamph. Vol. 127.
CAUSTON, H. Kent Staple. The Howard Papers; with a Biograph. Pedigree and Criticism. Lond., 1862. 8vo.
CAVADA, F. F. Libby Life: Experiences of a Prisoner of War in Richmond, 1863–4. N. Y., 1866. 12mo.
CAVALRY Tactics, Washington, 1854. 12mo.
CAVELIER, M. See Early Voyages on Mississippi.
—— Relation du Voyage Entrepris par feu M. Robert Cavelier, Sieur de la Salle pour Decouvrir dans le Golfe du Mexique l'Embouchure du Fleuve, Missisipy. N. Y., 1858. 4to.
CAVENDISH, Sir Henry. Debates of the House of Commons in 1774, on the Gov't of the Province of Quebec. Lond., 1839. 8vo.
CAVERNO, Rev. Chas. Social Science and Woman Suffrage. Trans. Wis. Acad. of Sciences, 1870–2.
CAVERT, M. P. The Study of the English Language and Literature at Geneva, 1866. Albany, 1866. 8vo. Addresses, etc. Vol. 19.
CAWOOD, Rev. John. The Church of England and Dissent. Lond., 1831. 12mo. 2d Ed. Eng. Religious Pamph. Vol. 72.
CAXTON SOCIETY. Publications of Chronicles and Other Writings Illustrative of the History and Miscellaneous Literature of the Middle Ages. viz.:
Chronicon Henrici de Silgrave. By C. HOOK.
Gaimar Geoffry Anglo-Norman Metrical Chronicle of the Anglo-Saxon Kings.
With Appendix, containing the Lay of Havelok the Dane, the Legend of Ernulph, and Life of Hereward the Saxon. Edited by T. WRIGHT, Esq., F. S. A.
La Revolte du Comte de Warwick contre le Roi Edouard IV. to which is added a French Letter concerning Lady Jane Grey and Queen Mary, from a Ms. at Bruges. Edited by DR. GILES.
Walteri Abbatis Dervenfis Epistolae.
Benedicti Abbatis Petriburgensis de Vita et Miraculis St. Thomæ Cantaur. By DR. GILES.
Galfridi le Baker de Swinbroke, Chronicon Angliæ temp. Edward II. et III. By DR. GILES.
Epistolæ Herberti de Losinga, primi Episcopi Norwicensis, et Oberti de Clara, et Elmeri Prioris Cantuariensis. By COL. ANSTRUTHER.

CAXTON SOCIETY, *continued.*
Anecdota Bedæ, Lanfranci, et aliorum (inedited Tracts, Letters, Poems, &c., Bede, Lanfranc, Tatwin, &c). By DR. GILES.
Radulphi Nigri Chronica Duo. By Col. ANSTRUTHER.
Memorial of Bishop Waynflete, Founder of St. Mary Magdalen College, Oxford. By Peter Heylyn. Edited by J. R. BLOXAM, D. D.
Robert Groffetete, Bishop of Lincoln, "Chasteau d'Amour;" to which is added, "La Vie de Sainte Marie Egyptienne," and an English Version (of the 13th Century) of the Chasteau d'Amour. By M. COOKE.
Galfredi Monumententis Historia Brittonum, nunc primum in Anglia novem codd. Mss. collatis. Edidit J. A. GILES.
Alani, Prioris Cantuariensis postea Abbatis Tewksberiensis, Scripta quae extant. Edita J. A. GILES.
Chronicon Angliæ Petriburgense Iterum post Sparkium cum cod. Mss. contulit J. A. GILES.
Vita Quorandum Anglo-Saxonum. Original Lives of Anglo-Saxons and Others who lived before the Conquest—in Latin. Edited by Dr. GILES.
Scriptores Rerum Gestarum Wilhelmi Conquestoris. In unum collecti. Ab J. A. GILES.

CAYLEY, Edw. Up the River Moisie. Read before the Québec Lit. and Hist. Soc., Apr. 1, 1863. Transactions, N. Ser. Vol. 1, Part 1.

CAYUGA Lake Academy, Aurora, N. Y. Acc. of the Celebra., July 22, 1857. N. Y. 8vo. n. d. N. York Hist. Discourses, etc. Vol. 2.

CEAN, Juan Augustin. Sumario de las Antiquedades Romanasque hay en Espana.

CECIL, E. Life of George Washington—for Young Persons. Boston, 1859. 18mo.

CELESIA, Emanule. The Conspiracy of Giauluigi Fieschi; or Genoa in the 16th Century. Translated by D. H. Wheeler. Lond., 1866. 8vo.

CELLULAR Iron Pavements. Advantages of. St. Louis, 1859. 8vo. Scientific Pamph. Vol. 14.

CELTS, (The) of the 19th Century. See GAULLE, C. de. Appeal to.

CEMETERIES. See BRIDGMAN, T. Memorials of Dead in Boston.
—— —— Northampton G. Yard Inscriptions.
—— —— Pilgrims of Boston.
—— Forest Hill Cemetery.
—— Mount Auburn.
—— See Epitaphs.

CENSUS of U. S. See U. S. Census.

CENTRAL AMERICA. See BERENDT, C. H. Explorations in.
—— —— BYAM, G. Ship Canal through C. A.
—— —— GALLATIN, A. Inhabitants of.
—— —— Map of. Published by Cong. Washington, 1856.
—— —— See SQUIER, E. G. Unexplored Regions of.
—— —— STEPHENS, J. L. Incidents of Travel.

CENTRAL AMERICA. VELASQUEZ, P. Memoir of Exped. to, 1848.
—— —— WELLS, W. V. Walker's Exped. to Nicaragua.
—— American Treaty. See Congress. Speeches.
—— Water-Line from the Ohio River to the Virginia Capes, connecting the Kanawha and James Rivers. Richmond, 1868. 8vo. Va. Misc. Pamph. Vol. 2.
—— Same, 2d Ed., 1869. Va. Misc. Pamph. Vol. 2.
CENTURIAL Jubilee, for Oct. 31, 1817, in Commem. of the Reformation. n. p. 1817. 8vo. Religious Pamph. Vol. 14.
CEREALS. See RUGGLES, S. B. Report on, 1869.
CEREMONIES attending the 2d Inaugura. of A. G. Curtin, Gov. of Penn., 1864. Rebell'n Pamph. Vol. 46.
CERTAIN Inducements to Well-Minded People. Lond., 1643. N. Y. Reprint, 1865. 4to.
CEYLON, and the Government of Lord Torrington. Lond., 1851. 8vo. Strangford Pamph. Vol. 59.
—— Mission. Brief Sketch of the Amer. Ceylon Mission. Jaffna, 1849. 12mo. Religious Pamph. Vol. 25.
CHADBOURNE, Paul A., M. D. Influence of History on Individual and National Action. Madison, 1868. 8vo. Wis. Hist. Soc. Addresses, Vol. 1. See Also Addresses and Orations, Vol. 23.
—— Relation of Nat. Science to Religion. An Address. In Norwegian. Madison, 1869. 8vo. Wis. Misc. Pamph. Vol. 4.
—— See Williams College.
CHADWICK, Edwin. Address on Railway Reform. Lond., 1865. 8vo. Eng. Misc. Pamph. Vol. 14.
CHALDEA. LOFTUS, W. K. Travels and Researches in.
CHALKLEY, Thomas. Journal of his Life, Travels, and Christian Experiences. 5th Ed. Lond., 1791.
CHALMERS, George. Introduction to the History of the Revolt of the Amer. Colonies. Boston, 1845. 2 vols. 8vo.
—— Polit. Annals of the present United Colonies from their First Settlement to the Peace of 1763. Lond., 1780. 4to.
—— Polit. Annals of the Province of Carolina; from the Polit. Annals of the United Colonies. CARROLL, B. R. Hist Coll. of S. C. Vol. 2.
—— State of the United Kingdom at the Peace of Paris, Nov. 20, 1815. Lond., 1816. 8vo. 2d Ed. Pamphleteer. Vol. 7.
CHALMERS, Jas. Naval Armor. Lond., 1865. 8vo. Eng. Polit. Pamph. Vol. 61.
CHALMERS, Thos., D. D. See MOFFATT, J. C. Life of.
—— On the Power, Wisdom, etc., of God, Manifested in External Nature. Lond., 1835. 2 vols. 8vo.
—— Remarks on the Present Position of the Ch. of Scotland. Glasgow, 1840. 8vo. Strangford Pamph. Vol. 19.
—— Speech at Edinburgh, Mar. 14, 1829, on the Catholic Question, and two Letters from Rev. Dan'l Wilson on the Same. Lond., 1829. 8vo. Eng. Polit. Pamph. Vol. 37.
—— See SPRAGUE, Rev. W. B.
CHALONER, Jas. Short Treatise on the Isle of Man. Douglas, 1864. 8vo.

CHAMBERLAIN, Henry. History and Survey of the Cities of Lond. and Westminster. Lond., 1770. 2 vols. Folio.

CHAMBERLAIN, Rev. N. H. Paper on N. England Architecture, read before the N. Eng. Hist. Genealog. Soc., Sept. 4, 1858. Boston, 1858. 8vo.

CHAMBERLAIN, T. C. Suggestions as to a Basis for the Gradation of the Vertebrata. Trans. Wis. Acad. of Sciences, 1870–2.

CHAMBERLAYNE, John. Magnae Britanniae Notitia; or the Present State of G. B.; with divers Remarks on the Ancient State thereof. Lond., 1726. 8vo.

CHAMBERS, A. H. Comments on some recent Political Discussions. Lond., 1819. 8vo. Pamphleteer, Vol. 15.

—— Thoughts on the Resumption of Cash Payments by the Bank, and on the Corn Bill. Lond., 1819. 8vo. Pamphleteer, Vol. 14.

CHAMBERS, Geo. Tribute to the Principles, etc., of the Irish and Scotch Early Settlers of Penn. Chambersburgh, 1856. 8vo. Penn. Misc. Pamph. Vol. 1.

CHAMBERS, H. C. Speech in Confed. Cong., Nov. 10, 1864, on the Employment of Negro Troops. Rebell'n Pamph. Vol. 113.

CHAMBERS, John. Biograph. Illustrations of Worcester, Eng. Worcester, 1820. 8vo.

CHAMBERS, John David. The New Bills for the Registration of Electors Critically Examined. Lond., 1836. 8vo. Eng. Polit. Pamph. Vol. 41.

CHAMBERS, Robt. Biograph. Dictionary of Eminent Scotsmen; with Supplement Vol. Edinburgh, 1859. 5 vols. 8vo.

—— Cyclopedia of Eng. Literature. Edinburgh. n. d. 2 vols. 8vo.

—— Life and Adventures of the Chevalier Chas. Stuart, and Hist. of the Rebellion in Scotland in 1745–6. Waldie's Circulating Libr. Vol. 2.

—— Life of Sir Walter Scott. N.Y., 1832. 8vo. Biograph. Pamph. Vol. 15.

CHAMBERS'S, W, Social Science Tracts. On Building Societies. Lond., 8vo. n. d. Scientific Pamph. Vol. 32.

—— Amer. Slavery. Lond., 1857. 8vo.

—— Hist. of Peebleshire. Edinburgh, 1864. 8vo.

CHAMBERS, W. & R. Encyclopedia; a Dictionary of Universal Knowledge for the People, with Maps and Wood Engravings. Lond., 1868. 10 vols. 8vo.

—— Miscellany of Useful and Entertaining Tracts. Phila., 1857. 10 vols. 12mo.

—— Papers for the People. Phila., 1856. 6 vols. 12mo.

—— Pocket Miscellany. Phila., 1857. 12 vols. 18mo.

—— Repository of Instructive and Amusing Tracts. Phila., 1856. 6 Vols. 12mo.

CHAMBERSBURG, Penn. See GARRARD, L. H. Colonial and Revolutionary Hist. of.

CHAMBRUN, Aldebert de. La Republique Reformiste et la Republique Revolutionnaire. Paris, 1848. 8vo. Strangford Pamph. Vol. 68.

CHAMPE, Sergeant. See LEE, Gen. Henry. Adventures.

CHAMPIGNY, Chevalier de. Present State of Louisiana. French's Hist. Coll. of La. Vol. 4.
CHAMPLAIN. Expeditions to Northern and Western N. Y. 1609-15. Doc. Hist. of N. Y. Vol. 3.
CHAMPLAIN, Saml. See MCGEE, Thos. D. On a Lately Discovered MS. of.
CHAMPLAIN, Le Sieur de. Voyages, ou Journal des Decouvertes de la Nouvelle France. Paris, 1830. 2 Vols. 8vo.
CHAMPLAIN Valley, N. Y. See Watson, W. C. Hist. of.
CHAMPLIN, Com. Stephen. See CLINTON, Judge. Vol. 1.
CHAMPNEY, Mrs. Susanna P. See WHITNEY, F. A. Obit. Disc. and Geneal.
CHANCELLORSVILLE and its Results; Maj.-Gen. Hooker in Command of the Army of the Potomac. (n. d.) Rebell'n Pamph. Vol. 12.
CHANDLER & Co.'s Business Directory of Chicago, Milwaukee and Green Bay, etc. Indianapolis, 1867. 8vo.
CHANDLER, Jos. R. Address at Celebra. of the Landing of the Pilgrims of Md., May 15, 1855. Baltimore. 8vo. Md. Misc. Pamph. Vol. 2.
—— See Girard Coll.
—— Oration at Phila., Dec. 22, 1845, at the 2d Annivers. of the Sons of N. England. Phila., 1846. 8vo. Addresses. Vol. 32.
—— Speech in Cong., Mar. 28, 1850, on the Admission of Cal. Congr. and Polit. Pamph. Vol. 86.
—— Speech in Cong., Apr. 8, 1852, on the Homestead Bill. Congr. and Polit. Pamph. Vol. 83.
—— Speech in Cong., Jan. 10, 1855, on the Temporal Power of the Pope. Speeches. Vol. 5. Congr. ann Polit. Pamph. Vol. 87.
CHANDLER, Morton & Culver. Memorial to Cong., on Cotton seized by Treasury Agents. Richmond, 1871. 8vo. Congr. and Polit. Pamph. Vol. 131.
CHANDLER, P. W. Amer. Criminal Trials. Boston, 1844. 2 vols. 12mo.
—— Oration at Boston, July 4, 1844. 8vo. Addresses. Vol. 2.
CHANDLER, T. P. Polit. Address at Brookline, Mass., Sept. 27, 1860. Rebell'n Pamph. Vol. 77.
CHANDLER, Z. Speech in U. S. Senate, Feb. 17, 1859, on Acquisition of Cuba. Congr. and Polit. Pamph. Vol. 87.
—— Speech in U. S. Senate, Apr. 19, 1869, on Relations with G. B. Congr. and Polit. Pamph. Vol. 122.
—— Speech in U. S. Senate, Feb. 21, 1870, on Case of Fitz John Porter. Congr. and Polit. Pamph. Vol. 119.
CHANGE for the Amer. Notes, in Letters from Lond. to N. Y. By an Amer. Lady. N. Y., 1843. 8vo.
CHANNING, Edw. T. Life of Wm. Ellery. Sparks' Amer. Biog. 1st Ser. Vol. 6.
CHANNING, G. G. Early Recollections of Newport, R. I., from 1793 to 1811. Newport, 1868. 8vo.

CHANNING, Walter, M. D. Ann. Address before the Mass. Temperance Soc'y, May 29, 1836, with Ann. Report. Boston, 1836. 8vo. Temp. Pamph. Vol. 2.

—— A Plea for Pure Water, with an Address to Citizens of Boston, by H. WILLIAMS. Boston, 1844. 8vo. Boston Misc. Pamph. Vol. 1.

CHANNING, W. E., D. D. Address at Seneca, Mass., Aug. 1, 1842, on Emancipation in the British West Indies. Lenox, 1842. 8vo. Sermon. Vol. 3.

—— Address before the Merc. Libr. Co. of Phila., May 11, 1841. Phila., 1841. 8vo. Addresses. Vol. 14.

—— See GANNETT, Rev. E. S. Obit. Sermon.

—— HAZARD, R. G. Essay on Character of.

—— Importance and Means of a Nat. Literature. Edinburgh, 1835. 12mo. Addresses. Vol. 38.

—— Lecture on War. Boston, 1839. 8vo. Addresses. Vol. 1.

—— Letter on Annexation of Texas. 6th. Ed. Boston, 1837. Congress. and Polit. Pamph. Vol. 102.

—— Letter to the Standing Comm. of the Proprietors of the Meeting-House, Federal St., Boston. Boston, 1840. 8vo. Religious Pamph. Vol. 16.

—— See Remarks on "Slavery, by W. E. CHANNING."

—— Selections from his Works. Boston, 1855. 12mo.

—— Self-Culture. Address at Boston, Sept., 1838. Two Copies. Boston, 1839. 12mo. London, (n. d.) 12mo. Addresses. Vol. 30.

—— Tribute to the Memory of Rev. Noah Worcester; Disc. at Boston, Nov. 12, 1837. Boston, 1837. 8vo. Serm. Vols. 21, 31.

CHANNING, Wm. F. The Amer. Fire-Alarm Telegraph. Boston, 1855. 8vo. Scientific Pamphlets. Vol. 2.

—— The Municipal Electric Telegraph and Fire Alarms. N. Haven, 1852. 8vo.

CHANNING, W. H. Memoir of James H. Perkins. Boston, 1851. 2 Vols. 12mo.

—— Religions of China; Address at Boston, May 27, 1870. Boston, 1870. 8vo. Religious Pamph. Vol. 8.

CHAPIN, Alonzo B., D. D. Glastenbury for 200 years; a Centen. Disc., May 18, 1853, with Hist. and Genealog. Statistics. Hartford, 1853. 8vo.

—— Address and Disc. at his Inaugura. as Prest. of Beloit Coll., July 24, 1850. Milwaukee, 1850. 8vo. Beloit Coll. Pamph.

—— Relations of Labor and Capital. Trans-Wis. Acad. of Sciences. 1870–2.

CHAPIN, Calvin, D. D. Sermon at the Funeral of John Marsh, D. D., at Wetherfield, Conn., Sept., 1821. Hartford, 1821. 8vo. Sermons. Vol. 51.

CHAPIN, Edwin H., D. D. Memoir of. Holden's Mag., Feb. 1859. Biograph. Pamph. Vol. 11.

CHAPIN, Orange. Chapin Genealogy; Descendants of Dea. Sam. Chapin, Springfield, 1642, with E. B. Clark's Centen. Disc. at Chicopee, and G. Bliss' Address at Springfield, 1828. Northampton, 1862. 8vo.

CHAPIN, Wm. Complete Reference Gazetteer of the U. S. N. Y., 1844. 8vo.

CHAPLIN, Fred. Remarks on Acts of Parl't, affecting Life Assurance. 1853. Lond. 12mo. Eng. Misc. Pamph. Vol. 12.

CHAPMAN, Dr. C. B. Introduct. Lecture at Ohio Coll. of Dental Surgery, 1856–7. Cincin., 1856. 8vo.

CHAPMAN, F. W. The Buckingham Family, Descendants of Thos. Buckingham, of Milford, Conn. Hartford, 1872. 8vo.

—— Chapman Family; or Descendants of Robert Chapman, one of the First Settlers of Saybrook, Conn., with Genealog. Notes of other Families. Hartford, 1854. 8vo.

—— Pratt Family, of Hartford, Conn. Hartford, 1864. 8vo.

—— The Trowbridge Family, Descendants of Thos. Trowbridge, of N. Haven, Conn. N. Haven, 1872. 8vo.

CHAPMAN, Isaac A. Sketch of the History of Wyoming, with a Statist. Acc. of the Valley and Adjacent Country. Wilkesbarre, 1830. 12mo.

CHAPMAN, Rev. Jas. Hist. Notices of St. Peter's Ch., in Perth-Amboy, N. J., 1825. Elizabethtown, 1830. 8vo. N. Jersey Hist. Discourses. Vol. 1.

CHAPMAN, John. Baroda and Bombay; their Polit. Morality. Narrative of the Removal of Col. Outram, etc. Lond., 1853. 8vo. Eng. Polit. Pamph. Vol. 50.

CHAPMAN, Dr. N. See PATTISON, G. S. Corres. with. 1821.

CHAPMAN, Silas. Maps of Wis., 1861–69, etc., on Rollers. Milwaukee, ——.

—— Map of the Co's of Kenosha, Racine, Milwaukee and Waukesha. Milwaukee, (v. d.)

—— Map of Lake Superior Country.

—— Maps of Dakota, Iowa, Minnesota, (v. d.)

—— Hand-Book of Wis. 2d Ed. Milwaukee, 1855. 18mo.

CHAPPELL, Edw. Narrative of a Voyage to Hudson's Bay. Lond., 1817. 8vo. Bound with "Welby's Visit to America."

CHAPPLE, W. Review of Part of Risdon's Survey of Devon, being the Gen. Descrip. of that Co., with Corrections and Additions. Exeter, 1785. 4to.

CHARACTER of Abraham Lincoln, and the Constitutionality of Emancipation. Boston, (n. d.) Rebellion Pamph. Vols. 8 and 27.

CHARITY, Noxious and Beneficient. From Westminster Rev., Jan. 1853. Eng. Misc. Pamph. Vol. 32.

CHARLEMAGNE. See JAMES, G. P. R. History of.

CHARLEROI. Paleontolog. and Archæolog. Soc. Documents and Reports. Vol. 4. Mons, 1869. 8vo.

CHARLES I., King of G. Britain. See HARRIS, W.

—— —— STILES, Rev. E. Hist. of Three Judges of.

CHARLES II. See SIDNEY, H. Diary of Times of.

CHARLES V., of Germany. See CORTES, Hernando. Dispatches.

—— —— ROBERTSON, W. Hist. of his Reign.

CHARLES XII., of Sweden. See VOLTAIRE.

CHARLES STEWART, Pretender. See HOOK, Col.

CHARLESTON, S. C. Book, a Miscellany in Prose and Verse. Charleston, 1845. 12mo.
—— Coll. Mag., Nov., 1854. Charleston, 1854. 8vo.
—— Magnolia Cemetery. Proceedings at Dedica. of, Nov. 19, 1850. Addresses, etc. Vol. 12.
—— See Confederate Memorial Day. 1871.
—— Early Reminiscences of. See CARDOZO, J. N.
—— GILMAN, Mrs. Letter of Mrs. Wilkinson on the Invasion of.
—— Proceedings of the State Rights and Free Trade Party. 1831–1832. Charleston, 1831–32. 12mo. Nullifica. Tracts.
—— See SMYTH, Rev. T. Manual of 2d Presb. Ch.
CHARLESTOWN, Mass. See BARTLETT, J. Hist. Sketch of.
—— First Church. Articles of Faith, Covenant, etc. Boston, 1842. 8vo. Mass. Hist. Discourses, etc. Vol. 8.
—— —— See BUDINGTON, Rev. W. I. Hist. of.
—— —— HUNNEWELL, J. F. Illustra. of Hist. of.
—— Harvard Church. See ELLIS, G. E. Annivers. Disc. 1865.
—— Pub. Library. Report for 1872. Charlestown, 1873. 8vo.
—— Report of Trustees of the City Schools, 1840. 8vo.
—— Reports of School Comm. for 1847 '49, '57, '59. 8vo.
—— Municipal Register, 1852. 8vo.
—— Mayor's Address, Jan., 1853. 8vo.
CHARLESTOWN, N. H. See CROSBY, J. Annals of.
CHARLEVOIX, Francoise X. Histoire de l'Isle Espagnole, ou de S. Dominigue. Paris, 1730. 4to.
—— Histoire et Description Generale de la Nouvelle France, avec le Journal Historique d'au Voyage fait dans l'Amerique Septentrionale. Paris, 1744. 3 Vols. 4to.
—— Hist. of New France, Translated by John G. Shea. Vols. 1 and 6. N. Y., Pr. Printed 1866–1872. 8vo.
—— Letters to Duchess of Lesdiguieres, giving an Account of a Voyage to Canada. Lond., 1763. 8vo. See also French's Hist. Coll. of La. Vol. 3.
CHARLOTTE, Princess of Wales. See KNIGHT, Charlotte. Autobiog.
—— Memoirs of the Life, Death and Funeral of. Lond., 1817. 8vo. Biograph. Pamph. Vol. 2.
—— Selections from One Hundred and Twelve Sermons on her Death. Lond., 1818. 8vo. Eng. Sermons. Vol. 36.
—— See THOMSON, Dr. A. F. Med Statement of her case.
CHARLTON, E. A. N. Hampshire as it is. Claremont, 1857. 8vo.
CHARREL, J. Traité des Maguaneries. Paris, 1848. 8vo.
CHASE, Benj. Hist. of Old Chester, N. H., 1719—1869. Auburn, N. H., 1869. 8vo.
CHASE, Rev. B. C. Half-Century Disc. at Camden, Me., on the Organization of Cong. Ch. Boston, 1855. 8vo. Maine Hist. Discourses, Vol. 1.
CHASE, Dr. Enoch. Address to the Old Settlers' Club, Milwaukee, July 4, 1872. Milwaukee, 1872. 8vo. Wis. Local Hist. Vol. 2.
CHASE, Francis. Gathered Sketches from the Early History of N. Hampshire and Vt. Claremont, 1856. 12mo.

CHASE, G. B. Genealog. Memoir of the Chase Family, of Bucks. Boston, 1869. 8vo. Genealog. Pamph. Vols. 2 & 4.

CHASE, Geo. W. Hist. of Haverhill, Mass., 1640—1860. Haverhill, 1861. 8vo.

CHASE, H. & SANBORN, C. W. The North and South; a Statist. View of Free and Slave States. Boston, 1856. 8vo.

CHASE, Lucien B. English Serfdom and Amer. Slavery. N. Y., 1854. 12mo.

—— History of the Polk Administra. N. Y.. 1850. 8vo.

—— Speech in Cong., June 26, 1846, on the Tariff. Washington, 1846. 8vo. Speeches, Vol. 1.

CHASE, Bishop Philander. Plea for the West. (In behalf of Kenyon Coll.) Phila., 1826. 8vo. Ohio Coll. Pamph.

—— Reminiscences. An Autobiography. Peoria, 1841-2. 8vo.

CHASE, Pliny E. Intellectual Symbolism; a Basis for Science. Trans. Amer. Philosoph. Soc., N. S. Vol. 12.

—— On the Comparative Etymology of the Yoruba Language. Trans. Amer. Philosoph. Soc., N. S. Vol. 13.

—— On the Mathematical Probability of Accidental Linguistic Resemblances. Trans. Amer. Philosoph. Soc. Vol. 13.

CHASE, S. B. Manual, or Exposition of the Independent Order of Good Templars. Chicago, 1864. 12mo. Masonic Pamph., etc. Vol. 1.

CHASE, Salmon P. Letter to the Hon. A. P. Edgerton on Politics in Ohio, Nov. 14, 1853. Speeches, etc. Vol. 3.

—— Speech at Toledo, May 30, 1851, before Dem. Mass. Conven. Congr. and Polit. Pamph. Vol. 90.

—— Speech in U. S. Senate, Apr. 14, 1852, on Public Lands. Congr. and Polit. Pamph. Vol. 84.

—— Speech in U. S. Senate, Feb. 3, 1854, on the Compromise Bill. Speeches, Vol. 5.

—— Speech in the Peace Conference of 1861. N. Y., 1863. 8vo. Rebell'n Pamph. Vols. 31 and 90.

—— Speeches during his Visit to Ohio, with Speeches at Indianapolis and Baltimore, Oct., 1863 Rebell'n Pamph. Vol. 36.

CHASE, Judge Sam'l. Answer and Pleas to the Articles of Impeachment Exhibited against him by the House of Repr. Phila., 1805. 8vo.

—— Trial of, for High Crimes and Misdemeanors. Washington, 1805. 2 vols. 8vo.

CHASE, Rev. Sam'l. Review of Jubillee Coll. Peoria, 1843. 12mo. Ill. Misc. Pamph. Vol. 2.

CHASE, Warren. The Amer. Crisis; or Trial and Triumph of Democracy. Boston, 1862. 12mo. Rebell'n Pamph. Vol. 102.

CHASTAIN, E. W. Speech in Cong., Mar. 5, 1852, on the Union Party of Ga. Congr. and Polit. Pamph. Vol. 88.

CHASTELLUX, Marquis De. Travels in N. America in 1780, '81, '82. Translated from the French. Lond., 1787. 2 vols. 8vo.

CHATEAUBRIAND, F. A. Buonaparte and the Bourbons, and the Necessity of Rallying around our Legitimate Princes, etc. Lond., 1814. 8vo. Pamphleteer, Vol. 3.

CHATEAUBRIAND, F. A. On the Censorship recently Established in France, 1822. Lond., 1824. 8vo. Pamphleteer, Vol. 24.
—— See PHILLIPART, Sir John. On the Libels published by him.
—— Travels in America and Italy. Lond., 1828. 2 vols. 8vo.
CHATHAM, Lord. See Speeches of Chatham, Burke, etc.
CHATHAM, Lord. Speech in House of Lords, Nov. 22, 1770, on the State of the Nation. 8vo. Eng. Polit. Pamph. Vol. 17.
CHATHAM Artillery. See Jones, C. C. Hist. Sketch of.
CHATHAM, Conn. See FIELD, D. D.
CHATHAM, Mass. Descrip. of. Mass. Hist. Soc. Coll. 1st Ser. Vol. 8.
CHATTERTON, Thos. See MATHIAS, Th. J. Poems of Th. Rowley.
CHAUCER, See CARPENTER, S. H. English of the XIV Century, Illustrated, etc.
CHAUMONOT, R. P. Pierre Joseph Marie. La Vie; Ecrite par lui—Même par Ordre de son Superieur, l'an., 1688. Avec Suplement et Continuation. N. Y., 1858. 4to. 2 vols.
CHAUNCEY, E. M. The Ancestry of Gen. Grant and their Contemporaries. N. Y., 1869. 12mo.
CHAUNCEY Family Memorials. See FOWLER, W. C.
CHAUNCEY, Nathan'l. See FOWLER, Wm. C. Character of, etc.
CHAUNCY, Chas. See FOWLER, W. C. Sketch of.
CHAUSSIER, M. Francois. Notice of. Paris, (n. d.) 8vo. Medical Pamph. Vol. 7.
CHAUTAUQUE Co., N. Y. See Warren, E. F. Sketches of.
CHEAP Cotton by Free Labor; by a Cotton Manufacturer. Boston, 1861. 8vo. Rebell'n Pamph. Vol. 62.
CHECKLEY, John. Speech upon his Trial at Boston, in 1724, with Introduction by Rev. E. H. Gillett. Morrisania, N. Y., 1868. 8vo. Boston Hist. Discourses, Vol. 2.
CHEDWORTH, Lord John. Charge to Grand Jury—County of Suffolk, Jan. 18, 1793. Ipswich, 1793? 4to. Law Pamph. Vol. 25.
CHEEVER, Ezekiel. Trial of, before the Church at N. Haven, 1649. Conn. Hist. Soc. Coll. Vol. 1.
CHEEVER, Geo. B. Defence of, concerning an Alleged Libel, in the Story of "Deacon Giles' Distillery." Salem, 1846. 12mo. Temp. Pamph. Vol. 3.
—— Journ of the Pilgrims at Plymouth in N. England, in 1620; reprinted from the Original Volume. N. Y., 1848. 12mo.
—— See N. Y. City. Ch. of the Puritans.
—— True Hist. of Deacon Giles' Distillery. N. Y., 1859. 8vo. Temp. Pamph. Vol. 3.
CHEEVER, Geo. F. The Prosecution of Ann Pudeator for Witchcraft, in 1692. Essex Institute Coll. Vol. 4.
—— Remarks on the Commerce of Salem from 1626 to 1740, with a Sketch of Philip English, his Prosecution for Witchcraft, &c. Essex Institute Coll. Vols. 1, 2, 3.
CHEEVER, Rev. Henry T. Life in the Sandwich Islands; or the Heart of the Pacific. N. Y., 1856. 12mo.
CHELMSFORD, Mass. See ALLEN, Geo. H. Centen. Address, 1871.
CHELSEA, Eng., Royal Hospital and Asylum. See SMITH, Thomas. Hand-Book, 1851.

CHELSEA, Mass. Mayor's Addresses, 1862, '67, '70.
—— Ann. Reports of Receipts and Expenditures for 1862 and '67.
—— Ann. Report of School Com. for 1859, '67, '69. Chelsea. 8vo.
—— Winnisimmet Congr. Ch. See LANGWORTHY, I. P. Hist. Disc., 1866.
CHELTENHAM, Eng., as it is. Cheltenham, n. d. 8vo. Guide Books. Vol. 23.
—— See Davies, Henry. Strangers' Guide, 1834.
—— GRIFFITH, J. K. Guide Books, 1818?
—— Guide. Lond., 1781. 8vo. Guide Books. Vol. 23.
—— See GRIFFITH, S. Y. Hist. Descrip., 1826.
CHEMISTRY. See BAYEN, P. Opuscules Chimiques.
—— BECQUEREL, M. Traite de Physique, etc.
—— Booth and Morfit. On Improvement in Chem. Arts.
—— Chymie Hydraulique.
—— COLVIN, Verplanck. New Phenomena in.
—— COOLEY, A. J. Cyclo. of Prac. Receipts.
—— DE LUC, J. A. Physique Terrestre.
—— DESAINS, E. Sur l'Absorption de l'Eau.
—— FONTANA, F. Opuscules Chymique.
—— POTT, J. H. Des Elemens.
—— PROUT, Wm. Chemistry and Nat. Theol.
—— RENWICK, J. Applications of, to the Arts.
—— SPIELMANN, J. R. Instituts de Chymie.
—— TENNETAR, M. Elemens de Chymie.
—— THOMPSON, Dr. R. D. Cyclopedia of.
—— VOELCKER, Dr. Aug. Chemistry of Food.
—— YOUMAN, E. L. Chemical Atlas.
CHENEY, Rev. Martin. See DAY, Rev. Geo. T.
CHEPSTOW, Town and Castle of. See HEATH, C.
CHEROKEE Indians. See Drake, S. G. Embassy of Sir A. Cumings.
—— —— JONES, C. Acc. of Cherokee Schools.
—— —— Memorial of Delegates of the Cherokee Nation to Pres't and Cong., 1866.
—— —— Reply of Southern Cherokees to said Memorial.
—— —— Comments on Objections of certain Cherokee Delegates, etc. 3 Pamphlets. Washington, 1866. 8vo. Indian Pamph. Vol. 4.
—— —— Reasons why the Pending Treaty should be Ratified. 1870. 8vo. Congr. and Polit. Pamph. Vol. 117.
—— —— See TIMBERLAKE, H. Memoir of Travels, 1765.
—— Land on Walldin Ridge, East Tenn. N.Y., 1848. 8vo. Tenn. Misc. Pamph. Vol. 1.
CHESAPEAKE and Ohio R. R. Co. 1st Ann. Report of Pres't and Directors, 1868. Richmond, 1868. 8vo.
CHESAPEAKE (Frigate) See LOWELL, J.
CHESHIRE, Ct. See DAVIS, C. H. S. Hist. of Wallingford, etc.
CHESHIRE, Eng. See Histor. Soc. of Lancashire and Cheshire.
—— Holmes Chapel. See BARLOW, T. W. Hist. of the Ch., 1853.
CHESTER, Eng. Diocesan Board of Educa. Report, adopted at Liverpool, Sept. 17, 1840. Warrington, 1840. 8vo. Educa. Pamph. Vol. 33.

CHESTER, G. J. Sketches in the U. S., Canada, West Indies, etc. Lond., 1869. 8vo.
CHESTER, H. Education and Advancement for the Working Classes. Speech at Hackney, Jan. 20, 1863. Lond. 8vo. Educa. Pamph. Vol. 28.
CHESTER, Jos. L. Paper on the Ancestry of Geo. Washington. N. Eng. Hist. and Gen. Reg. Vol. 21.
CHESTER, N. H. See BELL, C. Early Hist. of.
—— CHASE, B. Hist. of, 1719—1869.
CHESTER Co., Penn., Agr. Soc'y. See LEE, Z. C. Address, 1858.
—— —— Cabinet of Nat. Science. Constitution of. West Chester, 1832. 12mo. Scientific Pamph. Vol. 3.
—— —— —— 14th Ann. Rep't, West Chester, 1849. 12mo. Scient. Pamph. Vol. 3.
—— See DARLINGTON, Wm.
—— —— Horticult. Soc. DARLINGTON, Wm.
—— Med. Soc. DARLINGTON, Wm.
CHESTERFIELD, N. H. See MEAD, L. K. Descrip. of.
CHEVALIER, M. M. France, Mexico and the Confed. States. N. Y., 1863. 8vo. Rebellion Pamph. Vol. 1.
—— Society, Manners and Politics of the U. States. Boston, 1839. 8vo.
CHEVALIER, Prof. Thos. Remarks on Suicide. Lond., 1824. 8vo. Pamphleteer. Vol. 23.
CHEYENE Indians. See EVANS, Gov. John., on the Massacre of. 1865.
CHEYNE, John, M. D. Essay on Cynanche Trachealis, or Croup. Phila., 1813. 8vo. Med. Pamph. Vol. 6.
CHICAGO, Ill. Academy of Sciences. Transactions. Vol. 1. Part 1. Chicago, 1867. 4to.
—— Advance, Newspaper. 1868–9. 1 Vol.
—— and Alton R. R. Co. Case of—in McLean Co. Circuit Court. 1872. 8vo. Ill. Pamph. Vol. 2.
—— and N. Western R. R. Co. 1st–11th Ann. Reports. N. Y. and Chicago, 1860–1870. 8vo.
—— See BALESTIER, J. N. Annals of. 1840.
—— Biograph. Sketches of Leading Men.
—— Blanchard's Guide Map. 1868.
—— Board of Police. Report for 1871–2. Chicago, 1872. 8vo,
—— —— of Public Works. 1st to 11th Ann. Reports, inclusive. Chicago, 1862–1872. 8vo.
—— —— of Sewerage Coms. Reports June 30, 1860, and Dec. 31, 1860.
—— —— Rep. on Sewerage in Europ'n Cities. 1857. Chicago. 8vo.
—— —— of Trade. 1st–14th Ann. Statements of Trade and Commerce of Chicago. 1858–1871, except the 6th Report, for 1863–4. Chicago, 1859–72. 8vo.
—— Burlington & Quincy R. R. Co. Reports for 1865–6, 1869–70. Chicago, 1866–1870. 8vo.
—— Business Directory. 1856.
—— Cameron and Lincoln Club. Address to the People of the N. West. (n. d.) 8vo. Congr. and Polit. Pamph. Vol. 75.

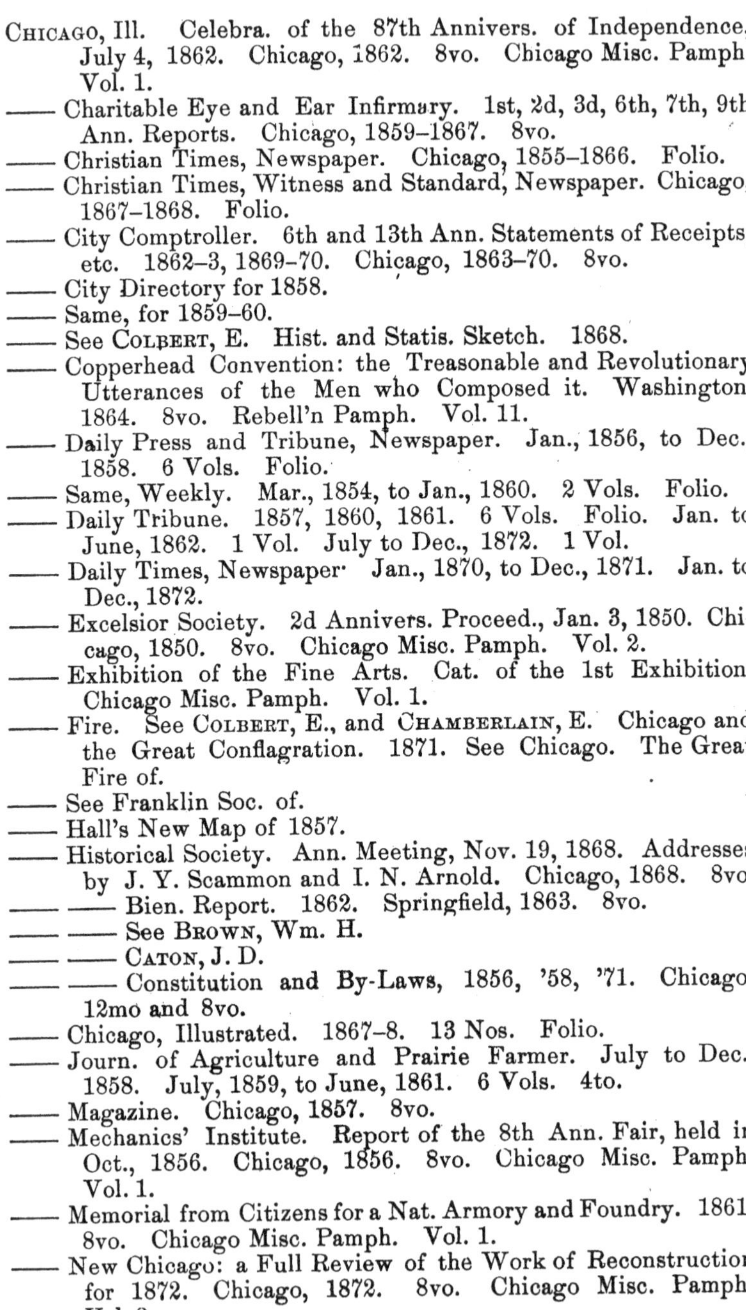

CHICAGO, Ill. Celebra. of the 87th Annivers. of Independence, July 4, 1862. Chicago, 1862. 8vo. Chicago Misc. Pamph. Vol. 1.

—— Charitable Eye and Ear Infirmary. 1st, 2d, 3d, 6th, 7th, 9th Ann. Reports. Chicago, 1859–1867. 8vo.

—— Christian Times, Newspaper. Chicago, 1855–1866. Folio.

—— Christian Times, Witness and Standard, Newspaper. Chicago, 1867–1868. Folio.

—— City Comptroller. 6th and 13th Ann. Statements of Receipts, etc. 1862–3, 1869–70. Chicago, 1863–70. 8vo.

—— City Directory for 1858.

—— Same, for 1859–60.

—— See COLBERT, E. Hist. and Statis. Sketch. 1868.

—— Copperhead Convention: the Treasonable and Revolutionary Utterances of the Men who Composed it. Washington, 1864. 8vo. Rebell'n Pamph. Vol. 11.

—— Daily Press and Tribune, Newspaper. Jan., 1856, to Dec., 1858. 6 Vols. Folio.

—— Same, Weekly. Mar., 1854, to Jan., 1860. 2 Vols. Folio.

—— Daily Tribune. 1857, 1860, 1861. 6 Vols. Folio. Jan. to June, 1862. 1 Vol. July to Dec., 1872. 1 Vol.

—— Daily Times, Newspaper· Jan., 1870, to Dec., 1871. Jan. to Dec., 1872.

—— Excelsior Society. 2d Annivers. Proceed., Jan. 3, 1850. Chicago, 1850. 8vo. Chicago Misc. Pamph. Vol. 2.

—— Exhibition of the Fine Arts. Cat. of the 1st Exhibition. Chicago Misc. Pamph. Vol. 1.

—— Fire. See COLBERT, E., and CHAMBERLAIN, E. Chicago and the Great Conflagration. 1871. See Chicago. The Great Fire of.

—— See Franklin Soc. of.

—— Hall's New Map of 1857.

—— Historical Society. Ann. Meeting, Nov. 19, 1868. Addresses by J. Y. Scammon and I. N. Arnold. Chicago, 1868. 8vo.

—— —— Bien. Report. 1862. Springfield, 1863. 8vo.

—— —— See BROWN, Wm. H.

—— —— CATON, J. D.

—— —— Constitution and By-Laws, 1856, '58, '71. Chicago. 12mo and 8vo.

—— Chicago, Illustrated. 1867–8. 13 Nos. Folio.

—— Journ. of Agriculture and Prairie Farmer. July to Dec., 1858. July, 1859, to June, 1861. 6 Vols. 4to.

—— Magazine. Chicago, 1857. 8vo.

—— Mechanics' Institute. Report of the 8th Ann. Fair, held in Oct., 1856. Chicago, 1856. 8vo. Chicago Misc. Pamph. Vol. 1.

—— Memorial from Citizens for a Nat. Armory and Foundry. 1861. 8vo. Chicago Misc. Pamph. Vol. 1.

—— New Chicago: a Full Review of the Work of Reconstruction for 1872. Chicago, 1872. 8vo. Chicago Misc. Pamph. Vol. 2.

CHICAGO, Ill. Northwestern Sanitary Fair. 1865. Catalogue of the Department of Arms and Trophies. Chicago, 1865. 8vo. Rebell'n Pamph. Vol. 107. Chicago Misc Pamph. Vol. 1.
—— See PEYTON, J. L. Statis. View, &c., 1855.
—— Public Schools. 3d to 16th Ann. Reports Inclusive, 1856–70, except the 14th Report. Chicago, 1857–70. 8vo. 18th Ann. Report. Chicago, 1872. 8vo.
—— R. R. Gazette, Newspaper. Chicago, 1868–73. 4to.
—— Rebuilt Chicago: A Complete Hist. of its Mercantile and Manufacturing Interests since the Fire, Illustrated. Chicago, 1873. Folio
—— (Ill.) Record, Newspaper. 1857–1859.
—— Reform School. 3d–15th Ann. Reports. 1858–1871. Chicago. 8vo.
—— Relief and Aid Soc. 1st Special Report. Chicago, 1871. 8vo. Annual Report. Chicago, 1872. 8vo. Chicago Misc. Pamph. Vol. 2.
—— River and Harbor Convention. Proceedings at Chicago, July 5, 1847. Chicago, 1847. 8vo. Chicago Misc. Pamph. Vol. 1.
—— St. Paul & Fond du Lac R. R. Co. Charter of. N. Y., 1855. 8vo.
—— See SHAW, Jas. Military Occupation of.
—— SHEA, J. G. Chicago from 1673 to 1725.
—— Sons of Penn. Organiz. and Proceed. of the 1st Ann. Festival, Feb. 22, 1850. Chicago, 1850. 8vo. Chicago Misc. Pamph. Vol. 2.
—— Standard, Newspaper. Chicago, 1869–1870. Folio.
—— Same. See Chicago Christian Times.
—— Statist. and Hist. Review of. Chicago, 1869. 8vo. Chicago Misc. Pamph. Vol. 2.
—— The Great Fire of; a full Acc. of its Origin and Progress; also of the Fires of Mich. and Wis. Indianapolis, 1871. 8vo.
—— to the Seaboard, by way of Port Huron and Lake Mich. R. R. Co. Port Huron, 1866. 8vo.
—— Trade and Commerce of. 1st–8th Ann. Reviews, 1852–1860. Chicago. 8vo.
—— See Chicago Board of Trade.
—— University of. Cat. for 1860–1.
—— First Circular of the Law School for 1859–60. Chicago. 8vo.
—— Water Commiss'rs. 13th and 15th Semi-Ann. Reports. Chicago, 1858–9. 8vo.
—— See WILKIE, F. B. Walks about Chicago, etc.
—— WING, J. The Great Union Stock Yards of.
—— WRIGHT, J. S. Chicago, Past and Present.
—— Y. M. C. A. 11th Ann. Report, Apr., 1868. Chicago, 1869. 8vo. Chicago Misc. Pamph. Vol. 2.

CHICHESTER, Rev. Edw. Oppressions and Cruelties of Irish Revenue Officers. Lond., 1818. 8vo. Eng. Polit. Pamph. Vol. 34.

CHICHESTER Cathedral. See CROCKER, Chas. Visit to.
—— Guide. Chichester, (n. d.) 12mo. Guide Books. Vol. 23.

CHICKAMAUGA, the Price of Chattanooga, with Descrip. of Plans, Marches and Battles. Phila., 1864. 8vo. Rebell'n Pamph. Vol. 69.

CHICKASAW Bapt. Assoc. Minutes of Meetings held 1838, 1840, 1841, 1843. Misc. Pamph. Vol. 1.

—— Indians. See Letters on the Chickasaw and Osage Missions. 1831.

CHICKERING, Jesse. Immigration into the U. S. Boston, 1848. 8vo. Pamphlets. Vol. 13.

—— Statist. View of the Popula. of Mass., 1765–1840. Boston, 1846. 8vo. Mass. Misc. Pamph. Vol. 2.

CHICOPEE, Mass. See CHAPIN, O. Chapin Geneal.

—— See CLARK, Rev. E. B. Centen. Disc. 1852.

CHIFFLET, J. J. Geminæ Matris Sacrorum Titulus Sepulcralis Explicatus. Antwerp, 1634. 4to. Latin Pamph. Vol. 1.

CHILD, Asa. Oration at Norwich, Conn., July 4, 1838. Norwich, 1838. 8vo. Addresses, etc. Vol. 29.

CHILD, John. New England's Jonas Cast up at London, 1847. Edited by W. T. R. MARVIN. Boston, 1869. 4to. Pr. Printed. See also Force's Hist. Tracts. Vol. 4. See also Mass. Hist. Soc. Coll. Vol. 4. 2d Ser.

CHILD, L. Maria. Biographies of Good Wives. 6th Ed. N. Y., 1855. 12mo.

—— Brief Hist. of the Condition of Women in Various Ages and Nations. 5th Ed. N. Y., 1854. 2 Vols. 12mo.

—— Hobomoh: a Tale of Early Times. Boston, 1824. 12mo.

CHILDE, John. See STUART, Gen. C. B. Life of.

CHILDS, Ebenezer. Recollections of Wis. since 1820. Wis. Hist. Soc. Coll. Vol. 4.

CHILDS, Geo. W. Nat'l Almanac and Ann. Record. 1863. Phila., 1863. 12mo.

CHILI. See Rambles in, etc. 1836.

—— WISE, Henry A., Jr. Los Gringos: Wanderings in Peru, etc. 1849.

CHILLICOTHE, (O.) Directory. Chillicothe, 1858. 8vo.

—— Lyceum and Mechanics' Institute. See LEONARD, B. G.

CHILTON (Wis.) Times, Newspaper. Sept., 1857, to Sept., 1859; Bound with Sauk & Juneau Co. Papers.

—— Same. 1860–73. Folio.

CHINA and Japan Order in Council, 1865. Lond., 1865. 8vo. Eng. Polit. Pamph. Vol. 61.

—— Apologiè des Dominicains de la Chiné.

—— British Policy in. See SCARTH, John.

—— British Relations with. 1836. See LINDSAY, H. H.

—— CALLERY, M. Hist. of Insurrec. in.

—— See Christianity in China.

—— Claims against. See U. S. House of Repr. Mess. from Pres't. 1868.

—— Digest of Dispatches on. Lond., 1840. 8vo. Strangford Pamph. Vol. 29.

—— See DOWNING, C. T. The Fan-Qui in China, in 1836–7.

CHINA. Eng. Trade with. See Assey, Chas. On the Trade to China. 1819.
—— FRANCIS, J. F. Descrip. of.
—— HAWKS, Rev. F. L. Expedit. to China and Japan.
—— Hist. of Paper Money in China. Amer. Oriental Soc. Journ. Vol. 1.
—— Its Population and Trade, and the Prospect of a Treaty. 1851. Amer. Oriental Soc. Journ. Vol. 1.
—— See LAY, G. T. Chinese as they are.
—— LOCKMAN, J. Travels of Jesuits.
—— MACKIE, J. M. Life, etc., of Tai-ping-wang.
—— MORRISON, Rev. R. Horae Sinicæ; or Chinese Literature.
—— —— Memoir of an Embassy from the British Gov't. 1816.
—— PARKER, Rev. P. Reports of Med. Miss. Soc. and Opthalmic Hospt. 1845–1847.
—— PETERS, J. R. Remarks upon the Gov't, Hist., etc., of the Chinese.
—— PUMPELLY, R. Geolog. Researches. 1862–65.
—— Religions of. See CHANNING, W. H.
—— Remarks on Occurrences in China, since the Opium Seizure in 1839. Lond., 1840. 8vo. Strangford Pamph. Vol. 27.
—— Report of the East India Comm. on Military Operations in 1839. Lond., 1843. 8vo. Strangford Pamph. Vol. 32.
—— Review of the Management of our Affairs in China since 1834. Lond., 1840. 8vo. Strangford Pamph. Vol. 29.
—— The Rupture with China, and its Causes, Incuding the Opium Question. Lond., 1840. 8vo. Strangford Pamph. Vol. 27.
—— See SHAW, Maj. S. Journals. 1847.
—— TALMAGE, Rev. J. V. N. Anti-Missionary Movement in 1871.
—— TAYLOR, B. Visit to India, China and Japan.
—— Ten Thousand Things respecting.
—— WILLIAMS, S. W. Present Position of.
CHINESE Culture, etc. See BROWN, Rev. S. R.
—— Indemnity Fund. Report from Comm. on For. Rela. of U. S. Senate. 1870. Congr. and Polit. Pamph. Vol. 66.
—— Museum, Boston. See PETERS, J. R. Descrip. Cat. of 1845–47.
—— Testament. See Bible.
—— Tracts and other Religious Pamphlets. Religious Pamph. Vol. 12.
CHINOOK Language. See GIBBS, Geo. Dictionary of.
CHIPMAN, Danl. Life of Col. Seth Warner, with Acc. of the Controversy between N. Y. and Vt. 1763–1775. Burlington, 1858. 12mo.
—— Memoir of Col. Seth Warner, with a Life of Col. Ethan Allen, by Jared SPARKS. Middlebury, 1848. 12mo.
CHIPMAN, N. P. Claims of Loyal Citizens for Property taken by U. S. during the Rebellion. Washington, 1870. 8vo. Congr. and Polit. Pamph. Vol. 116.
CHIPMAN, R. Manning. History of Harwinton, Conn. Hartford, 1860.

CHIPMAN, Saml. Report of an Examination of Poor-Houses, Jails, etc., in the State of N. Y., etc. Albany, 1835. 8vo. Temp. Pamph. Vol. 3.

—— The Temperance Lecturer, Showing the Taxes, Pauperism and Crime; also the Deaths from Intemperance. Albany, 1845. 8vo. Temp. Pamph. Vol. 2.

Chippewa Falls (Wis.) Democrat, Newspaper 1869–73.

—— Indians. See SUMMERFIELD, John. Sketch of Grammar of.

—— Language. See HOWSE, Jos. Cree and Chippewa Language.

—— —— SUMMERFIELD, J.

—— Land District, Wis. See OWEN, D. D. Geolog. Reconnoisance. 1848.

—— Union and Times, Newspaper. Chippewa Falls, 1867, 1868, 1870. Folio.

CHIPPEWAS of Minnesota. See WELSH, Wm.

CHIPS from a German Workshop. See MULLER, Max.

CHITTENDEN, L. E. Debates and Proceedings in Secret Sessions of the Conference Conven. at Washington, Feb. 1861. N. Y., 1864. 8vo.

CHITTY, Jos. Observa. on the Game Laws. Lond., 1816. 8vo. Pamphleteer. Vol. 9.

—— Treatise on Criminal Law. Phila., 1819. 4 Vols. 8vo.

CHIVALRY. See BULFINCH, T. The Age of.

—— JAMES, G. P. R. Hist. of.

—— MILLS, Chas. Hist. of.

—— Letters on Chivalry and Romance, 1762.

CHOATE, Rufus. See ADAMS, Nehemiah. Obit. Disc., 1859.

—— Cat. of his Private Library. Boston, 1859. 8vo. Bibliograph. Pamph. Vol. 72.

—— Opinion on Land Warrants, 1851. Mineral Pt., Wis., 1852. 8vo. Congr. and Polit. Pamph. Vol. 87.

—— See PARKER, E. G. Reminiscences of, 1860.

—— and NORTHEND, W. D. Arguments, etc., for a R. R. from Danvers to Malden. Boston, 1847. 8vo. Mass. R. R. Reports, etc. Vol. 3.

—— and RUSSEL, C. T. Arguments, etc., for a R. R. from Salem to Malden. Boston, 1846. 8vo. Law Pamph. Vol. 1.

—— Speech in U. S. Senate, May, 1842, on Remedial Justice in U. S. Courts. Washington, 1842. 8vo. Congr. and Polit. Pamph. Vol 24.

—— Speech in U. S. Senate, Mar. 14, 1842, on the Tariff. Washington, 1842. 8vo. Congr. and Polit. Pamph. Vol. 24.

CHOCTAW Claims. See PITCHLYNN, P. P.

—— Language. See BRINTON, D. G.

—— —— BYINGTON, Rev. C.

CHOICE Notes from Notes and Queries. Lond., 1858. 12mo.

CHOLERA. Acc. of the Rise and Progress of Indian or Spasmodic Cholera. N. Haven, 1832. 8vo. Med. Pamph. Vol. 9.

—— See FOX, Dr. Tilbury. Cholera Prospects, etc., 1865.

—— McBRIDE, Dr. A. Cause and Cure of.

—— Narrative of Rise and Progress of Malignant Cholera from 1817 to 1832. Lond., 1832. 8vo. 4th Ed. Med. Pamph. Vol. 19.

CHOLERA. Memorandum on. By Medical Conference at Ottawa, 1866. n. d. 8vo. Med. Pamph. Vol. 10.

—— Report on the Epidemic Cholera of 1848 and '49, by the Eng. Gen. Board of Health. Lond., 1850. 8vo. Med. Pamph. Vol. 14.

CHOULES, Rev. John O. Cat. of his Private Library. N. Y. n. d. 8vo. Bibliograph. Pamph. Vol. 61.

—— See HAGUE, Rev. Wm. Commem. Disc., 1856.

CHRISTIAN Alliance (The); its Constitution, List of Officers, and Address. N. Y., 1843. 8vo. Religious Pamph. Vol. 13.

CHRISTIAN, Edw. Explanation of the Law of Elections in the University of Cambridge. Cambridge, 1822. 8vo. Eng. Polit. Pamph. Vol. 56.

—— General Observations on Provident Banks, etc. Lond., 1820. 8vo. Pamphleteer, Vol. 17.

CHRISTIAN Examiner and Theolog. Review. Boston, 1824–66. 71 vols. 8vo.

—— Indians. See APESS, Wm.

—— —— See GOOKIN, Dan'l.

CHRISTIAN, Rev. L. H. Thanksgiving Disc. at Phila., Nov. 27, 1862. Rebell'n Pamph. Vol. 40.

—— Spectator. See EYRE, John.

CHRISTIANITY in China. History of Christian Missions and the Present Insurrection. Lond., 1853. 8vo. Eng. Religious Pamph. Vol. 52A.

—— Interested in the Dismissal of Ministers. A Vindication of the People, etc. Lond., 1821. 8vo. 2d Ed. Pamphleteer, Vol. 19.

CHRISTIE, Jonathan H. Letter to Hon. Robt. Peel, on the Laws of Real Property. Lond., 1827. 8vo. Law Pamph. Vol. 19.

CHRISTIE, Robt. Hist. of the late Province of Lower Canada, Parliamentary and Political. Quebec, 1848–53. 4 vols. 12mo.

—— Military and Naval Operations in the Canadas from 1807 to 1815. Quebec, 1818. 12mo.

CHRISTY, David. Cotton is King; or the Culture of Cotton and its Relation to Agriculture, etc. Cincin., 1855. 12mo.

CHRONICA Jocelini de Brakelonda. See Camden Scc. Publica.

CHRONICLE of Calais. See Camden Soc. Publica.

CHRONICLES of Casco Bay. Portland, 1850. 8vo. Maine Hist. Discourses, etc. Vol. 2.

—— ot the Great Rebellion. 1860–65. Phila., 1867. 8vo.

CHRONICON Monasterri de Bello numc primum Typis Mandatum. Lond., 1846. 8vo.

CHRONOLOG. Hist. of the Currency. From De Bow's Review, June, 1848. Banking and Currency Pamph. Vol. 3.

CHRONOLOGY. See HOLGATE, J. B. Chronolog. View of the World.

—— LEE, Noah. Chronol. of Christian Era.

—— London Chronolog. Institute.

—— MUNSELL, J. Everyday Book of.

—— PUTNAM, G. P. World's Progress.

CHUKRUBURTEE, T. Dictionary in Bengalee and English. Calcutta, 1827. 12mo.

CHURCH, Benjamin. History of King Philip's Indian War, with Notes by H. M. Dexter. Part 1. Boston, 1865. 4to.

CHURCH Educa. Directory for 1852. Lond. 8vo. Educa. Pamph. Vol. 29.

—— Establishments. See HULL, Wm.

—— —— See SPENCE, Jas.

—— Extension in the Diocese of London. Lond., 1853. 8vo. Eng. Religious Pamph. Vol. 91.

—— History. See BURNAP, G. W. Lectures on Hist. of Christianity.

—— —— D'AUBIGNE, J. H. M. Hist. of Reformation.

—— —— DUDLEY, D. Hist. of Council of Nice.

—— —— Eccles. Hist. of Mass.

—— —— MATHER, C. Magnalia Christi Americana.

—— —— MOSHEIM, John L. Compend of Ch. Hist.

—— —— SPENCER, J. A. Hist. of Reforma. in England.

—— —— SUICERI, J. H. Henrici Alting. Theologi, etc.

—— —— Testimony of the Fathers.

—— —— Baptist, Congrega., and other churches.

CHURCH, J. A. Mining School in the U. S. N. Y., 1871. 8vo. Educa. Pamph. Vol. 5.

CHURCH, Sam'l. Hist. Address at the 100th Annivers. of the 1st Ann. Town Meeting of Salisbury, Conn., Oct. 20, 1841. N. Haven, 1842. 8vo. Conn. Hist. Discourses, Vol. 7.

CHURCH, S. E. Speech at Batavia, Oct. 13, 1863. Rebell'n Pamph. Vol. 37.

CHURCH, Thos. History of Philip's Indian War, or the Great Indian War of 1675–6, with Notes by S. G. Drake. 2d Ed. Exeter, N. H., 1829. 12mo.

CHURCHILL, A. & J. Collection of Voyages and Travels; some now first printed from Original Manuscripts. Lond., 1704. 4 Vols. Folio.

CHURCHILL, John, Duke of Marlborough. See BUSH, Rev. R. W. England's two Great Captains.

CHURCHILL, J. Francis. Cause and Treatment of Pulmonary Phthisis. N. Y. 8vo. Med. Pamph. Vol. 1.

CHURCHMAN'S Year Book, for the Years 1870, '71, compiled by Dr. Wm. S. Perry. Hartford. 12mo. 2 vols.

CHURCH (The) Register. Vol. 2, 1868–9. Vol. 3, 1869–70. Nos. 1 and 5 wanting. Vol. 4, 1870–71. Vol. 5, 1871–72. Imperfect. Milwaukee, 1868–72. 8vo.

CHURCHWELL, Wm. M. Speech in Cong., Mar. 30, 1852, on the Homestead Bill. Congr. and Polit. Pamph. Vol. 83.

CHUTER vs. Bunn: Trial for Recovery of Amount of Guarantee. Lond., 1805. 8vo. Misc. Tracts, Vol. 2.

CHYMIE Hydraulique, pour Extraire les Sels Essentiels des Vegetaux Animaux et Mineraux, avec l'eau Pure. Paris, 1745. 18mo.

CIBBER, Colley. The Egotist; or, His own Picture Retouched. Lond., 1743. 8vo. Eng. Misc. Pamph. Vol. 23.

—— Two Letters to Mr. Pope. Lond., 1742, 1744. 8vo. Eng. Misc. Pamph. Vol. 23.

CIBOLA—"Seven Cities of." See SIMPSON, J. H. Coronado's March, 1530.

CICERO. Thoughts of Cicero on Religion, Man, Conscience, etc. Lond., 1773. 8vo. Eng. Misc. Pamph. Vol. 21.

CIESZKOWSKI, Aug. De la Pairie et de L'Aristocratie Moderne. Paris, 1844. 8vo. Strangford Pamph. Vol. 38.

CILGERRAN, Wales. See PHILLIPS, J. R. Hist. of, 1867.

CINCINNATI, O. Abstract of Laws regulating Municipal Elections. Cincin., 1859. 8vo. Cincin. Misc. Pamph. Vol. 1.

—— and Baltimore R. R. Co. Prospectus, 1869. 8vo. Ohio Misc. Pamph. Vol. 2.

—— Astronom. Soc. See ADAMS, J. Q. MANSFIELD, E. D.

—— —— Proceedings in Commem. of Prof. O. M. Mitchel. Cincin., 1862. 8vo. Cincin. Misc. Pamph. Vol. 1.

—— Auditor. 6th and 18th Ann. Reports on Receipts and Expenditures of Cincin. Cincin., 1859, 1871. 8vo.

—— Black Brigade. See CLARK, P. H. Hist. of.

—— —— Enrollment and Report of, 1864. Reb. Pamph. Vol. 48.

—— Board of Trade. Semi-Ann. Reports for 1868–9. 8vo.

—— —— Report of Comm. on Railroads, on the Cincin. and Chattanooga R. R. Co. Cincin., 1870. 8vo. Cincin. Pamph. Vol. 1.

—— —— Report of Comm. on River Navigation, on the Louisville Canal and Cincin. Bridge. Cincin., 1870. 8vo. Cincin. Pamph. Vol. 1.

—— Celebra. of the 45th Annivers. of the 1st Settlement of Cincin. and the Miami Country. Cincin., 1834. 8vo. Ohio Local Hist. Vol. 2.

—— Cemetery of Spring Grove. Reports, Forms, etc. Cincin., 1862. 8vo.

—— Chamber of Commerce. Review of the Trade and Commerce for 1850, '51, '52, '53,

—— —— Ann. Statements for 1855, '58.

—— —— Ann. Review of Commerce for 1865.

—— —— Ann. Report for 1866. Cincin., 1850—66. 8vo.

—— —— Memorial to Cong., on Bridging the Ohio and Mississipi Rivers. Cincin., 1868. 8vo. Cincin. Pamph. Vol. 1.

—— See Cist, C. Cincin. Miscellany.

—— —— Sketches and Statistics of.

—— CLARK, Jos. Plants in Vicinity of.

—— Coll. of Medicine and Surgery. Announcement for 1855–6. Cincin. 8vo.

—— Commercial Advertiser, Newspaper. Cincin., 1844–53. 2 Vols. Folio.

—— Common Schools. Report of Supt. on Organiza. of Grammar Schools, 1854.

—— —— Report of the Trustees and Visitors, June, 1856.

—— —— Report of Special Comm. of Board of Educa. on the University Project, 1869.

—— —— 40th and 41st Ann. Reports of the Board, 1869, '70.

—— Directories, 1819, 1849—1861. Cincin., 1819 1849–61. 11 vols. 8vo.

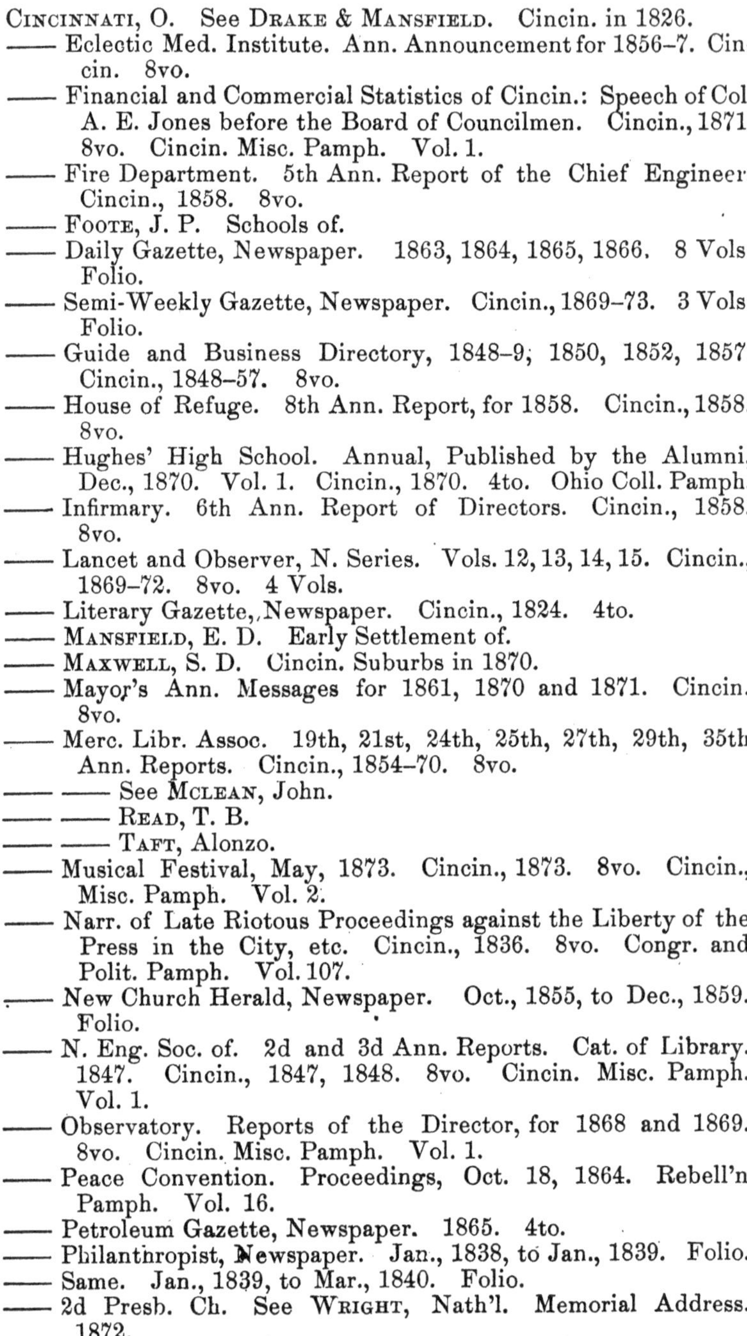

CINCINNATI, O. See DRAKE & MANSFIELD. Cincin. in 1826.
—— Eclectic Med. Institute. Ann. Announcement for 1856–7. Cincin. 8vo.
—— Financial and Commercial Statistics of Cincin.: Speech of Col. A. E. Jones before the Board of Councilmen. Cincin., 1871. 8vo. Cincin. Misc. Pamph. Vol. 1.
—— Fire Department. 5th Ann. Report of the Chief Engineer. Cincin., 1858. 8vo.
—— FOOTE, J. P. Schools of.
—— Daily Gazette, Newspaper. 1863, 1864, 1865, 1866. 8 Vols. Folio.
—— Semi-Weekly Gazette, Newspaper. Cincin., 1869–73. 3 Vols. Folio.
—— Guide and Business Directory, 1848–9, 1850, 1852, 1857. Cincin., 1848–57. 8vo.
—— House of Refuge. 8th Ann. Report, for 1858. Cincin., 1858. 8vo.
—— Hughes' High School. Annual, Published by the Alumni, Dec., 1870. Vol. 1. Cincin., 1870. 4to. Ohio Coll. Pamph.
—— Infirmary. 6th Ann. Report of Directors. Cincin., 1858. 8vo.
—— Lancet and Observer, N. Series. Vols. 12, 13, 14, 15. Cincin., 1869–72. 8vo. 4 Vols.
—— Literary Gazette, Newspaper. Cincin., 1824. 4to.
—— MANSFIELD, E. D. Early Settlement of.
—— MAXWELL, S. D. Cincin. Suburbs in 1870.
—— Mayor's Ann. Messages for 1861, 1870 and 1871. Cincin. 8vo.
—— Merc. Libr. Assoc. 19th, 21st, 24th, 25th, 27th, 29th, 35th Ann. Reports. Cincin., 1854–70. 8vo.
—— —— See MCLEAN, John.
—— —— READ, T. B.
—— —— TAFT, Alonzo.
—— Musical Festival, May, 1873. Cincin., 1873. 8vo. Cincin., Misc. Pamph. Vol. 2.
—— Narr. of Late Riotous Proceedings against the Liberty of the Press in the City, etc. Cincin., 1836. 8vo. Congr. and Polit. Pamph. Vol. 107.
—— New Church Herald, Newspaper. Oct., 1855, to Dec., 1859. Folio.
—— N. Eng. Soc. of. 2d and 3d Ann. Reports. Cat. of Library. 1847. Cincin., 1847, 1848. 8vo. Cincin. Misc. Pamph. Vol. 1.
—— Observatory. Reports of the Director, for 1868 and 1869. 8vo. Cincin. Misc. Pamph. Vol. 1.
—— Peace Convention. Proceedings, Oct. 18, 1864. Rebell'n Pamph. Vol. 16.
—— Petroleum Gazette, Newspaper. 1865. 4to.
—— Philanthropist, Newspaper. Jan., 1838, to Jan., 1839. Folio.
—— Same. Jan., 1839, to Mar., 1840. Folio.
—— 2d Presb. Ch. See WRIGHT, Nath'l. Memorial Address. 1872.

CINCINNATI Public Library. Catalogue. Cincin., 1871. 8vo.
—— —— 4th and 5th Ann. Reports. Cincin., 1871–72. 8vo.
—— See PURCELL, Archbishop. Silver Jubilee. 1858.
—— Record of the Distribution and Sale of Lots in the Town of Losantiville. Cincin., 1788–90. Cincin., 1870. 8vo. Ohio Hist. Discourses, etc. Vol. 2.
—— Southern Railway. Memorial of Trustees, and Speech of John C. Breckinridge in Ky. Gen. Assem. (n. p.) 1871. 8vo. Cincin. Misc. Pamph. Vol. 1.
—— —— The Ferguson Railway Act, Proceedings of Citizens, City Council, etc. Cincin., 1869. 8vo. Cincin. Misc. Pamph. Vol. 1.
—— See STEVENS, G. E. Summary of its Advantages, etc.
—— —— The Queen City, in 1869.
—— Superior Court. J. Bryant Walker *vs.* The Southern Railway, etc. Cincin., 1870. 8vo. Cincin. Misc. Pamph. Vol. 1.
—— —— Case of Habeas Corpus, *ex parte* Wm. Childs. 1851. Law Pamph. Vol. 9.
—— See TAFT, A. Railroads of.
—— Theolog. and Religious Library Assoc. 1st, 2d, 4th and 5th Ann. Reports of Directors. 1865–68. 8vo.
—— Times, Newspaper. Oct., 1840, to Oct., 1841. Folio. 2 Vols.
—— University of. By-Laws of Board of Directors. Cincin., 1871. 8vo. Report of Comm. on Reorganization, etc. (n. d.) 8vo.
—— —— See TAFT, A. Lecture on. 1872.
—— Wesleyan Female Coll. Catalogues. 1843–1862. 8vo.
—— Wholesale Business Directory for 1853. Cincin., 1853. 8vo.
CINCINNATUS, (The). Devoted to Scientific Agriculture, Horticulture, Education, etc. Cincin., 1857–60. 5 Vols. 8vo.
CIRENCESTER, Eng. Hist. of the Town of. Cirencester, 1833. 8vo. 3d Ed.
CIST, Chas. Cincinnati in 1841; its Early Annals and Future Prospects. Cincin., 1841. 12mo.
—— Cincinnati Miscellany; or Antiquities of the West. Cincin., 1845. 8vo.
—— Sketches and Statistics of Cincin. in 1851. Cincin., 1851. 12mo.
—— Same, in 1859. Cincin., 1859. 12mo.
CITIZEN of Nature; Letters from an American Indian to his Friend at Home. Lond., 1824. 12mo.
—— (The) Soldiers at North Point and Fort McHenry, Sept. 12 and 13, 1814. Baltimore (n. d.) 8vo.
CITIZENSHIP. See AYDELOTT, Rev. B. P. Address. 1840.
—— BATES, Edw. What Constitutes Citizenship?
—— THAYER, M. R. Address. 1862.
CIVIL ENGINEERING. See BLAKE, W. P. Report to Paris Exposition.
—— —— See Chicago R. R. Gazette.
—— Service of the U. S. From the N. Amer. Rev., Oct., 1867. Boston. 8vo. Congr. and Polit. Pamph. Vol. 72.
—— —— See JENCKS, M. Report on. 1868.

CIVIL Service Reform. See CLARKE, C. C. P. Commonwealth Reconstructed. 1872.

—— —— —— See Congress'l Speeches.

—— —— —— From the N. Y. Times, Dec. 3, 1870. Congr. and Polit. Pamph. Vol. 129.

—— —— —— From the Penn. Monthly. Phila., 1870. 8vo. Congr. and Polit. Pamph. Vol. 120.

—— —— —— See FISHER, J. F. Degradation of the Representative System.

—— —— —— Report of the Commission Appointed to Devise Rules, etc., for the Reform of the Civil Service. Washington, 1871. 8vo. Congr. and Polit. Pamph. Vol. 138.

—— —— —— See ROSENGARTEN, J. G.

CIVIL War; its Causes, Consequences, Crimes, and Compromises. 1861. Rebell'n Pamph. Vol. 76.

CIVILIZATION. See BUCKLE, H. T. Hist. of—in England.

—— CROWLEY, E. Art no Evidence of.

—— DEAN, A. Hist. of.

—— Lecture on the Origin of. 1854. Lond., (n. d.) 12mo. Eng. Misc. Pamph. Vol. 36.

—— LUBBOCK, Sir J. Origin of.

—— Mordacque, L. H. Names, etc., in Connection with.

CLAGETT, Wm. H. Speech in Cong., Jan. 28 and 29, 1873, on the Utah Bill. Washington, 1873. 8vo. Congr. and Polit. Pamph. Vol. 68.

CLAGETT WYSEMAN. See ATHERTON, C. H. Memoir of.

CLAIMS against the Gov't of the U. S.; Laws and Information Relating to. Congr. and Polit. Pamph. Vol. 76.

—— of American Citizens on the U. S. Gov't for French Spoliations. Baltimore, 1826. 8vo. Congr. and Polit. Pamph. Vol. 54.

—— of Loyal Citizens of the South. See Congress. Speeches.

—— of U. S. against G. Britain. Corres. Relating to. Washington, 1869. 5 Vols. 8vo.

CLAIRBORNE, J. F. H. Life and Corres. of Gen. John A. Quitman. N. Y., 1860. 12mo. 2 Vols.

CLANCARTY, Earl of. Objections to the Oath of Supremacy; Corres. with J. Napier. Dublin, 1851. 8vo. Strangford Pamph. Vol. 61.

CLAP, Otis. Letter to Abbott Lawrence and Robt. G. Shaw on the Present Condition and Future Growth of Boston. Boston, 1853. 8vo. Boston Misc. Pamph. Vol. 2.

CLAP, Roger. See Dorchester Antiq. Soc. Coll. Vol. 1.

CLAREMONT, N. H. War Hist. See WAITE, O. F. R.

CLARENDON, Earl. Hist. of the Rebellion and Civil Wars in England. Oxford, 1839. 7 Vols. 12mo.

—— Speech in the House of Lords, on Recent Communications with the French Gov't, Mar. 1, 1858. Lond. 8vo. Eng. Polit. Pamph. Vol. 56.

CLARION Co., Penn. Pocket Map of. (n. d.)

CLARK, Rev. Alex. The Unavailing Cry; a Sermon for the Times. Phila., 1863. 8vo. Rebellion Pamph. Vol. 70.

CLARK, Dr. Andrew. Observations on the Anatomy of the Skin of a Species of Muraena. Lond. (n. d.) 8vo. Med. Pamph. Vol. 14.

CLARK, Chas. John Noakes and Mary Styles; a Poem in the Essex Dialect. Lond., 1839. 12mo.

CLARK, C. C. P. Nova Instauratio Republicae: The Commonwealth Reconstructed. Oswego, 1872. 8vo. Congr. and Polit. Pamph. Vol. 68.

—— True Method of Representation in Large Constituencies. N. Y., 1873. 8vo. Congr. and Polit. Pamph. Vol. 140.

CLARK, Daniel. Speech in U. S. Senate, Feb. 14, 1866, on Suffrage for Loyal Black men. Congr. and Polit. Pamph. Vol. 137. Rebell'n Pamph. Vol. 34.

CLARK, Rev. Dorus. Fugitives from the Escritoire of a Retired Editor. Boston, 1864. 12mo.

CLARK, Rev. E. B. Centen. Disc. before the 1st Cong. Ch. in Chicopee, Mass., Sept. 26, 1852. Springfield, 1852. 8vo. Mass. Hist. Discourses. Vol. 11.

CLARK Geneal. See CLARK, John, and CLARKE, S. C.

CLARK, George. Voyage to America. See O'CALLAGHAN, E. B.

CLARK, Rev. Geo. F. An Enemy in Camp. Letter to the Officers and Privates of the Union Army. Boston, 1864. 12mo. Temp. Pamph. Vol. 3.

—— Hist. of Norton, Bristol Co., Mass., 1669–1859. Boston, 1859. 12mo.

CLARK, Gen. Geo. Rogers. See REYNOLDS, John. Sketch of Life of.

—— Sketch of his Campaign in the Illinois in 1778–9, including Maj. Bowman's Journ. of the taking of St. Vincent. Cincinnati, 1869. 8vo.

CLARK, Henry. Address before the Vt. Hist. Soc., July 7, 1859, on the 82d Annivers. of the Battle of Hubbardton. Rutland, 1859. 8vo. Vt. Hist. Soc. Addresses. Vol. 1.

CLARK, Henry G. Address before Suffolk Dist. Med. Soc., April 24, 1832. Boston, 1852. 8vo. Med. Pamph. Vols. 2 and 31.

CLARK, John. Ill News from N. England; or a Narrative of N. England's Persecution. 1652. Mass. Hist. Soc. Coll. 4th Ser. Vol. 2.

—— Record of Descendants of Hugh Clarke, of Watertown, Mass., 1640–1860. Boston, 1866. 8vo.

CLARK, Rev. Joseph. Hist. Disc. at Plymouth, Mass., May 10, 1855. Boston, 1855. 8vo. Mass. Hist. Discourses. Vol. 5.

—— Hist. and Theory of Revolutions. Phila., 1862. 8vo. Rebellion Pamph. Vol. 3.

CLARK, Jos. Cat. of Flowering Plants and Ferns, in the Vicinity of Cincin. Cincin., 1852. 12mo. Cincin. Misc. Pamph. Vol. 1.

—— Diary when in the Continental Army, from May, 1778, to Nov., 1779. N. J. Hist. Soc. Proceed. Vol. 7.

CLARK, J. H. Sight and Hearing; how Preserved, and how Lost. N. Y., 1856. 12mo.

—— The Iron-Hearted Regiment; or 115th Reg't of N. Y. Albany, 1865. 12mo.

CLARK, J. V. H. Lights and Lines of Indian Character, and Scenes of Pioneer Life. Syracuse, 1854. 12mo.

—— Onondaga; or Reminiscences of Earlier and Later Times; Historical Sketches relative to Onondaga. Syracuse, 1849. 2 Vols. 8vo.

CLARK, P. H. The Black Brigade of Cincin., O., with a Muster Roll of its Members. Cincin., 1864. 8vo.

CLARK, Rufus W. Address at the Commencement of Albany Med. Coll., May 28, 1863. Albany, 1863. 8vo. Addresses. Vol. 16.

—— Disc. before the Soc. for the Prevention of Pauperism, Boston, Jan. 8, 1854. Boston, 1854. 8vo. Addresses, Vol. 26.

—— Disc. Commem. of Heroes of Albany, Fallen during the Present War. Albany, 1864. 8vo. Rebell'n Pamph. Vol. 8.

—— Review of Rev. Moses Stuart's Pamphlet on Slavery. Boston, 1850. 8vo. Congr. and Polit. Pamph. Vol. 85.

CLARK, Sam'l. Narrative of the Signal Judgment upon the Papists in Black Friers, Lond., 1623. Lond., Reprinted, 1817. 4to. Eng. Religious Pamph. Vol. 38.

CLARK, S. A. History of St. John's Ch., Elizabeth, N. J. Phila., 1857. 12mo.

CLARK, Dr. Wm. C. The Schoolmaster; his Past, his Present, and his Future. Lond., 1859. 12mo. Educa. Pamph. Vol. 38.

CLARK, Wm. T. Speech in Congress, Feb. 8, 1871, on National Educa. 8vo. Congr. and Polit. Pamph. Vol. 119.

CLARKE, Edw. D. Travels in Various Countries of Europe, Asia and Africa, commencing Jan. 1, 1801. Part 1. Russia, Tartary and Turkey. Part 2. Greece, Egypt, and the Holy Land. N. Y., 1813. 2 Vols. 8vo.

CLARKE, Geo. R. Diplomatic Relations with Rome a Departure from the Act of Settlement. Lond., 1848. 8vo. Strangford Pamph. Vol. 48.

—— Observa. on the Socinian Endowment Bill, or Dissenters Chapels Bill. Lond., 1844. 8vo. Strangford Pamph. Vol. 35.

CLARKE, Rev. J. B. B. Remarks on Dr. Hook's Letter on a State Provision for Gen. Education. Lond., 1846. 8vo. Educa. Pamph. Vol. 32.

CLARKE, Jas. Freeman. Disc. concerning Theo. Parker, at Boston, June 3, 1860. Boston, 1860. 8vo. Sermons. Vol. 31.

—— Discourse on the Rendition of Anthony Burns. Boston, 1854. 8vo. Congr. and Polit. Pamph. Vol. 102.

CLARKE, J. H. Speech in U. S. Senate, Feb. 9, 1852, on Non-Intervention. Congr. and Polit. Pamph. Vol. 83.

CLARKE, Rev. Liscombe. Letter to H. Brougham on Winchester College. Lond., 1818. 8vo. Eng. Misc. Pamph. Vol. 27.

CLARKE, Mrs. M. A. Letter to the Hon. Wm. Fitzgerald. Lond., 1813. 8vo. Eng. Polit. Pamph. Vol. 31.

CLARKE, Manlius Stimson. See HUNTINGTON, Rev. F. D.

CLARKE, Dr. Sam'l. See Collection (A) of Queries, etc.

CLARKE, S. C. Record of Descendants of Thos. Clarke of Plymouth, Mass., 1623—1697; of Wm. Curtiss of Roxbury, 1632; of Rich'd Hull of N. Haven, 1639—1662, and of John Fuller, of Newtown, Mass., 1644–98. Boston, 1869. 8vo.

CLARKE, S C. Record of Descendants of John Fuller, of Newtown, Mass., 1644–98. Boston, 1869. 8vo. Genealog. Pamph. Vol. 2.

—— Record of Descendants of Richard Hull, of N. Haven, Ct., 1639–62. Boston, 1869. 8vo. Genealog. Pamph. Vol. 2.

CLARKE, Sidney. Remonstrance against the Treaty with the Osage Indians. Washington, 1868. 8vo. Indian Pamph. Vol. 4.

CLARKE, Thos. A. Essay on the Defence of Prisoners by Counsel. Lond., 1833. 12mo. Law Pamph. Vol. 10.

CLARKE, Thos. Brooke. Essay on the Powers of Parliament, the Right of Making Laws, etc. Dublin, 1781. 12mo. Eng. Polit. Pamph. Vol. 19.

CLARKE, Rev. Walter. Half Century Disc.—The 1st Ch. in Buffalo. Feb. 3, 1862. Buffalo, 1863. 8vo.

—— Oration July 4, 1862, at Buffalo, N. Y. Rebell'n Pamph. Vol. 100.

CLARKE, Capt. Wm. See LEWIS, Capt. M., and.

CLARKSFIELD, Ohio. See BARNUM, E. M. Memoirs of.

—— BENSON, B. Sketch of, 1858.

CLARKSON, Thos. Abolition of the African Slave Trade by the British Parliament. Abridged. Augusta, Me., 1830. 2 Vols. 18mo.

—— Not a Laborer Wanted for Jamaica, etc.; with Acc. of the Slave Trade. Lond., 1842. 8vo. Strangford Pamph. Vol. 30.

CLARKSON, Wm. Inquiry into the Cause of the Increase of Pauperism and Poor Rates. Lond., 1816. 8vo. Pamphleteer. Vol. 8.

CLASSIC and Historic Portraits. See BRUCE, J.

CLASSICAL (The) Journal, March, 1810, to Dec., 1829. Lond. 40 Vols. 8vo.

—— Literature. See ESCHENBURG, J. J. Manual of.

CLASSICS, Study of the. From De Bow's Review, 1861. Educa. Pamph. Vol. 7.

CLAUSSEN, Chevalier. The Flax Movement; its National Importance, etc. Lond. n. d. 8vo. Agr. Pamph. Vol. 9.

CLAVERACK, N. Y. See ZABRISKIE, F. N. Hist. of Dutch Ref. Ch.

CLAVERHOUSE. See GRAHAM, John. Memoirs of.

CLAVIS Poetica, Antiquae Linguae, Septentrionalis. Hafnae, 1864. 8vo.

CLAY, Cassius M. Address before Wis. State Agr. Soc., Oct., 1858. Transactions. 1858.

—— Speech at Washington Aug. 12, 1863, on our Relations with Foreign Powers. Rebell'n Pamph. Vol. 54.

—— Speech before the Law Department of Univers. of Albany, N. Y., Feb. 3, 1863. N. Y., 1863. 8vo. Addresses, etc. Vol. 21.

—— Writings of; including Speeches and Addresses, with a Memoir by Horace Greeley. N. Y., 1848. 8vo.

CLAY, Henry against Frontier Settlers. (Political Tract.) (n. d.) Congr. and Polit. Pamph. Vol. 69.

—— and the Administration; a Tract for the Times. Phila., 1850. 8vo. Congr. and Polit. Pamph. Vols. 100 and 104.

CLAY, Henry, and the Laboring Millions. (Political Tract.) (n. d.) 8vo. Congr. and Polit. Pamph. Vol. 69.
—— See BRECKINRIDGE, R. J. Oration on.
—— COLTON, C. Last Seven Years of his Life.
—— —— Life and Times of.
—— —— Private Corres. of.
—— Fifty Reasons why the Hon. H. Clay should be elected Prest. of the U. S. Baltimore, 1844. 8vo. Congr. and Polit. Pamph. Vol. 58.
—— See JACKSON, A. Letter to Carter Beverly, etc.
—— LATHROP, J. H. Eulogy on.
—— Lecture on the Present Crisis. at N. Y., Dec. 16, 1860, Mrs. C. and N. Hatch, Medium, Rebell'n Pamph. Vol. 31.
—— Life and Speeches. N. Y., 1842. 2 Vols. 8vo.
—— See Madison, Wis. Proceed. on Death of.
—— N. Y. City. Funeral Obsequies.
—— N. Y. State Auxiliary Monument Assoc.
—— Obit. Addresses on his Death, at Washington, June 30, 1852. Washington, 1852. 8vo.
—— See PRENTICE, G. D. Biog. of.
—— SARGENT, E. Life and Pub. Services of.
—— Speech in U. S. Senate, Dec. 26 and 30, 1833, on the Removal of the Deposits. Washington, 1833. 8vo. Speeches. Vol. 4.
—— Speech in U. S. Senate, Feb. 19, 1838, on U. S. Banks. Congr. and Polit. Pamph. Vol. 24.
—— Speech in U. S Senate, Mar. 1, 1842, on the Tariff. Washington, 1842. 8vo. Congr. and Polit. Pamph. Vol. 24.
—— Speeches in U. S. Senate, Jan. 29, Feb. 5 and 6, and July 22, 1850, on Compromise Bill. Congr. and Pol. Pam. Vol. 94.
CLAY, John. Free Trade Necessary to the Welfare of G. B. Lond., 1820. 8vo. Pamphleteer, Vol. 17.
CLAY Monument Assoc. Ceremonies at Laying the Corner Stone of the Nat. Monument to Henry Clay, near Lexington, with Dr. Breckinridge's Oration. Cincin., 1857. 8vo. Kentucky Misc. Pamph. Vol. 1.
CLAYTON-Bulwer Treaty. See Congress. Speeches.
CLAYTON, John. Letter to the Roy. Soc., 1688, respecting Virginia. See Force's Hist. Tracts, Vol. 3.
CLAYTON, J. M. See Addresses in Cong., on his Death.
—— Speech in U. S, Senate, Feb. 8, 1836, on National Defence. Congr. and Polit. Pamph. Vol. 90.
—— Speech in U. S. Senate, Apr. 23 and 24, 1846, on French Spoliations. Congr. and Polit. Pamph. Vol. 84.
—— Speech in U. S. Senate, Mar. 1 and 2, 1852, on the Kansas and Nebr. Bill. Congr. and Polit. Pamph. Vol. 92.
—— Speech in U. S. Senate, Mar. 17 and 19, 1856, on the Cent. Amer. Treaty. Congr. and Polit. Pamph. Vol. 83.
—— Speeches in U. S. Senate, Mar. 31, and Apr. 1, 1856, on Naval Affairs. Congr. and Polit. Pamph. Vol. 90.
—— and Others. Speeches in U. S. Senate, Jan. 26, 1855, on Claimants of the Brig, Gen. Armstrong. Congr. and Polit. Pamph. Vol. 90.

CLAXTON, Tim. Concise Decimal Tables for Facilitating Arithmetical Calculations. Boston, 1830. 8vo. Scientific Pamph. Vol. 17.

CLAYPOOLE, S. Amer. Daily Advertiser, Newspaper. Jan. to Dec. 1797. Folio.

CLEARFIELD Coal and Lumber Co. 1st Ann. Report, 1856. Phila., 1856. 8vo. Penn. Misc. Pamph. Vol. 2.

CLEAVELAND, Nehemiah. Address at Topsfield, Mass., Aug. 28, 1850, the 200th Anniversary of the Town. N. Y., 1851. 8vo.

CLEAVELAND, Parker. See WOODS, Rev. Dr. Eulogy on.

CLELAND, Rev. Thos. See Humphrey, E. P. Memoirs of.

CLEMENS, J. Speech in U. S. Senate, Dec. 24, 1851, on the Compromise. Congr. and Polit. Pamph. Vol. 94.

CLEMENS, Orion. City of Keokuk in 1856, with a Sketch of the Black Hawk War. Keokuk, 1856. 8vo.

CLEMENS, S. Speech in Cong., Jan. 22, 1861, on Slavery. Congr. and Polit. Pamph. Vol. 85.

CLEMENT, J. Memoir of Adoniram Judson; being a Sketch of his Life and Missionary Labors. N. Y., 1858. 12mo.

—— Noble Deeds of Amer. Women, with Biograph. Sketches. N. Y., 1858. 12mo.

CLENDENNING, John. Observa. on the History of Poison. Lond., 1830. 8vo. Strangford Pamph. Vol. 11.

CLERGY (The) and Homœopathy. Errors of the Clergy in Advocating the Doctrine of Hahnemann. Lond., 1853. 8vo. Med. Pamph. Vol. 22.

CLERK, D. J. Dissertatio de Stylis Veterum, et Diversis Chartarum Generibus. n. d. 4to.

—— Dissertatio de Monumentis quibusdam Romanis, in Boreali Magnae Brittaniae Parte, detectis Anno, 1731. Edinburgh, 1750. 4to.

CLEVELAND, Mr. —. Life and Adventures of Mr. Cleveland, Natural Son of Oliver Cromwell. Written by himself. 2d Ed. Lond., 1741. 3 Vols. 12mo.

CLEVELAND, Charles D. Compendium of Amer. Literature; with Biograph. Sketches. Phila., 1858. 8vo.

—— Compendium of Eng. Literature, from Sir John Mandeville to Wm. Cowper. Phila., 1848 and 1858. 8vo.

—— Eng. Literature of the 19th Century. Phila., 1853. 12mo.

CLEVELAND, C. F. Speech in Cong., Apr. 1, 1852, on the Homestead Bill. Congr. and Polit. Pamph. Vol. 83.

CLEVELAND, Rev. Edw. Sketch of the Early Settlement and History of Shipton, Canada East. 1858. 12mo.

CLEVELAND, Mrs. E. H., M. D. Introduct. Lecture to the Class of the Female Med. Coll. of Penn, for 1858–9. Phila., 1858. 8vo. Med. Pamph. Vol. 33.

CLEVELAND, Henry. Alex. H. Stephens in Public and Private; with Letters and Speeches before, during, and since the War. Phila., 1866. 8vo.

CLEVELAND, Henry R. Life of Henry Hudson. Spark. Amer. Biog. 1st Ser. Vol. 10.

CLEVELAND, John. Poems by J. C., with Additions never before Printed. Lond., 1657. 12mo.

—— Clevelandi Vindiciae. Lond., 1677. 12mo.

CLEVELAND, O., and W. Virginia Oil & Mining Co. Circular, 1865. Cleveland, 1865. 8vo. Ohio Misc. Pamph. Vol. 2.

—— Columbus, and Cincinnati, R. R. See WILLIAMS, C. Report on Prelim. Surveys, etc., 1846.

—— Ann. Statement of Trade and Commerce, 1866. Cleveland, 1867. 8vo.

—— as a Naval Depot. Report of Comm. of Citizens, 1863? 8vo.

—— Board of Educa. Report for 1858–9. Cleveland, 1860. 8vo.

—— Directory, including Ohio City, for 1837. Cleveland, 1837. 12mo.

—— 1st Presb. Ch. Manual of. Cleveland, 1842. 12mo. Ohio Hist. Discourses, etc. Vol. 2.

—— Med. Coll. Catalogue for 1853–4. Cleveland. 8vo.

—— True Democrat. See BRADBURN, G.

—— WHITTLESEY, C. Early Hist. of.

—— —— Location, Settlement and Progress of. 1843.

—— —— Sketch of. 1842.

CLEWS, Henry. Our Monetary Evils; Suggestions for their Remedy. N. Y., 1872. 8vo. Congr. and Polit. Pamph. Vol. 68.

CLIFFORD, Alfred. Letter on the Exclusion of Attorneys from the Inner Temple. Lond., 1821. 8vo. Eng. Polit. Pamph. Vol. 35.

CLIFFORD, Nathan. Speech in Cong., Apr. 28, 1842, on Apportionment. Washington, 1842. 8vo. Congr. and Polit. Pamph. Vol. 25.

—— Speech in Cong., July 11, 1842, on the Tariff. Washington, 1842. 8vo. Congr. and Polit. Pamph. Vol. 25.

CLIFFORD, Wm. Address to the Judges and Jurors Appointed to try Persons for Offences —— in G. B. Lond., 1832. 8vo. Law Pamph. Vol. 21.

CLINE, A. J. Secession Unmasked; an Appeal, etc. Rebellion Pamph. Vol. 85.

CLINGMAN, T. L. Speech in Cong., Aug. 21, 1852, on the Tariff. Congr. and Polit. Pamph. Vol. 92.

CLINTON, Chas. A. Biograph. Sketches of Clinton Family. N. Y., 1859. 8vo.

CLINTON, (Conn.) Cong. Church. 200th Annivers. of the Ch., held Nov. 13, 1867. N. Haven, 1868. 8vo. Conn. Hist. Discourses, etc. Vol. 7.

CLINTON, DeWitt. See CAMPBELL, W. W. Life and Writings of.

—— Disc. before N. Y. Hist. Soc., Dec. 6, 1811. N. Y., 1812. 8vo. N. Y. Hist. Soc. Addresses. Vol. 1. See also Collections. Vol. 2.

—— On certain Phenomena of the Great Lakes of America. N. Y., 1817. 4to. Scientific Pamph. Vol. 38.

—— Introduct. Disc. before the Literary and Philosoph. Soc. of N. Y., May 4, 1814. N. Y., 1815. 8vo. Scientific Pamph. Vol. 5.

—— See RENWICK, J. Life of.

CLINTON, DeWitt. Speech before N. Y. Legisla., Jan. 2, 1822. Congr. and Polit. Pamph. Vol. 89.
CLINTON, Geo. W. Address at the Closing of the N. Y. State Normal School, July 10, 1856. Albany, 1856. 8vo. Addresses. Vols. 8 and 16.
—— Address before the Buffalo Horticult. Soc., Sept. 3, 1845. Buffalo, 1846. 8vo. Agr. Pamph. Vol. 1.
—— Oration before Phi-Beta Kappa Soc. of Union Coll., July 21, 1857. Addresses. Vol. 6.
—— Paper before the Buffalo Hist. Soc., Dec. 5, 1870, on the late Com. Stephen Champlin.
—— Prelim. List of Plants of Buffalo, N. Y., and its Vicinity 1864. 8vo. Scientific Pamph. Vol. 16.
CLINTON Hall and Mercantile Libr. Associations. Celebration Commem. of the Removal of the Library to Astor Place, June 8, 1854, including Addresses of J. R. Brodhead and Gov. H. Seymour. N. Y., 1854. 8vo.
CLINTON, Sir Henry. Narrative Relative to his Conduct During his Command of Troops in N. America, in the Campaign of 1781. 6th Ed. Lond., 1783. 8vo.
CLINTON, Gen. Jas. See CAMPBELL, W. W. Life and Military Services of. 1839.
CLINTON River, Mich. Meeting of Citizens of Macomb County, at Mt. Clemens, Dec. 1, 1849., for the Improvement of the river. 8vo. Mich. Misc. Pamph. Vol. 1.
CLINTON, N. Y. See Hamilton College.
CLONCURRY, Valentine Lord. Personal Recollections and Correspondence. Dublin, 1849. 8vo.
CLOQUET, Jules. Recollections of the Private Life of Gen. Lafayette, with Illustrations. Lond., 1835. 8vo.
CLOUGH, Gibson. Journ. Report when on a Campaign against Canada, in 1759–60. Essex Institute Coll. Vol. 3.
CLOUGH, Rev. Simon. Acc. of the Christian Denom. in the U. S. Boston, 1827. 8vo. Sermons. Vol. 9.
CLOWNEY, William K. Speech in Cong., Feb. 26, 1834, on the Removal of the Deposits. Washington, 1834. 8vo. Speeches. Vol. 4.
CLUSERET, Gen. G. Mexico, and the Solidarity of Nations. N. Y., 1866. 8vo. 3d Ed.
CLUSKEY, M. W. Polit. Text Book, or Encyclopedia, for the Reference of Politicians and Statesmen of the U. S. 12th Ed. Phila., 1860. 8vo.
CLYMER, Hiester. Speech in Penn. Senate on Emancipation. 1862. Rebell'n Pamph. Vol. 32.
COAHOMA, Co., (Miss.) Massacre. See MEASON, C. F. H. Narrative. 1841.
COAL. See FYFE, A. Evaporating Power of.
—— Its Producers and Consumers. Pottsville, 1854. 8vo. Penn. Misc. Pamph. Vol. 2.
—— See JOHNSON, Walter R. Report on Amer. Coals. 1844.
—— NORWOOD, J. G., on Ill. Coal.

COAL Question, (The.) Review of Commiss'r Wells' Report on Coal. Phila., 1870. 8vo. Congr. and Polit. Pamph. Vol. 120.

—— See Statement of Facts on the Duty on Foreign Coal.

—— TAYLOR, R. C. Statistics of Coal.

—— WHITTLESEY, C. Origin of Mineral Coal.

COAST Survey (The American). Its Cost, Abuses and Power. From the N. Y. Times, Nov. 17, 1858. Congr. and Polit. Pamph. Vol. 125.

—— —— —— Reply to the Official Defence of its Cost, Abuses and Power. 1858. 8vo. Congr. and Polit. Pamph. Vol. 125.

—— —— See DAVIS, Lieut. C. H.

—— —— HASSLER, F. R. Papers Relating to.

—— —— Report of Amer. Assoc. for Advancement of Science on the Hist. and Progress of the Survey. 1858. Congr. and Polit. Pamph. Vol. 125.

—— —— Report from the House Comm. on the Coast Survey, 1843. Washington, 1843. 8vo. Coast Survey Misc. Reports.

—— —— Reports of Supt. of. See U. S. Sec. of Treasury.

COATES, Benj. Suggestions on Cotton Cultivation in Africa, in Reference to Slavery. Phila., 1858. 8vo. Congr. and Polit. Pamph. Vol. 125.

COATES, B. H. Biograph. Notice of Chas. Caldwell, M. D. Phila., 1855. 8vo. Addresses. Vol. 13.

—— Biograph. Sketch of the Late Thos. Say. Waldie's Circulating Libr. Vol. 5.

—— Disc. before the Hist. Soc. of Penn., April 24, 1834, on the Origin of the Indians. Penn. Hist. Soc. Memoirs. Vol. 3. Part 2.

—— Notice of Sam'l P. Griffitts, M. D. Penn. Hist. Soc. Memoirs. Vol. 2. Part 2.

COBB, Amasa. Speech in Cong., Mar. 2, 1868, on Impeachment of the President. Congr. and Polit. Pamph. Vol. 122.

COBB, Gen. David. See BAYLIES, Francis. Life and Character of.

COBB, Joseph B. Leisure Labors; or Miscellanies Historical, Literary and Political. N. Y., 1858. 12mo.

COBBETT, J. P., and DOUBLEDAY, Thos. Handy Book for Reformers, Containing Notes upon Duration of Parliament, Suffrage, etc. Lond., 1859. 8vo. Eng. Polit. Pamph. Vol. 57.

COBBETT, Wm. Brief Exposition of his Political Opinions. Lond., (n. d.) 12mo. Eng. Misc. Pamph. Vol. 4.

—— Gold Forever! Real Causes of the Fall of the Funds, etc. Lond., 1825. 12mo. Eng. Misc. Pamph. Vol. 4.

—— Hist. of the Amer. Jacobins, commonly denominated Democrats. Phila., 1796. 8vo. Congr. and Polit. Pamph. Vol. 95.

—— Letters on the Late War between the U. S. and G. B. N. Y., 1815. 8vo.

—— Life of Andrew Jackson, President of the U. S. Baltimore, 1834. 8vo. Congr. and Polit. Pamph. Vol. 111.

COBBETT, Wm. Life of, Written by Himself. Lond. (n. d.) 12mo. 7th Ed. Biograph. Pamph. Vol. 10.
—— A Peep into the Den of Sinecures, Pensions, and Grants. 1817. Eng. Polit. Pamph. Vol. 77.
—— Polit. Register, Newspaper. 1817–1821. Lond. 3 Vols. 8vo.
—— Porcupine's works, containing Various Writings and Selections, exhibiting a Faithful Picture of the U. S. of America. Lond., 1801. 12 Vols. 8vo.
—— The Queen's Answer to the Letter from the King to his People. From Cobbett's Register. Phila., 1821. 8vo. Eng. Polit. Pamph. Vol. 77.
COBBETT's Reasons for War against Russia in Defence of Turkey. Lond., 1854. 8vo. Strangford Pamph. Vol. 67.
COBURN, Rev. David N. Hist. Disc. at Ware, Mass., 1851, Commem. Disc. of the 1st Ch. in Ware, May 9, 1751. West Brookfield, 1851. 8vo. Mass. Hist. Discourses. Vol. 19.
COCHIN, M. Augustin. Acc. of the Reformatory Institution for Juvenile Offenders at Mettray, France. Lond., 1853. 8vo. Eng. Misc. Pamph. Vol. 18.
COCHRAN, A. W. Notes on Measures adopted by Gov't, between 1775 and 1786, to check the St. Paul's Bay Disease. Read before the Quebec Lit. and Hist. Soc'y, Mar. 6, 1841. Transactions, Vol. 4, Part 2.
COCHRANE, Lord. Calumnious Aspersions in regard to him Exposed and Refuted. Lond., 1814? 8vo. Eng. Misc. Pamph. Vol. 3.
—— Letter to Lord Ellenborough. Lond., 1815. 8vo. Eng Polit. Pamph. Vol. 32.
COCHRANE, Alex. B. Exeter Hall; or Church Polemics. Lond., 1841. 8vo. Strangford Pamph. Vol. 26.
—— Who are the Liberals? Lond., 1852. 8vo. Strangford Pamph. Vol. 63.
COCHRANE, Geo. On the Economy of the Law. Lond., 1855. 8vo. Law Pamph. Vol. 26.
COCK, Thos. Address before N. Y. Acad. of Medicine, Apr. 7, 1852. N. Y., 1852. Med. Pamph. Vol. 2.
COCKBURN, Lord. Life of Lord Jeffray; with a Selection from his Correspondence. Phila., 1857. 8vo.
COCKBURN, John. Narr. of Adventures among Spaniards in Amer. Lond., 1779. 8vo.
COCKE, Wm. A. Constitutional Hist. of the U. S., from the Adoption of the Articles of Confederation to the Close of Jackson's Administration. Vol. 1. Phila., 1858. 8vo.
CODMAN, John, D. D. See JENKS, Wm. Tribute to.
—— Sermon at Dorchester, Dec. 7, 1845, on the 37th Annivers. of his Ordination. Boston, 1846. 8vo. Mass. Hist. Discourses, Vol. 16.
—— See STORRS, Rev. R. S. Obit. Disc., 1847.
—— Address before the Special Comm. of House of Repr., of Navigation Interests, Mar. 19, 1870. Congr. and Polit. Pamph. Vol. 120.

CO-EDUCATION of the Sexes. From the Penn. School Journal, Sèpt., 1872. Educa. Pamph. Vol. 7.

—— —— From the Western Educa. Review, Mar., 1871, Educa. Pamph. Vol. 7.

COFFEE and the Coffee Trade. From De Bow's Review, Nov., 1846. Pamphlets. Vol. 14.

COFFIN, Chas. Life and Services of Maj. Gen. John Thomas. N. Y., 1844. 8vo. Biograph. Pamph. Vol. 1.

—— The Narragansett Townships. Maine Hist. Soc. Coll. Vol. 2.

COFFIN, Chas. C. Four Years of Fighting; a Volume of Personal Observation with the Army and Navy. Boston, 1866. 8vo.

COFFIN, Joshua. List of Descendants of Edw. Woodman, who settled in Newbury, Mass., 1635. Newburyport, 1855. 12mo. Genealog. Pamph. Vol. 11.

—— Sketch of the Hist. of Newbury, Newburyport, and West Newbury, from 1635 to 1845, with Genealogy of the First Settlers. Boston, 1845. 8vo.

—— The Toppans of Toppan's Lane. with their Descendants and Relations. Newburyport, 1862. 8vo. Genealog. Pamph. Vol. 8.

COFFIN, Paul, D. D. See WOODMAN, C. Memoir of, and Journals.

COFFINBERRY, S. C. Eulogy on the Late Elihu Mather, at Coldwater, Mich., Mar. 15, 1866. Coldwater, 1866. 8vo. Addresses. Vol. 21.

COGGESHALL. Hist. of Amer. Privateers, and Letters of Marque during the War of 1812. N. Y., 1861. 8vo.

COGGESHALL, Wm. T. Disc. before the Beta Theta Pi Soc. of Ohio Univers., June 22, 1858, on the Protective Policy in Literature. Columbus, 1859. 8vo. Addresses. Vol. 30.

—— Disc. on the Advantages of Local Literature, June 22, 1858. Columbus, 1859. 8vo. Addresses. Vol. 15.

—— Home Hits and Hints; a Book for the Fireside. N. Y., 1859. 12mo.

—— Lincoln Memorial. Journeys of Abr. Lincoln from Springfield to Washington, 1861, as Pres't Elect; and from Washington to Springfield, 1865, as President Martyred, with Acc. of Pub. Ceremonies. Columbus, 1865. 12mo.

—— Ohio's Prosperity; an Argument against Rebellion. (n. d.) 8vo. Rebell'n Pamph. Vol. 48.

—— Poets and Poetry of the West, with Biograph. and Critical Notices. N. Y., 1864. 8vo.

COGGSWELL, E. C. Hist. of New Boston, N. H. Boston, 1864. 8vo.

COGSWELL, Rev. Jonathan. Topograph. and Hist. Sketch of Saco Co., of York, District of Maine. 1815. Mass. Hist. Soc. Coll. Vol. 4. 2d Series.

COGSWELL, Jos. G. See VERAZZANO, John de.

—— and BANCROFT, Geo. Acc. of Round Hill School, Northampton, Mass., 1826. 8vo.

COGSWELL. Rev. Wm. Hist. of Atkinson, N. H. N. H. Hist. Soc. Coll. Vol. 6.

—— Individual and Family Names. N. Eng. Hist. and Gen. Register. Vol. 2.

COGGSWELL, Rev. Wm. N. H. Repository. Vol. 1. Gilmanton, 1845. 8vo.
COHASSET, Mass. See FLINT, Rev. J. Hist. and Descrip. of.
—— 2d Cong. Church. Articles of Faith and Covenant. Bingham, 1851. 12mo. Mass. Hist. Discourses, etc. Vol. 11.
COHEN, J. Barrett. Oration on the 1st Annivers. of S. C. Hist. Soc., June 28, 1856. Collections. Vol. 2.
COHEN, Solomon. Eulogy on the Life and Character of Stephen Elliott, D. D. Savannah, 1867. 8vo. Addresses. Vol. 21.
COINDET, M. John. Le Mont Blanc: Traduit de L'Anglais de M. Albert Smith. Lond., 1854. 12mo. Hist. Pamph. Vol. 8.
COINS. See Numismatics.
COKE, Lieut. E. T. A Subaltern's Furlough; Scenes in the U. S. and Canada, during 1832. Waldie's Circulating Libr. Vol. 2.
COLBATCH, Sir John. Methods to be taken in case of the Plague. Lond., 1721. 12mo. Med. Pamph. Vol. 27.
COLBERT, E. Hist. and Statist. Sketch of Chicago. Chicago, 1868. 8vo. Ill. Local Histories. Vol. 1.
—— and CHAMBERLAIN, E. Chicago and the Great Conflagration, Illustrated. Cincin., 1871. 12mo.
COLBURN, Jeremiah. Bibliog. of the Local History of Massachusetts. N. Eng. Hist. and Gen. Register. Vols. 21–25.
—— The First Coinage of America. Hist. Mag. Vol. 1.
COLBURN'S United Service Journal, and Naval and Military Magazine. Lond., 1829–1858. 88 Vols. 8vo.
COLBY, Geo. J. L. Address before the Essex, Mass., Agr. Soc., Oct. 1, 1862. South Danvers, 1862. 8vo.
COLCHESTER, Eng. See CROMWELL, Thos. Hist. and Descript. of.
COLCHESTER, Conn. See TAINTOR, C. M.
COLDEN, Lt. Gov. C. Corres. with Wm. Smith, Jr., concerning the Hist. of N. Y. N. Y. Hist. Soc. Coll., N. Ser. Vol. 2.
—— Hist. of the Five Indian Nations of Canada, which are dependant on the Province of N. Y. in America.
—— Hist. of the Five Indian Nations of N. Y., edited with Notes, by J. Gilmary SHEA. N. Y., 1866. 8vo.
—— State of the Lands in the Province of N. Y., 1732. Doc. Hist. Soc. of N. Y. Vol. 1.
COLDEN, Cadwallader D. Letter upon the Secret Order of Freemasonry. N. Y., 1829. 8vo. Masonic Pamph, etc. Vol. 1.
—— Life of Robert Fulton, with an Appendix. N. Y., 1817. 8vo.
—— Vindication of the Steamboat Right granted by the State of N. Y., in a Letter to Mr. Duer. N. Y., 1819. 8vo. Law Pamph. Vol. 5. N. Y. Misc. Pamph. Vol. 3.
COLE, Rev. Henry. Appeal to the People of Eng. to resist the Catholic Claims. Lond., 1829. 8vo. Strangford Pamph. Vol. 6.
COLE, Jas. E. Genealogy of the Family of Cole, of Co. of Devon. Lond., 1867. 8vo.
COLE, Thos. List of Infusorial Objects found near Salem, Mass., 1853. Scientific Pamphlets. Vol. 2.
—— See NOBLE, Rev. L. L. Life and Works of.
COLEBROOK, Conn. See LEE, Chauncey. Farewell Sermon. 1828.

COLEMAN, Edward. Trial of—for Conspiring the Death of the King, etc. Lond., 1678. Folio. Eng. Polit. Pamph. Vol. 1.

COLEMAN, Jas. Gen. Index to Printed Pedigrees, which are to be found in County and Local Histories, etc. Lond., 1866. 8vo.

—— Catalogue of Pedigrees hitherto Unindexed. Lond., 1867. 8vo.

—— Pedigree and Genealog. Notes of the Family of Penn, of England and America. Lond., 1871. 8vo.
See also Genealog. Pamph. Vol. 6.

COLEMAN, Lyman, D. D. Genealogy of the Lyman Family in G. Britain and America. 1631. Albany, 1872. 8vo.

—— See Review of Coleman's Antiquities.

COLERIDGE, Rev. Derwent. Letter on the Training-College for Schoolmasters, at Chelsea, Eng. Lond., 1842. 8vo. Educa. Pamph. Vol. 30.

COLES, Edward. Hist. of the Ordinance of 1787. Read before the Hist. Soc. of Penn., June 9, 1856. Phila., 1856. 8vo. Penn. Hist. Soc. Addresses. Vol. 1.

COLESON, Ann. Narra. of Captivity among the Sioux Indians in Minnesota. Phila., 1864. 8vo.

COLFAX, Schuyler. See PHELPS, C. A. Lives of Grant and Colfax. 1868.

—— Speech in Cong., June 21, 1856, on the Lecompton Constitution. Congr. and Polit. Pamph. Vol. 93.

—— Speech in Cong., Apr. 23, 1862, on Confiscation. Rebell'n Pamph. Vol. 66.

—— Speech in Cong., Apr. 14, 1864, on the Expelling of Mr. Long. Rebell'n Pamph. Vol. 34.

COLLAMER, Jacob. See Addresses in Cong. on his Death.

—— BARRETT, Jas. Memorial Address. 1868.

—— Speech in Cong., June 26, 1846, on the Tariff. Washington, 1846. 8vo. Speeches. Vol. 1.

—— Speech in U. S. Senate, Apr. 24, 1862, on Confiscating Rebel Property. Rebellion Pamph. Vol. 9. Congr. and Polit. Pamph. Vol. 121.

—— Speech in U. S. Senate, Feb. 6, 1865, on Reconstruction. Congr. and Polit. Pamph. Vol. 121.

COLLECTANEA Topographica et Genealogica. Lond., 1834–1843. 8 Vols. 8vo.

COLLECTION of Authentic Papers Relative to the Dispute between G. Britain and Amer, from 1764 to 1775. Ed. by J. ALMON. Lond., 1777. 8vo.

—— of Essays Relative to the Progress of Medical Science. Calcutta, India, 1833. 8vo. Med. Pamph. Vol. 14.

—— of Interesting Biography, containing the Life of Dr. S. Johnson, Mr. Elwes and Captain Cook. Lond., 1791. 12mo. Biograph. Pamph. Vol. 9.

—— of Memorials concerning divers Deceased Ministers and others of the People called Quakers in Penn. and N. J., to 1787. Phila., 1788. 8vo.

COLLECTION of Parliamentary Debates in England, 1712 to 1717, and 1740 to 1742. Lond., 1742. 2 Vols. 8vo.
—— of Scarce and Interesting Tracts, written by Persons of Eminence upon Important Subjects, during 1763–1770. Lond., 1888. 4 Vols. 8vo.
—— of Several Treatises, concerning the Penal Laws. Lond., 1688. Sm. 4to. Eng. Polit. Pamph. Vol. 65.
—— of the Substance of Several Speeches and Debates in Parliament, relating to the Popish Plot. Lond., 1681. Folio. Eng. Polit. Pamph. Vol. 63.
—— of Useful and Remarkable Events. Middlebury, Vt. (n. d.)
COLLEGE of Preceptors, London. Royal Charter of Incorporation, By-Laws, etc. Lond., 1853. 8vo. Educa. Pamph. Vol. 37.
—— —— Calendar. Lond., 1847. 8vo. Educa. Pamph. Vol. 30.
—— of Teachers. Transactions for 1834–5, '36, '37, '39, '40. Cincin., 1835–41. 5 Vols. 8vo.
—— of William and Mary. See HARTWELL, H. Present State of, etc. 1727.
—— —— History of. 1693–1870. Baltimore, 1870. 8vo.
COLLET, Henry. Treatise on the Laws of England concerning Estates, etc. Savoy, 1754. 8vo. Eng. Polit. Pamph. Vol. 13.
COLLIER & MATTHEWS' Invasion of Virginia, in 1779. Va. Hist. Register. Vol. 4.
COLLIER, Joshua. Reply to a Pamphlet on the "State of the Nation, at the Commencement of 1822." Lond., 1822. 8vo. 2d Ed. Pamphleteer. Vol. 21.
COLLIER, J. Payne. Bibliograph. and Critical Acc. of the Rarest Books in the English Language. N. Y., 1864. 4 Vols. 12mo.
—— Reasons for a New Edition of Shakespeare's Works. Lond., 1842. 8vo. 2d Ed. Strangford Pamph. Vol. 26.
COLLIER, Robt. Laird. The Social Evil; an Address. Chicago, 1871. 8vo. Addresses. Vol. 34.
COLLIN, John F. Speech in Cong., June 19, 1846, on the Tariff. Washington, 1846. 8vo. Speeches. Vol. 1.
COLLIN, Nicholas, D. D. Brief Acc. of the Swedish Mission in Racoon and Penn's Neck, N. J. N. J. Hist. Soc. Proceed. Vol. 3.
COLLINS' Line of Steamers. See Congress'l Speeches.
—— Map of the Crimea. Lond. (n. d.) Guide Books. Vol. 14.
COLLINS, Arthur. Supplement to the Four Volumes of the Peerage of England. Lond., 1750. 2 Vols. 8vo.
—— The Peerage of England, containing a Genealog. and Histor. Account of all the Peers of that Kingdom. 4th Ed. Lond., 1768. 7 Vols. 8vo.
COLLINS, Chas. Omaha Directory, with Hist. Statistics. Omaha, 1866. 12mo.
COLLINS, C. T. Letter on the proposed Exemption of Friends from Military Service. Rebell'n Pamph. Vol. 46.
COLLINS, S. H. Emigrant's Guide to the U. States. Hull, Eng. (n. d.) 12mo.

COLLINS, Wm. H. Third Address to the People of Maryland. 2d Ed. Baltimore, 1861. Rebell'n Pamph. Vol. 32.
COLLINSON, Peter. See DILLINGHAM, W. H. Tribute to.
COLLOT, Gen. Victor. Journey in N. America, containing a Survey of the Countries watered by the Mississippi, Ohio, Missouri and other Affluing Rivers. Paris, 1826. 4to, with an Atlas.
COLLYER, W. B., D. D. Oration before the Philosoph. Soc. of London, Nov. 22, 1815. Lond., 1816. 8vo. Addresses. Vol. 33. Scientific Pamph. Vol. 28.
COLMAN, Benj., D. D. Memoir of. N. Eng. Hist. and Gen. Register. Vol. 3.
COLMAN, Henry. European Agriculture and Rural Economy. Boston, 1844–1846. 2 Vols. 8vo.
—— European Life and Manners. Boston, 1850. 2 Vols. 12mo.
COLOMBIA, S. A. See DUANE, W. Visit to. 1822–23.
—— See HALL, Francis. Its Present State, etc.
COLONIAL Hist. of Eastern and Southern States. See TYSON, J. R.
—— —— of N. Y. See BRODHEAD, J. R.
—— (The) Intelligencer, or Aborigines' Friend, comprising the Transactions of Aborigines' Protection Soc. Lond., 1847–58. 5 Vols. 8vo.
—— Penny Postage; Statement of Facts, etc. London, 1853. 8vo. Eng. Polit. Pamph. Vol. 52.
—— Journal, No. 3. October, 1816. Lond., 1816. 8vo.
—— Policy of Great Britain considered, with relation to her North American Provinces and West India Possessions. Lond., 1816. 8vo.
—— Records of Conn. See TRUMBULL, J. H.
—— Trade with G. Britain. See Congress'l Speeches.
COLONIES (The) and G. Britain must be Incorporated, and form one Universal Empire. Lond., 1839. 8vo. Strangford Pamph. Vol. 17.
COLONIZATION. See African Repository.
—— Amer. Coloniz. Soc.
—— BROWN, I. V. Biog. of Finley, and Hist. of Coloniza.
—— Few Facts and Figures for Friends of Africa.
—— HANSON, R. D. Lecture, etc. 1831.
—— Indiana State Board of.
—— Liberia.
—— Mass. Coloniza. Soc.
—— Papers Relating to the Colonization Experiment at A'Vache, Hayti. 1864. Col. Pamph. Vol. 1.
—— See REESE, D. M. Letters to Wm. Jay.
—— Remarks on Coloniza. of the Western Coast of Africa. N. Y., 1850. 8vo. Col. Pamph. Vol. 1.
—— Same. N. Y., 1852. 8vo. Congr. and Polit. Pamph. Vol. 56.
—— See TRACY, Jos. State of Soc'y in Western Africa. 1845.
COLONNA Vittoria. See TROLLOPE, T. A. Life of.
COLOR (The) Guard. See HOSMER, Jas. K.

COLORADO Agricult. and Indust. Assoc. Proceed. of 3d and 4th Ann. Exhibitions, in 1868–69. Central City, 1870. 8vo.
—— Regulations, etc., for the 6th Exhibition to be held in 1871. Denver, 1871. 8vo. Col. Misc. Pamph. Vol. 1.
—— Biennial Message of the Governor, 1870. Central City, 1870. 8vo. Col. Misc. Pamph. Vol. 1.
—— FARRELL, N. E. Colorado, the Rocky Mountain Gem. 1868.
—— GILPIN, Gov. Wm. Notes on. 1870.
—— HAYDEN, F. V. Geolog. Survey. 1869.
—— HOLLISTER, O. J. Mines of Colorado.
—— Official Information published by Terr. Board of Immigration. Denver, 1872. 8vo. Col. Misc. Pamph. Vol. 1.
—— Reports of Territorial Officers. Central City, 1871. 8vo.
—— Resources of by the Board of Trade of Denver City. Brooklyn, N. Y., 1868. 8vo. Col. Misc. Pamph. Vol. 1.
—— See TAYLOR, B. Summer Trip, 1867.
—— VILLARD, H. Pike's Peak Gold Regions.
—— WALLIHAN, S. S. Gazeteer, 1871.
—— River Exploration. See DERBY, Lieut. Report, 1850–51.
—— —— IVES, Lieut. J. C. Report, 1857–8.
—— —— SITGREAVES, Capt. L. Report, 1853.
COLORED People's Nat. Lincoln Monument Assoc. Fourth of July Celebra. at Washington, 1865. Washington, 1865. 8vo. Congr. and Polit. Pamph. Vol. 125.
COLQUHOUN, John C. The Progress of the Ch. of Rome toward the Ascendancy in Eng., traced through the Parliamentary Hist. of nearly Forty Years. Lond., 1868. 8vo. Eng. Religious Pamph. Vol. 92.
COLQUITT, W. T. Speech in U. S. Senate, Feb. 17, 1846, on the Oregon Question. Congr. and Polit. Pamph. Vol. 139.
COLTON, Rev. C. C. Lacon; or Many Things in Few Words. Revised Ed. N. Y., 1849. 8vo.
COLTON, Calvin. Private Corres. of Henry Clay. N. Y., 1856. 8vo.
—— Public Economy for the U. S. 3d Ed. N. Y., 1853. 8vo.
—— Life of Henry Clay, the Great Amer. Statesman. N. Y., 1856. 2 Vols. 8vo.
—— Rights of Labor. 3d Ed. N. Y., 1847. 8vo. Congr. and and Polit. Pamph. Vol. 94.
—— Tour of the Amer. Lakes, and among the Indians of the N.-West Territory, in 1830. Lond., 1833. 2 Vols. 12mo.
—— Speeches of Henry Clay. N. Y., 1857. 2 Vols. 8vo.
—— Last Seven Years of the Life of Henry Clay. N. Y., 1856. 8vo.
COLTON, Chauncey, D. D. Essay on the Study of the Scriptures as a Part of Liberal Educa. N. Y., 1835. 8vo. Educa. Pamph. Vol. 5.
COLTON, G. W. Atlas of the World; with Descriptions by R. S. Fisher. N. Y., 1856. 2 Vols. 4to.
—— Map of the World, N. Y., 1854. Folded.
COLTON. Rev. Walter. Deck and Port; or Cruise of U. S. Frigate Congress to California. N. Y., 1852. 12mo.

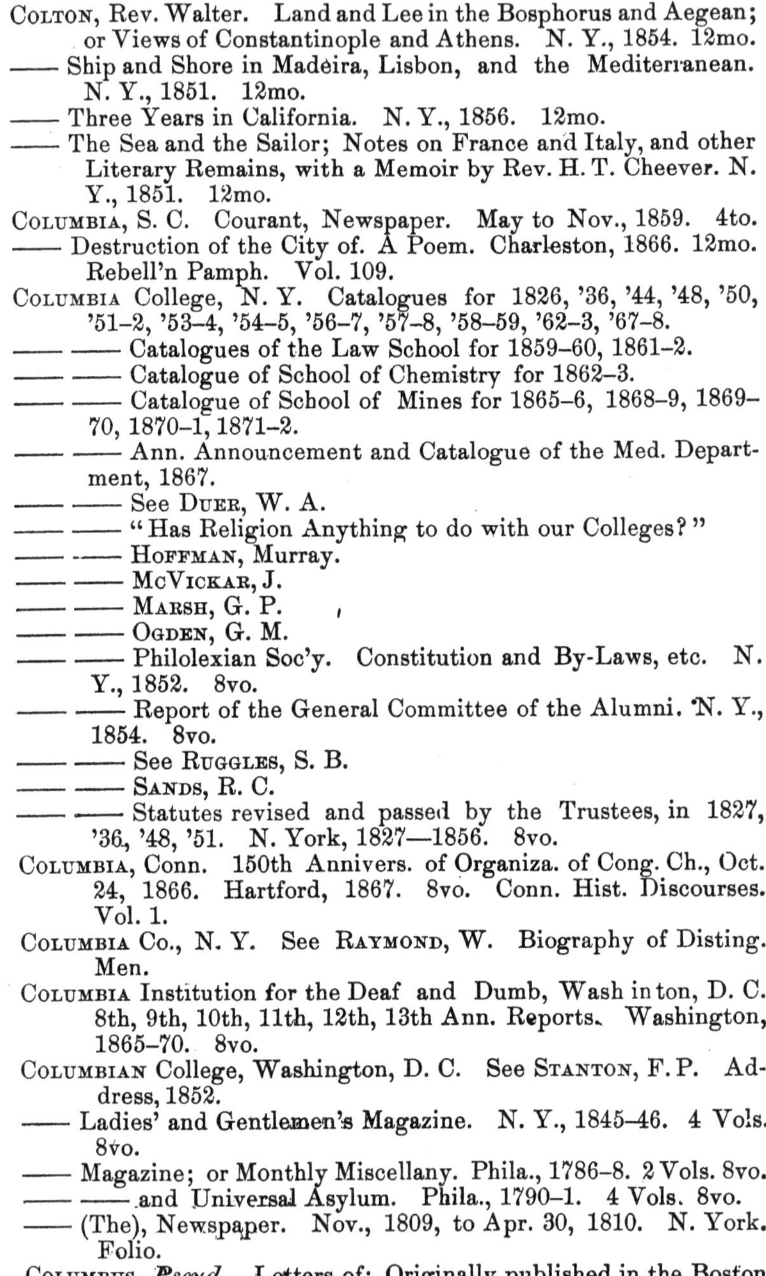

Colton, Rev. Walter. Land and Lee in the Bosphorus and Aegean; or Views of Constantinople and Athens. N. Y., 1854. 12mo.

—— Ship and Shore in Madèira, Lisbon, and the Mediterranean. N. Y., 1851. 12mo.

—— Three Years in California. N. Y., 1856. 12mo.

—— The Sea and the Sailor; Notes on France and Italy, and other Literary Remains, with a Memoir by Rev. H. T. Cheever. N. Y., 1851. 12mo.

Columbia, S. C. Courant, Newspaper. May to Nov., 1859. 4to.

—— Destruction of the City of. A Poem. Charleston, 1866. 12mo. Rebell'n Pamph. Vol. 109.

Columbia College, N. Y. Catalogues for 1826, '36, '44, '48, '50, '51–2, '53–4, '54–5, '56–7, '57–8, '58–59, '62–3, '67–8.

—— —— Catalogues of the Law School for 1859–60, 1861–2.

—— —— Catalogue of School of Chemistry for 1862–3.

—— —— Catalogue of School of Mines for 1865–6, 1868–9, 1869–70, 1870–1, 1871–2.

—— —— Ann. Announcement and Catalogue of the Med. Department, 1867.

—— —— See Duer, W. A.

—— —— "Has Religion Anything to do with our Colleges?"

—— —— Hoffman, Murray.

—— —— McVickar, J.

—— —— Marsh, G. P.

—— —— Ogden, G. M.

—— —— Philolexian Soc'y. Constitution and By-Laws, etc. N. Y., 1852. 8vo.

—— —— Report of the General Committee of the Alumni. N. Y., 1854. 8vo.

—— —— See Ruggles, S. B.

—— —— Sands, R. C.

—— —— Statutes revised and passed by the Trustees, in 1827, '36, '48, '51. N. York, 1827—1856. 8vo.

Columbia, Conn. 150th Annivers. of Organiza. of Cong. Ch., Oct. 24, 1866. Hartford, 1867. 8vo. Conn. Hist. Discourses. Vol. 1.

Columbia Co., N. Y. See Raymond, W. Biography of Disting. Men.

Columbia Institution for the Deaf and Dumb, Wash inton, D. C. 8th, 9th, 10th, 11th, 12th, 13th Ann. Reports. Washington, 1865–70. 8vo.

Columbian College, Washington, D. C. See Stanton, F. P. Address, 1852.

—— Ladies' and Gentlemen's Magazine. N. Y., 1845–46. 4 Vols. 8vo.

—— Magazine; or Monthly Miscellany. Phila., 1786–8. 2 Vols. 8vo.

—— —— and Universal Asylum. Phila., 1790–1. 4 Vols. 8vo.

—— (The), Newspaper. Nov., 1809, to Apr. 30, 1810. N. York. Folio.

Columbus, *Pseud.* Letters of; Originally published in the Boston Bulletin: with Two Letters of Col. Orne to Gen. Duff Green. Boston, 1829. 8vo. Congr. and Polit. Pamph. Vol. 134.

COLUMBUS, Christopher. See BARLOW, J. Vision of. A Poem.
—— CAMPE, J. H. Discov. of America.
—— DODGE, Robt. Memorials of, etc.
—— HELPS, A. Hist. of.
—— Hist. and Voyages of. Lond., 1777. 12mo.
—— LENOX, James. Bibliograph. Acc. of Voyages of.
—— IRVING, W. Life and Early Voyages of.
—— Lettre de Christophe Colomb sur la Decouverte du Nouveau-Monde. Paris, 1865. 8vo.
—— See SYLLACIUS, N. De Insulis Meridiana, etc.
COLUMBUS, Ohio. See STUDER, J. H. Hist. of, 1873.
COLUMBUS, Wis. Republican Journal, Newspaper. Jan., 1855, to Dec., 1863. Folio.
COLVIN, Verplanck. On Certain New Phenomena in Chemistry. Albany, 1872. 8vo. Scientific Pamph. Vol. 4.
COLVOCORESSES, G. M. Four Years in the Gov't Exploring Expedition commanded by Capt. Chas. Wilkes. N.Y., 1855. 12mo.
COLWELL, Chas. Fiery Facts; or the City Coal Tax exposed. Lond., 1861. 8vo. Eng. Misc. Pamph. Vol. 10.
COLWELL, S. The South; Letter from a Friend in the North, 1856. Rebell'n Pamph. Vol. 82.
—— The Five Cotton States and N. Y., 1861. Rebell'n Pamph. Vol. 87.
COLYER, Vincent. Brief Report of Services rendered by the Freed People to U. S. Army in N. Carolina in 1862. N. Y., 1864. 8vo. Rebell'n Pamph. Vol. 41.
—— Peace with the Apaches of N. Mexico and Arizona. Washington. 1872. 8vo. Indian Pamph. Vol. 4.
COMBE, Andrew, M. D. Principles of Physiology applied to Health, etc. Harper's Fam. Libr. N. Y., 1855. 18mo.
COMBE, Geo. Constitution of Man. N. Y., 1850. 8vo.
—— Same. Edinburgh, 1835. 8vo. 4th Ed. Scientific Pamph. Vol. 35.
—— Moral and Intellectual Science. N. Y., 1848. 8vo.
COMBES, M. Memoire sur l'Exploitation des Mines des Comptes de Cornwall et de Devon. Paris, 1834. 12mo.
COMBS, Gen. Leslie. Narr. of his Life; embracing Incidents in the Early Hist. of N.-W. Territory and the War of 1812. N. Y., 1852. 8vo.
—— Col. Wm. Dudley's Defeat opposite Fort Meigs, May, 5, 1813. Cincin., 1869. 8vo. Pamphlets War of 1812. Vol. 4.
COMETS. See BARTLETT, W. H. C.
—— HASKINS, R. W. Popular Essay on.
—— NULTY, E.
—— RITTENHOUSE, D. Observa. on a Comet, 1784.
—— STIRLING, Earl of.
COMING (The) Contraband; a Reason against the Emancipation Proclamation. N. Y., 1862. Rebell'n Pamph. Vol. 100.
COMINGS, Wm. F. Report of his Trial for Murder at Grafton, N. H., 1843. Boston, 1844. 8vo. Law Pamph. Vol. 24.
COMLY, Isaac. Sketches of the Hist. of Byberry, in Co. of Phila., Pa. Phila., 1827. 8vo.

COMLY, Isaac. See also Penn. Hist. Soc. Memoirs. Vol. 2, Part 1.
COMMENTARIES upon Martial Law, with Special Reference to its Regulation and Restraint. Lond., 1868. 8vo.
COMMERCE (The) and Navigation of the Valley of the Mississipi, and that appertaining to St. Louis considered. St. Louis, 1847. 8vo. St. Louis Misc. Pamph. Vol. 1.
COMMERCE and Navigation. See ANDREWS, I. D. Commerce of Brit. Colonies.
—— —— BARTON, W. On Freedom of Naviga. 1802.
—— —— BELLONI, Jerome. Dissertation on Commerce, 1752.
—— —— Causes of Reduction of Amer. Tonnage.
—— —— CHALMERS, T. Commercial Discourses.
—— —— Considera. on Abolishing Damages, etc.
—— —— Examinations of Pretensions of N. England.
—— —— See Free Trade—Tariff.
—— —— GEE, J. Trade and Naviga. of G. Britain, 1730.
—— —— HENSER, P. Handbuch sur Rauflente.
—— —— Hudson, C. Speech on Wheat Trade.
—— —— Inquiry into Commer. Policy of U. S.
—— —— Lectures on Progress of Commerce.
—— —— Memorial on Tariff of Duties, 1832.
—— —— National Board of Trade.
—— —— PICKERING, T. Speech on Embargo Act.
—— —— PITKIN, T. Statist. View of Commerce of U. S.
—— —— RAWLE, Wm. Lecture on the Influence of Commerce.
—— —— SHEFFIELD, John, Lord. Commerce of Amer. States, 1700–83.
—— —— Spoliation of Amer. Commeree.
—— —— Taxes, or Tribute Money, levied on Agriculture and Commerce.
—— —— U. S. Sec. of Treasury Reports on.
—— —— WHATELY, T. Trade and Finance of G. Britain, 1765.
COMMERCIAL Intercourse with and in States declared in Insurrection. Washington, 1863. 8vo. Rebell'n Pamph. Vol. 17.
—— Policy of England and Germany. Lond., 1845. 8vo. Strangford Pamph. Vol. 38.
—— —— of U. S. See Inquiry into, etc.
—— Regulations of Foreign Countries, with which the U. S. have Commer. Intercourse. Washington, 1819. 8vo.
—— Relations of U. S. See U. S. Sec. of State.
—— Travellers' Benevolent Institution, London. Report, Rules, etc., 1855. London. 12mo. Eng. Misc. Pamph. Vol. 15.
COMMON Sense vs. Judicial Legislation; Review of a Law recently Enacted by the Supreme Court of Mass. N. Y., 1871. 8vo. Law Pamph. Vol. 22.
COMMUCK, Thos. Indian Melodies. N. Y., 1845. 8vo.
COMONFORT, Gen. Manifesto in Defence of his Policy during his Administra. in Mexico. N. Y., 1858. 8vo. Congr. and Polit. Pamph. Vol. 56.
COMORO Islands. See PALMER, A. H.
COMPARISON of the Taxes of the City and County of N. Y., during 1836 and 1837. N.Y., 1838. 8vo. N. Y. City Pamph. Vol. 6.

COMPENDIOUS or Brief Examination of Complaints of Divers of our Countrymen, in these our Dayes. In Three Dialogues, 1581. Lond., 1815. 8vo. Pamphleteer. Vol. 5.
COMPLETE Refutation of Argument on the Subject of the Agricultural Petition. Lond., 1819. 8vo. Pamphleteer. Vol. 14.
COMPRESSED View of Points to be discussed, in Treating with the U. S. Lond., 1815. 8vo. Pamphleteer. Vol. 5.
COMPROMISE Bill. See Congressional Speeches—Compromise.
COMPTON, R. I. Notes on, 1803. Mass. Hist. Soc. Coll. Vol. 9. 1st Series.
COMPULSORY Education. See BLODGETT, Lorin.
—— —— BURROWES, T. H. Against Compuls. Educa.
—— —— Congressional Speeches—National Educa.
—— Enlistment of Amer. Citizens. See U. S. Messages of the Presidents.
COMSTOCK, Geo. F. Speech at Brooklyn, 1864. Rebell'n Pamph. Vol. 37.
COMSTOCK, Rev. G. S. Notes on Arakan, India. Amer. Oriental Soc. Journ. Vol. 1.
COMTE, M. See SPENCER, Herbert. Classification of the Sciences, etc.
CONANT, Roger. See FELT, J. B. Notice of.
CONCESSION and Compromises. See FISHER, J. T.
CONCHOLOGY. See ADAMS, C. B. Catalogue of Recent Shells, 1847.
—— Agassiz, L. Lake Superior.
—— GOULD, A. A. Shells from Pacific Coast.
CONCISE (A) Hist. of Spanish America. Lond., 1741. 8vo.
—— Statement of Facts on the Gen. Treatment of Law Clerks. Lond., 1832. 8vo. Law Pamph. Vol. 21.
CONCORAN, Col. Michael. Narr. of his Captivity in Richmond and other Southern Cities, 1862. Rebell'n Pamph. Vol. 88.
CONCORD, Mass. See EMERSON, R. W. Centen. Disc., 1835.
—— RANTOUL, R. jr. 75th Annivers. Address of Battle of.
—— Ann. Report of School Comm. for 1848–9. Charlestown, 1849. 8vo.
—— See RIPLEY, Rev. Ezra. Half Century Disc., 1828.
—— SHATTUCK, L. Hist. of.
CONCORD, N. H. See BOUTON, Rev. N. Centen. Celebra. of 1st Ch., 1830.
—— —— Hist. of, 1856.
—— —— 40th Annivers. Sermon, 1865.
—— Directory, 1860–1. 8vo.
—— MOORE, J. B. Hist. Sketch of.
—— Ann. Reports of Schools for 1865 and 1867. Concord, 1865, '67. 8vo.
—— 13th Ann. Report of Receipts and Expenditures for 1865. Concord, 1866. 8vo.
CONCORD, N. C., Presbytery. Minutes of Sessions held in Newton, 1872. Salisbury, 1872. 8vo.
CONDIT, Rev. J. B. Address at South Hadley, Mass., Aug. 6, 1846. N. Y., 1846. 8vo. Pamphlets, Vol. 3.

CONDUCT (The) of a Noble Lord Scrutinized. With Remarks on the Same. Lond., 1759. 8vo. Eng. Polit. Pamph. Vol. 70.

—— of a Rt. Hon. Gentleman in Resigning the Seals of his Office Justified, etc. Lond., 1761. 8vo. Eng. Polit. Pamph. Vol. 15.

—— of His Grace, the Duke of Argyll, for the Last Four Years reviewed. Lond., 1740. 8vo. Eng. Polit. Pamph. Vol. 68.

—— of the Late Administration Examined, relative to the Stamp Act: with Appendix of Authentic Doc's. Lond., 1767. Amer. Tracts, Vol. 2.

—— of the Ministry Impartially Examined. Lond., 1756. 8vo. Eng. Polit. Pamph. Vol. 70.

—— of the Opposition, and the Tendency to Modern Patriotism,—Reviewed. Edinburgh, 1734. 12mo. Eng. Polit. Pamph. Vol. 67.

—— of the "Paxton Men" Impartially Represented. Phila., 1764. 8vo.

—— of the War. See U. S. Sec. of War. Reports.

CONE, Rev. Spencer H. Life of, by his Sons. N. Y., 1857. 12mo.

CONFEDERATE Memorial Day at Charleston, S. C., May 10, 1871. Address by Rev. Dr. Girardeau, etc. Charleston, 1871. 8vo. Rebell'n Pamph. Vol. 107.

—— States of America. See Amer. War of Rebellion.

—— —— Constitution of—Adopted by Congress of C. S. A., Mar. 11, 1861. to which is added the Ordinance of Ratification, passed by La. State Conven., Mar. 21, 1861. N. Orleans, 1861. 18mo. Rebell'n Pamph. Vol. 9.

—— —— See DAVIS, Jeff.

—— —— President's Message and Accompanying Doc's., 1862. Richmond. 8vo. Rebell'n Pamph. Vol. 107.

CONFISCATION. See Congress'l Speeches.

CONFLICT of Jurisdiction between State and Federal Courts. Opinion in Case of Jos. Hollman vs. H. Fulton, on Habeas Corpus. Keokuk, 1869. 8vo. Rebell'n Pamph. Vol. 55.

CONGDON, C. T. The Warning of War; a Poem. N. Y., 1862. Rebell'n Pamph. Vol. 17.

CONGER, A. B. Address before the Rockland Co., N. Y., Agr. Assoc., Oct. 21, 1847. Agr. Pamph. Vol. 2.

CONGRATULATORY Letter to a Rt. Hon. Person, upon his Late Disappointment. Lond. n. d. 8vo.

—— With a Reply to the Same. Eng. Polit. Pamph. Vol. 68. Lond., 1743. 8vo. Eng. Polit. Pamph. Vol. 68.

CONGREGATIONAL Church. See Amer. Cong. Assoc.

—— —— Amer. Cong. Union.

—— —— —— Year Book, 1854–9.

—— —— Board of Publication. 25th Ann. Report, May, 1854. Boston, 1854. 12mo.

—— —— See Conn. Gen. Assoc.

—— —— Gen. Convention. Proceedings at Albany, 1852, and at Chicago, 1858. N. Y. and Chicago. 8vo.

CONGREGATIONAL Church. See GREENLEAF, Rev. J. Eccl. Hist. of Maine.
—— —— HAWES, Joel. Tribute to Pilgrims, etc.
—— —— Illinois Gen. Assoc.
—— —— KENNEDY, W. S. Hist. of in Western Reserve.
—— —— LAMB, D. Ministers in Addison Co., Vt.
—— —— LAMSON, Rev. A. Disc. on Congregationalism.
—— —— Mass. Gen. Assoc.
—— —— Mass. Gen. Conference.
—— —— MATHER, Cotton. Magnalia Christi Americana.
—— —— N. Y. Gen. Assoc.
—— —— PACKARD, T. Hist. of Franklin, Mass., Assoc.
—— —— PEET, Rev. S. Hist. of. in Wis.
—— —— WHITE, D. A. N. Eng. Congregationalism.
—— —— Wis. Convention Reports.
—— Churches in Mass. See Inquiry into the Right to Change the Constitution of, 1816.
—— Friends. Proceedings of the Yearly Meeting at Waterloo, N. Y., 1851. Auburn, 1851. 12mo. Religious Pamph. Vol. 17.
CONGRESS. Dictionary of. See LANMAN, C.
CONGRESS. History of. See BARNES, W. H. Hist. of 39th Congress.—Hist. of Congress (title gone), Vol. 1. 1789–93. WHEELER, H. G. Biograph. and Polit. Hist.
CONGRESSIONAL Banquet in Honor of Washington, Feb. 21, 1852. Congr. and Polit. Pamph. Vol. 89.
—— Debates. See Congressional Globe.
—— —— BENTON, T. H. Abridg. of Debates, 1789—1856.
—— Directories for the 3d Session 27th Congress, 1st Sess. 31st, 2d Sess. 32d, 3d Sess. 34th, 1st Sess. 35th, 2d Sess. 35th, 1st Sess. 36th, 2d Sess. 36th, 2d Sess. 37th, 2d Sess. 38th, 1st Sess. 39th, 2d Sess. 39th, 1st Sess. 40th, 3d Sess. 40th, 2d Sess. 41st, 3d Sess. 41st. Washington, 1842–70. 8vo.
—— Globe, containing Sketches of Debates and Proceedings from the 23d Congress, 1833, to 1st Session 42d Cong., 1871, inclusive, except the 2d Sess. 34th Cong., 1856–7, 1st Sess. 39th Cong., Part 3, and 2d Sess. 39th, 1866–7. Washington, 1834–71. 88 Vols 4to.
—— Library. See Library of Congress.
—— Speeches. Acquisition of Cuba. See BELL, H., 1853; BROOKS, Jas., 1853; CHANDLER, Z., 1859.
—— —— Admission of California. See BENNETT, H., 1850; BALDWIN, R. S., 1850; CALDWELL, G. A., 1856; CAREY, Jos., 1850; CHANDLER, J. R., 1850; CORWIN, M. P., 1850; DUER, W., 1850; DUNCAN, J. H., 1850; DURKEE, Chas., 1850; GREEN, J. S., 1850; HARRIS, T. L., 1850; HOWE, J. W., 1850; KING, J. A., 1850; McLANE, R. M., 1850; McWILLIE, W., 1850; PECK, L. B., 1850; PHELPS, J. S., 1850; PUTNAM, H., 1850; RICHARDSON, W. A., 1850; SEWARD, W. H., 1850; SYLVESTER, H., 1850; SMITH, T., 1850; STANTON, F. P., 1850; THOMAS, J. H., 1850; TOOMBS, R., 1850; WILMOT, D., 1850.

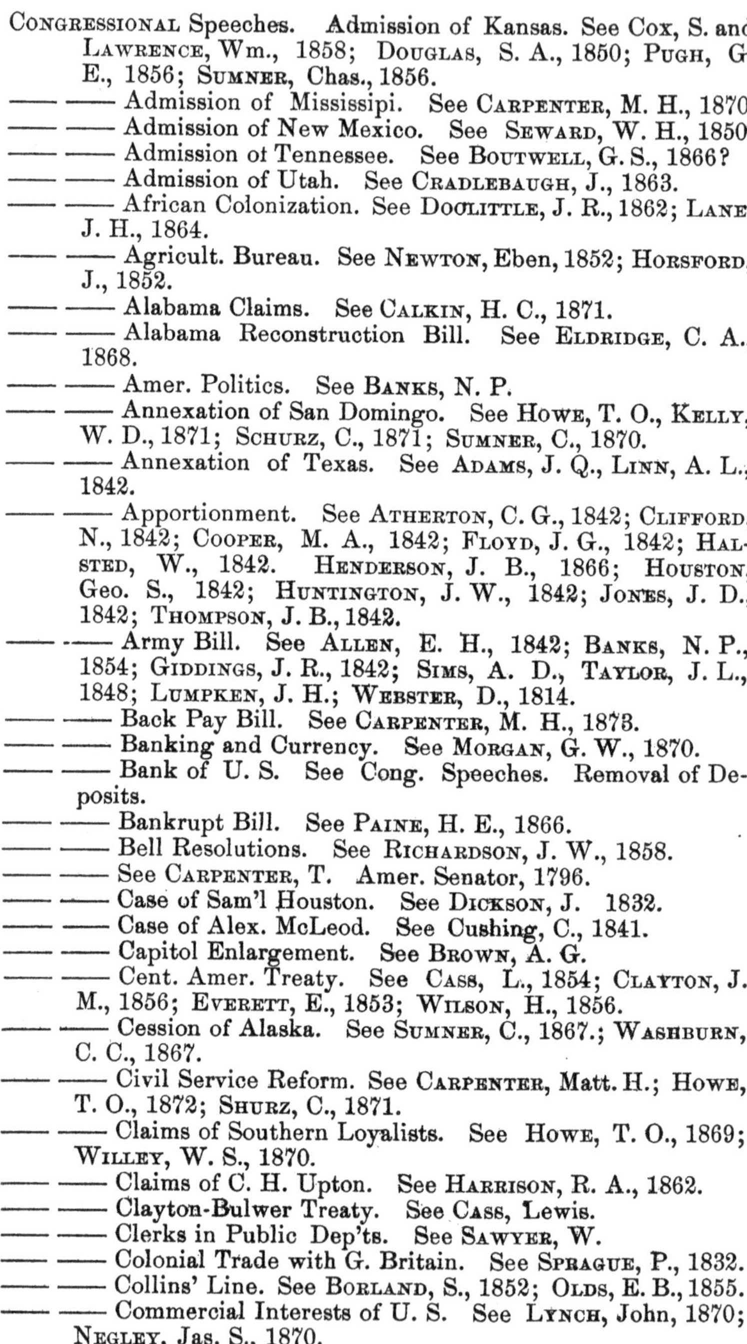

CONGRESSIONAL Speeches. Admission of Kansas. See COX, S. and LAWRENCE, Wm., 1858; DOUGLAS, S. A., 1850; PUGH, G. E., 1856; SUMNER, Chas., 1856.

—— —— Admission of Mississipi. See CARPENTER, M. H., 1870.

—— —— Admission of New Mexico. See SEWARD, W. H., 1850.

—— —— Admission ot Tennessee. See BOUTWELL, G. S., 1866?

—— —— Admission of Utah. See CRADLEBAUGH, J., 1863.

—— —— African Colonization. See DOOLITTLE, J. R., 1862; LANE, J. H., 1864.

—— —— Agricult. Bureau. See NEWTON, Eben, 1852; HORSFORD, J., 1852.

—— —— Alabama Claims. See CALKIN, H. C., 1871.

—— —— Alabama Reconstruction Bill. See ELDRIDGE, C. A., 1868.

—— —— Amer. Politics. See BANKS, N. P.

—— —— Annexation of San Domingo. See HOWE, T. O., KELLY, W. D., 1871; SCHURZ, C., 1871; SUMNER, C., 1870.

—— —— Annexation of Texas. See ADAMS, J. Q., LINN, A. L., 1842.

—— —— Apportionment. See ATHERTON, C. G., 1842; CLIFFORD, N., 1842; COOPER, M. A., 1842; FLOYD, J. G., 1842; HALSTED, W., 1842. HENDERSON, J. B., 1866; HOUSTON, Geo. S., 1842; HUNTINGTON, J. W., 1842; JONES, J. D., 1842; THOMPSON, J. B., 1842.

—— —— Army Bill. See ALLEN, E. H., 1842; BANKS, N. P., 1854; GIDDINGS, J. R., 1842; SIMS, A. D., TAYLOR, J. L., 1848; LUMPKEN, J. H.; WEBSTER, D., 1814.

—— —— Back Pay Bill. See CARPENTER, M. H., 1873.

—— —— Banking and Currency. See MORGAN, G. W., 1870.

—— —— Bank of U. S. See Cong. Speeches. Removal of Deposits.

—— —— Bankrupt Bill. See PAINE, H. E., 1866.

—— —— Bell Resolutions. See RICHARDSON, J. W., 1858.

—— —— See CARPENTER, T. Amer. Senator, 1796.

—— —— Case of Sam'l Houston. See DICKSON, J. 1832.

—— —— Case of Alex. McLeod. See Cushing, C., 1841.

—— —— Capitol Enlargement. See BROWN, A. G.

—— —— Cent. Amer. Treaty. See CASS, L., 1854; CLAYTON, J. M., 1856; EVERETT, E., 1853; WILSON, H., 1856.

—— —— Cession of Alaska. See SUMNER, C., 1867.; WASHBURN, C. C., 1867.

—— —— Civil Service Reform. See CARPENTER, Matt. H.; HOWE, T. O., 1872; SHURZ, C., 1871.

—— —— Claims of Southern Loyalists. See HOWE, T. O., 1869; WILLEY, W. S., 1870.

—— —— Claims of C. H. Upton. See HARRISON, R. A., 1862.

—— —— Clayton-Bulwer Treaty. See CASS, Lewis.

—— —— Clerks in Public Dep'ts. See SAWYER, W.

—— —— Colonial Trade with G. Britain. See SPRAGUE, P., 1832.

—— —— Collins' Line. See BORLAND, S., 1852; OLDS, E. B., 1855.

—— —— Commercial Interests of U. S. See LYNCH, John, 1870; NEGLEY, Jas. S., 1870.

CONGRESSIONAL Speeches. Compromise Bill. See BELL, John, 1850; BENTON, T. H., 1850; BRODHEAD, R., 1848; CADWALLADER, J., 1856; CHASE, S. P., 1854; CARTER, D. K., 1852; CLAY, H., 1850; CLEMENS, J., 1851; DAYTON, W. L., 1850; DODGE, A. C., 1850; DOUGLAS, S. A., 1851; DOWNS, S. W., 1850 and 1852; FOOTE, H. S., 1851.

—— —— Compromise Bill. See GOODRICH, J. Z., 1852; GREY, B. E., 1852; HARRIS, S. W., 1850; MCRAE, J. J., 1852; POLK, W. H., 1852; RIDDLE, G. R., 1852; SAGE, R., 1856; SEWARD, W. H., 1850; SOULE, P., 1850; STEPHENS, A. H., 1854; SUMNER, C., 1854; UPHAM, W., 1850; WASHBURN, I., 1852.

—— —— —— See Kansas and Nebraska.

—— —— Confiscation. See STEPHENS, T., 1867.

—— —— Contested Election. See BIRCH, J. H. 1864.

—— —— Continental Relations of U. S. See SEWARD, W. H., 1853.

—— —— Copyright. See ARCHER, S., 1872.

—— —— Cuban Affairs. See CARPENTER, Matt. H., 1869; LATHAM, M. S.

—— —— Daniel Webster. See ASHMUN, Geo.

—— —— Currency Bill, 1870. See HOWE, T. O.

—— —— Deficiency Bill. See BORLAND, S., 1852; RUSK, T. J., 1852.

—— —— Diplomatic System. See PERKINS, John, Jr.

—— —— Education. See PROSSER, Wm. F., 1870.

—— —— Election of Speaker. See VALLANDIGHAM, C. L., 1859.

—— —— Election of Presidential Electors. See DUNCAN, A., 1844.

—— —— Embargo. See HILLHOUSE, Jas., 1808; QUINCY, Josiah, 1809; PICKERING, T., 1808.

—— —— European Affairs. See CASS, L.

—— —— Executive Patronage. See NYE, Jas. W., 1866; WILSON, H., 1866.

—— —— Executive Policy. See GIDDINGS, J. R.

—— —— Extension of Boundaries. See HOOKER, Wm. H., 1869.

—— —— Finance. See BUNDY, H. S., 1867; MORRILL, J. S., 1867; VOORHIES, D. W., 1862.

—— —— Fortification Bill. See ADAMS, J. Q.

—— —— 14th Amendment. See EDMUNDS, G. F., 1871.

—— —— Freedmen's Bureau. See TRUMBULL, L., 1866.

—— —— French Intervention. See MCDOUGALL, J. A., 1863.

—— —— French Spoliations. See BRADBURY, J. W., 1852; CLAYTON, J. M., 1846; DAVIS, Tim., 1858; FELCH, A., 1852; SEWARD, W. H., 1851.

—— —— Fugitive Slave Bill. See BAYLEY, T. H., 1852; DURKEE, Chas., 1852; SEWARD, W. H., 1852; SUMNER, C., 1852, '54.

—— —— Galphin Claim. See FEATHERSTON, W. S., 1850.

—— —— Gen. Appropria. Bill, 1831. See BURGES, T.

—— —— Gov't Contracts. See STEVENS, Thad.

—— —— Grants of Lands to Hungarian Exiles, etc. See SEWARD, W. H., 1850.

—— —— Greek Question. See WEBSTER, D.

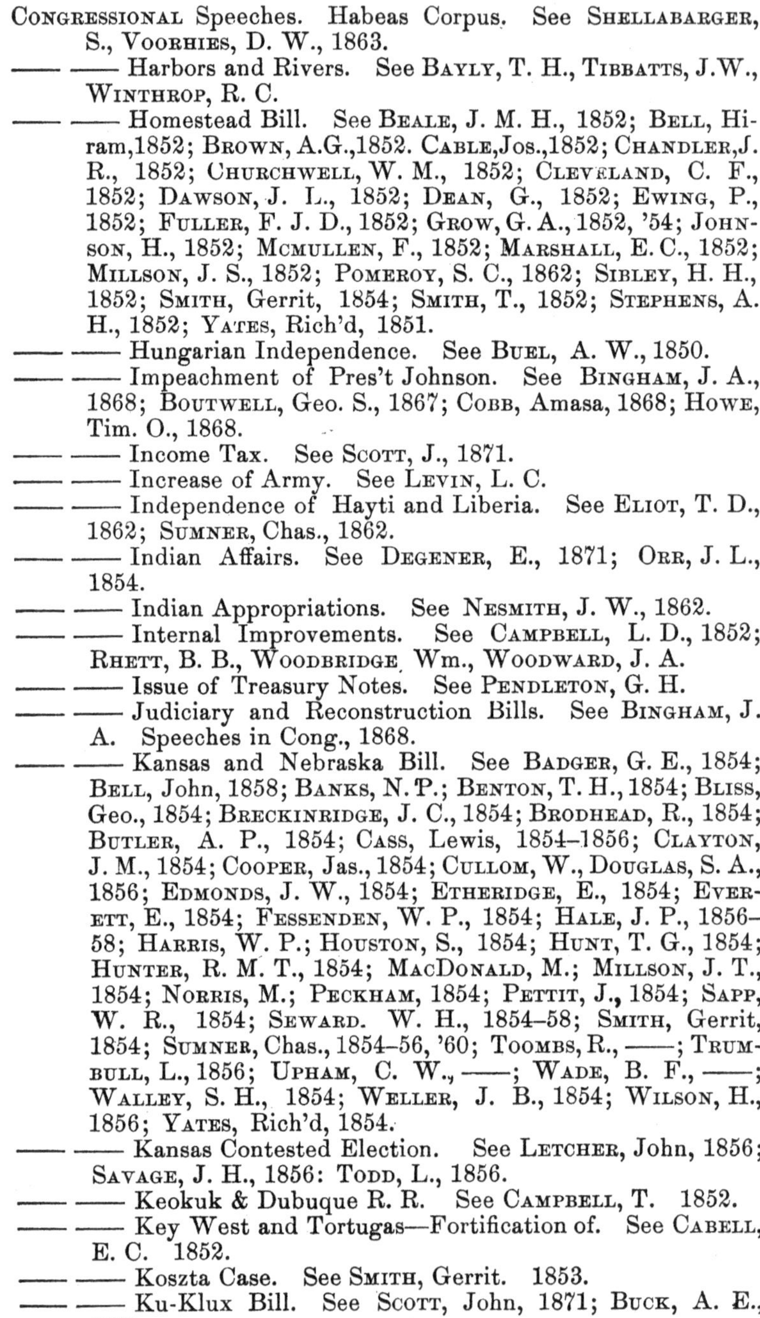

Congressional Speeches. Habeas Corpus. See Shellabarger, S., Voorhies, D. W., 1863.

—— —— Harbors and Rivers. See Bayly, T. H., Tibbatts, J.W., Winthrop, R. C.

—— —— Homestead Bill. See Beale, J. M. H., 1852; Bell, Hiram, 1852; Brown, A.G., 1852. Cable, Jos., 1852; Chandler, J. R., 1852; Churchwell, W. M., 1852; Cleveland, C. F., 1852; Dawson, J. L., 1852; Dean, G., 1852; Ewing, P., 1852; Fuller, F. J. D., 1852; Grow, G. A., 1852, '54; Johnson, H., 1852; McMullen, F., 1852; Marshall, E. C., 1852; Millson, J. S., 1852; Pomeroy, S. C., 1862; Sibley, H. H., 1852; Smith, Gerrit, 1854; Smith, T., 1852; Stephens, A. H., 1852; Yates, Rich'd, 1851.

—— —— Hungarian Independence. See Buel, A. W., 1850.

—— —— Impeachment of Pres't Johnson. See Bingham, J. A., 1868; Boutwell, Geo. S., 1867; Cobb, Amasa, 1868; Howe, Tim. O., 1868.

—— —— Income Tax. See Scott, J., 1871.

—— —— Increase of Army. See Levin, L. C.

—— —— Independence of Hayti and Liberia. See Eliot, T. D., 1862; Sumner, Chas., 1862.

—— —— Indian Affairs. See Degener, E., 1871; Orr, J. L., 1854.

—— —— Indian Appropriations. See Nesmith, J. W., 1862.

—— —— Internal Improvements. See Campbell, L. D., 1852; Rhett, B. B., Woodbridge, Wm., Woodward, J. A.

—— —— Issue of Treasury Notes. See Pendleton, G. H.

—— —— Judiciary and Reconstruction Bills. See Bingham, J. A. Speeches in Cong., 1868.

—— —— Kansas and Nebraska Bill. See Badger, G. E., 1854; Bell, John, 1858; Banks, N. P.; Benton, T. H., 1854; Bliss, Geo., 1854; Breckinridge, J. C., 1854; Brodhead, R., 1854; Butler, A. P., 1854; Cass, Lewis, 1854–1856; Clayton, J. M., 1854; Cooper, Jas., 1854; Cullom, W., Douglas, S. A., 1856; Edmonds, J. W., 1854; Etheridge, E., 1854; Everett, E., 1854; Fessenden, W. P., 1854; Hale, J. P., 1856–58; Harris, W. P.; Houston, S., 1854; Hunt, T. G., 1854; Hunter, R. M. T., 1854; MacDonald, M.; Millson, J. T., 1854; Norris, M.; Peckham, 1854; Pettit, J., 1854; Sapp, W. R., 1854; Seward. W. H., 1854–58; Smith, Gerrit, 1854; Sumner, Chas., 1854–56, '60; Toombs, R., ——; Trumbull, L., 1856; Upham, C. W., ——; Wade, B. F., ——; Walley, S. H., 1854; Weller, J. B., 1854; Wilson, H., 1856; Yates, Rich'd, 1854.

—— —— Kansas Contested Election. See Letcher, John, 1856; Savage, J. H., 1856: Todd, L., 1856.

—— —— Keokuk & Dubuque R. R. See Campbell, T. 1852.

—— —— Key West and Tortugas—Fortification of. See Cabell, E. C. 1852.

—— —— Koszta Case. See Smith, Gerrit. 1853.

—— —— Ku-Klux Bill. See Scott, John, 1871; Buck, A. E., 1871.

CONGRESSIONAL Speeches. Lecompton Constitution. See COLFAX, S., 1856; DOUGLAS, S. A., 1857–58; DURKEE, Chas., 1858.

—— —— Loan Bill. See BROWN, Chas., 1842; GENTRY, M. P., 1842; GRAHAM, W. A., 1842; KENNEDY, A., 1842; LANE, H. S., 1842; PRESTON, W. C., 1842; RAYNER, K., 1842; VINTON, S. F., 1848; WENTWORTH, J., 1866; WRIGHT, Silas, 1842.

—— —— McGarrahan Claim. See BECK, J. B., 1871; GARFIELD, J. A., 1871; KERR, M. C., 1871; SARGENT, A. A., 1871.

—— —— Maritime Rights. See SUMNER, Chas. 1862.

—— —— Mexican Indemnity. See GREY, Benj. E. 1852. HOUSTON, G. S. 1852.

—— —— Mexican Treaty. BAYLY, T. H.

—— —— Mexican War. See CALHOUN, J. C., 1848; HOLMES, E. B., 1846. MARSH, G. P., 1848; DOUGLAS, S. A,, ——; SEVERANCE. L., STEPHENS, A. H., THURMAN, A. G., TIBBATTS, J. W., WEBSTER, D., 1848; WINTHROP, R. C., 1847.

—— —— Missouri Compromise. See Cong. Speeches. Compromise Bill. 1850.

—— —— Missouri River Levees. See ALCORN, J. L. 1873.

—— —— Monroe Doctrine. See SMITH, Gerrit. 1854.

—— —— Nat. Currency. See HOWE, Tim. O. 1870.

—— —— Nat. Debt. See KELLEY, W. D. 1867.

—— —— Nat. Defence. See CLAYTON, J. M. 1836.

—— —— Nat. Educa. See CLARK, W. T., 1871; GARFIELD, J. A., 1866; MCNEELY, T. W., 1871; TOWNSEND, W., 1871.

—— —— Nat. Road Bill. See BARBOUR, P. P. 1830.

—— —— Naturalization Laws. See ADAMS, Stephen; ELDRIDGE, C. 1870.

—— —— Naval Affairs. See BUTLER, A. P., 1856; CLAYTON, J. M., 1856; CRITTENDEN, BUTLER and JONES, 1856; HOUSTON, S. 1856; KING, T. B., 1848; MILLSON, J. S., 1856; STANTON, F. P., 1852; STORER, B., 1836.

—— —— Navy Pension Fund. See ADAMS, J. Q.

—— —— Negro Suffrage. See CLARK, D. 1866.

—— —— Neutrality. See HOWE, T. O. 1870.

—— —— Newport and Cincinnati Bridge. See STEVENSON, J. E. 1871.

—— —— N. Y. Politics. See CUTTING and WALSH. 1854.

—— —— Non-Intervention. See JONES, J. C., 1852; SOULE, P., 1852; WELLS, John, 1852.

—— —— N. Amer. Fisheries. See SEWARD, W. H. 1852.

—— —— N. Pacific R. R. See WINDOM, Wm. 1869.

—— —— Oregon Question. See ASHLEY, C.; BELL, J. F., 1846; BENTON, T. H.; BREESE, S.; CRITTENDEN, J. J.; CUMMINS, J. D.; DICKINSON, D. S.; DIX, J. A.; DODGE, A. C., 1846; EVANS, Geo.; HILLIARD, H. W.; KING, T. B.; MCCLERNAND, J. A.; ROCKWELL, J. A.; SEDDON, J. A.; WINTHROP, R. C.; WICK, W. W., 1846; WOODWARD, W. A.

—— —— Organization of the House. See GIDDINGS, J. R., 1855; LARRABEE, C. H., 1859.

CONGRESSIONAL Speeches. Removal of Deposits. See ADAMS, J. Q. BENTON, T. H.; BINNEY, H., 1834; CALHOUN, J. C., CLAY, H., 1838; CLOWNEY, W. K., DICKSON, J., FORSYTH, J., GHOLSON, J. H., LEIGH, B. W., POLK, J. K., RIVES, W. C., WEBSTER, D., WILDE, R. H., WRIGHT, Silas.

—— —— Removal of Indians. See Speeches on that Subject. 1830.

—— —— Removals and Appointments to Office. See BRADBURY, J. W. 1850. SMITH, Truman. 1850. EWING, Thos. 1850.

—— —— Representation and Taxation· See PALMER, A. (n. d.)

—— —— Republican Economy, etc. See BLAINE, J. G. 1868.

—— —— Repub. Party in the South. See McKENZIE, L. 1871.

—— —— Revenue. See ASPER, J. F. 1871. CORWIN, T. 1837.

—— —— Rights of Neutrals. See LATHAM, M. S.

—— —— River and Harbor Improvements. See CAMPBELL, Thomson, 1852; EWING, Thos., FICKLIN, O. B., 1844; LOCKHART, Jas., 1852; ROCKWELL, J. A., 1846; STOCKTON, R. F., 1852.

—— —— Roman Catholic Church. See CHANDLER, J. R. 1855.

—— —— San Juan Island. See HOWARD, J. M. 1869.

—— —— Seizure of Arsenals at Harper's Ferry. See TRUMBULL, L. 1859.

—— —— Slavery. See BISSELL, W. H., 1850; BLISS, P., 1858; BUTLER, T. B., 1850; CABELL, E. C., 1850; CALHOUN, J. C., 1850; CAMPBELL, L. D., 1850; CLEMENS, S., 1861; CONWAY, M. F., 1861; DOUGLAS, S. A., 1860; FISHER, G. P., 1862; GRANGER, A. P., 1856; INGERSOLL, C. M., 1852; JOHNSON, Reverdy, 1864; JULIAN, G. W., 1850; GIDDINGS, J. R., MANN, H., 1848–52; MORTON, J., 1850; PALFREY, J. G., 1848; SAULSBURY, W., 1860; SCHOONMAKER, M., 1852; SUMNER, C., 1860; TAPPAN, M. W. 1856; TOWNSEND, N. S., 1852; UNDERWOOD, J. R., 1850; WADE, E., 1856; WEBSTER, D., 1850.

—— —— Slavery in Dist. of Columbia. See DICKSON, —., 1835; FESSENDEN, W. P., 1862; Hale, J. P., 1862; MOORE, Ely, 1839; SLADE, —., 1840; SEWARD, W. H., 1850.

—— —— Smithsonian Institution. See MARSH, Geo. P.

—— —— Soldiers' Bounties. See PAINE, H. E. 1868.

—— —— Spanish Spoliations. See SMART, E. K. 1852.

—— —— State Appropriations. See HOFFMAN, O. 1840.

—— —— State Banks. See STUART, J. T.. 1842.

—— —— State of Parties in Illinois. See DOUGLAS, S. A. 1858.

—— —— State of the Union. See BURLINGAME, Anson, 1856; RANTOUL, R., 1852; SCUDDER, Z., 1852; SEWARD, W. H., 1860; SKELTON, C., 1853; SMART, E. K., 1852; SMITH, Truman, WILLIAMS, T., 1864.

—— —— State Rights. See TEN EYCK, J. C., 1860.

—— —— Steamships. See KELLOGG, W. P., 1871; LATHAM, M. S.

—— —— Sub-Treasury Bill. See DAVIS, John, 1840; TALLMADGE, N. P., 1838; WEBSTER, Daniel, 1838.

CONGRESSIONAL Speeches. Suffrage. See SUMNER, C. 1866–69.

—— —— Suffrage in Dist. of Columbia. See KELLEY, Wm. D. 1866.

—— —— Tariff. See ASPER, J. F., BARRINGER, D. M., BAYLY, T. H., BENTON, C. H., BLAIR, A., 1870; BLANCHARD, J., BOYCE, W. W., BRODHEAD, R., CARROLL, J. H., CATTELL, A. G., 1867; CHASE, L. B., CLINGMAN, T. L., COLLAMER, J., COLLIN, J. F., COOPER, J., DIXON, J., EWING, T., 1832; FICKLIN, O. B., FOWLER, O., 1852; GENTRY, M. P., HARMANSON, J. H., HOUSTON, J. W., HUBBARD, E. W., HUDSON, C., INGERSOLL, J. R., JAMES, C. T., 1856; JENKINS, T., JONES, S., KAUFMAN, D. S., KELLY, W. D., 1870; LEWIS, D. H., MARSH, G. P., MCHENRY, J. H., NILES, J. M., OWEN, D. D., PERRY, Thos., ROCKWELL, J. A., ROOT, J. A., ROSS, Thos., SALTONSTALL, L., 1842; SEVERANCE, L., SLADE, W., 1841; STEWART, A., 1832; STROHM, J., THOMPSON, Jas., TIBBATTS, J. W., TOOMBS, R., WEBSTER, D., 1824; WELLER, J. B., 1841; WINTHROP, R. C., YOUNG, B. R.

—— —— Tariff Bills. 1841–2. See Congr. and Polit. Pamph. Vols. 24 and 25.

—— —— Temperance. See SMITH, Gerrit, 1854.

—— —— Territorial Affairs. See DIX, J. A., 1848; QUITMAN, J. A., 1856; STEVENS, J. J., 1858.

—— —— Test Oath—Constitutionality of. See BAYARD, Jas. A.

—— —— Texan Affairs. See HOUSTON, S.

—— —— Texas Boundary. See ASHMUN, G., 1850; BALDWIN, R. S., 1850; BENTON, T. H., 1850; GIDDINGS, J. R., 1850; HILLIARD, H. W., 1850; KAUFMAN, D. S., 1848; RUSK, T. J., 1850; STEPHENS, T., 1850.

—— —— —— Pacific R. R. See HOWARD, Jacob M., 1870.

—— —— Treasury Note Bill. See SUMNER, C. THOMPSON, Jacob, 1842; TIBBATTS, J. W.

—— —— Union Parties in Miss. See FREEMAN, J. D., 1852.

—— —— —— Party of Georgia. See CHASTAIN, E. W., 1852.

—— —— U. S. Bank. See CALHOUN, J. C.

—— —— U. S. Military Academy. See SMITH, Gerrit.

—— —— Utah Bill. See CLAGETT, W. H., 1873; HOOPER, W. H., 1870.

—— —— Veto Power. See ARCHER, Wm. S., 1842; BERRIEN, J. M., 1842; BUCHANAN, Jas., 1842; CALHOUN, J. C., 1842; PRESTON, W. C., 1842; WOODBURY, Levi, 1842.

—— —— Virginia Land Claims. See GOODE, P. G., 1842; HALL, Hiland, 1842.

—— —— Warehouse Bill. See DIX, John A.; SMITH, Truman.

—— —— Wheat Trade of U. S. See HUDSON, Chas.

—— —— Wilmot Proviso. See BIRDSALL, A., 1848.

—— —— Woodworth's Patent. See OTIS, Jno. 1850.

—— Temperance Soc. Annivers. Proceed., Feb. 27, 1838, in Hall of House of Repr. 8vo. Congr. and Polit. Pamph. Vol. 105.

CONGREVE, Sir Wm., on the Impracticability of the Resumption of Cash Payments. Lond., 1820. 8vo. Pamphleteer. Vol. 15.

CONIFERAE of the Rocky Mountains. See KNAPP, J. G.

CONINGTON, Henry. Reform at any Price! A Question about the Lond. Corporation Bill. Lond., 1856. 8vo. Eng. Polit. Pamph. Vol. 53.

CONKLING, Alfred. Opinion upon the Question of Copyright in the case of Little & Co. *vs.* Hall, Goulds & Banks. 1852. Law Pamph. Vol. 2.

CONKLING, Rev. C. Slavery Abolished; its Relation to the Gov't. 1862. Rebell'n Pamph. Vol. 74.

CONKLING, Henry. Inside View of the Rebellion. Cincin., 1864. 8vo. Rebell'n Pamph. Vol. 1.

CONKLING, Margaret C. Memoirs of the Mother and Wife of Washington. New Ed., Revised. N. Y., 1858. 12mo.

CONKLING, Roscoe. Speech in Cong., Apr. 29, 1862, on Gov't Contracts. Rebell'n Pamph. Vol. 66.

—— Speech in Cong., Jan. 6, 1862, on Battle of Ball's Bluff. Rebellion Pamph. Vol. 32.

—— Speech in U. S. Senate, Feb. 22, 1870, on 15th Amendment. 8vo. Congr. and Polit. Pamph. Vol. 119.

—— Speech in U. S. Senate, Feb. 19, 1872, on Sales of Arms to French Agents, etc. Congr. and Polit. Pamph. Vol. 129.

CONNECTICUT Acad. of Arts and Sciences. Memoirs. Vol. 1. Parts 1, 2, 3. N. Haven, 1810–13. 4to. Memoirs. Vol. 1. Pt. 4. N. Haven, 1816. 8vo.

—— Adjutant General's Ann. Reports for 1860, '63, '64, '65, '66, '67, '68, '69. Hartford, 1860–69. 8vo.

—— Alpha of the Phi Beta Kappa. Catalogue for 1838. N. Haven, 1838. 8vo.

—— and Passumpsie Rivers R. R. Co. 20th Ann. Report, July, 1865. Boston, 1865. 8vo. Conn. Misc. Pamph. Vol. 1.

—— Ann. Registers for 1833, '39, '42, '45, '47, '50, '55, '57, 60, '68. 10 Vols. 18mo.

—— Assoc., Boston. Festival at the Revere House, Boston, Jan. 14, 1857, with the Constitution, etc., of the Assoc. Boston, 1857. 8vo. Boston Misc. Pamph. Vol. 2.

—— Bank Commissioners. Report to Gen. Assembly. 1856. N. Haven, 1856. 8vo.

—— See BARBER, J. W. Conn. Hist. Coll.

—— Blue Laws of N. Haven Colony.

—— BUSHNELL, H. Hist. Estimate of. 1851.

—— CARPENTER and ARTHUR. Hist. of.

—— Catalogue of Volunteer Organizations in War of Rebellion. Hartford, 1869. 8vo.

—— Colonial Records. See TRUMBULL, J. H.

—— Comptroller's Reports, 1853, '56, '70. 8vo.

—— Correspondence with the British Gov't. Conn. Hist. Soc. Coll. Vol. 1.

—— See CROFFUT and MORRIS. Conn. in the War of Rebell'n.

—— DWIGHT, T. Hist. of.

—— EPISCOPACY in. See ELIOT, John. Papers on. 1722.

—— Episcopal Acad., Cheshire. Catalogue for 1848. N. Haven, 1849. 18mo.

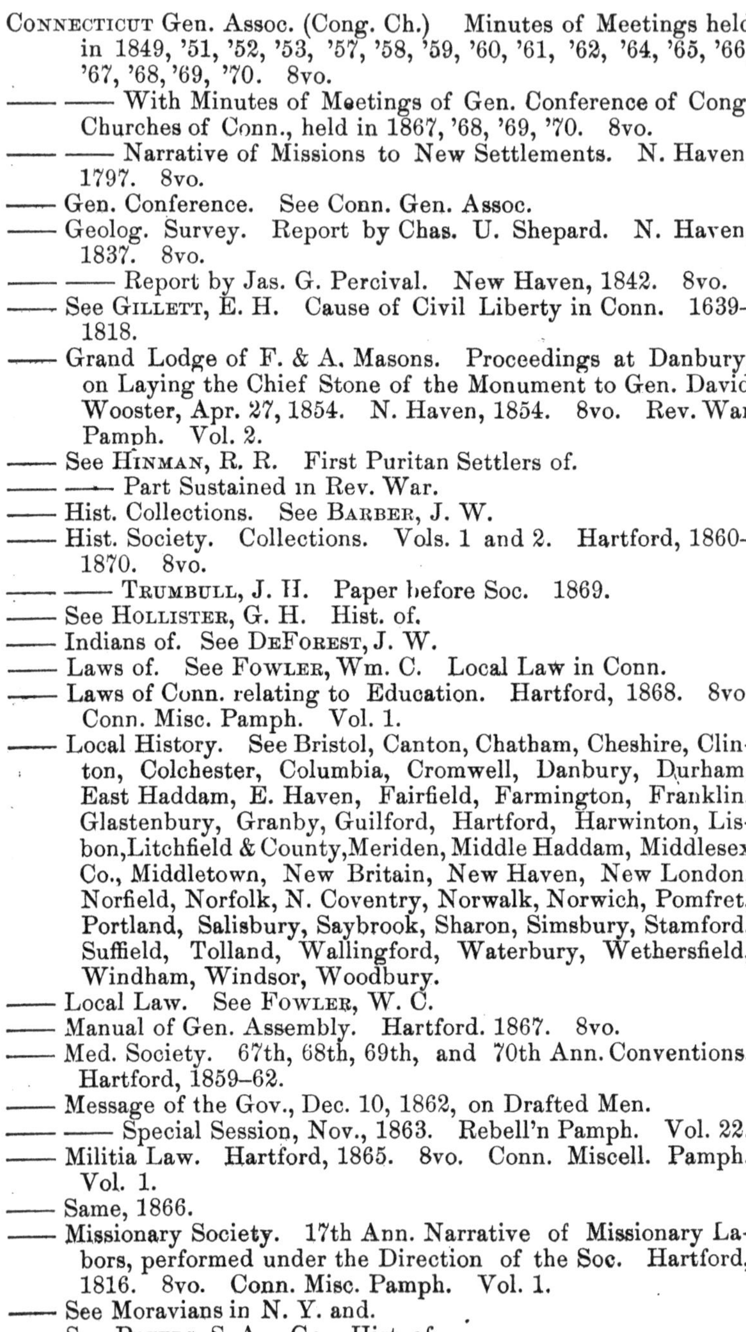

CONNECTICUT Gen. Assoc. (Cong. Ch.) Minutes of Meetings held in 1849, '51, '52, '53, '57, '58, '59, '60, '61, '62, '64, '65, '66, '67, '68, '69, '70. 8vo.

—— —— With Minutes of Meetings of Gen. Conference of Cong. Churches of Conn., held in 1867, '68, '69, '70. 8vo.

—— —— Narrative of Missions to New Settlements. N. Haven, 1797. 8vo.

—— Gen. Conference. See Conn. Gen. Assoc.

—— Geolog. Survey. Report by Chas. U. Shepard. N. Haven, 1837. 8vo.

—— —— Report by Jas. G. Percival. New Haven, 1842. 8vo.

—— See GILLETT, E. H. Cause of Civil Liberty in Conn. 1639–1818.

—— Grand Lodge of F. & A. Masons. Proceedings at Danbury, on Laying the Chief Stone of the Monument to Gen. David Wooster, Apr. 27, 1854. N. Haven, 1854. 8vo. Rev. War Pamph. Vol. 2.

—— See HINMAN, R. R. First Puritan Settlers of.

—— —— Part Sustained in Rev. War.

—— Hist. Collections. See BARBER, J. W.

—— Hist. Society. Collections. Vols. 1 and 2. Hartford, 1860–1870. 8vo.

—— —— TRUMBULL, J. H. Paper before Soc. 1869.

—— See HOLLISTER, G. H. Hist. of.

—— Indians of. See DEFOREST, J. W.

—— Laws of. See FOWLER, Wm. C. Local Law in Conn.

—— Laws of Conn. relating to Education. Hartford, 1868. 8vo. Conn. Misc. Pamph. Vol. 1.

—— Local History. See Bristol, Canton, Chatham, Cheshire, Clinton, Colchester, Columbia, Cromwell, Danbury, Durham, East Haddam, E. Haven, Fairfield, Farmington, Franklin, Glastenbury, Granby, Guilford, Hartford, Harwinton, Lisbon, Litchfield & County, Meriden, Middle Haddam, Middlesex Co., Middletown, New Britain, New Haven, New London, Norfield, Norfolk, N. Coventry, Norwalk, Norwich, Pomfret, Portland, Salisbury, Saybrook, Sharon, Simsbury, Stamford, Suffield, Tolland, Wallingford, Waterbury, Wethersfield, Windham, Windsor, Woodbury.

—— Local Law. See FOWLER, W. C.

—— Manual of Gen. Assembly. Hartford. 1867. 8vo.

—— Med. Society. 67th, 68th, 69th, and 70th Ann. Conventions. Hartford, 1859–62.

—— Message of the Gov., Dec. 10, 1862, on Drafted Men.

—— —— Special Session, Nov., 1863. Rebell'n Pamph. Vol. 22.

—— Militia Law. Hartford, 1865. 8vo. Conn. Miscell. Pamph. Vol. 1.

—— Same, 1866.

—— Missionary Society. 17th Ann. Narrative of Missionary Labors, performed under the Direction of the Soc. Hartford, 1816. 8vo. Conn. Misc. Pamph. Vol. 1.

—— See Moravians in N. Y. and.

—— See PETERS, S. A. Gen. Hist. of.

CONNECTICUT. PHELPS, R. H. Hist. of the Newgate of.
—— Poets of.
—— P. Episcopal Ch. See P. E. Ch. Doc. History.
—— Public and Private Acts and Resolves of Gen. Assembly, May, 1853.
—— Public Acts, May, 1856.
—— Public and Private Acts and Resolves, May, 1857, '58, '59.
—— Public Acts, May, 1860.
—— Public and Private Acts and Resolves, 1861–2.
—— Public Acts, 1863.
—— Public and Private Acts and Resolves, 1864–5.
—— Public Acts of Gen. Assembly, 1866, '67, '68, '69, '70.
—— Private Acts and Resolutions, May, 1867.
—— Public Acts passed at May Session of Gen. Assembly, 1872. Hartford, 1872.
—— Public Schools. Reports of Supt. of Common Schools, for 1849, '50, '51, '53, '55, '56, '60. Hartford, 1849–60. 8vo.
—— Quarter Master Gen'l. Report, May Session, 1863. Rebell'n Pamph. Vol. 92.
—— —— Report for the Year 1863–4. Hartford, 1864. 8vo. Rebell'n Pamph. Vol. 79.
—— Railroad Commiss'rs. Reports for 1854, '55, '56. 8vo.
—— Records of the Colony and Plantation of New Haven, from 1638 to 1649.
—— The Same from May, 1653, to the Union, together with the New Haven Code of 1656.
—— (Public) Records of Conn. from Aug., 1689, to Oct., 1716. Edited by C. J. Hoadly. Hartford. v. d. 8vo.
—— (Public) Records of the Colony from May, 1717, to Oct., 1725. Hartford, 1872. 8vo.
—— Register; or a State Calendar of Officers and Institutions for 1856. Hartford, 1856. 18mo.
—— River. Geology of the. See HITCHCOCK, Edw. Sketch of, 1822.
—— —— Valley. See SMITH, Alfred. Geol. of, etc., 1832.
—— School for Imbeciles. Reports, 1861, '65. Hartford, 1861, '65. 8vo.
—— Seal of. See HOADLY, C. J.
—— Sketches of 40 Years Since.
—— Soldiers' Relief Assoc. 1st Ann. Report, 1862. Rebell'n Pamph. Vol. 20.
—— State Agricult. Soc. Transactions for 1854–5–6–7–8–9. 6 Vols. 8vo. Hartford.
—— State Librarian. Reports on Registration of Births, etc., for 1856,–57–58–59–60. '69. Hartford and N. Haven, 1857–70. 8vo.
—— State Normal School. Ann. Report of Trustees, 1857, with Catalogue. Hartford, 1857. 8vo.
—— State Prison. Report of Directors, 1855. Hartford, 1855. 8vo.
—— State Reform School. 4th Ann. Report for 1856. N. Haven, 1856. 8vo.

CONNECTICUT. Statutes of the State of. N. Haven, 1854. 8vo.
—— See Steady Habits Vindicated, etc. 1805.
—— Their Majesties' Colony of Conn. in N. England Vindicated, etc., 1694. Conn. Hist. Soc. Coll. Vol. 1.
—— Theolog. Institute, East Windsor Hill. Gen. Catalogue, 1850 Hartford 1850. 12mo.
—— See TRUMBULL, Rev. B. Hist. of.
—— TRUMBULL, J. H. Colonial Records of.
—— Valley of. See DEANE, Jas. Fossil Footprints.
CONNELL, Geo. Speech in Penn. Senate, Feb. 15, 1863. Rebell'n Pamph. Vol. 36.
CONNERY, Jas. Essay on Charitable Economy, etc. Dublin, 1837. 12mo. Eng. Misc. Pamph. Vol. 12.
CONQUEST of Canaan. See DWIGHT, Timothy.
—— of Granada. See IRVING, W.
—— of Santa Fé and Subjection of New Mexico. Phila., 1847. 8vo. Mex. War Pamph. Vol. 2.
CONSEQUENCES (The) of Trade as to the Wealth and Strength of any Nation. Lond., 1740. 8vo. Eng. Misc. Pamph. Vol. 23.
CONSIDERATIONS (Farther) upon a Reduction of the Land Tax. Lond., 1751. 8vo. Eng. Polit. Pamph. Vol. 69.
—— in favor of the Construction of a Great State Road from Lake Erie to the Hudson River. Albany, 1827. 8vo. N. York Misc. Pamph. Vol. 1.
—— of the Police Report of 1816, with a few Words concerning Perpetual Motion. Lond., 1852. 8vo. Pamphleteer. Vol. 21.
—— on the State of the Poor in G. Britain. 2 Pamphlets. Lond., 1773. 12mo. Eng. Polit. Pamph. Vol. 17.
—— on British Commerce with India, America, etc. Lond., 1817. 8vo. Pamphleteer. Vol. 11.
—— on the Addresses lately presented to H. Majesty, on the Loss of Minorca. Lond., 1756. 8vo. Eng. Polit. Pamph. Vol. 71.
—— on the Consequences of the French Settling the Colonies on the Mississipi. Lond., 1720. 12mo.
—— on the Dissenters' Bill now pending in Parl't. Lond., 1779. 8vo. Eng. Polit. Pamph. Vol. 19.
—— on the Establishment of a Regency. Lond., 1788. 8vo. Eng. Polit. Pamph. Vol. 74.
—— on the Expediency of Abolishing Damages on Protested Bills of Exchange, etc. N. Y., 1829. 8vo. Banking and Currency Pamph. Vol. 2. Congr. and Polit. Pamph. Vol. 98.
—— on the Great Western Canal, from the Hudson to Lake Erie. Brooklyn, 1818. 8vo. 2d Edition. N. Y. Misc. Pamph. Vol. 1.
—— on the Intended Reform in Parliamentary Representation. Lond., 1785. 8vo. Eng. Polit. Pamph. Vol. 22.
—— on the Law of Forfeiture for High Treason, etc., regarding the Pretender's Sons. Lond., 1745. 8vo. Eng. Polit. Pamph. Vol. 12.

CONSIDERATIONS on the Legality of General Warrants, with a Postcript concerning Juries, Libels, etc. 2d Ed. Lond., 1765. Polit. Tracts. Vol. 2.
—— on the Military Establishments of G. Britain, etc. Lond. n. d. Sm. 4to. Eng. Polit. Pamph. Vol. 23.
—— on the Necessity of Establishing an Agricult. Coll. in the State of N. Y. Albany, 1819. 8vo. Agr. Pamph. Vol. 12.
—— on the Present German War. 4th Ed. With a Review of the Same. Lond., 1760. 8vo. Eng. Polit. Pamph. Vol. 14.
—— —— Another Answer to the Same. Lond., 1760. 8vo. 2d Ed. Eng. Polit. Pamph. Vol. 72.
—— on the Present German War, 1761. See Reasons in Support of the War, etc.
—— on the Proposal for Reducing the Interest on the Nat. Debt. Lond., 1750. 8vo. Eng. Polit. Pamph. Vol. 69.
—— on the Slavery Question; addressed to the Pres't of the U. S. 1862.
—— on the Use and Abuse of Antimonial Medicines in Fevers and other Disorders. Lond., 1773. 8vo. 2d Ed. Med. Pamph. Vol. 15.
—— Suggested by the Report of Her Majesty's Commissioners, respecting the Court of Chancery. Lond., 1826. 8vo. Law Pamph. Vol. 14.
—— upon Commissions of Bankrupts. Lond., 1727. 8vo. Eng. Polit. Pamph. Vol. 8.
—— upon the Present State of Our Affairs. Lond., 1739. 12mo. Eng. Polit. Pamph. Vol. 68.
—— upon Two Bills now before the House of Commons, relating to the Clergy of Ireland, 1731. Dublin, 1741. 8vo. Eng. Polit. Pamph. Vol. 11.
CONSPIRACY of Pontiac. See BRADSTREET, Gen.
—— —— PARKMAN, F.
—— —— Siege of Detroit, etc.
CONSTANT, Benj. On the Dissolution of the Chamber of Deputies. Lond., 1821. 8vo. From the French. Pamphleteer. Vol. 18.
CONSTANTINOPLE. See COLTON, Rev. W. Views of.
CONSTITUTION (The) and Mr. Motley. Phila., 1861. 12mo. Rebell'n Pamph. Vol. 28.
—— of Confederate States. Pamph. n. d.
—— of the U. States and the Several States. Phila., 1800. 12mo.
—— —— See MARSHALL, John.
—— —— with the Amendments thereto: Jefferson's Manual and Digest of the Rules of the House of Repr., and Joint Rules of both Houses. Washington, 1865. 8vo.
—— —— Same. Washington, 1871. 8vo.
—— —— A Pro-Slavery Contract; or Extracts from the Madison Papers, etc. 3d Ed. N. Y., 1856. 12mo. Congress. Pamph. Vol. 97.
—— —— Catechism of the Constitution. n. p. 1863. 8vo. Congr. and Polit. Pamph. Vol. 71.
—— —— FARRAR, T. Manual of.

CONSTITUTION of United States and Standing Rules of House of Representatives, and Rules of the Senate. Washington, 1852 12mo. Congress. Pamphlets. Vol. 56.

—— —— Proposed Amendments. Loyal Publica. Soc. N. Y., 1865. 8vo.

—— —— with Standing Rules of both Houses of Cong., 1852. Congr. and Polit. Pamph. Vol. 56.

CONSTITUTIONAL Law. See PARKER, Joel.

—— Reform. See JORDAN, Francis.

—— View of the India Question. Lond., 1858. 8vo. Eng. Polit. Pamph. Vol. 55.

CONSTRUCTION and Use of the Sea Quadrant; or Hadley's Quadrant. Lond., 1666. 8vo. Scientific Pamph. Vol. 30.

—— Ecônomique des Toits pour les Edifices de toutes Dimensions, Terrasses, etc. Bordeaux, 1819. 4to. Scientific Pamph. Vol. 38.

CONSULAR Service. See GREEN, John. Nature and Character of. 1848.

CONSULS, etc., of U. S. See U. S. Sec. of State.

CONTARET, Dr. D. E. Disinfecting Process. Testimonial in favor of. N. Y., 1857. Scientific Pamph. Vol. 17.

CONTEST in America, 1757. See MITCHELL, Dr. J.

—— See Amer. War, etc.

CONTINENTAL Monthly Mag. N. Y., 1862. 2 Vols. 8vo.

—— Soc. for the Diffusion of Religious Knowledge. Proceedings and Report, 1827–8. Lond., 1828. 8vo. Eng. Religious Pamph. Vol. 88.

CONTOSTAVLOS, Alex. Facts relative to the Building of the Two Greek Frigates. N. Y., 1826. 8vo. Hist. Pamph. Vol. 7.

CONTRAST (The); or Two Speeches—the one delivered by the President of the U. S., Dec. 2, 1817, and the other to the Borough Mongers of G. Britain, Jan. 27, 1818. Lond., 1818.

CONTRIBUTIONS to Amer. History. Phila., 1858. 8vo. Penn. Hist. Soc. Memoirs. Vol. 6.

CONTROVERSY between the 1st Parish in Cambridge and the Rev. Dr. Holmes. Cambridge, 1829. 8vo. Mass. Hist. Discourses, etc. Vol. 19.

CONVENTION between the Crowns of G. Britain and Spain, at the Pardo, Jan. 14, 1739. Articles of, etc., with "The Convention Vindicated." Lond., 1739. 8vo. Eng. Polit. Pamph. Vol. 11.

—— of Medical Delegates, at Northampton, Mass. Proceedings, June 20, 1827. Boston, 1827. 8vo. Med. Pamph. Vol. 12.

CONVERSATION (Imaginary) between President Jackson and the Ghost of Jefferson. Columbia, S. C., 1831. 12mo. Nullification Tracts.

CONWAY, Gen. See Counter-Address to the Public, etc. 1764.

—— GUTHRIE, W. Address on his Dismission from his Military Employments.

—— Speech in Parl't, May 5, 1780, on the Troubles in America. Lond., 1781. 8vo. Eng. Polit. Pamph. Vol. 73.

CONWAY, (Mass.) Centenn. Celebra. Northampton, 1867. 8vo.

CONWAY, M. F. Speech in Cong., Dec. 12, 1861, on the Rebellion. Rebell'n Pamph. Vols. 66 and 69. Congr. and Polit Pamph. Vol. 84.

CONWAY, Thos. W. The Freedmen of Louisiana. Final Report of the Bureau of Free Labor, etc. N. Orleans, 1865. 8vo. La. Misc. Pamph. Vol. 1.

CONWAY, Rev. W. Sermon in Westminster Abbey, Oct. 29, 1865, on the Death of Viscount Palmerston. Lond., 1865. 8vo. Eng. Sermons. Vol. 44A.

CONYGHAM, D. P. Sherman's March through the South, with Incidents of the Campaign. N. Y., 1865. 8vo.

CONYNGHAM, Redmond. Acc. of the Settlement of Dunkers, at Ephratah, Pa. Phila., 1826. 8vo. See Penn. Hist. Soc. Memoirs. Vol. 2. Part 1.

COOK, Dan'l P. See BROWN, Wm. H. Memoir of.

COOK, Eben. The Sot-Weed Factor; or a Voyage to Maryland. Lond., 1708. N. Y., 1865. 4to. Reprint.

COOK, Capt. Jas. See Collection of Interesting Biography. 1791.

COOK, Jas. M. See N. York Supreme Court.

COOK, Joel. The Siege of Richmond; Narra. of Military Operations of Maj. Gen. McClellan in May and June, 1862. Phila., 1868.

COOK, John Wilson, on the Hist. of Canada. Read before the Quebec Lit. and Hist. Soc., Feb. 21, 1866. Transactions. N. Series. Part 4.

COOK, Wm. A. Opinions and Practice of the Founders of the Republic in Relation to Arbitrary Arrests. Washington, 1864. 8vo. Rebell'n Pamph. Vol. 33.

—— Review of Hon. Geo. W. Woodward's Speech at Phila., 1863. 8vo. Rebell'n Pamph. Vol. 39.

COOK'S Scottish Tourist. Leicester, 1865. 8vo. Guide Books. Vol. 31.

—— Tours on the English and French Coasts. Lond., 1865. 8vo. Guide Books. Vol. 31.

COOKE, Edw. Address to the Public on Examining the Affairs of the Bank. Lond., 1819. 8vo. Eng. Polit. Pamph. Vol. 35.

—— on the High Price of Gold Bullion, etc. Lond., 1819. 8vo. Pamphleteer. Vol. 14.

—— Thoughts on the Expediency of Repealing the Usury Laws. Lond., 1818. 8vo. Pamphleteer. Vol. 13.

COOKE, Eleutheros. Oration before the Fire Lands Hist. Soc., at Norwalk, O., July 4, 1857. Fire Lands Pioneer. Vol. 1.

COOKE, G. A. Topograph and Statist. Descrip. of the Co. of Durham, Eng. Lond. (n. d.) 12mo. Guide Books. Vol. 3.

—— Topograph. and Statist. Descrip. of Wales. Part 2. Lond., (n. d.) 12mo. Guide Books. Vol. 27.

COOKE, G. A. Topograph. Survey of the County of Cornwall. Lond., (n. d.) 18mo. Pamph.

COOKE, H. T. Descriptive Guide to Guy's Cliff. Warwick, Eng., 1844. 12mo. Guide Books. Vol. 10.

COOKE, Jay. How to Organize a Nat. Bank under Sec. Chase's Bill. 1863. Rebell'n Pamph. Vol. 87.

COOKE, John E. Life of Gen. Robert E. Lee. New York, 1871. 8vo.

—— Personal Portraits; Scenes and Adventures of the War. N. Y., 1871. 8vo.

—— Recollections of Dr. J. W. Francis. From Hours at Home, April, 1866. Biograph. Pamph. Vol. 11.

—— Stonewall Jackson; a Military Biography. N. Y., 1866. 8vo.

COOKE, Rev. Parsons. Address at Laying the Corner Stone of the 1st Calvinistic Ch. in Hardwick, Mass., Sept., 1828. Brookfield, 1828. 8vo. Sermons. Vol. 53.

COOKE, Rev. Wm. The Sin of Drinking; Sermon at St. Stephen. Hammersmith, 1855. Lond., 1855. 8vo. Temp. Pamph. Vol. 3.

COOKVILLE, (Wis.) Waucoma Lodge, No. 65, I. O. O. F. Constitution, By-Laws, etc. Milwaukee, 1854. 18mo. Wis. Misc. Pamph. Vol. 1.

COOLEY, Arnold. Cyclopœdia of Six Thousand Practical Receipts in Arts, Manufactures and Trades. N. Y., 1857. 8vo.

COOLEY, J. E. Speech in U. S. Senate, Mar. 19, 1853, on Completion of Public Works. Congr. and Polit. Pamph. Vol. 88.

COOLIDGE, A. J., and MANSFIELD, J. B. Hist. and Descrip. of N. England, General and Local. Vol. 1. Maine, N. Hampshire and Vermont. Boston, 1860. 8vo.

COOMBE, Rev. P. Sermon at Phila., June 30, 1861, on the Divine Right of Civil Gov't. Rebell'n Pamph. Vol. 80. Rebell'n Pamph. Vol. 40.

COOMBS, Gen. Leslie. Narr. of his Life, embracing Incidents of the Hist. of the War of 1812. N. Y., 1852. 8vo.

COOPER, Rev. Mr. History of N. America to their becoming Free States. 1st Ed., Lond., 1789., 12mo.; and 2d Ed., Lansingburgh, 1795. 12mo.

COOPER, Chas. Purton. See Letters to. 1835.

COOPER, Rev. Jacob. The Loyalty demanded by the Present Crisis. Phila., 1864. 8vo. Rebell'n Pamph. Vol. 17.

COOPER, Rev. Jas. Disc. at Phila., Apr. 16, 1865, on Death of Pres't Lincoln. Rebell'n Pamph. Vol. 8.

COOPER, Jas. Remarks in Cong., Jan. 18, 1842, on the Treasury Note Bill. Washington, 1842. 8vo. Congr. and Polit. Pamph. Vol. 24.

—— Speech in Cong., Feb. 27, 1854, on the Kansas and Nebr. Bill. Cong. and Polit. Pamph. Vol. 93.

—— Speech in Cong., Feb. 17, 1855, on Duties on Railroad Iron. Speeches. Vol. 5.

COOPER, J. Fennimore. Hist. of the Navy of the U. States of America. N. Y., 1854. 8vo.

—— Lives of Distinguished Amer. Naval Officers. Vol. 1. Phila., 1846. 12mo.

—— Memorial of. N. Y., 1832. 8vo.

—— The Battle of Lake Erie; or Answers to Messrs. Burges, Duer & Mackenzie. Cooperstown, 1843. 12mo. Pamphlets War of 1812. Vol. 2.

COOPER, Jas. M. The Government and the Manufactuier. (n. d.) Rebell'n Pamph. Vol. 18.
COOPER, John. Topograph. Descrip. of Machias, in the Co. of Lincoln, Me. Mass. Hist. Soc. Coll. 1st Ser. Vol. 3.
COOPER, Lemuel P. Hist. Sketch of Croydon, N. H. N. H. Hist. Soc. Coll. Vol. 6.
COOPER, Mark A. Speech in Cong., Apr. 25, 1842, on Apportionment. Washington, 1842. 8vo. Congr. and Polit. Pamph. Vol. 25.
—— Speecn in Cong., July 6, 1842, on the Tariff. Washington, 1842. 8vo. Congr. and Polit. Pamph. Vol. 25.
COOPER, Peter. Dangers of a War of Commerce on all the Great Interests of our Country. N. Y., 1872. 8vo. Congr. and Polit. Pamph. Vol. 129.
—— See Cooper Union.
—— Letter on Emancipation. N. Y., 1863. 8vo. Rebell'n Pamph. Vols. 39 and 90.
—— Letter to Hon. Robert J. Walker, June 15, 1846, on the Tariff. 1846. Speeches. Vol. 1.
—— The Death of Slavery. Letter to Gov. Seymour. N. Y., 1863. 8vo. Rebell'n Pamph. Vols. 46 and 90.
COOPER, Rich'd. Lecture to the Working Classes at London, Feb. 6, 1854. Lond. 12mo. Eng. Polit. Pamph. Vol. 52.
COOPER, Saml. Introduct. Med. Address before University Coll., Oct. 1, 1844. Lond., 1844. 8vo. Med. Pamph. Vol. 29.
—— Resignation of the Professorship of Surgery, in University Coll., London. Lond., 1847. 8vo. Med. Pamph. Vol. 33.
COOPER, Thos. Analysis of an Essay on the Temperature of the Interior of the Earth, by M. Cordier. 1827. Silliman's Journ. Vol. 15.
—— Some Information Respecting America. 2d Ed. Lond., 1795. 8vo.
COOPER, Thompson. Men of the Time; a Dictionary on Contemporaries. Lond., 1872. 12mo.
CO-OPERATIVE Societies. See Articles on Social Science, etc.
COOPER Union, N. Y. Charter, Trust-Deed and By-Laws, with Letter of Peter Cooper. N. Y., 1859. 8vo. N. Y. Misc. Pamph. Vol. 2.
—— —— 1st Ann. Report of the Trustees, Jan. 1, 1860. N. Y., 1860. 8vo. N. Y. Misc. Pamph. Vol. 2.
COOPER, Wm. D. Glossary of Provincialisms in use in the Co. of Surrey. 2d Ed. Lond., 1853. 12mo.
COOPERSTOWN (N. Y.) Freeman's Journal, Newspaper. Oct., 1833, to Dec., 1844. Folio.
—— Same. Jan., 1845, to Dec., 1847. Folio.
—— Same. Feb., 1846, to July, 1851. Folio.
Coos County, N. H. See POWERS, Rev. G. Hist. Sketches of.
COOTE, Sir Eyre. Statement of Facts Relative to his Case. Lond., 1816. 8vo. Eng. Polit. Pamph. Vol. 77.
COOTE, Rich'd Holmes. Letter to his Majesty's Commissioners on the State of the Laws —— on the Proposed Gen. Registry. Lond., 1829. 8vo. Law Pamph. Vol. 14.

COPE, Gilbert. Genealogy of the Dutton Family of Pennsylvania, with Acc. of the Dutton's of Conn. Westchester, Pa., 1871. 8vo.

—— Record of the Cope Family as Established in America by Oliver Cope. 1682. Phila., 1861. 8vo.

COPHTS, or Jacobites. See ABUDACNUS, J. Hist. of. 1693.

COPIES and Extracts of Documents on the Subject of British Impressments of Amer. Seamen. Lond., 1812, 8vo.

—— of Original Letters from the Army of Bonaparte, in Egypt, Intercepted by Admiral Nelson. Lond., 1798. 8vo.

COPLEY, Josiah. Kansas and the Country beyond, on the Union Pacific R. R. Phila., 1867. 8vo.

COPPEE, H. Gen. Grant and his Campaigns. N. Y., 1865. 8vo.

COPPERHEAD Catechism, for the Instruction of Young Politicians. 1864. Rebell'n Pamph. Vol. 96.

—— Conspiracy in the Northwest. Rebell'n Pamph. Vol. 56.

—— Minstrel; a Collection of Democratic Poems and Songs. 1863. Rebell'n Pamph. Vol. 97.

COPPER Mines of Lake Superior. See FOSTER, J. W., and WHITNEY, J. D.

—— Region of Lake Superior. See FARMER, S., WHITTLESEY, C. Mines and Mining.

COPP'S Hill Burial Ground. See BRIDGMAN, Thomas.

COPWAY, Geo. Life, History and Travels of Kah-ge-ga-gah-bowh. Albany, 1847. 12mo.

—— Life, Letters and Speeches of Kah-ge-ga-gah-bowh. N. Y., 1850. 12mo.

—— Organization of a New Indian Territory. N. Y., 1850. 8vo. Congr. Pamph. Vol. 99.

—— Running Sketches of Men and Places in England, France, Germany, etc. N. Y., 1851. 12mo.

—— The Ojibway Conquest, a Tale of the Northwest—a Poem. N. Y., 1850. 12mo.

—— Traditional Hist. and Characteristic Sketches of the Ojibway Nation. Lond., 1850. 12mo.

COPYRIGHT. See ARCHER, S., Speech in Cong., 1872; CAREY, H. C., Letters on; GERHARD, F., Benefit of Copyright Law.

—— International. Meeting of Authors and Publishers, at the Rooms of the N. Y. Hist. Soc., 1868. N. Y., 1868. 8vo.

—— LIEBER, F., on International Copyright.

—— Observations on the Law of. Lond., 1838. 8vo. Strangford Pamph. Vol. 15.

—— See Plea for Authors. 1838.

—— The Question of Unreciprocated Foreign Copyright in G. B. Lond., 1851. 8vo. Strangford Pamph. Vol. 60.

CORBAUX, Fanny. The Rephaim and their Connection with Egyptian History. Lond., (n. d.) 8vo. Strangford Pamph. Vol. 64.

CORBIN, D. T. Argument in the Trial of the Ku-Klux, before the U. S. Circuit Court, Nov., 1871. Washington, 1872. 8vo. Congr. and Polit. Pamph. Vol. 138.

CORDER, Susanna. Origin, Principles, etc., of the Soc. of Friends. Lond., 1852. 12mo. Religious Pamph. Vol. 21.

CORDIER, M. L. Essay on the Temperature of the Interior of the Earth. Amherst, 1828. 12mo. Scientific Pamph. Vol. 6.

CORDNER, Rev. John. Oration before the N. Eng. Soc. of Montreal, Dec. 22, 1856. Montreal, 1857. 8vo. Canada Pamph. Vol. 2.

CORDOVA, J. DE. Texas: Her Resources and her Public Men. Phila., 1858. 8vo.

CORNARO, Lewis. Methods of Attaining a Long and Healthful Life. Lond., 1821. 8vo. 33d Ed. Pamphleteer. Vol. 18.

CORNHILL Magazine. Lond., 1850–1870. 22 Vols. 8vo.

CORN Laws, England. Address on the Corn Laws. Lond., 1846. 8vo. Strangford Pamph. Vol. 40.

—— —— See BROWN, W. K. "Protection to Agriculture." 1845.

—— —— Considerations on the Corn Question. Lond, 1821. 8vo. Pamphleteer. Vol. 17.

—— —— Corn and Consistency. Reply to Sir Robert Peel and the Corn Law Crisis. Lond., 1846. 8vo. Eng. Polit. Pamph. Vol. 45.

—— —— Dialogue on the Corn Laws, between a Gentleman and a Farmer. Manchester, (n. d.) 8vo. Eng. Polit. Pamph. Vol. 45.

—— —— See DRUMMOND, H., on the Corn Laws. 1841.

—— —— EDWARDS, D. O., on Agrarian Endowment.

—— —— GREG, W. R. Agriculture and the Corn Law. 1842.

—— —— HOPE, Geo. Prize Essay. 1842.

—— —— HULL, Wm. Remarks on. 1840.

—— —— HUME, J. D. Evidence, etc. 1839.

—— —— Inquiry into the Policy of the proposed Alterations in the Corn Laws. Lond., 1814. 8vo. Pamphleteer. Vol. 4.

—— —— See JAMES, G. P. R. Remarks on. 1841.

—— —— See London Anti-Corn Law Conference. 1842.

—— —— MORSE A. Prize Essay. 1842.

—— —— MOSELY, J. On the Repeal of. 1839.

—— —— NAISMITH, John. Propriety of Increasing Import Duty, etc. 1814.

—— —— Nature and Effect of the Corn Laws. Edinburgh, 1839. 8vo. Strangford Pamph. Vol. 19.

—— —— See NOEL, Rev. B. W. Plea for the Poor.

—— —— PARNELL, H. Substance of Speeches on.

—— —— PRESTON, R. Address to Manufacturers, etc. 1817.

—— —— Selections from Mrs. Loudon's Philanthropic Economy. Manchester, Eng., (n. d.) 8vo. Eng. Polit. Pamph. Vol. 45.

—— —— See SHARP, J. B. Anti-Corn Law League and the Cotton Trade. 1844.

—— —— STANHOPE, Earl. Letter on. 1827.

—— —— STANLEY, Lord. Speech in Parl't. 1846.

—— —— Ten Tracts issued by the Nat. Anti-Corn Law League. Manchester, 1842. 8vo Strangford Pamph. Vol. 33.

—— —— See THOMPSON, T. P. Selections from Works on. 1841.

—— —— WESTERN, Lord. Supplementary Letter on. 1841.

CORNELL University, Ithaca, N. Y. 1st Gen. Announcement. 1867.
—— —— Report of the Committee on Organization, 1866.
—— —— University Registers, 1869–70, 1870–71, 1871–2.
—— —— Report of Comm. on Organization, 1866.
—— —— University Register, 1870–1, 1871–2. Albany and Ithaca. 8vo.
CORNER, Wm. H. Cat. of his Private Library. Baltimore, 1866. 8vo. Bibliograph. Pamph. Vol. 6.
—— Cat. of Balance of his Library. 1869. Bibliograph. Pamph. Vol. 16.
CORNING, Erastus, and John F. WINSLOW *vs.* Peter A. BURDEN, before Circuit Court of the U. S. for Nor. Dist. of N. Y. 1850. Law Pamphlets. Vol. 3.
CORNISH Provincial Dialect. See Specimens of.
CORNPLANTER, (Indian Chief). See SNOWDEN, J. R. Cornplanter Memorial.
CORNWALL, Rev. N. E. Hist. Discourse at Trinity Church, Fairfield, Conn., Aug. 10, 1851, for the Jubilee of Soc'y for Propagating the Gospel. New Haven, 1851. 8vo. Conn. Hist. Discourses. Vol. 1.
CORNWALL, Eng. See COOKE, G. A. Topograph. Survey of.
CORNWALL, (Western) Eng. See HALLIWELL, J. O. Rambles in. 1861.
CORNWALLIS, Lord. Acc. of his Campaign in Virginia, in 1781. From his Answer to the Narr. of Sir H. Clinton. Va. Hist. Register. Vol. 6.
—— Correspondence. Lond., 1859. 3 Vols. 8vo.
CORONADO, Vasques de. See SIMPSON, J. H. Narrative of his March, etc.
CORONATION Guide. Lond., 1838. 12mo. Guide Books. Vol. 5.
—— of King George III. and Queen Charlotte. Lond., 1820. 8vo. Eng. Misc. Pamph. Vol. 28.
—— Services to be Observed at the Coronation of K. William IV. and Queen Adelaide. Lond., 1838. 12mo. Eng. Misc. Pamph. Vol. 28.
CORPORAL Punishment. See WYMAN, M. Progress in School Discipline.
—— —— Teachers' Miscellany, p. 70.
CORPORATIONS. On the Rights and Powers of Corporations. Notice of a Pamphlet by a Citizen of Boston. Boston, 1837. 8vo. Pamphlets. Vol. 13.
CORRESPONDENCE between the Colonies of New Netherlands and New Plymouth, A. D., 1627. From the Letter Book of Gov. Wm. Bradford. N. Y. Hist. Soc. Coll. 2d Ser. Vol. 1.
—— between the Session of 2d Presb. Ch., Albany, and Hon. John C. Spencer and others, respecting Charges preferred by G. M. West against Rev. W. B. Sprague, D. D. Albany, 1850. 8vo. Pamphlets. Vol. 3.
—— Orders, etc., between Maj.-Gen. D. Hunter, Maj.-Gen. J. G. Foster, and Brig. Gen. H. M. Naglee, Feb. and Mar., 1863. Rebell'n Pamph. Vol. 69.

CORRESPONDENCE relative to the Wreck of the Steamer Governor, and Search for the Ship Vermont, 1862. Rebell'n Pamph. Vol. 67.

—— respecting the "Alabama"; also respecting the "Maury," at N. Y., during the Crimean War. Lond., 1862. 8vo. Rebell'n Pamph. Vol. 45.

—— with the Editor of the "Times," relative to the American Question, 1812. Lond., 1813. 8vo. Pamphleteer. Vol. 2.

—— with Inhabitants of the Moon (?) Lond., 1800. Reprinted Cincin., 1868. Congr. and Polit. Pamph. Vol. 79.

CORRUPTIONS and Frauds of Lincoln's Administration. Rebell'n Pamph. Vol. 17.

CORRY, John. Hist. of Bristol, Civil and Ecclesiastical, with Biograph. Notices. Bristol, Eng., 1816. 2 Vols. 8vo.

CORTÈS, Ferdinand. Correspondance avec l'Empereur Charles-Quint, sur la Conquete du Mexique. En Suisse? 1779. 8vo.

—— Despatches addressed to the Emperor Charles V., with Introduction and Notes by Geo. Folsom. N. Y., 1843. 8vo.

CORTLAND Co., N. Y. See GOODWIN, H. C. Hist. of.

CORWIN, E. T. Hist. Disc. on Centen. Annivers. of Reformed Ch., Millstone, N. J. N. Y., 1869. 8vo.

—— The Corwin Genealogy in the U. S. N. Y., 1872. 8vo.

CORWIN, M. B. Speech in Cong., Apr. 9, 1850, on Admission of California. Congr. and Polit. Pamph. Vol. 86.

CORWIN, Thos. Speech in Cong., Jan. 12, 1837, on the Revenue. Congr. and Polit. Pamph. Vol. 90.

—— Speech in Cong., Jan. 21, 1861, on the State of the Union. Rebell'n Pamph. Vol. 61.

COSIN, Jas. Names of the R. Catholic Non-Jurors and Others who refused to take the Oaths to His Late Majesty, King George. Lond., 1745. Reprint, 1862. 8vo.

COSMOGONY. See ANDERSON, J. Course of Creation.

COST-BOOK System (The); its Principles and Practice. Lond., 1852. 8vo. Eng. Misc. Pamph. Vol. 14.

COSTA RICA. Concessions of Extensive Territory in Costa Rica, for the Opening a new Route between the Oceans, etc. Lond., 1850? 8vo.

COSTE, M. Voyage d'Exploration sur le Littoral de la France et de l'Italie, sur les Industries de Comaccio, du lac Fusaro. Paris, 1855. Folio.

COSTI, A. M. Memoir or the Trent Affair. Washington, 1865. 8vo. Rebell'n Pamph. Vol. 22.

COTHEAL, Alexander I. Grammatical Sketch of the Language of the Mosquito Indians. Amer. Ethnolog. Soc. Vol. 2.

COTHREN, Wm. Hist. of Ancient Woodbury, Conn., from the first Indian Deed in 1659, to 1854; with a Genealog. Hist. of the Early Settlers. Waterbury, 1854. 2 Vols. 8vo.

—— Second Centen. Celebra. of the Explora. of Ancient Woodbury, Conn., held July 4 and 5, 1859. Woodbury, 1859. 8vo. Conn. Hist. Discourses, etc. Vol. 2.

—— History of Ancient Woodbury, Conn., 1659–1872. Vol. 2. Supplementary. Woodbury, 1872. 8vo.

COTTAGE Hill Seminary, Poughkeepsie, N. Y. Catalogue for 1863–4. Poughkeepsie, 1863. 8vo.
COTTEN, Edw. R. Life of Hon. Nathan'l Macon, of N. Carolina. Baltimore, 1840. 12mo.
COTTER, Rich'd. Sketches of Bermuda or Somers' Islands. Lond., 1828. 8vo.
COTTON, A. J. Poems on Various Subjects; with an Autobiograph. Sketch and Condensed History of the Early Settlements in Indiana. Cincin., 1858. 8vo.
COTTON, Mrs. Ann. Acc. of our Late Troubles in Virginia, written in 1676.. Force's Hist. Tracts. Vol. 1.
COTTON, Bishop Geo. See BANERJEA, Rev. K. M. Obit. Sermon.
COTTON, Rev. Josiah. Vocabulary of the Mass. or Natick Indian Language. Mass. Hist. Soc. Coll. Vol. 2. 3d Ser.
COTTON. See BAINES, E. Hist. of Manufac. in G. Britain.
—— BARBER, Wm. J. The Cotton Question, 1866.
—— DUDLEY, J. G. Growth, Trade and Manufacture of.
—— PARROTT, Wm. W. Introduct. of into the U. S.
—— Tax. See KIMBALL, Israel. Constitutionality of, 1873.
COTTONIAN Library. See British Museum.
COTTU, M. On the Administra. of the Criminal Code in England, and the Spirit of the Eng. Gov't. Lond., 1820. 8vo. Pamphleteer. Vol. 16.
COUNCIL Bluffs, Iowa. See BURKE, W. S. Directory, 1866.
—— of Nice. See DUDLEY, D. Hist. of.
—— of Revision of N. Y. See STREET, A. B.
COUNSEL, G. W. Hist. and Descrip. of the City of Gloucester to the Present Time. Gloucester, Eng., 1829. 12mo.
COUNTER-Address to the Public on the late Dismission of a Gen. Officer. Lond., 1764. 8vo. Eng. Polit. Pamph. Vol. 15A.
COURAGE, Arch'd. Brief Survey of Aberdeen. Aberdeen, Scotl'd, 1856. 2d Ed. 12mo. Guide Books. Vol. 10.
COURIER du Bas Rhine, Newspaper. French. Hague, Cleves, etc. 1786–1794. 9 Vols. 4to.
COURSE of Creation. See ANDERSON, J., D. D.
COURTENAY, T. P. Letter to Wm. Sturges Bourne, on the Poor Laws. Lond., 1817. 8vo. Pamphleteer. Vol. 11.
COURTENAY, Sir W. Eccentric and Singular Productions of. Canterbury. n. d. 8vo. Strangford Pamph. Vol. 50.
—— Essay on the Character of. Canterbury, 1833? 8vo. Strangford Pamph. Vol. 8.
COURTNEY, L. H. Direct Taxation; an Inquiry. Lond., 1860. 8vo. Eng. Polit. Pamph. Vol. 58.
COVELL, Rev. L. and Rev. A. L. See BROWN, Mrs. D. C.
COVENTRY, Eng. Charter granted by King James I., in 1621. Coventry, 1816. 8vo. Hist. Pamph. Vol. 17.
—— See POOLE, Benj. Hist. and Antiquities.
COVENTRY, Geo. Critical Enquiry as to the Author of Junius Letters—Lord Geo. Sackville. Lond., 1825. 8vo.
COVENTRY, Sir W. The Character of a Trimmer. Lond., 1688. Sm. 4to. Eng. Polit. Pamph. Vol. 65.
COVENTRY, Vt. See WHITE, P. H. Hist. of.

COVINGTON and Ohio R. R. Laws and Acts of Incorporation, etc. Richmond, 1867. 8vo.
COVODE Investigation. Report of Select Comm. of U. S. House of R., 1863. Washington, 1863. 8vo.
COVODE, John. See Addresses in Cong., on his Death, 1871.
COW CHACE (The). See ANDRÉ, Maj. J.
COWAN, Edgar. Speeches in U. S. Senate, Mar. 4 and June 27, 1864, on Confiscation. Rebell'n Pamph. Vol. 34.
—— Speech in U. S. Senate, Mar. 2, 1866, on Representation of Southern States in Cong. Congr. and Polit. Pamph. Vol. 121.
COWARD'S (The) Convention. N. Y., 1864. 8vo. Rebell'n Pamph. Vol. 45.
COWELL, Benj. Spirit of '76 of R. Island; or Efforts of the Gov't and People in the War of the Revolution, with Biographies. Boston, 1850. 8vo.
COWELL, John. The N. England Patriot; a Comparison of Washington's and Jefferson's Administration. Boston, 1810. 8vo.
COWELL, J. W. La France et les Etats Confédérés. Paris, 1865. 8vo. Rebell'n Pamph. Vol. 38.
—— Letter to Capt. M. F. Maury, of Confed. Navy, on his Letter to Admiral Fitzroy. Lond., 1862. Rebell'n Pamph. Vol. 46.
COWEN, B. S. Speech in Cong., June 21, 1842, on the Tariff. Washington, 1842. 8vo. Congr. and Polit. Pamph. Vol. 24.
COWIE, Rev. Morgan. Letter on Educa. at Putney College. Lond. n. d. 8vo. Strangford Pamph. Vol. 52.
COWLEY, Chas. Hist. of Lowell, Mass. 2d Ed. Boston, 1868. 12mo.
—— Memories of Indians and Pioneers of the Region of Lowell. Lowell, 1862. 8vo. Mass. Hist. Discourses, etc. Vol. 20.
COWPER, Wm. See MEMES, J. S. Life of.
COX, C. C., M. D. Introduct. Lecture in the Phila. Coll. of Medicine, Nov. 4, 1848. Phila., 1848. 8vo. Med. Pamph. Vol. 33.
COX, Edw. W. Conservative Principles and Conservative Policy; Letter to the Electors of Tewkesbury. Lond., 1852. 8vo. Eng. Polit. Pamph. Vol. 49.
COX, Geo. Compendium of Photography. Lond. 12mo. n. d. Scientific Pamph. Vol. 24.
COX, Jos. Gen. Harrison at North Bend; Address before the Cincin. Literary Club, Feb. 4, 1871. Cincin., 1871. 8vo.
COX, Rev. Robt. Life of the Rev. John Wm. Fletcher. Lond., 1822. 12mo. Biograph. Pamph. Vol. 9.
COX, S. and LAWRENCE, Wm. Speeches in Cong., Apr. 28, 1858, on the Admission of Kansas. Congr. and Polit. Pamph. Vol. 93.
COX, Rev. Sam'l H. Address at Boston, May 30, 1849, in behalf of the Soc. for the Promotion of Collegiate and Theolog. Educa. at the West. N. York. 8vo.

COX, Rev. Sam'l H. Memoir of. From Holden's Mag., Oct., 1848. Biograph. Pamph. Vol. 11.

—— Sermon at Brooklyn, Oct. 1, 1843, on the Death of Mrs. M. L. Stafford. N. Y., 1843. 8vo. Sermons. Vol. 52.

COX, Samuel S. A Buckeye Abroad; or Wanderings in Europe and the Orient. Cincin., 1854. 12mo.

—— Eight Years in Cong., 1857–65. Memoirs and Speeches. N. Y., 1865. 8vo.

—— Speech in Cong., Jan. 31, 1862, in Vindica. of Gen. McClellan. Rebell'n Pamph. Vol. 32.

—— Speech in Cong., June 6, 1862, on Emancipation and its Results. Rebell'n Pamph. Vol. 32.

—— Speech in Cong., Dec. 15, 1862, on the State of the Union. Rebell'n Pamph. Vol. 67.

—— Speech before Dem. Union Assoc., Jan. 13, 1863. N. Y., 1863. 8vo. Rebell'n Pamph. Vol. 66.

—— Speech in Cong., Feb. 17, 1864, on Miscegenation or Amalgamation. Rebell'n Pamph. Vol. 32.

—— Speech in Cong., May 4, 1864, on Reconstruction. Rebell'n Pamph. Vol. 32.

—— Speech iu Cong., Jan. 26, 1865, on Admitting the Cabinet into the House of Repr. for Debate. Rebell'n Pamph. Vol. 30.

COX, Sandford C. Recollections of the Early Settlement of the Wabash Valley. La Fayette, 1860. 8vo.

—— The Evangelist, and Other Poems. Cincin., 1867. 12mo.

COX, Thos. Magna Brittania; Topograph. Hist. of Wiltshire, Eng. 1720. Folio.

COXE, Rev. A. C. Moral Reform suggested in a Pastoral Letter. Phila., 1869. 12mo.

COXE, Danl. Description of the Eng. Province of Carolana, by the Spaniards called Florida, and by the French La Louisiane; also of the Great River Mississipi, 1598. Lond., 1741. 12mo. Also in French's Hist. Coll. of La. Vol. 2.

COXE, Dr. John R. Cat. of his Private Library. Phila., 1864. 8vo. Bibliograph. Pamph. Vol. 72.

COXE, Rich'd S. Address on Gen. Wm. Henry Harrison, June 24, 1841. Washington, 1841. 8vo. Addresses. Vol. 35.

COXE, Tench. View of the U. States of America, in a Ser. of Papers Written between 1787 and 1794. Dublin, 1795. 8vo.

—— The Same. Phila., 1794. 8vo.

COYNER, D. H. The Lost Trappers; Scenes and Events in the Rocky Mountains. Cincin., 1859. 12mo.

COZZENS, Rev. Saml. W. Sermon on the Death of Hon. Wm. Reed, Feb. 26, 1837. Boston, 1837. Sermons. Vol. 1.

CRAAN, Guillaume B. See HEUSCHLING, X.

CRACOW, Poland. See KROLIKOWSKI, L. Hist. and Polit. Memoir of, 1840.

—— Relation de ce qui s'est passe au Meeting tenu a Londres le 2 Mars, 1847, au Sujet de Cracovie. Lond., 1847. 8vo. Strangford Pamph. Vol. 42.

CRADLEBAUGH, J. Speech in Cong., Feb. 7, 1863, on Admission of Utah. Congr. and Polit. Pamph. Vol. 86.

CRADOCK, Sir Mathew. See ROBERTS, David. Abstract of Disc. on.

CRAFT, Benj. Journal of the Siege of Boston. Essex Institute Coll. Vol. 3.

—— Journal of the Siege of Louisburg in 1745. Essex Institute Coll. Vol. 6.

CRAFT, Zachary. First Sitting of the Committee on the Proposed Monument to Shakespeare. Lond., 1823. 8vo. Pamphleteer. Vol. 22.

CRAIG, David. De Vita Animali quoad Calorum Externum. Dissertatio Physiologica. Edinburgh, 1816. 8vo. Latin Pamph. Vol. 7.

CRAIG, Maj. Isaac. See CRAIG, N. B. Life and Services of.

CRAIG, J. Duncan. Hand Book of Modern Provençal Language, Spoken in the South of France. Lond., 1863. 12mo.

CRAIG, Neville B. Braddock's Defeat. Va. Hist. Register. Vol. 5.

—— Hist. of Pittsburgh, Penn., with a Brief Notice of its Advantages for Commercial and Manufacturing Purposes. Pittsburgh, 1851. 12mo.

—— Memoirs of Maj. Robert Stobo, of the Virginia Reg't. Pittsburgh, 1854. 18mo.

—— Notices of the Settlement of the Country along the Monongahela and Upper Ohio Rivers. Olden Time. Vol. 1.

—— Sketch of the Life and Services of Isaac Craig, Maj. in the 4th Reg't of Artillery, during the Rev. War. Pittsburgh, 1854. 12mo.

—— Washington's First Campaign, Death of Jumonville, and the Taking of Fort Necessity; also, Braddock's Defeat. Pittsburgh, 1848. 8vo. Pamphlets—Early Amer. Wars.

CRAIK, Geo. L. Compendious Hist. of Eng. Literature, and of the Eng. Language. N. Y., 1863. 2 Vols. 8vo.

CRAM, Capt. T. J. Report on the Hydrographic Survey of L. Michigan, for 1841. Washington, 1842. 8vo. Wis. Misc. Pamph. Vol. 5.

—— Report on Internal Improvements in the Terr. of Wisconsin; with Maps. Washington, 1840. 8vo. Wis. Misc. Pamph. Vol. 5.

—— —— See also Senate Doc., No. 140, 1st Sess. 26th Cong., 1840.

—— Reports of the Survey of the Boundary Line between the State of Michigan and Terr. of Wisconsin, 1841–2. Wis. Misc. Pamph. Vol. 5.

—— Reports, Plans and Estimates for the Improvement of the Neenah, Wisconsin, and Rock Rivers; the Improvement of the Haven of Rock River; and the Construction of a Pier at the at the N. Extremity of Winnebago Lake. With numerous Maps. Senate Doc. No. 318. 1st Sess. 26th Cong., March, 1840.

—— Topographical Memoir and Report, relative to the Territories of Oregon and Washington. Ex. Doc. No. 114, 2d Sess. 35th Cong., 1859.

CRANCH, Chris. Pearse. Poem at Quincy, Mass., May 25, 1840, on the Bi-Centen. Annivers. of the Town. Boston, 1840. 8vo. Mass. Hist. Discourses, etc. Vol. 17.

CRANCH, Wm. Memoir of the Life, Character of John Adams, before Columbian Institute, Mar. 16, 1827. Washington, 1827. 8vo. Biograph. Pamph. Vol. 8.

—— Sketches of Alumni at the different Colleges in New Eng. N. Eng. Hist. and Gen. Register. Vol. 1.

CRANDAL, Wm. Lusk. Talks with the People of N. Y.: Report on the Public School Policy of N. Y., 1853. 8vo. N. Y. Misc. Pamph. Vol. 3.

CRANDALL, Chas. M. See HOUGH, F. B. Biograph. Notice of.

CRANE, Edw. Abstract of an Address on Transportation, at Boston, Feb., 1868. Boston, 1868. 8vo. Mass. Misc. Pamph. Vol. 2.

CRANE Genealogy. See APPLETON, W. S.

CRANE, L. H. D. See Wis. Legis. Manual.

CRANE, Wm. H. Memoirs of Vermillion, Ohio. Fire Lands Pioneer. Vol 1.

CRANIA AMERICANA. See MORTON, S. G.

CRAVEN, J. J. Prison Life of Jeff. Davis. N. Y., 1867. 12mo.

CRAWFORD, Co., Penn. See HUIDEKOPER, A. Early Hist. of.

—— —— See Penn. Surveyor Gen.

—— —— Teachers' Institute. Catalogue and Proceedings at Meadville, 1858. Meadville, 1858. 8vo. Educa. Pamph. Vol. 5.

CRAWFORD, J. Marshall. Mosby and his Men; or Adventures of the Partisan Ranger, Col. John S. Mosby, C. S. A. N. Y., 1867. 12mo.

CRAWFORD, Wm. H. Sketches of the Life and Character of. Albany, 1824. 8vo. Biograph. Pamph. Vol. 12.

CRAWFURD, G., and ROBERTSON, G. Gen. Descrip. of the Shire of Renfrew, with Acc. of the Noble and Ancient Families and Genealog. Hist. of House of Stewart. Paisley, 1818. 4to.

CRAYON (The). A Journal devoted to Graphic Arts and Literature. N. Y., 1855-60. 7 Vols. 4to.

CREASY, E. S. Rise and Progress of the Eng. Constitution, 3d Ed. N. Y., 1856. 12mo.

CREDIT FONCIER (The) and Mobilier of England, Limited. Second Report, to Sept. 30, 1865. London. 4to. Eng. Misc. Pamph. Vol. 11.

CREDIT MOBILIER. See ELDREDGE, C. A. Speech on. 1873.

—— —— Report of Select Comm. of U. S. House of Repr., Feb. 1873. Washington, 1873. 8vo.

CREE Language. See HOWSE, Jos. Grammar of the Cree and Chippewa Languages.

CREEK Indians. Congress. Report on the Georgia Controversy with. Washington, 1827. 8vo. Congress. Pamph. Vol. 39.

—— —— See HAWKINS, Benj. Sketch of Creek Country in 1798-9.

—— —— HODGSON, W. B. Creek Confederacy.

CREICHTON, Capt. John. See SWIFT, Jonathan. Memoir of.

CREIGH, Alfred. Hist. of Washington Co., Pa., from its First Settlement. 2d Ed. Revised. Harrisburg, 1871. 8vo.

CREMONY, John C. Life among the Apaches. San Francisco, 1868. 12mo.
CREOLE Grammar. See VAN NAME, Addison. Contributions to.
CRESAP, Capt. Michael. See JACOB's Biograph. Sketch.
—— MAYER, B.
CRESPEL, Emanuel. Travels in N. America, with a Narr. of his Shipwreck. Lond., 1797. 12mo.
—— Voyage au Nouveau Monde et Histoire Interessante de son Naufrage. Amsterdam, 1757. 18mo.
—— Voyage dans le Canada et son Naufrage en Revenaut en France. Frankfort, 1752. 18mo.
CRESWELL, John A. J. Oration on Henry Winter Davis, at Washington, 1866. Washington, 1866. 8vo. Addresses. Vol. 35.
CRETAN Refugees. See HOWE, S. G.
CRETE. See WOODFORD, S. L. Address at N. Y., 1868.
CREUXIUS, Franciscus. Historiæ Canadensis sell. Novæ Franciæ libri decem. Paris, 1664. 4to.
CREVIER, M. Histoire des Empereurs Romains Depuis auguste jusqua Constantin. Paris, 1749. 11 Vols. 12mo.
CRICHTON, Andrew, and WHEATON, H. Scandinavia, Ancient and Modern; or a Hist. of Denmark, Sweden and Norway. Harper's Fam. Lib. N. Y., 1860. 2 Vols. 18mo.
—— Hist. of Arabia, Ancient and Modern. Harper's Fam. Lib. N. Y., 1858. 2 Vols. 18mo.
CRIMEA. See COLLINS' Map of.
CRIMEAN War. See BRIGHT, John. Letter on.
—— —— COBBETT's Reasons for War, etc.
—— —— De la Conduite de la Guerre d'Orient. Expedition de Crimée. Brussels, 1855. 8vo. Strangford Pamph. Vol. 68.
—— —— DELAFIELD, Maj. R. Art of War in Europe. 1854–6.
—— —— "Diplomatic Mystifications," etc. 1854.
—— —— Inquiry into the Alleged Justice of the War. 1855.
—— —— "Is the War Just?" 1855.
—— —— JOHNSON, W. O. Diplomatic Hist. of the War in the East.
—— —— JOHNSTON's Map. 1859.
—— —— LAYARD, A. H. Prospects and Conduct of the War. 1854.
—— —— MCCLELLAN, G. B. Seat of War in Europe. 1855–6.
—— —— Observations on the War in the Crimea. Lond., 1855. 8vo. Hist. Pamph. Vol. 7.
—— —— See PORTER, J. G. V. England's Demands not Just, etc. 1855.
—— —— See SUVOROVE's Greek Dragoon, on the War in the East. 1856.
—— —— URQUHART, D. Recent Events in the East. 1854.
—— —— —— The Home Face of the "Four Points."
—— —— WRIGHT, H. P. Recollections of a Crimean Chaplain.
CRIMINAL Trials of England. Lond., 1832. 2 Vols. 12mo.

18

CRISIS (The), and the Remedy. N. Y., 1842. Cong. and Polit. Pamph. Vol. 92.

—— —— Addressed to the People of England and America. 16 Nos. Lond., 1775. 12mo.

—— —— Newspaper. Lond. Jan. to Oct., 1775. Folio.

—— —— A Periodical on the Slavery Controversy. 2 Nos. 1860–1863. Rebell'n Pamph. Vol. 75.

—— —— of the Quaker Contest in Manchester. Manchester, Eng., 1836. 12mo. Part 1. Religious Pamph. Vol. 21.

—— —— or the Origin of our Political Dissensions, by a Citizen of Vermont. Albany, 1815. 8vo. Pamph. War of 1812. Vol. 5.

CRITCHETT, Dr. G. Practical Remarks on Strabismus. Deptford, Eng., 1855. 12mo. Med. Pamph. Vol. 17.

CRITICAL and Social Essays from "The Nation." N. Y., 1857. 12mo.

—— History of the Religions and Customs of the Eastern Nations. Lond., 1685. 12mo. Religious Pamph. Vol. 18.

—— Review of the New Administration. Lond., 1765. 12mo. Eng. Polit. Pamph. Vol. 15A.

CRITICISM Criticised; Supplement to the Law Reporter for Jan., 1859. Boston. 8vo. Law Pamph. Vol. 1.

—— of Mr. Wm. B. Reed's Aspersions on Dr. Benjamin Rush, with an Incidental Consideration of Gen. Jos. Reed's Character. By a Member of the Phila. Bar. 8vo. Phila. 1867.

CRITTENDEN'S Phila. Commercial Coll. Catalogue, 1855–6. Phila., 8vo.

CRITTENDEN, J. J. Speech in U. S. Senate, April 16, 1846, on the Oregon Question. Washington, 1846. 8vo. Speeches. Vol. 1.

—— Speech in Cong., Apr. 11, 1862, on Slavery in Dist. of Columbia. Rebell'n Pamph. Vol. 32.

—— Speech in Cong., on Confiscation of Rebel Property, Apr. 23, 1862. Rebell'n Pamph. Vol. 67.

CROCKER, Chas. A Visit to Chichester Cathedral. Chichester, Eng., 1848. 12mo. Guide Books. Vol. 6.

CROCKETT, David. Life and Adventures. Phila., (n. d.) 8vo.

CROES, Rev. Robt. B. Annivers. Lecture before the Hist. Soc. of the Co. of Vigo, Indiana, Mar. 14, 1844. Cincin., 1845. 8vo. Ind. Hist. Discourses. Vol. 1.

CROFFUT, W. A., and MORRIS, J. M. Military and Civil Hist. of Conn. during the War of 1861–5. 3d Ed. N. Y., 1869. 8vo.

CROGHAN, Geo. Journ. of his Route from Fort Pitt to Vincennes and Detroit in 1765. "Olden Time." Vol. 1.

CROKER, John Wilson. Letters on the Naval War with America. Lond., 1813.

—— Resolutions on the Report of the Reform Bill, Mar. 14, 1832. Lond., 1832. 8vo. Strangford Pamph. Vol. 8.

—— Speech in Parl't, May 4, 1819, on the Catholic Question. Lond., 1819. 8vo. Strangford Pamph. Vol. 1.

—— Speech in Parl't, Sept. 21, 1831, on the Reform Bill. Lond., 1831. 8vo. Strangford Pamph. Vol. 7.

CROLY, Rev. George. Life and Times of his late Majesty, George the IV. Harper's Fam. Libr. N. Y., 1859.
—— The Divine Origin, Appointment and Obligation of Marriage. A Sermon. Lond., 1836. 8vo. Strangford Pamph. Vol. 12.
CROMBIE, Dr. A. Letters on the Present State of the Agricult. Interst, to Chas. Forbes. Lond., 1816. 8vo. Pamphleteer. Vol. 8.
—— Letter to D. Ricardo, on the Depreciation of Bank Notes. Lond., 1817. 8vo. Pamphleteer. Vol. 10.
CROMWELL, Conn. See FIELD, D. D.
CROMWELL, Oliver. See DEAN, John Ward. Reputed Embarkation of, for N. Eng.
—— See GUIZOT, M. Hist. of.
—— HEADLEY, J. T. Life of.
—— LAMARTINE, A. Life of.
—— Memoirs of the Protector, Oliver Cromwell, and of his Sons Richard and Henry. Lond., 1822. 2 Vols. 8vo.
—— RUSSELL, M. Life of.
—— VAUGHN, R. Protectorate of.
CROMWELL, Thos. Hist and Descrip. of the Ancient Town and and Borough of Colchester in Essex. Lond., 1825. 2 vols. 8vo.
—— CRONHELM, F. W. Thoughts as to a Plurality of Worlds. Lond., 1858. 8vo. Scientific Pamphl. Vol. 39.
CRONIQUES DE LONDON. See Camden Soc. Publications.
CRONISE, Titus. The Nat. Wealth of California; comprising its Early Hist., Geog., &c. San Francisco, 1868. 8vo.
CROOKSHANKS, John. See ERSKINE, Capt. Robt.
CROSBY, Alpheus. Address at Dartmouth Coll. on the Present Position of the Seceded States, July 19, 1865. Rebelln. Pamph. Vol. 37.
CROSBY, Rev. C. C. P. Hist. of West Boylston, Mass. Worcester Mag. Vol. 2.
CROSBY, Edw. N. Our Country vs. Party Spirit; a Rejoinder to Prof. Morse. Po'keepsie, 1863. 8vo. Rebelln. Pamph. Vol. 39.
CROSBY. Frank. Life of Abraham Lincoln; His Early Hist. and Polit. Career, Speeches, Messages, &c, Phila., 1865. 12mo.
CROSBY, H.. Œdipus Tyrranus of Sophocles. N. Y., 1859. 12mo.
CROSBY, Jaazaniah. Annals of Charlestown, in the Colony of Sullivan, N. H. N. H. Hist. Soc. Coll. Vol. 4.
CROSBY, Nathan. Ann. Obit. Notices of Eminent Persons who have died in the United Stetes in 1857 & 1858. Boston, 1858–9. 2 Vols. 8vo.
CROSS, A. B. Battle of Gettysburg and the Christian Commission. Rebell'n Pamph. Vol. 81.
CROSS, Edward. Speech in Cong. June 3, 1842, on the Army Appropriation Bill. Washington, 1842. 8vo. Congr. & Polit. Pamph. Vol. 25.
CROSS, Maj. O. Journal of the March of the Regt. of Mounted Riflemen, from St. Louis to Oregon, May 10 to Oct. 5, 1849. Ex. Doc. No. 1. 2d Sess. 31st Con., 1850–1.

CROWDER. Geo. A. Letters on Marriage with a Deceased Wife Sister. Lond., 1846. 8vo. 2d Ed. Strangford Pamph. Vol. 41.
CROWELL, Robert. Hist. of Town of Essex, Mass., from 1639 to 1868. Essex, 1868. 8vo.
CROWLEY, Edw. The Age we Live in; High Art no Evidence of High Civilization. Clapham, 1854. 8vo. Stranf. Pam. Vol. 68.
CROYDON, N. H. See COOPER, L. P. Historical Sketch of.
CRUCHLEY'S Map of Railways in England and Scotland. n. d.
CRUGER, Henry. See VAN SCHAACK, H. C. Memoir of.
CRUISE of the Brig Dolphin. See LEE, S. P.
CRUSADES. See BLOSS, C A. Heroines of the.
—— KEIGHTLEY, Thos. Scenes, Events and Characters for the Times of the Crusades.
CRUSIUS, Dr. Baumgarten. Eutropii Breviarium Historiae Romanae. Leipsic, 1824. 12mo. Latin Pamph. Vol. 9.
CRUSOE'S Island. See BROWNE, J. Ross, Rambles, &c.
CRYSTAL PALACE Co. Deed of Settlement, Royal Charters, and List of Shareholders, Jan. 1856. Lond. 8vo. Eng. Mis. Pamph. Vol. 8.
—— —— Description of the Building now Erecting at Sydenham. Lond. 8vo. n. d. Guide Book. Vol. 5.
—— —— GUIDES. Hand-Book to the Courts of Modern Sculpture. Hand-Book for the Mediaeval Courts. Hand-Book for the Assyrian Court. Hand-Book for the Greek Court. Lond., 1854. 8vo. Gude Books. Vol. 24.
—— —— The Nat. Hist. Department described. Lond., 1854. 12m. Guide Books. Vol. 2.
—— —— RUSKIN, John. On the Opening of 1854.
CUBA. See Congress. Speeches.
—— Correspondence on the proposed Tripartite Convention, relative to Cuba. Boston, 1853. 8vo. Congr. and Polit. Pamph. Vol. 135.
—— Expedition. See U. S. Sec. of Treasury.
—— See Gan-Eden or Pictures of.
—— LOPEZ, N.
—— or the Policy of England, Mexico and Spain, etc. Lond., 1830. 8vo. Strangford Pamph. Vol. 6.
—— See TAYLOR, R. C., on the Copper Region and Geol. of.
CUBAN Affairs. See U. S.—Message of President.
—— Question and Amer. Policy, in the Light of Common Sense. N. Y., 1869. 8vo. Congr. and Polit. Pamph. Vol. 113.
—— —— in England. Extracts from Opinions of the Press. Lond., 1871. 8vo. Congr. and Polit. Pamph. Vol. 113.
—— —— in the Spanish Parl't. Debate in the Cortes. Lond. 1872. 8vo. Hist. Pamph. Vol. 10.
CUBITT, Rev. Geo. Lectures against Socialism, at London. Lond. 1840. 8vo. Eng. Religious Pamph. Vol. 90.
CUDWORTH, W. H. Hist. of First Mass. Infantry. 1861–1864. Boston, 1866. 12mo.
CULL, Richd. Case of Precocious Musical Talent, as shown in EARNEST A. KELLNER. With Phrenolog. Remarks. Lond., n. d. 8vo. Scientific Pamph. Vol. 29.

CULLOM, Wm. Speech in Cong., April 11, 1854, on the Kansas and Nebr. Bill. Washington, 1854. 8vo. Speeches. Vol. 3.
CULTIVATOR, The. A Monthly Publication to Improve the Soil and the Mind. Vols. 5, 6, 7 and 8. Albany, 1838–41. Quarto.
CULVERWELL, Robert J. Guide to Health and Long Life. N. Y., 1859. 8vo. Med. Pamph. Vol. 1.
—— The Lakes of Cumberland, the Highlands, and North Wales. Lond., n. d. 12mo. Guide-Books. Vol. 8.
CUMBACK, Wm. Speech in Cong., May 28, 1856, on Grants of Pub. Lands to R. R's. Congress. and Political Pamph. Vol. 83.
CUMBERLAND, Eng. Dialect. See DICKINSON, W. Glossary of Words. See WHEELER, A. Dialogues and Poems.
CUMBERLAND, Richard. Memoirs, written by himself, with Acc. of his Life and Writings, with Notes by HENRY FLANDERS. Phila., 1856. 8vo.
CUMBERLAND University, Lebanon, Tenn. Catalogue of Officers and Students for 1859–60. Lebanon. 8vo.
CUMING, Sir Alex. See DRAKE, S. G. His Embassy to the Cherokees.
CUMING, F. Sketches of Tour to the Western Country, through Ohio and Kentucky, etc. Pittsburg, 1810. 16mo.
CUMMING, Kate. Journ. of Hospital Life in the Confed. Army. Louisville, 1866. 8vo.
CUMMINGS, Jas. J. The Sabbath: Patriarchal, Mosaic and Christian. A Lecture. Lond., 1856. 8vo. Religious Pamph. Vol 11.
CUNNINGHAM, Allen. Biograph. and Critical Hist. of the Literature of the last Fifty Years. 1834. Waldo's Circulating Libr. Vol. 3.
—— Lives of Most Eminent British Painters and Sculptors. Harpers' Fam. Lib. N. Y., 1859. 5 Vols. 18mo.
CUNNINGHAM, G. G. Lives of Eminent and Illustrious Englishmen, from the time of Alfred the Great. Glasgow, 1836–37. 8 Vols., bound in 16.
CUNNINGHAM, J. W. Cautions to Continental Travelers. Lond., 1823. 8vo. 2d Ed. Pamphleteer. Vol. 21.
—— Observations on Friendly Societies, and their Influence on Public Morals. Lond., 1823. 8vo. 2d Ed. Pamphleteer. Vol. 22.
CUNNINGHAM, Wm. See ADAMS, John. Corres. with, 1803–12.
—— PICKERING, Tim. Review of his Corres. with John Adams.
CURATES' APPEAL (The) to the Equity and Christian Principles of the British Legislature, etc., examined. Lond., 1820. 8vo. Pamphleteer. Vol. 17.
CURIOSITIES OF LITERATURE. See D'ISRAELI, J. C.
CURIOSITY HUNTER. Vol 1, No's 1–6. Rockford, 1872–73. 8vo.
CURIOUS OBSERVATIONS upon the Manners, Customs, Usages, etc., of the several Nations of Asia, Africa and America. Lond., 1760. 2 Vols. 8vo.
CURRENCY. See ADAMS, C. F. Reflections on, of U. S.
—— APPLETON, N. Remarks on and Banking.
—— Banking.
—— CAREY, H. B. Letters to S. Colfax, 1865.

CURRENCY. See HICKCOX, J. H. Hist. of N. Y. Bills of Credit, 1709–89.
—— KELLY, P. The Universal Cambist.
—— National (A) Currency.
—— NESMITH, J. On the Measure of Value.
—— New Financial Project, 1837.
—— —— System of Paper Money.
—— PHILLIPS, H. Sketches of Amer. Colonial Currency.
—— Present State of the, practically considered. Lond., 1847. 8vo. Strangford. Pamph. Vol. 45.
—— SAEZ, L. Valor de las Monedas.
—— SPOONER, L. New System of Paper. See Banking and Currency.
CURTIN, Gov. A. G. Political Portrait of, by one of his own party. 1863. Rebell'n Pamph. Vol. 23.
CURTIS, B. R. Argument submitted to Cong., in behalf of the Union Pacific R. R., 1870. Congr. & Polit. Pamph. Vol. 114.
—— Executive Power. Boston, 1862. 12mo. Rebell'n Pamph. Vols. 4, 56, 102, 108.
—— See SHATTUCK, G. O. Reply to Curtis.
CURTIS Genealogy. See CLARKE, S. S.
CURTIS, Geo. T. Address at Phila., Sep. 30, 1864, in favor of Nomination of Gen. McClellan. Rebell'n Pamph. Vol. 37.
—— Life of Daniel Webster. N. Y., 1870. 8vo. 2 Vols.
—— Oration at Boston, July 4, 1862. Boston. 8vo. Addresses. Vols. 2 and 15. Rebell'n Pamph. Vol. 35.
—— Reply to Hon. Stephen A. Douglas, on Popular Sovereignty. Boston, 1859. 8vo. Congr. and Polit. Pamph. Vol. 76.
CURTIS, Rev. Jonathan. Hist. Sketch of Epsom, N. H. Farmer & Moore's Hist. Coll. of N. H.
CURTIS, J. C. Memoirs of Fitchville, Ohio. Fire Lands Pioneer. Vol. 1.
—— Notes on Fitchville Township, Ohio. Fire Lands Pioneer. Vol. 9.
CURTIS, Nathaniel. Memoir of. N. Eng. Hist. and Gen. Register. Vol. 22.
CURTIS, Stephen. Objection to the Present Practice in regard to Unanimous Verdicts in Criminal Courts. Lond., 1834. 8vo. Law Pamph. Vol. 19.
CURTISS, Chas. G. See Buffalo Board of Trade.
CURTISS, Daniel S. Western Portraiture and Emigrants' Guide; a Description of Wis., Ill. and Iowa. N. Y., 1852. 12mo.
—— Same in German. N. Y., 1852. 12mo.
CURTISS, Geo. W. Address at N. Y., May 14, 1858, on the Right of Woman to the Elective Franchise. N. Y, Addresses, etc. Vol. 8. 8vo.
—— Lotus Eating; a Summer Book. N. Y., 1856. 12mo.
—— Nile Notes of a Howadji. N. Y., 1857. 12mo.
—— Prue and I. N. Y., 1857. 12mo.
—— The Howadji in Syria. N. Y., 1857. 12mo.
—— The Potiphar Papers. N. Y., 1856. 12mo.
CURWEN GENEALOGY. See VINTON, John A.

CURWEN, J. C. Speech in Parl't, May 28, 1866, on the Poor Laws. Lond., 1816. 8vo. 2d Ed. Pamphleteer. Vol. 8.

—— Speech in Parl't, Feb. 21, 1817, on the Poor Laws. Lond., 1817. 8vo. Pamphleteer. Vol. 10.

CURWEN, M. E. Sketch of the Hist. of the City of Dayton, Ohio. 2d Ed. Dayton, 1850. 12mo.

CURWEN, Samuel. Journal and Letters, 1775–84, with Biograph. Notices of Amer. Loyalists, by G. A. Ward. N. Y., 1845. 8vo.

CURZON, Robt. Monasteries of the East: Embracing Visits to Monasteries in the Levant. N. Y., 1854. 12mo.

CUSHING, Caleb. Claims of Citizens of the U. States on Denmark, examined. Boston, 1826. 8vo. Congr. and Polit. Pamph. Vols. 69, 134.

—— History of the Present State of Newburyport, Mass. Newburyport, 1826. 12mo.

—— Oration at Boston, July 4, 1833. 8vo. Addresses. Vol. 3.

—— Speech in Cong., June 24 and 25, 1841, on Case of Alex. McLeod. 8vo. Congr. and Polit. Pamph. Vol. 89.

CUSHING, Jonathan P. Address before the Va. Hist. and Philosoph. Soc., Feb. 4, 1833. Collections. Vol. 1.

CUSHING, Luther S. Reports of Controverted Elections in Mass., 1780–1852. Boston, 1853. 8vo.

CUSHING, Thos. Letters from 1767 to 1775. Mass. Hist. Soc. Coll. 4th Series. Vol. 4.

—— Memoir of Gideon F. Thayer. N. Eng. Hist. and Gen. Register. Vol. 19.

CUSHING, William. See FLANDERS, H. Lives of Chief Justices.

CUSHMAN Celebration. Proceedings at Plymouth, Mass., Aug. 15, 1855, in commem. of the embarkation of the Plymouth Pilgrims and Acc. of Elder Thos. Cushman. Boston. 1855. 8vo. Genealog. Pamph. Vol. 12.

CUSHMAN, Rev. David. The Ancient Settlement of Sheepscot, Maine. Me. Hist. Soc. Coll. Vol. 4.

CUSHMAN Genealogy. See CUSHMAN, H. W.

CUSHMAN, Henry W. See DAVIS, G. T. Biograph. Sketch of Green, Rev. B.

—— Hist. and Biograph. Genealogy of the Cushmans: the Descendants of Robt. Cushman, the Puritan, from 1617 to 1855. Boston, 1855. 8vo.

CUSHMAN, Rev. Robt. The Sin and Danger of Self-Love. Disc. at Plymouth in 1621, being the First Sermon preached in N. E. Reprint. N. A., 1847. 12mo.

CUSICK, David. Sketches of Ancient History of the Six Nations. Lockport, N. Y., 1848. 8vo. Indian Pamph. Vol. 2.

CUSTIS, Geo. W. P. Recollections of the Private Memoirs of Washington, with a Memoir of the Author by his Daug and Notes by B. J. Lossing. N. Y., 1860. 8vo.

CUSTOM HOUSE FRAUDS. See U. S. House of Repr. Report on.

CUTLER, Rev. Benj. C. Centen. Sermon at Quincy, Dec. 25, 1827. Cambridge, 1828. 8vo. Mass. Hist. Discourses. Vol. 19.

CUTLER Family Genealogy. See MORSE, A.

CUTLER, G. W. Poems: National and Patriotic. Phila., 1857. 8vo.

CUTLER, Wm. Life of Gen. Lafayette. N. Y., 1857, 12mo.

—— Life of Israel Putnam, Maj. Gen. in the Army of the Amer. Revolution. N. Y., 1857. 12mo.

CUTTING, F. B. and WALSH, M. Speeches in Cong. Jan. 17 and 20, 1854, on N. Y. Politics. Cong. and Polit. Pamph. Vol. 88.

CUTTS Hampden. Life and Public Services of the late Hon. Wm. Jarvis. N. Eng. Hist. and Gen. Register. Vol. 20.

CUTTS, J. Madison. Brief Treatise on Constitutional and Party Questions and Hist. of Polit. Parties. N. Y., 1866. 12mo.

CUVIER, M. See FLOURERNS, M. Memoirs of.

—— Memoirs of Dr. Jos. Priestly. Read before the Nat. Institute of France, June 27, 1805. Smithsonian Report,. 1858.

CUYAHOGA Valley (Ohio) Antiquities. See WHITTLESEY, Chas.

CYCLOPÆDIAS. See ENCYCLOPÆDIAS.

CYMRY of 1776. See JONES, Alex.

D.

DABLON, Rev. Claude. Relation de ce qui je'st passi de plus remarquable aux Missions des Peres de la Compagne de Jesus en la Nouvelle France. 1672–73. N. Y., reprint. 1861. 8vo.

Same. 1673, '79. N. Y., reprint. 1860. 8vo.

DABNEY, Rev. A. L. Life and Campaigns of Lieut. Gen. Thos. J. Jackson. N. Y. 1866. 12mo.

DACOTAH Co., MINN. See MITCHELL, W. H.

DAGGETT, John. Sketch of the Hist. of Attleborough, from its Settlement to the Present Time. Dedham. 1834. 8vo.

DAHKOTAH LAND AND LIFE. See NEILL, E. D.

DAHL, O. R. Key to Southern Prisons of U. S. Officers. N. Y., 1865. 12mo. Rebell'n Pamph. Vol. 4.

DAHLGREEN, Mrs. M. V. Thoughts on Female Suffrage, and in Vindication of Woman's True Rights. Washington, 1871. Congr. and Polit. Pamph. Vol. 128.

DALHGREN, J. A. Boat Armament of the Navy. Phila., 1856. 8vo.

DAKE, Orsamus C. See Nebraska Legends and Poems. N. Y., 1871. 12mo.

DAKOTA COUNTY, MINN. See MITCHELL, W. H. Sketch of. 1869.

—— Ann. Message of Gov. Jayne, Mar., 1862. Yankton, 1862. 8vo.

—— See ARMSTRONG, M. K. Hist. and Resources of. 1866.

—— Information Circular. 1870.

—— Commissioner of Emigration. 2d Bien. Report, 1872. Yankton. 1872–3. 8vo.

—— See FOSTER, J. S. History, and Emigrant's Guide. 1870.

—— Historical Soc'y. First Ann. Report, 1865. (Newspaper Article pasted in small blank-book.)

DAKOTA INDIANS. See LYNDE, Jas. W. The Religion of.
—— —— NEILL, E. D. Dahkotah Land and Dahkotah Life.
—— —— POND, G. H. Dakota Superstitions.
—— Language. See RIGGS, Rev. S. R. Gram. and Dict. of.
—— —— RŒHRIG, F. L. O. Language of. 1872.
DALE, Wm. A. Tweed. Manual of the Albany Lancaster School. Albany, 1820. 12mo. Educa. Pamph. Vol. 6.
DALEY, John *vs.* S. D. Van Schaick and others. Before N. Y. Court of Appeals. Law Pamph. Vol. 2.
DALL, Wm. H. Alaska and its Resources. Boston, 1870. 8vo.
DALLAS, Alex· Jas. See DALLAS, Geo. M.
DALLAS, Geo. M. Eulogy on Prest. Jas. K. Polk. Phila., 1849. 8vo. Addresses. Vol. 13.
—— Life & Writings of Alex. Jas. Dallas. Phila. 1871. 8vo.
—— See Penn. Grand Lodge.
—— Sketch of his Life, N. Y. 1844. 8vo. Congr. & Polit. Pamph. Vol. 76.
DALLIBA, Maj. Jas. Narr. of the Battle of Brownstown, Aug. 9, 1812, under Gen. Hull. N. Y. 1816. 8vo. Pamphlets War of 1812. Vol. 5.
DALY, Chas. P. Are the Southern Privateersmen Pirates? N. Y. 1862. 8vo. Rebell'n Pamph. Vol. 15.
DALRYMPLE, Sir Hew. See HAGUE, Thos. Letter on his late Appointment.
DALYRMPLE, Sir John. Memoirs of G. Britain and Ireland from Charles 2d to the Sea Battle of La Hogue. 2d. Ed. Lond. 1771. 3 Vols. 4to.
DALTON, Dr. Edward B. Memorial of. N. Y. 1872. 8vo.
D'ALTON, John. Illustrations, Historical and Genealogical of King James' Irish Army List, 1689. 2d. Ed. Enlarged. Lond. 1861. 2 Vols. 8vo.
DALTON, John. Meteorolog. Observations & Essays, Lond. 1793? 8vo. Scientific Pamph. Vol. 3.
D'ALVA, Fernando. Cruante's Horribles des Conquerants du Mexique. See Ternaux. Voyages. Vol. 8.
—— Histoire des Chichimèques, on des Anciens Rois de Tezcuco. 2 vols. See TERNAUX. Voyages. Vols. 12, 13.
DALZEL, Andrew. Chevalier's Tableau de la Plaine de Troye, illustrated and confirmed. Lond. 1797. 4to. Hist. Pamph. Vol. 22.
DALZELL, J. M. John Gray. of Mount Vernon; the Last Soldier of the Revolution. Washington. 1868. 8vo. Rev. War. Pamph. Vol. 2.
DAMASCUS and the July Massacres. From the Christian Examiner May, 1861. Hist. Pamph. Vol. 2.
D'AMERIE—Emery—Amory. From N. Eng, Register, Oct. 1869. Boston. 1869. 8vo. Genealog. Pamph. Vol. 4
DAMON, Saml. C. Hist. of Holden, Mass., 1667–1841. Worcester. 1841. 8vo. Mass. Hist. Discourses. Vol. 13.
DAMPIER, W. New Journey to South Seas, and Travels around the World, in Dutch. Amsterdam, 1715. 4to. 2 Vols.

DANA, Chas. A. The U. States Illustrated, Vol. 1. The East; or the Sea Board States; Vol. 2, The West, or the States of the Mississipi Valley. N. Y. n. d. 4to.

DANA, C. W. The Great West; or Garden of the World. Boston, 1861. 12mo.

DANA, Dan'l, D. D. Address at Ipswich Female Seminary, Jan. 15, 1834. Newburyport, 1834. 8vo. Addresses, Vol. 33.

—— Half Century Disc. at Newburyport, Mass, Nov. 19, 1844. Newburyport, 1845. 8vo.

—— Sermon before Andover Theolog. Sem., on Wm. Bartlett, Apr. 19, 1841. Andover, 1841. 8vo. Sermons, Vol. 33.

DANA, E. Descrip. of Bounty Lands of Illinois. Cincin., 1819. 12mo.

DANA, Jas. D. Notes on Oregon and Upper California. Silliman's Journ., Vol. 7, 2d Ser.

—— Science and Scientific Schools. Address before the Alumni of Yale Col., Aug., 1856. N. Haven, 1856. 8vo. Yale Coll. Pamph.

—— System of Mineralogy, comprising the most recent Discoveries. 2d Ed. N. Y., 1844. 8vo.

DANA, Rich'd H. Poem before the Porter Rhetorical Soc. in the Andover Theolog. Seminary, Sept. 22, 1829. Boston, 1829. 8vo. Pamph. Poetry, Vol. 25.

—— Poems and Prose Writings. N. Y., 1857. 2 Vols. 12mo.

DANA, Rich'd H., Jr. Address at Cambridge, Feb. 22, 1865, on the Life and Services of E. Everett. Cambridge, 1865. 8vo. Addresses, Vol. 31.

—— Enemy's Territory and Alien Enemies. Boston, 1864. 8vo. Rebellion Pamph., Vol. 6.

—— Remarks on the proposed Removal of Edw. G. Loring from the office of Judge of Probate. Boston, 1855. Addresses, Vol. 9.

—— Speech at Faneuil Hall, June 21, 1865, on Reorganiza. of the Rebel States. Rebell'n Pamph., Vol. 107.

—— Two Years before the Mast; a Personal Narrative of Life at Sea. Harpers Fam. Library. N. Y., 1860. 18mo.

DANA, Sam'l. Address on the Importance of a well regulated Militia. Charlestown, 1801. Addresses, Vol. 5. 8vo.

—— See ATHERTON, C. H., Memoir of.

—— Disc. on the Hist. of the 1st Ch. in Marblehead, delivered Jan. 7, 1816. Boston, 1816. 8vo. Mass. Hist. Discourses, Vol. 20.

DANBURY, Conn., Congr. Ch. Manual, compiled by Rev. R. S. Stone. Albany, 1853. 12mo. Conn. Hist. Discourses, &c. Vol. 6.

DANE Baptist Assoc., Wis. Minutes of Sessions held from 1850 to 1865 inclusive, and in 1867 and 1868. Watertown, &c., 1850–68. 8vo.

DANE Co., Wis., Agricult. Soc. Constitution and Premium List. Madison, 1857. 8vo. Dane Co. Pamph., Vol. 1.

—— —— —— Premium List for 1870. Madison, 1870. 8vo. Dane Co. Pamph., Vol. 1.

—— —— Almanac for 1872. 8vo. Dane Co. Pamph., Vol. 1.

—— —— Atlas.—See HARRISON & WARNER. 1873.

DANE Co. Bible Soc'y. Ann. Report for 1869–70 and 1870–71. Madison. 8vo. Dane Co. Pamph. Vol. 1.

—— —— Board of Supervisors. Journal of Sessions of Nov., 1857, and Jan., 1858. Madison, 1858. 8vo. Dane Co. Pamph. Vol. 1.

—— —— —— Report of Committee of Investigation on the Financial Affairs of Dane Co. Madison, 1860. 8vo. Dane Co. Pamph. Vol. 1.

—— —— Statistics of, with a Sketch of the Settlement, Growth, etc., of Madison. Madison, 1852. 8vo. Dane Co. Pamph. Vol. 1.

DANE Genealogy. See DANE, John.

DANE, John. Declaration of Remarkable Providences in the Course of My Life. With a Pedigree of the Dane Family. Boston, 1854. 8vo. Genealog. Pamph. Vol. 2. See also N. Eng. Gen. Register. Vol. 8.

DANE, Nathan. Sketch of. From the Boston Messenger. 1835. Biograph. Pamph. Vol. 17.

DANET, Peter. Phaedri Augusti Caesaris Liberti, Fabularum Aesopiarum Libri quinque, etc. Lond., 1702. (?) 8vo. Latin Pamph. Vol. 3.

DANFORTH Family Genealogy, from their First Arrival in N. England in 1634 to the 18th Century. Farmer & Moore's N. H. Hist. Coll. Vol. 2.

DANFORTH, Dr. Thomas. Oration at Boston, July 4, 1804. 8vo. Addresses, etc. Vol. 2.

DANFORTH, Gov. Thomas. State Papers. Mass. Hist. Soc. Coll. 2d Ser. Vol. 8.

DANGER, The, and Unreasonableness of a Toleration: in reference to Late Papers on Liberty of Conscience. Lond., 1685. Sm. 4to. Eng. Religious Pamph. Vol. 3.

—— of G. Britain and Ireland becoming Provinces to France. Lond., 1745–6. 8vo. Eng. Polit. Pamph. Vol. 12.

DANGERFIELD, J. Stenographic Lecture at the Royal Institution, Mar. 1, 1825. Lond., 1834. 2d Ed. Scientific Pamph., etc. Vol. 26.

DANGERFIELD, Thos. Answer to Elizabeth Cellier's "Malice Defeated;" etc. Lond., 1680. Fol. Eng. Polit. Pamph. Vol. 1.

—— Particular Narrative of the late Popish Design. Lond., 1679. Fol. Eng. Polit. Pamph. Vol. 63.

DANGERS of Europe from the Growing Power of France. Lond., 1702. Small 4to. Eng. Misc. Pamph. Vol. 1.

DANIEL, Justice. Opinion in the Wheeling Bridge Case. Richmond, 1852. 8vo. Penn. Misc. Pamph. Vol. 2.

DANIEL, Sir F. C. Memoir of. Lond., 1826. 8vo. Biograph. Pamph. Vol. 10.

DANIELL, Edw., M. D. Proposals for Establishing a General Medical Annuity Fund. Lond., 1845. 8vo. Med. Pamph. Vol. 33.

DANIELS, ——. Life of Stonewall Jackson; from Official Papers, Contemporary Narratives and Personal Acquaintance. N.Y., 1863. 12mo.

DANIELS, Edward. See Wis. Geolog. Survey.
DANISH Islands. See PARTON, Jas. Are we bound to pay for them?
—— —— St. Thomas Treaty.
—— Question. Letters to the Editor of the Times. Lond., 1848. 8vo. Strangford Pamph. Vol. 46.
DANKERS, J., and SLUYTER, P. Journal of a Voyage to N. Y. & a Tour in the Amer. Colonies in 1679–80. 8vo. Translated and Edited by H. C. Murphy. L. Island Hist. Soc. Memoirs. Vol. 1.
"DANUBIAN Principalities." See BRATIANO, D., Documents concerning, &c. 1849.
DANVERS, J. T. A Picture of Jefferson's Administration, (title page wanting.) N. Y., 1808. 8vo. Congr. & Polit. Pamph. Vol. 129.
DANVERS, Mass. Acc. of the Centenn. Celebra. in Danvers, June 16, 1852, with Proceedings in relation to the Donation of Geo. Peabody. Boston, 1852. 8vo.
—— Reports of School Committees for 1843–4, 1847–8, 1853.
—— Statements of Receipts and Expenditures for 1852 & 1853.
—— Address of Health Committee, 1849.
—— See OSGOOD, Geo. Histor. Sketch of N. Danvers.
DANVILLE, Vt. See DUDLEY, Rev. John, Half Cent. Disc. 1851.
DAPONT, Lorenzo. Hist. of the Florentine Republic, and the Age and Rule of the Medici. N. Y. 12mo,
—— Memoirs of, from the Antologia of Florence, 1828. N. Y. 1829. 8vo. Biograph. Pamph. Vol. 18.
—— Sketch of the Life of. N. Y., 1842. 12mo. Biograph. Pamph. Vol. 18.
DAPPER, O. Travels in Africa, Asia, Morea and Tartary, and Descriptive Accounts of the Islands of the Archipelago, Palestine, &c., in Dutch. Amsterdam, 1670–1688. 7 Vols. folio.
DARBOY, Archb'p Geo. Murder of, by Communists. See WASHBURNE, E. B.
DARBY, G. H. See U. S. Sec. of War.
DARBY, Wm. Emigrants' Guide to Western and S. Western States and Territories, N. Y., 1818. 8vo.
—— Geograph. Descrip. of the State of Louisiana, the Southern Part of Mississippi and Alabama. 2d Ed. enlarged. N. Y., 1817. 8vo.
—— Map of Louisiana. N. Y., 1816.
—— Memoir on the Geography and Natural and Civil Hist. of Florida, with a map. Phila., 1821. 8vo.
—— Tour from the City of N. Y. to Detroit, with maps. N. Y., 1819. 8vo.
—— View of the U. States, Historical, Geographical and Statistical. Phila., 1828. 12mo.
—— & DWIGHT, Theo. New Gazeteer of the United States.
—— States of N. America. Hartford, 1833. 8vo.
DARD, Mad. Shipwreck of the Medusa. Waldo's Cir, Libr. Vol. 2.
DARING Deeds of Amer. Generals. See JENKINS, John S.
DARK Day in N. England, 1780. See WILLIAMS, Saml.

DARLING, Rev. Henry. Slavery and the War: a Histor. Essay. Phila., 1833. 8vo. Rebellion Pamph. Vols. 3, 29, 67.

DARLINGTON Genealogy. Sesqui-Centen-Gathering of the Clan Darlington. Lancaster, 1853. 8vo. Genealog. Pamph. Vol. 7.

DARLINGTON, Wm., M. D. Address to Chester Co. Cabinet of Nat Science, Mar. 18, 1826. West Chester, Pa., 1826. 12mo. Scientific Pamph. Vol. 3.

—— Address before the Chester Co. Penn., Horticult. Soc., Sept. 11, 1846. Agr. Pamph. Vol. 14.

—— Address to the Chester Co. Med. Soc., West Chester, Penn., 1852. 8vo. Med Pamph. Vol. 2.

—— Agricult. Botany; an Enumeration and Description of Useful Plants. Phila., 1847. 12mo.

—— Disc. upon Agriculture before the Citizens of Oxford, Sept. 4, 1847. Agr. Pamph. Vol. 14.

—— Flora Cestrica: Catalogue of Flowering and Filicoid Plants of Chester Co., Penn. Westchester, 1837. 8vo.

—— Same. 3d Ed., 1853. 8vo.

—— Florula Cestrica: Catalogue of Phaenogamous Plants in Westchester, Penn. Westchester, 1826. 8vo.

—— Memorial of David Townsend. Westchester, 1858. 8vo. Addresses, etc. Vol. 13.

—— Memorials of John Bartram and Humphrey Marshall, with Notices of their Botanical Contemporaries. Phila., 1849. 8vo.

—— Plea for the Study of Nat. Hist. in the Common Schools. Lancaster, 1855. 8vo. Educa. Pamph. Vol. 3.

—— Reliquiæ Baldwinianæ: Selections from the Correspondence of Wm. Baldwin, M. D. Phila., 1843. 12mo.

—— Memorial of Westchester, Pa., 1763. 8vo. Addresses, etc. Vol. 13.

—— See Penn. Agric. Soc., 1825.

DARNELL, Elias. Journal of an Account of Hardships, etc., of Kentucky Vols. and Regulars, commanded by Gen. Winchester in 1812, '13. Phila. 12mo. 1854. Pamphlets War of 1812. Vol. 2.

DARTMOUTH College, Hanover, N. H. Catalogues for 1840, 1843–4, 1844–5, 1849–50.

—— —— Trien. Catalogue, 1843, 1855, 1864. Hanover. v. d. 12mo and 8vo.

—— —— See CROSBY, A. Address, 1865.

—— —— See EMERSON, R. W. Oration, 1838.

—— —— FARMER, J. Sketches of Graduates of.

—— —— FARRER, T. The Case of.

—— —— MCCLURE and Parish. History of.

—— —— PEABODY, A. P. Address, 1843.

—— —— Sketches of the History of, from 1779 to 1815, with a Review of the same. n. p. 8vo. 2 Pamphs. N. H. Hist. Discourses, etc. Vol. 3.

—— —— See TENNEY, Jona. Memo. of Class of 1843.

—— —— Vindication of the Official Conduct of the Trustees of. Concord, 1815. 8vo. Dartmouth College Pamphs.

DARTMOUTH, Mass. See New Bedford Centen. Celebra.

DAUBENY, Chas. Sketch of the Geology of Sicily, 1825. Silliman's Journ. Vol. 10.

D'AUBIGNE, J. H. M. Hist. of Reformation of the Sixteenth Century. N. Y., 1849. 4 Vols. 12mo.

DAUCHER, A. B. Isagoges in Lectionem Aristotelis, etc. Altdorf, 1658. 4to. Latin Pamph. Vol. 10.

DAUCKAERTZ, C. History of the Wars of Gustavus Adolphus, in Dutch. Amsterdam, 1642. Folio.

DAUGHTERS COLLEGE, near Harrodsburg, Kentucky. Ann. Announcement. 1863–4. Cincin., 1863. 8vo.

DAVENPORT, Bishop. Gazetter and Geograph. Dictionary of N. America and West Indies. Baltimore, 1833. 8vo.

DAVENPORT, A. Benedict. Hist. and Geneal. of the Davenport Family in England and America, 1086 to 1850. N. Y., 1851. 12mo.

DAVENPORT, City, Iowa. Directory for 1858 and 1859. Davenport, 1858. 12mo.

—— See WILKIE, F. B.

DAVENPORT, Rev. James R. Sermon on the 6th Annivers. of Grace Ch., Albany, Feb. 15, 1852. Albany, 1852. 8vo. N. Y. Hist. Discources. Vol. 1.

DAVENPORT, R. A. Perilous Adventures: or, Instances of Courage, Perseverance and Suffering. Harpers Fam. Library. N. Y., 1859. 18vo.

DAVID, J. C. Introduction to Universal Language, etc. Washington, 1838. 12mo. Educa. Pamph. Vol. 2.

DAVIDS, T. W. Annals of Evangelical Non-Conformity in the Co. of Essex, England. London, 1863. 8vo.

DAVIDSON, D. Connexion of Sacred and Profane History. N. Y., 1857. 12mo.

DAVIDSON, R. Excursion to Mammoth Cave and Barrens of Ky.; Early Settlement, etc. Lexington, 1840. 12mo.

DAVIDSON, Rev. Robt. Memoir of Lewis Morris, Gov. of N. Jersey, 1738–1746. N. J. Hist. Soc. Proceed. Vol. 4.

DAVIE, Wm. R. See HUBBARD, F. M. Life of.

DAVIES, Henry. Stranger's Guide through Cheltenham. Cheltenham, Eng., 1834. 2d Ed. Guide-Books. Vol. 7.

DAVIES, John. On the Temporal Augment, in Sanskrit and Greek. Hertford, Eng. 8vo. n. d. Educa. Pamph. Vol. 32.

DAVIES, John E., M. D. On Potentials and their Application to Physical Science. Trans. Wis. Acad. of Sciences, 1870–2.

DAVIES, Robert. Extracts from the Municipal Records of the City of York, during the Reigns of Edward IV, Edward V and Richard III. Lond., 1843. 8vo.

—— Pope: Additional Facts concerning his Maternal Ancestry. Lond., 1858. 12mo. Genealog. Pamph. Vol. 6.

DAVIES, Rev. Sam'l. Letters shewing the State of Religion in Virginia, particularly among the Negroes. Lond., 1757. 12mo. 2d Ed. Va. Misc. Pamph. Vol. 1.

DAVIES, W. H. A. Notes on Esquimaux Bay and the Surrounding Country. Read before the Quebec Lit. & Hist. Soc., Feb. 19, 1842. Transactions, Vol. 4, Part 1.

—— Notes on Ungava Bay & its Vicinity. Read before the Lit. & Hist. Soc. of Quebec, Dec. 3, 1842. Transactions, Vol. 4, Part 2.

DAVIES, A. Antiquities of America, the First Inhabitants of Central America, & the Discovery of N. England by the Northmen. Buffalo, 1849. 8vo. 21st Edition. Pamphlets. Pre. Columbian Discov.

—— Lecture on the Discovery of America by the Northmen. N. Y., 1839. 8vo. Pamphlets. Pre. Columbian Discov.

—— Lecture on Remarkable Discoveries in the East. Buffalo, 1852. 8vo. Archaeolog. Pamph. Vol. 2.

DAVIS, Amos. Speech in Cong. May 28, 1834, on the Contested Election of Moore vs. Letcher. Washington, 1834. 8vo. Speeches. Vol. 4.

DAVIS, Chas. H. Remarks on the Establishment of an American Prime Meridian. Cambridge, 1849. 8vo. Scientific Pamph. Vol. 42.

—— Report on Inter-Oceanic Communication at the Isthmus. Washington, 1870. 8vo. Sec. of Navy Misc. Rp'ts.

—— The Coast Survey of the U. States. Washington, 1851. 8vo.

DAVIS, C. H. S. Davis' Family Records. Nos. 1, 4, 5, 6, 7, 8. Newspaper, 1867. 8vo. Meriden, Ct. Genealog. Pamph. Vol. 1.

—— Hist. of Wallingford, Ct., from 1670 to the Present Time, including Meriden & Cheshire. Meriden. 1870. 8vo.

DAVIS, Emerson. Half Century: or Hist. of Changes & Events in the U. S., between 1800 & 1850. Boston, 1851. 12mo.

—— Hist. Sketch of Westfield, Mass. Westfield, 1826. 8vo. Mass. Hist. Discourses, &c. Vol. 12.

DAVIS, Dr. E. H. Report to the Ohio State Med. Soc., on Statistics of Calculous Disease in Ohio. Columbus, 1850. 8vo. Med. Pamph. Vol. 7.

DAVIS Family Genealogy. See DAVIS, C. H. S.

DAVIS, Garret. Resolutions offered by him in U. S. Senate, Jan. 5, 1862, on the power of the President of the U. S. Rebell'n Pamph., Vol. 54.

—— Speech in U. S. Senate, Jan. 23, 1862, on the War. Rebell'n Pamph., Vol. 99.

—— Speech in Cong., Feb. 16, 1864, on Bill to Equalize the Pay of Soldiers. Rebell'n Pamph., Vol. 34.

—— Speeches in Conven. to Revise the Constitution of Ky., Dec., 1849, in regard to Foreign Immigration. Frankfort, 1855. 8vo. Congr. and Polit. Pamph., Vol. 105.

DAVIS, Geo. Hist. Sketch of Sturbridge and Southbridge, Mass. W. Brookfield, 1856. 8vo.

DAVIS, Geo. T. Biogaph. Sketch of Hon. Henry W. Cushman. N. Eng. Hist. and Gen. Register, Vol. 18.

—— Biograph. Sketch of Isaac P. Davis. Mass. Hist. Soc. Proceedings, 1869–70.

DAVIS, Henry W. Address at Brooklyn, Nov. 26, 1861, on the Southern Rebell'n. Rebell'n Pamph., Vol. 99.

—— See CRESWELL, J. A. J., Oration on Life of. 1866.

—— Speech at Baltimore, Sep. 27, 1860. Rebell'n Pamph., Vol. 32.

—— Speech at Concert Hall, Phila., Sep. 24, 1863. Rebell'n Pamph., Vol. 32.

—— Speech in Cong., Jan. 14, 1864, on Confiscation. Rebell'n Pamph., Vol. 9.

—— Speech in Cong., Apr. 11, 1864, on the Expulsion of Mr. Long. Rebell'n Pamph., Vol. 9.

DAVIS, Isaac. Hist. Discourse at Semi-Centen. Celebra. of 1st Bapt. Ch., Worcester, Dec. 9, 1862. Worcester. 8vo. Mass. Hist. Discourses, Vol. 1.

DAVIS, Isaac P.—See DAVIS, Geo. T., Memoir of.

DAVIS, Jeff'n.—See Alfriend, H. F., Life of.

—— Bledsoe, A. T., Is Davis a Traitor?

—— Corres. with Pope of Rome. 1863. Rebell'n Pamph., Vol. 54.

—— See CRAVEN, J. J., Prison Life of.

—— Second Ann. Message of President of Confed. States to Congress. Lond., 1863. 8vo. Rebell'n Pamph., Vol. 39.

—— See POLLARD, E. A. Life of and Southern Confederacy.

—— and STONEWALL JACKSON. From authentic sources. Portaits, etc. N. Y., 1866. 12mo.

DAVIS, John. Disc. before the Mass. Hist. Soc., Dec. 22, 1813, on the Landing of the Pilgrims, 1620. Collections. Vol. 1. 2d Series.

—— See FRANCIS, Convers. Memoir of.

—— GANNETT E. S. Obt. Sermon, 1847.

—— KINNICUTT, Thos. Life and Character of.

—— Memoirs of. —— Amer. Antiq. Soc. Coll. Vol. 3.

—— Speeches in U. S. Senate, Jan. 23, 1840, on the Sub-Treasury Bill, etc. Congr. and Polit. Pamph. Vol. 92.

DAVIS, JOHN. Travels of Four Years and a half in U. States of America; 1798–1802. Lond., 1803. 8vo.

—— Travels in Lousiana and the Floridas. N. Y., 1806. 12mo.

DAVIS, John Francis. The Chinese; a General Description of the Empire of China and its Inhabitants. Harpers' Fam. Lib. N. Y. 2 Vols. 18mo.

DAVIS, M. On the Removal of Duty on Lumber imported from Canada. Washington, 1870. 8vo. Congr. and Polit. Pamph. Vol. 120.

DAVIS, Matthew L. Memoirs of AARON BURR; with Selections from his Correspondence. N. Y., 1857. 2 Vols. 18vo.

—— Private Journ. of AARON BURR during his Four Years Residence in Europe. N. Y., 1858. 2 Vols. 8vo.

DAVIS, Nathan M. See MITCHELL, Nahum. Memoir of.

DAVIS, Noah. Speeches in Cong., Mar. 7, 1870, on the Admission of Georgia. Congr. and Polit. Pamph. Vol. 119.

DAVIS, N. S., M. D. Address on the Free Medical Schools in Rush Medical Coll. Chicago, 1849. 8vo. Med. Pamph, Vol. 2.

DAVIS, N. S., M. D. Text Book on Agriculture. Binghampton, 1846. 18mo.

—— Valedict. Address before Graduating Class of Rush Medical Coll., 1853. 8vo. Med. Pamph. Vol. 2.

DAVIS, Paris M. Authentic History of the Late War between the U. States and G. Britain. N. Y., 1836. 12mo. Pamphlets, War of 1812. Vol. 1.

DAVIS, Robt. M. Public and Private Credit and Banking, and their Abuses. N. Orleans, 1869. 8vo. Congr. and Polit. Pamph. Vol. 79.

DAVIS, Rev. Solomon, Prayer Book in the Language of the Six Nations of Indians. N. Y., 1837. 12mo.

DAVIS, Thomas. Gen. View of the Agriculture of Wiltshire, Eng. Lond., 1813. 8vo.

DAVIS, T. T. Speech in Cong., Mar. 23, 1864, on Military and Post Roads. Rebell. Pamph. Vol. 34.

DAVIS, Tim. Speech in Cong., May 22, 1858, on French Spoliations. Cong. and Polit. Pamph. Vol. 84.

DAVIS, Wendell. Description of Sandwich, in the Co. of Barnstable, Mass. Mass. Hist. Soc. Coll. 1st Ser. Vol. 8.

DAVIS, Rev. Wm. The Difficulties of Education. A Lecture. Lond. 1848, 2d. Ed. Educa. Pamph. Vol. 30.

DAVIS, W. W. H. Hist. of 104th Pa. Regt., from Aug. 22, 1861, to Sept. 30, 1864. Phila. 1866. 8vo.

——Hist. and Geneal. of Hart Family of Warminster, Bucks Co., Pa. Doylestown, Pa. 1867. 8vo.

—— Sketch of Life and Character of John Lacey of Rev. Army. Doylestown. 1868. 8vo.

—— The Spanish Conquest of N. Mex. Doylestown, Pa. 1869. 8vo.

DAVISON, Alex. Observations on the 3d Report of the Commiss'rs of Military Enquiry. Lond. 1807. 8vo. Eng. Polit. Pamph. Vol 28.

DAVISON, James Wood. The Living Writers of the South. 12mo. N. Y., 1869.

DAVY, Sir Humphrey. Review of the Scientific Labors and Character of. Silliman's Journ. Vol. 17.

DAWES, M. The Deformity of the Doctrine of Libels, with a view of the Case of the Dean of St. Asaph, etc. Lond. 1785. 8vo. Eng. Polit. Pamph. Vol. 22.

—— England's Alarm. On the prevailing Doctrine of Libels, as laid down by the Earl of Mansfield, in a Letter etc. Lond., 1785. 8vo. Eng. Polit. Pamph. Vol. 22.

DAWES, Rev. Rich'd. Hints on an improved System of Na. Educa. Lond., 1855. 12vo. Educa. Pamph. Vol. 34.

DAWES, Sir Wm. Sermon at St. James's, in Lent, 1698. Lond., 1707. 12vo. 2d Ed. Eng. Sermons. Vol. 7.

DAWSON, B. F. Lands in Rock Co., Wis., to be sold by Auction, June 23, 1864. N. Y., 1864. 8vo. Wis. Misc. Pamph. Vol. 1.

DAWSON, Henry B. Acc. of Interment of Remains of Amer. Patriots who died in British Prison Ships during Amer. Revolution with notes. N. Y. repub., 1865. 8vo.

DAWSON, Henry B. Assault on Stoney Point by Gen. Anthony Wayne, July 16, 1779, with maps, notes and fac-similes. Morrisiana, 1863. 4to.

—— Battles of the U. States, by Sea and Land. N. Y., 1858. 2 Vols. 4to.

—— Correspondence with tho Comptroller, N. Y. city, concerning the Records of the Department of Finance. 1862. 8vo. N. Y. City Pamph. Vol. 6.

—— See FOEDERALIST, The.

—— Gleanings from Harvest Fields, of Amer. History. Vol. 4. being the Diary of David Howe, in Rev. War. N. Y., 1866. 4to.

—— Hist. Paper on the Battle of Bunker's Hill. Hist. Mag., 2d Ser. Vol. 3.

—— See JAY, John. Second Letter on his Introduction to the Foederalist.

—— Letter to Prest. of N. Y. Hist. Soc., on the Declara. of Independence by Mass. Bay Colony. May 1, 1776. n. p., 1862. 8vo. Rev. War. Pamph. Vol. 4. See also N. Y. Hist. Soc. Discourses.

—— Maj. Gen. Israel Putnam. Correspondence with the Editor of "The Hartford Daily Post" by "Selah," of that City, and H. B. Dawson. Morrisania, 1860. 8vo.

—— Records of the Trial of Joshua Hett Smith, for Complicity in the Treason of Benedict Arnold, 1780. Morrisania, 1866. 8va. Rev. War Pamph. Vol. 3.

—— The Citizen Genet. Hist. Mag. Vol. 10.

—— The Park in the City of New York and its Vicinity. Morrisiana, 1867. 8vo.

—— The Sons of Liberty in N. York. Papers before the N. Y. Hist. Soc., May 3, 1859. Po'keepsie, 1859. 8vo. N. Y. Hist. Soc. Addresses. Vol. 3.

DAWSON, J. L. Speech in Cong. Mar. 3, 1852, on the Homestead Bill. Cong. and Polit. Pamph. Vol. 83.

—— Speech in Cong. Feb. 24, 1864, on the State of the Union. Rebelln. Pamph. Vol. 34.

—— Speech in Cong., Jan. 9, 1855, on the Homestead Bill. Speeches. Vol. 5.

DAWSON, Moses. Sketches of the Life of Martin Van Buren. Cincinnati, 1840. 12mo.

DAWSON, W. W., M. D. Chloroform Deaths. Cincin. n. d. 8vo. Med. Pamph. Vol. 31.

DAY & BUSH. Les Merveilles de Londres avec une Carte. Lond. n. d. 12mo. Guide Books. Vol. 1.

DAY (The) Breaking, if not the Sun Rising of the Gospel with the Indians of N. England. Lond. 1647. Reprint. N. Y., 1865. Small. 4to.

DAY Genealogy. See DAY, Geo. E.

DAY, Geo. E. Genealogy. Register of the Descendants in the Male Line of Robt. Day, of Hartford, Conn. 2d Ed. Northampton, 1848. Genealog. Pamph. Vol. 9.

DAY, Rev. George T. Life of Rev. Martin Cheney. Providence, 1853. 8vo.

DAY, Sam. P. Down South; an Englishman's Experience at the American Seat of War. Lond., 1862. 2 vols. 12mo.

DAY, Sherman. Hist. Collections of the State of Penn. Phila., 1842. 8vo.

DAYS of the Week. Names of. See HARE, Rev. J. C.

DAY, T. Reflection on State of England and Independence of America. 3d Ed. Lond., 1783. Amer. Tracts. Vol. 5.

DAY, T. C. Speech in Cong., Apr. 23, 1856, on the Rebellion. Congr. and Polit. Pamph. Vol. 84.

DAYTON, W. L. Speech in the U. S. Senate, June 11 and 12, 1850, on the Compromise. Congr. and Polit. Pamph. Vol. 94.

DAYTON, O. See CURWEN, M. E. Hist. of.

——VAN CLEVE, J. W. Hist. of Settlement of.

D'BERNICRE, Ensign. Narr. of Occurrences, 1785. Mass. Hist. Soc. Coll. 2d Series. Vol. 3.

DEAD (The) Languages. From De Bow's Review, Mar. 1861. Educa. Pamph. Vol. 7.

DEAD Sea. See LYNCH, W. F., Report of Explora., 1849.

—— MONTAGUE, E. P., Expedition to.

DEAF & Dumb. Alphabetical Chart. Broadside, placed with Amer. Annals, Deaf and Dumb.

—— See Amer. Annals of 1848–52.

—— American Asylum, Hartford.

—— BECK, Dr. T. R. Statistics of, 1837.

—— CLARK, J. H., on the Preservation of Hearing.

—— DAY, G. E. Visit to European Institute, 1844.

—— LIBIER, F. On the Vocal Sounds of, Laura Bridgman.

—— Proceedings of 7th Convention of Amer. Instructors of Deaf & Dumb, held at Indianapolis, 1870. Indianapolis, 1870. 8vo.

—— Wisconsin Institution, Reports Other States.

DEAN, Amos. Address before Y. M. Assoc. of the State of N. Y., at Geneva, Sept. 2, 1841. Addresses Vols. 8, 12, 16.

—— Catalogue of his Library. N. Y., 1868. 8vo. Biograph. Pamph. Vol. 18.

—— Eulogy on Jesse Buel, at Albany, Feb. 5, 1840. Addresses, Vol. 11.

—— History of Civilization. Albany, 1848–9. 7 Vols. 8vo.

—— Principles of Medical Jurisprudence. Albany, 1854. 8vo.

—— The Philosophy of Human Life. Boston, 1839. 12mo.

DEAN, Ezra. Speech in Cong., Jan. 11, 1842, on the Treasury Note Bill. Washington, 1842. 8vo. Congr. & Polit. Pamph. Vol. 25

DEAN, G. Speech in Cong., Apr. 23, 1852, on the Homestead Bill. Cong. & Polit. Pamph. Vol. 87.

DEAN, John Ward. Brief Memoir of Rev. Giles Firmin, one of the Ejected Ministers of 1662. Boston, 1866. 8vo. Addresses, Vol. 15. See, also, N. Eng. Hist. Gen. Register. Vols. 20, 25.

—— Memoir of Hon. Dan'l Messinger of Boston. N. Eng. Hist. & Gen. Register. Vol. 16.

DEAN, John Ward. Mem. of Rev. Nathan'l Ward, and Genealogy. Albany, 1868. 8vo.

—— Sketch of the Life of Rev. Michael Wigglesworth. Albany. 1863. 8vo. Biograph. Pamph., Vol. 8.

—— The Story of the Embarkation of Cromwell and his Friends for N. England. Boston, 1866. 8vo. N. Eng. Pamph., Vol. 1. N. Eng. Register, Vol. 20.

DEAN, Chas. Gen. Washington's Head-Quarters in Cambridge. Paper before the Mass. Hist. Soc., Sept., 1872. Boston, 1873. 8vo. Reprinted from Proceedings.

—— See HALE, E. E.

—— Gov. Hutchinson's Hist. Publications. Mass. Hist. Soc. Proceed. 1855–58.

—— Hutchinson's History of Mass. Paper before the Mass. Hist. Soc. Hist. Mag., Vol. 1.

—— Memoir of Geo. Livermore. Mass. Hist. Soc. Proceed. 1867–69.

—— Notice of Sam'l Gorton. N. Eng. Hist. and Gen. Register. Vol. 4.

DEANE Genealogy.—See DEANE, W. R. & J. W.

DEANE, Jas., M. D.—See BOWDITCH, H. I.

—— Fossil Footprints of the Valley of the Connecticut. Memoirs of Amer. Acad. of Arts and Sciences, N. S., Vol. 4.

DEANE, Silas. Correspondence of. 1774–76. Conn. Hist. Soc. Coll., Vol. 2.

—— Papers in relation to the Case of. From the Original Manuscripts. Phila., 1855. 8vo.

DEANE, Wm. Reed. Memoir of Elkanah Watson. N. Eng. Hist. and Gen. Register, Vol. 17.

—— DEANE, Wm. Reed and J. Ward. Brief Memoirs of John and Walter Deane, two of the First Settlers of Taunton, Mass., and of the Early Generations of their Descendants. Boston, 1849. 8vo.

DE ANTIQUIS Legibus Liber.—See Camden Soc. Publications.

DEABBORN's Guide through Mount Auburn. Boston, 1854. 8vo.

DEARBORN, Benj. Copy of his Will, July 2, 1832. Boston, 1859. 8vo. Boston Misc. Pamph., Vol. 1.

DEARBORN, H. Acc. of the Battle of Bunker Hill. Hist. Mag., Vol. 8.

DEARBORN, H. A. S., & Gray, Thos. Address and Poem on 2d Centen. Annivers. of the Settlement of Roxbury, Mass., Oct, 8, 1830. Roxbury, 1830. 8vo. Mass. Hist. Discourses, Vols. 14 and 18.

—— Letters on the Internal Improvements and Commerce of the West. Boston, 1839. 8vo. Mass. Misc. Pamph., Vol. 2.

—— Sketch of the Life of the Apostle Eliot. Roxbury, 1850. 8vo. Biograph. Pamph., Vols. 6, 8.

—— See PUTNAM, Rev. Geo.

—— Variations of Level in the Great N. Amer. Lakes. 1829. Silliman's Journ., Vol. 16.

DEARBORN SEMINARY, Chicago. Constitution of. n. d. 8vo. Chicago Misc. Pamph. Vol. 2.

DEATH, The. Dissection, Will, and General Procession, of Mrs. Regency. Lond., 1789-80. Eng. Polit. Pamph. Vol. 74.

DEBATE at the East India House, Mar., 18, 1841, on the proposed Statute in honor of the Marquess Wellesley. Lond., 1841. 8vo. Strangford Pamph. Vol. 26.

DEBATE in the House of Repr., U. S., upon the Resolution of H. Dodge, of Wisconsin, to inquire into the Official Conduct of Gov. Doty, May 14, 1842. Washington, 1842. 8vo. Congr. and Polit. Pamph. Vol. 25.

DEBATES IN CONGRESS. See Discussion of Resolutions providing for the publication of. See BENTON, T. H. Congress. Annals of, etc.

DE BEAUCHESNE, A. Louis XVII: his Life; his Suffering; his Death: the Captivity of the Royal Family in the Temple. N. Y., 1853. 2 Vols. 12mo.

DEBERDT, Esther. See REED, Esther.

DEBODE, Baron. A Few Words on the French Claims. Lond., 1830. 8vo. Stranford Pamph. Vol. 6.

DEBOIS GALLAIS, M. F. Lepelle. Biography of Rosa Bonheur. Lond., 1856. 8vo. Biograph. Pamph. Vol. 4.

DEBOW, J. D. B. Amer. Legislation, Science, Art and Agriculture. From DeBow's Review. 1846. Congr. and Polit. Pamph. Vol. 112.

—— Review. Vols. 1—40. Jan. 1846 to Feb. 1870. N. Orleans, 1846-70. 40 Vols. 8vo. (A few volumes wanting.)

—— Statistical view of the U. S. See Census.

DEBRETT, John. Peerage of the United Kingdom of Great Britain and Ireland. 14th Ed. Lond., 1822. 2 Vols. 12mo.

—— Illustrated Peerage of same. Lond., 1865. 8vo.

DEBRUYN, C. Travels in Asia, Muscovy, Persia, etc. In Dutch, Amsterdam, 1698, 1771. 2 Vols. Folio.

DEBRY'S VOYAGES. Bibliograph. Description of Collection of "Grands Voyages" of DeBry. N. Y., 1869. 8vo. priv. pr.

DEBT—Imprisonment for. Disquisition on Imprisonment for Debt, as the Practice exists in N. Y., 1818. C. and P. Pam. Vol. 99.

—— FANE, C. On the Abolition of. 1838.

—— MONTAGUE, Basil. Enquiries respecting the Insolvent Debtors' Bill.

—— PARKER, Thos. Brief Enquiry into the Justice of.

DEBURY, Richard. Philobiblon; a Treatise on the Love of Books. collated and corrected, with notes by Sam'l. Hand. Albany, 1861. 12mo.

DECASSAGNAC, A. G. Recit Complet et Authentique des Evenements de Decembre, 1851, a Paris. Paris, 1851. 8vo. Hist. Pamph. Vol. 19.

DECATUR, Com. Stephen. Corres. with Com. James Barron, Washington, 1820. 8vo. Congr. and Polit. Pamph. Vol. 134.

—— See MACKENZIE, A. S. Life of.

—— WALDO, S. Putnam. Life and Character of.

DE CHARMILLY, Col. Venault. Narr. of his Transactions in Spain, &c.; being a Refutation of Calumnies against Him. Lond., 1810. 8vo. Eng. Polit. Pamph. Vol. 30.

DECIMAL Association, formed June 12, 1854. Proceedings. Lond., 1855. 8vo. Strangford Pamph. Vol. 67.

—— System of U. S. See Amer. Geol. and Statis. Soc.

DECLARATION of Archbishop of Canterbury, and the Bishops in and near London, testifying their Abhorrence of the Present Rebellion. Lond., 1715. 4to. Eng. Polit. Pamph. Vol. 66.

—— Of Amer. Independence. See FORCE, P. Notes on Lord Mahon's Hist.

—— —— Articles of Confederation, and Constitution of the U. S. Cincin., 1863. 8vo. Congr. and Polit. Pamph. Vol. 70.

—— England against the Holy Alliance; with Official Documents. Lond., 1821. 8vo. Pamphleteer. Vol. 18.

—— The Causes which Induce and Justify the Secession of S. Carolina from the Federal Union, and the Ordinance of Secession. Charleston, 1860. 8vo. Rebell. Pamph. Vol. 63.

—— Lords and Commons assembled at Westminster; presented to the Prince and Princess of Orange, Feb. 13, 1688–9. Lond., 1689. Fol. Eng. Polit. Pamph. Vol. 1.

—— Nobility and Gentry that Adhered to the Late King, in and about London. 1680 (?) Sm. 4to. Eng. Misc. Pamph. Vol. 1.

—— Rebels in the West of Scotland. 1678. Fol. Eng. Polit. Pamph. Vol. 1.

—— State of the Colonie and Affaires in Virginia, with the Names of Adventurers. 1620. Force's Hist. Tracts. Vol. 3.

DECLARATIONS of the King of Sweden, the Emperor of Russia, the King of Prussia and the King of England, in regard to the Conduct of the Common Enemy. Lond., 1803. 8vo. Eng. Polit. Pamph. Vol. 76.

DECLARATORY Considerations upon the Present State of the Affairs of England. Lond., 1679. Sm. 4to. Eng. Polit. Pamph. Vol. 6.

DE CONSTANT, M. Benj. On the Responsibility of Ministers. Lond., 1815. 8vo. Pamphleteer. Vol. 5.

—— On the Liberty of the Press. Lond., 1815. 8vo. Pamphleteer. Vol. 6.

DE COSTA, B. F. Notes on the Hist. of Fort George during the Colonial and Revolutionary Periods. N. Y., 1871. 8vo. N. Y. Hist. Discourses, etc. Vol. 4.

—— Sailing Directions of Henry Hudson, for his Use in 1608. Albany, 1869. 8vo.

—— Pre-Columbian Discovery of America. Albany, 1868. 8vo.

—— The Moabitish Stone. N. Y., 1871. 8vo.

—— The Northmen in Maine. Albany, 1870. 8vo.

DE COURCELLE' & DE TRACY'S Expedition against the Mohawk Indians. Papers relating to. 1665–6. Doc. Hist. of N. Y. Vol. 1.

DE COURCY, Henry. The Catholic Church in the U. States: pages of its History translated and enlarged, by John Gilmary Shea. 2d Ed. revised. N. Y., 1857. 12mo.

DE Couto, Jose Ferrer. Cuba may become Independent. A Political Pamphlet on Current Events. N. Y., 1872. 8vo. Congr. & Polit. Pamph. Vol. 130.

DE CUSTINE, Marquis. Russia, translated from the French. N. Y., 1854. 12mo.
DEDHAM, Mass. Ann. Report of the School Comm., for 1854–5. 1855. 8vo.
—— See HAVEN, S. F. Histor. Address, 1836.
—— LAMSON, Rev. A. Bi-Centen. Addresses.
—— MANN, H. Hist. Annals of.
—— Pulpit: Sermons of Pastors in 17th & 18th Century, with Centen. Disc. Boston, 1840. 8vo.
—— See WORTHINGTON, E. Hist. of.
DEERFIELD, Mass. See WILLARD, Sam'l. Hist. Disc., 1857.
—— WILLIAMS, S. W. Sacking of, in 1703–4.
—— Captive. See WILLIAMS, S. W.
DEERING, Rich'd. Louisville: her Commercial, Manufacturing & Social Advantages. Louisville, 1859. 8vo.
DEETH, S. G. Catalogue of his Library. N. Y. n. d. 8vo.
DEFECTION (The) farther Considered, wherein the Resigners, ——, are really Deserters. Lond., 1718. 8vo. Eng. Polit. Pamph. Vol. 67.
DEFENSE of the Christian Doctrines of the Soc. of Friends; a Reply to the Followers of Elias Hicks. Phila., 1825. 8vo.
—— Constitution: or an Answer to an Argument in the Case of Dudly Moor. Dublin, 1714. Sm. 4to. Eng. Polit. Pamph. Vol. 8.
—— Legislature of Mass: or the Rights of N. England Vindicated. Boston, 1808. 8vo. Congress. & Polit. Pamph. Vol. 97.
—— Minority in the House of Commons, on the Question of General Warrants. Lond., 1764. 8vo. Eng. Polit. Pamph. Vol. 72.
—— Rockingham Party, in their Late Coalition with Lord North. Lond., 1783. 12mo. Eng. Polit. Pamph. Vol. 20.
—— Great Lakes: its Necessity and the quickest and best way to accomplish it. 1862. Rebell'n Pamph. Vol. 98.
DEFINITE TREATY (The) of Aix la Chapelle, Dec. 18, 1748. Lond., 1749. Sm. 4to. Eng. Polit. Pamph. Vol. 10.
DEFOE, Daniel. Hist. of the Great Plague in London in 1665. Lond., 1840. 18mo.
DE FONTAINE, A. Book of Prudential Relations: or the Golden Bible of Nature and Reason. Boston, 1845. 8vo.
DE FONTAINE, F. G. Amer. Abolitionism from 1787 to 1861. Rebell'n Pamph. Vol 74.
DE FORD, Samuel T. Address before Brutus Fire Soc. in Newburyport, Jan. 6, 1831. Addresses. Vol. 12.
DE FOREST, Henry A. Notes of a Tour in Mt. Lebanon & to Lake Huleh. Amer. Oriental Soc. Journ. Vol. 2.
DE FOREST, John W. Hist. of the Indians of Connecticut to 1850. Hartford. 8vo. 1853.
DEFREES, John D. Speech in Cong. Aug. 1, 1864, on the Rebellion. Rebell'n Pamph. Vols. 9, 107.
DEGASPARIN, Count Agenor. Reconstruction; a Letter to Prest. Johnson, 1865. Rebellion Pamplets. Vol. 18.

DEGASPARIN, Count Agenor. Reply to the Loyal and National League of N. Y. 1864. French. Rebell'n Pamph. Vols. 14, 15.

—— The Uprising of a Great People: the United States in 1861. 12mo. Rebellion Pamph. Vol. 109.

—— Une Parole de Paix. Paris, 1862. 12mo. Rebell'n Pamph. Vol. 109.

DEGENER, Edward. Speech in Cong., Jan. 21, 1871, on Indian Affairs. 8mo. Congr. & Polit. Pamph. Vol. 119.

DE GERAMB, Baron. Letter to Earl Moira, on the Spaniards & Cadiz. Lond., 1810. 4mo. Eng. Polit. Pamph. Vol. 53*A*

DEGRAND, P. P. F. Address on the Advantages of Low Fares, & Low Rates, of Freight. Boston, 1840. 8vo. Pamphlets Vol. 13.

DE HASS, Wills. Hist. of the Early Settlement and Indian Wars of W. Virginia. Wheeling, 1859. 8vo.

DE JOINVILLE, Prince. The Army of the Potomac; its Organization, its Commander and its Campaign. N. Y., 1862. 8vo. Rebelln. Pamph. Vol. 12.

—— The same in French. ——

DE KALB, Baron. See Smith J. Spear.

DE KOLLI, Baron. Memoirs du Baron de Kolli; et de la Reine d'Etrurie. Paris, 1823. 8vo. Strangford Pamh. Vol. 3.

DE LA BECHE, H. T. Application of Geology to the ordinary Purposes of Life. N. Y. 1836. 8vo. Scientific Pamph. Vol. 11.

DE LA CUESTA, F. F. A. See Shea's Library of Linguistics.

DE LAET, Jean. L'Histoire du Nouveau Monde; ou Description des Indes Occidentales. Leyden. 1640. folio.

—— Extracts from the New World, or a Description of the West Indies. N. Y. Hist. Soc. Coll. New Ser. Vol. 1.

DELAFIELD, J. Jr. Brief Topograph. Description of Washington Co., Ohio. N. Y. 1834. 8vo.

DELAFIELD, John. Gen. View & Agricult. Survey of Seneca Co., N. Y. N. Y. Agr. Soc. Trans. 1850.

DELAFIELD, John J. Inquiry into the Origin of the Antiquities of America. New York. 1839. 4to.

DELAFIELD, Maj. Rich'd. Report on the Art of War in Europe in 1854, 55 & 56. Washington. 1860. 4to.

DELAMBRE, M. See Fourier, Joseph. Memoir of,

DE LA MOTTE, Francis H. Acc. of his Trial for High Treason, July 14, 1781. Lond., 12mo. Eng. Polit. Pamph Vol. 19.

DE LANCEY, Edw. F. Memoir of Jas. De Lancey, Lieut. Gov. of N. Y. Doc. Hist. of N. Y. Vol. 4.

DE LANCEY, Jas. See DE LANCEY, E. F. Memoir of.

DE LANCEY, Wm. H.. D. D. Sermon at the Centen. Celebra. of the Opening of St. Peter's Ch., Phila., Sept. 4, 1861. Phila., 1862. 8vo. Penn. Hist. Discourses. Vol. 1.

DELAPLAINE, Joseph. Repository of the Lives and Portraits of Distinguished American Characters. Phila., 1815. 4to. 1 vol.

—— Same. Phila., 1816–18. 3 vols. 4to.

DELAPLAINE, Joseph. The Author turned Critic, etc. A Reply to an Attack on Delaplaine's Repository. Phila., 1816. 8vo. Pamphlet.

DE LA RIVE, Prof. A. Michael Faraday—his Life and Works. Smithsonian Report, 1867.

DE LARRAY, M. History of England and Scotland in Dutch. Amsterdam, 1728. 4 Vols. folio.

DE LATUDE, Henri M. Life of; with some Acc. of the Bastile. Lond., 1814. 8vo. Pamphleteer. Vol. 3.

DELAWARE. See Cat. of Papers relating to, in State Paper Office.

—— FERRIS, B. Hist. of Early Settlements

——GRAHAM, J. D., on Mason & Dixon's Line.

—— HISTORICAL SOCIETY. Catalogue of, with its History, Constitution and By-Laws. Wilmington, 1871. 8vo. See SNOWDEN, J. R.

—— Laws passed by the Gen. Assembly, in 1859, 1863, 1866, 1867, 1869. 8vo.

—— Local Hist. See WILMINGTON. 8vo.

—— Message of Wm. Benton, Governor, to Legis., Jan. 6, 1863. n. d. Rebell'n Pamph. Vol. 65.

—— See VINCENT, Francis. Hist. of. Nos. 1–4.

DELAWARE Co., Penn. See SMITH, G. Hist. of.

DELAWARE Ohio Female Seminary. 1st Ann. Catalogue for 1850–1. Columbus, 1851. 8vo.

—— Indians. See Enquiry into Alienation from G. Britain, 1759.

—— River. See COLLIN, Rev. N. Observa. on the Climate adjoining.

DE LEON, E. La Verite sur les Etats Confederes a'Amerique. Paris, 1862. 8vo. Rebell'n Pamph. Vol. 20.

DELESSE, M. Memoire sur la Constitution Mineralogique et chimi que des Roches des Vosges. Grauwake. Paris, 1853. 8vo.

DELEUZE, M. Histoire et Description du Museum d'Histoire Naturelle. Paris, 1823. 8vo. Misc. Tracts. Vol. 4.

DELAVAN, E. C. Letter to the Bishops of the Episcopal Church, on the Adulteration of Liquors, etc. Albany, 1859. 8vo. Temp. Pamph. Vol. 3.

—— Speech at a Meeting of Friends of Mr. Fillmore, at Ballston, Aug. 9, 1856. Congr. and Polit. Pamph. Vol. 139.

—— Temperance of Wine Countries. Letter to Rev. Dr. Nott. N. Y., 1860. 8vo. Temp. Pamph. Vol. 3.

—— See TAYLOR, John, vs. Delavan. 1840.

DELAVAN, Wis. Messenger, Newspaper, Aug., 1856, to June, 1857. Folio.

—— Republican, 1868–72. 1 Vol.

DELGADO, Antonio. Memoria Historico—Critica Sabre el Gran Disco de Theodosio Encontrado en Almen draleso. Madrid, 1849. 4to.

DELIBERATE Thoughts on the System of our Late Treaties with Hesse-Cassell and Russia, in Russia, in regard to Hanover. Lond., 1756. 8vo. Eng. Polit. Pamph. Vol. 70.

DELICIAE Brittanicae. See BICKHAM, Geo.

DE L'ISLE. Barony & Viscountcy of. Lond. n. d. 8vo. Strangford Pamph. Vol. 53.

DELLA Correlazione delle Forze Chimiche colla Rifrangibilita delle Irradiazioni. Amer. Philos. Soc. Trans. N. S. Vol. 11.

DELMAR, A. Gold Money and Paper Money, 1863. Rebell'n Pamph. Vol. 93.

—— The Great Paper Bubble; or the Coming Financial Explosion. 1864. Rebell'n Pamph. Vols. 47, 87.

DE LOMENIE, Louis. Beaumarchais and his Times; Sketches of French Society in the 18th Century. N. Y., 1857. 12mo.

DELORME, E. N. Les Etats—Unis et L'Europe. Paris, 1863. 8vo. Rebell'n Pamph. Vol. 20.

DELPLA, A. French Drama; a Discussion on the Best Means of Improving the Theatre. Lond., 1818. 8vo. Pamphleteer. Vol. 12.

DE LUC, J. A. Introduction a la Physique Terrestre par les Fluides Expansibles. Chemistry. Paris, 1803. 2 Vols. 8vo.

DELUSIONS. Demonology, &c. See WITCHCRAFT.

DE MEYER, Leopold. Biography of. Lond., 1845. 8vo. Biograph. Pamph. Vol. 2.

DEMILT Dispensary. See N. Y. City.

DEMING, H. C. Speech in Cong., Jan. 19, 1866, on the State of the Union. Congr. & Polit. Pamph. Vol. 121.

—— See Wooster Monument.

DEMING, Leonard. Catalogue of Officers of Vermont, 1778–1851. Middlebury, 1851. 8vo.

—— Collection of Useful, Interesting & Remarkable Events. Middlebury, Vt. n. d. 12mo.

DEMOCRACY. See BURNAP, G. W. Origin and Causes of.

—— BUTLER, B. F. Address on Representative Democracy.

—— CAMP, G. S. Democracy.

—— CHASE, S. P. Letters on Ohio Politics.

—— Dem. Nat. Convent., 1852.

—— Dem. Text Book.

—— FESSENDEN, T. G. Democracy Unveiled.

—— GODWIN, P. Democracy, Constructive and Pacific.

—— Hist. of—in the U. S.

—— In America. See DE TOCQUEVILLE, A.

—— in U. States. See GILLETT, R. H.

DEMOCRAT'S Reasons (A) why HORACE GREELEY will be the next President. N. Y., 1872. 12mo. Congr. and Polit. Pamph. Vol. 130.

DEMOCRATIC and Republican Platforms, n. d. 8vo. Rebell'n Pamph. Vol. 39.

—— Catechism of Negro Equality, 1863. Rebell'n Pamph. Vol. 75.

—— Nat. Convention, 1852. Proceedings at Baltimore June, 1852. Congr. and Polit. Pamph. Vols. 41, 75.

—— —— Proceedings at Cincinnati, 1856. Congr. and Polit. Pamph. Vol. 69.

—— —— Official Proceedings at Charleston and Baltimore, 1860. Cleveland, 1860. Rebell'n Pamph. Vols. 45 and 77.

—— Opinions on Slavery, 1776–1863, n. d. Rebell'n Pamph. Vol. 46.

DEMOCRATIC Party—its Record from 1860 to 1865. Congr. and Polit. Pamph. Vol. 75.
—— Peace offered for Acceptance of Penn. Voters. Phil., 1864. 8vo. Rebell'n Pamph. Vol. 11.
—— Review. See U. S. Mag. and Dem. Review.
—— Songster. N. Y., 1864. 12mo. Rebell'n. Pamph. Vol. 48.
—— Text-Book: containing the Lives of PIERCE and KING. Phila. n. d. 8vo. Congr. and Polit. Pamph. Vols. 76 and 100.
DEMONOLOGY. See SCOTT, Sir W.
—— Witchcraft.
DE MONTALEMBERT, M. Debate on India, in the Eng. Parl't. Lond. 1858. 8vo. Eng. Polit. Pamph. Vol. 55.
—— See MOORE, G. H. On his late Review of the Gov't of Eng. 1859.
DE MONTENEY, Barclay. The Case of a Dêtenu. Lond., 1838. 8vo. Stangford Pamph. Vol. 16.
DEMPSEY & O'Toole. Mem. to Cong. in regard to Contract with the P. Office Department. 1870. With Appendix, 1871. 8vo. Congr. and Polit. Pamph., Vol. 131.
DEMPSTER, John W. General Table of Greek Verbs. Lond., 1843. 12mo. Educa. Pamph., Vol. 28, 30.
D'ENGHIEN, Duc.—See ROVIGO, Duc de. Extrait des Memoires, &c.
DENNISON, Rev. C. W. Winfield: How he came to be a Major General. Phila., 1865. 12mo.
DENISON, Maj. Gen. Dan'l.—See SLADE, D. D. Memoir of.
DENISON, Edmund B. Short Letter on the Bishop of Exeter's Speech on the Marriage Bill. Lond., 1851. 8vo. Strangford Pamph., Vol. 57.
—— The Validity of Marriages with a Wife's Sister, celebrated abroad. Lond., 1852. 8vo. Strangford Pamph., Vol. 62.
DENNISON, Geo. Fred. Notes of the Baptists, and their Principles in Norwich, Conn., from the Settlement of the Town to 1850. Norwich, 1858. 12mo.
DENISON University, Granville, O. Catalogue for 1856–7, 1857–8, 1858–9. Columbus and Newark. 8vo.
DENMAN, Capt. The Slave Trade, the African Squadron, and Mr. Hutt's Committee. Lond., n. d. 8vo. Strangford Pamph., Vol. 53.
DENMAN, Lord. Letter to Lord Brougham on the Slave Trade. London, 1848. 8vo. Strangford Pamph., Vol. 49.
—— Reasons for Legalizing Marriage with a Deceased Wife's Sister. Lond., 1852. 8vo. Strangford Pamph., Vol. 62.
DENMARK and England. 1848.—See DISRAELI, M. Speech in Parl't. 1848.
—— And its Relations.—See LEAVITT, Joshua.
—— Crichton, A. History of.
—— The Crown of Denmark disposed of through a Fraudulent Treaty, &c. Lond., 1853. 8vo. Strangford Pamph., Vol. 64.
—— See CUSHING, C. Claims of U. S. considered.
—— MEURSIUS, J. Historica Danica.

DENMARK. See PARTON, Jas. Danish Islands.
—— SINDING, P. C., Hist. of Scandinavia.
—— St. Thomas Treaty.
DENNIS, Jeffery. Address, with a Plan for the Relief of Distressed Seamen. Lond., 1818. 8vo. Eng. Misc. Pamph., Vol. 3.
DENNIS, Mass. Description of. Mass. Hist. Soc. Coll. 1st Ser., Vol. 8.
DENNY, Wm. H. Military Journ. of Maj. Ebenezer Denny, an officer in the Rev. and Indian Wars, with an Introduct. Memoir. Memoirs of Penn. Hist. Soc., Vol. 7.
DENONVILLE, M. de. Papers relating to his Expedition to the Genesee Country and Niagara. 1687. Doc. Hist. of N. Y. Vol 1.
—— Expedition against the Senecas. See MARSHALL, O. H.
DENSLOW, V. B. Fremont and McClellan. Their Polit. and Mil. Career reviewed. N. Y., 1862. 8vo. Rebelln. Pamph. Vol. 13.
DENSON, A. C. Westmoreland: or Secession Ferocity at the Breaking out of the Rebellion. St. Louis, 1865. 8vo.
DENT, Edw. J. On the Construction and Management of Chronometers, etc. Lond., 1850. 8vo. Scientific Pamph. Vol. 40.
DENTAL Register. Vols. 1–26 inclusive. Some Nos. missing. Cincin., 1847–72. 8vo.
DENTISTRY. See Ohio College of Dental Surgery, Cincinnati.
DENTON, Danl. Brief Description of N. York, formerly called New Netherlands. Lond., 1670. New Ed., with Introduction by G. Furman. N. Y., 1845. 8vo.
DENTON, Rev. W. The Christians in Turkey. Lond., 1863. 8vo. Eng. Polit. Pamph. Vol. 60.
DENVER City Colorado. Ann. Reports of the Board of Trade, for 1871, '72. Denver, 1872, '73. 8vo.
DE PEYSTER, Fred. Address before the N. Y. Hist. Soc., Nov. 21, 1865, on the Influence of Libraries. N. Y., 1866. 8vo. N. Y. Hist. Soc. Addresses. Vol. 4.
DE PEYSTER, Gen. J. Watts. Address at Madalin, N. Y., Nov. 28, 1866, on the Inaugura. of a Soldier's Monument. N. Y., 1867. 8vo. Rebell'n Pamph. Vol. 13.
—— Address to the Officers of the N. Y. State Troops, Jan. 19, 1858. Addresses. Vol. 32.
—— The Ancient Mediæval and Modern Netherlanders; Dutch and Flemings. Poughkeepsic, N. Y., 1859. 8vo. Hist. Pamph. Vol. 3.
—— Concurrent Resolution of N. Y. Legislature conferring on him the Commission of Brevet Maj.-Gen., of N. Y. Nat. Guard. Rebell'n Pamph. Vol. 22.
—— Decisive Conflicts of the Late Civil War. Parts 1, 3. N. Y., 1867. Rebell'n Pamph. Vol. 13.
—— Eulogy of Lennart Torstenson of the Swedish Artillery. N. Y. 1872. 4to. Pamph. Military Science.
—— See GUIZOT'S Meditations.
—— Hist. of Carausius, the Dutch Augustus and Emperor of Britain. Poughkeepsie, 1858. 8vo.

DE PEYSTER, Gen. J. Watts. The Eclaireur. A Periodical devoted to Military Science. 1853–4, 1854–5. 1860. Tivoli and Hyde Park. 3 Vols. 4to.

—— La Royale. Parts I–V1. The Grand Hunt of the Army of the Potomac, from Petersburg to High Bridge, under Gen. Humphries. N. Y., 1872. 4to. Rebellion Pamph. Vol. 110.

—— La Royale. Part VIII. The Last Twenty-four Hours of the Army of No. Virginia. N. Y., 1872. 4to. Rebell'n Pamph. Vol. 110.

—— Memorials of a Birthday Breakfast to Capt. F. H. Lahrbush, on his 100th Birthday. Rebell'n Pamph. Vol. 22.

—— Personal and Military History of Maj. Gen. Philip Kearny. N. Y., 1869. 8vo.

—— Practical Strategy as illustrated by Achievements of Marshal Traun. Catskill. 1863. 8vo. Pamph. Mil. Science.

—— Secession in Switzerland and in the U. States compared. Address before Vt. Hist. Soc., 1863. Vt. Hist. Soc. Addresses. Vol. 2. Another Copy, Rebllion Pamph. Vol. 3.

—— Suggestions on Winter Campaigns. Rebell'n. Pamph. Vol. 24.

—— The Dutch Battle of the Baltic, 1658. between the Hollanders and the Swedes. Poughkeepsie, 1858. 8vo. Hist. Pamph. Vol. 19.

DE RASIERES, Isaack. New Netherland in 1627. Letter to Sam'l. Blommaert. Translated by J. R Brodhead. N. Y., Hist. Soc. Coll. 2d Ser. Vol. 2.

DEPRADT, M. Abbe. Comparison between the Powers of England and Russia. Lond., 1824. 8vo. Pamphleteer. Vol. 24.

—— Vrai Systeme de l'Europe relativement a l'Amerique et a la Grece. Lond., 1825. 8vo. Pamphleteer. Vol. 25.

—— Les Six dernier mois de l'Amerique et du Brèsil. Avec pièces relatives a Saint Dominque et a l'Amerique. Paris, 1818. 12mo.

DEPUY, Henry W. Louis Napoleon and the Bonaparte Family. N. Y., 1856. 12mo.

—— Mishaps of an Indian Agent. Albany, 1863. 8vo. Indian Pamphlets. Vol. 5.

DEQUINCY, Quatremière. Historie de la viè et des Ouvrages de Rapahël. Troisieme Edition. Paris, 1835. 8vo.

DERBYSHIRE, Eng. See BATEMAN, Thos. Antiquities of. 1848.

—— See GLOVER, Stephen. Hist. and Gazetteer. 1831.

DERBY, Lieut. Report on a Reconnoissance of the Gulf of California and the Colorado River, in 1850–1. Sec. of War Misc. Reports.

DERBY, E. H. Abstract of Argument against Fitchburg, Mass., R. R. Bill, etc. n. d. 8vo. Law Pamph. Vol. 9.

—— Argument before a Joint Special Comm. of the Legis. of Mass., in behalf of the Troy and Greenfield R. R. Co. Boston, 1856. 8vo. Mass. R. R. Reports, etc. Vol. 2.

—— Agrèement in behalf of the Old Colony R. R. Co., before the Mass. Legisla. Comm., Apr. 7, 1848. Boston, 1848. 8vo. Mass. R. R. Reports, etc. Vol. 3.

DERBY, E. H. Argument in favor of a State Loan to the Vermont and Mass. R. R. Co., before Mass. Legisla. Comm. Boston, 1855. 8vo. Mass. R. R. Reports, etc. Vol. 3.

—— Review of the Speech of Thos. G. Cary, against a Loan for the Hoosac Tunnel, May, 1853. Boston, 1853. 8vo. Mass. R. R. Reports, etc. Vol. 2.

—— Two Month's Abroad: or, a Trip to England, France, Baden, Prussia, and Belgium in 1843. Boston, 1844. 8vo. Hist. Pamph. Vol. 3.

DERBY, John Barton. Polit. Reminiscences, including a Sketch of the Origin and Hist. of the "Statesman Party" of Boston. Boston, 1835. 8vo. Congr. and Poilt. Pamph. Vol. 134.

DERBY, Perly. The Hutchinson Family; Descendants of Barnard Hutchinson, of Carolam, Eng. Salem, 1870. 8vo.

DE REIMER, J. Description of City of Hague—in Dutch. Amsterdam, 1728. 4 vols. Fol.

DERENZY, Geo. W. Enchiridion: or a Hand for the One-Handed. Lond., 1823. 8vo. Pamphleteer. Vol. 22.

D'ERES, Chas. Dennis Ruscoe. Memoirs; with Acc. of his Eleven Years' Captivity by the Indians. Exeter, 1800. 12mo.

DE RHAM, Wm. Moore. See MCVICKAR, Rev. John. Address on his death. 1834.

DE RIVERO, M. E. Antiquedades Peruanas. Lima. 1841. 8vo. Archaeolog. Pamphlets. Vol. 1.

DERMER, Thos. Letter describing his Passage from Maine to Virginia, in 1619. N. Y. Hist. Soc. Coll. N. Ser. Vol. 1.

DE ROGNIAT, Baron. See SWETT, S. Abstract of his Considerations on the Art of War.

DERRIES, S. Hist. Chronicle, in Dutch. Leyden, 1702. 3 vols. Folio.

DERRY, N. H., See LONDONDERRY, N. H. Celebra.

DESAINS, E. Sur l'absorption de l'eau par les sels-secs. Thèse de Chimie. Paris, 1842. 4to.

DESCANT, A., on the Penny Postage. Lond., 1841. 8vo. 2d Ed. Eng. Polit. Pamph. Vol. 44.

DESCRIPTION of Battles and Sieges of Marlborough, Eugene and Prince of Savoy, in Dutch, illustrated by Maps and Engravings. Hague, 1739. 2 vols. Large folio.

—— of Pitcairn's Island and its Inhabitants; with Acc. of Mutiny of the Bounty. Harpers' Fam. Lib. N. Y., 1861. 18mo.

—— of the Country between Albany and Niagara in 1792. Doc. Hist. of N. Y. Vol. 2.

—— of Grand Fete given at N. Y., by Citizens of France, to Gen. La Fayette. N. Y., 1824. 8vo. N. Y. City Pamph. Vol. 3.

—— De la Colonne de la Place Vendôme. 1810 (?) 12mo. Guide Books. Vol. 12.

—— of a View of the City of Mexico and Surrounding Country, now Exhibiting in the Panorama, Lond., 1825. Lond. 8vo. Hist. Pamph. Vol. 15.

—— of Hagley, Envil and the Leasowes, Eng. Birmingham, n. d. 12mo. Guide-Books. Vol. 7.

DESCRIPTION of the Petroleum Region of California; with a Report on the Same by Prof. B. Silliman, Jr. N. Y., 1865. 8vo. Scientific Pamph. Vol. 16.
—— of the Largest Ship in the World, the Great Republic, of Boston; with Illustrated Designs of her Construction. Boston, 1853. 8vo. Scientific Pamph. Vol. 30.
—— of the New Palace of Westminster. Lond., 1848. 8vo. Guide-Books. Vol. 9.
DESCRIPTIVE Catalogue of Flags, Trophies and Relics belonging to N. Y. Bureau of Military Statistics. Albany, 1864. 8vo. Rebell'n Pamph. Vol. 16.
DE SEGUR, Gen. Count. Hist. of the Expedition to Russia undertaken by the Emperor Napoleon in the Year 1812. Harpers' Fam. Lib. N. Y., 1858. 2 vols. 18mo.
DESERET, State of. Constitution of the State of Deseret and Memorial to Cong., 1872. Salt Lake City, 1872. 8vo.
DESERTION (The) Discussed, in a Letter to a Country Gentleman. Lond., 1868. Sm. 4to. Eng. Polit. Pamph. Vol. 65.
DESLANDES, M. Essay on Maritime Power and Commerce. Lond., 1743. 8vo. Eng. Misc. Pamph. Vol. 23.
DESMET, P. J. Letter and Sketches of a Year's Residence among the Indian Tribes of the Rocky Mountain. Phila., 1843. 12mo.
—— Oregon Missions and Travels over the Rocky Mountains in 1845–46. N. Y., 1847. 12mo.
DES MOINES Bulletin, Newspaper. Legislative Supplement. Des Moines, Iowa, 1870. Folio.
—— River Land Grant. Farmers' Statement in Cong. in Reference to. (n. d.) 8vo. Congr. and Polit. Pamph. Vol. 131.
DESOR, E. Lacustrian Constructions of the Lake of Neuchatel. Smithsonian Report. 1865.
—— *vs.* Charles H. DAVIS. Trial for Breach of Contract, etc. Boston, 1852. 8vo. Law Pamph. Vol. 1.
DE SOTO, Ferdinand. See BIEDMA, L. H. Acc. of his Expedit. IRVING, T.
—— Letter to the Justice and Board of Magistrates in Santiago De Cuba, from Florida, 1539; also a Memoir of Hernando de Escalante Fontaneda, respecting Florida, 1575. Washington, 1854. 4to. Privately Printed.
—— See VEGA, G. de la.
—— WILMER, L. A. Life and Travels of.
DESPARD, Col. Edw. M. Acc. of his Trial for High Treason, in 1803. Lond. 8vo. Eng. Polit. Pamph. Vol. 27.
DESPOTISM in America. See HILDRETH, R.
DESPOTS as Revolutionists. To the German People. Berlin, 1859. 8vo. Eng. Polit. Pamph. Vol. 57.
DE STÆL, Madame. DE l'ALLEMAGNE Paris, 1820. 2 Vols. 8vo.
DESTRUCTION of the Gaspee. See STAPLES, W. R.
—— of Tea in Boston Harbor, Dec. 16, 1773. Three Letters. Mass. Hist. Soc. Coll. 4th Ser. Vol. 4.
DESULTORY Remarks on Extending Slavery into Missouri. Westchester, Penn., 1856. 8vo. Congress. and Polit. Pamph. Vol. 100.

De Tocqueville, Alexis. Democracy in America, with Notes by Francis Bowen. Boston, 1873. 2 Vols. 12mo.
—— The Old Regime and the Revolution. Translated by John Bonner. N. Y., 1856. 8vo.
Detroit & Milwaukee R. R. Co. See Howard, S and C.
—— Campbell, M. Life of Gen. Hull, etc.
—— Diary of the Siege of. Ellis, E. S. Life of Pontiac, etc.
—— Elmwood Cemetery. 5th Report of the Trustees, with Rules, etc. Detroit, 1868. 8vo. Ohio Hist. Discourses, etc. Vol. 1.
—— See Farmer, S. Pocket Map of.
—— 1st Congregational Ch. 25th Annivers. of Organization. Detroit, 1870. 8vo. Ohio Hist. Discourses, etc. Vol. 1.
—— See Foster, J. Hist. of Hull's Expedit. 1812.
—— Gazette, Newspaper. Apr., 1818, to July, 1828. Folio.
—— See Rameau, M. Notes, Historiques, etc. 1861.
—— Roberts, R. E. Sketches of. 1855.
—— Trowbridge, C. C. Detroit, Past and Present. 1864.
—— Walker, C. J. Sketch of Hist. of.
—— Whittlesey, Chas. Indian Affairs in 1706.
—— Woodmere Cemetery: Its Organization, Incorporation, etc., with an Address by Hon. C. J. Walker. Detroit, 1869. 8vo. Ohio Hist. Discourses, etc. Vol. 1.
De Tumultibus Americanis. 1776. See Amer. Tracts. 1776–1788.
De Vere, M. Schele. Americanisms: The English of the New World. N. Y., 1872. 12mo.
Devereux, J. E. Letter on the Trappist Question. Lond., 1840. 8vo. Strangford Pamph. Vol. 25.
Devil's Lake, Wis. See Eaton, J. H. Geology of the Region of. See Baraboo, Wis.
Devlin, J. Dacres. Helps to Hereford History, Civil and Legendary. Lond., 1848. 12mo.
Devoe, Capt. Jonathan. See Hildreth, S. P. Early Ohio Settlers.
De Voe, Col. Thos. F. Reminiscences of "Old Brooklyn." Read before the L. Island Hist. Soc., May 16, 1867. Hist. Mag. 2d Ser. Vol. 2.
De Vastey, Baron. Polit. Remarks on some French Works and Papers, Concerning Hayti. Lond., 1818. 8vo. Pamphleteer. Vol. 13.
De Vauban, M. Treatise on Fortifications, in French. Amsterdam, 1688. 8vo. Another Copy. Amsterdam, 1718. 8vo.
Devon, W. A. War Lyrics. N. Y., 1862. Rebell'n Pamph. Vol. 96.
Devonshire (Eng.) Celebrities. See Pridham, T. L.
Devonshire, Eng. See Chapple, W. Review of Survey of. 1785.
—— Lyson, D. and S. Hist. of. 1822.
—— Moore, Thos. Hist. of. 1829.
—— Polwhele, Rich'd. Hist. of. 1797.
—— Provincial Dialect. See Hogg, Nathan. Poems.
—— Tuckett, J. Devon. Pedigrees.

DE VRIES, David Peterson. Voyages from Holland to America, A. D., 1632 to 1644. Translated from the Dutch by H. C. Murphy. N. Y., 1853. 4to.
—— Extracts from same. N. Y. Hist. Soc. Coll. 2d Ser. Vol. 1.
DE VRYER, A. Hist. of the Duke of Marlborough, in Dutch. Amsterdam, 1738. 4 Vols. 4to.
DE WAILLY, Alfred. Hymnes de Callimaque Traduites en vers Francais avec le texte Grec in regard et des Notes, etc. Paris, 1842. 8vo.
DE WARVILLE, J. P. Brissot. New Travels in the U. States Performed in 1788. Translated from the French. Lond., 1792. 8vo.
DEWEES, Jacob. Address to the People of Penn. 1862. Rebell'n Pamph. Vol. 89.
—— Appeal to the Legisla. of Penn. on the War. 1862. Rebell'n Pamph. Vol. 74.
—— Appeal to the Legisla. of Penn. for a Nat. Convention. 1863. Rebell'n Pamph. Vol. 14.
—— To the Amer. Public. (State of the Country.) (n. d.) Rebell'n Pamph. Vol. 29.
DEWEES, Capt. Saml. See HANNA, John S.
DEWEES, W. B. Letters from an Early Settler in Texas. Louisville, 1854. 8vo.
DEWEY, Prof. Chester. Memoir of. From Holden's Mag., Jan., 1849. Biograph. Pamph. Vol. 11.
—— Sketch of the Geol. and Mineral. of the Western Part of Mass. 1824. Silliman's Journ. Vol. 8.
DEWEY, Rev. Orville. Lecture before N. Y. Merc. Libr. Assoc. 1852. Addresses. Vol. 11.
—— Memoir of. From Holden's Mag., Nov., 1848. Biograph. Pamph. Vol. 11.
DE WITT, F. Gen. Atlas of the World; no Title or Date. Folio.
DE WITT, John. See BARNWELL, R. G. Hist. of.
DE WITT, J. H. Zouave Light Infantry Tactics. Phila., 1861. Rebell'n Pamph. Vol. 104.
DE WITT, Rev. Wm. R. Memories of the Past; Sermon at Harrisburg, Pa., on his 70th Birthday. N. Y., 1862. 8vo. Penn. Hist. Discourses.
DE WOLF, Lyman E. The Grant Government a Cage of Unclean Birds. Chicago, 1872. 8vo. Congr. and Polit Pamph. Vol. 130.
DEXTER, Rev. Henry M. Disc. at Manchester, N. H., Dec. 22, 1847. Andover, 1848. 8vo. Sermons. Vol. 12.
—— Mourt's Relation; or Journal of the Plantation at Plymouth, Mass. Boston, 1865. 4to.
—— See CHURCH, Benj.
DEXTER, Thos. C. A. See HOLT, Judge J. Report on Care of.
D'HAUSSEZ, Baron. G. Britain in 1833. Waldie's Circulating Libr. Vol. 2.
DIAGRAM of the Ohio River at Cincinnati, and Reports, etc., in Relation to the Newport and Cincin. Bridge. Pittsburgh, 1871. 8vo. Congr. and Polit. Pamph. Vol. 138.

DIALECT of Leeds and its Neighborhood, with a Copious Glossary. Lond., 1862. 12mo.

DIALOGUE between a Gentleman of London and an Honest Alderman of the Country Party. Lond., 1747. 8vo. Eng. Polit. Pamph. Vol. 69.

—— between Sir R. L. Knight and T. O. D. (Dr. Oates.) Lond., 1689. Sm. 4to. Eng. Polit. Pamph. Vol. 9.

—— betwixt Philanthus and Timotheus—against the Vindicator of "Naked Truth." Lond., 1681. 4to. Eng. Polit. Pamph. Vol. 6.

—— in the Shades, between Mercury, a Nobleman, and a Mechanic. Lond., 1794. 8vo. Eng. Misc. Pamph. Vol. 26.

—— in the Manner of Plato, on the Pleasures of the Understanding. Lond., 1734. 8vo.

"—— of the Dead"; between Minos and Pluto. Also, "An Additional Dialogue of the Dead," between Pericles and Aristides. Lond., 1760. 8vo. Eng. Misc. Pamph. Vol. 2.

"DIALOGUES of the Dead." See Amer. Dialogues, etc.

—— on the Uses of Foreign Travel, considered as a Part of Education. Lond., 1764. 8vo. 2d Ed. Eng. Misc. Pamph. Vol. 22.

DIAMOND Cut Diamond; Observa. on N. Jeffreys' Review of the Conduct of the Prince of Wales. Lond., 1806. 8vo. Eng. Polit. Pamph. Vol. 28.

—— Rock (Capture of the). See BOSWELL, Capt.

DIARY of a Lady of Gettysburg, Penn., from June 15 to July 15, 1863. n. d. Rebell'n Pamph. Vol. 12.

—— of the Great Rebellion from Dec. 20, 1860, to Jan. 1, 1862. Washington, 1862. 12mo. Rebell'n Pamph. Vol. 104.

—— of the Siege of Detroit in the War with Pontiac; also a Narrative of the Principal Events of the Siege by Maj. Robt. Rogers; a Plan for Conducting Indian Affairs by Col. Bradstreet, and other Documents. Albany, 1860. 4to.

DIBBLE, Rev. Sheldon. Hist. and Gen. Views of the Sandwich Islands' Mission. N. Y., 1839. 12mo.

D'IBERVILLE, M. P. Le Moyne. Narr. of the Voyage made by Order of the King of France, in 1698, to take Possession of Louisiana. French's Hist. Coll. La. and Florida.

DIBS, Jeremiah. The Navigation Laws; Three Letters to Lord Russel. Lond., 1848. 8vo. Strangford Pamph. Vol. 49.

DICK, Thos., L. L. D. Celestial Scenery; or the Wonders of the Planetary System Displayed. Phila., 1856. 12mo.

—— Same. Harper's Fam. Libr. N. Y., 1858. 18mo.

—— Christian Philosopher; or the Connexion of Science and Philosophy with Religion. Phila., 1856. 12mo.

—— On the Improvement of Society by the Diffusion of Knowledge. Phila., 1856. 12mo.

—— Same. Harper's Fam. Libr. N. Y., 1855. 18mo.

—— On the Mental Illumination and Moral Improvement of Mankind. Phila., 1856. 12mo.

—— Practical Astronomer. Phila., 1856. 12mo.

—— Sidereal Heavens, and Other Subjects connected with Astronomy. Phila., 1856. 12mo.

DICK, Thos., L. L. D. Same. Harper's Fam. Libr. N. Y., 1860. 18mo.

—— The Solar System; with Moral and Religious Reflections. Phila. 1856. 12mo.

—— Works of; containing "Moral Improvement of Mankind," "Essay on Covetousness," "Celestial Scenery," "Sidereal Heavens," and "Practical Astronomer." Hartford, 1849. 8vo.

—— Works of. Four Volumes in One. Hartford, 1850. 8vo. Also, Phila., 1854. 10 Vols. 12mo.

DICKENS, Chas. American Notes for General Circulation. N. Y., 1842. 8vo.

—— See Change for the Amer. Notes; by an Amer. Lady.

DICKENSON, John. Letters from a Farmer in Penn. to the Inhabitants of the British Colonies. Boston, 1768. 8vo.

DICKERSON, Edw. N. The Navy of the U. States; an Exposure of its Condition and the Cause of its Failure. N. Y., 1864. 8vo. Rebell'n Pamph. Vol. 28.

DICKERSON, Mahlon. See REYNOLDS, J. N. Corres. with, 1837–8.

DICKESON, M. W. Amer. Numismatic Manual of the Currency or Money of the Aborigines, and Colonial State, and U. States Coins. 23 plates of fac-similes. 4to. Phila.

DICKINSON, Miss Anna E. See Addresses of, etc.

DICKINSON, D. S. Address to the Hermean Soc. of Geneva Coll., Aug. 2, 1848. Geneva, N. Y., 1848. 8vo. Addresses, Vol. 36.

—— Address before the Graduating Class of the Law Depart. of Hamilton Coll., July 21, 1858. Utica, 1858. 8vo. Hamilton Coll. Pamphs.

—— Speech at Breckinridge and Lane Mass Meeting, N. Y., July 18, 1860. Rebell'n Pamph. Vols. 39, 77.

—— Speech in U. S. Senate, Feb. 24, 1846, on the Oregon Question. Washington, 1846. 8vo. Speeches. Vol. 1.

—— The Union; Address before Literary Societies of Amherst Coll., July 10, 1861. Rebell'n Pamph. Vols. 35, 99.

DICKINSON Genealogy. See DICKINSON, J. T.

DICKINSON, J. T. Genealogy of the Lymans, Dickinsons and Partridges. Boston, 1865. 8vo. Genealog. Pamph. Vol. 2.

DICKINSON, Capt. T. Narr. of Operations at Cape Frio, on the Wreck of the Thetis. Waldie's Circulating Libr. Vol. 9.

DICKINSON, Wm. Glossary of Words and Phrases of Cumberland, Eng. Lond., 1859. 12mo.

DICKSON, D. Speech in Cong., Feb. 2, 1835, on Slavery in Dist. of Columbia. Congr. and Polit. Pamph. Vol. 85.

DICKSON, D. J. H. Observations on the Utility of Blood-letting and Purgatives in Fever. Edinburgh, 1816. 8vo. Med. Pamph. Vol. 19.

DICKSON, John. Speech in Cong., May 11, 1832, on the Case of Sam'l Houston. Congr. and Polit. Pamph. Vol. 88.

—— Speech in Cong., May 19, 1834, on the Removal of the Deposites. Washington, 1834. 8vo. Speeches. Vol. 4.

DICKSON, Dr. S. Henry. Oration at N. Haven, before the Phi Beta Kappa Soc., Aug. 17, 1842. N. Haven, 1842. 8vo. Yale Coll. Pamph.

DICKSON, Wm. Address at Cincin., O., 1863, on the War. Rebell'n Pamph. Vol. 6.

DICTIONARIES. See BOWEN, T. J. Grammar and Dict. of Yoruba Language.

—— Haydn's Dict. of Science, 1871.

—— PICKERING, John. Vocab. of Amer. Words and Phrases.

—— POOLE, W. F. Websterian Orthography.

—— WEBSTER, N. Amer. Dict. and Abridgements.

DICTIONARIUM Scoto-Cetticum; an Etymological Dictionary of the Gaelic Language, compiled and published by the Highland Soc. Edinburgh, 1828. 2 Vols. 4to.

DICTIONARY of American Books. See WEST, G. M.

—— of Americanisms. See BARTLETT, John R.

—— of Select and Popular Quotations; taken from the Latin, French, Greek, Spanish and Italian Languages. 6th Ed. Phila., 1858. 12mo.

Dictionnaire de l'Academie Françoise revu, Corrige et Augmente par l'Academie elle-même. Cinquieme Edition. Paris, 1814. 2 Vols. 4to.

—— Supplement to Same, 1825. 4to.

DIE Munition des Loyalisten. Phila., 1863. 8vo. Rebell'n Pamph. Vol. 11.

DIGBY, Lord. Speeches in the High Court of Parl't, and in the House of Commons, 1640, concerning Grievances, and the Trien. Parl't, 1641. Sm. 4to. Eng. Polit. Pamph. Vol. 6.

DIGEST of Decisions of Courts of Common Law and Admiralty. Vol. 1. 3d Ed. Boston, 1846. 8vo.

—— of the Commercial Regulations of the Different Nations with which the U. S. have Intercourse. Washington, 1824. 8vo.

DIKE Genealogy. See NOYES, Jacob.

DILLAWAY, C. K. Hist. of the Grammar School or Free School of 1645 in Roxbury, Mass. Roxbury, 1860. 12mo.

DILLE, Israel. Sketch of Ancient Earthworks. Smithsonian Report, 1866.

DILLINGHAM, W. H. Tribute to the Memory of Peter Collinson. Phila., 1852. 8vo. Addresses, etc. Vol. 13.

DILLON, John B. Hist. of Indiana from its Earliest Exploration by Europeans to the Close of the Terr. Gov't in 1816. Vol. 1. Indianapolis, 1843. 8vo.

—— Same. Another Edition. 1859. 8vo.

DILLON, John Jos. Two Memoirs upon the Catholic Question, occasioned by Recent Events. Lond., 1809. 4to. Eng. Polit. Pamph. Vol. 53A.

DILUCIDATOR (The); or Reflections upon Modern Transactions, by way of Letters from Amsterdam to London. Lond., 1689. Sm. 4to. Eng. Polit. Pamph. Vol. 65.

DIMAN, J. L. Oration at Providence, July 4, 1866. Providence, 1866. 8vo. Addresses. Vol. 35.

DIMSDALE, Thos. The Vigilantes of Montana; Capture, Trial and Execution of H. Plummer's Road Agents' Band. Virginia City, 1866. 12mo.

DIPLOMATIC (The) Correspondence of the U. States of America, from the Definite Treaty of 1783, to the Adoption of the Constitution, 1789. Washington, 1833. 7 Vols. 8vo.
—— Correspondence of the U. S. See U. S. Sec. of State.
—— Mystifications and Popular Credulity. [With reference to the War in the East.] Lond., 1854? 8vo. Strangford Pamph. Vol. 67.
—— System of U. S. See Congressional Speeches.
—— Year; being a Review of Mr. Seward's Foreign Corres. of 1862. Phila., 1863. 2d Ed. Rebell'n Pamph. Vols. 3, 17.
DIRECTORIES. See Albany Directory, 1813, '40, '45, '47, '50–55, '58, '60.
—— ALLEN, T. S. Mineral Point, 1859.
—— Baltimore, Md., 1858.
—— Boston, 1789, 1831–2, '32–3, '36–69.
—— Brooklyn, 1846–7, '49–50, '53–4, '58–9, '64–5.
—— Buffalo, 1838–71.
—— Cambridge, Mass., 1856.
—— CHANDLER—Business Direct. of Chicago, etc., 1867.
—— Chicago, 1856, 1858, 1859, '60.
—— Chillicothe, O., 1858.
—— Cincinnati, O. 1819, '49, '50, '51, '52, '53, '54, '55, '56, '57, '59, '60, '61.
—— Cleveland, O., 1837–8.
—— Concord, N. H., 1860–1.
—— Council Bluffs, 1866.
—— Davenport City, 1858–59.
—— Dubuque and Sioux City Guide and Directory, 1856 and 1868.
—— EDWARDS. Wisconsin and Western States, 1868.
—— Fond du Lac, 1857–8.
—— Galena, Ill., 1848–9.
—— Green Bay, Wis., 1872–3.
—— HALL, E. H. Northern Counties Ill.
—— Hartford, Ct., 1848, '49, '51, '58.
—— HAWES, G. W. Kentucky State Gaz. and Direct., 1859.
—— Illinois Business Directory, 1860.
—— Jersey City and Hoboken Directories, 1866–7, 1870–1.
—— KIMBALL and JAMES. Mississippi Valley, 1844.
—— London, Eng., 1760–1817, 1856–57.
—— LYFORD, W. G. Baltimore, Md., 1836.
—— Lynn, Mass., 1860.
—— Madison, Wis., 1855, '58, '66, '68, '70–1.
—— Milwaukee, Wis., 1847, '48–58, '60, '63.
—— Mineral Point, Wis., 1859.
—— MITCHELL, J. L, Tenn. Gaz. and Business Direc., 1860–1.
—— Mobile, Ala., 1844.
—— Moline, Ill., 1858–9.
—— MONTAGUE, W. L. Mo. and Ill., 1854.
—— N. Haven, Ct., 1845–6, 1848–9, 1854–5, 1867.
—— N. York, 1786, '91, 1826, '34–71. (Some Vacancies.)
—— Ohio State Business Direc., 1853.
—— Omaha, Neb., 1866.

DIRECTORIES. Oshkosh, Wis., 1857.
—— Peoria, Ill., 1844.
—— Phila., 1845, '49, '58, '61.
—— Providence, R. I., 1855.
—— Racine, Wis., 1858.
—— Richmond, Ind., 1857.
—— Richmond, Va., 1869.
—— Rock Co., Wis., 1858.
—— Rock Island, Ill., 1858–9.
—— St. Louis, 1857, '58, '59.
—— St. Paul, 1856–7, 1858–9, 1863, 1864, 1866, 1867.
—— Salem, Mass., 1837, '46, '51.
—— Taunton, Mass., 1859.
—— Toronto City, 1837.
—— WALLIHAN, S. S. Rocky Mountains, 1871.
—— Washington, D. C., 1834.
—— Watertown, N. Y., 1840.
—— Westchester, Penn., 1857.

DIRECTORY of the Monongahela and Youghiogheny Valleys. Pittsburg, 1860. 8vo.

DISBROW and SULLIVAN. Advertisement to Supply the City of N. Y. with Rock Water, etc. N. Y., 1832. 8vo. N. Y. City Misc. Pamph. Vol. 1.

DISCIPLINE (The), Harmony and Efficiency of the Navy. Washington, 1870. 8vo. Congress. Pamph. Vol. 114.

DISCOURSE on the Neutral Relations of G. Britain during the Present War. Lond., 1758. 4to. Eng. Polit. Pamph. Vol. 10.

—— on the Unreasonableness of a New Separation on Account of the Oaths, etc. Lond., 1689. Sm. 4to. Eng. Polit. Pamph. Vol. 9.

—— upon the Modern Affairs of Europe, in relation to the French Monarchy. Hague, 1680. Sm. 4to. Eng. Polit. Pamph. Vol. 6.

DISCOVERY of Newe Brittaine, began Aug. 27, 1650, from Fort Henry in Va. Lond., 1651. (MS. Copy.)

—— of the Popish Plot; Examinations of Dr. Titus Oates before the High Court of Parl't, etc. Lond., 1679. 8vo. Eng. Polit. Pamph. Vol. 6.

DISCUSSION of Resolutions providing for the Publica. of the Debates of Congress, etc. Washington, 1869. 8vo. Congr. and Polit. Pamph. Vol. 117.

DISPASSIONATE Inquiry into Reasons alleged by Mr. Madison for Declaring War. N.Y., 1812. 8vo. Congr. and Polit. Pamph. Vol. 96.

D'ISRAELI, Benj. Speech in Parl't Apr. 19, 1848, on the Danish Question. Lond., 1848. 8vo. Strangford Pamph. Vol. 46.

—— Speech in Parl't, Aug. 30, 1848, on the Labours of the Session. Lond. 8vo. n. d. Strangford Pamph. Vol. 55.

—— Speech in Parl't, June 30, 1851, on the Financial Policy of the Gov't. Lond., 1851. 8vo. Eng. Polit. Pamph. Vol. 48.

—— Vindica. of the Eng. Constitution in a Letter to a Noble Lord. Lond., 1835. 8vo. Strangford Pamph. Vol. 12.

D'ISRAELI, J. C. Curiosities of Literature and Literary Character. Illustrated, with Curiosities of Amer. Litera. by Rufus W. Griswold. N. Y., 1847. 8vo.

DISSENT and the Church of England. See JAMES, J. A..

—— Anti-Monarchical and Aggressive on the Established Church. Lond., 1836. 8vo. Eng. Rel. Pamph. Vol. 47.

DISSENTER (The) Exposed to Himself and the Ch., with a View to Conformity. Lond., 1834. 8vo. Eng. Rel. Pamph. Vol. 46.

DISSENTER'S (The) Apology; or their Principles and Conduct Justified. Lond., 1639. 8vo. Eng. Rel. Pamph. Vol. 15.

DISSENTERS. Appeal to the Prot. Dissenters to Unite with the Catholics for the Removal of their Disabilities. Lond., 1813. 8vo. Pamphleteer. Vol. 1.

—— See BINNEY, Rev. T. Duty of Dissent, 1831.

—— Case of the Prot. Dissenters, with reference to the Corporation and Test Acts, 1787. With Review of the Same, 1790. Lond. 8vo. Two Pamphlets. Eng. Polit. Pamph. Vol. 23.

—— Case of the Dissenters, in a Letter to the Lord Chancellor. Lond., 1834. 8vo. 5th Ed. Strangford Pamph. Vol. 21.

—— See CAWOOD, Rev. John. Church of Eng. and Dissent, 1831.

—— Claim of Right to a Capacity for Civil Offices. Lond., 1717. 12mo. Eng. Rel. Pamph. Vol. 11A.

—— Chapels Bill, 1844. See CLARKE, G. R. Observa. on.

—— —— Debate in House of Commons, June 6, 1844, on the 2d Reading of the Bill. Lond., 1844. 8vo. Strangford Pamph. Vol. 35.

—— —— Debate on, in House of Lords, May 3, 1844. Lond., 1844. 8vo. 2d Ed. Strangford Pamph. Vol. 37.

—— —— See EVANS, J. C. Letter on. 1844.

—— —— Letter to Sir Robert Peel from the Gen. Assembly of the Presb. Ch. in Ireland, on the Bill. Lond., 1844. 8vo. Strangford Pamph. Vol. 35.

—— See LEE, Saml. Dissent Unscriptural and Unjustifiable. 1834.

—— Letter to Members of Parl't, etc. 1834.

—— WHEWELL, Wm. Admission of, to Academ. Degrees. 1834.

—— WOODSWORTH, Rev. C. Admission of, to Univers. of Cambridge. 1834.

DISSERTATION on the State of the Nation, respecting its Agriculture. Lond., 1817. 8vo. Pamphleteer. Vol. 11.

DISTANCES from Places in the U. States. Washington, 1867. 4to.

DISTINGUISHED Men of Modern Times. Harper's Fam. Libr. N. Y., 1858. 2 Vols. 18mo.

DISTRICT of Columbia. 1st Report of the Women's Christian Association. Washington, D. C., 1871. 8vo.

—— See HOUGH, Dr. F. B. Census of. 1867.

—— Congress. Report on an Alleged Hostile Organization in the Dist. of Col. Washington, 1861. 8vo. Rebell'n Pamph. Vol. 39.

—— See MARTIN, J. Descrip. of.

—— Reform School. Report of Trustees. 1870. Washington, D. C., 1870. 8vo.

—— Slavery in. See Congress'l Speeches.

DISTURNELL, John. Great Lakes; or Inland Seas of America—a Guide for Tourists. N. Y., 1865. 12mo. Guide Books. Vol. 28.

—— Same. N. Y., 1868. 12mo.

—— Railway and Steamship Guide. N. Y., 1865. 12mo.

—— Same. N. Y., 1853. 12mo. Guide Books. Vol. 28.

—— Influence of Climate: Paper before the Amer. Geograph. and Statist. Soc., with Map. N. Y., 1866. 4to. Scientific Pamph. Vol. 38.

—— U. States Nat. Register and Calendar for 1851–2. N. Y. 12mo.

—— U. S. Registers or Blue Books for 1865, '66 and '68. N. Y. 8vo.

DITSON, G. L., M. D. The Caucasian Mountains and their Inhabitants. Albany Institute Trans. Vol. 6.

DIVING, on Hydraulic Principles. See HOUGH, H. G.

DIVORCE. From DeBow's Review, Sept., 1846. Law Pamph. Vol. 23.

—— Dissertatio de Divortio. Jena, 1737. 4to. Latin Pamph. Vol. 4.

DIX, John A. Speech in Cong., Feb. 18 and 19, 1846, on the Oregon Question. Washington, 1846. 8vo. Speeches. Vol. 1.

—— Speech in Cong., June 26, 1848, on Terr. Affairs. Congr. and Polit. Pamph. Vol. 86.

—— Speech in Cong., on Terr. Affairs. (n. d.) 8vo. Congr. and Polit. Pamph. Vol. 86.

—— Speech in Cong., June 19, 1846, on the Warehouse Bill. Washington, 1846. 8vo. Speeches. Vol. 1.

—— Speeches and Occasional Addresses. N. Y., 1864. 2 Vols. 8vo.

DIX, John Ross. Hand-Book for Lake Memphremagog. Boston, (n. d.) 12mo. Guide Books. Vol. 16.

—— Pulpit Portraits; or Pen-Pictures of Distinguished Amer. Divines. Boston, 1854. 12mo.

DIXON, B. Homer. Surnames. Boston, 1857. 8vo. Pr. Printed.

DIXON, Hepworth. John Howard and the Prison World of Europe. N. Y., 1856. 12mo.

DIXON, James. Speech in Cong., June 30, 1846, on the Tariff. Washington, 1846. 8vo. Speeches. Vol. 1.

DIXON, Nathan F. Speech in the Case of R. H. Ives vs. C. T. Hazard, et al. Providence, 1859. 8vo. R. I. Misc. Pamph. Vol. 1.

DIXON, W. H. New America. Illustrations from Photographs. (Mormon Country.) Phila., 1867. 12mo.

—— William Penn: An Historical Biography, from New Sources, with an Extra Chapter on the "Macaulay Charges." Phila., 1851. 12mo.

DOANE, G. W., D. D. 1st Ann. Address before the N. Jersey Hist. Soc., Jan. 15, 1846. Burlington, 1848. 8vo.

—— Baccalaureate Address at Burlington Coll., 1857. Burlington, Vt., 1857. 8vo. Addresses. Vol. 26.

—— See OGILBY, Rev. F. Obit. Sermon.

DOANE, Rev. Wm. C. Oration at Burlington, N. J., Feb. 22, 1862. Rebell'n Pamph. Vol. 82.
DOBELL, Sydney. Parliamentary Reform; a Letter to a Politician. Lond., 1865. 8vo. Eng. Polit. Pamph. Vol. 61.
DOBSON, Mr. Chronolog. Annals of the War. 1755–63. Oxford, 1763. 8vo.
DOBSON, Mrs. Life of Petrarch. Vol. 2. 5th Ed. Lond., 1803. 8vo.
DOCUMENTARY Hist. of N. York. See O'CALLAGHAN, E. B.
—— of the P. Episcopal Ch., Connecticut. N. Y., 1863. 2 Vols. 8vo.
—— of Vermont. 1790–1832. N. Y., 1870. 8vo.
DODD, Bethuel L., and BURNETT, J. R. Genealogies of the Male Descendants of Daniel Dod, of Branford, Conn., 1646–1864. Newark, N. J., 1864. 8vo.
DODD Genealogy. See DODD, B. L., and BURNETT, J. L.
DODD, Geo. Curiosities of Industry: Glass and its Manufacture. Lond., 1852. 8vo. Scientific Pamph. Vol. 35.
DODD, Geo. H. On Diseases of Cattle. N. Y., 1852. 12mo.
DODD, Rev. Stephen. East Haven (Conn.) Register, Containing a History of the Town from 1644 to 1800, with Names, Births, Marriages and Deaths of First Settlers, etc. N. Haven, 1824. 12mo.
—— Revolutionary Memorials. See CASE, Rev. W.
DODD, Rev. Wm., LL. D. Trial of, with Acc. of his Confinement and Execution. Edinburgh, 1777. 8vo. Bound with "Views of N. America."
DODGE, A. C. Speech in Cong., Feb. 7, 1846, on the Oregon Question. Congr. and Polit. Pamph. Vol. 86.
—— Speech in Cong., May 28, 1850, on the Compromise. Congr. and Polit. Pamph. Vol. 94.
DODGE Co. (Wis.) Board of Supervisors. Journals of Proceedings, 1863, '64, '65. Beaver Dam, 1864–66. 8vo. Wis. Misc. Pamph. Vol. 2.
—— Citizen, Newspaper. Beaver Dam, 1864–70. Folio.
DODGE and Washington Counties, Wis. See PERCIVAL, J. G. Report on the Iron of.
DODGE, Gen. Henry. See Debate in House or Repr., U. S., May 14, 1842.
—— Journ. of Expedition to Rocky Mountains in 1835. Washington, 1836. 8vo. Another Copy. See Congr. and Polit. Pamph. Vol. 50.
—— See WHEELOCK, T. B. Campaign of. 1834.
—— Report as Supt. of Indian Affairs, on the Condition of the Indian Tribes of Wis. 1840. Senate Doc. No. 1. 2d Sess. 26th Cong. Vol. 1. p. 330, et al.
—— See SMITH, J. Y. Seventeen Letters to.
DODGE, J. R. The Red Men of the Ohio Valley, an Aboriginal Hist., from 1650 to 1795. Springfield, Ohio, 1860. 12mo.
—— West Virginia: Its Farms and Forests, Mines and Oil Wells. Phila., 1865. 12mo.

DODGE, Robt. Memorial of Columbus, read to the Maryland Hist. Soc., Apr. 3, 1851. Baltimore, 1851. 8vo. Md. Hist. Soc. Addresses. Vol. 2.

DODGE, Thos. H. Practical Suggestions to Inventors, Patentees, Assignees, and others interested in Inventions. 1858. Scientific Pamph Vol. 15.

DODGE, Wm. C. Memorial to the Sec. of War, on Strengthening the Army and Crushing the Rebellion. Washington, 1864. 8vo. Rebell'n Pamph. Vol. 9.

DODGE, Wm. S. Oration at Sitka, Alaska, July 4, 1868. San Francisco, 1868. 8vo. Addresses. Vol. 15.

DODGEVILLE, Wis. Chronicle, Newspaper. Dodgeville, 1863–70. Folio.

DODSLEY, J. See Annual Register; Historical Register.

DOES War Help Christianity? Reprinted from the "Herald of Peace." Lond., (n. d.) 8vo. Religous Pamph. Vol. 16.

DOLBY, Wm. Hist. of Ireland, Illustrated. N. Y., 1845. 2 Vols. 4to.

DOLE, Benj. Examination of Mr. Rantoul's Report for Abolishing Capital Punishment in Mass. Boston, 1837. 8vo. Mass. Reports, 1837.

DOLE, Geo. T. Yale Revisited, Poem before the Phi Beta Kappa Soc. of Yale Coll., July 22, 1868. N. Haven, 1869. 8vo. Yale Coll. Pamph.

DOMENECH Abbé M. Seven Years' Residence in the Great Deserts of N. America. Plates and Maps. Lond., 1862. 2 Vols. 8vo.

DOMESDAY Book. See ALLEN, Prof. Wm. F. Rural Population of England, as Classified in.

—— ELLIS, Sir H. Gen. Introduc. to.

—— HENSHALL, S.

—— MORTON, J. Northamptonshire, etc.

—— of Norfolk. See MUNFORD, Geo. Analysis of.

—— Seu Liber Censualis Willelmi Primi Reges Angliæ. Lond., 1783. 2 Vols. Folio.

—— Same. Addimenta ex Codic Antiquiss. Lond., 1816. 1 Vol. Folio.

—— Same. Indices. Lond., 1816. 1 Vol. Folio.

DOMESTIC Economy. See BLAKE, Rev. J. L. Farmers' Every Day Book and.

—— DUSSARD, M. Art de Fabriquer les Savons.

—— KLEIN, P. Sur les Fourneaux Economique.

—— PELOUZE, M. Art du Blanchissage.

—— Industry. See Gen. Convention of Agriculturists, etc. 1827.

DOMINICA. See ATWOOD, Thos. Hist. of.

—— San Domingo.

DONALDSON, John. Agricult. Biography: British Agricult. Authors, from 1480 to the Present Time. Lond., 1854. 8vo. Biograph. Pamph. Vol. 2.

DONALDSON, Thos. Address before the Md. Hist. Soc., Mar. 29, 1849. Amer. Colonial History. Baltimore, 1849. 8vo. Md. Hist. Soc. Addresses. Vol. 2.

DONALDSON, Thos. L. Plan for Promotion of Art, Science and Literature. Lond., 1838. 8vo. Strangford Pamph. Vol. 15.

DONALSON, Israel. Narr. of his Captivity by the Indians in 1791. Amer. Pioneer. Vol. 1.

DONGAN, Gov. Thos. Report on the Province of N. Y. 1687. Doc. Hist. of N. Y. Vol. 1.

DONIPHAN'S Expedition. See EDWARDS, F. S.; HUGHES, J. T.; RICHARDSON, W. H.; WISLIZENUS, A.

DONLEVY, John. Exercises on Phonography, or Writing by Sound. N. York, 1845. 8vo. Educa. Pamph. Vol. 6.

DONNAVAN, C. Adventures in Mexico during a Captivity of Seven Months, Cincin., 1847. 8vo. Mex. War Pamph. Vol. 2.

DONNE, Dr. John. See WALTON, I.

DONNE, W. Bodham. Corres. of King George III. with Lord North, 1778 to 1783. Lond., 1867. 2 Vols. 8vo.

DONNELLY, Ignatius. Speech in Cong., Feb. 1, 1866, on the Freedmen's Bureau. Speeches. Vol. 5. Rebell'n Pamph. Vol. 5.

DOOLITTLE, Jas. R. Speech in U. S. Senate, Dec. 14, 1859, on the Rebellion. Rebell'n Pamph. Vol. 9.

—— Speech in U. S. Senate, Feb. 16, 1867, in Vindication of his Course. Washington, 1867. 8vo. Congr. and Polit. Pamph. Vols. 71 and 122.

—— See SMITH, J. Y. Review of his Speech at Madison, 1865, on Reconstruction.

—— Speech in U. S. Senate, Jan. 17, 1866, on Reconstruction. Congr. and Polit. Pamph. Vol. 121. Rebell'n Pamph. Vol. 57.

—— Speech in Cong., Apr. 11, 1862, on African Coloniza. Congr. and Polit. Pamph. Vol. 83.

—— Reply to Senators Morton, Trumbull and others, in U. S. Senate, Feb. 24, 1868. Congr. and Polit. Pamph. Vol. 122.

DOOLITTLE, Mark. Hist. Sketch of the Cong. Ch. in Belchertown, Mass., for 114 Years: with Genealogies. Northampton, 1852. 12mo.

DOOR Co. (Wis.) Advocate, Newspaper. Sturgeon Bay, 1862–70. Folio.

—— See Resources of Brown, Door, etc. 1870.

DORAN, Dr. Monarch's Retired from Business. N. Y., 1857. 2 Vols. 12mo.

DORCHESTER, Eng. Guide to. (n. d.) 12mo. Guide Books. Vol. 10.

DORCHESTER (Mass.) Antiq. and Hist. Soc. Collections. No. 1. Memois of Roger Clap. 1630. No. 2. BLAKE, J. Annals of Dorchester. 1750. No. 3. Journ. of Rich'd Mather. 1635. His Life and Death. 1670. Boston, 1846–50. 3 Vols. 12mo.

—— See BLAKE, J. Annals of.

—— CODMAN, J. Annivers. Disc. 1845.

—— DRAKE, Saml. G. Recovery of Materials for Early Hist. of.

—— Epitaphs from the Old Burying Ground. Boston Highlands, 1869. 8vo. Mass. Hist. Discourses, etc. Vol. 7.

DORCHESTER. See EVERETT, E. Oration 1835, etc., at Celebra. 225th Annivers.
—— HARRIS, Rev. J. M. Chronolog. and Topog. Acc. of.
—— Hist. of. By a Comm. of the Dorchester Antiq. and Hist. Soc. Boston, 1859. 8vo.
—— Memorial of the Proprietors of the New South Meeting House in Dorchester to the Boston Assoc., with their Report. Boston, 1813. 8vo. Mass. Hist. Discourses, etc. Vol. 8.
—— Reports of Receipts and Expenditures for 1843, '46, '48, '50, '51, '52, '54, '55, '57, '59, '65, '66, '68.
—— Reports of School Comm. for 1842, '47, '48, '49, '50, '51, '54, with Regulations adopted Apr., 1853, '57, '66, '67.
—— Report of Special Comm. on Schools. 1845.
—— Rules, etc., of the Board of Health. 1855.
—— 1st Ch. See HARRIS, Rev. T. M. Memorials of.
—— 2d Ch. See ALLEN, Wm. 40th Annivers. Disc. 1848.
—— Proceedings of 2d Ch. and Parish. Boston, 1812. 8vo. Mass. Hist. Discourses, etc. Vol. 18.
—— Taxable Valuation of the Polls and Estates, and Amount of Tax for 1849, '50, '53, '55, '61, '65, '69. Boston, 8vo.
DORE. By a Stroller in Europe. N. Y., 1857. 12mo.
DORR, Rev. Benjamin. See Belmont Hospt.
—— Hist. Acc. of Christ Ch. Phila., from 1695 to 1841. Phila., 1859. 12mo.
—— Memoir of John Fanning Watson, the Annalist of N. Y. and Phila. Phila., 1861. 8vo.
—— Notes of Travel in Egypt, Holy Land, Turkey and Greece. Phila., 1856. 12mo.
—— The American Vine. Fast Day Sermon. Phila., 1861. 8vo. Sermons. Vols. 15, 25, 70.
—— See WALLACE, J. W. Commem. Disc.
DORR, H. C. The Two Donkeys; a Fable for the People. San Francisco, 1863. 8vo. Rebell'n Pamph. Vol. 72.
DORR, Thos. Wilson. Report of Trial of, for Treason. Providence, 1844. 8vo. R. I. Misc. Pamph. Vol. 1.
DORREGO, M. Asesinato del Gobernador de la Provincia de Buenos Ayres. Lond., 1829. 8vo. Strangford Pamph. Vol. 6.
DORSET, Eng., Antiquities. See WARNE, C. The Celtic Tumuli.
—— Dialect. See BARNES, W. Grammar and Glossary.
—— —— BARNES, W. Poems.
DORSEY, Sarah A. Recollections of Brig. Gen. Henry Allen, of Confed. States Army. N. Y., 1866. 12mo.
DOTY, Gov. Jas. D. See Debate in House of Repr., U. S., May 14, 1842.
—— MEDILL, Wm. Speech in Cong., Apr. 5, 1852.
DURANT, Thos. J. Letter to Henry Winter Davis. N. Orleans, 1864. 8vo. Congr. and Polit. Pamph. Vol. 67.
DOSTIE, A. P. The Political Position of Thos. J. Durant. N. Orleans, 1865. 8vo. Congr. and Polit. Pamph. Vol. 67.
DOUAY, Rev. Anastatius. See SHEA, J. G. Discov. of Mississipi Valley.

DOUGHERTY, Daniel. Address before Senate of Union Coll., July 20, 1863. Phila., 1863. 8vo. Rebell'n Pamph. Vol. 6.

DOUGLAS, Fred. Speech at Mass. Anti-Slavery Soc., at Boston, 1862. Rebell'n Pamph. Vol. 37.

—— See Addresses of, etc.

—— My Bondage and My Freedom; with an Introduction by Dr. James M'Cune Smith. N. Y., 1857. 12mo.

DOUGLAS, Sir Howard. On the Defence of England; Naval, Littoral, and Internal. Lond., 1860. 8vo. Eng. Polit. Pamph. Vol. 58.

—— On Naval Operations in the Black Sea, and the Siege of Sevastopol. Lond., 1855. 8vo. Eng. Polit. Pamph. Vol. 53.

DOUGLAS, Rev. Jas. Opening Address before the Quebec Lit. and Hist. Soc., Session of 1865–6. Transactions, N. Ser. Part 4.

—— The Belief of the Ancient Egyptians respecting a Future State. Read before the Quebec Lit. and Hist. Soc. Transactions, Vol. 5. Part 1.

—— The Gold Fields of Canada; Paper before Quebec Lit. and Hist. Soc., 1863. Quebec, 1863. 8vo. Scientific Pamph. Vol. 14.

DOUGLAS, James S. Modern Mysteries; Address delivered at Waukesha. Waukesha, 1854. 8vo. Wis. Misc. Pamph. Vol. 3.

DOUGLAS, Capt. Joseph. See Case (A) of Individual Sacrifice, etc.

DOUGLAS Monument Assoc. Organization, Constitution, By-Laws, etc. Chicago, 1862. 8vo. Chicago Misc. Pamph. Vol. 1.

DOUGLAS, S. A. Address before N. Y. State Agr. Soc., 1851. Albany. 8vo. Agr. Pamph. Vol. 5.

—— See CURTIS, Geo. T. Reply to, on Popular Sovereignty, 1859.

—— Douglas Monument Assoc.

—— His Record on the Tariff. Rebell'n Pamph. Vol. 77.

—— See FLINT, H. M. Life and Speeches.

—— Letter to Dr. Gwin, on Territorial Affairs, 1859. Congr. and Polit. Pamph. Vol. 85.

—— Letter of Thos. B. Bryant, on his Views of the Rebellion, 1863. Rebell'n Pamph. Vol. 67.

—— Letter to Gov. Matteson on River and Harbor Improvements. Washington, 1854. Congress. and Polit. Pamph. Vol. 86.

—— See Polit. Debates with A. Lincoln, 1858.

—— Polit. Record of, on Slavery. Rebell'n Pamph. Vol. 77.

—— See READ, Prof. Dan'l. Eulogy on.

—— Remarks on the Kansas, Utah, and the Dred Scott Decision. Chicago, 1857. Rebell'n Pamph. Vol. 41.

—— Speech in U. S. Senate, May 13, 1846, on the Mex. War. Washington, 1846. 8vo. Speeches. Vol. 1.

—— Speech at Chicago, Oct. 23, 1843, on the Compromise. Congr. and Polit. Pamph. Vol. 94.

—— Speech in U. S. Senate, Dec. 23, 1851, on the Compromise. Congr. and Polit. Pamph. Vol. 93.

—— —— Jan. 30, 1854, on Kansas and Nebr. Bill. Congr. and Polit. Pamph. Vol. 93.

—— —— Mar. 3, 1854, on the Kansas and Nebr. Bill. Washington, 1854. 8vo. Speeches. Vol. 3.

DOUGLAS, S. A. Speech in U. S. Senate, Mar. 20, 1856, on the Kansas and Nebr. Bill. Congr. and Polit. Pamph. Vol. 93.

—— —— Dec. 9. 1857, on the Lecompton Constitution. Congr. and Polit. Pamph. Vol. 93.

—— —— Mar. 22, 1858, on the Lecompton Constitution. Congr. and Polit. Pamph. Vol. 93.

—— —— Apr. 29, 1858, on Admission of Kansas. Congr. and Polit. Pamph. Vol. 88.

—— —— June 15, 1858, on State of Parties in Ill. Congr. and Polit. Pamph. Vol. 88.

—— —— May 15, 1860, on Slavery. Rebell'n Pamph. Vol. 77.

—— The Dividing Line between Federal and Local Authority. N. Y., 1859. 8vo. Congr. and Polit. Pamph. Vol. 76.

DOUGLASS, D. B. Further Statement of his Removal from the Presidency of Kenyon College. Albany, 1845. 8vo. Ohio Coll. Pamph.

DOUGLASS, Dr. Wm. Letters to Cadwallader Colden. Mass. Hist. Soc. Coll. 4th. Ser. Vol. 2.

DOUGLASS, William. Summary, Historical and Political, of British Settlements in N. America. Lond., 1755. 2 Vols. 8vo.

DOVER Bapt. Assoc., Va. Minutes of 75th Ann. Meeting, held at Colosse, Va., 1858. Richmond, 1858. 8vo.

DOVER, Eng. See BATCHELLER, W. Descriptive Picture and Guide of, 1837.

DOVER Harbor, Eng. See WORTHINGTON, Lieut. B.

DOVER, Mass. See SANGER, Rev. Ralph. 30th Annivers. Disc., 1842.

DOVER, N. H. See ROOT, Rev. David. Bi Centen. Sermon, 1838.

DOVER, Lord. Life of Frederick the Second, King of Prussia. 2d Ed. Lond., 1833. 2 Vols. 8vo.

—— Same. N. Y., 1859. 2 Vols. 18mo. Harpers' Fam. Libr.

DOW Genealogy. See STILES, H. R.

DOW, Jos. Hist. Address at Hampton, N. H., Dec. 25, 1838, on the 200th Annivers. of the Town. Concord, 1839. 8vo. N. Y. Hist. Discourses. Vol. 1.

DOWLEY, M. F. History and Honorary Roll of 12th Reg't N. G. S. N. Y. N. Y., 1869. 12mo.

DOWLING, Rev. John. History of Romanism; from the Earliest Corruptions of Christianity to the Present Time. 11th Ed. N. Y., 1846. 8vo.

—— Same. N. Y., 1855. 8vo.

DOWNES, John. Occultations Visible in the U. States during 1851-52-53. Smithson, Contr. Vols. 2, 3, 6.

—— U. States Almanac, 1843. Phila., 1843. 8vo.

DOWNING, A. J. Cottage Residences; a Series of Designs for Rural Cottages and Cottage Villas. 3d Ed. N. Y., 1847. 8vo.

—— Fruits and Fruit Trees of America. Revised and Corrected by Chas. Downing. N. Y., 1859. 12mo.

DOWNING, C. T. The Fan-Qui in China, 1836-7. Waldie's Circulating Libr. Vol. 11.

"DOWN SOUTH." See DAY, S. P.

DOWNS, Solomon W. Biography of. Washington, 1852. 8vo. Congr. and Polit. Pamph. Vol, 56.
—— Speeches in U. S. Senate, Feb. 18–19, and May 22, 1850, and Jan. 10, 1852, on the Compromise. Congr. and Polit. Pamph. Vol. 94.
—— Speech in U. S. Senate, May 15, 1852, on Public Lands. Congr. and Polit. Pamph. Vol. 84.
DOWSE, Thos. See EVERETT, Edw.
DOYLE, Sir Chas. Wm. Memoir of. n. d. 8vo. Biograph. Pamph. Vol. 2.
DOYLE, Sir John. Speech at the India House, upon the Hyderabad Papers, Mar. 4, 1825. Lond., 1825. 8vo. Strangford Pamph. Vol. 1.
DOYLE, Martin. Hints on Emigration to Upper Canada. Dublin, 1831. 12mo. Canada Pamph. Vol. 3.
DRAGOON Campaigns to the Rocky Mountains. N. Y., 1836. 12mo.
DRAKE, Benj., and MANSFIELD, E. D. Cincinnati in 1826. Cincin., 1827. 12mo.
—— Life of Black Hawk, the Great Indian Chief of the West. Cincin., 1854. 12mo.
—— Life of Tecumseh and of his Brother "The Prophet"; with Hist. Sketch of the Shawanee Indians. Cincin., 1852. 12mo.
—— See TODD, C. S. and DRAKE. Life of Gen. Harrison.
DRAKE, C. D. Address at Washington, Mo., July 4, 1862, on the Rebellion. n. d. Rebell'n Pamph. Vol. 66.
—— Address at St. Louis, Sept. 17, 1862, on the War of Slavery, etc. St. Louis, 1862. 8vo. Rebell'n Pamph. Vols. 3, 66.
—— Speech on the Rebellion, at St. Louis, Apr. 14, 1862. St. Louis, 1862. 8vo. Rebell'n Pamph. Vol. 66.
—— Speech at St. Louis, Jan., 1863, on Emancipation. Rebell'n Pamph. Vols. 6 and 66.
—— Speech before Nat. Union Assoc., 1864. Cincin., 1864. 8vo. Rebell'n Pamph. Vol. 6.
—— Speech in U. S. Senate, Dec. 10, 1867, on the President's Message. Congr. and Polit. Pamph. Vol. 121.
—— Speech in U. S. Senate, Dec. 15, 1870, in Reply to Carl Schurz, on Polit. Disabilities, etc. 8vo. Congr. and Polit. Pamph. Vol. 119.
DRAKE, Dr. Daniel. Geolog. Acc. of the Valley of the Ohio. Amer. Philos. Soc. Trans. N. S. Vol. 2.
—— See GROSS, S. D.
—— Inaug. Disc. on Med. Educa. at Ohio Med. Coll., Nov. 11, 1820. Cincin., 1820. 8vo. Pamphlets. Vol. 4.
—— Introduct. Lecture at Transylvania Univers., Nov. 7, 1823. Lexington, 1823. 8vo. Pamphlets. Vol. 4.
—— See MANSFIELD, E. D.
—— Pioneer Life in Kentucky; a Series of Reminiscential Letters, with Notes by C. D. Drake. Cincin., 1870. 8vo.
—— Systematic Treatise on Diseases of the Interior Valley of N. America. Cincin., 1850. 8vo.
DRAKE Family Genealogy. See DRAKE, S. G. Drakes of Hampton, N. H.

DRAKE, F. D. Sketch of the Settlement of Oxford, O., Previous to 1815. Fire Lands Pioneer. Vol. 3.

DRAKE, Francis S. Dictionary of American Biography, including Men of the Time. Boston, 1872. 8vo.

DRAKE, Saml. A. Old Landmarks and Historic. Personages of Boston. Boston, 1873. 12mo.

DRAKE, Saml. G. Address before the N. Eng. Hist. and Gen. Soc., Jan. 20, 1858. N. Eng. Hist. and Gen. Register. Vol. 12.

—— Address before N. Eng. Hist. and Gen. Soc., Jan. 20, 1858. Boston. 8vo.

—— Annals of Witchcraft in N. Eng. Boston, 1869. 4to.

—— Biography and History of the Indians of N. America. 3d Ed. Boston, 1834. 8vo.

—— Same. 11th Ed. Boston, 1851. 8vo.

—— Catalogue of his Private Library, chiefly relating to America and Amer. Indians. Boston, 1845. 8vo. Bibliograph. Pamph. Vol. 44.

—— See CHURCH, T.

—— Early Hist. of Georgia, embracing the Embassy of Sir Alex. Cuming to the Cherokee Country in 1730, with Map. Boston, 1872. 4to. See also N. Eng. Reg. Vol. 26.

—— Genealog. Chart of the Family of Drake, of Hampton, N. H. Boston. Sheet from Genealog. Pamph. Vol. 7.

—— Hist. and Antiq. of Boston, from its first Settlement in 1630, to 1700. Boston, 1856. 8vo.

—— Hist. of the Five Years' French and Indian War in N. England and Parts Adjacent. 1744–1747. Albany, 1870. 4to.

—— Indian Biography. Boston, 1832. 12mo.

—— Indian Captivities; or True Narratives of Captives, etc. N. Y., 1857. 12mo. and 8vo. 1856.

—— Memoir of Sir Walter Raleigh. N. Eng. Hist. and Gen. Register. Vol. 16.

—— Memoir of the Rev. Cotton Mather, D. D. N. Eng. Hist. and Gen. Register. Vol. 6.

—— Notes on the Indian Wars in N. England. N. Eng. Hist. and Gen. Register. Vols. 12 and 15.

—— Notice of Wm. T. Harris. Boston, 1855. Sm. 4to. Addresses. Vol. 31.

—— Old Indian Chronicle; a Collection of Rare Tracts on the King Philip Indian War. Boston, 1867. 4to.

—— Recovery of Materials for the Early Hist. of Dorchester, Mass. Boston, 1851. 8vo. Mass. Hist. Discourses, etc. Vol. 15.

—— Researches among the British Archives for Information of Founders of N. England. Boston, 1860. 4to.

—— See SHEPPARD, J. H. Memoir of.

—— See Witchcraft Delusion, etc.

DRAKE, Rev. W. Hist. and Descrip. Guide to the Ruins of Kenilworth Castle. Warwick, Eng. 12mo. (n. d.) Guide Books. Vol. 8.

DRAMA. See Amer. Dramatic Fund Assoc.
—— BOADEN, J. Life of Kemble and Hist. of Stage.
—— Collection of Old Plays—Comedies, Tragedies, Operas, etc. Pamphlets. 16 Vols. 8vo.
—— See DELPLA, A. French Drama, etc.
—— EDGEWORTH, M. Comic Dramas.
—— English Drama under the Stuarts.
—— Fall of Brit. Tyranny. 1776.
—— Federalism Triumphant.
—— FOOTE, S. Englishman in Paris.
—— —— —— Returned from Paris.
—— HOGARTH, Geo. Memoirs of the Musical Drama.
—— JONES, G. Tecumseh, the Prophet.
—— LAWRENCE, Jas. Dramatic Emancipation, etc.
—— LUDVIGH, S. Der fall Von Ungarn.
—— O'CONWAY, M. J. Knights Templars.
—— PONTEACH.
—— SHAKSPEARE, W.
—— SIMMS, W. G. Michael Bonham.
DRAPER Family History. See DRAPER, F. P.
DRAPER, Fernando P. Acc. of the Silver Wedding of Mr. and Mrs. F. P. Draper, of Westford, N. Y., June 16, 1871, with Hist. Essays on the Draper and Preston Families. Albany, 1871. 8vo. Genealog. Pamph. Vol. 12.
DRAPER, James. Hist. of Spencer, Mass., with a Brief Sketch of Leicester to 1753. 2d Ed., Enlarged. Worcester. (n. d.) 8vo.
DRAPER, Dr. J. W. Address to the Alumni of the Univers. ot N. Y., June 28, 1853. 8vo. Addresses. Vol. 7.
—— Hist. of the Amer. Civil War. N. Y., 1867–70. 3 Vols. 8vo.
—— Thoughts on the Future Civil Policy of America. N, Y., 1865. 8vo.
DRAPER, Lyman C. Adventures of Capt. Robt. Stobo, with some Notice of La Force and Van Braam. "Olden Time." Vol. 1. Va. Hist. Register. Vol. 5.
—— Ann. Reports on the Condition and Improvement of the Common Schools and Educa. Interests of Wisconsin, 1858–9. Madison. 2 Vols. 8vo.
—— Madison, the Capital of Wisconsin: Its Growth, Progress, Condition, Wants and Capabilities. Madison, 1857. 8vo. Madison City Pamph. Vol. 1.
—— The Expedition against the Shawanoe Indians in 1756. Va. Hist. Register. Vol. 5.
—— —— See Wis. State Histor. Soc. Collec.
DRAPER, Col. Wm. Answer to the Spanish Arguments Claiming the Galeon, etc. Lond., 1764. 8vo. Eng. Polit. Pamph. Vol. 15A.
DRAYTON, John. Memoirs of the Amer. Revolution as far as relates to S. Carolina. Charleston, 1821. 2 Vols. 8vo.
—— View of S. Carolina as respects her Natural and Civil Concerns. Charleston, 1820. 8vo.

DRAYTON, Col. Wm. See GRIMKE, Thos. S. Oration at Charleston, etc.

"DRED Scott Case." See BENTON, T. H. Examination of.

—— HOWARD, B. C.

—— U. S. Supreme Court. Opinions of Chief Justice Taney and others.

DRENNAN, Wm. Letter to Hon. Chas. Jas. Fox. Dublin, 1806. 8vo. Eng. Polit. Pamph. Vol. 27.

DRESDEN Assoc. for Exploration of the World. 2d Ann. Report. Dresden, 1865. 8vo. Hist. Pamph. Vol. 7.

DRESSER, G. J. Instructions for Collecting War Claims of Soldiers. Chicago, 1862. 8vo. Rebell'n Pamph. Vol. 9.

DRESSER, Horace E. Battle Record of Amer. Rebellion. N. Y., 1865. 8vo. Rebell'n Pamph. Vols. 1 and 69.

DREUILLETTES, Gabrielis. Epistola ad Dominum Joannen Winthrop. N. Y., 1869. 8vo.

—— Narré du Voyage faict pour la Mission des Abnaquiois, et des Connaissances tirèz de la Nouvelle Angleterre, 1650–1. Albany, 1855. 12mo.

DRISLER, H. Reply to Bishop Hopkins' "Bible View of Slavery." 1863. Rebell'n Pamph. Vols. 16, 40, 90.

DRUCE Family. Genealog. Acc. of the Family of Druce, of Goreing, in the Co. of Oxon. Lond., 1735. 4to. Reprint. 18 —. 4to.

DRUIDS. See FELLOWS, John. Exposition of Mysteries, etc.

DRUMMOND, Henry. Future Destinies of the Celestial Bodies. Lond., 1755. 8vo. Scientific Pamph. Vol. 25.

—— On Government by the Queen, and Attempted Gov't from the People. Lond., 1842. 8vo. Strangford Pamph. Vol. 39.

—— on the Corn Laws. Lond., 1841. 8vo. Strangford Pamph. Vol. 39.

—— Speech in Parl't, Mar. 27, 1851, on the Ecclesiastical Titles Bill. Lond. 8vo. Eng. Polit. Pamph. Vol. 49.

DRYDEN, Sir H. E. L. Antiquities and Hist. of Steeple Aston, Oxfordshire. Deddrington, 1845. 8vo.

DRYDEN, John. See Scott W. Prose Works.

DUANE, Jas. See JONES, S. W. Memoir of.

DUANE, Wm. Canada and the Continental Congress, delivered before the Hist. Soc. of Penn., Jan. 31, 1850. Phila., 1850. 8vo. Penn. Hist. Soc. Addresses. Vol. 1.

—— A Visit to Colombia in 1822 and 1823. Phila., 1826. 8vo.

DUBLIN House of Recovery and Fever Hospital Reports for 1808 and 1815. Dublin, 1809. 16mo. 8vo. Eng. Misc. Pamph. Vol. 26.

—— Magazine for 1763 and 1764. Dublin. 2 Vols. 8vo.

—— Model Schools. See TAYLOR, W. C. Visit to. 1847.

—— Society of United Irishmen. Declaration, 1791. 8vo. Eng. Polit. Pamph. Vol. 24.

—— Statistical Soc. See PARE, Wm. Paper. 1854.

—— University of. See STOKES, Dr. Wm.

—— —— See TODD, J. H. See Maynooth College.

DUBLIN, N. H. See LEONARD, Rev. L. W. Hist. of.

Du Boulay, John. England's Advantages: Lecture before the Shaftesbury Literary Institution. Shaftesbury, 1857. 12mo. Eng. Polit. Pamph. Vol. 54.
Dubuque, Iowa. Hand-Book of the Cong. Ch., of Dubuque, May, 1869. No. 2. Dubuque, 1869. 12mo.
—— Board of Educa. 2d Ann. Report, 1857. Dubuque, 1858. 8vo. Iowa Misc. Pamph. Vol. 1.
—— Directory and Advertiser. Dubuque, 1856–57. 8vo.
—— and Sioux City R. R. Guide, Directory and Gazetteer. Dubuque, 1868. 8vo.
Dubuque, Julian. Land Claim. Abstract and Argument of Platt Smith for Defendant, Dec., 1852, and Opinion of Justice Wayne, Dec., 1852. Iowa Misc. Pamph. Vol. 1.
Ducachet, H. W. Tribute to the Memory of Jacob Dyckman, M. D. N. Y., 1823. Addresses. Vol. 11.
Ducatel, J. T. See Maryland Geolog. Survey, 1835–6.
Duden, Gottfried. Bericht über eine Reise nach den Westlichen Staaten Nord Amerikas, 1824–7. 2d Ed. Bonn., 1834. 8vo.
Dudley, Dean. Dudley Genealogies and Family Records. Boston, 1848. 8vo.
—— Hist. of the Council of Nice; a World's Christian Convention, A. D., 325. Boston, 1860. 8vo.
Dudley Genealogy. See Dudley, D.
Dudley, Rev. H. B. Short Address to the Lord Primate of Ireland, on Commutation of Tythes, etc. Lond., 1808. 8vo. Pamphleteer. Vol. 6.
Dudley, Rev. John. Half Century Sermon at Dedica. of Cong. Meeting House, Danville, Vt., Dec. 20, 1851. Hanover, 1852. 8vo. Vt. Hist. Discourses. Vol. 1.
Dudley, J. G. Paper on the Growth, Trade, and Manufacture of Cotton. Amer. Geograph. and Statist. Soc. Bulletin. Vol. 1.
Dudley Papers. Mass. Hist. Soc. Coll. 4th Series. Vol. 2.
Dudley, Rev. J. L. Disc. on the Death of Gen. Jos. K. F. Mansfield, 1862, at Middletown, Conn. Rebell'n Pamph. Vol. 88.
Dudley, Mass. See Bates, Rev. Joshua. Hist. Disc., 1853.
Dudley Observatory. See Albany, University of.
—— Annals of. Vol. 1. Albany, 1866. 8vo.
—— Correspondence between the Officers of the Board of Trustees and the Director of the same Institution, 1858. Scientific Pamph. Vol. 1.
—— See Everett, E.
—— Report of the Astronomer in Charge, 1863. Scientific Pamph. Vol. 17.
—— and the Scientific Council. Statement of the Trustees, 1858. Scientific Pamph. Vol. 1.
—— —— Reply to Same, by B. A. Gould, Jr., 1859. Scientific Pamph. Vol. 1.
—— —— Letter to the Trustees, by Geo. H. Thacher, 1858. Scientific Pamph. Vol. 1.
—— —— Defence of Dr. Gould by Scientific Council. Scientific Pamph. Vol. 1.

DUDLEY and the Scientific Council. Address to Citizens of Albany, 1858. Scientific Pamph. Vol. 1.

—— Inauguration, Aug. 28, 1856. Albany, 1856. 8vo. Scientific Pamph. Vol. 1.

—— Report of the Astronomer for 1863.

DUDLEY, Robt., Earl of Leicester. Correspondence during the Gov't of the Low Countries. Camden Soc. Publica.

DUDLEY, Gov. Thos. Life of. Mass. Hist. Soc. Proceedings, 1869–70.

—— Letter to the Countess of Lincoln, respecting N. England, March, 1631; with Notes by John Farmer. Force's Hist. Tracts. Vol. 2.

DUDLEY, Rev. Thos. P. Battle and Massacre at Frenchtown, Mich., Jan., 1813. Western Reserve Hist. Soc. Tracts.

DUDLEY, Col. Wm. See COMBS, Capt. Leslie. Official Report on his Defeat, etc.

DUELLING. See BOSQUETT, A. Treatise on.

—— BUCKINGHAM, Jas. S.

—— Discourse concerning, 1687.

DUER, John. Discourse on Life, Character, etc., of Jas. Kent, before the N. Y. Bar, Apr. 12, 1848. N. Y. 8vo. Addresses. Vol. 22.

DUER, Wm. Speech in Cong., Apr. 10, 1850, on the Admission of Cal. Congr. and Polit. Pamph. Vol. 86.

DUER, Wm. A. Address before the Literary Societies of Columbia Coll., July 24, 1848. Scientific Pamphlets. Vol. 1.

—— Lectures on the Constitutional Jurisprudence of the U. States. Harpers' Fam. Libr. N. Y., 1838. 18mo.

—— Life of Wm. Alexander, Earl of Stirling, Maj. Gen. in the Army of the U. S. during the Revolution. N. J. Hist. Soc. Coll. Vol. 2.

DUFFIELD, Rev. Geo., Jr. Hist. Sermon on Fast Day at Phila., 1861. Rebell'n Pamph. Vol. 80.

DUKE, B. W. Hist. of Morgan's Cavalry. Cincin., 1867. 8vo.

DUKE, R. T. W. Speech in Virginia Legislature, Feb. 13, 1873, on the James River and Kanawha Canal. Washington, 1873. 8vo. Va. Misc. Pamph. Vol. 2.

DUKE'S Co., Mass. Descrip. of, 1807. Mass. Hist. Soc. Coll. Vol. 3. 2d Ser.

DUKE'S Co., N. York. See HOUGH, G. B. Papers relating to.

DUKINFIELD, Sir H. R. Letter to the Inhabitants of St. Martin in-the-Fields. Lond., 1847. 8vo. 2d Ed. Eng. Misc. Pamph. Vol. 5.

DU LAC, M. Perrin. Travels through the Louisianas and among the Savage Nations of the Missouri, 1801–3. From the French. Lond., 1807. 8vo.

—— Same. Lyons, 1805. 8vo. French.

DULANEY, Daniel. Considerations on Imposing Taxes in the British Colonies, for Raising a Revenue, etc. Lond. Re-printed, 1766. 8vo.

—— Same. 2d Ed. 1766. Amer. Tracts. Vol. 1.

DULUTH, Minn. Report of Select Comm. of Minn. Legisla., on Duluth as a Harbor, etc. St. Paul, 1870. 8vo.

DULWICH College, Eng. See Appeal for a Charitable Trusts Act of Parliament, etc., 1852.

DUMARESQ Family History. Sketch of. Albany, 1863. 8vo. Genealog. Pamph. Vol. 7.

DUMMER, Jer. Defence of the N. England Charters. Lond. n. d. Amer. Tracts. Vol. 1.

DUMONT, M. Hist. of Louisiana, from the French. French's Hist. Coll. of La. Vol. 4.

DUMORTIER, B. C. Belgium and the 24 Articles. Translated by Chas. White. Brussels, 1838. 8vo. Hist. Pamph. Vol. 17.

DUNBAR, Rev. Elijah. Eccles. Hist. of Peterborough, N. H. Farmer and Moore's Coll. Vol. 1.

—— Topograph. and Hist. Acc. of Peterborough, N. H. Farmer and Moore's Coll. Vol. 1.

DUNBAR, Reuben. See THOMPSON, Mrs. M. Phrenolog. Character of.

—— Trial of, for Murder of Stephen V. and David L. Lester. Albany, 1850. 8vo. N. Y. Pamph. Vol. 2.

DUMBARTON, N. H. See BURNHAM, Rev. A. W. Centen. Address, 1865.

—— STARKS, C. Hist. of.

DUMBARTONSHIRE, Scotland. See IRVING, Jos. Hist. of, 1860.

DUNCAN, A. Speech in Cong., Mar. 6, 1844, on Election of Presidential Electors. Congr. and Polit. Pamph. Vol. 87.

DUNCAN, Arch'd. The British Trident; or Register of Naval Actions. Lond., 1805–9. 6 Vols. 12mo. Vol. 1 wanting.

DUNCAN, Francis. Our Garrisons in the West; or Sketches of British N. America. Lond., 1864. 8vo.

DUNCAN, Garnett. Speech in Cong., July 24, 1848, on Executive Power. Rebell'n Pamph. Vol. 32.

DUNCAN, Rev. Henry. Sacred Philosophy of the Seasons. N. Y., 1856. 2 Vols. 12mo.

DUNCAN, John. Travels in Western Africa in 1845–1846. 2d Ed. Lond., 1847. 2 Vols. 8vo.

DUNCAN, J. H. Speech in Cong., June 7, 1850, on Admission of Cal. Congr. and Polit. Pamph. Vol. 86.

DUNCAN, John M. Travels through Part of U. S. and Canada, in 1818–19. Glasgow, 1823. 2 Vols. 12mo.

DUNCAN, W., M. D. Tabulated Mortuary Record of Savannah, Ga., 1854–69. Savannah, 1870. 8vo. Georgia Misc. Pamph. Vol. 1.

DUNCOMB, John. Collections toward the Hist. and Antiq. of Hereford. Hereford, 1804. 2 Vols. 4to.

DUNDAS, Sir David. Hunterian Oration before the Roy. Coll. of Surgeons, Feb. 14, 1818. Lond., 4to. Med. Pamph. Vol. 28.

DUNDAS, Henry. Speech in Parl't, Apr. 23, 1793, on India Affairs. Lond. 4to. Eng. Polit. Pamph. Vol. 5.

DUNGLISON, Robley, M. D. Introduct. Lecture, delivered in Jefferson Med. Coll., Oct. 19, 1848. Phila., 1848. 8vo. Med. Pamph. Vol. 31.

DUNKERS. See CONYNGHAM, R.

DUNKIRK, Eng. See STEELE, Rich'd. Importance of, 1713.

DUNLAP, Andrew. Oration at Salem, Mass., July 5, (4th) 1819, before the Assoc. of the Essex Reading Room. Salem, 1819. 8vo. Addresses. Vol. 29.

DUNLAP, John. Amer. Daily Advertiser, Newspaper. Jan. and Feb., 1792. Phila. Folio.

—— See Penn. Packet.

DUNLAP, Wm. Address before the Nat. Academy of Design, Apr. 18, 1831. N. Y., 1831. 8vo. Art Pamph. Vol. 6.

—— Hist. of the N. Netherlands, Province of N. York, and State of N. York, to the Adoption of the Fed. Constitution. N. Y., 1839. 2 Vols. 8vo.

DUNLAVY, John. The Nature and Character of the True Ch. of Christ proved, etc. (Shakers.) N. Y., 1847. 12mo. Religious Pamph. Vol. 21.

DUNLEVY, A. H. History of Miami Baptist Assoc., from 1797 to 1836. Cincin., 1869. 12mo.

DUNLOP, Alex. Answer to the Dean of Faculty's Letter on the Ch. of Scotland. Edinburgh, 1839. 8vo. Strangford Pamph. Vol. 19.

DUNLOP, Anthony. Sketches on Polit. Economy. Lond., 1818. 8vo. Pamphleteer. Vol. 11.

DUNLOP, Jas. Memoir of the Controversy between Wm. Penn and Lord Baltimore, on the Boundaries of Penn. and Md., 1825. Penn. Hist. Soc. Memolrs. Vol. 1, Part 1. "Olden Time." Vol. 1.

DUNMORE'S (Lord) War. Papers and Letters in reference to. "Olden Time." Vol. 2.

DUNN, Henry. Calm Thoughts on the Recent Minutes of the Committee of Council on Educa., etc. Lond., 1847. 8vo. Educa. Pamph. Vol. 33.

—— National Educa.; Apology for the Bible in Schools. Lond., 1838. 8vo. Educa. Pamph. Vols. 29, 40.

—— Sketch of the Lives of Jos. Lancaster and Wm. Allen. Lond., 1848. 12mo. Biograph. Pamph. Vol. 16.

DUNN, John. Hist. of the Oregon Territory and British N. Amer. Fur Trade. Lond., 1844. 8vo.

DUNN, Robt. Evidence in Support of the Unity of the Human Species. Lond., 1861. 8vo. Scientific Pamph. Vol. 3.

DUNN, Wm. The Soul of Mr. Pitt; developing that Eighteen Millions of Taxes may be taken off, etc. Lond., 1819. 2d Ed. Eng. Polit. Pamph. Vol. 35.

—— The Vansittart Plan of Finance. Lond., 1820. 8vo. Pamphleteer. Vol. 16.

DUNNELL, Henry G. True Genealogies of the Dunnell and Dwinell Families of N. England. N. Y., 1862. 8vo. Genealog. Pamph. Vol. 9.

DUNNINGTON, F. C. Letter to Ex-President Johnson, 1872. Congr. and Polit. Pamph. Vol. 130.

DUNSKY, H. D. Statement on the Timber and Deal Trade, as regards Europe and the Brit. Amer. Colonies. Lond., 1821. 8vo. Pamphleteer. Vol. 18.

DUNSTABLE, Mass. See Fox, C. J. Hist. of.

DUNSTER Papers. Mass. Hist. Soc. Coll. 4th Ser. Vol. 2.
DUNTON, John. Journal in Mass. 1686. Mass. Hist. Soc. Coll. 2d Ser. Vol. 2.
—— Summer's Ramble through Ten Kingdoms. Lond., 1685. Boston reprint, 1867. 4to. See Prince Soc. Publica.
DU PONCEAU, Peter S. Discourse before the Hist. Soc. of Penn., June 3, 1837. Memoirs. Vol. 4. Part 1.
—— Discourse on the Early Hist. of Penn., before the Amer. Philos. Soc., June 6, 1821. Phila., 1821. 8vo.
—— English Phonology: Analysis of Component Sounds of the English Language. Amer. Philos. Soc. Trans. N. S. Vol. 1.
—— Hist. of the Treaty of Wm. Penn with the Indians in 1682. Penn. Hist. Soc. Memoirs. Vol. 3. Part 2.
—— Notes, etc., on Eliot's Indian Grammar. Mass. Hist. Soc. Coll. 2d Ser. Vol. 9.
—— Sketch of Life of. Amer. Oriental Soc. Journ. Vol. 1.
DUPONT, Chevalier. Voyages and Adventures, translated from the French. Lond., 1772. 4 Vols. 18mo.
DUPPA, B. F. Educa. of the Peasantry in England. Lond., 1834. 12mo. Educa. Pamph. Vol. 8.
—— Industrial Schools for the Peasantry. Lond., 1837. 12mo. Educa. Pamph. Vol. 31.
DU PRATZ, Le Page. Hist. of Louisiana or the Western Parts of Virginia or Carolina, from the French. Lond., 1763. 2 Vols. 12mo.
—— Same. Lond., 1784. 8vo.
DURAND, Elias. Biograph. Memoir of the Late Francois André Michaux. Amer. Philos. Soc. Trans. N. S. Vol. 11.
—— Sketch of the Botany of the Basin of the Great Salt Lake of Utah. Amer. Philos. Soc. Trans. N. S. Vol. 11.
DURANT, Thos. J. See Dostie, A. P. Polit. Position of 1865.
DURBIN, John, D. D. Memoir of. From Holden's Mag., May, 1859. Biograph. Pamph. Vol. 11.
DURFEE, Rev. Calvin. Commem. Disc. before Cong. Ch. in Great Barrington, Mass., May 13, 1866, with Appendix. Boston, 1866. 8vo. Mass. Hist. Discourses. Vol. 2.
—— Hist. of Williams Coll. Boston, 1860. 8vo.
—— Sketches of the Class of 1825 of Williams Coll. N. Y., 1865. 8vo. Williams Coll. Pamphs.
DURFEE, Job. Discourse before the R. I. Hist. Soc., Jan. 13, 1847. Providence, 1847. 8vo. R. I. Hist. Soc. Addresses. Vol. 1.
—— See DURFEE, Thos. Complete Works of.
—— HAZARD, R. G. Character and Writings of.
DURFEE, Thos. Complete Works of Hon. Job Durfee, LL. D., Ch. Justice of R. I. Providence, 1849. 8vo.
DURHAM, Conn. See FOWLER, W. C. History of.
—— —— Dedica. Sermon. 1847.
DURHAM, Eng. See BAGG, S. C. Antiquities and Legends of. 1866.
—— HUTCHINSON, Wm. Hist. and Antiquities. 1825.
—— RAINE, Jas. Hist. and Antiq. of N. Durham. 1852.
DURHAM, N. H. See BURT, Rev. F. Civil and Eccles. Hist. of.

DURKEE, Chas. Speech in Cong., June 10, 1850, on the Admission of Cal. Congr. and Polit. Pamph. Vol. 86.

—— Speech in Cong., Aug. 6, 1852, on the Fugitive Slave Bill. Cong. and Polit. Pamph. Vol. 84.

—— Speech in U. S. Senate, Mar. 20, 1858, on the Lecompton Constitution. Congr. and Polit. Pamph. Vol. 93.

DURRIE, Dan'l S. Bibliography of Wisconsin, from Hist. Mag., July, 1869.

—— Early Outposts of Wisconsin: Green Bay for Two Hundred Years. Annals of Prairie du Chien. Madison, 1873. 8vo. Wis. Local Hist. Vol. 2.

—— Bibliographia Genealogica Americana; an Alphabetical Index to Amer. Genealogies and Pedigrees, contained in State, County and Town Histories, Printed Genealogies and kindred Works. 8vo. Albany. 1868.

—— Steele Family. A Genealog. Hist. of John and George Steele, Settlers at Hartford, Conn., 1835–6, and their Descendants, with Genealog. Information respecting other Families of the Name; enlarged edition. Sup. royal 8vo. Albany. 1862.

—— Holt Genealogy. A Genealog. Hist. of the Holt Family in the U. States; more particularly the Descendants of Nicholas Holt, of Newbury and Andover, Mass., 1634–1644, and of Wm. Holt, of N. Haven. 8vo. Albany. 1864.

—— Capt. Jonathan Carver and the "Carver Grant." Wis. State Hist. Soc. Coll. Vol. 6.

—— Utility of the Study of Genealogy; read before the Exec. Comm. of the State Hist. Soc. of Wis., July 9, 1862. 8vo. Addresses. Vol. 15.

DURYEE'S Brigade. See HOUGH, F. B.

DUSSANCE, H. Treatise on Coloring Matter derived from Coal Tar. Phila., 1863. 12mo.

—— Treatise on Perfumery. Phila., 1864. 8vo.

—— Treatise on the Fabrication of Matches. Phila., 1834. 12mo.

DUSSARD, M. Art de Fabriquer les Savons mis a la portée des Menages. Paris, 1829. 24mo.

DUSSELDORF Academy of Art. Catalogue of Paintings by Artists of. N. Y., 1859. (?) 8vo. Art Catalogues. Vol. 1.

DUTCH Slave Trade. See Voyages of St. John and Arms of Amsterdam.

DUTCHER, L. L. Hist. Disc. on the Rise and Progress of the 1st Cong. Ch., St. Albans, Vt. St. Albans, 1860. 8vo. Vt. Hist. Discourses. Vol. 1.

DUTCHESS Co., N. Y., and Poughkeepsie Sanitary Fair. Report of. 1864. Rebell'n Pamph. Vol. 18.

—— Census of 1744, and other Papers. 1660–1766. See N. Y. Doc. Hist. Vol. 1.

DUTENS, M. Memoirs of a Traveller, now in Retirement. Written in 1775–1805. Waldie's Circulating Libr. Vol. 10.

DUTTON Genealogy. See COPE, Gilbert.

DUTTON, Rev. Saml. W. S. Address at the Funeral of Hon. Simeon Baldwin, May 28, 1851. N. Haven, 1851. 8vo. Sermons. Vol. 51.

DUTY (The) of Adopted Citizens at the Present Time. German. 1863. Rebell'n Pamph. Vol. 91.
—— of Allegiance Settled, etc., in Answer to Dr. Sherlock's "Case of Allegiance." Lond., 1691. Sm. 4to. Eng. Polit. Pamph. Vol. 64.
—— of Conservative Whigs in the Present Crisis. Letter to Hon. Rufus Choate. Boston, 1856. 8vo. Congr. and Polit. Pamph. Vol. 135.
DUXBURY, Mass. See ALLEN, S. M. On Miles Standish.
—— BRADFORD, A. Notes on the Town of.
DUYCKINCK, E. A. Nat. Portrait Gallery of Eminent Americans. N. Y., 1862. 2 Vols. 4to.
—— and G. L. Cyclopœdia of Amer. Literature, embracing Personal and Critical Notices of Authors. N. Y., 1855. 2 Vols. 8vo., and Supplement, 1866. 1 Vol. 8vo.
—— Hist. of the War for the Union. N. Y., 3 Vols. 4to. (n. d.)
DWIGHT, Benj. W. Acc. of the Great Storm at Catskill, N. Y., July 26, 1819. Silliman's Journ. Vol. 4.
—— Hist. of the Descendants of Elder John Strong, of Northampton, Mass. Albany, 1871. 2 Vols. 8vo.
—— Modern Philology: Its Discoveries, History and Influence. N. Y., 1859. 8vo.
DWIGHT, Rev. Edw. S. Address in Saco, Oct. 12, 1862, on the 100th Annivers. of the 1st Ch. Saco, 1862. 8vo. Maine Hist. Discourses. Vol. 2.
DWIGHT, Henry E. Acc. of the Kaatskill Mountains. Silliman's Journal. Vol. 2.
DWIGHT, M. A. Grecian and Roman Mythology. 2d Abridged Ed. N. Y., 1855. 12mo.
DWIGHT, N. Lives of the Signers of the Declara. of Independence. N. Y., 1852. 12mo.
DWIGHT, Rev. Sereno E. The Greek Revolution. Address at Boston, Apr. 1, 1824. Boston, 1824. 8vo. Hist. Pamph. Vol. 7.
DWIGHT, T. Amer. Monthly Magazine. Vols. 1, 2, 3. N. Y., 1845–47. 3 Vols. 8vo.
DWIGHT, Theo. Jr. Hist. of Conn., from the First Settlement to the Present Time. Harpers' Fam. Libr. N. Y., 1859. 18mo.
—— Hist. of the Hartford Convention, with a Review of the Policy of the U. S. Gov't, leading to the War of 1812. N. Y., 1833. 8vo.
—— Remarks on Docs. accompanying Pres't Madison's late Message. (n. d.) or title. Miscell. Tracts. Vol. 1.
—— Sketch of the Polynesian Language. Amer. Ethnolog. Soc. Vol. 2.
—— The Character of Thos. Jefferson, as Exhibited in his own Writings. Boston, 1839. 12mo.
—— Travels in America. Glasgow, 1848. 12mo.
DWIGHT, Timothy. See SPRAGUE, W. B. Life of.
—— The Conquest of Canaan; a Poem. Hartford, 1785. 12mo.
—— Travels in N. England and N. York. N. Haven, 1821. 4 Vols.

DWIGHT, Rev. Wm. T. Address before the Alumni of Yale Coll., Aug. 14, 1844. N. Haven, 1844. 8vo. Yale Coll. Pamph.
—— Oration at Portland, Me., July 4, 1861. Rebell'n Pamph. Vol. 30.
DWINELL Genealogy. See DUNNELL.
DWINNELL, Rev. S. A. Wisconsin as it was and as it is. 1836 Compared with 1866. Milwaukee, 1867. 8vo. Wis. Misc. Pamph. Vol. 6.
DYCKMAN, Jacob. See DUCACHET, H. W. Tribute to.
DYE, John S. The Adder's Den; or Secrets of the Great Conspiracy. N. Y., 1864. 8vo. Rebell'n Pamph. Vol. 17.
DYEING. See Dyer and Color-Maker's Companion.
—— LOVE, T. On Cleaning, Dyeing and Scouring.
—— NAPIER, J. Chemistry Applied to.
—— SMITH, D. Dyer's Instructor.
—— ULRICH, M. L. Treatise on.
DYER (The) and Color-Maker's Companion. Phila., 1855. 12mo.
DYER, Gen. A. B. Proceedings of Court of Inquiry in regard to the Case of ——. Part 2. Washington, 1868. Congr. and Polit. Pamph. Vol. 69.
DYER, Chas. E. See HURLBUT, H. H. Reply to his Old Settlers Address.
—— Hist. Address before the Old Settlers Soc. of Racine Co., Wis., with Constitution. List of Members, etc. Racine, 1871. 8vo. Wis. Local Hist. Vol. 2.
DYER, David. Hist. of Albany Penitentiary. Albany, 1867. 8vo.
—— Impressions of Prison Life in G. Britain, Submitted to the Inspectors and Supt. of Albany Penitentiary. Albany, 1868. 8vo., with Reports of the Penitentiary.
DYER, Geo. Dissertation on the Theory and Practice of Benevolence. Lond., 1819. 8vo. Pamphleteer. Vol. 13.
—— Four Letters on the English Constitution. Lond., 1818. 8vo. 4th Ed. Pamphleteer. Vol. 12.
DYER, J. C. Democracy: What is it? Let us Inquire. Manchester, 1859. 8vo. Eng. Polit. Pamph. Vol. 56.
DYLKS, Jos. C. See TANEYHILL, R. H. The Leatherwood God.
DYMOND, Jonathan. Essays on the Principles of Morality, and on the Private and Political Rights and Obligations of Mankind. N. Y., 1854. 12mo.
—— Accordancy of War with the Principles of Christianity. N. Y. and Phila. 8vo. Religious Pamph. Vol. 5.
—— Oaths: their Moral Character and Effects. Phila., 1835. 12mo. Religious Pamph. Vol. 5.
DYSON, Jeremiah. The Case of the late Election for the Co. of Middlesex Considered. Scarce Tracts. Vol. 3.

E.

EAGER, Sam'l W. Outline Hist. of Orange County, N. Y., with Biograph. and Genealog. Sketches of Early Settlers. Newburg, 1846–7. 8vo.
EAGER, W. See Mass. Supreme Court.
EARLE, J. M. Rept. on Indians of Mass. Boston, 1861. 8vo.
EARLE, Thos. Treatise on Rail Roads and Internal Communications. Phila., 1830. 8vo.
EARLY History of Western Penn. and of the West and Western Expeditions and Campaigns. 1754–1833. Pittsburg, 1846. 8vo.
EARLY, Gen. Jubal A. Memoir of the Last Year of the War for Independence in the Confed States. Lynchburg, 1867. 8vo.
—— The Campaigns of Gen. Robt. E. Lee. Address delivered Jan. 19, 1872. Baltimore, 1872. 8vo. Rebellion Pamph. Vol. 110.
EARLY Voyages up and down the Mississippi, by Cavelier St. Cosme, Le Sueur, Gravier, Guignas, with Introduction and Notes by John Gilmary Shea. Albany, 1861. 4to.
EAST Boston. See SUMNER, Gen. W. H. Hist. of.
EASTBURN, Rev. Jas. See GREEN, A. Memoirs, etc.
EASTBURN, Bishop Manton. Sermon at Boston, Feb. 18, 1843, on the Death of Bishop ALEX. GRISWOLD. Boston, 1843. 8vo. Sermons. Vol. 43.
EASTBURN, Robert. See GREEN, Ashbel. Residence among Canadian Indians. 1758.
EASTERN, R. R. Co. Act of Incorporation, By-Laws, etc., 1836. 21st Ann. Rept. 1856. See LORING, C. G. See Mass. Supreme Judicial Court.
EAST Haddam, Conn. 1st Ch. Extracts from Records of Early Hist. of the Ch. (Newspaper Cuttings.) Conn. Hist. Discourses, etc. Vol. 1.
—— —— See FIELD, D. D. Hist. of. 1814.
—— —— PARSONS, Isaac. 25th Annivers. 1841.
EASTHAM, Mass. Descrip. of. Mass. Hist. Soc. Coll. 1st series. Vol. 8.
—— See PRATT, E. Comprehen. Hist. of.
EASTHAMPTON Book of Laws. 1665. N. Y. Hist. Soc. Coll. Vol. 1.
EASTHAMPTON, Mass. See LYMAN, P. W. Hist. of.
—— WILLISTON, Rev. Payson. Half Century Sermon. 1839.
—— WRIGHT, L. Hist. Sketch of. 1851.
—— GARDINER, D. Chronicles of.
EAST Haven, Conn. See DODD, Rev. S. E. Haven Register.
EAST India College. See MALTHUS, Rev. T. R. Statements, etc.
EAST India Co. See Acc. of the Subversion of the Legal Govt. of Madrass, etc.
—— —— Appeal to Eng. against the new Stamp Act. 1828.
—— —— Edinburgh (The) Reviewer refuted, etc. 1831.
—— —— Hints on the Renewal of the Charter of. 1813.
—— —— India Reform Tracts. 1852.

EAST India Co. Letter from Mahommed Ali CHAN, to the Court of Directors, etc. Lond., 1777. 4to. Eng. Polit. Pamph. Vol. 4.

—— —— See MACLEAN, Dr. Chas. Remarks on Evidence given before Parl't. 1813.

—— —— —— Consequences of Opening Trade to Private Ships.

—— —— Papers and Proceedings relative to the Payment of the Private Debts of the Nabob of Arcot. 1796. 4to. Eng. Polit. Pamph. Vol. 66.

—— —— Papers respecting a Renewal of the Co.'s Exclusive Trade. 6 Papers. 1793. 4to. Eng. Polit. Pamph. Vol. 5.

—— —— See PIGOT, Lord. Letter to the Court of Directors. 1776.

—— —— Report of Select Comm. on the Participation of Ireland in the Indian and China Trade. 4to. Eng. Polit. Pamph. Vol. 5.

—— —— Report of the Committee of Warehouses, on Extending the Trade in Bengal Raw-Silk. 1794. Lond., 1795. 4to. Eng. Polit. Pamph. Vol. 5.

—— —— Short Hist. of the Company, and of their Trade. 1793. 1793. 4to. Eng. Polit. Pamph. Vol. 5.

EASTMAN, Ira A. Speech in Cong., Dec. 28 and 29, 1841, on the Tariff. Washington. 1841. 8vo. Congr. & Polit. Pamph. Vol. 25.

EASTMAN, Luke. Masonic Melodies. Boston. 1818. 8vo.

EASTMAN, L. R. Genealogy of the Eastman Family — from N. E. Hist. & Genealog. Register. 1867. Genealog. Pamph. Vol. 1.

EASTMAN, Mrs. Mary. Dahcota; or Life and Legends of the Sioux around Fort Snelling, illustrated. 1849. 12mo.

EASTMAN, Saml. C. Bibliograph of New Hampshire. Descriptive Catalogue of Books and Pamphlets relating to the Hist. and Statistics of N. H. Norton's Literary Letter. N. Ser. No. 1. 1860.

EASTON, Jas. Hist. of the Cathedral Ch. of Sarum or Salisbury, with an Hist. Acc. of Old Sarum. Salisbury, Eng. 1825. 12mo. Guide Books. Vol. 19.

EASTON, John. Narrative of Causes of Philip's Indian War of 1675 and 1676, with Introduction and Notes by F. B. Hough. Albany, 1858. 4to.

EASTON, Md. Peoples Monitor. Newspaper. Jan. 1813 to Dec. 1813.

EASTON, Penn., High School. Catalogue for 1854. Easton. 1854. 8vo.

EAST TENNESSEE RELIEF Asso. Report. Knoxville, 1865. 8vo. Rebell'n Pamph. Vol. 23.

EATON, Amos Geolog. & Agricult. Survey of Rensselaer Co. N. Y. Albany, 1822. 8vo. N. Y. Misc. Pamph. Vol. 5.

—— Manual of Botany for the Northern and Middle States of America. 3d Ed. Albany. 1822. 8vo.

EATON, Rev. Asa. Hist. Acc. of Christ Ch., Boston: a Discourse delivered Dec. 28, 1823. Boston, 1824. 8vo. Mass. Hist. Discourses. Vol. 17.

See also Boston Hist. Discourses. Vol. 1.

EATON, Cyrus. Annals of the Town of Warren, Me., with the Early Hist. of St. Georges' Broad Bay, and Settlements on the Waldo Patent, with Genealogies. Hallowell, 1851. 12mo.

—— History of Thomaston, Rockland and S. Thomaston, Maine, with Gencalogies. Hallowell, 1863. 2 vols. 12mo.

EATON, Edw. B. California and the Union. Lond., 1863. Rebell'n Pamph. Vol. 53.

EATON, F. B. Hist. of Candia; once known as Charmingfare, with Notices of some of the Early Settlers. Manchester, 1852. 8vo.

EATON, Horace, M. D. Address before the Alumni of Castleton Med. Coll., June 18, 1845. Albany, 1845. 8vo. Med. Pamph. Vol. 2.

EATON, Jas. H. Report on the Geology of the Region about Devil's Lake. Trans. Wis. Acad. of Sciences, 1870–72.

EATON, John H. Life of Gen. Andrew Jackson. Phila., 1824. 8vo.

EATON, Gov. Theophilus. See BAILEY, J. B. Memoir of.

EATON, Gen. William. See FELTON, C. C. Life of.

—— Life of, principally collected from his Manuscripts. Brookfield, 1813. 8vo.

EAU CLAIRE, Wis. Free Press. Newspaper. Eau Claire, 1867–1870. Folio.

EBRINGTON, Viscount. Letter to Lord Palmerston on Representative Self-Government for the Metropolis. Lond., 1854. 8vo. Strangford Pamph. Vol. 66.

ECCLESIASTICAL Commissions. Royal and Parliamentary. From the British Critic. 1838. Lond. n. d. 8vo. Strangford Pamph. Vol. 66.

—— —— See SMITH, Sidney; WORDSWORTH, C.

—— Hist. of Mass. and the Old Colony of Plymouth. Mass. Hist. Soc. Coll. Vols. 7, 9 & 10. 1st Ser.

—— Register; a Statistical View of the Principal Religious Denominations. 1831. n. p. 8vo. Religious Pamph. Vol. 20.

ECHOES from the South; comprising Speeches, Proclamations and Public Acts Emanating from the South during the Late War. N. Y. n. d. 8vo.

ECKFELDT, J. R., & DU BOIS, Wm. E. New Varieties of Gold and Silver Coins, Counterfeit Coins and Bullion. N. Y., 1852. 8vo. 2d Ed.

ECKLEY, Jos., D. D. See LATHROP, John, D. D. Obt. Disc., 1811.

ECLAIREUR (The.) See DE PEYSTER, Gen. J. W.

ECLECTIC Magazine. N. Y., 1847. 2 Vols. 8vo.

ECLIPSE of 1869. See HOUGH, G. W.

—— —— See U. S. Naval Observatory.

ECONOMY, Pa. See BAKER, R. L. Description of.

ECUADOR. Esposicion que dirife al Congresso del Ecuador, en 1855. Quito, 1856. Folio.

EDDIS, Wm. Letter from America, Historical and Descriptive, comprising Occurences from 1769 to 1777. Lond., 1792. 8vo.

EDDY, Rev. Danl. C. Address before the Amer. Baptist Hist. Soc., at Phila., on the Unitarian Apostacy. Phila., 1864. 8vo.

EDDY, Capt. Josh. See EDDY, Zach. Memoirs of.

EDDY, Rev. Rich'd. Hist. of 60th Regt. N. Y. Volunteers. Phila., 1864. 12mo.

EDDY, Zach. Memoirs of Capt. Joshua Eddy. N. Eng. Hist, and Gen. Register. Vol. 8.

EDEN, R. C. The Sword and Gun; a Hist. of the 37th Wis. Vol. Infantry. Madison, 1865. 12mo.

EDEN, Robert H. Observations on the Bill now pending in Parlt. for the Consolidation and Amendment of the Bankrupt Laws. Lond., 1824. 8vo. Eng. Polit. Pamph. Vol. 37. Law Pamph. Vol. 15.

EDEN, Wm. Four Letters to the Earl of Carlisle, on Polit. Affairs. Lond., 1779. 8vo. Eng. Polit. Pamph. Vol. 19.

—— View of his Treaty of Commerce with France; signed at Versailles, Sept. 20, 1786. Lond., 1787. 8vo. Eng. Polit. Pamph. Vol. 22.

EDES, H. H. Memorial of Josiah Barker, of Charlestown, Mass. Boston, 1871. 8vo. Genealog. Pamph. Vol. 2.

EDGE, Fred. M. An Englishman's View of the Battle between the Alabama and the Kearsage. N. Y., 1864. 12mo. Rebell'n Pamph. Vol. 47.

—— Letter to Lord Russell on the Destruction of the American Carrying Trade. London, 1864. 8vo. Rebell'n Pamph. Vol. 39.

—— Major Gen. McClellan, and the Campaign on the Yorktown Peninsula. Loyal Publica. Soc. N. Y., 1865. 8vo. Rebell'n Pamph. Vol. 90A.

EDGERTON, J. K. Speech in Cong., Feb. 20, 1865, on Reconstruction. Cong. and Polit. Pamph. Vol. 121.

EDGERTON Papers. See Camden Soc. Publica.

EDGEWORTH, Maria. Comic Dramas. Boston. 1817. 12mo.

EDINBURGH Academ. Institution. See MILTON, John. His Plan of Educa., etc.

—— Advertiser. July 1, 1783, to July 4, 1786. 5 Vols. 4to.

—— Annual Register. Edinburgh, 1808 to 1825. 23 Vols. 8vo. (Vol. for 1822, wanting.

—— Encyclopedia—edited by Sir David Brewster. Philadelphia, 1832. 18 Vols. 4to.

—— Evening Courant, Newspaper. Jan., 1727 to Dec., 1727. 4to.

—— Chronicle, Mar. 1759 to Sep. 1759. 4to.

—— Same. March, 1760, to Oct., 1760. 4to.

—— Advertiser. Jan. to Dec., 1765. 4to.

—— —— June, 1772, to June, 1773. 2 Vols. 4to.

—— —— Jan. to Dec. 1779. 4to.

—— Philosoph. Journal. Jan., 1819, to Apr., 1824. Edinburgh. 10 Vols. 8vo.

—— Review. Oct., 1802, to Apr., 1868. Edinburgh, 1802–68. 127 Vols. 8vo.

—— —— Gen. Index, from 1802 to 1812, Edinb'gh, 1812. 1 vol. 8vo.

—— Reviewer refuted. Concerning the East India Company and the China Question. Lond., 1831. 8vo. Strangford Pamph. Vol. 11.

EDINBURGH Royal College of Physicians. Charter and Regulations of. Edinburgh, 1829. 8vo. Med. Pamph. Vol. 13.
—— Royal Infirmary of. See HERDMAN, Dr. John.
—— Royal Physical Society. Proceedings, 1844–1866. Edinburgh, 1858–67. 3 Vols. 8vo.
—— Royal Society. Transactions. Edinburgh, 1788–1818. 8 Vols. in 10 4to.
—— Society for Promoting the Educa. of the Poor in Ireland. 1st Report. Edinburgh, 1815. 8vo. Educa. Pamph. Vol. 28.
—— Society for the Suppression of Beggars, etc. Report for 1815. Edinburgh, 1815. 8vo. Eng. Misc. Pamph. Vol. 18.
—— Views in Edinburgh and its Vicinity. Lond., 1820. 2 Vols. 8vo. Vol. 1.
EDMANDS, J. W. Speech in Cong., May 20, 1854, on the Kansas and Nebr. Bill. Congr. and Polit. Pamph. Vol. 93.
EDMEADS, Rev. W. National Establishment, National Security; or Thoughts on Commuting the Tithes. Lond., 1816. 8vo. Pamphleteer. Vol. 7.
EDMONDS, Francis, W. Defence in regard to his Connection with the Mechanics' Bank. N. Y., 1855. 8vo. N. Y. City Misc. Pamph. Vol. 5.
EDMONDS, J. W. Address on the Constitution and Code of Procedure of N. Y., 1848. Congr. and Polit. Pamph. Vol. 96.
EDMONSTON, Thos. Etymolog. Glossary of the Shetland and Orkney Dialect. Lond., 1866. 8vo. Pub. in "Trans. of Philolog. Soc." 1866.
EDMONDS, Geo. F. Speech in U. S. Senate, Apr. 14, 1871, on the 14th Amendment. Congr. and Polit. Pamph. Vol. 119.
—— See Vermont Hist. Soc.
EDMUNDSON, William. Journal of his Life, Travels, Suffering and Labors of Love in the Work of the Christian Ministry. 2d Ed. Lond., 1774. 8vo.
EDOM, The, of the Prophecies. From the London Quarterly for July, 1837. Waldies Circulating Libr. Vol. 10.
EDSON Genealogy. See NOYES, J.
EDUCATION. See ADAMS, J. Q. Discourse on.
—— American Annals of.
—— —— Educa. Year Book, 1858.
—— —— Institute of Instruction.
—— BACHE, A. D. Educa. in Europe.
—— BARNARD, H. Educa. & Employment of Children in Factories, &c.
—— Nat. Educa. in Europe.
—— BOTT, A. Prussian System of.
—— BOTTA, E. Educa. in Sardinia.
—— BOUTWELL, G. S. Educa. Topics.
—— British & Foreign Sch. Soc. Manual.
—— BROOKS, Rev. C. Moral Educa.
—— BUTLER, J. D. Incentives to Mental Culture.
—— CALTHROP, S. R. Lecture before Amer. Inst. of Instr., 1859.
—— CAMPBELL & HADLEY, Teacher's Miscellany.
—— Canada. Reports on.

EDUCATION. College of Teachers. Trans., 1834–40.
—— Common School Jour., 1839.
—— Common Schools in U. S. & Europe.
—— CRANDALL, Wm. L. Talks with the People of N. Y.
—— EMERSON, J.. Female Educa.
—— FOOTE, J. P. Schools of Cinncinnati.
—— FOSTER, B. F. Educa. Reform.
—— GEHANT, V. Le Livre des principes.
—— Hibernian School Soc.
—— HOYT, J. W. On University Progress.
—— In England. Recent Measures for the Promotion of Educa. Lond., 1839. 8vo. Strangford. Pamph. Vol. 17.
—— LIEBER, F., on Educa. and Crime.
—— MANSFIELD, E. D. Amer. Educa.
—— MAYHEW, I. Popular Educa.
—— MOLINEAUX, Maj. E. L. Physical & Military Exercises in Pub. Schools
—— National Convention, 1849.
—— National Tèachers Assôciation.
—— N. Y., Board of Education, and other States.
—— N. Y., Free School Society.
—— Of the Middle Classes. Oxford and Lond., 1862. 8vo. Educational Pamph. Vol. 37.
—— See OGDEN, John. Science of.
—— Ohio Journal of Education.
—— Ohio Teacher.
—— OLIVER, H. K. Lecture on Teacher's Morals, etc.
—— Papers for the Teacher.
—— PARSONS, E. Address on Education.
—— POWELL, Baden. Educa. Secular and Religious.
—— RANDALL, S. S. Mental Culture and Popular Educa.
—— READ, Danl. Address on, 1851.
—— SMITH, H. I. Hist. of.
—— Society for Promotion of Collegiate and Theol. Ed. at the West.
—— —— Promoting Man. Labor in Schools.
—— —— Support of Gaelic Schools. See Sup'ts Reports of Various States.
—— TAFT, C. P. The German University and the Amer. College.
—— TAPPAN, H. P. Dis. at Ann Arbor, 1858.
—— Thonghts on the Establishment of a Nat. University.
—— TREMENHEERE, H. S. Pub. Schools in U. S. and Canada, 1852.
—— TURNER, J. B. On Industrial Universities.
—— U. S. Dep't of Edca. Reports.
—— WAYLAND, F. Address before Amer. Instit. of Instruct, 1854.
—— WICKERSHAM, J. P. Education in Reconstruction.
—— Wis. Journ. of Educa.
—— Wis. Teachers' Assoc.
EDUCATIONAL Aphorisms and Suggestions, Ancient and Modern. From Barnard's Amer. Journ, of Educa. 1860. Hartford. n. d. 8vo. Educa. Pamph. Vol. 4.
—— Commission for Freedmen. 1st Ann. Report, 1863. Boston, 1863. 8vo. Rebell'n Pamph. Vol. 74.

EDWARD VI. See TYTLER, P. F. England under his Reign.
EDWARD, David B. Hist. of Texas; or Emigrants' and Farmers' Guide, with Map. Cincin. 1836. 12mo.
EDWARDS, A. Descriptive Gazetteer and Commercial Directory of Mississippi River. St Louis, 1866. 8vo.
EDWARDS, Brian. Thoughts on the Late Proceedings of Govt. respecting the Trade of the West India Islands with the U. S. 2d ed. Lond., 1784. 8vo.
EDWARDS, B. B. Inquiry into the State of Slavery in Ancient Greece. Edinburgh, 1835. 12mo. Hist. Pamph. Vol. 8.
EDWARDS' Business Directory of Wisconsin and Western States, 1868. Chicago, 1868. 8vo.
EDWARDS, David O. Proposal for an Agrarian Endowment in lieu of the Poor Law and Corn Law. Lond., 1846. 8vo. Eng. Polit. Pamph. Vol. 46.
EDWARDS, Edward. Memoirs of Libraries; including a Hand Book of Library Economy. Lond., 1859. 2 Vols. 8vo.
EDWARDS, Frank S. A Campaign in New Mexico with Col. Doniphan. Phila., 1848. 8vo. Mex. War Pamph. Vol. 1.
EDWARDS, Dr. Geo. Plan and Documents in reference to Universal Wealth. Abundance of Commerce, Arts, &c. Part I. Lond. 1819. 8vo. Eng. Polit. Pamph. Vol. 34.
EDWARDS, Henry. Colonization of Palestine. Lond., 1846. 12mo. Eng. Religious Pamph. Vol. 90.
—— "Union," the Patriot's Watchword at the Present Crisis. Manchester, 1842. 8vo. Eng. Polit. Pamph. Vol. 44.
EDWARDS, Isaac. Temperance Oration at Guilderland, N. Y. July, 4, 1844. 8vo. Addresses. Vol. 3.
EDWARDS, J., D. D. Temperance Manual. N. Y. n. d. 12mo. Temp. Pamph. Vol. 3.
EDWARDS, Rev. J. E. The Confederate Soldier; Memorial Sketch of Geo, N. and B. W. Harris, Privates in Confederate Army. N. Y., 1868. 12mo.
EDWARDS, John N. Shelby and his Men; or the War in the West. Cincin., 1867. 8vo.
EDWARDS, Rev. Jonathan. Life of the late Rev. David Brainerd, Missionary to the Indians. Boston, 1749. 12mo.
—— See MILLER, S. Life of.
—— Narrative of the Surprising Work of God, in the Conversion of Many Hundred Souls in Northampton, Mass. 2d ed. Lond., 1738. 12mo.
—— —— Another Copy. Worcester, 1832. 12mo.
—— Language of Muhhekaneew Indians. Mass. Hist. Soc. Coll. Vol. 10. 2d Ser.
—— —— Another Copy. Lond., 1789. 8vo.
EDWARDS, Dr. Justin. HALLOCK, W. A. Life and Labors.
EDWARDS, Rev. Morgan. Materials for a Hist. of the Baptists in R. Island. R. I. Hist. Soc. Coll., Vol. 6.
EDWARDS, N. W. Hist. of Ill., and Life and Times of Gov. Ninian Edwards. Springfield, 1870. 8vo.
EDWARDS, Richard.—See ST. LOUIS Agric. and Mech. Assoc.

EDWARDS, Wm. H. Voyage up the River Amazon, including a residence at Para. N. Y., 1847. 12mo.

EELLS, Sam'l. Oration before the Alpha Delta Phi Soc. of N. Haven, Aug. 15, 1839, on Social Advancement. Cincin., 1839. 8vo. Addresses, Vol. 37.

EFFECT of an Ordinance of Secession upon a State of the U. S., by which the same is adopted. n. d. Rebell'n Pamph., Vol. 18.

EFFECT of Secession on the Commercial Relations between the North and South. 1861. Rebell'n Pamph., Vol. 47.

EGGLESTON, Rev. N. H. Religion in Politics. Disc. before the Cong. Ch. in Madison, Wis., Nov., 1856. Madison, 1856. 8vo. Wis. Misc. Pamphlets, Vol. 4.

EGYPT.—See ABBOTT, H. Cat. of Egypt. Antiquities.
—— CURTIS, G. W. Nile Notes of a Howadji.
—— CURZON, R. Monasteries of the Levant.
—— DORR, Rev. B. Travels.
—— GLIDDON, G. R. Ancient Egypt.
—— KENRICK, J. Ancient Egypt, under Pharoahs.
—— MARTINEAU, H. Eastern Life.
—— MILLARD, D. Travels in Egypt and Holy Land.
—— MORTON, Dr. S. G. Ethnography of.
—— RUSSELL, M. Ancient and Modern Egypt.
—— SPENCER, J. A. Egypt and Holy Land.
—— THOMAS, J. Travels in.
—— WILKINSON, I. G. Thebes and Gen. View of Egypt.
—— WILSON, R. T. British Exped. to.

EGYPTIAN Monuments; a Series of Drawings, 5 Nos. Lond., n. d. oblong folio.
—— Mysteries and Religious Dogmas.—See FELLOWS, John.
—— Society. Rules and Regulations of. Alexandria, n. d. 8vo. Hist. Pamph., Vol. 19.

EGYPTIANS, Religion of.—See DOUGLAS, Rev. J.

EICHHORN, Prof. J. G. Life and Writings of John D. Michaelis. Edinburgh, 1835. 12mo. Eng. Misc. Pamph. Vol. 19.

EIGHTEENTH Century. See Literary Hist. of.
—— —— SCHLOSSER, F. C. Hist. of, to French Republic.

ELBA. Isle of. See Island Empire.

ELDER, Wm. Biography of Elias Kent Kane. Phila., 1858. 8vo.
—— Debt and Resources of the U. States; and the Effect of Secession upon Trade and Industry. Phila., 1863. 8vo. Rebellion Pamph. Vol. 108.
—— —— Same in German. Rebellion Pamph. Vol. 87.
—— How our National Debt can be paid. Phila., 1865. 8vo. Rebellion Pamph. Vol. 10.
—— How the Western States can become the Imperial Power in the Union. Phila., 1865. 8vo. Rebellion Pamph. Vols. 10, 41. Addresses. Vol. 15.
—— Lecture at Boston, on Emancipation. Phila., 1856. 8vo. Addresses. Vol. 17.
—— The Western States: their Pursuits and Policy. Phila., 1865. 8vo. Pamphlets. Vol. 14.

ELDON, Lord. See BENTHAM, J.
—— WELLESLEY, W. L. Two Letters to. 1827.
ELDORADO. See BULLFINCH, Thos. Oregon and. 1866.
ELDRIDGE, Chas. A. Speech in Cong., Apr. 12, 1864, on Resolution to Expel Mr. Long. Rebell'n Pamph. Vol. 9.
—— Speech in Cong., Dec. 10, 1867, on Confiscation. Rebell'n Pamph. Vol. 34.
—— Speech in Cong., Mar. 28, 1868, on Reconstruction in Alabama. Congr. and Polit. Pamph. Vol. 122.
—— Speech in Cong., June 9, 1870, on Naturalization and Immigration. Congr. and Polit. Pamph. Vol. 119.
—— Speech in Cong., Feb. 15, 1871, against the Bayonet at the Ballot Box. Congr. and Polit. Pamph. Vol. 129.
—— Speech in Cong., Feb. 26, 1873, on the Credit Mobilier. Washington, 1873. 8vo. Congr. and Polit. Pamph. Vol. 68.
ELECTRIC Communications. From Chambers' Papers for the People. n. d. 12mo.
ELECTRICITY. See BRAE A. E. Electrical Communica. in Railway Trains.
—— HALES, Chas. Theory of Electric Expulsion Examined.
—— HAÜY, Abbe. Theorie de l'Electricité.
—— HENRY, J. Contributions to Magnetism and E.
—— REID and BAIN. Elements of Chemistry and E.
—— See SHERWOOD, H. H., on Magnet. Organiza. of Human System.
ELECTRO-MAGNETISM. See GRIGLIETTA, C. Brief Essay on.
—— SILLIMAN, Benj. Davenport's Invention.
ELÉMENS d' Oryctologie ; ou Distribution Methodique des Fossiles. Neuchatel. 1783. 8vo.
ELEMENTS of Discord on Secessia. N. Y. 1863. 8vo. Rebell'n Pamph. Vols. 45, 90.
—— of Spanish and English Conversation. Mexico, 1847.
ELEUSINIAN Mysteries. See OUVAROFF. Essai sur les Mysteries D'Eleusis.
ELFORD, Sir Win. Remarks on the Obnoxious Parts of the Game Law. Lond., 1817. 8vo. 2d Ed. Pamphleteer. Vol. 10.
ELGIN, Lord. Letters to the Editor of the Edinburgh Review, on "The Remains of John Tweddell.". Lond., 1816. 8vo. Hist. Pamph. Vol. 16.
—— See WEST, Benj. Mem. on his Pursuits in Greece.
ELGIN, Ill., History of. From the Chicago Republican. Chicago, 1867. 8vo. Ill. Local Histories. Vol. 2.
—— Watch Factory. See RICHARDSON, A. D.
ELGIN, N. Y., Botanic Garden. See HOSACK, D.
ELIOT, Andrew. Letters to Thos. Hollis. 1766–1771. Mass. Hist. Coll. 4th Ser. Vol. 4.
—— Remarks on the Bishop of Oxford's Sermon on Episcopacy in the Colonies. 1741. Mass. Hist. Soc. Coll. 2d. Ser. Vol. 2.
ELIOT, Chas. Wm. See Harvard Coll.
ELIOT, Francis, P. Letters on the Polit. & Financial State of the Country. Lond., 1814. 8vo. Pamphleteer. Vols. 3, 4.
—— —— Same, Lond., 1815. Pamphleteer. Vol. 5.
—— —— " " 1816. " " 7.

ELIOT. John, D. D. Biograph. Dictionary, containing a Brief Acc. of the First Settlers, etc., of N. England. Boston, 1809. 8vo.
—— See DEARBORN, H. A. S. Sketch of Life of.
—— DUPONCEAU, Peter S. Notes on his Indian Grammar.
—— FRANCIS, C. Life of.
—— FREEMAN, Jas. Character of.
—— Hist. Acc. of. See Mass. Hist. Soc. Coll. Vol. 8. 1st Ser.
—— Papers respecting the Episcopal Controversy in Conn. 1722. Mass. Hist. Soc. Coll. 2d Ser. Vol. 2.
—— The Christian Commonwealth; or, The Civil Policy of the Rising Kingdom of Jesus Christ. Mass. Hist. Soc. Coll. 3d Ser. Vol 9.
—— The Day-Breaking, if not the Sun-Rising of the Gospel with the Indians of N. Eng. 1647. Mass. Hist. Soc. Coll. Vol. 5. 3d Ser.
—— The Glorious Progress of the Gospel amongst the Indians in N. Eng. Mass. Hist. Soc. Coll. Vol. 5. 3d Ser.
—— The Indian Grammar begun, etc. 1666. Mass. Hist. Soc. Coll. 2d Ser. Vol. 9.
ELIOT, Samuel A. Sketch of the Hist. of Harvard Coll., and of its Present State. Boston, 1848. 12mo.
ELIOT, Thomas D. Speech in Cong., June 3, 1862, on Representatives to Hayti and Liberia. N. Y., 1870. 8vo. Cong. and Polit. Pamph. Vol. 121.
—— Speech in Cong., Feb. 10, 1864, on Establishing a Bureau of Freedmen's Affairs. Rebellion Pamph. Vols. 9, 32.
ELIS, Alex. J. Three Pamphlets on Phonetics. Lond., 1849. 12mo. Educa. Pamph., etc. Vol. 39.
ELIZABETH, N. J. Christ Church. See HOFFMAN, Rev. E. A. Statistics and Ann. Address. 1856.
—— St. John's Church.
—— CLARK, S. A.
—— RUDD, J. C.
ELIZABETH, Queen. The Last End and Character of. Canadian Mag. Vol. 1.
—— Last Speech and Thanks to Her Last Parliament, after Her Delivery from the Popish Plots, etc., Nov. 30, 1601. Lond., 1679. Folio. Eng. Polit. Pamph. Vol. 1.
—— See Review of Prescott's Ferdinand and Isabella, and Queen Elizabeth.
—— Sketch of the Life of. n. d. 12mo. Biograph. Pamph. Vol. 3.
—— STRICKLAND, A. Queens of Eng.
—— WRIGHT, Thos. Queen Elizabeth and Her Times.
ELKHORN, Wis., Conservator. Magazine No. 1, with an Hist. Acc. of the Village. Elkhorn, 1857. 8vo.
—— Independent. Newspaper. Aug. 1857 to Dec. 1860 (bound with Delavan & Geneva. Papers.) Same 1861–73. Folio.
ELLENBOROUGH, Lord. See COCHRANE, Lord. Letter, &c.
—— India & Lord ELLENBOROUGH. 1844.
ELLERMAN, Chas. F. Sanitary Reform & Agricult. Improvement. Lond. 1848. 8vo. Strangford Pamph. Vol. 47.
ELLERY, Wm. See CHANNING, E. T. Life of.

ELLET, Chas. Army of the Potomac and its Mismanagement. Washington. 1851. 8vo. Rebell'n Pamph. Vols. 8 & 82.
—— Physical Geography of the Mississippi Valley, and the Improvement of the Ohio and other Rivers. Smithson. Contrib. Vol. 2.
—— Military Incapacity and what it costs the Country. 1862. 8vo. Rebell'n Pamph. Vols. 38, 82.
ELLET, CHAS. Jr. Remarks on the Wheeling Bridge Suit. 1852. Phila. 1852. 8vo. Penn. Misc. Pamph. Vol. 2.
—— Report on a Suspension Bridge across the Potomac, addressed to Mayor and Council of Georgetown. Phila. 1852. 8vo. Pamph.
—— The Mississippi and Ohio Rivers; containing Plans for the Protection of the Delta from Inundation. Phila. 1853. 8vo.
ELLET, Mrs. E. F. Domestic History of Amer. Revolntion. N. Y. 1850. 12mo.
—— Pioneer Women of the West. N. Y. 1854. 12mo.
—— The Queens of Amer. Society. 5th Ed. N. Y. 1870. 8vo.
—— Women of the Amer. Revolution. 6th Ed. N. Y. 1854. 3 Vols. 12mo.
—— Women Artists in all Ages and Countries. N. Y. 1859. 12mo.
ELLICOTT, Andrew. Journal 1796–1800; with Acc. of the Determination of the Boundary between the U. States and the Possessions of His Catholic Majesty in America. Phila. 1803. 4to.
—— Miscell. Observations relative to the Western part of Penn. Amer. Philos. Soc. Trans. Vol. 4.
ELLICOTT'S MILLS, Md. See TYSON, Martha. Hist of.
ELLIOT, Adam. Modest Vindica. of Titus OATES. Lond. 1682. Folio. Eng. Polit. Pamph. Vol. 2.
ELLIOT GENEALOGY. From N. E. Hist. Register. Genealog. Pamph. Vol. 1.
ELLIOT, J. H. Credit in the Life of Commerce; being a Defense of of the British Merchant, &c. Lond. 1845. 8vo. Eng. Polit. Pamph. Vol. 45.
ELLIOT, Rob't. Specimen of Bishop Burnet's Posthumous History. Lond. n. d. 3d. Ed. Eng. Rel. Pamph. Vol. 10.
ELLIOTT, Chas. Boileau.—Letters from the North of Europe; or a Journal of Travels in 1830. Waldie's Circulating Libr. Vol. 2.
ELLIOTT, Chas. W.—N. England History, from the Discovery by the Northmen, A. D. 986, to A. D. 1776. N. Y., 1857. 2 Vols. 8vo.
ELLIOTT, E. B.—International Coinage. n. p. 1869. 8vo. Banking and Currency Pamph. Vol. 3.
ELLIOTT, E. B. Letters on the Credit of the U. S. Govt., addressed to the Sec. of the Treasury. 2 Pamphlets. Washington, 1872. 8vo. Congr. and Polit. Pamph. Vol. 129.

ELLIOTT, Com. Jesse D.—Biograph. Notice of, containing a Review of the Controversy between him and the late Com. Perry. Phila., 1835. 12mo.

—— Speech in Hagerstown, Md., Nov, 14, 1843. Phila., 1844. 8vo. Pamphlets, War of 1812. Vol. 5.

ELLIOTT, Jonathan.—Debates, Resolutions, and other Proceedings, in Cönvention, on the Adoption of the Federal Constitution, in 1787. Washington, 1827. 8vo. Vol. 1.

—— Same. 2d Ed. Washington, 1854. 8vo. 4 Vols.

ELLIOTT, Rev. Stephen.—Addresses at Savannah Med. Coll., 1853. Savannah, 1853. 8vo. Med. Pamph., Vol. 2.

—— COHEN, Solomon.—Eulogy on. 1867.

—— A High Civilization the Moral Duty of Georgians. Disc. before the Georgia Hist. Soc., Feb. 12, 1844. Savannah, 1844. 8vo. Ga. Hist. Soc. Pamph.

—— Reply to a Resolution of the Georgia Hist. Soc., read before the Society Feb. 12, 1866. Savannah, 1866. 8vo. Ga. Hist. Soc. Pamph.

ELLIOTT, Thos. B.—Address before the Wis. Legislature, Feb., 1856, in behalf of the Insane of the State. Madison, 1856. 8vo. (Bound with Message and Docs.)

ELLIS, Mr.—New Britain. Narr. of a Journey to a Country on the Vast Plain of the Missouri, inhabited by a People of British Origin. Lond., 1820. 8vo.

ELLIS, Mrs.—A Voice from the Vintage, or the Force of Example. N. Y., 1843. 8vo. Temp. Pamph., Vol. 3.

ELLIS, Albert G.—Acc. of the Advent of the N. Y. Indians into Wisconsin. Wis. Hist. Soc. Coll., Vol. 2.

—— The "Upper Wisconsin" Country. Wis. Hist. Soc. Coll., Vol. 2.

ELLIS, Alex J.—Early English Pronunciation, with especial reference to Shakspeare and Chaucer, Pub. in "Philolog. Soc. Trans." 1869, '70.

—— The Ethnical Alphabet, or Alphabet of Nations. Bath. n. d. 8vo. Strangford Pamph., Vol. 49.

—— Two Alphabets in Phonetic Characters. Lond., 1849. 12mo.

ELLIS, Chas. M.—Hist. of Roxbury, Mass. Boston, 1847. 8vo. Mass. Hist. Discourses, etc. Vol. 14.

—— The Power of the Commander-in-Chief to declare Martial Law and decree Emancipation, as shown from B. R. Curtis. Boston, 1862. 8vo. Congr. and Polit. Pamph., Vol. 125.

ELLIS, Edw. S.—Life of Pontiac the Conspirator, with Acc. of the Siege of Detroit. Lond., 1861. 12mo. Indian Pamph., Vol. 3.

—— Life and Times of Col. Dan'l Boone. N. Y. n. d. 12mo.

—— Life of Tecumseh, the Shawnee Chief. N. Y., 1861. 12mo. Indian Pamph. Vol. 3.

ELLIS, Rev. Geo. E. Introduct. Disc. in Harvard Ch., Charleston, Mar. 15, 1840. Boston, 1840. 8vo. Sermons. Vol. 28.

—— Disc. in Harvard Ch., Charlestown, Mar. 12, 1865, on 25th Annivers. of his Ordination. Charlestown, 1865. 8vo. Mass. Hist. Discourses Vols. 8 & 16.

ELLIS, Rev. Geo. E. 50th Annivers. Disc. in New South Ch., Boston, Dec. 25, 1864. Boston, 1865. 8vo. Boston Hist. Disc. Vol. 1.

—— Life of Wm. Penn. Sparks' Amer. Biog.. 2d Ser. Vol. 12.

—— Disc. at Charlestown, Mass., Feb. 22, 1857, on Washington. Charlestown, 1857. 8vo. Sermons. Vol. 3.

—— Life of Anne Hutchinson; with a Sketch of the Antinomian Controversy in Mass. Sparks' Amer. Biog. 2d Ser. Vol. 6.

—— Life of John Mason of Conn. Sparks' Amer. Biog. 2d Ser. Vol. 3.

—— Memoirs of Jared Sparks, LL. D. Mass. Hist. Soc. Proceed., 1867–69.

—— Memoir of Luther V. Bell, M. D. Mass. Hist. Soc. Proceed., 1863–64.

—— The Nation's Ballot & its Decision: Disc. at Cambridgeport, Nov. 13, 1864. Boston, 1864. 8vo. Sermons. Vol. 37.

ELLIS, Sir Henry. Gen. Introduction to the Domesday Book. Lond., 1833. 2 Vols. 8vo.

ELLIS, Henry. Voyage de la Baye de Hudson fait en 1746 et. 1747, pour la Decouverte du Passage de Nord-Ouest Paris, 1749. 2 Vols. 12mo.

ELLIS, Rev. John. Topograph. Descrip. of Topsham, Lincoln Co., Maine. Mass. Hist. Soc. Coll. 1st Ser. Vol. 3.

ELLIS, Dr. Rufus. Last Sermon preached in First Church, Boston, May 10, 1868. With Appendix. Boston, 1868. 8vo. Boston Hist. Discourses Vol. 1.

—— Memoir of Hon. Sam'l Howe. Boston, 1850. 12mo. Biograph. Pamph. Vol. 5.

ELLIS, Thos. Metropolitan Sewage; or the Conversion of Lord Torrington. Lond., 1863. (?) 8vo. Eng. Misc. Pamph. Vol. 10.

ELLIS, Thos. T. Leaves from the Diary of an Army Surgeon. N. Y., 1863. 12mo.

ELLIS, Wm. L. Hurtspierpoint; its Lords and Families. Lond. n. d. 8vo.

—— Notices of the Ellises, of England, Scotland and Ireland, from the Conquest to the Present Time. Pr. printed. Lond., 1866. 8vo.

—— Plea for the Antiquity of Heraldry; with an Attempt to expound its Theory. 1853. 8vo.

ELLSWORTH, E. E. Manual of Arms for Zouave Cadets. Chicago, 1861. 18mo.

ELLSWORTH, Henry L. Improvements in Agriculture, Arts, &c., of the U. States. N. Y., 1843. 8vo. Agricult. Pamph. Vol. 1.

ELLSWORTH, Henry W. Valley of the Upper Wabash, Indiana, with Hints on its Agricult. Advantages. N. Y., 1838. 12mo.

ELMER, Ebenezer. Jour. of an Expedition to Canada in 1776. N. J. Hist. Soc. Proceed. Vols. 2, 3.

ELMER, L. Q. C. Constitution and Govt. of the Province and State of N. Jersey; with Biograph. Sketches of Governors, 1776 to 1845, and Reminiscences of the Bar for Half a Century, forming Vol. 7, N. J. Hist. Soc. Coll. Newark, 1872. 8vo

ELMES, Jas. The Fine Arts in relation to Architecture. Letter to Thos. Hope. Lond., 1814. 8vo. Pamphleteer. Vol. 3.
ELMORE, F. H. See Addresses in Cong. on his Death.
ELOQUENCE. See GRIMKE, T. S. Grecian & Amer.
—— MOORE, Frank. Amer. Eloquence.
—— WILLISTON, E. B. Eloquence of U. S. See Speeches, &c.
ELRINGTON, Rev. Chas. R. Suggestions to the Clergy concerning Nat. Educa. in Ireland. Dublin, 1847. 8vo. 4th Ed. Educa. Pamph. Vol. 32.
ELSE, Dr. Jos. Essay on the Cure of Hydrocle, &c. Lond., 1770. Med. Pamph. Vol. 24.
ELTON, Romeo. Life of Roger Williams, the Earliest Legislator and True Champion of Liberty of Conscience. Providence, 1853. 12mo.
—— Literary Remains of Dr. Jona. Maxcy. N. Y., 1844. 8vo.
—— Memoir of John Callender, and Notices of some of his Contemporaries. R. I. Hist. Soc. Coll. Vol. 4.
ELWES, John. See Collection of Interesting Biography. 1791.
—— TOPHAM, Edwd. Life of.
ELY, Alfred. Journ. while a Prisoner of War at Richmond. N. Y., 1862. 12mo.
EMANCIPATION and its Results. N. Y. n. d. Rebell'n Pamph. Vol. 19.
EMBARGO Act. See PICKERING, J. Corres. with Gov. Sullivan.
—— —— Letter of, respecting.
—— —— Speech on, in U. S. Senate 1808.
—— Reasons of Gov't for Laying an Embargo.
—— Reply of Majority of Representatives of Mass. in Cong., &c. 1808.
—— SULLIVAN, Gov. See AMER. War, 1812.
EMERSON, Rev. Brown. Semi-Centen. Disc. in South Ch., Salem, Mass., Apr. 24, 1855; with Appendix. Boston, 1855. 8vo. Salem Hist. Disc., Vol. 2.
—— Sermon in South Ch., Salem, Mass., on the 38th Anniver. of his Ordination. Salem, 1843. 8vo. Salem Hist. Discourses. Vol. 2.
—— Another copy. Sermons, Vol. 7.
EMERSON, G. Cotton in the Middle States, with Directions for its Easy Culture. Phila., 1862. Rebell'n Pamph., Vol. 72.
EEERSON, Geo. B. Hist. and Design of the Amer. Institute of Instruction. Boston, 1849. 12mo. Educa. Pamph., Vol. 6.
—— Moral Education. Lecture before the Amer. Institute of Instruction. 1842. Boston, 1842. 8vo. Educa. Pamph., Vol. 7.
EMERSON, Jos. Address at 10th Annivers. of Beloit Coll., Wis. Beloit, 1857. 8vo. Beloit Coll. Pamph.
—— Address before the Archæon Union of Beloit Coll., Feb. 28, 1862. Beloit, 1862. 8vo. Beloit Coll. Pamph.
—— Female Education. A Disc. at the Dedica. of the Seminary Hall in Saugus, Jan. 15, 1822. Boston, 1822. 8vo. Educa. Pamph., Vol. 3.
EMERSON, Ralph Waldo. From the Continental Monthly, Jan., 1862. Biograph. Pamph., Vol. 11.

EMERSON, Ralph Waldo. Histor. Disc. at 2d Centen. Celebra. at Concord, Mass., Sept. 12, 1835. Concord, 1835. 8vo. Mass. Hist. Discourses, Vol. 8.

—— Oration before the Literary Societies of Dartmouth Coll., July 24, 1838. Boston, 1838. 8vo. Dart. Coll. Pamph.

—— Representative Men. Boston, 1850. 12mo.

EMERSON'S Magazine. Oct., 1857, to Dec., 1858, inclusive. Vols. 5, 6, 7. N. Y. 8vo.

EMERY Family.—See D'AMERIE.

EMERY, Robt. "About Jamaica;" its Past, Present and Future. Lond., 1844? 8vo. Pamphlets—West Indies, &c.

EMERY, S. H. Ministry of Taunton, Mass., with an Introduction by Francis Baylies. Boston, 1853. 2 Vols. 8vo.

EMIGRANTS, The, Guide, or Pocket Geography of the Western States and Territories. Cincin., 1818. 18mo.

EMIGRATION.—See BROMWELL, W. J., Hist. of, to the U. S. 1819–55.

—— MARCUS, M. Address on.

—— N. Y. Commiss'rs' Reports, and other State Reports.

—— STURZ, J. J. Suggestions for Encouragement of.

—— CHICKERING, J. Immigra. in U. S. 1848.

—— To America, canidly considered, in a Series of Letters, from a Resident to his Friend in England. Lond., 1798. Sm. 8vo. bound with Williamson's Genesee Country.

—— See U. S. Sec. of Interior. Reports of Commiss'r of Emigration.

—— WILLIS, W. On the Scotch and Irish Emig. to Maine.

EMMET Monument, N. Y. Report in relation to. N. Y., 1833. 12mo. N. Y. City Misc. Pamph. Vol. 5.

EMMET, Thos. Addis. See MADDEN, R. R. Life of.

—— Memoir of. N. Y., 1829. 12mo. Biograph. Pamph. Vol. 16.

EMMITSBURG, Md. See Mount St. Mary's College.

EMMONS, D., M. D. Description of some of the Bones of the Zeuglodon Cetoides of Prof. Owen. n. d. 8vo. Scientific Pamph. Vol. 42.

—— Strictures upon the Report of Select Comm. on the State Work on Nat. Hist. n. d. 8vo. N. Y. Misc. Pamph. Vol. 5.

EMMONS, Nathan'l., D. D. See WILLIAMS, Thos. Obit. Sermon, 1840.

EMORY, W. H. See Fremont, J. C.

—— Notes of a Military Reconnoissance from Fort Leavenworth, Mo., to San Diego, Cal. Washington. 1848. 8vo.

—— Paper on the Mexican Boundary. Amer. Geograph. and Statistical Society Bulletin. Vol. 1.

EMPEROR'S ANSWER (The) to the French Kings' Manifesto, 1688. Lond., 1688. Sm. 4vo. Eng. Polit. Pamph. Vol. 7.

ENCKE'S Comet. Report on Observations during its Return in 1871. By Profs. Hall and Harkness. Washington. 1872. 4to.

ENCYCLOPEDIA, American: A Popular Dict. of Arts, Sciences, Literature, History, etc. Phila., 1835. 13 Vols. 8vo.

—— Brittanica: A Dict. of Arts, Sciences and General Literature. 8th Ed. Edinburgh, 1860. 21 Vols., and one Vol. Index. 4to.

ENCYCLOPEDIA Perthensis: or Universal Dict. of Arts, Sciences, Literature, etc., 370 maps and plates. Edinburgh, 1816. 23 Vols. 8vo.

—— See Amer. Cyclopedia.

—— Chambers, W. & R.

—— COOLEY, A. J. Cyclo. of Prac. Receipts.

—— DUYCKINCK, E. A. & G. L. Cyclo. of Amer. Literature.

—— Edinburgh Encyclo.

—— FROST, J. Pict. Family Encyclo.

—— KNIGHT, C. Cyclo. of Industry.

—— Netherlands Encyclo.

—— REES, A. Cyclo.

—— WILLICH, A. F. M. Domestic Encyclo.

ENCYCLOPEDIE Dictionaire Universal Raisonne. Yverdon. 142 Vols. 4to.

END, (The) of the Irrepressible Conflict by a Merchant of Phila. Phila., 1860. 8vo. Congr. and Polit. Pamph. Vol. 100.

ENDECOTT, Gov. John. Memoirs of. N. E. Hist. and Gen. Register. Vol. 1.

ENDERBY, Chas. Our Money Laws the Cause of the National Distress. Lond., 1847. 8 vo. Strangford Pamph. Vol. 45.

—— Redress of National Grievances. Lond., 1859. 8vo. Eng. Polit. Pamph. Vol. 57.

—— The Auckland Islands—their Climate, Soil and Productions. Lond., 1849. 8vo. Strangford Pamph. Vol. 51.

ENDICOTT, Chas. M. Account of Leslie's Retreat at Salem, Feb. 26, 1775. Salem, 1856. 8vo. Rev. War Pamph. Vol. 2.

—— History of the Salem and Danvers Aqueduct. Essex Institute Collections. Vol. 2.

—— Narr. of the Piracy and Plunder of the Ship Friendship of Salem, near Sumatra, Feb., 1831. Essex Institute Colls. Vol. 1.

ENFIELD, N. H. Topograph. Descrip. of. N. H. Hist. Soc. Coll. Vol. 1.

ENGLAND and Napoleon III. The Truth on the Italian Question. Lond., 1860. 8vo. Eng. Polit. Pamph. Vol. 58.

—— Army of. List of Officers of Army and Marines. 1794, 5, 9, 1801, 3, 6, 8, 9. Lond., 1794–1809. 8 Vols. 8vo.

—— Bank of. See G. Britain—House of Commons. Reports from Secret Comm. 1819.

—— —— G. Britain—House of Lords· Reports of Secret Comm. 1819.

—— —— PAYNE, D. B. Address to Proprietors of Bank Stock.

—— —— Representation agreed upon by the Directors, May 20, 1819. London. 8vo. Pamphleteer. Vol. 14.

—— BANKS, See Sir T. C. Baronia Anglica. Concentrata.

—— Collections of Papers relating to the Present Juncture of Affairs, 1688, 1689. Lond., 1688, '9. 12mo. Eng. Polit. Pamph. Vol. 7.

—— See Commercial Policy of Eng. and Germany. 1845.

—— Constitution of. See CREASY, E. S. Rise and Progress of the.

—— —— Disraeli, Vindica. of. 1835.

ENGLAND, Constitution of. DYER, G. Four Letters on.
—— County Families of. See TYMMES S. Family Topographer of Eng. Counties. WALFORD, Edw.
—— Co. Genealogies. See BERRY, W. Berkshire, Buckingham, Surrey, Kent and Hants.
—— See Criminal Trials of.
—— Education. See RICHSON, C. Pauper Educa. considered. 1850.
—— —— Recent Measures for the Promotion of. Lond., 1839. 8vo. Strangford Pamph. Vol. 17.
—— Enslaved by her own Slave Colonies. Lond., 1823. 8vo. Eng. Mis. Pamph. Vol. 4.
—— History of. See Con -Test. 1756–57.
—— —— DE LARREY, M. Hist. of. 1728.
—— —— DE PEYSTER, J. W. Hist. of Carcausius.
—— —— DONNE, W. B. Corres. of Geo. 3d and Lord North.
—— —— See English Histor. Soc.
—— —— FISHER, Geo. Companion and Key to Eng. Hist. 1832.
—— —— FROISSART, J. Chronicles of Eng. etc.
—— —— FROUDE, A. Hist. from Fall of Wolsey to Death of Elizabeth.
—— —— GEORGE, J.W. H. Hist. of Rebellion. 1685.
—— —— GRANGER & NOBLE. Biograph. Hist.
—— —— G. Britain—State Papers and Chronicles.
—— —— Greatest of the Plantagenets.
—— —— HALLIWELL, J. O. Letters of Kings of England.
—— —— HANSARD, T. C. Parliamentary Hist. of. 1066–1803.
—— —— HUME, D. Hist. from Invasion of Caesar to 1688.
—— —— JESSE, J. H. Hist. of Pretenders.
—— —— Junius. Letters, etc.
—— —— KEIGHTLEY, T. Hist. to 1839.
—— —— KNIGHT, C. Hist. from B. C. 55 to A. D. 1867.
—— —— LAPPENBERG, J. M. Eng. under Anglo-Saxon and Norman Kings.
—— —— LINGARD, John. Hist. from Roman Invasion to 1688.
—— —— LODGE, E. Illustra. of British Hist.
—— —— MACAULAY, T. B. Hist. from Accession of Jas. II.
—— —— MANCHESTER, Duke of. Court and Society.
—— —— POLWHELE, Rev. R. Letters of Cromwell, Chas. II., etc.
—— —— RAPIN, P. Hist. 1722.
—— —— —— Abridg't of Hist. 1747.
—— —— RUSSELL, P., and PRICE, O. England Displayed. 1769.
—— —— RUSSELL, W. A. New Hist.
—— —— ST. JOHN, J. A. Hist. of the Four Conquests.
—— —— Salmasius—Defenso Regia pro Carolo I.
—— —— Sarcastic Notes on the Long Parliament.
—— —— STRICKLAND, A. Tales of Eng. Hist.
—— —— —— Queens of England.
—— —— TURNER, S. Hist. of, from the Earliest Period through the Reign of Elizabeth.
—— —— TYTLER, P. F. Reign of Edward VI and Mary.
—— —— WACE, Master. Chronicles of Norman Conquest.
—— —— WRIGHT, Thos. Essays on the History of, in Middle Ages.

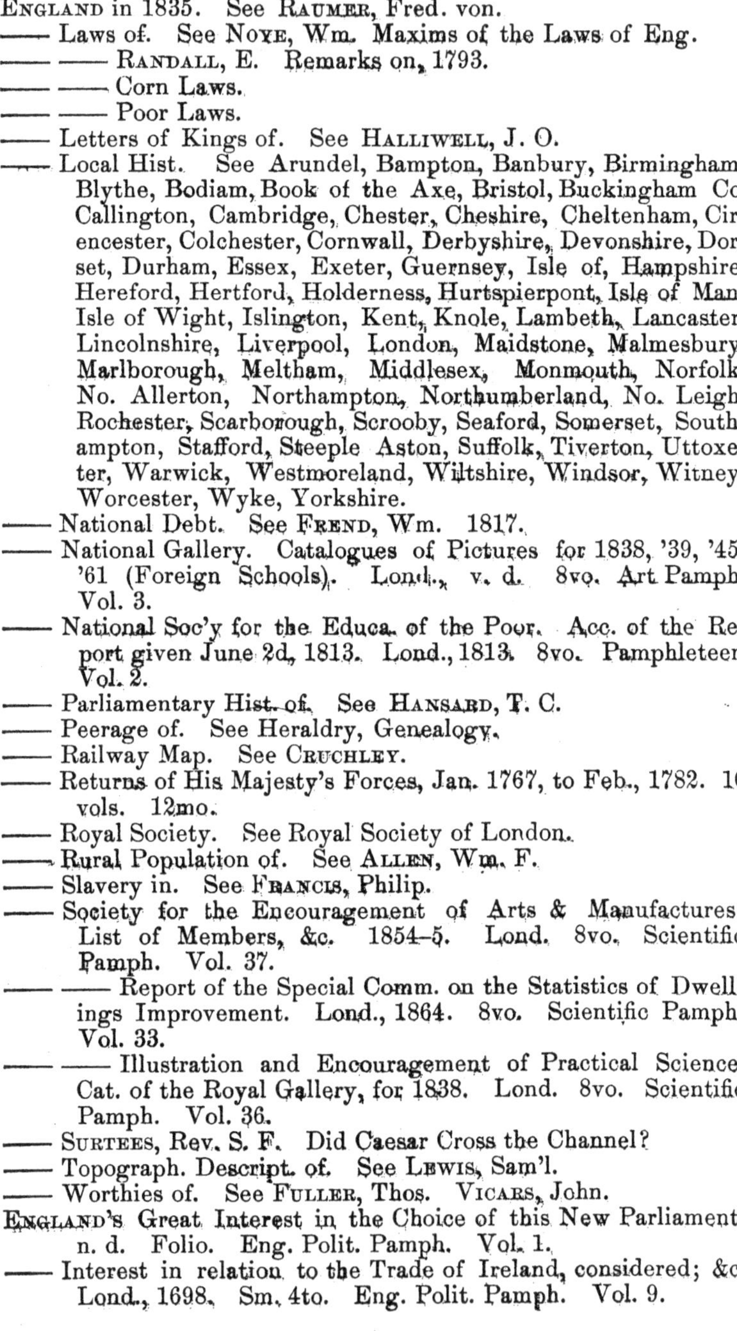

ENGLAND in 1835. See RAUMER, Fred. von.
—— Laws of. See NOYE, Wm. Maxims of the Laws of Eng.
—— —— RANDALL, E. Remarks on, 1793.
—— —— Corn Laws.
—— —— Poor Laws.
—— Letters of Kings of. See HALLIWELL, J. O.
—— Local Hist. See Arundel, Bampton, Banbury, Birmingham, Blythe, Bodiam, Book of the Axe, Bristol, Buckingham Co, Callington, Cambridge, Chester, Cheshire, Cheltenham, Cirencester, Colchester, Cornwall, Derbyshire, Devonshire, Dorset, Durham, Essex, Exeter, Guernsey, Isle of, Hampshire, Hereford, Hertford, Holderness, Hurtspierpont, Isle of Man, Isle of Wight, Islington, Kent, Knole, Lambeth, Lancaster, Lincolnshire, Liverpool, London, Maidstone, Malmesbury, Marlborough, Meltham, Middlesex, Monmouth, Norfolk, No. Allerton, Northampton, Northumberland, No. Leigh, Rochester, Scarborough, Scrooby, Seaford, Somerset, Southampton, Stafford, Steeple Aston, Suffolk, Tiverton, Uttoxeter, Warwick, Westmoreland, Wiltshire, Windsor, Witney, Worcester, Wyke, Yorkshire.
—— National Debt. See FREND, Wm. 1817.
—— National Gallery. Catalogues of Pictures for 1838, '39, '45, '61 (Foreign Schools). Lond., v. d. 8vo. Art Pamph. Vol. 3.
—— National Soc'y for the Educa. of the Poor. Acc. of the Report given June 2d, 1813. Lond., 1813. 8vo. Pamphleteer. Vol. 2.
—— Parliamentary Hist. of. See HANSARD, T. C.
—— Peerage of. See Heraldry, Genealogy.
—— Railway Map. See CRUCHLEY.
—— Returns of His Majesty's Forces, Jan. 1767, to Feb., 1782. 10 vols. 12mo.
—— Royal Society. See Royal Society of London.
—— Rural Population of. See ALLEN, Wm. F.
—— Slavery in. See FRANCIS, Philip.
—— Society for the Encouragement of Arts & Manufactures. List of Members, &c. 1854–5. Lond. 8vo. Scientific Pamph. Vol. 37.
—— —— Report of the Special Comm. on the Statistics of Dwellings Improvement. Lond., 1864. 8vo. Scientific Pamph. Vol. 33.
—— —— Illustration and Encouragement of Practical Science. Cat. of the Royal Gallery, for 1838. Lond. 8vo. Scientific Pamph. Vol. 36.
—— SURTEES, Rev. S. F. Did Caesar Cross the Channel?
—— Topograph. Descript. of. See LEWIS, Sam'l.
—— Worthies of. See FULLER, Thos. VICARS, John.
ENGLAND'S Great Interest in the Choice of this New Parliament. n. d. Folio. Eng. Polit. Pamph. Vol. 1.
—— Interest in relation to the Trade of Ireland, considered; &c. Lond., 1698. Sm. 4to. Eng. Polit. Pamph. Vol. 9.

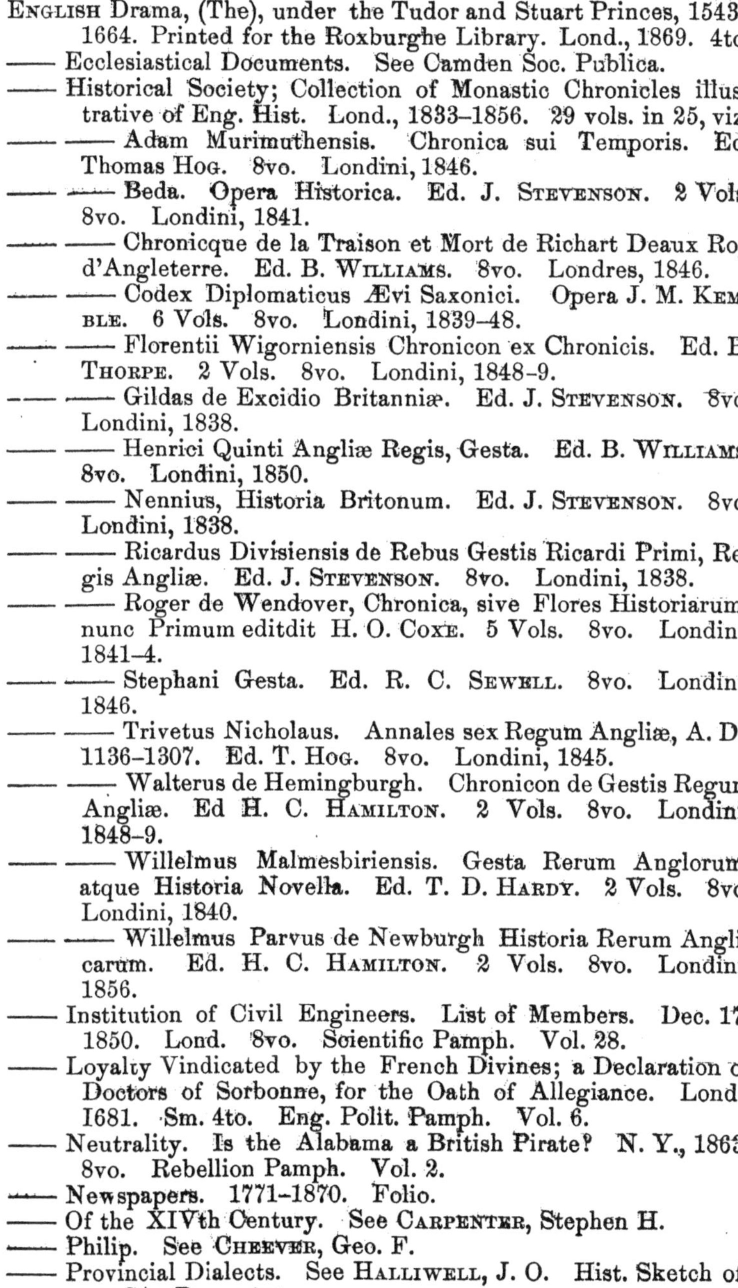

ENGLISH Drama, (The), under the Tudor and Stuart Princes, 1543–1664. Printed for the Roxburghe Library. Lond., 1869. 4to.
—— Ecclesiastical Documents. See Camden Soc. Publica.
—— Historical Society; Collection of Monastic Chronicles illustrative of Eng. Hist. Lond., 1833–1856. 29 vols. in 25, viz:
—— —— Adam Murimuthensis. Chronica sui Temporis. Ed. Thomas HOG. 8vo. Londini, 1846.
—— —— Beda. Opera Historica. Ed. J. STEVENSON. 2 Vols. 8vo. Londini, 1841.
—— —— Chronicque de la Traison et Mort de Richart Deaux Roy d'Angleterre. Ed. B. WILLIAMS. 8vo. Londres, 1846.
—— —— Codex Diplomaticus Ævi Saxonici. Opera J. M. KEMBLE. 6 Vols. 8vo. Londini, 1839–48.
—— —— Florentii Wigorniensis Chronicon ex Chronicis. Ed. B. THORPE. 2 Vols. 8vo. Londini, 1848–9.
—— —— Gildas de Excidio Britanniæ. Ed. J. STEVENSON. 8vo. Londini, 1838.
—— —— Henrici Quinti Angliæ Regis, Gesta. Ed. B. WILLIAMS. 8vo. Londini, 1850.
—— —— Nennius, Historia Britonum. Ed. J. STEVENSON. 8vo. Londini, 1838.
—— —— Ricardus Divisiensis de Rebus Gestis Ricardi Primi, Regis Angliæ. Ed. J. STEVENSON. 8vo. Londini, 1838.
—— —— Roger de Wendover, Chronica, sive Flores Historiarum; nunc Primum editdit H. O. COXE. 5 Vols. 8vo. Londini, 1841–4.
—— —— Stephani Gesta. Ed. R. C. SEWELL. 8vo. Londini, 1846.
—— —— Trivetus Nicholaus. Annales sex Regum Angliæ, A. D., 1136–1307. Ed. T. HOG. 8vo. Londini, 1845.
—— —— Walterus de Hemingburgh. Chronicon de Gestis Regum Angliæ. Ed H. C. HAMILTON. 2 Vols. 8vo. Londini, 1848–9.
—— —— Willelmus Malmesbiriensis. Gesta Rerum Anglorum, atque Historia Novella. Ed. T. D. HARDY. 2 Vols. 8vo. Londini, 1840.
—— —— Willelmus Parvus de Newburgh Historia Rerum Anglicarum. Ed. H. C. HAMILTON. 2 Vols. 8vo. Londini, 1856.
—— Institution of Civil Engineers. List of Members. Dec. 17, 1850. Lond. 8vo. Scientific Pamph. Vol. 28.
—— Loyalty Vindicated by the French Divines; a Declaration of Doctors of Sorbonne, for the Oath of Allegiance. Lond., 1681. Sm. 4to. Eng. Polit. Pamph. Vol. 6.
—— Neutrality. Is the Alabama a British Pirate? N. Y., 1863. 8vo. Rebellion Pamph. Vol. 2.
—— Newspapers. 1771–1870. Folio.
—— Of the XIVth Century. See CARPENTER, Stephen H.
—— Philip. See CHEEVER, Geo. F.
—— Provincial Dialects. See HALLIWELL, J. O. Hist. Sketch of.
—— —— See PHILOLOGY.

ENGLISH Universities. In the N. Amer. Review. An Essay. Albany, 1854. 8vo. Educa. Pamph. Vol. 3.
ENGLISHWOMAN in America. See MAURY, S. M.
—— In Russia; Impressions of Society and Manners of the Russians at Home, by a Lady. N. Y., 1856. 12mo.
ENLOE Mining Property. Geological Report by B. F. Shumard. St. Louis, 1867. 8vo. Mo. Misc. Pamph. Vol. 1.
ENQUIRY into the Alienation of the Delaware and Shawanese Indians. Lond. 1759. Phil'a, reprint. 8vo.
—— Into the Causes of Popular Discontents in Ireland. Dublin. 1805. 8vo. Eng. Polit. Pamph. Vol. 76.
—— Into the Measures of Submission to the Supreme Authority, &c. n. d. Sm. 4to. Eng. Misc. Pamph. Vol. 1.
—— Into the Origin of Disease, &c. Lond. 1859. 8vo. Med. Pamph. Vol. 27.
—— Into Present System of Medical Educa. Albany. 1830. 8vo. Med. Pamph. Vol. 5.
ENTAIL; its History & Influence. See BEALE, Jas.
ENTICK, John. Gen. Hist. of the Late War in Europe, Asia, Africa and America. Lond. 1763. 5 Vols. 8vo.
ENTOMOLOGY. See AGASSIZ, Louis, on the Classifica. of Insects.
—— FITCH, A. Noxious Insects of N. Y.
—— HARRIS, T. W. Insects Injurious to Vegeta.
—— HOY, P. R. Insects Injurious to Agriculture.
—— JAEGER, B. N. Amer. Insects.
—— LE BARON, Wm. Noxious Insects of Illinois.
—— LE CONTE, J. L. The Coleoptera of Kansas & N. Mexico.
—— LEWIS, W. G. Cateehism of.
—— Nat. Hist. of Insects.
—— WESTWOOD, J. O. Address before Entomolog. Soc. of Lond. 1835.
EPHESUS. See AKERMAN, J. Y. Coins of Ephesus.
EPHRATA, Penn. See CONYNGHAM, R. Settlement of the Dunkers.
EPISCOPACY in Connecticnt. 1722. See ELIOT, John.
—— In the Colonies. 1741. See ELIOT, Rev. Andrew.
EPISCOPAL CHURCH. See Protestant Episcopal Ch.
EPITAPHS. See ALDEN, Tim. Coll. of Amer. Epitaphs. 1814.
—— BARTON, W. S. Epitaphs from Worcester Common. Mass.
—— BOOTH, J. Metrical Epitaphs. 1868.
—— See Baltimore, Cambridge.
—— CANSICK, F. P. Coll. of. from St Pancras. Ch.
—— See Dorchester, Mass.
—— HARRIS, W. T. & E. D. Watertown, Mass., Epitaphs.
—— NEVE, John Le. Inscriptions, &c. 1700–1715.
—— NORFOLK, H. E. Gleanings in Grave Yards.
—— WEBB, T. Select Collection of.
EPPS, Dr. John. Counteraction Viewed as a Means of Cure, &c. Lond. 1832. 8vo. Med. Pamph. Vol 24.
EPSOM, Eng. Description of. Lond. 1711. 12mo. Guide-Books. Vol. 11.
EPSOM, N. H. See CURTIS, Rev. J. Hist. Sketch of.

EQUALITY as Consistent with the British Constitution. Dialogue between a Manufacturer and his Workman. Lond. 1792. 8vo. Eng. Polit. Pamph. Vol. 24.
— of All Men before the Law claimed and defended; in Speeches by Kelley, Phillips, and Douglas. Boston, 1865. 8vo. Congr. and Polit Pamph. Vol. 71.
— the Constitution. Lond., 1819. 8vo. Pamphleteer. Vol. 14.
ERICSSON'S Caloric Engine. Description of the Trial Excursion, Jan. 18, 1853. N. Y., 1853. 8vo. Congr. and Polit. Pamph. Vol. 56.
ERIE CANAL. See BARTON, J. L. Commerce of the Lakes, &c., 1847.
— Congress. Reports on Surveys of Routes for the Canal. 1837–38. N. Y. Misc. Pamph. Vol. 8.
— See Considerations on the Great Western Canal. 1818.
— Letter from the Sec. of War, on the Construction of the Canal. 1836. Washington, 1836. 8vo. N. Y. Misc. Pamph. Vol. 8.
— See PROSSER, E. S. Enlargement of the Locks on.
— Remarks on the Importance of the contemplated Canal. 1814.
— WATSON, E. Hist. of.
— WRIGHT, B. H.
ERIE County, N. Y. Proceedings of Board of Supervisors for 1871. Buffalo, 1872. 8vo. N. York Miscell. Pamph. Vol. 6.
ERIE Pa., Academy, Catalogue for, 1846. Erie, 1847. 8vo.
— County, Penn. See SANFORD, L. G. Hist. of.
ERRORS of the British Minister in the Negotiation with the Court of Spain. Lond., 1790. 8vo. Eng. Polit. Pamph. Vol. 23.
ERSKINE, D. See CANNING, Sec. Geo. Corres. with,
ERSKINE, Lord. Appeal to the People of G. Britain, on the Subject of Confederate Greece. Lond., 1824. 8vo. Pamphleteer. Vol. 23.
— Sketch of the Character of the late Lord Erskine. Lond., 1824. 8vo. Pamphleteer. Vol. 23.
— Speech in the House of Lords, Mar. 8, 1808, against the Legality of the Orders in Council. Lond., 1808. 8vo. Eng. Polit. Pamph. Vol. 29.
— See Speeches of, &c.
— The Defences of the Whigs. Lond., 1820. 8vo. Pamphleteer. Vol. 15.
ERSKINE. Capt. Robt. On the alleged Conduct and Treatment of John Crookshanks. Lond., 1759. 8vo. Eng. Polit. Pamph. Vol. 70.
ERSKINE, Hon. Thos. See PAINE, T. Letter Respecting the Prosecution of Thos. Williams.
— Speech at Guildhall, Dec. 18, 1793, on the Liberty of the Press. Edinburgh, 1793. 12mo. Eng. Polit. Pamph. Vol. 25.
— Speech at Westminster, June 24, 1797, in the Cause of the King vs. Williams, for Publishing Paine's Age of Reason. Lond. 8vo. Eng. Rel. Pamph. Vol. 28.
— View of the Causes and Consequences of the Present War with France. Phila., 1797. 8vo. 10th ed. London, 1797. 8vo. Congr. & Polit. Pamph. Vol. 96.

ESCANO. Gen. Don Antonio. Quadrado. Elogio Historico.
ESCHENBURG, J. J. Manual of Classical Literature translated, with additions by N. W. Fiske. Phila., 1836. 8vo.
—— —— Same. 4th ed. Phila., 1854. 8vo.
ESOPUS War. 1663. See KREGIER, Martin.
ESPINASSE, Isaac. Letter to Members of the New Parl't on Defects in the Gen. Statute Law. Lond., 1827. 8vo. Law Pamph. Vol. 17.
ESPY, Prof. Jas. P. Introduction to his Theory of Storms. No title. Scientific Pamph. Vol. 13.
—— Second, Third and Fourth Reports on Meteorology made to the Sec. of the Navy, with charts. Washington, 1850;'57. oblong. 4to.
ESPY, Josiah. Tour in Ohio, Kentucky, and Indiana Terr., in 1805. Ohio Valley Hist. Miscellanies.
ESQIMAUX Bay. See DAVIES, W. H. A. Notes on, etc.
—— Indians in Greenland. See Kaladit Okalluktualliat.
ESSAY on Crimes and Punishments, translated from the Italian. Edinburgh, 1778. 12mo.
—— on Matter. Phila., 1784. 8vo. Scientific Pamph. Vol. 40.
—— on the Credibility of Swedenborg. 2d Ed. Lond., 1835. 12mo.
—— on the Inequality of our Present Taxes. Lond., 1746. 8vo. Eng. Misc. Pamph. Vol. 24.
—— on the Interests and Resources of the Empire of the King of G. Britain and Ireland, etc. Dublin, 1783. 8vo. Eng. Polit. Pamph. Vol. 21.
—— on the Origin and Progress of Government. Lond., 1785. 8vo. Eng. Polit. Pamph. Vol. 22.
—— on the Relation of Cause and Effect, controverting the Doctrine of Mr. Hume. Lond., 1824. 8vo.
—— on the Usefulness of Mathematical Learning. Lond., 1745. 8vo. 3d Ed. Educa. Pamph. Vol. 28.
—— toward Instruction for the Indians by the Bishop of Sodor and Man. Lond., 1754. 12mo.
—— towards an Indian Bibliography. Catalogue of Books on Amer. Indians, in the Library of Thos. W. Field. N. Y., 1873. 8vo.
ESSAYS. ADDISON, J. Spectator. See ALISON, A. Miscell. Essays.
—— BACON, F. Essays.
—— BAYNE, Peter. Essays in Biography and Criticism.
—— BEATTIE, C. On Truth, etc., and Moral Dissertations.
—— British Essayists.
—— BROUGHAM, Lord. Dissertations, etc.
—— COBB, J. B. Leisure Labors.
—— Critical Social Essays.
—— DANA, R. H. Prose Writings.
—— FOSTER, J. Essays.
—— GILMER, F. W. Sketches and Essays.
—— HAMILTON, Eliz'th. Popular Essays.
—— JONES, W. A. Essays on Authors, etc.
—— LANMAN, C. Essays for Summer Hours.

ESSAYS. MASCERES, Baron. Polit. and Hist. Essays.
—— SHARP, Richd. Letters and Essays.
—— on the Present Crisis, in the Condition of the Amer. Indians. Boston, 1829. 8vo.
—— on Political Organization: published by the Union League of Phila. Phila., 1868. 8vo. Congr. Polit. Pamph. Vol. 126.
—— PRESCOTT, W. H. Biog and Crit. Miscell.
ESSEX, Earl of. How he Killed himself in the Tower of London, July 13, 1683. Lond., 1683. Fol. Eng. Polit. Pamph. Vol. 2.
ESSEX, Robt., Earl of. Arraignment, Trial and Condemnation of, etc., Feb. 19, 1600. Lond., 16?9. Folio. Eng. Polit. Pamph. Vol. 1.
ESSEX, Co., Eng. See CLARKE, C. Poem in Essex Dialect.
—— WRIGHT, Thos. Hist. and Topog. of 1836.
—— Archaeolog. Society. Transactions. Vols. 1–4. Colchester, 1858–69. 4 vols, 8vo. & part 1, Vol. 5. 1870.
—— See LETHIEULLIER, T. Antiq. of Co. Essex. 1747.
ESSEX Co. Mass., Agricult. Soc'y. Premiums awarded in 1825, and List of Premiums offered in 1826. Salem. 1826. 8vo.
—— Agricult. Essays. Danvers. 1847. 8vo.
—— —— See CABOT, J. S. Address. n. d.
—— —— Reports of committees, etc., for 1829 & 1830. Pamphlets. Vol. 6.
—— —— See SALTONSTALL, L. Address. 1843.
—— —— Transactions for 1849. Boston. 1849. 8vo.
—— —— Trustees Account of the Cattle Show, etc., 1820. Salem. 1821. 8vo
—— Mass. Declaration by its Delegates assembled in Conven. at Ipswich, July 21, 1812. Salem, 1812. 8vo. Congr. & Polit. Pamph. Vol. 123.
—— Natural History Society. Journal. Vol. 1. Salem, 1836, 8vo. 3 Nos.
—— —— Journal. 1836–1852. Salem. 1852. 8vo.
—— See SPALDING, S. J. Contribu. to Eccles. Hist. 1865.
—— View of Jurisdiction of Court of Probate.
—— N. J. Soc. for Promo. of Agriculture. Constitution. 1845. Newark. 12mo. Agr. Pamph. Vol. 7.
—— N. Y. Military & Civil Hist. See WATSON, W. C.
ESSEX INSTITUTE. Act of Incorporation. Constitution and By-Laws. Salem. 8vo. 1855.
—— —— See BRIGGS, G. W. ENDICOTT, C. M. FELT, J. B. GOODELL, A. C. PHIPPEN. G. D. RANTOUL, R. S. STONE, L. R. UPHAM, C. W.
—— —— Historical Collections. Vols. 1–10. Salem. 1859–1869.
—— —— Hist. Notice of; with By-Laws, etc. Salem, 1856. 8vo.
—— —— Proceedings. Vols. 1, 2, 3. Salem. 1856, 58, 64. 8vo.
ESSEX, Mass. See CROWELL, R. Hist. of.
—— FELT, J. B. Hist. of
—— NEWHALL, J. R. Essex Memorial.

ESSEX, Mass. Valuation of Essex for 1853, and Auditor's Rept. Mar. 1854.
—— Vt. See BUTLER, L. C. Memorial Record of. 1866.
ESTES, L. C, Antiquities on the Banks of the Mississippi River & Lake Pepin. Smithsonian Report. 1866.
ESTRADA, D. Alvaro F. Representation to Ferdinand VII, King of Spain, in Défence of the Cortes. Lond., 1819. 8vo. Pamphletéer. Vol. 14.
ESTVAN, B. War Pictures from the South. N. Y. 1863. 12mo.
'ETAT Present de la Pensilvanie, ou l'on trouve le detail de ce quis'y est passi' depuis la de faite du Gen. Braddock jusqu'a' la prise d'Oswego. Paris, 1756. 12mo.
ETHERIAL INTONATIONS. pertaining to an Initiation into the Mysteries of the O. E. O. 1001. Janesville, 1850. 8vo. Wis. Misc. Pamph. Vol. 8.
ETHERIDGE, E. Speech in Cong., May 17, 1854, on the Kansas and Nebr. Bills. Congr. and Polit. Pamph. Vol. 93.
ETHERIZATION in Surgery, etc. See Anaesthetics.
ETHICS. See Moral Philosophy.
ETHIOPIA. See HARRIS, W. C. Highlands of.
ETHNICAL PHILOSOPHY. See MACINTOSH, Sir, J.
ETHNOGRAPHY. See HAYDEN, F. V. Indian Tribes of Missouri River.
—— MORTON, Dr. S. G. On Egyptian Ethnog.
ETHNOLOGY. See Amer. Ethnolog. Soc. Antiquities.
—— ARNOLD and SAMUELS. The Living World.
—— BARTLETT, J. R. Progress of.
—— CALDWELL, C. Unity of the Human Race.
—— EWBANK, T. The Position of our Species.
—— FEULING, J. B. Place of Indian Languages in the Study of.
—— HALE, Wm. H. Origin and Primal Condition of Man.
—— JOHNES, A. J. Philolog. Proof of the Unity of Human Race.
—— LANGTON, John. Paper on Skulls.
—— LUBBOCK, Sir John. Social and Religious Condition of the Lower Races of Man.
—— LUNT, Rev.Wm. P. Lecture before the Quincy Lyceum, 1850.
—— MATILE, G. A. On the Study of.
—— MEIGS, J. A. Human Crania.
—— MORGAN, L. H. Systems of Consanguinity.
—— MORTON, S. G. Catalogue of Skulls.
—— —— Crania Americana.
—— NOTT & GLIDDON. Indigenous Races.
—— —— Types of Mankind.
—— RETZIUS, A. Form of the Human Skull.
—— SIMON, Mrs. Ten Tribes identified with Aborigines.
—— WILLIAMS, J. Essays.
—— WILSON, Danl. Lectures on.
—— WOOD, J. G. Uncivilized Races of Men.
ETNA, Mt. See JOHNSON, S. L. Ascent of.
ETON, Eng. College. List of, 1853. Eton. 12mo. Hist. Pam. Vol. 18.
—— Remarks on the Present Studies and Management of Eton School. Lond., 1834. 8vo. Educa. Pamph. Vol. 35.

EULER, Leonard. Letters on Natural Philosophy, with Notes and a Memoir by David Brewster. Harpers' Fam. Lib. N. Y., 1858. 2 Vols. 18mo.

EUROPE and America, in 1839. Lond., 1839. 8vo. Strangford Pamph. Vol. 23.

—— History of, etc. See ALISON, A., History of 1789–1852.

—— —— Annals of Europe. 1739–43.

—— —— BARBER, J. W., European Hist. Collections.

—— —— ENTICK, J. Hist. of Late War, in.

—— —— EVERETT, A. H. Gen. Survey of.

—— —— FROISSART, Sir John. Chronicles etc.

—— —— KOCH, C. W. Hist. of Revolution in Europe.

—— —— Memoirs of Present State of. 1692–3.

—— —— PRADT, M. de. Europe, after Congress at Aix La Chalette.

—— —— Present State of. 1692, 1704, '57.

—— —— RUSSELL, W., Hist. of Mod. Europe.

—— —— UNGEWITTER, F. H. Past and Present Condition.

—— —— ZIMMERMAN, E. A. W. Polit. Survey.

—— Travels in. See BELTRAMI, Pilgrimage in. 1828.

—— —— BROWN, W. W. Sketches of Places, etc., abroad.

—— —— COLMAN, H. European Life and Manners.

—— —— COPWAY, G. Running Sketches.

—— —— COX, S. S. Buckeye abroad.

—— —— DERBY, E. H. Two Months Abroad in 1843.

—— —— DORÉ.

—— —— ELLIOTT, C. B. Letters from the North. 1830.

—— —— FIELD, H. M. Summer Pictures, etc.

—— —— OSSOLI, Margaret Fuller. At Home and Abroad.

—— —— SILLIMAN, B. Visit to Europe. 1851.

—— —— SMITH, J. J. Summer Jaunt across the Water.

—— —— TAYLOR, B. Views Afoot.

—— —— WILLIS, N. P. Pencillings by the Way.

EUROPEAN Agriculture. See COLMAN, H.

—— Magazine and Lond. Review. 1782 to 1823. Lond. 84 vols. 8vo.

EUSTACE, Maj. Gen. J. S. Exile of Maj.-Gen. Eustace, a Citizen of the U. S., from G. Britain, by order of the Duke of Portland. Lond., 1797. 8vo. Hist. Pamph. Vol. 6.

EUSTAPHIEVE, M. The Resources of Russia in the Event of a War with France. Lond., Reprinted, 1812. 8vo. Hist. Pamph. Vol. 7.

EUSTIS, Dr. Wm. Letter on the Assassination Plot in N. Y., in 1776. With notes by Rev. E. F. Slafter. Boston, 1869. 8vo. N. York Hist. Discourses, etc. Vol. 4.

EUSTIS, Gov. Wm. See SHARP, Rev. Danl. Obit. Sermon. 1825.

EVANGELICAL Alliance. See KING, Rev. Dr. Hist. Sketch of.

—— —— M'NEILE. Rev. Hugh. Reasons for not joining the. 1846.

—— —— Statement of Proceedings at Liverpool, etc.

—— —— British Organization. Report presented to the Conference at London, Oct., 1855. Lond., 1856. 8vo. Eng. Regious Pamph. Vol. 57.

EVANGELICAL Biography; Lives of Eminent Christians. Vols. 2, 3, 4. Lond., 1807. 8vo.

—— Lutheran Ch.—Hartwick Synod. Minutes of Ann. Sessions of 1851, '52, '56, '64, '66, '67. Albany, N. Y., 1851–'67. 8vo.

—— ——Synod of N. York. Minutes of the 3d & 4th Ann. Sessions. Albany, 1869, 70. 8vo.

—— —— Ministerium—N. York,&c. Minutes of the 55th, 61st, 66th, 67th, 68th, 70th, Synods, held in 1850–1865. Albany, 1850–1865. 8vo.

EVANS, Maj. Gen. De Lacy. Claims of Naval Officers to Honorary Distinctions: Speeches in House of Commons, June 21, 1849. Lond. 8vo. Eng. Misc. Pamph. Vol. 31.

EVANS, Geo. Speech in the U. S. Senate, Mar. 17 & 18, 1842, on the Tariff. Washington, 1842. 8vo. Cong. & Polit. Pamph. Vol. 24.

—— Speech in Cong. March 9 and 10, 1846, on the Oregon Bill. Washington, 1846. 8vo. Speeches. Vol. 1.

EVANS, Geo. W. Geographical, Histor. & Typograph. Descrip. of Van Diemen's Land. Lond., 1822. 8vo. Hist. Pamph. Vol. 18.

EVANS, James C. Letter to Lord Lyndhurst, on the Dissenters' Chapels Bill. Lond., 1844. 8vo. 3d Ed. Strangford. Pamph. Vol. 35.

EVANS, Gov. John. Reply to a Report on the Massacre of the Cheyenne Indians. Denver, 1865. 8vo. Colorado Misc. Pamph. Vol. 1.

EVANS, John. The Coins of the Ancient Britons; with Engravings. Lond., 1864. 8vo.

EVANS, Lewis. Analysis of Map of Middle British Colonies in America; with Map. Phila., 1755. 4to.

EVANS, Sebastian. Sonnets on the Death of the Duke of Wellington. Cambridge, 1852. 8vo. Strangford. Pamph. Vol. 63.

EVANSVILLE, Wis. Citizen and Review. Newspaper. Evansville, 1866–70. Folio.

—— Seminary Catalogues for 1864–5, 1866–7. Janesville. 8vo.

EVARTS, Jeremiah. See WOODS, Leonard. Obit. Sermon. 1831.

EVARTS, W. M. Speech at Auburn, N. Y., Oct. 16, 1860. Rebellion Pamph. Vol. 77.

EVELIN, Geo. See STREETER, Sebastian F.

EVENING Schools and District Libraries. An Appeal to Philadelphians. Phila., 1850. 8vo. Phila. Misc. Pamph. Vol. 1.

EVENTS in the Indian History, Acc. of American Indians, Biographies of Chiefs, &c. Phila., 1842. 8vo.

EVERARD, Edmund. Depositions, &c., concerning the Popish Plot. Lond., 1679. Folio. Eng. Polit. Pamph. Vol. 63.

EVERETT, A. H. America; or a Gen. Survey of the Polit. Situation of the several Powers of the Western Continent. Phila., 1827. 8vo.

—— Europe; or a Gen. Survey of the Present Condition of the Principal Powers. Boston, 1822. 8vo.

—— Life of Joseph Warren. Spark's Amer. Biog. 1st Ser. Vol 10.

—— Life of Patrick Henry. Spark's Amer. Biog. 2d Ser. Vol. 1.

EVERETT, Edw. Address at Charlestown, Mass., Aug. 1, 1826, in Commemora. of John Adams and Thos. Jefferson. Boston, 1826. 8vo. Addresses, Vol. 24.

—— Address at the Consecration of the Nat. Cemetery at Gettysburg, Nov. 19, 1863, with other exercises. Boston, 1864. 8vo. Rebellion Pamph. Vol. III.

—— Address at Fanueil Hall, Oct. 19, 1864. Boston, 1864. 8vo. Rebell'n Pamph. Vol. 8.

—— Address at Lexington, Apr. 19, (20th) 1835. Charlestown, 1835. 8vo. Addresses, etc. Vol. 24.

—— Address at N. Y., July 4, 1861. N. Y., 1861. 8vo. Rebell'n Pamph. Vols. 61, 68.

—— Address before Amer. Coloniza. Soc., Jan. 18, 1853. 8vo. Addresses. Vol. 1. Congr. and Polit. Pamph. Vol. 85.

—— Address before Amer. Institute, N. Y., Oct. 14, 1831. 8vo. Addresses. Vol. 10.

—— Address before Boston Union Club, Apr. 9, 1863. Rebell'n Pamph. Vol. 36.

—— Address before N. Y. State Agr. Soc., at Buffalo, Oct. 9, 1857. Albany, 1857. 8vo. Addresses. Vol. 20. Agr. Pamph. Vol. 12.

—— Address in the Academy of Music, N. Y., July 4, 1861. N.Y., 1861. 8vo. Addresses. Vol. 27.

—— Address (in connection with Gov. J. A. Andrew and Others), Aug. 27, 1862, at Boston, in Aid of Recruiting. Addresses. Vol. 9.

—— See Amer. Antiq. Soc.

—— Boston. Thursday Eve. Club. Proceedings on his Death, 1865.

—— See DANA, R. H.

—— Disc. at Inaugura. of Dudley Observatory, Aug. 28, 1856. Albany, 1856. Scientific Pamph. Vol. 1.

—— Eulogy on J. Q. Adams, at Boston, Apr. 15, 1848. Boston, 1848. 8vo. Addresses. Vol. 31.

—— Eulogy on Thos. Dowse, of Cambridgeport, before the Mass. Hist. Soc., Dec. 9, 1858. Boston, 1859. 8vo.

—— See HOLT, J. On the Present Crisis.

—— The Discovery and Colonization of America; Lecture before the N. Y. Hist. Soc., June 1, 1853. Boston, 1853. 8vo. N. Y. Hist. Soc. Addresses. Vol. 3.

—— —— See also Addresses and Orations. Vol. 1.

—— Life of Gen. Geo. Washington. N. Y., 1860. 12mo.

—— Life of John Stark. Spark's Amer. Biog. 1st Ser. Vol. 1.

—— See Mass. Hist. Soc.

—— Memoir of John Lowell, Jr.; delivered at Boston, Dec. 31, 1839. Boston, 1840. 8vo. Biograph. Pamph. Vol. 6.

—— The Monroe Doctrine; with a Letter from John Q. Adams on the same Subject, 1869. Rebell'n Pamph. Vols. 15 and 90.

—— See N. Eng. Hist. Gen. Soc. Tribute to.

—— Oration at Battlefield of Gettysburg, Nov. 19, 1863. 2 Editions. Rebell'n Pamph. Vol. 81.

EVERETT, Edw. Oration at Boston, July 4, 1860. Rebell'n Pamph. Vol. 99. Addresses. Vol. 2.
—— Oration at Cambridge, before the Soc. of Phi Beta Kappa, Aug. 27, 1824. Addresses. Vol. 11.
—— Oration at Charlestown, June 17, 1850, on the 75th Annivers. of the Battle of Bunker Hill; with Acc. of the Celebra. Boston, 1850. 8vo. Addresses. Vol. 24.
—— Oration at Dorchester, Mass., July 4, 1855, at the Dorchester Festival. Boston, 1855. 8vo. Mass. Hist. Discourses. Vol. 7.
—— —— Another Copy. Addresses. Vol. 3.
—— Oration at Plymouth, Mass., Dec. 22. 1824. Boston, 1825. 8vo. Addresses. Vol. 9.
—— Orations and Speeches on Various Occasions. Boston, 1836. 8vo.
—— Remarks at the Plymouth Festival, Aug. 1, 1853. Boston. 8vo. Addresses, etc. Vol. 4.
—— Remarks at Fanueil Hall, July 4, 1853. 8vo. Addresses, etc. Vol. 3.
—— Speech in Support of the Memorial of Harvard, Williams, and Amherst Colleges, at Boston, Feb. 7, 1849. Cambridge, 1849. 8vo. Addresses, etc. Vol. 30.
—— Speech at Danvers, Oct. 9, 1856, in honor of Geo. Peabody. Boston. 8vo. Addresses. Vol. 6.
—— Speech, Mar. 21, 1853, in U. S. Senate, on the Cent. Amer. Treaty. Speeches. Vol. 5.
—— Speech in U. S. Senate, Feb. 8, 1854, on the Nebr. and Kansas Bill. Washington, 1854. 8vo. Speeches. Vol. 3. Congr. and Polit. Pamph. Vol. 93.
—— See Tribute to Memory of.
—— WARREN, G. W. Address before Bunker Hill Monument Assoc., 1865.
—— and Others. Remarks in U. S. Senate, Mar. 14, 1854, on the Memorial of the N. Eng. Clergy, against the Nebraska Bill. Congr. and Polit. Pamph. Vol. 139.
EVERETT, Edw. F. Genealogy of the Everett Family. Boston, 1860. 8vo. From N. Eng. Register, July, 1860. Genealog. Pamph. Vol. 11.
EVERETT Genealogy. See EVERETT, E. F.
EVERETT, Rev. O. C. Report of the Ministry at Large in Charlestown, Mass. Charlestown, 1854. 12mo. Mass. Misc. Pamph. Vol. 4.
EVERETT, R. L. Why the Malt Tax should be repealed. Leicester, 1864. 8vo. Eng. Polit. Pamph. Vol. 60.
EVERY Man his own Law Maker; or the Englishman's Guide to Parl. Reform. Lond., 1785. 8vo. Eng. Polit. Pamph. Vol. 22.
—— his own Lawyer. Lond., 1765. 8vo.
EWBANK, Thos. Aboriginal Ingenuity; the Tepiti. N. Y.? 1865. 8vo. Indian Pamph. Vol. 5.
—— Cursory Thoughts on some National Phenomena. N. Y. n. d. Scientific Pamph. Vol. 13.
—— Descript. and Hist. Acc. of Hydraulic and other Machines for Raising Water. N. Y., 1847–8. 8vo.

EWBANK, Thos. Inorganic Forces destined to supersede Amer. Slavery. N. Y., 1860. 8vo. Scientific Pamph. Vol. 11.

—— N. American Rock-writing and other Aboriginal Modes of Recording and Transmitting Thought. Morrisania, 1866. 8vo. Archaeolog. Pamph. Vol. 1.

—— —— See also Hist. Magazine. Vol. 10.

—— The Position of our Species in the Path of its Destiny. n. d. Scientific Pamph. Vol. 11.

—— The World a Workshop; Physical Relationship of Man to the Earth. N. Y., 1855. 12mo.

EWER, Rev. T. C. Disc. on the National Crisis, at N. Y., May 5, 1861. Rebell'n Pamph. Vol. 71.

"EWING Investigation." Report of Select Comm. of U. S. House of R., 1850. Congr. Pamph. Vol. 41.

EWING, Andrew. Oration at Memphis, Jan. 8, 1859, on the Inaugura. of the Bust of Gen. Andrew Jackson. Nashville, 1859. 8vo. Addresses. Vol. 31.

EWING, Presley. Speech in Cong., Apr. 24, 1852, on the Homestead Bill. Congr. and Polit. Pamph. Vol. 83.

EWING, Thos. Letter to Gov. Stanton, on the Conduct of the Battle of Shiloh. Columbus, O., 1862. 8vo. Rebell'n Pamph. Vol. 48.

—— Speech in U. S. Senate, Feb. 17 and 20, 1832, on the Tariff. Congr. and Polit. Pamph. Vol. 92.

—— Speech in U. S. Senate, Jan. 7, 1851, on Removals from Office. Congr. and Polit Pamph. Vol. 89.

—— Speech in Cong., Jan. 13, 1854, on Tariff. Washington, 1854. 8vo. Speeches. Vol. 3.

—— See STANTON, B. Letter in Reply to, 1862.

EWING, Gen. Thos., Jr. Speech at Convention of Union Soldiers and Sailors at N. Y., 1868. Rebell'n Pamph. Vol. 57.

EWING, Wm. Remarks in Tenn. Legisla., Dec. 5, 1859, on Slavery. Congr. and Polit. Pamph. Vol. 85.

EXAMEN des Recherches Philosophique sur America l'Amerique, et les Americains et de la Defense de cet Ouvrage. Berlin, 1771. 2 Vols. 18mo.

EXAMINATION into the Principles, Conduct, and Designs of the Minister. Lond., 1783. 8vo. Eng. Polit. Pamph. Vol. 20.

—— of Mr. Cobbett's Objections to the Bill for the Relief of the Unitarians. Lond., 1813. 8vo. Pamphleteer. Vol. 2.

—— of Precedents and Principles on Impeachments. Lond., 1790. 8vo. Eng. Polit. Pamph. Vol. 23.

—— of the Currency Question. Lond., 1830. 8vo. Strangford Pamph. Vol. 6.

—— of the President's Reply to the N. Haven Remonstrance. N. Y., 1801. 8vo. Congr. and Polit. Pamph. Vol. 123.

—— of the Pretensions of N. England to Commercial Pre-eminence. Phila., 1814. 12mo.

—— of the Scruples of those who refuse to take the Oath of Allegiance. Lond., 1689. Small 4to. Eng. Religious Pamph. Vol. 7.

EXAMINER (The) Examined; or Logic Vindicated. Addressed to the Junior Students of Oxford. Oxford, 1809. 8vo. Eng. Misc. Pamph. Vol. 26.

EXCLUSION (The) of the Queen from the Liturgy considered. Lond., 1821. 8vo. Pamphleteer. Vol. 18.

EXCURSION through the U. States and Canada during 1822–3. Lond., 1824. 8vo.

—— to the Highlands of N. Hampshire and Lake Winnipiseogee. Andover, 1833. 12mo.

EXECUTIVE Patronage. See Congress'l Speeches.

—— Policy. See Congress'l Speeches.

—— Power. See CURTIS, B. R. Davis Resolutions, 1862.

—— —— ELLIS, C. M.

—— —— SHATTUCK, G. O. Reply to Curtis.

—— —— WHITING, Wm. War Powers of the President.

EXETER, Eng. See BRITTON, J. Cathderal Ch. at, 1826.

EXETER College, Eng. Vindica. of the Soc. of Exeter Coll., in reply to Dr. W. King and Others. Lond., 1755. 4to. Eng. Polit. Pamph. Vol. 4.

EXETER, N. H. See NASON, E. Record of Events in 1862, and Names of Soldiers.

—— SMITH, Jere. Address at 2d Centen. Celebra.

—— TENNEY, Dr. S. Topograph. Descript. of.

EXILES in Virginia; with Observa. on the Conduct of the Soc. of Friends during the Rev. War: comprising the Gov't Official Papers, 1777–78. Phila., 1848. 8vo.

—— of Floridà. See GIDDINGS, J. R.

EXODUS of the Western Nations. See BURY, Viscount.

EXPEDIENCY (The) of Securing our Amer. Colonies by Settling the Country adjoining the Mississippi and the Country upon the Ohio, considered. Edinburgh, 1763. 8vo. MS. Copy.

EXPLANATION of a Map of the Federal Lands between Penn., West Line, and the Rivers Ohio and Scioto, and Lake Erie. Salem, 1787. 12mo.

EXPOSITION of the Case of the Assistant Surgeons of the Royal Navy. Lond., 1850. 8vo. 3d Ed. Med. Pamph. Vol. 25.

—— of the Causes and Character of the Late War with G. Britain. Lond., reprint, 1815. 8vo.

EXPOSURE of Misstatements and Misrepresentations contained in Mr. Marryatt's Pamphlet on the Slave Trade. Lond., 1816. 8vo. Eng. Misc. Pamph. Vol. 27.

EXTRACT from a MSS. Coll. of Annals relative to Virginia. Washington, 1838. 8vo. Force's Hist. Tracts. Vol. 2.

EXTRACTS from the Report of His Majesty's Commiss'rs for Inquiring into the Administration of the Poor Laws, 1834. Boston, 1835. 8vo. Congr. and Polit. Pamph. Vol. 104.

EXTRAIT du Livre d'Or de la R. Loge de Temple de Minerve. Paris, 1829. 8vo.

EXTRAMURAL Sepulture. Report on a Gen. Scheme, presented to Parliament, 1849. Lond., 1850. 8vo. Eng. Misc. Pamph. Vol. 31.

EXTRA Official State Papers, addressed to Lord Rawdon, on Promoting the Prosperity of the British Empire. Lond., 1789. 8vo.

EYRE, John. The Christian Spectator; being a Journey from England to Ohio, Travels in America, etc. Albany, 1832. 16mo.

F.

FABENS, Jos. W. Facts about Santo Domingo, with Map. 1862. Rebell'n Pamph. Vol. 75.

FABER, M. Sketches of the Internal State of France. Phila., 1812. 12mo.

FABER, Hector. Canadian Literature. Read before the Quebec Lit. and Hist. Soc., Mar. 21, 1866, (in French.) Transactions. N. Ser. Part 4.

FACTORY System of England. Observations on. Lond., 1844. 8vo. Strangford Pamph. Vol. 37.

FACTS and Documents relating to Ex Parte Councils held at Rehoboth, Nov., 1825. Providence, (n. d.) 8vo. Mass. Hist. Discourses, etc. Vol. 1.

—— and Figures from the Standpoint of a Departmental Clerk. 1867. Rebell'n Pamph. Vol. 15.

—— and Reasons why a Convention should be called to Revise the Constitution. Boston, 1852. 8vo. Mass. Misc. Pamph. Vol. 1.

—— Concerning the Freedmen; their Capacity and their Destiny. 1863. Rebell'n Pamph. Vol. 75.

—— for the People. Nos. 1 and 2. Gov. Barstow on Know-Nothingism, etc. Two Campaign Documents. 1855. Wis. Misc. Pamph. Vol. 1.

—— —— A Dem. Campaign Document. 1857. 8vo. Wis. Misc. Pamph. Vol. 1.

—— —— The Abolition Leaders Convicted of Disunion, etc. (n. d.) Rebell'n Pamph. Vol. 52.

—— Important to be known by Manufacturers and Mechanics. N. Y., 1831. 8vo. Cong. and Polit. Pamph. Vol. 98.

—— in Relation to the Consumption of Fuel for Generating Steam. Boston, 1852. 8vo. Scientific Pamphlets. Vol. 2.

—— relative to Canadian Indians, with a Report on the same Subject. Lond., 1838–1839 8vo.

FADEN, Wm. N. American Atlas. Lond., 1777. Folio.

FAGGING: Is it Inseparable from the Discipline of a Public School. Lond., 1847. 8vo. Educa. Pamph. Vol. 30.

FAHNESTOCK, Geo. W. Centen. Memorial of Christian and Anna Maria Wolf, March 25, 1863, with Genealogies, etc. Phila., 1863. 4to.

FAIR Exposition of the Principles of the Whig Club. Dublin, 1790. 12mo. Eng. Polit. Pamph. Vol. 23.

FAIRBAIRN, Robt. B., D. D. Plea for the Endowment of St. Stephen's College. Albany, 1870. 8vo. Sermons. Vol. 48.

FAIRBANKS, Geo. R. Hist. of Florida from its Discovery, in 1512, to the Close of the Florida War, in 1842. Phila., 1871. 12mo.

—— Introduct. Lecture before the Florida Hist. Soc., Apr. 15, 1857, on the Early History of Florida. St. Augustine, 1857. 8vo.

FAIRFAX Family. See NEILL, E. D. Fairfax's of England and Amer.

FAIRFAX'S New Leamington Guide. Leamington, Eng., 1832. 12mo. Guide Books. Vol. 6.

FAIRFIELD, Conn. See CORNWALL, Rev. N. E. Hist. Disc. 1851.

FAIRFIELD Co., Ohio. SANDERSON, G. Hist. of.

FAIRFIELD (N. Y.) Academy. Catalogue for 1849-50. Utica, 1850. 8vo.

FAIRFIELD, Ohio. See FOOTE, Sam'l. Memoirs of.

FAIRFIELD, Sumner Lincoln. Poems and Prose Writings, in 2 Vols. Vol. 1. Phila., 1841. 8vo.

FAIR Haven, Conn. See New Haven.

FAIRHOLT, F. W. The Home of Shakespeare, illustrated and described. N. Y., 1848. 8vo. Hist. Pamph. Vol. 4.

FAIRMOUNT (Ohio) Theolog. Sem. Catalogue for 1854-5. Cin. 8vo.

FAITH of the Church of Jesus Christ of Latter-Day Saints. N. Y., 1838. 8vo. Pamph.

FALCONER, Richard. Voyages, Travels, Adventures and Escapes. Lond., 1801. 12mo.

FALCONER, Thos. On the Discov. of the Mississippi, and on the S.-Western, Oregon, and N.-Western Boundary of the U. States. Lond., 1844. 12mo.

FALKLAND Islands. See MACKINNON, L. B. Acc. of. 1840.

FALL (The) of British Tyranny; or Amer. Liberty Triumphant; a Tragi-Comedy. Phila., 1776. Amer. Tracts. Vol. 4.

FALL River, Mass. See FOWLER, O. Hist. of.

—— R. R. Co. 8th Ann. Report of Directors, Jan., 1854. Fall River, 1854. 8vo. Mass. R. R. Reports. Vol. 3.

FALLS of Niagara. See KALM, Peter.

—— —— MAUDE, J. Visit to, in 1800.

—— St. Anthony. See LONG, Maj. S. H. See Minnesota.

FAMILIAR, A. Epistle to Robt. J. Walker. Lond., 1863. 8vo. Rebell'n Pamph. Vol. 14.

FAMILY (The) of St. Richard, the Saxon. Lond., 1844. 8vo. Biograph. Pamph. Vol. 3.

FAMIN, Abbé. Cours Abrégé de Physique Experimentale a la Porteé de tout le Monde. Paris, 1791.

FANCY Ball (The). A Letter from the Portfolio of a Young Lady of Albany. Albany, 1846. 8vo. Albany Misc. Pamph. Vol. 2.

FANE, C. Bankruptcy Reform: Letters to Sir Robert Peel. Lond., 1838. 8vo. Strangford Pamph. Vol. 15.

—— Letter to His Majesty's Attorney-General on Imprisonment for Debt. Lond., 1837. 8vo. Eng. Polit. Pamph. Vol. 42.

—— Ministry of Justice: Its Necessity as an Instrument of Law Reform. Lond., 1848. 8vo. Strangford Pamph. Vol. 56.

FANE, C. Observation on the Proposed Abolition of Imprisonment for Debt. Lond., 1838. 8vo. Strangford Pamph. Vol. 16.
—— Tenant Right: Its Necessity for Promoting Good Farming. (n. d.) 8vo. Strangford Pamph. Vols. 54 and 55.
FANNING, David. Narrative, with Acc. of his Adventures in N. Carolina, 1775 to 1783. N. Y., 1865. 8vo.
FANNING, Edmund. Voyages around the World, with Sketches of Voyages to the South Seas, etc. N. Y., 1823. 8vo.
FAR (The) West; or a Tour beyond the Mountains. N. Y., 1838. 2 Vols. 12mo.
FARADAY, Prof. Michael. See DE LA RIVE, A. Memoir of.
—— Practical Prevention of Dry Rot in Timber; Lecture at London, 1833. Lond., 1834. 8vo. Agr. Pamph. Vol. 10.
FARGO, F. F. Personal Sketches of Members of Assembly in N. Y. Legislature, for 1873. Buffalo, 1873. 8vo. N. Y. Misc. Pamph. Vol. 5.
FARIBAULT, G. B. Catalogue d'Ouvrages Sur l'Histoire de l'Amerique, et un particulier sur celle du Canada. Quebec, 1837. 8vo.
FARMER, John. Acc. of the Penacook Indians in N. Hampshire. N. H. Hist. Soc. Coll. Vol. 1.
—— and MOORE, J. B. Collections; Topographical, Historical and Biographical, relating principally to N. Hampshire. 2 Vols. Concord, 1822–3. 8vo.
—— Churches and Ministers in N. Hampshire. Mass. Hist. Soc. Coll. 2d Ser. Vols. 8, 9 and 10. 3d. Ser. Vols. 1, 2 and 3.
—— Genealog. Register of First Settlers in N. England. Lancas- Mass., 1829. 8vo.
—— Hist. Memoir of Billerica, Mass. Amherst, N. H., 1816. 8vo. Mass. Hist. Discourses. Vol. 7.
—— Hist. Sketch of Amherst, N. H. N. H. Hist. Soc. Coll. Vol. 5. See also Mass. Hist. Soc. Coll. 2d Ser. Vol. 2.
—— Memoir of. N. Eng. Hist. and Gen. Register. Vol. 1.
—— Memoir of the Narraganset Townships. Mass. Hist. Soc. Coll. 3d Ser. Vol. 2.
—— Memorials of Graduates of Harvard University, from 1642. Concord, N. H., 1833. 8vo. Harvard Coll. Pamph. See also N. H. Hist. Soc. Coll. Vol. 4.
—— Notes on the Co. of Hillsborough, N. H., 1816. Mass. Hist. Soc. Coll. Vol. 7. 2d Ser.
—— Sketches of Early Hist. of Billerica, Mass. Farmer & Moore's N. H. Hist. Coll. Vol. 2.
—— Sketches of Graduates of Dartmouth Coll., from 1769. N. H. Hist. Soc. Coll. Vols. 3, 4.
—— See Moore, J. B. Memoir of.
FARMER, John, of Michigan. Map of Territories of Ouisconsin and Mich. Detroit, 1836.
FARMER, S. Guide Map of City of Detroit. Detroit, 1862.
—— Map of the Copper Region of Lake Superior. Detroit, 1859.
—— Map of Wisconsin on Rollers. Detroit, 1866. 8vo.
—— R. R. and Township Map of Mich., 1863. Detroit, 1863.

FARMER'S (The) Guide. For the Use of Small Farmers of Ireland. Dublin, 1841. 12mo. Agr. Pamph. Vol. 3.

—— Library, Comprising PETZHOLD, A., on Agric. Chemistry; THAER, A. D., Principles of Agriculture; and STEVENS, H., Book of the Farm. N. Y., 1848. 3 Vols. 8vo.

FARMINGTON, Conn. See PORTER, N. Centenn. Address. 1841.

—— PORTER, Rev. Noah. Half Cent. Disc. 1856.

FARNHAM, Eliza. Life in Prairie Land. N. Y., 1846. 12mo.

FARNHAM, Luther. A Glance at Private Libraries. Boston, 1855. 8vo.

FARNHAM, Thos. J. Hist. of Oregon Territory, with Map. N. Y., 1844. 8vo. Oregon Pamph. Vol. 1.

—— Life, Adventures and Travels in California, and Travels in Oregon. N. Y., 1857. 8vo.

—— Travels in the Great Western Prairies, Rocky Mt's. and Oregon Terr'y.
N. Y., 1843. 8vo. Pamphlets Amer. Travel. Vol. 1.

FARNSWORTH, Dr. H. Oration on Music, at Cooperstown, N. Y., Apr., 1794. Cooperstown, 1795. 12mo. Addresses. Vol. 33.

FARNSWORTH, John F. Speech at St. Charles, Ill., on the Presidential Campaign. n. d. Chicago, 1872. 8vo. Congr. & Polit. Pamph. Vol. 130.

FAROE Islands. See Hist. and Descript. Acc. of.

FARR, Dr. W. Application of Statistics to Naval and Military Matters. 1850. 8vo. Scientific Pamph. Vol. 33.

FARRAGUT and our Naval Commanders. New York, 1867. 8vo.

FARRAR, C. C. S. The War; its Causes and Consequences. Cairo, Ill., 1864. 12mo.

FARRAR Family. Memoir of, from N. E. Hist. & Gen. Register. Oct., 1852. Genealog. Pamph. Vol. 2.

FARRAR, Thos. Manual of the Constitution of the U. S. Boston, 1869. 8vo.

FARRAR, Tim. Case of the Trustees of Dartmouth Coll. against William H. Woodward. Portsmouth, 1819. 8vo.

FARRELL, Ned. E. Colorado, the Rocky Mountain Gem. Chicago, 1868. Col. Misc. Pamph. Vol. 1.

FARWELL, Gov. Leonard J. Sketch of the Career of. Chicago, 1871. 8vo. Wis. Misc. Pamph. Vol. 7.

FARWELL, W. B. Oration before the Soc. of Cal. Pioneers, on the 9th Annivers. of the Admission of Cal. San Francisco, 1859. 8vo. Cal. Hist. Discourses. Vol. 1.

FATAL Consequences (The) of Ministerial Influence, Occasioned by the Late Petition of Six Noble Peers, &c. Lond., 1736. 8vo. Eng. Polit. Pamph. Vol. 68.

FAUCHET, Jos. Political Dispatch, No. 10, to the U. S. Phila., 1795. 8vo. Congr. & Polit. Pamph. Vol. 72.

FAUDEL, Henry. A Few Words on Jewish Disabilities. Lond., 1848. 8vo. Strangford Pamph. Vol. 45.

FAULKNER, T. C. Hist. of the Revolution in the Southern States. N. Y., 1861. 8vo. Rebellion Pamph. Vol. 108.

FAUNA Americana. See HARLAND, Richard.

FAUQUIER White Sulphur Springs. See STRINGFELLOW, Rev. T.

FAWKES (The) of York in the 16th Century; including Notices of the Early Hist. of Guy Fawkes, the Gunpowder Plot Conspirator. Westminister, 1850. 12mo. Genealog. Pamph. Vol. 6.

FAXON Genealogy. See VINTON Memorials.

FAY, Maj. H. A. Collection of Official Accounts in detail of all Battles between the U. States and G. Britain. 1812–15. N. Y., 1817. 8vo.

FEARING, Hon. Paul. See HILDRETH, S. P. Early Ohio Settlers.

FEARN, J. Essay on External Perception. Lond., 1815. 8vo. Pamphleteer, Vol. 5.

—— Letter to Prof. Stewart, on Objects of General Terms, and Axiomatical Laws of Vision, &c. Lond., 1818. 8vo. Pamphleteer, Vol. 12.

—— Review of the First Principles of B'p Berkeley, Dr. Reid, and Prof. Stewart, &c. Lond., 1813. 8vo. Pamphleteer. Vol. 3.

FEARON, Rev. Henry. On the Importance of Teaching Common Things. Lond., 1856. 8vo. Educa. Pamph., Vol. 33.

FEARON, Henry B. Narr. of a Journey through the Eastern and Western States of America, with Remarks on Mr. Birbeck's "Notes" and "Letters." Lond., 1819. 8vo.

FEATHERSTON, W. S. Speech in Cong., July 2, 1850, on the Galphin Claim. Congr. and Polit. Pamph., Vol. 90.

FEATHERSTONAUGH, G. W. A Canoe Voyage up the Minnay Sotor; with Acc. of the Lead and Copper Deposites in Wisconsin. Lond., 1847. 2 Vols. 8vo.

—— Excursion through the Slave States. N. Y., 1844. 8vo.

—— Geological Report of an Examina. made in 1834 of the Elevated Country between the Missouri and Red Rivers. Washington, 1835. 8vo.

—— Report of a Geological Reconnoisance made in 1835, from the Seat of Government by the way of Green Bay and the Wisconsin Territory, to the Coteau de Prairie, Minn. Washington, 1836.

FEDERAL Gov't. See FREEMAN, E. A. Hist. of,

FEDERMAN, N. Voyage aux Indes de la Mer Océane, 1529–30. See TERNAUX, H. Voyages. Vol. 1.

FELCH, Alpheus. Speech in U. S. Senate, Feb. 3 and 4, 1852, on Public Lands. Cong. and Polit. Pamph., Vol. 84.

—— —— Apr. 12 and 14, 1852, on French Spoliations. Congr. and Polit. Pamph., Vol. 84.

FELDBORG, A. Anderson. Appeal to the Eng. Nation in behalf of Norway. Lond., 1814. 8vo. Pamphleteer, Vol. 4.

FELLOWS, John. Exposition of the Mysteries, or Religious Dogmas, &c., of the Ancient Egyptians, Pythagoreans and Druids. With an Inquiry into Freemasonry. N. Y., 1835. 8vo.

—— The Veil Removed; or Reflections on Gen. D. Humphrey's Life of Israel Putnam. N. Y., 1843. 12mo.

FELT, Amos. Notes on the Organization of the Township of Perkins, O. Fire Lands Pioneer, Vol. 9.

FELT, Lieut. Geo. H.—Proceedings of a Court of Enquiry, convened at the request of. N. Y., 1863. 8vo. Rebell'n. Pamph., Vol. 8.

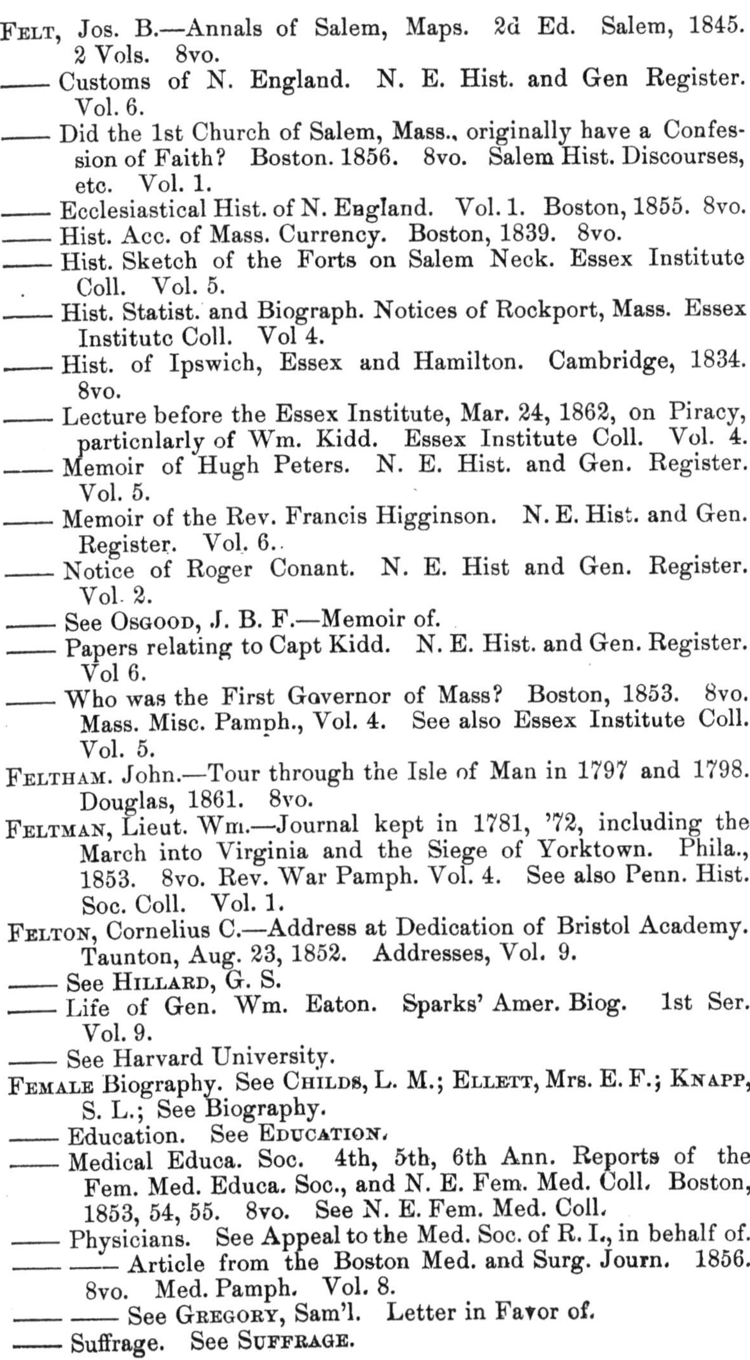

FELT, Jos. B.—Annals of Salem, Maps. 2d Ed. Salem, 1845. 2 Vols. 8vo.

—— Customs of N. England. N. E. Hist. and Gen Register. Vol. 6.

—— Did the 1st Church of Salem, Mass., originally have a Confession of Faith? Boston. 1856. 8vo. Salem Hist. Discourses, etc. Vol. 1.

—— Ecclesiastical Hist. of N. England. Vol. 1. Boston, 1855. 8vo.

—— Hist. Acc. of Mass. Currency. Boston, 1839. 8vo.

—— Hist. Sketch of the Forts on Salem Neck. Essex Institute Coll. Vol. 5.

—— Hist. Statist. and Biograph. Notices of Rockport, Mass. Essex Institute Coll. Vol 4.

—— Hist. of Ipswich, Essex and Hamilton. Cambridge, 1834. 8vo.

—— Lecture before the Essex Institute, Mar. 24, 1862, on Piracy, particnlarly of Wm. Kidd. Essex Institute Coll. Vol. 4.

—— Memoir of Hugh Peters. N. E. Hist. and Gen. Register. Vol. 5.

—— Memoir of the Rev. Francis Higginson. N. E. Hist. and Gen. Register. Vol. 6.

—— Notice of Roger Conant. N. E. Hist and Gen. Register. Vol. 2.

—— See OSGOOD, J. B. F.—Memoir of.

—— Papers relating to Capt Kidd. N. E. Hist. and Gen. Register. Vol 6.

—— Who was the First Governor of Mass? Boston, 1853. 8vo. Mass. Misc. Pamph., Vol. 4. See also Essex Institute Coll. Vol. 5.

FELTHAM. John.—Tour through the Isle of Man in 1797 and 1798. Douglas, 1861. 8vo.

FELTMAN, Lieut. Wm.—Journal kept in 1781, '72, including the March into Virginia and the Siege of Yorktown. Phila., 1853. 8vo. Rev. War Pamph. Vol. 4. See also Penn. Hist. Soc. Coll. Vol. 1.

FELTON, Cornelius C.—Address at Dedication of Bristol Academy. Taunton, Aug. 23, 1852. Addresses, Vol. 9.

—— See HILLARD, G. S.

—— Life of Gen. Wm. Eaton. Sparks' Amer. Biog. 1st Ser. Vol. 9.

—— See Harvard University.

FEMALE Biography. See CHILDS, L. M.; ELLETT, Mrs. E. F.; KNAPP, S. L.; See Biography.

—— Education. See EDUCATION.

—— Medical Educa. Soc. 4th, 5th, 6th Ann. Reports of the Fem. Med. Educa. Soc., and N. E. Fem. Med. Coll. Boston, 1853, 54, 55. 8vo. See N. E. Fem. Med. Coll.

—— Physicians. See Appeal to the Med. Soc. of R. I., in behalf of.

—— —— Article from the Boston Med. and Surg. Journ. 1856. 8vo. Med. Pamph. Vol. 8.

—— —— See GREGORY, Sam'l. Letter in Favor of.

—— Suffrage. See SUFFRAGE.

FENDALL, Philip R. Argument on Trial of Geo. A. Gardiner for False Swearing. Washington, 1853. 8vo. Law Pamph. Vol. 5.

FENDLER, Aug. Acc. of a Collection of Plants from Sante Fe, New Mexico, with Descriptions, &c., by Asa Gray, M. D. Memoir of Amer. Acad. of Arts and Sciences. Vol. 4, N. S.

FENELON, Archbishop. Lives of Ancient Philosophers; with notes by Rev. John Cormack. Harpers' Fam. Lib. N. Y., 1858. 18mo.

FENIAN Brotherhood. Extract from Proceedings of the 9th Gen. Conven., N. Y., 1870. 8vo. Congr. and Polit. Pamph. Vol. 128.

FENNER, Rev. David. Sermon at Lond., Mar. 12, 1823. Battle, 1823. 8vo. Eng. Sermons. Vol. 59.

FENWICK, Lady. Re-interment of the Remains of Lady Alice Apsley Boteler Fenwick, Old Saybrook, Conn., Nov. 23, 1870. 12mo. Conn. Hist. Discourses, etc. Vol. 7.

FENWICKE, John. See JOHNSON, R. G. Memoir of.

FERDINAND and Isabella. See PRESCOTT, W. H. Hist. of Reign of.

FERGUSON, Adam. Hist. of the Progress and the Termination of the Roman Republic. Phila., 1830. 8vo.

—— Same, abridged. N. Y., 1859. 18mo. Harpers' Fam. Lib.

—— Practical Notes during a Tour in Canada, and a Portion of the U. S. in 1831. Edinburgh, 1833. 12mo.

FERGUSON, Dr. Robt. Lecture before the Med. Classes of King's Coll., Lond., Oct. 1, 1836. Med. Pamph. Vol. 29:

FERGUSSON, James. Illustrations of the Rock Cut Temples of India. Lond., 1845. Large 4to.

FERMENTATION (The) of Europe. Lond., 1848 (?) 8vo. Eng. Misc. Pamph. Vol. 18.

FERNANDEZ, Martin, de Navarrete. Discurso Leido. a la real Academia de la Historia. Nov. 24, 1837, and Nov. 27, 1840. Madrid, 1838. 1841. 8vo.

FERRALL, S. A. Ramble of Six Thousand Miles in the U. S. Lond., 1832. 12mo.

FERREE, Rev. P. V. The Heroes for the War of the Union. 1st. Ser. Cinn., 1834. 12mo.

FERRIBAULT, Pelagie. See Reply to Objections of Sec. of War against the Claims of.

FERRIS, Benj. Hist. of the Original Settlements on the Delaware, from its Discov. by Hudson, to the Coloniza. under Penn, with a Hist. of Wilmington. Wilmington, 1846. 8vo.

FERRIS, Jacob. States and Territories of the Great West: their Geography, History, Resources, etc. N. Y.. 1856. 12mo.

FERRY, Orris S. Speech in Cong., May 16 and 17, 1870, on the 15th Amendment. Cong. and Polit. Pamph. Vol. 119. 8vo.

FERUSSAC, Baron de. Bulletin genéral et universel des Announces et des Nouvelles Scientifiques. Paris, 1822. 8vo. Miscell. Tracts. Vol. 4.

FESSENDEN, Thos. G. Address before the Charlestown Temperance Soc., Jan. 31. 1831. Charlestown, 1831. 8vo. Temp. Pamph. Vol. 3.

FESSENDEN, Thos. G. Democracy Unveiled; or, Tyrrany Stripped of the Garb of Patriotism. 2d Ed. Boston, 1805. 12mo.
Same, 3d Ed. N. Y. 1806. 2 Vols. in 1. 12mo.

FESSENDEN, Wm. Pitt. See Memorial Addresses.
—— See PREBLE, G. H. Memoir of.
—— Speech in Cong., May 31, 1842, on the Army Appropriation Bill. Washington, 1842. 8vo. Congr. and Polit. Pamph. Vol. 24.
—— Speech in Cong., March 3, 1854, against the Repeal of the Missouri Compromise. Washington, 1854. 8vo. Speeches. Vol. 3. Cong. and Polit. Pamph. Vol. 93.
—— Speech in Cong., Dec. 4, 1856, on the President's Message. Cong. and Polit. Pamph. Vol. 90.
—— Speech in Cong., Feb. 12, 1862, on the Issue of U. S. Notes. Rebell'n Pamph. Vol. 9.
—— Speech in Cong., April 1, 1862, on Slavery in District of Columbia. Cong. and Polit. Pamph. Vol. 85.

FESTIVAL OF THE SONS OF NEW HAMPSHIRE, with Speeches of Webster, Woodbury, Wilder and others. Boston, Nov. 7, 1849. Boston, 1850. 8vo.
—— (Second) OF THE SONS OF NEW HAMPSHIRE, Nov. 2, 1853, at Boston. Boston, 1854. 8vo.

FESTIVALS, GAMES AND AMUSEMENTS. See SMITH, Horatio.

FEULING, Prof. J. B. On the Place of Indian Languages in the Study of Ethnology. Transac. Wis. Academy of Sciences. 1870–2.
—— Phocylidis Pœma Admonitorum. Andover, 1869. 12mo.

FEUTRY, M. Manuel Tironien ou recueil d' Abbreviations faciles et Intelligibles. Paris, 1775. 12mo.

FEW Plain Words to the Rank and File of the Union Armies. 1864. Rebell'n Pamph. Vol. 46.
—— Weeks (A) in Paris during the Residence of the Allied Sovereigns in that Metropolis. Boston, 1814. 12mo.
—— Words for Honest Penn. Democrats, n. d. Rebell'n Pamph. Vol. 20.
—— —— in behalf of the Loyal Women of the U. States. N. Y. 1863. 8vo. Rebell'n Pamph. Vols. 19 & 20.
—— —— on Strikes and Combinations among Workmen. Lond., 1848. 12mo. Eng. Misc. Pamph. Vol. 12.

FICHTE: a Biography. From Chambers' Papers for the People. Vol. 9. Biograph. Pamph. Vol. 18.

FICKLIN, O. B. Speech in Cong., Jan. 10, 1844, on River and Harbor Improvements. Congress. and Polit. Pamph. Vol. 84.
—— Speech in Cong., July 1, 1846, on the Tariff. Washington, 1846. Speeches. Vol. 1.

FIDDES, Rev. Rich'd. Proposals for Printing the Life of Cardinal Wolsey, with Extracts Vindicating him, etc. n. d. Fol. Eng. Polit. Pamph. Vol. 2.

FIEDLER, Franciscus. Casp. Barthii. Observationes ad D. Juneii Juvenalis Scholia vetera et ad aliquot Catulli, Tibulli, Ovidii, etc. Vesaliæ, 1827. 8vo. Latin Pamph. Vol. 7.

FIELD, Justice. Constitutionality of the Legal Tender Act Considered. Washington, 1872. 8vo. Banking and Currency Pamph. Vol. 4.

FIELD, David D., D.D. Centen. Address with Hist. Sketches of Cromwell, Portland, Chatham, Middle Haddam and Middletown, Conn. Middletown, 1853. 8vo.

—— Genealogy of the Brainerd Family in the U. S. N. Y., 1857. 8vo.

—— Hist. Sketch of the Cong. Ch. in Stockbridge, Mass. N. Y., 1853. 8vo. Mass. Hist. Discourses, etc. Vol. 1.

—— History of Pittsfield, Mass. Hartford, 1844. 8vo. Mass. Hist. Discourses, etc. Vol. 10.

—— History of the Towns of Haddam and East Haddam, Conn. Middletown, 1814. 8vo. Conn. Hist. Discourses, etc. Vol. 4.

—— Statist. Acc. of the Co. of Middlesex, Conn. Middletown, 1819. 8vo. Conn. Hist. Discourses, etc. Vol. 4.

FIELD, Geo. Aesthetics, or the Analogy of the Sensible Sciences indicated. Lond. 1820. 8vo. Pamphleteer. Vol. 17.

—— Analogy of the Physical Sciences indicated. Lond., 1819. 8vo. Pamphleteer. Vol. 15.

—— Brief Outline of the Universal System. Lond., 1816. 8vo. Pamphleteer. Vol. 9.

—— Ethics, or the Analogy of the Moral Sciences indicated. Lond., 1824. 8vo. Pamphleteer. Vol. 23.

—— The Third Organon attempted; or Elements cf Logic and Subjective Philosophy. Lond., 1818. Pamphleteer. Vol. 12.

FIELD, Henry M. Summer Pictures; from Copenhagen to Venice. N. Y., 1859. 12mo.

FIELD, Osgood. Genealog. Sketch of the Family of Field of the West Riding of Yorkshire. Albany, 1863. 8vo, Genealog. Pamph. Vol. 7.

FIELD, Rich'd S. Addresss on Jos. C. HORNBLOWER, LL. D., before the N. J. Hist. Soc., Jan. 16, 1865. Proceedings. Vol. 10.

—— See HART, Chas. H. Necrolog. Notice of.

—— The Provincial Courts of N. J., with Sketches of the Bench and Bar. Dis. before the N. J. Hist. Soc. Collections. Vol. 3.

FIELD, Thos. W. See Essay, (An,) towards an Indian Bibliography.

—— The Battle of Long Island; Introductory Narr. with Authentic Docs. L. I. Hist. Soc. Memoirs. Vol. 2.

—— Hist. and Antiq. Scenes in Brooklyn and Vicinity. Brooklyn, 1868. Sm. 4to.

FIELDING, HENRY. Enquiry into the causes of the late Increase of Robbers, etc. Lond., 1851. 8vo.

FIECHI, Giauluigi, See CELESIA, E. Conspiracy of.

FIGGINS, Vincent. Specimen of Book and Newspaper Types from his Foundry. Lond., 1838. 4to.

FILDER, Wm. Remarks on the Report of the Crimean Commissioners, on the Supplies of the British Army, etc. Lond., 1856. 8vo. Hist. Pamph. Vol. 17.

FILLMORE Co., Minn. See BISHOP, J. W. Hist. of. 1858.

FILLMORE, Millard. See BARRE, W. L. Life and Pub. Services of. 1856.

—— Speech in Cong., June 9. 1842, on the Tariff. Washington, 1842. 8vo. Congr. and Polit. Pamph. Vol. 24.

FILSON, John. Discovery, Settlement and Present State of Kentucky. 1784. Imlay's America. P. 306.

—— Histoire de Kentucke, Nouvelle Colonie a l'ouest de la Virginie, traduit de l'Anglois par. M. Parraud. Paris. 1785. 8vo.

FINANCE. See Banking and Currency.

—— CAMPBELL, A. True Amer. System of.

—— CAREY, H. C. The Finance Minister, the Currency and the Public Debt. 1868.

—— ELDER, Dr. Wm. Debt and Resources of the U. S.

—— MORING, H. E. Suggestions on. 1869.

—— PAINE, Thos. Decline and Fall of English System.

—— PRICE, R. An Appeal on the Subject of.

—— REED, Henry. The Public Debt. n. d.

—— Review of the late Report of the Sec. of the Treasury. 1867.

—— RICHARDSON, D. M. Resumption of Specie Payments. 1866.

—— RUGGLES, A. G. Nat. System of.

—— SANDS, N. Letter to Sec'y of Treasury. 1869.

—— U. S. Sec. of Treasury. Reports.

—— Views of Our Nat. Finances, etc. 1868.

—— WHATELY, T. Considerations on Trade and Finance of G. B. 1865.

—— WOLCOTT, A. Our Nat. Currency. 1866.

FINCH, John. Effect of the Physical Geog. of the World on the Boundaries of Empires. Silliman's Journ. Vols. 14, 16.

—— Essay on the Mineralogy and Geology of Lawrence Co., N. Y. 1830. Silliman's Journ. Vol. 19.

—— In the Celtic Antiquities of America. Silliman's Jour. Vol. 7.

—— On the Forts around Boston, erected during the War of Independence. Silliman's Journ. Vol. 8.

FINDDAY, A. G. Modern Atlas. London. 1850. Sm. Folio.

FINCK, Hugo. Acc. of Antiquities in the State of Vera Cruz, Mexico. Smithsonian Report. 1870.

FINLAY, Hugh. Journal during his Survey of the P. Offices between Falmouth and Casco Bay, Mass., and Savannah in Georgia. 1773–74. Brooklyn, pr. printed. 1863. 4to.

FINLAYSON, Jas. Surnames and Sirenames; the Origin and History of Family and Hist. Names. London. n. d. 8vo.

FINLAYSON, W. F. Hist. of the Jamaica Case; with Acc. of the Rebellion of Negroes. 2d Enlarged Ed. Lond. 1869. 8vo.

—— Justice to a Colonial Governor; or Considerations on the Case of Mr. Eyre. Lond. 1868. 8vo.

—— Rept of Case of Mc Queen *vs.* E. J. Eyre

—— Review of Authorities as to the Repression of Riot or Rebellion. Lond. 1868. 12mo.

—— The Catholic Hierarchy Vindicated by the Law of England. Lond. 1851. 8vo. Strangford Pamph. Vol. 61.

FINLEY, Rev. Jas. B. Autobiography; or Pioneer Life in the West. Cincin. 1867. 12mo.

FINLEY, Rev. J. B. Life among the Indians. Cincin. 1868. 12mo.
—— Sketches of Western Methodism. Cincin. 1854. 12mo. See FINLEY. Rev. Robert. See BROWN, I. V. Biog. of.
FINNEY, Rev. C. G. & BEMAN, N. S. S. See Troy, N. Y., 1st Presb. Ch., &c.
FIRE LANDS GRANT. Abstract of the Record Hist. of. Firé Lands Pioneer. Vol. 4.
—— —— Hist. Soc'y. See BETTS, Rev. Xenophon; BRONSON, S. A; COOKE, E.; GURLEY, L. B; HARTUPEE, Prof.; LEWIS, C. F.; ROOT, J. M.; SEYMOUR, John; SHERMAN, John; SMITH, S. D.; STEWART, G. T.; WALKER, J. B.; WHITTLESEY, C.; WHITTLESEY, E.; WICKHAM, C. P.
—— —— Pioneer. Published under the Supervision of the Fire Lands Hist. Soc. Sandusky. &c. 1858–68. Vols. 1–9. 9 Vols. in 2. 8vo.
FIRMIN, Rev. Giles. See DEAN, John Ward. Memoir of.
FIRST (the) Duty of the Citizen. The Grandeur of the Struggle and its Responsibilities. 1863. Rebell'n Pamph. Vol. 91.
—— Organization of Colored Troops in the State of N. Y., to aid Supressing the Rebellion. N. Y., 1864. 8vo. Rebell'n Pamph. Vol. 39.
—— Reader for Southern Schools. Raleigh, 1864. 12mo. Rebellion Pamph. Vol. 109.
—— Settlers of Virginia; a Hist. Novel. N. Y., 1806. 8vo.
FIRTH, Wm. The Case of Ireland set at rest; a Letter to Hon. Rob't Peel. Lond., 1825. 8vo. Pamphleteer. Vol. 25.
FISCH, Dr. Geo. Nine Months in the U. S. During the Crisis. Lond., 1863. 8vo.
FISH, Artificial Propagation of. See Marsh, G. P.
FISH, Hamilton. Corres. with Hon. J. A. Hamilton, on the Election of Fremont, 1856. 8vo. Congr. & Polit. Pamph. Vol. 135.
FISHER, Prof. Alex. M. See KINGSLEY, J. L. Eulogy on.
FISHER, Geo. Companion and Key to the Hist. of England, with Geneal. of British Sovereigns. Lond., 1832. 8vo.
FISHER, Prof. Geo. P. Discourse on the Hist. of the Ch. of Christ in Yale Coll., Nov. 22, 1857, with Appendix. New Haven, 1858. 8vo. Conn. Hist. Discourses. Vol. 5. See also Yale Coll. Pamphlets.
—— Life of Benj. Silliman, M. D. N. Y., 1866. 2 Vols. 12mo.
—— Speech in Cong., Mar. 11, 1862, on Slavery. Congr. & Polit. Pamph. Vol. 94.
FISHER, J. B. Catalogue of his Library. Phila., 1866. 8vo. Bibliograph. Pamph. Vol. 58.
FISHER, Joshua Francis. Concessions and Compromises. Phila., 1860. 8vo. Rebell'n Pamph. Vol. 60 and 106.
—— Degradation of the Representative System, and its Reform. Phila., 1863. 8vo. Congr. & Polit. Pamph. Vol. 128. Rebell'n Pamph. Vol. 85.
—— Discourse Before the Hist. Soc. of Penn., April 9, 1836, on the the Private Life, etc., of Wm. Penn. Hist. Soc. of Penn. Memoirs. Vol. 3. Part 2.

FISHER, Joshua Francis. Inedited Letters of Wm. Penn; from the Originals. Hist. Soc. of Penn. Memoirs. Vol. 4. Part 1.

—— Narr. of Sir Wm. Keith's Coming to the Gov't of Penn., etc. Penn. Hist. Soc. Memoirs. Vol. 2. Part 2.

—— Acc. of the Early Poets and Poetry of Penn. Hist. Soc. of Penn. Memoirs. Vol. 2. Part 2.

FISHER, J. S. Description of Amer. Medals. Mass. Hist. Soc. Coll. Vol. 6. 3d Series.

FISHER, R. S., & COLBY, C. Amer. Statis. Annual. N. Y., 1854. 12mo.

—— Progress of the U. States. N. Y., 1854. 8vo.

FISHER, Samuel W., D. D. Address before the Graduating Class of the State Normal School, Jan. 29th, 1863. Albany, 1863. 8vo. Addresses. Vol. 16.

—— See Hamilton College.

—— Hist. Discourse before Hamilton College, July 16, 1862. n. d. n. p. 8vo. N. Y. Hist. Discourses. Vol. 2.

—— Lecture before Y. M. Asso., Albany, Dec. 3, 1844. Addresses. Vol. 7.

—— The Supremacy of Mind: Lecture at Albany, Dec., 1844. Albany, 1845. 8vo. Pamphlets. Vol. 3.

FISHER, Sydney G. The Science of Government. From Amer. Monthly Mag. 1838. 8vo. Congr. and Polit. Pamph. Vol. 139.

—— A Nat. Currency. From N. American Review, July, 1854. Phil'a., 1864. 12mo.

FISHERIES. See ADAMS, J. Q. The Fisheries and the Mississippi.

—— SABIN, L. Report on Amer. Fisheries, 1853.

FISHES OF NEW YORK. See MITCHELL, S. L.

FISK, Capt. J. L. Report of his Expedition to Rocky Mountains. Washington, 1864. 8vo. Congr. Pamph. Vol. 61.

FISHKILL, N. Y., 1st R. D. Ch. See KIP, Rev. F. M. 150 Annivers. Disc. 1866.

FISK, Rev. Elisha. Annivers. Sermons, in 1st Cong. Ch., Wrentham, June 14, 1846. Boston. 12mo. n. d. Mass. Hist. Discourses. Vols. 1 and 16.

—— Half Cent. Disc. in Wrentham, Mass., June 12, 1849. Boston, 1850. 8vo. Mass. Hist. Discourses. Vols. 16 and 18.

——See STORRS, Rev. R. S. Obit. Disc. 1851.

FISKE, A. A. Genealogy of Fiske Family. Chicago, 1867. 12mo.

FISKE, Rev. Nathan. Hist. Acc. of the Settlement of Brookfield, in the Co. of Worcester. Mass. Hist. Soc. Coll. 1st Ser. Vol. 1.

FISHER, L. F., M. D. Local History of Camden, N. J. Camden, 1858. 12mo.

FITCH, Asa, M. D. Hist. Topograph. & Agricult. Survey of Washington Co., N. Y. N. Y. Agr. Soc. Trans., 1848–49.

—— 1st and 2d Reports on Noxious and other Insects of N. Y. State. Albany, 1856. 1865. 8vo.

FITCH Genealogy. See STILES, H. R.

FITCH, John. Annals of Army of Cumberland. Phila., 1864. 8vo.
—— Reply to Jas. Rumsey on the Priority of his Steamboat Invention, 1788. Doc. Hist. of N. Y. Vol. 2
—— See RUMSEY, Jas., WESTCOTT, T., WHITTLESEY, C.
FITCHBURG, Mass., R. R. Co. 11th, 12th, 13th, 14th, 15th, 16th, 24th, 26th, 27th, & 29th Ann. Reports. Charlestown & Boston, 1853–71. Mass. R. R. Reports. Vol. 1.
—— —— See Mass. Supreme Judicial Court.
—— FORREY, R. C. Hist. of.
FITCHVILLE, Ohio. See CURTIS, J. C. Memoirs of.
—— OSBORN, Eben. Obit. Record of Pioneers.
FITTS, Jas. H. Genealogy of the Fitts or Fitz Family. Clinton, 1869. 8vo. Genealog. Pamph. Vol. 3.
FITZ, Rev. Dan'l. 30th Annivers. Disc., Ipswich, Mass.. June 29, 1856, Boston, 1856. 8vo. Mass. Hist. Discourses. Vol. 3.
FITZGERALD, Lord Edward. See MOORE, T. Life of.
FITZGERALD, Jas. E. Examina. of the Charter and Proceedings of the Hudson Bay Co., with reference to Vancouver's Island. Lond., 1849. 12mo.
FITZHARRIS, Edw. Examina. relating to the Popish Plot. Lond., 1681. Folio. Eng. Polit. Pamph. Vol. 63.
FITZ-JAMES, Duke of. The Proposed Law relative to Periodical Journals. Lond., 1818. 8vo. Pamphleteer, Vol. 11.
FITZPATRICK, Wm. John. Note to the Cornwallis Papers, embracing a Narr. of the Career of Francis Higgins, &c. Dublin, 1859. 8vo. Eng. Polit. Pamph., Vol. 57.
FITZWILLIAM, Earl. Protest in the House of Lords, May 8, 1795. Lond., 1795. 12mo. Eng. Polit. Pamph., Vol. 25.
FITZWYGRAM, Rev. John. Hints on the Improvement of Village Schools. Lond., 1859. 8vo. Educa. Pamph., Vol. 33.
FIVE, (The) Cotton States and N. York. N. Y., 1861. 8vo. Rebell'n Pamph., Vol. 14.
FLAG, (The) of Truce. A Sermon. Baltimore, 1862. 12mo. Rebell'n Pamph., Vol. 100.
FLAGG, Edmund. Venice: the City of the Sea, from the Invasion by Napoleon, 1797, to 1849. N. Y., 1853. 2 Vols. 12mo.
FLAGG, Wm. J. Speech in Ohio Legisla. on the Expulson of Hon. O. Dresel, 1863. Rebell'n Pamph., Vol. 36.
FLANDERS, Henry. Lives and Times of the Chief Justices of the Supreme Court of the U. S., viz: John Jay, John Rutledge, Wm. Cushing, Oliver Ellsworth and John Marshall. Phil'a, 1858. 2 Vols. 8vo.
—— Must the War go on? Phil'a, 1863. 8vo. Rebell'n Pamph., Vols. 1, and 76.
FLANDREAU, Thos. H. Address before the Utica Temperance Societies. 1842. Utica, 1842. 8vo. Temp. Pamph., Vol. 5.
FLATBUSH, L. I. See STRONG, Rev. T. M. Hist. of.
FLAX. See CAMERON, A. Cultivation of, and Preparation of Flax Cotton. 1852.
—— Culture. See CLAUSSEN, Chevalier.
—— —— Manual of, and Prize Essays, &c. N. Y., 1865. 8vo. Agric. Pamph., Vol. 5.

FLEETWOOD, Rev. John. Life of Christ; and the Lives of his Holy Evangelists and Apostles. N. Y., 1858. 12mo.

FLEMING, Aug. Catalogue of his Library. N. Y., 1866. 8vo. Bibliograph Pamph., Vol. 21.

FLETCHER, Judge. Charge to the Grand Jury of the Co. of Wexford, Eng., July, 1814. Lond. 8vo. Pamphleteer, Vol. 4.

FLETCHER, Calvin. See TRASK, Wm. B. Biograph. Sketch of.

FLETCHER, Ebenezer. See BUSHNELL, C. I. Revolu. War. Narr.

FLETCHER, Edw. H. Fletcher Genealogy; Descendants of Robert Fletcher, of Concord, Mass. Boston, 1871. 8vo.

FLETCHER, Edw. Taylor. The Twenty Years' Siege of Candia. read before the Literary and Hist. Soc. of Quebec, Jan. 19, 1853. Transactions. Vol. 4. Part 3.

FLETCHER Genealogy. See FLETCHER, E. H.

FLETCHER, Jas. Hist. of Poland; from the Earliest Period to the Present Time. Harpers' Fam. Libr. N. Y., 1859. 18mo.

FLETCHER, Rev. John Wm. See COX, Rev. Robt. Life of.

FLETCHER, Jos. Education: National, Voluntary and Free. Lond., 1851. 8vo. Educa. Pamph. Vol. 33.

FLEURY, Andrew H. de. Memoirs of the Life and Administration of. Lond., 1743. 12mo. Eng. Relig. Pamph. Vol. 82.

FLINT, Austin, M. D. Introduct. Lecture at the Rush Med. College, 1844. Chicago, 1844. 8vo. Med. Pamph. Vol. 2.

FLINT, Charles L. Grasses and Forage Plants. 4th Revised Ed. Boston, 1859. 12mo.

FLINT, H. M. Life of Stephen A. Douglas, with his Speeches and Reports. Phila., 1865. 12mo.

FLINT, Rev. Jacob. Hist. and Description of Cohasset, in the Co. of Norfolk, Mass., 1821. Mass. Hist. Soc. Coll. 3d Ser. Vol. 2.

FLINT, Jas. Letters from America, with Observations on the Climate and Agriculture of the Western States. Edinburgh, 1822 8vo.

FLINT, Jas., D. D. Disc. at Salem, Mass., on the Death of John Brazer, D. D., Mar. 14, 1846. Salem, 1846. Sermons. Vol. 5.

—— Sermon at Salem, July 21, 1850, on the Death of Pres't Taylor, and Hon. Nathaniel Silsbee. Salem, 1850. Sermons. Vol. 5.

—— Sermon at Marblehead, Mass., Feb. 11, 1849, on the Death of Rev. John Bartlett. Salem, 1849. 8vo. Sermons. Vol. 3.

—— Discourses on Leaving the Old Ch. of the East Society in Salem, Dec. 28, 1845, and at the Dedica. of the New, Jan. 1, 1846. Salem, Mass., 1846. 8vo. Mass. Hist. Discourses. Vol. 17.

—— Another Copy. Sermons. Vol. 5.

FLINT, John. and STONE, John H. Genealog. Register of the Descendants of Thos. Flint, of Salem. Andover, 1860. 8vo.

FLINT, Timothy. A Condensed Geography and History of the Western States, or the Mississippi Valley. Cincin., 1828. 2 Vols. 8vo.

FLINT, Timothy. Address before the Cincin. Temp. Soc. Western Monthly Review. Vol. 2.
—— History and Geography of Mississippi Valley. Cincin., 1833. 8vo.
—— Indian Wars of the West, with Biograph. Sketches of Pioneers. Cincin., 1833. 12mo.
—— Journal of, from the Red River to the Ouachita or Washita, in La., in 1835. Waldie's Circulating Libr. Vol. 7.
—— Life and Adventures of Daniel Boone. New Ed. Cincin., 1868. 12mo.
—— See Western Monthly Review.
FLORENCE, Italy. Galerie Imperiale et Royale de Florence. Florence, 1816 and 1844. 8vo. Guide Books. Vol. 14.
FLORENCE, Ohio. Memoirs of. Fire Lands Pioneer. Vol. 2.
FLORENTINE Republic. See DAPONT, Lorenzo.
FLORIAN, M. Hist. of the Moors of Spain, with Acc. of the Rise and Decline of the Mahommedan Empire. Harpers' Fam. Libr. N. Y., 1860. 18mo.
FLORIDA. Acts and Resolutions of the Gen. Assembly, passed at the 8th and 9th Sessions, 1856–1858.
—— Acts, etc., adopted at an Adjourned Session, Nov., 1859. 8vo.
—— See BARTRAM, W. Travels in Ga., Florida, etc.
—— BIEDMA, L. H. De Soto's Exped. to.
—— BILL, L. Winter in.
—— BRINTON, Danl. G. Notes on.
—— COXE, D. Descript. of. 1741.
—— DARBY, W. Geog. and Hist. of.
—— DAVIS, J. Travels in La. and Florida. 1806.
—— DE SOTO, H. Letter from. 1539.
—— FAIRBANKS, Geo. R. Hist. of, to 1842.
—— —— Lecture on Early Hist. of. 1857.
—— FORBES, J. G. Hist. and Topograph. Sketches.
—— FRENCH, B. F. Hist. Collec. of La. and Flor.
—— GARCILASSO. Conquête de la.
—— GIDDINGS, J. R. Exiles of.
—— HACKLEY, R. S. Titles, etc., of his Lands in East Florida.
—— HILTON, W. Relation of a Voyage to. 1664.
—— Hist. Society. Constitution and By-Laws. N. Y., 1856. 18mo.
—— See FAIRBANKS, G. R. Address. 1857.
—— Histoire de la Conqueste.
—— House and Senate Journals. Tallahassee, 1858–9. 4 Vols.
—— HUTCHINS, T. Topograph. Descrip. of. 1784.
—— IRVING, T. Conquest of.
—— Its Climate, Soil and Productions, with a Sketch of its History, Nat. Features and Social Condition. Jacksonville, 1869. 8vo. Florida Misc. Pamph. Vol. 1.
—— Joint Resolutions of Gen. Assembly on M. VATTEMARE's Internat. Exchanges. Tallahassee, 1853. 8vo.
—— See LATOUR, A. L. Memoir of War. 1814–15.
—— LAUDONNIERE, René. French Coloniza. of.

FLORIDA. Legislative Journals of the Adjourned Session, Nov., 1859. 8vo.
—— Local Hist. Seee St. Augustine.
—— Ann. Messages of Gov. H. Reed, 1869, '70, '71, '72. Tallahassee, 1869–72. 8vo. Florida Pamph. Vol. 1.
—— Original Memoirs on the Floridas. Baltimore, 1821. 8vo. Florida Misc. Pamph. Vol. 1.
—— PIERCE, Jas. Notices of the Floridas and the Indian Tribes. 1824.
—— RATTENBURG, J. F. Cession of the Floridas, etc. 1819.
—— Recueill de Pieces sur la Floride.
—— SIMMS, W. G. Huguenots in.
—— SMITH, Buckingham. Relation of De Vacca.
—— Vega. Hist. of Conquest of Florida, by De Soto.
—— Virginia Richly Valued. 1609.
—— Vue de la Colonie Espagnal.
—— War in Florida; Exposition of its Causes, and Hist. of the Campaigns under Generals Clinch, Gaines and Scott. Baltimore, 1836. 12mo.
—— See SPRAGUE, John T. Origin, Progress and Conclusion of. 1848.
—— See WHITING, Major Henry. Cursory Remarks upon E. Florida. 1838.
—— WILLIAMS, J. L. View of W. Florida.
FLOUR of Bone. Fertilizing Properties of. N. Y., 1866. 8vo. Agr. Pamph. Vol. 11.
FLOURENS, M. Memoir of Cuvier, with a Hist. of his Works. Smithsonian Report, 1868.
FLOWER, Richard. Letters from the Illinois, 1820–21, with Acc. of the Eng. Settlement at Albion. With M. Birbeck's Letter, etc. Lond., 1822. 8vo. Ill. Local Histories, etc. Vol. 2.
FLOYD, John G. Speech in Cong., Apr. 27, 1842, on Apportionment. Washington, 1842. 8vo. Congr. and Polit. Pamph. Vol. 25.
FLUCTUATIONS in Gold, Stocks, Exchange and Gov't Securities. Nat. Bank Statements, from 1863 to '68. N. Y., 1868? 8vo. Banking and Currency Pamph. Vol. 3.
FLUSHING, L. I., Institute. Catalogue for 1846. Flushing, 1846. 8vo.
FOBES, Rev. Perez. Topograph. Descript. of Raynham, in the Co. of Bristol, Mass. Mass. Hist. Soc. Coll. 1st Ser. Vol. 3.
FŒDERALIST (The); with Hist. Introduction and Notes by H. B. Dawson. Morrisania, N. Y., 1864. 8vo.
—— See JAY, John. Second Letter on Dawson's Introduction.
FOGG, Thos. B. Memorial Sermon in Old Trinity Ch., Brooklyn, Conn., on the 100th Annivers. of its Opening, Apr. 12, 1871. Hartford. n. d. 8vo. Conn. Hist. Discourses. Vol. 7.
FOLGER, Walter, Jr. and MACY, Zacheus. Topograph. Descript. of Nantucket. Mass. Hist. Soc. Coll. 1st Ser. Vol. 3.
FOLKESTONE, Eng. See Monument in Folkestone Ch.
FOLLANSBEE Family. See SMITH, Columbus. Report to Follansbee Assoc.

FOLLANSBEE, Joshua. The Case of, before a Naval Court Martial, at Phila., 1863. Rebell'n Pamph. Vol. 26.
FOLLEN, Rev. Chas. See CHANNING, Rev. Wm. E. Obit. Disc.
—— Funeral Oration at Boston, Nov. 17, 1832, on the Death of Gaspar Spurzheim, M. D. Boston, 1832. 8vo. Sermons. Vol. 35.
—— Suggestions on Landscape Gardening. Boston, 1859. 8vo. Agr. Pamph. Vol. 14.
FOLSOM, Chas. Titi Livii Patavina Historiarum. Boston, 1842. 12mo.
FOLSOM, Geo. See Despatches of Hernando Cortes.
—— Disc. before Maine Hist. Soc., Sept. 6, 1846. Collections. Vol. 2.
—— Hist. Sketch of the N. Y. Hist. Soc. N. Y. Hist. Soc. Coll. N. S. Vol. 1.
—— Hist. of Saco and Biddeford, Me., with Notices of other Early Settlements. Saco, 1830. 12mo.
—— Particulars concerning the Directors General or Governors of New Netherlands. N. Y. Hist. Soc. Coll. N. S. Vol. 1.
FOND DU LAC, Wis., Commonwealth, Newspaper, 1860–65. Folio. 1869–72. Folio.
—— Co., Wis. Bible Society. Ann. Report for 1869. Wis. Misc. Pamph. Vol. 6.
—— See MITCHELL, Martin. Hist. of, 1854.
—— Directory Business Advertiser for 1857–8. Fond du Lac, 1857. 12mo.
—— Fountain City Herald, Newspaper. Nov., 1852, to Feb., 1856. Folio.
—— Same. Jan., 1855, to Sept., 1856. Folio.
—— Same, Daily. July, 1854, to Oct., 1854. Folio.
—— Same, Daily. Mar., 1856, to Sept., 1856. Folio.
—— Journal, Newspaper. Jan., 1850, to June, 1853. Folio.
—— MCKENNEY, T. L., on the Indian Treaty at.
—— Reporter, Newspaper. 1861–6. 4to.
—— Saturday Reporter, Newspaper. 1867–70. Folio.
—— Union, Newspaper. June, 1853, to Dec., 1855. Folio.
—— Same. Jan., 1856, to May, 1858. Folio.
—— Weekly Commonwealth, Newspaper. Sept., 1856 to Dec., 1859. Folio.
FONDEY, Wm. H. Oration before the Y. M. Assoc. at Albany, July 4, 1858. Albany, 1858. 8vo. Addresses, etc. Vol. 18.
FONTAINE, Rev. Jas. See MAURY, A. Autobiog. of.
FONTANA, F. Opuscules Physique et Chimiques. Paris, 1784. 8vo.
FONTHILL Abbey, Eng. See Britton, John.
—— RUTTER, J.
FOOD and its Digestion. See TOWNSEND, H. Paper on.
FOOT, Adoniram. See PARSONS, E. B. Memorial Sermon.
FOOT, Jos. I. Hist. Disc. on Brookfield, Mass., with Capt. Wheeler's Narr. of the Burning of the Town by Indians. W. Brookfield, 1843. 12mo. Mass. Hist. Discourses. Vol. 4.
FOOT, Dr. Lyman. Remarks on Indian Summers. With Diary of the Weather, kept at Fort Winnebago in 1835. Silliman's Journ. Vol. 30.

FOOTE Genealogy. See GOODWIN, N.
—— See PARSONS, E. B.
FOOTE, H. S. Speech in U. S. Senate, Dec. 18 and 19, 1851, on the Compromise Bill. Congr. and Polit. Pamph. Vol. 94.
—— Texas and the Texans; or the Advance of the Anglo-Americans to the S. West. Phila., 1841. 2 Vols. 12mo.
—— War of the Rebellion; Observa. on the Causes of the War. N. Y., 1866. 12mo.
FOOTE, John P. The Schools of Cincinnati and Vicinity. Cincin., 1855. 8vo.
FOOTE, Saml. Memoirs of Fairfield, Ohio. Fire Lands Pioneer. Vol. 5.
FOOTE, Solomon. See Addresses on the Death of.
—— See Vermont Hist. Soc.
FOOTE, Wm. H., D. D. Sketches of Virginia, Historical and Biographical. Phila.. 1850. 8vo.
—— Same. 2d Ser., 1855. 8vo.
FORBES, Alex. Hist. of Upper and Lower California, from their first Discovery. Lond., 1839. 8vo.
FORBES, James Grant. Sketches, Historical and Topographical, of the Floridas. N. Y., 1821. 8vo.
FORBES, John, M. D. On Etherization in Surgery and Practical Medicine. Lond., 1847. 8vo. Med. Pamph. Vol. 5.
FORBES, P. S. Letter to the Chairman of the Joint Comm. on Commerce, of Cong., on Navigation Interests, 1870. 8vo. Congr. and Polit. Pamph. Vol. 118.
FORBES, S. D. Camp Randall and Environs. n. d. 12mo. Madison Misc. Pamph. Vol. 1.
FORCE in Nature and its Effects upon Matter. Cincin., 1869. 8vo. Scientific Pamph. Vol. 20.
FORCE, Peter. Documentary History. See U. S. Sec. of State.
—— Nat. Calendar and Annals of the U. S. for 1823. Washington. 1823. 12mo.
—— Paper before Nat. Institute, July, 1853, on "Grinnell Land." Scientific Pamph. Vol. 14.
—— See Librarian of Congress. Report on Libr'y of, 1867.
—— Tracts and Other Papers, relating to the Origin, Settlement and Progress of the Colonies in N. A. to 1776. Washington, 1836–46. 4 Vols. 8vo.
—— The Declaration of Independence, or Notes on Lord Mahon's History. Lond., 1855. 8vo. Rev. War Pamph. Vol. 1.
FORD, Capt. David. Journ. of an Expedition in 1794, to Aid in Suppressing the "Whiskey Rebellion." N. J., Hist. Soc. Proceed. Vol. 8.
FORD, H. A. Hist. of Putnam and Marshall Counties, Ill. Lacon, Ill., 1860. 12mo.
FORD, Henry A., M. D. Observations on the Fevers of the West Coast of Africa. N. Y., 1856. 12mo. Med. Pamph. Vol. 6.
FORD, Gov. Thos. Hist. of Illinois, from 1818 to 1847, with a full Acc. of the Black Hawk War, and the Rise, etc., of Mormonism. Chicago, 1854. 12mo.

Foreign Evangelical Society. 2d and 9th Ann. Reports, May, 1841–1848. N. Y., 1841–8. 8vo.
—— Missionary Chronicle of Presb. Ch. See Missionary Chronicle.
Forest Hill Cemetery, Roxbury, Mass. See Roxbury, Mass.
—— Home Cemetery. See Milwaukee, Wis.
Forlorn (The) Hope of the United Kingdom, etc. Part 1. Lond., 1819. 8vo. Eng. Polit. Pamph. Vol. 34.
Form of Prayer to be used in Lond. and Westminster, June 5, 1669, for the Success of the War against France. Lond., 1689. Sm. 4to. Eng. Relig. Pamph. Vol. 79.
—— —— and Thanksgiving for Apr. 25, 1723, for Preservation from the Late Plague in France. Lond., 1723. Sm. 4to. Eng. Relig. Pamph. Vol. 93.
—— —— to be used in Churches and Chapels in G. Britain, Dec. 13, 1776, on Acc. of the War with America. Lond., 1776. 4to. Eng. Rel. Pamph. Vol. 22.
—— —— and Thanksgiving, for July 7, 1814, on the End of the War with France. Lond., 1814. 4to. Eng. Rel. Pamph. Vol. 96.
—— —— and Thanksgiving to be used throughout England and Ireland, Jan. 18, 1816, for the Conclusion of the War with France. Lond., 1816. 4to. Eng. Rel. Pamph. Vol. 38.
—— —— and Thanksgiving, on the Deliverance of Queen Caroline from the late Conspiracy. Lond., 1820. 8vo. Eng. Rel. Pamph. Vol. 87.
—— —— to be used throughout England and Ireland, Mar. 21, 1832, being the day for a Gen. Fast, etc. Lond., 1832. 8vo. Eng. Rel. Pamph. Vol. 45.
—— —— to be used throughout England and Ireland, May 24, 1847, being the day for a Gen. Fast. Lond., 1847. 4to. Eng. Rel. Pamph. Vol. 32.
—— —— to be used throughout England and Ireland, Apr. 26, 1854, and Mar. 21, 1855, for the Restoration of Peace, etc. Lond., 1854–1855. 8vo. Eng. Rel. Pamph. Vol. 57.
—— —— to be used throughout England and Ireland, Oct. 7, 1857. on Peace in India. Lond., 1857. 8vo. Eng. Rel. Pamph. Vol. 57.
—— —— and Thanksgiving to be used throughout England and Wales, June 21, 1840, on the Preservation of the Queen from a late Treasonable Attempt. Lond., 1840. 8vo. Eng. Rel. Pamph. Vol. 49.
Forman, Chas. Protesilaus; or the Character of an an Evil Minister. Lond., 1730. 8vo. Eng. Polit. Pamph. Vol. 11.
Formation of Character considered, with reference to our Institutions and State of Society. From the Christian Review, 1838. 8vo. Congr. and Polit. Pamph. Vol. 139.
Forney, John W. Eulogy on the Hon. Stephen A. Douglas, at Washington, July 3, 1861. Rebell'n Pamph. Vol. 35.
—— Speech at Mifflintown, Penn., Sept. 8, 1863. Rebell'n Pamph. Vol. 36.
Forrest, Edwin. Oration at N. Y., July 4, 1838. 8vo. Addresses. Vols. 3 and 29.

FORREST, Lieut. Gen. N. B. See JORDAN and PRYOR. Campaigns of.

FORREST, Wm. S. Hist. and Descript. Sketches of Norfolk (Va.) and Vicinity, including Portsmouth and the adjoining Counties during a Period of 200 Years. Phila., 1853. 8vo.

FORRY, Dr. Saml. Meteorology: A Description of the Atmosphere and its Phenomena. N. Y., 1843. 4to. Scientific Pamph. Vol. 38.

FORSHEY, Caleb G. Memoir on the Physics of the Mississippi River and Improvements in Louisiana. N. Orleans, 1850. 8vo. La. Misc. Pamph. Vol. 1.

FORSTALL, Edmund J. Analytical Index of Public Documents relative to Louisiana, deposited at Paris. French's Hist. Coll., La. Part 1.

FORSTER, Jacob. Pedigree of Jacob Forster, Sr., of Charlestown, Mass. Charlestown, 1870. 12mo. Genealog. Pamph. Vol. 1.

FORSTER, John Reinhold. Hist. of Voyages and Discoveries made in the North, translated from the German, with Maps. Lond., 1786. 4to.

FORSTER, Mark. Arithmetical Trigonometry. Lond., 1690. 12mo.

FORSTER, Nathaniel See SIMMS, J. R. Biog. of.

FORSTER, Thos. Causes and Mitigation of Pestilential Fever. Lond., 1824. 8vo. 2d Ed. Pamphleteer. Vol. 24.

—— Application of the Organology of the Brain to Education. London, 1815. 8vo. Pamphleteer. Vol. 5.

—— Observations on the Phenomena of Insanity, being a Supplement to Observations on the Influence of the Atmosphere. Lond., 1819. 8vo. Pamphleteer. Vol. 15.

—— Observations on the Influence of the Atmosphere on Human Health and Diseases, particularly Insanity. Lond., 1819. 8vo. 2d Ed. Pamphleteer. Vol. 14.

—— Observations on the Brumal Retreat of the Swallow. Lond., 1814. 8vo. 4th Ed. Pamphleteer. Vol. 4.

—— Sketch of the New Anatomy and Physiology of the Brain and Nervous System of Drs. Gall and Spurzheim, in relation to Phrenology, etc. Lond., 1815. 8vo. Pamphleteer. Vol. 5.

FORSTER, Wm. See ALLINSON, W. J.

FORSTER, W. E. William Penn and Thos. B. Macaulay. Reply to Macaulay's History. Phila., 1850. 8vo. Biograph. Pamph. Vol. 15.

FORSYTH, John. Speech in U. S. Senate, Jan., 1834, on the Removal of the Deposites. Congr. and Polit. Pamph. Vol. 139. Speeches. Vol. 5.

FORSYTH, William. Hist. of the Captivity of Napoleon at St. Helena, from the Letters and Journals of the late Sir Hudson Lowe. N. Y., 1853. 2 Vols. 12mo.

FORT Duquesne. Hist. Incidents connected with the Capture of Fort Duquesne. "Olden Time." Vol. 1.

—— —— See Registres des Baptesmes. 1753–6.

—— Edward (N. Y.) Collegiate Institue. Catalogue for 1855–6. Albany. 8vo.

FORT George, N. Y. See DECOSTA, B. F. Notes on the Hist. of.
—— Griswold, Conn. Storming of. See HARRIS, W. W.
—— Harmer, Ohio. Account of. Amer. Pioneer. Vol. 1.
—— Meigs, Ohio. See COMBS, Capt. Leslie. Official Report of Col. Dudley's Defeat. 1813.
—— —— WILLIAMS, Saml. Two Western Campaigns.
—— Necessity. See CRAIG, N. B. Taking of.
FORTNIGHTLY Review. Edited by Geo. H. LEWES. Lond., 1865–70. 14 Vols. 8vo.
FORT Oswego, N. York. See Oswego.
—— Pillow Massacre. Report of Joint Congress. Committee on the. Washington, 1864. 8vo.
—— Popham Celebration. See Popham and Gorges.
—— Pownall Maine. See PIKE, Rich'd. Building and Occupancy of.
—— Pulaski. See GILMORE, Q. A. Report of Siege and Reduction.
—— St. Philip Canal, Louisiana. Address to Chambers of Commerce, Boards of Trade, and Congress, in behalf of. N. Orleans. 1872. 8vo. La. Misc. Pamph. Vol. 1.
—— Snelling, Minn. See NEILL, E. D.
—— Stanwix. Papers relating to. 1758. Doc. Hist. of N. Y. Vol. 4.
—— —— Treaty of, in 1784. "Olden Time." Vol. 2.
—— Stephenson. Defence of. See WHITTLESEY, E. Address. 1858.
—— Wayne, Ia. See BRICE, W. A. Hist. of.
—— —— See WILLIAMS, J. L. Sketch of 1st Presb. Ch. 1860.
—— William Henry. See STICKNEY, M. A. Massacre at. 1757.
—— Winnebago. See FOOT, Lyman. Weather Diary. 1835.
—— —— River Times, Newspaper. July, 1850, to Sept., 1853. Folio. See Portage City, Wis.
—— —— See RUGGLES, D. Geology, etc., of the Region of. 1835.
FORWARD or Backward. N. Y., 1863. 8vo. Rebellion Pamph. Vol. 1.
FOSBROKE, Rev. Thos. D. Encyclopædia of Antiquities and Elements of Archæology. Lond., 1825. 2 Vols. 4to.
—— Original Hist. of the City of Gloucester, Eng. Lond., 1819. Folio.
FOSDICK, Rev. David. Scriptural Temperance. A Sermon. Boston, 1846. 8vo. Sermons. Vol. 1.
FOSDICK, Rev. David Jr. Sermon, Sept. 5, 1855, at the Dedica. of a New Meeting House belonging to the "South Groton Christian Union." Boston, 1855. 8vo. Sermons. Vol. 46.
FOSSILS. See WARD, H. A. Catalogue of Casts of Fossils.
FOSTER, Alfred D. See SMALLEY, E. Obit. Sermon. 1852.
FOSTER, A. and WOODBURY, P. P. Topograph. and Hist. Sketch of Bedford, Hillsborough Co., N. H. N. H. Hist. Soc. Coll. Vol. 1.
FOSTER, B. F. Education Reform; a Review of Wyse on National Education. N. Y., 1837. 8vo. Educa. Pamph. Vol. 1.

FOSTER, Chas. J. The University of London a Parliamentary Constituency. Lond. n. d. 8vo. Strangford Pamph. Vol. 63.

FOSTER Family of Charlestown, Mass. From the N. E. Hist. and Gen. Register, 1871. Genealog. Pamph. Vol. 2.

FOSTER, Frank. The Age we Live in; or Doings of the Day. Lond., 1863. 12mo. 2d Ed. Hist. Pamph. Vol. 19.

FOSTER, G. G. N. York by Gas-Light. N. Y., 1850. 8vo. N. Y. Local Hist. Vol. 5.

—— N. York in Slices; by an Experienced Carver. N. Y., 1849. 8vo. N. Y. Local Hist. Vol. 5.

FOSTER, G. L. The Past of Ypsilanti; Discourse on leaving the Old Presb. Ch. Edifice, Sept. 20, 1857. With Appendix. Detroit, 1857. 8vo. Mich. Hist. Discourses. Vol. 1.

FOSTER, Jas. Acc. of the Behaviour of the late Earl of Kilmarnock on the Day of his Execution. Lond., 1746. 8vo. Eng. Misc. Pamph. Vol. 24.

FOSTER, Jas., D. D. See BULKLEY, Rev. C.

FOSTER, James. The Capitulation; Hist. of the Expedition of Wm. Hull, Brigadier Gen. of the N. Western Army. Chillicothe, 1812. 12mo. Pamphlets War of 1812. Vol. 3.

FOSTER, Jas. S. Outlines of Hist. of Territory of Dakotah, and Emigrants' Guide; with Sectional Map. Yankton, 1870. 8vo.

FOSTER, John. Essay on the Evils of Popular Ignorance. N. Y., 1856. 12mo.

—— Essays on Decision of Character and other Subjects. N. Y., 1858. 12mo.

FOSTER, J. W. The Mississippi Valley; its Physical Geography, &c. Chicago, 1869. 8vo.

—— Report on the Mineral Resources of the Ill. Central R. R. N. York, 1856. 8vo. Ill. Misc. R. R. Reports, etc.

—— and WHITNEY, J. D. Report on the Geol. aud Topog. of a Portion of the Lake Superior Land District. Washington, 1850–1. 2 Vols. 8vo. 1 Vol. Maps.

FOSTER, John Y. N. Jersey in the Rebellion; a History of the Services of the Troops of that State in the Union Cause. Newark, 1868. 8vo.

FOSTER, L. F. S. Speech in U. S. Senate, Apr. 26, 1864, on the Fugitive Slave Bill. Rebell'n Pamph. Vol. 9.

FOSTER, Sidney. Description of a Pictorial Model of London in the Olden Time. London, 1844. 8vo. Hist. Pamph. Vol. 15.

FOULKE, Wm. P. Notes respecting the Indians of Lancaster Co., Pa. Hist. Soc. of Penn. Memoirs, Vol. 4. Part 2.

—— Remarks on Cellular Separation. Phila., 1861. 8vo. Med. Pamph. Vol. 1.

—— Remarks on Penal System of Penn., with reference to County Prisons. Phila., 1855. 8vo. Placed with Penn. Journals of Prison Discipline.

—— The Right Use of History; Disc. before the Penn. Hist. Soc. Phila., 1856. 8vo. Penn. Hist. Soc. Addresses. Vol. 1.

FOUR Grand Questions Proposed and briefly Answered, on Religious Toleration, etc. Lond., 1689. Sm. 4to. Eng. Relig. Pamph. Vol. 7.

—— Letters from the Country Gentleman, on the Petitions. Lond., 1780. 8vo. Eng. Polit. Pamph. Vol. 19.

—— —— to "The Morning Advertiser," on the Admiral, the First Lord, and the Anglo-Carthaginians, Sept., 1855. Lond. 8vo. Eng. Polit. Pamph. Vol. 53.

—— Papers from Boston Courier. See Radicalism in Religion, etc.

—— Years of a Liberal Government. Lond., 1834. 8vo. Eng. Polit. Pamph. Vol. 40.

FOURIER, M. Jos. Hist. Eulogy on Laplace, 1829. Silliman's Journ. Vol. 25.

—— Memoir of Delambre. Smithsonian Report, 1864.

FOURS d'un Nouveau Systeme pour la Carbonisation des Différents Combustibles. Paris, 1845. 8vo.

FOWLE, Wm. B. See NASON, Elias. Sketch of Life of.

FOWLE, Wm. F. Catalogue of his Private Library. Cambridge, 1864. 8vo. Bibliograph. Pamph; Vol. 17.

FOWLER, D. W. Genealog. Memoir of Descendants of Capt. Wm. Fowler. Milwaukee, 1870. 8vo. Genealog. Pamph. Vol. 3.

FOWLER, F. W. Reminiscences of Milan Township, Ohio. Fire Lands Pioneer. Vols. 1, 2.

FOWLER Genealogy. See FOWLER, W. C.

—— —— See FOWLER, D. W.

FOWLER, Orin. Hist. of Fall River, with Notices of Freetown and Tiverton. Fall River, 1862. 8vo. Mass. Hist. Discourses. Vol. 13.

—— Speech in Cong., Dec. 31, 1850, on Reduction of Postage. Congr. and Polit. Pamph. Vol. 90.

—— Speech in Cong., Mar. 31, 1852, on the Tariff. Congr. and and Polit. Pamph. Vol. 92.

FOWLER, O. S. Lecture on Temperance considered Physiologically and Phrenologically. Phila., 1841. 8vo. Temp. Pamph. Vol. 3.

—— Religion, Natural and Revealed; or the Nat. Theology and Moral Bearings of Phrenology and Physiology. N. Y., 1844. 8vo. Tenth Ed.

FOWLER, Saml. P. Biograph. Sketch and Diary of Rev. Jos. Green, of Salem. Essex Institute Coll. Vols. 8, 10.

FOWLER, Wm. C. Conditions of Success in Genealogical Investigations, illustrated in the Character of Nathan'l Chauncey. Boston, 1866. 8vo. Pamph.

—— Hist. of Durham, Conn., 1662–1866. Hartford, 1866. 8vo.

—— Local Law in Mass. and Conn., Historically considered. Albany, 1872. 8vo.

—— Memorials of the Chaunceys, including President Chas. Chauncey, and his Ancestors and Descendants. Boston, 1858. 8vo.

—— —— See also N. E. Hist. and Gen. Register. Vols. 10 and 11.

—— Sermon at Dedica. of the South Cong. Ch. in Durham, Conn., Dec. 29, 1847. Amherst, 1848. 8vo. Conn. Hist. Discourses. Vol. 1.

FOWLER, Wm. C. The Sectional Controversy—the Causes of the War, etc. N. Y., 1868. 8vo.

—— William Fowler the Magistrate, and One Line of his Descendants. 1869? n. p. 8vo. Genealog. Pamph. Vol. 2.

FOWLER, Wm. W. Hints to Genealogists, derived from Eng. Local Nomenclature. N. Eng. Hist. and Gen. Register. Vols. 22, 23.

FOX, Chas. J. History of Dunstable, Nashua, etc., N. H. Nashua, 1847. 8vo.

—— Speech in Parliament, Mar. 24, 1795, on the State of the Nation. Lond., 1795. 8vo. Eng. Polit. Pamph. Vol. 75.

FOX, Ebenezer. Revolutionary Adventures. Boston, 1838. 12mo.

FOX, Geo. See JANNEY, S. M. Life of.

—— Journal or Hist. Acc. of his Life, Travels, Sufferings, etc., in the Ministry; with a Preface by Wm. Penn. Lond., 1765. Folio.

—— and BURNYEAT, John. A New England Fire Brand Quenched; being an Answer to a Slanderous Book, entitled, Geo. Fox Digged out of his Burrows by Roger Williams, etc. Lond., 1679. 4to.

FOX, Jos. Comparative View of the Plans of Education of Dr. Bell and Mr. Lancaster. Lond., 1808. 8vo. Educa. Pamph. Vol. 29.

FOX LAKE, Wis. Gazette, Newspaper. April, 1858, to Dec., 1863. Folio.

—— —— and Beaver Dam Argus, Newspapers. 1864–6. Folio.

Fox River Improvement. See Wisconsin and Fox River Improvement.

—— Survey. See PETITVAL, J. B. Report, 1839.

—— Valley R. R. Exhibit of the Present Condition of the R. R. Milwaukee, 1857. 8vo.

FOX, Dr. Tilbury. Cholera Prospects; compiled from Personal Observations in the East. Lond., 1865. 8vo. Med. Pamph. Vol. 18.

FRAAS, Dr. Geschichte Landwirth Schaft. Prague, 1852. 8vo.

FRAMINGHAM, Mass. See BARRY, W. Hist. of.

—— Report of the School Comm. for 1853–54. Boston, 1854. 8vo.

FRANCE. Academie des Sciences. Compte Rendus des Seances de l'Academie des Sciences. Paris, 1839. 2 Vols. 4to.

—— Administrative Changes since 1848. See SANFORD, H. S.

—— Algiers. Rapport sur le Governement et l'Administration des Tribus Arabes de l'Algerie. Paris, 1851. 8vo.

—— —— Rapport sur les Operations Militaire en Algerie. Paris, 1850. 8vo.

—— —— Rapport sur la Situation de l'Algerie en 1853. Paris, 1854. 8vo.

—— —— Tableau de la Situation des Establissements Francais dans l'Algerie, 1850–2. 1 Vol, 1852–4. 2 Vols. Paris. 3 Vols. 4to.

—— See Analysis of Corres. between France and U. S.

—— ANDREWS, J. Hist. of the War, 1775–83.

—— Annuaire Historique, 1837.

FRANCE. BECHARD, F. De la Reform Administrative et Electorale, 1848.
—— CASS, L. France; its King, etc.
—— CHAMBRUN, Aldebert de. La Republique Reformiste, etc., 1848.
—— Chemin de Fer de l'Ouest. Rapport du Conseil d'Administration. Sevres, 1852. 4to.
—— Colonies. Commission Instituee par Decision Royale, pour l'examen des Questions relatives a l'Esclavage, et, a la Constitntion Politique des Colonies. Paris, 1840. 4to.
—— —— See JEFFREYS, T.; PALAIRET, J.
—— —— State of French and Brit. Colonies in America. 1755.
—— COLTON, Rev. W. Notes on France and Italy.
—— Commerce and Agriculture. Annuaire des Eaux de la France pour 1851. Paris, 1851. 4to.
—— —— Commission de Pisciculture. Travaux et Rapports. Paris, 1850. 8vo.
—— —— Compte rendu de l'Execution du decret relatif a l'Enseignement Professionel de l'Agriculture. Paris, 1850. 4to.
—— —— Documents relatifs a la Question de la Boucherie. Paris, 1856. 4to.
—— —— Notice Historique et Statistique sur l'Industrie tulliere a a la Calais et a Saint-Pierre-les-Calais.
—— —— Rapports sur le Rouissage du lin le Drainage, la Nouvelle. Exploitation de la Tourbe, etc. Paris, 1850.
—— —— Recherches Scientifiques en Orient Enterprises par les Ordres du Gouverment pendant les Annees. 1853-1854. par Albert GANDRY. Paris, 1855. 4to.
—— —— See RODET, D. L. Du Commerce Exterieur, etc. 1825.
—— —— Tableau General du Commerce de la France avec ses Colonies et les Puissances Etrangeres, pendant les annees, 1855-1856. Paris. 2 Vols. 4to.
—— —— Tableau General des Mouvements du Cabotage, pendant l'annee 1855. Paris, 1856. 4to.
—— Commission Departmentale Faisant Fonctions de Conseil General du Department de la Seine. Session de 1848. Proces Verbal. Paris, 1849. 8vo.
—— Compagnie du Chemin de Fer de Graissessac a Beziers Department de l'Herault. Paris, 1856. 4to.
—— Compte Rendu au Roi de l'Execution des Lois des 18 et 19 Juillet 1845, sur le Regime des Esclaves. Paris, 1847. 4to.
—— Constitution. La Revision de la Constitution. Paris, 1848. 8vo. Strangford Pamph. Vol. 61.
—— See COSTE, M. Voyage d'Exploration, etc.
—— De la Roche Bitumineuse dite Asphalte. 1838. Paris, 1838. 4to.
—— Deliberation du Conseil de la Compagnie des Canaux. Paris, 1823. 4to.
—— DE LOMENIE, L. Beaumarchais and his Times.
—— Des Institutions de Credit Foncier et Agricole dans les divers Etats de l'Europe. Paris, 1851. 8vo.

FRANCE. Diplomata et Chartae Merovingicae Aetatis in Archivo Franciæ Asservata. Paris, 1848. 4to.
—— Documents relatifs aux Canaux. Paris, 1840. 4to.
—— Education. See THIERS, M. Rapport sur la Loi D'Instruction, etc. 1844.
—— ERSKINE, T., on War with G. Britain.
—— Etude des Getes Houillers et Metalliferes du Bocage Vendeen, faite en 1854 et 1855, par H. FOURNEL. Atlas. Paris, 1836. Folio. Text. 1 Vol. 4to.
—— Establissement des Invalides de la Marine. Paris, 1831. 8vo.
—— Explication de la Carte Geologique de la France. Paris, 1841. 2 Vols. 4to.
—— Exposition, 1855. Catalogue de la Collection des Produits Agricoles Vegetaux et Animaux de l'Angleterre. Paris, 1855. 4to.
—— —— Catalogue des Objets exposes dans la Section des Etats-Unis d'Amerique. Paris, 1855. 8to.
—— —— Catalogue des Produits Naturels Industriel et Artistiques Exposes dans la Section Mexicaine. Paris, 1855. 8vo.
—— —— Des Institutions de Prevoyance fondees par les Industries du Haut-Rhin. Mulhouse, 1854. 8vo.
—— —— Le Portugal et ses Colonies. Paris, 1855. 8vo.
—— FABER, M. Internal State of. 1812.
—— —— Compte Rendu, par M. NECKER, Directeur-General des Finances. Paris, 1781. 4to.
—— HARPER, R. G. Observa. on Dispute between U. S. and.
—— Hist. of. See FROISSART, Sir. J. Chronicles of England, France, etc.
—— —— SISMONDI, J. C. L. S. Histoire des Francaise.
—— —— SMUCKER, S. M. Scenes in French Hist.
—— —— THIERS, M. A. Hist. of Consulate and Empire.
—— See HOLMES, Rev. A. French Protestants in Mass.
—— International Exchange. Contributions de l'Agence Centrale des Exchanges Internationaux au Concours Agricole Universel de 1856. Paris, 1856. 4to.
—— Its King, Court and Gov't, by an American. N. Y., 1848. 8vo. 3d Ed. Hist. Pamph. Vol. 9.
—— See LABAUME, E. Campaign against Russia. 1815.
—— LEFRANC, P. La Republique et les Partis. 1848–52.
—— Letter on the Situation of France. 1815.
—— MACLEAN, Dr. C. Excursion in France, etc., in 1801–1803.
—— MARTEAU, M. Considerations sur L'Etablissement de la Republique. 1848.
—— Memoire sur le Canal Lateral a la Garonne, Etablissant la Jonction Definitive des deux mers. Par A. DOIN. Paris, 1835. 4to.
—— Memoire sur le Projet d'un Chemin de Fer de Paris a Rouen au Havre, et a Dieppe, par M. DEFONTAINE. Paris, 1837. 4to.
—— Memoire sur le Projet d'un Chemin de Fer de Lyon a Marseille. Par M. F. KERMAINGAUT. Paris, 1837. 4to.
—— Memoire sur le Projet d'un Chemin de Fer de Paris d'Orleans. Paris, 1837. 4to.

FRANCE. Memoires des Commissaires du Roi.
—— Memo. of Henry the Great aud Court of.
—— Deliberation sur les Halles Centrales. Paris, 1851. 4to.
—— Notice sur les Travaux Publics Executes Depuis. 1830. Paris, 1847. 4to.
—— See Orators of.
—— PARDOE, Miss. Recollections of the Rhone and the Chartreuse. 1835.
—— POWNALL, Gov. Antiquities of the Provincia Romana of Gaul.
—— Rapport Addresse A. M. le Ministre des Travaux Publics sur les Chemins de Fer. Paris, 1843. 4to.
—— Rapport du Jury Central sur les Produits de l'Industrie Francaise Exposes en. 1834. Paris, 1836. 3 Vols. 8vo.
—— Same for 1839. Paris. 3 Vols. 8vo.
—— Same for 1844. Paris. 3 Vols. 8vo.
—— Rapport par l'Academie Royal de Medecine sur les Vaccinations. 1838–39. Paris, 1841. 8vo. 2 Vols.
—— Rapport sur l'Ensemble des Dispositions Administrative Auxquelles a donne lieu la Guerre d'Orient. Paris, 1856. 8vo.
—— Rapport sur les Questions Coloniales, a la Suite d'un Voyage fait aux Antilles et aux Guyanes. Paris, 1843–4. 2 Vols. Folio.
—— Rapport sur les Vaccinations Pratiquees en France. 1840. Paris, 1842.
—— Rapport sur l'Etat actuel des Prisons. Oct., 1823. Lond., 1825. 8vo. Pamphleteer. Vol. 25.
—— Rapport sur l'Exposition de 1839. Bruxelles, 1841. 2 Vols. 8vo.
—— Recherches et Considerations relatives aux Intérêts Materiels de la France. Des Chemins de Fer. Paris, 1839. 8vo.
—— Recueil des Documents Statistiques, tome 1. Routes Royal, Routes Departementales. Paris, 1837. 1 Vol. 4to.
—— Renseignements sur la Fabrication des Monnaies Fran Caise. Paris, 1853. Small Folio.
—— SESLLIUS, C. P. Republica sive Status Regni Galliae.
—— Statistics: Archives Statistiques du Ministre des Travaux Publiques, de l'Agriculture et de Commerce; publies par le Ministre Secretaire d'Etat de ce Department. Paris, 1837. 1 Vol. Folio.
—— —— Compte rendu de la Deuxieme Session du Congres International de Statistique. 1855. Paris, 1856. 4to.
—— —— Statistiques de la France; Publiee par le Ministre des travaux Publiques, de l'Agriculture et du Commerce. Paris, 1837–55. 8 Vols. Folio. Contents: Territoire et Population. 1837–55. 2 Vols. Agriculture. 1840–42. 4 Vols. Commerce Exterieur. 1838. 1 Vol. Administration Publique. Vol. 1. 1843.
—— See STURT, Chas. Condition of, in 1809.
—— SWAN, Col. Progress of Commerce with U. S. 1790.
—— Tables Nouvelles pous Abreger divers Calculs relatifs aux Profets de Routes. Paris, 1838. 4to.

FRANCE. Theses de Physique et de Chimie presentees a la Faculte des Sciences de Paris. 1847–1849. Paris. 2 Vols. 4to.

—— See TUSSAUD, Madame. Memoirs and Reminiscences.

—— U. States. Messages of the President. 1797–1799.

—— WELLESLEY, W. De la France Contemporaine. 1849.

FRANCHERE, Gabriel. Narr. of a Voyage to the N. West Coast of America in 1811–14; or the First American Settlement on the Pacific. N. Y., 1854. 12mo.

FRANCIS I, King of France. Life and Times of. Lond., 1829. 2 Vols. 8vo.

FRANCIS, Convers, D. D. Disc. at Plymouth, Mass., Dec. 22, 1832, on the Landing of the Fathers. Plymouth, 1832. 8vo. Addresses. Vol. 24.

—— Three Discourses beforc the Cong. Soc. in Watertown, on Leaving the Old Meeting-House, etc. Cambridge, 1836. 8vo. Mass. Hist. Discourses. Vol. 1.

—— Hist. Sketch of Watertown, Mass., to the Close of the 2d Century. Cambridge, 1830. 8vo. Mass. Hist. Discourses, etc. Vcl. 18.

—— Life of John Eliot, the Apostle to the Indians. Sparks Amer. Biog. 1st Ser. Vol. 5.

—— Life of Sebastian Rale, Missionary to the Indians. Sparks Amer. Biog. 2d Ser. Vol. 7.

—— Memoir of Gamaliel Bradford, M. D. Mass. Hist. Soc. Coll. 3d Ser. Vol. 9.

—— Memoir of Hon. John Davis. Mass. Hist. Soc. Coll. 3d Ser. Vol. 10.

—— See NEWELL, Rev. Wm.

FRANCIS, Geo. H. The Late Sir Robt. Peel Bart; a Critical Biography. Lond., 1852. 12mo. Biograph. Pamph. Vol. 5.

FRANCIS, John W., M. D. Address at N. Y. Acad. of Medicine, 1847. N. Y., 1847. 8vo. Med. Pamph. Vol. 2.

—— Address on Induction of Dr. Valentine Mott as Prest. of N. Y. Acad. of Medicine, Feb. 7, 1849. N. Y., 1849. 8vo. Med. Pamph. Vol. 2.

—— Address before Philolexian Soc. of Columbia Coll., May 15, 1831. Addresses. Vol. 12.

—— Catalogue of his Private Library. N. Y., 1862. 8vo. Bibliograph. Pamph. Vol. 57.

—— See COOKE, John Esten. Recollections of.

—— Disc. on Nat. History, at N. Y., 1841. Addresses. Vol. 10.

—— Hist. Disc. before the N. York Hist. Soc., on their 53d Anniver., Nov. 17, 1857. With Acc. of other Exercises. N. Y., 1857. 8vo. N. Y. Hist. Soc. Discourses. Vol. 3.

—— Old New York; or Reminiscences of the Past Sixty Years; an enlarged ed. of his Annivers. Disc. before N. Y. Hist. Soc., Nov. 17, 1857. Boston, 1858. 12mo.

—— Letter on the Cholera Asphyxia. N. Y., 1832. 8vo. Med. Pamph. Vol. 4.

—— Reminiscences of Saml. Latham Mitchill, M. D. N. Y., 1859. 8vo. Biograph. Pamph. Vols. 1 and 11.

—— Sketch of David Hosack, M. D. Hist. Mag. Vol. 4.

FRANCIS, Sir Philip. Letter to Earl Grey, on the Policy of G. Britain and the Allies toward Norway. Lond., 1814. 8vo. 3d Ed. Pamphleteer. Vol. 4.
FRANCIS, Philip. Proceedings of the House of Commons on the Slave Trade, and State of the Negroes in the West Indies. Lond., 1796. 8vo. Eng Polit. Pamph. Vol. 25.
FRANCIS, Valentine M. The Fight for the Union; a Poem. N.Y., 1863. 8vo. Rebell'n Pamph. Vol. 23.
FRANK, Michael. Early Hist. of Kenosha. Wis. State Hist. Soc. Coll. Vol. 3.
FRANKFORT, Ky. Commonwealth, Newspaper. Apr., 1854, to Dec., 1859. 2 Vols. Folio.
FRANKLAND, Sir Chas. See NASON, E. Hist. of.
FRANKLIN Co., N. Y. Proceedings of Board of Supervisors, 1861. Malone, 1861. 8vo.
FRANKLIN, Dr. Benj. Autobiography. See GREEN, S. A. Story of a Famous Book.
—— Familiar Letters to B. Franklin, from his Family and Friends, 1751–90. N. Y., 1859. Sm. 4to.
—— See GILPIN, H. D. On the Character of.
—— His Examination before the House of Commons, 1766, in Support of the Repeal of the Amer. Stamp Act. Scarce Tracts. Vol. 2. Amer. Tracts. Vol. 2.
—— Life of, written by himself, with his Miscell. Essays. N. Y., 1858. 12mo.
—— See M'NEILE, Rev. Hugh. Lecture on the Life of, 1841.
—— Memoirs of; with his Social Epistolary Correspondence, Philosoph., Polit., and Moral Letters and Essays. Phila., 1834. 2 Vols. 8vo.
—— Memoirs, written by himself, with a Selection from his Essays, Letters and Writings. Harpers' Fam. Libr. N.Y., 1860. 2 Vols. 18mo.
—— See PARTON, Jas. Life of.
—— Remarks for the Information of those who wish to Settle in America. Imlay's America, p. 481.
—— Report on Animal Magnetism. 2d. Ed. Phila., 1837. 8vo. Scientific Pamph. Vol. 10.
—— See SPARKS, J. Life and Writings of.
—— WELD, H. H. Life of.
FRANKLIN, Conn., Cong. Ch. Celebra. of the 150th Annivers. of the Primitive Organization of, Oct. 14, 1868. N. Haven, 1869. 8vo. Conn. Hist. Discourses, etc. Vol. 6.
—— —— See WOODWARD, A. Hist. Address, 1868.
—— NOTT, Rev. Saml. Half Century Sermon, 1832.
FRANKLIN Co., Mass. See HOLLAND, J. G.
—— Agr. Society. Transactions for 1856 and 1857. Greenfield, 1857–8. 8vo. Agr. Pamph. Vol. 13.
FRANKLIN, Mass., Assoc. of Congrega. Ministers. See PACKARD, T. Hist. of Churches.
FRANKLIN Co., N. Y. See HOUGH, F. B. Hist. of St. Lawrence and Franklin Co's.
—— Agr. Soc'y. See TITUS, J. H. Address, 1853.

FRANKLIN Co., Ohio. See MARTIN, W. T. Hist. of.
FRANKLIN Institute, Phila. Charter and By-Laws. Phila., 1864. 12mo.
—— —— Journal. Phila., 1831–53. 6 Vols. 8vo.
—— —— Report on the School of Design for Women. Phila., 1852. 8vo. Phila. Misc. Pamph. Vol. 2.
FRANKLIN, Jas. Philosoph. and Polit. Hist. of the Thirteen U. States. Lond., 1774. 18mo.
FRANKLIN, Sir John. His Melancholy Fate, as disclosed in Dr. Rae's Report, etc. Lond., 1854. 8vo. Pamphlets—Amer. Travel. Vol. 1.
—— See MCCLINTOCK. Narr. of Discovery of his Fate, etc.
—— MARKHAM, C. R. Franklin's Footsteps.
FRANKLIN, O. See Licking Co. Pioneers.
FRANKLIN, Wm. See WHITEHEAD, Wm. A.
FRANKLIN, Maj. Gen. W. B. Reply to the Report of Joint Comm. of Cong. on the Conduct of the War. N. Y., 1863. 8vo. Rebell'n Pamph. Vols 2, 81.
—— Reply to the Joint Comm. of Cong. on the Conduct of the War, on the First Battle of Fredericksburg. N. Y., 1867. 8vo. 2d Ed. Rebell'n Pamph. Vol. 107.
FRANKLIN, Penn. See M'CALMONT, J. S. On the Early Settlement of.
FRANKKIN Society of Chicago. Publications: No. 1. SHEAHAN, J. W. The Printer, 1869. No. 2. Boss, H. R. Early Newspapers in Illinois, 1870.
FRANKLIN Memorial. See Memorial of, etc.
FRASER, Jas. B. Hist. and Descript. Acc. of Persia, from the Earliest Ages to the Present Time. Harpers' Fam. Libr. N.Y., 1860. 18mo.
—— Mesopotamia and Assyria from the Earliest Ages to the Present Time.. Harpers' Fam. Libr. N. Y., 1856. 18mo.
—— Military Memoir of Lieut. Col. Jas. Skinner, C. B. Lond., 1851. 2 Vols. 12mo.
FRASER's Magazine for Town and Country. Lond., 1830–65. 72 Vols. 8vo.
—— N. Series. Vol. 2. July–Dec., 1870. 8vo.
FRAZEE, L. J., M. D. The Mineral Waters of Ky. Louisville, 1872. 8vo. Ky. Misc. Pamph. Vol. 1.
FRASER, Col. Malcolm. Extract from a Manuscript Journal, relating to the Siege of Quebec in 1759. n. d. 8vo. Pamphlets Early Amer. Wars.
FREAKE, A. Use of the Humulus Lupulus in Gout, etc. Lond., (n. d.) 8vo. 2d Ed. Med. Pamph. Vol. 22.
FREDERICK II. of Prussia. See ABBOTT, J. S. C. Hist. of.
—— See DOVER, Lord. Life of.
—— Hist. of, in Dutch. Amsterdam, 1758. 14 Vols. 8vo.
—— See MACAULEY, Lord. Life of.
FREDERIC VII. of Denmark. Sur la Construction des Salles Dites des Geants. From the Memoires of the Roy. Soc. of No. Antiquaries, 1857.
FREDERICK, Md. Female Seminary. 11th Ann. Catalogue, 1856. Frederick, 1856. 8vo.

FREDERICKSBURG, Battle of. See FRANKLIN, W. B., Maj. Gen.
FREE, John, D. D. Essay towards an Hist. of the Eng. Tongue. Lond., 1773. 8vo. 3d Ed.
FREEDLEY, Edwin T. Philadelphia and its Manufactures; a Hand-Book of the Manufacturing Industry of Phila. in 1857. Phila., 1858. 12mo.
FREEDMEN. See ALVORD, J. W. Letter on the Condition of, 1870.
—— Facts concerning the Freedmen. Their Capacity and their Destiny. Boston, 1863. 8vo. Rebell'n Pamph. Vol. 107.
FREEDMEN'S Bureau. See Bureau of Freedmen, etc.
—— U. S. Sec. of War.
FREEDOM and Slavery in U. S. See NOEL, B. W.
—— of the Press. See Liberty of, etc.
FREELON, T. W. Oration before the Soc. of Cal. Pioneers, on the Seventh Annivers. of the Admission of Cal. San Francisco, 1857. 8vo. Cal. Hist. Discourses. Vol. 1.
FREEMAN, Chas. Account of Limerick, Me. Me. Hist. Soc. Coll. Vol. 1.
FREEMAN, Edw. A. Hist. of Federal Government from the Foundation of the Achaian League to the Disruption (?) of the U. S. Vol. 1. Lond., 1863. 8vo.
FREEMAN, Frederick. Hist. of Cape Cod. Annals of Barnstable Co., Mass. Boston, 1858. 2 Vols. 8vo.
FREEMAN, Rev. Jas. Character of Rev. John Eliot: Disc. at Boston, Mar. 7, 1813. Boston, 1813. 8vo. Sermons. Vol. 31.
FREEMAN, Rev. John. See SMITH, S. R. Memoir of.
FREEMAN, J. D. Speech in Cong., Mar. 18, 1852, on Union Parties in Mississippi, etc. Congr. and Polit. Pamph. Vol. 89.
—— Speech in Cong., Aug. 13, 1852, on Pub. Lands. Congr. and Polit. Pamph. Vol. 84.
FREEMAN, Saml, Emigrants' Hand-Book, and Guide to Wisconsin. Milwaukee, 1851. 8vo. Wis. Misc. Pamph. Vol. 1.
FREEMAN, S. C. Suggestive Manual on the Theory and Practice of Education. Lond., 1850. 8vo. Educa. Pamph. Vol. 33.
FREEMANTLE, Col. Three Months in Southern States, Apr.—June, 1863. N. Y., 1864. 12mo.
FREE MASONRY. See Secret Societies.
—— See Masonry.
FREE Military School for Applicants for Command of Colored Troops. Phila., 1864. Rebell'n Pamph. Vol. 14.
—— Negroism; or Results of Emancipation, 1862. Rebell'n Pamph. Vol. 74.
—— People of Colour. Minutes and Proceedings of the 3d Ann. Convention for the Improvement of. N. Y., 1833. 8vo. Congr. and Polit. Pamph. Vol. 103.
FREEPORT, Maine. Topograph. and Hist. Sketch of. Mass. Hist. Soc. Coll. Vol. 4. 2d Series.
FREE Religious Assoc. Proceedings at Boston, May, 1872. Boston, 1872. 8vo. Religious Pamph. Vol. 8.
FREETOWN, Mass. See FOWLER, O. Notices of.
FREE Trade. See Amer. Free Trade League.

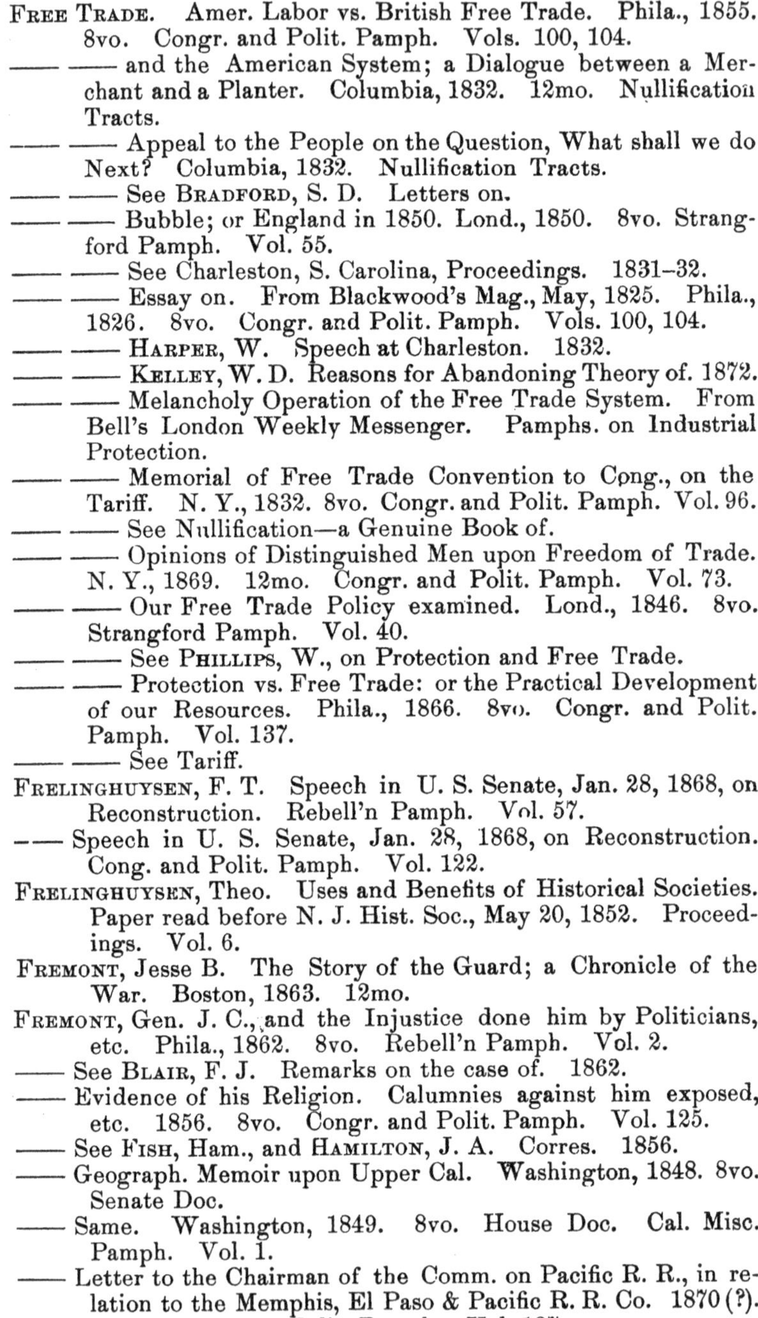

FREE TRADE. Amer. Labor vs. British Free Trade. Phila., 1855. 8vo. Congr. and Polit. Pamph. Vols. 100, 104.

—— —— and the American System; a Dialogue between a Merchant and a Planter. Columbia, 1832. 12mo. Nullification Tracts.

—— —— Appeal to the People on the Question, What shall we do Next? Columbia, 1832. Nullification Tracts.

—— —— See BRADFORD, S. D. Letters on.

—— —— Bubble; or England in 1850. Lond., 1850. 8vo. Strangford Pamph. Vol. 55.

—— —— See Charleston, S. Carolina, Proceedings. 1831–32.

—— —— Essay on. From Blackwood's Mag., May, 1825. Phila., 1826. 8vo. Congr. and Polit. Pamph. Vols. 100, 104.

—— —— HARPER, W. Speech at Charleston. 1832.

—— —— KELLEY, W. D. Reasons for Abandoning Theory of. 1872.

—— —— Melancholy Operation of the Free Trade System. From Bell's London Weekly Messenger. Pamphs. on Industrial Protection.

—— —— Memorial of Free Trade Convention to Cong., on the Tariff. N. Y., 1832. 8vo. Congr. and Polit. Pamph. Vol. 96.

—— —— See Nullification—a Genuine Book of.

—— —— Opinions of Distinguished Men upon Freedom of Trade. N. Y., 1869. 12mo. Congr. and Polit. Pamph. Vol. 73.

—— —— Our Free Trade Policy examined. Lond., 1846. 8vo. Strangford Pamph. Vol. 40.

—— —— See PHILLIPS, W., on Protection and Free Trade.

—— —— Protection vs. Free Trade: or the Practical Development of our Resources. Phila., 1866. 8vo. Congr. and Polit. Pamph. Vol. 137.

—— —— See Tariff.

FRELINGHUYSEN, F. T. Speech in U. S. Senate, Jan. 28, 1868, on Reconstruction. Rebell'n Pamph. Vol. 57.

—— Speech in U. S. Senate, Jan. 28, 1868, on Reconstruction. Cong. and Polit. Pamph. Vol. 122.

FRELINGHUYSEN, Theo. Uses and Benefits of Historical Societies. Paper read before N. J. Hist. Soc., May 20, 1852. Proceedings. Vol. 6.

FREMONT, Jesse B. The Story of the Guard; a Chronicle of the War. Boston, 1863. 12mo.

FREMONT, Gen. J. C., and the Injustice done him by Politicians, etc. Phila., 1862. 8vo. Rebell'n Pamph. Vol. 2.

—— See BLAIR, F. J. Remarks on the case of. 1862.

—— Evidence of his Religion. Calumnies against him exposed, etc. 1856. 8vo. Congr. and Polit. Pamph. Vol. 125.

—— See FISH, Ham., and HAMILTON, J. A. Corres. 1856.

—— Geograph. Memoir upon Upper Cal. Washington, 1848. 8vo. Senate Doc.

—— Same. Washington, 1849. 8vo. House Doc. Cal. Misc. Pamph. Vol. 1.

—— Letter to the Chairman of the Comm. on Pacific R. R., in relation to the Memphis, El Paso & Pacific R. R. Co. 1870 (?). 8vo. Congr. and Polit. Pamph. Vol. 137.

FREMONT, Life, Explorations and Pub. Services of. N. Y., 1856. 12mo. Biog. Pamph. Vol. 13.
—— Life of. N. Y., 1856. 8vo. Congr. and Polit. Pamph. Vol. 76.
—— See MAGOON, Jas.
—— PILSEN, Col. J.
—— Report of the Exploring Expedition to the Rocky Mountains in 1842, and to Oregon and N. California in 1843–44. Washington, 1845. 8vo. 2 copies. Senate Doc. and House Doc.
—— See SHANKS, J. P. C.
—— and EMORY, W. H. Notes of Travel in Cal. N. Y., 1849. 8vo. Cal. Misc. Pamph. Vol. 1.
FREMONT'S Romanism Established. Acknowledged by Archbishop Hughes. n. d. 8vo. Congr. and Polit. Pamph. Vol. 135.
—— See UPHAM, C. W. Life and Pub. Services.
FREMONT, Ohio. See WHITTLESEY, E. Defence of Fort Stephenson.
FRENCH & English Languages. Comparison of. See WILKIE, Rev. D.
—— And German War 1870. See MCCABE, J. D. History of.
—— And Indian War. See Amer. Wars, 1754, &c.
FRENCH, Benj. B. Address on the Antiquity & Advantages of Freemasonry. Washington, 1869. 8vo. Addresses. Vol. 21.
FRENCH, B. F. Hist. Collections of Louisiana; embracing Rare and Valuable Documents relating to the Nat., Civil and Polit. Hist. of that State. Phila. and N. Y., 1846–53. 4 Vols. 8vo. *Part* 1. Hist. Documents, 1678-1691. *Part* 2. Translations from De Soto, Coxe, Marquette, &c. *Part* 3. La Harpe's Establishment of the French in La.; Charlevoix Journal, etc. *Part* 4. Dumont and Champigny's Memoirs, &c.
—— Hist. Collections of La. and Florida. N. Series. Vol. 1. N. Y. 1869. 8vo.
FRENCH, Maj. Christopher. Journal of, 1776. Conn. Hist. Soc. Coll. Vol. 1.
FRENCH, Daniel. Cobbett on the Gridiron! Lond., 1829. Cong. & Polit. Pamph. Vol. 99.
FRENCH Genealogy. See VINTON, J. A. Memorials.
FRENCH, (The) in Africa. Lond., 1838. 8vo. Strangford Pamph. Vol. 17.
—— Intervention. See Congress'l Speeches.
—— —— in Mexico. See MCDOUGALL, J. A.
—— Intrigues (The) discovered. With Methods & Arts to Retrench the Potency of France, &c. Lond., 1681. Fol. Eng. Polit. Pamph. Vol. 2.
FRENCH, Rev. Jonathan. Hist. Sketch of North Hampton, N. H. 1815. Mass. Hist. Soc. Coll. Vol. 4. 2d Ser.
—— List of Cong. Ministers in the Eastern part of Rockingham Co., N. H., from its Settlement, &c. N. E. Hist. & Gen. Register. Vol. 1.
FRENCH, J. H. Hist. and Statist. Gazeteer of the State of N. Y. Syracuse, 1860. 8vo.
FRENCH Neutrals in Maine. Me. Hist. Soc. Coll. Vol. 6.
—— —— Penn. See REED, Wm. B.

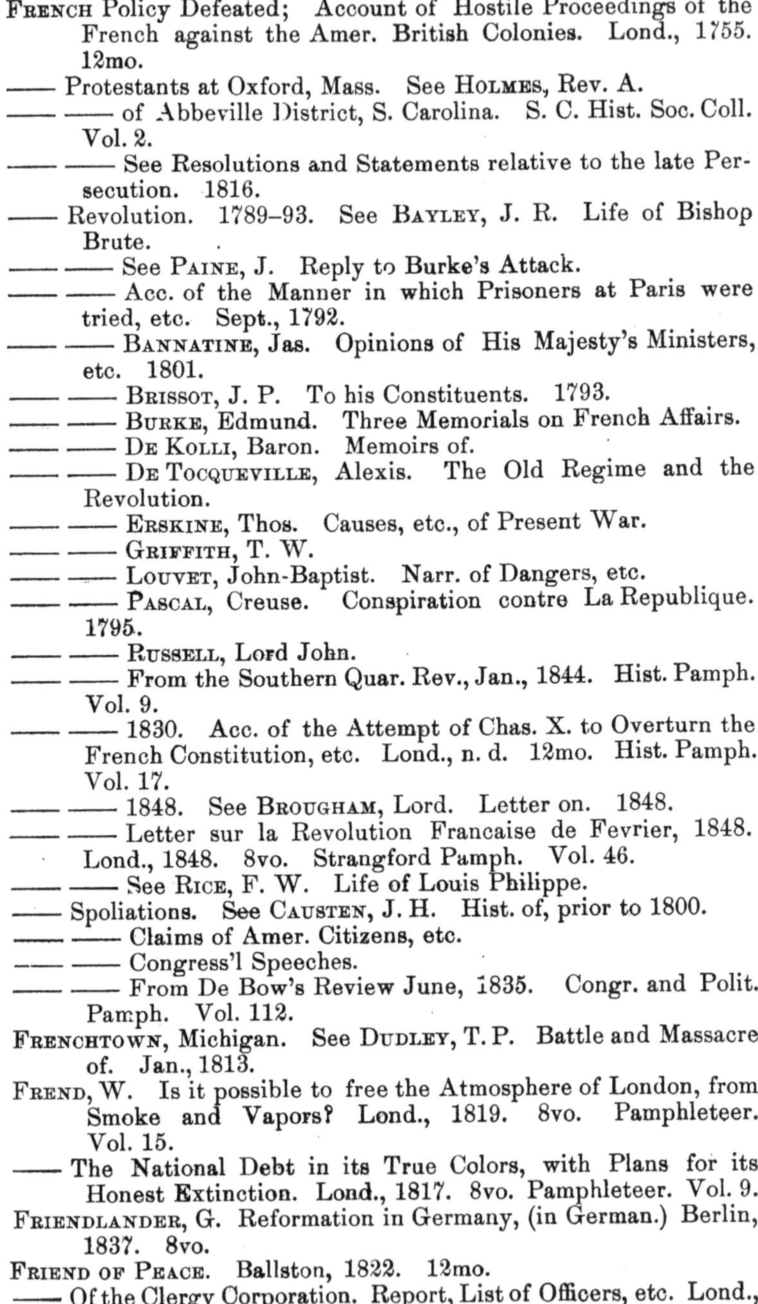

FRENCH Policy Defeated; Account of Hostile Proceedings of the French against the Amer. British Colonies. Lond., 1755. 12mo.

—— Protestants at Oxford, Mass. See HOLMES, Rev. A.

—— —— of Abbeville District, S. Carolina. S. C. Hist. Soc. Coll. Vol. 2.

—— —— See Resolutions and Statements relative to the late Persecution. 1816.

—— Revolution. 1789–93. See BAYLEY, J. R. Life of Bishop Brute.

—— —— See PAINE, J. Reply to Burke's Attack.

—— —— Acc. of the Manner in which Prisoners at Paris were tried, etc. Sept., 1792.

—— —— BANNATINE, Jas. Opinions of His Majesty's Ministers, etc. 1801.

—— —— BRISSOT, J. P. To his Constituents. 1793.

—— —— BURKE, Edmund. Three Memorials on French Affairs.

—— —— DE KOLLI, Baron. Memoirs of.

—— —— DE TOCQUEVILLE, Alexis. The Old Regime and the Revolution.

—— —— ERSKINE, Thos. Causes, etc., of Present War.

—— —— GRIFFITH, T. W.

—— —— LOUVET, John-Baptist. Narr. of Dangers, etc.

—— —— PASCAL, Creuse. Conspiration contre La Republique. 1795.

—— —— RUSSELL, Lord John.

—— —— From the Southern Quar. Rev., Jan., 1844. Hist. Pamph. Vol. 9.

—— —— 1830. Acc. of the Attempt of Chas. X. to Overturn the French Constitution, etc. Lond., n. d. 12mo. Hist. Pamph. Vol. 17.

—— —— 1848. See BROUGHAM, Lord. Letter on. 1848.

—— —— Letter sur la Revolution Francaise de Fevrier, 1848. Lond., 1848. 8vo. Strangford Pamph. Vol. 46.

—— —— See RICE, F. W. Life of Louis Philippe.

—— Spoliations. See CAUSTEN, J. H. Hist. of, prior to 1800.

—— —— Claims of Amer. Citizens, etc.

—— —— Congress'l Speeches.

—— —— From De Bow's Review June, 1835. Congr. and Polit. Pamph. Vol. 112.

FRENCHTOWN, Michigan. See DUDLEY, T. P. Battle and Massacre of. Jan., 1813.

FREND, W. Is it possible to free the Atmosphere of London, from Smoke and Vapors? Lond., 1819. 8vo. Pamphleteer. Vol. 15.

—— The National Debt in its True Colors, with Plans for its Honest Extinction. Lond., 1817. 8vo. Pamphleteer. Vol. 9.

FRIENDLANDER, G. Reformation in Germany, (in German.) Berlin, 1837. 8vo.

FRIEND OF PEACE. Ballston, 1822. 12mo.

—— Of the Clergy Corporation. Report, List of Officers, etc. Lond., 1864. 8vo. Eng. Misc. Pamph. Vol. 34.

FRIENDLY Address to the Laboring Part of the Community, concerning Public Affairs, etc. Lond., 1803. 8vo. Eng. Polit. Pamph. Vol. 27.

—— Observations addressed to Sculptors and Artists, on certain works in the Palace of Industry, etc. Lond., 1851. 12mo. Pamph. on Art. Vol 2.

FRIENDS' REVIEW. A Religious, Literary and Misc. Journal. Vol. 11. Phila., 1858. 8vo.

FRIEND'S Society of. Acc. of Proceedings in House of Commons, on the Petition of Quakers, on the Tithe Bill. Lond., 1737. 12mo. Eng. Polit. Pamph. Vol. 11.

—— —— Address to the Citizens of the U. S. on Slavery. Phila., 1837. 8vo. Religious Pamph. Vol. 5.

—— —— See ALLINSON, Wm. J. Quakerism Vital.

—— —— BARCLAY, Robt. Life and Writings of.

—— —— BISHOP, G. N. England Judged.

—— —— Brief Sketch of Efforts of the Phila. Yearly Meeting in behalf of the Indians. Phila. 1866. 8vo. Indian Pamph. Vol. 2.

—— —— See Collection of Memorials of Deceased Ministers. 1787.

—— —— Congregational Friends.

—— —— CORDER, Susanna. Origin and Principles of.

—— —— Crisis of the Quaker Contest in Manchester. 1836.

—— —— DYMOND, J. Essays, etc.

—— —— Epistle from the Yearly Meeting held in Phila., in 1861. Phila., 1861. 8vo. Religious Pamph. Vol. 5.

—— —— Epistles from Yearly meetings held at London, from 1675 to 1759. Lond., 1760. 4to.

—— —— Epistles from Yearly Meetings held in London in 1815, 1820, 1821, 1828. Do., held in N. Y. 1820, Baltimore 1828, N. York, 1829. 7 pamphlets. Folio.

—— —— Gen. Epistle from the Yearly Meeting, held in London, 1870. N. Bedford, 1871. 12mo. Religious Pamph. Vol. 5A.

—— —— See FOX, Geo. Journ. of Life, &c. Friends' Review, 1858.

—— —— GRIFFITH, J. Life and Ministerial Labors.

—— —— JANNEY, S. M. Life of G. Fox, &c.

—— —— Memorial and Remonstrance in relation to the Indians of the State of N. Y. N. Y., 1840. 8vo.

—— —— Memorial of Deceased Friends, of N. E. Yearly Meeting. N. Bedford, 1868. 8vo. Religious Pamph., Vol. 5A.

—— —— Narr. of Proceedings of Yearly Meeting of Friends of N. Y. on the Condition of N. Y. Indians. N. Y., 1839. 8vo.

—— —— See Narr. of Events in Ireland. 1804.

—— —— NORRIS, J. S. Early Friends of Md.

—— —— PENN, W. Works of.

—— —— Proceedings of Comm. of Friends of Penn. and N. J., 1795, for the Improvement of the Indians. London, 1806. 8vo. Indian Pamph., Vol. 3.

—— —— See ROGERS, Rev. J. Persuasive to Conformity.

—— —— SCOTT, J. Life and Gospel Labors.

FRIEND'S Society of. Some acc. of the Conduct of, towards the Indian Tribes in N. J. and Penn. Lond., 1844. 8vo.

—— —— See STODDART, John. Life of Thos. Wilson.

—— —— Summary of the Hist., Doctrines and Discipline of. Lond., 1790. 8vo. Religious Pamph., Vol. 5.

—— —— Testimony of Friends on the Continent of America. Phila., 1830. 8vo. Religious Pamph., Vol. 5.

—— —— See WILSON, Thos. Labors in the Ministry. 1784.

FRIES, John. Two Trials of, for Treason and Insurrection in the Counties of Bucks, Northampton and Montgomery, Penn., 1799. Phila., 1800. 8vo.

FRISBIE, Barnes. Hist. of Middletown, Vt., in Three Discourses delivered in Feb. and Mar., 1867. Rutland, 1867. 8vo. Vt. Hist. Discourses. Vol. 2.

FRITOT, Albert. Science du Publiciste; on traite des principes Elementaires du Droit. Paris, 1820. Vols. 1, 2, 3, 7, 8, 11. 6 vols. 8vo.

FRITSCHIUS, Ahasuerus. Dissertatio de Vitiis Eruditorum. Leipsic, 1676. 4to. Latin Psmph. Vol. 1.

FROBISHER, Sir Martin. Memoirs of. 1536–1594. N. E. Hist. and Gen. Qegister. Vol. 3.

FROISSART, Sir John. Chronicles of England, France and Spain. Lond., 1812. 2 vols. 4to.

FROMENT, Charles. Etudes sur la Revolution Belge. Ghent, 1834. 8vo. Strangford Pamph. Vol. 11.

FRONTENAC, Count de. Papers relating to his Expedition against the Onondagoes. 1696. Doc. Hist. of N. Y. Vol. 1.

FROST, Chas. Considerations on Making a Remuneration to Witnesses in Civil Actions, for Loss of Time, &c. Lond., 1815. 8vo. Pamphleteer. Vol. 7.

—— See PARSONS, Usher. Memoir of.

FROST Family, of Elliot, York Co., Maine. n. d. Small 4to. Genealog. Pamph. Vol. 8.

FROST, John. Border Wars of the West; embracing Individual Adventures among the Indians. Auburn, 1854. 8vo.

—— Heroic Women of the West. Phila., 1854. 8vo.

—— Incidents and Narratives of Travel in Europe, Asia, Africa and America. Auburn, 1855. 8vo.

—— Indian Wars of the U. S., from the Earliest Period to the Present Time. N. Y., 1856. 8vo.

—— Pictorial Family Encyclopœdia of Hist., Biography and Travels. N. Y., 1857. 8vo.

—— Universal Naval Hist. N. Y. and Hartford, 1854. 8vo.

—— Wild Scenes of the Hunter's Life: or the Hunting and Hunters of all Nations. N. Y., 1858. 12mo.

FROST, Mrs. J. B. Rebellion in the U. S.; or War of 1861. Boston, 1862. Vol. 1. 8vo.

FROTHINGHAM, N. L., D. D. Farewell Sermon in the 1st Ch., Boston, Mar. 10, 1850. Boston, 1850. 8vo. Sermons. Vol. 34.

—— See HEDGE, F. H. Memoir of.

FROTHINGHAM, N. L., D. D. Sermon at 1st Church, Boston, on the 20th Annivers. of his Ordination, Mar. 15, 1835. Boston, 1835. 8vo. Boston Hist. Discourses. Vol. 1.

—— Sermon at 1st Ch., Boston, on the Close of their 2d Century, Aug. 29, 1830. Boston, 1830. 8vo. Boston Hist. Discourses. Vol. 1.

—— Bi-Centen-Sermon at Boston, on the Celebra. of the Establishment of the Thursday Lecture. Boston, 1833. 8vo. Mass. Hist. Discourses. Vol. 17. See also Boston. Hist. Discourses. Vol. 1.

—— Funeral Sermon on the Death of Jos. Kean. D.D., Apr., 1818. Boston, 1818. 8vo. Sermons. Vol. 1.

—— Memoir of Thad. M. Harris, D. D. Mass. Hist. Soc. Coll. 4th Ser. Vol. 2.

—— Memoir of Wm. P. Lunt, D. D. Sermons, etc. Vol. 29. Mass. Hist. Soc. Proceed. 1855–58. Coll. 4th Ser. Vol. 4.

—— Sermon at Boston, Feb. 25, 1838, on the Death of Jos. P Bradlee. Boston, 1838. 8vo. Sermons. Vol. 43.

—— Sermon at Boston, Apr. 10, 1842, after the Funerals of the Rev. Dr. Harris, and the Hon. Dan'l. Sargent. Boston, 1842. 8vo. Sermons. Vol. 43.

—— Sermon at Boston, Aug. 6, 1843, on the Death of Rev. F. W. P. Greenwood, D. D. Boston, 1843. 8vo. Sermons. Vols. 32, 43.

—— Sermon at Boston, Jan. 7, 1849, on the Death of Hon. Peter C. Brooks. Boston, 1849. 8vo. Sermons. Vol. 32.

—— Sermon on the Death of John Adams, at Boston, July 9, 1826. Boston, 1826. 8vo. Sermons. Vol. 31.

FROTHINGHAM, Richard. The Rise of the Republic of the U. States. Boston, 1872. 8vo.

FROUDE, Jas. Anthony Hist. of England from the Fall of Wolsey to the Death of Queen Elizabeth. N. Y., 1871. 12 Vols. 12mo.

—— See BURKE Rev. T. N. Reply to. 1872.

FRUITS. See Downing, A. J. Fruit Trees of America.

—— HOOPER, E. J. Western Fruit Book.

FRY, Emilie L. Petition for a Divorce; Memorial of John Grigg, Speeches, etc. Phila., 1859. 8vo. Law Pamph. Vol. 5.

FRY, J. See Albany Directory.

FRY, Jos. Storrs. Concise History of Tithes, with an Inquiry into their warrant from the Gospel. Lond., 1820. 8vo. Pamphleteer. Vol. 15.

FRY, Joshua & JEFFERSON, Peter. Map of the settled portion of Virginia and Maryland. Lond., 1775. In cover.

FRY, Wm. T. Facts and Evidence relating to the Opium Trade with China. Lond., 1840. 8vo. Strangford Pamph. Vol. 23.

FUGITIVE SLAVE LAW. Proceedings of U. S. Senate on the Fugitive Slave Bill and Slavery in the Dist. of Columbia. Boston, 1850. 8vo. Congr. and Polit. Pamph. Vol. 56.

—— —— Report of Comm. of U. S. Senate on the Repeal of the. Washington, 1864. 8vo. Rebell'n Pamph. Vol. 9.

FUGITIVE SLAVE LAW. See Congress. Speeches.
—— —— And Its Victims. N. Y., 1861. 12mo. Congr. and Polit. Pamph. Vol. 136.
—— —— See HARRIS, T. L. Letter on Repeal of. 1851.
—— —— SPEAR, S. T. Sermon. 1850.
—— —— SPENCER, Rev. J. S. Sermon. 1850.
—— —— FUGITT, Rev. Jas. P. Is Slaveholding Constitutional and Scriptural. Baltimore, 1862. 12mo. Rebell'n Pamph. 109.
FULLER GENEALOGY. See CLARKE, S. C. J. Fuller's Descendants. NOYES, J.
FULLER, H. Causes and Consequences of the Civil War in America. Lond., 1861. 8vo. Rebell'n Pamph. Vol. 19.
FULLER, H. M. Speech in Cong., May 10, 1856, on Political Parties, etc. Congr. and Polit. Pamph. Vol. 89.
FULLER, Rich'd. Address before Amer. Coloniza. Soc., at Washington, Jan. 21, 1851. Baltimore, 1851. 8vo. Coloniza. Pamph. Vol. 1.
FULLER, Sam'l., D. D. Disc. at Litchfield, Conn., Sept. 19, 1849, on the Death of Maj. Gen. Francis Bacon. N. Y., 1849. 8vo. Sermons, Vol. 22.
—— Memorial to Peter Smith Byers, at Andover, Mass., March 21, 1856. 8vo. Sermons, Vol. 3.
—— Two Sermons at Rensselaerville, N. Y., Apr. 24, 1842, on the Death of Rev. Sam'l Fuller his Father. Andover, 1843. 8vo. N. Y., Hist. Discourses. Vol. 1.
FULLER, S. M. Summer on the Lakes in 1843. Boston, 1844. 12mo.
FULLER, Thos. Hist. of the Worthies of England. Lond., 1840. 3 Vols. 8vo.
FULLER, T. J. D. Speech in Cong., Mar. 30, 1852, on the Homestead Bill. Cong. and Polit. Pamph., Vol. 83.
FULTON CITY, Ill. Sketches of Early Hist. and Present Advantages of Fulton City, with a Sketch of Whiteside Co. Fulton, 1856. 8vo. Ill. Local Histories, Vol. 1.
FULTON Co. Teachers' Institute, held at Gloversville, N. Y., Oct., 1865. Gloversville, 1866. 8vo. Educa. Pamph., Vol. 5.
FULTON, Justin D. R. Catholic Element in Amer. History. N. Y. 1857. 12mo.
FULTON, Robert. See COLDEN, C. D. Life of.
—— RENWICK, J. Life of.
FURBER, Geo. C. The Twelve Months' Volunteer and War in Mexico. Cincin., 1857. 8vo.
FURNEAUX, Rev. Philip. Essay on Toleration; with reference to the Act of Toleration. Lond., 1773. 8vo. Eng. Polit. Pamph., Vol. 17.
FURMAN, Gabriel. Notes, Geographical and Historical, relating to the Town of Brooklyn, with Notes and a Memoir. Brooklyn, 1865. 4to.
FURNESS, Wm. H. Discourse at Phila., June 29, 1862. Rebell'n Pamph., Vols. 40 and 63.
—— Discourse at Phila., Jan. 10, 1864. Rebell'n Pamph., Vol. 70.

FURNISS, Wm. H. Discourse on the Death of Jos. Sill. Phila., n. d. Rebell'n Pamph., Vol. 40.

FURNIVALL, Fred. J. Early Eng. Poems and Lives of the Saints, from MSS. in the British Musuem, pub. in Trans. of Philolog. Soc. 1858.

FURTHER and still more Important Suppressed Documents. n. d. Congr. and Polit. Pamph., Vol. 98.

—— Queries on the Present State of N. E. Affairs. Lond., 1689. N. Y. reprint, 1865. Sm. 4to.

FUR Trade. See DUNN, John. Oregon Terr'y and British N. Amer. Fur Trade. 1844. NEILL, E. D. Hist. of, in N. West.

FUTURE, The, of the Country, by a Patriot. n. d. Rebell'n Pamph., Vol. 8.

FYFE, Dr. Andrew. Use of Chlorine as an Indication of the Illuminating Power of Coal Gas, &c. Edinburgh, 1842. 8vo. Scientific Pamph., Vol. 34.

—— Evaporative Power of Coal. From the Edinburgh Philos. Journ., 1841. 8vo. Scientific Pamph., Vol. 25.

G.

GABELL, Rev. H. See LOWTH, Rev. Robt. Correspondence.

GAELIC Language. See Dictionarium Scoto—Cellicum.

GAFFIELD, Thos. Action of Sunlight on Glass. N. Haven, 1867. 8vo. Scientific Pamph. Vol. 19.

GAGE, Thos. Hist. of Rowley, Mass., including Bradford, Boxford and Georgetown, from 1639, with Rev. Jas. Bradfcrd's 2d Centenn. Address, Sept. 5, 1839. Boston, 1840. 8vo.

GAGE, Gen. Thos. Letters to Peyton Randolph, Oct. 20, 1774. Congr. & Polit. Pamph. Vol. 58.

GAIL, G. W. Suggestions for Taxing Tobacco. Baltimore, 1865. 8vo. Rebell'n Pamph. Vol. 7.

GAILLARD Genealogy. See GAILLARD, W.

GAILLARD, W. Hist. and Pedigrees of the House of Gaillard or Gaylord, in France, England and the U. S. Photographic Portraits and Views. 8vo. Cincin. n. d.

GAIMAR, Geoffrey. Anglo-Norman Chronicle. See Caxton Soc. Publica.

GAINES, Myra Clark. See PASCHAL, Geo. W. Argument in Case of.

GALAXY (The). Apr., 1867, to Apr., 1871. 7 Vols. All incomplete but Vol. 8, July–Dec., 1869. N. Y. 8vo.

GALE, Genealogy. See GALE, Geo.

GALE, Geo. Gale Family Record. Galesville, Wis., 1866. 8vo.

—— Genealogy of the Gale Family. n. d. n. p. 8vo. Genealog. Pamph. Vol. 7.

—— The Upper Mississippi; or Hist. Sketches of the Mound Builders. Chicago, 1857. 12mo.

GALE, S. Essay on the Nature and Principles of Public Credit. Lond., 1784. 8vo.

GALENA & Chicago Union R. R. Co. 4th and 5th Ann. Reports. 1851. Docs. in relation to the Chicago, Fulton & Mississippi R. R. Bridge. 1858. Chicago. 8vo. Ill. Misc. R. R. Reports, &c.

—— Directory and Miner's Ann. Register for 1848, 1849. Galena, 1849. 8vo. Ill. Local Histories, &c. Vol. 1.

—— Miners Journal. Newspaper. Sept. 1829, to Dec. 1830, folio.

—— Northwestern Gazette and Advertiser. Newspaper. Nov. 1834 to Nov., 1837, folio.

GALERM, John B. See REED, Wm. B.

GALESVILLE, Wis., Transcript. Newspaper. Galesville. 1860–1866. Folio.

—— —— Record and Journal. Newspaper. Galesville. 1867–1873. Folio.

—— —— University. Catalogue for 1863–4. Galesville. 8vo.

GALFREDI Monumentensis Historia Brittonum. See Caxton Soc. Publica.

GALIANO, Prof. Antonio. Introduct. Lecture before the University of London, Nov. 1828. Lond. 1829. 8vo. 2d Ed. Educa. Pamph. Vol. 35.

GALICIA La Verie sur les Evenement de Gallicie. Paris, 1847. 8vo. Strangford Pamph. Vol. 68.

GALILEO and the Roman Inquisition ; a Defence of the Catholic Church. Cincin., 1859. 8vo. Scientific Pamph. Vol. 23.

—— See BREWSTER, D.

GALAGHER, Jas. The Western Sketch Book. Cincin. 12mo.

GALAGHER, Wm. D. Ann. Disc. before the Hist. Soc. of Ohio, Apr., 1850, on the 62d Annivers. of the Settlement of the State. Cincin., 1850. 8vo.

GALLAND, I. Iowa Emigrant, containing a Map and a Gen. Descrip. of the Territory. Chillicothe, 1840. 8vo.

GALLATIN, Albert. Hale's Indians of N. West America, and Vocabularies. Amer. Ethnonolog. Soc. Trans. Vol. 2.

—— Inaug. Address before N. Y. Hist. Soc., Feb. 7, 1843. N. Y., 1843. 8vo. N. Y. Hist. Soc. Addresses. Vol. 2.

—— Memoir of. Amer. Antiq, Soc. Proceed. 1813–1855.

—— Memoir on the N. Eastern Boundary, with a Speech on the same subject by DAN'L WEBSTER, before N. Y. Hist. Soc., 1834. 8vo. N. Y. Hist. Soc. Addresses. Vol. 2.

—— Notes on the Semi-Civilized Nations of Mexico, Yucatan and Cent. America. Amer. Ethnolog. Soc. Trans. Vol. 1.

—— Peace with Mexico. N. Y., 1847. 8vo. Congr. and Polit. Pamph. Vols. 80 and 96.

—— Suggestions on the Banks and Currency of the several U. S. 1841. Congr. and Polit. Pamph. Vol. 98.

—— Synopsis of the Indian Tribes within the U. S., East of the Rocky Mountains, and in British and Russian America. 1836. Amer. Antq'n Soc. Coll. Vol. 2.

—— The Oregon Question. N. Y., 1846. 8vo. Cong. & Polit. Pamph. Vol. 56.

GALLATIN, Albert. Views of the Public Debt. Receipts & Expenditures of the U. S. Phila., 1801. 8vo. 2d Ed. Congr. & Polit. Pamph. Vol. 123.

GALLATIN, JAS. Letter to Hon. Saml. Hooper on Nat. Finances and the Treasury. N. Y. 1862. 8vo. Rebell'n Pamph. Vol. 28.

—— The National Debt, Taxation, Currency and Banking System of the U. S. 1864. Rebell'n Pamph. No. 87.

—— The Public Debt, Banking, Currency, & Finances of the U. S. Letters to Hon. Jas. R. Doolittle. N. Y. 1866. 8vo. Banking and Currency Pamph. Vol. 3.

—— Two Letters to Hon. S. P. Chase. N. Y. 1861. 8vo. Rebell'n Pamph. Vol. 14.

GALLAUDET, Rev. Thos. H. See BARNARD, H. Obit. Dis. 1852.

—— HUMPHREY, Rev. H. Life and Labors of.

GALLERY OF PORTRAITS; with Memoirs, published by the Soc. for the Diffusion of Useful Knowledge. Lond. 1833–34. 3 Vols. 8vo.

GALLOWAY, Earl of. Abuse and Reform of the Monitorial System of Harrow School. Lond., 1854. 8vo. Strangford Pamph. Vol. 66.

GALLOWAY, A. An Insight to the Assessed Taxes, giving the Exemptions and the manner of claiming the same, etc. Lond. 1850. 8vo. Eng. Polit. Pamph. Vol. 49.

GALLOWAY, Jos. Amer. Tracts: 1. Candid Examina. of Mutual Claims of G. Britain and the Colonies. N. Y. 1775. 8vo. N. Y. 1775. 8vo.

2. Reply to an Address to the Author of "a Candid Examina. of Claims of G. Britain. N. Y. 1775. 8vo.
3. His Examination before House of Commons. 2d Ed. N. Y. 1780. 8vo.
4. Letters to a Nobleman on the Conduct of the War. 2d Ed. N. Y. 1779 with map.
5. Letter to Lord Howe on his Naval Conduct in the Amer. War. Lond. 1779. 8vo.
6. Cool Thoughts on the Consequences of Amer. Independence. Lond. 1780. 8vo.
7. Histor., and Polit. Reflections on the Amer. Rebellion. Lond. 1780. 8vo.

GALPHIN CLAIM. See Congr'l Speeches.

GALT, John. Life of Lord Byron. Harpers' Fam. Lib. N. Y. 1859. 18mo.

GALUSHA, Jonas. See Vermont Hist. Soc.

GALVANIC Battery. See HOUGH, G. W. Remarks. 1868.

GALVANISM. See ELECTRICITY.

GALVESTON & Texas Red River R. R. Facts to Establish the Importance of. N. Y., 1854. 8vo. Texas Misc. Pamph. Vol. 1.

—— Bay & Texas Land Co. Address. N. Y., 1831. 8vo. Texas Misc. Pamph. Vol. 1.

—— Chamber of Commerce. Memorial to Congress for the Improvement of Galveston Bay. Galveston, 1870. 8vo. Congr. and Polit. Pamph. Vol. 116.

GALVESTON 1st Semi-Ann. Report of the Pub. Schools. Galveston, 1847. 8vo. Texas Misc. Pamph. Vol. 1.

—— Title to the City of. N. Y., 1847. 8vo. Texas Misc. Pamph. Vol. 1.

GALWAY, N. Y., 2d Bapt. Ch. Confession of Faith. n. d. 12mo. Religious Pamph. Vol. 19.

GAMBLE, R. L. Speech in Congress, July 7, 1842, on the Tariff. Washington, 1842. 8vo. Congr. and Polit. Pamph. Vol. 24.

GAMING. See ABITOL M. English Gaming Law of 1854.

—— Danger to British Freedom by the Proposed Bill to Suppress Gaming Houses. Lond., 1854. 8vo. Strangford Pamph. Vol. 66.

GAMMELL, Wm. Address before the R. Island Hist. Soc., at the Opening of their Cabinet, Nov. 20, 1844. Providence, 1844. 8vo. R. I. Hist. Soc. Addresses. Vol. 1.

—— Life of Roger Williams. Spark's Amer. Biog. 2d Ser. Vol. 4.

—— Life of Sam'l Ward, Gov. of R. Island. Spark's Amer. Biog. 2d Ser. Vol. 9.

GAN-EDEN; or Pictures of Cuba. Boston, 1854. 12mo.

GANILH, Ch. Gen. Reflections on the Financial Situation of France, in 1816. Translated from the French. Paris, 1816. 8vo. Pamphleteer. Vol. 7.

GANNETT, Caleb. Sketch of Life and Character of. Mass. Hist. Soc. Coll. 2d Ser. Vol. 8.

GANNETT, Rev. E. G. Funeral Address on Rev. Wm. E. Channing, Oct., 1842. Boston, 1843. 8vo. Sermons. Vol. 1. Vol. 30.

—— Dis. delivered at the Funeral of Rev. Wm. B. O. Peabody, Springfield, Mass., June 1, 1847. Springfield, 1847. 8vo. Sermons. Vol. 30.

—— Disc. on the Death of Josiah Quincy, at Boston, July 10, 1864. Boston, 1864. 8vo. Sermons. Vol. 31.

—— 40th Annivers. Disc. in the Arlington St. Ch., Boston, July 3, 1864. Boston, 1864. 8vo.

—— Mr. Parker and his Views. From the Christian Examiner. Boston, 1845. 8vo. Religious Pamph. Vol. 8.

—— Obit. Sermon on the Death of Hon. Nathan Appleton. Boston, 1861. 8vo. Sermons. Vol. 2.

—— Sermon at the Funeral Obsequies of Hon. Chas. Paine. Northfield, 1853. 8vo. Sermons. Vols. 1 and 51.

—— Sermon before the Boston Y. M's Total Abstinence Soc., Nov. 8, 1846. Boston, 1846. 8vo. Sermons. Vol. 44.

—— Sermon at Boston, July 19, 1840, on the Arrival of the Brittania. Boston, 1840. 8vo. Vol. 41.

—— Sermon at the Arlington St. Ch., Boston, July 3, 1864, at the close of the 40th Year of his Ministry. Boston, 1784. 8vo. Boston Hist. Discourses. Vol. 2.

—— Sermon on the Death of John Davis, at Boston, Jan. 24, 1847. Boston, 1847. 8vo. Sermons. Vol. 31.

GANTT, Gen. E. W. Address at Little Rock, Ark., Oct. 7, 1863. Rebell'n Pamph. Vol. 31.

GARDEN, Alexander. Anecdotes of the Amer. Revolution. Brooklyn. Reprint. 1865. 3 Vols. 4to.

GARDENING. Essay on Design in Gardening. Lond., 1768. 12mo. Agr. Pamph. Vol. 15.

—— See JOHNSON, G. W. Dictionary of.

—— PERFECT, Thos.

GARDINER, Absalom. Centen. Address at Wales, Mass., Oct. 3, 1862. 8vo. Springfield, 1865. 8vo.

GARDINER, David. Chronicles of the Town of Easthampton, in the Co. of Suffolk, N. Y. N. Y., 1871. 8vo.

GARDINER, Geo. A. See FENDALL, P. R.

GARDINER Investigation. Report of the Select Comm. of U. S. House of R. 1852. Congress Pamph. Vol. 41.

GARDINER, Rev. John S. J. Fast Day Disc. at Boston, July 23, 1812, on the Declar. of War against G. Britain. Boston, 1812. 8vo. Sermons. Vol. 40.

—— Sermon at Boston, Dec. 9, 1804, on the Death of Bishop Saml. Parker. Boston, 1804. 8vo. Sermons. Vol. 43.

GARDINER, Lion. Biograph. Sketch of. Mass. Hist. Soc. Coll. 3d. Ser. Vol. 10.

—— Hist. of the Pequot War, 1638. Cincin. Reprit, 1860. 4to.

GARDINER, Robert H. Hist. of the Kennebec Purchase; or Proceedings under the Grant to the Colony of Plymouth, of Lands on the Kennebec. Maine Hist. Soc. Coll. Vol. 2.

—— Memoir of Benj. Vaughan, M.D., L.L.D. Maine Hist. Soc. Coll. Vol. 6.

GARDNER Absalom. Centen. Address in Wales, Mass., Oct. 5, 1862. With a "Roll of Honor." Springfield, 1866. 8vo. Mass. Hist. Discourses. Vol. 12.

GARDNER, Chas. K. Dictionary of all Officers who have been Commissioned, or have been appropriated and served in the Army of the U. S. from 1789–1853. N. Y., 1853. 12mo.

GARDNER, Daniel. Treatise on the Law of the Amer. Rebellion. N. Y., 1862. 8vo. Rebellion Pamph. Vol. 3.

GARDNER, Rev. Francis. Half Century Sermon in Leominster, Dec. 27, 1812. Leominster, 1813. 8vo. Mass. Hist. Disc. Vol. 16.

GARDNER, Dr. W. H. Ethnology of the Indians of the Red River of the North. Smithsonian Report, 1870.

GARDWELL, Godek. Currency: The Evil and the Remedy. N. Y., 1844. 8vo. 5th Ed. Banking and Currency Pamph. Vol. 3.

GARFIELD, Jas. A. Addresses before the Literary Societies of the Eclectic Institute at Hiram, O., June 14, 1867. Cleveland, 1867. 8vo. Addresses. Vol. 19.

—— Oration on the Life and Character of Gen. Geo. H. Thomas, before the Soc. of the Army of the Cumberland, Nov. 25, 1870. Cincin., 1871. 8vo. Rebell'n Pamph. Vol. 107.

—— Speech in Cong. on Confiscation, Jan. 28, 1864. Rebell'n Pamph. Vol. 9.

—— Speech in Cong., Mar. 24 & 31, 1864, on Raritan & Atlantic R. R. Cong. & Polit. Pamph. Vol. 92.

GARFIELD, Jas. A. Speech in Cong., June 8, 1866, on National Education. Addresses, &c. Vol. 19.

—— Speech in Congress, Feb. 20, 1871, on the McGarrahan Claim. 8vo. Cong. & Polit. Pamph. Vol. 132.

GARFIELD, Rich'd. On the General Establishment of Register Offices for the Register of Deeds, etc., 1818. 8vo Pamphleteer. Vol. 12. Eng. Misc. Pamph. Vol. 4.

GARIBALDI, Guiseppe. Life of. Lond. n. d. 8vo. Biograph. Pamph. Vol. 4.

GARLAND, Hugh A. Life of John Randolph of Roanoke. 9th Ed. N. Y., 1854. 8vo.

—— Oration at N. Y., July 27, 1840, on the Independent Treasury Bill. Addresses. Vol. 12.

GARNEAUX, F. X. Hist. of Canada, from its Discovery to the Union 1840–1. Montreal, 1860. 2 Vols. 8vo.

GARNET, Rev. H. Trial & Execution of Father H. Garnet, for the Powder-Treason, 1616.(?) Lond., 1679. Fol. Eng. Polit. Pamph. Vol. 1.

GARNETT, Jas. M. Constitutional Charts; or Comparative Views of the Legislative Departments in the Constitutions of the different States. Richmond, 1829. 4to.

GARNETT, S. Ann. Cursory Family Sketches, Tompkins Family, pr. printed. Albany, 1870. 8vo.

GARRARD, Lewis H. Chambersburg in the Colony and the Revolution; a Sketch. Phila., 1856. 8vo.

GARRATT, Alfred C. Electro-Physiology and Electro-Therapentics. 2d Ed. Boston, 1860. 8vo.

GARRETT, John W. Address to the Directors of the Baltimore & Ohio R. R. Co. Baltimore, 1868. 8vo. Ind. Misc. Pamph. Vol. 1.

—— Necessity for, and Advantages of a First Class Railway between Baltimore, Phila. and N. Y. Baltimore, 1871. 8vo. Md. Misc. Pamph. Vol. 1.

GARRISON, John. Autobiography of. Pioneer Settler of Sandusky. Fire Lands Pioneer. Vol. 6.

GARRISON, Wm. L. Address before the Free People of Color, April, 1833. 8vo. Cong. & Polit. Pamph. Vol. 103.

—— The Abolitionists and their Relations to the War. Speech at N. Y., 1862. Rebell'n Pamph. Vol. 99.

—— Selection from his Speeches, &c. Boston, 1852. 8vo.

GARRISON, W. P. The Benson Family of Newport, R. I., with Appendix concerning the Benson Family in America. N. Y., printed 1872. 8vo.

GARRISONS, (Our), in the West. See DUNCAN, Francis.

GARWOOD, Rev. John. Lecture at London, Jan. 30, 1840, on the Authority of the Bible. (Against Socialism.) Lond., 1840. 8vo. Eng. Rel. Pamph., Vol. 90.

GASCOIGNE, Geo. Complete Poems; with Notes by W. C. Hazlitt. Roxburghe Libr. Lond., 1869. 4to.

—— Complete Works, with a Memoir by W. C. Hazlitt. Vol. 2. 1870. Roxburghe Libr. Lond., 1870. 4to.

GASKELL, P. Prospects of Industry. Brief Exposition of the Condition of the Laboring Classes. Lond., 1835. 8vo. Eng. Misc. Pamph., Vol. 25.

GASPARIN, A. America before Europe. N. Y., 1862. 8vo. See DEGASPARIN, A.

GASPEE. Destruction of the. 1772. See STAPLES, Wm. R. Dcc. Hist. of.

GASS, Pat'k. Journ. of Voyages and Travels under Capt's Lewis and Clarke, through the Interior Parts of America in 1804–6. Lond., 1808. 8vo.

GASSAWAY, Rev. S. G. See ARNETT, Rev. W. W.

GATLING'S Battery Gun. Descrip. of. Hartford, 1857. 8vo. Rebell'n Pamph., Vol. 16.

GAULLE, Chas. de. The Celts of the 19th Century; An Appeal to Living Representatives of the Celtic Race. Tenby, 1865. 8vo.

GAULTER, Dr. Henry. Origin and Progress of the Malignant Cholera in Manchester. Lond., 1833. 8vo. Med. Pamph., Vol. 24.

GAVAZZI, Rev. Alessandre. See KING, J. W. Biog. of.

—— Lectures in N. Y. on Romanism, with Acc. of his Life. 3d Ed. N. Y., 1856. 12mo.

—— Oration on the Abuses and Corruptions of the Church of Rome. Lond., n. d. 8vo, Eng. Rel. Pamph., Vol. 63.

GAVIN, Hector, M. D. Habitations of the Industrial Classes. Address at Crosby Hall, Nov. 27, 1850. Lond. 8vo. Eng. Misc. Pamph., Vol. 31.

GAWLER, Col. Geo. Emancipation of the Jews indispensable for the Maintenance of the Protestant Profession. Lond., 1847. 8vo. Strangford Pamph., Vol. 45.

GAY, Rev. Ebenezer. Disc. at Hingham, Mass., Aug. 26, 1871, on his 85th Birthday. Reprint. Hingham, 1846. 8vo. Mass. Hist. Discourses Vol. 2.

GAY, Geo. H. Remarks on the Treatment of Wounds received in Battle. Boston, 1862. 8vo. Med. Pamph. Vol. 1.

GAY, Dr. Martin. Claims of Chas. T. Jackson, M. D., to the Discovery of the Use of Sulphuric Ether in Surgical Operations. Boston, 1847. 8vo. Med. Pamph. Vol. 12.

GAYARRE, Chas. Address to the People of Louisiana on the State of Parties. N. Orleans, 1855. Congr. & Polit. Pamph. Vol. 81.

—— Hist. of Louisiana;* The Spanish Domination. N. Y., 1854. 8vo.

—— Influence of the Mechanic Arts on the Human Race, in two Lectures. N. Y., 1854. 12mo. Scientific Pamph. Vol. 12.

—— Louisiana; its Colonial Hist. and Romance. N. Y., 1851. 8vo.

—— Louisiana; its Hist. as a French Colony. Third Ser. of Lectures. N. Y., 1852. 8vo.

GAYLORD Genealogy. See GAILLARD, W.

GAZE, Henry. Paris; How to See it for Five Guineas. Lond., 8vo. n. d. Guide Books. Vol. 12.

GAZETTEER of the State of N. Y. Albany, 1842. 8vo.

GAZETTEERS. See BECK, L. C. Illinois and Missouri.

—— BLOIS, J. T. Mich. Gazeteer, 1840.

GAZETTEERS. BROOKS, R. General Gaz. 1815-16.
—— BROWN, S. R. Western Gaz.
—— DAVENPORT, B. Gaz. and Geograph. Dict. 1833.
—— Dubuque, Sioux City, Guide, Directory and Gaz. 1868.
—— HAWES, G. W. Ohio Gaz. and Business Directory. 1859.
—— HUNT, J. W. Wisconsin Gaz.
—— Indiana Gaz.
—— JENKINS, O. Ohio Gaz. 1841.
—— Lippincott's Gaz. of the World.
—— Manning & Darby, U. S. Gaz., 1843.
—— MITCHELL, J. L. Tenn. State Gaz. 1860-1.
—— N. Amer. and West India. 1776.
—— PECK, J. M. Illinois Gaz.
—— SALMON, Mr., Modern Gaz.
—— WETMORE, A. Missouri Gaz. 1837.

GEARY, John W. Corres. with Vice-Admiral Porter, on the Foreign Commerce of the U. S., 1870. 8vo. Congr. and Polit. Pamph. Vol. 120.

GEE, Joshua. Trade and Navigation of G. Britian Considered. Lond., 1767- 12mo. 2d Ed. Lond., 1730. 8vo.

GEER, J. J. Beyond the Lines: or, A Yankee Prisoner Loose in Dixie. Phila., 1863. 12mo.

GEHAUT, Victor. Le Livre des Principes: ou Plan Nouveau d'Education d'accordance la Raison et les Traditions Catolique. Paris, 1849. 12mo.

GEISLER, A. F. Sketches of Character and Events of 157 English Officers who excelled during the last Amer. War; and also of some Officers of German troops who assisted in said War. In German, Dresden, 1784. 12mo.

GANDRON, Le Lieur. Quelques Particuarites du Pays Des Hurons en la Nouvelle France. Paris, 1660. Albany, reprint. n. d. Sm. 4to.

GENEALOGY. See ABBOT, A. E. Register of Abbot Family.
—— ADAM, W. Geneal. of Adam Family.
—— ADAMS, G. Geneal. of Adams Family.
—— ADAMS, Josiah. Haven Geneal.
—— ALDEN, E. Alden Geneal.
—— ALLEN, A. W. Allen and Witter Families.
—— ALLEN, Jos. Allen Geneal.
—— AMES, Ellis. Descendants of Wm. Ames.
—— ANDERSON, W. Geneal. and Surnames.
—— —— The Scottish Nation.
—— ANDREWS, A. Geneal., etc., of New Britain, Conn.
—— ANGELL, A. F. Geneal. of Angell Family.
—— ANTHON, C. E. Narr. of Settlement of Geo. C. Anthon in America.
—— APPLETON, W. S. Crane's of Chilton.
—— —— Oliver Family.
—— Archer Family. Memorials.
—— Baird Geneal. Collections.
—— BAKER, N. M. Geneal. of Edw. Baker.
—— BALDWIN, B. A. Descendants of N. Baldwin.

GENEALOGY. BARRY, J. S. Stetson Family.
—— —— Hist. and Geneal. of Hanover, Mass.
—— BARRY, W. Hist. of Framingham, with Genealogies.
—— BELLOWS, H. W. Bellows' Hist. and Geneal.
—— BENEDICT, H. M. Benedict Geneal.
—— BERGEN, T. G. Bergen Geneal.
—— —— VanBrunt Geneal.
—— BERRY, W. Co. Genealogies. Kent, Surry, Buckingham, Berkshire and Essex.
—— —— Hertfordshire Pedigrees.
—— BILL, L. Geneal. of Bill Family.
—— BINNEY, C. J. F. Hist. and Geneal. of Prentiss Family.
—— BIRNIE, J. Birnie and Hamilton Families.
—— BLAKE, S. Blake Family.
—— BOLLES, J. A. Bolles Geneal.
—— BOLLING, R. Memo. and Geneal. of Bolling, of Va.
—— BOLTON, R. Hist. and Geneal. of Westchester Co., N. Y.
—— BOND, Dr. H. Early Settlers of Watertown, Mass.
—— BOUTELLE, J. A. Burke and Alvord Families.
—— BRIGHT, J. B. Brights of Suffolk, Eng.
—— BRONSON, H. Hist. and Geneal. of Waterbury, Conn.
—— BROOKS, C. Hist. of Medford, with Family Registers.
—— BROWN, O. Memorandum of Preston Family.
—— BUCKMINSTER, L. N. Hastings Geneal.
—— BURGESS, E. Burgess Memorial.
—— BURKE, Sir B. Genealog. and Herald. Dict. of Landed Gentry of G. B. and Ireland.
—— —— Geneal. Dict. of British Peerage.
—— —— BURKE, J. and J. B. Genealog. Hist. of Extinct Eng. Baronetcies.
—— —— Heraldic Illustrations. Pedigrees, etc.
—— —— The Patrician. 1846–8.
—— BURNHAM, R. H. Burnham Geneal.
—— BUTLER, C. Hist. and Geneal. of Groton, Pepperell and Shirley, Mass.
—— Calendarium Genealogicum.
—— CAMPBELL, C. Spotswood Family of Scotland and Va.
—— CAUSTON, H. K. S. Howard Papers.
—— CHAPIN, Rev. A. B. Glastenbury Geneal.
—— CHAPIN, O. Chapin Geneal.
—— CHAPMAN, F. W. Buckingham Family.
—— —— Chapman Family.
—— —— Pratt Family.
—— —— Trowbridge Family.
—— CHASE, G. B. Chase Geneal.
—— CLARK, J. Clark Geneal.
—— CLARKE, S. C. Curtiss Geneal.
—— —— Hull Family.
—— —— Record of Thos. Clarke.
—— CLARK, S. E. Fuller Geneal.
—— CLINTON, C. A. Biograph. Sketches of Clinton Family.
—— COFFIN, J. Descendants of E. Woodman.

GENEALOGY. COFFIN, J. Toppan Family.
—— COLE, J. E. Geneal. of Cole, of Co. of Devon.
—— COLEMAN, Jas. Catalogue of Pedigrees hitherto unindexed.
—— —— Gen. Index to Printed Pedigrees.
—— —— Penn Pedigrees.
—— COLEMAN, L. Geneal. of Lyman.
—— COLLINS, A. Peerage of Eng.
—— Collectanea Topographica Genealogica.
—— COPE, G. Dutton Geneal.
—— —— Record of Cope Family.
—— CORWIN, E. T. Geneal. of Corwin.
—— COTHREN, W. Hist. and Geneal. of Ancient Woodbury, Conn.
—— CUSHMAN, H. W. Cushman Family.
—— D'AMERIE, Emery, Amory.
—— Danforth Family. Genealog. Acc. of.
—— Darlington Family.
—— DAVENPORT A. B. Davenport Family.
—— DAVIS. C. H. S. Davis Family Records.
—— DAVIS, W. H. H. Hart Family, of Pa.
—— DAY, G. E. Register of Day Family.
—— DEANE, W. R. and J. W. Dean Family.
—— DEBRETT, J. Peerage of G. Britain.
—— DERBY, P. Hutchinson Family.
—— DICKINSON, J. T. Dickinson Family.
—— —— Lyman Family.
—— —— Partridge Family.
—— DODD, B. L. and BURNETT, J. R., Descendants of Danl. Dod.
—— DODD, Rev. S. East Haven Register.
—— DOOLITTLE, M. Geneal. of Early Settlers of Belchertown, Mass.
—— DRAKE, S. G. Chart of Drake Family.
—— DRAPER, F. P. Draper Geneal.
—— —— Preston Family.
—— Druce Family.
—— DUDLEY, D. Dudley Geneal.
—— Dumaresq Family.
—— DURRIE, D. S. Index to Amer. Pedigrees.
—— —— Holt Family.
—— —— Steele Family.
—— —— Utility of the Study of.
—— DUNNELL, H. G. Dunnell Geneal.
—— DWIGHT, B. W. Strong Family Geneal.
—— EASTMAN, L. R. Eastman Geneal.
—— EAGER, S. W. Hist. of Orange Co., N. Y., with Genealogies.
—— EATON, C. Annals, etc., of Warren, Me.
—— —— Hist. of Thomaston, Me., and Genealogies.
—— EDES, H. H. Memorial of Josiah Barker.
—— Elliott Family.
—— ELLIS, W. S. Notices of the Ellises.
—— EVERETT, E. H. Everett Family.
—— FAHNESTOCK, G. W. Wolff Memorial.

GENEALOGY. FARMER, J. Genealog. Register of N. E. Settlers.
—— Farrar Family.
—— FIELD, Rev. D. D. Brainerd Family.
—— FIELD, O. Field Family.
—— FISKE, A. A. Geneal. of Fiskes.
—— FITTS, J. H. Fitts or Fitz Family.
—— FLETCHER, E. H. Fletcher Geneal.
—— FLINT and Stone. Flint Genealog. Register.
—— FORSTER, Jacob. Pedigree.
—— Foster Family, of Charlestown, Mass.
—— FOWLER, D. W. Fowler Geneal.
—— FOWLER, Wm. C. Conditions of Success in Genealog. Investigations, etc.
—— —— Memorial of Chauncey.
—— —— Wm. Fowler, the Magistrate.
—— FOWLER, W. W. Hints to Genealogists.
—— Frost Family of Elliot, Maine.
—— GAILLARD, W. Hist. and Pedigrees of the Gaillards or Gaylords.
—— GALE, G. Gale Family Records.
—— GARRISON, W. P. Benson Family.
—— GIBSON, Mrs. E. B. Bordley Family.
—— GILMAN, A. Gilman Family.
—— Gilpin Geneal.
—— GLOVER, A. Glover Memorials and Genealogies.
—— GOODWIN, N. Foot Family.
—— —— Genealog. Notes of Early Settlers of Conn.
—— —— Olcott Geneal.
—— GOULD, B. A. Ancestry and Posterity of Zacheus Gould.
—— Grant Family.
—— GRANT, M. Old Church Record.
—— GREEN, R. H. Todd Family Geneal.
—— GRFFFIN, A. First Settlers of Southold, R. I.
—— GRIFFIN, N. Gathering of his Descendants.
—— GUILD, C. Geneal. of Guild Family.
—— GUILD, J. Ancestry, ete., of Zacheus Gould.
—— HALE, M. Lawrence Family.
—— HALL, Rev. E. Hist. Records of Norwalk, Conn.
—— HARRIS, E. D. Bascom Geneal.
—— —— Brattle Geneal.
—— —— Vassal Family.
—— HARRIS, L. M. Morey Family.
—— —— Metcalf Family.
—— —— Robt. Harris and Descendants.
—— Heacock Family.
—— HERRICK, J. Herrick Genealog. Register.
—— HILL, M. L. Lithgow Family.
—— HINMAN, R. R. Early Conn. Settlers.
—— —— Hinman Geneal.
—— HOLDEN, F. A. Capron Geneal.
—— HOLGATE, J. B. Amer. Geneal.
—— HOSMER, J. B. Hosmer Family.

GENEALOGY. HOTTEN, J. C. Hand Book of Eng. Family Hist.
—— HOWELL, G. R. Hist. of Southampton and Genealogies.
—— HOYT, D. W. Hoyt Family.
—— HUDSON, C. Hist. and Geneal. of Marlboro, Mass.
—— HUNT and WYMAN. Hunt Family Geneal.
—— HUNTER, J. Genealog. Notices of N. E. Settlers.
—— —— Suffolk, Eng., Emigrants.
—— HUNTINGTON, E. B. Huntington Geneal.
—— HURLBUT, H. H. Descendants of Saml. Hurlbut.
—— Hutchinson and Oliver Families.
—— JACKSON, F. Hist. and Geneal. of Newton, Mass.
—— JANES, Rev. F. Janes Geneal.
—— Jenner Family.
—— JEWETT, J. A. Appleton Memorial.
—— JONES, David S. Jones Family of Queen's Co., N. Y.
—— JONES, H. G. Levering Family.
—— JONES. Waldo Family.
—— JUDD, S. Thos. Judd and Descendants.
—— KELLOGG, Rev. A. S. White Family Memorials.
—— KILBOURNE, P. K. Kilbourne Geneal.
—— KINGMAN, B. N. Bridgewater Families.
—— KIP, Bishop Wm. J. Family of Kip.
—— LAPHAM, J. A. Lapham Pedigree.
—— LAWRENCE, J. Descendants of.
—— LAWRENCE, Thos. Lawrence Family.
—— LEONARD, Rev. L. W. Hist. of Dublin with Family Registers.
—— LELAND, S. Leland Genealog. Record.
—— LINCOLN, S. Notes on Lincolns of Mass.
—— LITTELL, John. Passaic Valley Settlers.
—— LOCKE, John G. Locke Geneal.
—— LODGE, E. Geneal. of British Peerage.
—— LOOMIS, E. Loomis Geneal.
—— LOWER, M. A. Genealog. Mem. of Scrase Family.
—— LUDLOW and WILLINK.
—— LUDWIG, M. R. Ludwig Geneal.
—— Lyman Anniversary. Reunion, etc.
—— MACY, S. Macy Geneal.
—— MAKEPEACE, W. Makepeace Family.
—— MARSHALL, G. W. Index to Pedigrees in Heraldic Visitations.
—— MARVIN, T. R. Descendants of R. Marvin.
—— MESSINGER, G. W. Hinckley Family.
—— —— Geneal. of Messinger.
—— MEYRICK, S. R. Welsh Heraldry and Geneal.
—— Miscellanea Genealogica et Heraldica.
—— MITCHELL, N. Hist. and Geneal. of Bridgewater, Mass.
—— MONTGOMERY, T. H. Montgomery Family.
—— MOODY, C. C. P. Moody Family.
—— MORGAN, N. H. Morgan Geneal.
—— Morse's Register of Brigham, Hapgood, Pettee, Hewin's and Willis Families.
—— MORSE, Rev. A. Brigham Family.

GENEALOGY. MORSE, Rev. A. Cutler Family.
—— —— Goulding Family.
—— —— Grout Geneal.
—— —— Richards Family.
—— MUDGE, A. Mudge Geneal.
—— Munsell Family, of Windsor, Ct.
—— NASH, S. Nash Family.
—— NEAL, T. A. Neal Record.
—— NEILL, E. D. Fairfaxes of Eng. and America.
—— New Baronetage of Eng.
—— NEWCOMB, J. B. Bearse Family.
—— N. E. Hist. and Genealog. Register.
—— N. Y. Genealog. and Biograph. Record.
—— NICHOLS, J. G. Topographer and Genealogist.
—— NORTH, J. W. Hist. and Geneal. of Augusta, Me.
—— NORTON. A. B. Descendants of Chas. Norton, of Guilford, Conn.
—— NOYES, J. Noyes, Dike, Fuller, and Edson Families.
—— Odin Pedigree.
—— Paine Family Register.
—— PEABODY, W. S. Peabody Geneal.
—— PEASE, D. Pease Geneal.
—— PEASE, F. S. Descendants of I. Lawrence.
—— PECK, I. Geneal. of Peck Family.
—— Peerage of Ireland.
—— Penn. Pedigree and Geneal.
—— PHELPS, N. A. Hist. and Geneal. of Simsbury, Conn.
—— PHOENIX, S. W. Descendants of J. Phoenix.
—— Plummer Hall Dedica., with Memoir of Plummer Family.
—— POOR, A. Bailey Family.
—— —— Hist. and Genealog. Researches.
—— Pope Family Geneal.
—— PREBLE, G. H. Preble Geneal.
—— PRENDERGAST, J. P. Acc. of M. de Prendergast.
—— PRESCOTT, W. Prescott Memorial.
—— RAWSON, S. S. Rawson Geneal.
—— READ, J. W. Read Geneal.
—— REDFIELD, J. H. Redfield Geneal.
—— ROCKWOOD, E. L. Rockwood Family.
—— Rogers Family of Dowdeswell, Eng.
—— ROLLINS, J. R. Rawlins Family.
—— ROOT, J. P. Root Genealog. Record.
—— SANBORN, N. B. Sanborn Geneal.
—— SANFORD, E. Kings Family of Raynham, Mass.
—— SAVAGE, Jas. Genealog. Dict. of N. E. Settlers.
—— SAWIN, Thos. E. Summary Notes of John Sawin, etc.
—— SCRANTON, Rev. E. Scranton Geneal.
—— SEARS, E. H. Pictures of Olden Time and Sears Geneal.
—— SHATTUCK, L. Memorials of the Whites.
—— —— Shattuck Memorials.
—— SHELDON, H. O. Sheldon Magazine.
—— SIBLEY, J. L. Hist. of Union, with Geneal.

GENEALOGY. SILL, Rev. G. G. Descendants of John Sill.
—— SIMMS, C. S. Stemmata Rosellana.
—— SIMS, Rich'd. Index to Pedigrees in Herald's Visitations.
—— —— Manual for Genealogists.
—— SLAFTER, E. F. Shafter Memorial.
—— SMITH, Columbus. Report of Booth Assoc.
—— —— Report to Brown Assoc.
—— —— Report to Follansbee Assoc.
—— —— Report to Gibson Assoc.
—— —— Report to Jennings Assoc.
—— SMITH, H. O. Report to Wilson Assoc.
—— SMITH, Nathan'l, Jr. Register of Descendants of.
—— SPRAGUE, H. Sprague Geneal., 1828.
—— STEBBINS, R. B. Wilbraham Hist. and Geneal.
—— STICKNEY, M. A. Stickney Family.
—— STILES, H. R. Conn. Family of Stiles.
—— —— Dow Family.
—— —— Fitch Geneal.
—— —— Hist. and Geneal. of Windsor, Conn.
—— —— Josselyn Family.
—— —— Mass. Family of Stiles.
—— —— Stranahan Family.
—— STODDARD, A. Descendants of.
—— STODDARD. E. W. A Stoddard's Descendants.
—— STONE, R. C. Geneal. of Stone.
—— SUMNER, W. H. Sumner Family.
—— SWAN, B. F. Boothe Family.
—— TAINTOR, C. M. Geneal. of Taintor Family.
—— TEMPLE, J. H. Hist. of Whately and Geneal.
—— THACHER, J. Thacher Biog. and Geneal.
—— THAYER, E. Geneal. of 14 Allied Families.
—— THOMAS, E. L. Olmsted Family of N. E.
—— THOMAS, John. Descendants.
—— THOMPSON, B. F. Hist. of Long Island, with Geneal.
—— THORNTON, J. W. Bowles Pedigree.
—— THURSTON, C. M. Thurston Family.
—— Tuthill Family Meeting.
—— Tuttle Family.
—— Upham Geneal.
—— Varnum Family Geneal.
—— Vernatti Family.
—— Vickery or Vickers Genealogy.
—— VINTON, J. A. Genealogies of.
—— —— Adams, Alden, Allen.
—— —— Boylston,
—— —— Curwen,
—— —— Faxon, French,
—— —— Giles, Gould, Green,
—— —— Hayden, Holbrook, Holmes,
—— —— Jennison,
—— —— Leonard,
—— —— Marshall, Miles, Mills,

GENEALOGY. VINTON, J. A. Penniman,
—— —— Richardson, Robinson,
—— —— Sampson,
—— —— Thayer,
—— —— Vinton,
—— —— Webb, White.
—— WALFORD, E. Eng. County Families.
—— WALKER, J. B. R. Walker Memorial.
—— WALWORTH, R. H. Hyde Family.
—— WARD, A. H. Hist. and Geneal. of Shrewsbury.
—— —— Rice Family Geneal.
—— WATSON, Thos. Watson Family.
—— WENTWORTH, J. Wentworth Family.
—— Wentworths of N. H.
—— WETMORE, J. C. Family Geneal.
—— WHITING, W. Memoir and Geneal. of S. Whiting.
—— WHITMAN, E. Whitman Family.
—— WHITMORE, W. H. Amer. Genealogist.
—— —— Hand-Book of Geneal.
—— —— Hutchinson and Oliver Geneal.
—— —— Origin of the Founders of the 13 Colonies.
—— WHITNEY, F. A. Champney Family.
—— —— Park Family.
—— Whittlesey Family Memorial.
—— Wilder Family Hist.
—— WILKINSON, Rev. I. Wilkinson Memoirs.
—— WILLARD, J. Descendants of Maj. S. Willard.
—— WILLIAMS, S. W. Williams' Geneal.
—— WILLIS, W. McKinstry Family.
—— —— Smith & Dean's Journals, with Geneal.
—— WINCHELL, A. Winchell Geneal.
—— WOODMAN, J. H. Descendants of J. Woodman.
—— WORCESTER, J. F. Worcester Family.
—— WYNKOOP, R. Wynkoop Genealogy.
—— YALE, E. Yale Family.

GENERAL Convention of Agriculturists and others friendly to Domestic Industry of the U. S. 1827. (n. d.) 8vo. Pamphlets. Vol. 14.

GENESEE and Alleghany Canal. Proceedings of Citizens of N. Y., on the Construction of a Canal from Rochester to Olean. N. Y., 1835. 8vo. N. Y. Misc. Pamph. Vol. 1.
—— Country, N. Y. See DENONVILLE, M. de. Expedition to. 1687.
—— —— MUNRO, Robt. Description of. 1804.
—— —— WILLIAMSON, Chas. Settlement of. 1799.
—— Tract, N. Y. Acc. of the Soil, Timber, and other Productions of the Genesee Tract, in N. Y. Imlay's America, p. 458.
—— Co., Mich. Sheep-Breeders and Wool-Growers' Assoc. Constitution, By-Laws, etc. 1866. 12mo. Agr. Pamph. Vol. 5.
—— Farmer and Gardener's Journal. Vol. 1. Rochester, 1831. 4to.
—— GENET, E. C. See DAWSON, H. B. Paper on.
—— —— Vindica. of his Memorial on the upward forces of Fluids. N. Haven, 1827. 8vo. Scientific Pamph. Vol. 11.

GENEVA Arbitration. The Case of G. Britain as laid before the Tribunal at Geneva. Washington, 1872. 3 Vols.

—— —— The Counter Case of G. Britain, as laid before the Tribunal of Arbitration. Washington, 1872. 8vo.

—— —— See Alabama Claims.

GENEVA College, Geneva, N. Y. Catalogues for 1829–30, 1838–9, 1841–2, 1843–4.

—— —— Ann. Circular of the Medical Institution of the College. 1840. Geneva. 4to.

—— —— Journals of House of Convocation, 1849, 1850, 1851. Geneva, 1851. 8vo. Syracuse, 1849. 8vo.

—— See DICKINSON, D. S. Address. 1848.

—— —— HENRY, C. S. Discourse. 1840.

—— See Hobart College.

—— Presb. Ch. See WINSLOW, Hubbard. History of. 1859.

GENEVA, Wis. Express, Newspaper, Oct., 1855, to Aug., 1856. Folio.

—— Lake Geneva Seminary. 2d Ann. Catalogue, 1870–71. Elkhorn. 8vo.

GENIN, Sylvester. Selections from his Works in Poetry, Prose and and Hist. Design. N. Y., 1855. 8vo.

GENIN, Thos. H. Oration at St. Clairsville, Ohio, Feb. 22, 1823. 8vo. Addresses. Vol. 6.

GENIUS (Infirmities of.) See MADDEN, R. R.

GENLIS, Countess de. Memoirs of the Marchioness de Bonchamps, on La Vendee. Waldie's Circulating Libr. Vol. 12.

GENOA, Italy. See Celesia, E. Conspiracy of Fieschi, etc.

GENTLEMAN'S Magazine and Hist. Chronicle, from 1731 to 1833. 154 Vols. (Vol. 2, 1826, wanting.) London. 8vo.

—— —— Selections from Gent. Mag., 1809–11. 4 Vols. 8vo.

—— Monthly Intelligencer. See London Magazine.

GENTRY, M. P. Speech in Cong., July 11, 1842, on the Tariff. Washington, 1842. 8vo. Congr. and Polit. Pamph. Vol. 24.

—— Speech in Cong., Mar. 28, 1842, on the Loan Bill. 8vo. Congr. and Polit. Pamph. Vol. 24.

—— Speech in Cong., July 2, 1846, on the Tariff. Washington, 1846. 8vo. Speeches. Vol. 1.

—— Speech in Cong., June 14, 1852, on the Presidency. Congr. and Polit. Pamph. Vol. 89.

GEODESY (The) of Britain; or the Ordnance Survey of England, Scotland and Ireland. 1859. Lond. 8vo. Eng. Polit. Pamph. Vol. 57.

GEOGHEGAN, Edw. Observations on Effects of Blood-Letting. Lond., 1833. 8vo. Med. Pamph. Vol. 18.

GEOGRAPHY. See BOWEN, E. Geog. of America.

—— BUTLER, S. Geographia Classica.

—— CALLICOT, T. C. Cyclopedia of.

—— DAVIES, B. Modern Geog.

—— ELLETT, C., on Physical Geog. of Mississippi Valley.

—— FLINT, T. Geog. of Western States.

—— GORDON, P. Geog. Anatomized. 1749.

GEOGRAPHY. Great Lakes of N. A.
—— GUTHRIE, W. Geograph. Grammar.
—— LAURENT, P. E. Manual of Ancient Geog.
—— LIPPINCOTT & Co., Gazetteer.
—— MALTE-BRUN'S Geog.
—— Memoires Geographiques.
—— MORDEN, R. Geography Rectified.
—— MORSE, J. Amer. Univers. Geog.
—— —— Amer. Geog.
—— PRESCOTT, T. H. Vol. of the World.
—— PUTZ, W. Hand-Book of Geog.
—— Royal Geograph. Soc.
—— SCHOOLCRAFT, H. R. Geog. of the Western Country.
—— SOMERVILLE, M. Physical Geog.
GEOLOGICAL Magazine; or Monthly Journal of Geology, Edited by T. Ruper JONES. London, 1864–71. 8 Vols. 8vo.
—— Surveys of States. See Arkansas, 1857–60;
—— —— California, 1851, '54, '56.
—— —— Connecticut, 1837–42.
—— —— Illinois, 1852, '58, '66–70.
—— —— Indiana, 1837.
—— —— Iowa, 1839, '48, '52, '55–57, '70.
—— —— Kentucky, 1854–59.
—— —— Maine, 1838.
—— —— Maryland, 1836.
—— —— Massachusetts, 1830, '31, '38.
—— —— Michigan, 1849–50.
—— —— Minnesota, 1852.
—— —— Nebraska, 1852.
—— —— N. Hampshire. 1841, '69, '71.
—— —— N. Jersey, 1868.
—— —— Ohio, 1838, '39, '70, '71, '73.
—— —— Penn., 1838–42.
—— —— R. Island, 1839.
—— —— Tennessee, 1855.
—— —— Vermont, 1858 '61.
—— —— Wisconsin, 1835, '39, '48, '52. '54, '55, '56, '57, '58.
GEOLOGY. See AIKIN, Wm. E. A. Geol. of Country between Baltimore and Ohio River. 1834.
—— ANDERSON, J. Course of Creation.
—— Assoc. of Amer. Geologists.
—— BADDELEY, Lieut. Geol. of Labrador Coast.
—— —— Geol. of Saugenay Co., Canada.
—— BALL, John. Geol. of Country West of Rocky Mts. 1834.
—— BAYFIELD, H. W. Geol. of Lake Superior.
—— BEAUMONT, L. E. Observationes Geologiques.
—— BRAINERD, Jehu. Origin of Quartz, Pebbles, etc.
—— BUCKLAND, W. Geol. and Nat. Theol.
—— BURNET, Rev. J. Geol. and Christianity.
—— Canada Geolog. Survey, 1863 to 1866.
—— Catalogue of Amer. Minerals.
—— COCKBURN, Wm., D. D. Bible Defended, etc.

GEOLOGY. DAUBENY, C. Geol. of Sicily. 1825.
—— DRAKE, Dr. D. Geol. Acc. of Ohio Valley.
—— FEATHERSTONHAUGH, G. W., on the Country between Missouri and Red Rivers.
—— FOSTER & WHITNEY. Lake Superior Land District.
—— Geolog. Magazine. 1864–71.
—— GIBSON, J. B. Geol. of the Lakes and Miss. Valley. 1833.
—— HALL, J. Geol. of Western States. 1841.
—— —— Notes on Minn.
—— HARLAN, Dr. R. Fossil Bones in Tertiary Formation in La.
—— HAYDEN, Dr. F. V. Geolog. Sketch of the Estuary and Deposites of Bad Lands in Nebr.
—— —— Geol. of the Upper Missouri.
—— —— Report on Wyoming, etc. 1872.
—— HILDRETH, S. P. Valley of the Ohio. 1836.
—— HITCHCOCK, E. Element. Geol.
—— —— Illustra. of Surface Geol.
—— HOLMES, F. S. Fossils in S. Carolina.
—— —— Phosphate Rocks of S. C. 1871.
—— JACKSON, C. T. and ALGER, A. Geology, etc., of Nova Scotia.
—— JAMES, E. P. Sandstone Formations of the Valley of the Mississippi.
—— LATROBE, B. H. Sand Hills at Cape Henry, Va.
—— LEA, Isaac. Oolitic Formation in America.
—— LEE, C. A. Elements of.
—— LIEBIG & KOPP. Reports on the Progress of.
—— LYELL, Chas. Geolog. Observations and Travels in N. America.
—— —— Eight Lectures on. 1842.
—— MARCOU, Jules. Amer. Geol.
—— —— Reply to Jas. D. Dana.
—— MARTIN, D. S., on Studying Minerals.
—— MEEK, F. B. and HAYDEN, F. V. Palæontology of the Upper Missouri.
—— MURCHISON, R. I. Siluria; the Oldest Rocks with Organic Remains.
—— OSBORN, A. Field Notes on Geol., 1858.
—— PAINE, M. Theoretical Geol.
—— Pa. Geolog. Soc., 1834–5.
—— Rapport sur la Geologie de l'Amerique Meridionale.
—— Relics from the Wreck of a Former World.
—— ROGERS, W. B. and H. D. Contribu. to Geol. of Va.
—— SAULT, W. D. On Astronom. and Geolog. Phenomena.
—— SCHOOLCRAFT, H. R. Geol. of the Sources of the Mississippi.
—— —— Geol. of the Western Country.
—— STANSBURY, H. Append. to Gr. Salt Lake Exped.
—— STRUVER, H. Method des Fossiles.
—— TAYLOR, R. C. Geol. of N. E. Part of Cuba.
—— PUMPELLY, H. Geolog. Researches in China and Japan.
—— TUOMEY, M. and HOLMES, F. S. Fossils of S. Carolina.
—— U. S. Geolog. Explora. of 40th Parallel.

GEOLOGY. WHITTLESEY, Chas. Fresh Water Glacial Drift of the N. Western States.
—— —— Geol. of Ohio.
—— —— On Ohio and N. Y. Rocks.
—— WINCHELL, A. and MARCY, O. Fossils found at Chicago in Niagara Limestone.
—— WOOD, H. C. On the Flora of the Coal Period.
—— WOODS, Henry. Fossil Skull of an Ox from Welksham, Eng., 1838.
GEORGE III. of England. See BROUGHAM, Lord. Statesmen of Time of, etc.
—— —— DONNE, W. B. Corres. with Lord North.
—— —— HOLT, Edw. Pub. and Domestic Life.
—— —— HUISH, R. Pub. and Priv. Life of.
—— —— RAY, Dr. On Insanity of.
—— —— Sketch of the Life of. n. d. 8vo. Biograph. Pamph. Vol. 18.
GEORGE IV. See CROLY, Rev. G. Life and Times of.
—— and Queen Caroline. See BROUGHAM, Lord.
GEORGE, Anita. Annals of the Queens of Spain. N. Y., 1850. 2 Vols. 12mo.
GEORGE, Julia W. H. Hist. of the Eng. and Scotch Rebellions of 1685. N. Y., 1851. 12mo.
GEORGETOWN, D. C., Academy. Catalogue of Pupils for 1869–70. Georgetown, 1870. 8vo.
—— College, Med. Depart. Addresses at 22d Ann. Commencement, 1871. Washington, 1871. 8vo. Med. Pamph. Vol. 33.
—— See ELLET, Chas. Report on Suspension Bridge, 1852.
—— Washington Federalist, Newspaper. Dec., 1808. Folio.
GEORGETOWN, Me. Topograph. Description of. Mass. Hist. Soc. Coll. 1st Ser. Vol. 1.
GEORGETOWN, Mass. See BRAMAN, Rev. Isaac. Semi-Centen. Sermon, 1847.
GEORGIA. Acc. showing the Progress of the Colony from its first Establishment. 1741.
—— See Force's Hist. Tracts. Vol. 1.
—— Ga. Hist. Coll. Vol. 2.
—— Admission of. Congress. Report on, 1870. Congr. and Polit. Pamph. Vol. 116.
—— A New Voyage to Georgia—with Acc. of the Indians, and a Poem to Jas. Oglethorpe, 1737. Ga. Hist. Coll. Vol. 2.
—— Antiquities of. See JONES, Chas. C., Jr. Ancient Tumuli of Ga.
—— —— —— Indian Remains in So. Georgia.
—— See ARTHUR and CARPENTER. Hist. of.
—— BARD, Saml. Polit. Situation of, 1870.
—— BARTRAM, W. Travels in Carolina and Ga.
—— before the Senate Judiciary Comm., Washington, D. C., Feb. 9, 1870. Congr. and Polit. Pamph. Vol. 114.
—— Brief Acc. of Causes that have retarded the Progress of the Colony, 1743. Ga. Hist. Coll. Vol. 2.

GEORGIA. Brief Acc. of the Establishment of the Colony under Gen. Jas. Oglethorpe, in 1733. Force's Hist. Tracts. Vol. 1.
—— Comptroller Gen. Ann. Reports, 1866, '69. Macon, 1866. Atlanta, 1869. 8vo.
—— Constitution adopted by the Constitutional Convention of Mar. 11, 1868. Augusta, 1868. 8vo. Ga. Misc. Pamph. Vol. 1.
—— Description of, by One of the First Settlers, 1741. Force's Hist. Tracts. Vol. 2.
—— See DRAKE, S. G. Early Hist. of.
—— Gold Mines. See PHILLIPS, Wm. Essay on, 1833.
—— HARRIS, T. M. Memorials of Oglethorpe.
—— Hist. Acc. of S. C. and Ga., 1779.
—— Hist. Society. See COHEN, S.
—— —— Collections. Vols. 1, 2. Savannah, 1840, 1842. 8vo.
—— —— Collections. Vol. 3, Part 1. Savannah, 1848. 8vo.
—— —— Constitution, By.Laws, and List of Members. Savannah, 1871. 8vo.
—— —— See ELLIOTT, Stephen, Jr.
—— —— JONES, Chas. C.
—— —— LAW, Wm.
—— —— SPALDING, Thos.
—— —— STEVENS, W. B.
—— —— WARD, J. E.
—— See HOLCOMBE, H. Georgia Analyt. Repository.
—— Impartial Inquiry into the State and Utility of the Province of Georgia. Lond., 1741. Ga. Hist. Soc. Coll. Vol. 1.
—— See JONES, C. C. Monumental Remains of.
—— McCALL, H. Hist. of.
—— MARTYN, Benj. Enquiry into the State of, 1741.
—— Special Message of Gov. Bullock to Legislature, 1870. Atlanta, 1870. 8vo. Ga. Misc. Pamph. Vol. 1.
—— Veto Message of Gov. Conley, 1871. Atlanta, 1871. 8vo. Ga. Misc. Pamph. Vol. 1.
—— MILLER, S. F. Bench and Bar of.
—— MOORE, F. Voyage to, in 1735.
—— New and Accurate Account of the Provinces of S. Carolina and Georgia. Lond., 1733. Ga. Hist. Soc. Coll. Vol. 1.
—— OGLETHORPE, Gov. Acc. of, 1732.
—— Proceedings of the Provisional Legislature of Ga., 1870. Atlanta, 1870. 8vo. Ga. Misc. Pamph. Vol. 1.
—— Reasons for establishing the Colony of Georgia, with regard to the Trade of G. Britain. Lond., 1733. Ga. Hist. Soc. Coll. Vol. 1.
—— Reconstruction of. See Congress'l Speeches.
—— —— U. S. Senate. Report from Comm. on Judiciary, 1870.
—— Remrrks on Election of U. S. Senators from Ga., 1870.
—— Scenes, Characters, Incidents, etc., in the First Half Century of the Republic. 2d Ed. N. Y., 1854. 12mo.
—— —— Another Ed. N. Y.,, 1856. 12mo.
—— SHERWOOD, A. Gazetteer of, 1829.
—— Senatorial Election. See MILLER, H. V. M.
—— —— NORWOOD, T. M.

GEORGIA State Agricult. Society. Premium List for the Fair of 1870. Atlanta, 1870. 8vo. Ga. Misc. Pamph. Vol. 1.
—— State of the Province of Ga., attested upon Oath, in the Court of Savannah, in 1740. Force's Hist. Tracts. Vol. 1. Ga. Misc. Pamph. Vol. 2.
—— STEVENSON, M. F. Geol. and Mineral. of, 1871.
—— STEVENS, W. B. Hist. of.
—— STROBEL, P. A. Salzburgers and Descendants. Hist. of Colony, etc.
—— Supt. of Public Works. Ann. Report for 1871. Atlanta, 1871. 8vo. Ga. Misc. Pamph. Vol. 1.
—— Supreme Court. Can a Negro hold Office in Georgia? Decision in Case of R. W. White vs. J. C. Clements. Atlanta, 1869. 8vo. Congr. and Polit. Pamph. Vol· 101.
—— TAILFER, P. Narr. of Colony, 1741.
—— University of. See INGERSOLL, J. R. Address, 1847.
—— VON RECK. Journ. of a Voyage to, 1734.
—— WHITE, Rev. G. Hist. Collections of.
—— —— Statistics of.
—— WRIGHT, R. Mem. of Gen. Jas. Oglethorpe, 1867.
GEORGIAN (The) Era; Memoirs of Most Eminent Persons in G. Britain from the Access. of George I. to the Demise of George IV. Lond., 1832. 4 Vols. 8vo.
GERARD, Jas. W. Banquet given to him by the N. Y. Bar. N.Y., 1869. 8vo. N. Y. City Pamph. Vol. 6.
—— London and N. Y.; their Crime and Police. N. Y., 1853. 8vo. N. Y. City Misc. Pamph. Vol. 3.
GERHARD, Fred. Illinois as it is: its History, Geography, Statistics, etc., with Maps. Chicago, 1857. 12mo.
—— On the Benefits of International Copyright. N. Y., 1868. 8vo. Scientific Pamph., etc. Vol. 16.
—— Will the People of the U. S. be benefited by an International Copyright Law? N. York, 1868. 8vo. Congr. and Polit. Pamph. Vol. 74.
GERKEN, C. H. Musical Compass; or a System of the Harmonies. Baltimore, 1847. 8vo. Scientific Pamph. Vol. 14.
GERMAINE, Geo. The Rights of G. Britain asserted against the Claims of America. Amer. Tracts. Vol. 4. Phila., 1776.
GERMAN Democratic Central Club. Corres. with the German Dem. Union Party of N. Y., 1863. Rebell'n Pamph. Vol. 46.
—— Universities. See ROBINSON, E.
—— —— See TAFT, C. P.
GERMANY. See BRACE, C. L. Home Life in.
—— Commercial Policy of Eng. and Germany, 1845.
—— Considerations on the Present War, 1761.
—— HADLEY, Rev. E. The Pantheism of.
—— HEADLEY, J. T. Letters from Alps and Rhine.
—— KOHLRAUSCH, F. Hist. of.
—— Letter to the People of Eng., on the War, 1760.
—— MURRAY, J. Hand Book of.
—— ROBERTSON, W. Reign of Chas. V.

GERMANY Unmasked; or Facts explanatory of her Real Views in Wresting Schleswig from Denmark. Lond., 1848. 8vo. Strangford Pamph. Vol. 47.

GERRY, Elbridge. See AUSTIN, J. T. Life of.

GERSTAECKER, Frederick. Wild Sports in the Far West. Boston, 1859. 12mo.

GEST, E. Report of the Preliminary Surveys of the Western Division of the Ohio and Mississippi R. R. Cincin., 1851. 8vo. Ohio Misc. Pamph. Vol. 2.

GESTA Regum Brittaniæ. See MICHEL, F.

GETTYSBURG (Battle of.) See JACOBS, A. Rebel Invasion of Md., etc.

—— National Cemetery. See EVERETT, Edw. Address. 1863.

—— —— Proceedings and 6th Ann. Report, Nov. 30, 1869. Gettysburg, 1870. 8vo. Rebell'n Pamph. Vol. 107.

GEYER, H. S. Speech in U. S. Senate, Feb. 24 and 25, 1852, on Pub. Lands. Congr. and Polit. Pamph. Vol. 84.

GHIRARDINI, A. Studj Sulla Lingua Umana Sopra. Alcune Antiche Inscrizoni. Milán, 1869. 8vo.

GHOLSON, J. H. Speech in Cong., Mar. 10, 1834, on Removal of the Deposits. Washington, 1835. 8vo. Sheeches. Vol. 4.

GHOLSON, W. T. Speeches on the Nat. Debt, and on Reconstruction. Cincin., 1868. 8vo. Congr. and Polit. Pamph. Vol. 80.

GIBBES, Dr. Geo. S. Outline of a new Theory of Medicine. Bath, Eng., 1815. 8vo. Med. Pamph. Vol. 16.

GIBBES, R. W. Document. History of the Revolution, chiefly in S. Carolina. Vol. 1. 1764–76. N. Y., 1855. 8vo. Vol. 2. 1776–82. N. Y., 1857. 8vo. Vol. 3. 1781–2. Columbia, 1853. 8vo.

GIBBON, Edw. See EVANS, John, on Infidelity of, etc.

—— Hist. of the Decline and Fall of the Roman Empire, with Notes by Rev. H. H. Milman. N. Y., 1856. 6 Vols. 8vo.

—— Life of Mahomet, with Notes by Dean Milman and Dr. Wm. Smith. N. Y., 1860. 18mo.

GIBBONS, Chas. Speech at Phila., Oct. 5, 1860, in Reply to Hon. W. B. Reed. Phila., 1860. 8vo. Rebell'n Pamph. Vol. 77.

GIBBONS, J. A. The Kanawha Valley; its Resources and Developments. Charleston, 1872. 8vo.

GIBBONS, J. S. The Public Debt of the U. States. Taxation and Finances. N. Y., 1867. 12mo.

GIBBS, Geo. Alphabet Vocabularies of the Clallam and Lummi. N. Y., 1863. 4to. Shea's Library of Linguistics.

—— Dictionary of the Chinook Jargon, or Trade Language of Oregon. N. Y., 1863. 4to.

—— —— Alphabet Vocabulary of Do. N. Y., 1863. Shea's Library of Linguistics.

—— Memoirs of the Administrations of Washington and John Adams, edited from the Papers of Oliver Wolcott. N. Y., 1846. 2 Vols. 8vo.

GIBBS, Geo. Notes on the Tinneh or Chepewyan Indians of British and Russian America. Smithsonian Report. 1866.

—— Language of the Aboriginal Indians of America. Smithsonian Report. 1870.

GIBBS, Oliver, and YOUNG, C. E. Sketch of the City of Prescott and Pierce Co., Wis. Wis. Hist. Soc. Coll. Vol. 3.

—— and YOUNG, C. E. 1st Ann. Review of Pierce Co., Wis. Prescott, 1856. 12mo. Wis. Local Hist. Vol. 1.

—— The St. Croix Valley, Wis. 1859. 8vo. Wis. Misc. Pamph. Vol. 4.

GIBBS, W. aud GENTH, F. A. Researches on the Ammonia-Cobalt Bases. Smithsonian Contributions. Vol. 9.

GIBSON, Mrs. E. B. Biograph. Sketches of the Bradley Family of Md. Phila., 1865. 8vo. Genealog. Pamph. Vol. 1.

GIBSON Family. See SMITH, Columbus. Report to the Gibson Assoc.

GIBSON, Hugh. See ALDEN, T. Acc. of his Captivity. 1756–59.

GIBSON, John B. Geology of the Lakes and the Miss. Valley. 1833. Silliman's Journ. Vol. 29.

GIBSON, Capt. J. W. Letter Descriptive of the Battle of Buena Vista. Lawrenceburgh, 1847. 1847. 12mo. Mex. War Pamph. Vol. 2.

GIBSON, Lyman. *vs.* Josias PENNINGTON, before N. Y. Court of Appeals. Law Pamph. Vol. 2.

GIBSON, Walter M. The Prison of Weltervreden, and a Glance at the East Indian Archipelago. N. Y., 1855. 12mo.

GIBSON, Wm. S. Notices of Northumbrian Castles, Churches and Antiquities. 3d Ser. Lond., 1854. 8vo. Hist. Pamph. Vol. 14.

GIDDINGS, Edw. Cause of the Rise and Fall of the Lakes. Lockport, 1838. 8vo. Scientific Pamph. Vol. 10.

GIDDINGS, J. R. Exiles of Florida; or Crimes Committed by the Gov't against the Maroons. Columbus, O., 1858. 12mo.

—— Hist. of the Rebellion; its Authors and Causes. N. Y., 1864. 8vo.

—— Remembrances of the Skirmish with the Indians on the Peninsula, in the War of 1812. Fire Lands Pioneer. Vol. 1.

—— Speech in Cong., June 3, 1842, on the Reduction of the Army to the Basis of 1821. Washington, 1842. 8vo. Congr. and Polit. Pamph. Vol. 24.

—— Speech in Cong., Aug. 13, 1850, on the Texas Boundary. Cong. and Polit. Pamph. Vol. 83.

—— Speech in Cong., June 23, 1852, on Slavery. Congr. and Polit. Pamph. Vol. 85.

—— Speech in Cong., Dec. 11, 1854, on Executive Policy. Speeches. Vol. 5.

—— Speech in Cong., Dec. 18, 1855, on Organization of the House. Congr. and Polit. Pamph. Vol. 87.

—— Speeches in Congress. Boston, 1853. 8vo.

GIERLOW, John. Elements of the Danish and Swedish Languages. Cambridge, 1847. 12mo.

GIFFORD, Archer. The Aborigines of N. Jersey. N. J. Hist. Soc. Proceed. Vol. 4.

GIFFORD, Rev. Rich'd. Outlines of an Answer to Dr. Priestley on Matter and Spirit. Lond., 1781. 8vo. Scientific Pamph. Vol. 39.

GIBSON, John H. Gov. Geary's Administration in Kansas, with a Hist. of the Territory, to Jan., 1857. Phila., 1857. 12mo.

GILBERT, Amos. Memoirs of Francis Wright, the Pioneer Woman, in the Cause of Human Rights. Cincin., 1855. 12mo.

GILBERT, David, M. D. Valedictory Address before the Med. Depart. of Penn College, Mar. 5, 1852. Phila., 1852. 8vo. Med. Pamph. Vol. 33.

GILBERT, Davies. Plain Statement of the Bullion Question. Lond., 1819. 8vo. 2d Ed. Pamphleteer. Vol. 14.

GILBERT, Dr. J. P. Treatise on Deafness and Diseases of the Eye and Ear. Albany, 1858. 8vo. Med. Pamph. Vol. 10.

GILBERT, T. Considerations on the Better Relief and Employment of the Poor. Lond., 1787. 12mo. Eng. Polit. Pamph. Vol. 22.

—— Heads of a Bill for the Relief and Employment of the Poor, etc. Manchester, 1786. 12mo. Eng. Polit. Pamph. Vol. 22.

GILBERT, W. B. Antiquities of Maidstone, Eng., with Acc. of the Corpus Christi Fraternity. Maidstone, 1865. 12mo.

GILCHRIST, John Jas. Digest of the Reports of Cases Argued and Determined in the Supreme Court of Judicature of N. Hampshire. Vols. 1 and 12. Concord, 1846. 8vo.

GILCHRIST, Octavius. Letter to the Rev. Wm. L. Bowles, in Answer to a late Pamphlet. Lond., 1820. 8vo. Eng. Polit. Pamph. Vol. 35.

GILES, Rev. Chas. Convention of Drunkards; a Satirical Essay on Temperance. N. Y., 1840. 18mo.

GILES, Rev. Chauncey. The Problem of Amer. Nationality; Disc. on Fast Day, Apr. 30, 1863. Cincin., 1863. 8vo. Rebell'n Pamph. Vol. 2. Rebell'n Pamph. Vol. 6.

GILES Family Genealogy. See VINTON, J. A.

GILES, John. Memoir of Odd Adventures, Strange Deliverances and Captivities. Originally pub. 1736. Cincin., 1869. 8vo. Indian Pamph. Vol. 4.

GILES, J. A. Hist. of Witney, with Notices of Neighboring Parishes. Lond., 1852. 8vo.

—— Hist. of the Parish and Town of Bampton and the Districts and Hamlets belonging to it. New Ed. Bampton, 1848. 8vo.

GILES, Rev. John E. Lecture against Socialism, at Leeds, Sept. 23, 1838. Lond., 1839. 8vo. Eng. Rel. Pamph. Vol. 90.

GILES, Wm. F. Ann. Address before the Maryland Hist. Soc'y, Dec. 17, 1866. Baltimore, 1867. 8vo. Md. Hist. Soc. Addresses. Vol. 2.

GILFILLAN, C. W. Speech in Cong., Apr. 1, 1870, on the Public Debt. Congr. and Polit. Pamph. Vol. 84.

GILFILLAN, Geo. Bards of the Bible. N. Y., 1851. 12mo.

GILFILLAN, Rev. Jas. The Sabbath Viewed in the Light of Reason. Revelation and History. N. Y., 1862. 12mo.
GILL, Julia. Legends of N. England. N. Y. 18mo.
GILL, Rev. W. Manx and English, and English and Manx Dictionary. Douglas, 1866. 8vo.
GILLESPIE, W. M. Manual of the Principles and Practice of Road-Making, including Railroads. 8th Ed. N. Y., 1855. 8vo.
GILLESPY, John C. Hist. of Green Lake Co., Wis., with Biograph. Sketches, etc. Berlin, 1860. 12mo. Wis. Local Hist. Vol. 1.
GILLETT, E. H., D. D. Hist. Sketch of the Cause of Civil Liberty in Conn., 1639–1818. Hist. Mag. 2d Ser. Vol. 4.
—— and Others. Sketches of the Presb. Churches in this Country before the Revolution. Hist. Mag. 2d Ser. Vol. 3.
GILLETT, R. H. Democracy in the U. States. Boston, 1853. 8vo.
GILLIES, John. Hist. of Ancient Greece; its Colonies and Conquests. N. Y., 1858. 8vo.
GILMAN, Arthur. Genealogy of the Gilman Family in England and America. Albany, 1864. 4to.
—— The Gilman Family of N. Hampshire. Albany, 1869. 4to.
GILMAN, Caroline. Letters of Eliza Wilkinson during the Invasion of Charleston, S. C., by the British in the Rev. War. N. Y., 1839. 12mo.
GILMAN, D. C. Our National Schools of Science. Boston, 1867. 8vo. Addresses, etc. Vol. 14.
GILMAN, Hon. Jos. See HILDRETH, S. P. Early Ohio Settlers.
GILMANTON, N. H. See LANCASTER, D. Hist. of.
—— PRESCOTT, Dr. W. Sketch of Hist. of.
—— Academy. See SANBORN, E. D.
GILMER, Francis W. Geolog. Formation of the Natural Bridge in Va. Amer. Philos. Soc. Trans. N. S. Vol. 1.
—— Sketches, Essays and Translations. Baltimore, 1828. 8vo.
GILMER, John H. Argument before the Senate of Va., Jan., 1866, on Negro Evidence, etc. Richmond, 1866. 8vo. Va. Misc. Pamph. Vol. 1.
—— Corres with Sec. of Treasury of U. S. Richmond, 1869. 8vo. Congr. and Polit. Pamph. Vol. 70.
GILMER, Thos. W. Speeches in Cong., Mar. 9, and May 26 and 30, 1842, on the Army Bill. Washington, 1842. 8vo. Congr. and Polit. Pamph. Vol. 24.
GILMOR, Harry. Four Years in the Saddle. N.Y., 1866. 12mo.
GILMORE, Gen. Q. A. Offic'l Rep't of U. S. Engineering Dep't, of the Siege and Reduction of Fort Pulaski. Maps, etc. N. Y., 1862. 8vo.
GILPIN Family. Genealogy, with Notice of the West Family. Lima, Pa., 1870. 8vo. Genealog. Pamph. Vol. 2.
GILPIN, Henry D. Address at Phila., Dec. 4, 1856, on B. Franklin. Phila., 1857. 8vo. Addresses, etc. Vol. 13.
—— See Pennsylvania Geolog. Survey, 1839.
GILPIN, Rev. Wm. Memoirs of Josias Rogers, Esq., Commander of H. M. Ship Quebec. Lond., 1808. 8vo.

GILPIN, Gov. Wm. Notes on Colorado, its Physical Geography, etc. Lond., 1870? 12mo. Colorado Misc. Pamph. Vol. 1.

GIRAFFI, Alessandro. Rise and Fall of Masaniello, at Naples, 1647. Translated from the Italian by Jas. Howell. Waldie's Circulating Libr. Vol. 2.

GIRALDUS Cambrensis de Instructione Principum, Libri 3. Lond., 1843. 8vo.

GIRARD, Chas. Bibliography of Amer. Nat. Hist. for 1851. Washington, 1852. 8vo. Bibliograph. Pamph. Vol. 22.

—— Contributions to the Nat. Hist. of the Fresh Water Fishes of N. America. No. 1. A Monograph of the Cottoids. Smithson. Contrib. Vol. 3.

—— Publications of Learned Societies and Periodicals in the Library of the Smithsonian Institution, Dec. 31, 1854.

—— Same. May, 1856. Smithson. Contr. Vols. 7, 8.

GIRARD College, Phila. Addresses on Opening the College, Jan. 1, 1848, by J. R. Chandler and J. Jones. Phila., 1848. 8vo.

—— —— Ann. Reports, 1848–64. Phila., 1848–65. 8vo.

—— —— See AREY, H. W. Hist. of.

—— —— Ceremonies on Inaugura of Prof. R. S. Smith as President, 1863. Phila., 1863. 8vo.

—— —— Description of, contained in a final Report of the Building Committee, and other Documents. Phila., 1850. 8vo.

—— —— Digest of Acts of Assembly and Ordinances of Councils relating to the College, 1851.

—— —— See GIRARD, Stephen.

—— —— Magnetic and Meteorological Observations, 1840—1845. Washington, 1845. 3 Vols. 8vo.

—— —— See TYSON, J. R.

GIRARD, Stephen. See STIMPSON, S. Biography of.

—— The Will of, with Short Biogra. Phila., 1832. 8vo. Biograph. Pamph. Vols. 2 and 12.

—— See U. S. Supreme Court.

—— Will and Biography of. Phila., 1848. 8vo. Girard College Pamph's.

GIRARDEAU, J. L., D. D. See Confederate Memorial Day at Charleston, 1871.

GIRDLESTONE, Rev. Chas. Letters on the Unhealthy Condition of the Lower Class of Dwellings in Large Towns. Lond., 1845. 8vo. Sanitary Reform Pamph. Vol. 1.

GIZEH, Pyramid of. See Pyramids.

GLADSTONE, W. E. Two Letters to the Earl of Aberdeen, on the State Prosecutions of the Neapolitan Gov't. Lond., 1851. 8vo. 11th Ed. Eng. Polit. Pamph. Vol. 49.

GLAISHER, Jas. Philosoph. Instruments and Processes, as represented in the Great Exhibition, 1852. 8vo. Scientific Pamph. Vol. 25.

GLANVILLE, Jos. Blow at Modern Sadducism. Lond., 1668. 12mo.

GLASTENBURY, Conn. See CHAPIN, Rev. A. B. 200th Celebra.

GLAZIER, W. W. Capture, Prison Pen and Escape. Albany, 1866. 12mo.

GLEANINGS from the Poets, for Home and School. Boston, 1857. 12mo.

GLEIG, Rev. G. R. Hist. of the Bible. Harpers' Fam. Libr. N. Y., 1859. 2 vols. 18mo.

GLEN COVE, L. I., N. Y. See SCUDDER, H. J. 2d Centen. Annivers. 1868.

GLENDALE, Ohio, Fem. College. 3d, 4th and 5th Ann. Catalogues, 1857, 8, 9. Cincin. 8vo.

GLIDDON, Geo. R. Ancient Egypt: her Monuments, Hieroglyphics, History and Archæology. Phila., 1847 (?). 4to.

GLOSSARY of Provincial Words, used in Teesdale in the Co. of Durham, Eng. Lond., 1849. 12mo.

—— of Yorkshire Words and Phrases. Lond., 1855. 12mo.

GLOUCESTER Co., N. J. See MICKLE, Isaac. Reminiscences of.

—— Eng. See COUNSEL, G. W. Hist. and Descrip. of. 1829.

—— —— See FOSBROOKE, Rev. T. D. Hist. of the City of. 1819.

—— Mass. See BABSON, J. J. Hist. of.

GLOVER, Mr. ——. Evidence delivered to a Comm. of the House of Commons, concerning the Trade to Germany, &c. Lond., 1794. 8vo. Eng. Polit. Pamph. Vol. 72.

GLOVER, Anna. Glover Memorials and Genealogies. Boston, 1867. 8vo.

GLOVER, Fred. R. A. Harbours of Refuge; not "Dangerous Decoys," "Ship Traps," nor "Wrecking Pools." Lond., 1859. 8vo. Eng. Misc. Pamph. Vol. 33.

GLOVER, Rev. Geo. Present State of Pauperism in England. Lond., 1817. 8vo. Pamphleteer. Vol. 10.

—— Character and Tendency of the Property Tax, &c. Lond., 1816. 8vo. 2d Ed. Pamphleteer. Vol. 8.

GLOVER, Gen. John. See UPHAM, W. P. Memoir of.

GLOVER, Stephen.—Hist. and Gazetteer of the Co. of Derby, Eng. Derby, 1831. 2 Vols. 4to.

GLOVER, Vt.—See PERKINS, Rev. S. K. B.—Semi-Centen. Disc., 1867.

GLOVER, Wm.—Lord Brougham's Law Reforms and Courts of Local Jurisdiction. Lond., 1834. 8vo. Eng. Polit. Pamph. Vol 78.

GOADBY, Henry.—Text Book of Vegetable and Animal Physiology. N. Y., 1858. 8vo.

GOD Bless Abraham Lincoln. A Solemn Discourse by a Local Preacher. N. J. Rebelln. Pamph. Vol. 40 and 65.

GODDARD, Wm. G.—Address at Providence, R. I., May 14, 1841, on the Death of Wm. H. Harrison. Providence, 1841. 8vo. Adddresses. Vol. 24.

—— Addresses to the People of R. Island, on the Change in the Civil Gov't. Providence, 1843. 8vo. R. I. Misc. Pam. Vol. 1.

—— Address to Phi. Beta Kappa Society of R. Island, Sept. 7, 1836. Vol. 11. Addresses, etc.

GODEY, L. A.—The Lady's Book. Phila., 1839–43. 5 Vols. 8vo.

GODFREY, William C.—Narr. of the last Grinnell Arctic Exploring Exped. in search of Sir John Franklin. 1853–5. Phila, 1857. 12mo.

GODMAN, John D.—Amer. Nat. History. 2d Ed. Phila. 1831. 3 Vols. 8vo.
—— Rambles of a Naturalist with a Biograph Sketch of the Author by Dr. Drake. Waldie's Circulating Libr. Vol. 1.
GODWIN, Parke.—Cyclopædia of Universal Biography. N. Y., 1854. 12mo.
—— Democracy, Constructive and Pacific. N. Y., 1844. 8vo. Cong. and Polit. Pamph. Vol. 99.
GODWYN, Thomas.—Moses and Aaron; Civil and Ecclesiastical. Rites used by the Ancient Hebrews. 10th Ed. Lond., 1671. 4to.
GOERRES, Prof.—Germany and the Revolution. Lond., 1820. 8vo. Pamphleteer. Vol. 15.
GOETHE, John Wolfgany Von.—See BOILEAU, D. Remarks on Hayward's Transla, of Faust.
GOFFE, Wm.—Plan for seizing and carrying to N. Y., Wm. Goffe, the Regicide. Albany, 1855. 12mo.
—— See ROBBINS, C.—Regicides sheltered in N. England. N. Eng. Pamph. Vol. 1.
GOGGIN, Wm. L. Speech in Cong., June 10, 1842, on the Public Lands. Washington, 1842. 8vo. Congr. and Polit. Pamph. Vol. 24.
GOIN, John W. An Apprentice System for the U. S. Merchant Service. N. Y., 1853. 12mo. Pamphlets. Vol. 13.
GOLD Districts. From the Amer. Quarterly Review, Mar., 1832. Hist. Pamph. Vol. 3.
—— See CARY, Thos. G. Gold from Cal.
—— JACOB, W. Inquiry into Precious Metals.
—— KENT, E. N. Instructions for Collecting and Testing Gold.
—— Mines of the Gila. See WEBBER, C. W.
—— MITCHELL, E. Gold Mines of N. Carolina. 1828. MURCHISON, R. I. Distribution, etc., of.
—— OLMSTEAD, D. Gold Mines of N. Carolina. 1825.
—— PHILLIPS, Wm. On the Georgia Gold Mines. 1833.
—— ROTHE, C. E. Gold Mines of S. Carolina. 1828.
—— VILLARD, H. Pike's Peak Gold Regions.
GOLDEN AGE, Newspaper. Mar. 1871 to June, 1872, bound with the "Revolution." 1870.
—— Campaign Tracts. Six Pamphlets, viz.:
1. The Phila. Failure, by THEO. TILTON.
2. The New Departure, by G. W. JULIAN.
3. A Democrat's Reasons, etc.
4. What I know of Horace Greeley, by OLIVER JOHNSON.
5. Self-Condemned, by THEO. TILTON.
6. Mr. Greeley's Answer to the Union League.
} N. Y., 1872, 12mo. Cong. and Political Pamph. Vol. 130.
GOLDSBOROUGH, Chas. W. U. S. Naval Chronicle. Vol. I. Washington, 1824. 8vo.
GOLDSBOROUGH, W. W. The Maryland Line in the Confed. States Army. Baltimore, 1869. 12mo.

GOLDSMID, Benj. Statement of the Circumstances and Manner of his Death. Lond., 1808. 8vo. Hist. Pamph. Vol. 18.

GOLDSMID, Francis H. Arguments against the Enfranchisement of the Jews, considered. Lond., 1831. 8vo. Eng. Relig. Pamph. Vol. 44. Same 2d Ed. 1833. Strangford Pamph. Vol. 8.

—— Reply to Arguments against the Removal of Jewish Disabilities. Lond., 1848. 8vo. Eng. Rel. Pamph. Vol. 51. See also Strangford Pamph. Vol. 45.

GOLDSMITH, Lewis. On the Appointment of Hon. Geo. Canning to the Foreign Department. Lond., 1822. 8vo. Strangford Pamph. Vol. 27.

GOLDSMITH, Oliver. Hist. of the Earth and Animated Nature. New ed. Phila., 1858. 4 Vols. in 2—8vo.

—— See Irving, W. Life of and Selec. of Works.

—— Irving W. Biog. of.

—— Miscellaneous Works, with Acc. of his Life and Writings, Edited by Washington Irving. Phila., 1849. 8vo.

—— See PRIOR, Jas. Life of.

GONSON, Sir John. Five Charges to Several Grand Juries, in 1728–9. Lond. n. d. 8vo. Eng. Polit. Pamph. Vol. 67.

GONZAGA College, Washington, D. C. Catalogue of Officers, etc., for 1867–8. Washington, 1868. 8vo.

GOOCH, D. W. Argument before the Comm. on Naval Affairs of Cong. on Purchase of Tools for Phila. Navy Yd. Washington, 1869. 8vo. Congr. and Polit. Pamph. Vol. 117.

—— Speech in Cong., May 3, 1864, on Secession and Reconstruction. Rebell'n Pamph. Vol. 9.

GOOD, Dr. John M. Letter to Sir John C. Hippisley, on the Tread-Wheel in Prison Discipline. Lond., 1824. 8vo. 2d ed. Pamphleteer. Vol. 23.

—— Treatise on Self Knowledge. Phila., 1818. 18mo.

GOODALL, Nathan. See Hildreth, S. P. Early Ohio Settlers.

GOODE, Pat. G. Speech in Cong., June 24, 1832, on Va. Land Claims. Washington, 1842. 8vo. Cong. and Polit. Pamph. Vol. 25.

GOODELL, A. C. Biograph. Sketch of Thos. Maule of Salem. Essex Institute Coll. Vol. 3.

—— Notice of Alonzo Lewis. Essex Institute Coll. Vol. 3.

—— The Difference between the Nonconformists of Mass. Bay & the Separatists of Plymouth Colony, discussed. Essex Institute Coll. Vol. 4.

GOODHUE, Josiah F. History of Shoreham, Vt., from 1761 to the Present Time. Middlebury. 1861. 8vo. Vt. Hist. Discourses, etc. Vol. 2.

—— Sermon on. Rev. Thos. A. Merrill, at Middlebury, June 6, 1855. Middlebury, 1856. 8vo. Sermons. Vol. 51.

GOODLOE, Dan'l R. The Southern Platform : or Manuel of Southern Sentiment on Slavery. Boston, 1858. 8vo. Rebell'n Pamph. Vol. 8. Congr. & Polit. Pamph. Vol. 102.

GOODMAN, Alfred T. First White Children born on Ohio Soil. Western Reserve Hist. Soc. Tracts.

GOODMAN, Afred T. Judges of the Supreme Court of Ohio, under the First Constitution. 1803–1852. Western Reserve Hist. Soc. Tracts.

—— See Western Reserve Hist. Soc'y.

GOODMAN COUNTRY : to His Worship the City of London. n. d. Folio. Eng. Polit. Pamph. Vol. 1.

GOODMAN, Godfrey. Court of King James the First. Lond. 1839. 2 vols. 8vo.

GOODMAN, Rev. J. R. Penn. Biography; or Memoirs of Eminent Pennsylvanians. For Schools. Phila. 1839. 12mo.

GOOD News from N. England: with an exact Relation of the first Planting that Country: etc. 1648. Trans. Hist. Soc. Coll. 4th Series. Vol. 1.

GOOD QUEEN ANNE Vindicated, and the Conduct of the Whig Ministry and the Allies exposed. Lon'd. 1748. 8vo. Eng. Polit. Pamph. Vol. 69.

GOODRICH, Chas. A. Lives of the Signers of the Declaration of Amer. Independence. N. Y. 1829. 12mo.

—— Another Ed. Boston. 1834. 12mo.

—— Religious Ceremonies and Customs practised by all Nations. Hartford. 1834. 12mo.

—— See Worcester, Mass. 1st Ch.

GOODRICH, Rev. Chauncey E. Sermon on Death of Amariah Brigham, M. D., preached in Utica, N. Y., 1849. Utica. 1858. 8vo. 2d Ed. Sermons. Vol. 52.

GOODRICH, C. R. Progress of Science and Mechanism; illustrated by Examples in the N. Y. Exhibition. 1853–4. N. Y. 1854. 4to.

GOODRICH, Frank B. The Tribute Book : a Record of the Munificence, Sacrifice and Patriotism of the Amer. People during the War for the Union. N. Y. 1865. 8vo.

GOODRICH, J. Z. Speech in Cong., May 27, 1852, on tne Compromise Bill. Congr. & Polit. Pamph. Vol. 94.

GOODRICH, S. G. Popular Biography; embracing Eminent Characters of all Nations. N. Y. 1850. 12mo.

—— Recollections of a Lifetime; or Men and Things I have Seen. N. Y., 1857. 2 Vols. 12mo.

GOODWIN.—See Arms of Goodwin & Bradbury.

GOODWIN, Dan'l R. Inaug. Address as Provost of the University of Penn., Sept. 10, 1860. Phila., 1860. 8vo.

GOODWIN, Rev. Harvey. Address at Cambridge, Oct. 29, 1855, on Educa. for Working Men. Cambridge, Eng. 12mo. Educa. Pamph., Vol. 38.

GOODWIN, H. C. Ithaca, as it was and is. Ithaca, 1853. 8vo. N. Y. Hist. Discourses, etc., Vol. 2.

—— Pioneer History; or Cortland County and the Border Wars of N. Y. N. Y., 1859. 12mo.

GOODWIN, Isaac. Oration at Lancaster, Mass., Feb. 21, 1826, in Commem. of the 150th Annivers. of the Destruction of that Town by the Indians. Worcester Mag., Vol. 2.

GOODWIN, Nathaniel. Descendants of Thos. Olcott, one of the first Settlers of Hartford, Conn. Hartford, 1845. 8vo. Genealog. Pamph., Vol. 11.

—— Genealog. Notes; or Contributions to the Family Hist. of some of the first Settlers of Conn. and Mass. Hartford, 1856. 8vo.

—— The Foote Family; or the Descendants of Nathan'l Foote, one of the first Settlers of Wethersfield, Conn. Hartford, 1849. 8vo.

GOODWIN, Philo A. Biography of Andrew Jackson, President of the U. States. N. Y., 1833. 12mo.

GOODWIN, Thos. S. The Nat. Hist. of Secession. N. Y., 1864. 12mo.

GOODYEAR, Wm. H. Memoranda for Lectures on the Hist. and Development of Art. N. Y., 1872. 8vo. Art Pamph., Vol. 6.

GOOKIN, Dan'l. Hist. Acc. of the Christian Indians in New Eng., in 1685–77. Am. Antq. Soc. Coll., Vol. 2.

—— Hist. Collections of the Indians of New England. Boston, 1792. 8vo. See also Mass. Hist. Soc. Coll., 1st Ser., Vol. 1.

GORDON, Sir Cosmo. Life and Genius of Lord Byron. Lond., 1824. 8vo. Pamphleteer, Vol. 24.

GORDON, Rev. Jas. B. Hist. and Geograph. Memoir of the N. Amer. Continent. Dublin, 1820. 4to.

GORDON, J. E. British Protestantism. 2 Letters. Lond., 1847. 8vo. Strangford Pamph., Vol. 44.

GORDON, Pat'k. Geography Anatomized. Lond., 1744. 8vo. Another ed. Lond., 1749. 8vo.

GORDON, Rev. R. A. Observations on Village-School Educa. Oxford, n. d. 8vo. Educa. Pamph. Vol. 28.

GORDON, Sam'l. Speech in Cong., Jan. 13, 1842, on the Treasury Note Bill. Washington, 1842. 8vo. Congr. and Polit. Pamph. Vol. 25.

GORDON, Thos. F. Hist. of N. Jersey from its First Discovery to the Adoption of the Federal Constitution. Boston, 1834. 8vo.

—— Hist. of Spanish Discoveries in America prior to 1520. Phila., 1831. 2 vols. 12mo.

—— Hist. of Penn., from its Discovery by Europeans to the Declara. of Independence in 1776. Phila., 1829. 8vo.

GORDON, Wm. See LORING, Jas. S. Paper on.

—— Hist. of the Rise, Progress and Establishment of the U. States. Lond., 1788. 4 vols. 8vo.

GORE, Montague. Lectures on the Character of the Duke of Wellington at Wells, 1852. Lond., 1852. 8vo. Strangford Pamph. Vol. 63.

—— Lecture on Military Educa. in France. Lond., 1856. Educa. Pamph. Vol. 37.

—— The Dwellings of the Poor, and Means of Improving them. Lond., 1851. 8vo. Srangford Pamph. Vol. 57.

GEORGES, Sir Ferdinando. Brief Relation of the Advancement of Plantations in America, especially N. England, 1658. Mass. Hist. Soc. Coll. 3d Ser. Vol. 6.

GEORGES, Sir Ferdinando. Brief Relation of the Original Undertakings of Advancement of Plantations in America, especially in N. England. Lond., 1658. Maine Hist. Soc. Coll. Vol. 2.

GORHAM, Geo. C. Speech at Platt's Hall, San Francisco, July 10, 1867. Cal. Misc. Pamph. Vol. 1.

GORHAM, Maine. See PIERCE, Josiah. Centen. Address. 1836.

—— —— History of.

GRAHAM, John, M. D. See PALFREY, Rev. John G. Obit. Sermon.

GORRIE, Rev. P. D. Lives of Eminent Methodist Ministers. N. Y., 1857. 12mo.

GORTON, John. Gen. Biograph'l Dictionary. New Ed. with Supplementary Vol. Lond., 1851. 4 vols. 8vo.

GORTON, Sam'l. See DEANE, Chas. Notice of.

GORTON, Rev. S. Letter to Nathan'l Morton, 1669. Force's Hist. Tracts. Vol. 4.

—— Simplicities, Defence against Seven Headed Policy, 1646. See Force's Hist. Tracts. Vol. 4.

—— Same, ed. by W. K. Staples. R. I. Hist. Soc. Coll. Vol. 2. Providence, 1835. 8vo.

—— See MACKEE, J. M. Life of.

GOSNOLD, Capt. Bartholomew. See ARCHER, Wm. Relation of his Voyage to Va.

—— BRERETON, M. John. Relation of his Discovery of Va.

—— Documents relating to his Voyage to America in 1602. Mass. Hist. Soc. Coll. 3d Ser. Vol. 8.

GOSPEL of Slavery; a Primer of Freedom. N. Y., 1864. 12mo. Rebell'n Pamph. Vol. 24.

GOSS, C. C. Statist. Hist. of First Century of Amer. Methodism. N. Y., 1866. 12mo.

GOSS, E. H. The Melrose Memorial; Annals of Melrose, Mass., in the Rebellion. Boston, 1868. 4to.

GOUDA, Holland. Explanation of the Famous Glass-Work in St. John's Ch. Gouda. 12mo. n. d. Scientific Pamph. Vol. 24.

GOUGE, H. A. New System of Ventilation. 2d Ed. N. Y., 1867. 8vo. Scientific Pamph. Vol. 16.

GOUGE, Wm. M. Short Hist. of Paper Money and Banking in the U. S. N. Y., 1835. 8vo. Cong. & Polit. Pamph. Vol. 75.

GOULD, Aug. A., M. D. Origin, Progress and Present Condition of the Boston Soc. of Nat. Hist. n. d. 8vo.

—— Description of Shells from the Gulf of Cal. and Pacific Coasts. n. d. Scientific Pamph. Vol. 14.

GOULD, B. A. Ancestry and Posterity of Zacheus Gould of Topsfield, Mass. Salem, 1872. 8vo. Genealog. Pamph. Vol. 14.

—— Oration before the Conn. Beta of Phi Beta Kappa, at Trinity Coll., Hartford, July 15, 1856. Hartford, 1858. 8vo. Addresses. Vol. 19.

—— Reply to the Statement of the Trustees of the Dudley Observatory. Albany, 1859.

GOULD, CHAS. A Financial Scheme for the Gov't. From Bankers' Mag., Mar., 1862. Rebell'n Pamph. Vol. 39.

GOULD, Chas. His Appeal from the Session of Madison Square Presb. Ch., N. York. N. Y., 1864. 8vo. N. Y. Hist. Discourses, etc. Vol. 1.

GOULD Genealogy. See VINTON, J. A.

GOULD, John. Papers relative to the Case of, and the Period of Usurpation in N. England. Mass. Hist. Soc. Coll. 3d Ser. Vol. 7.

GOULD, Nathan'l. Instructions for Navigating the St. Lawrence. Lond., 1832, 33. 8vo. Strangford Pamph. Vol. 11.

—— Letter on the Insurrection in Canada. Leeds, 1838. 8vo. Strangford Pamph. Vol. 14.

—— Sketch of the Trade of British America. Lond., 1833. 8vo. Strangford Pamph. Vol. 11.

GOULD, Maj. Wm. Journ. kept during an Expedition into Penn., in 1794. N. J. Hist. Soc. Proceed. Vol. 3.

GOULDEN'S Hand-Book and Guide through Canterbury. Canterbury, Eng. 12mo. n. d. Guide-Books. Vol. 1.

GOULDING Genealogy. See MORSE, Rev. A.

GOURAUD, Francis Fauvel. Phreno-Mnemotechnic Dictionary; being a Philosoph. Classification of all Homophonic Words in the Eng. Language. Part I. N. Y., 1844. 8vo.

GOURGAUD, General. See GROUCHY, Marshal De.

GOURLEY, D. D. Sanitary Reform of the British Army. Lond., 1858. 8vo. Eng. Misc. Pamph. Vol. 18.

GOVERNMENT Aid to American Shipping Interests. The Bounty Plan of Gen. E. A. Merritt. N. Y., 1870. 8vo. Congr. and Polit. Pamph. Vol. 120.

GOVERNMENT. See BROWNE, P. A., on U. S. Naturalization Laws.

—— Collection of Scarce Tracts.

—— DRUMMOND, H. Gov't by the Queen and Gov't by the People. 1842.

—— FISHER, S. G. Science of.

—— Hospital for the Insane, Washington. 5th to 14th Ann. Reports, inclusive. Washington, 1861. 8vo.

—— LIEBER, F., on Self Gov't.

—— NAVARRO, J. Etudes Législatives. 1836.

—— See Politics and Government

—— PRICE, R. Observations on the Principles of.

—— SMITH, Gerrit. True Office of.

—— SMITH, Leveson. On Mill's Essay on.

—— Treatise on. 1698.

GOWANS, Wm. Catalogue of Books belonging to his Estate. Nos. 1–16. N. Y., 1871–2. 8vo. Bibliograph. Pamph. Vols. 24–26.

GRAFTON, Mass. See BRIGHAM, Wm. Centen. Address, 1835.

—— WILLSON, E. B. Hist. Disc. 1846.

GRAHAM, C. True Philosophy of Mind. Louisville, 1869. 8vo.

GRAHAM, Isabella. Life and Writings of. N. Y., n. d. 12mo.

GRAHAM, Sir Jas. See Observations on his System of Favoritism, etc., toward the Navy.

GRAHAM, Jas. Life of Gen. Danl. Morgan of the Va. Line of the U. S. A. N. Y., 1858. 12mo.

GRAHAM, Jas. Speech in Cong., Apr. 4, 1842, on the Branch Mints. Washington, 1842. 8vo. Congr. and Polit. Pamph. Vol. 24.

GRAHAM, J. A. Descriptive Sketch of the Present State of Vermont. London, 1797. 8vo.

GRAHAM, Col. Jas. J. Memoir of Gen. Saml. Graham, with Notices of his Campaign, from 1779 to 1801. Edinburgh, 1862. 12mo.

GRAHAM, John. Lord Viscount Dundee (or Claverhouse). Memoirs of. n. d. 12mo. Biog. Pamph. Vol. 16.

GRAHAM, John A. Memoirs of John Horne Tooke—with Proofs of his Identity with Junius. N. Y. 1828. 8vo.

GRAHAM, Col. J. D. A Lunar Tidal Wave in Lake Michigan. Chicago, 1860. 8vo. Scientific Pamph. Vol. 11.

—— A Lunar Tidal Wave in the N. Amer. Lakes. Cambridge. 1861. 8vo.

—— On the Latitude and Longitude of Milwaukee, Pr. du Chien, Racine and Madison, Wis. Wis. Hist. Soc. Coll. Vol. 4. Same, corrected copy, 1860. Scientific Pamph. Vol. 14.

—— Report on the Boundary Line between the U. S. and Mexico. 1852. Washington, 1853. 8vo.

—— Reports on the Harbor Improvements of Lake Michigan and St. Clair for 1855 and 1856; embracing portions of the Report for 1855 which relates to the Lake Michigan Harbors within the States of Ill. and Wis. Parts 1 and 2. Washington. 8vo.

—— Ann. Report on the Harbors of Lakes Michigan, St. Claire, Erie, Ontario and Champlain, for 1858. Washington, 1859. 8vo. Wis. Misc. Pamph. Vol. 5. Same for 1857, bound as volume.

—— Report on the Improvement of the Navigation of the St. Clair River. 1855. Sec. of War Misc. Reports.

—— Report on the Military and Hydrograph. Chart of the Extremity of Cape Cod, including Provincetown and Truro, etc. Washington, 1838. Folio.

—— Report on the Intersection of the Boundary Lines of the States of Md., Penn. and Delaware. Washington, 1850. 8vo.

GRAHAM, Gen. Saml. See GRAHAM, Jas. J. Memoirs of.

GRAHAM, William A. British Invasion of N. Carolina in 1780–81. A Lecture before the N. Y. Hist. Soc., Jan., 1852. Rev. Hist. of N. Carolina.

—— Speech in U. S. Senate, Apr. 13, 1842, on the Loan Bill. Washington, 1842. 8vo. Congr. and Polit. Pamph. Vol. 24.

—— Speech in the U. S. Senate, June 3, 1842, on the Apportionment Bill. Washington, 1842. 8vo. Congr. and Polit. Pamph. Vol. 24.

GRAHAME, Jas. History of the Rise and Progress of the U. S. of North America till the British Revolution in 1768. Lond., 1827. 2 Vols. 8vo.

—— History of the U. S. from the Plantation of the Amer. Colonies to Assumption of Nat. Independence. Boston, 1845. 4 Vols. 8vo.

GRAHAME, Jas. See QUINCY, Josiah. Vindica. of.

GRAINGER, Rich'd D. Observations on the Cultivation of Organic Science, being the Hunterian Oration of 1848. Lond. 8vo. Med. Pamph. Vol. 17.

GRAMMAR, Chinese. See MORRISON, R. Grammar of Eng. Language for Chinese.

—— Schools considered with reference to a Lease lately decided by the Chancellor. Lond., 1820. 8vo. Pamphleteer. Vol. 16.

GRANBY, Conn. See PHELPS, N. A. Hist. of.

GRAND ARMY OF THE REPUBLIC. Manual of, together with Memorial Day in the Department of Michigan, May, 1869. Lansing, 1869. 8vo. Rebellion Pamph. Vol. 56.

—— —— Proceedings of National Encampment at Washington, May 11 and 12, 1870. Washington, 1870. 8vo. Rebellion Pamph. Vol. 56.

—— —— Rules and Regulations for the Gov't of, May 1869 and 1870. Boston, 1869–70. 12mo. Rebellion Pamph. Vol. 56.

—— —— Departm't of Mass. By-Laws and Rules of Order, 1869. Proceedings at New Bedford, 1870. Mass. Misc. Pamph. Vol. 4.

—— —— Departm't of Minn. Proceedings of Encampments for 1869, '70 and '71. St. Paul, 1871. 8vo. Rebellion Pamph. Vol. 56.

—— —— Departm't of N. J. Proceedings of 6th Semi-Ann. Encampment, held at N. Brunswick, 1870. Newark, 1870. 8vo. Rebellion Pamph. Vol. 56.

—— —— Departm't of N. York. Semi-Annual Encampment, July 19, 1871. N. Y., 1871. 8vo. Rebellion Pamph. Vol. 56.

GRAND JUNCTION R. R. Co. See Mass. Supreme Judicial Court.

GRAND (The) Magazine of Universal Intelligence. Lond., 1758. 8vo.

GRAND RAPIDS, Wis. Wood County Reporter. Newspaper. Feb. 1858 to May, 1859. Folio.

GRANGER, A. P. Speech in Cong., Apr. 1856, on Slavery. Congr. and Polit. Pamph. Vol. 84.

GRANGER, Rev. J. Biograph. History of England from Egbert the Great to the Revolution. 5th Ed., with a continuation to the end of the Reign of George I, by Rev. M. Noble. Lond., 1806 and 1824. 9 Vols. 8vo.

GRANT, Mrs. Anne. Memoir and Corres. of Mrs. Grant of Laggan. 2d Ed. Lond., 1845. 3 Vols. 12mo.

—— Memoirs of an Amer. Lady: with Sketches of Manners and Scenery in America before the Revolution. N. Y., 1846. 12mo.

GRANT, Rev. Brewin. "Gladstone and Justice to Ireland." The Liberal Cry Examined, etc. Sheffield, 1868. 8vo. Eng. Misc. Pamph. Vol. 36.

GRANT COUNTY, Wis. Witness. Newspaper. 1863–6, 1870–2. Folio.

—— Herald, 1869–73.

GRANT, E. B. Boston Railways: their Condition & Prospects Boston, 1866. 8vo. Boston Misc. Pamph. Vol. 2.

GRANT FAMILY GENEALOGY. From "Lives of GRANT & COLFAX." Cincin., 1868. 8vo. Genealog. Pamph. Vol. 14.

—— —— CHAUNCEY, E. M. Ancestry of Gen. GRANT & their Contemporaries.

GRANT, John Peter. Essays Illustrating Elementary Principles of Wealth & Currency. Lond., 1812. 8vo. Eng. Misc. Pamph. Vol. 18.

GRANT, MATT. Old Church Record.—from Stiles' History of Ancient Windsor, Conn. Albany. 1860. 8vo. Conn. Hist. Discourses, &c. Vol. 3.

GRANT, ROB'T. MACAULAY, T. B., and others. Speeches in Parl't on Jewish Disabilities. Lond., 1833. 8vo. Strangford Pamph. Vol. 8.

GRANT, T. H. The Future Commercial Policy of British America. read before the Quebec Lit. & Hist. Soc., Mar. 20, 1867. Transactions N. S. Part 5.

GRANT, Gen. U. S., and his Cabinet, 1869 See MARTIN, E. W.

—— and the Presidency. Letter to Hon. E. B. WASHBURNE. N. Y., 1868. 8vo. Congr. & Polit. Pamph. Vol. 122.

—— See BADEAU, A. Military Hist. of.

—— CHAUNCEY, E. M. Ancestry of.

—— Chicago Tribune Campaign Doc's, 1872.

—— COPPEE, H. GRANT & his Campaigns.

—— DE WOLF, L. E. On the Grant Gov't, 1872.

—— Golden Age Compaign Tracts, 1872.

—— His Life and Services as a Soldier. n. d. Reb. Pamph. Vol. 95.

—— See HOWLAND, Edw. GRANT as a Soldier & Statesman, 1868.

—— PHELPS, C. A. Life and Services of, 1868.

—— Report of the Armies of the U. States, 1864–5. Washington, 1865. 8vo. Congr. & Polit. Pamph. Vols. 67, 81.

—— See SCHURZ, Carl, and GRANT, U. S. Reports on S. Carolina, &c., 1865.

—— STOWE, Mrs. H. B. Extracts from "Men of Our Times."

GRANVILLE, Dr. A. B. Letter to W. Huskisson on the Quarantine Bill. Lond., 1825. 8vo. Pamphleteer, Vol. 25.

GRANVILLE College, O. See WILLIAMS, Rev. S. Address, 1848.

—— Cong. Church. See LITTLE, Rev. Jacob. 27th New Year's Sermon. 1854.

—— Female Academy Catalogue for 1857–8. Newark, O. 8vo.

GRAPHIC Illustrations of the Life and Times of Sam'l Johnson, LL.D. Lond., 1836. 8vo.

GRATIOT, Gen. C. Report from Comm. on Judiciary of U. S. Senate on his Memorial. Washington, 1852. 8vo. Congr. and Polit. Pamph. Vol. 41.

GRATTAN, Henry. See Speeches of, &c.

GRAVE CREEK Mound. See SCHOOLCRAFT, H. R.

—— TOMLINSON, A. B.

GRAVES, A. J. Women in America; or the Moral and Intellectual Condition of American Female Society. Harpers Fam. Lib. N. Y., 1855. 18mo.

GRAVES, Wm. Two Letters on the Conduct of Rear Admiral Graves. July—Dec., 1781. Morrisania, 1865. 8vo.

GRAVESVILLE, Wis. Calumet Republican, Newspaper. Aug. to Dec., 1859. Folio. (Bound with Sauk and Juneau Co. Papers.)

GRAVIER, R. P. Jacques. Relation ou Journal de son Voyage en 1700 depuis le pays des Illinois jusqu'à l'Embouchure de Mississippi. N. Y., 1859. 4to. Shea's Ed.

—— Relation de cé qui s'est passé dans la Mission de l'Immaculee Conception au Pays des Ilinois. 1693–94. N. Y., 1857. Shea's Ed.

—— See Early Voyages on Mississippi.

GRAVITATION, Law of. See BURR, T. W. Lecture. 1856.

GRAY, Alonzo. Elements of Chemistry. 12th Ed. N. Y., 1846. 12mo.

—— Same. 40th Ed. N. Y., 1857. 12mo.

GRAY, Asa. Botanical Excursion to the Mountains of N. Carolina. 1841. Silliman's Journ., Vol. 42.

—— Botanical Text Book. N. Y., 1842.

—— Same. N. Y., 1853. 8vo.

—— How Plants Grow; a Simple Introduction to Structural Botany. N. Y., 1859. Sm. 4to.

GRAY, F. C. Remarks on the Early Laws of Mass. Bay; with the Code adopted in 1641, called the "Body of Liberties." Mass. Hist. Soc. Coll. 3d Ser. Vol. 8.

GRAY, Rev. F. T. Extract from a Funeral Sermon on Amos Lawrence of Boston, Jan., 1853. Boston, 1853. 12mo. Sermons, Vol. 2.

—— See Letters to the Friends of, &c.

—— Pastoral Letter to the Ch. at Pitts St. Chapel, Boston, Dec. 31, 1838. Boston, 1839. 12mo.

—— See PEABODY, E. Obt. Sermon. 1855.

—— Two Sermons in the Bulfinch St. Ch., Boston, Nov. 29, 1841. With Hist. Appendix. Boston, 1841. 8vo. Boston Hist. Discourses Vol. 2.

GRAY, Hugh. Letters from Canada, written during a Residence in 1806–1808. London, 1809. 8vo.

GRAY, John. New Method of Observing the Meridian Altitudes of the Heavenly Bodies, and their Use in Naviga. Lond., 1763. 8vo. Scientific Pamph. Vol. 30.

GRAY, John. (Last Revolutionary Soldier.) See DALZELL, J. M.

GRAY, John C. Address before Mass. Soc. for Promoting Agriculture. Oct. 20, 1830. Pamphlets. Vol. 6.

GRAY, John F., M. D. The Policy of Chartering Colleges of Medicine; Introduct. Lecture before the N. Y. School of Medicine. N. Y., 1833. 8vo. Med. Pamph. Vol. 2.

GRAY, Robert, D. D. Discourse at Bishop Wearmouth Church, May 17, 1812, on the Assassination of Hon. Spencer Perceval. Sunderland, 1812. 8vo. Eng. Sermons, Vol. 32. A.

GRAY, S. Remarks on the Production of Wealth; Letter to Rev. T. R. Malthus. Lond., 1820. 8vo. Pamphleteer. Vol. 17.

GRAY, Rev. Dr. Thos. Half Century Sermon at Jamaica Plain, Apr. 24, 1842. Boston, 1842. 8vo. Mass. Hist. Discourses Vols. 6, 15.

GRAY, Thos. Jr. See DEARBORN, H. A. S. and GRAY, T.

GRAY, W. H. Hist. of Oregon, 1792—1849, drawn from Personal Observation and Authentic Information. Portland, O, 1870. 8vo.

GRAYDON, Alex. Memoirs of his own Time, with Reminiscences of Men and Events of the Revolution. Ed. by J. S. Littell. 8vo. Phila. 1846.

—— Memoirs of My Life. Harrisburg, Pa.; 1811. 12mo.

GRAYDON, Wm. J. James Louis Petigru — a Biograph. Sketch. N. Y., 1866. 12mo.

GRAYSON, E. P. See Argument in his Defence.

GRAZEBROOK, H. S. The Heraldry of Smith; a Collection of Arms borne by most Families of that Name. Lond., 1870. 4to.

GREAT Barrington, Mass. See DURFEE, Rev. C. Commem. Disc., 1866.

—— TODD, Rev. John. Centen. Sermon 1843.

GREAT Britain. Acts passed in the Reign of Queen Anne, from 1706 to 1715. 31 Pamphlets. Lond., Folio. Eng. Polit. Pamph. Vol. 3.

—— Acts passed in the Reign of Geo. III, from 1793–1819, and An Act, Cap. 140, in the Reign of Geo. IV, 1826. Folio. Eng. Polit. Pamph. Vol. 5.

——A griculture. See Corn Laws.

—— —— Reports on the State of thè Agricult. Interest of the United Kingdom. 1850. Lond. 8vo. Strangford Pamph. Vol. 55.

—— Army. See Hist. Records of British Army.

—— —— List of Officers of Army & Marines, 1794, 1795, 1799, 1801, 1802, 1803, 1808, 1809.

—— —— Royal Military Chronicle. 1810–13.

—— CALENDAR of State Papers. Lond. 1865—1870. 61 vols. 4to.:

—— —— Calendarum Genealogicum; for the Reigns of Henry III, and Edward I. 2 vols. 4to.

—— —— State Papers of Reign's of Edward VI, Mary and Elizabeth. 1547—1590. 2 vols. 4to.

—— —— Same of Queen Elizabeth continued. 1591—1601. 3 vols. 4to.

—— —— Same of Reign of James I. 1603—1625. 4 vols. 4to.

—— —— Same of Reign of Charles I. 1825—1638. 12 vols. 4to.

—— —— Same of Reign of Charles II. 1660—1667. 7 vols. 4to.

—— —— Same relating to Scotland. 1509—1587. 2 vols. 4to.

—— —— Same relating to Ireland. 1509—1585. 2 vols. 4to.

—— —— Same Colonial Series. 1574—1616. 2 vols. 4to.

—— —— Same Reign of Henry VIII. 1509—1523. 5 vols. 4to.

—— —— Same Reign of Edward VI. 1547—1553. 1 vol. 4to.

—— —— Same Reign of Queen Mary. 1553—1558. 1 vol. 4to.

—— —— Foreign Series of Reign of Queen Elizabeth, 1558-1563. 6 Vols. 4to.

—— —— Treasury Papers. Vol. 1. 1557-1696. 4to.

GREAT Britain. Calendar of State Papers—Carew Papers, 1515–1603. 4 Vols. 4to.
—— —— Calendar of Letters relating to England and Spain, 1485–1525; with Supplement. 3 Vols. 4to.
—— —— Calendar of State Papers relating to English Affairs in Archives of Venice, 1202–1526. 3 Vols. 4to.
—— —— Syllabus in English, or Rymer's Fœdera. Vol. 1. 1066–1377. 4to.
—— See Publications of Comm'rs of Pub. Records. P. 441.
—— Chronicles and Memorials during the Middle Ages. Lond., 1858–1869. 100 Vols. 8vo.
—— Colonies. Case of the Free-Labour British Colonies. Lond., 1852. 8vo. Strangford Pamph. Vol. 63.
—— —— See LYTTLETON, Lord. Colonial Empire of G. B., 1850.
—— —— See British Colonies in America. Canada. Amer. War of Revo., etc.
—— Commissioners of Pub. Records. Reports, 1800–1819. Lond., 1819. Folio. 1837. Appendix to Reports. Lond., 1819. Folio.
—— Conquest of by Saxons. See HAIGH, D. H.
—— Constitution of. Introduct. Lessons on the British Constitution. Lond., 1854. 12mo. Eng. Polit. Pamph. Vol. 52.
—— —— See England.
—— Defences of. See KENNEDY, S. SMITH Toulmin.
—— Extra Official State Papers, 1789.
—— Finances and Trade of the United Kingdom, at the beginning of 1852. 8vo. Strangford Pamph. Vol. 62.
—— High Court of Chancery. New Orders from Apr. 3, 1828, to May 5, 1837. Lond., 1837. 12mo. Law Pamph. Vol. 10.
—— HISTORY OF, &c. See BARNES, W. Notes on Ancient Britain.
—— —— BYRNE, Wm. Brittania Depicta.
—— —— Chronicles and Memorials during the Middle Ages. Lond., 1858–69. 100 Vols. 8vo.
—— —— DALRYMPLE, Sir John. Memoirs of G. B., 1771.
—— —— HAIGH, D. H. Conquest of Britain by the Saxons.
—— —— Land (The) We Live in.
—— —— POSTE, B. Brittania Antiqua.
—— —— —— Brittanic Researches.
—— —— —— Materials for Early Hist.
—— House of Commons. Alphabet. List of Members in 1821 and '22, with the Votes of each, etc. Lond., 1823. 8vo. Pamphleteer. Vol. 21.
—— —— Analysis of the House, as at present Constituted, with the Votes of each member, etc. 1822-3. Lond., 1823. 8vo. Pamphleteer. Vol. 22.
—— —— Bill entitled, An Act for preventing Occasional Conformity. 1703. Fol. Eng. Polit. Pamph. Vol. 2.
—— —— Debate on the Distillery Laws, Apr. 17, 1830, including Speeches of Drummond, Brownlow and others. Lond., 1830. 8vo. Eng. Polit. Pamph. Vol. 37.
—— —— Declaration of the Commons Concerning the Rebellion in Ireland, etc. Lond., 1643. Small 4to. Eng. Polit. Pamph. Vol. 6.

GREAT Britain. HOUSE OF COMMONS. Draught of a Bill for the Recovery of Debts. Lond., 1739. 8vo. Eng. Polit. Pamph. Vol. 10.

—— —— See Electors' Remembrancer.

—— —— LLOYD, C.—Defense of, Gen. Warrants.

—— —— Reasons and Narratlve of Proceedings betwixt the Two Houses, Delivered by the Commons to the Lords on the Tryal of the Lords in the Tower. May 26, 1679. Fol. Eng. Polit. Pamph. Vol. 1.

—— —— Report of Commiss'rs on the Pub. Accounts, with Resolutions of the House, etc., 1711. Lond., 1712. Fol. Eng. Polit. Pamph. Vol. 3.

—— —— Report from Comm. on the King's Bench, Fleet and Marshalsea Prisons, etc., 1814. 8vo. Pamphleteer. Vol. 6.

—— —— Report of Comm. on Petitions of Share Holders in the Mine Adventure, etc. Lond., 1710. Fol. Eng. Polit. Pamph. Vol. 3.

—— —— Report of Comm. appointed on the Employment of Chimney Sweeps. Lond., 1817. 8vo. Pamphleteer. Vol. 10.

—— —— Report from Select Comm. on the Earl of Elgin's Collection of Sculptured Marbles, etc. Lond., 1818. 8vo. Pamphleteer. Vol. 8.

—— —— Report from Comm. on Laws Relating to the Manufacture, etc., of Bread. Lond., 1815. 8vo. Pamphleteer. Vol. 6.

—— —— Report from Comm. on Mad Houses. Lond., 1815. 8vo. Pamphleeteer. Vol. 6.

—— —— 1st and 2d Reports from Secret Comm. on the Resumption of Cash Payment. Lond., 1819. 8vo. Pamphleteer. Vol 14.

—— —— Report on Abuses in the P. Office. Lond., 1787. 8vo. Eng. Polit. Pamph. Vol. 73.

—— —— Report of Comm. of Secrecy in regard to the Soc. of United Irishmen. 1799. 8vo. Eng. Polit. Pamph. Vol. 75.

—— —— Report of Select Comm. on Gaols, &c., 1819. Lond., 1820. 8vo. Pamphleteer. Vol. 15.

—— —— Report on a General Scheme for Extramural Sepulture. 1850. 8vo. Eng. Polit. Pamph. Vol. 48.

—— —— Representations to the Queen, with Her Majestie's Answers. Lond., 1711. Fol. Eng. Polit. Pamph. Vol. 3.

—— —— Resolutions relative to the National Debt and the Sinking Fund, 1822. Lond., 1823. 8vo. Pamphleteer. Vol. 21.

—— —— Resolutions for Impeachment of Sir Wm. Scroggs and others, Dec. 23, 1680. Fol. Eng. Polit. Pamph. Vol. 2.

—— —— See TOWNSHEND, C. Defence of the Minority on Gen. Warrants.

—— —— Votes of the House in 1710, 11, 12, 13. Fol. Eng. Polit. Pamph. Vol. 3.

—— House of Lords. Addresses, &c., of the Lords, presented to Her Majesty, Mar. 1 and 22, 1707; &c. Lond., 1707, '8. Fol. Eng. Polit. Pamph. Vol. 2.

GREAT Britain. HOUSE OF LORDS. Jurisdiction of, in the Point of Impositions. Lond., 1676. 12mo. Eng. Polit. Pamph. Vol. 6.

—— —— Minutes of the Decision in 1783, in the Case of the B'p of Lond. vs. L. D. Fytche. Salisbury. 8vo. Eng. Polit. Pamph. Vol. 21.

—— —— 1st and 2d Reports from the Secret Comm. on the Resumption of Cash Payments. Lond., 1819. 8vo. Pamphleteer. Vol. 14.

—— —— Representation to Her Majesty, Mar. 14, 1704, on certain Proceedings of the Commons. Lond., 1704. Fol. Eng. Polit. Pamph. Vol. 2.

—— in 1833. See D'HAUSSEZ, Baron.

—— Memoires des Commissaires du Roi.

—— Memoirs of. See DALRYMPLE, Sir John. 1771.

—— MISCELLANEOUS. See Analysis of Correspond. between G. B. and U. States.

—— —— Antonini Iter Britanniarum. 1709.

—— —— Appeal to G. B. on Disputes with America.

—— —— BURKE, E. Acc. of a Short Administration. 1765.

—— —— CHALMERS, G. Estimate of the Strength of G. B.

—— —— CHAMBERLAYNE, J. Magnae. Brittaniae Notitia.

—— —— Claims of U. S., &c.

—— —— Collection of Scarce Tracts. 1753–1770.

—— —— CAVENDISH, Sir H. Parlia. Debates on Canada. 1774.

—— —— Colonial Policy of G. B.

—— —— DAY, T. Reflections on Present State of. 1783.

—— —— DOWDESWELL, W. Address to Electors of G. B.

—— —— DUNCAN, A. British Trident.

—— —— DYSON, J. Middlesex Election Case considered.

—— —— FRANCIS P. Letter from the Cocoa Tree. 1762.

—— —— Geodesy, (The) of Britain. 1859.

—— —— HARTLEY, D. The Budget.

—— —— Key to Orders in Council.

—— —— JOHNSON, B. P, Report on World's Fair. 1851.

—— —— KEITH, Sir W. Papers and Tracts.

—— —— Letter to Sir. Geo. Saville.

—— —— LLOYD, C. True History of a Late Short Administration.

—— —— LLOYD, D. Protestant Martyrs, etc.

—— —— —— Reasons for Refusing to take part in the New Administration. 1765.

—— —— See LOLME, J. L. de. The British Empire in Europe. 1787.

—— —— MACAULEY, C. Address on Amer. Affairs.

—— —— Miscellanies; Copy of Magna Charta, etc.

—— —— MOGG, E. Paterson's Roads.

—— —— Newcastle (Duke of). Letter to Sec. of Prussian Embassy. 1752.

—— —— Observa. on State of the Nation. 1769.

—— —— People's Answer to Court Famphlet.

—— —— Political Essays concerning. 1772.

—— —— PRICE, R. Appeal on Nat. Debt.

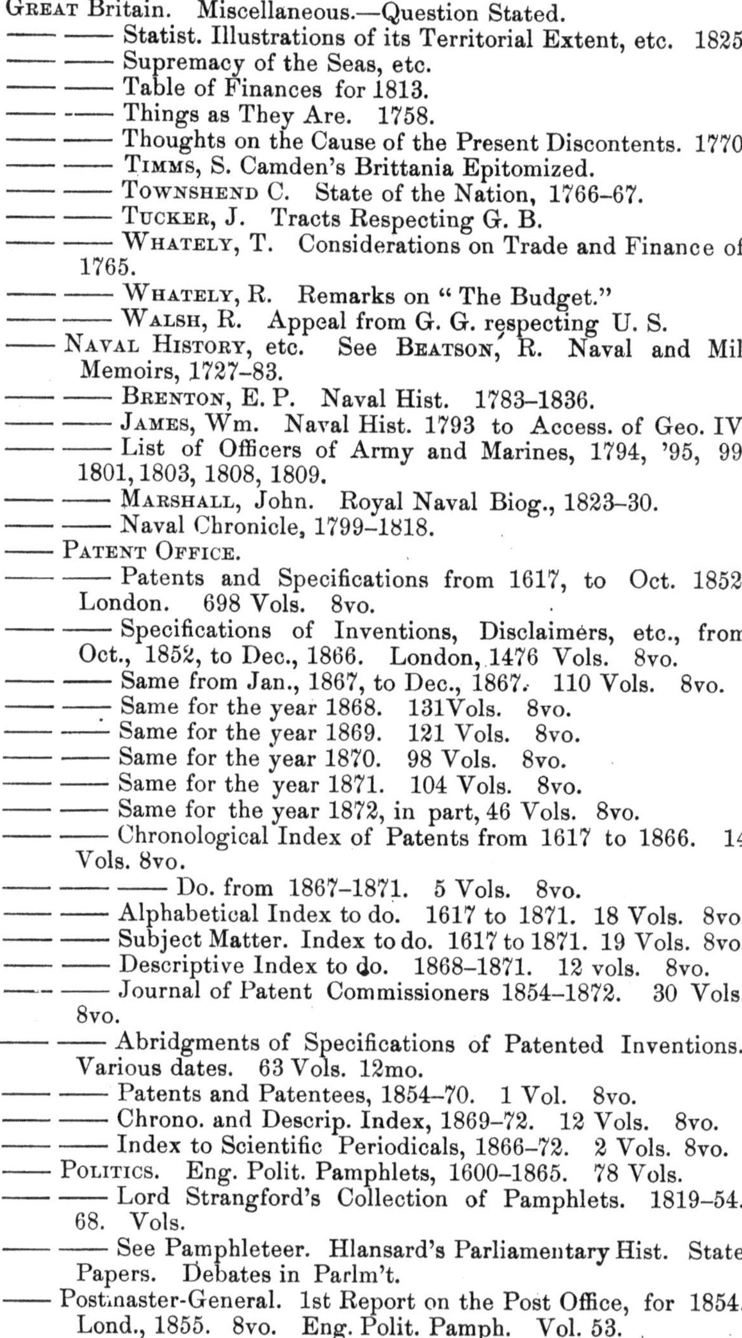

GREAT Britain. Miscellaneous.—Question Stated.

—— —— Statist. Illustrations of its Territorial Extent, etc. 1825.

—— —— Supremacy of the Seas, etc.

—— —— Table of Finances for 1813.

—— —— Things as They Are. 1758.

—— —— Thoughts on the Cause of the Present Discontents. 1770.

—— —— TIMMS, S. Camden's Brittania Epitomized.

—— —— TOWNSHEND C. State of the Nation, 1766–67.

—— —— TUCKER, J. Tracts Respecting G. B.

—— —— WHATELY, T. Considerations on Trade and Finance of. 1765.

—— —— WHATELY, R. Remarks on "The Budget."

—— —— WALSH, R. Appeal from G. G. respecting U. S.

—— NAVAL HISTORY, etc. See BEATSON, R. Naval and Mil. Memoirs, 1727–83.

—— —— BRENTON, E. P. Naval Hist. 1783–1836.

—— —— JAMES, Wm. Naval Hist. 1793 to Access. of Geo. IV.

—— —— List of Officers of Army and Marines, 1794, '95, 99, 1801, 1803, 1808, 1809.

—— —— MARSHALL, John. Royal Naval Biog., 1823–30.

—— —— Naval Chronicle, 1799–1818.

—— PATENT OFFICE.

—— —— Patents and Specifications from 1617, to Oct. 1852. London. 698 Vols. 8vo.

—— —— Specifications of Inventions, Disclaimers, etc., from Oct., 1852, to Dec., 1866. London, 1476 Vols. 8vo.

—— —— Same from Jan., 1867, to Dec., 1867. 110 Vols. 8vo.

—— —— Same for the year 1868. 131 Vols. 8vo.

—— —— Same for the year 1869. 121 Vols. 8vo.

—— —— Same for the year 1870. 98 Vols. 8vo.

—— —— Same for the year 1871. 104 Vols. 8vo.

—— —— Same for the year 1872, in part, 46 Vols. 8vo.

—— —— Chronological Index of Patents from 1617 to 1866. 14 Vols. 8vo.

—— —— —— Do. from 1867–1871. 5 Vols. 8vo.

—— —— Alphabetical Index to do. 1617 to 1871. 18 Vols. 8vo.

—— —— Subject Matter. Index to do. 1617 to 1871. 19 Vols. 8vo.

—— —— Descriptive Index to do. 1868–1871. 12 vols. 8vo.

—— —— Journal of Patent Commissioners 1854–1872. 30 Vols. 8vo.

—— —— Abridgments of Specifications of Patented Inventions. Various dates. 63 Vols. 12mo.

—— —— Patents and Patentees, 1854–70. 1 Vol. 8vo.

—— —— Chrono. and Descrip. Index, 1869–72. 12 Vols. 8vo.

—— —— Index to Scientific Periodicals, 1866–72. 2 Vols. 8vo.

—— POLITICS. Eng. Polit. Pamphlets, 1600–1865. 78 Vols.

—— —— Lord Strangford's Collection of Pamphlets. 1819–54. 68. Vols.

—— —— See Pamphleteer. Hlansard's Parliamentary Hist. State Papers. Debates in Parlm't.

—— Postmaster-General. 1st Report on the Post Office, for 1854. Lond., 1855. 8vo. Eng. Polit. Pamph. Vol. 53.

GREAT Britain. Public Debt. Proposal for the Partial Liquidation of the. Lond., 1850. 8vo. Strangford Pamph. Vol. 54.

—— —— See MORGAN, W. Facts respecting.

—— PUBLICATIONS OF THE COMMISSIONERS OF PUBLIC RECORDS AND ROLLS OFFICE viz.:

—— Ancient, The. Kalendars and Inventories of the Treasury of His Majesty's Exchequer. 3 Vols. 8vo. 1836.

—— Abbreviat. Placitorum. Richard I. Edw. II. Folio, Lond., 1811.

—— Ancient Laws and Institutes of England, comprising Laws enacted under the Anglo Saxon Kings from Aethelbirht to Cnut; the Laws of Edward the Confessor, William the Conqueror and Henry I: etc. Folio Lond. 1840.

—— Alphabetical Index to Statutes of the Realm, from Magna Carta, to the End of the Reign of Queen Anne. Folio. Lond. 1824.

—— Ancient Laws and Institutes of Wales, comprising Laws enacted by Howell the Good, up to the Conquest of Edward I. Folio. Lond. 1841.

—— Acts (The) of the Lords of Council in Civil Causes; or Acta Dominorum Concilii. A. D. 1478–1495. Folio. Lond. 1839.

—— Acts (The) of the Lords Auditors of Causes and Complaints; or Actor Dominorum Auditorum. A. D., 1466–1494. Folio. 1839.

—— Acts (The) of the Parliaments of Scotland from A. D. 1124 to the Union with England. 1423. 1 vol. Lond. Folio. 1844.

—— Chronological Index to Statutes of the Realm, from Magna Carta. to the End of the Reign of Queen Anne. Folio. Lond. 1828.

—— Calendar of rhe Proceedings in Chancery in the Reign of Queen Anne. Folio. Lond. 1828.

—— Calendar of the Proccedings in Chancery in the Reign of Queen Elizabeth. Vol. 3. Lond. 1832. Folios.

—— Calendar of State Papers (see p. 436–7.) London. 66 vols. 4to.

—— Catalogue of the MSS. in the Harleian Library in the British Museum. Vol. 4. Folio. Lond. 1812.

—— Chronicles and Memorials of G. B. during the Middle Ages. Lond. 100 vols. 8vo.

—— Ducatus Lancastriae. Calendar to the Pleadings from 14th to end of Reign of Queen Elizabeth. Folio. Lond. 1834.

—— Domesday Book; Libri Censualis Vocati. Indices. Folio. Lond. 1811.

—— The same. Additamenta, excodic antiquiss. Folio. Lond. 1816.

—— Documents illustrative of English History in the 13th and 14th centuries, selected from the Records in the Department of the Queen's Remembrancer of the Exchequer. Folio. Lond. 1844.

—— Documents and Records illustrating the History of Scotland, and the Transactions between the Crowns of Scotland and England. Lond. 8vo. 1837.

GREAT Britain. PUBLICATION, of Rolls Office. Excerpta e Rotulis Finium, in Turri. Londin. Asservatis. Henry III. 1216–1272. 2 Vols. 8vo. 1835.

—— Fines. Sive Pedes Finium. Sive Finales Concordiæ in curia Domini Regis. 7 Rich. 1 —— 16 John. (1195–1214) In counties. 2 Vols. 8vo. 1835–1844. Lond.

—— General Report of the Board of Commissioners of Public Records from 1831 to 1837. Lond. 1837. Folio.

—— Hand Book to the Public Records, by F. S. Thomas, Secretary of the Public Record Office. Lond. 1853.

—— Issues of the Exchequer, containing Payments made out of His Majesty's Revenue, extracted from the Pell Records. Henry III–Henry VI. 4to. Lond. 1837.

—— Same. 44 Edw. III. 1370. 4to. 1835.

—— Same. Temp. Jac. I. 4to. 1836.

—— Liber Munerum Publicorum Hiberniæ, 1152–1827; or the Establishment of Ireland from the 19th of King Stephen to the 7th of George IV. 2 Vols. Folio. Lond., 1852.

—— Modus Tenendi Parliamentum; an Ancient Treatise on the Mode of Holding the Parlm't of England. Lond. 1846. 8vo.

—— Monumenta Historica Brittanica; or Materials for the History of Britain, from the Earliest Period to the Reign of King Henry VII. Vol. 1. Folio. Lond., 1848.

—— Proceedings and Ordinances of the Privy Council of England from 10 Richard 11 to 33 Henry VIII. 7 Vols. 8vo. 1834–37.

—— Rotuli Chartarum in Turri Londinensi Asservati. A. D., 1199–1216. Folio. Lond., 1837.

—— Rotuli de Oblatis et Finibus in Turri Londinensi Asservati Temp Regis Johannis. 8vo. Lond., 1835.

—— Rotuli Normanniæ in Turri Londinensi Asservati. A. D., 1200–1205; also from 1417 to 1418. 8vo. Lond., 1835.

—— Rotuli de Liber ate ac de Misis et Præstitis. 8vo. Lond., 1844.

—— Rotulorum Originalium in Curia Scaccarii Abbreviatio. Henry III — Edward III. 2 Vols. Folio. Lond., 1805–1810.

—— Rotuli Litterarum Patentium in Turri Londinensi Asservati. A. D., 1201 to 1216. Folio. Lond., 1835.

—— Rotuli Litterarum Clausarum in Turri Londinensi Asservati. 2 Vols. Folio. Lond., 1843–1844.

—— Rotuli Curiae Regis. Rolls and Records of the Court held before the Kings' Justiciars or Justices. 6 Ric. 1. 1 John. 2 Vols. 8vo. Lond., 1835.

—— State Papers, temp Henry VIII. 11 Vols. 4to. Lond., 1830–52.

—— The Great Rolls of the Pipe. of the 2d, 3d, and 4th years of the Reign of King Henry 11. 1155–1158. 8vo. Lond., 1844.

—— —— The same — for the 1st year of the Reign of King Richard I. 1189–1190. 8vo. Lond., 1844.

—— Valor Ecclesiasticus, temp Henry VIII. Auctoritate Regia Institutis. Vols 5 & 6. Folio. Lond.. 1825, 1834.

GREAT Britain. Registrar General. Ann. Reports from 1839 to 1845 inclusive. Lond. 7 vols. 8vo.
—— Relations with U. S. Correspondence on. Boston, 1862. Rebellion Pamph. Vols. 23, 25.
—— Sec. of Treasury. Report on the Bank of the U. S., etc. Lond, 1820. Pamphleteer. Vol. 17.
—— Society for the Liberation of Religion from State Patronage and Control. Letter to the Dissenters of the United Kingdom. Lond., 1863. 8vo. Eng. Religious Pamph. Vol. 60.
—— State of at the Commencement of 1822. Lond., 1822. 8vo. 4th Ed. Strangford Pamph. Vol. 4. Do. 6th Ed. Pamphleteer. Vol. 20.
—— Trade and Navigation of. See GEE, J. 1767.
—— Statement of Trade, etc, with Foreign Countries for 1869. Lond., 1870. 4to.
—— Treaties with U. S. See Succinct Acc. etc.
—— Treaty between Her Majesty and the States General, Oct. 1709. Lond., 1712. Eng. Polit. Pamph. Vol. 3.
—— Treaty of Peace with France, 1796. Papers relating to the Negotiation, etc. Lond., 1796. 8vo. Eng. Polit. Pamph. Vol. 25.
—— War with France. See ERSKINE, T.
—— Wars with U. S. See Amer. War of Revolution, etc.
GREAT Eastern Steamship—Two Pamphlets describing the. Lond., n. d. 12mo. Hist. Pamph. Vol. 8.
GREATEST (The) of the Plantagenets ; an Historical Sketch. Lond., 1860. 8vo.
GREAT (The) Issue to be decided in Nov., 1860. Rebell'n Pamph. Vol. 77.
—— Lakes: or Inland Seas of N. America. N. Y., 1865. 12mo.
—— Plague of London, 1665. See DEFOE, D.
—— Salt Lake. See STANSBURY, H. Exped. to.
—— Surrender to the Rebels in Arms. Rebell'n. Pamph. Vol. 46.
—— Truths by Great Authors: A Dictionary of Aids to Reflection. Phila., 1858. 8vo.
—— West. See DANA, C. W.
—— —— HOWE, H.
—— Western Sanitary Fair. Hist. of. Cincin., 1864. 8vo.
GREBLE, J. T. See BRAINERD, Rev. Dr.
GREECE, See Appeal in behalf of the Greeks, etc. 1823.
—— BLAQUIERE, E. Report on the Greek Confederation, 1823.
—— Considerations sur la Guerre Actuelle entre les Grecs et les Turcs.
—— CONTOSTAVLOS, Alex. Building of the Two Greek Frigates.
—— DE PRADT, M. Vrai Systeme de l'Europe relativement a l'Amerique et a la Grece. 1825.
—— EDWARDS, B. B. Slavery in Ancient Greece.
—— ERSKINE, Lord. Appeal in behalf of. 1824.
—— HUGHES, Rev. T. S. Considerations on the Greek Revolution. 1823.
—— GILLIES, S. Hist. of.

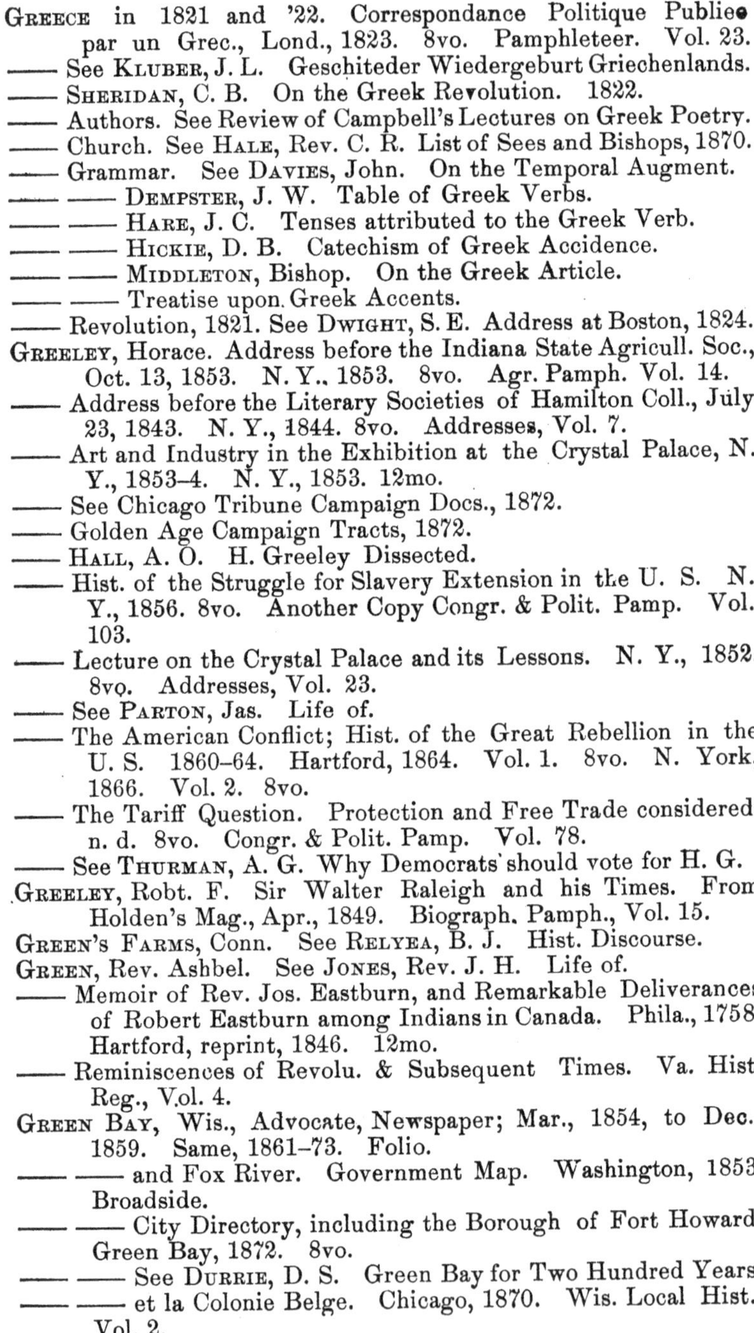

Greece in 1821 and '22. Correspondance Politique Publiee par un Grec., Lond., 1823. 8vo. Pamphleteer. Vol. 23.

—— See Kluber, J. L. Geschiteder Wiedergeburt Griechenlands.

—— Sheridan, C. B. On the Greek Revolution. 1822.

—— Authors. See Review of Campbell's Lectures on Greek Poetry.

—— Church. See Hale, Rev. C. R. List of Sees and Bishops, 1870.

—— Grammar. See Davies, John. On the Temporal Augment.

—— —— Dempster, J. W. Table of Greek Verbs.

—— —— Hare, J. C. Tenses attributed to the Greek Verb.

—— —— Hickie, D. B. Catechism of Greek Accidence.

—— —— Middleton, Bishop. On the Greek Article.

—— —— Treatise upon Greek Accents.

—— Revolution, 1821. See Dwight, S. E. Address at Boston, 1824.

Greeley, Horace. Address before the Indiana State Agricull. Soc., Oct. 13, 1853. N. Y., 1853. 8vo. Agr. Pamph. Vol. 14.

—— Address before the Literary Societies of Hamilton Coll., July 23, 1843. N. Y., 1844. 8vo. Addresses, Vol. 7.

—— Art and Industry in the Exhibition at the Crystal Palace, N. Y., 1853–4. N. Y., 1853. 12mo.

—— See Chicago Tribune Campaign Docs., 1872.

—— Golden Age Campaign Tracts, 1872.

—— Hall, A. O. H. Greeley Dissected.

—— Hist. of the Struggle for Slavery Extension in the U. S. N. Y., 1856. 8vo. Another Copy Congr. & Polit. Pamp. Vol. 103.

—— Lecture on the Crystal Palace and its Lessons. N. Y., 1852. 8vo. Addresses, Vol. 23.

—— See Parton, Jas. Life of.

—— The American Conflict; Hist. of the Great Rebellion in the U. S. 1860–64. Hartford, 1864. Vol. 1. 8vo. N. York, 1866. Vol. 2. 8vo.

—— The Tariff Question. Protection and Free Trade considered. n. d. 8vo. Congr. & Polit. Pamp. Vol. 78.

—— See Thurman, A. G. Why Democrats should vote for H. G.

Greeley, Robt. F. Sir Walter Raleigh and his Times. From Holden's Mag., Apr., 1849. Biograph. Pamph., Vol. 15.

Green's Farms, Conn. See Relyea, B. J. Hist. Discourse.

Green, Rev. Ashbel. See Jones, Rev. J. H. Life of.

—— Memoir of Rev. Jos. Eastburn, and Remarkable Deliverances of Robert Eastburn among Indians in Canada. Phila., 1758. Hartford, reprint, 1846. 12mo.

—— Reminiscences of Revolu. & Subsequent Times. Va. Hist. Reg., Vol. 4.

Green Bay, Wis., Advocate, Newspaper; Mar., 1854, to Dec., 1859. Same, 1861–73. Folio.

—— —— and Fox River. Government Map. Washington, 1853. Broadside.

—— —— City Directory, including the Borough of Fort Howard. Green Bay, 1872. 8vo.

—— —— See Durrie, D. S. Green Bay for Two Hundred Years.

—— —— et la Colonie Belge. Chicago, 1870. Wis. Local Hist., Vol. 2.

GREEN BAY Gazette, Newspaper; 1866–1873. Folio.
—— —— Intelligencer, Newspaper; Dec. 1833 to Oct., 1835. 1844.
—— —— Milwaukee & Chicago R. R. First Report of Chief Engineer, 1852. Milwaukee, 1852. 8vo.
—— —— Newspapers, 1861–67, '68.
—— —— Report of the Survey of Green Bay made by Capt. W. G. Williams of U. S. Topograph. Engineers. Ex. Doc., No. 170, 1st Sess. 29th Congress. 1846.
—— —— See WHITTLESEY, Chas. Water Level at.
GREEN, Beriah. Valedict. Address to the Senior Class of Oneida Institute, Sept. 12, 1838. Whitesboro, N. Y., 1838. 8vo. Addresses, Vol. 21.
GREEN County, Wis. See STEWART, J. W. Early Hist. of.
GREEN Genealogy. See VINTON, J. A. Memorial.
GREEN, Jas. D. Remarks on the Connection of the City of Cambridge with the Cambridge Water Works. Boston, 1858. 8vo. Mass. Misc. Pamph. Vol. 4.
GREEN, John. Nature and Character of the Consular Service. Lond., 1848. 8vo. Strangford Pamph. Vol. 56.
GREEN, Rev. John B. Address at the Funeral of Hon. Henry W. Cushman, in Bernardston, Mass., Nov. 24, 1863. Boston, 1864. 8vo. Sermons, Vols. 14 and 51.
GREEN, Rev. Jos. See FOWLER, S. P. Biograph. Sketch of.
GREEN, J. H. Secret Band of Brothers: or the Amer. Outlaws. Phila., 1848. 12mo.
GREEN, Jos. Henry, M. D. Suggestions respecting the Intended Medical Reform. Lond., 1834. 8vo. Med. Pamph. Vol. 29.
GREEN, J. S. Speech in Cong., Apr. 4, 1850, on Admission of Cal. and N. Mexico. Congr. and Polit. Pamph. Vol. 86.
GREEN Lake County, Wis. See GILLESPY, J. C. Hist. of.
GREEN, N. W. Fifteen Years Among the Mormons; Narr. of Mrs. Mary E. V. Smith. N. Y., 1858. 12mo.
GREEN, R. H. Todd Genealogy and connected Families. N. Y., 1867. 8vo.
GREEN Saml. A., M. D. School Histories and Some Errors in Them. Boston, 1872. 8vo. Educa. Pamph. Vol. 7.
—— The Story of a Famous Book: an Account of Dr. Ben. Franklin's Autobiography. Boston, 1871. 8vo.
GREEN, Wm. Notes on the Country in the Neighbourhood of the Falls of Montmorency. Quebec Lit. and Hist. Soc. Trans. Vol. 1.
GREEN, Rev. Wm. L. Plea for the Supremacy of Christ: Two Sermons on the Presb. Ch., Madison, Wis., Mar. 18, 1860. (Slavery Question). Madison, 1860. 8vo. Sermons. Vol. 25.
GREENBACKS: The Evils and Remedy for using Promises to pay as a Measure of Value. Rebell'n Pamph. Vol. 87.
GREENE, Albert G. Catalogue of his Library. N. Y., 1889. 8vo. Bibilograph. Pamph. Vol. 2.
GREENE, Chas. S. Thrilling Stories of the Great Rebellion; with Acc. of the Death of Prest. Lincoln. Phila., 1864. 12mo.
GREENE, Geo. W. Disc. before the R. I. Hist. Soc., Feb. 1, 1849. Providence, 1849. 8vo. R. I. Hist. Soc. Addresses. Vol. 1.

GREENE, Geo. W. Historical View of Amer. Revolution. Boston, 1865. 8vo.
—— Life of Gen. Nathaniel Greene. Sparks' Amer. Biog. 2d. Ser. Vol. 10. Same. N. Y., 1871. 3 Vols. 8vo.
—— Nathaniel Greene. Examina. of Statements in Bancroft's Hist., etc. Boston, 1866. 8vo. Biograph. Pamph. Vol. 12.
GREENE, Griffin. See HILDRETH, S. P. Early Ohio Settlers.
GREENE, J. G. J. Evils Resulting from the Existing System of Laws Relating to Real Property. Lond., 1850. 8vo. Eng. Polit. Pamph. Vol. 48.
GREENE, John P. Facts Relative to the Expulsion of the Mormons from Missouri. Cinn., 1839. 8vo. Mormon Pamph. Vol. 1.
GREENE, Nathaniel. See CALDWELL, C. Memoirs of Life.
—— Compendious Hist. of Italy. Harpers' Fam. Libr. N. Y., 1860. 18mo.
—— See GREENE, G. W. Examina. of Statements in Bancroft's Hist.
—— —— Life of.
—— JOHNSON, Wm. Life and Corres.
—— Presentation to the U. S. of his Statue. 1870.
—— SIMMS, W. G. Life of.
GREENE, Samuel D. The Broken Seal; or Reminiscences of the Morgan Abduction, etc. Boston, 1870. 12mo.
GREENE, Samuel G. See ARNOLD, S. G. Address. R. I. Hist. Soc.
GREENE, Wm. See LEE, Henry. Campaign of 1781.
GREENFIELD, Eliz. T., or the "Black Swan." Brief Memoir of. Lond., 1853. 8vo. Strangford Pamph. Vol. 64.
GREENFIELD, Mass. See WILLARD, D. Hist. of.
GREENFIELD, O. See SIMMONS, C. B. Memoir of. 1858.
GREENHOW, Robert. Hist. of Oregon and Cal., and the other Territories on the N.-West Coast of N. America. 2d revised Ed. Boston, 1845. 8vo.
—— Memoir Historical and Political on the N.-West Coast of N. America and Adjacent Territories, with Map. Senate Doc. No. 174. 1st Sess., 26th Congress. Feb., 1840.
GREENLAND. See Hist. and Descrip. Acc. of.
GREENLEAF, Rev. Jonathan. See Sketches of the Eccles. Hist. of Maine. Portsmouth, 1821. 8vo.
GREENOUGH, Wm. W. Address at the Dedica. of the East Boston Branch of the Pub. Library, Mar. 22, 1871. Boston, 1871. 8vo.
—— Oration at Boston, July 4, 1849. Boston, 1849. 8vo. Addresses, etc., Vol. 26.
GREENWAY Boarding School for Boys, near Springfield, O. Circular. 1861–2, 1864–5. Springfield. 8vo.
GREENWICH Royal Hospt. for Seamen. Papers relating to Operations performed by Wm. Adams, for the Cure of Cataract and Egyptian Ophthalmia. Lond., 1814. 8vo. Med. Pamph. Vol. 22.

GREENWICH, N. Y., Cong. Ch. Manual. Albany, 1860. 12mo. N. Y. Hist. Discourses, etc. Vol. 4.

GREENWICH, Ohio. See MEAD, M. E. Memoirs of.

GREENWOOD, Rev. F. W. P. See FROTHINGHAM, N. L. Obit. Sermon.

—— Sermon on the Death of John Lowell, LL. D., at Boston, Mar. 22, 1840. Boston, 1840. 8vo. Sermons. Vol. 32.

GREENWOOD, Isaac J. First American Built Vessels in the British Navy. N. E. Hist. and Gen. Reg. Vol. 20.

GREENWOOD, John. Personal Recollections of Aaron Burr, and some of his Cotemporaries of the N. Y. Bar. Read before the L. Island Hist. Soc., Sept. 24, 1863. Hist. Mag. Vol. 7.

GREG, W. R. Agriculture and the Corn Law. Prize Essay. Manchester, 1842. 8vo. Strangford Pamph. Vol. 31.

GREGG, Francis. Suggestions for some Alteration of the Bankrupt Law. Lond., 1831. 8vo. Law Pamph. Vol. 19.

GREGG, Col. John I. Hist. of 16th Regt. Penn. Cavalry, for 1863. Rebell'n Pamph. Vol. 81.

GREGOIRE, H. Inquiry concerning the Intellectual and Moral Faculties and Literature of the Negroes. Brooklyn, 1810. 8vo.

GREGOR, Rev. Walter. The Dialect of Banffshire; with a Glossary of Words not in Jamieson's Scottish Dictionary. Lond., 1866. 8vo. Pub. in Trans. of Philolog. Society, 1866.

GREGORY's Commercial and Agricult. Colleges, Chicago. Circular and Catalogue, 1856. Chicago, 1856. 8vo.

GREGORY, Jas. J. H. Paper before the Essex Institute, Apr. 24, 1857, on Indian Relics from Marblehead, etc. Proceedings. Vol. 2.

GREGORY, John. Industrial Resources of Wisconsin. Chicago, 1853. 12mo.

GREGORY, Dr. Olinthus. Oration before the Philos. Soc. of Lond., June 12, 1817. Lond., 1819. 8vo. Pamphleteer. Vol. 13.

GREGORY, Sam. Letter to Ladies in Favor of Female Physicians. Boston, 1850. 8vo. Med. Pamph. Vol. 12.

GREGSON, Matt, Portfolio of Fragments relative to the Hist., Antiq., Topog. and Genealogies of the Co. Palatine and Duchy of Lancaster. 3d Ed. Lond., 1869. 8vo.

GRENNELL, Geo., Jr. Oration at Northampton, Mass., on the Anniversary of Amer. Independence, 1811. Misc. Tracts. Vol. 1.

GRENVILLE, Lord. Letter to the Earl of Fingal, on the Claims of the R. Catholics. Lond., 1812. 8vo. New Ed. Eng. Polit. Pamph. Vol 31.

—— Same, 1815. 8vo. Lond. 3d Ed. Pamphleteer. Vol. 5.

—— and HOWICK, Lord. See Letters addressed to them on their Removal from Office, etc.

GRENVILLE, Geo. See Letter to, in Reply to his Speech respecting John Wilkes.

—— Speech in House of Commons on Expelling Mr. Wilkes. Lond., 1769. Scarce Tracts. Vol. 3.

GRENVILLE, Pascoe. Speech in Parl't, Apr. 28, 1814, on the Application of the Sinking Fund. Lond., 1817. 8vo. Pamphleteer. Vol. 9.

GRESHAM, Sir Thos. See BURGON, John W. Life and Times of.
GREUVE, F. C. de. Brieven in Antwoord op de Brieven Van den Hooglebraar. ph. W. Van Heusde, etc. Groningen, 1838. 8vo.
GREVILLE, Robt. K. Letter to the Marquess of Clanricarde, on Sabbath Desecration in the P. Office Department. Edinburgh, 1850. 8vo. Strangford Pamph. Vol. 53.
GREW, Henry. Address before the Peace Soc. of Hartford, Conn., 1828. Congr. and Polit. Pamph. Vol 96.
GREY, Earl. See Letter to, etc., 1832.
—— Speech in Parl't, Aug. 10, 1848, on Emigration to Australia, and in Reply to Lord Monteagle. Lond., 1848. 8vo. Eng. Polit. Pamph. Vol. 47.
GREY, Lord, of Wilton. Life of. See Camden Soc. Publica.
GREY, Benj. E. Speech in Cong., Feb. 9, 1852, on the Mexican Indemnity. Congr. and Polit. Pamph. Vol. 83.
—— Speech in Cong., May 17, 1852, on the Compromise. Congr. and Polit. Pamph. Vol. 83.
GREY, Lady Jane. See BARTLETT, D. W. Life of.
GREY, Rev. Zachary. Impartial Examination of the 2d Volume of Neal's Hist. of the Puritans. Lond., 1736. 8vo.
GRIDLEY, Rev. John. Hist. of Montpelier, Vt.; Disc. at Montpelier, Dec. 8, 1842. Montpelier, 1843. 8vo. Vt. Hist. Discourses. Vol. 2.
GRIFFIN, Aug. Griffin's Journal: First Settlers of Southold; the Names of the Heads of those Families, First Proprietors of Orient. Orient, L. I., 1857. 12mo.
GRIFFIN, G. W. Memoir of Col. Chas. S. Todd. Phila., 1872. 8vo.
GRIFFIN, John Jos. System of Crystallography, with its Application to Mineralogy. Glasgow, 1841. 8vo.
GRIFFIN, Nathan. Gathering of Descendants of Nathan Griffin at the Old Homestead, at Stockton, Me. Belfast, Me., 1863. 18mo. Genealog. Pamph. Vol. 2.
GRIFFIN, Richd. The Grievances of the Poor Law Medical Officers elucidated, etc. Lond., 1858. 8vo. Med. Pamph. Vol. 17.
GRIFFITH, John. Journal of his Life, Travels and Labors in the Work of the Ministry. Lond., 1779. 8vo.
GRIFFITH, J. K. General Cheltenham Guide. Cheltenham, Eng., 1818. 12mo. Guide Books. Vol. 23.
GRIFFITH, S. Y. New Hist. Description of Chettenham. Lond., 1826. 4to.
GRIFFITH, Thos. W. Hist. Sketch of the Revolution in Paris, and Battle of the 10th of Aug. (n. d.) 12mo. Hist. Pamph. Vol. 6.
GRIFFITH, Wm. Hist. Notes of the Amer. Colonies and Revolution. 1754–1775. Burlington, N. J., 1843. 8vo.
GRIFFITHS, Julia. Autographs for Freedom. Auburn, 1854. 12mo.
GRIFFITTS, Saml. P., M. D. See COATES, B. H. Notice of.
GRIGLIETTA, C. Brief Essay on Electro-Magnetism. Phila., 1838. 8vo. Med. Pamph. Vol. 5.

GRIGNON, Aug. Seventy-Two Years' Recollections of Wisconsin. Wis. Hist. Soc. Coll. Vol. 3.

GRIGSBY, H. B. Disc. before Va. Hist. Soc., Dec. 15, 1853, on the Va. Convention of 1829–30. Va. Hist. Reporter. Vol. 1. Another Copy Bound with Va. Hist. Soc. Coll. Vol. 1.

GRIMKÉ, Thos. S. Extracts from Newspapers relative to the Decease of. Phila., 1834. 12mo. Biograph. Pamph. Vol. 13.

—— Oration on Grecian and American Eloquence, at Oxford, O., Sept. 23, 1834. Cincin., 1834. 8vo. Addresses, etc. Vol. 38.

—— Oration at Charleston, S. C., before the Washington Soc., July 4, 1833, with the Farewell Address of Hon. Wm. Drayton. Charleston, 1833. 8vo. Addresses. Vol. 29.

GRINDLAY, Capt. Melville. Present State of the Question as to Steam Communication with India, etc. Lond., 1837. Svo. 1st and 3d Editions. Eng. Polit. Pamph. Vol. 42.

GRINNELL Land. See FORCE, Peter.

GRISCOM, John. Address before Newark Mechanic's Assoc., Jan. 1825. Addresses. Vol. 10.

GRISCOM, John H. Animal Mechanism and Physiology. Harpers' Fam. Libr. New York. 18mo.

—— The Uses and Abuses of Air, with Remarks on Ventilation. 3d Ed. N. Y., 1854. 12mo.

GRISWOLD, Bishop Alex. V. See EASTBURN, Bishop M. Obit. Sermon. 1843.

GRISWOLD, Roger, and LYON, Matt. Report of Comm. of U. S. House of R., on the Expulsion of. 1798. Congr. and Polit. Pamph. Vol. 123.

GRISWOLD, Rufus W., D. D. Catalogue of his Private Library. N. Y., 1859. 8vo. Bibliograph. Pamph. Vol. 57.

—— See D'ISRAELI, J. C. Curiosities of Literature.

—— Poets and Poetry of America to the Middle of the 19th Century. Phil., 1850. 8vo.

—— The Republican Court; or Amer. Society in the Days of Washington, with Portraits. N. Y., 1855. 4to.

GRISWOLD, Mrs. S. M. A Woman's Pilgrimage to the Holy Land. Hartford, 1872. 12mo.

GRISWOLD, Wayne. Kansas: Her Resources and Developments, or the Kansas Pilot, etc. Cincin., 1871. 8vo. Kansas Misc. Pamph. Vol. 1.

GROSH, A. B. Odd-Fellows Manual. Phila., 1853. 12mo.

GROSS, C. H. Reply to H. Binney on the Habeas Corpus. 1862. Rebellion Pamph. Vol. 27.

GROSS, S. D., M. D. Disc. on Danl. Drake, M. D., at the University of Louisville, Jan. 27, 1853. Louisville, Ky., 1853. 8vo. Biograph. Pamph. Vol. 7.

GROSSE, Francis. Glossary of Provincial and Local Works used in England. Lond., 1839. 8vo.

GROSSETETE, Robt. Works of. See CAXTON Soc. Publica.

GROSVENOR, L. Address at a Meeting of the Descendants of Maj. Gen. Israel Putnam, at Putnam, Ct., 1855. Boston, 1855. 8vo. Rev. War Pamph. Vol. 5.

GROTE, Geo. Life, Teachings and Death of Socrates. N. Y., 1860. 18mo.
GROTON Heights, Conn. Battle of. See HARRIS, W. W.
GROTON, Mass. See BUTLER, C. Hist. of.
—— By-Laws relating to Schools. 1805. Cambridge, 1806. 8vo.
—— Same. Boston, 1828. 8vo.
—— By-Laws in relation to Truant Children. 1856–1865. 8vo.
—— Public Library. Catalogues of. 1855, '62, '68.
—— Report on Establishing a High School. 1856.
—— Ann. Reports of Receipts and Expenditures for 1861, '62, '63, '64, '67, '70. Groton and Boston, 1863–70. 8vo. and 12mo.
—— Reports of School Comm. for 1853–4, 1854–5, 1857–8, 1860–1, 1861–2, 1862–3, 1863–4, 1864–5, 1867–8, 1868–9, 1869–70. Boston, 1854–1870. 8vo.
—— Result of an Eccles. Council at Groton, July 17, 1826. Boston, 1827. 8vo. Mass. Hist. Discourses, etc. Vol. 2.
—— Soapstone Quarry and Manufactory. Statement regarding Property, Location, Value, etc. Boston, 1864. 8vo. Mass. Misc. Pamph. Vol. 4.
GROUCHY, Marechal de. Observations sur la Relation de la Campagne de 1815, Publiée par le Gen. Gourgaud. Phila., 1818. 8vo. Hist. Pamph. Vol. 6.
GROUT Genealogy. See MORSE, Rev. A.
GROUT, Rev. Lewis. Essay on the Phonology and Orthography of the Zulu Dialects in S. Africa. Journ. Amer. Oriental Soc. Vol. 3.
——The Zulu and other Dialects of S. Africa. Amer. Oriental Soc. Journ. Vol. 1.
GROUX, Eugéne. Fissura Sterni Congenita. Observation and Experiments in the Case of Eugéne Groux. Hamburg, 1859. 4to. Med. Pamph. Vol. 34.
GROVER, Rev. H. M. A Notice from Stonehenge. Part I. Lond., 1847. 8vo. Hist. Pamph. Vol. 14.
GROW, G. A. Speech in Cong., Mar. 30, 1852, on the Homestead Bill. Congr. and Polit. Pamph. Vol. 83.
—— Speech in Cong., Feb. 21, 1854, on the Homestead Bill. Congr. and Polit. Pamph. Vol. 83.
—— Speech in Cong., Feb. 29, 1860. Rebell'n Pamph. Vol. 77.
GRUND, Francis J. Americans in their Moral, Social and Political Relations. Lond., 1837. 8vo.
GRUYER, L. A. Du Spiritualisme au XIX me. Siècle; ou Examinen de la Doctrine de Maine de Biran. Bruxelles, (n. d.) 8vo.
GUANO. Account of the Manure Guano, with Instructions for using it, etc. Liverpool, 1843. 8vo. Strangford Pamph. Vol. 31.
—— See NESBIT, J. C.
—— LEE, Dan'l. Treatise on Peruvian Guano.
—— Statements made in Cong., on Duty on Importation of Peruvian Guano. Agr. Pamph. Vol. 3.
—— See SHEPPARD, J. H. Treatise on Use of, etc.
—— TESCHEMACKER, J. E. Essay on.

GUATEMALA. See THOMPSON, G. A. Official Visit to, 1829.

GUENYVEAU, M. D' l'Etat de la Fabrication du Fer et de l'avenir des Forges. Paris, 1838. 8vo.

GUERNSEY, A. H. The Campaigns of Robt. E. Lee. From the Galaxy, May, 1871. Rebell'n Pamph. Vol. 112.

GUERNSEY, Isle of. See BERRY, Wm. Hist. of, 1815.

GUERNSEY, O. and WILLARD, J. F. Hist. of Rock Co., Wis., and of the Rock Co. Agricult. Soc. and Mechanics' Institute. Janesviile, 1856.

GUEST, W. E. Ancient Indian Remains near Prescott, C. W. Smithsonian Report, 1856.

GUIANA. See APTHORP, G. H. Topog. Descript. of Surinam.

—— PREMIUM, B. Eight Years in.

—— British. See HANCOCK, John. Climate, Soil, and Productions of, 1840.

—— —— PECK and PRICE. Report as Delegates to, in 1840.

—— —— SCHOMBURGH, R. H. Description of, 1840.

GUIDE to the White Mts. and Lakes of N. Hampshire. Concord, 1850. 12mo. N. H. Hist. Discourses, etc. Vol. 1.

GUIDE BOOKS. See BICKHAM, Geo. Curiosities of Kensington, Hampton Court, etc.

—— —— Brit. Amer. Guide Book.

—— —— DARBY, W. Emigrants' Guide, 1818.

—— —— DISTURNELL, J. Railway and Steamship Guide.

—— —— Emigrants' Guide to Western States.

—— —— Northern Traveller, 1830.

—— —— REDPATH. Jas. Guide to Hayti, 1861.

—— —— SPOFFORD, H. G. Tourist Guide, 1824.

—— —— View of Valley of the Mississippi, 1834.

—— —— See Directories.

—— —— 31 Pamphlet Volumes. American and Foreign.

GUIGNAS. See Early Voyages on Mississippi.

GUILD, Calvin. Genealogy of Descendants of John Guild. Providence, 1867. 12mo.

GUILD, R. A. Hist. Sketch of Brown University. n. p. 1858. 8vo.

—— The Librarian's Manual; a Treatise on Bibliography, comprising a Select and Descriptive List of Bibliograph. Works. N. Y., 1858. 4to.

GUILFORD, Conn. See RUGGLES, Rev. T. Hist. of Sketch of.

GUILFORD, Earl of. Speech at the Wellington Festival, Aug. 30, 1839. Dover, 1839. 8vo. Strangford Pamph. Vol. 19.

GUILFORD, Nathan. Memoir of. From the Western Review, 1852. Biograph. Pamph. Vol. 11.

GUILLEMARD, Robt. Adventures of a French Serjeant during his Campaigns in Italy, Spain, etc., from 1805 to 1823. Waldie's Circulating Libr. Vol. 9.

GUINEA, Africa. See Relation of De Bontauban, 1698.

GUINNESS, H. G. The Duty of Christians in the Present Crisis. Phila., 1861. 8vo. Rebell'n Pamph. Vol. 47.

GUIZOT, M. Hist. of Oliver Cromwell and the Eng. Commonwealth. Phila., 1854. 2 Vols. 12mo.

GUIZOT, M. Washington. Lond., 1840. 12mo.
—— See WELLESLEY, W. De la France Contemporaine.
—— Meditations on the Immortality of the Soul. Translated by Gen. J. Watts de Peyster. 1864? 8vo. Religious Pamph. Vol. 13.
GULF STREAM. See Bache, A. D. Paper on, 1856.
GUNN, Rev. Alex. Sermon at N. Y., Jan. 26, 1812, on the Death of Rev. Dr. J. N. Abeel. N. Y., 1812. 8vo. Sermons. Vol. 17.
GUNN & Co's Index to Advertisements which have appeared in Newspapers since 1600 for Next of Kin, Heirs at Law, Unclaimed Money, etc. Lond., 1864–9. 6 Nos. 8vo.
GUNNISON, J. W. The Mormons or Latter Day Saints in the Valley of the Great Salt Lake. Phila., 1852. 12mo.
GUNPOWDER PLOT. See FAWKES of York, and Hist. of Guy Fawkes.
—— Treason (The); with a Discourse on its Discovery, etc. Also King James' Speech to both Houses of Parliament, and other Papers. Originally published in 1609. Lond., 1850. 8vo. Eng. Polit. Pamph. Vol. 49.
—— —— See GARNETT, Rev. H. Trial of, 1679.
GURLEY, Rev. L. B. Fifty Years Ago and Now. Ann. Address before the Fire Lands Hist. Soc., June 11, 1862. Fire Lands Pioneer. Vol. 4.
GURLEY, Ralph R. Life of Jehudi Ashman, late Colonial Agent in Liberia. N. Y., 1835. 8vo.
—— Memorial to Cong. for the Purchase of Catlin's Collection of Indian Portraits, 1848. 8vo. Indian Pamph. Vol. 1.
—— Report in regard to Liberia. Washington, 1850. Sec. of State Misc. Rep'ts.
GURNEY, Goldsworthy. Acc. of the Invention of the Steam Jet, or Blast, and its Application to Steamboats, etc. Lond., 1859. 8vo. Scientific Pamph. Vol. 28.
GURNEY, Hudson. Letter to Dawson Turner, on Norwich, Eng., and the Venta Icenorum. Norwich, 1847. 8vo. Hist. Pamph. Vol. 15.
GURNEY, Jos. J. Notes on a Visit made to Prisons in Scotland and the North of England, with Elizabeth Fry. Lond., 1819. 8vo. 2d Ed. Pamphleteer. Vol. 15.
—— Observations on the Views and Practices of the Soc. of Friends. N. Y., 1840. 8vo.
GUROWSKI, Adam. America and Europe. N. Y., 1857. 8vo.
—— Diary from Mar. 4, 1861, to Nov. 12, 1862. Boston, 1862. 12mo.
—— Diary from Nov. 18, 1862, to Oct. 18, 1863. N. York, 1864. 12mo.
GUSTAVUS ADOLPAUS. See DANCKDERTZ, C. Hist. of.
GUTHRIE, S. S. See BUFFALO, N. Y., Board of Trade.
GUTHRIE, Wm. Address to the Public on the Late Dismission of a General Officer (Gen. Conway), 1764; also a Counter-Address on the Same, by Hon. Horace Walpole. Scarce Tracts. Vol. 1.

GUTHRIE, Wm. Geograph., Hist. and Commercial Grammar; and Present State of the several Kingdoms of the World. 13th Ed. Lond., 1792. 8vo.
GUTZLAFF, Rev. Chas. On the Chinese System of Writing. Amer. Philos. Soc. Trans. N. S. Vol. 7.
GUY, Wm. Aug. On the Diurnal Variations of the Pulse in Disease. Edinburgh? n. d. 8vo. Med. Pamph. Vol. 14.
—— On the Health of Towns. Lond., 1846. 2d Ed. 8vo. Sanitary Reform Pamph. Vol. 1.
—— On the Value of the Numerical Method as applied to Science. Lond.? 1839. 8vo. Scientific Pamph. Vol. 28.
GUYANA. See BRETT, W. H. Indian Tribes of.
—— News of Sir Walter Raleigh, and Acc. of, 1617.
GUYLFORDE, Sir Richard. Pilgrimage to the Holy Land, A.D., 1506. See Camden Soc. Publica.
GUYOT, Arnold. See Manual of Geograph. Teaching.
—— PHELPS, Wm. F.
GWIN, Wm. M. Speech in Cong., May, 1842, on Navy Appropriation. Washington, 1842. 8vo. Congr. and Polit. Pamph. Vol. 25.
—— Speech in Cong., July 8, 1842, on the Tariff. Washington, 1842. 8vo. Congr. and Polit. Pamph. Vol. 25.
—— Speech in Cong., Aug. 2, 1852, on Pub. Lands. Congr. and Polit. Pamph. Vol. 86.
—— Speech in Cong., April 10, 1854, on the Pacific R. R. Washington, 1854. 8vo. Speeches. Vol. 3.
GYPSUM. See SHEPPARD, J. H. Treatise on.

H.

HABEAS Corpus. See BINNEY, H., on the Privilege of.
—— BULLITT, J. C. Review of Mr. Binneys Pamphlet.
—— Congress'l Speeches.
—— MARSHALL, J. A. Amer. Bastile.
—— Remarks on Mr. Binney's Treatise.
—— Reply to same.
—— Rebellion Pamph. Vol. 73.
—— SHELLABARGER, S. Speech in Congress.
HABERDASHER, O. M. *Pseud.* Plain Reasons for Removing a Certain Great Man from His M——y's Presence and Councils. Lond., 1759. 8vo. Eng. Polit. Pamph. Vol. 14.
HABERSHAM, R. W. Speech in Cong., June 22, 1842, on the Tariff. Washington, 1842. 8vo. Congr. and Polit. Pamph. Vol. 25.
HACKLEY, Prof. Notes on Astronomy. N. Y., 1855. 12mo. Scientific Pamph. Vol. 12.
HACKLEY, Richd. S. Titles, and Legal Opinions thereon, of Lands, in E. Florida, belonging to R. S. Hackley. Brooklyn, 1822. 8vo. Florida Misc. Pamph. Vol. 1.
HADDAM, Conn. See FIELD, D. D. Hist. of. 1814.

HADLEY, Mass. Celebration of the 200th Annivers. of the Settlement of Hadley, June 8, 1859, with Address by F. D. Huntington, D. D. Northampton, 1859. 8vo. Mass. Hist. Discourses. Vol. 13.

—— See HOPKINS, Rev. Saml. Half Century Disc. 1805.

—— WOODBRIDGE, Rev. John. Half Century Sermons. 1860.

HADLEY'S Quadrant. See PATTERSON, R.

HAGER, Albert D. Address on the Marbles of Vermont, before the Vt. Hist. Soc., Oct. 29. 1858. Burlington, 1858. 8vo. Vt. Hist. Soc. Addresses. Vol. 1.

—— See Vt. Geolog. Survey. 1861.

HAGUE, Holland. See DE REIMER, J. Descrip. of.

—— Description Succincte de La Haye et de ses Environs. La Haye, 1823. 12mo. Guide-Books. Vol. 27.

HAGUE, Jas. D. Mining Industry of U. S. Geolog. Explora.

HAGUE, Thos. Letter to the Duke of York, on Circumstances leading to the Appointment of Sir Hew Dalrymple, etc. Lond., 1808. 8vo. Eng. Polit. Pamph. Vol. 29.

HAGUE, Rev. Wm. Disc. on Rev. John A. Choules, at Newport, R. I., Feb. 24, 1856. N. Y., 1856. 8vo. Sermons. Vol. 30.

—— Life and Character of Adoniram Judson, late Missionary to Burmah. Boston, 1851. Sermons. Vol. 3.

HAIGH, D. H. The Conquest of Britain by the Saxons. Lond., 1861. 8vo.

—— The Anglo-Saxon Sagas; Examina. of their Value as Aids to History. Lond., 1861. 8vo.

HAINES, Andrew M. Original Papers relating to Saml. Haines and his Descendants. Boston, 1869. 8vo. Genealog. Pamph. Vol. 2.

HAINES, Elijah M. Completion of all the Gen. Laws of Illinois, relative to Township Organization. Chicago, 1857. 8vo. Ill. Misc. Pamph. Vol. 1.

HAINES Genealogy. See HAINES, A. M.

HAINES, Jas. Petition to Cong. in relation to Letters Patent of Jonathan Haines. Washington, 1870. 8vo. Congr. and Polit. Pamph. Pol. 118.

HAKE, Gordon, M. D. Vital Force: Its Pulmonic Origin and General Laws of its Metamorphoses. 1854. 8vo. Med. Pamph. Vol. 4.

HAKEWILL, Henry. Roman Remains discovered in the Parishes of N. Leigh and Stonesfield, Oxfordshire. Lond., 1836. 8vo. Archæolog. Pamph. Vol. 2.

HAKLUYT, Richard. Collections of the Early Voyages, Travels and Discoveries of the Eng. Nation. Vol. 5. Lond., 1812. 4to.

HALDEMAN, Prof. S. S. Description of several New and Interesting Animals. Albany, 1847. 8vo. Scientific Pamph. Vol. 42.

—— Elements of Latin Pronunciation. Phila., 1851. 12mo.

HALDIMAND Papers. Negotiations between Vt. and Fred. Haldimand. 1779-83. Vt. Hist. Soc. Coll. Vol. 1.

HALE, Rev. Dr. Benj. Sermon on Dr. David Bates Douglas, at Geneva College, Dec. 16, 1849. Geneva, N. Y., 1850. 8vo. Sermons. Vol. 32.

HALE, Chas. Review of Proceedings of the Nunnery Committee of the Mass. Legislature, in reference to the Catholic School in Roxbury. Boston, 1855. 8vo. Mass. Misc. Pamph. Vol. 2.

HALE, Rev. Chas. R. List of Sees and Bishops in the Holy Eastern Ch. Phila., 1870. 8vo. Religious Pamph. Vol. 20.

—— Same. Hartford, 1872. 8vo. Religious Pamph. Vol. 24.

HALE, C. S. Geology of South Alabama. Silliman's Journ. Vol. 6. 2d Ser.

HALE, Edw. E. and DEANE, Chas. Notes on Roanoke Island and James River. Amer. Antiq. Soc. Proceed. 1862–5.

—— Hist. of Kansas and Nebraska. Map. Boston, 1854. 12mo.

—— The Name of California. Amer. Antiq. Soc. Proceed. 1862–65.

—— Kansas and Nebraska; the History, Geograph. and Phys. Characteristics of those Territories. Boston, 1854. 12mo.

—— Letters on Irish Emigration. Boston, 1852. 8vo. Congr. and Polit. Pamph. Vol. 124.

HALE, Rev. John. See RANTOUL, Robt. Memoir of.

HALE, John P. Speech in Cong., Jan. 6, 1848, on the Increase of the Army in Mexico. Washington, 1848. 8vo. Mex. War Pamph. Vol. 2.

—— Speech in Cong., Feb. 26, 1856, on the Kansas and Nebr. Bill. Congr. and Polit. Pamph. Vol. 93.

—— Speech in Cong., Jan. 19 and 21, 1858, on the Kansas and Nebr. Bill. Congr. and Polit. Pamph. Vol. 93.

—— Speech in Cong., Feb. 7, 1862, on the Purchase of Vessels. Rebell'n Pamph. Vol. 62.

—— Speech in Cong., Mar. 18, 1862, on Slavery in Dist. of Columbia. Congr. and Polit. Pamph. Vol. 85.

—— Speech in Cong., May 23, 1864, on Frauds in Naval Contracts. Washington, 1864. 8vo. Congr. and Polit. Pamph. Vol. 71.

HALE, Sir Matt. See WILLIAMS, J. B. Life, Character and Writings.

—— THIRLWALL, Rev. T. Works, Moral and Religious.

HALE, M. Spring Water vs. River Water, for supplying the City of N. Y. N. Y., 1835. 8vo. N. York City Misc. Pamph. Vol. 1.

HALE, Mercy. Genealog. Memoir of Families of Lawrence. Boston, 1856. 8vo. Genealog. Pamph. Vol. 9.

HALE, Nathan. See STUART, I. W. Life of.

HALE, Salma. Address before the N. H. Hist. Soc., June 11, 1828. Collections. Vol. 3.

—— Annals of the Town of Keene, N. H., 1734–90, Keene, 1851. 8vo.

—— —— See also N. H. Hist. Soc. Coll. Vol. 2.

—— Hist. of the U. States from First Settlement of the Colonies to the Close of War with G. Britain, 1815. Lond., 1826. 8vo.

—— Hist. of the U. States from the First Settlement as Colonies to the Close of Madison's Administra. Harpers' Fam. Libr. N. Y., 1857. 2 Vols. 18mo.

HALE, Wm. H. Present State of the Inquiry into the Origin and Primal Condition of Man, 1871. Albany Institute Trans. Vol. 7.

HALES, Chas. Theory of Electric Repulsion examined. Lond., 1837. 8vo. Scientific Pamph. Vol. 32.

HALHED, Nathan'l B. Letters to Lord Loughborough, on the Confinement of Rich'd Brothers. Lond., 1795. 8vo. Eng. Rel. Pamph. Vol. 27.

—— Speeches in Parl't, Mar. 31 and Apr. 21, 1795, on the Confinement of Rich'd Brothers. Lond., 1795. 8vo. Eng. Rel. Pamph. Vol. 27.

—— Authenticity of the Prophecies of Rich'd Brothers, and his Mission to the Jews. Lond., 1795. 8vo. 2d Ed. Eng. Rel. Pamph. Vol. 27.

HALIBURTON, Judge. Rule and Misrule of the English in America. N. Y., 1851. 8vo.

HALIBURTON, Thos. C. Hist. and Statist. Acc. of Nova Scotia, with Maps and Engravings. Halifax, 1829. 2 Vols. 8vo.

HALIFAX, Mass. See Topog. and Hist. of. Mass. Hist. Soc. Coll. 2d Ser. Vol. 4.

HALIFAX, Nova Scotia, Baptist Ch. Origin and Formation of. Halifax, 1828. 8vo. Pamphlet.

HALKETT, John. Hist. Notes on the Indians of N. America. Lond., 1825. 8vo.

HALL, A. Oakey. See Albany Y. M. Assoc.

—— Argument in Case of the People of State of N. Y. vs. John A. Dix and Five Others. Rebell'n Pamph. Vol. 25. 1864.

—— Horace Greeley decently Dissected; a Letter to Jos. Hoxie, Esq., 1862. Rebell'n Pamph. Vol. 88.

HALL, Capt. Basil. Selections from Fragments of Voyages and Travels, 1831. 2d and 3d Series. Waldie's Circulating Libr. Vol. 2.

—— Travels in N. America in 1827–8. Edinburgh, 1829. 3 Vols. 12mo.

HALL, Benj. H. Bibliography of Vermont; a Descriptive Catalogue of Books and Pamphlets relating to Vermont. Norton's Literary Letter. N. S. No. 2. 1860.

—— College Words and Customs. Cambridge, 1856. 12mo.

—— Hist. of Eastern Vermont, from its Earliest Settlement to the Close of the Eighteenth Century. N. Y., 1858. 8vo.

—— The "Westminster Massacre." Read before the N. Y. Hist. Soc., Mar. 1, 1859. Hist. Mag. Vol. 3.

HALL, Rev. B. M. Sermon on the Fugitive Slave Law. Schenectady, 1850. 8vo. Sermons. Vol. 11.

HALL, Rev. C. See SMITH, Rev. A. D. Life and Character of, 1854.

HALL, Chas. W. Court Martial of, at Cincinnati, Oct., 1863. Cincin., 1863. 8vo. Rebell'n Pamph. Vol. 5.

HALL, David, D. D. Half Century Sermon at Sutton, Mass., Oct. 24, 1779. Worcester, 1781. 12mo. Mass. Hist. Discourses. Vol. 20.

HALL, Rev. Edwin. Ancient Hist. Records of Norwalk, Conn., with a Plan of the Ancient Settlement, and a Genealog. Register. Norwalk, 1847. 12mo.
HALL, E. B., D. D. Disc. before R. Island Hist. Soc., Feb. 6, 1855, on the Life and Times of John Howland. Providence, 1855. 8vo. R. I. Hist. Soc. Addresses. Vol. 1.
—— Disc. on the Death of Wm. Ellery Channing, Oct. 12, 1842. Providence, 1842. 8vo. Sermons. Vol. 22.
—— Discourses on the Hist. of the 1st Cong. Ch. in Providence, June 19, 1836. Providence, 1836. 8vo. R. I. Hist. Discourses. Vol. 1.
HALL, E. H. and Co. New Map of Chicago, Ill., 1857.
—— The Northern Counties' Gazetteer and Directory for 1855–6; a Guide to Northern Ill. Chicago, 1855. 8vo.
HALL, Francis. Colombia, S. A. Its Present State in respect to Climate, Soil, Productions, etc. Phila., 1825. 12mo. S. Amer. Pamph. Vol. 1.
—— Travels in Canada and the U. States. Lond., 1818. 8vo.
HALL, Fred. Statist. Acc. of the Town of Middlebury in N. Y. Mass. Hist. Soc. Coll. Vol. 8. 2d. Ser.
HALL, Henry. Evacuation of Ticonderoga, in 1777. Read before the Vt. Hist. Soc., July 17, 1862. Hist. Mag. 2d. Ser. Vol. 6.
HALL, Hiland. Early Hist. of Vermont, to 1791. Albany, 186·8 8vo.
—— Speeches in Cong., June 16 and 25, 1842, on the Va. Bounty Land Claims. Washington, 1842. 8vo. Congr. and Polit. Pamph. Vol. 24.
—— Vindication of Vol. 1 of the Collections of the Vt. Hist. Soc. from the Attacks of the N. Y. Hist. Magazine. Montpelier, 1871. 8vo. Vt. Hist. Soc. Addresses, etc. Vol. 2.
—— Why the Early Inhabitants of Vt. disclaimed the Jurisdiction of N.Y. Address delivered Dec. 4, 1860. Bennington, 1872. 8vo. N. Y. Hist. Soc. Addresses.
HALL, Judge Jas. Letters from the West, containing Sketches of Scenery, Manners and Customs, etc. Lond., 1828. 8vo.
—— Memoir of the Public Services of Gen. Wm. Henry Harrison. Phila., 1836. 12mo.
—— Memoirs of Thomas Posey, Gov. of Indiana. Sparks Amer. Biog. 2d Ser. Vol. 9.
—— Notes on the Western States. Phila., 1838. 12mo.
—— Romance of Western History; or Sketches of History, Life and Manners in the West. Cincin., 1869. 12mo.
—— Sketches of History, Life and Manners in the West. Phila., 1835. 2 Vols. 12mo.
—— Statistics of the West at the Close of 1836. Cincin., 1836. 12mo.
—— The West; its Commerce and Navigation. Cincin., 1848. 12mo.
—— The West; its Soil, Surface, etc. Cincin., 1848. 12mo.
—— The Wilderness and the War Path. N. Y., 1846. 12mo.
HALL, Prof. Jas. and WHITNEY, J. D. See Iowa Geolog. Survey, 1855–7.

HALL, Prof. Jas. and WHITNEY, J. D. Notes on the Geology of the Western States, 1841. Silliman's Journ. Vol. 42.

—— Notes upon the Geology of some Portions of Minn., from St. Paul to the Western Part of the State. Trans. Amer. Philos. Soc. N. S. Vol. 13.

—— Report of the Geolog. Survey of Wisconsin. Vol. 1. 1862.

—— Report on Building-Stones. Albany, 1868. 8vo. Scientific Pamph. Vol. 18.

HALL, Rev. John. Hist. of the Presb. Ch. in Trenton, N. J. N.Y., 1859. 8vo.

HALL, J. Prescott. Disc. before the N. E. Soc., in the City of N. Y., Dec. 22, 1847. N. Y., 1848. 8vo. Addresses. Vol. 7.

HALL, Rev. Nathan'l. Address at Dorchester, Mass., Apr. 7, 1842, at the Funeral of Rev. Thaddeus M. Harris. Boston, 1842. 8vo. Sermons. Vols. 6 and 30.

—— See CAPEN, Nahum. Politics and the Pulpit, 1855.

—— Disc. at Dorchester, Mass., May 10, 1864. Rebell'n Pamph. Vol. 40.

—— Two Sermons at Dorchester, Dec. 11, 1859, on Slavery, and on the Execution of John Brown. Boston, 1859. 8vo. Sermons. Vol. 37.

HALL, Newman. The American War. Boston, 1862. 12mo. Rebell'n Pamph. Vols. 4, 100 and 102.

HALL, Judge N. K. Opinion on Habeas Corpus, in Case of Rev. J. D. Benedict. Buffalo, 1862. 8vo. Law Pamph. Vol. 8.

—— Same. Buffalo, 1863. 8vo. Rebell'n Pamph. Vol. 26.

HALL, Rev. Robt. Apology for the Freedom of the Press and for General Liberty. Lond., 1793. 8vo. Misc. Tracts. Vol. 4.

HALL, T. Dwight. Hudson, and its Tributary Region. Hudson, Wis. 1857. 8vo. Wis. Local Hist. Vol. 1. See also Wis. Hist. Soc. Coll. Vol. 3.

HALL, Willis. Address, Aug. 14, 1844, before the Soc. of Phi Beta Kappa, in Yale Coll. N. Haven, 1844. 8vo. Yale Coll. Pamph.

HALL, Wm. Abominations of Mormonism Exposed Cincin., 1852. 12mo.

HALL, Wm., of Eng. Proceedings of Gen. Court-Martial, held at Gibralter, May, 1801, for his Trial. Lond., 1801. 4to. Eng. Misc. Pamph. Vol. 38.

HALL, W. P. Speech in Cong., Dec. 11, 1851, on Public Lands. Congr. and Polit. Pamph. Vol. 85.

HALLECK, Fitz-Greene. Catalogue of his Private Library. N. Y., 1868. 8vo. Bibliograph. Pamph. Vol. 16.

—— Selections from the British Poets. Harpers' Fam. Libr. N. Y., 1857. 2 Vols. 18mo.

—— See WILSON, J. G. Life and Letters of.

HALLECK, Gen. H. W. See Men of the Time.

—— His Report reviewed in the Light of Facts. N. Y., 1862. Rebell'n Pamph. Vol. 17.

HALLEY, Ebenezer. Sermon at Troy, on the Death of Pres't Taylor. Troy, 1850. 8vo. Sermons. Vol. 20.

—— The Pantheism of Germany. Sermon at Saratoga Springs, Oct. 9, 1850. Albany, 1850. 8vo. Pamphlets. Vol. 3.

HALLIWELL, J. O. Collection of Letters illustrative of the Progress of Science in Eng., from the Reign of Elizabeth to Charles II. Lond., 1841. 8vo.

—— Dictionary of Archaic and Provincial Words, Obsolete Phrases, etc. 6th Ed. Lond., 1868. 2 Vols. 8vo.

—— Hist. Acc. of the New Place, Stratford-on-Avon, the last Residence of Shakspeare. Lond., 1864. Folio.

—— Hist. Sketch of Provincial Dialects of Eng. Albany, 1863. 8vo.

—— Letters of Kings of England, from Originals in the Royal Archives. Lond., 1846. 2 Vols. 12mo.

—— Manuscript Rarities of the University of Cambridge. Lond., 1841. 8vo.

—— Notes of Family Excursions in North Wales. Lond., 1860. Sm. 4to.

—— Rambles in Western Cornwall by the Footsteps of Giants, with Notes on Celtic Remains of Land's End Dist., and the Isle of Scilly. Lond., 1861. 4to.

—— Roundabout Notes on Ancient Circles of Stones in the Isle of Man. Lond., 1863. Sm. 4to.

—— See SHAKSPEARE, Wm.

—— The Connection of Wales with the Early Science of Eng. Lond., 1840. 8vo. Scientific Pamph. Vol. 42.

—— The Archæologist and Journal of Antiquarian Science. Vol. 1. Sept., 1841—Feb., 1842. Lond., 1842. 8vo.

HALLOCK, Jeremiah. See YALE, C. Life of.

HALLOCK, William A. Sketch of the Life and Labors of Justin Edwards, D. D. N. Y., 1855. 12mo.

HALLOWEL, Me. Cultivator, Newspaper. Dec., 1839, to Dec., 1840. Folio.

HALSEY, Rev. Le Roy, J. Literary Attractions of the Bible. 3d Ed. N. Y., 1859. 12mo.

HALSTEAD, M. Hist. of the Nat. Polit. Conventions of 1860. Columbus, O., 1860. Rebell'n Pamph. Vol. 77.

HALSTED, Wm. Speech in Cong., May 2, 1842, on the Apportionment Bill. Washington, 1842. 8vo. Congr. and Polit. Pamph. Vol. 24.

HAMBURG, Germany. See Acc. of the Management of the Poor in. 1796.

—— International Agricult. Exhibition. 1862. See WRIGHT, J. A.

—— Plan of City of,—in Covers. 1842.

HAMERSLY, Lewis R. Records of Living Officers of the U. S. Navy, with Hist. of Naval Opera. during the Rebellion. 1861–5. Phila., 1870. 8vo.

HAMILTON Academy, Hamilton, N. Y. Catalogues for 1851–2, 1852–3. Hamilton. 8vo.

HAMILTON, Alex. Collection of Facts and Documents relative to the Death of,—with Comments. 8vo. N. Y., 1804.

—— See HAMILTON, J. C. Hist. of the Republic.

—— Hamilton Club Series.

HAMILTON, Alex. Letter concerning the Public Conduct and Character of John Adams. Boston, 1809. 8vo. Congr. and Polit. Pamph. Vol. 123.
—— Letter on Banks and Currency. N. Y., 1839. 8vo. Congr. and Polit. Pamph. Vol. 99.
—— Narr. of the Western Insurrection; or Opposition to Excise Law in Penn., in 1794. "Olden Time." Vol. 2.
—— Official and other Papers of. Vol. 1. N. Y. and Lond., 1842. 8vo.
—— See OTIS, H. G. Eulogy on. 1804.
—— RENWICK, J. Life of.
—— SMUCKER, S. M. Life and Times of.
HAMILTON, A. H. Summer Guide to the Amusements of London, for 1848. Lond. 12mo. Guide Books. Vol. 4.
HAMILTON, Gen. A. J. Letter to the President of the U. States. N. Y., 1863. 8vo. Rebell'n Pamph. Vols. 17 and 90.
—— Memorial to Cong. on the Texas Election Frauds. Austin, 1870. 8vo. Congr. and Polit. Pamph. Vol. 116.
—— Speech at Cooper Institute, N. Y., Oct. 3, 1862, on the Condition of the South. Rebell'n Pamph. Vol. 37.
HAMILTON Club Series. 4 Vols. 4to. No. 1. WILLIAMS, John. Life of Alex. Hamilton. N. Y., 1865.
2. HAMILTON, Alex. Observations on certain Documents in the Hist. of the U. S. for 1796.
3. The Hamiltoniad; or an Extinguisher for the Royal Faction of N. Eng.
4. Letters to Alex. Hamilton; King of the Federals. 1866.
HAMILTON COLLEGE, Clinton, N. Y. Catalogues for 1853–4, 1854–5, 1860–1, 1864–5, 1868–9.
—— —— Catalogus Senatus Academici, etc., 1855. Clinton and Utica. 8vo.
—— —— See DICKINSON, D. S. Address, 1858.
—— —— FISHER, S. W. Hist. Disc., 1862.
—— —— Public Exercises at Inaug. of Pres't S. W. Fisher, 1858. Utica, 1858. 8vo. Addresses, etc. Vol. 26.
—— —— Same at Inaug. of Pres't S. G. Brown, 1867. Utica, 1867. 8vo. Ham. Coll. Pamph's.
HAMILTON, Eliz'th. Popular Essays. Boston, 1817. 12mo.
HAMILTON, Dr. Frank H. Address at Fairfield Med. Coll., Dec. 3, 1839. Albany, 1839. 8vo. Med. Pamph. Vol. 2.
—— Disc. before the Auburn Fem. Seminary, May 30, 1838. Auburn, 1838. 8vo. Addresses. Vol. 38.
HAMILTON, Gail. Courage! a Tract for the Times. Rebell'n Pamph. Vol. 67.
HAMILTON Genealogy. See BIRNIE, J. Acc. of.
HAMILTON, Henry P. Practical Remarks on Popular Educa. in Eng. and Wales. Lond., 1847. 8vo. Educa. Pamph. Vol. 30.
—— The Privy Council and the National Society. Lond., 1850. 8vo. Strangford Pamph. Vol. 54.
HAMILTON, H. W. Rural Sketches of Minn. and Northern Wis. Milan, O., 1850. 8vo. Wis. Misc. Pamph. Vol. 7.

HAMILTON, Rev. Jas. Can the Church accept the Gov't Plan of Education? Letter to Rev. Dr. Hook. Lond., 1847. 8vo. Strangford Pamph. Vol. 42.

HAMILTON, Gov. Jas. Corres. with Hon. John C. Calhoun, on State Interposition. Charleston, 1832. 12mo. Nullification Tracts.

HAMILTON, Jas. List of the Hamilton Papers. Penn. Hist. Soc. Memoirs. Vol. 2. Part 1.

—— Life of Rear-Admiral John Paul Jones. Phila., 1858. 12mo.

HAMILTON, Dr. Jas. Letter to Sir Wm. Garrow, on the Bill for Regulating the Practice of Surgery. Lond., 1818. 8vo. 2d Ed. Pamphleteer. Vol. 12.

—— Reply to Dr. Gregory. Edinburgh, 1793. 8vo. Med. Pamph. Vol. 21.

HAMILTON, Jas. A. See FISH, Hamilton. Corres. on Election of Fremont, 1856.

—— Reminiscences of; or, Men and Events at Home and Abroad during Three Quarters of a Century. 8vo. N. Y., 1869.

—— The Constitution Vindicated. N. Y., 1864. 8vo. Rebell'n Pamph. Vols. 15, 28.

HAMILTON, J. C. Coercion Completed and Treason Triumphant, 1864. Rebell'n Pamph. Vol. 36.

—— Hist. of the Republic of the U. States of America, as traced in the Writings of Alex. Hamilton. Phila., 1864. 7 Vols. 8vo.

—— The Slave Power; its Heresies and Injuries to the Amer. People. N. Y., 1864? 8vo. Congr. and Polit. Pamph. Vol. 136. Rebell'n Pamph. Vol. 37.

HAMILTON, J. H. Letter to the Inhabitants and Congregation of St. Michael's Pimlico, with Reports of the Parochial Charities for 1858. Lond., 1858. 8vo. Eng Misc. Pamph. Vol. 9.

—— Same, for 1855. Eng. Misc. Pamph. Vol. 8.

HAMILTON, John. Remonstrance, addressed to the Legislature and Others, on the Scottish Ch. Question. Edinbnrgh, 1841. 8vo. Strangford Pamph. Vol. 27.

HAMILTON, Mass. See FELT, J. B. Hist. of.

HAMILTON, N. Y., Fem. Seminary. Catalogue for 1858–9. Utica, 1859. 8vo.

HAMILTON, Schuyler. Hist. of the National Flag of the U. S. Phila. 1852. 12mo.

HAMILTON, Capt. S. Presentation of a Sword to him, by H. Carey. n. d. 12mo. Congr. and Polit. Pamph. Vol. 90.

HAMILTON, T. Men and Manners in America. Phila., 1833. 8vo.

HAMILTON, Wm. R. Address to the Royal Geograph. Soc. of London, May 21, 1838. Lond. 8vo. Scientific Pamph. Vol. 40.

—— Second Letter to the Earl of Elgin on the Construction of the New Houses of Parliament. Lond., 1836. 8vo. Strangford Pamph. Vol. 12.

HAMILTON, Rev. W. T. Eloquence; its Characteristics and its Power: Oration before the Literary Societies of Oglethorpe University, Nov. 18, 1846. Charleston, S. C., 1847. 8vo. Addresses. Vol. 26.

HAMLIN, A. C. Martyria, or the Andersonville Prison. Boston, 1866. 12mo.
HAMLIN, H. Speech in Cong., Mar. 9–10, 1858, on the Lecompton Constitution. Congr. and Polit. Pamph. Vol. 93.
HAMMATT, Abraham. Ipswich Grammar School. Extract from an Address on the 200th Annivers. of the School, 1850. N. E. Hist. and Gen. Reg. Vol. 6.
HAMMOND, Chas. Address before the Citizens of Union, Conn., and Neighboring Towns, July 4, 1853. Worcester, Mass., 1853. 8vo. Addresses, etc. Vol. 27.
HAMMOND, Jabez D. Hist. of Polit. Parties in the State of N. Y., from the Ratification of the Fed. Constitution to Dec., 1840. Syracuse, 1852. 2 Vols. 8vo.
Same, Vol. 3, from Jan., 1841, to Jan., 1847. Syracuse, 1852. 8vo.
—— Life and Times of Silas Wright, late Gov. of the State of N. Y. Syracuse, 1848. 8vo.
HAMMOND, John. Leah and Rachel; or the Two Fruitful Sisters, Virginia and Maryland, 1656. Force's Hist. Tracts. Vol. 3.
HAMMOND, Capt. M. M. Memoir of. N. Y., 1858. 12mo.
HAMMOND, S. H. Speech in N. Y. Legisla., Feb., 1860. Rebell'n Pamph. Vol. 77.
—— Wild Northern Scenes; or Sporting Adventures with the Rifle and the Rod. N. Y., 1858. 12mo.
HAMMOND, Wm. A. Causes which led to his Dismissal as Surgeon Gen. of U. S. Army, 1863. Rebell'n Pamph. Vol. 17.
HAMOR, Ralph. True Discourse on the Present State of Virginia to June 18, 1614. Lond., 1615. N. Y. Reprint, 1869. 4to.
HAMPDEN Club, London. Full Report of Proceedings, Lond., June 15, 1816, on Parl. Reform. Lond. 8vo. Eng. Polit. Pamph. Vol. 33.
HAMPDEN Co., Mass. See HOLLAND, J. G.
HAMPDEN, Mass., Agric. Soc. See COLMAN, H.
HAMPDEN, Prof. R. D. Inaug. Lecture before the Univers. of Oxford, Mar. 17, 1836. Lond., 1836. 8vo. Edu. Pamph. Vol. 35.
HAMPSHIRE Co., Mass., Bar. See BLISS, Geo. Hist. Address, 1826.
—— —— Geology. See NASH, Alanson. Notices of, 1827.
—— —— See HOLLAND, J. G.
HAMPSHIRE, Eng. See WOODWARD, B. W. Gen. Hist. of. n. d.
HAMPSHIRE, Mass. See Address to the People of, 1809.
—— Gazette, Newspaper. Aug., 1808, to Dec., 1808. Folio.
HAMPSHIRE Missionary Society. Reports of Trustees, 1805, 1806. Northampton, 1805–6. 8vo. N. H. Misc. Pamph. Vol. 1.
HAMPTON Court Guide Books. Five Pamphlets. 8vo and 12mo. n. d. Guide Books. Vol. 5.
HAMPTON, N. H. See DOW, J. Hist. Address, 1838.
—— FRENCH, Rev. J. Hist. Sketch of.
HAMPTON, Va., Normal and Agricult. Institute. Report on, by Pres't Hopkins and others, 1869.
—— Catalogue, 1870–71.
HANAFORD, J. L. Hist. of Princeton, Worcester Co., Mass., from 1739. Worcester, 1852. 12mo.

HANAFORD, Mrs. P. A. Sketch of Rev. Stillman Barden. Essex Institute Coll. Vol. 7.

HANCOCK, Dr. Henry. Short Acc. of a Case of Disease of the Appendix Caeci Lond., 1848. 8vo. Med. Pamph. Vol. 29.

HANCOCK, John. Essays on the Elective Franchise. Phila., 1865. 8vo. Rebell'n Pamph. Vol. 57.

—— Ten Chapters in the Life of. Now first published since 1789. N. Y., 1857. 8vo.

—— Se THACHER, Peter. Obit. Disc., 1793.

HANCOCK, John, M. D. Observations on the Climate, Soil and Productions of British Guiana. Lond., 1840. 8vo. 2d Ed. Strangford Pamph. Vol. 23.

HANCOCK, Maj. Gen. W. S. His Civil Record during his Administra. in La. and Texas. 1871. 8vo. Congr. and Polit. Pamph. Vol. 138.

—— Reports on Indian Affairs, 1866-7. Rebell'n Pamph. Vol. 55.

—— See DENISON, C. W. How he became Maj. Gen.

HAND Book of Iowa. Chicago, 1869. 12mo

—— —— of Minnesota. Chicago, 1867. 12mo.

—— —— of Stevens' Point and the Upper Wisconsin. Stevens' Point, 1857. 12mo.

—— —— of Travel in U. S. See APPLETON.

—— —— of Young Artists and Amateurs in Oil Painting. N. Y., 1856. 12mo.

HAND, Saml. See DE BURY. Philobiblon.

HANDEL. See CALCOTT, Wm. H. Facts in the Life of.

HANDLEY, Benj. Facts, showing the Mode of Administering the Law by Country Magistrates; Case of the Writer and Rev. Wm. Waters. Lond., 1839. 8vo. Law Pamph. Vol. 20.

HANDLEY, Henry. Letter to Earl Spencer, on the Formation of a National Agricult. Institution. Lond., 1838. 8vo. Strangford Pamph. Vol. 15.

HANFORD, Levi. See BUSHNELL, C. I. Revolu. Life and Adventures.

HANGER, Col. Geo. Life, Adventures and Opinions of. Lond., 1801. 2 Vols. 8vo.

HANKY, Vaceslava. Dalimilova Chronika Ceska. Prague, 1853. 18mo.

—— Rukopis Kralodvorsky. Prague, 1851.

HANN, R. The Prophecies of Joanna Southcott. Lond., 1809. 12mo. Eng. Rel. Pamph. Vol. 86.

HANNAFORD, E. Hist. of the Campaign of the 6th Reg't of Ohio Vol. Infantry. Cincin., 1868. 8vo.

HANNAH, John S. Hist. of Life and Services of Capt. Samuel Dewees. Baltimore, 1844. 12mo.

HANNIBAL. See ARNOLD, T. Life of.

HANNIBAL & St. Joseph R. R. Co. Circular in regard to Lands of the Co. Hannibal, 1863. 8vo. Mo. Misc. Pamph. Vol. 1.

HANNINGTON, C. M. Registration made Easy; Plan for a Gen. Register. Lond., 1831. 8vo. Law Pamph. Vol. 19.

HANOVER College, Ind. See WOOD, Jas., D. D.

HANOVER, Mass. See BARRY. J. S. Hist. Sketch of.

HANOVER, M. D. Practical Treatise on the Law of Horses. Cincin., 1872. 8vo.

HANSARD, L. J. Proposition on the National Debt. Lond., 1845. 8vo. Strangford Pamph. Vol. 40.

HANSARD, T. C. Parliamentary Hist. of England, from 1066 to 1803. Lond., 1806–1820. 36 Vols. 8vo.

HANSON, Rev. John H. The Lost Prince; Facts tending to prove the Identity of Louis XVII, of France, and the Rev. Eleazer Williams. N. Y., 1854. 12mo.

HANSON, J. W. Hist. Sketch of the Old 6th Reg't of Mass. Volunteers, during 1861–4. Boston, 1866. 12mo.

HANSON, R. D. Lecture on Colonization, before the Literary Assoc., at the London Tavern, Dec. 5, 1831. Lond., 1832. 8vo. Eng. Polit. Pamph. Vol. 38.

HANTS Co., England. See BERRY, W. Genealogies.

HANWAY, Castner, and others. Hist. of their Trial for Treason, at Phila., 1851. Phila., 1852. 8vo. Phila. Misc. Pamph. Vol. 1.

HAPGOOD Genealogy. See MORSE, A.

HARBAUGH, H. A Tract for the Times. The Religious Character of Washington. 1863. Rebell'n Pamph. Vol. 47.

HARBISON, Massy. Narrative from Indian Barbarity, with Acc. of Indian Barbarities, 1790–94. Pittsburgh, 1828. 12mo.

HARBOR Defences. Report from Select Comm. of U. S. House of Repr., on Harbor Defences of the Great Lakes and Rivers. 1862. Rebell'n Pamph. Vol. 20.

HARBORS and Rivers. See Congressional Speeches.

HARDEE, W. J. Rifle and Light Infantry Tactics. Phila., 1861. 2 Vols. 18mo.

HARDIN, J. J. Speech in Cong., Mar. 21, 1844, on the Public Life of M. Van Buren. Cong. and Polit. Pamph. Vol. 88.

HARDING, Lt. Col. Hist. of Tiverton, in the County of Devon. Tiverton, 1845. 2 Vols. 8vo.

HARDING, Wm. Universal Stenography; or a Practical System of Short-Hand Writing. Lond., 1823. 12mo. Scientific Pamph. Vol. 26.

HARDINGE, Emma. America and her Destiny; an Inspirational Discourse by the Spirits. N. Y., 1861. 8vo. Rebell'n Pamph. Vol. 66.

—— Funeral Oration on Abraham Lincoln, Apr. 16, 1865, at Cooper Institute, N. Y. N. Y., (n. d.) 8vo. Addresses. Vol. 31.

HARE, Julius C. Education the Necessity of Mankind: a Sermon. Lond., 1851. 8vo. Educa. Pamph. Vol. 36.

—— On Certain Tenses attributed to the Greek Verb. On English Preterites and Genitives. 2 Pamphlets. (n. d.) 8vo. Strangford Pamph. Vol. 13.

—— On English Orthography. (n. d.) 8vo. Strangford Pamph. Vol. 16.

—— On the Names of the Days of the Week. Strangford Pamph. Vol. 16.

—— Vindica. of Niebuhr's Hist. of Rome. Cambridge, 1829. 8vo. Strangford Pamph. Vol. 11.

HARE, J. I. C. Opinion on the Constitutionality of Act of Cong. on Legal Tender Currency. 1862. Rebell'n Pamph. Vol. 87.

HARE, Prof. Robt. Introduct. Lecture on Chemistry, in the Univers. of Penn., Nov. 7, 1843. Phila., 1843. 8vo. Scientific Pamph. Vol. 40.

HARE, Thos. Minority Representation in Europe. 1871. 8vo. Cong. and Polit. Pamph. Vol. 114.

—— Thoughts on the Dwellings of the People, etc. Lond., 1862. 12mo. Eng. Misc. Pamph. Vol. 15.

HAREWOOD Iron and Mining Co., St. Lawrence Co., N. Y. Report of Directors. Boston, 1864. 8vo. N. Y. Misc. Pamph. Vol. 5.

HARGRAVE, Mr. Argument in the Case of Jas. Sommersett, a Negro, showing the Unlawfulness of Slavery in England. London, 1788. 4to. Law Pamph. Vol. 25.

HARIOT, Thos. Brief and True Report of the Newfoundland of Virginia. Fac Simile Reprint of Ed. of 1590. N. Y., 1872. Folio.

HARLAN, Jas. Speech in Cong., Apr. 14, 1856, on the Kansas Legislative Petition. Congr. and Polit. Pamph. Vol. 139.

—— Speech in Cong., July 11, 1862, on the "Service of the Militia." Rebell'n Pamph. Vol. 9.

—— Speech in Cong., Apr. 6, 1864, on Prohibiting Slavery in the U. S. Rebell'n Pamph. Vol. 9.

—— Speech in Cong., on Maintaining the Constitution, etc. 1864. 8vo. Congr. and Polit. Pamph. Vol. 121.

—— Speeches in Cong., Feb. 14th, 15th and 28th, 1872, on Sale of Arms to French Agents. Congr. and Polit. Pamph. Vol. 129.

HARLAN, Richd. Fauna Americana; a Descript. of Mammiferous Animals inhabiting N. America. Phila., 1825. 8vo.

HARLEIAN Manuscripts. See British Museum.

HARMANSON, John H. Speech in Cong., June 24, 1846, on the Tariff. Washington, 1846. 8vo. Speeches. Vol. 1.

HARMON, Daniel W. Journ. of Voyages and Travels in the Interior of N. America to the Pacific Ocean. Andover, 1820. 8vo.

HARMONY Grove Cemetery, Salem, Mass. See WHITE, D. A. Address at Consecra. of. 1840.

HARPER, Jas. Sketch of Life of. N. Y., (n. d.) 8vo. Biograph. Pamph. Vol. 7.

HARPER, L. Prelim. Report on the Geology and Agriculture of Mississippi. Jackson, 1857. 8vo.

HARPER, Robt. G. Letter to his Constituents. Washington, 1801. 8vo. Congr. and Polit. Pamph. Vols. 69 and 123.

—— Observations on the Dispute between the U. S. and France. Lond., 1797. 8vo.

—— Observations on the N. American Land Co., lately instituted in Phila. Lond., 1796. 8vo.

HARPER, William. Speech before the Charleston State Rights and Free Trade Assoc., April 1, 1832. Charleston, 1832. 8vo. Nullification Tracts.

HARPER, Wiliiam. The Remedy by State Interposition, or Nullification, explained and Advocated. Charleston, 1832. 12mo. Nullification Tracts.

HARPERS' Ferry Invasion. See Congressional Speeches.

—— —— Report of Comm. of U. S. Senate, with Accompanying Testimony. Washington, 1860. 8vo.

HARPERS' Family Library. N. Y., 1860. 187 Vols. 18mo.

HARPERS' New Monthly Magazine. June, 1850—Dec., 1872. 45 Vols. 8vo. N. Y.

HARPERS' Pictorial Hist. of the Rebellion. N. Y., 1868. 2 Vols. 4to.

HARRINGTON, Rev. Jos. See WHITING, W. Memoirs of.

HARRIS, Alex. Biograph. History of Lancaster Co., Pa., being a Hist. of Early Settlers and Eminent Men of that Co. Lancaster, 1872. 8vo.

HARRIS, B. G. Speech in Cong., Apr. 9, 1864, on the Expulsion of Mr. Long. Rebell'n Pamph. Vol. 32.

HARRIS, E. D. Acc. of some Descendants of Capt. Thos. Brattle Boston, 1867. 4to.

—— Genealog. Record of Thos. Bascom and his Descendants. Boston, 1870. 8vo.

—— The Vassals of N. Y. and their immediate Descendants. Albany, 1862. 8vo. Genealog. Pamph. Vol. 7.

HARRIS, Judge I. Opinion in Case of the People vs. Wm. P. Van Rensselaer et al., concerning the Manor of Rensselaerwyck. Albany, 1852. 8vo. N. Y. Misc. Pamph. Vol. 5.

HARRIS, John, Sr. See BRECK, Saml. Hist. Anecdote of.

HARRIS, John. Complete Collection of Voyages and Travels. Lond., 1744. 2 Vols. Folio.

HARRIS, J. Morrison. Disc. before Md. Hist. Soc., May 19, 1846, on the Life and Character of Sir Walter Raleigh. Baltimore, 1846. 8vo. Md. Hist. Soc. Papers. Vol. 1.

—— Papers upon California, before the Md. Hist. Soc., Mar., 1849. Baltimore, 1849. 8vo. Md. Hist. Soc. Papers. Vol. 2.

HARRIS, Gen. Lord. See LUSHINGTON, S. R. Life and Pub. Services of.

HARRIS L. M. Robert Harris and his Descendants, with Notice of the Morey and Metcalf Families. Boston, 1861. 8vo.

HARRIS, Sam'l. Inaug. Address as Prest of Bowdoin College, Aug. 6, 1867. Brunswick, 1867. 8vo. Addresses. Vol. 18.

HARRIS, S. R. Facts concerning the South Boundary of the Western Reserve. Fire Lands Pioneer. Vol. 8.

HARRIS, S. W. Speech in Cong., June 10, 1850, on the Compromise. Congr. and Polit. Pamph. Vol. 94.

HARRIS, T. L. Letter on the Repeal of the Fugitive Slave Law 1851. Congr. and Polit. Pamph. Vol. 87.

—— Speech in Cong., Mar. 25, 1850, on the Admission of Cal. Congr. and Polit. Pamph. Vol. 86.

HARRIS, Thaddeus M., D. D. Biograph. Memorials of Jas. Oglethorpe, Founder of the Colony of Ga. Boston, 1841. 8vo.

—— Chronolog. and Topograph. Acc. of Dorchester, Mass. Mass. Hist. Soc. Coll. 1st Ser. Vol. 9.

HARRIS, Thaddens M., D. D. See FROTHINGHAM, N. L. Memoir of.
—— HALL, Rev. Nathan'l. Address at his Interment.
—— Journ. of a Tour into the Terr'y Northwest of the Alleghany Mts., made in 1803, with a Geograph. and Hist. Acc. of the State of Ohio. Boston, 1805. 8vo.
—— Memorials of the 1st Ch. in Dorchester. Discourses delivered July 4, 1830. Boston, 1830. 8vo. Mass. Hist. Discourses. Vol. 8.
—— Tribute of Respect to Hon. Jas. Bowdoin, in a Sermon at Dorchester, Oct. 27, 1811. Boston, 1811. 8vo. Sermons. Vol. 45.
HARRIS, Thaddeus W., M. D. Treatise on some of the Insects injurious to Vegetation. 3d Ed. Boston, 1862. 8vo.
HARRIS, Wiley P. Speech in Cong., Apr. 24 and 26, 1854, on the Kansas and Nebraska Bill. Washington, 1854. 8vo. Speeches. Vol. 3.
HARRIS, Wm. Hist. and Critical Acc. of the Life and Writings of Charles I, King of G. Britain. Lond., 1758. 8vo.
HARRIS, Wm. C. The Highlands of Ethiopia, from the first Lond. Ed. N. Y., 1844. 8vo.
—— The Wild Sports of Southern Africa; Narr. of an Expedition from the Cape of Good Hope to the Tropic of Capricorn, in 1836. Waldie's Circulating Libr. Vol. 14.
HARRIS, Wm. S. Hist. Sketch of Poplar Tent Church, Cabarrus Co., N. C. Charlotte, N. C., 1873. 8vo.
HARRIS, Wm. Thaddeus. See DRAKE, S. G. Notice of.
—— and E. D. Epitaphs from the Old Burying Ground in Cambridge, Mass., with Notes. Cambridge, 1845. 12mo.
—— Epitaphs from Old Burial Ground, Watertown, Mass. Boston, 1869. 4to.
—— The Theory of Amer. Education. St. Louis, (n. d.) 8vo. Educa. Pamph. Vol. 7.
—— What Shall we Study? St. Louis, (n. d.) 8vo. Educa. Pamph. Vol. 7.
HARRIS, W. W. The Battle of Groton Heights; Narr. of the Storming of Ft. Grisworld, and Burning of N. London. 1781. N. Lond., 1870. 8vo.
HARRISBURG (Penn.) Nat. Democratic Union Club. Address. Phila., 1860. Rebell'n Pamph. Vol. 77.
—— Presb. Ch. See DEWITT, W. R. 70th Annivers. Disc. 1862.
—— ROBINSON, T. H. Hist. Discourse. 1868.
—— Portsmouth, Mountjoy & Lancaster R. R. Co. Report of Pres't, etc. 1856. Phila., 1856. 8vo. Penn. Misc. Pamph. Vol. 3.
—— Union, Newspaper. Harrisburg, 1860–61. Folio.
HARRISON & Warner. Atlas of Dane Co., Wis. Madison, 1873. 4to.
—— —— Railroad and Sectional Map of Wisconsin, 1873.
HARRISON, J. Scott. Pioneer Life at North Bend; Address before the Whitewater and Miami Valley Pioneer Assoc., at Cleves, Ohio, Sept. 8, 1866. Cincin., 1867. 8vo. Ohio Hist. Discourses. Vol. 2.
—— Another Copy. See Addresses. Vol. 19.

HARRISON, Rev. Matt. Rise, Progress and Present Structure of the Eng. Language. 2d Ed. Phila., 1856. 12mo.

HARRISON, Rich'd A. Oration, July 4, 1863, at Pleasant Valley, Ohio. Lond., O., 1863. 8vo. Rebell'n Pamph. Vol. 2. Addresses, etc. Vol. 17.

—— Speech in Cong., Jan. 28, 1862, on the Suppression of the Rebellion. Rebell'n Pamph. Vol. 9.

—— Speech in Cong., Feb. 27, 1862, on Claims of C. H. Upton. Congr. and Polit. Pamph. Vol. 87.

HARRISON, Wm. Bibliotheca Monensis: a Bibliograph. Acc. of Books relating to the Isle of Man. Douglas, 1861. 8vo.

—— Substance of his Speech before Select Comm. of the House of Commons, on East India Shipping. 1814. Lond. 8vo. Eng. Polit. Pamph. Vol. 31.

HARRISON. Pres't Wm. H. See Cox, Jos. Address at Cincin. 1871.

—— COXE, R. S. Address on Life of. 1841.

—— BACON, L. Discourse on Death of.

—— Biography of—in German. Phila., 1840. 8vo. Biograph. Pamph. Vol. 1.

—— See CARPENTER, H. S. Eulogy on.

—— Discourse on the Aborigines of the Valley of the Ohio. Ohio Hist. and Philos. Soc. Trans. Vol. 1. Part 2.

—— See GODDARD, Wm. G. Address on his Death. 1841.

—— HALL, J. Memoirs of Pub. Services.

—— Incidents in the Life of. Albany, 1839. 8vo. Congr. and Polit. Pamph. Vol. 124.

—— See JACKSON, J. R. Biography of.

—— JONES, G. Life and Hist. of.

—— LABAREE, Benj. Sermon on Death of. 1841.

—— MANSFIELD, E. D. Eulogy on. 1841.

—— MONTGOMERY, H. Life of.

—— Outlines of Life and Pub. Services of. Washington, 1840. 8vo.

—— Plain Reasons why he should be elected President. 1840. N. Y. 8vo. Congr. and Polit. Pamph. Vol. 124.

—— See Putnam, Geo. Discourse on. 1841.

—— Sketch of Life and Pub. Services of. Columbus, O., 1840. 8vo.

—— Same. N. Y., 1836. 8vo. Biograph. Pamph. Vol. 7.

—— Sketch of the Life of. Western Monthly Mag. Vol. 3.

—— See SPRAGUE, P. Character and Services of.

—— Tippecanoe Text-Book.

—— TODD, C. S. and DRAKE, B. Life of.

—— VAN RENSSELAER, Rev. C. Discourse on. 1841.

—— WHITNEY, Rev. G. Discourse on. 1841.

HARROW SCHOOL. See GALLOWAY, Earl of. Monitorial System of, 1854.

HARSHA, David A. The Most Eminent Orators and Statesmen of Ancient and Modern Times. N. Y., 1855. 8vo.

—— The Principles of Hydropathy, or the Invalid's Guide, etc. Albany, 1852. 12mo. Med. Pamph. Vol. 5.

HART, Adolphus M. Hist. of the Discovery of the Valley of the Mississippi. St. Louis, 1852. 12mo.

HART, Chas. Henry. Biograph. Sketch of Abraham Lincoln, late Pres't of the U. S. Albany, 1870. 8vo. Biograph. Pamph. Vol. 7.

—— Memoir of Wm. H. Prescott. N. E. Hist. and Gen. Reg. Vol. 22.

—— Necrological Notice of Hon. Rich'd Stockton Field: read before the Numismatic and Antiqua. Soc. of Phila., Oct. 6, 1870. Phila., 1870. 8vo. Biograph. Pamph. Vol. 8.

—— Tribute to the Memory of Hon. Wm. Willis: read before the Numismatic and Antiqua. Soc. of Phila., Mar. 3, 1870. Phila. 1870. 8vo. Biograph. Pamph. Vol. 8.

HART Family Genealogy. See DAVIS, W. H. H.

HART, Rev. Seth. Sermon in St. George's Ch., Hempstead, Sept. 21, 1823, with Sketch of the Hist. of the Ch. N. Y., 1823. 8vo. N. Y. Hist. Discourses. Vol. 1.

HARTFORD, Conn. See ALDEN, J. D. Dedica. of Charter Oak Hall, 1856.

—— Branch of the Amer. Tract Soc. Speeches of Chief Justice Williams and others, Jan. 9, 1859, on the Policy of the Parent Soc. in regard to Slavery. Hartford, 1859. 8vo.

—— Conn. Courant, Newspaper. Hartford, 1803—1809. 2 Vols. Folio.

—— Convention, 1814. See DWIGHT, T.

—— —— Proceedings of a Convention of Delegates, from Mass., Conn., and R. Island, etc., convened at Hartford, Dec. 15, 1814. Hartiord, 1815. 8vo. Conn. Misc. Pamph. Vol. 1.

HARTFORD Deaf and Dumb Institution. See Amer. Asylum, etc.

—— City Directory. Hartford, 1848. 12mo.

—— Same. WELLS, 1849, '51.

—— Same. GEER, 1858.

—— 1st Ch. See HAWES, Joel. Centen. Disc., 1836.

—— —— Papers relating to the Controversy in the Ch., 1656–59. Conn. Hist. Soc. Coll. Vol. 2.

—— 4th Cong. Ch. Unanimous Remonstrance against the Policy of the Amer. Tract Soc. on Slavery. Hartford, 1855. 12mo.

—— See HAWES, Rev. J. 2d Centen. Disc. 1835.

—— in the Olden Time; its First Thirty Years. By Scaeva. Hartford, 1853. 8vo.

—— North Church. See BUSHNELL, Horace. Commem. Discourse, 1853.

—— See PORTER, Wm. S. Hartford in 1640.

—— Proceedings at Dedication of Charter Oak Hall, 1856. Hartford, 1856. 8vo.

—— Report of Special Committee relative to War Debt Bonds, 1862. Rebell'n Pamph. Vol. 65.

—— Retreat for the Insane. Reports for 1841, 53, 54, 55, 56, 58, 59, 60, 61, 62. Hartford, 1842–63. 8vo.

—— Soldiers Aid Assoc. 1st Ann. Report, 1863. Rebell'n Pamph. Vol. 84.

—— —— 2d Ann. Report, 1863. Rebell'n Pamph. Vol. 78.

HARTFORD. See Trinity College, Hartford.
HARTLAND, Ohio. See WALDRON, E. J. Memoir of.
HARTLEY, Cecil B. Life and Times of Col. Daniel Boone, comprising the Hist. of the Early Settlement of Ky. Phila., 1859. 12mo.
HARTLEY, David. Letters on the Amer. War; addressed to the Mayor and Corporation of Kingston-upon-Hull. 6th Ed. Lond., 1779. Amer. Tracts. Vol. 5.
—— The Budget; inscribed to the Man who thinks himself Minister. Lond., 1764. Scarce Tracts. Vol. 1.
HARTLEY, Rev. J. Progress of the Reformation on the Continent; or Sketches of the Papal and Reformed Churches. London, 1837. 8vo. Eng. Rel. Pamph. Vol. 48.
HARTPENCE, Rev. A. Our National Crisis: Sermon at Holmesbury, Penn., Sept., 1862. Rebell'n Pamph. Vol. 29.
HART, C. J. and AGASSIZ, L. Scientific Results of a Journey in Brazil, and Geology and Physical Geography in Brazil. Boston, 1870. 8vo.
HARTUPEE, Prof. Dawn and Development of the Religious Interests of the Reserve and Fire Lands. Address before the F. L. Hist. Soc. Fire Lands Pioneer. Vol. 7.
HARTWELL, Henry, and others. The Present State of Virginia and the College of William and Mary. Lond., 1727. 8vo. Va. Misc. Pamph. Vol. 1.
HARTWICK Synod. See Evangel. Luth. Ch.
—— Theolog. and Classical Seminary. Ann. Catalogues, 1849, '58, '72. Albany, 8vo.
HARVARD College. Addresses at the Inaugura. of Chas. Wm. Eliot, as Pres't, Oct. 19, 1869. Cambridge, 1869. 8vo. Harvard Coll. Pamph.
—— —— Addresses at the Inaugura. of C. C. Felton, as Pres't, July 19, 1860. Cambridge, 1860. 8vo. Harvard College Pamph.
—— —— Alumni Assoc. See WHITE, D. A. Address, 1844.
—— —— See WINTHROP, R. C. Address, 1852.
—— —— Alumni Hall. Appeal to the Alumni and others in behalf of. Cambridge, 1866. 8vo.
—— —— See ANDREW, J. A. Address, 1864.
—— —— Arrangement of Lectures and Recitations for the 2d Term of 1839–40. Cambridge, 1840. 8vo.
—— —— Astronom. Observatory. Part 1. BOND, Wm. C. Hist. and Descript. of the Astronom. Observatory, 1856. 4to.
—— —— —— Part 2. BOND, W. C. Results of Astronom. Observations, made 1852–3. 1855. 4to.
—— —— Catalogue of Officers and Students for 1833–4, 1834–5, 1835–6, 1837, 1838–9, 1841–2, 1842–3, 1845–6, 1846–7, 1847–8, 1848–9, 1867–8. Cambridge, 1833–48. 8vo.
—— —— Catalogue of the Library. Cambridge, 1830–34. 6 Vols. 8vo.
—— —— Catalogue of the Law Library. 4th Ed. Cambridge, 1846. 8vo.
—— —— Triennial Catalogues for 1813, '21, '24—66, '72. 8vo.

HARVARD College. Christian Union. Constitution, etc., of. Boston, 1859. 12mo.
—— —— Divinity School. Catalogue of the Alumni. Cambridge, 1844. 8vo.
—— —— —— Order of Exercises at the 37th Ann. Visitation, July 19, 1853. Cambridge, 1853. 8vo.
—— —— See ELIOT, S. A. Sketch of the Hist. of.
—— —— Extracts from the Laws relating to the Library, Feb., 1860. 8vo.
—— —— See FARMER, J. Memorials of Graduates of, 1833.
—— —— Hasty Pudding Club. Cat. of Officers and Members. Cambridge, 1850. 12mo.
—— —— See HEDGE, Levi.
—— —— HILL, Rev. T. Address, 1853.
—— —— Iadma. See THAXTER, A. W. Poem, 1850.
—— —— Law Department. Catalogue of Students for 1842, '45, '58. Cambridge. v. d. 12mo.
—— —— —— PARKER, Joel. Law School of Harvard.
—— —— Letter of the Librarian to the Committee of the Assoc. of the Alumni, appointed to visit the Library. Cambridge, 1859. 8vo.
—— —— Medical Department. Ann. Circulars for 1846, 1849–50, 1856–7.
—— —— —— Ann. Announcements, 1857–8, 1860, 1861, 1870, 1871.
—— —— —— Catalogue of Students attending the Winter Session, 1862–3. Boston. 8vo.
—— —— —— See HOLMES, O. W. Benefactors of.
—— —— Memorial Biographies. Cambridge, 1867. 2 Vols. 8vo.
—— —— Memorial concerning the recent History and the Constitutional Rights and Privileges of Harvard Coll., presented to the Legislature, Jan. 17, 1851. Cambridge, 1851. 8vo.
—— —— Museum of Comparative Zoology. Charter, By-Laws, etc., 1859. Boston, 1859. 8vo.
—— —— —— Ann. Reports of Trustees, 1862–70. Boston, 1863–71. 8vo.
—— —— Nat. Hist. Soc. See HILL, Rev. Thos.
—— —— Orders and Regulations of the Faculty, passed July, 1857 and 1860. Cambridge. 8vo.
—— —— See PALMER, Jos. Necrology of Alumni, 1851–62.
—— —— Peabody Museum. 1st, 2d, 3d, 4th, 5th Ann. Reports of the Trustees, 1868–72. Boston, 1868–72. 8vo.
—— —— See PEABODY, Wm. B. O. Disc. on Death of J. A. Emery. 1842.
—— —— See PEIRCE, B. Hist. of.
—— —— Phi Beta Kappa. Catalogues of the Fraternity. Cambridge, 1814, '46, '53.
—— —— —— See HILL, Rev. Thos. Address. 1858.
—— —— —— MARSH, G. P. Discourse. 1847.
—— —— —— PUTNAM, G. Oration, 1844.
—— —— —— SUMNER, Chas. Address. 1846.

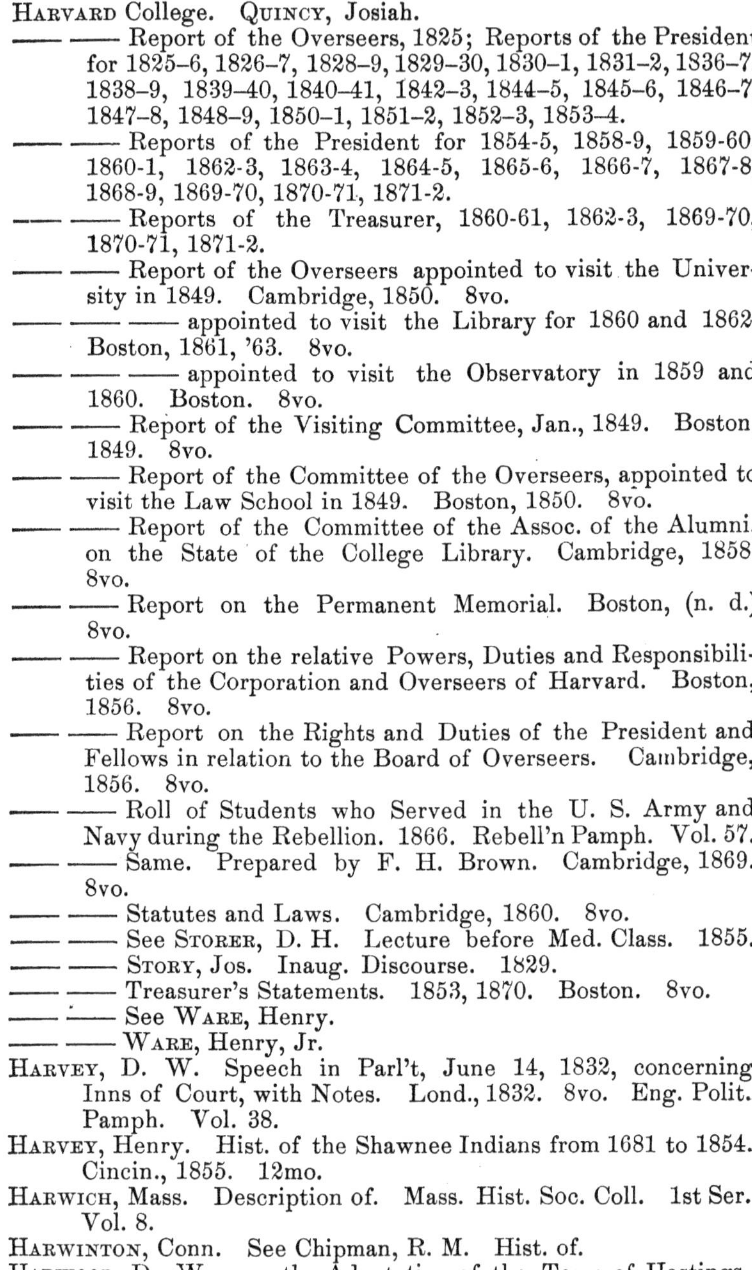

HARVARD College. QUINCY, Josiah.

—— —— Report of the Overseers, 1825; Reports of the President for 1825–6, 1826–7, 1828–9, 1829–30, 1830–1, 1831–2, 1836–7, 1838–9, 1839–40, 1840–41, 1842–3, 1844–5, 1845–6, 1846–7, 1847–8, 1848–9, 1850–1, 1851–2, 1852–3, 1853–4.

—— —— Reports of the President for 1854-5, 1858-9, 1859-60, 1860-1, 1862-3, 1863-4, 1864-5, 1865-6, 1866-7, 1867-8, 1868-9, 1869-70, 1870-71, 1871-2.

—— —— Reports of the Treasurer, 1860-61, 1862-3, 1869-70, 1870-71, 1871-2.

—— —— Report of the Overseers appointed to visit the University in 1849. Cambridge, 1850. 8vo.

—— —— —— appointed to visit the Library for 1860 and 1862. Boston, 1861, '63. 8vo.

—— —— —— appointed to visit the Observatory in 1859 and 1860. Boston. 8vo.

—— —— Report of the Visiting Committee, Jan., 1849. Boston, 1849. 8vo.

—— —— Report of the Committee of the Overseers, appointed to visit the Law School in 1849. Boston, 1850. 8vo.

—— —— Report of the Committee of the Assoc. of the Alumni, on the State of the College Library. Cambridge, 1858. 8vo.

—— —— Report on the Permanent Memorial. Boston, (n. d.) 8vo.

—— —— Report on the relative Powers, Duties and Responsibilities of the Corporation and Overseers of Harvard. Boston, 1856. 8vo.

—— —— Report on the Rights and Duties of the President and Fellows in relation to the Board of Overseers. Cambridge, 1856. 8vo.

—— —— Roll of Students who Served in the U. S. Army and Navy during the Rebellion. 1866. Rebell'n Pamph. Vol. 57.

—— —— Same. Prepared by F. H. Brown. Cambridge, 1869. 8vo.

—— —— Statutes and Laws. Cambridge, 1860. 8vo.

—— —— See STORER, D. H. Lecture before Med. Class. 1855.

—— —— STORY, Jos. Inaug. Discourse. 1829.

—— —— Treasurer's Statements. 1853, 1870. Boston. 8vo.

—— —— See WARE, Henry.

—— —— WARE, Henry, Jr.

HARVEY, D. W. Speech in Parl't, June 14, 1832, concerning Inns of Court, with Notes. Lond., 1832. 8vo. Eng. Polit. Pamph. Vol. 38.

HARVEY, Henry. Hist. of the Shawnee Indians from 1681 to 1854. Cincin., 1855. 12mo.

HARWICH, Mass. Description of. Mass. Hist. Soc. Coll. 1st Ser. Vol. 8.

HARWINTON, Conn. See Chipman, R. M. Hist. of.

HARWOOD, Dr. Wm., on the Adaptation of the Town of Hastings, Eng., for Invalids. Lond., 1829. 8vo. Hist. Pamph. Vol. 15.

HAS Religion anything to do with our Colleges? (On Unitarian Professorships in Columbia Coll.) (n. d.) 8vo. Columbia Coll. Pamph.

HASKINS, R. W. Art and Artists. Buffalo, 1851. 8vo. Art Pamph. Vol. 6.

—— Effects upon the Civilized World, of a Material Increase in the Quantity of the Money Metals. (n. p.) 1850. 8vo. Banking and Currency Pamph. Vol. 3.

—— Examination of the Hypothesis of Central Heat in the Earth. Buffalo, 1869. 8vo. Scientific Pamph. Vol. 3.

—— Exposition of "Hazlitt's Translation of Guizot's Hist. of Civilization." Buffalo, 1846. 8vo. Educa. Pamph., etc. Vol. 2.

—— Popular Essay upon Comets. Buffalo, 1842. 12mo. Scientific Pamph. Vol. 21.

—— See SELLSTEDT, L. G. Paper on.

HASKINS, Rev. S. M. Sermon at Williamsburgh, N. Y., on the 30th Annivers. of the Rectorship, 1869. N. Y. 8vo. Sermons. Vol. 26.

HASSLER, F. R. Papers on Subjects connected with the Survey of the Coast of the U. S. Amer. Philos. Soc. Trans. N. S. Vol. 2.

HALSTED, Fred. Letters addressed to Pres't Lincoln and others, on the War. Rebell'n Pamph. Vol. 74.

HASTINGS (Eng.) Guide. See POWELL, P. M. 1825.

—— and St. Leonard's Guide. See Ross's Guide. 1851.

—— See HARWOOD, Wm. Its Adaptation for Residence of Invalids.

HASTINGS Genealogy. See BUCKMINSTER, L. N.

HASTINGS, Sam'l D. Address before the Hastings Invincibles, at Madison, Wis., Nov. 9, 1862. Madison, 1862. 8vo. Wis. Misc. Pamph. Vol. 2.

—— Address at Sparta, Wis., July 4, 1863. Madison, 1863. 8vo. Wis. Misc. Pamph. Vol. 1.

—— Oration at Beaver Dam, July 4, 1865. Madison. 8vo. Wis. Misc. Pamph. Vol. 2.

—— Present Condition of the Common Jails of the Country. Trans. Wis. Acad. of Sciences. 1870–2.

—— Proceedings of State Treasurer Hastings' Reunion, Dec. 28, 1865. Madison, 1865. 8vo. Wis. Misc. Pamph. Vol. 3.

—— Remarks before the Board of Trustees of the Wis. State Hospt. for the Insane, June 4, 1868, on the Investigation of Affairs of the Hospt. Wis. Misc. Pamph. Vol. 2.

HASTINGS, Warren. Defence before the House of Commons, upon the Charges of High Crimes, etc. 1786. Calcutta, 1787. 8vo. Eng. Polit. Pamph. Vol. 23.

—— See Letter to E. Burke, in Reply to his Ninth Report, etc.

HASWELL, Anthony. Memoirs of Capt. Matt. Phelps, of Harwinton, Conn., particularly in two Voyages from the Connecticut to the River Mississippi, 1773 to 1780. Bennington, 1802. 12mo.

HATCH, Davis. See HOWARD, J. M. Report on his Memorial.

HATCH, I. P. Speech on the Niagara Ship Canal. See HAYES, J. D.

HATCH, Gen. J. P. See Men of the Time.

HATCH, Wm. S. Chapter of the History of the War of 1812, in the N.-West, embracing the Surrender of the N. W. Army at Detroit. Cincin., 1872. 12mo.

HATCHETT, Chas., on the Spikenard of the Ancients. (n. d.) Lond. 4to. Scientific Pamph. Vol. 37.

HATFIELD, R. G. American House Carpenter; a Treatise on the Art of Building. 7th Ed. N. Y., 1857. 8vo.

HATHERELL, Jas. W., D. D. Maynooth: Its Adoption by the State Considered. Lond., 1845. 8vo. Strangford Pamph. Vol. 39.

HATHEWAY, Maj.-Gen. S. G. See RANDALL, H. S. Obituary of.

HATTON, Sir Christopher. See NICOLAS, Sir Harry. Life and Times.

HAUKE, John S. Letter to Glenni W. Scofield, on Lands claimed by Land-Grant Corporations. Washington, 1872. 8vo. Congr. and Polit. Pamph. Vol. 129.

HAUPT, H. Remarks at a Public Meeting in Boston, June 9, 1857. for prosecuting the work on the Hoosac Tunnel. 8vo. Addresses. Vol. 6.

HAÜY, Abbé. Exposition Raisonnee de la Theorie de Electricité et du Magnetism. Paris, 1787. 8vo.

HAUTEFEUILLE, L. B. Quelques Question de Droit International Maritime, apropos de la Guerre d'Amerique. Paris, 1861. 8vo. Rebell'n Pamph. Vol. 17.

HAVE we the Best Possible Ambulance System? Boston, 1864. 8vo. Rebell'n Pamph. Vols. 5 and 10.

HAVELOCK, Gen. H. See BROCK, Rev. W. Biography of.

HAVEN Genealogy. See ADAMS, Josiah. Descendants of Rich'd Haven.

HAVEN, Henry P. Biograph. Sketch of Miss Frances M. Caulkins. N. E. Hist. and Gen. Register. Vol. 23.

HAVEN, Jos., D. D. Moral Philosophy, including Theoretical and Practical Ethics. Boston, 1859. 8vo.

HAVEN, S. F. Archæology of the U. States. Smithsonian Contrib. Vol. 8.

—— Hist. Address at Dedham, Mass., Sept. 21, 1836, on the 2d Centen. Celebra. of the Town. Dedham, 1837. 8vo. Mass. Mass. Hist. Discourses. Vol. 7.

HAVERFORD School, near Phila. Acc. of, with Constitution, By-Laws, etc. Phila., 1835. 8vo.

—— College, Penn. Catalogue of Officers and Students for 1866–7. Phila., 1866. 12mo.

—— —— Report of the Managers, Apr. 14, 1860. Phila., 1860. 8vo.

HAVERHILL, Mass. See CHASE, Geo. W. History of.

—— Hist. Sketch of, with Biograph. Notices. Mass. Hist. Soc. Coll. Vol. 4. 2d Ser.

—— See HOSFORD, Rev. B. F. Disc. at Re-Dedica. of Centre Ch., 1860.

HAVERHILL, Mass. MYRICK, B. L. Hist. of.
—— Ann. Report of Receipts and Expenses, 1840–41. Haverhill, 1841. 8vo.
HAVERSHAM, Lord. Memoirs of, from 1640 to 1710. Lond., 1711. Sm. 4to. Eng. Polit. Pamph. Vol. 9.
HAWAIAN Islands. See HUNNEWELL, J. F. Bibliog. of.
HAWES, G. W. Kentucky State Gazeteer and Business Directory, 1859–60. Louisville, 1859. 8vo.
—— Ohio State Gazeteer and Business Directory for 1859–60. Cincin., 1860. 8vo.
HAWES, Rev. Joel. Centen. Disc. at Hartford, Conn., June 26, 1836. Hartford, 1836. 8vo. Conn. Hist. Discourses. Vol. 1.
—— 2d Century Disc. at Hartford, Conn., Nov. 9, 1835. Hartford, 1835. 12mo.
—— The North and South; or Four Questions Considered. 1861. Fast Day Sermon. Rebell'n Pamph. Vol. 82.
—— Tribute to the Memory of the Pilgrims, and a Vindicaiion of Congregational Churches in N. England. Hartford, 1830. 12mo.
HAWKESWORTH, Dr. John. See Adventurer (The).
HAWKINS, Alfred. Picture of Quebec, with Hist. Recollections. Quebec, 1834. 12mo.
HAWKINS, Col. Benj. Sketch of the Creek Country in 1798–99. Ga. Hist. Soc. Coll. Vol. 3. Part 1.
HAWKINS, Caesar H. Hunterian Oration before the Royal Coll. of Surgeons, Feb. 14, 1849. Lond., 1849. 8vo. Med. Pamph. Vol. 29.
HAWKINS, Chris. See BUSHNELL, C. I. Adventures in Rev. War.
HAWKINS, Henry. Reform of Parliament the Ruin of Parliament. Lond., 1813. 8vo. Pamphleteer. Vol. 1.
HAWKINS, Rev. W. G. Life of John H.W.Hawkins. Boston, 1863, 12mo.
HAWKINS Zouave Reg't. See WHITNEY, J. H. E. Hist. of.
HAWKS, Rev. F. L. Contributions to the Eccles. Hist. of the U. States. Vol. 1. P. Episcopal Ch. in Virginia. Vol. 2. P. Episcopal Ch. in Maryland. N. Y., 1836 and 1839. 2 vols. 8vo.
—— Hist. of N. Carolina. Fayetteville, 1859. 2 Vols. 8vo.
HAWKS, Rev. Dr. Francis L. Narrative of the Expedition of an American Squadron to the China Sea and Japan in the Years 1852, 3 and 4, under Com. M. C. Perry, U. S. N. Washington, 1856. 3 Vols. 4to.
—— The Mecklenburg Declaration of Independence; a Lecture before the N. Y. Hist. Soc., Dec. 16, 1852. Revolu. Hist. of N. Carolina.
HAWKSLEY, Dr. Thos. Charities of London, and some Errours in their Administration. Lond., 1869. 8vo. Eng. Misc. Pamph. Vol. 11.
HAWLES, Sir John. The Englishman's Right; a Dialogue between a Barrister at Law and a Juryman, on the Office, etc., of Juries. Lond., 1763. 12mo. Eng. Polit. Pamph. Vol. 15A.
—— The Juryman's Preceptor, and Englishman's Right. Lond., 1812. 12mo. Law Pamph. Vol. 10.

HAWLEY, Gideon. Address before Albany Academy, Aug. 6, 1835. 8vo. Addresses. Vol. 8.

HAWLEY, Rev. Gideon. Journey to Oghquaga, in 1753. Doc. Hist. of N. York. Vol. 3.

HAWLEY, R. Remarks before Comm. of House of Repr., Mar. 14, 1872, on the Salt Duty. Washington, 1872. 8vo. Congr. and Polit. Pamph. Vol. 140.

HAWLEY, Seth C. Address before the Y. M. Assoc. of Buffalo, Mar. 22, 1836. Buffalo, 1836. 8vo. Addresses. Vol. 37.

HAWLEY, Uriah. Memoirs of Birmingham, Ohio. Fire Lands Pioneer. Vol. 2.

HAWTHORNE, Nathan'l. Life of Franklin Pierce. Boston, 1852. 12mo.

HAWTREY, Rev. Stephen. Letter with Acc. of St. Mark's School, Windsor, and Remarks on Educa. Lond., 1859. 12mo. 3d Ed. Educa. Pamph. Vol. 34.

HAY, Wm. Deformity: an Essay. Lond., 1754. 2d Ed. Med. Pamph. Vol. 21.

HAYCRAFT, Saml. Speech in Ky. Senate, Feb. 15, 1860, on the Erection of a Monument to Dan'l Boone. Louisville, 1860. 8vo. Ky. Misc. Pamph. Vol. 1.

HAYDEN Family Genealogy. See HAYDEN. J. H.

—— —— See VINTON, Rev. J. A.

HAYDEN, Dr. F. V. Contributions to the Ethnography and Philology of the Indian Tribes of the Missouri River. Trans. Amer. Philos. Soc. N. S. Vol. 12.

—— Geolog. Sketch of the Estuary and Fresh Water Deposit of the Bad Lands of the Judith, Nebraska. Amer. Philos. Soc. Trans. N. S. Vol. 11.

—— On the Geology and Nat. History of the Upper Missouri, 1861. Trans. Amer. Philos. Soc. N. S. Vol. 12.

—— U. S. Geolog. Survey of Colorado and N. Mexico. Washington, 1869. 8vo.

—— Preliminary Report of U. S. Geolog. Survey of Montana and Adjacent Territory. Washington, 1872. 8vo.

—— Preliminary Report of U. S. Geolog. Survey of Wyoming and Portions of Contiguous Territory. Washington, 1872. 8vo.

HAYDEN, J. H. Genealogy of the Hayden Family, from Stiles Hist. of Windsor, Conn. Albany, 1859. 8vo. Genealog. Pamph. Vol. 7.

HAYDEN, Sydney. Washington and his Masonic Compeers. 3d Ed. N. Y., 1866. 12mo.

HAYDN'S Dictionary of Science. Edited by G. F. Rodwell. Lond., 1871. 8vo.

HAYES, Geo. E. Geology of Buffalo, read before the Buffalo Hist. Soc., Mar. 15, 1869. Buffalo, 1869. 8vo.

—— Remarks on the Geology of Western N. York, 1836. Silliman's Journ. Vol. 31.

—— Same, 1839. Silliman's Journ. Vol. 35.

HAYES, Isaac I. Physical Observations in the Arctic Seas, 1860–1. Smithsonian Contrib. Vol. 15.

HAYES, J. D. The Niagara Ship Canal and Reciprocity. Buffalo, 1865. 8vo. N. Y. Misc. Pamph. Vol. 6.

HAYES, John L. Address before the Nat. Assoc. of Wool Manufacturers, Sept. 6, 1865. Cambridge, 1865. 8vo.

—— Protective Tariff abroad, and Remarks at the Indianapolis Convention. Cambridge, 1870. 8vo.

—— Statement of Facts relative to Canada Wools. Boston, 1866. 8vo.

HAYNE, Robert Y. Letter of, to a Committee of the State's Rights and Free Trade Party, and a Reply to Col. Drayton's late Address. Charleston, 1832. 12mo. Nullifica. Tracts.

HAYNES, D. C. The Baptist Denomination; its History, Doctrines, and Ordinances. N. Y., 1857. 12mo.

HAYTI and Liberia. Independence of. See Congress'l Speeches.

—— Papers relating to the Colonization Experiment at A'Vache, Hayti, 1864? Pamph. on Coloniza. Vol. 1.

—— See REDPATH, J. Guide to.

—— SMITH, J. Mc. C. Lecture on Haytien Revolutions.

HAYWARD, A. Remarks on the Law regarding Marriage with the Sister of a Deceased Wife. Lond., 1845. 8vo. Law Pamph. Vol. 20.

—— Report of Proceedings before the Judges, as Visitors of the Inns of Court, on his Appeal. Lond., 1848. 8vo. Strangford Pamph. Vol. 56.

HAYWARD. Annals of Queen Elizadeth. See Camden Society Publica.

HAYWARD, Chas. Life of Sebastian Cabot. Sparks Amer. Biog. 1st Ser. Vol. 9.

HAYWARD, John. N. England Gazeteer. Concord, N. H., 1839. 8vo.

HAYWOOD, John. Civil and Political Hist. of Tennessee to 1796. Knoxville, 1823. 8vo.

HAZARD, Eben. Documents extracted from his Hist. Collections, relating to N. Y. N. Y. Hist. Soc. Coll. Vol. 1.

—— Thoughts on Currency and Finance, 1863. Rebell'n Pamph. Vol. 87.

HAZARD, Erskine. History of the Introduction of Anthracite Coal into Phila., with a Letter from Jesse Fell on the Same Subject. Penn. Hist. Soc. Memoirs. Vol. 2. Part 1.

HAZARD, Rowland G. Disc. before the R. Island Hist. Soc., Jan. 18, 1848, on Chief Justice Durfee. Providence, 1848. 8vo. R. I. Hist. Soc. Addresses. Vol. 1.

—— Essay on the Philosoph. Character of Channing. Boston, 1845. 8vo. Addresses, etc. Vol. 25.

HAZARD, Saml. Annals of Penn., from the Discovery of the Delaware, 1609–82. Phila., 1850. 8vo.

—— The Register of Penn., Jan., 1828, to Dec., 1836. Phila. 16 Vols. 8vo.

HAZARD, Thos. R. Report on the Poor and Insane in R. Island, made to the Gen. Assembly, 1851. Providence, 1851. 8vo.

HAZEL Green, Wis., Collegiate Institute. 1st Ann. Catalogue, 1857. Galena, Ill., 1857. 8vo.

HAZELTON, Gerry W. Speech in Cong., Mar. 16, 1872, on the Fox and Wisconsin Rivers Improvement. Congr. and Polit. Pamph, Vol. 129.

HAZEN, Edw. Popular Technology; or Professions and Trades. Harpers' Fam. Libr. N. Y., 1859. 2 Vols. 18mo.

HAZEN, N. W. Memorial Discourse on Wm. Symmes, at Andover, 1859. Essex Institute Coll. Vol. 4.

HAZLITT, Wm. Life of Napoleon Buonaparte. 3 Vols. in 1. Phila., 1854. 8vo.

—— See Talvi's Hist. of Colonization.

HEACOCK (The) Family; Jonathan and Ann Heacock, who settled in Chester Co., Pa., in 1711, and their Descendants. n. p. 1869. 8vo. Genealog. Pamph. Vol. 2.

HEACOCK, W. J. Speech in N. Y. Legislature, Apr. 6, 1863, on a Vigorous Prosecution of the War, 1863. Rebell'n Pamph. Vol. 112.

HEAD, Sir Francis. A Faggot of French Sticks; or Paris in 1851. N. Y., 1852. 12mo.

—— A Narrative. (Canadian Affairs.) 3d Ed. Lond., 1839. 8vo.

—— Bubbles from the Brunnens of Nassau. Waldie's Circulating Libr. Vol. 4.

—— The Emigrant in Canada. 2d Ed. Lond., 1846.

—— The Life and Adventures of Jas. Bruce, the African Traveller. Harpers' Fam. Libr. N. Y., 1859. 18mo.

HEAD, Geo. Forest Scenes and Incidents in the Wilds of N. America. Lond., 1829. 12mo.

HEAD, John W. Reports of Cases Argued and Determined in the Supreme Court of Tenn. during 1858. Nashville, 1860. 2 Vols. 8vo.

HEADLEY, Joel T. Grant and Sherman; their Campaigns and Generals. N. Y., 1865. 8vo.

—— Letters from Italy, the Alps, and the Rhine. N. Y., 1854. 12mo.

—— Life of Oliver Cromwell. N. Y., 1857. 12mo.

—— Lives of Winfield Scott and Andrew Jackson. N. Y., 1852. 12mo.

—— Napoleon and His Marshals. 22d Ed. N. Y., 1858. 2 Vols. 12mo.

—— The Second War with England. N. Y., 1853. 2 Vols. 12mo.

—— The Chaplains and Clergy of the Revolution. N. Y., 1864. 12mo.

—— Washington and his Generals. N. Y., 1858. 2 Vols. 12mo.

HEADLEY, P. C. Life of Gen. Lafayete. N. Y., 1857. 12mo.

—— Life of Mary Queen of Scots. N. Y., 1858. 12mo.

—— Life of Napoleon Bonaparte. N. Y., 1858. 12mo.

—— Life of the Empress Josephine, First Wife of Napoleon. N. Y., 1858. 12mo.

HEALTH of Towns' Assoc. Address to the Inhabitants of Manchester & Salford. Lond. n. d. 8vo. Sanitary Reform Pamph. Vol. 1.

—— —— Evidence concerning the Value &c., of Metropolitan Sewage Manure. Lond., 1847. 8vo. Sanitary Reform Pamph. Vol. 1.

HEALTH of Towns' Assoc. Report of the Committee on Lord Lincoln's Bill. Lond., 1847. 8vo. Sanitary Reform Pamph. Vol. 1.

—— —— Sanitary Condition of the City of London; a Letter to Lord Ashley. Lond., 1848. 8vo. Sanitary Reform Pamph. Vol. 1.

—— Examination of the Act for establishing Cemeteries around the Metropolis. Lond., 1843. 8vo. Strangford Pamph. Vol. 31.

HEAP, G. H. Central Route to the Pacific, from the Valley of the Mississippi to the Coasts of the Pacific. Phila., 1854. 8vo.

HEARN, John. Guide to Salisbury & Vicintiy; comprising Old and New Sarum. Salisbury, Eng., 1839. 12mo. Guide Books, Vol. 18.

HEART, Jonathan. Observations on the Ancient Works of Art, etc., of the Western Country. Amer. Philos. Soc. Trans. Vol. 3.

HEAT, Internal. See Cooper, Thos. Analysis of Cordier's Essay.

—— Cordier, L. Essay on. 1828.

—— Haskins, R. W. Hypothesis of Central Heat in the Earth.

HEATH, Chas. Hist. and Descript. accounts of the Ancient and Present State of the Town and Castle of Chepstow, etc. 7th ed. Monmouth, 1821. Miscell. Tracts. Vol. 3.

HEATH, Maj. Gen. Wm. Memoirs of; with Anecdotes & Details of Skirmishes during Revolu. War. Boston, 1798. 12mo.

HEATHFIELD, Richard. Elements of a Plan for the Liquidation of the Public Debt, United Kingdom. Lond., 1820. 8vo. Pamphleteer. Vol. 15.

—— Further Observations on Liquidating the Public Debt of the United Kingdom. Lond., 1820. 8vo. 2d ed. Pamphleteer. Vol. 16.

—— Addenda to his Second Pamphlet on the Liquidation of the Public Debt. Lond., 1820. 8vo. Pamphleteer. Vol. 17.

—— Observations on the Public Debt, and on Agriculture, Trade, etc., of the United Kingdom. Lond., 1822. 8vo. Pamphleteer. Vol. 20.

HEBER, Reginald. Narr. of a Jour. Through the Upper Provinces of India, from Calcutta to Bombay. 1824–5. Phila., 1829. 2 Vols. 8vo.

HEBERLE, J. M. Bibliotheca Historica. Katalog. des Historischen Bucher—Lagers. Koln, 1855. 8vo.

HEBREW Chronology. See Michaelis, J. D.

—— Grammar. Lond., 1785. 8vo. Educa. Pamph. Vol. 40.

—— —— See Pinnock's Catechism.

HEBRIDES. See JOHNSON, S. Voyage to.

HERRON Cemetery Assoc. Washington, N. Y. By-Laws, Rules, etc. Albany, 1872. 8vo. N. Y. Misc. Pamph. Vol. 7.

HECKEWELDER, Rev. John. Names which the Delaware Indians had given to Rivers, Streams, Places, etc.; also Names of Indian Chiefs, with Biographical Sketches. Amer. Philos. Soc. Trans. N. S. Vol. 4.

HECKEWELDER, Rev. John. Narr. of the Mission of the United Brethren among the Delaware and Mohegan Indians from 1740 to 1808. Phila., 1820. 8vo.

—— See RAWLE, Wm. Vindica. of his Hist. of the Indian Nations.

—— RONDTHALER, Rev. E. Life of.

HEDGE, Rev. F. H. Disourse at Brookline, Mass., Sept. 26, 1861. Rebell'n Pamph. Vol. 102.

—— Memoir of N. L. Frothingham, D.D. Mass. Hist. Soc. Proceed. 1869-70.

HEDGE, Prof. Levi. Eulogy on Jos. McKean, D. D., before the University at Cambridge, April 22, 1818. Cambridge, 1818. 8vo. Harvard Coll. Pamph.

HEDINGER, J. M. Short Description of Castleton, in Derbyshire. Stockport, Eng., 1824. 12mo. Guide-Books. Vol. 7.

HEERMANS, J. War Powers of the President. N. Y., 1863. 8vo. Rebell'n Pamph. Vols. 15 and 90.

HELE, Rev. Rich'd. Notice of. Lond., 1844. 12mo. Biograph. Pamph. Vol. 4. Hist. Pamph. Vol. 19.

HELLWALD, Fred. Von. The American Migration. Smithsonian Report. 1866.

HELPER, Hinton R. Compendium of the Impending Crisis of the South. N. Y., 1860. 12mo. Rebellion Pamph. Vols. 11, 21.

HELPS, Arthur. Hist. of Christopher Columbus, the Discoverer of America. Lond., 1869, 12mo.

—— Life of Las Casas, the Apostle of the Indies. Phila., 1868. 12mo.

—— Life of Pizarro: with some Account of his Associates in the Conquest of Peru. 2d Ed. Lond., 1869. 12mo.

—— The Spanish Conquest in America; and its relation to the Hist. of Slavery. Lond., 1855. 4 Vols. 8vo.

HEMANS, Felicia. Memoir of her Life and Writings, by her Sister; with an Essay on her Genius by Mrs. Sigourney. N. Y., 1855. 12mo.

—— Sketch of Life of. Western Monthly Mag. Vol. 3.

HEMENWAY, Abby M. Vermont Quarterly Gazetteer; a Hist. Magazine. 5 Nos. Ludlow. 1860-63.

—— Vermont His. Gazetteer. Vol. 1. 11 Nos., comprising the Counties of Addison, Bennington, Caledonia Chittenden and Essex. Burlington, Vt., 1860. 1868.

—— Same. Nos. 12–24, embracing the Co's of Franklin and Grand Isle, Lamoille and Orange. Burlington, 1871. 8vo.

HEMP for the Navy. Report of Comm. of U. S. House of R. on Proposals of G. W. Billings. Washington, 1850. 8vo. Congr. and Polit. Pamph. Vol. 58.

HEMPSTEAD, N. Y., St. George's Church. See HART, Rev. Seth. Sermcn, with Hist. Sketch, etc. 1823.

HENDERSON, J. B. Speech in Cong., Mar. 27, 1862, on Slavery. Rebell'n Pamph. Vol. 7.

—— Speech in Cong., Feb. 13 and 14, 1866, on Apportionment. Congr. and Polit. Pamph. Vol. 121.

HENDERSON, Thos. Hints on the Medical Examination of Recruits for the Army. Phila., 1840. 8vo.

HENDERSON, Thos. J. Official Report of the Trial of Hon. Albert Jackson, Judge of 15th Judicial Circuit of Missouri. Jefferson, 1859. 8vo.

HENDERSON, Wm. A. Lecture to the Knoxville Board of Trade, Jan. 7, 1873, on Gov. John Sevier. Knoxville, Tenn., 1873. 8vo. Tenn. Misc. Pamph. Vol. 1.

HENDRICKSON, John, Jr. See WELLS, D. A.

HENDRY, A. W. Early Polit. Divisions of the Fire Lands; with a Sketch of Early Laws. Fire Lands Pioneer. Vol. 3.

HENING, Wm. W. Statutes at Large; being a Collection of all the Laws of Virginia, from 1619 to 1793. N. Y. & Phila., 1823. 13 vols. 8vo.

HENKLE, M. M. Address before Transylvania University on the Dignity and Claims of Agricult. Science. Frankfort, 1843. 8vo. Agr. Pamph. Vol. 1.

HENNEPIN Co., Minn. See STEVENS, J. H. Early Hist. of.

HENNEPIN, Louis. Acc. of the River Mississippi, with an Acc. of M. de la Salle's undertaking to discover said River by way of the Gulf of Mexico. See French's Hist. Coll., La. Vol. 1.

—— Description de la Louisiane, Nouvelle Decouverte au Sud-Ouest de la Nouvelle France. Paris, 1683. 12mo.

—— Same. Paris, 1688. 12mo.

—— Discovery of the River Mississippi and the adjacent Country. Amer. Antiq. Soc. Coll. Vol. 1.

—— Nouvelle Decouverte d'un tres grand pays situè dans l'Amerique entre le Nouveau-Mexique et la Mer Glaciale. Utrecht, 1697. 12mo.

—— New Discovery of a Vast Country in America; with a continuation, embracing De la Salle's Attempts upon the Mines of St. Barbe. Lond., 1698. 12mo.

—— See SHEA, J. G. Discovery of Mississippi River.

HENNEQUIN, Amedee. La Suisse en 1847. Paris, 1848. 8vo. Strangford Pamph. Vol. 59.

HENNINGSEN, C. F. Letter in Reply to Victor Hugo on the Harpers Ferry Invasion. 1860. Rebell'n Pamph. Vol. 17.

—— The Past and Future of Hungary. Cincin., 1852. 8vo. Hist. Pamph. Vol. 1.

HENRY IV. of France. Memoirs of the Court of France during his Reign. London, 1824. 2 vols. 8vo.

HENRY VIII. of England. See HERBERT, Edw. Life and Reign of.

—— Love Letters of Henry VIII. and Anna Boleyn.

HENRY of Monmouth. See TYLER, J. Endell. Life and Character of.

HENRY, Prince of Portugal. See MAJOR, R. H. Life of.

HENRY, Alex. Narrative of his Captivity by the Indians. (Included in Schoolcraft's Amer. Indians.)

—— Travels and Adventures in Canada and the Indian Territories, between 1760 and 1776. N. Y., 1809. 8vo.

HENRY, C. S., D.D. Disc. before the Literary Societies of Geneva College, Aug. 5, 1840. N. Y., 1840. 8vo. Addresses, etc., Vol. 36.

—— Epitome of the Hist. of Philosophy. Harpers' Fam. Libr. N. Y., 1859. 2 Vols. 18mo.

—— Patriotism and the Slaveholders' Rebellion. An Oration. N. Y., 1861. 8vo. Rebell'n Pamph., Vol. 62.

HENRY, Dr. Jas. Dialogue between a Bilious Patient and a Physician. Lond., 1843. 8vo. Med. Pamph., Vol. 18.

HENRY, J. Sketches of Moravian Life. Phila., 1859. 8vo.

HENRY, Jas., Jr. Address upon Education and Common Schools, at Cooperstown, Sept. 21, 1843. Albany, 1843. 8vo. Addresses, Vol. 15.

HENRY, John J. Hardships and Sufferings of the Heroes who traversed the Wilderness in the Quebec Campaign of 1775. Lancaster, Pa., 1812. 12mo.

HENRY, Prof. Jos. Acc. of the Smithsonian Institution; read before the Amer. Assoc. for the Advancement of Educa., Aug. 10, 1853. Newark, 1854. 8vo. Addresses, Vol. 15.

—— Eulogy on Prof. Alex. Dallas Bache. Smithsonian Report, 1870.

HENRY, J. P. Resources of the State of Arkansas, with Descrip. of Counties, Railroads and the City of Little Rock. Little Rock, 1872. 8vo. Ark. Misc. Pamph., Vol. 1.

HENRY, Patrick. See ALEXANDER, Arch'd. Reminiscences of.

—— EVERETT, A. H. Life of.

—— TATOR, H. H. Oration on.

—— WIRT, Wm. Life and Character.

HENRY, Capt. W. S. Campaign Sketches of the War with Mexico. N. Y., 1847. 12mo.

HENSER, P. Praktisches Handbuck sur rauflente. Elberfeld. 1851 8vo.

HENSHALL, Sam'l. Domesday; or an Actual Survey of South Britain. Part I. Kent, Sussex and Surrey. London, 1799. 4to.

—— Hist. of the Co. of Kent, Eng. Lond. 1798. 4to.

HENSHAW, Joshua. Sketch of the Life of. N. Eng. Hist. and Gen. Reg. Vol. 22.

HENSLOW, J. S. Address to Landlords on the Establishment of a Spade Tenantry from Among the Labouring Classes. Lond., 1845. 8vo.

HENSON, Josiah. His Life, as Narrated by Himself. Boston, 1849. 12mo. Biograph. Pamph. Vol. 5.

HEPWORTH, Rev. Geo. H. Disc. on the Death of Rev. Theo. Parker. Boston, 1860. Sermons. Vols. 3 and 44.

—— The Whip, Hoe and Sword, in 1863. Boston, 1864. 12mo.

HERALD of the New Jerusalem. Vol. 1. 1854. N. Y., 12mo.

HERALDIC JOURNAL. Boston, 1865–68. 4 Vols. 8vo.

HERALDRY. See ANDERSON, W. Notes on Heraldry.

—— Arms of Goodwin and Bradbury.

—— Book of Family Crests.

—— BOUTELLE, Chas. English Heraldry.

HERALDRY. BURKE, Sir B. Dict. of Landed Gentry of G. B.
—— —— Geneal. and Herald. Dict. of British Peerage.
—— BURKE, J. & J. B. Dict. of Extinct Baronetcies.
—— —— Encyclopædia of.
—— —— Heraldic Illustrations.
—— ELLIS, W. G. Plea for Antiquity of.
—— GRAZEBROOK, H. S. Heraldry of Smith.
—— LOWER, M. A. Curiosities of.
—— MEYRICK, S. R. Welsh Heraldry.
—— Miscellanea Genealogica et Heraldica.
—— SLOANE—Evans W. S. Grammar of.
—— WHITMORE, W. H. Elements of.
—— See Genealogy.

HERBERT, A. Cyclops Christianus; an Argument to disprove the supposed Antiquity of Stonehenge and other Methalithic Erections in England. Lond., 1849. 8vo.

HERBERT, Edw. Lord. The Life and Reign of King Henry the 8th. n. d. Lond., 1650, folio.

HERBERT, Rev. Geo. See WALTON, Isaac.

HERBERT, Henry W. Captains of the Old World. N. Y., 1852. 12mo.

—— Captains of the Roman Republic, as compared with the Great Modern Strategists. N. Y., 1854. 12mo.

—— Memoirs of Henry the 8th of England, with the Fortunes and Character of his Six Wives. N. Y., 1858. 12mo.

—— The Cavaliers of England; or Times of the Revolutions of 1642 & 1688. 2d Ed. N. Y., 1852. 12mo.

HERBERT, Sidney. Sanitary Condition of the Army, from the Westminster Review for Jan., 1859. Lond. 8vo. Eng. Polit. Pamph. Vol. 56.

HERCULANEUM Rolls. Correspondence relative to a Proposition made by Dr. Sickler, on their Development. Lond., 1817. 4to. Pamphlet.

HERDMAN, Dr. John. History and Statutes of the Royal Infirmary of Edinburgh. Edinburgh, 1778. 4to. Med. Pamph. Vol. 28.

HEREFORD, Eng. See DEVLIN, J. D. Helps to Hereford History, 1848.

—— DUNCOMB, J. Hist. and Antiq. of.

HERIOT, Geo. Hist. of Canada from its First Discovery. Lond., 1844. 8vo.

—— Travels through the Canadas, with Acc. of the Products, Commerce and Inhabitants of those Provinces, also a View of the Manners and Customs of Indian Nations. Lond., 1807. 4to.

HERKIMER, Co. N. York. See BENTON, N. S. Hist. of.

HERMES, Brittanicus. See BOWLES, Rev. W. L. Celtic Deity Tentates.

HERNDON, Lieut. Wm. L. Report of the Exploration of the Valley of Amazon. 2 Vols., and 2 Vols. Maps. Washington, 1853. 8vo.

HEROIC Incidents of the Civil War in America, 1862. Rebell'n Pamph., Vol. 76.

HEROINES of History. See HEWITT, M. E.

HERON, Robt. M. Industry for Ireland founded upon a System of Local Superintendence. Lond., n. d. 8vo. Strangford Pamph. Vol. 49.

HERPETOLOGY. See BAIRD, S. F. Cat. of N. A. Reptiles.

—— LEIDY, J. Cretaceous Reptiles of the U. S.

——STANSBURY, H. Append. to Expedition to Gr. Salt Lake.

HERRICK, Jedediah. Geneal. Register of the Family of Herrick, 1629–1846. Bangor, 1846. 8vo.

HERRICK, W. B. Remedial Properties of Alimentary Substances. Chicago, 1851. 8vo. Med. Pamph. Vol. 4.

HERRING, Jas., and LONGACRE, J. B. Nat. Portrait Gallery of Distinguished Americans. N. Y., 1834. 4 Vols. 8vo.

HERTFORD, Eng. See TURNOR, L. Hist. of. 1830.

HERTZ, Henry. Case of, in U. S. Dist. Court at Phila. Phila., 1855. 8vo. Law Pamph. Vol. 5.

HERVEY, Rev. Jas. See ROMAINE, Rev. Wm. Sermon on his Death.

—— The Works of. With Acc. of his Life, Character and Writings. Lond., 1807. 6 Vols. 8vo.

—— The Whole Works of. With a Memoir. Lond., 1819. 6 Vols. 12 mo.

HARVEY, Jas. B. Catalogue of his Private Library. N. Y., 1870. 8vo. Bibliograph. Pamph. Vol. 61.

HERSCHEL, Wm. See ARAGO, Francis. Memoir of.

HERSEY, Chas. Reminiscences of the Military Life and Sufferings of Col. Tim. Bigelow. Worcester, 1860. 8vo. Biograph. Pamph. Vol. 7.

HERTFORDSHIRE, Eng. See BERRY, W. Pedigrees of.

HERVEY, Rev. Henry M. Hist. Sketches of the Presb. Churches, (O. S.) in Licking Co., Ohio ; read before the Licking Co. Pioneer Assoc. Licking Co. Pioneer Addresses. Newark., O., 1869. 8vo.

HESPERIAN (The). Edited by Mrs. F. H. DAY, containing Sketches of Early Settlers of California. Vol. 2. San Francisco, 1859. 8vo.

—— Magazine. Columbus, O., 1838. 2 vols. 8vo.

HEUSCHLING, X. Bibliographie Historique de la Statistique en France. Brusselles, 1851. 4to.

—— Same. —— En Allemagne. Brusselles. 1845. 4to.

—— Essai sur la Statistique Génerale de la Belgique. Supplement. Brusselles, 1844. 4to.

—— Le Baron de Reiffenberg ; Notice Biographique. Cologne, 1850. 8vo.

—— Notice Biographique sur Guillaume Benjamin Craan. Cologne, 1850. 8vo.

HEWINS Genealogy. See MORSE, A.

HEWITT, Abram S. Statistics and Geography of the Production of Iron ; Paper read before the Amer. Geogr. and Statist. Soc., 1856.

HEWITT, Mary E. Heroines of History. N. Y., 1857. 12mo.

HEYWOOD, J. H., and BARRETT, S. F. Discourses on the Death of Jas. H. Perkins. Cincin., 1850. 8vo.

HEYWORTH, Lawrence. Fiscal Policy. Direct and Indirect Taxation, contrasted. Liverpool, n. d. 8vo. Eng. Polit. Pamph. Vol. 45.

—— Economic Fiscal Legislation. Lond., 1845. 8vo. Eng. Polit. Pamph. Vol. 45.

H. H. D. Betrayal of the Cause of Freedom, by Hon. W. SEWARD, Sec. of State. Broadside, 1866. Rebell'n Pamph. Vol. 9.

HIBBARD, Rev. B. Memoir of Life and Travels. N. Y., 1843. 12mo.

HIBERNIAN Magazine ; or Compendium of Entertaining Knowledge. 1783—1787. Dublin. 2 vols. 8vo.

—— 1774 and 1784. Defective. 1 vol. 8vo.

—— Society (London) for Establishing Schools, etc. Ann. Reports. Lond., 1808, 1814, 1815. 8vo. Educa. Pamph. Vol. 28.

HICKCOX J. H. Hist. Acc. Amer. Coinage. Albany, 1858. 8vo.

—— Hist. of Bills of Credit or Paper Money issued by N. Y. 1709–1789. Albany, 1866. 8vo. See also Albany Trans. Vol. 5.

HICKEY. Jos.—See Letter on His Acquital, etc. 1751.

HICKEY, W. Constitution of the U. States. Declaration of Independence. Articles of Confederation. Electorial Votes for Presidents, etc. 6th Ed. Phila., 1853. 12mo.

—— Same. 7th Ed. Phila., 1854.

HICKOK, Laurens P. Rational Cosmology, or Eternal Princlples and Necessary Laws of the Universe. N. Y., 1858. 8vo.

—— System of Moral Science. 3d Ed. N. Y., 1858. 12mo.

HICKS, Elias. Acc. of his Life, Ministry, Last Sickness, and Death. n. d. 8vo. Religious Pamph. Vol. 5.

HICKS, Matt., and JENKINS, Peter. Pseud. Letters to Isaac Tomkins, on his " Thoughts upon the Aristocracy." Lond., 1835. 8vo. Eng. Polit. Pamph. Vol. 41.

HIEROGLYPHICS. See Rosetta Stone.

HIGGINS, Jas., M. D. 3d Report as Agricultural Chemist of Maryland. Baltimore, 1853. 8vo. Md. Misc. Pamph. Vol. 1.

HIGGINS, W. Mullinger. The Earth: Its Physical Condition and Remarkable Phenomena. Harpers Fam. Libr. N. Y., 1858. 18mo.

HIGGINSON Letters. Mass. Hist. Soc. Coll. 3d Ser. Vol. 7.

HIGGINSON, Rev. Francis. See FELT, J. B. Memoir of.

HIGGINSON, Thos. W. Ought Woman to Learn the Alphabet? Boston, 1869. 12mo. Congr. and Polit. Pamph. Vol. 128.

—— Woman and her Wishes; an Essay. Boston, 1853. 8vo. Congr. and Polit. Pamph. Vol. 128.

HIGHER (The), Law tried by Reason and Authority. N. Y., 1851. 8vo. Law Pamph. Vol. 9.

HIGHLAND Immigration. See CALLAGHAN, E. B. A.

HIGHLANDS. Geology of the. See PIERCE, Jas.

—— of New Hampshire. See Excursion to.

HILDEBRAND. See KING, Rev. T. Starr. Lecture on. 1857.

HILDRETH, Rich'd. Archy Moore, the White Slave; or Memoirs of a Fugitive. N. Y., 1857. 12mo.

—— Despotism in America. Boston, 1854. 12mo.

HILDRETH, Rich'd. Hist. of the U. States of America. N. Y., 1854. 6 Vols. 8vo.

—— Lives of Atrocious Judges; with Appendix containing the Case of Passmore Williamson. N. Y., 1856. 12mo.

HILDRETH, Sam'l P. Facts relating to certain Parts of Ohio; in Answer to Inquiries of Caleb Atwater. 1819. Silliman's Journ. Vols. 10, 11.

—— Geology, Minerology, Topography, &c., of Parts of Ohio. Letter to Caleb Atwater, 1819. Silliman's Journ. Vol. 10.

—— Journal of some Emigrants from N. Eng. to Muskingum, in 1788. Amer. Pioneer. Vol. 2.

—— History of a Voyage from Marietta to N. Orleans, in 1805. Amer. Pioneer. Vol. 1.

—— Biograph. and Hist. Memoirs of Early Pioneer Settlers of Ohio, with Narratives of Occurrences in 1775.

——Biograph. Sketches of Early Physicians of Marietta, Ohio. N. E. Hist. & Gen. Reg. Vol. 3.

—— Brief Hist. of the Floods in the Ohio River from 1772 to 1832. Ohio Hist. Soc. Journ. Part 1, Vol. 1.

—— Contribution to the Early Hist. of the N. West, including the Moravian Missions in Ohio. Cincin. 1864. 16mo.

——Observations on the Bituminous Coal Deposits & Geology of of the Valley of the Ohio. 1836. Silliman's Journ. Vol. 29

—— Observations on the Climate and Productions of Washington Co., Ohio. 1827. Silliman's Journ. Vol. 12.

—— Pioneer History: Acc. of the first Examination of the Ohio Valley, and the Early Settlement of the N. West Territory. Cincin., 1848. 8vo.

—— Results of Meterol. Observa. made at Marietta, Ohio, 1826–1859. Smithsonian Contrib. Vol. 16.

HILDYARD, Rev. Jas. The University System of Private Tuition examined, etc. Two Papers. 1844, 1845. Lond., 8vo. Educa. Pamph. Vol. 31.

HILL, Dr. The Story of Elizabeth CANNING considered. Lond., 1853. 8vo. Eng. Misc. Pamph. Vol. 25.

HILL, Alonzo, D. D. Disc. on the Life & Character of Rev. Aaron BANCROFT, at Worcester, Mass., Aug. 22, 1838. Worcester, 1839 8vo. Sermons. Vol. 30.

—— Disc. on the Life & Character of Rev. Nathaniel THAYER, at Lancaster, Mass., June 29, 1840 Worcester 1840. Sermons. Vol. 39.

—— Sermon at Worcester, Mass., Apr. 23, 1854, on the Death of Hon. John DAVIS. N. Y., 1854. 8vo. Sermons. Vol. 51.

—— Sermon at Worcester, Mass., Mar. 28, 1867, on the 40th Annivers. of his Settlement. Cambridge, 1867. 8vo.

HILL, Arthur. Hints on Discipline, appropriate to Schools. Lond., 1855. 8vo. Educa. Pamph. Vol. 29.

HLLL, A. J. Constantine Beltrami. Minn. Hist. Soc. Coll. Vol. 2.

—— The Geography of Perrot; so far as it relates to Minn. and adjacent Regions. Minn. Hist. Soc. Coll. Vol. 2.

HILL, Geo. C. Daniel Boone, the Pioneer of Kentucky. A Biography. Phil'a., 1863. 12mo.

HILL, Geo. C. Benedict ARNOLD. A Biography. Boston, 1858. 12mo.
—— Capt. John SMITH,. A Biography. Boston, 1858. 12mo.
—— Gen. Isræl PUTNAM. A Biography. Boston, 1858. 12mo.
HILL, Hamilton A., & others. Arguments in favor of the Freedom of Immigration at the Port of Boston. Boston, 1871. 8vo Boston Miscell. Pamph. Vol. 3.
—— Commercial Associations; their Uses & Opportunities. Boston, 1869. 8vo. Pamphlets. Vol. 13.
—— Relations of the Business Men of the U. S., to the National Legislation. Boston, 1870. 8vo. Congr. & Polit Pamph. Vol. 128.
—— Steam Navigation between Boston and Europe. 1867 Scientific Pamph. Vol. 15.
HILL, Ira. Antiquities of America Explained Hagerstown, 1831. 8vo.
HILL, J. B. Hist. of the Town of Mason, N. H. 1749–1858. Boston, 1858. 8vo.
HILL, Joshua. His. Union Record: a Letter in reply to his Enemies. Washington, 1870. 8vo. Congr. & Polit. Pamph. Vol. 120.
—— Letter on the Election of U. S. Senators. Madison, Ga., 1866. 12mo. Cong. and Polit. Pamph. Vol. 74.
HILL, L. L. Photographic Researches and Manipulations. N. Y., 1851. 8vo. Scientific Pamph. Vol. 14.
HILL, Mark L. Acc. of the Lithgow Family. Maine Hist. Soc. Coll. Vol. 5.
HILL, Nicholas. Argument in the Albany Bridge Case, before U. S. Circuit Court, N. Y., Sept., 1858. Albany, 1859. 8vo. Law Pamph. Vol. 8.
HILL, Rev. Rowland. Serious Investigation of the Nature and Effects of Parochial Assessments on Places of Worship. Lond., 1811. 8vo. Eng. Polit. Pamph. Vol. 31.
—— See SIDNEY, E. Sketch of Life of.
HILL, Rev. Thos. Address before the Phi Beta Kappa Soc. of Harvard Coll., July 22, 1858. Cambridge, 1858. 8vo. Harvard Coll. Pamph.
—— Ann. Address before the Harvard Nat. Hist. Soc., May 19, 1853. Cambridge, 1853. 8vo. Harvard Coll. Pamph.
—— Religion in Public Instruction: Baccalaureate Address at Antioch College, June 20, 1860. Boston. 8vo. Antioch Coll. Pamph.
HILLARD, George S. Life of Capt. John Smith. Spark's Amer. Biog. 1st Ser. Vol. 2.
—— Memoir of C. C. Felton. Mass. Hist. Soc. Proceed., 1867–69.
—— Memoir of Jos. Story, LL. D. Mass. Hist. Soc. Proceed., 1867–69.
HILLARY, Sir Wm. Appeal for the Formation of a Nat. Institution for Preservation from Shipwreck. Lond., 1824. 8vo. 2d Ed. Pamphleteer. Vol. 23.
—— Plan for the Construction of a Steam Life Boat. Lond., 1825. 8vo. 2d Ed. Pamphleteer. Vol. 25.

HILLARY, Sir Wm. Sketch of Ireland in 1824: the Source of her evils considered. Lond., 1825. 8vo. 2d Ed. Pamphleteer. Vol. 25.

—— Suggestions for the Improvement and Embellishment of the Metropolis Lond., 1824. 8vo. Pamph. Vol. 24.

HILLHOUSE, Jas. Speech in Cong., Nov. 29, 1808, on the Embargo. Cong. and Polit. Pamph. Vol. 123.

HILLHOUSE, Jas. A. Oration at N. Haven, Aug. 19, 1834, in Commem. of Gen. La Fayette. N. Haven, 1834. 8vo. Addresses. Vol. 31.

HILLIARD, G. S. Life and Campaigns of Gen. Geo. B. McClellan. Phila., 1865. 12mo.

HILLIARD, H. W. Speech in Cong., Jan. 6, 1846, on the Oregon Question. Cong. and Polit. Pamph., Vol. 139. Speeches, Vol. 1.

—— Speech in Cong., Aug. 28, 1850, on the Texas Boundary. Cong. and Polit. Pamph., Vol. 83.

HILLSBOROUGH & Cincin. R. R. Co. See BALDWIN, W. H.

HILLSBOROUGH Co., N. H. See FARMER, J. Notes on.

HILTON, Wm. Relation of a Discovery made on the Coast of Florida, 1664. See FORCE's Hist. Tracts, Vol. 4.

HINHCLIFFE, Henry John. Proposal of a Method for Abridging Conveyances, etc. Lond., 1833. 8vo. Law Pamph., Vol. 18.

HINCHLIFFE, John. Speech in Ill. Legisla. on Protection to Miners, Feb. 15, 1872. Springfield, 1872. 8vo. Ill. Misc. Pamph., Vol. 2.

HINCKLEY Genealogy. See MESSINGER, G. W.

HINCKLEY, Thos. Letters and Papers. 1676-1679. Mass. Hist. Soc. Coll., Vol. 5, 4th Ser.

HIND, Henry Y. Narr. of the Canadian Red River Exploring Expedition, 1857. Lond., 1860. 2 Vols. 8vo.

HIND, J. Russell. The Solar System; a Treatise on the Sun, Moon and Stars. N. Y., 1852. 8vo. Scientific Pamph., Vol. 10.

HINDERWELL, Thos. Hist. and Antiquities of Scarborough, Eng., and Vicinity, 2d Ed. York, 1811. 8vo.

HINDOOS. See WARD, F. D. W. India and Hindoos.

HINDOSTAN. See SCRAFTON, Luke. Reflections on the Govt. of, etc.

HINDU Philosophy. See HOISINGTON, H. R.

—— Worship. See MORTON, Rev. W.

HINE, L. A. Progress-Pamphlets, (Part 2d) Science and Man. Cincin., O., 1853. 8vo. Scientific Pamph., Vol. 21.

HINES, David T. Life, Adventures and Opinions; Letters to Friends in S. Carolina. N. Y., 1840. 12mo.

HINES, Rev. Gustavus. History of the Oregon Mission; Adventures among the Indians, West of the Rocky Mts. Buffalo, 1850. 12mo.

—— Oregon; its History, Condition and Prospects. Buffalo, 1851. 12mo.

HINGHAM, Mass. Agricult. and Horticultural Soc'y Transactions. 1858—1861. Boston, 1861. 8vo. Agr. Pamph. Vol. 13.

—— See GAY, Rev. E. Discourse on his 85th Birthday, 1781.

HINGHAM, Mass. RICHARDSON, Rev. Joseph. Semi-Centen. Sermon, 1856.

—— STEARNS, O. Address at Dedication of Loring Hall, 1852.

HINMAN, Royal R. Catalogue of the First Puritan Settlers of the Colony of Conn. Nos. 1–5. Hartford, 1852–6. 8vo. Another Ed. Hartford, 1846. 8vo. With an Index.

—— Family Record of Descendants of Serg't Edw. Hinman, of Stratford, Conn., 1650. Hartford, 1856. 8vo.

—— Hist. Collection from Official Records, Files, etc., of the part Sustained by Conn., in the War of the Revolution. Hartford, 1842. 8vo.

HINMAN, Rev. S. D. Journal as Missionary to the Santee Sioux Indians, and Taopi, by Bishop Whipple. Phila., 1869. 12mo. Indian Pamph. Vol. 2.

HINTON, John Howard. Hist. and Topog. of the U. S. of N. America, with additions, &c., by Sam'l L. Knapp and John O. Choules. Boston, 1846. 2 Vols. 4to.

HINTS for the Cultivation of the Peat Bogs in Ireland, in a Letter to the Rev. T. Malthus. Lond., 1816. 8vo. Pamphleteer, Vol. 9.

—— on the Present State of the Question, relative to the Renewal of the East India Co.'s Charter. Lond., 1813. 8vo. Pamphleteer, Vol. 2.

—— on the Unlimited Diffusion of Useful Knowledge. Edinburgh, 1834. 8vo. Eng. Misc. Pamph. Vol. 29.

—— to People in Power on the Present Melancholy Situation of our Colonies in N. America. Lond., 1783. 8vo.

HISTORIE de la Conqueste de la Floride par les Espagnols sous Ferdinand de Soto. Paris, 1685. 18mo.

—— du Fils d'un Roi, Prisonnier a la Bastille, trouvee sous les debris de cette Foretresse. Paris, 1789. 12mo. Biograph. Pamph. Vol. 14.

—— du Parlement de Tournay. See PINAULT, M.

—— Naturelle et Politique, et de l'Establishmet des Quakers dans cette contree traduite de l'allemand. Paris, 1768. 2 Vols. 12mo.

HISTORIAE Romanae Epitomae. Amsterdam, 1630. 18mo.

HISTORIC Society of Lancashire and Cheshire. Proceedings and Papers. Liverpool, 1848–1854. 7 vols. 8vo.

—— —— Transactions. Lond. and Liverpool, 1855–1864. 10 vols. 8vo.

HISTORICAL Account of the Antiquity and Unity of the Britanick Churches. Lond., 1692. 4to. Eng. Rel. Pamph. Vol. 8.

—— —— of the Circumnavigation of the Globe, and the Progress of Discovery in the Pacific. Harpers' Fam. Lib., 1859. 18mo.

—— —— of the Rise and Progress of the Colonies of S. Carolina and Georgia. 2 vols. in 1. Lond., 1779. 8vo.

—— and Descriptive Acc. of Iceland, Greenland and the Faroe Islands. Harpers' Fam. Libr. N. Y., 1854. 18mo.

—— and Literary Curiosities. See SMITH, J. J.

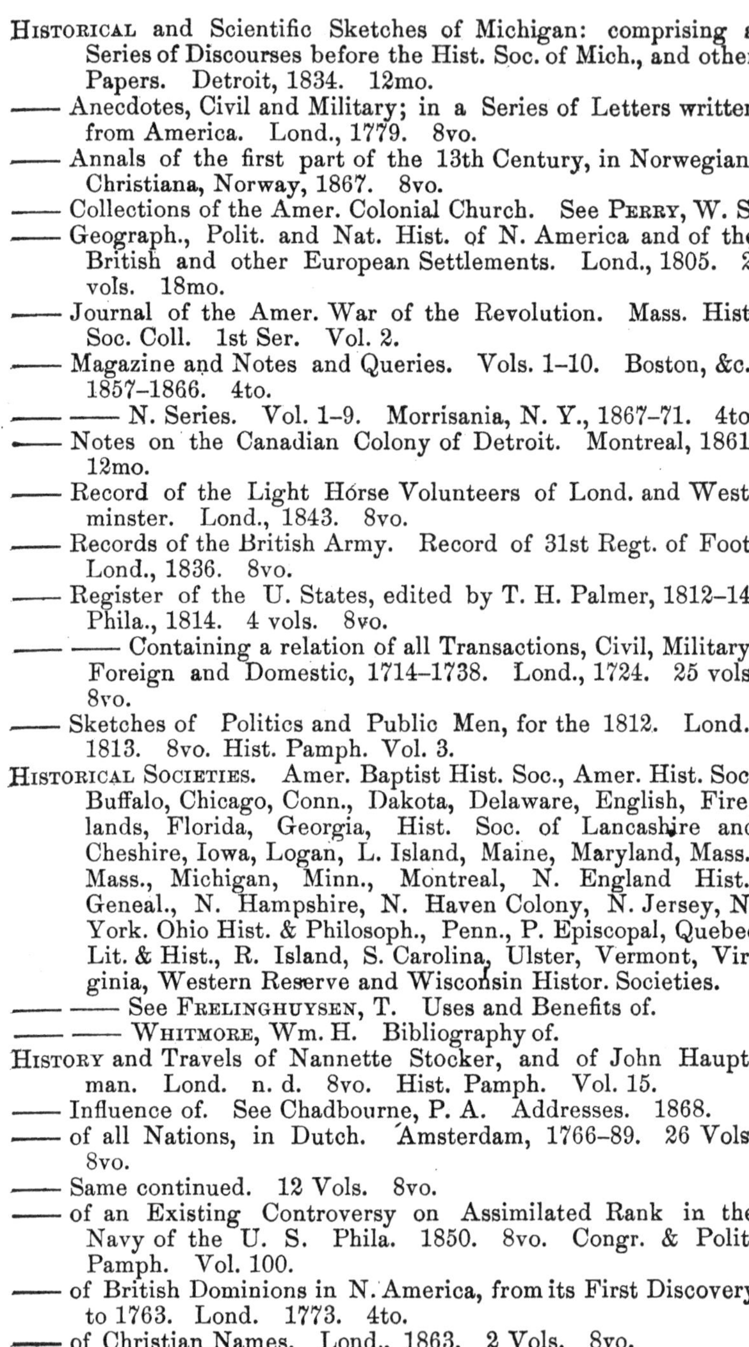

HISTORICAL and Scientific Sketches of Michigan: comprising a Series of Discourses before the Hist. Soc. of Mich., and other Papers. Detroit, 1834. 12mo.

—— Anecdotes, Civil and Military; in a Series of Letters written from America. Lond., 1779. 8vo.

—— Annals of the first part of the 13th Century, in Norwegian. Christiana, Norway, 1867. 8vo.

—— Collections of the Amer. Colonial Church. See PERRY, W. S.

—— Geograph., Polit. and Nat. Hist. of N. America and of the British and other European Settlements. Lond., 1805. 2 vols. 18mo.

—— Journal of the Amer. War of the Revolution. Mass. Hist. Soc. Coll. 1st Ser. Vol. 2.

—— Magazine and Notes and Queries. Vols. 1–10. Boston, &c., 1857–1866. 4to.

—— —— N. Series. Vol. 1–9. Morrisania, N. Y., 1867–71. 4to.

—— Notes on the Canadian Colony of Detroit. Montreal, 1861. 12mo.

—— Record of the Light Hórse Volunteers of Lond. and Westminster. Lond., 1843. 8vo.

—— Records of the British Army. Record of 31st Regt. of Foot. Lond., 1836. 8vo.

—— Register of the U. States, edited by T. H. Palmer, 1812–14. Phila., 1814. 4 vols. 8vo.

—— —— Containing a relation of all Transactions, Civil, Military, Foreign and Domestic, 1714–1738. Lond., 1724. 25 vols. 8vo.

—— Sketches of Politics and Public Men, for the 1812. Lond., 1813. 8vo. Hist. Pamph. Vol. 3.

HISTORICAL SOCIETIES. Amer. Baptist Hist. Soc., Amer. Hist. Soc. Buffalo, Chicago, Conn., Dakota, Delaware, English, Firelands, Florida, Georgia, Hist. Soc. of Lancashire and Cheshire, Iowa, Logan, L. Island, Maine, Maryland, Mass., Mass., Michigan, Minn., Montreal, N. England Hist.-Geneal., N. Hampshire, N. Haven Colony, N. Jersey, N. York. Ohio Hist. & Philosoph., Penn., P. Episcopal, Quebec Lit. & Hist., R. Island, S. Carolina, Ulster, Vermont, Virginia, Western Reserve and Wisconsin Histor. Societies.

—— —— See FRELINGHUYSEN, T. Uses and Benefits of.

—— —— WHITMORE, Wm. H. Bibliography of.

HISTORY and Travels of Nannette Stocker, and of John Hauptman. Lond. n. d. 8vo. Hist. Pamph. Vol. 15.

—— Influence of. See Chadbourne, P. A. Addresses. 1868.

—— of all Nations, in Dutch. Amsterdam, 1766–89. 26 Vols. 8vo.

—— Same continued. 12 Vols. 8vo.

—— of an Existing Controversy on Assimilated Rank in the Navy of the U. S. Phila. 1850. 8vo. Congr. & Polit. Pamph. Vol. 100.

—— of British Dominions in N. America, from its First Discovery to 1763. Lond. 1773. 4to.

—— of Christian Names. Lond., 1863. 2 Vols. 8vo.

HISTORY of Congress from May 4, 1789 to March 3, 1793. Phila., 1843. 8vo.
—— —— See WHEELER, H. G.
—— of Democracy in the United States of America. Boston. 1852. 8vo.
—— of Federal Gov't. See Freeman, E. A.
—— of our National Debts and Taxes, from 1688 to 1751. Lond. 8vo. Eng. Polit. Pamph. Vols. 13, 69.
—— of the Amer. Revolution. Published by Soc. for the Diffusion of Useful Knowledge. Columbus, 1834. 12mo.
—— of the Civil War in America. Vol. 1. 1775–77. Lond. 1780. 8vo.
—— of the Late War between the U. States and G. Britain. Wheeling, 1831. 18mo. Pamphlets War of 1812. Vol. 2.
—— of the Morvian Mission among the Indians of N. America. Lond., 1838. 12mo.
—— of the Negotiations in reference to the Eastern and N. Eastern Boundaries of the U. S. N. Y. 1841. 8vo.
—— of the Picts, or Roman-British Wall and of the Roman Stations. Engravings. Lond. 1849. 8vo.
—— of the Rebel Steam Ram "Atlanta," now on Exhibition in Phila., 1863. 12mo. Rebell'n Pamph. Vols. 6 and 106.
—— Revolutions in Europe, from the Subversion of the Roman Empire in the West, 406, to the Downfall of Bonaparte. Hartford, 1844. 12mo.
—— of the Rise, Progress and Suppession of several Late Insurrections in Ireland. Dublin. Reprinted. 1760. Eng. Polit. Pamph. Vol. 72.
—— of the U. States for 1796; including particulars relative to the Federal Govt. Previous to that Period. Washington, 1797. 8vo.
—— of the War on America between G. Britain and her Colonies to the Conclusion in 1783. Dublin, 1779-1785. 3 Vols. 8vo.
—— of the War with America, France, Spain and Holland. 1775-83. Lond., 1787. 8vo.
—— of the Yellow Fever in N. Orleans, in 1853. Phila. and St. Louis, 1854. 8vo. La. Misc. Pamph. Vol. 1.
—— of 39th Congress. See BARNES, Wm. H.
—— of Self-Defence, in Requital to the Hist. of Passive Obedience. Lond., 1689. Sm. 4to. Eng. Rel. Pamph. Vol. 79.
—— —— See Passive Obedience.
—— Romance of. See REED, Wm. B. Lecture on.
—— Study of. See STANLEY, A. P. Lecture on. 1854.
HITCHCOCK. C. H. See N. H. Geolog. Survey. 1869-71.
HITCHCOCK, E. Memoirs of the Bloomsgrove Family. Boston, 1790. 2 Vols. 8vo.
—— Address at his Inaugura. to the Presidency of Amherst College. 1845. Amherst. 8vo. Addresses. Vol. 1.
—— Attempt to Describe the Animals that made the Fossil Footmarks of the U. States, and especially of N. England. Memoirs of Amer. Acad. of Arts and Sciences. Vol. 3. N. S.

HITCHCOCK, E. Catalogues of Animals and Plants of Mass., with Index. Amherst, 1835. 8vo.

—— Illustrations of Surface Geology:

Part 1. On the Conn. Valley in N. England.

Part 2. On the Erosions of the Earth's Surface. Smithson. Contrib. Vol. 9.

—— See Massa. Geolog. Survey. 1830-1. 1838.

—— Sketch of the Geology, Mineralogy and Scenery of the Region of the River Conn. 1822. Silliman's Journ. Vols. 6, 7.

—— See Vermont Geolog. Servey. 1858.

HITCHCOCK, Rev. Enos. Disc. on Gen. Geo. Washington, at Providence, Feb. 22, 1800. Providence, 1800. 8vo. Sermons. Vol. 12.

—— See TAPPAN, Rev. David. Obit. Disc. 1803.

HITCHCOCK, Peter. Speech in Ohio Legislature, March 4, 1863, on Loyalty to the Gov. Rebell'n Pamph. Vol. 36.

HITCHCOCK, Rob't. Visit of the Lord High Admiral to the Port of Plymouth, in July, 1827. Plymouth. 12mo. Eng. Miscel. Pamph. Vol. 28.

HITCHCOCK, R. D. Address in Behalf of the Inebriate Asylum. 1855. Temperance Pamph. Vol. 1.

HLUBEK, Dr. F. X. Die Ernahrung der Pflaurzen und die Statif des Landbanes. Prague, 1841.

HITTELL, John S. Resources of California. 2d Ed., with Appendix on Oregon and Washington Territories. San Francisco, 1866. 12mo.

—— 19th Anniversary Oration before the Soc. of Cal. Pioneers. San Francisco, 1869. 8vo. Cal. Hist. Discourses. Vol. 1.

HOADLY, Bishop. Refutation of B'p Sherlock's Arguments against a Repeal of the Test and Corporation Acts. Lond., 1787. 8vo. Eng. Rel. Pamph. Vol. 26.

HOADLY, Chas. J. See Connecticut. Records of Colony.

—— The Public Seal of Conn. Conn. Hist. Soc. Coll. Vol. 1.

HOAR, Sam'l, Memoir of. Mass. Hist. Soc. Proceed., 1860–62.

HOARE, Rev. G. T. Notes on North Italy, and the Seat of War, in 1859. Lond., 1860. 12mo. Hist. Pamph. Vol. 5.

HOARE, Henry. See Corr. Relating to the Formation of a Church Institution in Lond.

HOARE, Sir Richard C. Hist. of Modern Wiltshire. Lond., 1822. Folio.

HOBART COLLEGE, Geneva, N. Y. Registers for 1862–3, 1865–6. 1872–3. Geneva, 1862–65–72. 8vo.

HOBART, B. Hist. of Town of Abington, Mass. Boston, 1866. 12mo.

HOBART, B'p John H. See Onderdonk, Rev. B. T. Obit. Sermon. 1830.

—— SCHRŒDER, Rev. J. F. Character of.

HOBART, Mrs. Jane Louisa. See KEDSIE, Rev. A. S.

HOBART, Nathaniel. Life of Emanuel Swedenborg, with acc. of his Writings. 2d ed. Boston, 1845. 12mo.

HOBBS, Thos. Considerations upon his Reputation, Loyalty, Religion, etc. Written by himself. Lond., 1680. 12mo. Eng. Misc. Pamph. Vol. 12.

HOBBS, Wm. New Discovery for finding the Longitude. Lond., 1714. 4to.
HOBBS, W. F. Landlord, Tenant and Labourer; in a Series of Papers affecting their Interests. Lond., 1859. 8vo. Eng. Polit. Pamph., Vol. 57.
HOBHOUSE, John C. Speech in the House of Commons, Apr. 17, 1821, on Parl. Reform. Lond., 1821. 8vo. Eng. Polit. Pamph., Vol. 35.
HOBOKEN, N. J. See Jersey City and Hoboken Directory, 1866–7. 1870–1.
HODGE, Mrs. A. H. The Boys in Blue; or Heroes of the Rank and File. N. Y., 1867. 8vo.
HODGE, Chas. England and America. From the Princeton Review of Jan., 1862. Rebell'n Pamph., Vol. 19.
HODGE, Jas. T. On the Wisconsin and Missouri Lead Region. Amer. Journ. of Science, Vol. 43, No. 1.
HODGES, Rich'd M. Semi-Centen. Disc. before 1st Cong. Ch., Bridgewater, Mass., Sept. 17, 1871, with Hist. Notes. Cambridge, 1871. 8vo.
HODGINS, J. G. The School-house; its Architecture, etc. Toronto, 1858. 8vo.
HODGINS, Thos. Canada Educa. Directory for 1857–8. Toronto, 1857. 8vo.
HODGKIN, Dr. Thos. Address to the Harveian Soc'y, Oct. 2, 1847, on Med. Reform. Lond., 1847. 8vo. Med. Pamph., Vol. 29.
HODGMAN, S. A. The Nation's Sin and Punishment; or the Hand of God in the Overthow of Slavery. N. Y., 1864. 12mo.
HODGSON, A. Remarks during a Journal in 1819–21, through N. America. N. Y., 1823. 8vo.
HODGSON, Rev. John. Notes upon Life Assurance, with reference to the Clergy Mutual Assurance Soc. Westminster, 1868. 8vo. English. Misc. Pamph., Vol. 13.
HODGSON, Thos. Classified Index to the Lond. Catalogue of Books published in G. Britain 1816 to 1851. Lond., 1853. 8vo.
HODSON, Wm. B. Grammatical Sketch and Specimens of the Berber Lauguage; with four letters on Berber Etymologies. Amer. Philos. Soc. Trans. N. S. Vol. 4.
—— The Creek Confederacy. Georgia Hist. Soc. Coll. Vol. 3. Part 1.
HOE, Rich'd M. Memorial to Congress for an Extension of Letters. Patent. Washington, 1868. (?) 8vo. Congr. & Polit. Pamph. Vol. 126.
HOEFER, Ferd. Premier Memoire sur les Ruines de Ninive. Paris, 1850. 8vo.
HOFFMAN, Chas. F. The Administration of Jacob LEISLER; a Chapter in Amer. History. Sparks' Amer. Biog. 2d Ser. Vol. 3.
—— The Pioneers of N. York. Annivers. Disc. before the St. Nicholas Soc. of Manhattan. Dec. 6, 1847. N. Y., 1848. 8vo. N. Y. Hist. Disc. Vol. 3.
—— Wild Scenes in Forest and Prairie. N. Y., 1843. 12mo. Same in 2 Vols. N. Y., 1843. 12mo.

HOFFMAN, Chas. F. Winter in the West. 2d Ed. N. Y., 1835. 2 Vols. 12mo.

HOFFMAN, Rev. E. A. Parish Statistics of Christ Ch. Elizabeth, N. J., & Ann. Address. 1856. N. Y., 1856. 8vo. N. Jersey Hist. Disc. Vol. 1.

HOFFMAN, John T. Public Papers. 1869–72. N. Y., 1872. 8vo.

HOFFMAN, Murray. Address to the Graduating Class of the Law School of Columbia Coll. May, 1861. N. Y., 1861. 8vo. Columbia Coll. Pamph.

—— Treatise upon the Estate and Rights of the Corporation of the City of N. Y. N. Y., 1853. 8vo.

HOFFMAN, O. Speech in Cong., Feb. 12, 1840, on State Appropriations. Congr. & Polit. Pamph. Vol. 88.

HOGARTH, Geo. Memoirs of the Musical Drama. Waldie's Circulating Libr. Vol. 13.

—— Musical History, Biography & Criticism; a General Survey of Music from the earliest period. Waldie's Circulating Libr. Vols. 11, 12.

HOGE, Rev. Wm. J. Discourse at N. Y., July 21, 1861, on the Resignation of his Charge. Rebell'n Pamph. Vol. 29.

HOGG, Nathan. Poetical Letters tu es Brither Jan., in the Devonshire Dialect. 5th Ed. Lond., 1865. 12mo.

—— New Series of Poems in the Devonshire Dialect. 4th Ed. Enlarged. Lond., 1866. 12mo.

HOISINGTON, Rev. Henry R. Brief Notes on the Tamil Language. Journ. Amer. Oriental Soc. Vol. 3.

—— The Tattuva—Kattalei, Siva—Gnana—Potham, and Siva—Pirakasam; Treatises on Hindu Philosophy, translated from the Tamil. N. Haven, 1854. 8vo.

HOLBROOK, Genealogy. See VINTON, J. A.

HOLCOMB Jas. P. Sketches of Polit. Issues and Controversies of the Revolution. Disc. before Va. Hist. Soc., Jan. 1856. Va. Hist. Soc. Coll. Vol. 1.

HOLCOMBE, Henry. Georgia Analytical Repository. Savannah, 1802. 8vo.

HOLDEN, Fred. A. Genealogy of the Descendants of Banfield Capron. 1660—1859. Boston, 1859. 12mo.

HOLDEN, H. Narr. of Shipwreck of Ship Mentor on Pellew Island, 1832. Cooperstown, 1841. 12mo.

HOLDEN, Mass. See DAMON, S. C. Hist. of, 1667—1841.

HOLDERNESS, Eng. See POULSON, Geo. Hist. and Antiq.

HOLDSWORTH, A. H. Letter to a Friend, on the present Situation of the Country. Lond., 1816. 8vo. Pamphleteer. Vol. 8.

—— A Second Letter to the same. Pamphleteer. Vol. 9.

HOLFORD, Geo. Thoughts on the Criminal Prisons of England. Lond., 1821. 8vo. 2d ed. Pamphleteer. Vol. 18.

HOLGATE, Jerome B, Amer. Genealogy of Early Settlers of N. America. N. Y., 1851. 4to.

—— Conversations on the present Age of the World in connection with Prophecy. Albany, 1853. 12mo.

HOLIDAYS ABROAD. See KIRKLAND, C. M.

—— See MANNERS, Lord J. Plea for.

HOLKAM, Eng. See RIGBY, Edw. Agriculture, etc. 1819.
HOLKHAM House, Holkham, Eng. Description of, with Acc. of, the Paintings, Statues, &c. Wells, 1860. 12mo. 6th Ed. Guide Books. Vol. 3.
HOLLAND. See ANDREWS, J. Hist. of the War. 1775–1783.
—— BATTY, Lt. Col. Tour through South Holland, 1832?
—— Book of the Laws. Hague and Amsterdam, 1658–1796. 9 Vols. Folio.
—— History of, in Dutch. Amsterdam, 1752–59. 21 Vols. 8vo.
—— DE PEYSTER, J. W. Battle of the Baltic.
—— LAFAYETTE, Madame. Memoires de.
—— Mercury. Newspaper (in Holland Language), 1650–90. Harlem, 1651–1691. 40 Vols. 4to.
—— —— See European Mercury, 1691–1756.
—— Monthly Mercury. Newspaper. Amsterdam, 1756–1790. 69 Vols. 4to.
—— —— And Polit. History. Amsterdam, 1801–1806. 6 Vols. 4to.
—— See MESSLER, Rev. A. Hollanders in N. Jersey.
—— See MOTLEY, J. L. Rise of Dutch Republic.
—— Society of Knowledge. Publications. Harlem, 1758–1778. 24 Vols. 8vo.
HOLLAND, Rev. F. W. Rutland Co., Vt., Insurrection, 1786. N. Eng. Reg. Vol. 26.
HOLLAND, John. Life and Ministry of Rev. John Summerfield, with an Introduction by Jas. Montgomery. N. Y., n. d.
HOLLAND, John G. Life of Abraham Lincoln. Springfield, 1866. 8vo.
HOLLAND, Josiah Gilbert. Hist. of Western Massachusetts, the Counties of Hampden, Hampshire, Franklin and Berkshire. Springfield, 1855. 2 Vols. 12mo.
HOLLAND, Purchase. N. Y. See TURNER, O.
HOLLAND, Wm. M. Life and Polit. Opinions of Martin Van Buren. Hartford, 1835. 12mo.
HOLLES, ——. Duke of Newcastle. Letter to M. Michell, in answer to his Memorial and other Papers. Lond., 1753. 4to. Eng. Polit. Pamph. Vol. 66.
HOLLES, D., STAPLETON, P. and others. Vindica. and Answer to a late printed Pamphlet, etc. Lond., 1647. Sm. 4to. Eng. Polit. Pamph. Vol. 6.
HOLLEY, Alex. L. Oration before the Theta Delta Chi Fraternity, June 1, 1855. Providence, 1855. 8vo. Addresses. Vol. 34.
HOLLEY, Rev. Horace. See CALDWELL, C. Disc. on his Genius and Character.
HOLLEY, Mrs. Mary A. Observations, Historical, Geographical and Descriptive of Texas. Baltimore, 1833. 12mo.
HOLLEY, O. L. N. Y. State Ann. Register for 1843. 1845–6. N. Y., 1843, 1846. 12mo.
HOLLEY, Robt. D. D. Lecture on the Pilgrim Fathers ; illustrative of the Govt. Prize Picture by CHARLES LACY. Manchester. 4to, n. e. Addresses, etc. Vol. 4.

HOLLINGSWORTH, Rev. N. J. Claims of Dr. Bell and Jos. Lancaster, in reference to Improvements in Educa. Practices. Lond., 1812. 4to. Educa. Pamph. Vol. 40.

HOLLIS, THOS. See ELIOT, Andrew. Letters to.

—— Memoir of. Lond., 1780. 4to.

HOLLISTER, G. H. Hist. of Connecticut from the First Settlement of the Colony. 2d Ed. Enlarged. Hartford, 1857. 2 vols. 8vo.

—— Oration at Litchfield, Con., July 4, 1842. Hartford, 1842. 8vo. Adresses. Vol. 29.

HOLLSTER, Dr. H. Contributions to the Hist. of the Lackawana Valley. N. Y., 1867. 12mo.

HOLLISTER, Hiel. Pawlet, Vt., for One Hundred Years. Albany, 1866. 8vo.

HOLLISTER, O. J. The Mines of Colorado. Springfield, Mass., 1867. 8vo.

HOLLOWAY, J. N. Hist. of Kansas from the First Exploration of the Mississippi Valley. La Fayette, 1868. 8vo.

HOLM, Thos. C. Extract from his Work on New Sweedland, translated from the Swedish. N. Y. Hist. Soc. Coll. Vol. 2.

—— Kort beskrifning om Provincien Nya Swerige uti America, som nu fortiden af the engelske Kallas Pennsylvania. Stockholm, 1702. 4to. The same translated into English by P. S. DUPONCEAU, LL. D. Hist. Soc. of Penn. Memoir. Vol. 3. Part 1.

HOLMAN'S Dollar Magazine. N. Y., Sep. 1848 to July, 1849.

HOLMES, Abiel, D. D. Address before the Amer. Antiquarian Soc., Oct. 24, 1814. Boston, 1814, 8vo. Proceedings. 1813–55.

—— Annals of America from its Discovery by Columbus to 1826. 2d Ed. Cambridge, 1829. 2 vols. 8vo.

—— See Controversy between the 1st Parish in Cambridge and Dr. HOLMES.

—— Hist. of Cambridge Mass. Mass. Hist. Soc. Coll. Vol. 7. 1st series.

—— See JENKS, Rev. W., Memoir of.

—— Memoir of the French Protestants whe Settled in Oxford, Mass., 1686. Worcester Mag. Vol. 2. See also, Mass. Hist. Soc. Coll., 3d Ser. Vol. 2.

HOLMES Chapel, Cheshire, Eng. See BARLOW, T. W. Hist. of the Ch. at. 1853.

HOLMES, E. Report of an Exploration and Survey of the Aroostook Territory in 1838. Augusta, 1839. 8vo.

HOLMES, Elias B. Speech in Cong. June 18, 1846, on the Mexican War. Washington, 1846. 8vo. Speeches, Vol. 1. Cong. & Polit. Pamph. Vol. 88.

HOLMES Family Genealogy. See VINTON, J. A.

HOLMES, Francis S. Phosphate Rocks of S. Carolina & the Great Carolina Marl Bed. Charleston, 1870. 8vo. S. C. Misc. Vol. 1.

—— Post Pleiocene Fossils of S. Carolina. Charleston, 1858–60. Folio.

HOLMES, F. S. Remains of Domestic Animals Discovered among the Post Pleiocene Fossils in S. Carolina. Charleston, 1858. 8vo. Scientific Pamph. Vol. 4. See also S. C. Pamph. Vol. 1.

—— See TUOMEY, M. & HOLMES, F. S., Fossils of S. Carolina.

HOLMES, Rev. John, Hist. Sketches of the Missions of the United Brethren for propagating the Gospel among the Heathen. Dublin. 1818. 8vo.

HOLMES, John S. See Boston. Report of Celebra. July 4, 1858.

HOLMES, Mead. A Soldier of the Cumberland. Phila., 1864. 12mo.

HOLMES, Oliver W. Astræa; the Balance of Illusions; a Poem before the Phi Beta Kappa Soc. of Yale Coll., Aug. 14, 1850. Boston, 1850. 8vo. Yale Coll. Pamphlets.

—— Oration at Boston, July 4, 1863. Rebell'n Pamph. Vols. 68, 91.

—— The Benefactors of the Med. School of the Harvard University; with a Biograph. Sketch of the late Dr. Geo. Parkman. Boston, 1850. 8vo. Harvard Coll. Pamph.

HOLSTEIN, H. L. V. D. Memoirs of Gilbert M. La Fayette. 2nd ed. Geneva, 1835. 12mo.

HOLT, Edw. Public and Domestic Life of George III. Lond., 1820. 2 Vols. 8vo.

HOLT, Rev. Edwin. Disc. at Dedica. of North Church in Portsmouth, N. H., Jan. 31, 1838. Portsmouth, 1838. 8vo. N. H. Hist. Discourses. Vol. 2.

HOLT Genealogy. See DURRIE, D. S.

HOLT, Judge Jos. Address to the People of Kentucky, July 13, 1861. N. Y., 1861. 18mo. Rebell'n Pamph. Vols. 11, 99.

—— Letter on the Assassination of President Lincoln, 1866. Rebell'n Pamph. Vol. 112.

—— Letters on the Policy of the Gen'l Gov't. Louisville, 1861. 8vo. Rebell'n Pamph. Vol. 66.

—— Letters to the People of Kentucky on the present Crisis, with Letters from Hon. E. Everett and Com. Chas. Stewart on the same subject. Phila., 1861. 8vo. Rebell'n Pamph. Vol. 1.

—— Report on the Case of Thos. C. A. Dexter. N. Y., 1867. 8vo. Rebell'n Pamph. Vol. 67.

—— Review of the Proceedings, Findings and Sentence of a Gen. Court Martial for the trial of Maj. Gen. Fitz John Porter, 1863, with a Reply to the same by Reverdy Johnson. Rebell'n Pamph. Vol. 88.

HOLTON, Isaac F. New Granada: Twenty Years in the Granada Andes, with Maps. N. Y., 1857. 8vo.

HOLTON Library, Brighton, Mass. See Brighton.

HOLYOKE, Edw. A. See BRAZER, Rev. J. Obit. Disc., 1829.

—— Memoir of. Boston, 1829. 8vo.

HOMANS, Dr. C. D. A Case of Hydrophbia. Read before the Boston Soc. for Med. Observation, Mar. 6, 1854. 8vo. Med. Pamph. Vol. 8.

HOMANS, I Smith. Plain Words to England and her Manufacturers. N. Y., 1862. Rebell'n Pamph. Vol. 19.

—— Merchants' and Bankers' Almanac. N. Y., 1862, 1864. 2 Vols. 8vo. 1868, 1869. 2 Vols. 8vo.

HOME, Francisco. Methodus Materiæ Medicæ. Edinburgh, 1781. 12mo. Med. Pamph. Vol. 15.

HOME, Henry, Lord Kames. Elements of Criticism: revised, with additions by Rev. Jas. R. Boyd. N. Y., 1857. 12mo.

HOME, John. Hist. of the Rebellion in 1745. Lond., 1802. 4to.

"HOME of the Badgers." See Sketches of the West, &c.

"HOME of the Crows." See CARRINGTON, M. I.

HOMER, Rev. Jona. Description and History of Newton in the Co. of Middlesex. Mass. Hist. Soc. Coll. Vol. 5. 1st Ser.

HOMERSHAM, Sam'l Collet. Review of the Report of the General Board of Health, on the Supply of Water to the Metropolis. Lond., 1850. 8vo. Eng. Misc. Pamph. Vol. 6.

HOMERUS. The Iliad of Homer. Lond., 1728. 12mo.

HOMES, Henry A. Observations on the Design and Import of Medals. Albany, 1863. 8vo. Scientific Pamph. Vol. 11. See also Albany Institute Trans. Vol. 4.

—— Our Knowledge of California and the North-West Coast, One Hundred Years Since. Albany, 1870. 8vo. Cal. Mis., Vol. 1. See also Albany Institute Trans. Vol. 6.

—— Palatine Emigration to England in 1709. Albany, 1871. 8vo. Hist. Pamph. Vol. 4. See also Albany Institute Trans. Vol. 7.

HOMESTEAD Bill. See Congr. Speeches.

HOMESTEADS for Actual Settlers on the Public Domain. Act of Cong., approved Apr. 20, 1862. Rebell'n Pamph. Vol. 20.

HOMŒOPATHY. See Amer. Institute of.

—— at Taunton. The Case of Jas. D. Blake and the Royal Coll. of Surgeons. Lond., 1848. 8vo. Med. Pamph. Vol. 13.

—— See MILLER, Dr. A. Letters on. 1849.

—— N. Y. Homœopath. Soc.

—— RANSFORD, Chas. Reasons for embracing.

—— REED, D. M. Reasons for embracing.

—— SHIPMAN, Dr. G. E. An Appeal unto Caesar, etc.

—— —— N. W. Journal of.

HONDURAS. See SQUIER, E. G. Honduras: Descriptions, &c. 1870.

HONE, Philip. Address before Mercantile Libr. Assoc., Boston, Oct. 3, 1843. Addresses. Vol. 12.

HONEST (An.) and Useful Scheme for the Year 1748; or an Easy Method of Equipping and Maintaining 16 Men of War. Lond, 1748. 8vo. Eng. Polit. Pamph. Vol. 69.

—— (The) Grief of a Tory, Expressed in a Letter from Wiltshire to the Monitor. Also, a Second Letter by the Same. Lond., 1759. 8vo. Eng. Polit. Pamph. Vol. 70.

HOOD, Geo. Hist. of Music in N. England: with Biograph. Sketches of Reformers and Psalmists. Boston, 1846. 12mo.

HOOK, Rev. Walter F. Letter to the Bishop of St. David's on Gen. Education. Lond., 1846. 8vo. 3d Ed. Educa. Pamph. Vol. 32.

HOOK, W. H. Lecture on the Backward March of Amer. Society. Madison, Wis., 1869. 8vo. Addresses. Vol. 34.

HOOKE, Col. Secret Negociations in Scotland in Favour of the Pretender in 1707. Written by himself. Polit. Tracts. Vol. 3.

HOOKER, Edw., D. D. The Preservation of Manuscripts. Paper Before the Vt. Hist. Soc., Feb. 19, 1863. N. E. Hist. and Gen. Reg. Vol. 17.

HOOKER, John. Letter to his Friends of the Democratic Party on the Present War. n. d. Rebelllon Pamph. Vol. 9.

—— Letter to the Democratic Party on the Issues of the Day. n. d. Rebellion Pamph. Vol. 6.

HOOKER, Gen. Jos. See Men of the Times.

HOOKER, Rev. Rich'd. See Walton, I. Life of

HOOKER, Rev. Thos. Abstracts of Two Sermons. Conn. Hist. Coll. Vol. 1.

—— Letter in Reply to Gov. Winthrop. 1638. Conn. Hist. Soc. Coll. Vol. 1.

HOOKER, Sir W. J. Guide to the Royal Botanic Gardens of Kew. London, 1850. 8vo. 7th Ed. Guide Books. Vol. 10.

HOOLE, Sam'l. Anecdotes respecting the late Mr. John Hoole. Lond., 1803. 8vo. Miscell. Tracts. Vol. 2.

HOOPER, E. J. Western Fruit Book. 3d Revised Ed. Cincin., 1858. 12mo.

HOOPER, Sam'l. Speech in Cong., Apr. 6, 1864, on the National Currency Bill. Rebell'n Pamph. Vol. 32.

HOOPER, Wm. H. Speeeh in Cong., Feb. 25, on Extension of Boundaries. Utah, etc. 8vo. Cong. and Polit. Pamph. Vol. 83.

—— Speech in Cong., Mar. 23, 1870, on the Utah Bill. 8vo. Cong. and Polit. Pamph. Vol. 119.

HOOKER, Wm. J. On the Botany of America. Silliman's Journ. Vol. 9.

HOOSAC Tunnell. See BIRD, F. W.; CARY, T. G.; DERBY E. H. PIPER, J. J.

—— Report of the Hearing of the Troy and Greenfield R. R. Co. Petitioners for a Loan, etc. Boston, 1853. 8vo. Mass. R. R. Reports, &c. Vol. 2.

HOP Culture. Practical Details as given by experienced cultivators. N. Y., 8vo. Agr. Pamph. Vol. 11.

HOPE, A. J. B. The Amer. Disruption—in Three Lectures. Lond. 1862. 8vo. Rebell'n Pamph. Vol. 53.

—— Letter to Sir Robert Inglis, on Marriage with a Deceased Wife's Sister. Lond., 1850. 8vo. Strangford Pamph. Vol. 57.

—— Modern Memoir Writing. Oration delivered Dec. 14, 1840. Cambridge, 1840. 8vo. Strangford Pamph. Vol. 43.

—— On the Comparative Greatness of the Duke of Buckingham and Cardinal Richelieu. 1840. 8vo. n. p. Strangford Pamph. Vol. 27.

—— The Gov't Scheme of Academical Education in Ireland considered. Lond., 1845. 8vo. Strangford Pamph. Vol. 43.

HOPE, Geo. Agriculture and the Corn Law. Prize Essay. Manchester, 1842. 8vo. Strangford Pamph. Vol. 31.

HOPWELL, O. See Licking Co. Pioneers.

—— SMUCKER, I.

HOPKINS, Rev. A. T. Sermon at Utica and Rome. N. Y., 1834. Utica, 1834. 8vo. Sermons, Vol. 27.

HOPKINS, B. F. See Madison (Wis.) Mutual Insurance Co. Proceedings on his Death.

HOPKINS, Edw. A. Memoir on the Geog., Hist., Productions and Trade of Paraguay. Amer. Geograph. and Statist. Soc. Bulletin, Vol. 1.

HOPKINS, Fred. W. Eulogy on Col. Truman B. Ransom. Hanover, Vt. 1848. 8vo. Vt. Hist. Soc. Addresses, &c. Vol. 1.

HOPKINS Grammar School, N. Haven. See BACON, L. W. Hist. Disc., 1860.

HOPKINS, Bishop J. H. Bible View of Slavery n. d. 8vo. Congr. & Polit. Pamph. Vol. 85.

—— Disc. at Albany, Aug. 24, 1856, before Amer. Assoc. for the Advancement of Science. 8vo. Addresses, Vol. 7.

—— See DRISLER, H. "Bible View of Slavery" examined.

—— His Letter on Slavery ripped up, etc. N. Y., 1863. 12mo. Rebellion Pamph. Vol. 41.

—— Letter to Rev. M. A. DeWolf Howe, D. D., 1863. Rebellion Pamph. Vol. 54.

—— See NEWMAN, Louis C. Bible View of Slavery reconsidered.

—— Remarks on his Letter on Slavery.

—— Review of his Bible View of Slavery.

—— Vindication of his Views on Slavery.

HOPKINS, Mark., D. D. Address at Boston, May 26, 1852, before the Soc. for the Promotion of Collegiate and Theolog. Education at the West. Boston. 1852. 8vo.

—— Baccalaureate Sermon, at Williamstown, Mass., Aug. 18, 1850. Boston, 1850. 8vo. Williams' College Pamphs.

—— Discourse commem. of Amos Lawrence, at Williams' Coll. Feb. 21, 1853. Boston. 1853. 8vo. Addresses Vols. 4 and 25.

—— Oration before the N. England Soc. of N. Y., Dec. 22, 1853. N. Y., 1854. 8vo. Addresses, Vol. 34.

HOPKINS, Rev. Sam'l. Half Century Dis. at Hadley, Mass., Mar. 3, 1805. Northampton, Mass., 1805. 8vo. Mass. Hist. Dis. Vol. 2.

—— The Puritans of the Church, Court and Parliament of England. Boston, 1860. 3 Vols. 8vo.

HOPKINS, Stephen. Hist. Acc. of the Planting and Growth of Providence, R. I. Mass. Hist. Soc. Coll. 2d. Ser. Vol. 9.

HOPKINS, Wm. Speech in Penn. Legisla., Apr. 9, 1863, on the State of Country. Rebell'n Pamph. Vol. 36.

HOPKINSON, Francis. The Miscellaneous Essays and Occasional Writings of, with Portraits. 3 Vols. Phila., 1792.

HOPKINGTON, Mass. Ann. Report of School Comm., 1863–4. Milford, 1864. 8vo.

—— See Howe, Rev. N. Century Sermon, 1815.

—— STIMSON, J. Topog. Descript. of.

—— Webster, Rev. J. C. 25th Annivers. Dis. 1863.

HOPLEY, Thos. Wrongs which Cry for Redress. A Letter to the Men & Women of the United Kingdom. Lond., 1860. 8vo. Eng. Misc. Pamph. Vol. 33.

HOPPIN, Rev. Jas. M. See Plummer Hall Decica. Salem, 1858.

HOPPIN, Nicholas, D. D. Annivers. Sermon at Christ Ch., Cambridge, Nov. 25, 1860. Boston, 1861. 8vo. Mass. Hist. Discourses. Vol. 16.

HORATIUS, Quintus Flaccus. Opera. Edited by J. PINE. Lond., 1733 2 Vols. 8vo.

HORDYNSKI, Joseph. Hist. of the late Polish Revolution and Events of the Campaign. Boston, 1832. 8vo.

HORICON, Wis. Argus. Newspaper, 1854–61.

HORN, Mrs. Captivity by Camanche Ind. See Authentic Nar. of.

HORN, Adam or Hellman. The Confession of, &c., With Account of his Trial for Murder. Baltimore. 1843. 8vo. Law Pamph. Vol. 24.

HORNBLOWER, Joseph C. Address before the N. Jersey Hist. Soc., January 21, 1847. Collections. Vol. 2.

—— See FIELD, Rich'd S. Life & Character of.

HORNBY, Thos. Dissertation on Lime, & its Use and Abuse in Agriculture. Lond., 1842. 8vo. Agr. Pamph. Vol. 14.

HORNE, Geo. Answer to N. B. HALHED on the Pretended Mission of Rich'd BROTHERS to the Jews. Oxford. 8vo. n. d. Eng. Rel. Pamph. Vol. 27.

HORNE, Thos. H. Protestant Memorial for the 3d Century of the Reformation, Oct. 4, 1835. Lond., 1835. 12mo. 2d Ed. Eng. Rel. Pamph. Vol. 73.

HORSFORD, Prof. E. N. Service Pipes for Water. Investigation made at the suggestion of Physicians of Boston. Cambridge, 1849. 8vo. Scientific Pamph. Vol. 40.

HORSFORD, J. Speech in Cong., June 24, 1852, on Establishment of an Agricult. Bureau. Cong. & Polit. Pamph. Vol. 87.

HORSMANDEN, Dan'l. The N. Y. Conspiracy; or Hist. of the Negro Plot, with a Journal of Proceedings against the Conspirators, 1741-2. N. Y., 1810. 8vo.

—— The Negro Conspiracy in the City of N. York, in 1741. No. 1. N. Y., 1851. 8vo. N. Y., Hist. Discourses, &c. Vol. 3.

HORTICULTURE. See Boston Hist. School for Women.

—— HOSACK, D. Address before N. Y. Hort. Soc. 1824.

—— KEMP, E. Landscape Gardening.

—— KERN, G. M. Landscape Cardening.

—— LOUBAT, A. Amer. Vine Dresser's Guide.

—— M'MAHON, B. Amer. Gardeners Calendar.

—— N. York Hort. Soc.

—— SALISBURY, Wm. Cottager's Companion.

—— THOMAS, J. J. Amer. Fruit Cultur't.

HORTON, R. W. Lecture at the Lond. Mechanics Institution, Jan. 19, 1831. Lond., 1831. 8vo. Eng. Polit. Pamp. Vol. 37.

HOSACK, David. Biograph. Memoir of Hugh Williamson, M. D., LL.D. N. Y. 1819. 8vo. N. Y. Hist. Soc. Addresses. Vol. 1. Same collections, Vol. 3.

—— —— Catalogue of Plants in Botanic Gardens at Elgin, N. Y., in 1806. N. Y., 1811. 8vo. 2d Ed. Agr. Pamph. Vol. 2.

—— —— FRANCIS, J. W. Sketch of.

HOSACK, D. Inaugural Address before the N. Y. Hist. Soc. Feb. 20, 1820. N. Y. Hist. Soc. Addresses. Vol. 1. Coll. Vol. 3.

—— Inaug. Disc. before the N. Y. Horticult. Soc. Aug. 31, 1824. N. Y. 1824. 8vo. Agr. Pamph. Vol. 1

—— Introduct. Lect. before the Coll. of Physicians and Surgeons, Nov. 7, 1825. N. Y. 1825. 8vo. Med. Pamph. Vol. 31.

—— Observations on the Medical Character: to the Graduates of Coll. of Physicians & Surgeons of N. Y. 1826. 8vo. Med. Pamph. Vol. 9.

HOSEASON, John C. The Steam Navy; and the Application of Screw Propellers to Sea-Going Line of Battle Ships. Lond. 1853. 8vo. Eng. Misc. Pamph. Vol. 32.

HOSFORD, Rev. B. F. Disc. at Re-Dedica. of the Center Ch., Haverhill, Mass., Jan. 27, 1860. Boston, 1860. 8vo. Mass. Hist. Disc. Vol. 2.

HOSKINS, Nathan. Hist of Vermont from its Discovery aud Settlement to 1830 Vergennes, 1831 12vo

HOSMER, Rev. Dr. G. W. See Buffalo, 1st Unitarian Ch.

—— Report of Delegates from Gen. Aid Soc. for the Army at Buffalo, 1862. Rebell'n Pamph. Vol. 84.

—— The Physiognomy of Buffalo — Ann. Address before Buffalo Hist. Soc. Jan. 13, 1864. 8vo. N. Y. Hist Discourses. Vol. 2.

HOSMER, H. L. Early Hist. of the Maumee Valley. Toledo, 1858. 8vo. Ohio Hist. Discourses etc. Vol. 1.

HOSMER, H. P. Mary Palmer, the Indian Captive of the Genesee. Rochester, 1847. 8vo. Indian Pamph. Vol. 5.

HOSMER, Jas. B. Genealogy of the Hosmer Family. Hartford, 1861. 8vo. Genealog. Pamph. Vol. 10.

HOSMER, Jas. K. The Color Guard; a Corporal's Notes of Military Service in the 19th Army Corps. Boston, 1864. 12mo.

HOSMER, William. The Young Man's Book; or Self Education. N. Y., 1856. 12mo.

—— The Young Ladies' Book; or Principles of Female Education. N. Y., 1856. 12mo.

HOSMER, Wm. H. C. Poetical Works. N. Y., 1854. 2 vols. 12mo.

—— See SCHOOLCRAFT, H. R. Address before Iroquois.

HOSPITAL Life in Confed. Army. See CUMMING, Kate.

—— Scenes after the Battle of Gettysburg. July, 1863. Rebell'n Pamph. Vol. 81.

—— Transports; Memoir of the Embarkation of the Sick and Wounded from Virginia in the Summer of 1862. Boston, 1863. 12mo.

HOTALING, Sam'l. Speech before the Y. Men's Repub. Union, at N. Y., Oct. 29, 1860. Rebell'n Pamph. Vol. 36.

HOTCHKIN, Rev. Jas. H. Hist. of the Purchase and Settlement of Western N. Y., and of the Rise, Progress and Present State of the Presb. Ch. N. Y., 1848. 8vo.

HOTCHKISS, Rev. F. W. Half Century Sermon at Saybrook, Conn., Sept. 22, 1833. Hartford, 1838. 8vo. Conn. Hist. Disc. Vol. 3.

HOTCHKISS, Rev. F. W. Valedict. Address before the 1st Ch. & Congregation in Saybrook, Conn., Jan. 7, 1838. Hartford, 1838. 8vo. Conn. Hist. Disc. Vol. 7.

HOTCHKISS, Jed., and Allen, W. Battle Fields of Virginia, with Maps, etc. N. Y., 1867. 8vo.

HOTTEN, John C. Hand Book of Topog. and Family Hist. of Eng. and Wales. Lond., n. d. 8vo.

HOUDON Statue of Washington. See WASHINGTON: his Person as represented by the Artists.

HOUGH, F. B. Agricult. Statistics of the State of N. Y., by Counties, from the Census of 1865. Albany, 1867. 8vo. Agr. Pamph., Vol. 12.

—— Biograph. Notice of Dr. Chas. Milford Crandall. Albany, 1868. 8vo. Addresses, etc., Vol. 14.

—— Biograph. Notice of Dr. Sylvester D. Willard. Albany, 1866. 8vo. Addresses, etc., Vol. 20.

—— Census of N. Y. for 1865. Albany, 1867. 4to.

—— Census Report of the Dist. of Columbia. 1867? Cong. and Polit. Pamph., Vol. 81.

—— Communication relative to the 9th Census. 1869. 8vo. Congr. and Polit. Pamph., Vol. 70.

—— Constitution of State of N. Y., with Constit. Provisions of other States. Albany, 1867. 4to.

—— Essay on the Climate of the State of N. Y. Albany, 1857. 8vo. Addresses, etc., Vol. 14.

—— Hist. of Duryee's Brigade in the Campaign in Va. and Md. Albany, 1864. 8vo.

—— Hist. of Jefferson Co., N. Y., from the Earliest Period to the Present Time. Albany, 1854. 8vo.

—— Hist. of Lewis Co. in the State of N. Y. Albany, 1860. 8vo.

—— Hist. of St. Lawrence and Franklin counties, N. Y., from the Earliest Period to the Present Time. Albany, 1853. 8vo.

—— Hist. of the Census in N. Y., and Plan for the State Census of 1865. Albany Institute Trans., Vol. 5.

—— N. Y. Civil List, containing the Names and Origin of the Civil Divisions, and the Names and Dates of the Election of State and Co. Officers, from the Revolution to the present time. Albany, 1855. 12mo.

—— Notices of Peter Penet among the Oneida Indiana. Lowville, 1866. 4to. See also Albany Institute Trans., Vol. 5.

—— Papers relating to Pemaquid and Parts adjacent, in Maine. Maine Hist. Soc. Coll., Vol. 5.

—— Papers relating to the Island of Nantucket, with Documents relating to the Original Settlement of that Island, Martha's Vineyard and Islands adjacent. Albany, 1856. 4to. Privately printed.

—— Prize Essay on Medical and Vital Statistics. Albany, 1867. 8vo. Med. Pamph. Vol. 8.

—— Proceedings of Commissioners of Indian Affairs for the Extinguishment of Indian Titles. Albany, 1861. 2 vols. Sm. 4to.

—— Proceedings of N. E. Delegates at Boston, Aug., 1780, for Prosecuting the War. Albany, 1867. 4to.

HOUGH, F. B. Statistics of City and Co. of N. Y. N. Y., 1866. 8vo.

—— Washingtoniana; or Memorials of the Death of Washington. Pr. printed. Albany, 1865. Small folio.

HOUGH, G. W. Descript. of an Automatic Registering and Printing Barometer. Albany, 1865. 8vo. Scientific Pamph. Vol. 16.

—— Remarks on the Galvanic Battery. Read before the Albany Institute, Nov., 1868. 8vo. Scientific Pamph. Vol. 20.

—— Velocity of the Electric Current over Telegraph Wire. Read before the Albany Institute, June, 1869. Scientific Pamph. Vol. 20. Albany Institute Trans. Vol. 6.

—— The Total Eclipse of Aug. 7, 1869. Read before the Albany Institute, Oct., 1869. Scientific Pamph. Vol. 20. Albany Institute Trans. Vol. 6.

HOUGH, H. G. Diving; described on Hydraulic and Hydrostatic Principles. 1813. Scientific Pamph. Vol. 16.

HOUGHTON, Geo. F. See BUTLER, J. D.

HOUGHTON, Rev. Wm. A. Centen. Sermon, June 7, 1846, before the 1st Ch. in Northborough, Mass. Worcester, 1847 (?). Mass. Hist. Discourses. Vol. 20.

HOULTON, Rev. Rob't. Indisputable Facts relative to the Suttonian Art of Inoculation. Dublin, 1768. 8vo. Med. Pamph. Vol. 26.

HOULTON, R. The Lottery Inquisitor, with an Examination of the Lottery Scheme for 1805. Lond., 1805. 8vo. Misc. Tracts. Vol. 2.

HOUSTON, G. S. Speech in Cong., Jan. 24, 1852, on Mexican Indemnity. Congr. and Polit. Pamph. Vol. 88.

—— Speech in Cong., April 27, 1842, on Apportionment. Washington, 1842. 8vo. Congr. and Polit. Pamph. Vol. 25.

HOUSTON, John W. Speech in Cong., July 2, 1846, on the Tariff. Washington, 1846. 8vo. Speeches. Vol. 1.

HOUSTON, Gen. Sam'l. Case of. See Congressional Speeches.

—— Life of. Illustrated. N. Y., 1835. 12mo.

—— Life of. Washington. n. d. 8vo. Congr. and Polit. Pamph. Vol. 87.

—— Speech in Cong., Sept. 9, 1850, in Reply to Articles in the "Southern Press." Congr. and Polit. Pamph. Vol. 90.

—— Speeches in Cong., Feb. 14 and 15, and Mar. 3, 1854, on the Kansas and Nebraska Bill. Washington, 1854. 8vo. Speeches. Vol. 3.

—— Speech in Cong., Aug. 1, 1854, on Texan Affairs. Speeches. Vol. 5.

How can the Church Educate the People? Letter to the Archbishop of Canterbury. Lond., 1844. 8vo. Educa. Pamph. Vol. 32.

HOW, David. Diary in Rev. War, 1776. See DAWSON, H. B.

HOW, Henry K. The Battle of Trenton. A Poem. N. Brunswick, 1856. 8vo. Rev. War Pamph. Vol. 3.

How our National Debt can be Paid. Phila., 1865. 8vo. Rebellion Pamph. Vol. 7.

How shall we vote on the Water Act? Boston. n. d. 8vo. Boston Misc. Pamph. Vol. 1.
—— the War was Commenced; an Appeal to the Documents. N. Y., 1863. 8vo. Rebell'n Pamph. Vol. 17.
—— the Act in Baltimore in 1862. Rebell'n Pamph. Vol. 73.
—— to Enjoy London: or the Elegant Economist. Lond., 1837. 12mo. Guide Book. Vol. 1.
—— to get Fat; or the Means of Preserving the Medium between Leanness and Obesity. Lond., 1855. 8vo. 2d Ed. Med. Pamph. Vol. 14.
HOWARD, B. C. Report of Decision of Supreme Conrt of U. S. in the case of Dred Scott. Washington, 1857. 8vo. Rebell'n Pamph. Vol. 96. Another Copy. N. Y., 1857. 8vo.
HOWARD, Chas. and others. Memorial to Cong. for Arbitrary Arrests. 1862. Rebell'n Pamph. Vol. 20.
HOWARD, F. K. Fourteen Months in Amer. Bastiles. Baltimore, 1863. 8vo. Rebell'n Pamph. Vols. 12, and 73.
HOWARD, Jacob M. Speech in Congr. June 22 and 23, 1870, on Texas Pacific R. R. 8vo. Congr. & Polit. Pamph. Vol. 119.
HOWARD, John. See DIXON, H. Life of.
—— Sketch of his Life. n. d. Lond. 12mo. Biograph. Pam. Vol. 3.
HOWARD, J. M. Report to Cong. on Memorial of Davis Hatch on San Domingo affairs. Washington, 1869. 8vo.
—— Speech in Cong. on the Confiscation of Rebel Property. Rebell'n Pamph. Vol. 9.
—— Speech in Cong., Apr. 16, 1869, in regard to San Juan Island. Congr. & Polit. Pamph. Vol. 122.
HOWARD, Gen. O. O. Statement before Comm. of Cong., in Reply to Fernando Wood, etc. N. Y., 1870. 8vo. Congr. & Polit. Vol. 114.
HOWARD Papers. See CAUSTON, H. K. G.
HOWARD, Percy. Barbarities of the Rebels. Providence, 1863. Rebell'n Pamph. Vols. 1, 6, 69.
HOWARD, S. and C. Abridged Statement of Differences with the Detroit & Milwaukee R. R. Co. Mich. Misc. Pamph. Vol. 1.
HOWE, Geo. D. D. Early Hist. of Presbyterianism in S. Carolina. Sermon at Charleston, Nov. 15, 1854. Columbia, 1855, 8vo. S. C. Hist. Discourses Vol. 1.
—— Early Presbyterian Immigration into S. Carolina. Disc. before the Gen. Assem. May 7th, 1858. Columbia, 1858. 8vo. S. C. Hist. Disc. Vol. 1.
—— The Scotch Irish, and their first Settlements on the Tyger River in S. C. A Centen. Disc. Columbia, 1861. 8vo. S. C. Hist. Discourses Vol. 1.
HOWE, Henry. Hist. Collections of Ohio. Cincin., 1852. 8vo.
—— Hist. Collections of the Great West; containing the Most Important Events in Western History. 2 Vols. in 1. Cincin. 1853. 8vo.
—— Hist. Collections of Virginia; its History and Antiquities, with Maps and Engravings. Charleston, S. C., 1852. 8vo.
—— The Times of the Rebellion in the West; showing the part taken in the War by each Western State. Cincin., 1867. 8vo.

HOWE, Henry. Travels and Adventures of Celebrated Travelers in the principal Countries of the World. Cincin. 8vo. 1853.

HOWE, Rev. Jas. H. Oration at North East, N. Y., July 4, 1845. Poughkeepsie, N. Y. 12mo. Addresses. Vol. 29.

HOWE, J. W. Speech in Cong., June 5, 1850, on the Admission of Cal. Cong. and Polit. Pamph. Vol. 86.

HOWE, M. A. DeWolf. Letter relative to his reply to Bishop Hopkins, 1863. Rebell'n Pamph. Vol. 54.

HOWE, Rev. Nathan'l. Century Sermon at Hopkinton, Mass., Dec. 24, 1815, with a Memoir of the Author, by E. Nason. Boston, 1851. 8vo. 4th Ed. Mass. Hist. Discourses. Vol. 2.

HOWE, Sam'l. See ELLIS, Rev. Rufus. Memoir of.

HOWE, S. G. Essay on Separate and Congregate Systems of Prison Discipline. Boston, 1846. 8vo. Mass. Misc. Pamph. Vol. 1.

—— Letter on the Sanitary Condition of Troops in the neighborhood of Boston. Washington, 1861. Rebell'n Pamph. Vol. 62.

—— Letter to the Commissioners of Mass., for the State Reform School for Girls. Boston. 1854 8vo.

—— Letter to the Gov. of Mass., on the Teaching and Training of Idiots. Boston, 1851. 8vo.

—— The Cretan Refugees and their Amer. Helpers. Boston, 1868. 8vo. Hist. Pamph. Vol. 1.

HOWE, Tim. O. Address before the Amer. Iron Assoc. at Chicago, May 24, 1865. Chicago, 1865. 8vo. Addresses. Vol. 16.

—— Address before the Wis. State Teachers' Assoc., at Whitewater, Aug. 2, 1865. Madison, 1865. 8vo. Wis. Misc. Pamph. Vol. 1.

—— Speech at Madison, Mar. 29, 1860, on the State and National Governments—their Mutual Relations. Madison. 8vo. Wis. Misc. Pamph. Vol. 1. See also Rebell'n Pamph. Vol. 10.

—— Speech in Cong., Aug. 2, 1861, on Approving certain Acts of the President of the U. S. Rebell'n Pamph. Vol. 9.

—— Speech in Cong., Feb. 12, 1862, on the Pub. Debt. Congr. and Polit. Pamph. Vol. 88.

—— Speech in Cong., April 4, 1864, on Amendment to the Constitution. Rebell'n Pamph. Vol. 9.

—— Speech in Cong., Jan. 10, 1866, on Reconstruction. Rebell'n Pamph. Vols. 7 & 9.

—— Same, June 5, 1866. Rebell'n Pamph. Vols. 7 and 34.

—— Same, Jan. 31, 1868. Congr. and Polit. Pamph. Vols. 84 and 122.

—— Speech in Cong. on Impeachment of the Pres't, 1868. Congr. Polit. Pamph. Vol. 84.

—— Speech in Cong. Jan. 14 and 15, 1869, on Claims of Loyal Citizens of the South during the Rebellion. Congr. and Polit. Pamph. Vol. 89.

—— Speech in Cong. Jan. 24, 1870, on the Currency. Congr. and Polit. Pamph. Vols. 84 and 119.

—— Speech in Cong. Feb. 2, 1870, on Neutrality. Congr. and Polit. Pamph. Vol. 119.

HOWE, Tim. O. Speech in Cong. Mar. 27 and 28, 1871, on the San Domingo Question. Congr. and Polit. Pamph. Vol. 119.

—— Speech in Cong. Mar. 8, 1872, on Civil Service Reform. Congr. and Polit. Pamph. Vol. 138.

HOWE, Gen. Sir Wm. Narr. befors Comm. of House of Commons, Apr. 29, 1779, on his Conduct in America. 2d Ed. Lond., 1780. 4to.

HOWELL, B. C., D. D. The Early Baptists of Virginia. Address before the Amer. Baptist Hist. Soc., at N. Y., 1856. Phila., 1857. 8vo.

HOWELL, E. Catalogue of Ancient and Modern Books. Liverpool, 1870. 8vo.

HOWELL, Geo. R. Early Hist. of Southampton, L. I., with Geneologies. N. Y., 1866. 12mo.

HOWISON, John. Sketches of Upper Canada. Edinburgh, 1821. 8vo.

HOWISON, Lieut. N. M. Report on the Soil, Climate, etc., of Oregon. Washington, 1847. 8vo. Congr. and Polit. Pamph. Vol. 80.

HOWISON, Rob't R. Hist. of Virginia from its First Settlement by Europeans, to the present time. Phila. 2 vols. 8vo. 1846.

HOWITT, E. Letters from the U. S. in 1819—Indian Character, etc. Nottingham, Eng., 1820. 12mo.

HOWITT, Wm. Hist. of Priest-craft in all Ages and Nations. N. Y., 1855, 12mo.

HOWLAND, C. H. Remarks in Senate of Missouri, Jan. 13, 1865, on Equal Rights, etc. 8vo. Congr. and Polit. Pamph. Vol. 105.

HOWLAND, Edw. Grant as a Soldier and Statesman, a Hist. of his Military and Civil Career. Lond., 1868. 8vo.

HOWLAND, John. See HALL, E. B. Hist. Disc. on.

—— HALL, E. B. Life and Times of.

—— STONE, Rev. E. M. Life and Recollections. of.

HOWSE, Jas. Grammar. of the Cree Language; with an Analysis of the Chippewa Dialect. Lond., 1844. 8vo.

HOWSHIP, Dr. John. Hunterian Oration before the Royal Coll. of Surgeons, Feb. 14, 1833. Lond. 8vo. Med. Pamph. Vol. 13.

HOWSON, H. The American Jute; Paper before the Franklin Institute. Phila., Oct. 16, 1862. Agr. Pamph. Vol. 2.

HOXIE, Jos. H. Greeley decently dissected in a Letter to A. Oakey Hall. N. Y., 1862. 8vo. Rebellion Pamph. Vol. 7.

HOY, P. R., M. D. Deep-Water Fauna of L. Michigan. Trans. Wis. Acad. of Sciences, 1870–2.

—— Insects Injurious to Agriculture. Aphides. Trans. Wis. Acad. of Sciences, 1870–2.

HOYT, Albert H. Memoir of Wm. Plumer, Senior. N. E. Hist. and Gen. Reg. Vol. 25.

HOYT, David W. Genealog. Hist. of John Hoyt of Salisbury, and David Hoyt of Deerfield, Mass., and their Descendants. Boston, 1857. 8vo.

HOYT, E. Antiquarian Researches; comprising a Hist. of Indian Wars, in the Country bordering Conn. River, and parts adjacent. Greenfield, 1824. 8vo.

HOYT Genealogy. See HOYT, D. W.
HOYT, Geo. H. Kansas and the Osage Swindle. Washington, 1868. 8vo. Indian Pamph. Vol. 4.
HOYT, Rev. Jas. The Mountain Society; a Hist. of the 1st Presb. Ch. Orange, N. J. N. Y., 1860. 12mo.
HOYT, Dr. John W. Address on University Progress, before the Nat. Teachers' Assoc., at Trenton, N. J., 1869. N. Y., 1870. 8vo.
—— Report to the Nat. Teachers' Assoc., on an Amer. University. 1869. 8vo. Educa. Pamph. Vol. 5.
—— Reports on the London and Paris International Exhibitions of 1862 and 1867. Madison, 1869. 8vo. Wis. Misc. Pamph. Another Copy. Congress. Pamph. Vol. 106.
—— See Wis. Acad. of Sciences. Vol. 3.
HOYT, Jos. G. Address at his Inaugura. as Chancellor of Washington University, St. Louis, Oct. 4, 1859. St. Louis, 1859. 8vo. Mo. Coll. Pamph.
HUBARD, Edmund W. Speech in Cong., June 25, 1846, on the Tariff. Washington, 1846. 8vo. Speeches. Vol. 1.
HUBBARD, Edwin. Ancestral Register. 2 ruled sheets. Pamph. and Circular. Chicago, 1870.
HUBBARD, Fordyce M. Life of Wm. Richardson Davie. Sparks' Amer. Biog. 2d Ser. Vol. 12.
HUBBARD, G. G. Report on Postal Telegraph, 1869. Washington, 1869. 8vo. Congr. and Polit. Pamph. Vol. 127.
HUBBARD, Jere. Acc. of the Town of Wells, Me. Maine Hist. Soc. Coll. Vol. 1.
HUBBARD, Rev. Wm. Gen. Hist. of N. England, from the Discovery to 1680. 2d Ed. 1848. Mass. Hist. Soc. Coll. Vols. 5 and 6. 2d Ser.
—— Hist. of the Indian Wars in N. England, 1677, Revised, with Notes, etc., by Sam'l G. Drake. N. Y., 1865. 2 Vols. 4to.
—— Narra. of the Indian Wars in N. England from 1607 to 1677. Boston, 1775. 12mo.
HUBBARD, Wm. J. Argument before the Joint Special Com. of Mass. Legis. on the Boston Water Question. Boston, 1845. 8vo, Boston Misc. Pamph. Vol. 1.
HUBBARDTON, Vt. See CLARK, H. Hist. Address.
HUBBELL, Levi. Address before the State Agricult. Soc., Wis., Oct., 1852. Transactions, 1852.
—— Oration before the Y. M. Association of Albany, July 4, 1835. Albany, 1835. 8vo. Addresses, etc. Vol. 37.
—— Trial of Impeachment, by the Senate of Wisconsin, June, 1853, Madison, 1853. 8vo.
—— See KILBOURN, Byron. Review of Trial of.
—— RYAN, E. G. Argument in Case of.
HUBBELL, Seth. Narrative of his Sufferings in his Beginning a Settlement at Wolcott, Vt. Danville, 1826. 12mo. Vt. Hist. Discourses, etc. Vol. 3.
HUBBELL, Wheeler. Reply to a Pamphlet headed "Bureau of Ordnance and Hydrography, Apr., 1862." Washington, 1862. 8vo. Rebell'n Pamphlets. Vol. 61.

HUBBELL, Wheeler. The Way to Secure Peace and Establish Unity as one Nation. 1863. Rebell'n Pamph. Vol. 72.
HUBLEY, Bernard. Hist. of the Amer. Revolution. Vol. 1. Northumberland, Pa., 1805. 8vo.
HUDSON, Chas. Character of Abraham Lincoln. (n. d.) Rebell'n Pamph. Vol. 8.
—— Hist. of the Town of Lexington, Mass. Boston, 1868. 8vo.
—— Hist. of the Town of Marlborough, Mass., from 1657 to 1861, with a Genealogy of Early Settlers. Boston, 1862. 8vo.
—— Hist. of Westminster. Mendon, Mass., 1832. 8vo. Mass. Hist. Discourses, etc. Vol. 12.
—— Non-Resistance. Boston, 1848. 8vo. Rebell'n Pamph. Vol. 8.
—— Speeches in Cong., Dec. 27th and 28th, 1841, and July 8, 1842, on the Tariff. Washington, 1842. 8vo. Cong. and Polit. Pamph. Vol. 24.
—— Speech in Cong., Feb. 26, 1846, on the Wheat Trade. Washington, 1846. 8vo. Speeches. Vol. 1.
—— Speech in Cong., June 29, 1846, on the Tariff. Washington, 1846. 8vo. Speeches. Vol. 1.
HUDSON, Henry. Acc. of his Several Voyages. N. Y. Hist. Soc. Coll. Vol. 1.
—— See ASHER, Dr. G. M. Sketch of.
—— CLEVELAND, H. R. Life of.
—— DECOSTA, B. F. Sailing Directions of. 1608.
—— JUET, Rob't.
—— READ, J. M. Hist. Inquiry relative to.
HUDSON, H. N. Lectures on Shakspeare. 2d Ed. N. Y., 1857. 2 Vols. 12mo.
HUDSON, J. C. Letter on the Employment of Children as Chimney Sweeps. Lond., 1823. 8vo. Pamphleteer. Vol. 22.
HUDSON, N. H. See Londonderry Celebration.
HUDSON, N. Y. Balance and Columbian Repository, Newspaper. Jan., 1805, to Dec., 1805. 4to.
—— Same. Jan. to April, 1804. 4to.
—— 1st Presb. Ch. Manual. Hudson, 1852. 12mo. N. Y. Hist. Discourses, etc. Vol. 4.
—— See MILLER, S. B. Hist. Sketches.
—— Rural Repository, Newspaper. 1825.
HUDSON (O.) Observatory. See LOOMIS, E.
—— Proceedings on the 56th Anniversary of Settlement. Hudson, 1856. 8vo. Ohio Hist. Discourses, etc. Vol. 1.
HUDSON River Baptist Assoc. North. 11th and 17th Anniversaries, held in 1861 and 1867. Cohoes, 1861; Albany, 1867. 8vo.
—— —— Institute, Claverack, N. Y. Catalogue for 1864–5. N. Y. 1865. 8vo.
HUDSON, Rev. Tim. B. Address before the Phi Delta Soc'y of Oberlin College, Apr. 5, 1858, with a Biographical Notice of Prof. Hudson. Oberlin Coll. Pamphs.
HUDSON, Wis. See HALL, T. D. Acc. of.
—— North Star, Newspaper. Nov., 1854, to Aug. 1859. Folio.
—— Star and Times, Newspaper. 1866–1872. Folio.

HUDSON'S Bay. See CHAPPELL, E. Voyage to. 1817.
—— —— ELLIS, H. Voyage. 1746-7.
—— —— ROBSON, J. Six Years' Residence in.
—— —— WILLIS, W. Indians of.
—— —— Co. See FITZGERALD, J. E.
—— —— Territories. See MARTIN, R. M.
HUGHES, Capt. Elias. See SMUCKER, Isaac.
HUGHES, Rev. Henry. What am I? Lecture against Socialism, delivered at London. Lond., 1840. 8vo. Eng. Rel. Pamph. Vol. 90.
HUGHES, Jas. Speech in the Indiana Senate Chamber, Jan. 15, 1869, on the Baker-Cumback Correspondence. Congr. and Polit. Pamph. Vol. 122.
HUGHES, Archbishop John. Life of. Phila., 1864. 8vo. Biograph. Pamph. Vol. 6.
—— Sermon at N. Y., Aug. 17, 1862, on the Civil War in America. Phila., 1862. 8vo. Rebell'n Pamph. Vol. 3.
—— Sermon at the Cathedral of St. Patrick, N. Y., 1863. Rebell'n Pamph. Vol. 54.
HUGHES, John T. Doniphan Expedition, with Acc. of the Conquest of N. Mexico. Cincin., 1847. 8vo. Mex. War Pamph. Vol. 2.
HUGHES, Rev. Jos. Disc. at Bristol, Mar. 6, 1831, on the Death of Rev. Rob't Hall. Lond., 1831. 8vo. Eng. Sermons. Vol. 38.
—— Hist. of the Township of Meltham, near Huddlesfield, in the West Riding of the Co. of York, Eng. Lond., 1866. 12mo.
HUGHES, Mary. Life of Wm. Penn, Abridged. Lond., 1822. 12mo.
HUGHES, Rev. T. S. Address to the People of England, in the Cause of the Greeks. Lond., 1822. 8vo. 2d Ed. Pamphleteer. Vol. 21.
—— Considerations on the Greek Revolution. Lond., 1823. 8vo. Pamphleteer. Vol. 22.
HUGHES, W. Remarks on Geography as a Branch of Popular Educa., especially in Normal Schools. Lond., 1847. 8vo. Educa. Pamph. Vol. 32.
HUGUENOTS. See BRAWNING, W. S. Hist. of—in 6th Century.
—— SIMMS, W. G. Huguenots in Florida.
HUIDEKOPER, Alfred. Incidents in the Early Hist. of Crawford Co., Penn. Hist. Soc. of Penn. Vol. 4. Part 2.
HUIDEKOPER, Fred. Letter to Rev. H. W. Bellows, on the Meadville Theolog. School. N. Y., 1847. 12mo. Placed with Catalogue of School.
HUIDEKOPER, H. J. Obituary of. From the Christian Examiner. Boston, 1854. 8vo. Biograph. Pamph. Vol. 8.
HUISH, Rob't. Public and Private Life of His Late Majesty, George III., with Portraits. Lond., 1821. 4to.
—— The Last Voyage of Capt. Sir John Ross to the Arctic Regions, for the Discovery of a Northwest Passage, in 1829-33. Lond., 1836. 8vo.
HULL Genealogy. See CLARK, S. C. Descendants of R. Hull.

HULL, Isaac. Proceedings of the Court of Inquiry into his Official Conduct as Commandant of U. S. Navy Yard at Charleston. Washington, 1822. 8vo.

HULL, John. Memoirs and Diaries of. Amer. Antiquarian Soc. Coll. Vol. 3.

—— Plans and Suggestions for Improving the Condition of the Laboring Poor. Lond., 1835. 12mo. 5th Ed. Eng Misc. Pamph. Vol. 15.

HULL, Gen. Wm. See CAMPBELL, M. Revolu. Services and Life of.

—— Defence before the Gen. Court-Martial, March, 1814. Boston, 1814. 12mo. Pamphlets War of 1812. Vol. 1.

—— From the N. E. Register, Jan., 1857. Pamphlets War of 1812. Vol. 4.

—— Memoirs of the Campaign of the N. W. Army of the U. S. in 1812. Boston, 1824. 8vo. Pamphlets War of 1812. Vol. 4.

—— See SUMNER, W. H. Vindication of.

HULL, Wm. Remarks on the Corn Laws, in connection with the Prussian League. Lond., 1840. 8vo. Strangford Pamph. Vol. 23.

HUMASON, W. L. From the Atlantic Surf to the Golden Gate. Two Days and Nights among the Mormons. Hartford, 1869. 8vo. Mormon Pamph. Vol. 1.

HUMBOLT, Alexander Von. See AGASSIZ, Louis. Address on the Centen. Annivers. of his Birth.

—— Travels and Researches in America and Asiatic Russia, condensed by W. Macgillivray. Harpers' Fam. Libr. N. Y., 1855. 18mo.

—— and Bonpland. Travels in S. America in Dutch. Harlem, 1815. 6 Vols. 8vo.

—— Centennial. See Iowa Institute of Science and Arts. Celebration. 1869.

HUME, David. His Life, written by Himself. Lond., 1777. 12mo. Biograph. Pamph. Vol. 3.

—— Hist. of England from the Invasion of Julius Cæsar to the Abdication of James II. 1688. Boston, 1849. 6 Vols. 12mo.

HUME, Jos. See McMASTERS, S. Y.

—— Speech in Parl't, Mar. 10, 1835, on the Malt Tax. Lond. 8vo. Eng. Polit. Pamph. Vol. 41.

HUME, J. D. Evidence before the Comm. of the House of Commons, on the Corn Law, in 1839. Manchester, 1842. 8vo. Eng. Polit. Pamph. Vol. 44.

HUME, Rob't M. Letter on the Delay in the Masters' Offices in Chancery. Lond., 1832. 8vo. Law Pamph. Vol. 21.

HUMPHREY, David. Letters to Sir Jos. Banks on ths Sea Serpent seen in Gloucester Bay. N. Y., 1817. 12mo.

HUMPHREY, E. P. and CLELAND, T. H. Memoirs of Rev. Thos. Cleland. Cincin., 1859. 12mo.

HUMPHREY, Rev. Heman, D. D. Address at Amherst, Mass., 1829, on the Amer. Indians. Amherst, 1830. 12mo. Addresses, etc. Vol. 1.

HUMPHREY, Rev. Heman, D. D. Fast Day Sermon at Amherst, Apr. 8, 1841, on the Death of Prest. Harrison. Amherst, 1841. 8vo. Sermons. Vol. 36.

—— Life and Labors of Rev. T. H. Gallaudet. N. Y., 1857. 12mo.

—— Sermon at Dedica. of the College Chapel in Amherst, Mass., Feb. 28, 1827. Amherst, 1827. 8vo. Sermons. Vol. 27.

—— See TODD, Rev. John. Obit. Sermon.

—— Valedict. Address at Amherst Coll., 1845. Amherst, 1845. 8vo. Addresses. Vol. 1.

HUMPHREY, Henry B. Catalogue of the Library sold at Boston. Boston, 1871. 8vo.

HUMPHREYS, Maj. Gen. A. A. See DE PEYSTER, J. W. La Royale.

—— Preliminary Report of Explorations and Surveys, principally in Nevada and Arizona, couducted by Lt. G. M. Wheeler, 1871. Washington, 1872. 4to.

—— Report on the Levees of the Mississippi River, 1866. Sec. of War Miscell. Reports.

HUMPHREYS, David. Miscell. Works, including his Essay on the Life of Gen. I. Putnam. N. Y., 1790. 12mo.

HUMPHREYS, Jas. Letter to Edw. B. Sugden, on Alterations in the Eng. Laws of Real Property. Lond., 1827. 8vo. Law Pamph. Vol. 15.

HUMPHREYS, W. H. Letter to R. G. Payne, on the Proposed Modification of the Usury Law. n. d. 8vo. Congr. and Polit. Pamph. Vol. 76.

HUN, Dr. E. R. Paper before the Albany Institute, Jan. 5, 1869, on the Trichina Spiralis. Albany, 1869. 8vo. Med. Pamph. Vol. 12. Albany Institute Trans. Vol. 6.

HUN, Thos., M. D. Address before the Med. Soc. of the State of N. Y., Feb. 4, 1863. Albany, 1863. 8vo. Med. Pamph. Vol. 31.

—— Lecture before Albany Med. Coll., Oct. 3, 1848. 8vo. Addresses. Vol. 7 and 19.

HUNDRED Boston Orators. See LORING, J. S.

HUNGARIAN Independence. See Report on the Termination of the Hungarian Struggle, etc., 1850.

—— —— See Congress'l Speeches.

HUNGARY. See BRAWL, C. L. Hungary in 1851.

—— HENNINGSEN, C. F. Past and Future of. 1852.

—— LUDVIG, S. Kossuth; oder der Fall von Ungarn.

—— PAGET, J. Hungary and Transylvania.

—— PRAGAY, J. War in Hungary.

HUNNEWELL, Tas. F. Bibliography of the Hawaiian Islands. Boston, 1869. 4to.

—— Illustrations of the Hist. of the 1st Ch. in Charleston. N. E. Hist. and Gen. Reg. Vol. 24.

HUNT, Chas. H. Life of Edw. Livingston. With an Introduction by Geo. Bancroft. N. Y., 1864. 8vo.

HUNT, Cornelius E. The Shenandoah; or the Last Confederate Cruiser. N. Y., 1867. 12mo.

HUNT, Rev. D. Hist. of Pomfret, Conn.: Disc. in 1st Ch., Pomfret, Nov. 19, 1840. Hartford, 1841. 8vo. Conn. Hist. Discourses. Vol. 2.

HUNT, E. B. Union Foundations: a Study of Amer. Nationality, as a Fact of Science. N. Y., 1863. 8vo. Rebell'n Pamph. Vols. 6 and 65.

HUNT, Freeman. Merchants' Magazine and Commercial Review, 1839–61. N. Y. 44 Vols. 8vo.

HUNT Genealogy. See HUNT, W. L. G. and WYMAN, T. B.

HUNT, G. J. Hist. Reader; containing the War with G. Britain, 1812–15. N. Y., 1819. 12mo. Pamphlets War of 1812. Vol. 3.

HUNT, Harriot K. Glances and Glimpses; or 50 Years Social, including 20 Years Professional, Life. Boston, 1856. 12mo.

HUNT, Henry. To the Radical Reformers of England, Ireland and Scotland. Lond., 1820–3. 8vo. 4 Papers. Eng. Polit. Pamph. Vol. 35.

HUNT, Henry, M. D. Visit to the Red Sulphur Spring of Va., in 1837. Boston, 1839. 8vo. Va. Misc. Pamph. Vol. 1.

HUNT, J. The Amer. Union shown to be the "New Heaven and the New Earth," and its predicted Restoration to Life within four Years from its Death. N. Y., 1865. 8vo. Rebell'n Pamph. Vol. 23.

HUNT, Jas. Annivers. Address before the Anthropolog. Soc. of Lond., Jan. 5, 1864. Lond., 1864. 8vo. Scientific Pamph. Vol. 6.

—— On Physio-Anthropology, its Aims and Method. n. d. 8vo. Scientific Pamph. Vol. 6.

HUNT, Dr. J. G. Address before the Nat. History Club of Phila., Dec. 3, 1868. Phila. 8vo. Phila. Misc. Pamph. Vol. 2.

HUNT, John Warren. Wisconsin Gazetteer, containing the Names, Location, etc., of Counties, Cities, Towns, Villages, Post-Offices etc. Madison, 1853. 8vo.

—— See Wisconsin Almanac, 1856–7.

HUNT, Leigh. A Book for a Corner. N. Y., 1852. 12mo.

HUNT, Nathan. Brief Memoir of. Lond., 1854. 8vo. Biograph. Pamph. Vol. 4.

HUNT, Rob't. Hand-Book to the Official Catalogues: an Explanatory Guide to the Great Exhibition of 1851. Part 2. Lond., 12mo. n. d. Guide Books. Vol. 10.

—— Synopsis of the Contents of the Great Exhibitions of 1851 and '62. Lond. 12mo. Guide Books. Vol. 5.

HUNT, Theo. G. Speech in Cong., Mar. 23, 1854, on the Kansas and Nebr. Bill. Washington, 1854. 8vo. Speeches. Vol. 3. Congr. and Polit. Pamph. Vol. 3.

HUNT, Washington. Speech in Cong., June 20, 1842, on the Tariff. Washington, 1842. 8vo. Congr. and Polit. Pamph. Vol. 24.

HUNT, Wm. Amer. Biograph. Panorama. Albany, 1849. 8vo.

HUNT, Wm. G. See Western Review.

HUNT, W. L. G. and WYMAN, T. B. Genealogy of the Name and Family of Hunt. Boston, 1862–3. 4to.

HUNTER, Gen. D. Letter to Sec. of War on Negro Volunteers, 1862. Rebell'n Pamph. Vol. 100.

HUNTER, John D. Manners and Customs of Several Indian Tribes West of the Mississippi. Phila., 1823. 12mo.

HUNTER, Rev. Jos. Collections concerning the Ch. of Protestant Separatists at Scrooby, in Nottinghamshire—The Founders of New Plymouth. Lond., 1854. 8vo.

—— Collections concerning the Early History of the Founders of N. Plymouth. Mass. Hist. Soc. Coll. 4th Ser. Vol. 1.

—— Same. Lond., 1849. 8vo. N. Eng. Pamph. Vol. 1.

—— Diary of Ralph Thoresby, F. R. S., with his Correspondence. 1677–1724. Lond., 1830. 4 Vols. 8vo.

—— Genealog. Notices of Persons and Families who, in the Reign of Charles I, Emigrated to N. England from the Co. of Suffol. Mass. Hist. Soc. Coll. 3d Ser. Vol. 10.

—— Pope: His Descent and Family Connections. Lond., 1857. 12mo. Genealog. Pamph. Vol. 6.

HUNTER, Robt. M. T. Disc. before the Va. Hist. Soc., Dec. 14, 1854. Richmond, 1855. 12mo. Bound with Va. Hist. Soc. Coll. Vol. 1.

—— Oration at Inaugura. of Crawford's Equestrian Statue of Washington, at Richmond, Va., Feb. 22, 1858. Richmond, 1858. 8vo. Addresses. Vol. 32.

—— Speech in Cong., July 4, 1842, on the Tariff. Washington, 1842. 8vo. Congr. and Polit. Pamph. Vol. 25.

—— Speech in Cong., Feb. 24, 1854, on the Kansas and Nebr. Bill. Washington, 1854. 8vo. Speeches. Vol. 3. Congr. and Polit. Pamph. Vol. 93.

HUNTER, Wm. Sovereignty, Allegiance and Secession. Memphis, 1868. 8vo. Rebell'n Pamph. Vol. 57.

HUNTINGDON, Lady. See KNIGHT, H. C. Lady Huntington and her Friends.

HUNTINGFORD, Geo. I., D. D. The Petition of the Eng. Roman Catholics considered. Lond., 1812. 8vo. Eng. Polit. Pamph. Vol. 76.

HUNTINGTON Co., Penn. See ADAMS, J. Account of.

HUNTINGTON, D. Gen. View of the Fine Arts, Critical and Historical. 5th Ed. N. Y., 1854. 12mo.

HUNTINGTON, E. B. Geolog. Memoir of the Huntington Family in this Country. Stamford, 1863. 8vo.

—— History of Stamford, Conn. Stamford, 1866. 8vo.

HUNTINGTON, F. D., D. D. See Hadley, Mass., Bi-Centen. Celebra. 1859.

—— Sermon on the 50th Annivers. of the Boston Female Asylum, Sept. 20, 1850. Boston, 1850. 8vo. Sermons. Vol. 34.

—— Unconscious Tuition. From Barnard's Amer. Journ. of Educa. (n. d.) 8vo. Educa. Pamph. Vol. 3.

HUNTINGTON, Geo. C. Hist. Sketch of Kelley's Island. Fire Lands Pioneer. Vol. 4.

HUNTINGTON, J. W. Speech in Cong., Mar. 21, 1842, on the Resolutions of Mr. Clay. Washington, 1842. 8vo. Congr. and Polit. Pamph. Vol. 24.

—— Speech in Cong., May 31, 1842, on Apportionment. Washington, 1842. 8vo. Congr. and Polit. Pamph. Vol. 24.

HUNTT, Dr. Henry. Visit to the Red Sulphur Spring of Va. Boston, 1839. 8vo. Va. Misc. Pamph. Vol. 1.

HURD, John R. National Bank, or no Banks. N. Y., 1852 8vo.

HURLBUT, E. P. Essays on Human Rights and their Polit. Guarantees, with Preface and Notes by Geo. Combe. Edinburgh, 1847. 8vo. Eng. Polit. Pamph. Vol. 46.

—— Secular View of Religion in the State, and the Bible in the Pub. Schools. Albany, 1870. 8vo. Religious Pamph. Vol. 14.

HURLBUT Genealogy. See HURLBUT, H. H.

HURLBUT, H. H. Early Days at Racine, Wisconsin. Reply to C. E. Dyer's Address before the Old Settlers' Soc. Racine, 1872. 8vo. Wis. Local Hist. Vol. 2.

—— Paper read at a Family Meeting of Descendants of Samuel Hurlbut. Racine, Wis., 1861. 8vo. Genealog. Pamph. Vol. 11.

HURON, Ohio. See WEST, E. W. Memoir of.

HURTSPIERPONT: its Lords and Families. See ELLIS, Wm. S. Ancient and Modern Hist.

HURWITZ, Hyman. Introduct. Lecture before the University of Lond., Nov. 11, 1828. Lond., 1829. 8vo. 2d Ed. Educa. Pamph. Vol. 35.

HUSKISSON, Wm. See Select Speeches of, etc.

—— Speech in Parl't, Mar. 25, 1813, on the Finances of G. B. London, 1813. 8vo. Pamphleteer. Vol. 2.

HUSSEY, Rev. Arthur. Notes on the Churches in the Co's of Kent, Sussex and Surrey, mentioned in the Domesday Book. Lond., 1852. 8vo.

HUTCHINS, Thos. Description Topographique de la Virginie, de la Pennsylvanie, du Maryland, et de la Caroline. Septentrionale. Paris, 1781. 8vo.

—— Hist. Narr. and Topograph. Description of Louisiana and W. Florida. Phila., 1784. 8vo.

—— New Map of Western Parts of Va., Penn., Md., N. C. Lond., 1778. In cover.

—— Topograph. Description of Va., Penn., Md., and N. Carolina. Lond., 1778. 8vo.

HUTCHINSON, Rev. Aaron. Sermon at Windsor, July 2, 1777, at the Convention for forming the State of Vt. Vt. Hist. Soc. Coll. Vol. 1.

HUTCHINSON, Abijah. See HUTCHINSON, K. M. Memoir of.

HUTCHINSON, Anne. See ELLIS, G. E. Life of.

—— LAWRENCE, Eugene. Paper on.

HUTCHINSON, C. C. Resources of Kansas: 15 Years Experience. with Maps and 40 Illustrations. Topeka, 1871. 12mo.

HUTCHINSON Family Genealogy. See DERBY, P. Hutchinson Family of Cowlan, Eng.

—— —— WHITMORE, W. H.

HUTCHINSON, Rev. Francis. Hist. Essay on Witchcraft. Lond., 1718. 8vo.

—— —— Another Copy. 2d Ed. Lond., 1720. 8vo.

HUTCHINSON, Col. John. See HUTCHINSON, Lucy. Memoir of.

HUTCHINSON, I. W. Hist. of Adventures in the Camps of the Army of the Potomac, 1864. Rebell'n Pamph. Vol. 20.

HUTCHINSON, K. M. Memoir of Abijah Hutchinson, a Soldier of the Revolution. Rochester, 1843. 12mo. Rev. War Pamph. Vol. 5.

HUTCHINSON, Lucy. Memoir of Life of Col. John Hutchinson, Gov. of Nottingham Castle. Lond. n. d. 8vo.

HUTCHINSON, Simon. On the Drainage of Land, on Hydraulic and Pneumatic Principles. Grantham, Eng., 1851. 8vo. Agr. Pamph. Vol. 9.

HUTCHINSON, Gov. Thos. Collection of Original Papers relative to the History of the Colony of Mass. Bay. 1769. Boston, reprint, 1865 2 Vols. 4to. See Prince Society Publica.

—— Papers of. Mass. Hist. Soc. Coll. 2d Ser. Vol. 10. 3d Ser. Vol. 1.

—— See DEANE, Chas. Hist. Publications of.

—— Hist of the Colony of Mass. Bay, 1628 to 1749. 2d Ed. Lond., 1760. 2 Vols. 8vo.

—— Hist. of Province of Mass. Bay, 1749 to 1774. Lond., 1828. 8vo.

—— Memoir of. N. E. Hist. and Gen. Reg. Vol. 1.

—— Proceedings of His Majesty's Privy Council, upon an Address ot Mass. Bay for his Removal, and Lieut. Gov. Oliver, in 1774. Scarce Tracts. Vol. 4.

—— The Witchcraft Delusion of 1692, with Notes by Wm. F. Poole. Boston, 1870. 4to.

—— —— See also N. E. Hist. and Gen. Reg. Vol. 24.

HUTCHINSON, Rev. Wm. Address at Oswego, Dec. 25, 1838, on Claims of Foreign Powers in the U. States. Oswego, 1839. 8vo. Addresses. Vol. 38.

—— Hist. and Antiq. of the Co. Palatine of Durham. Durham, 1825. 3 Vols. 8vo.

HUTCHISON, Rev. Aeneas B. Monograph on the Hist. and Restoration of Callington Ch., Cornwall. Lond., 1861. 4to.

HUTTON, Wm. Life of, written by himself. Lond., 1841. 8vo. Biograph. Pamph. Vol. 15.

HYATT, H. S. Manufacturing, Agricultural and Industrial Resources of Iowa. Des Moines, 1873. 8vo.

HYDE, Fanny. Report of the Trial of, for Murder. N. Y., 1872. 8vo. Law Pamph. Vol. 24.

HYDE Genealogy. See WALWORTH, R. H.

HYDE, Wm. Address at the Opening of the New Town Hall, Ware, Mass., Mar. 31, 1847, with Hist. Sketches. Brookfield, 1847. 8vo. Mass. Hist. Discourses. Vol. 12.

HYDRAULICS. See EWBANK, T. Hydraulics and Mechanics.

—— POLONCEAU, A. R. Travaux Hydrauliques.

HYDROPATHY. A Few Pages on Hydropathy, or the Water Cure. Lond., 1843. 8vo. Strangford Pamph. Vol. 31.

—— See HARSHA, D. A. Principles of, 1852.

HYDROPHOBIA. See HOMANS, C. D. Case of, 1854.

—— LAYARD, Dan'l P. Essay on the Bite of a Mad Dog, 1763.

—— PINCKARD, Dr. G. Case of, 1808.

HYDROPHOBIA. POWELL, Dr. R. Case of, 1808.

HYPERCRITIC (The). Lond., 1783. 8vo. Eng. Misc. Pamph. Vol. 20.

I.

ICE (Manufacture of). See TWINING, A. C.
ICELAND. See BARROW, John, Jr. Visit to, in 1834.
—— Hist. and Descript. Acc. of Iceland, Greenland, etc.
—— PFEIFFER, I. Journey to Iceland.
ICHTHYOLOGY. See AUSTIN, F. W. G. Fishes of the St. Lawrence.
—— SMITH, S. V. C. Fishes of Mass.
—— STORER, D. H. Fishes of Mass.
IDAHO. See ARMSTRONG, M. K. Hist. and Resources of. 1866.
—— Proceedings of the Grand Lodge of Idaho, A. F. & A. M., at 1st Ann. Communication. 1867. Portland, 1868. 8vo.
IDE, Rev. Geo. B. Disc. at Phila., May 19, 1864, on the Freedmen. Rebell'n Pamph. Vol. 48.
IDES (The) of March; or Abraham Lincoln, as a Private Citizen, being a Sequel to the End of the Irrepressible Conflict. Phila., 1861. 8vo. Rebell'n Pamph. Vol. 23.
IDIOCY. See Insanity.
—— Mass. School for Idiotic Children—other States.
IDYL (An) for the People. N. Y., 1863. Rebell'n Pamph. Vols. 89 and 97.
IKIN, Rev. W. D. Sermon at Hammersmith, Apr. 20, 1856, in aid National and Sunday Schools. Hammersmith, 1856. 8vo. Eng. Sermons. Vol. 45.
ILFRACOMBE (Eng.) Guide. Ilfracombe, 1830. 12mo. Guide Books. Vol. 22.
ILIFF, Rev. Geo. An Eng. Education: what it means, and how it may be carried out. Lond., 1859. 12mo. 2d Ed. Educa. Pamph. Vol. 34.
ILLINOIS. Acts of 30th Gen. Assembly. 1842–3 Springfield. 8vo.
—— Adjt.-General. Ann. Reports, 1861–5. Springfield. 8 Vols. 8vo.
—— and Indiana Med. and Surg. Journal. Vol. 1. N. Ser. 1846–7. Vol. 2. N. Ser. 1847–8, except No. 1. Indianapolis and Chicago. 8vo.
—— and Michigan Canal. Memorial of Legisla. of Ill. to Cong., on Improvement of. Washington, 1868. 8vo. Congr. and Polit. Pamph. Vol. 67.
—— —— Report of Trustees for 1840, 1857 and 1858. Springfield, 1859. 8vo.
—— —— Rules, By-Laws, etc., of Trustees. Chicago, 1848. 8vo.
—— and Oubache Land Companies. Memorial to Cong., 1802. (n. d.) 8vo. Indian Pamph. Vol. 2.
—— and St. Louis Bridge Co. Reports of Chief Engineer, Oct., 1870. St. Louis, 1871. 8vo. Mo. Pamph. Vol. 1.
—— Ann. Reports of Public Officers and State Institutions for 1867. Springfield, 1867. 8vo.
—— Antiquities. See WALBRIDGE, T. C. Mound Structures of S. Ill.

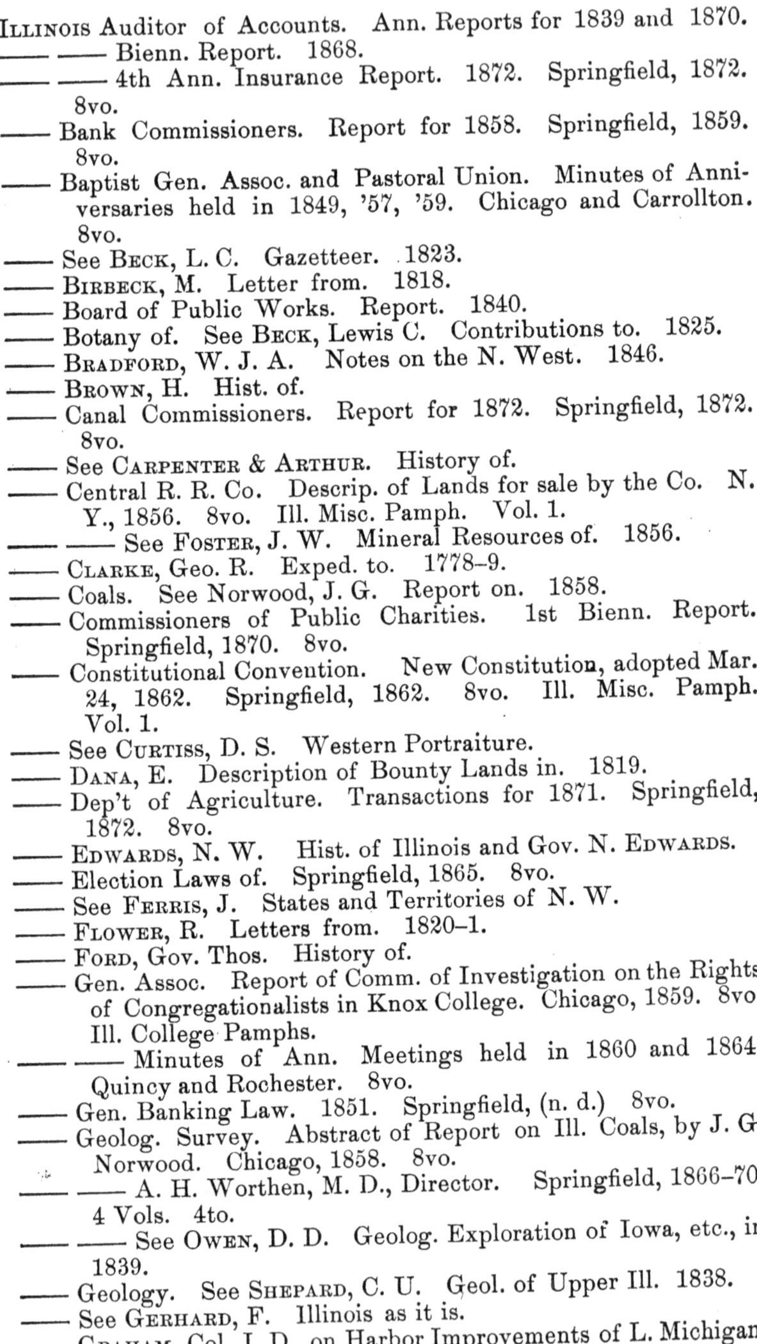

Illinois Auditor of Accounts. Ann. Reports for 1839 and 1870.
—— —— Bienn. Report. 1868.
—— —— 4th Ann. Insurance Report. 1872. Springfield, 1872. 8vo.
—— Bank Commissioners. Report for 1858. Springfield, 1859. 8vo.
—— Baptist Gen. Assoc. and Pastoral Union. Minutes of Anniversaries held in 1849, '57, '59. Chicago and Carrollton. 8vo.
—— See Beck, L. C. Gazetteer. 1823.
—— Birbeck, M. Letter from. 1818.
—— Board of Public Works. Report. 1840.
—— Botany of. See Beck, Lewis C. Contributions to. 1825.
—— Bradford, W. J. A. Notes on the N. West. 1846.
—— Brown, H. Hist. of.
—— Canal Commissioners. Report for 1872. Springfield, 1872. 8vo.
—— See Carpenter & Arthur. History of.
—— Central R. R. Co. Descrip. of Lands for sale by the Co. N. Y., 1856. 8vo. Ill. Misc. Pamph. Vol. 1.
—— —— See Foster, J. W. Mineral Resources of. 1856.
—— Clarke, Geo. R. Exped. to. 1778–9.
—— Coals. See Norwood, J. G. Report on. 1858.
—— Commissioners of Public Charities. 1st Bienn. Report. Springfield, 1870. 8vo.
—— Constitutional Convention. New Constitution, adopted Mar. 24, 1862. Springfield, 1862. 8vo. Ill. Misc. Pamph. Vol. 1.
—— See Curtiss, D. S. Western Portraiture.
—— Dana, E. Description of Bounty Lands in. 1819.
—— Dep't of Agriculture. Transactions for 1871. Springfield, 1872. 8vo.
—— Edwards, N. W. Hist. of Illinois and Gov. N. Edwards.
—— Election Laws of. Springfield, 1865. 8vo.
—— See Ferris, J. States and Territories of N. W.
—— Flower, R. Letters from. 1820–1.
—— Ford, Gov. Thos. History of.
—— Gen. Assoc. Report of Comm. of Investigation on the Rights of Congregationalists in Knox College. Chicago, 1859. 8vo. Ill. College Pamphs.
—— —— Minutes of Ann. Meetings held in 1860 and 1864. Quincy and Rochester. 8vo.
—— Gen. Banking Law. 1851. Springfield, (n. d.) 8vo.
—— Geolog. Survey. Abstract of Report on Ill. Coals, by J. G. Norwood. Chicago, 1858. 8vo.
—— —— A. H. Worthen, M. D., Director. Springfield, 1866–70. 4 Vols. 4to.
—— —— See Owen, D. D. Geolog. Exploration of Iowa, etc., in 1839.
—— Geology. See Shepard, C. U. Geol. of Upper Ill. 1838.
—— See Gerhard, F. Illinois as it is.
—— Graham, Col. J. D., on Harbor Improvements of L. Michigan.

ILLINOIS. HAINES, E. M. Compilation of Township Laws.
—— HALL, E. H. Gazetteer, etc., of Northern Ill.
—— Hospital for Insane. Ann. Reports, 1847 to 1862. Springfield. 8vo.
—— Incorporation Laws Passed by Gen. Assembly at the Session of 1836–7. Vandalia, 1837. 8vo.
—— Indians. See CATON, J. D.
—— in 1837; Sketch of the Situation, Boundaries, Face of the Country, etc., of the State of Ill. Phila., 1837. 8vo.
—— in the Rebellion. See WILSON, J. G. Sketches of Ill. Officers. 1862.
—— Industrial University. Report of Comm. on Courses of Study and Faculty for the University. Springfield, 1867. 8vo.
—— —— 1st, 2d and 3d Ann. Reports. Springfield, 1868–70. 8vo.
—— —— Ann. Report of the Regent, 1870. Champaign, 1870. 8vo.
—— Institution for Feeble-Minded Children. 1st, 2d, 3d, 4th Reports of Directors of the Experimental School. 1866–1868.
—— —— 8th Ann. Report of the Institution, etc., 1872. Springfield, 1866–72. 8vo.
—— Journals of Senate at 1st and 2d Sessions of 5th Gen. Assembly. Vandalia, 1826. 8vo.
—— Journals of Senate and House of Repr. of 4th Gen. Assembly. Vandalia, 1824. 8vo.
—— Journal of House of Repr. of 5th Gen. Assembly, 1st Session. Vandalia, 1826. 8vo.
—— Journal of Senate and House of Repr. of 6th Gen. Assembly, 1st. Session. Kaskaskia, 1829. 8vo.
—— Manual of the House of Repr. for 1832–3, 1834–5, 1836–7, 1838–9.
—— Journal of the Senate for 1832–3, 1834–5, 1836–7, 1838–9.
—— Journals of the Senate and House of Repr. 1857. Springfield, 1857. 2 Vols. 8vo.
—— Journals of the Senate and Assembly. Springfield, 1867. 3 Vols. 8vo.
—— Journal. Extra Session, 1867. 1 Vol. 8vo.
—— See KINZIE, Mrs. J. H. Wau-bun; or Early Day in the Northwest.
—— Laws of Ill. passed by the Gen. Assembly, 1831, '35, '36, '37, '39, '40, '41, '42, '43, '45, '47, '49, '50, '53, '54, '57, '59, '63, '67, '69, '72.
—— See LE BARON, W. 2d Report on Noxious Insects of.
—— Legislative Report on Improvement of the Ill. and Little Wabash Rivers. Springfield, 1872. 8vo.
—— —— on Gov. Palmer's Messages of Nov. 15 and Dec. 9, 1871. Springfield, 1872. 8vo.
—— Local History. See Chicago, Elgin, Fulton City, Galena, Morris, Ogle Co., Peoria, Putnam Co., Marshall Co., Springfield, Stephenson Co.
—— Manual of 25th Gen. Assembly, 1867. Springfield, 1867. 12mo.

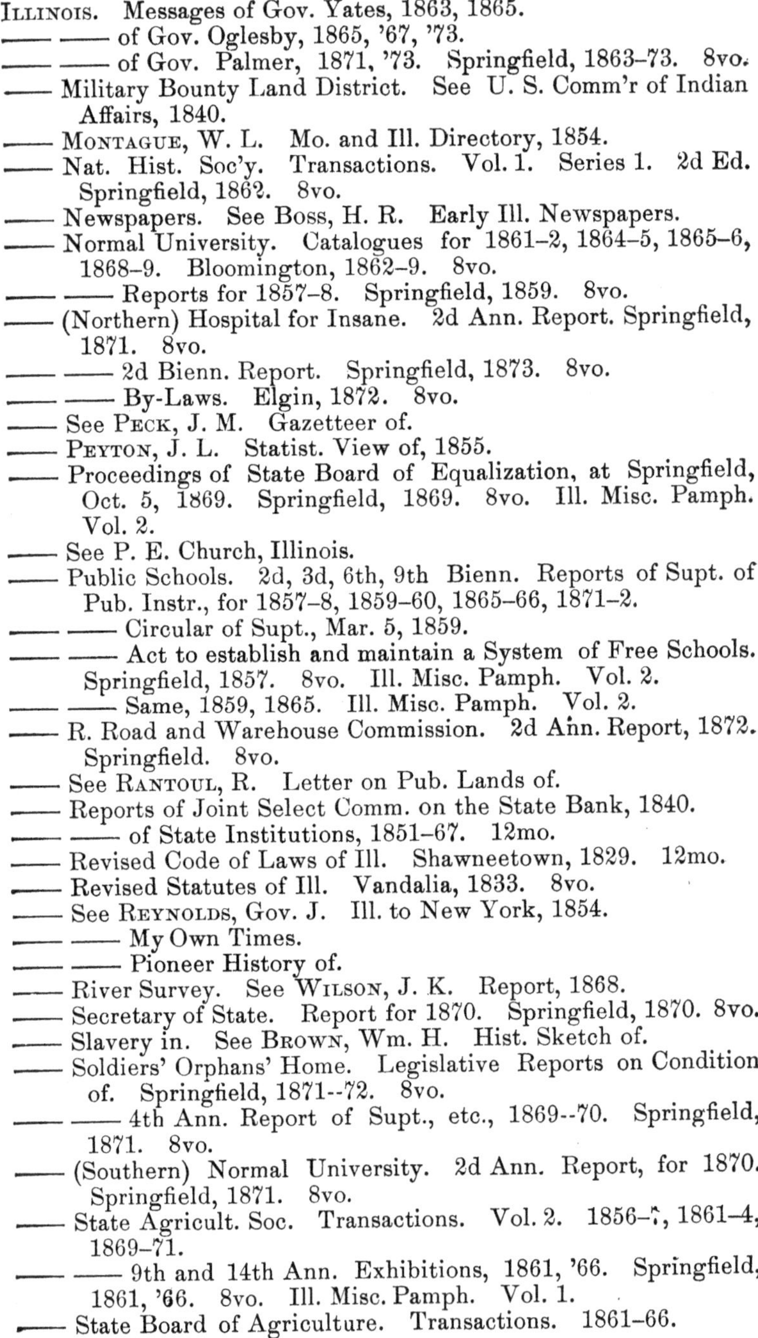

ILLINOIS. Messages of Gov. Yates, 1863, 1865.
—— —— of Gov. Oglesby, 1865, '67, '73.
—— —— of Gov. Palmer, 1871, '73. Springfield, 1863–73. 8vo.
—— Military Bounty Land District. See U. S. Comm'r of Indian Affairs, 1840.
—— MONTAGUE, W. L. Mo. and Ill. Directory, 1854.
—— Nat. Hist. Soc'y. Transactions. Vol. 1. Series 1. 2d Ed. Springfield, 1862. 8vo.
—— Newspapers. See Boss, H. R. Early Ill. Newspapers.
—— Normal University. Catalogues for 1861–2, 1864–5, 1865–6, 1868–9. Bloomington, 1862–9. 8vo.
—— —— Reports for 1857–8. Springfield, 1859. 8vo.
—— (Northern) Hospital for Insane. 2d Ann. Report. Springfield, 1871. 8vo.
—— —— 2d Bienn. Report. Springfield, 1873. 8vo.
—— —— By-Laws. Elgin, 1872. 8vo.
—— See PECK, J. M. Gazetteer of.
—— PEYTON, J. L. Statist. View of, 1855.
—— Proceedings of State Board of Equalization, at Springfield, Oct. 5, 1869. Springfield, 1869. 8vo. Ill. Misc. Pamph. Vol. 2.
—— See P. E. Church, Illinois.
—— Public Schools. 2d, 3d, 6th, 9th Bienn. Reports of Supt. of Pub. Instr., for 1857–8, 1859–60, 1865–66, 1871–2.
—— —— Circular of Supt., Mar. 5, 1859.
—— —— Act to establish and maintain a System of Free Schools. Springfield, 1857. 8vo. Ill. Misc. Pamph. Vol. 2.
—— —— Same, 1859, 1865. Ill. Misc. Pamph. Vol. 2.
—— R. Road and Warehouse Commission. 2d Ann. Report, 1872. Springfield. 8vo.
—— See RANTOUL, R. Letter on Pub. Lands of.
—— Reports of Joint Select Comm. on the State Bank, 1840.
—— —— of State Institutions, 1851–67. 12mo.
—— Revised Code of Laws of Ill. Shawneetown, 1829. 12mo.
—— Revised Statutes of Ill. Vandalia, 1833. 8vo.
—— See REYNOLDS, Gov. J. Ill. to New York, 1854.
—— —— My Own Times.
—— —— Pioneer History of.
—— River Survey. See WILSON, J. K. Report, 1868.
—— Secretary of State. Report for 1870. Springfield, 1870. 8vo.
—— Slavery in. See BROWN, Wm. H. Hist. Sketch of.
—— Soldiers' Orphans' Home. Legislative Reports on Condition of. Springfield, 1871--72. 8vo.
—— —— 4th Ann. Report of Supt., etc., 1869--70. Springfield, 1871. 8vo.
—— (Southern) Normal University. 2d Ann. Report, for 1870. Springfield, 1871. 8vo.
—— State Agricult. Soc. Transactions. Vol. 2. 1856–7, 1861–4, 1869–71.
—— —— 9th and 14th Ann. Exhibitions, 1861, '66. Springfield, 1861, '66. 8vo. Ill. Misc. Pamph. Vol. 1.
—— State Board of Agriculture. Transactions. 1861–66.

ILLINOIS State Business Directory, 1860. Chicago, 1860. 8vo.
—— State House Commissioners. Report for 1869–70. Springfield, 1871. 8vo.
—— —— Investigation. Report of the Comm. of Investiga. on the Affairs of the New State House. Springfield, 1871. 8vo.
—— State Penitentiary. Reports by the Commissioners for 1863–4, '65–6, '67–8, '70. Springfield, 1865, '7, '9. 8vo.
—— State Reform School. Ann. Report, 1870. Springfield, 1871. 8vo.
—— State Sanitary Commissioner. Report on Condition of Troops, Hospitals, etc., 1864. 8vo. Rebell'n Pamph. Vol. 48.
—— State Treasurer. Ann. Report, 1870. Springfield, 1870. 8vo.
—— Temperance Law of the State of Ill., passed in 1872. Springfield, 1872. 8vo. Ill. Misc. Pamph. Vol. 2.
—— War Record of the State of Ill. to Oct. 1, 1863. Proclamation of Gov. Yates, and Report of Adj. Gen. Fuller, Feb. 1, 1864. Springfield, 1864. 8vo. Rebell'n Pamph. Vol. 108.
—— See WELBY, A. Visit to Eng. Settlements, 1821.
—— WILSON, J. G. Ill. Officers in the War of Rebellion.
—— WOODS, John. Two Years Residence in, 1822.
ILLUSTRATED (The) Exhibitor and Magazine of Art. Vol. 1. Lond. 1852. 8vo.
ILLUSTRATIONS and Expositiosn of the Principles of the People's Co-Operative Equal Rights Party. n. d. 8vo. Congr. and and Polit. Pamph. Vol. 104.
IMISON, John. Treatise on the Mechanical Powers. Lond. 8vo. n. d. Scientific Pamph. Vol. 25.
IMLAY, Gilbert. Topograph. Descrip. of the Western Territory of N. America; with the Discovery and Present State of Ky. by John Filson, the Adventures of Daniel Boone, and Acc. of the Indian Nations, etc. 2d Ed. Lond., 1793. 8vo.
—— Same. 3d Ed. Lond., 1797. 8vo.
IMPARTIAL Enquiry into the Causes of the Present Fears and Dangers of the Government. Lond., 1692. Sm. 4to. Eng. Polit. Pamph. Vol. 65.
IMPERIAL Guide throughout the United Kingdom. Lond. n. d. 8vo. Guide Books. Vol. 9.
IMPORTANCE of the Study of Anatomy. From the Westminster Review. Boston, 1825. Med. Pamph. Vol. 7. 8vo.
IMPORTANT Question (The) concerning Invasions, Subsidies for Foreign Troops, etc. Lond., 1755. 8vo. Eng. Polit. Pamph. Vol. 14.
IMPRESSMENT of Seamen. See ADAMS, John. Correspondence, etc.
—— BUTLER, Chas. On the Legality of.
—— Copies and Extracts of Doc's on Impressment, 1812.
—— LLOYD, J. Letter to T. H. Perkins on.
—— Right (The) and Practice of Impressment.
—— URQUHART, Thos. Letter to W. Wilberforce, 1824.
IMPRISONMENT for Debt. See Debt.
"IN AND OUT," or the Right Men in the Wrong Place; a Letter to the New Members of the Palmerston Parl't of 1857. Lond., 8vo. Eng. Polit. Pamph. Vol. 54.

INAUGURATION of the Perry Statue at Cleveland, O., Sept. 10, 1860, with a Hist. of the Battle of L. Erie by Geo. Bancroft. Cleveland, 1861. 8vo. Pamphlets War of 1812. Vol. 4.

—— of the Statue of Dan'l Webster, Sept. 17, 1859. Boston, 1859. 8vo. Boston Misc. Pamph. Vol. 1.

INCIDENTS and Sketches connected with the Early Hist. and Settle ment of the West. Cincin. n. d. 8vo.

INCOME Tax. See Congress'l Speeches.

—— —— Remarks upon the Legality of the. n. d. n. p. Congr. and Polit. Pamph. Vol. 128.

INDEPENDENT (The) Whig. A Defence of Primitive Christianity. Hartford, 1816. 8vo.

INDIA Affairs. See ANDERSON, Geo. Gen. View of the Variations, etc., 1784–92.

—— —— BRUCE, John. Speech in House of Commons, 1813.

—— —— Case of the Governor and of the Council of Madras, 1777. Lond., 1777. 4to. Eng. Polit. Pamph. Vol. 5.

—— —— See CHAPMAN, John. Baroda and Bombay; their Political Morality, etc.

—— —— DE MONTALEMBERT, M. Debate in the Eng. Parl't in 1858.

—— —— DUNDAS, Henry. Speech in House of Commons, 1793.

—— —— See East India Co.

—— —— HARRISON, Wm. Speech on East India Shipping, 1814.

—— —— HASTINGS, Marquess of. Administration of the Gov't, 1813–23.

—— —— Intercepted Correspondence from India, 1805.

—— —— JEPPHI, Recos. Ministerial Almanack, etc.

—— —— KINLOCH, C. W. Mutinies in the Bengal Army.

—— —— Letter from Fort St. George, Oct. 10, 1776, on India Affairs. n. d. Folio. Eng. Polit. Pamph. Vol. 4.

—— —— Letter to Sir Chas. Forbes, on the Suppression of Public Discussion in India, 1824.

—— —— Second Setter on the Same, 1824.

—— —— Letter to the Earl of Buckinghamshire, on Open Trade to India, 1813.

—— —— Letters on the New System of E. India Shipping, 1803.

—— —— Letters to Edmund Burke, on Evidence relating to.

—— —— MACLEAN, Dr. C. Affairs of Asia and the Liberties of Britain, 1806.

—— —— Mutiny of the Bengal Army.

—— —— Reports on the Administra. of Justice in Bengal, Bahar, and Orissa. Lond., 1783–4. 8vo. Eng. Polit. Pamph. Vol. 20.

—— —— See PRICE, Jos. Letter to Sir Philip J. Clerke.

—— —— Series of Facts, shewing the Polit. State of India, etc.

—— —— WARING, Scott. Present State of the East India Co., 1808.

—— Agr. and Horticult. Soc. Code of By-Laws, Mar. 30, 1850. Calcutta. 8vo. Agr. Pamph. Vol. 11.

—— Ancient and Modern. Lond. n. d. 12mo. Hist. Pamph. Vol. 20.

INDIA and Lord Ellenborough. Lond., 1844. 8vo. 3d Ed. Strangford Pamph. Vol. 38.
—— See Asiatic Register, 1800.
—— British India: her Claims, etc.
—— BUCKINGHAM, J. S. Plan for the Future Gov't of.
—— FERGUSON, Jas. Rock-Cut Temples of.
—— GIBSON, W. M. Prison of Weltevreden, etc.
—— GRINDLAY, Capt. Melville. Steam Communication with, 1837.
—— HEBER, R. Journey through N. Provinces, 1824–5.
—— Hist. Sketch of Missions, 1862.
—— JACOB, John. Native Army of, 1858.
—— Life in India.
—— MACKENZIE, Mrs. C. Six Years in.
—— MACKENZIE, R. War with Tippoo Sultain.
—— MINTURN, R. B. N. Y. to Delhi.
—— MURRAY, H. Hist. and Descript. Acc. of.
—— OVIEDO, F. de. Historia General y Natural.
—— Reform Tracts, Nos. 1–5. Lond., 1852? 8vo. Strangford Pamph. Vol. 64.
—— See RIEDEL, H. Oude Historie.
—— See Sepoy Mutiny.
—— TAYLOR, B. Visit to India, China and Japan.
—— WARD, F. D. W. India and Hindoos.
—— WRIGHT, Caleb. India and its Inhabitants.
INDIAN River Navigation; or, Steam Navigation upon the Rivers of India. Lond., 1850. 8vo. Strangford Pamph. Vol. 58.
—— Summer. Essay on, read before the Md. Acad. of Sciences, 1833. Silliman's Journ. Vol. 27.
—— —— See FOOT, Lyman. Remarks on, 1835.
INDIANA. Act to provide for a Gen. System of Common Schools and Libraries. Indianapolis, 1852. 8vo. Ind. Misc. Pamph. Vol. 1.
—— Acts of 42d Gen. Assembly. Indianapolis, 1863. 8vo.
—— See Addresses to Legislature on Educa., etc., 1849–52.
—— Adjutant Gen. Reports on the War of the Rebellion, Roster of Officers, etc. Indianapolis, 1869. 8 Vols. 8vo.
—— Agricult. Reports, 1859–60. Indianapolis, 1860–1.
—— Auditor of State. Ann. Reports for 1853, '57, '68, '69. Indianapolis, 1854–70. 8vo.
—— Baptist Gen. Assoc. Minutes of 20th Annivers., held at Ebenezer, 1852. Indianapolis, 1852. 8vo.
—— Colonization Soc. 11th and 12th Ann. Reports for 1845, 1846. Indianapolis. 8vo and 12mo. Ind. Misc. Pamph. Vol. 1.
—— Conspirators. See Review of Decision of U. S. Court.
—— Constitution of, and the Address of the Constitutional Convention. New Albany, 1851. 8vo. Ind. Miscell. Pamph. Vol. 1.
—— See COX, S. C. Settlement of Wabash Valley.
—— DILLON, J. B. History of, 1859.
—— Documents of Gen. Assembly for 1844–5, '45–6, '48–9, '49–50, '50–1, '51–2, '53. 7 Vols. Indianapolis. 8vo.
—— See ELLSWORTH, H. W. Valley of the Wabash.

INDIANA. FERRIS, J. States and Territories of G. West.
—— Gazetteer; or Topograph. Dictionary Indianapolis, 1850. 12mo.
—— Geolog. Survey. Report of a Geolog. Reconnoissance made in 1837, by D. D. Owen. Indianapolis, 1853. 8vo. Doc. Journal of Ind. 1853.
—— Hospital for Insane. Reports for 1853 and 1865. Indianapolis, 1853–66. 8vo.
—— Institute for the Blind. Ann. Reports for 1853–79. Indianapolis, 1853–70. 8vo.
—— Institution for Deaf and Dumb. Ann. Reports for 1853–54. Indianapolis, 1853. 8vo.
—— See LAW, J. Colon. Hist. of Vincennes.
—— Laws of the Territory passed at the 1st Session of the 2d Gen. Assembly. 1807. Vincennes, 1807. 8vo.
—— Laws of the State. 1846–49, '53, '55, '61, '63. Indianapolis.
—— Local Hist. See COTTON, A. J. Poems, with Hist. of Early Settlements in Ind.
—— —— See Fort Wayne, Indianapolis, Montgomery, Wayne Co.
—— Medical College. Catalogues, 1845–6, 1846–7, 1847–8. Chicago, and La Porte. 1846–48. 8vo.
—— See KNAP, M. L. Address. 1847.
—— Memorial of Bondholders of State Bank for 1844–1845.
—— Message of Gov. Wright, Jan., 1853. Indianapolis, 1853. 8vo.
—— Message of Gov. to Legislature, Jan. 6, 1865. Rebell'n Pamph. Vol. 23.
—— Message of Gov. Morton, Jan. 11, 1867. Indianapolis, 1867. 8vo.
—— Normal Acad. of Music. Ann. Catalogue. 1865–66. Indianapolis, 1866. 8vo.
—— Revised Statutes of the State of Ind., passed at the 27th and 36th Sessions of the Gen. Assembly. Indianapolis, 1852. 2 Vols. 8vo.
—— —— in the German Language. Indianapolis, 1853. 2 Vols.
—— Rules and Regulations for the Gov't of the Militia of the State of Ind. Indianapolis, 1853. 8vo. Ind. Misc. Pamph. Vol. 1.
—— School Laws of the State of Ind., with forms. 1844, '53, '55. Indianapolis. 8vo.
—— Secretary of State. Ann. Report for 1853. Indianapolis, 1853. 8vo.
—— See SMITH, O. H. Early Trials and Reminiscences.
—— State Agricult. Soc'y. See GREELEY, H. Address. 1853.
—— State Bank. Report of, for 1853. Indianapolis, 1853. 8vo.
—— State Board of Agriculture. Reports for 1851–2, '53, '54, '55, '59, '60. Indianapolis, 1852–61. 8vo.
—— —— Rules, etc., for the 9th Ann. Fair. 1860. Indianapolis, 1860. 8vo. Ind. Misc. Pamph. Vol. 1.
—— —— of Colonization. Report of the Secretary for 1853. Indianapolis, 1853. 8vo.

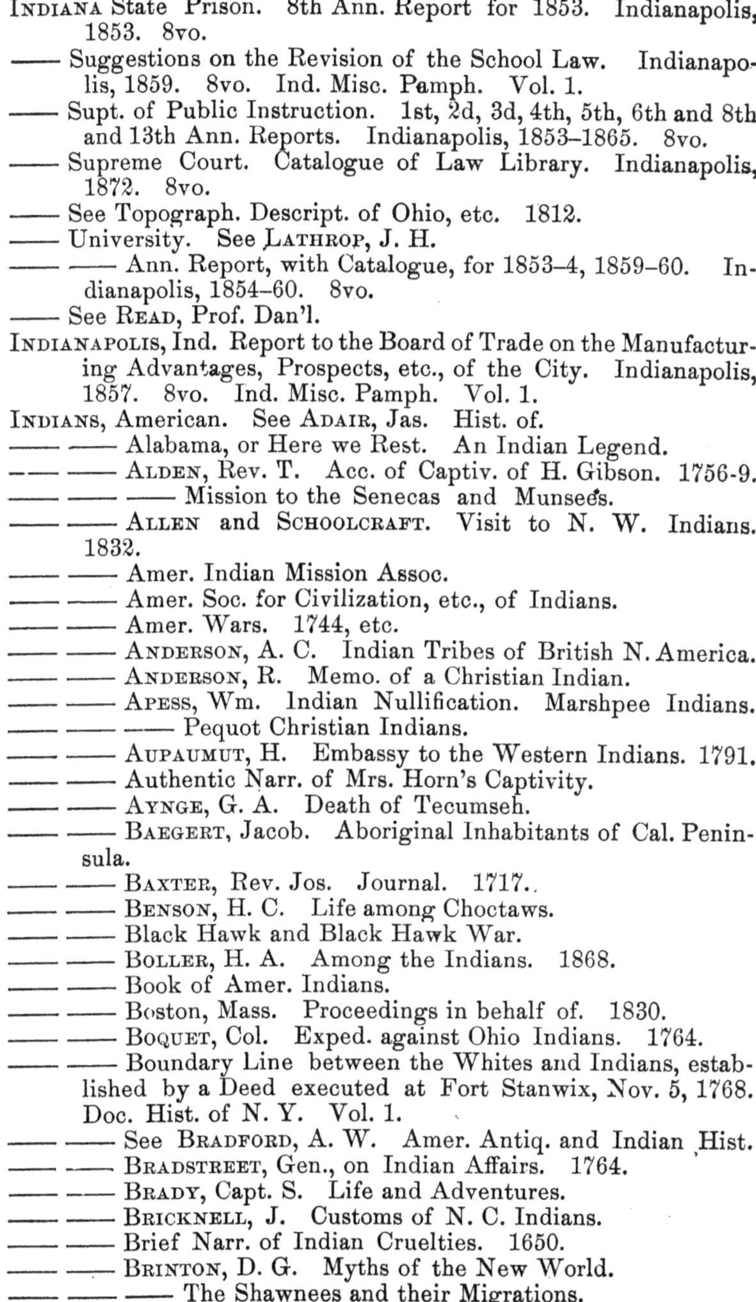

INDIANA State Prison. 8th Ann. Report for 1853. Indianapolis, 1853. 8vo.

—— Suggestions on the Revision of the School Law. Indianapolis, 1859. 8vo. Ind. Misc. Pamph. Vol. 1.

—— Supt. of Public Instruction. 1st, 2d, 3d, 4th, 5th, 6th and 8th and 13th Ann. Reports. Indianapolis, 1853–1865. 8vo.

—— Supreme Court. Catalogue of Law Library. Indianapolis, 1872. 8vo.

—— See Topograph. Descript. of Ohio, etc. 1812.

—— University. See LATHROP, J. H.

—— —— Ann. Report, with Catalogue, for 1853–4, 1859–60. Indianapolis, 1854–60. 8vo.

—— See READ, Prof. Dan'l.

INDIANAPOLIS, Ind. Report to the Board of Trade on the Manufacturing Advantages, Prospects, etc., of the City. Indianapolis, 1857. 8vo. Ind. Misc. Pamph. Vol. 1.

INDIANS, American. See ADAIR, Jas. Hist. of.

—— —— Alabama, or Here we Rest. An Indian Legend.

—— —— ALDEN, Rev. T. Acc. of Captiv. of H. Gibson. 1756-9.

—— —— —— Mission to the Senecas and Munsees.

—— —— ALLEN and SCHOOLCRAFT. Visit to N. W. Indians. 1832.

—— —— Amer. Indian Mission Assoc.

—— —— Amer. Soc. for Civilization, etc., of Indians.

—— —— Amer. Wars. 1744, etc.

—— —— ANDERSON, A. C. Indian Tribes of British N. America.

—— —— ANDERSON, R. Memo. of a Christian Indian.

—— —— APESS, Wm. Indian Nullification. Marshpee Indians.

—— —— —— Pequot Christian Indians.

—— —— AUPAUMUT, H. Embassy to the Western Indians. 1791.

—— —— Authentic Narr. of Mrs. Horn's Captivity.

—— —— AYNGE, G. A. Death of Tecumseh.

—— —— BAEGERT, Jacob. Aboriginal Inhabitants of Cal. Peninsula.

—— —— BAXTER, Rev. Jos. Journal. 1717.

—— —— BENSON, H. C. Life among Choctaws.

—— —— Black Hawk and Black Hawk War.

—— —— BOLLER, H. A. Among the Indians. 1868.

—— —— Book of Amer. Indians.

—— —— Boston, Mass. Proceedings in behalf of. 1830.

—— —— BOQUET, Col. Exped. against Ohio Indians. 1764.

—— —— Boundary Line between the Whites and Indians, established by a Deed executed at Fort Stanwix, Nov. 5, 1768. Doc. Hist. of N. Y. Vol. 1.

—— —— See BRADFORD, A. W. Amer. Antiq. and Indian Hist.

—— —— BRADSTREET, Gen., on Indian Affairs. 1764.

—— —— BRADY, Capt. S. Life and Adventures.

—— —— BRICKNELL, J. Customs of N. C. Indians.

—— —— Brief Narr. of Indian Cruelties. 1650.

—— —— BRINTON, D. G. Myths of the New World.

—— —— —— The Shawnees and their Migrations.

INDIANS, American. BRISBIN, J. S. Belden, the White Chief.
—— —— British Trade with N. Amer. Indians.
—— —— BROWNE, J. Ross. Adventures in the Apache Country.
—— —— BROWNELL, C. D. W. Ind. Races of America.
—— —— BRYANT, C. S. Indian Massacres in Minn.
—— —— BULKLEY, Rev. J., on Indian Titles to Land.
—— —— BURDER, G. Welch Indians.
—— —— Captivity of Mrs. E. Hanson.
—— —— CATLIN, Geo. Fourteen Ioway Indians.
—— —— —— Illustra. of Manners and Customs.
—— —— —— Last Rambles among Indians.
—— —— —— Life among Indians.
—— —— —— Notes of Eight Years' European Travel.
—— —— —— O-kee-pah. A Ceremony of the Mandans.
—— —— —— N. American Indians.
—— —— CAXTON, J. D. The Last of the Illinois, etc.
—— —— Cherokees.
—— —— Chickasaws.
—— —— Choctaws.
—— —— CHURCH, T. Hist. of Philip's War. 1675.
—— —— CLARK, J. V. H. Lights and Lines of Ind. Character.
—— —— COATES, B. H., on the Origin of.
—— —— COLDEN, C. Hist. of Five Nations.
—— —— COLESON, A. Captivity with Sioux.
—— —— Colonial Intelligence, or Aborigine's Friend. 1847–58.
—— —— COLTON, C. Tour among Indians in N. W. Terr. 1830.
—— —— COLYER, Vincent. Peace with Apaches. 1872.
—— —— COMMUCK, Thos. Indian Melodies.
—— —— Congress Report on Intercourse with the Indian Tribes. 1851. Congress. Pamph. Vol. 41.
—— —— —— on the Management of Indians in British America, by the British Gov't. 1870. Congress. Pamph. Vols. 105 and 116.
—— —— —— on the Passage of a Gen. Law concerning Indians. 1865. Congress. Pamph. Vol. 137.
—— —— —— on the Removal of the Indians. 1830. Indian Pamph. Vol. 1.
—— —— See Congress'l Speeches.—Ind. Appropriations, etc.
—— —— COPWAY, G. Life, Hist. and Travels.
—— —— —— Life, Letters and Speeches.
—— —— —— Organiza. of Indian Territory.
—— —— —— Ojibway Conquest.
—— —— —— Tradit. Hist. and Sketches of Ojibway Nation.
—— —— Correspondence, etc., relating to Expeditions against the Indians. Salem, Oregon, 1855. 8vo. Congr. and Polit. Pamph. Vol. 85.
—— —— CREMONY, J. C. Life among the Apaches.
—— —— CUSICK, D. Sketches of Ancient Hist. of the Six Nations.
—— —— See Dakota Indians.
—— —— Day Breaking on N. E. Indians. 1647.
—— —— DEFOREST, J. W. Hist. of the Indians of Conn.

INDIANS, American. DEHASS, W. Indian Wars of Virginia.
—— —— D'ERES, C. D. R. Memoirs and Captivity.
—— —— DESMET, P. J. Indian Tribes of Rocky Mountains.
—— —— Documents relative to the Indian Trade. Washington, 1822. 8vo. Indian Pamph. Vol. 1.
—— —— See DODGE, J. R. Red Man of Ohio Valley.
—— —— DRAKE, B. Life, etc., of Black Hawk.
—— —— —— Life of Tecumseh and Hist. of Shawanoe Indians.
—— —— DRAKE, S. G. Biog. and Hist. of N. A. Indians.
—— —— —— Book of Indians.
—— —— —— Cat. of Priv. Libr'y.
—— —— —— Indian Biography.
—— —— —— Indian Captivities.
—— —— —— Notes on Indian Wars in N. Eng.
—— —— EARLE, J. M. Report on Mass. Indians. 1861.
—— —— EASTMAN, Mrs. M. Dahcota, or Legends of Sioux.
—— —— EASTON, J. Narr. of Philip's Indian War.
—— —— ELLIS, A. G., on Advent of N. Y. Indians in Wis.
—— —— Inquiry into Alienation of Delaware Ind. 1759.
—— —— Essay on Religious Instruction of.
—— —— Essay towards an Indian Bibliography.
—— —— Essays on Condition of.
—— —— EVANS, Gov. John. Massacre of the Cheyenne Indians.
—— —— Events in Indian Hist. 1842.
—— —— EWBANK, T. Aboriginal Ingenuity.
—— —— Examination of an Article in N. Amer. Review, for Jan., 1826, respecting the Indians of America. From the N. York Review, May, 1826. Indian Pamph. Vol. 4.
—— —— Extracts from Reports of Missions to the Cherokees, Creeks, etc., 1835. 8vo. Indian Pamph. Vol. 2.
—— —— See Facts relative to Canadian Indians. 1838–9.
—— —— FARMER, J. Acc. of Penacook Indians in N. H.
—— —— FARMAR, S. F. Religion of Indian Tribes.
—— —— FINDLAY, J. B. Life among the Indians.
—— —— FLINT, T. Indian Wars.
—— —— FOULKE, W. P. Indians of Lancaster Co., Penn.
—— —— See Friends (Soc'y of.)
—— —— FROST, J. Border Wars of the West.
—— —— —— Indian Wars of U. S.
—— —— GARDNER, W. H. Ethnology of Indians of the Valley of the Red River of the North.
—— —— GALLATIN, A. Indians of N. W. America.
—— —— —— Synopsis of the Indian Tribes. 1836.
—— —— GIBBS, Geo. Chepewyan Indians of British America.
—— —— GIFFORD, A. Aborigines of N. Jersey.
—— —— GILES, John. Adventures and Captivities.
—— —— GOOKIN, D. Christian Indians of N. Eng. 1675–7.
—— —— Hist. Coll. of N. Eng. Indians.
—— —— GREGORY, J. J. H. Indian Relics from Marblehead, Mass.
—— —— GURLEY, R. R. Memorial to Cong., for Purchase of Catlin's Indian Portraits, etc.

INDIANS, American. HALKETT, J. Hist. Notes respecting.
—— —— HALL, James. The Wilderness and War Path.
—— —— HARRISON, M. Indian Barbarity.
—— —— HARRISON, W. H. Address on Aborigines of Ohio Valley.
—— —— HARVEY, H, Hist. of Shawnee Indians.
—— —— HAWKINS, Benj. Creek Country in 1788–9.
—— —— HAYDEN, F. V. Ethnography and Philology of Mo. In-Indians.
—— —— HECKEWEDDER, J. Mission among Indians.
—— —— —— Names of Rivers in Delaware Language, with Acc. of Indian Chiefs.
—— —— HENRY, A. Narr. of his Captivity.
—— —— HERIOT, G. Manners and Customs of.
—— —— HINES, Rev. G. Adventures among.
—— —— HINMAN, S. D. Journal as Missionary to the Santee Sioux, 1869.
—— —— Hist. of Moravian Missions among Amer. Indians.
—— —— HODGSON, Wm. B. The Creek Confederacy.
—— —— HOSMER, H. P. Mary Palmer, the Captive of the Genesee.
—— —— HOUGH, F B. N. Y. Indian Treaties.
—— —— —— Peter Penet among the Oneidas.
—— —— HOYT, E. Hist. of Indian Wars.
—— —— HUBBARD, Rev. W. Indian Wars N. E., 1677.
—— —— HUMPHREY, Rev. H. Address on.
—— —— HUNTER, John D. Manners and Customs of Ind. Tribes.
—— —— IMLAY, G. Description of the Western Terr'y, etc.
—— —— Indian Battles, Captivities, and Adventures, from the earliest period to the present time. Edited by John Frost. N. Y., 1858. 12mo.
—— —— Indian Battles, Murders, Sieges, and Forays in the South West. Nashville, 1853. 8vo. Indian Pamph. Vol. 5.
—— —— Indian Narratives: or Hist. of Indian Wars from Landing of Pilgrim Fathers, 1620, to Gen. Wayne's Victory, 1794, with acc. of Burning of Royalton, and Capture of Mrs. Johnson, Zadoc Steele and others. Claremont, 1854. 12mo.
—— —— Indian Traditions, Customs, etc. From Memoirs of Rev. David Zeisberger and other Missionaries. "Olden Time." Vol. 1.
—— —— Indian Treaties made by Mass. with the Indians, 1735, '49, '52. Maine Hist. Soc. Coll. Vol. 4.
—— —— Indian Treaty made at Easton, Penn., in 1758. Amer. Pioneer. Vol. 1.
—— —— Indians (The); or Narratives of Massacres and Depredations on the Frontier, in Wawasink and Vicinity, during the Revolution. Rondout, N. Y., 1846. 8vo. Indian Pamph. Vol. 2.
—— —— See Iroquois Indians.
—— —— IRVING, J. J. Indian Sketches.
—— —— JAMESON, Mrs. Rambles among the Red Men.
—— —— JARVIS, S. F. On Religion of Indian Tribes.

INDIANS, American. JEFFRIES, C. Wabash Captives.
—— —— JOHNSON, W. R. Descript. of Ind. Engraving.
—— —— JOHNSTON, Chas. Narr. of Captivity.
—— —— JOHNSTON, John. State of Indians in Ohio, 1819.
—— —— JONES, Calvin. Acc. of the Cherokee Schools. n. d.
—— —— JONES, C. C. Hist. Sketch of Tomo-chi-chi.
—— —— JONES, D. Visits to Indian Tribes.
—— —— JONES, N. W. Indian Bulletins, 1867–8.
—— —— JONES, P. Hist. of Ojibway Indians.
—— —— Journal de la Guerre du Miscissippi, 1739.
—— —— Journal of a Tour in the Indian Terr'y in 1844.
—— —— Journals of Treaties, 1754, '75, '93.
—— —— KENNEDY, Jas. Probable Origin of.
—— —— KETCHUM, W. Seneca Indians.
—— —— KIDDER, F. Abenaki Indians.
—— —— —— Indians of N. Carolina.
—— —— —— Lovewell's Expedition.
—— —— KNIGHT, Dr. and SLOVER, John. Narr. of Perils, etc., among the Indians.
—— —— LAFITAU, J. F. Moeurs des Sauvages.
—— —— LANG, J. D. and Taylor, S. Visit to Indians west of Miss. River, 1843.
—— —— See Language, Indian.
—— —— LAPHAM, J. A. Indians of Wis.
—— —— LARIMER, S. L. Life among the Sioux.
—— —— LE BEAU, C. Voyages parmi le Sauvages de l'Amerique.
—— —— Letters on Chicksaw and Osage Indians, 1831.
—— —— Letters on Indian Antiquities. Western Review. Vols. 1, 2.
—— —— See Little Osage Captive.
—— —— LONG, J. Voyages and Travels among.
—— —— McCOY, I. Hist. of Bapt. Indian Missions.
—— —— —— Indian Reform, etc., 1827.
—— —— McFARLAND, A. Massacre at Concord, 1746.
—— —— McINTOSH, J. Origin of the N. A. Indians.
—— —— McKENNEY and HALL. Hist. of.
—— —— McKENNEY, T. L. On the Chippewas, and Treaty at Fond du Lac.
—— —— —— Travels among Northern and Southern Indians.
—— —— See Mandan Indians.
—— —— MARKHAM, Wm. Conference with Delawares, etc., 1694.
—— —— MARSHALL, O. H. Exped. against Seneca Indians, 1687.
—— —— MARSHE, W. Jour. of Treaty with Six Nations.
—— —— MARTIN, H. Acc. of the Dyes used by them.
—— —— MASON, J. Hist. of Pequot War.
—— —— MERCER, Maj. Asiatic Origin of.
—— —— MOORE, W. V. Indian Wars.
—— —— MORGAN, S. H. League of the Iroquois.
—— —— MORSE, Rev. J. Report on Indian Affairs, 1822.
—— —— MORSE, R. E. Chippewas of L. Superior.
—— —— MORTON, S. G. Aboriginal Race of America.
—— —— —— Ethnography of Amer. Indians.

Indians, American. Narr. of Capture and Escape of Frances and Almira Hall, 1833.
—— —— Narr. of Ind. Wars in Virginia, 1675.
—— —— Narr. of Mrs. Johnson's Captivity.
—— —— Narr. of Massacres in Penn., 1764.
—— —— See Navajo Indians.
—— —— Neil, E. D. Dakotah Land and Life.
—— —— —— On the Effort to Civilize the Aborigines.
—— —— —— Relations of the Gov't to the.
—— —— N. York City. Board for Preservation, etc., of the Indians.
—— —— Niles, Rev. S. Indian and French Wars.
—— —— Noble, Frances. Narr. of her Captivity.
—— —— Ojibwa New Testament.
—— —— Origin of the Tradition of Hiawatha.
—— —— Orton, J. R. Camp Fires of Red Men.
—— —— See Osage Indians.
—— —— Papers relating principally to the Conversion and Civilization of the Six Nations. 1642—1776. Doc. Hist. of N. Y. Vol. 4.
—— —— Papers relating to Indian Troubles in Maine, 1702–1704. Me. Hist. Soc. Coll. Vol. 3.
—— —— Papers relating to the Iroquois and other Indian Tribes. 1666–76.
—— —— Parkman, F. Conspiracy of Pontiac.
—— —— Penhallow, S. Hist. of N. E. Wars, 1703–26.
—— —— See Plea for the Indians.
—— —— See Pocahontas.
—— —— See Ponteach; a Tragedy.
—— —— See Pontiac.
—— —— See Pottawatomies.
—— —— Proceedings or an Indian Council, 1842.
—— —— Progress of Gospel among N. E. Ind., 1659.
—— —— Rau, Chas. Indian Pottery.
—— —— Remarks on the Indians of N. America, in a Letter to an Edinburgh Reviewer. Lond., 1822. 8vo. Indian Pamph. Vol. 4.
—— —— Review of an Article in the N. Amer. Rev., 1830.
—— —— Ruttenber, E. M. Indians of Hudson River.
—— —— St. Clair, A. Narr. of Campaign against, 1791.
—— —— Schermerhorn, J. F. Report on the Western Indians, 1814.
—— —— Schoolcraft, H. R. Address before Confedera. of Iroquois, 1847.
—— —— —— Algic Researches.
—— —— —— Amer. Indians.
—— —— —— Hist. and Statist. Information of.
—— —— —— Myth of Hiawatha.
—— —— —— Notes on the Iroquois.
—— —— —— Oneota, or Red Race.
—— —— —— Thirty Years Residence among.
—— —— —— Western Scenes and Reminiscences.

INDIANS, American. Seminole War.
—— —— Seneca Indians.
—— —— Shawnee Indians.
—— —— SHEA, J. G. Hist. of Cath. Missions.
—— —— —— Indian Tribes of Wis.
—— —— SHEPHERD, T. Clear Sunshine of Gospel. N. E. Indians. 1648.
—— —— SHORT, Dr. C. W. Descript. of Indian Fort in Ky.
—— —— SIGOURNEY, L. H. Traits of the Aborigines.
—— —— SIMON, Mrs. Ten Tribes of Israel identified with.
—— —— Sketches of the Character, Manners, etc., of. Western Monthly Review. Vol. 1.
—— —— See SMITH, Col. Jas. Captivity with Indians. 1753–59.
—— —— Soc'y for Converting and Civilizing the Indians.
—— —— Speech delivered by an Indian Chief, etc. 1789.
—— —— SPENCER, O. M. Indian Captivity.
—— —— SQUIER, E. G. Traditions of Algonquins.
—— —— Statement of the Indian Relations, with a Reply to an Article in the N. A. Review, on the Removal of the Indians. N. Y., 1830. 8vo. Indian Pamph. Vol. 5.
—— —— See Stockbridge Indians.
—— —— STOCKWELL, Q. Acc. of his Captivity.
—— —— STONE, W. L. Life of Brant and Indian Wars.
—— —— —— Uncas and Miantonomoh.
—— —— Stories of Indians during the Revolution.
—— —— STRATTON, R. B. Captivity of Oatman Girls.
—— —— STREETER, S. F. Fall of the Susqnehannocks.
—— —— STUART, Col. John. Memoir of Indian Wars.
—— —— SULLIVAN, J. Hist. of Penobscot Indians.
—— —— SWAN, J. G. Indians of Cape Flattery.
—— —— SYMMES, Rev. T. Acc. of Lovewell's Fight.
—— —— TANNER, J. Captivity and Adventures.
—— —— —— Manners and Customs of Indians.
—— —— THATCHER, B. B. Indian Biography.
—— —— Tracts relative to their Conversion to Christianity.
—— —— Traits of Indian Life and Character.
—— —— Treaty with Six Nations. 1745.
—— —— TURNER, G. Traits of Indian Character.
—— —— TYSON, J. R. Discourse on.
—— —— See U. S. Sec. of Interior. Reports of Commiss'rs of Indian Affairs.
—— —— See U. S. Senate. Report from Com. on Fur Trade. 1829.
—— —— U. S. Senate. Report cf Joint Special Comm. 1867.
—— —— VETROMILE, Rev. E. Abenaki Indians.
—— —— See Virginia. Indian Relics.
—— —— WADSWORTH, Rev. B. Journey to Five Nations. 1694.
—— —— WEISER, C. Narr. of his Journey to N. Y. and Ohio. 1737 and 1748.
—— —— WELSH, W. Visit to Brulé Sioux Indians, etc. 1870.
—— —— WEST, J. Journal of a Mission to.
—— —— —— Mission of Canada Indians and other Provinces. 1827.

INDIANS, American. WHEELOCK, E. Indian Charity School. 1763–75.
—— WHITFIELD, H. Progress of Gospel among N. E. Ind.
—— —— State of N. England. 1651.
—— —— WHITTLESEY, C. Indian Titles in Ohio.
—— —— —— Relation of Tribes to the Whites during the Revolution.
—— —— WILLIAMS, Rev. E. Life of Te-ho-ra-gwa-ne-gen.
—— —— WILLIAMS, S. W. Indian Wars at Deerfield, Mass.
—— —— WILLIAMSON, Wm. D. Indians in N. Eng. 1839.
—— —— WILLIS, W. Indians of Hudson Bay.
—— —— Winnebagoe Indians.
—— —— WITHERS, A. S. Chronicles of Border Warfare.
—— —— WORSLEY, I. View of.
—— —— Wyandots.
—— —— See Amer. Wars, 1744, etc., French and Indian.
INDICTMENT, (The). Arraignment, Trial and Judgment-at-Large, of Twenty-Nine Regicides, the Murderers of His Majesty, King Charles I. Lond., 1724. 8vo.
INDULGENCE to Tender Consciences shown to be most Reasonable and Christian. Lond., 1687. 4to. Eng. Rel. Pamph. Vol. 5.
INDUSTRIAL Instruction in England. A Report made to the Belgian Gov't by Chevalier de Cocquiel. Lond., 1853. 8vo. Educa. Pamph. Vol. 38.
—— Resources. See DEBOW, J. D. B.
—— Universities. See TURNER, J. B.
INDUSTRY. See Plain Sense on National Industry.
—— SCROPE, G. P. Rights of.
—— SULLIVAN, Sir E. Protection to Native Industry.
—— See Commerce and Navigation.
INEDITED Tracts, illustrating the Manners, Opinions and Occupation of Englishmen in the 16th and 17th Centuries. Printed for Roxburghe Library. Lond., 1868. 4to.
INFALLIBILITY, (Papal). See WENINGER, Rev. F. X.
INGALLS, E. S. The Iron Mines of Menominee Co., Michigan. Menominee, 1871. 32 mo. Mich. Hist. Discourses, etc. Vol. 1.
INGALLS, Henry A. See BURNAP, G. W. Memoir of.
INGERSOLL, Chas. An Undelivered Speech on Executive Arrests. Phila., 1862. 8vo. Rebell'n Pamph. Vol. 73.
—— Letter to a Friend in a Slave State. Phila., 1862. 8vo. Rebellion Pamph. Vols. 37 and 60.
—— Speech in Case of Kneedler vs. Lane—Conscription Case. Rebell'n Pamph. Vol. 54.
INGERSOLL, Chas. J. Hist. Sketch of Second War between the U. S. and G. B. Phila., 1849. 8vo.
—— Opinion of the U. S. Bank and the Question of Vested Rights. 1836. 8vo. Law Pamph. Vol. 9.
—— Speech in Cong., Apr. 14, 1842, on the Appropriation Bill. Washington, 1842. 8vo. Congr. and Polit. Pamph. Vol. 25.
INGERSOLL, C. M. Speech in Cong., Mar. 31, 1852, on Slavery. Congr. and Polit. Pamph. Vol. 85.

INGERSOLL, E. Personal Liberty and Martial Law. Phila., 1862. 8vo. Rebell'n Pamph. Vols. 27 and 60.

INGRAHAM, E. D. Events which preceded the Capture of Washington by the British, Aug. 24, 1814. Phila., 1849. 8vo.

INGERSOLL, Jos. R. Address before the Literary Societies of the University of Georgia, Aug. 5, 1847. Athens, 1847. 8vo. Addresses. Vol. 36.

—— See BROWN, D. P. Eulogium on.

—— Manual of Maratime Law. Phila., 1809. 8vo.

—— Memoir of the late Sam'l Breck. Phila., 1863. 8vo. Penn. Hist. Soc. Addresses. Vol. 1.

—— Secession, a Folly and a Crime. 1861. Rebell'n Pamph. Vol. 85.

—— Secession Resisted. Phila., 1861. Rebell'n Pamph. Vol. 76.

—— Speech in Cong., July 2, 1846, against the proposed Tariff. Washington, 1842. 8vo. Speeches. Vol. 1.

INGHAM, S. D. Observations on the Currency of the U. S. Trenton, 1851. 8vo.

INGHAM University, Leroy, N. Y. Ann. Synopsis, 1858. Rochester, 1858. 8vo.

INGLE. Rev. John. Queen's Letters and State Services; the one to be Obeyed, the other to be Resisted. Lond., 1847. 8vo. Eng. Polit. Pamph. Vol. 46.

INGLEDEW, C. J. D. Hist. and Antiq. of N. Allerton, in the Co. of York. Lond., 1858. 8vo.

INGLIS, Rev. Chas. Memorial concerning the Iroquois, or Five Nations, in the Province of N. Y. 1771. Doc. Hist. of N. Y. Vol. 4.

INQUIRY into the Alleged Justice and Necessity of the War with Russia. Lond., 1855. 8vo. Strangford Pamph. Vol. 67.

—— into the Commercial Policy of the U. S.; or the Right Principles of Revenue Laws and Internat. Commerce. Boston, 1845. 8vo. Speeches. Vol. 1.

—— into the Miscarriages of the Four Last Years Reign. Lond., 1714. 8vo. Eng. Polit. Pamph. Vol. 8.

—— into the Right and Duty of compelling Spain to relinquish her Slave Trade. Lond., 1816. 8vo. Pamphleteer. Vol. 7.

—— into the Right to Change the Ecclesiastical Constitution of Cong. Churches of Mass. Boston, 1816. 8vo. Religious Pamph. Vol. 16.

INQUISITION. History of the Spanish Inquisition. Western Monthly Review. Vol. 2.

—— See IVES, I. M. Two Lectures on.

INSANITY. See Amer. Jour. of Insan.

—— Appeal for the Insane.

—— Boston Lunatic Asylum Reports.

—— ELLIOTT, T. B. Address in behalf of Insane.

—— HAZAN, T. R. Report on Insanity of R. I.

—— Mass. report on Insanity. 1854.

—— N. York Commiss'rs Public Charities.

—— SUKE, Dr. D. H. Moral Management of the Insane. 1854.

—— Waterston, R. C. Condition of the Insane in Mass. 1843.

INSANITY. WILKINS, E. T. Insanity and Insane Asylums.
—— Wisconsin Hospital Reports. See other States.
INSTANCE (An) of the Church of England's Loyalty. Lond., 1667. Sm. 4to. Eng. Polit. Pamph. Vol. 65.
INSTITUTE of British Architects. Report of Proceedings, June 15, 1835, with List of Members and Donors. Lond. 12mo. Scientific Pamph. Vol. 30.
—— of Reward for Orphans of Patriots. Journal. Vol. 1. Nos. 1, 2 and 3. N. Y., 1864. 8vo. Rebell'n Pamph. Vol. 5.
—— —— 5th Ann. Report, 1866. Rebell'n Pamph. Vol. 9.
INSTITUTIONS de Physique. Paris, 1740. 8vo.
INSTRUCTIONS for Field Artillery. Phila., 1854. 12mo.
—— for Heavy Artillery. Washington, 1863. 12mo.
—— for Officers on Outposts and Patrol Duty. N. Y., 1862. 12mo. Rebell'n Pamph. Vol. 105.
—— —— Same. 1863. Rebell'n Pamph. Vol. 11.
INSURANCE against Robbery; or the present System of the Police considered, etc. Lond., 1814. 8vo. Pamphleteer. Vol. 3.
—— See Amer. Life Underwriters' Convention. 1859.
—— BARD, W. Letter on Life Ins. 1832.
—— CORNARO, L., on Longevity.
—— MACLAY, I. W., on Longevity.
—— National Ins. Convention. 1871.
—— N. Y. Bank Department.
—— NORTON, C. B. Hand-Book of Life Ins.
—— TUCKETT, H. G. Present State of Life Ins. in U. S., 1851.
—— WARD, S. Doctrine of Probabilities.
INSURRECTIONS in Massachusetts. See MINOT, G. R.
INTELLECTUAL Philosophy. See ABERCROMBIE, A. Intellec. Powers.
—— —— BEATTIE, J. Moral Science and Philos. of Human Mind.
—— —— BROWN, T. Lectures on.
—— —— COMBE, G. Moral and Intell. Science.
—— —— GRAHAM, C. True Philos. of Mind.
—— —— LOCKE, J. On the Understanding.
—— —— MAHAN, Rev. I. System of.
—— —— Observa. sur " des Causes, Conditionelles des Idees."
—— —— UPHAM, T. C. Mental Philos.
—— Repository and New Jerusalem Magazine. Dec., 1844—Nov., 1845. Incomplete. Lond. 8vo.
—— Symbolism. See CHASE, Pliny E.
INTEMPERANCE. See Temperance.
INTERCEPTED Corres. from India, containing Dispatches from Marquis Wellesley, etc. Lond., 1805. 8vo. Eng. Polit. Pamph. Vol. 27.
INTEREST (The) of G. Britain considered with regard to her Colonies, and the Acquisition of Canada and Guadaloupe. Lond., 1760. 8vo.
—— Another Copy. Lond., 1770. 8vo.
INTERESTING Detail of the Operations of the Amer. Fleet in the Mediterranean in 1804. Springfield, Mass., 1804. 8vo.
INTERIOR Causes of the War. N.Y., 1863. 8vo. Rebell'n Pamph. Vol. 15.

INTERNAL Revenue Frauds. Report from Select Comm. of U. S. House of R., 1867. Washington, 1867. 8vo. Congr. and Polit. Pamph. Vol. 67.
—— —— Law as it affects Savings Banks in Cal. San Francisco, 1870. 8vo. Congr. and Polit. Pamph. Vol. 114.
—— —— Report from Comm. of Ways and Means of U. S. House of R., on a Bill to provide, etc., 1862. Washington, 1862. 8vo. Rebell'n Pamph. Vol. 46.
—— —— See U. S. House of Repr. Bill to provide, 1864.
—— —— U. S. Sec. of Treasury. Reports of Commissioners.
INTERNATIONAL Assoc. for obtaining a Uniform Decimal System. Reports of Gen. Meetings held in 1857, '58, '59, '60, '61, '62, '63. Lond., 1857–64. 8vo. Eng. Misc. Pamph. Vol. 16.
—— Coinage. See ALEXANDER, J. H.
—— —— International Monetary Conference at Paris, 1867.
—— Congress on the Prevention and Repression of Crime. Proceedings at N. Y., 1872. N. Y., 1872. 8vo.
—— Exchange. Joint Resolutions of the Gen. Assembly of Florida, etc. Tallahassee, 1853. 8vo. Florida Pamph. Vol. 1.
—— —— See VATTEMARE, Alex.
—— Exhibition, 1862. Official Catalogue of the Fine Art Department. Lond. 8vo. Guide Books. Vol. 11.
—— Law vs. the Trent and San Jacinto, from Hunt's Merchants' Mag., Jan., 1862. Rebell'n Pamph. Vol. 62.
—— Monthly Magazine, Aug., 1850, to July, 1851. N. Y., 1850–1. 3 Vols. 8vo.
—— Ocean Telegraph Co. Statement of its Extortionate Charges for Messages between Cuba and the U. States. Washington, 1870. 8vo. Congr. and Polit. Pamph. Vol. 120.
—— Rights of Peace and War. From De Bow's Review, Mar., 1846. Law Pamph. Vol. 23.
—— Tourist Guide for 1871--2. Chicago. 12mo. Guide Books. Vol. 28.
INTER-OCEANIC Communication—Isthmus of Panama. See DAVIS, Admiral C. H. Report, 1870.
—— See Nicaragua Ship Canal.
—— See STEVENS, S. The New Route, 1871.
INTERVENTION. Few Thoughts on. Phila., 1852. 8vo. Rebell'n Pamph. Vol. 19.
—— In European Affairs. See BOARDMAN, H. A.
INTRODUCTION (The) of Paper Money involves the Abolishment of of Taxation. n. d. Rebell'n Pamph. Vol. 8.
—— to the Index to the Public General Statutes of the United Kingdom, 1801–28. Lond., 1829. 4to. Eng. Polit. Pamph. Vol. 53A.
INTRODUCTORY and Historical Description of the Diorama of Venice. Glasgow, 1841. 8vo. Guide Books. Vol. 14.
INVENTIONS. See Belgium. Patents.
—— G. Britain. Commissioner of Patents.
—— U. S. Commissioner of Patents.
IONIAN (The) Islands under British Protection. Lond., 1851. 8vo. 2d Ed. Strangford Pamph. Vol. 63.

IOWA. Acts of Gen. Assembly, 7th, 9th, 10th, 11th, 12th Sessions. Iowa City and Des Moines, 1858–68. 8vo.
—— Adjutant General. Reports for 1861, 1863–66. Des Moines. 8vo.
—— Adjutant and Inspector General. Reports, Jan. 1, 1869, and Jan. 1, 1870. Des Moines, 1870. 8vo.
—— Acts and Resolutions of the 13th Gen. Assembly. Des Moines, 1870. 8vo.
—— Annals of. Published under the auspices of the Iowa Hist. Soc. Iowa City, 1863–71. 5 Vols. 8vo.
—— Auditor of State. Report to 14th Gen. Assembly. Des Moines, 1871. 8vo.
—— See BRADFORD, W. J. A. Notes on the N. West.
—— Census Returns for 1859, '65, '67, '68, '69. Des Moines. 8vo.
—— College. Grinnell, Iowa. Catalogue, 1867–8. Davenport, 1867. 8vo.
—— Constitutional Convention, with Census Returns for 1856. Iowa City, 1857. 8vo.
—— County, Wis., I. O. G. T. Proceedings of 2d Convention, held at Arena, Sept., 1867. Dodgeville, 1867. 8vo. Wis. Misc. Pamph. Vol. 6.
—— See CURTISS, D. S. Western Portraiture.
—— FERRIS, J. States and Territories of G. West.
—— The Free Lands of; being an Accurate Description of the Sioux City Land District, etc. Des Moines, 1869. 8vo.
—— See GALLAND, I. Iowa Emigrant, 1840.
—— Gen. Assoc. Minutes of their Session in Muscatine, June, 1859. Burlington, 1859. 8vo. Iowa Misc. Pamph. Vol. 1.
—— Geolog. Survey. See OWEN, D. D. 1839, '48, '52.
—— —— Report of Jas. Hall and J. D. Whitney, embracing Results of Investigations made in 1855, '56, '57. Vol. 1. Parts 1 and 2. Albany, 1858.
—— —— Report, 1866–9, by Chas. A. White. Des Moines, 1870. 2 Vols. Roy. 8vo.
—— Grand Lodge. Catalogue of Library of, June 1, 1873. Davenport, 1873. 8vo.
—— Hand Book of Iowa, 1869.
—— Hospital for Insane. 1st and 3d Bienn. Reports, Dec., 1861, Nov., 1865. Des Moines, 1862, '66. 8vo.
—— See HYATT, H. S. Resources of, 1873.
—— Insurance Department. 1st Ann. Report, 1868–9. Des Moines, 1870. 2 Vols. 8vo.
—— Institute of Science and Arts. Celebration of the Humboldt Centennial and Opening of the Institute, at Dubuque, Sept. 14, 1869. Dubuque, 1869. 8vo. Iowa Misc. Pamph. Vol. 1.
—— Journal of the House of Repr., Extra Sess., 1847–8. 8vo. Legislative Journals, 1858.
—— House and Senate Journals, 1868. Des Moines, 1868. 8vo.
—— Journals of the Senate and Assembly. Des Moines, 1870. 2 Vols. 8vo.
—— Laws. Statute Laws of the Territory, enacted at the First Sess of Legislative Assembly, 1838–9. Dubuque, 1839. 8vo.

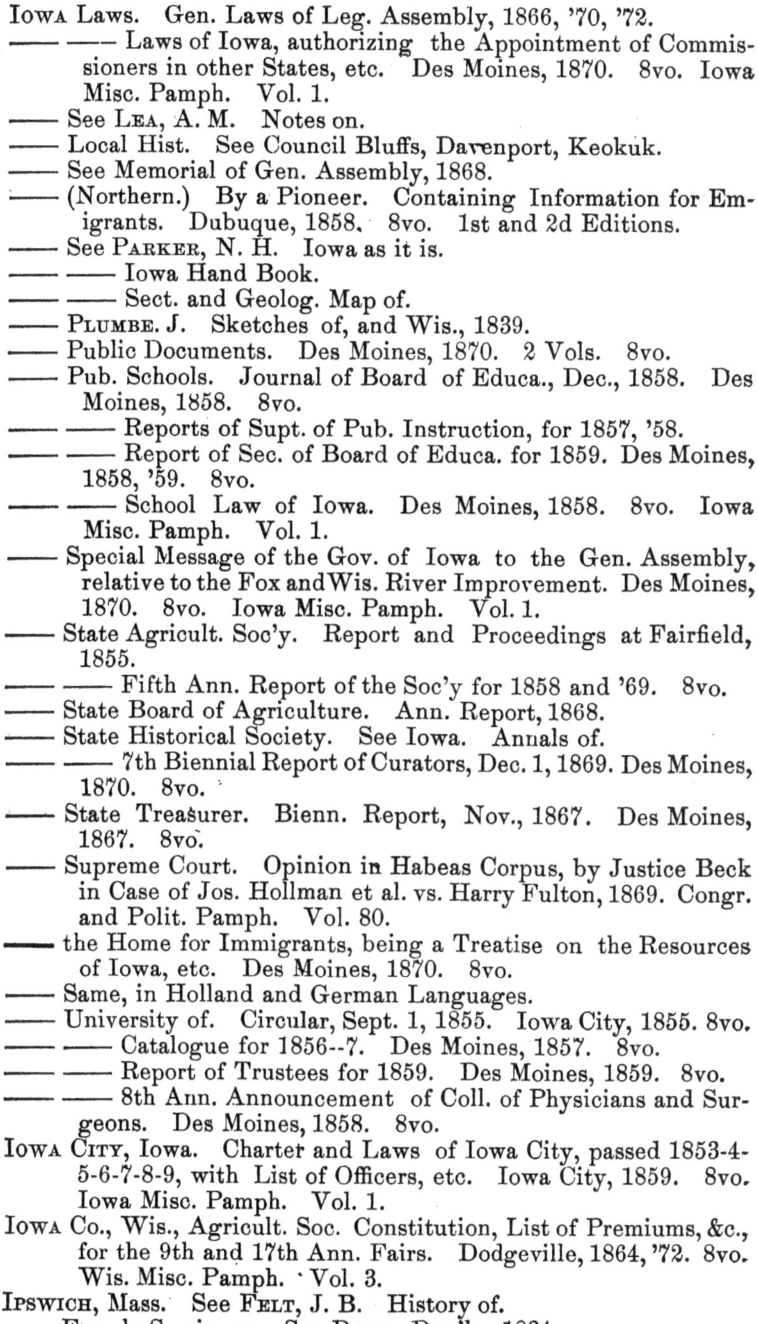

IOWA Laws. Gen. Laws of Leg. Assembly, 1866, '70, '72.
—— —— Laws of Iowa, authorizing the Appointment of Commissioners in other States, etc. Des Moines, 1870. 8vo. Iowa Misc. Pamph. Vol. 1.
—— See LEA, A. M. Notes on.
—— Local Hist. See Council Bluffs, Davenport, Keokuk.
—— See Memorial of Gen. Assembly, 1868.
—— (Northern.) By a Pioneer. Containing Information for Emigrants. Dubuque, 1858. 8vo. 1st and 2d Editions.
—— See PARKER, N. H. Iowa as it is.
—— —— Iowa Hand Book.
—— —— Sect. and Geolog. Map of.
—— PLUMBE. J. Sketches of, and Wis., 1839.
—— Public Documents. Des Moines, 1870. 2 Vols. 8vo.
—— Pub. Schools. Journal of Board of Educa., Dec., 1858. Des Moines, 1858. 8vo.
—— —— Reports of Supt. of Pub. Instruction, for 1857, '58.
—— —— Report of Sec. of Board of Educa. for 1859. Des Moines, 1858, '59. 8vo.
—— —— School Law of Iowa. Des Moines, 1858. 8vo. Iowa Misc. Pamph. Vol. 1.
—— Special Message of the Gov. of Iowa to the Gen. Assembly, relative to the Fox and Wis. River Improvement. Des Moines, 1870. 8vo. Iowa Misc. Pamph. Vol. 1.
—— State Agricult. Soc'y. Report and Proceedings at Fairfield, 1855.
—— —— Fifth Ann. Report of the Soc'y for 1858 and '69. 8vo.
—— State Board of Agriculture. Ann. Report, 1868.
—— State Historical Society. See Iowa. Annals of.
—— —— 7th Biennial Report of Curators, Dec. 1, 1869. Des Moines, 1870. 8vo.
—— State Treasurer. Bienn. Report, Nov., 1867. Des Moines, 1867. 8vo.
—— Supreme Court. Opinion in Habeas Corpus, by Justice Beck in Case of Jos. Hollman et al. vs. Harry Fulton, 1869. Congr. and Polit. Pamph. Vol. 80.
—— the Home for Immigrants, being a Treatise on the Resources of Iowa, etc. Des Moines, 1870. 8vo.
—— Same, in Holland and German Languages.
—— University of. Circular, Sept. 1, 1855. Iowa City, 1855. 8vo.
—— —— Catalogue for 1856--7. Des Moines, 1857. 8vo.
—— —— Report of Trustees for 1859. Des Moines, 1859. 8vo.
—— —— 8th Ann. Announcement of Coll. of Physicians and Surgeons. Des Moines, 1858. 8vo.
IOWA CITY, Iowa. Charter and Laws of Iowa City, passed 1853-4-5-6-7-8-9, with List of Officers, etc. Iowa City, 1859. 8vo. Iowa Misc. Pamph. Vol. 1.
IOWA Co., Wis., Agricult. Soc. Constitution, List of Premiums, &c., for the 9th and 17th Ann. Fairs. Dodgeville, 1864, '72. 8vo. Wis. Misc. Pamph. Vol. 3.
IPSWICH, Mass. See FELT, J. B. History of.
—— Female Seminary. See DANA, Dan'l. 1834.

IPSWICH, Mass. See FITZ, Rev. D. Annivers. Discourse, 1856.
—— Grammar School. See HAMMATT, Abraham.
—— KIMBALL, Rev. D. T. Centen. Discourse, 1834.
—— —— Half Century Discourse, 1856.
—— —— Last Sermon in the Old Meeting-House, 1846.
—— —— Sketch of Eccles. History of, 1820.
IREDELL, Jas. See MCREE, G. J. Life and Corres. of.
IRELAND. Convict Prisons. 6th Ann. Report of Directors. Dublin, 1860. 8vo. Eng. Misc. Pamph. Vol. 33.
—— See DOLBY, Wm. Hist. of.
—— DUDLEY, Rev. H. B. Address to the Lord Primate, on the Tithes, etc., 1808.
—— Education. See ELRINGTON, Rev. C. R. Few Suggestions, etc., 1847.
—— —— HOPE, A. J. B. New Gov't Scheme considered, etc.
—— —— NEWLAND, H. Education of the Poor, 1845.
—— —— Report of the Commiss'rs of Nat. Educa. in Ireland, for 1864. Dublin, 1865. 8vo. Educa. Pamph. Vol. 40.
—— See Enquiry into the Causes of the Popular Discontents, 1805.
—— Essay on Native Annals and other Sources for Illustrating the History and Topography of Ireland. n. d. Strangford Pamph. Vol. 40.
—— See FIRTH, Wm. The Case of Ireland set at rest, etc., 1825.
—— See G. Britain. State Papers and Chronicles.
—— her Church and her People; by a Tory. Lond., 1841. 8vo. Strangford Pamph. Vol. 26.
—— See HERON, R. M. Industry for Ireland, etc.
—— HILLARY, Sir Wm. Sketch of, in 1824.
—— Historical and Archæolog. Assoc. of. Journal, Vol. 1. 3d Ser. 1868--9, complete except No. 8.
—— —— Journal, Vol. 1. 4th Ser. 1870--1, complete.
—— —— —— Vol. 2. 4th Ser. 1872, wants all but Nos. 9, 10, 11.
—— See Irish Union. 1798.
—— KELLY, Rev. M. Cambrensis Eversus.
—— LELAND, Thos. History of.
—— Letters on the State of. Lond., 1847. 8vo. Strangford Pamph. Vol. 43.
—— Same, 1825. Eng. Polit. Pamph. Vol. 37.
—— See MCAULEY, A. Pensions on the Irish Establishment.
—— MACNEVEN, Dr. On Irish Repeal.
—— Ministerial Policy in Ireland in 1844 and 1848.
—— Moderation recommended to the Friends of. 1754.
—— O'BRIEN, W. S. Speech on Irish Discontents. 1843.
—— Observations on the People, the Land and the Law, in 1851. Dublin, 1852. 8vo. 3d. Ed. Strangford Pamph. Vol. 67.
—— See O'CONNEL, John. Argument for. 1844.
—— Peerage of. See Peerage of Ireland.
—— Poor Laws. See MCCULLAGH, W. T. Letter to Irish Peers. 1838.
—— —— SCROPE, G. D. Letters on. 1846.
—— —— —— Remarks on Poor-Relief Bill. 1847.
—— —— SHREWSBURY, Lord, Thoughts on Poor-Relief Bill. 1847.

IRELAND Poor Laws. STANLEY, Wm. Poor Law of. 1837.
—— PRENDERGAST, J. P. Cromwellian Settlement of.
—— —— The Tory War of Ulster.
—— Rebellion of 1643. See G. Britain—House of Commons—Declaration, etc. 1643.
—— Recent Scenes and Occurrences in Ireland. Lond., 1823. 8vo. Strangford Pamph. Vol. 4.
—— Remarks on some of the Evils of Ireland. Lond., 1825. 8vo. Pamphleteer. Vol. 25.
—— See ROGERS, J. W. Employment of the Irish Peasantry. 1847.
—— RONEY, C. P. How to spend a Month in.
—— SCROPE, G. P. How is Ireland to be Governed? 1846.
—— —— The Irish Difficulty, etc. 1849.
—— SHREWSBURY, Earl of. On Pacification of. 1844.
—— Sketch of the State of Ireland, Past and Present. Lond., 1822. 8vo. New Ed. Strangford Pamph., Vol. 67.
—— See SLIGO, Marquis of. Present State of. 1847.
—— STEPHENS, Geo. Political Prophecy Fulfilled, etc. 1839.
—— TAYLOR, W. C. History of.
—— The Case of, in 1823; an Argument for the Repeal of the Union. Lond., 1823. 8vo. Strangford Pamph., Vol. 21.
—— The Source of her Troubles; and the Policy required. Lond. 1835. Svo. Eng. Polit. Pamph., Vol. 41.
—— Thoughts on Present Disturbances in Southern Districts. Lond., 1824. 8vo. Pamphleteer, Vol. 24.
I RELAND, Rev. John. Letter to H. Brougham on the Croydon Charities. Lond., 1819. 8vo. Pamphleteer, Vol. 14.
RELAND, Dr. John. The Plague of Marseilles in 1720. Lond., 1834. 4to. Hist. Pamph., Vol. 14.
RISH Bar. Sketches of. See SHEIL, R. L.
—— Church. See GRANT, Rev. B. Gladstone and Justice to Ireland. 1868.
—— —— RYAN, John. Letter to Protestants of Ireland. 1834.
—— —— PEEL, Sir Robt. Speech in House of Commons. 1835.
—— —— SHEE, Wm. The Ch. of Rome in Ireland. 1848.
—— —— The Reform Association to the Reformers of England, Scotland and Wales. Lond., 1835. 8vo. Eng. Polit. Pamph., Vol. 78.
—— Corporation Bill. 1840. See BUTT, Isaac. Speech. 1840.
—— Epitome of the Case of Irish Corporations. Dublin, 1839. 8vo. Strangford Pamph., Vol. 18.
—— Emigration. See HALE, E. E.
—— Municipal Reform. See BUTT, Isaac. Speech, 1840.
—— —— Epitome of the Case of Irish Corporations. 1839.
—— Narratives, 1641 and 1690. See Camden Soc. Publica.
—— Oratory; with its Effects on Catholic Emancipation considered. Lond., 1817. 8vo. Pamphleteer. Vol. 10.
—— Patriot. Dan'l O'Connell's Legacy to the Irish Americans. 1863. Rebell'n Pamph. Vol. 91.
—— Tithe Bill. 1834. See Mahony, Mr. Letters on. 1834.

IRISH Union. Statement of the Origin and Progress of the Irish Union, delivered to the Irish Government by Messrs. Emmet, O'Connor and McNevin; with Acc. of their Examination before the House of Lords, 1798. Pamphlets. Vol. 9.

IRONS, Rev. Wm. J. The Theory of Development examined; with special reference to Mr. Newman's Essay. Lond., 1846. 8vo. Scientific Pamph. Vol. 28.

IRONTON, Ohio. See LAWSON, A. Iron Industries of. 1871.

IROQUOIS Indians. See INGLIS, Rev. Chas. Memorial concerning. 1771.

—— Letters on the Iroquois by Skenandoah, addressed to Albert Gallatin. "Olden Time." Vol. 2.

—— See MORGAN, L. H.; SCHOOLCRAFT, H. R.

—— Or the Bright Side of Indian Character. N. Y., 1855. 12mo.

—— Papers relating to the Iroquois and other Indian Tribes, 1666 -1676. Doc. Hist. of N. Y. Vol. 1.

IRVING, Geo. V., and MURRAY, Alex. The Upper Ward of Lanarkshire described and delineated. Glasgow, 1864. 3 vols. 8vo.

IRVING, John T. Indian Sketches, taken during an Expedition to the Pawnee Tribes. Phila., 1835. 2 vols. 12mo.

IRVING, Jos. Hist. of Dunbartonshire, Civil, Ecclesiastical and Territorial; with Genealog. Notices of Families in the Co. 2d Ed. Dunbarton, 1860. 4to.

IRVING, Prof. Roland. Age of the Quartzites, Schists and Conglomerates of Sauk Co., Wis. Trans. Wis. Acad. of Sciences. 1870–2.

IRVING, Theo. The Conquest of Florida by Hernando de Soto. N. Y., 1857. 12mo.

IRVING, Washington. Abbotsford and Newstead Abbey. Phila., 1835. 12mo.

—— Adventures of Captain BONNEVILLE, U. S. A., in the Rocky Mountains and the Far West. N. Y., 1857. 12mo.

—— Astoria; or Anecdotes of Enterprise beyond the Rocky Mountains. Authors Revised Ed. N. Y., 1857. 12mo.

—— Bracebridge Hall; or the Humorists, by Geoffrey Crayon. N. Y., 1857. 12mo. Another Ed., N. Y., 1856. 12mo.

—— Chronicle of the Conquest of Granada. Phila., 1833. 2 Vols. 12mo.

—— Crayon Miscellany. N. Y., 1857.

—— Hist. of N. York, by Diedrich Knickerbocker. N. Y., 1856. 12mo. Another Ed. N. Y., 1856. 12mo.

—— Letters of Jonathan OLDSTYLE. Gent. N. Y., 1824. 8vo. Pamph.

—— Life of Geo. WASHINGTON. N. Y., 1856–7. 4 Vols. 12mo.

—— Life of Oliver GOLDSMITH; with a selection from his writings. Harpers' Fam. Libr. N. Y., 1858. 2 Vols. 18mo.

—— Life and Voyages of Christopher COLUMBUS. Abridged. N. Y., 1829. 12mo.

—— MAHOMET and his Successors. N. Y., 1857. 2 Vols. 12mo.

—— Spanish Papers and other Miscellany, not heretofore published. N. Y., 1867. 2 Vols. 12mo.

IRVING Tales of a Traveler by Geoffrey Crayon. Authors Revised Ed. N. Y., 1856. 12mo.
—— Wolfert's Roost; and other papers now first collected. N. Y., 1856. 12mo.
IRWIN, Wm. W. Speeches in Cong., July 11, and Aug. 12, 1842, on the Tariff. Washington, 1842. 8vo. Congr. & Polit. Pamph. Vol. 24.
Is a Member of the Legislature, or a Justice of the Supreme Court, eligible to the office of U. S. Senator? Geneva, N. Y., 1867. 12mo. Congr. and Polit. Pamph. Vol. 80.
Is Cotton our King? From Continental Monthly Mag., Mar., 1862. Rebell'n Pamph. Vol. 67.
ISABELLA, Queen. See PRESCOTT, W. H.
—— See Review of PRESCOTT's Ferdinand and Isabella.
ISLAND The, Empire; or the Scenes of the First Exile of the Emperor, Napoleon, 1. Phila., 1855. 12mo.
ISLE of Man. See CHALONER, Jas. Short Treatise on. 1864.
—— —— HALLIWELL, J. O. Ancient Stone Circles.
—— —— Manx Society Publications.
—— —— ROBERTSON, D. Jour. 1794, and Review of Manx History.
—— —— WOODS, Geo. Past and Present State, 1811.
—— of Wight. See ALBINS Companion to, 1823.
—— —— BRANNON, G. Pleasure Visitor's Companion. 1848.
—— —— WOODWARD, B. W. Hist. of Southampton etc.
ISLES of Shoals, N. H. Descrip. and Hist. Acc. of. Mass. Hist. Soc. Coll. Vol. 7. 1st Ser.
ISLINGTON, Middlesex Co., Eng. See NELSON, J. Hist. of St. Mary Islington. 1811.
Is the War Just? Letter to Lord Palmerston on the War in the East. Lond., 1855. 8vo. Strangford Pamph. Vol. 67.
ITALIAN Church Reformation Commission Report. Oct. 1872. Hartford, 1872. 8vo. Religious Pamph. Vol. 24.
—— Freedom. See N. Y. City. Proceedings of Public Demonstration, etc. 1847.
ITALY See BECKFORD, Wm. Sketches of, etc.
—— By an Exile. Waldie's Circulating Libr. Vol. 14.
—— See CARNE, John. Letters from Switzerland and Italy. 1833.
—— CHATEAUBRIAND, Viscount. Travels in.
—— COLTON, Rev. W. Notes on France and Italy.
—— COSTE, M. Voyage d'Exploration, &c.
—— GREENE, N. Compend. History of.
—— HEADLEY, J. T. Letters from.
—— HOARE, G. T. North Italy, and the Seat of War. in 1859.
—— MAZZINI, Jos. Italy, Austria and the Pope. 1845.
—— SPALDING, W. Italy and Italian Islands.
—— WHEELER, D. H. Brigandage in S. Italy.
—— WILLIS, N. P. Summer Cruise in Mediterranean.
ITASCA Lake. See SCHOOLCRAFT, H. R. Expedition to.
ITHACA, N. Y. See BOWEN, G. F. Ithaca in 1850.
—— GOODWIN, H. C. Ithaca as it was and is. 1853.

IVES, Chas. G. Discourses on his 50th Annivers. as Deacon in the Cong. Ch. in Bristol, Conn., Feb. 2, 1859. Hartford, 1859. 8vo. Conn. Hist. Discourses Vol. 6.

IVES, Rev. I. M. Two Lectures on the Inquisition. Milwaukee, 1853. 8vo. Sermons Vol. 17.

IVES, Lieut. Jos. C. Report upon the Colorado River of the West, explored in 1857 and 1858. Washington, 1861. 4to.

J.

JACKSON, Gen. Andrew. See COBBETT, Wm. Life of. 1834.

—— Conversation (Imaginary) between Jefferson and.

—— Corres. with J. C. Calhoun, on the Seminole War. 1831. 8vo. Congr. and Polit. Pamph. Vol. 74.

—— See EATON, J. H. Life of.

—— EWING, A. Oration at Memphis. 1859.

—— Farewell Address to the People of the U. S., Mar. 4, 1837. Republished 1863. Rebell. Pamph. Vol. 68.

—— See GOODWIN, P. A. Biog. of.

—— HEADLEY, J. T. Lives of Scott and Jackson.

—— JENKINS, J. S. Life and Pub. Services of.

—— KENDALL, A. Life of.

—— Letter to Carter Beverley, and Mr. Clay's Reply. Mr. Clay's Speech at the Lexington Dinner. Gen. Jackson's Reply to Mr. Clay, and Mr. Buchanan's Letter in reply to the preceding. Portsmouth, 1827. 8vo. Congr. and Polit. Pamph. Vol. 134.

—— Linn, L. F. Speech on the Bill to Indemnify him, etc. 1842.

—— Memoirs of Gen. Jackson, with Letter of Sec'y Adams in Vindica. of the Execution of the Arbuthnot and Ambrister, etc. N. Y., 1824. 8vo. Congr. and Polit. Pamph. Vol. 111.

—— See MERRICK, P. Eulogy at Boston. 1845.

—— Narr. of his First Invasion of Florida, and Defence of N. Orleans. N. Y., 1827. 8vo. Congr. and Polit. Pamph. Vol. 111.

—— Official Record of Proceedings of the Court Martial which Tried, and the Orders of Gen. Jackson for Shooting Six Militia Men. Albany, 1828. 8vo. Congr. Pamph. Vol. 92.

—— See PARTON, Jas. Life of.

—— Presentation of his Sword to Cong., Feb. 26, 1855. Washington, 1855. 8vo. Addresses. Vol. 16.

—— Proclamation to the People of S. Carolina, Dec. 10, 1832. Reprinted 1863. Same in German Language. Rebell'n Pamph. Vol. 68.

—— Protest [of the Prest. of the U. S.] against the recent Unconstitutional Proceedings of the U. S. Senate. Read in Senate, April 17, 1834. Speeches. Vol. 5.

JACKSON, Gen. Andrew. See Reflections upon his Qualifications for the Presidency, 1828. N. Y. 8vo. Congr. and Polit. Pamph. Vol. 111.
—— Reminiscenses; or an extract from the Catalogue of his "Juvenile Indiscretions," n. d. 8vo. Congr. and Polit. Pamph. Vol. 111.
—— See SAYLER, M. Eulogy of. 1863.
—— SNELLING, W. J. Life and Actions.
—— TENNESSEE, The. Farmer.
—— Truth's Advocate and Monthly Anti-Jackson Expositor.
—— Virginia Anti-Jackson Convention. 1827.
—— WALKER, A. Jackson and N. Orleans.
—— WRIGHT, SILAS. Speech on the Bill to indemnify him, etc. 1842.
—— YANCEY, Wm. L. Oration at Baltimore. 1846.
—— And Gen. G. Washington on Negro Soldiers, 1863. Same in German. Rebell'n Pamph. Vol. 91.
JACKSON, Chas. Narr. of his Sufferings and Escape, with Acc. of Atrocities committed in June, 1798, at Wexford, Ireland, by the Rebels. Lond., 1799. 8vo. Eng. Polit. Pamph. Vol. 26.
JACKSON, Chas. T. and ALGER, Francis. Mineralogy and Geology of part of Nova Scotia. 1828. Silliman's Journ. Vols. 14, 15.
—— See GAY, Dr. M. Claims of, etc.
—— Mass. Geolog. Survey. 1838.
—— Maine —— —— 1838.
—— Mich. —— —— 1849.
—— MORTON, Dr. W. T. G. Anaesthetic Discovery Controversy.
—— N. Hampshire Geolog. Survey. 1841.
—— R. Island Geolog. Survey. 1839.
—— Report on the Claims of, in regard to the Ether Discovery. 1852. Med. Pamph. Vol. 1.
JACKSON, David T. Petition to Cong., Feb. 15, 1869. N. Y., 1869. 8vo. Congr. and Pollt. Pamph. Vol. 120.
JACKSON DEMOCRATIC ASSOC. Proceedings at Washington, Jan. 8, 1852. Congr. and Polit. Pamph. Vol. 69.
JACKSON, Francis. History of the Early Settlement of Newton, Middlesex Co., Mass., 1639–1800; with a Genealogy. Register of its Inhabitants. Boston, 1854. 12mo.
JACKSON, Rev. Henry. Account of the Churches of R. Island of the R. Island Bapt. State Convention, Nov., 1853. Providence, 1854. 8vo.
—— Hist. Discourse delivered at the 250th Anniversary of the first Baptist Church in America, Providence, R. I., 1854. 8vo. Sermons. Vol. 25. Another Copy, R. I. Hist. Discourses. Vol. 1.
—— Hist. Disc., at Central Bapt. Church, Newport, R. I., Jan. 8, 1854. Newport, 1854. 8vo. R. I. Hist. Disc. Vol. 1.
JACKSON, Dr. John. Oration before the Hunterian Soc., Feb. 10, 1864. Lond., 1864. 8vo. Med. Pamph. Vol. 13.
JACKSON, John D., M. D. The Black Arts in Medicine. Cincin., 1870. 8vo. Med. Pamph. Vol. 31.

JACKSON, John W. View of the Polit. Situation of Province of Upper Canda. Lond., 1809. 8vo. Canada Pamph. Vol. 1.
JACKSON, James C. Tobacco; and its Effect upon the Health and Character. Dansville, 1864. 8vo. Temp. Pamph., etc. Vol. 6.
JACKSON, J. R. Biog. of General Harrison. In German. Phila., 1840. 8vo. Congr. and Polit. Pamph. Vol. 135.
JACKSON, Mich. Map of the City, on Rollers. Jackson, 1871.
JACKSON, Patrick Tracy. See LOWELL, John A. Memoir of.
JACKSON, Tatlow. Authorites cited antagonistic to H. Binney on Habeas Corpus. Phila. 1862. 8vo. Rebll'n Pamph. Vol. 27.
—— Martial Law: What is it? And who can declare it? Phila., 1862. 8vo., Rebell'n Pamph. Vol. 27.
JACKSON, Thos. The Centenary of Wesleyan Methodism: Sketch of Rise and Progress of the Church in the World. N. Y., 1839. 12mo.
JACKSON, Gen. Thos. J. ("Stonewall.") See ADDEY, M. Life of.
—— COOK, Esten. Military Biography. 1866.
—— DABNEY, A. L. Life and Campaigns of.
—— DANIELS, — Life of. 1863.
—— DAVIS, JEFF., and STONEWALL JACKSON.
—— Life of. Richmond, 1864. 12mo. 2d Ed.
JACKSON, Wm. A. Col. 18th Reg. N. Y. Vol. Rebellion Pamph. Vol. 88.
JACOB, Gen. Jno. Tracts on the Native Army of India, its Organization and Discipline. Lond., 1858. 8vo. Engligh Polit. Pamph. Vol. 55.
JACOB, J. J. Biograph. Sketch of the late Michael Cresap. Cinn., 1866, 4to. Reprint.
JACOB, W. Inquiry into the Causes of Agricult. Distress. Lond., 1817. 8vo. Pamphleteer. Vol. 10.
—— Hist. Inqniry into the Production and Consumption of the Precious Metals. Phila., 1832. 8vo.
JACOBINISM. See WOOLLASTON, Rev. R. Origin and Arts of.
JACOBITES, or Cophts. See ABUDACNUS, J. Hist. of. 1693.
JACOBS, Geo. See STONE, L. R. Trial of, for Witchcraft. 1692.
JACOBS, M. Notes on the Rebel Invasion of Md. and Pa., and the Battle of Gettysburg. Phila., 1864. 12mo.
JACOBS, Rev. Peter. Journal from Rice Lake to Hudson's Bay Co. 1852. N. Y., 1857. 12mo.
JACOBUS, M. W., D.D. Popery against Common School Education. Phila., n. d. 12mo. Religious Pamph. Vol. 22.
JÆGER, Prof. B. The Life of N. Amer. Insects. Illustrated. Nos. 1, 2, 3, 4, 6. N. Y., 1853–4. Scientific Pamphlets. Vol. 2.
JAGGER, Wm. Imformation, with respect to the Institution of Slavery. N. Y., 1856. 8vo. Congress. and Polit. Pamph. Vol. 58.
JALAPA. State Documents relating to the Conferences at Jalapa, between the Mexican and French Ministers. Lond., 1839. 8vo. Strangford Pamph. Vol. 17.
JALLABERT, M. Experiences Sur l 'Electricité: avec quelques conjectures sur la Cause de ses Effets. Paris, 1749. 18mo.

JAMAICA. See African Slave Trade in.
— BURGE, W. Speech on Gov't of. 1839.
— EMERY, Rob't. About Jamaica, &c.
— FINLAYSON, W. F. Hist of the Jamaica Case.
— — Justice to Gov. Eyre.
— — Rep't of Case of Queen vs. E. J. Eyre.
— House of Assembly. Reports from Comm. on the Slave Trade &c. Lond., 1789. 4to. Eng. Polit. Pampe. Vol. 10.
— See MEREWETHER, Serjeant. Speech on Gov't of. 1839.
— PHILLIPPO, J. M. Past and Present State of. 1843.
— PIM, Bedford. The Negro and Jamaica.
— SLIGO, Lord, Present State of. 1839.
— The Case of the Agent of Jamaica on behalf the Legislature &c. Lond., 1839. 8vo. Strangford Pamph. Vol. 18.
— under the Apprenticeship System. Lond., 1838. 8vo. Strangford Pamph. Vol. 14.
JAMAICA, Long Island. See OGDEN, J. DePeyster. 50th Annivers. Address. 1842.
JAMAICA PLAIN, Mass. See GRAY, Rev. Thos. Half Cent. Sermon, 1842.
JAMES I. Army List, 1689. See D'ALTON, John. Illustrations, Historical and Genealogical.
— See GOODMAN, G. Court of.
JAMES, Chas. T. On the Comparative Cost of Steam and Water Power. Newburyport, 1844. 8vo. Scientific Pamph. Vol. 40.
— Speech in Cong. March 20, 1856, on the Tariff. Cong. and Polit. Pamph. Vol. 92.
JAMES, Edwin. Acc. of an Expedition from Pittsburgh, Pa., to the Rocky Mountains, in 1819 and '20, under Command of Maj. Stephen H. Long. Phil'a, 1823. 2 vols. 8vo.
— Suggestions for a Uniform System of Bankruptcy. 1864. Rebell'n Pamph. Vol. 87.
JAMES, G. P. R. Hist. of Charlemagne. Harpers' Fam. Libr. N. Y., 1860. 18mo.
— Hist. of Chivalry. Harpers' Fam. Libr. N. Y., 1859. 18mo.
— Hist. of the Life of Rich'd Cœur de Lion. Lond., 1842. 2 Vols. 8vo. Another Ed. Paris, 1842. 8vo.
— Life and Times of Louis XIV. Lond., 1839. 4 Vols. 8vo.
— Some Remarks on the Corn Laws. Lond., 1841. 8vo. Strangford Pamph., Vol. 26.
JAMES, Henry. Essay on the Currency, in relation to the Distressed State of the Country. London, 1820. 8vo. Pamphleteer, Vol. 17.
— Oration at Newport, R. I., July 4, 1861. Boston, 1861. 8vo. Addresses, Vol. 27.
JAMES, John A. Dissent and the Church of Eng.; or, a Defence of the Principles of Nonconformity. Lond., 1830. 8vo. Eng. Rel. Pamph., Vol. 88.
— See RALEIGH, Rev. A. Sermon on Death of.
JAMES, John H. Address before the Ohio Hist. and Philosoph. Soc., Dec. 26, 1835, on the Prevailing Systems of Education. Journal, Part 1, Vol. 1.

JAMES, J. H., Jr. On Military Commissions for Trial of Citizens. Cincin., 1869. 8vo. Law Pamph., Vol. 9.

JAMES, Sam'l. Thoughts on Middleclass Education. Lond., 1853. 8vo. Educa. Pamph., Vol. 29.

JAMES River and Kanawha Canal. See CENTRAL (The) Water Line, etc.

—— —— DUKE, R. T. W. Speech in Va. Legisla. 1873.

—— —— Nat. Board of Trade. Report on Transportation through Va. 1869.

—— —— Reports on the Survey of. Richmond, 1871. 8vo. Va. Misc. Pamph., Vol. 2.

—— —— 21st Ann. Report, 1855. Richmond, 1855. 8vo. Va. Misc. Pamph., Vol. 2.

JAMES, Thos. vs. Moses Patten and Samuel Patten. Law Pamph. Vol. 2.

JAMES, Thos. C., M. D. Brief Acc. of the Discovery of Anthracite Coal on the Lehigh. Penn. Hist. Soc. Memoirs. Vol. 1. Part 2.

—— See TYSON, J. R. Memoir of.

JAMES, Wm. Full and Correct Acc. of the Late War between G. Britain and the U. States. Lond., 1818. 2 Vols. 8vo.

—— Inquiring into the Merits of Naval Transactions between G. Britain and the U. States with Acc. of Ships of War Captured and destroyed since June 18, 1812. Halifax, S. C., 1816. 8vo.

—— Naval Hist. of G. Britain from Declaration of War by France 1793, to Accession of George IV. New Ed. Lond., 1837. 6 Vols. 8vo.

JAMESON, Mrs. Memoirs of Celebrated Female Sovereigns. Harpers' Fam. Libr. N. Y., 1858. 2 Vols. 18mo.

—— Relative Position of Mothers and Governess. Lond. n. d. 8vo. 2d Ed. Eng. Misc. Pamph. Vol. 14.

—— Sketches in Canada, and Rambles among the Red Men. Lond., 1852. 8vo.

JAMESON, D. D. Practical Measures. Lond., 1844. 8vo. Strangford Pamph. Vol. 37.

JAMESTOWN, N. York, 1st Cong. Ch. 50th Anniversary Celebra. 1866. 8vo. N. Y. Hist. Discourses, etc. Vol. 1.

JAMIESON, Rob't. Commerce with Africa. Suggestions for Development of Resources of Western Central Africa. Lond., 1859. 8vo. Eng. Misc. Pamph. Vol 32.

JANES, Fowler, Kirtland & Co. Memorial to Cong., concerning Work on the Dome of the Capitol. n. d. 8vo. Congr. and Polit. Pamph. Vol. 112.

JANES, Rev. Fred. Janes' Family Genealogy. N. Y., 1868. 8vo.

JANESVILLE, Wis. Free Press. Newspaper. Jan., 1854, to Mar., 1857. Folio.

—— Democratic Standard. Newspaper. April, 1854, to Oct., 1858. 2 Vols. Folio.

—— Daily Gazette. Newspaper. 1852.–1873. Folio.

—— Its Business, Manufactories, Water Power, etc. From the Janesville Democrat, 1866. Wis. Local Hist. Vol. 2.

JANESVILLE School Commissioners. 1st Ann. Report. Janesville, 1857. 8vo. Wis. Misc. Pamph. Vol. 1.

—— Times and Republican. Newspaper. Janesville, 1859–1861. Folio.

JANIN, Jules. The American in Paris, during the Summer. N. Y., 1844. 8vo. Hist. Pamph. Vol. 6.

JANNEY, Sam'l M. Life of Geo. Fox; with Dissertations on his Views of the Doctrines, &c., of the Christian Ch. Phila., 1853. 8vo.

—— Life of Wm. Penn; with Selections from his Correspondence and Autobiography. 2d Ed. revised. Phila., 1853. 8vo.

JANSE, Anneke. Acc. of, and of her Family, with her Will in Dutch and English. Albany, 1870. 12mo. Geneal. Pamph. Vol. 14.

JANSSEN, Sir S. T. Letter to the Lord Mayor and others, on Rebuilding the Jail of Newgate. Lond., 1767. 8vo. Eng. Misc. Pamph. Vol. 2.

JANVIER, F. De Haes. The Sleeping Sentinel. Phila., 1863. 12mo. Rebell'n Pamph. Vol. 102.

JAPAN Expedition. See ALLEN, Thos. Address. 1852.

—— —— HAWKS, Rev. F. L.

—— See Manners and Customs of Japanese.

—— PALMER, A. H. Origin of Mission to.

—— PUMPELLY, R. Geolog. Researches.

—— TAYLOR, B. Visit to India, China and Japan.

—— TOMES, R. Americans in Japan.

JAQUES, John D. See ANTHON, John. Court Martial of.

JAQUITH, Geo. W. See WHITCOMB, Rev. W. C. Obit. Disc.

JARDINE, L. J., M. D. Letter from Penn. to a Friend in England, with Information on America, 1794. Bath, 1795. 8vo. pamph.

JARVES, J. J. Descriptive Catalogue of Old Masters. Cambridge, Mass., 1863. 8vo. Art Catalogues. Vol. 1.

JARVIS, Dr. Edw. See Assoc. of Med. Supt's of Amer. Institute for the Insane.

—— Influence of Distance from & Nearness to an Insane Hospt. on its Use by the People. n. d. 8vo. N. Y. Misc. Pamph. Vol. 7.

—— Discourse on the Religion of the Indian Tribes of N. America. N. Y. Hist. Soc. Coll. Vol. 3. Another Copy, N. Y., 1820. 8vo.

JARVIS, Wm. See CUTTS, Hampden. Life and Services of.

JAVA LITERARY & SCIENTIFIC SOCIETY. See RAFFLES, T. S. Discourse, 1815.

JAY, John. Ch. Justice.

—— See FLANDERS, H. Lives of Chief Justices.

—— JAY, Wm. Life of.

—— RENWICK, J. Life of.

—— Sketch of Life of. Western Monthly Magazine. Vol. 2.

JAY, John. Caste & Slavery in the Amer. Ch., by a Churchman. N. Y., 1843. 8vo. Congr. Pamph. Vol. 103.

—— Seeond Letter on Dawson's Introduction to the Federalist. N. Y., 1864. 8vo. Congr. & Polit. Pamph. Vol. 125.

JAY, John. Statist. View of Amer. Agriculture; Address before the Amer. Geograph. & Statist. Soc. N. Y., 1859. 8vo. Ad dresses. Vol. 17.

—— The Great Conspiracy; Address at Mt. Kisco, N. Y., July 4, 1861. Rebell'n Pamph. Vol. 98.

JAY, Wm. Causes and Consequences of the Mexican War. 2d. Ed. Boston, 1849. 12mo.

—— Examina. of the Mosaic Laws of Servitude. N. Y., 1854. 8vo. Addresses. Vol. 8.

—— Life of John JAY. With Selections from his Corres. & Miscell. Papers. N. Y. 1833. 2 Vols. 8vo.

—— Miscel. Writings on Slavery. Boston, 1853. 8vo.

—— Table of Killed and Wounded in the War of 1812. N. Y. Hist. Soc. Coll. N. S. Vol. 2.

—— War and Peace; the Evils of the First, and a Plan for preserving the Last. Lond., 1842. 8vo. Strangford Pamph. Vol. 31.

JEBB, J. Practical Treatise on Strengthening and Defending Outposts, &c. Chatham, 1836. 8vo. Scientific Pamph., etc. Vol. 31.

JEE, Rev. Thos. Practical Observations on the Management of the Poor. Lond., 1817. 8vo. Pamphleteer Vol. 9.

JEFFERSON Co., N. York. See HOUGH, F. B. Hist. of.

—— —— Journal of Board of Supervisors, 1870. Watertown, 1870. 8vo.

—— Medical College, Phila. Ann. Announcement, 1854–5. Phila., 1854. 8vo.

JEFFERSON, Thos. Administration. See DANVERS, J. T. Picture of his Admiuistration.

—— —— LOWELL, John. N. Eng. Patriot.

—— See Conversation (Imaginary) between Jackson and.

—— DWIGHT, T. Character of.

—— His Pretensions to the Presidency examined. 1796. 8vo. Congr. & Polit. Pamph. Vol. 110.

—— Inaugural Address, March 4, 1801. Phila., 1861. 8vo. Rebell'n Pamph. Vol. 31.

—— See LEE, H. Observations on the Writings of.

—— Letters on his Official Conduct.

—— Memoirs of. Containing a Concise History of the U. S., from the Acknowledgement of their Independence. With a View of French Influence and French Principles. 2 Vols. 8vo. 1809.

—— See MITCHELL, S. L. Discourse on Life of.

—— Notes on the State of Virginia. Lond., 1787. 8vo.

—— —— first hot pressed. Ed. Phila., 1801. 8vo.

—— —— Same, New Ed. Richmond, 1853. 8vo.

—— —— Appendix to same, relative to the Logan Murder. Phila., 1800. 8vo.

—— —— See Observations upon Passages tending to Subvert Religion, etc. 1804.

—— PIERSON, H. W. Private Life of.

—— RANDALL, H. S. Life of.

—— RANDOLPH, T. J. Memoir and Corres.

JEFFERSON, Thos. RAYNOR, B. L. Life, Writings and Opinions of.
—— Report of Cases, determined in Gen. Court of Va., from 1730 to 1740, and from 1768 to 1772. Charlotteville, 1829. 8vo.
—— See SMUCKER, S. M. Life of.
—— TATOR, H. H. Oration on.
—— The Writings of; being his Autobiography, Correspondence, Reports, Messages and other Writings, Edited by H. A. WASHINGTON. Washington, 1853. 9 vols. 8vo.
—— TUCKER Geo. Life of.
—— Vindications against certain Charges by "GROTIUS."
—— WEBSTER, Dan'l. Address.
JEFFERSON, Wis. Banner. Newspaper. Jefferson, 1864-1873. Folio.
JEFFERYS, Thos. Amer. Atlas. Lond. 1776 and 1778. Folio. 2 copies.
—— Nat. and Civil Hist. of the French Dominions in N. and S. America. Lond., 1760. Folio.
JEFFERYS, Nathan'l. See Antidote to Poison, or a Reply to his Attack on the Prince of Wales.
—— Brief Remarks in regard to his Attack on the Prince of Wales.
—— Diamond Cut Diamond, etc.
—— Letter to him on his "Review of the Conduct of the Prince of Wales."
JEFFREY, Lord Francis. See COCKBURN, Lord. Life and Corres. of.
JEFFRIES, C. Wabash Captives; Narr. of Adventures of Jas. Brady and others, among the Indians on the Wabash. La Fayette, 1846. 8vo. Indian Pamph. Vol. 5.
JEFFRIES, John, M. D. Annivers. Address before the Suffolk Dist. Med. Soc., Apr. 27, 1850. Boston, 1850. 8vo. Med. Pamph. Vol. 31.
JEFFRIES, J. C. See SAYLER, M. Speech on his Death. 1863.
JEKYLL, Sir. Jos. Argument in the Case of Evelyn vs. Evelyn. Lond., 1819. 8vo. Law Pamph. Vol. 12.
JENCKES, T. A. Report on the Civil Service Bill. 1868. Washington, 1868. 8vo.
—— Speech in Cong., June 1, 1864, on the Bankrupt Law. Rebellion Pamph. Vol. 32.
JENNISON, Robt. Narr. of the Late Popish Plot. Lond., 1679. Folio. Eng. Polit. Pamph. Vol. 63.
JENKINS, Rev. J. Thoughts for the Crisis. Phila., 1861. 12mo. Rebell'n Pamph. Vol. 70.
JENKINS, John S. Daring Deeds of Amer. Generals. Illustrated. 12mo. N. Y., 1857.
—— Hist. of the War between the U. S. and Mexico. Auburn, 1849. 12mo.
—— Hist. of Political Parties, in the State of N. Y. to 1849. 2d. Ed. Auburn, 1849. 12mo.
—— Jas. K. Polk, and a Hist. of his Administration, embracing the Annexation of Texas, the Difficulties with Mexico, etc. 12mo. Buffalo, 1850.
—— Life and Pub. Services of Gen. Andrew Jackson, with the Eulogy by Hon. Geo. Bancroft. N. Y., 1858. 12mo.

JENKINS, J. S. Life of John C. Calhoun. Auburn, 1850. 12mo.
—— Lives of the Governors of the State of N. Y. Syracuse, 1852. 8vo.
JENKINS, Tim. Speech in Cong., June 30, 1846, on the Tariff. Washington, 1846. 8vo. Speeches. Vol. 1.
—— Speech in Cong., Apr. 14, 1852, on Public Lands. Congr, and Polit. Pamph. Vol. 84.
JENKINS, Warren. Ohio Gazetter and Travellers Guide. Columbus, 1841. 12mo.
JENKS, G. S. Sanitary State of the Town of Brighton. Lond., 1840. 8vo. Eng. Misc. Pamp. Vol. 30.
JENKS, R. W. The Brachial Telegraph: a New Method of Conversing and Signalizing. N. Y., 1852. 8vo. Scientific Pamph. Vol. 16.
JENKS, Wm., D. D. Address before the Amer. Antiq. Soc., Oct. 23, 1813. Boston, 1813. 8vo. Proceedings, 1813–55.
—— Address before the N. E. Hist. and Genealog. Soc., March 1, 1852. Boston, 8vo. Addresses, Vol. 9. N. E. Register. Vol. 6.
—— See BLAGDEN. G. W. Memoir of.
—— Memoir of Abiel Holmes, D. D. Mass. Hist. Soc. Coll. 3d. Ser. Vol. 7.
—— Paper read before the N. E. Hist. and Gen. Soc., Aug. 1, 1855. N. E. Hist. and Reg. Vol. 10.
—— Tribute to the Memory of Rev. Chas. Lowell and Rev. John Codman. Mass. Hist. Soc. Proceed. 1860–62.
JENNER, Dr. Edw. Facts respecting Variolous Contagion. Lond., 1808. 4to. Med. Pamph. Vol. 28.
—— Letter to Dr. C. H. Parry, on Artificial Eruptions, in certain Diseases. Lond., 1822. 4to. Med. Pamph. Vol. 28.
JENNER FAMILY GENEALOGY. From N. E. Hist. and Gen. Reg. 1865. Genealog. Pamph. Vol. 1.
JENNINGS FAMILY. See SMITH, Columbus. Report to the Jennings Assoc.
JENNINGS, Rev. Eben. Address at Plainfield, Mass., July 4, 1836. Northampton, 1836. 8vo. Addresses. Vol. 29.
JENNINGS, Hargrave. War in London; or Peace in London: Remonstrance addressed to the People of England. Lond., 1859. 8vo. Eng. Misc. Pamph. Vol. 9.
JENNINGS, Rev. I. Memorials of a Century: Early Hist. of Bennington, Vt., and 1st Ch. Boston, 1869. 12mo.
JENNINGS, Paul. A Colored Man's Reminiscences of J. Madison. Brooklyn, 1865. 4to.
JENNINGS, W. J. St. Louis and its Lumber Trade. St. Louis, 1871. 12mo. St. Louis Pamph. Vol. 2.
JENNISON Family Genealogy. See VINTON, J. A.
JEPPHI, Recos. A Ministerial Almanac, exhibiting the Nature and Value of the Patronage about to be transferred from the East India Co. to the Crown. Lond., 1783. 8vo. Eng. Polit. Pamph. Vol. 21.
JERAULD, Charlotte A. Poetry and Prose, with a Memoir by Henry Bacon. Boston, 1850. 12mo.

JERDAN, Wm. Plan of a National Assoc. for the Encouragement of Authors, etc. Lond., 1839. 8vo. Strangford Pamph. Vol. 18.
JERMON, J. W. Abram Lincoln and S. Carolina. Phila., 1861. Rebell'n Pamph. Vol. 99.
JERRARD, J. H. Evidence before the Educa. Comm. of the House of Commons, Mar. 28 and 29, 1836. 8vo. Educa. Pamph. Vol. 29.
JERRMANN, Edw. Pictures from St. Petersburg. N. Y., 1852. 8vo. Guide Books. Vol. 15.
—— St. Petersburg; its People; their Character and Institutions. N. Y., 1855. 12mo.
JERROLD, W. B. The English Official Guide to the Universal Exhibition. Paris, 1855. 8vo. 2d Ed. Guide Books. Vol. 12.
JERSEY City and Hoboken, N. J. City Directories, 1866–7, 1870–1 Jersey City, 1866, '71. 8vo.
JERSEY, Isle of. See BERRY, W. Hist. of Guernsey, etc.
JERUSALEM. See Anglican (The,) Bishopric of Jerusalem, 1843.
—— MORRISON, W. The Recovery of. 1871.
—— PALMER, W. A. Foundation of a Protestant Bishopric at. 1841.
—— PERCEVAL, A. P. Mission of Bishop Alexander, 1843.
—— Statement of Proceedings relating to a Bishopric at Jerusalem etc. 1841.
—— Delivered. See TASSO, T.
—— Topog. of. See WILLIAMS, Rev. Geo. Defence of "Jerusalem explored."
JERVIS, Rev. W. G. Startling Facts Respecting the Poverty and Distress of more than 400 Clergymen of the United Ch. of England and Ireland. Lond., 1860. 8vo. 2d Ed. Eng. Rel. Pamph., Vol. 59A.
JESSE, John Heneage. Memoirs of the Pretenders and their Adherents. Phila., 1846. 2 Vols. 18mo.
JESSUP, Wm. Address before the N. Y. State Agr. Soc., at Watertown, Oct. 3, 1856. Albany, 1856. 8vo. Agr. Pamph., Vol. 12.
JESUIT Missions and Relations. See BANDORY. Oeuvres Diverses.
—— —— BIARD. Missio Canadensis. 1612.
—— —— —— Relation de la Nouvelle France. 1616.
—— —— BIGOT. Mission Abnaquise. 1685.
—— —— —— Relation. 1701.
—— —— BRESSANY. Relations Abregee.
—— —— See CANADA.
—— —— Canadicæ Missionis Relatio. 1611–13.
—— —— CHAUMONOT. La Vie et Suite. 1688.
—— —— CREUXIUS, F. Historiæ Canadensis.
—— —— DABLON, C. Relations. 1672–79.
—— —— DREULETTE. Nouvelle Angleterre. 1650–51.
—— —— GRAVIER. Relations. 1693–94, 1700.
—— —— JCGUES. Jesuit Missions in N. A.
—— —— KIP, W. I. Early Jesuit Missions.

JESUIT Missions. LALLEMANT, Chas. Letters, etc. 1625. 26, 29, 42, 43, 45, 46, 59, 63, 64.
—— —— LAW, J. Missionaries of N. West.
—— —— LE MERCIER. Deux Lettres. 1655.
—— —— —— Relation. 1664, 65, 66, 67.
—— —— Lettres Edifiantes et Curieux.
—— —— LINCOLN, Gov. Acc. of Missions in Maine.
—— —— LOCKMAN, J. Travels of Jesuits.
—— —— MARQUETTE. Recit des Voyages. 1674–5.
—— —— —— Relations. 1676–77.
—— —— MINET. Relation. 1690–91.
—— —— O'CALLAGHAN. Relations. 1611–72.
—— —— RAGNEAU. Relation. 1645–46.
—— —— Relatio Rerum Gestarum in Novo Francica. 1613–14.
—— —— Relation de ce qui s'est passee en la Nouvelle France. 1626.
—— —— Relation de ce qui passee de plus remarquable aux Missions en la Nouvelle France. 1676.
—— —— Relations de la Mission du Mississippi. 1700.
—— —— Relations des Jesuites. 3 Vols.
—— —— Travels of Several Missionaries, etc.
—— —— VIMONT. Relation. 1643–44.
—— —— See SHEA'S Cramoisy Series.
JESUITES POLICY, (The,) to Suppress Monarchy; &c. Lond., 1678. Sm. 4to. Eng. Rel. Pamph. Vol. 1.
JESUITS. See BELON, Peter. The King-Killing Doctrine of. 1679.
—— Brief Acc. of the Jesuits, showing their Dangerous Character, &c. Lond., 1815. 8vo. Pamphleteer. Vol. 6.
—— See PARKMAN, F. Discovery of the Great West.
—— Jesuits of America.
—— Pioneers of France in the New World.
—— WATERWORTH, Rev. W. Origin, Progress, &c., of.
JEWELL, Gov. The Presidential Campaign. Speech at N. Y. Sept. 11, 1872. Hartford, 1872. 8vo. Congr. & Polit. Pamph. Vol. 130.
JEWELRY. See ROSET, H. Jewelry & Precious Stones.
JEWETT, Chas. C. Notices of Public Libraries in the U. S. Washington, 1851. 8vo. Bibliograph. Pamph. Vols. 22 and 50.
—— Report on the Constitution of Catalogues of Libraries. Washington, 1853. 8vo. Bibliograph. Pamph. Vol. 50.
JEWETT, Isaac, A. Memorial of Sam'l APPLETON of Ipswich, Mass., with Genealog. Notices. Boston, 1850. 8vo.
JEWETT, Wm. Cornell. Mediation in America, with his Correspondence. Six Pamphlets. Lond., 1865. Rebell'n Pamph. Vol. 45.
—— Mediation Position of France, in connection with a Congress of Nations. 1863. Rebell'n Pamph. Vol. 55.
JEWISH Admission into Parliament, considered. Lond., 1849. 12mo. Strangford Pamph. Vol. 49.
—— Antiquities. See JOSEPHUS, Flavius.
—— Chronicle, published under the direction of the Amer. Soc. for Ameliorating Condition of the Jews. N. Y., 1844–45. 8vo.

JEWISH Disabilities Bill. Protest by a Believing Jew, Lond., 1854. 8vo. Strangford Pamph. Vol. 66.
—— —— See CAMPBELL, W. F. Vindication of the House of Lords. 1848.
—— —— FAUDEL, H. Few Words on. 1848.
—— —— GAWLER, G. Emancipation Indispensable, etc. 1847.
—— —— GOLDSMID, F. H. Arguments on Removal of. 1831. 1848.
—— —— GRANT, Robert and others. Speeches in Parl't. 1833.
—— —— MAGILL, D. Claims of the Jews. 1851.
—— —— ROTHSCHILD, Baron de. Exclusion of, from Parl't.
—— —— RUSSELL, Lord John. Speech in House of Commons, in 1847.
—— —— Short Statement on behalf of Jewish subjects. Lond., 1835. 8vo. Strangford Pamph. Vol. 10.
—— —— Scriptural Reasonings in Support of Jewish Claims. 1850.
—— —— OWEN, B. Ought Baron de Rothschild to sit in Parl't? 1847.
—— —— WHATELY, Archb'p R. Speech on. 1833.
—— —— High Priesthood (Chronolog. Succession of). See London Chronolog. Institute. Proceedings, 1860, '61.
JEWITT, Rev. E. R. Address before Toledo Division, No. 220, Sons of Temperance, Dec. 25, 1847. Toledo, 1848. 8vo. Temp. Pamph. Vol. 6.
JEWITT, John R. Narr. of his Adventures and Sufferings among the Savages of Nootka Sound. Middletown, 1815. 12mo. Another Copy. Ithaca, 1851. 12mo.
JEWS. See Amer. Soc. of Meliorating Condition of.
—— GODWYN, T. Moses and Aaron.
—— HEIGHWAY, O. W. T. Leilia Ada.
—— Jewish Chronicle.
—— JOSEPHUS, F. History of.
—— LEVI, D. Letter to Dr. Priestley respecting.
—— London Soc. for Promoting Christianity among the Jews.
—— McCAUL, Alex., D. D.
—— MILLS, A. Ancient Hebrews.
—— MILMAN, H. H. Hist. of.
—— Nederlandsch. Israelietisch Jaarboekje, 1856.
—— SMITH, E. View of the Hebrews.
JOAN OF ARC, or the Maid of Orleans. From Michelet's Hist. of France. N. Y., 1860. 18mo.
—— See BARTLETT, D. W. Life of.
JOGUES, Rev. Isaac. Description of N. Netherland in 1644. Doc. Hist. of N. York. Vol. 4.
—— Novum Belgium. Description de Nieuw Netherland. N. Y., 1862. 8vo.
—— Novum Belgium in 1643–4 with a Fac Simile of the Original MSS, N. Y., 1862. 4to.
JOHNES, Arthur J. Philolog. Proofs of the Original Unity and Recent Origin of the Human Race. London, 1846. 8vo.
JOHNS, Henry T. Life with 49th Mass. Volunteers. Pittsfield, 1864, 12mo.

JOHNSON's Guide to the Sights of London. Southport, n. d. 8vo. Guide Books. Vol. 9.

JOHNSON, Mrs., of Charlestown, N. H. Narr. of her Captivity, Sufferings, etc. Farmer & Moore's N. H. Hist. Coll. Vol. 1.

JOHNSON, A. B. Thoughts on the approaching State Convention. Utica, 1846. 12mo. N. Y. Misc. Pamph. Vol. 8.

JOHNSON, Andrew. His Impeachment; his Suspension from Office while on Trial, etc. 1868. 8vo. Congr. & Polit. Pamph. Vol. 122.

—— His Southern Record, etc., 1872. Congr. & Polit. Pamph. Vol. 130.

—— Life and Times, written from a National Stand Point. N. Y., 1866. 8vo.

—— See LOGAN, J. A. Argument on Impeachment of.

—— National Johnson Club.

—— Speech in Cong. Apr. 29, 1852, on the Homestead Bill. Congr. and Polit. Pamph. Vol. 83.

—— Speech in U. S. Senate, Jan. 31, 1862, on Expulsion of Mr. Bright. Rebell'n Pamph. Vol. 66.

—— Trial of, on Impeachment. Washington, 1863. 3 Vols. 8vo.

JOHNSON, Benj. P. Report on the Exhibition of the Industry of all Nations, held 1851, in London. Albany, 1852. 8vo.

JOHNSON Cave. Speech in Cong., July 21, 1842, on the Navy Bill. Washington, 1842. 8vo. Congr. and Polit. Pamph. Vol. 25.

JOHNSON, Edw. "Wonder-Working Providence of Sions Savior in N. Eng." Hist. of N. E. 1628–1652. Mass. Hist. Soc. Coll. 2d Ser. Vols. 2, 3, 4, 7, 8.

JOHNSON, Edwin F. Northern Pacific R. R. Co. Report to the Board of Directors, Nov., 1867. Hartford, 1867. 8vo.

—— Railroad to the Pacific. Northern Route. Its Gen. Character, etc. N. Y., 1854. 8vo. 2d Ed.

JOHNSON, Geo. Dictionary of Modern Gardening. Lond., 1846. 12mo.

JOHNSON, Henry. Description of his Volutor. Lond., 1859. 8vo. Scientific Pamph. Vol. 34.

JOHNSON, Rev. John B. Farewell Sermon in North Dutch Ch., Albany, N. Y., Sept. 26, 1802. 8vo. Sermons, Vol. 27.

JOHNSON, Oliver. What I know of Horace Greeley. N. Y., 1872. 12mo. Congr. and Polit. Pamph. Vol. 130.

JOHNSON, Mrs. Jas. See Narrative of her Captivity, etc.

JOHNSON, Jos. Traditions and Reminiscences of the Amer. Revolution in the South, with Biograph. Sketches, etc. Charleston, 1851. 8vo.

JOHNSON, Rebecca. vs. Thomas Caruley, before N. Y. Court of Appeals. Law Pamph. Vol. 25.

JOHNSON, Reverdy. See Letter to.

—— Opinion in U. S. Senate, on the Rights of the Central Branch of the Union Pacific R. R. Co. 1868. Congr. and Polit. Pamph. Vol. 113.

—— Reply to Sir Roundell Palmer on the Washington Treaty and the Alabama Claims. Baltimore, 1871. 8vo. Rebellion Pamph. Vol. 108.

JOHNSON, Reverdy. Reply to the Review of Judge Advocate Gen. Holt, in the Case of Maj. Gen. Fitz John Porter. 1863. Rebell. Pamph. Vols. 1, 6, 22, 37.

—— Speech at Brooklyn McClellan Central Assoc., Oct. 21, 1864. Rebell'n Pamph. Vol. 36.

—— Speech in U. S. Senate, Apr. 5, 1864, on Slavery. Congr. and Polit. Pamph. Vol. 121. Rebell'n Pamph. Vols. 9, 32, 34.

JOHNSON, Col. R. M. Biog. of Col. Rich'd M. Johnson, of Kentucky. Boston, 1834. 12mo.

—— Review of his Report on Sabbath Mails. 1829. 8vo. Congr. and Polit. Pamph. Vol. 58.

JOHNSON, Rob't. Lecture at Kensington Hall, July 17, 1850, on Female Education. Lond., 1851. 8vo. Educa. Pamph. Vol. 29.

JOHNSON, Rob't G. Memoir of John Fenwicke, Chief Proprietor of Salem Tenth, N. J. N. J. Hist. Soc. Proceed. Vol. 4.

JOHNSON, R. W. Address to Citizens of Arkansas, Jan. 29, 1850. Washington, 1850. Congr. and Polit. Pamph. Vol. 90.

JOHNSON, Dr. Sam'l. See BOSWELL, J. Life of.

—— Collection of Interesting Biography. 1791.

—— Graphic Illustrations, &c.

—— Letter to. 1770.

—— Life and Writings; selected and arranged by Rev. Wm. P. Page. Harpers Fam. Libr. N. Y., 1860. 2 vols. 18mo.

—— Lives of the Most Eminent Eng. Poets, with Critical Observations. N. Y., 1857. 2 vols. 12mo.

JOHNSON, S. M. Letter to the President, on the Title to Yerba Buena Island. Washington, 1870. 8vo. Congr. and Polit. Pamph. Vol. 118.

—— The Dual Revolutions: Anti-Slavery and Pro-Slavery. 1863. Rebell'n Pamph. Vol. 73.

JOHNSON, Prof. S. W. See Conn. State Agr. Soc.

JOHNSON, Sidney L. Ascent of Mount Etna. Waldie's Circulat. Libr. Vol. 3.

JOHNSON, Theo. F. California and Oregon; or Sights in the Gold Region. 4th Ed. Phila., 1865. 12mo.

—— Sights in the Gold Regions. N. Y., 1849. 12mo.

JOHNSON, Walter R. Lecture on Schools of the Arts, before the Amer. Institute of Instruction, 1835. Waldie's Circulating Lib. Vol. 11.

—— Report on American Coals, made to the Navy Department of the U. S. Washington, 1844. 8vo.

JOHNSON, Sir Wm. Journals of of his Scouts, 1775–6. Doc. Hist. of N. Y. Vol. 4.

—— Manuscripts of. Doc. Hist. of N. Y. Vol. 2.

—— See STONE, W. L. Life and Times of.

JOHNSON, Wm. Sketches of the Life and Correspondence of Maj. Gen. Nathaniel Greene. Charleston, 1822. 2 Vols. 4to.

—— Life of Gen. Greene. See LEE, Henry.

JOHNSON, W. M. Hints in Photograpy. Milwaukee, 1864. 8vo. Scientific Pamph. Vol. 21.

JOHNSON, Wm. Otis. Diplomatic History of the War in the East. From N. Amer. Rev., Oct., 1855. Boston, 1855. 8vo. Hist. Pamph. Vol. 7.

JOHNSTON'S Map of the Seat of War in North Italy, 1859. Edinburgh. Guide-Books. Vol. 9.

JOHNSTON, Alex. Some Acc. of the Society of the Cincinnati. Penn. Hist. Soc. Memoirs. Vol. 6.

JOHNSTON, Chas. Narr. of Incidents attending the Capture, Detention and Ransom of Chas. Johnston, of Botetourt Co., Va.,, I790. N. Y., 1827. 12mo.

JOHNSTON, Jas. F. The Suspending Power and the Writ of Habeas Corpus. Phila., 1862. 8vo. Rebell'n Pamph. Vol. 27.

JOHNSTON, Jas. F. W. Catechism of Agricult., Chemistry and Geology. Lond., 1845. 12mo. 15th Ed. Scientific Pamph. Vol. 26.

JOHNSTON, John. Acc. of Present State of the Indian Tribes inhabiting Ohio. 1819. Amer. Antiq. Soc. Trans. Vol. 1.

JOHNSTON, Wm. Address on the Life and Pub. Services of Hon. Edwin M. Stanton, at Cincinnati, Jan. 7, 1870. Cincin.,

JOHNSTON, Wm. J. Sketches of the Hist. of Stephenson Co., Ill., 1870. 8vo. Addresses. Vol. 21.

and the Early Settlement of the N. West. Freeport, 1854. 8vo. Illinois Local Histories. Vol. 2.

JOHNSTONE, Gov. Speech on the Question of Recommitting the Address declaring the Colony of Mass. Bay in Rebellion. Lond., 1775. 8vo. Congr. and Polit. Pamph. Vol. 74.

JOHSTONE, Dr. John. Address at the Birmingham School of Medicine and Surgery, Oct. 6, 1834. Birmingham, 1834. 8vo. Med. Pamph. Vol. 29.

JOHNSTONE, Dr. J. Treatise on the Malignant Angina, or Putrid Sore Throat. Worcester, 1779. 8vo. Med Pamph. Vol. 16.

JOHONNOT, Jas. Country School Houses: containing Elevations, Plans and Specifications. N. Y., 1859. 8vo.

JOIGNEAUX, P. Traite des Amendments et des Engrais. Paris, 1848. 24mo.

JOINVILLE, Prince de. The Army of the Potomac, translated by W. H. Hurlbert. N. Y., 1862. 8vo. Rebell'n Pamph. Vol. 60.

JOLIET, Sieur. See MARQURTTE, Père.

JONES, ALEX. The Cymry of '76: or Welshmen and their Descendents of the Amer. Revolution. N. Y., 1855. 8vo.

JONES, Alfred. Principle of Privy Council Legislation. Lecture before the United Assoc. of Schoolmasters of G. B., at London., 1859. Edinburgh, 12mo. Educat. Pamph. Vol. 39.

JONES, A. D. Illustrated Amer. Biography. N. Y., 1853. 8vo.

JONES, Gen. Calvin. Account of the Cherokee Schools. From the Port Folio. Vol. 12. n. d. 8vo. Indian Pamph. Vol. 2.

JONES, Rev. Chas. C. Hist. Address before Liberty Independent Troop, Feb. 22, 1856. Savannah, 1856. 8vo. See Geo. Hist. Discourses. Vol. 1.

—— Hist. Sketch of Chatham Artillery. Albany, 1867. 8vo.

—— Hist. Sketch of Tomo-chi-chi, Mico of the Yamacraws. Albany, 1868. 8vo.

JONES, Chas. C. Jr. Ancient Tumuli on the Savannah River. pr. Printed. N. Y., 1868. 8vo. Ga. Miscell. Pamph. Vol. 1.
—— Indian Remains in So. Georgia. Address before the Georgia Hist. Soc., Feb. 12, 1859. Savannah, 1859. 8vo.
—— Monumental Remains of Georgia. n. d. 8vo.
—— Reminiscences of the Last Days, Death and Burial of Gen. Henry Lee. Albany, 1870. Sm. 4to.
JONES, David. Journal of Two Visits to some Nations of Indians. Reprinted. N. Y., 1865. Sm. 4to.
JONES, David S. Memorial of, with Appendix, containing Genealog. Notices of the Jones Family of Queens Co. N. Y., 1849. 12mo.
JONES, Electa F. Stockbridge, Past and Present. Springfield, 1854. 12mo.
JONES, Evan. Dissent and Morality of Wales. Lond., 1849. 8vo. Strangford Pamph. Vol. 56.
JONES, Evan R. Personal Recollections of the Amer. War. Newcastle-on-Tyne, Eng., 1872. 8vo. Rebell'n Pamph. Vol. 110.
JONES Family Genealogy. See JONES, David S. Jones Family of Queens Co., N. Y.
JONES, George. Count Johannes. Hist. of Ancient America, anterior to the time of Columbus: proving the Identity of the Aborigines with the Tyrians and Israelites. 3d ed. Lond., 1843. 8vo.
—— Jubilee Oration on the Life, Character and Genius of Shakspeare, at Stratford-on-Avon, April 23, 1836. Lond., 1844. 8vo.
—— Life and Hist of Gen. Wm. H. Harrison, late Pres't of the U. S. Lond., 1844. 8vo.
—— Tecumseh and the Prophet of tne West: an original Hist. Tragedy. Lond., 1844. 8vo.
JONES, Henry. Strange Phenomena of N. England in the 17th Century; including Salem Witchcraft. N. Y., 1846. 8vo. N. Eng. Pamph. Vol. 1.
JONES, Horatio Gates. Address before the Hist. Soc. of Penn., Feb. 9, 1869, on Andrew Bradford. Phil'a, 1869. 8vo.
—— The Levering Family; or a Geneal. Account of Wigard Levering and Gerhard Levering, of Roxborough Township, Penn. Phil'a, 1858. 8vo.
JONES, Hugh. Present State of Virginia. Lond., 1724. N. Y. reprint, 1865. 4to.
JONES, Rev. Isaac. Sermon at Centennial of Epis. Ch. in Litchfield, Conn., Nov. 5, 1845. Litchfield. 1846. 8vo. Conn. Hist. Discourses. Vol. 1.
JONES, I. D. Remarks in Cong., June 16, 1842, on the Apportionment Bill. Washington, 1842. 8vo. Congr. and Polit. Pamph. Vol. 24.
JONES, Dr. J. Exposure of the Hamiltonian System of teaching Languages. Lond., 1826. 8vo. Educa. Pamph. Vol. 35.
JONES, Joel. See Girard College.
JONES, Rev. John. The Slain in Liverpool during 1864, by Drink. Liverpool, 1865. 8vo. Temp. Pamph. Vol. 3.

JONES, Rev. J. A. Hist. of the Iniquitous "Schism Bill" of 1714. Lond., 1843. 12mo. Eng. Polit. Pamph. Vol. 78.

JONES, J. C. Speech in U. S. Senate, Mar. 18, 1852, on Non-Intervention. Congr. and Polit. Pamph. Vol. 83.

JONES, J. Paul. See HAMILTON, J. Life of. 1858.

—— Life of. With Acc. of his Service in the Amer. Revolution. Illustrated. 12mo. Phila., 1869.

—— Life and Adventures of. N. Y., 1869. 8vo. Biograph. Pamph. Vol. 4.

—— See MACKENZIE, A. S. Life of. 1841.

—— SHERBURNE, J. H. Life and Character of. 1825.

JONES, J. Seawell. Defence of the Revolutionary His. of N. Carolina from Aspersions of Thos. JEFFERSON. Boston, 1834. 8vo.

JONES, Dr. Jos. Researches, Chemical and Physiological, concerning N. Amer. Vertebrata. Smithson. Contrib. Vol. 8.

JONES, Rev. Jos. H. Life of Ashbel Green. N. Y., 1849. 8vo.

JONES, Maurice C. A Red Rose from the Olden Time; Annals of Rose Inn on the Barony of Nazareth, in the Days of the Province. Phila. 1872. 4to. Pamph.

—— Notes respecting Family of Waldo—Printed for Private Circulation. Edinburgh, 1863. 8vo.

JONES, Nathan'l. See WHITEHAD, Wm. A.

JONES, Rev. N. W. Indian Bulletin (No. I.) for 1867. N. Y., 1867. 8vo. Indian Pamph. Vol. 1.

—— Indian Bulletin (No. II.) for 1868; containing an Acc't of Chinese Voyages to the N. W. Coast of America, and the Interpretation of 200 Indian Names. N. Y., 1869. 8vo. Indian Pamph. Vol. 2.

JONES, Owen. The Alhambra Court in the Crystal Palace. Lond., 1854. 12mo. Guide-Books. Vol. 10.

JONES, Rev. Peter. Hist. of the Ojebway Indians with reference to their Conversion to Christianity. Lond., n. d. 8vo.

JONES, Pomroy. Annals and Recollections of Oneida County, N.Y. Rome, 1854. 8vo.

JONES, Rev. Rich'd. Remarks on the Manner in which Tithe should be assessed, etc. Lond., 1838. 8vo. Strangford Pamph. Vol. 16.

—— Remarks on the Proposed Commutation of Tithes. Lond., 1833. 8vo. Strangford Pamph. Vol. 8.

JONES, R. D. Opening Address before the N. Y. State Teachers' Assoc., at Utica, Aug. 1, 1855. Albany, 1855. 8vo. Educa. Pamph. Vol. 5.

JONES, Saml., D. D. Century Sermon before the Phila. Baptist Assoc., Oct. 6, 1807. Phila,, 1807. 8vo, Penn. Hist. Discourses. Vol. 1.

JONES, Sam'l W. Memoir of Hon. Jas. Duane. Doc. Hist. of N. Y. Vol. 4.

JONES, Seaborn. Speech in Cong., June 18, 1846, on the Tariff. Washington, 1846. 8vo. Speeches. Vol. 1.

JONES, Comm. Thos. Ap. Catesby. Proceedings of his Court Martial. 1851. Congr. and Polit. Pamph. Vol. 28.

JONES, T. Richer. Slavery sanctioned by the Bible. 1861. Rebellion Pamph. Vol. 74.

JONES, T. Wharton. Report on the Present State of the Knowledge of the Nature of Inflammation. Lond., (n. d.) 8vo. Med. Pamph. Vol. 19.

JONES, U. J. Hist. of the Early Settlement of the Juniata Valley, embracing an Acc. of the Early Pioneers, 1785. 8vo. Phila., 1856. 8vo.

JONES, Sir Wm. Dialogue between a Gentleman and a Farmer. Lond., 1785 8vo. Eng. Polit. Pamph. Vol. 22.

JONES, W. Alfred. Characters and Criticisms. N. Y., 1857. 2 Vols. 12mo.

—— Essays upon Authors and Books. N. Y., 1849. 12mo.

—— Paper on Long Island, read before the L. I. Hist. Soc., Nov. 5, 1863. Hist. Mag. Vol. 8.

JONES, Wm. C. Report on Land Titles in California. Washington, 1850. 8vo. Sec. of Interior Reports.

JONES, Rev. Wm. Henry. Lecture before the Bradford Literary Institution. Bradford, Eng., 1852. Eng. Misc. Pamph. Vol. 20.

JOPLIN, T. General Principles and Practice of Banking, in England and Scotland. Lond., 1824. 8vo. Pamphleteer. Vol. 24.

JORDAN, Francis. Constitutional Reform. From the Penn Monthly, Mar., 1872. Phila., 1872. 8vo. Congr. and Polit. Pamph. Vol. 140.

JORDAN, Sam'l. The Restorer of the Union of the U. S. to its Original Purity, etc. Augusta, Ga., 1866. 8vo. Congr. and Polit. Pamph. Vol. 126.

JORDAN, Thos. and PRYOR, J. P. Campaigns of Lieut.-Gen. N. B. Forrest, and of Forrest's Cavalry. N. Orleans, 1868. 8vo.

—— The South: its Products, Commerce and Resources. Lond., 1861. 8vo. Rebell'n Pamph. Vol. 38.

JOSEPH II., of Austria. Letters written by him to distinguished Princes and Statesmen, etc. Lond., 1821. 8vo. Pamphleteer. Vol. 19.

JOSEPHUS, F. See BASNAGE, J. Continuation of History.

—— Genuine works of.—translated by Wm. Whiston, containing Six Books of the Antiquities of the Jews. N. Y., 1825. 6 Vols. 18mo.

—— Works translated by Wm. Whiston. Baltimore, (n. d.) 8vo.

JOSEPHINE, Empress. See ABBOTT, J. S. C. Corres. of Napoleon.

—— HEADLEY, P. C. Life of.

—— MEMES, J. S. Life of.

JOSSELYN Genealogy. See Stiles, H. R.

JOSSELYN, John. Acc. of Two Voyages to N. England, 1675. Mass. Hist. Soc. Coll. 3d Ser. Vol. 3.

—— New England's Rarities discovered in Beasts, Birds, etc. Lond., 1672. Boston reprint, 1865. 4to.

—— Two Voyages to N. England in 1638. Lond., 1663. Boston Reprint, 1865. 4to.

JOURNAL de la Guerre du Micissippi Contre les Chicachas en 1739. N. Y., 1859. 4to.

—— d'un Voyage a la Louisiane fait en 1720, par MXXX. Paris, 1768. 12mo.

—— d'un Voyage fait dans l'Interieur de l'Amerique Septentrionale. Paris, 1790. 2 Vols. 8vo.

—— Same. Avec Carte et Figures. Paris, 1793. 2 Vols. 8vo.

—— (The) of a Naturalist. Phila., 1850. 12mo.

—— of a Nobleman, being a Narr. of his Residence at Vienna, during the Congress. Waldie's Circulating Libr. Vol. 1.

—— of a Tour in the "Indian Territory," performed under the direction of the P. Episcopal Ch., in 1844. N. Y., 1844. 8vo. Indian Pamph. Vol. 3.

—— of a Young Lady of Virginia. 1782. Baltimore, 1871. 4to. Published for the Lee Memorial Assoc. of Richmond.

—— of an English Traveller, from 1814 to 1816; or Memoirs of the Princess of Wales and her Court, etc. Lond., 1817. 8vo. Pamphleteer. Vol. 10.

—— of Man. See Buchanan's Journal.

—— of Pilgrims at Plymouth. See CHEEVER, G. B.

—— of Proceedings of the Grand Division of the Sons of Temperance of the State of N. York, for 1842–5. N. Y., 1845. 8vo.

—— of Proceedings of the Congress held at Albany in 1754, for the purpose of treating with the Six Nations of Indians. Mass. Hist. Soc. Coll. Vol. 5. 3d Ser.

—— of Sloop Mary, from Quebec. Albany, 1866. 4to.

—— of the Campaign on the Coast of France, 1758. Lond., 1758. 12mo. Eng. Polit. Pamph. Vol. 14.

—— of the Treaty held at Albany in Aug., 1775, with the Six Nations, by Commissioners of the United Colonies. Mass. Hist. Soc. Coll. Vol. 5. 3d Ser.

JOURNEY across the Continent of N. America, by an Indian Chief, about the middle of the last Century. Quebec Lit. and Hist. Soc. Trans. Vol. 1.

JOUTEL, M. Hist. Journal of M. de la Salle's last Voyage to the River Mississippi. See French's Hist. Coll. of La. Vol. 1.

—— Journal Historique du dernier Voyage que feu M. de la Salle, fit daus le Golfe de Mexique, pour trouver l'Embouchure et le cours de la Riviére de St. Louis. Paris, 1713. 12mo.

JOY, Walter. See STEELE, O. G. Memorial of.

JUBILEE College. Appeal for the Endowment of 1856. Ill. Misc. Pamph. Vol. 2.

—— —— See CHASE, Rev. S. Review of. 1843.

—— of the Constitution. See ADAMS, John Q.

JUBINAL Achille. Une lettre de Montaigne Accompagnee de quelques Recherches a son sujet precedee d'un Avertissement suivie de plusieurs fac simile. Paris, 1850. 8vo.

JUDD, Norman B. Speech in Congr., Jan. 17, 1870, on the Apportionment Bill. Cong. and Polit. Pamph. Vol. 119.

JUDD, Sylvester. Thomas Judd and his Descendants. Northampton, 1856, 8vo. Genealog. Pamph. Vol. 9.

JUDICIAL Decisions upon the Cases of Habeas Corpus brought by the late Officers of the Bank of the U. S. Phila., 1842. 8vo. Rebell'n Pamph. Vol. 27.

JUDSON, Adoniram. See Clement, J. Memoir of.

—— HAYNE, Rev. W. Disc. on Life and Character.

—— WAYLAND, F. Life and Labors of.

JUDSON, Mrs. Ann H., etc. See WILLSON, A. M. Lives of.

JUDSON, Eliza E. Address in Memory of Ann Preston, M. D., before the Woman's Medical Coll. of Penn., March 11, 1873. Phila., 1873. 8vo. With Reports of the Coll.

JUET, Rob't. Extract from the Journal of the Voyage of the Half Moon, under Hudson, in 1609. N. Y. Hist. Soc. Coll. N. S. Vol. 1.

JULIAN, Geo. W. Select Speeches, in Cong. during the Rebellion. Cinn., 1867. 8vo. Rebell'n Pamph. Vol. 110.

—— Speech in Cong., May 14, 1850, on Slavery. Congr. and Poli. Pamph. Vol. 85.

—— —— Jan. 21, 1871, on Grants to Railroads. 8vo. Cong. and Polit. Pamph. Vol. 119.

—— The New Departures. From a Speech at Williamsport, Ind., July 24, 1872. Golden Age Campaign Tracts. Cong. and Polit. Pamph. Vol. 130.

JUMPERTS, Henry. Career, Tragedy and Trial of, at Chicago, 1849. for Murder. Chicago, 1859. 12mo. Law Pamph. Vol. 24,

JUNEAU County, Wis. Newspaper. 1862–66.

JUNEAU, Wis. Dodge County Gazette. Newspaper. June, 1852 to Sept., 1853. Folio.

—— Burr Oak. Newspaper. Oct., 1853 to Dec. 1854. Folio.

JUNIATA County, Pa. See BANKS, A. Early Hist. of.

—— Valley. See JONES, U. J. Hist. of the Settlement of.

JUNIUS *pseud.* A Plain Tale for the new Parliament; or a Sketch of the Hist. of England, from 1794 to the present time. Part 1. Lond., 1796. 8vo. Miscell. Tracts. Vol. 4.

—— See BARBER, E. H. Authorship of.

—— BRITTON, J. Authorship Elucidated in Col. Barre.

—— BUSBY, Thos. Arguments as to DeLolme.

—— COVENTRY, Geo. Critical Enquiry, &c.

—— See GRAHAM, John A. John Horne Tooke Identified as Junius.

—— Including Letters by the same writer under other signatures. Edited by John WADE. Lond., 1865. 2 Vols. 12mo.

—— Letter to Hon. Brigadier General, Commander in Chief of his Majesty's forces in Canada. Lond., 1760. Lond., 1841. 12mo.

—— The Letters of. From the Galaxy, May, 1873.

—— Papers on Junius; a volume of newspaper and magazine cuttings.

—— Posthumous Works of Junius; with an Enquiry respecting the Author, and Sketch of Life of John Horne Tooke. N. Y., 1829. 8vo.

—— Supplement to Junius Identified. Lond., 1817. 8vo. 2d Ed.

JUNIUS. "Touching the Identity of Junius." From Dublin University Mag. Va. Hist. Reg. Vol. 5.
—— Two Letters to People of England in favor of Americans. Lond., n. d.
—— Unmasked; or Lord Geo. SACKVILLE proved to be Junius. Boston, 1828. 12mo.
—— See WATERHOUSE, B. Essay on, and Sketch of Lord CHATHAM.
—— Tracts. N. Y., 1844. 8vo. Congr. & Polit. Pamph. Vol. 95 and 124.
JURIES. See HAWLES, J. The Englishman's Right, &c., 1763.
—— LAURIE, P. Use and Abuse of Grand Juries, 1832.
—— SOMERS, J. Trust, Power and Duty of Grand Juries, 1766.
—— WILLMORE, G. Is Trial by Jury Worth Keeping? 1850.
JURYMAN, The, charged; or, a Letter to a Citizen of London. Lond., 1864. Sm. 4to. Eng. Polit. Pamph. Vol. 65.
JUSTE, Theodore. Un Tour en Hollande, 1839. Bruxelles, 1859. 12mo. Guide Books, &c. Vol. 27.
JUSTICE to Ireland; a Letter to the Marquis of Chandos, Nov. 9, 1837. Lond. 8vo. Eng. Polit. Pamph. Vol. 42.
JUTE, American. See HOWSON, H. Paper before Franklin Institute. 1862.

K.

KAIN, J. H. Mineralogy and Geology of Part of Va. and Tenn., 1819. Silliman's Journ. Vol. 1.
KALADIT Okalluktualliat; or Esquimaux Legends. Printed and bound at Noungme, Greenland, 1858. 2 Vols. 8vo.
KALAMAZOO Co., Mich., Agr. Soc. See CASS, Lewis. Address, 1850.
—— Theolog. Seminary and College. Catalogue, 1855–6. Kalamazoo, 1856. 8vo.
KALENDAR for 1853, being the 16th—17th Year of H. M. Queen Victoria and the 2d 3rd of H. I. Majesty Hien Fung. Shanghæ, 1853. 8vo.
KALM, Peter. Acc. of Niagara Falls. See BARTRAM, J.
—— Travels into N. America, 1748–9. 2d Ed. Lond., 1772. 2 Vols. 8vo.
KANAWHA Valley, Va. See GIBBONS, J. A. Resources and Developments, 1872.
—— STROTHER, D. H. Capitol of W. Va., etc., 1872.
KANE, E. K. Access to an Open Polar Sea; Paper read before Amer. Geograph. and Statist. Soc. 1852.
—— See Miscell. Papers of the Society. See also Society Bulletin. Vol. 1.
—— Arctic Explorations; the 2d Grinnell Expedition in Search of Sir John Franklin. Phila., 1858. 2 Vols. 8vo.
—— The Grinnell Expedition in Search of Sir John Franklin. New Ed. Phila., 1856. 8vo.

KANE, E. K. See ELDER, W. Biog. of.
—— Astronom. Observations in the Arctic Seas, 1853–55. Smithson. Contrib. Vol. 12.
—— Magnetic Observations in the Arctic Seas. 1853–55. Smithson. Contrib. Vol. 10.
—— Meteorolog. Observations in the Arctic Seas. 1853–55. Smithson. Contrib. Vol. 11.
—— Tidal Observations in the Arctic Seas, made in 1853–5. Smithson. Contrib. Vol. 13.
KANE, J. K. Address on the Patent Laws. Washington, 1849. 8vo. Addresses. Vol. 14.
KANE, Thos. L. Discourse before Penn. Hist. Society on the Mormons, Mar. 26, 1850. Phila., 1850. 8vo. Penn. Hist. Soc. Addresses. Vol. 1.
KANSAS. Adjutant General. Report for 1864–65. Leavenworth and Topeka, 1865–66. 2 Vols. 8vo.
—— Affairs, 1856. See U. S. House of Repr. Reports from Select Comm. 1856.
—— and Nebraska Bill. See Congress'l Speeches.
—— and the Constitution. Boston, 1856. 8vo. Congr. and Polit. Pamph. Vol. 77.
—— Auditor of State. 7th Ann. Report of, for 1867. Topeka, 1867. 8vo.
—— See BEECHER, H. W. Defence of.
—— BOYNTON, C. B. and MASON, T. B. Journey through Kansas. 1855.
—— BREWERTON, G. D. The War in.
—— COPLEY, Josiah. Kansas and the Country beyond.
—— Emigrant Aid Co. Organization, Objects. etc., of, with Descrip. of Kausas. Boston, 1854. 8vo. 2d Ed. Kansas Misc. Pamph. Vol. 1.
—— See GIHON, J. H. Gov. Geary's Administration.
—— GRISWOLD. Wayne. Resources, Etc., of. 1871.
—— HALE, E. History of, and Nebraska.
—— HOLLOWAY, J. N. Hist. of. 1868.
—— Homes for all. Published by the North Missouri R. R. Co. St. Louis, 1869. 8vo. Kansas Misc. Pamph. Vol. 1.
—— See HUTCHINSON, C. C. Resources of.
—— In 1856: Account of Outrages in Kansas, Etc. Washington, 1856. 8vo. Congr. and Polit. Pamph. Vol. 99.
—— Laws. Statutes of the Territory. Shawnee M. L. School. 1855. 8vo.
—— —— Gen. Laws passed at 1st Sess. of Legislature. Lawrence, 1861. 1863, '64, '65 and 1870.
—— LE CONTE, J. L. The Coleoptera of K. and N. Mexico.
—— Meek & Hayden. Organic Remains in N.E. Kansas. 1858. Scientific Pamph. Vol. 16.
—— Ann. Message of Gov. Harvey, 1871. Topeka, 1871. 8vo.
—— Pacific Railway. Hand-Book. St. Louis, 1870. 8vo. Guide Books. Vol. 16.
—— —— Emigrants' Guide to the Lands of. Chicago, 1871. 8vo. Kansas Misc. Pamph. Vol. 1.

KANSAS Pacific Railway. Report of Surveys in 1867–8. Phila., 1869. 8vo.
—— Papers transmitted to the U. S. Senate on the Sale of Shawnee Indian Lands in Kansas. Washington, 1870. 8vo.
—— See PHILLIPS, W. Conquest of.
—— Public Documents for 1862 and 1863. Lawrence, 1862, 3. 8vo.
—— Reports from Select Comm. of U. S. House of R., on Troubles in Kansas, 1856. Washington, 1856. 8vo. Congr. and Polit. Pamph. Vol. 139.
—— See ROBINSON, Mrs. S. T. L. Interior and Exterior Life.
—— Struggle (The) of 1856, in Congress and in the Presidential Campaign. N. Y., 1857. 8vo. Congr. and Polit. Pamph. Vol. 135.
—— See SUMNER, Chas. Outrages in Kansas. 1855.
—— Supt. of Pub. Instruction. 4th Ann. Report, for 1864. Topeka, 1865. 8vo.
—— See SWALLOW & HAWN. Rocks of Kansas. 1858.
—— WALKER, Gov. R. J. Inaug. Address, 1857.
—— Washington Terr. and Oregon Newspapers. Various. 1856–62.
—— See WEBB, T. H. Information for Immigrants.
KANT, Immanuel. See WIRGMAN, Thos. Principles of his Philosophy.
KAPP, Friedrich. Immigration and the Commissioners of Emigration of the State of N. Y. N. Y., 1870. 8vo.
—— Life of Fred. Wm. Von Steuben, Maj. Gen. in Revolutionary Army, with an Introduction by Geo. Bancroft. N. Y., 1859. 12mo.
KAUFMAN, David S. Speech in Cong. June 29, 1846, on the Tariff. Washington, 1846. 8vo. Speeches Vol. 1.
—— Speech in Cong. June 27, 1848, on Texas Boundary. Congr. and Polit. Pamph. Vol. 83.
KAY, Jos. See SPALDING, Bishop. Review of his Work on Education.
KAZINSKI, Count Louis. Two Lectures on Turkey and Russia. Manchester, N. H., 1854. 8vo. Addresses, Vol. 13.
KEACH, Rev. Israel. Address at Bennington, Aug. 15, 1829, on the 52d Annivers. of the Bennington Battle. Bennington, 1829. 8vo. Rev. War Pamph. Vol. 5.
KEARNEY, Gen. Phil. Se De PEYSTER, Gen. J. W. Personal and Military Hist.
—— See Men of the Time.
—— Official Report of the Battle of Seven Pines. Phila, 1863. Rebell'n Pamph. Vol. 12.
KEARSAGE and Alabama. See Story (The) of.
KEATING, Wm. H. Narr. of an Expedition to the Source of St. Peter's River, Lake Winnepeek, etc., under command of Maj, Stephen H. Long. Phila., 1824. 2 Vols. 8vo.
—— Same, Lond., 1825. 2 Vols. 8vo.
KEBLE, Rev. John. Letter to Sir Brook W. Bridges, on the Representation of the University of Oxford. Lond., 1852. 8vo. Eng. Polit. Pamph. Vol. 49.

KEBLE's enlarged Penny Guide Book to Margate, etc. Margate, Eng., 1867. 8vo. Guide Books, Vol. 8.

KEDZIE, Rev. A. S. Sermon on the Death of Mrs. Jane Louis Hobart. Detroit, 1853. 8vo. Wis. Miscell. Pamph. Vol. 4.

KEEVE, N. H. See HALE's S. Annals of.

KEIGHTLEY, Thomas. Hist. of England from the Earliest Period to 1839. Harpers' Fam. Lib. N. Y., 1855. 2 Vols. 18mo.

KEILEY, A. M. In Vinculis; or the Prisoner of War, being the Experience of a Rebel in Two Federal Pens. N. Y., 1866. 12mo.

KEIM, B. R. Sheridan's Troopers on the Borders, a Winter Campaign on the Plains. Phila., 1870. 2to.

KEITH, Lord. Sketch of the Life of. n. d. 8vo. Biograph. Pamph. Vol. 18.

KEITH, Rev. Geo. Geography and Navigation completed; New Theory and Method of ascertaining true Longitude. Lond. 1709. 4to.

—— Journal of Travels from N. Hampshire to Caratuck on the Continent of N. America. Lond., 1706. 4to.

KEITH, Sir Wm. Biograph. Sketch of. Penn. Hist. Soc. Memoirs, Vol. 1, Part 2.

—— Collection of Papers and other Tracts on various Subjects; including a Discourse on the Amer. Colonies. 1728. Lond., 1740. 12mo.

—— Collection of Papers and other Tracts on the Liberty of the Subject, Medium of Commerce, etc. 2d Ed. Lond., 1749. 12mo.

—— See FISHER, J. F. Narr., etc., of coming to Pa.

—— Hist. of British Plantations in America: Part I, containing a Hist. of Va. Lond., 1738. 4to.

KEITH, Wm., M. D. Hospital Statistics of Stone in the Bladder. Aberdeen, 1849. 8vo. Med. Pamph., Vol. 5.

KELDERMANS, J. B. Dissertatio Philologica de Origine atque Usu Nummorum apud Hebræos, etc. Utrecht, 1750. 4to. Latin Pamph., Vol. 4.

KELLER, Dr. Abstract of his Fifth Report on Lacustrian Settlements. Smithsonian Report, 1863.

KELLEY's Island. See HUNTINGTON, G. C. Hist. Sketch of.

KELLEY, Wm. D. Address at the Colored Department of the House of Refuge, Dec. 31, 1849. Phila., 1850. 8vo.

—— Dangers and Duties of the Hour. Address at Phila., Mar. 15, 1866. Washington, 1866. 8vo. Congr. and Polit. Pamph., Vol. 137.

—— See NORTHROP, Geo., and KELLEY, W. D. Joint Debates.

—— Reasons for Abandoning the Theory of Free Trade. Phila., 1872. 8vo. Congr. and Polit. Pamph. Vol. 68.

—— Speech in the Case of U. States vs. Wm. Smith, for Piracy. n. d. Rebell'n Pamph. Vol. 53.

—— Speeches at N. Orleans, Montgomery, Ala., and his Address to his Constituents. Rebell'n Pamph. Vol. 36.

—— Speech in Cong. on the "Trent Case," Jan. 7, 1862. Rebell'n Pamph. Vol. 66.

KELLEY, Wm. D. Speech in Congr., Jan. 31, 1862, on the Administration. Rebell'n Pamph. Vol. 61, 66.

—— —— May 9, 1862, on the Employment of Slaves in Navy Yards. Rebell'n Pamph. Vol. 34.

—— —— June 3, 1862, on the Recognition of Hayti and Liberia. Rebell'n Pamph. Vol. 68.

—— —— Dec. 19, 1862, on the State of the Union. Rebell'n Pamph. Vol. 67.

—— —— Feb. 24, 1863, on the Conscription Bill. Rebell'n Pamph. Vol. 66.

—— —— Feb. 23, 1864, on Freedmen's Affairs. Rebell'n Pamph. Vol. 32.

—— —— June 15, 1864, on Slavery. Rebell'n Pamph. Vol. 34.

—— —— Jan. 16, 1865, on Reconstruction. Rebell'n Pamph. Vols. 34, 37.

—— —— Mar. 7, 1866, on Trade with British America. Rebell'n Pamph. Vol. 32.

—— —— Jan. 3, 1867, on the National Debt. Congr. and Polit. Pamph. Vols. 84, 121. Rebell'n Pamph. Vol. 32.

—— —— Jan. 11, 1870, on the Report of the Special Commissioner of Revenue. Congr. and Polit. Pamph. Vol. 119.

—— —— Mar. 25, 1870, on the Tariff. 8vo. Congr. and Polit. Pamph. Vol. 119.

—— —— Jan. 27, 1871, on the Annexation of San Domingo. 8vo. Congr. and Polit. Pamph. Vol. 119.

—— The New Northwest: an Address on the Northern Pacific R. R. Phila. 8vo. 1871. Pacific R. R. Pamphs.

KELLO, John. Reasons for a Refusal to Sign a Report presented to the K——g's H——d S——y, Dec. 15, 181; in a Letter to Rev. John Clayton, Jr. Lond., 1813. 8vo. Eng. Polit. Pamph. Vol. 31.

—— Valedict. Address to Members of the King's Head Soc. Lond., 1813. 8vo. Educa. Pamph. Vol. 32.

KELLOGG, Allyn S. Memorials of Elder John White, of Hartford, Conn., and his Descendants. Hartford, 1860. 8vo.

KELLOGG, Chas. Family Meeting of Descendants of Chas. Kellogg, of Kelloggsville, N. Y. With Genealog. Items. Boston, 1858. 8vo. From N. Eng. Register. Genealog. Pamph. Vol. 7.

KELLOGG, F. W. Speech in Cong., May 25, 1864. On Reciprocity. Rebell'n Pamph. Vol. 34.

KELLOGG, Martin. Memoir of Bronson, Ohio. Fire Lands, Pioneer. Vols. 1, 3.

KELLOGG, Robert H. Life and Death in Rebel Prisons. Hartford, 1865. 12mo.

KELLOGG, Wm. P. Speech in Congr., Feb. 2, 1871, on a Steamship Line to Mexico. 8vo. Congr. and Polit Pamph. Vol. 119.

KELLY, Jas. Amer. Catalogue of Books, pub. in the U. S., Jan. 1861, to Jan. 1866. N. Y., 1866. 8vo.

—— Same. Jan., 1866, to Jan., 1871. N. Y., 1871. 8vo.

KELLY, John. Life and Adventures of. St. Louis, 1853. 8vo. Biograph. Pamph. Vol. 12.

KELLEY, John. Hist. Sketch of the Town of Hampstead, State of N. Hampshire.

KELLY, Rev. John. Practical Grammar of the Ancient Gaelic or Language of the Isle of Man, usually called Manx. Douglas, 1859. 8vo.

KELLY, Rev. Matt. Cambrensiis Eversus Seu Potius Historica Fides in Rebus Hibernicis Giralde Cambrensi Abrogata. Dublin, 1848. 3 Vols. 8vo.

KELLY, P. The Universal Cambist. and Commercial Instructor: being a Treatise on Exchanges, Coins, Weights and Measures of all nations. 2 Vols. in 1. Lond., 1835. 4to.

KELLY, Robt. Address on the Life and Character of Prof. Edward C. Ross, at N. Y., July 22, 1851. 8vo. Sermons, etc. Vol. 10.

KELSEY, John. Lives and Reminiscences of the Pioneers of Rochester and Western N. Y. Rochester, 1854. 8vo. N. Y. Hist. Discourses, etc. Vol. 3.

KELSO, Isaac. Stars and Bars; The Reign of Terror in Missouri. Boston, 1863. 12mo.

KEMBLE, Frances Ann. Francis the First. An Historical Drama. Lond., 1832. 8vo. Dramas. Vol. 12.

—— Poems. Boston, 1869. 12mo.

—— Views of Judge Woodward and Bishop Hopkins on Slavery, illustrated. 1863. Rebell'n Pamph. Vols. 74 and 91.

KEMBLE, J. P. Biograph. Sketch of. Canadian Mag. Vol. 1.

—— See BOADEN, J. Memoirs of.

KEMP, Edward. How to lay out a Garden; intended as a Guide to Choosing and Improving an Estate. N. Y., 1858.

KEMP. Nine Days Wonder. See Camden Society Publica.

KEMPER Hall, Kenosha, Wis. 1st Announcement, 1871–2. Louisville, 1871. 12mo.

KENDAL, Rev. Sam'l. Century Sermon at Weston, Mass., Jan. 12, 1812. Cambridge, 1813, 8vo. Mass. Hist. Discourses. Vol. 12.

KENDALL, Amos. Full Exposure of Dr. C. T. Jackson's Pretentions to the Invention of the Telegraph. Washington, 1852. 8vo. Congr. Pamph. Vol. 56.

—— Life of Gen. Andrew Jackson. N. Y., 1843. 7 Nos. all published.

KENDALL, Edw. A. Travels through Northern Parts of the U. S. in 1807, 1808. N. Y., 1809. 3 Vols. 8vo.

KENDALL, G. W. Narr. of the Texan Santa Fe Expedition. N. Y., 1856. 1 Vol. 12mo.

KENILWORTH Castle, Eng. See BECK'S Guide.

—— Concise Hist. and Descrip. of Warwick, Eng., 1822. 12mo. Guide Books, Vol. 23.

—— Same, 1834. Guide Books. Vol. 2.

KENNARD, Jas. H., D. D. See WINTER, Thos. Memorial of.

KENNEBEC Co., Maine. See BOARDMAN, S. L. Agriculture and Industry of. 1867.

—— Indians. See BAXTER, Rev. Jos.

—— Purchase, Me. See GARDINER, R. H.

—— River. See STRACHEY, W. Acc. of Popham's Colony.

KENNEDY, Andrew. Speech in Cong., March 18, 1842, on the Loan Bill. Washington, 1842. 8vo. Congr. & Polit. Pamph. Vol. 25.

KENNEDY, Benj. H. Ministerial Scheme of National Educa. Oxford, 1839. 8vo. Strangford Pamph. Vol. 17.

KENNEDY, Jas. Description of Curiosities in Wilton House. Salisbury, 1774. 12mo. Art Catalogues, etc. Vol. 5.

KENNEDY, James. Modern Poets and Poetry of Spain. Lond., 1852. 8vo.

—— Probable Origin of the Amer. Indians, with particular reference to that of the Caribs. Lond., 1854. 8vo. Indian Pamph. Vol. 3.

—— Sketch of Medical Monopolies with a Plan of Reform. Lond., 1836. 8vo. Med. Pamph. Vol. 18.

KENNEDY, J. C. G. See U. S. Census.

KENNEDY, John P. Address to the Horticult. Soc. of Maryland, June 12, 1833. Baltimore, 1833. 8vo. Agr. Pamph. Vol. 4.

—— Disc. on Geo. Calvert, Lord Baltimore, before Md. Hist. Soc. Dec. 9, 1845. 8vo. Md. Hist. Soc. Papers. Vol. 1.

—— See Mass. Hist. Soc.

—— Memoirs of the Life of Wm. Wirt, Attorney Gen. of the U. S, New ed. Phil'a, 1830. 2 Vols. 12mo.

—— See Peabody Institute.

—— Remarks of U. S. Catholic Magazine, &c.

—— See Review of his Discourse on Lord Baltimore. 1846.

—— The Border States: their Power and Duty on the present Conditon of the Country. Phil'a, 1861. 8vo. Rebell'n Pamph. Vol. 72.

—— The Great Drama: an Appeal to Maryland. Baltimore, 1861. 8vo. Rebell'n Pamph. Vol. 65.

KENNEDY, Pat'k. Journal up the Illinois River in 1773. Imlay's America, p. 506.

KENNEDY, Gen. Shaw. Notes on the Defence of G. Britain and Ireland. Lond., 1859. 8vo· Eng. Polit. Pamph. Vol. 57.

KENNEDY, T. L. The Privileges of the Writ of Habeas Corpus under the Constitution. Phil'a, 1862. 8vo. Rebell'n Pamph. Vol. 27.

KENNEDY, Wm. Texas: its Geography, Nat History and Topography. N. Y., 1844. 8vo. Texas Misc. Pamph. Vol. 1.

—— Texas: The Rise, Progress and Prospects of the Republic of Texas. Lond., 1841. 2 Vols. 8vo.

KENNEDY, Wm. S. The Plan of Union: or Hist. of the Presb. and Congrega. Churches of the Western Reserve; with Biograph. Sketches of the Early Missionaries. Hudson, Ohio, 1856. 12mo.

KENNET, Dr. White. His Conduct from 1681, to the Present Time. Being a Supplement to his Letters to the B'p of Carlisle, etc. Lonn., 1717. 12mo. Eng. Rel. Pamph. Vol. 11.

KENOSHA, Wis. Charter, By-Laws of the Council and Ordinances of the City of Kenosha. Kenosha, 1852.

—— Same. Kenosha, 1858.

—— Democrat. Newspaper. Mar., 1854, to Dec., 1856. Folio.

KENOSHA, Wis. See FRANK M. Early History. of.
—— LATHROP, Rev. J. Early History of.
—— Mayor's 3d Inaug. Address, Apr. 17, 1854. Kenosha, 1854. 8vo. Wis. Misc. Pamph. Vol. 1.
—— See MYGATT W. Settlement of.
—— Revised Charter and Ordinances of the City, etc. Kenosha, 1858. 8vo. Wis. Miscell. Pamph. Vol. 1.
—— Telegraph. Newspaper. Apr., 1848, to June, 1852. Folio.
—— Tribune and Telegraph. Apr., 1854 to Dec., 1870. Folio.
—— See Southport American.
—— Times. Newspaper. July, 1857, to Dec. 1859. Folio.
—— —— 1861, 1862. Folio.
KENRICK, John. Ancient Egypt under the Pharaohs. 2d Ed. N. Y., 1853. 2 Vols. 12mo.
—— Papers on Archaeology and History, communicated to Yorkshire Philosoph. Soc. Lond., 1864. 8vo.
—— Roman Sepulchral Inscriptions; their Archaeology, Language and Religion. Lond., 1858. 12mo.
KENT, Rev. Aratus. Address at Inaugura. of Rev. Aaron L. Chapin as Prest. of Beloit College, Wis. Milwaukee, 1850. 8vo.
KENT COUNTY, Eng. See HENSHALL, S. Domesday—Kent, Sussex and Surrey. 1799.
—— —— —— History of. 1798.
—— —— HUSSEY, A. Notes on Churches. 1852.
—— —— Kentish Society.
—— —— LARKIN, L. B. Domesday Book. 1869.
—— —— SMITH, J. R. Bibliotheca Cantiana. 1837.
—— —— Sussex Baptist Assoc. Circular Letters, 1780, '87, '89, '90, '91, '95. Eng. Rel. Pamph. Vol. 85.
—— East Indiaman. Narrative of her Loss by Fire in the Bay of Biscay, Mar. 1, 1825. Edinburgh, 1825. 12mo. Historical Pamph. Vol. 17.
KENT, Edw. N. Instructions for Collecting and Testing Gold: for the use of Visitors to the Gold Region of Cal. N. Y., 1848. 12mo. Cal. Misc. Pamph. Vol. 2.
KENT ISLAND. See STREETER, S. F. Geo. Evelin, the First Commander of.
KENT, James. Annivers. Disc. before the N. Y., Hist. Soc. Dec. 6, 1828. N. York, 1829. 8vo. N. Y. Hist. Soc. Addresses. Vol. 1. See also Collections Vol. 1. N. Ser.
—— See DUER, J. Life and Character of.
KENTISH DIALECT. See MICHEL, D. Ayenbite of Inwyt.
KENTON, Simon. See Harpers' Magaz. Vol. 28. MCCLURG, Sketches of Western Adventure. MCDONALD, J. PRITTS, J. THOMAS, F. W. Sketches of Character.
KENTUCKY. Acts of the General Assembly passed at the December Session, 1849. Frankfort, 1850. 8vo.
—— Adjutant General. Reports 1861–1866. Frankfort, 1866. 2 Vols. 8vo.
—— Agricult. and Mechanical College. Report, Feb. 7, 1872. 8vo. Ky. Coll. Catalogues, etc.
—— See ALLEN, W. B. History of. 1872.

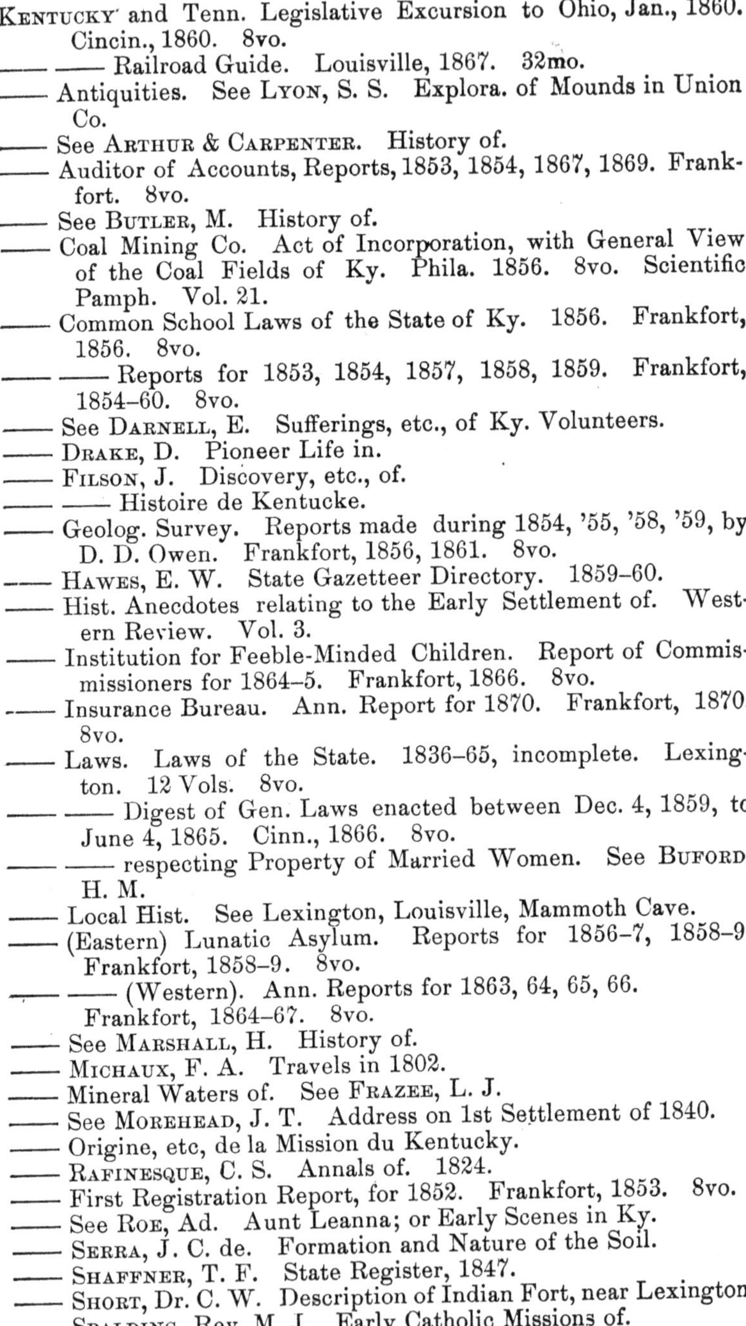

Kentucky and Tenn. Legislative Excursion to Ohio, Jan., 1860. Cincin., 1860. 8vo.

—— —— Railroad Guide. Louisville, 1867. 32mo.

—— Antiquities. See Lyon, S. S. Explora. of Mounds in Union Co.

—— See Arthur & Carpenter. History of.

—— Auditor of Accounts, Reports, 1853, 1854, 1867, 1869. Frankfort. 8vo.

—— See Butler, M. History of.

—— Coal Mining Co. Act of Incorporation, with General View of the Coal Fields of Ky. Phila. 1856. 8vo. Scientific Pamph. Vol. 21.

—— Common School Laws of the State of Ky. 1856. Frankfort, 1856. 8vo.

—— —— Reports for 1853, 1854, 1857, 1858, 1859. Frankfort, 1854–60. 8vo.

—— See Darnell, E. Sufferings, etc., of Ky. Volunteers.

—— Drake, D. Pioneer Life in.

—— Filson, J. Discovery, etc., of.

—— —— Histoire de Kentucke.

—— Geolog. Survey. Reports made during 1854, '55, '58, '59, by D. D. Owen. Frankfort, 1856, 1861. 8vo.

—— Hawes, E. W. State Gazetteer Directory. 1859–60.

—— Hist. Anecdotes relating to the Early Settlement of. Western Review. Vol. 3.

—— Institution for Feeble-Minded Children. Report of Commissioners for 1864–5. Frankfort, 1866. 8vo.

—— Insurance Bureau. Ann. Report for 1870. Frankfort, 1870. 8vo.

—— Laws. Laws of the State. 1836–65, incomplete. Lexington. 12 Vols. 8vo.

—— —— Digest of Gen. Laws enacted between Dec. 4, 1859, to June 4, 1865. Cinn., 1866. 8vo.

—— —— respecting Property of Married Women. See Buford, H. M.

—— Local Hist. See Lexington, Louisville, Mammoth Cave.

—— (Eastern) Lunatic Asylum. Reports for 1856–7, 1858–9. Frankfort, 1858–9. 8vo.

—— —— (Western). Ann. Reports for 1863, 64, 65, 66. Frankfort, 1864–67. 8vo.

—— See Marshall, H. History of.

—— Michaux, F. A. Travels in 1802.

—— Mineral Waters of. See Frazee, L. J.

—— See Morehead, J. T. Address on 1st Settlement of 1840.

—— Origine, etc, de la Mission du Kentucky.

—— Rafinesque, C. S. Annals of. 1824.

—— First Registration Report, for 1852. Frankfort, 1853. 8vo.

—— See Roe, Ad. Aunt Leanna; or Early Scenes in Ky.

—— Serra, J. C. de. Formation and Nature of the Soil.

—— Shaffner, T. F. State Register, 1847.

—— Short, Dr. C. W. Description of Indian Fort, near Lexington.

—— Spalding, Rev. M. J. Early Catholic Missions of.

KENTUCKY State Treasurer. Ann. Report for 1868. 8vo.
—— University, Lexington. Announcement for 1865–6.
—— —— Catalogues for 1866, 67, 68, 69, 70, 72.
—— —— Trien. Catalogue of Transylvania Uuiversity. 1822.
—— —— See Winchell, A. Address. 1866.
KENYON College, Gambier, Ohio. Catalogues of the Theological Seminary, for 1836, 1842–3, 1851–2. Gambier. 8vo.
—— —— See CHASE, Bishop. Plea for the West. 1826.
KENYON, Rev. H. B. See BACKUS, Rev. J. S. On Secret Societies.
KEOGH, Rev. Jas. Catholic Principles of Civil Govt. Cincin., 1862. 8vo. Rebell'n Pamph. Vol. 3.
KEOKUK, Iowa. See CLEMENS, O. Sketch of, 1856.
—— and Dubuque R. R. See Congress'l Speeches.
—— See N. Western Review and Reporter.
—— Its Commerce, etc. Keokuk, 1856. 8vo.
KEPLER, John. See BERTRAND, M. Life and Works of.
—— BREWSTER, D. Martyrs of Science.
KER, H. Bellenden. Report to the House of Commons, 1837, on the Law of Partnership. Lond., 1837. 8vo. Law Pamph. Vol. 21.
—— The Question of Registry or no Registry, considered. In a Letter to Hon. Rob't Peel. Lond., 1830. 8vo. Law Pamph. Vol. 19.
KER, John. Memoirs of, containing his Secret Transactions and Negotiations in Scotland, England, and the Courts of Vienna and Hanover. Lond., 1726. 3 vols. 8vo.
KERATRY, M. Du Beau dans les Arts d'Imitation avec un examen raisonne des productions des diverses ecoles de peinture et de Sculpture. Paris, 1822. 2 Vols. 12mo.
KERCHEVAL, Sam'l. Hist. of the Valley of Virginia. Winchester, 1833. 12mo. Do. 2d Ed. Revised and extended. Woodstock, 1850. 8vo.
KERN, G. M. Practical Landscape Gardening with reference to Rural Residences. 3d Ed. Cincin., 1855. 12mo.
KERR, Henry. Travels through the Western Interior of the U. S. from 1808 to 1816; with a particular Description of Mexico. Elizabethtown, N. J. 1816. 8vo.
KERR, Rev. John. The Metric System; its Prospects in this Country. Lond., 1863. 8vo. Eng. Misc. Pamph. Vol. 16.
KERR, M. C. Speech in Cong., Feb. 18, 1871, on the McGarrahan Claim. 8vo. Congr. and Polit. Pamph. Vol. 132.
KERR, Peter. See PASCHAL, G. W. Argument in his Case.
KERRISON, Rob't M. Inquiry into the State of the Medical Profession in England, etc. Lond., 1814. 8vo. Med. Pamph. Vol. 23.
—— Letter to Sir Rob't Peel, on the Supply of Water to the Metropolis. Lond., 1828. 8vo. Eng. Misc. Pamph. Vol. 4.
—— Observations on the Bill now before Parliament, for "Better Regulating the Medical Profession." Lond., 1815. 8vo. Pamphleteer Vol. 6.
KERVYN, H. Verslag Voorge dragen aen het raedgevend Komite. Ghent, 1850. 8vo.

KETCHUM, Hiram. Gen. McClellan's Peninsular Campaign. N. Y. 1864. 8vo. Rebell'n Pamph. Vol. 19.

—— Oration at New Haven, July 4, 1851. N. Haven, 1851. 8vo. Addresses, Vol. 27.

KETCHUM, Wm. Hist. of the City of Buffalo and the Seneca Indians. Buffalo, 1864–5. 2 Vols. 8vo.

KETTELL, Thos. P. Constitutional Reform; a series of articles contributed to the Democratic Review. N. Y., 1846. 8vo.

—— Southern Wealth and Northern Profits. N. Y., 1861. 8vo. Rebell'n Pamph. Vol. 33.

KEW, Eng. See HOOKER, W. J. Kew Gardens.

KEWAUNEE (Wis.) Enterprise. Newspaper. Kewaunee, 1859–1863.

KEY of the Historian's Common-Place Book and Companion to the Study of History. Lond., 1844. 8vo. Hist. Pamph. Vol. 20.

—— to the Orders in Council. London, 1812. 8vo. Miscell. Tracts. Vol. 4.

KEY, Francis S. Poems; with an Introductory Letter by Chief Justice TANEY. N. Y., 1857. 12mo.

KEY, Philip Barton. See SICKLES, Dan'l E. Trial. 1859.

KEY, T. Hewitt. A Bonus or not a Bonus in London Life Association? Lond., 1856. 8vo. Eng. Miscell. Pamph. Vol. 8.

KEY West and Tortugas (Fortification of). See Congr. Speeches.

KEYES, Emerson W. Address before the Cortland Co., N. Y., Teachers' Institute, Oct. 25, 1858. Homer, 1859, 8vo. Educa. Pamph. Vol. 5.

—— The Educational System of the State of N. Y. Address at Lockport, Aug. 5, 1858. Albany, 1858. 8vo. N. Y. Miscell. Pamph. Vol. 5.

KEYSER, Rudolph. The Religion of the Northmen; translated by Barclay Pennock. N. Y., 1854. 12mo.

KIDD, Dr. John. On the Adaptation of External Nature to the Physical Condition of Man. Lond., 1836. 8vo.

KIDD, Capt. Wm. See CAMPBELL, W. W. Hist. Sketch of.

—— Tracts relating to his History. Waldie's Circulating Libr., Vol. 1.

—— See FELT, J. B. Lecture on and Papers relating to.

KIDDER, D. P., and FLETCHER, J. C. Brazil and the Brazilians; portrayed in Hist. and Descript. Sketches. Phila., 1857. 8vo.

KIDDER, Francis. Hist. of Boston Massacre, March 5, 1770. Albany, 1870. 8vo.

—— Military Operations in East Maine and Nova Scotia in the Revolution. Albany, 1868, 4to.

KIDDER, Fred. The Abenaki Indians; their Treaties of 1713 and 1717. Portland, 1859. 8vo. Indian Pamph., Vol. 5.

—— Expedition of Capt. John Lovewell and his Encounters with the Indians. Boston, 1865. 8vo.

—— Hist. Sketch of the Indians who inhabited the Eastern part of N. Carolina, from 1524 to the present time. Hist. Mag., Vol. 1.

—— Hist. of 1st N. H. Reg't in Revolu. War. Albany, 1868. 8vo.

—— and others. Hist. of New Ipswich, N. H. With Genealogies. Boston, 1852. 8vo.

KIDDLE, Henry. Manual of Astronomy and the Use of the Globes. N. Y., 1857. 12mo.

KILBOURN, Byron. See Milwaukee & Miss. R. R. Co.

—— Review of the Report of the Court convened for the Trial of Levi Hubbell. Milwaukee, 1858. 8vo.

KILBOURN City, Wis., Mirror, Newspaper. 1860–61, 1868–70. Folio.

KILBOURNE, P. K. Litchfield, Conn., Biograph. History. N. Y., 1851. 8vo.

—— Sketches and Chronicles of Town of Litchfield, Conn. Hartford, 1859. 8vo.

—— Biograph. Hist. of the Co. of Litchfield, Conn. N. Y., 1851. 8vo.

—— Sketches and Chronicles of Town of Litchfield, Conn. Hartford, 1859. 8vo.

—— Hist. and Antiquities of the Name and Family of Kilbourn. New Haven, 1856. 8vo.

KILGORE, Damon Y. Address in favor of Female Suffrage. From the Legal Gazette. 1872. Congr. and Polit. Pamph. Vol. 128.

—— Closing Argument in Case of the Commonwealth of Penn. vs. Rev. S. M. Landis. Phila., 1870. 8vo. Law Pamph. Vol. 13.

—— Legislative Wrongs to Labor and how to Right Them. Address at Phila., 1873. Phila., 1873. 8vo. Congr. and Polit. Pamph. Vol. 68.

—— Oration at Phila., July 4, 1869, on the Dangers which Threaten the Republic. Phila., 1869. 8vo. Addresses. Vol. 23.

—— The Questions of To-day. Oration at Wilbraham, Mass., June 29, 1870. N. Y., 1870. 8vo. Addresses. Vol. 28.

KILKENNY and S. East of Ireland Archaeolog. Soc'y. Proceedings and Papers. Vol. 2, New Series, 1858–9, complete; Vols. 3, 4, New Series, 1860–4, incomplete; Vol. 5, New Series, 1864–7, complete; Vol. 6, New Series, 1867–8, incomplete. Dublin, 1858–67. 8vo.

—— —— See IRELAND. Histor. and Archaeolog. Assoc. of.

"KILLING no Murder." See ALLEN, W.

KIMBALL & JAMES. Business Directory for the Mississippi Valley, for 1844. Cincin., 1844. 8vo.

KIMBALL, Rev. David T. Centen. Discourse before 1st Ch. in Ipswich, Mass., August 10, 1834. Boston, 1834. 8vo. Mass. Hist. Discourses. Vol. 3.

—— Dedica. Sermon at Ipswich, Feb. 4, 1847. Boston, 1847. 8vo. Sermons. Vol. 39.

—— 50th Annivers. Disc. at Ipswich, Mass., Oct. 8, 1856. Boston, 1857. 8vo. Mass. Hist. Discourses. Vol. 3. Another Copy. Vol. 15.

—— Last Sermon in the Old Meeting-House, Ipswich, Mass., Feb. 22, 1846. Boston, 1846. 8vo. Mass. Hist. Discourses. Vol. 3.

—— Sketch of the Eccles. History of Ipswich, Mass. Substance of a Discourse, etc. Haverhill, 1823. 8vo. Mass. Hist. Discourses. Vol. 3.

KIMBALL, Israel. Argument in favor of the Constitutionality of the Cotton Tax. Washington, 1873. 8vo. Congr. and Political Pamph. Vol. 68.

KIMBALL, Jas. Notes of his Journey to the West in 1817. Essex Institute Collections. Vol. 8.

KIMBALL, M. G. Discourse at Free Masons' Hall, St. Louis, Mar. 21, 1869. St. Louis, 1869. 12mo. Sermons. Vol. 26.

KIMBALL Union Academy, Plainfield, N. H. Catalogue for 1846–7. Hanover, 1847. 8vo.

KIMBER, Thos. New Sartor Resartus: being a Critical Analysis of a Pamphlet entitled "A Review of Mr. Seward's Diplomacy." Rebell'n Pamph. Vol. 82.

KINDER, Thos. The Case of, as regards the Parras Estates, (Mexico.) Lond., 1837. 8vo. Strangford Pamph. Vol. 17.

KINDERHOOK (N. Y.) Academy. Circular, 1849. Albany. 8vo.

KING, Rev. Dr. Hist. Sketch of the Evangelical Alliance. Lond. n. d. Eng. Rel. Pamph. Vol. 62.

KING or Kings Genealogy. See SANFORD, E.

KING, Chas. Address before the Queens Co. Agr. Soc., at Flushing, L. I., Sept. 29, 1852. Jamaica, 1852. 8vo. Agr. Pamph. Vol. 2.

—— Disc. before N. J. Hist. Soc., May 7, 1845. Proceedings. Vol. 1.

—— Hist. of the N. Y. Chamber of Commerce. Discourse, Nov. 21, 1848, before N. Y. Hist. Soc. Collections. 2d Ser. Vol. 2.

—— Progress of the City of N. Y. during the last Fifty Years; Lecture at N. Y., Dec. 29, 1851. N. Y., 1852. 8vo. N. Y. Hist. Discourses, Vol. 2. See also Addresses, Vol. 8.

—— The Battle of Monmouth Court House. N. J. Hist. Soc. Proceedings. Vol. 4.

KING, Clarence. Geolog. Contributions. See U. S. Explora. of 40th Parallel.

KING, Dan'l P. See UPHAM, C. W. Memoir ot.

KING, John. Letter to Thos. Paine, Apr. 9, 1793. Lond. 8vo. Eng. Polit. Pamph. Vol. 24.

KING, J. A. Speech in Cong., June 4, 1850, on Admission of California. Congr. and Polit. Pamph. Vol. 86.

KING, J. W. Biography of Alessandro GAVAZZI. Lond., 1857. 8vo. Biograph. Pamph. Vol. 3.

—— The Silent Dead, or Roll of Honor of Muskingum, Ohio. Zanesville, 1866. 8vo. Rebell'n Pamph. Vol. 108.

KING PHILIP's Indian War. See CHURCH, Benj.

—— —— CHURCH, T.

—— —— DRAKE, L. G.

—— —— EASTON, John.

—— —— MATHER, Cotton and Increase.

—— —— See "Sudbury Fight," 1676.

KING, Thos. B. California; the Wonder of the Age, &c. N. Y., 1850. 8vo. Cal. Misc. Pamph. Vol. 1.

—— Lettre a son Excell M Le Ministre du Commerce. Paris, 1861. 8vo. Rebell'n Pamph. Vol. 38.

KING, Thos. B. Speech in Cong., Feb. 9, 1846, on the Oregon Question. Congr. & Polit. Pamph. Vol. 86.

—— —— July 19, 1848, on Naval affairs. Congr. and Polit. Pamph. Vol. 90.

KING, Rev. Thos. Starr. See BARTOL, C. A. Disc. in Memory of. 1864.

—— BRADLEE, C. D. Life and Character of.

—— Lecture on Hildebrand before the Y. M. C. Union, Boston. Boston, 1857. 8vo. Addresses. Vol. 36.

—— Sermon at Boston, Oct. 31, 1852, on the Death of Dan'l Webster. Boston, 1852. 8vo. 2d Ed. Sermons. Vol. 32.

KING, Dr. W. See Exeter College.

—— His Apology; or Vindication of himself, etc. Oxford, 1755. 4to. Eng. Polit. Pamph. Vol. 4.

KING, Wm. Rufus. See Democratic Text Book.

—— Addresses in Cong. on his Death. 1853.

KINGDOM'S Intelligence and other English Papers, 1652–1654.

KINGMAN, Bradford. History of No. Bridgewater, Mass. With Genealogies. Boston, 1866. 8vo.

KING'S Chapel Burial Ground. See BRIDGMAN, T.

—— College Lond. See SEDDON, Felix. Address. 1835.

—— —— TODD, R. B. Resources of, for Medical Educa. 1852.

—— Co., N. Y. Ann. Report of Superintendents of the Poor. 1854, Williamsburgh, 1854. 8vo.

—— —— Assessment Rolls of the Five Dutch Towns of. 1675. Doc. Hist. of N. Y. Vol. 4.

—— —— Papers relating to. 1698–1715. Doc. Hist. of N. Y. Vol. 3.

—— —— See STRONG, Rev. T. M. Hist, of Flatbush.

—— Evidence (The) Vindicated, as to the Imputation of Perjury. Lond., 1680. Fol. Eng. Polit. Pamph. Vol. 6.

KINGSLAND, Dalston and Shacklewell Ragged School. 16th Ann. Report. Lond., 1854. 8vo. Educa. Pamph. Vol. 29.

KINGSLEY, Jas. L. Eulogy on Prof. Alex. M. Fisher of Yale Coll. N. Haven, 1822. 8vo. Addresses. Vol. 37.

—— Life of Ezra Stiles, Prest. of Yale Coll. Spark's Amer. Biog. 2d Ser. Vol. 6.

KINGSLEY, Vine, W. French Intervention in America. N. Y., 1863. 8vo. Rebellion Pamph. Vol. 1.

KING'S Mountain. Celebration of the Battle of, with Address of Hon. J. S. Preston, Oct., 1855. Yorkville, S. C., 1855. 8vo.

—— Mountain. Battle of. See SHELBY, Isaac.
Rev. War Pamph. Vol. 5.

KINGSTON, Mass. Description of. Mass. Hist. Soc. Coll. Vol. 3. 2d Series.

KINGSTON Royal Gazette. Newspaper. Jan. to Dec., 1782. 4to.

KINGSTON, S. C. See WALLACE, J. A. Hist. of the Williamsburg Ch. 1856.

KINLOCK, Chas. W. Mutinies in the Bengal Army. Lond., 1858. 8vo. Eng. Polit. Pamph. Vol. 55.

KINNE, Asa. Laws of States and Territories of the U. S. on Imprisonment for Debt. N. Y., 1842. Congr. and Polit. Pamph. Vol. 96.

KINNICUTT, Thos. Notice of John Davis, read before the Amer. Antiq. Soc., Apr. 26, 1854. Boston. 8vo. Addresses. Vol. 22.

KINZIE, Mrs. John H. Wau-bun, the Early Day in the N. West, with illustrations. N. Y., 1856. 8vo.

KIP Family Genealogy. See KIP, W. I.

KIP, Rev. F. M. Discourse at Celebra. of 150th Annivers. of the 1st R. D. Church, Fishkill, with Hist. Appendix. N. Y., 1866. 8vo. N. York Hist. Discourses Vol. 1.

KIP, Leonard. California Sketches, with Recollections of the Gold Mines. Albany, 1850. 12mo. Pamphlets, Vol. 2.

KIP, Bishop W. I. A Few Days at Nashotah. Albany, 1849. 8vo. Wis. College Pamphs.

—— Early Jesuit Missions in N. America: compiled and translated from Letters of the French Jesuits, with notes. N. Y., 1846. 12mo.

—— Historical Notes on the Family of Kip of Kipsburg and Kip's Bay. N. York. Albany, pr. printed, 1871. 8vo. Genealog. Pamph. Vol. 12.

KIPPIS, Andrew, D. D. Biographia Brittanica; or Lives of the most Eminent Persons in G. B. and Ireland. 2d Ed. Lond., 1789–93. 5 Vols. folio.

—— Vindica. of the Protestant Dissenting Ministers with regard to their late application to Parl't. 2d Ed. Lond., 1773. Polit. Tracts. Vol. 1.

KIRBY, Rev. Wm. On the Power and Wisdom of God in the Creation of Animals. Lond., 1835. 2 Vols. 8vo.

KIRK, Jas. B., M. D. Practical Observations on Cholera Asphyxia. N. Y., 1832. 8vo. Med. Pamph. Vol. 4.

KIRK, Rev. John. Catholic Principle in reference to God and the King. 1680. London, 1818. 8vo. Pamphleteer Vol. 13.

KIRKE, Edmund. Down in Tennessee and Back by way of Richmond. N. Y., 1864. 12mo.

—— My Southern Friends. New York, 1863. 12mo.

KIRKE, Henry. The First Eng. Conquest of Canada, Nova Scotia New Foundland. London, 1871. 8vo.

KIRKLAND, Mrs. C. M. A New Home—Who'll follow? or Glimpses of Western Life. 5th Ed. New York, 1855. 12mo.

—— Holidays Abroad; or Europe from the West. N. Y., 1854. 2 Vols. 12mo.

—— Memoirs of Washington. N. Y., 1859. 12mo.

KIRKLAND, Chas. P. Two Letters to P. Cooper on the Treatment of Rebels, and the Restoration of the Rebel States. N. Y., 1865. 8vo. Rebellion Pamph. Vol. 18.

—— Letter to Hon. B. R. Curtis on Emancipation. N. Y., 1863. 8vo. Rebellion Pamph. Vol. 67.

KIRKLAND, John T., D. D. Disc. at Bosion, Apr. 18, 1823, on the Death of Hon. Geo. Cabot. Boston, 1823. 8vo. Sermons, Vol. 35.

—— Disc. in Commemora. of John Adams and Thos. Jefferson, before Amer. Acad. of Arts and Scienees, Oct. 30, 1826. Memoirs of Academy. Vol. 1. N. S.

KIRKLAND, John T., D. D. See PALFREY, John G. Discourse on, 1840.
—— PARKMAN, F. Obit. Sermon, 1840.
—— Sermon at Boston, June 22, 1798, on the Death of Rev. Jeremy Belknap. Boston. 8vo. (Imperfect.) Sermons. Vol. 43.
—— See YOUNG, Rev. Alex. Obit. Discourse.
KIRKLAND, Sam'l. See LOTHROP, S. K. Life of.
KIRKSTALL Abbey, Near Leeds, Eng. Hist. of. Leeds, 1831. 8vo. Hist. Pamph. Vol. 8.
KISSINGEN AND BROCKET. Brief Acc. of Mineral Waters of Frankfort, Ky. 1842. 12mo. Med. Pamph. Vol. 9.
KITCHI—GAMI: Wanderings around Superior. See KOHL, J. C.
KITCHIN, Thos. General Atlas. Lond., 1783. Folio.
KITTO, John. See RYLAND, J. E. Memories of.
—— THAYER, W. M. Life of.
—— The Lost Senses: Deafness and Blindness. N. Y., 1852. 12mo.
KITTREDGE, Jonathan. Address upon the Effects of Ardent Spirits at Lyme, N. H., 1827. Canandaigua, 1828. 8vo. Temp. Pamph. Vol. 6.
KLEIN, Pierre. Notice sur les Fourneaux Economiques pour la Vente de portions d'aliments a cinq centimes. Paris, 1856. 8vo.
KLIPPART. J. H. Address before Ohio Agr. Convention, Jan. 3, 1866. Columbus, 1866. 8vo. Agr. Pamph. Vol. 3.
KLUBER, Johann L. Pragmatische Geschichte der Nationaten und Politischen Wiedrgeburt Griechenlands. Frankfort-on-Main. 1835. 8vo.
KNAPP, Rev. Fred N. Dis. at the Funeral of John Pierce, D. D., at Brookline, Mass., Aug. 27, 1849. Boston, 1849. 8vo. Sermons. Vol. 46.
KNAPP, H. S. History of Ashland Co., Ohio. Phila., 1843. 8vo.
KNAPP, Judge J. G. Ancient Lakes of Wisconsin. Trans. Wis. Acad. of Sciences, 1870–2.
—— Coniferal of the Rocky Mountains. Trans. Wis. Acad. of Sciences. 1870–2.
KNAPP, M. L., M. D. Address to the Graduating Class of the Indiana Med. Coll., Feb. 18, 1847. Chicago, 1847. 8vo.
—— Address before Rock Island Med. School, Nov. 7, 1848. Chicago, 1849. 8vo. Med. Pamph. Vol. 31.
—— Cause, Nature, Cure and Prevention of Epedemic Cholera. N. Y., 1855. 8vo. Med. Pamph. Vol. 1.
—— Essay on Cholera Infantum. Cincin., 1855. 8vo. Med. Pamph. Vol. 3.
KNAPP, Sam'l L. Female Biography. N. Y., 1834. 8vo.
KNEELAND, Abner. Review of his Trial, Conviction and Imprisonment for Blasphemy. Boston, 1838. 12mo. Religious Pamph. Vol. 14.
KNICKERBOCKER MAGAZINE. Vol. 1. Vol. 3, No. 2. Vol. 5, 4 Nos. Vol. 6, 3 Nos. Vols. 7–18, 19 except No. 3. Vols. 20–25, 29. 30, 31 except No. 2. 32, 33, 34, 36–48, 51, 52, 53, 57 except No. 2, 61 except Nos. 2 & 6. Vol. 62, except 3 Nos. N. York. 1833–63. 8vo.

KNIGHT, Dr. and SLOVER, John. Narr. of their Perils and Sufferings among the Indians during the Revolu. War. Cincin. 1867. 12mo.

KNIGHT, Chas. Cyclopedia of the Industry of all Nations. Lond., 1851. 8vo.

—— Gallery of Portraits: with Memoirs. Vols. 1-6 in 3 Vols. Lond. 1833-36. 8vo.

—— Half-Hours with the Best Authors, with Biograph. and Critical Notices. N. Y., 1856. 4 Vols. 12mo.

—— Hist. of England with Illustrations on Steel and Wood. Lond., 1862. 8 vols. 8vo.

KNIGHT, Cornelia. Autobiography of Miss C. Knight, late Companion to the Princess Charlotte of Wales. 2d ed. Lond., 1851. 2 Vols. 8vo.

KNIGHT, F. W. The Parochial System vs. Centralization. Lond., 1854. 8vo. Strangford Pamph. Vol. 66.

KNIGHT, Helen C. Lady Huntington and her Friends; or the Revival of the Work of God in the Days of Wesley, etc. N. Y., n. d. 12mo.

KNIGHT, Dr. J. Eulogium on Nathan Smith, M. D., late Professor in Yale Coll. N. Haven, 1828. 8vo. Yale Coll. Pamph.

KNIGHT, Rev. J. and SPAULDING, Rev. L. English and Tamil Dictionary; or manual Lexicon for Schools. Madras, 1844. 8vo.

KNIGHT, Dr. Thos. Experiments and Observations made upon the Human Calculus. Lond., 1749. 12mo. Med. Pamph. Vol. 20.

KNIGHTLEY, Thos. The Crusaders; or Scenes, Events and Characters from the Crusades. Waldie's Circulating Lib. Vols. 7, 8.

KNIGHTON, Lady. Memoirs of Sir Wm. Knighton, Bart., Keeper of the Privy Purse during the Reign of King George 4. Phil'a, 1838. 8vo. Another ed., Lond., 1838. 4to.

KNIGHTON, Sir Wm. See Knighton, Lady, Memoirs of.

KNIGHTHOOD. See BURKE, Sir B. Book of Orders of.

—— BURKE, J. & J. B. Dict. of Extinct Baronetcies.

—— See Heraldry.

KNIGHTS of Golden Circle. See Authentic Exposition, etc.

—— of Malta. See VERTOT, L'abbe. History of.

—— Templar. Proceedings of Grand Encampment of Knights Templar for the U. S., at Baltimore, 1871. Davenport, 1871. 8vo.

KNOEPFEL'S Schoharie Cave, N. Y. Acc. of, with Hist. of its Discovery, etc. N. Y., 1853. 8vo. N. Y. Hist. Discourses, etc., Vol. 2.

KNOLE, Kent Co., Eng. See BRIDGMAN, J. Hist. and Topograph. Sketch, 1817.

KNOWLTON, Col. Thos. See WOODWARD, Ashbel. Sketch of.

KNOW Nothing Party. See American Party.

KNOX College, Galesburg, Ill. See BAILEY, J. W.

—— —— See Illinois Gen. Assoc. Report on the Rights of Congregationalists, etc.

KNOX Co., Ohio. See NORTON, A. B. Hist. of, 1779—1862.

KNOX, Gen. Henry. Plan for the Gen. Arrangement of the Militia of the U. S. Mass. Hist. Soc. Proceed., 1862–63.

KNOX, Capt. John. Hist. Journal of Campaigns in North America, 1757–60. Lond., 1769. 2 Vols. 4to.

KNOX, John P. Hist. Account of St. Thomas, W. I., and Notices of St. Croix and St. John. N. Y., 1852. 8vo.

KNOX, Thos., and LANE, John. Trial and Conviction of, for endeavoring to bring discredit upon the evidence of Dr. Oates, etc. Lond., 1680. Folio. Eng. Polit. Pamph., Vol. 1.

KNOX, Dr. Vicesimus. Remarks on a Bill now before Parliament, tending to degrade Public Schools. Lond., 1821. 8vo. 2d Ed. Pamphleteer, Vol. 19.

KNOXVILLE, Tenn., Industrial Assoc. See TEMPLE, O. P. Address. 1869.

KOCH, Albert. Description of the Missourium, or Missouri Leviathan; with a Catalogue of the Fossil Collection. Lond. 8vo. n. d. Scientic Pamph., Vol. 34.

KOHL, J. G. Hist. of Discovery of Maine. See Maine Hist. Soc.

—— Kitchi-Gami; Wanderings around Lake Superior. Lond., 1860. 8vo.

—— See Maine Documentary History.

KOHLRAUSCH, Frederick. History of Germany, from the Earliest Period to the Present Time. N. Y., 1856. 8vo.

KOKOREFF, B. A. The Trade of Russia considered from a European point of view. Lond., 1859. 12mo. Eng. Misc. Pamph. Vol. 33.

KOORDISTAN. See SMITH, Azariah. Contribution to the Geography of.

KOSS, Dr. F. A. Milwaukee. Milwaukee, 1872. 8vo.

KOSSUTH, Louis. See CASS, Lewis. Speech on. 1851.

—— SEWARD, W. H. Speech on. 1851.

—— Proceedings at Washington, in honor of Kossuth. Jan. 7, 1852. Congr. and Polit. Pamph. Vol. 87.

KOSTER, Henry. On the Amelioration of Slavery. Lond., 1816. 8vo. Pamphleteer. Vol. 8.

KOSZTA, Case. See Congress'l Speeches.

—— See U. S. Sec. of State. Correspondence relative to.

KRANTZOVIUS, Irenaeus. Some Thoughts concerning Happiness. Lond., 1738. 8vo. Eng. Misc. Pamph. Vol. 23.

KREGIER, Capt. Martin. Journal of the Second Esopus War. Doc. Hist. of N. Y. Vol 4.

KROLIKOWSKI, Lewis. Memoir Historical and Political on the State of the Free City of Cracow. In French. Paris. 1840. 8vo. Strangford Pamph. Vol. 24.

KU KLUX KLAN. See Congressional Speeches.

—— CORBIN, D. T. Argument in the Trial of. 1871.

—— U. S. Senate. Reports of Select Comm. 1871.

KURIOSITI KABINET. Periodical devoted to Stamp Collecting, etc. written in Phonetic Language. Vol. 1. Nos. 1--12. N. Y., 1870--1. 8vo.

L.

LA BARRE, M. de. Papers relating to his Expedition to Hungry Bay, Jefferson Co., N. Y., 1684. Doc. Hist. of N. Y. Vol. 1.
LABAREE, Rev. Benj. Sermon on the Death of Gen. Harrison, at Middlebury, Vt. Middlebury, 1841. 8vo. Sermons. Vol. 54.
LABARRE, John E. Memoirs of Sherman, Ohio. Fire Lands Pioneer. Vol. 5.
LABAT, J. B. Nouveau Voyage aux Isles de l'Amerique. Paris, 1722. 6 Vols. 12mo.
LABAUME, Eugene. Narr. of the Campaign in Russia. 3d Ed. Lond., 1815. 8vo.
LABELYE, Chas. Short Acc. of Methods used in Laying the Foundation of Westminster Bridge. Lond., 1739. 8vo. Eng. Misc. Pamph. Vol. 13.
LABORDE, Alex. View of Spain. Lond., 1809. Vols. 2 and 4.
LABOULAYE, Prof. E. On the Presidential Election, 1864. Rebell'n Pamph. Vol. 52.
—— Lès Etats Unis et La France. Paris, 1862. 8vo. Rebell'n Pamph. Vol. 20.
—— Separation: War Without End. 1863. Rebellion Pamph. Vols. 45, 90.
—— Upon Whom Rests the Guilt of the War. 1863. Rebellion Pamph. Vol. 85.
—— Why the North Cannot Accept of Separation. N. Y., 1863. 8vo. Rebell'n Pamph. Vols. 1, 10, 76.
LABRADOR. See BADDELEY, Lieut. Geology. of the Coast of.
—— ROBERTSON, Sam'l. Notes on the Coast of.
L'ACADEMIE Imperiale des Science. Recueil des Actes. 1856. Bordeaux, 1857. 8vo.
LACEY, Gen. E. See MOORE, Dr. M. A. Life of, etc.
LACEY, Gen. John. See DAVIS, W. H. H.
LACKAWANA VALLEY, Penn. See HOLLISTER, H. Contribution to Hist. of.
LACON. See COLTON, C. C.
LA CROSSE Valley, Wis., Baptist Assoc. Minutes of Meetings held in 1859, 61, 62. Sparta, etc. 1859—62. 8vo.
—— & Milwaukee R. R. Co. Compilation of Acts of Wis. Legislature affecting the Co., by MOSES M. STRONG. Milwaukee, 1856. 8vo. With Reports of the Co.
—— —— 1st, 2d, 3d and 4th Ann. Reports of the Directors, 1852, 53, 55, 56. Milwaukee, 1853–6. 8vo.
—— —— 1st, 2d and 3d Ann. Reports of the Receiver. 1860, 61, 62. Milwaukee, 1861–3. 8vo.
—— See CARR, Rev. Spencer. Brief Notice of.
—— Newspapers. 1867–70. Folio.
—— Democrat and The Republican. Newspapers. La Crosse. 1860–66. Folio.
—— Independent Republican. Newspaper. May, 1855 to Dec., 1859. 2 Vols. Folio.

LA CROSSE. See McMILLAN, M. Early Settlement of.
—— National Democrat. Newspaper. April 1853 to May 1854 Folio. Same, Sept. 1856 to Nov. 1859. Folio.
LACUSTRINE Deposits. See LAPHAM, I. A.
LADD, Wm. Annals of Bakerstown, Poland and Minot, Maine. Maine Hist. Soc. Coll. Vol. 2.
—— See BECKWITH, G. C. Obit. Notice of.
LADIES, (The), Magazine. Savannah, Geo., 1819. 8vo.
—— Society for the Promotion of Educa. at the West. Hist. and Formation of. Boston, 1846. 8vo. Boston Miscell. Pamph. Vol. 5. 3d Ann. Rep't, 1849. Same. Vol. 5.
—— The, Wreath. Periodical. June 1849 to Nov. 1850.
LADY's Magazine. Vols. 1, 2, 3, 4, 5, 7. Lond., 1770–1776. 8vo. Same, 1766. 1 Vol. Also July and August 1783.
LA FAYETTE College,— Easton, Pa. See ROBINSON, T. H. Address. 1867.
—— —— Announcement of Pardee Scientific Course for 1866. 8vo.
—— —— Catalogue for 1870–71. 8vo.
LA FAYETTE. Gen. and Louis Philippe. See SARRANS, B.
—— ADAMS, J. Q. Oration. 1835.
—— Amer. Milit. Biogr.
—— CLOQUET, J. Recollec. of Private Life.
—— CUTTER, W. Life of.
—— Description of Fete at N. Y., 1824.
—— HEADLEY, P. C. Life of.
—— HILLHOUSE, J. A. Oration on. 1834.
—— HOLSTEIN, H. L. V. D. Memoirs of.
—— Memoirs, Correspondence and Manuscripts of. Lond., 1837. 3 Vols. 8vo.
—— Same in French. Paris, 1837. 3 Vols. 8vo.
—— Memoirs of. Embracing Details of his Public and Private Life. Hartford, 1825. 12mo.
—— Of the Private Life of. From Fraser's Mag. Apr., 1836. Biograph. Pamph. Vol. 12.
—— See SUMNER, Gen. W. H. Reminiscences of.
—— WALN, R. Life of.
LAFAYETTE, Madame. Memoires de Holland: Histoire particulière en forme de Roman. Paris, 1856. 18mo.
LA FAYETTE, Ind. See WETHERILL, C. M., on Artesian Well at.
LA FAYETTE, Wis., Baptist Assoc. Minutes of 6th, 7th, 8th, 9th Meetings, held in 1852, 53, 54, 55. Lancaster. 8vo.
LAFITAU, J. F. Moeurs des Sauvages Ameriquains comparees aux Moeurs des premier temps. Paris, 1724. 4to.
LA GUERRE Civile aux Etats-Unis Impuissance du Nord, l'Independence du Sud Inevitable. Paris, 1862. 8vo. Rebell'n Pamph. Vol. 46.
—— En Amerique et L'Esclavage. Paris, 1861. 8vo. Rebell'n Pamph. Vol. 33.
LAHRBUSH, Capt. F. H. See DE PEYSTER, Gen. J. W.
LA HARPE, Benard de. JournalHistorique de l'Establissement des Francaise a La Louisiane. Paris, 1831. 8vo.
—— Same, translated. See French's Hist. Coll. of La. Vol. 3.

LA HONTAN, Baron. New Voyages to N. America, trans. from the French. Lond., 1703. 2 Vols. 8vo.
—— Voyages dans l'Amerique Septentrionale. Amsterdam, 1728. 2 Vols.
—— Same. Troisieme, 1731. 3 Vols. 18mo.
LAIRD, John. Dissertatio Medica Inauguralis de Stomacho, ejusque Morbis, etc. Edinburgh, 1783. 8vo. Miscell. Tracts. Vol. 4.
LAKE Champlain. See PALMER, P. S. Hist. of.
—— Papers relating to the French Seigniories on Lake Champlain. Doc. Hist. of N. Y. Vol. 1.
—— Commerce. See BARTON, J. L. Sketch of Commerce of Lakes and Erie Canal.
—— Erie, Battle of. See Battle of L. Erie Monument Assoc.
—— —— CALVERT, G. H. Anniversary Oration. 1853.
—— —— COOPER, J. Fenimore. Answer to Burges and others.
—— —— Inaugura. of Perry's Statue.
—— —— PARSONS, Usher. 45th Annivers. Address. 1858.
—— —— —— Sketches of Officers in the Battle.
—— Forest (Ill.) Academy. Catalogue for 1869–70. L. Forest, 1870. 8vo.
—— Harbors. Congress. Reports on Harbor Defences of the Great Lakes and Rivers, 1862. Rebell'n Pamph. Vol. 20.
—— —— See GRAHAM, J. D.
—— Levels. See DEARBORN, H. A. S. Variations of Level in the Great N. A. Lakes.
—— —— GRAHAM, J. D. Lunar Tidal Waves.
—— —— WHITING, Maj. H. Supposed Tides of N. Amer. Lakes, 1831.
—— —— WHITTLESEY, C. Surface of the No. Lakes.
—— Memphremagog. See DIX, J. R. Hand Book for.
—— Michigan. See CRAM, T. J. Report on Survey, 1841.
—— —— GRAHAM, J. D. Report on Harbors, etc., 1855–58.
—— —— HOY, P. R. Water Fauna of.
—— —— WHITTLESEY, C. Water Level at Green Bay.
—— Shore Baptist Assoc. Wis. Minutes of 1st and 4th Anniversaries. 1856, 59. Sheboygan and Milwaukee. 8vo.
—— Superior. See AGASSIZ, L. Phys. Character, Vegetation, etc. of.
—— —— Bayfield; H. W. Outline of Geology of.
—— —— Copper Mines. See FOSTER & WHITNEY Report.
—— —— —— FARMER S. Map of Copper Region.
—— —— —— SCHOOLCRAFT, H. R. Report on.
—— —— FOSTER & WHITNEY. Geology and Topog. of.
—— —— Government Map of Mineral Lands Ceded to the U. S. by Treaty of 1842. Broadside, n. d.
—— —— KOHL, J. G. Wanderings around L. Superior.
—— —— LANMAN, C. Canoe Voyage around.
—— —— Miner, Newspaper. Ontonagon and Superior City, 1857–8.
—— —— See MORSE, R. E. Chippewas of.
—— —— PITEZEL, J. H. Missionary Life at.
—— —— Reports on the Mineral Region, with a correct Map of the same, and a Chart of the Lake. Buffalo, 1846. 12mo.

LAKE Superior. See RITCHIE, J. S. Wis. and Lake Superior. 1857.
—— —— Ship Canal. Report from Comm. of U. S. Senate, Apr. 3, 1844, in relation to a Ship Canal at St. Mary's Falls. Washington, 1844. 8vo. Wis. Misc. Pamph. Vol. 5.
—— —— See WHITTLESEY, C., on Railway Commu. with.
—— Surveys. See MEADE, Capt. G. G. Reports. 1859–1861.
—— —— WILLIAMS, W. G. Report. 1842.
—— Winnipiseogee. See Excursion to.
LAKEY, Chas. D. Are the American Life Insurance Companies Solvent? Congr. and Polit. Pamph. Vol. 80.
LALANNE, Leon. Collection de Tables pour Abréger les calculs relatifs a la Reduction des Projets de Routes et de Chemins de toutes largeurs. Paris, 1843. 4to.
LALLEMANT, Pere Chas. Copie de Trois Lettres escrittes in 1625-26. Albany. Reprinted 1870. 8vo.
—— Lettre au Pere Hierosme l'Allemant son frere. 1626. Paris, 1627. 8vo. Albany, 1870 or 1871. Fac simile reprint.
—— Lettre au R. P. Supérieur du Collége des Jesuites a Paris, 22d November, 1629. Paris, 1632. 8vo. Albany, reprint 1870. 8vo.
LALLEMANT, R. P. Hierosme. Lettres Envoiees de la Nouvelle, France, 1659. Albany, 1854. 12mo. Lenox's Ed.
—— Relation de ce qui s'est passe de plus remarquable aux Missions des Peres de la Compagnie de Jesus en la Nouvelle France, es Annees, 1663–64. Paris, 1665. 12mo.
—— Relation de ce qui s'est passe de plus Remarquable es Missions de la Compagnie de Jesus en la Nouvelle France es Annees, 1645–46. Paris, 1647. 12mo.
—— Relation de ce qui s'est passe de plus Remarquable en la Mission des Peres de la Compagnie de Jesus, aux Hurons Pais de la Nouvelle, France, 1642–3. Paris, 1644. 12mo.
LAMARTINE, Alphonse. Life of Christopher Columbus. N. Y., 1860. 18mo.
—— Life of Mary Queen of Scots. N. Y., 1860. 18mo.
—— Life of Oliver Cromwell. N. Y., 1860. 18mo.
—— A Pilgrimage to the Holy Land in 1832–3. Waldie's Circulating Libr. Vol. 6.
LAMAS, Andres. Notice sur la Republique Orientale de L'Uruguay. Paris, 1851. 8vo. Strangford Pamph. Vol. 62.
LAMB, Chas. Works of. See TALFOURD, T. N.
LAMB, Rev. Dana. Complete List of Congrega. Ministers and Churches in Madison Co., Vt. Boston, 1839. 8vo. Vt. Hist. Discourses, etc. Vol. 1.
LAMB, Gen. John. See LEAKE, I. Q. Memoirs of.
LAMB, R. Memoirs of his own Life. Dublin, 1811. 8vo.
—— Original and Authentic Journal of Occurrences during the late Amer. War to 1783. Dublin, 1809. 8vo.
LAMBERT, John. Travels through Canada and the U. S. of N. America, in 1806, 1807 and 1808, with Maps and Engravings. 2d Ed. Lond., 1814. 2 Vols. 8vo.
LAMBERT, Wm. Abstracts of Calculations to ascertain the Longitude of the City of Washington, D. C. Amer. Philos. Soc. Trans. N. Ser. Vol. 1.

LAMBERT, Wm. Collection of Precedents, consisting of Proceedings and Decisions on Questions of Order and Appeals in the House of Repr. of the U. S. Washington, 1811. 8vo.

LAMBETH (Eng.) Asylum for Female Orphans. Account of. Lond., 1866. 12mo. Eng. Misc. Pamph. Vol. 11.

—— See TAUSWELL, John. Hist. and Antiq. of. 1858.

LAMBRECHTSEN, N. C. Short Description of the Discovery and subsequent History of New Netherlands, translated from the Dutch. 1818. N. Y. Hist. Soc. Coll. 2d Ser. Vol. 1.

LAMBTON, John G. Speech in Parl't, on the State of Representation, with a Bill for Parliam'ry Reform. Lond., 1822. 8vo. Pamphleteer. Vol. 21.

LAME, Rev. J. S. Maryland Slavery and Maryland Chivalry. Phila., 1858. 8vo. Rebell'n Pamph. Vol. 22.

LAMON, Ward H. Life of Abraham Lincoln, to his Inauguration. Boston, 1872. 8vo.

LAMSON, Rev. Alvan. Discourse at Dedham, Mass., Dec. 21, 1851, on John Robinson. Boston, 1852. 8vo. Sermons. Vol. 6.

—— Discourse at Dedham, Feb. 4, 1852, on Rev. John White. Boston, 1852. 8vo. Sermons. Vol. 6.

—— History of the 1st Ch. and Parish of Dedham, Mass., Nov. 18, 1838, on the Completion of its 2d Century. Dedham, 1839. 8vo. Mass. Hist. Discourses. Vol. 8.

LAMSON, Rev. Wm. Portsmouth: its Advantages and Needs. A Thanksgiving Sermon preached in 1854. Portsmouth, 1855. 8vo. N. H. Hist. Discourses. Vol. 3.

LANARKSHIRE, Ccotland. See IRVING and MURRAY. The Upper Ward Described. 1864.

LANCASHIRE, Eng. See Hist. Soc. of Lancashire and Cheshire.

—— Dialect. See BAMFORD, Saml.

LANCASTER Co., Eng. See BAINES, Edw. Hist. of. 1868.

—— GREGSON, M. Port Folio of Hist. Fragments. 1869.

LANCASTER Co., Penn. See HARRIS, Alex. Biograph. Hist. of. 1872.

—— RUPP, I. D. History of.

—— MOMBERT, J. I. Authentic Hist. of. 1869.

LANCASTER, D. Hist. of Gilmanton, from the First Settlement to the Present Time. Gilmanton, 1845. 8vo.

LANCASTER, Jos. See DUNN, Henry. Life of.

LANCASTER, Mass. See GOODWIN, I. Oration on 150th Annivers. of Destruction of the Town.

—— Memorial Hall. See THAYER, C. T. and BUSWELL, H. F. Dedication of.

—— See THAYER, Nathan'l. Dedica. Sermon, 1817.

—— —— Last Sermon in the Old Meeting-House, 1816.

—— WILLARD, J. History of.

—— —— 200th Annivers. Address.

LANCASTER, Wis., Herald, Newspaper. June, 1845, to Dec., 1858. Folio.

—— Institute. 1st Ann. Catalogue, 1859. Lancaster. 8vo.

LANCELOT, Francis. The Queens of England and their Times, from Matilda, Queen of William the Conqueror, to Adelaide, Queen of William the 4th. N. Y., 1859. 2 Vols. 12mo.

LAND (The) We Live In. A Pictorial and Literary Sketch Book of the British Empire. 34 Nos. Imperfect. n. d.
LANDED Gentry of G. Britain. See BURKE, Sir B.
LANDER, Richard and John. Journal of an Expedition to Explore the course and termination of the Niger. Harpers' Fam. Libr. N. Y., 1858. 2 Vols. 18mo.
LANDING at Cape Anne, Mass. See THORNTON, J. Wingate.
LANE, Ebenezer. See NEWTON, Alfred. Life and Character of.
—— The Moravian Missions. Address before the Fire Lands Hist. Soc., Mar. 12, 1862. Fire Lands Pioneer. Vol. 3.
—— See NEWTON, Rev. A. Life of.
LANE, Henry S. Remarks in Cong., Mar. 28, 1842, on the Loan Bill. Washington, 1842. 8vo. Congr. and Polit. Pamph. Vol. 24.
—— Speech in U. S. Senate, Feb. 8, 1866, on Reconstruction. Congr. and Polit. Pamph. Vol. 137.
LANE, J. H. Speech in U. S. Senate, Feb. 16, 1864, on African Colonization. Congr. and Polit. Pamph. Vol. 87.
LANE Theolog. Seminary; its History, Condition aud Claims. Cincin., 1870. 18mo.
LANG, Geo. S. Money. 1868. 8vo. Congr. and Polit. Pamph. Vol. 74.
LANG, John, D. and TAYLOR, Sam'l, Jr. Report of a Visit to Indians west of Mississippi River. N. Y., 1843. 8vo. Indian Pamph. Vol. 3.
LANGE, Dan'l A. Isthmns of Suez Canal Question, viewed in its Political Bearings. Lond., 1859. 8vo. Eng. Polit. Pamph. Vol. 58.
LANGHORN, Rich'd. Trial, and Speech at his Execution, July 14, 1679. Lond., 1679. Fol. Eng. Polit. Pamph. Vol. 1.
LANGRISH, Browne. Physical Experiments upon Brutes. Lond., 1746. 12mo. Med. Pamph. Vol. 20.
LANGTON, John. Address before the Quebec Lit. and Hist. Soc., 1862. Transactions. Vol. 1. N. S. Part 1.
—— On the Age of Timber Trees, and the Supply of Timber for Canada. Read before the Quebec Lit. and Hist. Soc., Jan. 15, 1862. Transactions. Vol. 5. Part 1.
—— On the Measurement of Heads in Ethnological Investigations. Quebec Lit. and Hist. Soc. Trans. N. S. Part 4.
LANGUAGE. See BUNSEN, C. C. History applied to Language.
—— THORNTON, W. Cadmus: a Treatise on written Language.
—— AFRICAN. See HODGSON, W. B. Berber Dialect.
—— —— BRYANT, Rev. J. S. Zulu Language.
—— —— GROUT, Henry. Zulu Language, etc.
—— —— WILSON, Rev. J. L. Negro Dialects of Africa.
—— CHINESE. See ANDREWS, S. P. Discoveries in Chinese.
—— —— GUTZLAFF, Rev. C. Chinese System of Writing.
—— DANISH. See GIERLOW, J. Dan. and Swed. Grammar.
—— ENGLISH. See BARNES, W. Anglo-Saxon Delectus.
—— —— —— English Roots and Stems.
—— —— BARTLETT, J. R. Dict. of Americanisms.
—— —— BOSWORTH, Jos. Anglo-Saxon and Eng. Dictionary.

LANGUAGE. ENGLISH. CARPENTER, S. H. English of 14th Century.
—— —— CRAIK, G. L. Hist. of Eng. Litera. and Language.
—— —— DE VERE, S. Americanisms: English of the New World.
—— —— DU PONCEAU, P. S. Analysis of Sounds of Eng. Lang.
—— —— FREE, John. Essay on Hist. of, 1773.
—— —— HALLIWELL, J. O. Eng. Provincial Dialects.
—— —— HARRISON, Rev. M. Rise and Progress of.
—— —— PHILLIPPS, Sir T. Fragments of Aelfric's Grammar and Glossary.
—— —— PICKERING, J. Vocabulary of Amer. Words and Phrases.
—— —— STEARNS, E. J. Eng. Pronunciation.
—— —— TRENCH, R. C. English Past and Present.
—— —— —— Glossary of Eng. Words.
—— —— VERNON, E. J. Guide to Anglo-Saxon.
—— —— WELCH, A. S. Analysis of Eng. Sentence.
—— —— WILKIE, Rev. D. Comparison of English and French Languages.
—— FRENCH. See CRAIG, J. D. Hand Book to Provencal Lang.
—— —— FEUTRY, M. Manuel Tironiem.
—— —— KEETELS, J. G. New Method of Learning the.
—— —— WILKIE, Rev. D. Comparison of English and French Languages.
—— GAELIC. See Dictonarium Scoto-Celticum.
—— —— KELLY, Rev. J. Grammar of Ancient Gaelic.
—— INDIAN. See BOWEN, T. S. Grammar of Yoruba Lang.
—— —— BRINTON, D. G. Grammar of Choctaw Lang.
—— —— BRUYAS, Jas. Mohawk Lang.
—— —— BYINGTON, C. Choctaw Grammar.
—— —— COTHEAL, A. I. Lang. of Mosquito Ind.
—— —— COTTON, Rev. J. Natick Vocab.
—— —— DAVIS, Rev. S. Prayer Book in Ind. Language.
—— —— DU PONCEAU, P. S. Notes on Eliot's Indian Grammar.
—— —— EDWARDS, J. On the Muhhekaneew Indians.
—— —— ELIOT, Rev. J. Indian Grammar.
—— —— FEULING, J. B. Place of Indian Languages in Study of Ethnology.
—— —— GALLATIN, A. Vocab. of N. W. Indians.
—— —— GIBBS, Geo. Chinook Jargon.
—— —— —— Lang. of Aborigines.
—— —— HECKEWELDER, Rev. J. Names of Rivers, Places, etc., in the Delaware Lang.
—— —— HOWSE, Jos. Cree Language.
—— —— LIEBER, O. M. Vocab. of Catawba Lang.
—— —— LINCOLN, Gov. Remarks on.
—— —— LONG, J. Vocab. of Chippeway Lang.
—— —— LUDEWIG, H. E. Literature of Amer. Aborig. Lang.
—— —— MCKENNEY, T. L. Vocab. of Chippewa Lang.
—— —— MENGARINI, G. Selish or Flat Head Grammar.
—— —— NASON, Elias. Indebtedness of the English to the Indian Languages.
—— —— NAXERA, E. On the Othomi Language.
—— —— Ojibwa New Testament.

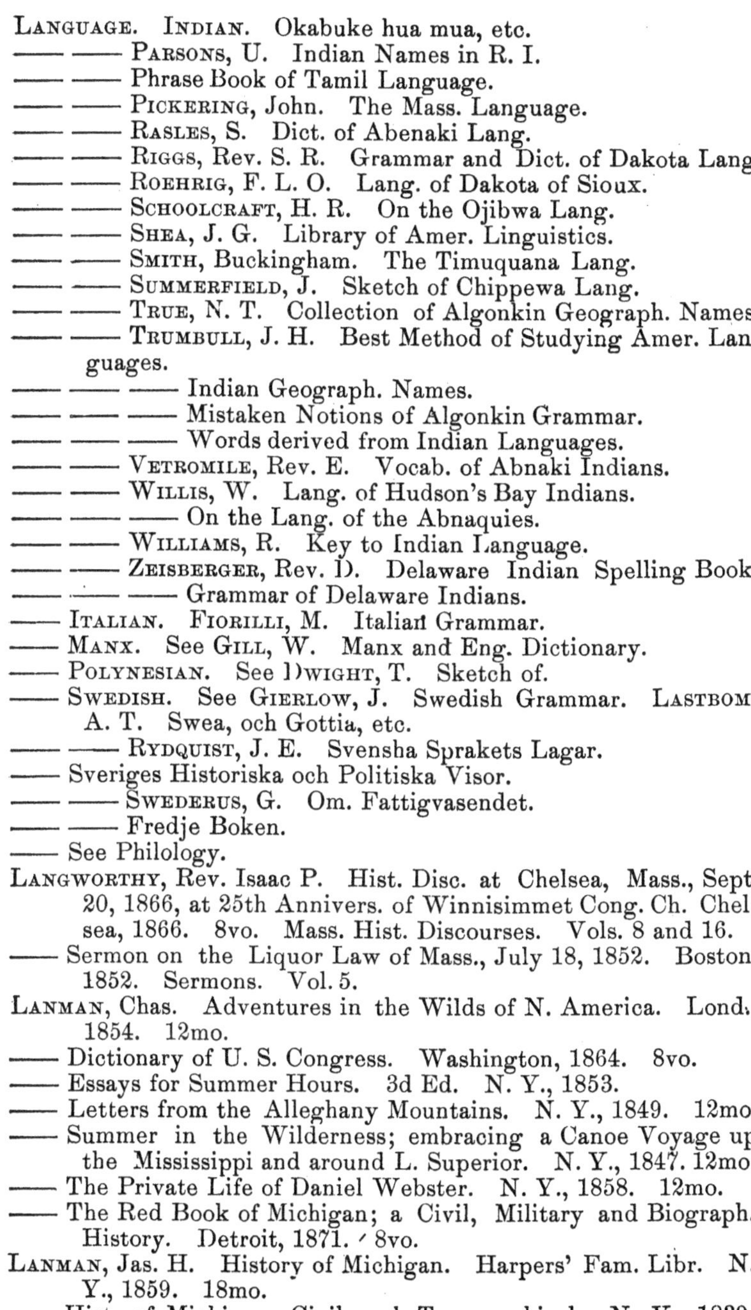

LANGUAGE. INDIAN. Okabuke hua mua, etc.
—— —— PARSONS, U. Indian Names in R. I.
—— —— Phrase Book of Tamil Language.
—— —— PICKERING, John. The Mass. Language.
—— —— RASLES, S. Dict. of Abenaki Lang.
—— —— RIGGS, Rev. S. R. Grammar and Dict. of Dakota Lang.
—— —— ROEHRIG, F. L. O. Lang. of Dakota of Sioux.
—— —— SCHOOLCRAFT, H. R. On the Ojibwa Lang.
—— —— SHEA, J. G. Library of Amer. Linguistics.
—— —— SMITH, Buckingham. The Timuquana Lang.
—— —— SUMMERFIELD, J. Sketch of Chippewa Lang.
—— —— TRUE, N. T. Collection of Algonkin Geograph. Names.
—— —— TRUMBULL, J. H. Best Method of Studying Amer. Languages.
—— —— —— Indian Geograph. Names.
—— —— —— Mistaken Notions of Algonkin Grammar.
—— —— —— Words derived from Indian Languages.
—— —— VETROMILE, Rev. E. Vocab. of Abnaki Indians.
—— —— WILLIS, W. Lang. of Hudson's Bay Indians.
—— —— —— On the Lang. of the Abnaquies.
—— —— WILLIAMS, R. Key to Indian Language.
—— —— ZEISBERGER, Rev. D. Delaware Indian Spelling Book.
—— —— —— Grammar of Delaware Indians.
—— ITALIAN. FIORILLI, M. Italian Grammar.
—— MANX. See GILL, W. Manx and Eng. Dictionary.
—— POLYNESIAN. See DWIGHT, T. Sketch of.
—— SWEDISH. See GIERLOW, J. Swedish Grammar. LASTBOM, A. T. Swea, och Gottia, etc.
—— —— RYDQUIST, J. E. Svensha Sprakets Lagar.
—— Sveriges Historiska och Politiska Visor.
—— —— SWEDERUS, G. Om. Fattigvasendet.
—— —— Fredje Boken.
—— See Philology.

LANGWORTHY, Rev. Isaac P. Hist. Disc. at Chelsea, Mass., Sept. 20, 1866, at 25th Annivers. of Winnisimmet Cong. Ch. Chelsea, 1866. 8vo. Mass. Hist. Discourses. Vols. 8 and 16.
—— Sermon on the Liquor Law of Mass., July 18, 1852. Boston, 1852. Sermons. Vol. 5.

LANMAN, Chas. Adventures in the Wilds of N. America. Lond., 1854. 12mo.
—— Dictionary of U. S. Congress. Washington, 1864. 8vo.
—— Essays for Summer Hours. 3d Ed. N. Y., 1853.
—— Letters from the Alleghany Mountains. N. Y., 1849. 12mo.
—— Summer in the Wilderness; embracing a Canoe Voyage up the Mississippi and around L. Superior. N. Y., 1847. 12mo.
—— The Private Life of Daniel Webster. N. Y., 1858. 12mo.
—— The Red Book of Michigan; a Civil, Military and Biograph. History. Detroit, 1871. 8vo.

LANMAN, Jas. H. History of Michigan. Harpers' Fam. Libr. N. Y., 1859. 18mo.
—— Hist. of Michigan, Civil and Topographical. N. Y., 1839. 8vo.

LANSDOWNE Manuscripts. See British Museum.

LANSING, John V. Frogs, and their Contributions to Science. Albany, 1869. Scientific Pamph. Vol. 18. Albany Institute Trans. Vol. 6.

—— Therapeutical Skepticism. Address before the Albany Med. College. 1869. Albany, 1869. 8vo. Albany Coll. Pamphs.

LAPHAM Family Pedigree. See LAPHAM, I. A.

LAPHAM, I. A., LL.D. Catalogue of Plants found in the Vicinity of Milwaukee, Wis. Milwaukee, 1838. 18mo.

—— Communica. to Gov. N. Dewey, on the subject of a State Penitentiary. 1848. Wis. Misc. Pamph. Vol. 1.

—— Documentary History of the Milwaukee and Rock River Canal. Milwaukee, 1840. 8vo. Wis. Misc. Pamph. Vol. 7.

—— Geograph. and Topograph. Description of Wis. Milwaukee, 1844. 12mo.

—— Same. 2d Ed., Enlarged. Milwaukee, 1846. 12mo.

—— Geological Formation of Wisconsin. Trans. Wis. State Agr. Society. Vol. 1, p. 122. 1851.

—— Geological Map of Wisconsin. N. Y., 1855.

—— KNAPP, J. G. and CROCKER, H. Report on the Disastrous Effects of the Destruction of Forest Trees in Wisconsin. Madison, 1867. 8vo. Wis. Misc. Pamph. Vol. 2.

—— Lapham Family Records. Tabular Pedigree. Genealog. Pamph. Vol. 7.

—— Meteorological Observations made at Milwaukee. Trans. Wis. State Agr. Soc. Vol. 1, p. 306, 1851; and Vol. 2, p. 449, 1852. Also Am. Almanac, 1852; p. 102.

—— Map of the City of Milwaukee, first published 1845. Reprinted with addition almost every year since. 1861.

—— Map of the State of Wisconsin, 6 miles to an inch, 1849; and several later Editions.

—— on the Classification of Plants. Trans. Wis. Acad. of Sciences. 1870–72.

—— on the Climate of the Country bordering upon the Great N. Amer. Lakes. Scientific Pamph. Vol. 19. n. d.

—— On Lacustrine Deposits, in the vicinity of the Great Lakes, usually confounded with Drift. Silliman's Journ. Vol. 3. 2d Ser.

—— on the Flora and Fauna of Wisconsin. Wis. State Agr. Soc. Trans. 1852.

—— on the Geology of the Southeastern portion of the State of Wis., being the part not surveyed by the U. States Geologists. In Foster & Whitney's Rep't. on the Geol. of the L. Superior Land District. Part 2, p. 167. 1851.

—— on the Man-Shaped Mounds of Wisconsin. Wis. Hist. Soc. Coll. Vol. 4.

—— and others. Paper on the Number, Locality and Times of Removal of the Indians of Wisconsin, with an Appendix on the Chronology of Wisconsin. Milwaukee, 1870. 8vo. Wisconsin Misc. Pamph. Vol. 2.

—— Another Copy. See Indian Pamph. Vol. 4.

LAPHAM, Increase A. and SOLOMON, Edw. Address at Dedication of Rooms of State Hist. Soc. of Wis., Jan. 24, 1866. Madison, 1866. 8vo. Wis. Hist. Soc. Addresses. Vol. 1.
—— Another Copy. See Indian Pamph. Vol. 4.
—— on the Penokee Iron Range. Trans. Wis. State Agr. Society. Vol. 5, p. 391. 1860.
—— on the Public Land Surveys, and the Latitude and Longitude of Places in Wisconsin. Coll. State Hist. Soc. of Wis. Vol. 4, p. 359. 1859.
—— The Antiquities of Wisconsin, surveyed and described. Smithson. Contrib. Vol. 7.
—— The Forest Trees of Wisconsin. Wis. State Agricul. Soc. Transactions. 1855.
—— The Grasses of Wisconsin, and the adjacent States. Wis. State Agr. Soc. Trans. 1853. p. 397.
—— The Plants of Wisconsin. Proceedings of the Am. Assoc. for the Advancement of Science. Vol. 2. Cambridge. p. 19.
LA PHYSIQUE Experimentale et Raisonnee. Paris, 1756. 18mo.
LAPLACE, Marquis de. See FOURIER, M. Hist. Eulogy on. 1829.
LAPPENBERG, J. M. Hist. of England under the Anglo-Saxon Kings. Lond., 1845. 2 Vols. 8vo.
—— Hist. of England under the Norman Kings, from the Battle of Hastings to the Accession of House of Plantagenet. Oxford, 1857. 8vo.
LARDNER, Dionysius. See ARAGO, M. Lectures on Astronomy. 1845.
—— The Steam Engine explained and illustrated, with Additions and Notes, by Jas. Renwick. N. Y., 1856. 8vo.
LARIMER, Mrs. S. L. The Capture and Escape; or Life among the Sioux. Phila., 1870. 12mo.
LARKIN, Rev. L. B. The Domesday Book of Kent, with translation, notes and appendix. Lond., 1869. Folio.
LA ROYALE. See DE PEYSTER, J. W.
LARRABEE, C. H. Speech in Cong., Dec. 17, 1859, on Organization of the House. Congr. and Polit. Pamph. Vol. 87.
LARRABEE, W. C. Inaug. Address as Principal of Oneida Conference Seminary, Nov. 10, 1831. Cazenovia, N. Y. 12mo. Addresses. Vol. 23.
LA SALLE, M. de. Last Expedition and Discoveries in America. translated from the French of the Chevalier de Tonti. Lond., 1698. 12mo.
—— See LA TONTY, Sieur De.
—— Memoir of, Discoverer of Louisiana, and the Mississippi. See French's Hist. Coll. of La. Vol. 1.
—— See SPARKS, J. Life of.
LAS CASAS, Barthelemi. Eveque de Chiapa. Œuvres. Paris, 1822. 8vo.
—— See HELPS, A. Life of.
LAS CASES, Count de. Memoirs of the Life, Exile and Conversations of the Emperor Napoleon. N. Y., 1855. 4 Vols. 12mo.
LASELL Female Seminary. Auburndale, Mass. Circular, 1859–60. Boston. 8vo.

LASTBOM, Aug. T. Swea, och Gotha Hofdinga-Minne. Sedan, 1720. Upsala, 1842–3. 2 Vols. 8vo.

LATE (The) Occurrences in N. America, and Policy of G. Britain considered. Lond., 1766. Amer. Tracts. Vol. 1.

LATHAM, Dr. John. On Rheumatism and Gout; a Letter to Sir G. Baker. Lond., 1796. 8vo. Med. Pamph. Vol. 26.

LATHAM, Milton S. Speech in Cong., June 14, 1854, on the Rights of Neutrals—Cuba. Washington, 1854. 8vo. Speeches. Vol. 3.

—— Speech in Cong., Jan. 9, 1855, on the Establishment of Mail Steamships between California and China. Speeches. Vol. 5.

LATHROP, Chas. C. Answer to Allegations made against his Appointment as Collector of the Port of N. Orleans, 1862. Rebell'n Pamph. Vol. 88.

LATHROP, Rev. John. See PARKMAN, F. Obit. Sermon, 1816.

—— Sermon at Boston, Apr. 30, 1811, at the Interment of Rev. Jos. Eckley. Boston, 1811. 8vo. Sermons. Vol. 43.

LATHROP, John H., LL. D. Address before the State Agricult. Soc. of Wisconsin, Oct., 1851. Milwaukee, 1851. 8vo. Wis. Misc. Pamph. Vol. 3.

—— Eulogy on the Death of Henry Clay, at Madison, July 19, 1852. Madison, 1852. 8vo. Madison City Pamph. Vol. 1.

—— Inaug. Address, delivered in the Assembly Hall, Madison, Wis. Jan. 16, 1850, as Chancellor of the University. Madison, Wis., 1850. 8vo. Wis. University Pamphs.

—— Inauguration of, as President of Indiana State University. Indianapolis, 1861. 8vo. Addresses. Vol. 36.

—— Topograph. Description of Wisconsin, for the use of State Emigration Agency. Madison, 1852. 8vo.

—— Wisconsin. 1851. 8vo. (2 Copies.) Wis. Misc. Pamph. Vol. 3.

LATHROP, Rev. Jos., D. D. See SPRAGUE, Wm. B. Obit. Sermon, 1821.

LATIMER, John. Local Records; or Hist. Register of Events which have occurred in Northumberland and Durham, Newcastle and Berwick, 1832-57. Newcastle, 1857. 8vo.

LATIN Language. See MERRILL, T. A. Essay on the Study of.

LA TONTY, Sieur De. Memoir of La Salle's Discovery of the Mississippi, etc. French's Hist. Coll. La. Vol. 1.

LATOUR, A. L. Hist. Memoir of the War in W. Florida and Louisiana in 1814–15. Phila., 1816. 8vo.

LATROBE, Benj. Succinct View of the Moravian Missions among the Heathen. Lond., 1771. 8vo. Eng. Rel. Pamph. Vol. 22.

LATROBE, Chas. J. Rambler in N. America. New York, 1835. 2 Vols. 12mo.

LATROBE, J. H. B. Address at Laying the Corner-Stone of the City Hall in Baltimore, Oct. 18, 1867. Baltimore, 1867. 8vo. Baltimore Pamph. Vol. 1.

—— History of Mason and Dixon's Line; Address before the Penn. Hist. Soc., Nov. 8, 1854. Phila., 1855. 8vo. Penn. Hist. Soc Addresses. Vol. 1.

LATROBE, J. H. B. Memoir of Benj. Banneker, read before the Md. Hist. Soc., May 1, 1845. Baltimore, 1845. 8vo. Md. Hist. Soc. Papers. Vol. 1.

—— Three Great Battles, viz. Buena Vista, The Seven Days' Battle, and Gettysburg. Baltimore. n. d. 8vo. Rebell'n Pamph. Vol. 108.

LATUDE, Henry Masers de. Memoirs during his 35 Years Confinement in various Prisons in France. Waldie's Circulating Libr. Vol. 4.

LAUDERDALE, Earl of. Sketch of an Address to His Majesty, on the Grievances of the Nation, 1821. Edinburgh, 1825. 8vo. Strangford Pamph. Vols. 4, 5.

LAUDONNIERE, Rene. Hist. of the First Attempt of the French (Huguenots) to Colonize Florida. French's Hist. Coll. La. and Florida.

LAUGEL, A. The U. States during the War. N. Y., 1866. 8vo.

LAUGHING (The) Philosopher; being a Letter on the Madness of Democritus. Lond., 1736. 8vo. Eng. Misc. Pamph. Vol. 23.

LAURENS, Henry. Correspondence of. N. Y., 1861. 4to.

—— See MOORE, Frank. Correspondence of.

—— Narrative of his Capture and Confinement in the Tower of London. S. C. Hist. Soc. Trans. Vol. 1.

LAURENT, Emile. Etudes sur les Societes de prevoyance ou de Secours Mutuels. Paris, 1856. 12mo.

LAURENT, M. Histoire de l'Empire Ottoman. Paris, 1724. 4 Vols. 8vo.

LAURENT, Peter E. Manual of Ancient Geography, with indexes. New Ed. Oxford, Eng., 1840. 8vo.

LAURIE, Peter. Use and Abuse of Grand Juries. Lond., 1832. 8vo. Law Pamph. Vol. 21.

LAURIE, Rev. Thos. Hist. Sketch of the Syria Mission. N. York, 1862. 8vo. Amer. Board For. Miss. Pamph's.

LAUSITZ Society for Advancement of Science. See NEWMAN, E. G. Neues Lausiksches Magazine.

LAVALETTE, Count. Memoirs written by himself. 2d Ed. Lond., 1831. 2 Vols. 8vo.

LAW and Law Literature. See Abstract of Laws of N. England, 1641.

—— —— ADAMS, J. Q. Argument in Armistad Case.

—— —— Albany and Schenectady R. R. Co. vs. Mayor of City of Albany.

—— —— ALLEN, F. Early Lawyers of Maine.

—— —— Amer. Law Register, 1852–3.

—— —— Another Letter to Mr. Almon, respecting Libel, 1770.

—— —— Argument in Case of Bank of U. S.

—— —— ARRINGTON, A.W. Argument—Hough vs. Western Trans. Co.

—— —— ASHMEAD, J. W. Speech in Case of U. S. vs. Hanway.

—— —— BALDWIN, R. S. Argument in Armistad Case.

—— —— BEARDSLEE, G. W. Case of B. Langdon before Comm'r of Patents.

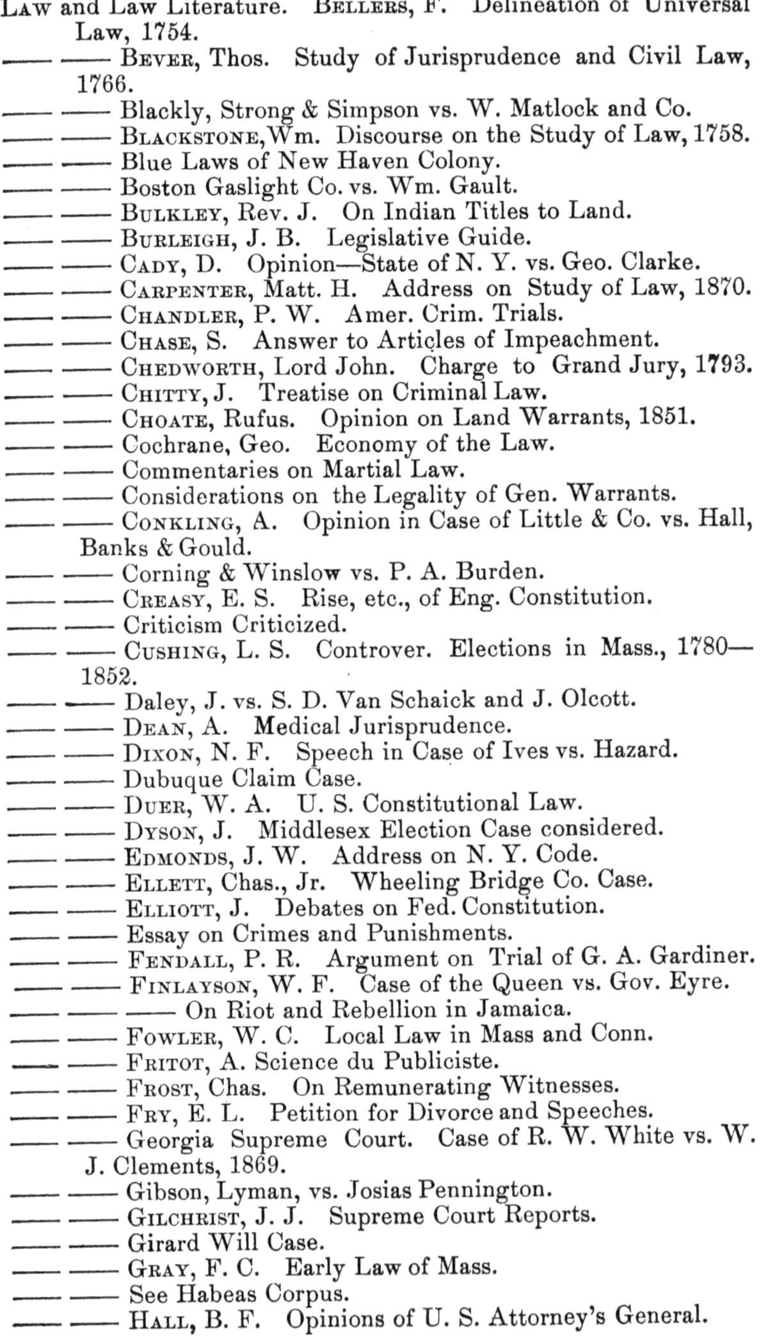

Law and Law Literature. Bellers, F. Delineation of Universal Law, 1754.

—— —— Bever, Thos. Study of Jurisprudence and Civil Law, 1766.

—— —— Blackly, Strong & Simpson vs. W. Matlock and Co.

—— —— Blackstone, Wm. Discourse on the Study of Law, 1758.

—— —— Blue Laws of New Haven Colony.

—— —— Boston Gaslight Co. vs. Wm. Gault.

—— —— Bulkley, Rev. J. On Indian Titles to Land.

—— —— Burleigh, J. B. Legislative Guide.

—— —— Cady, D. Opinion—State of N. Y. vs. Geo. Clarke.

—— —— Carpenter, Matt. H. Address on Study of Law, 1870.

—— —— Chandler, P. W. Amer. Crim. Trials.

—— —— Chase, S. Answer to Articles of Impeachment.

—— —— Chedworth, Lord John. Charge to Grand Jury, 1793.

—— —— Chitty, J. Treatise on Criminal Law.

—— —— Choate, Rufus. Opinion on Land Warrants, 1851.

—— —— Cochrane, Geo. Economy of the Law.

—— —— Commentaries on Martial Law.

—— —— Considerations on the Legality of Gen. Warrants.

—— —— Conkling, A. Opinion in Case of Little & Co. vs. Hall, Banks & Gould.

—— —— Corning & Winslow vs. P. A. Burden.

—— —— Creasy, E. S. Rise, etc., of Eng. Constitution.

—— —— Criticism Criticized.

—— —— Cushing, L. S. Controver. Elections in Mass., 1780—1852.

—— —— Daley, J. vs. S. D. Van Schaick and J. Olcott.

—— —— Dean, A. Medical Jurisprudence.

—— —— Dixon, N. F. Speech in Case of Ives vs. Hazard.

—— —— Dubuque Claim Case.

—— —— Duer, W. A. U. S. Constitutional Law.

—— —— Dyson, J. Middlesex Election Case considered.

—— —— Edmonds, J. W. Address on N. Y. Code.

—— —— Ellett, Chas., Jr. Wheeling Bridge Co. Case.

—— —— Elliott, J. Debates on Fed. Constitution.

—— —— Essay on Crimes and Punishments.

—— —— Fendall, P. R. Argument on Trial of G. A. Gardiner.

—— —— Finlayson, W. F. Case of the Queen vs. Gov. Eyre.

—— —— —— On Riot and Rebellion in Jamaica.

—— —— Fowler, W. C. Local Law in Mass and Conn.

—— —— Fritot, A. Science du Publiciste.

—— —— Frost, Chas. On Remunerating Witnesses.

—— —— Fry, E. L. Petition for Divorce and Speeches.

—— —— Georgia Supreme Court. Case of R. W. White vs. W. J. Clements, 1869.

—— —— Gibson, Lyman, vs. Josias Pennington.

—— —— Gilchrist, J. J. Supreme Court Reports.

—— —— Girard Will Case.

—— —— Gray, F. C. Early Law of Mass.

—— —— See Habeas Corpus.

—— —— Hall, B. F. Opinions of U. S. Attorney's General.

LAW and Law Literatnre. HANOVER, M. D. On Law of Horses.
—— —— HEAD, J. W. Tenn. Sup. Court Reports.
—— —— HENDERSON, T. J. Jackson's Impeachment Trial.
—— —— HOFFMAN, M. Treatise on the Estate and Rights of N. Y. City.
—— —— HOWARD, B. C. Report of "Dred Scott" Case.
—— —— Indiana Revised Statutes.
—— —— INGERSOLL, J. R. Manual of Maritime Law.
—— —— James, Thos. vs. M. and S. Patten.
—— —— JEFFERSON, T. Cases determined in Gen. Court of Va.
—— —— JOHNSON, Pres't A. Impeachment Case.
—— —— JOHNSON, R. vs. Thos. Caruley.
—— —— KETTELL, T. P. Constitutional Reform.
—— —— KINNE, A. Laws on Imprisonment for Debt.
—— —— LAMBERT, W. Precedents.
—— —— LAWRENCE, A. and A. vs. City of New York.
—— —— LAWRENCE, W. B. Visitation and Search.
—— —— LEGRAND, P. Legislation des portions Menageres.
—— —— Lemmon Slave Case.
—— —— LESTER, J. vs. S. R. GAY and others.
—— —— Letter on Libels, Warrants and the Seizure of Papers.
—— —— Letter to Mr. Almon in matter of.
—— —— LEWIS, E., on Legal and Judicial Oaths.
—— —— LLOYD, C. Defence of House of Commons on Gen. Warrants.
—— —— MCARTHUR, A. H. and others vs. F. S. Low.
—— —— MCAULEY, A. Inquiry into the Legality of Pensions.
—— —— MACKELDY, F. Lehrbuck des Heutigen Romischen Rechts.
—— —— Mass. Private and Special Statutes. 1822–59.
—— —— Mass. Supreme Court. Trial of Prof. Webster for Murder of Dr. Parkman. 1850.
—— —— Monthly Law Reporter.
—— —— N. Y. Code of Procedure.
—— —— —— Criminal Code.
—— —— —— People of, vs. James M. Cook.
—— —— NOTT, Eliphalet, vs. J. S. Thayer.
—— —— NOYE, W. Maxims of Laws of England.
—— —— OGDEN, S. G. vs. ASTOR, et al. 1850.
—— —— PALEY, W. Treatise on Principal and Agent.
—— —— See Parliamentary Reform.
—— —— Precedents in Trespass.
—— —— PRINCE, J. H., on Barring Dower.
—— —— Quebec. Code of Laws.
—— —— Remarks, etc., on Marine Losses.
—— —— Rensselaer Co. Ins. Co. vs. J. and J. M. Waggoner.
—— —— Review of Duponceau on Fed. Jurisdic.
—— —— RIVES, M. De la Propriete du cours et du lit des revieres.
—— —— ROBERTSON, Geo. Scrap Book on Law and Politics.
—— —— Rules, etc., in Bankruptcy. 1842.
—— —— RUSSELL, C. W. Argument in Wheeling Bridge Co. Case.

LAW and Law Literature. WOODWORTH, W. Planing Machine Patent, etc.

—— —— See Politics and Government.

—— Study of. Reflections on the Natural and Acquired Endowments requisite, etc. Dublin, 1764. 12mo. Law Pamph. Vol. 26.

LAW, Gen. E. M. Address before the Students of Davidson College, on Gen. R. E. Lee's Birthday. 1871. 8vo. Rebell'n Pamph. Vol. 110.

LAW, Geo. Sketch of Events in his Life, published in advance of his Biography. N. Y., 1855. Biograph. Pamph. Vol. 1.

LAW is a Bottomless Pit: exemplified in the Case of the Lord Strutt, John Bull, etc. Lond., 1712. 12mo. Eng. Polit. Pamph. Vol. 8.

LAW, Judge John. Jesuit Missionaries in the N. West; Lecture at Cincinnati, Jan., 1855. Wis. Hist. Soc. Coll. Vol. 3.

—— The Capture of Vincennes in 1779. From an Address delivered before the Vincennes Hist. and Antiquarian Soc'y, Feb. 22, 1839. Va. Hist. Register. Vol. 6.

—— The Colonial History of Vincennes, under the French, British and American Governments. Vincennes, 1858. 8vo.

LAW (The) of Slavery in the U. States. Boston, 1863. 12mo. Rebell'n Pamph. Vol. 4.

LAW REFORM.—England. See SMITH, Wm. Remarks on. 1840.

LAW, Wm. Oration before the Georgia Hist. Soc., Feb. 12, 1840. Ga. Hist. Coll. Vol. 1.

LAWRENCE, Abbott. See APPLETON, N. Memoir of.

—— Letters to Wm. C. Rives, of Virginia. Boston, 1846. 8vo. Va. Misc. Pamph. Vol. 1.

—— Letters on Free Trade. See BRADFORD, S. D.

—— Memoir of. N. E. Hist. and Gen. Reg. Vol. 10.

LAWRENCE Academy, Groton, Mass. Catalogues for 1850 to 1868 inclusive, except for 1867.

—— Same for 1871–2. Lowell, etc., 1850–1872. 8vo.

—— —— Catalogue of Library. Lowell, 1850. 8vo. Bibliograph. Pamph. Vol. 69.

—— —— Jubilee of Lawrence Academy, at Groton, July 12, 1854, with Gen. Catalogue. N. Y., 1855. 8vo. Lawrence Acad. Catalogues, etc. Another Copy Mass. Hist. Discourses, etc. Vol. 13.

—— —— Memorial soliciting Aid for rebuilding Academy. 1868. Groton, 1868. 8vo. Lawrence Acad. Catalogues, etc.

—— —— Programmes of Ann. Exhibitions. 1858–1865. Groton, 1858–65. 8vo. Lawrence Acad. Catalogues, etc.

LAWRENCE, Amos. See GRAY, Rev. F. T. Funeral Sermon on.

—— HOPKINS, Mark. Commem. Discourse. 1853.

—— et al., Plaintiffs in error vs. the Mayor, Aldermen and Commonalty of City of N. Y. 1843. Law Pamphlets. Vol 2.

—— See LAWRENCE, W. R. Extracts from his Diary and Corres.

—— LOTHROP, Rev. S. K. Obit. Sermon.

LAWRENCE Co., N. Y. See FINCH, J. Essay on Mineralogy of, 1830.

LAWRENCE, Eugene. Anne Hutchinson: Paper before the N. Y. Hist. Soc., Feb. 5, 1867. Hist. Mag. 2d Ser. Vol. 1.

—— Lives of the British Historians. N. Y., 1855. 2 Vols. 12mo.

—— N. York during the Revolutionary Struggle. Extracts from a Paper before the N. Y. Hist. Soc., Jan. 6, 1857. Hist. Mag. Vol. 1.

LAWRENCE Genealogy. See HALE, Mercy.

—— —— LAWRENCE, John.

—— —— PEASE, F. S.

LAWRENCE, Geo. Border and Bastile. N. Y. n. d. 12mo.

LAWRENCE, Jas. Dramatic Emancipation; or Strictures on the State of the Theatres, and the Degeneration of the Drama. Lond., 1813. 8vo. Pamphleteer. Vol. 2.

—— On the Nobility of the British Gentry; for the Use of Foreigners in G. B., and Britons abroad. Lond., 1824. 8vo. Pamphleteer. Vol. 23.

LAWRENCE, John. Genealog. Memoir of the Family of John Lawrence, of Watertown, 1636. Boston, 1847. 8vo. Genealog. Pamph. Vol. 9.

—— Genealogy of the Family of John Lawrence, of Wisset, Suffolk, Eng. Boston, 1869. 8vo.

LAWRENCE, Luther. See MILES, H. A. Obit. Sermon, 1839.

LAWRENCE, Mass. See WHITING, Lyman. Dedica. Sermon, 1848.

—— 6th and 12th Ann. Reports of the Public Schools for 1852–53, and 1857. Lawrence, 1853, '59. 8vo.

—— See Pemberton Mills.

LAWRENCE, Rev. Nathan'l. Hist. Sketch of Tyngsborough, Middlesex, Mass. Mass. Hist. Soc Coll. Vol. 4. 2d Ser.

LAWRENCE, Robt. F. N. Hampshire Churches; Hist. of Congregational and Presbyterian Churches. Claremont, 1856.

LAWRENCE, Thos. Hist. Genealogy of the Lawrence Family, 1635–1858. N. Y., 1858. 8vo.

LAWRENCE University, Appleton, Wis. Ann. Catalogues for 1853–4, 1854–5, 1855–6, 1857–8, 1859–60, 1860–1, 1863–4, 1864–5, 1866–7, 1867–8, 1868–9, 1869–70, 1871–2.

—— —— Catalogues of the Library, 1859, '70.

—— —— Catalogue of Appleton Library of. Chicago, 1869. 8vo.

—— —— Circular of Endowment Agent, 1864–5. Milwaukee. 8vo. Wis. Misc. Pamph. Vol. 2.

—— See SMITH, Reeder. Appeal in Behalf of, 1859.

LAWRENCE, W., M. D. Hunterian Oration at the Royal Coll. of Surgeons, Feb. 14, 1846. Lond., 1846. 8vo. Med. Pamph. Vol. 29.

LAWRENCE, Wm. See LOTHROP, Rev. S. K.

LAWRENCE, W. Speech in Cong., Dec. 22, 1869, on Reconstruction of Georgia. Congr. and Polit. Pamph. Vol. 122.

—— Speech in Cong., Mar. 5, 1870, on the Admission of Georgia. Congr. and Polit. Pamph. Vol. 119.

LAWRENCE, Wm. B. Annivers. Discourse before the N. Y. Hist. Soc., Apr. 19, 1832, on the Origin and Nature of Representative Institutions in U. S. N. Y., 1832. 8vo. N. Y. Hist. Soc. Discourses. Vol. 2.

LAWRENCE, Wm. B. Visitation and Search; Hist. Sketch of the British Claim to exercise a Maritime Police over the Vessels of all Nations. Boston, 1858. 8vo.

LAWRENCE, Wm. R. Extracts from the Diary and Correspondence of the late Amos Lawrence; with a Brief Acc. of his Life. Boston, 1855. 8vo.

LAWS of England, respecting Wills; with Instructions for making a Will or Testament. Lond., 1813. 12mo. Law Pamph. Vol. 10.

—— of Reproduction. See BROOKS, Rev. C.

—— of War and Martial Law. Boston, 1863. 12mo. Rebell'n Pamph. Vol. 4.

LAWSON, A. The Iron Industries of Ironton, and the Hanging Rock Iron Region of Ohio. Cincin., 1871. 8vo.

LAWSON, Jas. A. Five Lectures on Political Economy, before the University of Dublin, in 1843. Lond., 1844. 8vo. Strangford Pamph. Vol. 56.

LAWSON, John. History of Carolina. Lond., 1714. Raleigh, reprint, 1860. 12mo.

LAWSON, M. Substance of a Speech at the Boroughbridge Election, June 20, 1818. Cambridge. 8vo. Eng. Polit. Pamph. Vol. 34.

LAWSON, Dr. Thos. Meteorological Register, 1826–30. 8vo. Congr. and Polit. Pamph. Vol. 72.

LAWTON (The) or New Rochelle Blackberry; its Origin, Culture, etc. N. Y., 1857. 8vo. Agr. Pamph. Vol. 11.

LAY, G. T. The Chinese as they are; their Moral and Social Character, with Notes by E. G. Squier. Albany, 1843. 8vo.

LAYARD, Austen H. Discoveries among the Ruins of Nineveh and Babylon; with Travels in Armenia, etc. 2d Ed. N.Y., 1856. 12mo.

—— Prospects and Conduct of the War. Speech in Parl't, Dec. 12, 1854. Lond., 1854. Strangford Pamph. Vol. 67.

LAYARD, Dr. Dan'l P. Essay on the Bite of a Mad Dog. Lond., 1763. 8vo. 2d Ed. Med. Pamph. Vol. 15.

LEA, Lieut. Albert M. Notes on Wisconsin Territory; particularly with reference to the Iowa Dist., on Black Hawk Purchase, with a Map. Phila., 1836. 18mo. Another Copy. Wis. Misc. Pamph. Vol. 2.

LEA, Isaac. Contributions to Geology in Alabama, N. Jersey, and N. York. Phila., 1833. 8vo.

—— A Synopsis of the Family of the Naiades. 3d Ed. Phila., 1852. 4to.

—— On the Fossil Footmarks in the Red Sandstone of Pottsville, Penn. Amer. Philos. Soc. Trans. N. S. Vol. 10.

LEACH, Geo. Psalms of Freedom for the Amer. Christian Patriot, 1861. Rebell'n Pamph. Vol. 96.

LEACH, John. Journal, kept during his Confinement in Boston Gaol, in 1775. n. d. 8vo. Rev. War Pamph. Vol. 4.

LEAD Mines. See U. S. Secretary of War. Report of J. Flanagan. 1842.

LEAGUE (The) for the Union. Speeches of Geo. Bancroft and Jas. Milliken. Phila., 1863. Rebell'n Pamph. Vol. 83.

LEAGUE Island as a Naval Station. Advantages of League Island for a Naval Station. Phila., 1866. 8vo. Rebell'n Pamph. Vol. 59.

—— —— Majority and Minority Reports of Board of Officers appointed to Examine proposed Sites for a Naval Yard. Washington and Phila., 1862. 8vo. Rebell'n Pamph. Vol. 59.

—— —— Majority and Minority Reports of Naval Committee of U. S. House of Repr., 1864. Phila. and Washington, 1864. 8vo. Rebell'n Pamph. Vol. 59.

—— —— Reports of the Sec. of the Navy, and the Commission by him appointed, on the proposed Navy Yard at League Island. Phila., 1863. 8vo. Rebell'n Pamph. Vol. 59.

—— —— Report of the Naval Commission to examine League Island. Phila., 1863. 8vo. Rebell'n Pamph. Vol. 59.

—— —— Reply to a Pamphlet entitled "Advantages of League Island for a Naval Station." N. London, 1866. 8vo. Rebellion Pamph. Vol. 59.

—— —— See New London.

—— of the Iroquois. See MORGAN, L. H.

LEAKE, Isaac Q. Memoirs of the Life and Times of Gen. John Lamb, an Officer of the Revolution. Albany, 1850. 8vo.

"LEATHERWOOD God." See TANEYHILL, R. H.

LEAVITT, Judge. Decision in the Vallandigham Habeas Corpus Case. 1863. Rebell'n Pamph. Vol. 91.

LEAVITT, Joshua. Denmark and its Relations. Read before the Amer. Geograph. and Statist. Soc., Mar. 3, 1864. N. York, 1864. 8vo. Hist. Pamph. Vol. 1.

—— Another Copy. See Papers of Society.

—— Moral and Social Benefits of Cheap Postage. N. Y., 1849. 8vo. Congr. and Polit. Pamph. Vol. 76.

—— Remarks and Statistics on Cheap Postage and Postal Reform. Boston, 1848. 8vo. Congr. and Polit. Pamph. Vol. 124.

—— The Finance of Cheap Postage. N. Y., 1849. 8vo. Congr. and Polit. Pamph. Vol. 76.

—— The Monroe Doctrine. N. Y., 1863. 8vo. Congr. and Polit. Pamph. Vol. 74. Rebell'n Pamph. Vol. 8.

LEAVITT, O. S. Memorial to Cong., on the Finances. Loveland, O., 1871. 8vo. Congr. and Polit. Pamph. Vol. 114.

LEAVITT, T. H. Facts about Peat as an Article of Fuel. Boston, 1865. 8vo.

LEAVITT, Wm. Materials for the History of Ship-Building in Salem. Essex Institute Coll. Vols. 6 and 7.

LEBANON Co., Pa. See RUPP, I. D. History of.

LEBANON, N. H. See ALLEN, Rev. D. H. Centen. Sermon. 1861.

LEBANON Springs, N. Y. Sketch of its Attractions as a Summer Resort, etc. 2 Pamphs. Pittsfield, 1871–2. 12mo. N. Y. Local Hist. Vol. 5.

LEBARON, Wm., M. D. 1st and 2d Ann. Reports on Noxious Insects of Illinois. Springfield, 1871–2. 8vo.

LEBEAU, C. Avantures: ou Voyage Parmi les Sauvages de l'Amerique Septentrionale avec une Description du Canada. Amsterdam, 1738. 2 Vols. 18mo.

LECHFORD, Thos. Plain Dealing; or News from N. England, with introduction by J. H. Trumbull. Boston, 1867. 4to. See also Mass. Hist. Soc. Coll. 3d Ser. Vol. 3.

LECKIE, G. F. Essay on the Practice of the British Government. Lond., 1817. 8vo. Pamphleteer. Vol. 11.

LECLERC, Chas. Bibliotheca Americana. Paris, 1867. 8vo.

LECLERC, M. Life and Character of John Locke, Author of the Essay concerning Human Understanding. Lond., 1706. Sm. 4to. Biograph. Pamph. Vol. 10.

LECLERC, J. History of the United Netherlands, in Dutch. Amsterdam, 1730. 4 Vols. Folio.

LECLERCQ, Chrestien. Nouvelle Relation de la Gaspesie; qui Contient les Moeurs, et la Religion des Sauvages Gaspesieus Porte Croix, etc. Paris, 1691. 12mo.

LECOMPTON Constitution. See Congress'l Speeches.

LECTURES on the Progress of Arts and Science, resulting from the Great Exhibition in London. N. Y., 1856. 12mo.

LEDERER, John. Discoveries, from Virginia to Carolina, from Mar. 1669, to Sept. 10, 1670, with Map. Lond., 1672. MS. Copy bound. 4to.

LEDIARD, Thos. Charge to the Grand Jury at Westminster, Oct. 16, 1754. Lond., 1754. 8vo. Eng. Polit. Pamph. Vol. 70.

LEDUC, W. G. Minnesota Year Book for 1851-1852. St. Paul, 1852. 12mo.

LEE, Arthur. See LEE, R. H. Life and Corres. of.

—— Extracts from his Journal, kept during his Expedition to the N. Western Indians, in 1784. "Olden Time." Vol. 2.

LEE, Gen. Chas. Memoirs of Life of. N. Y., 1792. 12mo.

—— Life and Memoirs of, with his Political and Military Essays and Letters. N. Y., 1813. 12mo.

—— Same. Dublin, 1792. 8vo.

—— See MOORE, G. H. Treason of.

—— Proceedings of Gen. Court-Martial for the Trial of, July 4, 1778. N. Y., 1864. 4to.

LEE, Chas. A. Elements of Geology. Harpers' Fam. Libr. N. Y., 1858.

—— Valedictory Addresses to Graduates of Geneva Med. College, Jan. 26, 1847, and Jan. 23, 1849. N. Y., 1847. 8vo. Buffalo, 1849. 8vo. Med. Pamph. Vol. 2.

LEE, Chauncey, D. D. Farewell Sermon, Colebrook, Conn., Feb. 1828. Hartford, 1828. 8vo. Conn. Hist. Discourses. Vol. 8.

LEE, Dr. Dan'l. Treatise on Peruvian Guano. Washington, 1854. 8vo. Agr. Pamph. Vol. 3.

LEE, Dr. Edwin. Homburg and Nauheim, being part of the "Baths of Germany, France and Switzerland." Lond., 1865. 12mo. 3d Ed. Hist. Pamph. Vol. 8.

—— Remarks upon Medical Organization and Reform. Lond., 1846. 8vo. Strangford Pamph. Vol. 41.

LEE, H. Observations on the Writings of Thos. Jefferson, with particular reference to the Attack on the Memory of the late Gen. Henry Lee.

LEE, Gen. Henry. Campaigns of 1781 in the Carolinas, with Remarks on Johnson's Life of Gen. Greene. Phila., 1824. 8vo.

—— Funeral Oration on Gen. Geo. Washington, at Washington. 1799. Boston. 8vo. Addresses. Vol. 6.

—— Champe's Adventure. N. Y., 1864. 12mo.

—— See JONES, C. C., Jr. Last Days, Death and Burial.

—— Memoirs of the War in the Southern Department of the U. S., with Revisions and Biography by Gen. Robt. E. Lee. N. Y., 1870. 8vo.

LEE, Henry. Exposition of Evidence in support of the Memorial to Cong., on the Tariff of Duties. Boston, 1832. 8vo. Congr. and Polit. Pamph. Vol. 139.

LEE Memorial Association of Richmond. See Journal of a Young Lady of Virginia. 1782.

LEE, Noah. Treatise on the Chronology of the Christian Era. Adrian, Mich., 1857. 8vo. Scientific Pamph. Vol. 42.

LEE, Rev. Rich'd H. Letter on the Protest of Phila. Clergy against Bishop Hopkins' Slavery Views. 1863. Rebell'n Pamph. Vol. 54.

LEE, Richard Henry. Life of Arthur Lee, with his Correspondence. Boston, 1829. 2 Vols. 8vo.

LEE, Gen. Robert E. See COOKE, J. E. Life of. 1871.

—— EARLY, Gen. J. A. Campaigns of.

—— Early Life, Campaigns and Pub. Services, with a Record of the Campaigns and Heroic Deeds of his Companions in Arms. N. Y., 1871. 8vo.

—— See GUERNSEY, Gen. A. H. Campaigns of.

—— LAW, Gen. E. M. Address on Birthday of. 1871.

—— McCABE, Jas. B. Life and Campaigns.

—— WILCOX, C. M. Campaigns of.

LEE, Saml. Contemplations on Mortality. Boston, 1698. 18mo.

LEE, Sam'l, D. D. Dissent Unscriptural and Unjustifiable: in a Letter to Dr. John Pye Smith. Cambridge, 1834. 8vo. Eng. Rel. Pamph. Vol. 46A.

LEE, Lieut. S. P. Reports and Charts of the Cruise of the U. S. Brig, Dolphin. Washington, 1854. 8vo. 1 Vol. Maps.

LEE, T. J. Tables and Formulae, useful in Surveying, Geodesy, and Practical Astronomy. 2d Ed. Washington, 1853. 8vo.

LEE, Z. Collins. Address before the Chester Co., Penn., Horticult. Soc., June, 1858. West Chester, 1858. 8vo. Agr. Pamph. Vol. 14.

LEECH, D. D. T. See U. S. Post Office Directories.

LEEDS Co., Eng. See Dialect of.

—— Report of a Meeting of the Magistrates, Clergy, etc., to Establish the Working Man's Provident Soc'y, etc., 1856. Leeds, 8vo. Eng. Misc. Pamph. Vol. 13.

LEEDS, Geo., D. D. Sermon at Boston, Apr. 13, 1862, on the Death of Rev. Chas. Mason, D. D. Boston, 1862. 8vo. Sermons. Vol. 44.

LEEDS, S. P. Address at the Funeral of Capt. Lorenzo D. Gove, at Dartmouth College. Hanover, 1863. 8vo. Rebell'n Pamph. Vol. 64.

LEES, Dr. F. R. Argument for the Legislative Prohibition of the Liquor Traffic. Lond., 1864. 8vo. Temp. Pamph. Vol. 4.

LEFEVRE, Dr. Geo. W. Nature and Treatment of the Cholera Morbus, now prevailing in St. Petersburg. Lond., 1831. 8vo. Med. Pamph. Vol. 24.

LEFFERTS, Marshall. The Electric Telegraph; its Influence and Geograph. Distribution. Amer. Geograph. and Statistic. Soc. Bulletin. Vol. 2.

LEFRANC, Pierre. La Rěpublique et les Partis, 1848–1852. Paris, 1851. 12mo.

LEGAL Tender Act. Constitutionality of. See FIELD, Justice.

—— —— POTTER, C. N.

—— —— Treasury Notes a Legal Tender.

LEGARÉ, Hugh S. Writings of, containing Extracts from his Correspondence, Orations, Speeches, etc. Edited by his Sister. Charleston, 1846. 2 Vols. 8vo.

LEGENDS for Rhine Tourists; or Stories of the Ruins from Mayence to Cologne. Bonn., 1850. 8vo.

LEGENDRE, M. See BEAUMONT, Elie de. Memoir of.

LEGGE, Henry Bilson. See BUTLER, Dr. Acc. of.

LEGGETT, Maj. Abraham. Narrative, written by himself, with Notes by C. I. Bushnell. N. Y., 1865. 8vo. Rev. War Pamph. Vol. 4.

LEGRAND, J. C. Letter to Reverdy Johnson, on the Proceedings at Maryland Institute, Jan., 1861. Rebell'n Pamph. Vols. 17 and 73.

—— Oration on the Landing of the Pilgrims of Md., May 10, 1843. Baltimore, 1843. 8vo. Md. Misc. Pamph. Vol. 2.

LE GRAND, Louis. Military Hand Book. N. Y., 1862. Rebell'n Pamph. Vol. 101.

LEGRAND, Pierre. Legislation des Portions Menagères ou parts de Marais. Lille, 1850. 8vo.

LEHIGH Coal and Navigation Co. Reports, 1856, '57, '60. Phila., 8vo. Penn. Misc. Pamph. Vol. 2.

—— —— See Penn. Supreme Court.

LEHIGH Co., Pa. See RUPP, I. D. Hist. of.

—— University, South Bethlehem, Pa. Ann. Register, 1870–1. n. p. 8vo.

—— —— See STILLMAN, P. Address, 1872.

LEHMANN, Rev. G. W. Hist. of the Baptist Churches in Germany and adjacent Countries, since 1834. Berlin, 1869. 32mo. Religious Pamph. Vol. 22.

LEIBNITZ, G. M. Von. See MACKIE, J. M. Life of.

LEICESTER Academy. See WASHBURN, A. H. Dedica. Address, 1853.

—— WASHBURN, Emory. History of.

LEICESTER, Mass. See WASHBURN, E. Topog. and Hist. Sketches of.

LEIDY, Jos. Cretaceous Reptiles of the U. S. Smithson. Contrib. Vol. 14.

LEIFCHILD, John. A Christian Antidote to Unreasonable Fears at the Present Crisis; Reply to Rev. W. Thorp's Speech against Catholic Emancipation. 2d Ed. Lond., 1829. Misc. Tracts. Vol. 3.

LEIGH, Benj. Watkins. See MACFARLAND, W. H. Address, 1851.

—— Speeches on the Removal of the Deposites, in U. S. Senate, Mar. 12 and 18, 1834. Speeches. Vol. 5.

LEIGH, C. C., JOHNSON, C. P. and others. Speeches in N. Y. Legislature, Feb., 1855, on the U. S. Senatorial Question. Albany, 1855. 8vo. Congr. and Polit. Pamph. Vol. 135.

LEILA Ada. See HEIGHWAY, O. W. T.

LEIPSIC, Germany. See SHOBERL, Fred. Narrative of Events, Oct., 1813.

LEISLER, Jacob. See HOFFMAN, C. F. Administration of.

—— Papers relating to his Administration, 1689–91. Doc. Hist. of N. Y. Vol. 2.

LEISZ, Dr. Fred. Property in Invention and Patent Law. Lond., 1864. 8vo. Eng. Polit. Pamph. Vol. 60.

LELAND, Chas. G. Centralization; or State Rights. N. Y., 1863. 8vo. Rebell'n Pamph. Vol. 6.

LELAND Genealogy. See LELAND, Sherman.

LELAND, P. W. Is the North Right? a Word about Slavery. n. d. 8vo. Congr. and Polit. Pamph. Vol. 85.

LELAND, Sherman. Leland Magazine; or Genealog. Record of Henry Leland and his Descendants, 1653 to 1850. Boston, 1850. 8vo.

LELAND, Thos. Hist. of Ireland from the Invasion of Henry II. 3d Ed. Dublin, 1774. 3 Vols. 8vo.

LE MERCIER, Rev. Andrew. Brief Memoir of. N. E. Hist. and Gen. Reg. Vol. 13.

LE MERCIER, R. P. Francois. Copie de deux Lettres Envoiees de la Nouvelle France, 1655. Albany, 1854. 12mo. Lenox's Ed.

—— Relation de ce qui s'est passe en la Nouvelle France es Annees, 1664, 1665, 1666, 1667. Paris, 1666. 12mo. 2 Vols.

LEMMON Slave Case. See N. Y. Court of Appeals.

LEMOINE, J. M., on the Birds of Canada. Read before the Quebec Lit. and Hist. Soc., April 25, 1866. Trans. N. Ser. Part 4.

—— on the History of Literature. Read before the Quebec Lit. and Hist. Soc., Dec. 6, 1865, (in French). Trans. N. Ser. Part 4.

—— The Sword of Brig.-Gen. Rich'd Montgomery: a Memoir. Quebec, 1870. 12mo.

LENDRICK, Wm. E. Phases in Politics. Lond., 1858. 8vo. Eng. Polit. Pamph. Vol. 56.

LENDRUM, John. Concise and Impartial History of the Amer. Revolution. Trenton, 1811. 12mo.

LENOX, Jas. Bibliograph. Acc. of the Voyages of Columbus, (extracts) from his larger Work on the 2d Voyage. Hist. Mag. Vol. 5.

LEOMINSTER, Mass. See GARDNER, Francis. Half Century Sermon. 1812.

—— WILDER, D. History of.

LEONARD, Benj. G. Introduct. Discourse before Chillicothe Lyceum and Mechanic's Institute, 1833. Addresses. Vol. 11.

LEONARD Genealogy. See VINTON, J. A.

LEONARD, J. A. Sketches of Whitewater, Walworth Co., Wis. Wis. Hist. Soc. Coll. Vol. 2.

LEONARD, Rev. Levi W. Hist. of Dublin, N. H., and Proceedings at the Centen. Celebration, June 17, 1852, with a Register of Families. Boston, 1855. 8vo.

LÉOPARD, P. S. Coup D'Oeil Historique sur les Bourbons de Naples. Paris, 1847. 8vo. Strangford Pamph. Vol. 48.

LEPANTO. Naval Battle of. See ROSELL, C.

LE PLAY, F. le. Description de l'affinage par Cristallisation. Paris, 1837. 8vo.

—— Memoire sur la Fabrication de l'Acier en Yorkshire. Paris, 1843. 8vo.

LESCARBOT, Marc. Histoire de la Nouvelle France; Contenant les Navigations decouvertes et habitations faites par les Francois es Indes Occidentales et Nouvelle France, with 3 Maps. Paris, 1609. 12mo.

—— Same. Troisieme Ed. 1618. 12mo.

LESLEY, J. P. Notes on a Map of five Types of Earth-Surface, between Cincinnati and the Atlantic Sea Board. Trans. Amer. Philos. Soc. N. S. Vol. 13.

LESLIE, Prof. Narr. of Discovery and Adventure in the Polar Seas and Regions. Harpers' Fam. Libr. N. Y., 1859. 18mo.

LESQUEREUX, Leo. Fossil Plants of the Coal Measures of the U. S. Pottsville, 1858. 8vo. Scientific Pamph. Vol. 10.

—— on California Mosses. Trans. Amer. Philos. Soc. N. S. Vol. 13.

—— on the Species of Fossil Plants from the Tertiary of the State of Mississippi Trans. Amer. Philos. Soc. N. S. Vol. 13.

LESTER, C. Edwards. Artists of America; or Biograph. Sketches of Amer. Artists, with Portraits. N. Y., 1846. 8vo.

—— Life and Voyages of Americus Vespucius, and the Discovery of the New World. N. Haven, 1854. 8vo.

LESTER, Jas. vs. Stephen R. Gay, Geo. W. Kniffin and Sam'l Gates, before N. Y. Supreme Court. 1853. Law Pamph. Vol. 2.

L'ESTRANGE, Roger. A Word concerning Libels and Libellers. Lond., 1681. Sm. 4to. Eng. Polit. Pamph. Vol. 6.

—— Dialogue betwixt 'Zekiel and Ephraim. Lond., 1680. Sm. 4to. Eng. Polit. Pamph. Vol. 6.

LE SUEUR. See Early Voyages on the Mississippi.

LETCHER, Gov. John. Message to the Virginia Legislature. 1862. Rebell'n Pamph. Vol. 31.

—— Speech in Cong., May 18, 1854, on the Tariff. Congr. and Polit. Pamph. Vol. 92.

—— —— Mar. 13, 1856, on Kansas Contested Election. Congr. and Polit. Pamph. Vol. 93.

LETCHER, M. E. Account of a Recent Exploration of the Mammoth Cave, Ky. (?) N. Y., 1839. 12mo. Ky. Misc. Pamph. Vol. 1.

LETHERMAN, Jona. Sketch of the Navajo Tribe of Indians, in New Mexico. Smithsonian Report. 1855.

LETHIEULLIER, S. Letter to Dr. Chas. Lyttleton, relating to Antiquities found in the Co. of Essex. Read at the Soc. of Antiquaries, Nov. 27, 1746. (n. d.) 4to.

LETTER to Mr. Gale, relating to the Shrine of St. Hugh, the Crucified Child, at Lincoln, 1736. 4to. Lond. Hist. Pamph. Vol. 21.

—— addressed to a Republican Member of the House of Repr. of the State of Mass., in regard to a petition for a "College of Physicians." Boston, 1812. 8vo. Mass. Misc. Pamph. Vol. 3.

—— addressed to Two Great Men on the Prospect of Peace, etc. Lond., 1760. 8vo. Eng. Polit. Pamph. Vol. 15.

—— (another) to Mr. Almon, in matter of Libel, with a Postscript, upon Contempt of Court and Attachment. Lond., 1770. Scarce Tracts. Vcl. 4.

—— (A Second) to a late Noble Commander of the British Forces in Germany. Lond., 1759. 8vo. Eng. Polit. Pamph. Vol. 14.

—— concerning Libels, Warrants, the Seizure of Papers, with a view to some late Proceedings, and a Defence of them by the Majority. Lond., 1764. Scarce Tracts. Vol. 1.

—— from a Gentleman in Scotland to his Friend in England, against the Sacramental Test. Lond., 1709. Sm. 4to. 3d Ed. Eng. Misc. Pamph. Vol. 1.

—— from a Jew to a Christian, occasioned by the Recent Attacks on the Bible. Lond., 1820. 8vo. Pamphleteer. Vol. 16.

—— from a Magistrate to Mr. Wm. Rose, of Whitehall, on Mr. Paine's Rights of Men. Lond., 1791. 8vo.

—— from a Manufacturer to his Son, upon Radical Reform. Lond., (n. d.) 8vo. Eng. Miscell. Pamph. Vol. 6.

—— from a Member of the House of Commons to a Chief Magistrate of a Borough, on the Votes of Oct. 16, 1749. Lond., 1749. 8vo. Eng. Polit. Pamph. Vol. 12.

—— from an Aged and Retired Citizen of Boston to a Member of Cong., on Coercive Measures in Aid of Temperance. Boston, 1848. 8vo. 2d Ed. Temp. Pamph. Vol. 3.

—— from an Officer on board the Royal George Man of War, containing an Account of the Battle between the English and French, Nov. 20, 1759. Lond., 1759. 8vo. Hist. Pamph. Vol. 6.

—— from an Officer Retired to his Son in Parl't, on Amer. Affairs. Lond., 1776. 8vo. Eng. Polit. Pamph. Vol. 18.

—— from "Candor" to the Public Advertiser. Lond., 1764. 8vo. Eng. Polit. Pamph. Vol. 15A.

—— from L—t G—l B—gh to the Se—y of S—te, with His M—y's Instructions for the late Expeditions on the Coast of France. Dublin, 1758. 8vo. Eng. Polit. Pamph. Vol. 14.

—— from the King to his People, 1820. Lond. n. d. 10th Ed. 8vo.

—— —— Second Letter from same, 1821. Lond., 1821. 8vo. Strangford Pamph. Vol. 4.

—— from the Missionaries at Constantinople, in Reply to Charges by Rev. Horatio Southgate. Boston, 1844. 8vo. Religious Pamph. Vol. 13.

LETTER of the Bishop of Orleans to the Clergy of his Diocese on Slavery. French. 1862. Rebell'n Pamph. Vol. 75.
— on American History. Phila., 1847. 8vo.
— on Currency Matters, to the People of the U. S. 1841. N. Y. 8vo. Cong. and Polit. Pamph: Vol. 98.
— on the Acquittal of Joseph Hickey, from the Charge of Perjury. Lond., 1751. 12mo. Eng. Polit. Pamph. Vol. 13.
— on the Administration of the Parliamentary Grant, for the Promotion of Education in G. B. Lond., 1864. 8vo. Eng. Polit. Pamph. Vol. 60.
— on the Public Conduct of Mr. John Wilkes. Lond., 1768. Scarce Tracts. Vol. 3.
— on the Rebellion, to a Citizen of Washington. Phila., 1862. Rebell'n Pamph. Vol. 15.
— on the Situation of France, written from Dresden to a Friend in Paris. Lond., 1815. 8vo. Pamphleteer. Vol. 6.
— on the Tone and Matter of Judge Fletcher's printed Charge. Lond., 1815. 8vo. Pamphleteer. Vol. 5.
— on the True Principles of Advantageous Exploration. Lond., 1818. 8vo. 2d Ed. Pamphleteer. Vol. 12.
— to a Bishop on the subject of Relief in the matter of Subscription. Lond., 1772. 12mo. Eng. Polit. Pamph. Vol. 17.
— to Jos. Hume, upon the late Debate on Portugal, in the British House of Commons. Lond., 1847. 8vo. Strangford Pamph. Vol. 44.
— to Earl Grey, on his Renunciation of the English Monarchy. Lond., 1832. 8vo. Strangford Pamph. Vol. 7.
— to Dr. Candlish, of Edinburgh, on the Jewish Sabbath and Sunday. Lond., 1847. 8vo. Religious Pamph. Vol. 11.
— to Lord Braxfield, on his promotion to be one of the Judges of the High Court of Justiciary. Edinburgh, 1780. 12mo. Law Pamph. Vol. 26.
— to Members of Parliament, on the Dissenters' Petitions, and on Church Grievances. Lond., 1834. 8vo. Strangford Pamph. Vol. 21.
— to the Duke of Wellington, on the State of the English Navy. Lond., 1840. 8vo. Strangford Pamph. Vol. 20.
— to the Electors from Westminster, from a Protectionist. London, 1848. 8vo. Strangford Pamph. Vol. 47.
— to the Lord Advocate on Scottish Reform Bill. Edinburgh, 1832. 8vo. Strangford Pamph. Vol. 8.
— to a Celebrated Young Nobleman on his late Nuptials. Lond., 1777. 4to. Eng. Misc. Pamph. Vol. 24A.
— to Admiral Sir Isaac Coffin, on the inadequacy of Courts Martial in their present form. Lond., 1819. 8vo. Pamphleteer. Vol. 14.
— to a Gentleman in the Country, from his Friend in London, giving an Acc. of the Death of Admiral Byng. Lond., 1757. 8vo. Eng. Polit. Pamph. Vol. 71.
— to Albert Gallatin on the Doctrine of Gold and Silver, and the Evils of the present Banking System. N. Y., 1815. 8vo. Congr. and Polit. Pamph. Vol. 98.

LETTER to a Member of Parliament on the Present State of Affairs. Lond., 1741. 8vo. Eng. Polit. Pamph. Vol. 11.

—— to a Member of Parliament, on the Importance of the Amer. Colonies, and making them useful to the Mother Country. Lond., 1757. 12mo.

—— to a Member of Parliament, on the proposed Register Bill. Lond., 1831. 8vo. Law Pamph. Vol. 12.

—— to a Member of Parliament, relative to the Case of Admiral Byng. Lond., 1756. 8vo. Eng. Polit. Pamph. Vol. 71.

—— to an English Friend on the Amer. War. N. Y., 1863. 8vo. Rebell'n Pamph. Vol. 22.

—— to a Noble Lord, on the Nature and Prospects of Political Party. Lond., 1858. 8vo. Eng. Polit. Pamph. Vol. 55.

—— to Chas. O'Conor.—The Destruction of the Union is Emancipation. Phila., 1862. Rebell'n Pamph. Vol. 17.

—— to Cottagers, from a Conservative Bee-Keeper. Oxford, 1838. 8vo. Agr. Pamph. Vol. 10.

—— to Dr. Sherlock, in Vindication of his "Case of Allegiance." Lond., 1691. Sm. 4to. Eng. Polit. Pamph. Vol. 64.

—— to Edmund Burke, in Reply to Insinuations in the 9th Report, affecting the Character of Warren Hastings. Lond., 1783. 8vo. Eng. Polit. Pamph. Vol. 20.

—— —— on his late Charges against the Gov.-General of Bengal. Lond., 1783. 8vo. Eng. Polit. Pamph. Vol. 21.

—— to Fred. J. Robinson, on the present Depressed State of Agriculture. Lond., 1821. 8vo. Pamphleteer. Vol. 18.

—— to Henry Brougham, on the Best Method of restoring decayed Grammar Schools. Lond., 1818. 8vo. Pamphleteer. Vol. 13.

—— to Hon. Reverdy Johnson, on the Proceeding at the Meeting at Maryland Institute, Jan. 10, 1861. Baltimore, 1861. 8vo. Rebell'n Pamph. Vol. 7.

—— to Hon. Robert Peel, upon Delays in the Court of Chancery. Lond., 1825. 8vo. Law Pamph. Vol. 12.

—— to Hon. S. A. Eliot, on the Fugitive Slave Bill. Boston, 1851. 8vo. Congr. and Polit. Pamphlets. Vol. 102.

—— to Hon. Wm. Pitt, on his Apostacy from the Cause of Parliamentary Reform. Lond., 1822. 8vo. 3d Ed. Pamphleteer. Vol. 21.

—— to John, Lord Eldon, on the Rumor of an intended Royal Divorce. Lond., 1816. 8vo. Eng. Polit. Pamph. Vol. 33.

—— to John Manners, Marquis of Granby. Lond., 1759. 8vo. Eng. Polit. Pamph. Vol. 70.

—— to Lord Byron, protesting against the Immolation of Gray, Cowper and Campbell, at the Shrine of Pope. Lond., 1821. 8vo. Pamphleteer. Vol. 18.

—— to Lord Howe on his Naval Conduct in the War. Amer. Tracts. 1776–1783.

—— to Lord Robert Bertie, relating to his Conduct in the Mediterranean, and his Defence of Admiral Byng. Lond., 1757. 8vo. Eng. Polit. Pamph. Vol. 71.

LETTER to Louis Kossuth, concerning Freedom and Slavery in the U. S. Boston, 1852. 8vo. Congr. and Polit. Pamph. Vol. 133.

—— to Members of Cong., on the Pay of Clerks in Gov't offices. 1851. Congr. Pamph. Vol. 50.

—— to Michael A. Taylor, on the Judges of the Court of Chancery. Lond., 1829. 8vo. Law Pamph. Vol. 16.

—— to Mr. Jas. Parkinson, in Answer to his Examination of Dr. Sherlock's "Case of Allegiance." Lond., 1691. Sm. 4to. Eng. Polit. Pamph. Vol. 64.

—— to Nathan'l Jefferys, on his Pamphlet entitled "A Review of the Conduct of the Prince of Wales." Lond., 1806. 8vo. Eng. Polit. Pamph. Vol. 27.

—— to Rev. Dr. Marsh, on the Intentions of the Dissenters, with Dr. Marsh's Reply to the same. Lond., 1813. 8vo. Pamphleteer. Vol. 6.

—— to Sam'l C. Cox, in regard to the Practice of the Court of Chancery. Lond., 1824. 8vo. Law Pamph. Vol. 12.

—— to Sam'l Johnson, LL. D. Lond., 1770. 8vo. Eng. Polit. Pamph. Vol. 72.

—— to Sir Chas. Forbes, on the Suppression of Public Discussion in India, etc. Lond., 1824. 8vo. Pamphleteer. Vol. 24.

—— to Sir Geo. Grey, on Medical Registration and Med. Corporations. Lond., 1852. 8vo. 2d Ed. Med. Pamph. Vol. 22.

—— to Sir George Saville Bart, on the Qualifications of the Earl of Shelburne as Prime Minister. n. d. Amer. Tracts. Vol. 5.

—— to Sir Robt. Ladbroke, in favor of the Confinement of Criminals in Separate Apartments. Lond., 1771. 8vo. Eng. Misc. Pamph. Vol. 26.

—— to Sir Wm. Scott, on the Abuse of Charities. Lond., 1818. 8vo. 4th Ed. Eng. Misc. Pamph. Vol. 27.

—— to the Author of the Bank of England Case, under Marsh & Co.'s Commission. Lond., 1825. 8vo. Eng. Misc. Pamph. Vol. 28.

—— to the Authors of the Answers of the "Case of Allegiance by Dr. Sherlock. Lond., 1691. Sm. 4to. Eng. Polit. Pamph. Vol. 64.

—— to the Citizens of London, on a Dissenter Serving the Office of Sheriff of the City. Lond., 1739. 8vo. Eng. Polit. Pamph. Vol. 11.

—— to the Committee of Ways and Means of House of Repr., on Tariff on Lumber. Washington, 1870. 8vo. Congr. and Polit. Pamph. Vol. 116.

—— to the Duke of Wellington, on creating Peers for Life. Lond. 1830. 8vo. Eng. Polit. Pamph. Vol. 77.

—— to the Earl of Buckinghamsire, on Open Trade to India. Lond., 1813. 8vo. Pamphleteer Vol. 1.

—— to the Editor of the Pamphleteer, on a Reform in Parliament. Lond., 1815. 8vo. Pamphleteer Vol. 6.

—— to the Editor of the Letters on "The Spirit of Patriotism," etc. Lond., 1749. 8vo. Eng. Miscell. Pamph. Vol. 24.

LETTER to the Electors of Westminster, from a Protectionist. Lond., 1848. 8vo. 2d Ed. Eng. Polit. Pamph. Vol. 47.

—— to the Electors of Westminster, from an Aristocrat. Lond., 1850. 8vo. Eng. Miscell. Pamph. Vol. 6.

—— to the Friends of Rev. F. T. Gray, and the Bulfinch St. Society. Boston, 1842. 8vo. Bost. Hist. Discourses Vol. 2.

—— to the Gov. of Mass., on his late Proclamation, of Aug. 20, 1861. Boston, 1861, 8vo. Mass. Miscell. Pamph. Vol. 4.

—— to the Governors of the Small-Pox Hospital, on the present state of that Charity. Lond., 1808. 8vo. Med. Pamph .Vol. 19.

—— to the Hon. Geo. Canning, Lond., 1818. 8vo. Eng. Polit. Pamph. Vol. 34.

—— to Hon. John Letcher, in relation to the Rock River Valley Union R. R. Co., and its application for a grant of the Public Lands. Milwaukee, 1854. 12mo.

—— to the House of Peers, on the Present Crisis. Lond., 1831. 8vo. Eng. Polit. Pamph. Vol. 38.

—— to the Lord Chancellor of the Chancery Bar. Lond., 1820. 8vo. Eng. Polit. Pamph. Vol. 35.

—— —— on the Mode of Swearing, by laying the hand upon and kissing the Gospels. Berwick. 12mo. n. d. Eng. Misc. Pamph. Vol. 6.

—— —— on the Present State of the Law of Lunacy. Lond. 1838. 8vo. Eng. Polit. Pamph. Vol. 42.

—— to the Officers of the British Navy. Lond., 1757. 8vo. Eng. Misc. Pamph. Vol. 25.

—— to the People of England on the Necessity of putting an immediate End to the War, etc. Lond., 1760. 12mo. Eng. Polit. Pamph. Vol. 15.

—— to the Real Freeholders of Scotland, upon the Bill for Regulating Qualifications. Edinburgh, 1775. 8vo. Eng. Polit. Pamph. Vol. 73.

—— to Rt. Hon. George Grenville, on the Publication of his Speech for Expelling Mr. Wilkes, 1769. Scarce Tracts. Vol. 3.

—— to the Rt. Hon. J—— P——, Speaker of the House of Commons in Ireland. 1767. 8vo. Eng. Polit. Pamph. Vol. 72.

—— to the Rt. Hon. Lord B——y, being an Inquiry into his Defence of Minorca. With an Answer to the same. Lond., 1757. 8vo. Eng. Polit. Pamph. Vol. 70.

—— to the Trustees of Columbia College, N. Y., 1856. 8vo. Columbia Coll. Pamph.

—— to Thos. Harley, on the printing of Newgate State Tracts. Lond., 1768. 4to. Eng. Polit. Pamph. Vol. 10.

—— to W. W. Pole, on the Disappearance of the Gold Coin, and the Resumption of Cash Payments. Lond., 1818. 8vo. Pamphleteer. Vol. 12.

—— vindicating the Proceedings of the last Session of Parliament; with the State of the Plot, etc., 1697.? Folio. Eng. Polit. Pamph. Vol. 1.

LETTERS addressed to Lord Grenville and Lord Howick, on their Removal from the Councils of the King, etc. Lond. 1807. 8vo. Eng. Polit. Pamph. Vol. 28.

LETTERS addressed to the Earl of Liverpool, and Hon. Nicholas Vansittart, on the Resumption of Cash Payments. Lond., 1820. 8vo. Pamphleteer. Vol. 16.

—— addressed to Thos. Jefferson, Esq., President of the U. S., concerning his Official Conduct and Principles, by Tacitus. Phila., 1802.

—— against the Extension of the Excise Laws. Lond., 1733. 12mo. Eng. Polit. Pamph. Vol. 11.

—— from a Farmer in Penn., to the Inhabitants of the British Colonies. Boston, 1768. 8vo.

—— from Distinguished Citizens of Tenn., on the Buying and Selling of Human Beings. N. Y., 1828. 8vo. Congr. and Polit. Pamph. Vol. 111.

—— from Europe, touching the Amer. Contest. N. Y., 1864. 8vo. Rebell'n Pamph. Vol. 3.

—— from the Farmer, to the Free-Men of Dublin, 1794. 9 Papers. Dublin, 1749. 8vo· Eng. Polit. Pamph. Vol. 12.

—— from the Slave States. See STIRLING, Jas.

—— Intercepted on board the Admiral Alpin, captured by the French, and inserted in the Moniteur, etc., 1804. Lond. 8vo. Eng. Polit. Pamph. Vol. 27.

—— of Hon. Jos. Holt, Hon. Edw'd Everett and Comm. Chas. Stewart, on the Rebellion, 1861. Rebell'n Pamph. Vol. 99.

—— of Loyal Soldiers upon McClellan and the Chicago Platform. 1864. Rebell'n Pamph. Vol. 46.

—— of the British Spy. See WIRT, W.

—— of Vetus, published in the London Times, 1812–14. Lond., 1812–14. 8vo.

—— of Wyoming, on the Presidential Election, in favor of Andrew Jackson. Phila., 1824. 8vo. Congr. and Polit. Pamph. Vol. 111.

—— on Chivalry and Romance. Lond., 1762. 12mo.

—— on Indian Antiquities. Western Review. Vols. 1, 2.

—— on Monetary Science. Revised and Reprinted from Douglas Jerrold's Weekly Paper. Lond., 1848. 8vo. 2d Ed. Scientific Pamph. Vol. 34.

—— on Public House Licensing. Lond., 1816. 8vo. Pamphleteer. Vol. 7.

—— on the Chickasaw and Osage Missions. Boston, 1831. 18mo.

—— on the French Nation: by a Sicilian Gentleman. Translated. Lond., 1749. 8vo. Eng. Polit. Pamph. Vol. 12.

—— on the Necessity of Cheapening Transport between the West and the Ocean. Milwaukee, 1868. 8vo. Congr. and Polit. Pamph. Vol. 137.

—— on the New System of East India Shipping, etc. Lond., 1803. 8vo. Vol. 27.

—— (Original,) to an Honest Sailor. Lond., n. d. 8vo. Eng. Mis. Pamph. Vol. 24.

—— relating to the Suppression of Monasteries. See Camden Soc. Publica.

—— to a Nobleman on the Conduct of the War, 1779. See Amer. Tracts, 1776–1783.

LETTERS to Edmund Burke, on Evidence relating to East India Affairs. Lond., 1782. 8vo. 2 Papers. Eng. Polit. Pamph. Vol. 19.

—— to Ladies, on the formation of a Martha Washington Soc'y. N. Y., 1860. 8vo. Congr. and Polit. Pamph. Vol. 80.

—— to the English Public on the Condition, Abuses, etc., of the National Universities. Lond., 1836. 8vo. Educa. Pamph. Vols. 28, 40.

—— to the Prince of Wales, on an Application to Parliam't to Discharge Certain Debts. Lond., 1795. 12mo. 4th Ed. Eng. Polit. Pamph. Vol. 25.

—— to the Right Hon. Earl of B. 2 Papers. Lond., 1761, '62. 8vo. Eng. Polit. Pamph. Vol. 15.

—— written in London by an American Spy from 1764 to 1785. Lond., 1786. 8vo.

LETTRE a La Majeste l'Empereur Napoleon III, sur l'influence Francaise en Amerique. Paris, 1858. 8vo. Rebell'n Pamph. Vol. 52.

LETTRES Edifiantes et curieux ecrites des Missions Etrangeres, par quelque Missionaries de la Compagnie de Jesus. Paris, 1717–49. 27 Vols. 18mo.

—— Same. Toulouse, 1810, '11. 26 Vols. 18mo.

LETTSOM, Dr. John C. Reflections on the General Treatment and Cure of Fevers. Lond., 1772. 8vo. Med. Pamph. Vol. 25.

LEVANT Company, [of England.] Account of. Lond., 1825. 8vo. By-Laws. Lond., 1819. 8vo. Strangford Pamph. Vol. 1.

LEVERETT, Mass. See North Leverett.

LEVERETT Papers. See Mass. Hist. Soc. Coll., 4th Ser., Vol. 2.

LEVERING Genealogy. See JONES, H. G.

LEVERSON, M. Richard. On the Uses and Functions of Money. N. Y., 1868. 8vo. Banking and Currency Pamph., Vol. 4.

LEVETT, Christopher. Voyage to New England, 1623–4. Mass. Hist. Soc. Coll., 3d Ser., Vol. 8. Maine Hist. Soc. Coll., Vol. 2.

LEVI, David. Letters to Dr. Priestley, in Answer to his Letters to the Jews. Lond., 1789. 8vo. Miscell. Tracts., Vol. 2.

LEVIATHAN, Missouri. See Missourium.

LEVIN, Lewis C. Speech in Cong., Apr. 7, 1846, on the Bill to raise a Regiment of Mounted Riflemen. Washington, 1846. 8vo. Speeches, Vol. 1.

LEVINS, Peter. Manipulus Vocabulorum of the Eng. Language, 1570, with an Alphabetical Index by H. B. Wheatley. Pub. by Philolog. Soc. Lond., 1867. 4to.

LEVY, David. Speech in Cong., June 12, 1842, on the Army Appropriation Bill. Washington, 1842. 8vo. Cong. and Polit. Pamph. Vol. 25.

LEWES, Eng. See LOWER, M. A. Hand Book, 1852.

LEWES, Geo. H., Biograph. Hist. of Philosophy, from its origin in Greece to the present day. N. Y., 1857. 2 Vols. 8vo.

—— Life of Maximilian Robespierre, with extracts from his unpublished correspondence. Phila., 1849. 12mo.

LEWES, Geo. H. The Physiology of Common Life. Lond. 8vo. n. d. Scientific Pamph., Vol. 25.

LEWIN, Malcom. Has Oude been worse Governed by its Native Princes than our Indian Territories by Leadenhall Street? Lond., 1857. 8vo. 2d Ed. Eng. Polit. Pamph., Vol. 54.

LEWIS, Alonzo. See GOODELL, A. C. Notice of.

—— and NEWHALL, J. R. History of Lynn, including Lynnfield, Saugus, Swampscott and Nahant. Boston, 1865. 8vo.

LEWIS, C. F. Address before the Fire Lands Hist. Soc., June 12, 1861. Fire Lands Pioneer, Vol. 2.

LEWIS Co., N. Y. See HOUGH, F. B. Hist. of.

—— Proceedings of Board of Supervisors, 1863. Lowville. 8vo.

—— See STEPHENS, W. H. Hist. Notes of Settlement of No. 4, etc.

LEWIS, Dixon H. Speech in Cong., July 13, 1846, on the Tariff. Washington, 1846. 8vo. Speeches. Vol. 1.

LEWIS, Enoch. Observations on Legal and Judicial Oaths. Phila., 1846. 8vo. Law Pamph. Vol. 5.

LEWIS, J. W. Life, Labors and Travels of Elder Chas. Bowles. Watertown, N. Y., 1852. 12mo.

LEWIS, Matt. G. Journal of a West India Proprietor, kept during a Residence in Jamaica. 1815--17. Waldie's Circulating Libr. Vol. 3.

LEWIS, Capts. Meriwether, and CLARKE, Wm. Hist. of the Expedition to the Sources of the Missouri, across the Rocky Mountains to the Pacific Ocean, performed, 1804–6. Phila., 1814. 2 Vols. 8vo.

—— Same. Dublin, 1817. 2 Vols. 8vo.

—— Same, abridged. Harpers' Fam. Libr. 1852. 2 Vols. 12mo.

—— Same. Lond., 1807. 8vo.

LEWIS, Sam'l. Topographical Dictionary of Wales. Lond., 1833. 2 Vols. 4to.

—— Topographical Dictionary of England. Lond., 1831. 5 Vols. 4to.

LEWIS, Sam'l B. Reminiscences concerning the Early Hist. of Norwalk, O. Fire Lands Pioneer. Vol. 1.

LEWIS, Tayler. State Rights: a Photograph from the Ruins of Ancient Greece. Albany, 1864. 12mo. Rebell'n Pamph. Vol. 24.

LEWIS, W. G. Catechism of Entomology; or the Nat. Hist. of Insects. Lond., 1825. 12mo. Scientific Pamph. Vol. 26.

LEWIS, Wm. H., D.D. Position of the P. Episcopal Church, with reference to other Protestant Denominations. N. Y., 1853. 12mo. Religious Pamph. Vol. 3.

LEWIS, Dr. Winslow. Address before the N. Eng. Hist. Genealog. Soc., Jan., 1, 1862. Boston. 8vo. Addresses. Vol. 9.

—— Ann. Addresses before the New Eng. Historic-Genealogical Soc., Jan. 7, 1863, Jan. 6, 1864. Boston, 1863--4. 8vo.

LEXINGTON, Battle of. See Narrative of the Excursion and Ravages of the King's Troops under Gen̄. Gage, etc.

LEXINGTON, Ky. See PETER, R. Sketch of Hist. of. 1854.

—— RAUCK, G. W. Hist. of. 1872.

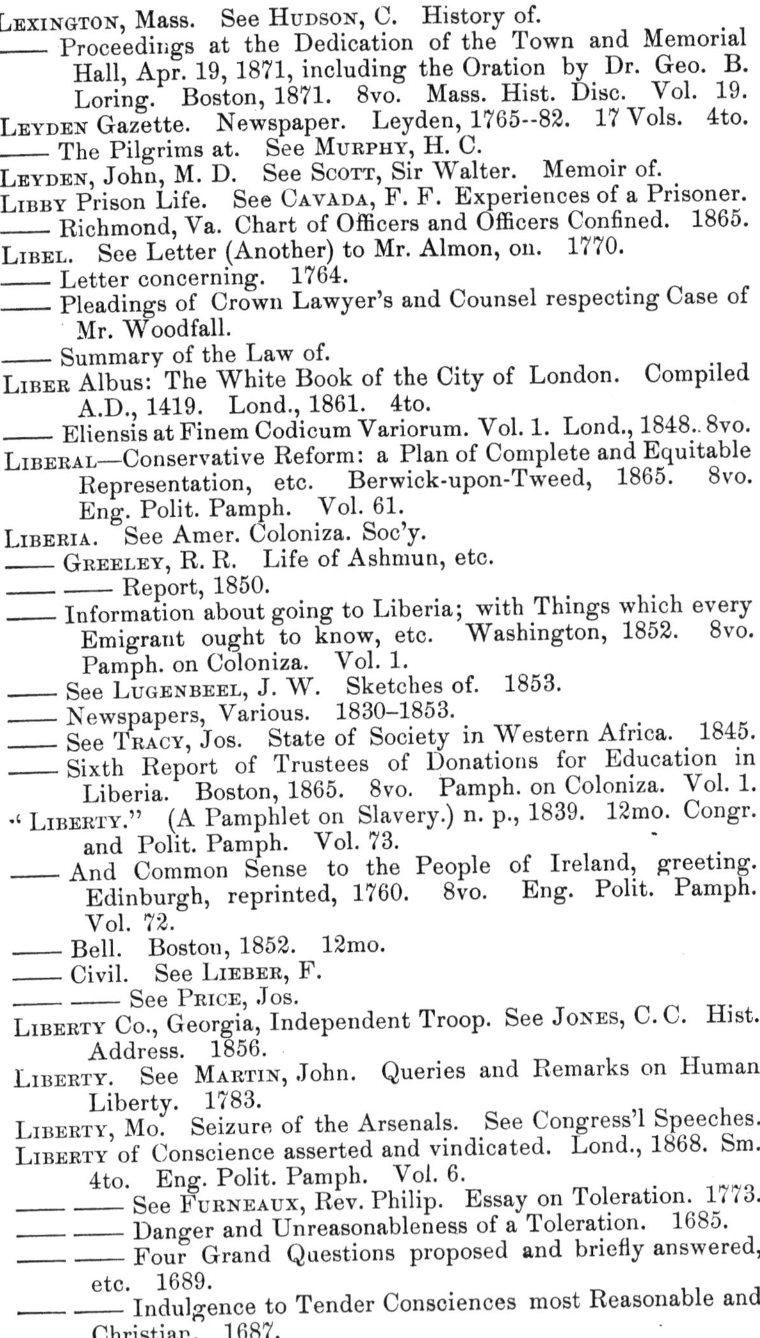

LEXINGTON, Mass. See HUDSON, C. History of.
—— Proceedings at the Dedication of the Town and Memorial Hall, Apr. 19, 1871, including the Oration by Dr. Geo. B. Loring. Boston, 1871. 8vo. Mass. Hist. Disc. Vol. 19.
LEYDEN Gazette. Newspaper. Leyden, 1765--82. 17 Vols. 4to.
—— The Pilgrims at. See MURPHY, H. C.
LEYDEN, John, M. D. See SCOTT, Sir Walter. Memoir of.
LIBBY Prison Life. See CAVADA, F. F. Experiences of a Prisoner.
—— Richmond, Va. Chart of Officers and Officers Confined. 1865.
LIBEL. See Letter (Another) to Mr. Almon, on. 1770.
—— Letter concerning. 1764.
—— Pleadings of Crown Lawyer's and Counsel respecting Case of Mr. Woodfall.
—— Summary of the Law of.
LIBER Albus: The White Book of the City of London. Compiled A.D., 1419. Lond., 1861. 4to.
—— Eliensis at Finem Codicum Variorum. Vol. 1. Lond., 1848. 8vo.
LIBERAL—Conservative Reform: a Plan of Complete and Equitable Representation, etc. Berwick-upon-Tweed, 1865. 8vo. Eng. Polit. Pamph. Vol. 61.
LIBERIA. See Amer. Coloniza. Soc'y.
—— GREELEY, R. R. Life of Ashmun, etc.
—— —— Report, 1850.
—— Information about going to Liberia; with Things which every Emigrant ought to know, etc. Washington, 1852. 8vo. Pamph. on Coloniza. Vol. 1.
—— See LUGENBEEL, J. W. Sketches of. 1853.
—— Newspapers, Various. 1830–1853.
—— See TRACY, Jos. State of Society in Western Africa. 1845.
—— Sixth Report of Trustees of Donations for Education in Liberia. Boston, 1865. 8vo. Pamph. on Coloniza. Vol. 1.
"LIBERTY." (A Pamphlet on Slavery.) n. p., 1839. 12mo. Congr. and Polit. Pamph. Vol. 73.
—— And Common Sense to the People of Ireland, greeting. Edinburgh, reprinted, 1760. 8vo. Eng. Polit. Pamph. Vol. 72.
—— Bell. Boston, 1852. 12mo.
—— Civil. See LIEBER, F.
—— —— See PRICE, Jos.
LIBERTY Co., Georgia, Independent Troop. See JONES, C. C. Hist. Address. 1856.
LIBERTY. See MARTIN, John. Queries and Remarks on Human Liberty. 1783.
LIBERTY, Mo. Seizure of the Arsenals. See Congress'l Speeches.
LIBERTY of Conscience asserted and vindicated. Lond., 1868. Sm. 4to. Eng. Polit. Pamph. Vol. 6.
—— —— See FURNEAUX, Rev. Philip. Essay on Toleration. 1773.
—— —— Danger and Unreasonableness of a Toleration. 1685.
—— —— Four Grand Questions proposed and briefly answered, etc. 1689.
—— —— Indulgence to Tender Consciences most Reasonable and Christian. 1687.

LIBERTY of Conscience. See MILTON, John. Unlawfulness of Compulsion.
—— —— WILD, Rob't. Letter on His Majesty's Declaration. 1672.
—— of the Press. DE CONSTANT, B. H. 1815.
—— —— ERSKINE, Thos. Speech. 1792.
—— —— HALL, Rev. Rob't. Apology for, etc.
—— —— See LIBELS.
—— —— MARBLE, M. Letter to Pres't Lincoln. 1864.
—— —— SLACK, H. J. Defence of Free Press of Eng. 1858.
—— —— VON GENTZ, F. Reflections on, in G. Britain. 1820.
LIBRARIAN of Congress. Ann, Reports for 1867, 68, 71, 72. Special Report on the Library of Peter Force, 1867. Washington, 1867–72. 8vo.
LIBRARIES. See Catalogues of Public Libraries.
—— DE PEYSTER, F. Influence of.
—— FARNHAM, Luther. Glance at Private Libraries. 1855.
—— JEWETT, C. C. Pub. Libraries of U. S.
—— RANDALL, H. S. Report on School Libraries.
—— RHEES, W. J. Manual of Public Libraries.
LIBRARY of Congress. Catalogue. Washington, 1815. 4to.
—— —— Same to June, 1849. 8vo.
—— —— Same to Nov. 1857. 8vo.
—— —— Alphabetical Catalogue. Authors, Washington, 1864. 8vo.
—— —— Catalogue of Additions. Dec. 1, 1864 to Dec. 1, 1865. Washington, 1866. 8vo.
—— —— Catalogue of Books added from December 1, 1866 to Dec. 1, 1870. Washington, 1871. 8vo. 4 Vols.
—— —— Catalogue of Books added for 1871. Washington, 1872. 8vo.
LIBRARY (The). A Poem. Lond., 1781. 4to. Poetry. Vol. 23.
LICKING Co., Ohio, Pioneers. Celebration at Clay Lick., July 4, 1869; with an Address by Dr. COULTER, and Hist. Sketches of Licking, Bowling Green, Franklin, Hopewell, &c, by Isaac SMACKER. Newark, 1869. 8vo.
—— —— See HERVEY, H. M.
—— —— PARK, Sam'l.
—— —— SCOTT, J. M.
—— —— WINTER, J.
—— —— SMUCKER, Isaac.
LIDDELL, Henry G. Life of Julius Cæsar. N. Y., 1860. 18mo.
LIEBER, Francis. Amendments to the Constitution submitted to the Consideration of the Amer. People. N. Y., 1865. 8vo. Rebell'n Pamph. Vol. 6.
—— Essays on Property and Labor. Harpers' Fam. Libr. N. Y., 1859. 18mo.
—— Instructions for the Government of Armies of the U. S. in the Field. N. Y., 1863. 12mo. Rebell'n. Pamph. Vol. 11.
—— Lincoln or McClellan; an appeal to Germans in America. Same in German and Dutch. Rebelln. Pamph. Vol 96.
—— Memorial to Cong. in relation to Proposals for a Work on the Statistics of the U. S. 1836. 8vo. Congr. & Polit. Pamph. Vol 124.

LIEBER, Francis. No Party Now, but all for Our Country. N. Y., 1863. 8vo. Rebelln. Pamph. Vols. 45, 90, 91.

—— Notes on the Fallacies of American Protectionists. N. Y., 1870. 12mo. Congr. & Polit. Pamph. Vol. 73.

—— On Civil Liberty and Self Government. Phila., 1853. 2 Vols. 12mo.

—— On Guerrilla Parties considered with reference to the Usages of War. N. Y., 1862. 8vo. Rebelln. Pamph. Vol. 100.

—— On International Copyright. N. Y., 1840. 8vo. Pamph.

—— On the Vocal Sounds of Laura Bridgman; compared with the Elements of Phonetic Language. Smithson. Contrib. Vol. 2.

—— Plantations for Slave Labor the Death of the Yeomanry. Rebelln. Pamph. Vol. 74.

—— Remarks on the Relation between Education and Crime. Phila. 1835. 8vo. Educa. Pamph. Vol. 3.

—— Slavery Plantations and the Yeomanry. N. Y., 1863. 8vo. Rebell. Pamph. Vols. 45, 90.

—— The Arguments of Secessionists. 1863. Rebelln. Pamph. Vols. 17, 90.

—— Two Lectures on the Constitution of the U. S., with an Address on Secession, written in 1851. N. Y., 1861. 8vo. Rebelln. Pamph. Vol. 27.

LIEBER, Oscar M. Vocabulary of the Catawaba Language, with Remarks on its Grammar, etc. S. C. Hist. Coll. Vol. 2.

LIEBIG, Dr. Justus. Annals of Pharmacy and Practical Chemistry. n. d. 8vo. Med. Pamph. Vol. 19.

—— Chemistry in its Application to Agriculture and Physiology. Phila. 1843. 8vo. Agr. Pamph. Vol 1.

—— & KOPP, H. Annual Reports of the Progress of Chemistry and Allied Sciences, Physics, Mineralogy and Geology. 1847–50. London, 1849–53. 4 Vols. 8vo.

LIFE and Liberty in America. See MACKAY, Chas.

—— Illustrated. Newspaper. Oct., 1857, to Oct., 1858. Oct., 1858, to Oct., 1859. N. Y. 2 Vols. 4to.

—— In India; or Madras, the Neilgherries and Calcutta. Phila., 1855. 18mo.

—— In the South from the Commencement of the War: by a Blockaded British Subject. Lond., 1863. 2 Vols. 8vo.

—— In the Union Army: by a Two Year's Volunteer in the 15th N. Y. Vol. Regt. 1864. Rebell'n Phamph. Vol. 81.

—— Insurance. See Insurance.

—— Of a Political Trickster; or the Duplicity and Treachery of J——, A. N——, of Milwaukee exposed. Milwaukee, 1857, 8vo.

—— Of Gen. Jacob Brown, with Short Memoirs of Generals Ripley and Pike. N. Y. 18mo.

LIGHT (The) and Dark of the Rebellion. Phila., 1863. 12mo.

LIGHTHOUSE Board. List of Lighthouses, Lighted Beacons and Floating Lights of the U. S., (with Coast Survey Reports.) Washington, 1849 and 1858. 8vo.

—— System in England. See REDMAN, J. B. Remarks on. 1843.

LIGHTHOUSES. See REDMAN, J. B. System of G. Britain. 1843.
—— See U. S. Sec. of Treasury—Reports of Supt. of Coast Survey.
LIGHTNING. See BROOKS, D. Facts relating to, etc.
LIGHTON, Wm. B. Autobiog. and Reminiscences of. New and Revised Edition. Albany, 1854. 8vo.
LIGON, T. W. Speech in Cong., Feb. 8, 1848, on the Public Debt. Congr. and Polit. Pamph. Vol. 90.
LIGONIER, J., and others. Report on the Conduct of Maj. Gen. Stuart, and Col. Cornwallis and Earl of Effingham. Lond., 1757. 8vo. Eng. Polit. Pamph. Vol. 70.
LIMERICK, Maine. See FREEMAN, C. Account of.
LINCOLN, Abraham. 1864. Rebell'n Pamph. Vol. 52.
—— See ABBOTT, A. N. Assassination of.
—— Address before Wis. State Agricult. Soc., Sept., 1859. Transactions. 1859.
—— See ARNOLD, I. N. Hist. of, etc.
—— BANCROFT, Geo. Memorial Address.
—— BARRETT, J. H. Life, Messages, etc., of.
—— BROCKETT, L. P. Life and Times.
—— CARPENTER, F. B. Six Months at the White House.
—— Character of, etc.
—— COGGESHALL, Wm. T. Lincoln Memorial. 1865.
—— Colored People's National Lincoln Monument Assoc.
—— CROSBY, F. Life of. 1865.
—— GREENE, C. S. Death of, etc.
—— HARDINGE, Emma. Funeral Oration on.
—— His Opinions upon Slavery and its Issues. Washington. n. d. 8vo. Congr. and Polit. Pamph. Vol. 136.
—— See HOLLAND, J. G. Life of.
—— HUDSON, C. Character of.
—— Letters on Questions of National Policy. 1863. Rebellion Pamph. Vols. 4 and 96.
—— Letter to Erastus Corning and others on the Vallandigham Habeas Corpus Case. 1863. Rebell'n Pamph. Vol. 91.
—— Life of. Tribune Tracts No. 6. N. Y. n. d. Rebell'n Pamph. Vol. 77.
—— Message to Cong., Dec. 3, 1861. Rebell'n Pamph. Vol. 53.
—— See N. York City Athenæum Club. Proceedings on Death of.
—— N. Y. City Obsequies, etc.
—— On Vallandigham and "Arbitrary Arrests." 1863. Rebell'n Pamph., Vol. 53.
—— Opinions on Slavery and its Issues. n. d. Rebell'n Pamph., Vol. 46.
—— See Pittman's Acc. of Assassination.
—— Polit. Debates with Hon. S. A. Douglas. 1858.
—— POORE, B. P. The Conspiracy Trial for the Murder of the President.
—— Proceedings of Clergy of Dist. of Columbia on his Death. Apr. 17, 1865. Washington, 1865. 8vo. Rebell'n Pamph. Vol. 111.
—— See SHEA, J. G. Lincoln Memorial. 1865.

LINCOLN, Abraham. Speech at Cooper Institute, Feb. 27, 1860. Rebell'n Pamph., Vol. 77.

—— Speech at Repub. State Convention, June 16, 1858. Rebell'n Pamph., Vol. 77.

—— The Assassination of, and the attempted Assassination of Wm. H. Seward, Sec. of State ; F. W. Seward, ass't Sec., on the 14th of April, 1865. Expressions of Condolence and Sympathy, etc. Washington, 1867. 4to.

—— See TOWNSEND, G. A. Life, Capture, etc., of J. Wilkes Booth.

—— Treatment of Gen. U. S. Grant and Gen. Geo. B. McClellan. A Dem. Campaign Doc. Rebell'n Pamph., Vol. 22.

—— Trial of, by the Great Statesmen of the Republic. 1863. Rebell'n Pamph., Vol. 89.

—— and Grant, U. S. Views on Peace and War. 1864. Rebell'n Pamph., Vol. 15.

—— and Johnson Ratification Meeting at Washington, D. C., June 15, 1864, with Speeches of Hon. J. M. Edmunds, Hon. W. D. Kelley and others. Rebell'n Pamph., Vol. 31.

LINCOLN'S, Mr., Arbitrary Arrests. Rebell'n Pamph., Vol. 18.

LINCOLN, Gen. Benj. See BOWEN, F. Life of.

—— Journal of a Treaty held 1793, with the Indian Tribes N. W. of the Ohio, by Commissioners of the U. S. Mass. Hist. Soc. Coll. Vol. 5. 3d Ser.

—— Notices of the Life of. Mass. Hist. Soc. Coll. 2d Ser. Vol. 3.

—— Observations on the Climate, Soil and Value of the Eastern Counties in the District of Maine, in 1789. Mass. Hist. Soc. Coll. 1st Ser. Vol. 4.

LINCOLN (The) Catechism, 1863. Same in German. Rebell'n Pamph. Vol. 97.

LINCOLN, Eng. Cathedral. See WINSTON, C.

LINCOLN Genealogy. See LINCOLN, S.

LINCOLN, Hosea H. Address before the Amer. Institute of Instruction, Aug. 31, 1867. Boston, 1867. 12mo. Educa. Pamph. Vol. 6.

LINCOLN, John L. 50th Annivers. Address before the 1st Bapt. Sunday School, Providence, May 30, 1869. Providence, 1869. 12mo.

LINCOLN, Gov. Levi. Memorial of. Boston, 1868. 8vo.

—— Remarks on the Indian Languages, and Acc. of the Catholic Missions in Maine. Me. Hist. Soc. Coll. Vol. 1.

—— See WASHBURN, E. Memoir of.

LINCOLN, Mass. See SHATTUCK, E. History of Concord, etc.

LINCOLN, Robt. W. Lives of the Presidents of the U. S., and of Signers of Declaration of Independence. N. Y., 1835. 8vo.

LINCOLN, Solomon. Notes on the Lincoln Families of Mass. Boston., 1865. 8vo. Genealog. Pamph. Vols. 3 and 7.

LINCOLN, Wm. Address before the Amer. Antiq. Soc., Oct. 23, 1835, on the Death of C. C. Baldwin. Worcester, 1835. 8vo. Proceedings, 1813–55.

—— Hist. of Worcester, Mass., to Sept. 1836. Worcester, 1837. 8vo.

—— Same, Worcester, 1862. 8vo.

LINCOLN, Wm. See WILLARD, Jos. Memoir of.

LINCOLNIANA; In Memoriam. pr. printed. Boston, 1865. 4to.

—— Or the Humors of Uncle Abe. N. Y., 1864. 12mo. Rebell'n Pamph, Vol. 47.

LINCOLNSHIRE, Eng. General View of the Agriculture of. 2d Ed. Lond., 1813. 8vo.

LINDLEY, Prof. John. Introductory Lecture before the University of Lond., April 30, 1829. 8vo. Educa. Pamph. Vol. 35.

LINDSAY, H. H. Letter to Lord Palmerston on British Relations with China. Lond., 1836. 8vo. 3d Ed. Strangford Pamph. Vol. 24.

LINDSAY, Lord. Travels in Egypt, Syria, etc., in 1836–7. Waldies Circulating Libr. Vol. 13.

LINDSAY, W. S. Letters on the Navigation Laws. Lond., 1849. 8vo. Strangford Pamph. Vol. 49.

LINSLEY, Chas. See PHELPS, E. J. Life and Character of.

LINGARD, John, D. D.History of England from the First Invasion by the Romans to the Accession of William and Mary in 1688. 6th revised Ed. Lond., 1855. 10 Vols. 12mo.

LINGARD, John. Philosophic and Practical Inquiry into the Nature and Constitution of Timber. Lond., 1820. 8vo. Pamphleteer. Vol. 16. See also Agr. Pamph. Vol. 9.

—— Reply to Observations of the Edinburgh Review, on Anglo Saxon Antiquities. Lond., 1816. 8vo. Pamphleteer. Vol. 7.

LINN, Arch'd L. Speech in Cong., Apr. 13, 1842, on the Annexation of Texas. Washington, 1842. 8vo. Congr. and Polit. Pamph. Vol. 24.

LINN, E. A. and SARGENT, N. Life and Public Services of Dr. Lewis F. Linn, for Ten Years U. S. Senator from Missouri. N. Y. 1857. 8vo.

LINN, L. F. Speech in U. S. Senate, Jan. 1841, on the prospective Pre-emption Bill. Congr. and Polit. Pamph. Vol. 84.

—— —— Aug. 11, 1841, on National Defences. Washington, 1842. 8vo. Congr. and Polit. Pamph. Vol. 25.

—— —— May 14, 1842, on the Bill to indemnify Gen. Jackson. Washington, 1842. 8vo. Congr. and Polit. Pamph. Vol. 25.

LINNAEUS, M. Natural History, in Dutch. Amsterdam, 1761–83. 37 Vols. 8vo.

LINTNER, G. A., D. D. Early History of the Lutheran Church in the State of N. Y. Albany, 1867. 8vo. N. Y. Hist. Discourses, Vol. 4.

LIPPINCOTT, J. B. & Co. Complete Pronouncing Gazetteer, or Geograph. Dictionary of the World. Phila., 1858. 8vo.

LIPSCOMBE, Dr. Geo. History and Antiquities of the Co. of Buckingham; maps and plates. Lond., 1847. 4 Vols. 4to.

LISBON, Spain. See COLTON, Rev. W. Ship and Shore: Visits to, etc.

LISBON, Conn. See NELSON, Rev. Levi. Half Century Sermon. 1854.

LISLE, SEMPLE, J. G. Life of. A Narrative of his alternate vicissitudes of splendor and misfortune. 2d Ed. Lond., 1800. 8vo.

LIST of Money Order Offices of the U. States, July 31, 1871. n. p. n. d. 8vo. Congr. and Polit. Pamph. Vol. 127.

—— Persons residents of the State of Wisconsin, reported as Deserters from the Military and Naval Service of the U. S. Madison, 1868. 8vo. Rebell'n Pamph. Vol. 112.

—— Publications of Learned Societies: France, Italy, Spain, G. Britain and Ireland. Smithson. Contrib. Vol. 8.

LITCHFIELD, Conn. See JONES, Rev. Isaac. Centen. Sermon, 1845.

—— KILBOURNE, P. K. Biograph. Hist.

—— —— Sketches and Chronicles of.

—— See WOODRUFF, Geo. C. Hist. of. 1845.

LITCHFIELD County, Conn., Centen. Celebration, held at Litchfield, Aug. 13 and 14, 1851. Hartford, 1851. 8vo.

—— North and South Consociations. Centen. Annivers. Proceedings, July 7 and 8, 1852. Hartford, 1852. 8vo. Conn. Hist. Discourses, etc. Vol. 6.

—— North Assoc. and Consociation. Hist. Sketch; Statistics and Rules. Hartford, 1852. 8vo. Conn. Hist. Discourses, etc. Vol. 6.

—— See KILBOURNE, P. K. Biogr. History of.

LITERARY Garland. Vols. 1 and 2. N. Y., 1838–40. 2 Vols. 8vo.

—— History of the 18th Century: consisting of Authentic Memoirs and Letters of Eminent Persons. Lond., 1817. 8 Vols. 8vo.

—— Magazine and British Review. Lond., 1788–1794. 12 Vols. 8vo.

LITERATURE, English. See CHAMBERS, R. Cyclopedia of.

—— —— CLEVELAND. C. Cyclopedias.

—— —— CRAIK, Geo. L. History of.

—— —— JONES, W. A. Essays upon Authors and Books.

—— —— SHAW, T. B. Manual of.

—— (The) of American Numismatics; Paper before Amer. Numismatic Soc. Nov., 1859. Norton's Literary Letter No. 3, 1859.

LITHGOW Family. See HILL, M. L.

LITTELL, E. Living Age. Magazine. April, 1844, to June 30, 1873. Boston. 116 Vols. 8vo.

—— The Museum of Foreign Literature and Science. July, 1822, to Dec., 1842. Phil'a, 45 Vols. 8vo.

LITTELL, John. Family Records; or Genealogy of the First Settlers of Passaic Valley. Feltville, N. J. 8vo. 1857.

LITTELL, J. S. See GRAYDON, Alex., Memoirs.

LITTLE, Rev. Jacob. Twenty-seventh New Year's Sermon preached in the Cong. Ch.. Granville, Ohio, 1854. Granville, 1854. 8vo. Ohio Hist. Discourses. Vol. 2.

LITTLE Osage Captive an Authentic Narrative. York, Eng. 1824. 18mo.

LITTLE ROCK, Ark. See HENRY, J. P. Arkansas & Little Rock. 1872.

LITTLE, Wm. Hist. of Warren, N. H. A Mountain Hamlet among the White Hills of N. H. Manchester, 1870. 8vo.

LIVERMORE, A. A. The War with Mexico Reviewed. Boston, 1850. 12mo.

LIVERMORE, Geo. See DEANE, Chas. Memoir of.

LIVERMORE, Geo. Hist. Research on the Opinions of the Founders of the Republic on Slavery. Mass. Hist. Soc. Proceed. 1862–63. Supplementary Note & Index to same. Boston, 1863. 8vo. Mass. Miscell. Pamph. Vol. 5.

LIVERPOOL, Eng. See BROOKE, R. History, 1775–1800.

—— Health of Towns' Advocate. Part 1. Lond., 1846. 8vo. Sanitary Reform Pamph. Vol. 1.

—— Map of the City and Vicinity. n. d.

—— Royal Institution. See ROSCOE, Wm. Disc. at the Opening of, 1817.

—— East Indian Assoc. Report of Committee of, on the Trade with India. Liverpool, 1828. 8vo. Strangford Pamph. Vol. 6.

LIVERMAN'S (A.) Reply to Sir Crisp Gascoigne's Address. (Case of E. Canning). Lond., 1754. 8vo. Eng. Misc. Pamph. Vol. 25.

LIVES and Voyages of Drake, Cavendish and Dampier, with a view of Earlier Discoveries in the South Seas. Harpers' Fam. Libr. N. Y., 1858. 2 Vols. 18mo.

—— of Atrocious Judges. See HILDRETH, R.

—— of Sir Walter Raleigh and Capt. John Smith, with Acc. of the Governors of Virginia, to 1781, Shepherds-Town, Va. 1817. 12mo. Biograph. Pamph. Vol. 5.

—— of the Presidents. See LOSSING, B. J.

LIVINGSTON, Rev. Dr. David. Outlines of his Missionary Journeys and Discoveries in Central South Africa. With a Map. London, 1857. 8vo. Eng. Misc. Pamph. Vol. 9.

LIVINGSTON, Edw. See HUNT, C. H. Life of.

—— Report to the Gen. Assembly of Louisiana on a Penal Code for the State. N. Orleans, 1822. 8vo. La. Pub. Docs.

LIVINGSTON, John. Law Register of U. S. N. Y., 1853. 8vo. Another Copy, Law Pamph. Vol. 7.

LIVINGSTON Manor. N. Y. Papers relating to. 1680–1795. Doc. Hist. of N. Y. Vol. 3.

LIVINGSTON, Warren. See DOANE, B'p Geo. W. Baccalaureate Address, etc. 1857.

LIVINGSTON, Wm. See SEDGWICK, Theo.

LIVING (The) World. See ARNOLD & SAMUELS.

LIVY. See FOLSOM, C. Titi Livii.

LLOYD, Chas. An Honest Man's Reasons for declining to take part in the New Administration. Lond., 1765. Also, a Candid Answer to the same ascribed to Sir Grey Cooper Bart. Scarce Tracts. Vol. 2.

—— A True History of a Late Short Administration. 1765. Scarce Tracts. Vol. 2.

—— Defence of the Majority in the House of Commons on General Warrants, being an Answer to the Defence of the Minority. Scarce Tracts. Vol. 1.

LLOYD, David. Memoirs of the Lives, Actions, Sufferings and Deaths of Personages that suffered by Death, Sequestration or otherwise for the Protestant Religion from 1637 to 1660, and continued to 1666, with the Life and Martyrdom of K. Charles 1. Lond., 1668. Folio.

LLOYD, Rev. H. Introductory Lectures on Physical and Mechanical Science, delivered in 1834. Dublin. 8vo. Scientific Pamph. Vol. 32.

LLOYD, Jas. Letter to Hon. Thos. H. Perkins, on Impressments. n. d. Miscell. Tracts. Vol. 1.

LLOYD, Jas. T. Steam Boat Directory and Disasters on Western Waters. Cincin., 1856. 8vo.

LLOYD, W. A. List, with Descriptions, Illustrations and Prices, of whatever relates to Aquaria. Lond., 1858. 8vo. Scientific Pamph. Vol. 32.

LLOYD'S List of Subscribers, July, 1812; with Rules and Regulations, &c. Lond. 8vo. Eng. Polit. Pamph. Vol. 34.

LLWYFO, Llew. Gemau Llwyfo; Sel Detholion o brif Gyfansoddiadan a Chanenon. (Welsh Poetry.) Utica, 1868. 12mo.

LOANS by Private Individuals to Foreign States, entitled to Gov't Protection. Lond, 1842. 8vo. Eng. Polit. Pamph. Vol. 44.

LOCAL Loiterings and Visits in the Vicinity of Boston. Boston, 1846. 12mo.

LOCK Asylum. Eng. Acc. of the Nature and Intention of. Pimlico, 1835. 8vo. Eng Misc. Pamph. Vol. 5.

LOCKE, John. Essay Concerning Human Understanding. 6th Ed. Lond., 1710. 2 Vols. 8vo.

—— See LE CLERC, M. Life and Character of.

—— On the Conduct of the Understanding. Harpers' Fam. Libr. N. Y., 1860. 18mo.

—— Observations on Terrestial Magnetism. 1845–47. Smithsonian Contr. Vol. 3.

LOCKE, John Goodwin. Genealog. and Hist. Record of the Descendants of Wm. LOCKE of Woburn. Boston, 1853. 8vo.

LOCKE, J. L. Sketches of the Hist. of the Town of Camden, Me., 1605–1809. Hallowell, 1859. 12mo.

LOCKE, Wm. Henry. The Story of the Old Penn. 11th. Phil'a, 1868. 12mo.

LOCKHART, John G. Hist. of Napoleon Bonaparte. Harpers' Fam. Libr. N. Y., 1858. 2 Vols. 18mo.

—— Life of Napoleon Bonaparte. N. Y.. 1858. 12mo.

—— Memoirs of the Life of Sir Walter Scott. N. Y., 1837. 7 Vols. 12mo.

LOCKHART, Jas. Speech in Cong., July 22, 1852, on River and Harbor Improvements. Congr. and Polit. Pamph. Vol. 83.

LOCKMAN, John. Travels of the Jesuits in the Various Parts of the World, particularly China and the East Indies. 2d Ed. Lond., 1762. 2 Vols. 12mo.

LOCKWOOD, Belva A., and others. Memorial to Cong. in support of the Right of Women to Vote, Washington, 1871. 8vo. Cong. and Polit. Pamph. Vol. 128.

LOCKWOOD, Henry. Memoirs of Norwalk, Ohio. Fire Lands Pioneer. Vol. 1.

LOCKWOOD, Jas. H. Early Times and Events in Wisconsin. Wis. Hist. Soc. Coll. Vol. 2.

LOCOMOTIVE Sketches with Pen and Pencil, over the Great Central Route from Phila. to Pittsburg. Phila., 1854. 12mo.

LODGE, Edmund. Genealogy of the Existing British Peerage; containg the Family History of the Nobility. Lond., 1859. 8vo.

—— Illustrations of British History, Biography and Manners in the Reign of Henry VIII, Edward VI, Mary, Elizabeth and James I. Lond., 1838. 3 Vols. 8vo.

—— Portraits of Illustrious Personages of G. Britain. Vols. 1–10. Lond., 1840. Roy. 8vo.

LODWICK, Chas. N. York in 1692. Letter to Messrs. Lodwick and Hooker, May 20, 1692. N. Y. Hist. Soc. Coll. N. S. Vol. 2.

LOEWE, Dr. L. Dictionary of the Circassian Language. Lond., 1854. 8vo. Contained in "Proceedings of Philolog. Soc. Vol. 6. 1852–53."

LOFTUS, Wm. K. Travels and Researches in Chaldaea and Susiana; with acc. of Excavations at Warka and Shush, in 1849–52. N. Y., 1857. 8vo.

LOGAN, Hist. Society. See American Pioneer.

LOGAN, the Mingo Chief. Letters and Papers concerning. Amer. Pioneer. Vol. 1.

—— See MAYER, B. Logan and Cresap.

—— Papers and Letters concerning the Authenticity, etc. of his celebrated Speech. "Olden Time." Vol. 2.

LOGAN, Jas. See PENN, Wm. Corres. with.

LOGAN, John A. Speech at Duquoin, Ill., July 31, 1863. Cincin. 8vo. Congr. and Polit. Pamph. Vo. 105.

—— Speech in Congr. July 12, 1867, on Reconstruction. Rebell'n Pamph. Vol. 34.

—— —— July 16, 1868, on the Principles of the Democratic Party. Congr. and Polit. Pamph. Vol. 122.

LOGAN, John H. Hist. of the Upper Country of S. Carolina. Charleston, 1859. Vol. 1. 8vo.

LOGANIAN Library. Catalogue with short Acc. of the Institution. Phila. 1837. 8vo.

LOGIC. See BARRON, W. Elements of.

—— MAHAN, A. Science of.

LOGIER, J. B. See Exposition of his Musical System, etc.

LOLME, J. L. de. The British Empire in Europe. Part 1. Lond., 1787. 4to. Eng. Misc. Pamph. Vol. 24 a.

LOMBARD University, Galesburg, Ill. Catalogue for 1859–60. Galesburg, 1860. 8vo.

LONDON, C. W. Directory for 1856 and 1857. Lond., 1856. 12mo.

LONDON, Eng. and Croydon Railway Company. Lond., 1839. 12mo. Guide Books. Vol. 19.

—— Anthropological Soc'y. See HUNT, Jas.

—— —— PIM, Bedford.

—— Anti-Corn Law Conference, 1842. Report of the Statistical Committee, March, 1842. Lond. 8vo. Strangford Pamph. Vol. 28.

—— Assoc. for Promoting the Welfare of the Blind. Report for 1860, '61. Lond. 8vo. Eng. Misc. Pamph. Vol. 9.

—— Assoc. for Relief of the Manufacturing and Laboring Poor. 2d Report. Lond., 1815. 8vo. Pamphleteer. Vol. 6.

LONDON, Eng. See BARTLETT, D. W. What I saw in Lond. 1852.
—— Board of Works for the Strand Dist. Statement of Accounts, Proceedings of the Board, etc., for 1856-7. Lond. 8vo. English Misc. Pamph. Vol. 8.
—— See BREWER, J. N. Lond. and Middlesex. 1810.
—— British Mercury. Newspaper, Feb., 1712, to June 14, 1715. Lond., 1712-1715. Folio.
—— See CHAMBERLAIN, H. Hist. and Survey of. 1770.
—— Chatham and Dover Railway Guide. Aug., 1867. Lond. 8vo. Guide Books. Vol. 9 and 18.
—— Chronicle (A) of Lond. from 1089 to 1483. Written in the 15th century. Lond. 1827. 4to.
—— —— Newspaper. Jan. 1758 to Dec. 1762. 9 Vols. 4to.
—— —— Same. Jan.-Dec. 1772.
—— —— Same. Jan. 1791 to Dec. 1794. 4 Vols. 4to.
—— Chronological Institute Transactions. Vols. 1 and 2. 1852-1861. Lond. 8vo. Scientific Pamph. Vol. 36.
—— City Corruption and Mal-Administration, displayed. Lond. 1739. 8vo. Eng. Polit. Pamph. Vol. 11.
—— City of, London Club. Rules, etc. Lond. 12mo. n. d. Eng. Misc. Pamph. Vol. 10.
—— Clare Market Ragged Schools. 8th Report. Lond. 1859. 12mo. Eng. Misc. Pamph. Vol. 33.
—— Companion to Newspaper. Mar. 1833 to Jan. 1834. Folio.
—— Corresponding Soc'y. Acc. of Proceedings at a Gen. Meeting held June 29, 1795. Lond. 8vo. Eng. Polit. Pamph. Vol. 74.
—— —— Address on Parliamentary Reform. Lond. 1792. 8vo. Eng. Polit. Pamph. Vol. 74.
—— —— Same. 1793. Eng. Polit. Pamph. Vol. 24.
—— —— Address and Resolutions. July, 1794. Lond. 8vo. Eng. Polit. Pamph. Vol. 74.
—— —— Vindication of. Lond. n. d. 8vo. Eng. Polit. Pamph. Vol. 74.
—— Description of the Monument erected in Memory of the Great Fire in 1666; with Acc. of the Fire. Lond. 1805. 8vo. Hist. Pamph. Vol. 14.
—— Diocese of. Statistics of Church Education in the. Lond. 1866. 8vo. Eng. Rel. Pamph. Vol. 61.
—— Directories for 1760, '63, '65, '68, '77, '79, '80, '84, '90, '92, '97. 1802. 1817.
—— Domestic Mission Soc. Report, with Proceedings May 17, 1837. Hackney, 1837. 12mo. Eng. Rel. Pamph. Vol. 48A.
—— See EBRINGTON, Viscount. On Metropolitan Gov't. 1854.
—— Emancipation Society. Proceedings of, an Anti-Slavery Meeting, at Spafields' Chapel, Oct. 14, 1859. Lond. 8vo. Eng. Misc. Pamph. Vol. 9.
—— Exhibition, 1851. Brief Survey of Objects of Graphic Art exhibited by the Printing Establishment at Vienna. Lond. 8vo. Guide Books. Vol. 11.
—— —— See GLAISHER, Jas. Lecture on the Philos. Instruments.
—— —— JOHNSON, B. P. Report on.

LONDON Exhibition, 1851. Lectures on Scientific Subjects, Jan. and Feb., 1852. 4 Papers. 8vo. Scientific Pamph. Vol. 36.

—— —— Report of Central Committee. Washington, 1850. 8vo Scientific Pamph. Vol. 18.

—— Faculty of Physic, Charter of Incorpora. granted by Henry VIII., 1518. Lond., n. d. 8vo. Med. Pamph. Vol. 23.

—— Field Lane Ragged School. 11th Ann. Report. Lond., 1853. 8vo. Eng. Misc. Pamph. Vol. 32.

—— Fish Assoc., 1st Report of Committee. 1813. Pamphleteer. Vol. 1. 2d Report of Same. Pamphleteer. Vol. 2.

—— Gazette. Newspaper. Apr. 1680 to June 1681. Folio.

—— Loyal Protestant. Newspaper. June 1681 to August 1682. Folio.

—— —— Same, from June 30, 1767 to Jan. 1, 1811. 55 Vols. Small Folio.

—— General Board of Health. Information concerning Drainage of Town Sites, etc. Lond., 1852. 8vo. Eng. Misc. Pamph. Vol. 7.

—— General Evening Post. Newspaper. Jan. 1757 to August 1759. Folio.

—— Governesses' Benevolent Institution. Report and List of Subscribers, for 1865. Lond., 1866. 8vo. Eng. Miscellan. Pamph. Vol. 11.

—— Guardian Soc. Address. Lond., 1817. 8vo. Pamphleteer. Vol. 11.

—— —— Report of Committee. Lond., 1835. 8vo. Eng. Miscel. Pamph. Vol. 5.

—— See HAWKSLEY, Dr. Thos. Charities of.

—— HILLARY, Sir Wm. Improvement and Embellishment of the Metropolis. 1824.

—— Horticultural Soc. Proceedings, August 21, and Nov. 6, 1838. Lond., 1838. 8vo. Agr. Pamph. Vol. 9.

—— Hospital for Disease of the Throat. 3d Ann. Report. Lond., 1866. 8vo. Med. Pamph. Vol. 14.

—— Hospital for the Maintenance of Deserted Children. Acc. of, By-Laws, etc. Lond., 1749. 8vo. Educa. Pamph. Vol. 34.

—— Hospital. Statement of Facts Addressed to the Governors of. Lond., 1833. 8vo. Med. Pamph. Vol. 27.

—— Illustrated News, May, 1842, to Dec., 1871. Lond., 1843–71. 59 Vols. Folio.

—— Infirmary for Diseases of the Eye. Report, occasioned by the Statements of Sir Wm. Adams. Lond., 1818. 8vo. Med. Pamph. Vol. 22.

—— Institution. Catalogue of the Library of — systematically classed; with a Hist. and Bibliograph. Acc. of the establishment. Lond., 1835–52. 4 Vols. 8vo.

—— International Exhibition, 1862. Catalogues of Canada Products, etc. With Acc. of the Eastern Townships of Lower Canada. Lond., etc., 1862. 8vo.

—— —— See HOYT, Dr. J. W. Report on.

—— Leader; a Political and Literary Review. July, 1857, to Dec. 1857. 4to.

LONDON. See Liber Albus; the White Book of the City. 1419

—— Light Horse Volunteers. See Hist. Record of.

—— List of the Brokers of the City, 1815. London. 8vo. Eng. Misc. Pamph. Vol. 3.

—— Literary Fund. Address of the Committee for the Anniversary Festival, May 10, 1843. London. 8vo. Eng. Misc. Pamph. Vol. 22.

—— —— Report of the Anniversary, Annual Reports, etc., 1854. Lond. 8vo. Eng. Misc. Pamph. Vol. 7.

—— —— Same. 1864. Vol. 10.

—— —— Report of the Annivers. Dinner, May 11. 1842. Lond. 8vo. Eng. Misc. Pamph. Vol. 5.

—— Literary Gazette, and Journal of Belles Lettres, Arts, Politics, etc. 1817–1839. 23 Vols. 4to.

—— Magazine, Apr., 1732, to Dec., 1783. 52 Vols. 8vo.

—— See MAITLAND, W., and ENTICK, J. Hist. of. 1772.

—— Mesmeric Infirmary. 6th Report of the Meeting, June 8, 1855. Lond., 1855. 8vo. Med. Pamph. Vol. 27.

—— Metropolitan Board of Works. Report of Main Drainage Committee. Lond., 1863. 8vo. Eng. Misc. Pamph. Vol. 10.

—— Metropolitan Police Criminal Returns, 1863. Lond., 1864. 8vo. Eng. Misc. Pamph. Vol. 10.

—— Midnight Meeting Movement, etc. 5th and 6th Ann. Reports, 1864–'5, 1865–'6. Lond. 12mo. Eng. Misc. Pamph. Vol. 11.

—— Missionary Society. Sermons before the Soc'y, May 11, 12, 13, 1814. With Report. Lond., 1815. 8vo. Eng. Sermons. Vol. 34.

—— —— —— May 10, 11, 12, 1815. With Report. Lond., 1815. 8vo. Eng. Sermons. Vol. 34.

—— —— Report, May 12, 1864. Lond., 1864. 8vo. Eng. Rel. Pamph. Vol. 59A.

—— —— Transactions to the end of 1812. Vol. 3. Lond., 1813. 8vo. Eng. Rel. Pamph. Vol. 35.

—— Monitor (The); or British Freeholder. Newspaper. Aug., 1755 to July, 1757. Apr. 28, 1759 to Jan. 1, 1763. Lond. Sm. Folio.

—— Monument of. History of the Monument of London. Lond., n. d. 12mo. Guide Books. Vol. 19.

—— Morning Herald. May—Dec., 1805. 3 Vols. Folio. Echo and Post, 1807–1809. 2 Vols. Folio. Newspapers. 1790–1802. 1 vol. Folio.

—— New Broad St. Day and Infant Schools. Report of the Committee, Feb. 13, 1844. 8vo. Educa. Pamph. Vol. 32.

—— New Hospital for the Paralysed and Epileptic. Account of Inaugura. Ceremony, July 25, 1866. Lond. 8vo. Med. Pamph. Vol. 14.

—— North Briton. Newspaper. Lond., 1869. 2 Vols. Fol.

—— Observer (The) and The Rehearsal. Newspaper. Aug., 1704—Oct., 1707, and The Rehearsal, Oct. 1707—Mar. 1708, with The Examiner, Aug., 1710—June, 1711. Lond. Folio. 2 Vols.

LONDON Open Air Mission. 13th Ann. Report. Lond., 1866. 8vo. Eng. Rel. Pamph. Vol. 92.

—— Orphan Working School. Circular. 1855. Lond. 8vo. Eng. Misc. Pamph. Vol. 8.

—— Packet and Lloyds Evening Post. Nov., 1808 to Dec. 30, 1814. 6 Vols. Folio.

—— Parthenon. Newspaper. Oct., 1836 to July, 1837. 4to.

—— Pathological Soc'y. Report of the Proceedings. 1850–51. Lond. 8vo. Med. Pamph. Vol. 18.

—— Peace Society. Series of Tracts. Lond., 1833 and 1835. 8vo. Eng. Rel. Pamph. Vol. 46.

—— See PETTY, Sir Wm. Growth of Lond. 1682.

—— Poor Men's Guardian Society. Ann. Report. Lond. 1847. 8vo. Eng. Misc. Pamph. Vol. 6.

—— Porcupine (The). Newspaper. Oct. to Dec., 1800. Folio.

—— Post Office Lond. Directory for 1846. 47th Annual Publication. 2,074 pp. Lond., 1846. Roy. 8vo.

—— Principal Streets and Places in Lond., and its Environs. Lond., 1856. 8vo. Guide Books. Vol. 18.

—— (Southwest,) Protestant Institute Report. Lond., 1858. 8vo. Eng. Rel. Pamph., Vol. 58.

—— Public Records. Analyt. Indexes to Vols. 2 and 8 of the Records known as the Remembrancia, preserved among Archives of the City of Lond. 1580–1664. Lond., 1870. 8vo.

—— Publishers' Circular, and Record of British and Foreign Literature. Dec., 1858, to Dec., 1859. 4to.

—— Pure Literature Society. Report for 1866. Lond. 8vo. Eng. Misc. Pamph., Vol. 14.

—— Quarterly Review, Feb., 1809, to Oct., 1867. Lond., 122 Vols. 8vo.

—— Ragged Schools. Plea for. Lond., 1850. 8vo. Strangford Pamph., Vol. 54.

—— Royal Gazette, Newspaper. May and June, 1761. 4to.

—— Royal Society of. See Royal Society.

—— St. James Chronicle, or British Evening Post, Sept., 1774, to Nov., 1774. Folio.

—— Sanitary Condition of. See Health of Towns Assoc.

—— Shakespeare Society. Reports of the Council of the Ann. Meetings of 1847, 1848, 1850. 8vo. Eng. Misc. Pamph., Vol. 22.

—— Society for Encouragement of Arts, Manufactures and Commerce. Transactions. Lond., 1806–1827. 45 Vols. 8vo.

—— —— for Improvement of Prison Discipline. Report for 1832. Lond., 1832. 8vo.

—— —— for Protection of Young Females. Ann. Report, 1863. Lond. 8vo. Eng. Misc. Pamph., Vol. 10.

—— —— for Promoting Christian Knowledge. Report. Lond., 1823. 8vo. Eng. Rel. Pamph., Vol. 41A.

—— —— for Promotion of Christianity among the Jews. Series of Discourses before and in aid of the Society. 1810–1831. Eng. Sermons, Vols. 63, 64.

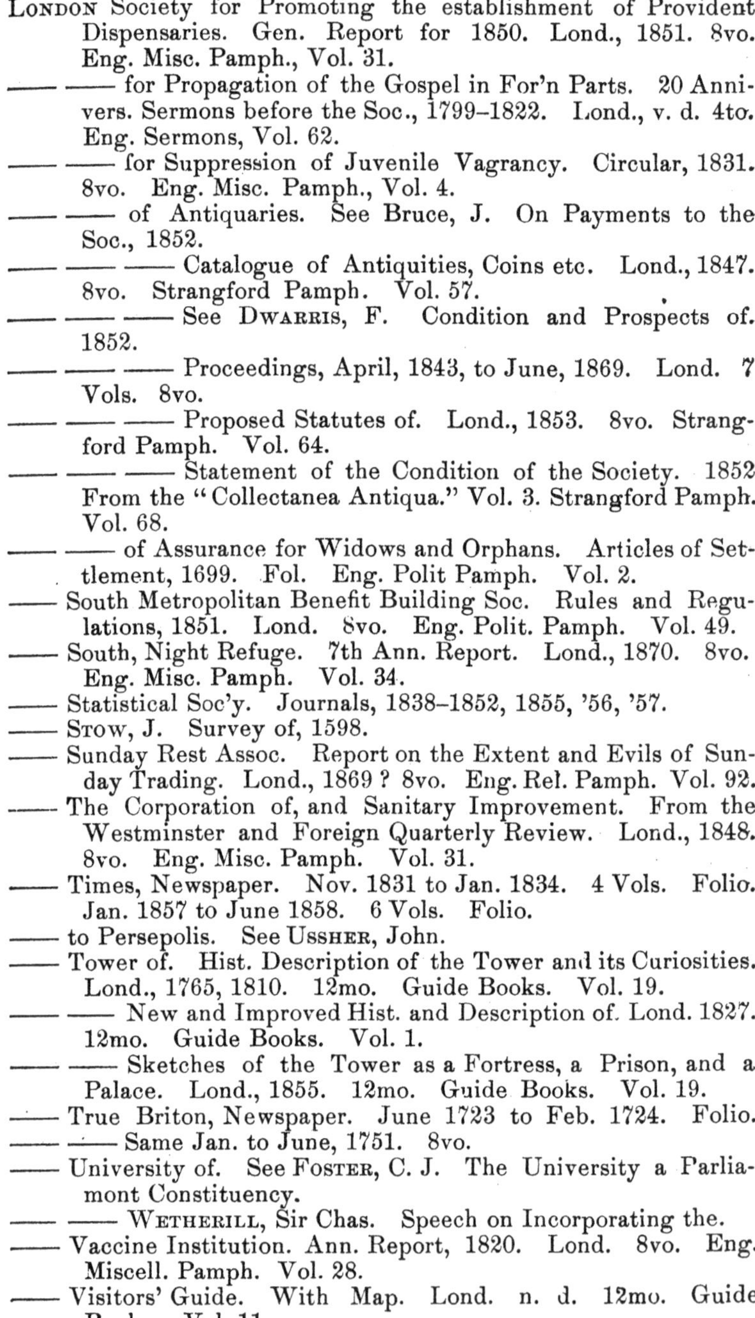

LONDON Society for Promoting the establishment of Provident Dispensaries. Gen. Report for 1850. Lond., 1851. 8vo. Eng. Misc. Pamph., Vol. 31.

—— —— for Propagation of the Gospel in For'n Parts. 20 Annivers. Sermons before the Soc., 1799–1822. Lond., v. d. 4to. Eng. Sermons, Vol. 62.

—— —— for Suppression of Juvenile Vagrancy. Circular, 1831. 8vo. Eng. Misc. Pamph., Vol. 4.

—— —— of Antiquaries. See Bruce, J. On Payments to the Soc., 1852.

—— —— —— Catalogue of Antiquities, Coins etc. Lond., 1847. 8vo. Strangford Pamph. Vol. 57.

—— —— —— See DWARRIS, F. Condition and Prospects of. 1852.

—— —— —— Proceedings, April, 1843, to June, 1869. Lond. 7 Vols. 8vo.

—— —— —— Proposed Statutes of. Lond., 1853. 8vo. Strangford Pamph. Vol. 64.

—— —— —— Statement of the Condition of the Society. 1852 From the "Collectanea Antiqua." Vol. 3. Strangford Pamph. Vol. 68.

—— —— of Assurance for Widows and Orphans. Articles of Settlement, 1699. Fol. Eng. Polit Pamph. Vol. 2.

—— South Metropolitan Benefit Building Soc. Rules and Regulations, 1851. Lond. 8vo. Eng. Polit. Pamph. Vol. 49.

—— South, Night Refuge. 7th Ann. Report. Lond., 1870. 8vo. Eng. Misc. Pamph. Vol. 34.

—— Statistical Soc'y. Journals, 1838–1852, 1855, '56, '57.

—— STOW, J. Survey of, 1598.

—— Sunday Rest Assoc. Report on the Extent and Evils of Sunday Trading. Lond., 1869 ? 8vo. Eng. Rel. Pamph. Vol. 92.

—— The Corporation of, and Sanitary Improvement. From the Westminster and Foreign Quarterly Review. Lond., 1848. 8vo. Eng. Misc. Pamph. Vol. 31.

—— Times, Newspaper. Nov. 1831 to Jan. 1834. 4 Vols. Folio. Jan. 1857 to June 1858. 6 Vols. Folio.

—— to Persepolis. See USSHER, John.

—— Tower of. Hist. Description of the Tower and its Curiosities. Lond., 1765, 1810. 12mo. Guide Books. Vol. 19.

—— —— New and Improved Hist. and Description of. Lond. 1827. 12mo. Guide Books. Vol. 1.

—— —— Sketches of the Tower as a Fortress, a Prison, and a Palace. Lond., 1855. 12mo. Guide Books. Vol. 19.

—— True Briton, Newspaper. June 1723 to Feb. 1724. Folio.

—— —— Same Jan. to June, 1751. 8vo.

—— University of. See FOSTER, C. J. The University a Parliamont Constituency.

—— —— WETHERILL, Sir Chas. Speech on Incorporating the.

—— Vaccine Institution. Ann. Report, 1820. Lond. 8vo. Eng. Miscell. Pamph. Vol. 28.

—— Visitors' Guide. With Map. Lond. n. d. 12mo. Guide Books. Vol. 11.

LONDON Weekly Amusement—Magazine. Nov. 1734 to Sept. 1735. 3 Vols. 8vo. And from Dec. 1763 to to June, 1767. 7 Vols. 8vo.
—— Westminster Magazine. Vol. 5. Jan. to Dec. 1777.
—— Zoological Society. See SCLATER, Philip L.
—— —— List of Fellows of, 1831. Scientific Pamph. Vol. 34.
—— —— Reports of Council and Auditors, 1850–51. Lond., 1850–51. 8vo. Strangford Pamph. Vol. 60.
—— —— Same, 1852. Strangford Pamph. Vol. 62.
LONDONDERRY, Lord. Letter to Lord Brougham [on his Sketches of Statesmen of George III.] Lond., 1839. 8vo. Strangford Pamph. Vol. 17.
—— Speech in House of Lords, on Spanish Affairs, June 19, 1838, with Notes, etc. Lond., 1838. 8vo. Strangford Pamph. Vol. 16.
LONDONDERRY, N. H. Celebration; Exercises at 150th Anniversary of Settled Part of Old Nutfield, comprising the Towns of Londonderry, Derry. Windham, Manchester, Hudson and Salem. N. H. Manchester, 1870. 8vo.
—— PARKER, Rev. E. L. Century Sermon, 1819.
—— —— History of.
LONG, Chas. Causes of the Present High Price of Bread. Lond. 1817. 8vo. 2d Ed. Pamphleteer, Vol. 10.
LONG, Geo. Lecture before the University of London, Nov. 4, 1828. Lond., 1829. 8vo. 2d Ed. Educa. Pamph. Vol. 35.
LONG Island (Battle of.) See FIELD, T. W.
—— —— See L. I., Hist. Soc.
—— —— See WARD, S.
—— Bible Soc'y. 52d and 53d Ann. Reports, 1867, '68. 8vo.
—— Hist. Soc'y. By-Laws and Certificate of Incorporation. Brooklyn, 1863. 8vo.
—— —— See FIELD, T. W.
—— —— GREENWOOD, John.
—— —— JONES, W. A.
—— —— MURPHY, H. C.
—— —— 1st–6th An. Reports, inclusive. Brooklyn, 1864–1869. 8vo.
—— See JONES, W. A. Paper on. 1863.
—— Papers Relating to. See Doc. Hist. of N. Y. Vol. 1.
—— See PRIME, N. S. Hist. of.
—— Reports of Engineers upon the Practicability of, etc. N. Y., 1834. 12mo.
—— Rate Lists, 1675, '76 '83. Doc. Hist. of N. Y. Vol. 2.
—— See THOMPSON, B. F. Hist. of.
—— WOOD, Silas. Early Settlement of.
LONG, J. Voyages and Travels of an Indian Interpreter and Trader among the N. Amer. Indians, with a Vocabulary of the Chippewa and other Indian Language. Lond., 1791. 4to.
—— Voyages chez different Nations Savages de l' Amerique, Septentrionale. trad. de l' Anglois. Paris, 1794. 8vo.
—— Hist. Sketches of the Town of Warner. N. H., 1832. Republished, 1870. 8vo. N. H. Hist. Discourses, etc. Vol. 3. See also N. H. Hist. Soc. Coll. Vol. 3.

LONG Parliament. List of Unanimous Voters in the Parliament, dissolved in 1670, n. d. Folio. Eng. Polit. Pamph. Vol. 1.

LONG, S. H. Report on the Improvement of Red River. 1841. War Depart. Misc. Rep'ts.

—— Voyage in a Six-oared Skiff to the Falls of Saint Anthony in 1817. Minn. Hist. Soc. Coll. Vol. 2.

—— See JAMES, E. KEATING, W. H.

LONGEVITY. See CORNARO, Lewis. Methods of Attaining, &c.

—— Extract from Lord Bacon's Writings on. pub. by Amer. Pop. Life Insurance Co., N. Y. n. d. 8vo. Ins. Pamph. Vol. 1.

—— See MACLAY, I. W. Relations of different Professions &c. to.

LONGFELLOW, Henry W. Poets and Poetry of Europe with Introduction and Biograph. Notices. Phila., 1847. 8vo.

LONGLEY, John Observations on the Trial by Jury; particularly on Unanimous Verdicts. Lond., 1812. 8vo. Pamphleteer. Vol. 5.

LONGVIEW ASYLUM. 1st, 9th, 10th, 11th Ann. Reports. Columbus, 1860–70. 8vo.

LOOMIS, ELIAS. Descendants of Jos. Loomis. N. Haven, 1870. 8vo.

—— Elements of Astronomy. N. Y., 1869. 12mo.

LOOMIS Genealogy. See LOOMIS, E.

LOPER, R. E. Letter to Sec. of War against Aspersions of the Senate Comm. Phila., 1863. Rebell'n Pamph. Vol. 17.

LOPEZ, Marcial Antonio. Discurso leido a la Real Academia de la Historia. Nov. 27, 1846. Madrid, 1847. 4to.

—— Discurso leido a la Real Academia de la Historia. Nov. 30. 1849. Madrid, 1850. 8vo.

LOPEZ, Gen. Narciso. Life of, with Hist. of the Attempted Revolution in Cuba. N. Y., n. d. Biograph. Vol. 1.

LORD, Chas. F. J. Letter to Sir Thomas M. Wilson on Sources of Disease, &c. Lond., 1847. 8vo. Sanitary Reform Pamph. Vol. 1.

LORD, Eleazar. National Currency: a Review of the National Banking Law. N. Y., 1863. 12mo. Rebell'n Pamph. Vol. 23.

—— Six Letters on the Necessity of a National Currency. N. Y., 1862. 12mo. Rebell'n Pamph. Vol. 102.

LORD, Jas. The Protestant Character of the British Constitution. Lond., 1847. 8vo. Strangford Pamph. Vol. 44.

LORD, J. L. & H. C. Defence of Dr. C. T. Jackson's Claim to the Discovery of Etherization. Boston, 1848. 8vo. Scientific Pamph. Vol. 18.

LORD, O. P. Speech at Boston, Oct. 8, 1856, on Fremont's Principles. Congr. & Polit. Pamph. Vol. 89.

LORIMER, J. Letter to Dr. H. WILLIAMS on the Climate and Productions of W. Florida. Amer. Philos. Soc. Trans. Vol. 1.

LORING, Rev. Amasa. A History of Shapleigh, Maine. Portland, 1854. 8vo. Me. Hist. Discourses, &c. Vol. 2.

LORING, Chas. O. Argument on behalf of the Eastern R. R. Co., before the R. R. Comm. of the Mass. Legislature. Boston, 1845. 8vo. Mass. R. R. Reports, &c. Vol. 1.

LORING, Chas. O. England's Liability for Indemnity. Boston, 1864. 8vo. Rebell'n Pamph. Vol. 3.

—— Memoir of Hon. Wm. STURGIS. Mass. Hist. Soc. Proceed. 1863–64.

—— Neutral Relations of England and the U. S. Boston, 1863. 8vo. Rebell'n Pamph. Vol. 1.

—— See PARSONS, Theop. Memoir of.

LORING, Geo. B. Address before the Merrimack Co. Agr. Soc., Sept. 28, 1864. Concord, 1864. 8vo. Addresses. Vol. 14.

—— See Lexington, Mass. Town Hall Dedication. 1871.

LORING, Jas. S. Hundred Boston Orators appointed by the municipal authorities and other public bodies, from 1770 to 1852. 2d Ed. Boston, 1853. 8vo.

—— Our First Historian of the Amer. Revolution (Wm GORDON). Paper before the N. Eng, Hist. Gen. Soc'y, May 2, 1860. Hist. Mag. Vol. 6.

LOS GRINGOS. See WISE, H. A., Jr.

LOSKIEL. Geo. H. Geschichte der Mission der Evangerlischen Bruder unter den Indianern in Nordamerica. Barby, 1789 8vo.

—— Hist. of the Mission of the United Brethren among the Indians of N. Amer. Lond., 1794. 8vo.

LOSSING, Benson J. Biograph. Sketches of the Signers of the Declaration of Amer. Independence. N. Y., 1857. 12mo.

—— See CUSTIS, G. W. C. Private Memoirs of Washington.

—— Diary of George Washington, 1789–91, embracing the opening of the first Congress, and his Tour through N. Eng., L. I., and other states, with his Journal of a Tour to Ohio in 1753. N. Y., 1860. 12mo.

—— Eminent Americans; comprising Brief Biographies of 330 persons. N. Y., 1857. 8vo.

—— Hist. of the U. States, for Families and Libraries. N. Y., 1857. 8vo.

—— Life of Gen. Philip Schuyler. N. Y., 1873. 12mo. 2 Vols.

—— Lives of the Presidents of the U. S. N. Y., 1847. 8vo. Biograph. Pamph. Vol. 2.

—— Our Countrymen; or Brief Memoirs of Eminent Americans. N. Y., 1855. 12mo.

—— Outline History of the Fine Arts. Harpers' Fam. Libr. N. Y., 1854. 18mo.

—— Pictorial Description of Ohio. N. Y., 1848. 8vo. Ohio Misc. Pamph. Vol. 3.

—— Pictorial Field Book of the Revolution; or Illustrations by Pen and Pencil of the Hist. etc., of the War for Independence. N. Y., 1855. 2 Vols. 8vo.

—— Pictorial Field Book of War, 1812. N. Y., 1868. 8vo.

—— Pictorial History of the Civil War of the U. States. Phil'a 1866. 3 Vols. 8vo.

—— 1776; or the War of Independence; a Hist. of the Anglo Americans, from the Union of the Colonies against the French, to the Inaugura. of Washington. N. Y., 1840. 8vo.

—— The League of the States. N. Y., 1863. 8vo. Rebell'n Pamph. Vols. 8, 67.

LOSSING, Benson J. Washington; a Biography profusely illustrated. N. Y., 1856. 3 Vols. (bound in 10). 8vo.
—— Washington's Life Guard. Paper before the N. Y. Hist. Soc. Jan. 5, 1858. Hist. Mag. Vol. 2.
"Lost Cause." See POLLARD, E. A.
"LOST Cause Regained." See POLLARD, E. A.
—— Senses. See KITTO, John.
—— Trappers. See COYNER, D. H. Scenes in Rocky Mts.
LOTHIAN, East, Scotland. See SOMERVILLE, R. View of. Agr. of. 1813.
LOTHROP, Rev. Jason. Sketch of the Early Hist. of Kenosha Co., Wis., and the Western Emigration Company. Wis. Hist. Soc. Coll. Vol. 2.
LOTHROP, Sam'l K. D. D. Address at the Opening of the Rooms of the Amer. Unitarian Assoc. Boston. Boston, 1854. 8vo. Sermons, Vol. 2.
—— Centen. Address before the Independent Co. of Cadets. Boston, 1841. 8vo. Mass. Hist. Discourses. Vol. 17.
—— Hist. of Battle Street Church. Boston, 1851. 8vo.
—— Life of Samuel Kirkland, Missionary to the Indians. Sparks' Amer. Biog. 2d Ser. Vol. 15.
—— Memoir of Nathan'l I. Bowditch. Mass. Hist. Soc. Proceedings. 1860–62.
—— Memoir of Sam'l Appleton. Mass. Hist. Soc. Proceedings. 1855–58. Collections 4th Ser. Vol. 3.
—— Proceedings of an Eccles. Council, in the Case of the Proprietors of the Hollis Street Meeting House, and Rev. John Pierpont. Boston, 1841. 8vo.
—— Sermon on the Death of Amos Lawrence, Jan. 9, 1853. Sermons. Vols. 2 and 19.
—— Sermon on the Death of Daniel Webster. Boston, 1852. 8vo. Sermon. Vol. 5.
—— Sermon at Boston, Nov. 5, 1848, on the Death of Harrison Gray Otis. Boston, 1848. 8vo. Sermons. Vol. 31.
LOTTERI, T. C. Atlas Minor. Augsburg, n. d. Folio.
LOTTERIES. See HOULTON, R. The Lottery Inquisitor.
—— STANSBURY, A. O. Lawfulness of.
LOUBAT, Alphonse. American Vine Dressers Guide. New and revised evition. N. Y., 1872. 12mo.
LOUDON PARK CEMETERY. Sketch of, with Address at its Dedica., by Hon. C. F. Mayer. Baltimore, 1853. 8vo. Baltimore Pamph. Vol. 1.
LOUIS XIV. See JAMES, G. P. R. Life and Times.
—— SAINT SIMON, Duke of. Anecdotes of his Court.
LOUIS XVII. See DE BEAUCHESNE, A. Life, etc., of.
LOUIS PHILIPPE. See RICE, F. W. Life of.
LOUISBURG, Siege of. 1745. See CRAFT, Benj. Journal.
LOUISIANA. Acc. of Louisiana, being an Abstract of Documents, in the Departments of State and Treasury. Phila., 1803. 8vo. La. Misc. Pamph. Vol. 1.
—— Address of Citizens of La. to the People of the U. S. Washington, 1872. 8vo. La. Misc. Pamph. Vol. 2.

LOUISIANA. Addresses of the Republican State Campaign Committee, 1868, 1871. N. Orleans, 1868, '71. 8vo. La. Misc. Pamph. Vol. 1.

—— and Reconstruction. See DURANT, Thos. J. Letter to 1869, '70. 8vo.

—— Affairs in 1873. Message of President and Papers, on the Condition of Affairs in La. Washington, 1873. 8vo. La. Misc. Pamph. Vol. 2.

Henry Winter Davis. 1864.

—— Auditor of Accounts. Reports for 1867, '68, '69. N. Orleans,

—— Board of Public Works. Ann. Report to Gen. Assembly, for 1869. N. Orleans, 1870. 8vo.

—— See BOSSU, Mr. Travels, 1771.

—— BRACKENRIDGE, H. M. Views of 1811.

—— BRADBURY, J. Travels in U. S. and Upper La.

—— BRAGDON, O. D. Facts for People of 1872.

—— BULLARD, H. A. La. Histor. Researches, 1845.

—— BUNNER, E. Hist. of. 1846.

—— See CARPENTER, Matt. H. Speech at N. Orleans. 1873.

—— CHAMPIGNY, Chev. Present State of.

—— CHAILLOUIX. P. F. Journal of Travels.

—— Constitutional Convention, 1864. Official Journal. English and French.

—— Debates in the Convention. N. Orleans, 1864. 8vo.

—— See CONWAY, T. W. Freeemen of. 1865.

—— COXE, D. Descrip. of. 1741.

—— DARBY, W. Geograph. Descrip. of.

—— —— Map of.

—— DAVIS, John. Travels, 1806.

—— D'IBERVILLE, M. P. De Moyne.

—— DU LAC, M. P. Travels through.

—— —— Voyages dans les deux Louisianes. 1801–5.

—— DUMONT, M. History of.

—— DU PRATZ, L. P. Hist. of.

—— ELECTIONS. Congress. Reports on the La. Contested Election Cases. 1870. Congr. and Polit. Pamph. Vol. 131.

—— —— Legislative Report on the Conduct of. 1868. Supplementary Report on the Conduct of. 1869. Congr. and Polit. Pamph. Vol. 80. Rebell'n Pamph. Vol. 41.

—— See FLINT, Rev. Tim. Journal, 1835.

—— FORSHEY, C. G. Internal Improvements, etc. 1850.

—— FORSTALL, E. J. Index of Pub, Documents in Paris relative to.

—— FRENCH, B. F. Hist. Collections.

—— GAYARRE, C. History of.

—— HENNEPIN, L. Description de la.

—— —— Discovery in America. French and English.

—— Hist. Soc'y. See BULLARD, H. A.

—— HUTCHINS, T. Topograph. Descrip. of.

—— Inaug. Address of Gov. Kellogg to Gen. Assembly. N. Orleans, 1873. 8vo. La Misc. Pamph. Vol. 2.

—— Insane Asylum. Jackson. Ann. Report, 1859. Baton Rouge, 1859. 8vo.

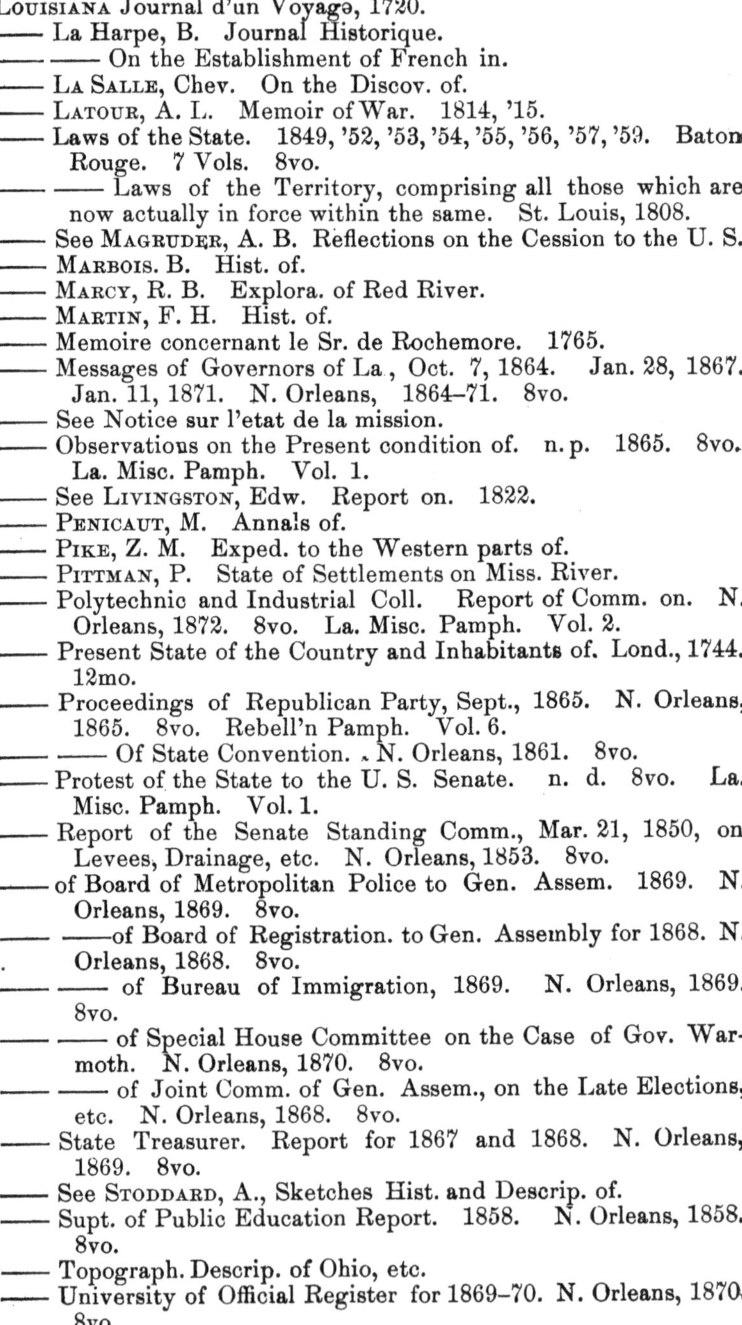

LOUISIANA Journal d'un Voyage, 1720.

—— La Harpe, B. Journal Historique.

—— —— On the Establishment of French in.

—— LA SALLE, Chev. On the Discov. of.

—— LATOUR, A. L. Memoir of War. 1814, '15.

—— Laws of the State. 1849, '52, '53, '54, '55, '56, '57, '59. Baton Rouge. 7 Vols. 8vo.

—— —— Laws of the Territory, comprising all those which are now actually in force within the same. St. Louis, 1808.

—— See MAGRUDER, A. B. Reflections on the Cession to the U. S.

—— MARBOIS. B. Hist. of.

—— MARCY, R. B. Explora. of Red River.

—— MARTIN, F. H. Hist. of.

—— Memoire concernant le Sr. de Rochemore. 1765.

—— Messages of Governors of La., Oct. 7, 1864. Jan. 28, 1867. Jan. 11, 1871. N. Orleans, 1864–71. 8vo.

—— See Notice sur l'etat de la mission.

—— Observations on the Present condition of. n. p. 1865. 8vo. La. Misc. Pamph. Vol. 1.

—— See LIVINGSTON, Edw. Report on. 1822.

—— PENICAUT, M. Annals of.

—— PIKE, Z. M. Exped. to the Western parts of.

—— PITTMAN, P. State of Settlements on Miss. River.

—— Polytechnic and Industrial Coll. Report of Comm. on. N. Orleans, 1872. 8vo. La. Misc. Pamph. Vol. 2.

—— Present State of the Country and Inhabitants of. Lond., 1744. 12mo.

—— Proceedings of Republican Party, Sept., 1865. N. Orleans, 1865. 8vo. Rebell'n Pamph. Vol. 6.

—— —— Of State Convention. N. Orleans, 1861. 8vo.

—— Protest of the State to the U. S. Senate. n. d. 8vo. La. Misc. Pamph. Vol. 1.

—— Report of the Senate Standing Comm., Mar. 21, 1850, on Levees, Drainage, etc. N. Orleans, 1853. 8vo.

—— of Board of Metropolitan Police to Gen. Assem. 1869. N. Orleans, 1869. 8vo.

—— ——of Board of Registration. to Gen. Assembly for 1868. N. Orleans, 1868. 8vo.

—— —— of Bureau of Immigration, 1869. N. Orleans, 1869. 8vo.

—— —— of Special House Committee on the Case of Gov. Warmoth. N. Orleans, 1870. 8vo.

—— —— of Joint Comm. of Gen. Assem., on the Late Elections, etc. N. Orleans, 1868. 8vo.

—— State Treasurer. Report for 1867 and 1868. N. Orleans, 1869. 8vo.

—— See STODDARD, A., Sketches Hist. and Descrip. of.

—— Supt. of Public Education Report. 1858. N. Orleans, 1858. 8vo.

—— Topograph. Descrip. of Ohio, etc.

—— University of Official Register for 1869–70. N. Orleans, 1870. 8vo.

LOUISIANA. See Voyage a la Louisiane.
—— Vue de la Colonie Espagnole.
LOUISVILLE, Ky. See CASSEDAY, B. Hist. of.
—— DEERING, Rich'd. Advantages of. 1859.
—— Dollar Farmer: a Monthly publication on Practical and Scientific Agriculture. Louisville, 1842–43. 4to.
—— See M'MURTRIE, H. Sketches of.
—— Medical Institute. Ann. Catalogue for 1839–40. Louisville, Ky., 1840. 8vo.
LOUVERTURE, Touissaint. History of. Lond., 1814. 8vo. New Ed. Pamphleteer. Vol. 4.
LOUVET, John-Baptist. Narr. of Dangers to which he has been exposed, since May 31, 1793. With Hist. Memorandums. Lond., 1795. 8vo. Eng. Polit. Pamph. Vol. 25.
LOVATT, Matt. See RUGGIERI, Dr. Cesar. Narr. of his Crucifixion.
LOVE, Alfred H. Appeal in Vindication of Peace Principles, in Reply to Wm. J. Mullen. Phila., 1862. 8vo. Congr. and Polit. Pamph. Vol. 137.
LOVE Letters (The) of Henry VIII. to Anna Boleyn; with Letters of Contemporaries, etc. Lond., 1823. 8vo. Pamphleteer. Vol. 21.
LOVE, Thos. Art of Cleaning, Dyeing, Scouring and Finishing. Phila., 1860. 12mo.
LOVE, W. D. Loss. Wisconsin in the War of the Rebellion. Chicago, 1866. 8vo.
LOVEDAY, John. Observations upon Shrines. 1754. 4to. Lond. Hist. Pamph. Vol. 21.
LOVEJOY, Rev. ELIJAH P. See BEECHER, Rev. E. Acc. of his Death at Alton.
LOVEJOY, J. C. Letter to Hon. Owen Lovejoy, on Slavery. Boston. 1859. 8vo.
LOVEJOY, O. See Addresses in Cong. on his Death.
LOVELL, Dr. Jos. Meteorological Register. 1822–25. 8vo. Congr. and Polit. Pamph. Vol. 32.
LOVEWELL, Capt. John. Adventures with the Indians, 1725. N. E. Hist. and Gen. Reg. Vol. 7.
LOVEWELL'S Expedition to Indians. See KIDDER, Francis.
LOWE, Ex. Gov. Letter to Virginia Legislature, Dec. 16, 1861.
LOWE, Rev. Chas. Sermon at Charleston, S. C., Apr. 23, 1865, on the Death of Lincoln. Boston, 1865. 12mo. Sermons, Vol. 46.
—— The Condition and Prospects of the South. Sermon at Somerville, Mass., June 4, 1865. Boston, 1865. 8vo. Sermons, Vol. 37.
LOWE, Sir Hudson. See FORSYTH, W. Captivity of Napoleon.
LOWE, John. Letter to Geo. Canning on Recognizing the Independence of S. America. Lond., 1823. 8vo. Pamphleteer, Vol. 21.
—— On the Recognition of Columbia by G. Britain. Lond., 1823. 8vo. Pamphleteer, Vol. 22.
LOWE, P. P. Oration at Dayton, O., July 4, 1839. Congr. and Polit. Pamph., Vol. 80.

LOWELL, Chas., D. D. See Boston—West Church. Proceedings on his Decease. 1861.
—— Discourse in West Ch., in Boston, Aug. 3, 1845, with Hist. Appendix. Cambridge, Mass., 1845. 8vo. Boston Hist. Discourses. Vol. 1.
—— See JENKS, Wm. Tribute to Memory of.
—— Memoir of John Pierce, D. D. Mass. Hist. Soc. Coll. 4th Ser. Vol. 1.
—— 25th Annivers. Discourse, West Ch., Boston, Jan. 2, 1831. Boston, 1831. 8vo. Boston Hist. Discourses. Vol. 2.
LOWELL, J. Enquiry into the Question of the Chesapeake, and the Necessity and Expediency of War. Boston, 1807. 8vo. Congr. and Polit. Pamph. Vol. 123.
LOWELL, Jas. Russell. The President's Policy, from the N. Amer. Rev., Jan. 1864. Rebell'n Pamph. Vol. 23.
LOWELL, John. See GREENWOOD, Rev. F. W. P. Obit. Sermon.
—— The New England Patriot; Companion of the Washington and Jefferson Administrations. Boston, 1810. 8vo. Congr. and Polit. Pamph. Vol. 112.
—— Perpetual War the Policy of Mr. Madison; an Examination of his late Message. Boston, 1812. 8vo. Congr. and Polit. Vol. 123.
LOWELL, John, Jr. See EVERETT, Edw. Memoir of.
LOWELL, John A. Memoir of Pat'k Tracy Jackson. N. Y., 1848. 8vo. Biograph. Pamph. Vol. 6.
—— Reply to a Pamphlet recently circulated by Edward Brooks. Boston, 1848. 8vo. Mass. Misc. Pamph. Vol. 1.
LOWELL, Joshua A. Speech in Cong., May 30, 1842, on Army Appropriation. Washington, 1842. 8vo. Congr. and Polit. Pamph. Vol. 25.
—— Speech in Cong., June 9, 1842, on British Colonial Trade. Washington, 1842. 8vo. Congr. and Polit. Pamph. Vol. 25.
LOWELL, Mass. Btll of Mortality of the City, 1851–59. 8vo.
—— Charter, with Amendments and Revised Ordinances, etc., of the city. 1846.
—— Church of the Pilgrims. Statement in regard to the Moral Exposure and Spiritual Wants of Lowell. 1850. 8vo. Mass. Misc. Pamph. Vol. 3.
—— City School Library Catalogue. Lowell, 1858. 8vo.
—— See COWELL, Chas. Hist. of.
—— —— Indians and Pioneers of.
—— Ministry at Large. Ann. Reports, 1856, 1865.
—— School Committee. Reports for 1849, '51, '53, '55, with Rules of Committee, 1843.
LOWER, Mark A. Bodiam and its Lords. new ed. Lond., 1871. 8vo.
—— Contributions to Literature: Historical, Antiquarian and Metrical. Lond., 1834. 8vo.
—— Curiosities of Heraldry: with Illustrations from old English writers. Lond., 1844. 8vo.
—— Essay on Family Nomenclature, Historical, Etymological, etc. Lond., 1849. 2 Vols. 12mo.

LOWER, Mark A. Genealog. Memoir of the Family of Scrase. Lond., 1856. 8vo. Genealog. Pamph., Vol. 6.
—— Hand Book for Lewes, Historical and Descriptive. Lewes, Eng., 1852. 12mo. 2d Ed. Guide Books, Vol. 20.
—— Memorials of the Town, Parish and Cinque-Port of Seaford. Historical and Antiquarian. Lond., 1855. 8vo.
—— Patronymica Britannica; a Dictionary of Family names of the United Kingdom. Lond., 1860. 8vo.
—— The Chronicle of Battle Abbey from 1066 to 1176, now first translated. Lond., 1851. 8vo.
—— The Sussex Martyrs; their Examinations and Burnings in the time of Queen Mary, including the personal Narratives of Rich'd Woodman, with notes. Lewes. n. d. 12mo.
—— The Worthies of Sussex; with Biographical Sketches. Lond., 1865. Quarto.
LOWNDES, Wm. T. Bibliographers Manual of Eng. Literature. Lond., 1834. 4 Vols. 8vo. Another Ed., Lond., 1857–64. 10 Vols. 12mo. Appendix to same, containing Publications of Learned Societies of G. B. Lond., 1864. 12mo.
LOWREY, Grosvenor P. English Neutrality: Is the Alabama a British Pirate. N. Y., 1863. 8vo. Rebell'n Pamph. Vol. 6.
—— The Commander-in-chief; a Defence of the Proclamation of Emancipation. N. Y., 1863. Rebell'n Pamph. Vol. 100.
LOWTH, Rev. Rob't. Correspondence with Rev. H. Gabell. Oxford, 1819. 8vo. Eng. Polit. Pamph. Vol. 35.
LOWVILLE (N. Y.) Academy. Catalogue for 1861–2. Utica. 8vo.
—— Rural Cemetery. Dedication Services, Oct. 9, 1867. Lowville, 1868. 8vo. Sermons, etc. Vol. 21.
—— Semi-Centen. Anniversary. Lowville, 1859. 8vo.
LOXLEY, Capt. Journal of the Campaign to Amboy, 1776. Hist. Soc. of Pa. Coll. Vol. 1.
LOYAL Leagues of the U. S. Proceedings of Convention at Utica, 1863. Vol. 83.
—— National League. Letter to Count A. Gasparin, E Laboulaye, H. Martin and other Friends of America in France. Rebell'n Pamph. Vol. 72.
—— —— Letter to Messrs. John Bright, Rich'd Cobden and other Friends in England. Rebell'n Pamph. Vol. 72.
—— —— Opinions of Prominent Men, concerning the Great Questions of the Times. 1863. Rebell'n Pamph. Vol. 83.
—— —— Proceedings at Organization at N. Y., Mar. 20, 1863. Rebell'n Pamph. Vol. 83.
—— —— Resolutions on Annivers. of the Assault on Fort Sumter. 1863. Rebell'n Pamph. Vol. 52.
—— Protestant's Vindication. Lond., 1680. Folio. Eng. Polit. Pamph. Vol. 1.
—— Publication Soc. Proceedings at 1st Annivers. Meeting, 1864. Rebell'n Pamph. Vol. 45.
—— Same, at 2d Anniver., 1865. Rebell'n Pamph. Vol. 90 A.
—— —— Publications Nos. 1–40, 49, 57, 64, 65, 67, 68, 70, 72, 78, 80, 81, 83. Rebell'n Pamph. Vols. 90 and 90 A.

LOYALISTS, The, Ammunition. 1863.

—— —— Same, in German Language. Rebell'n Pamph. Vol. 91.

—— of the Revolution. See CASE AND CLAIM OF, etc,

—— —— SABINE, Lorenzo. WARD, G. A. WILMOT, J. E.

LOYALTY AND DISLOYALTY. Phila., n. d. Rebell'n Pamph. Vol. 65.

—— for the Times. A Voice from Kentucky. 1864. Rebell'n Pamph. Vol. 46.

LUBBOCK, Sir John. North American Archælogy. Smithson. Report, 1862.

—— Origin of Civilization and Primitive Condition of Man. N. Y., 1870. 8vo.

—— Pre-Historic Times, Illustrated by Ancient Remains. N. Y., 1872. 8vo.

—— Social and Religious Condition of the Lower Races of Man. An Address. Smithson. Report. 1869.

LUCAS, Lord. Speech in the House of Peers, Feb. 22, 1670, on the Subsidy Bill. Lond., 1670. Small 4to. Eng. Political Pamph. Vol. 6.

LUCUBRATIONS during a Short Recess, by a Member of Parliament. With a Reply to the same. Lond., 1782. 8vo. Eng. Polit. Pamph. Vol. 19.

LUDEWIG, Herman E. Bibliothaca Glottica. Literature of Amer. Aboriginal Languages, with additions and corrections, by Prof. W. W. Turner. Edited by Nicholas Trübner. Lond., 1848. 8vo.

—— Catalogue of his Library. N. Y., 1858. 8vo. Bibliograph. Pamph. Vol. 21.

—— The Literature of American Local History: a Bibliographical Essay. N. Y., 1846. 8vo. Bibliog. Pamph. Vol. 50.

LUDLOW and Willink Hall, of St. Stephen's College. Proceedings at Laying the Corner Stone, June 13, 1866, with Genealog. Cambridge, 1866. 8vo. Genealog. Pamph. Vol. 4.

LUDLOW, Edward. Letter on the Tyranny of Chas. I., compared with that of Jas. II. Amsterdam, 1691. Sm. 4to. Eng. Polit. Pamph. Vol. 9.

LUDWIG, M. R. Ludwig Genealogy; Sketch of Jos. Ludwig, wife and family. Augusta, Geo., 1866. 12mo.

LUGENBEEL, J. W. Sketches of Liberia. Washington, 1853. 8vo. 2d Ed. Pamph. on Colonization. Vol. 1.

LUMLEY'S Bibliographic Advertiser. 6th Series. Nov., 1846 to Dec., 1847. Lond. 4to.

LUMPKIN, John H. Speech in Cong. May 18, 1846, on Army Appropriation. Washington, 1846. 8vo. Speeches. Vol. 1.

LUND, Dr. Edw. Introductory Address before the Manchester Royal School of Medicine and Surgery. 1860. Lond. 8vo. Med. Pamph. Vol. 13.

LUNDY, Rev. J. P. Loyalty to Government; Speech at Holmesburg, Penn., Apr. 21. 1861. Rebell'n Pamph. Vol. 100.

LUNENBURG, Mass. Topograph. and Hist. Sketch of. Mass. Hist. Soc. Coll Vol. 1. 2d Ser.

—— TORREY, R. C. Hist. of Lunenberg to 1764.

LUNIER, Dr. L. Project of a System of Statistics, applicable to the study of Mental Diseases. Translated by T. M. FRANKLIN, M. D. Utica, 1869. 8vo. Med. Pamph. Vol. 4.

LUNT, Geo. Origin of the Late War—to the Revolt of the Southern States. N. Y., 1867. 12mo.

—— Three Eras of New England, and other Papers Critical and Biographical. Boston 1867. 12mo.

LUNT, Paul. Diary, May to December, 1775. Edited by Dr. S. A. GREEN. Boston, 1872. 8vo. Rev. War Pamph. Vol. 4.

LUNT, Rev. Wm. P. Address before the Citizens and Schoools of Quincy, Mass., July 4, 1838. Quincy, 1838. 8vo. Sermons, Vol. 29.

—— Bi-Centen. Sermons before 1st Cong. Ch., Quincy, Mass., Sept. 29, 1839. Boston, 1840. 8vo. Sermons. Vol. 29. See See also Mass. Hist. Discourses. Vol. 5.

—— Discourse at Quincy, Mar. 11, 1848, at the Interment of John Quincy Adams. Boston, 1848. 8vo. Addresses, Vol. 4. Sermons. Vol. 29.

—— —— Nov. 25, 1852, Commem. of Dan'l Webster. Boston, 1852. 8vo. Sermons, Vol. 29. Addresses, Vol. 4.

—— —— Jan. 8, 1854, on the Death of Thos. Greenleaf. Boston, 1854. 8vo. Sermons, Vol. 29.

—— —— on the 20th Annivers. of his Installation; June 3, 1855. Boston, 1855. 8vo. Sermons, Vol. 29.

—— Discourses on 200th Annivers. of Cong. Ch. at Quincy, Mass. Boston, 1840. 8vo.

—— See FROTHINGHAM, Rev. N. L. Memoir of.

—— Lecture before Quincy Lyceum. Feb. 7, 1870. Boston. 8vo. Addresses, Vol. 4.

—— See ROBBINS, Rev. C. Commem. Discourse.

LUSHINGTON, Mrs. Chas. Narr. of a Journey from Calcutta to Europe by way of Egypt, in 1827 and 28. Waldie's Circulating Libr. Vol. 1.

LUSHINGTON, S. R. Account of his Refusal of Church Rates. Lond., 1841. 8vo. Strangford Pamp. Vol. 26.

—— Life and Services of Gen. Lord Harris G. C. B. during his Campaigns in America, the West Indies and India. Lond., 1840. 8vo.

LUTHER, Martin. See BUNSEN, Chev. Life of.

LUTHERAN CHURCH IN MAINE. See POHLMAN, Rev. Dr. Hist. or Address. 1869.

—— In N. Jersey. See COLLIN, Rev. N. Swedish Missions in N. J.

—— In N. York. LINTNER, G. A. Hist. of, 1867. Hartwick Synod. N. Y. Evangel. Luth. Synod.

LYCOMING COAL CO. Brief Description of Property of belonging to the Co. Poughkeepsie. 1828. 8vo. Penn. Miscell. Pamph. Vol. 2.

LYELL, Chas. 8 Lectures on Geology, at the Broadway Tabernancle, N. Y. N. Y., 1842. 8vo. Scientific Pamph. Vol. 40.

—— Geological Evidences of the Antiquity of Man and on the Origin of Species. 2d Ed. Phila., 1870. 8vo.

LYELL, Chas. Travels in North America in the years 1841–2; with Geological Observations on the United States. Canada and Nova Scotia. New York, 1856. 2 Vols. in 1.

LYFORD, W. G. Baltimore Md. Address Directory. Baltimore, 1836. 12mo.

LYLE, Rev. J. K. Catalogue of his Library. Cincinnati, 1872. 8vo. Bibliograph. Pamph. Vol. 37.

LYMAN Anniversary; Proceedings of the Re-union of the Lyman Family held at Mount Tom and Springfield, Mass., Aug. 30 and 31, 1871. Albany, 1871. 8vo. Genealog. Pamph. Vol. 12.

LYMAN Genealogy. See COLEMAN, L.

—— —— DICKINSON, J. T.

—— —— Lyman Anniversary Reunion. 1871.

LYMAN, Jos., D. D. Sermon at Northampton, at the Interment of the late Caleb Strong, Nov. 11, 1819. 8vo. Sermons. Vol. 54.

LYMAN, P. W. Hist. of East Hampton, Mass., with Genealog. Record of Families. Northampton, 1866. 12mo.

LYMAN, S. P. Daniel Webster, his Life and Times, including most of his Speeches, etc. Phila., 1852. 2 vols. in 1.

—— Speech at Ithaca, July 11, 1839, on the N. Y. and Erie R. R. N. York, 1839. 8vo. N. Y. Misc. Pamph. Vol. 8.

LYMAN, Theo., Jun. See Boston—Supreme Judicial Court—Trial for Libel. 1828.

—— Oration at Boston, July 4, 1829. Boston. 8vo. Addresses. Vol. 29.

LYME, Ohio. See SMITH, Chas. Memoirs of.

LYMNE, Kent Co., Eng. Antiquarian Excavations on the Site of the Roman Station at Lymne. Lond. 1850. 8vo. Strangford Pamph. Vol. 55.

LYNCH, Anne C. The Rhode Island Book. Providence, 1841. 12mo.

LYNCH, Jas. Address before the Amer. Institute of the City of N. Y., Oct. 1829. 8vo. Adresses. Vol. 33.

LYNCH, John. Speech in Congr., May 11, 1870, on Amer. Commerce. 8vo. Congr. and Polit. Pamph. Vol. 119.

LYNCH, W. F. Naval Life; or Observations Afloat and Ashore. The Midshipman. N. Y., 1851. 12mo.

—— Report of Examination of the Dead Sea. Washington, 1849. 8vo. Congr. and Polit. Pamph. Vol. 28.

—— See also Senate Doc. 34, 2d Sess. 30th Cong. 1849.

LYND, Jas. W. The Religion of the Dakotas. Minn. Hist. Soc. Coll. Vol. 2.

LYNDHURST, (Lords) Brougham and Local Courts. From Blackwood's Mag. Lond., 1834. 8vo. Eng. Polit. Pamph. Vol. 78.

LYNE, Francis. Tribunals of Commerce. Letter to the Bankers of Lond. Lond., 1854. 8vo. Strangford Pamph. Vol. 65.

LYNN, Mas. 1st Ann. Report of Receipts and Expenditures for 1850–51. Lynn, 1851. 8vo.

—— Ann. Reports of School Comm. for 1849–50, and 1851–2. Lynn, 1850, '52. 8vo.

LYNN, Mass. Directory for 1860. Lynn. 1860. 18mo.
—— See LEWIS, A. and Newhall, J. R. Hist. of
—— Mayor's Inaugural Address to City Council, May, 1850. Lynn. 1850. 8vo.
LYNNFIELD, Mass. See Lewis, A, and Newhall, J. R. Hist. of.
LYON, Matt. See White, Pliny H. Life and Services of.
LYON, Gen. Nathanl. See Peckham, Jas. Gen. Lyon and Missouri in 1861.
—— The Last Political Writings of; with a Sketch of his Life and Military Services. N. Y. 1861. 12mc.
—— See WOODWARD, A. Life of.
LYON, SIDNEY S. Report of an Exploration of Ancient Mounds in Union Co., Ky. Smithsonian Report. 1870.
LYSONS, Rev. D. and S. Magna Brittania: Topograph. Acc. of the several counties of G. Britain. Vol. 2. Part 1. Cambridgeshire. Lond. 1808. 4to.
—— Same. Vol. 6. Devonshire. 2 Vols. Lond. 1822. 4to.
LYTTLETON, Lord. Speech in the House of Lords, July 27, 1840, on Ecclesiastical Duties' and Revenues' Bill. Lond., 1840. 8vo. Strangford Pamph. Vol. 27.
—— The Colonial Empire of G. Britain. A Lecture. Lond., 1850. 8vo. Strangford Pamph. Vol. 54.
LYTTON, Sir E. Bulwer. Confessions of a Water-patient. Lond. 12mo. n. d. Med. Pamph. Vol. 26.

www.ingramcontent.com/pod-product-compliance
Lightning Source LLC
LaVergne TN
LVHW021057110826
845150LV00001B/101

* 9 7 8 1 4 2 5 5 6 6 5 6 2 *